CollegeBoard

International Student Handbook 2012

2012

International Student Handbook

CollegeBoard

Twenty-fifth Edition

The College Board, New York

The College Board

The College Board is a mission-driven not-for-profit organization that connects students to college success and opportunity. Founded in 1900, the College Board was created to expand access to higher education. Today, the membership association is made up of more than 5,900 of the world's leading educational institutions and is dedicated to promoting excellence and equity in education. Each year, the College Board helps more than seven million students prepare for a successful transition to college through programs and services in college readiness and college success — including the SAT® and the Advanced Placement Program®. The organization also serves the education community through research and advocacy on behalf of students, educators and schools.

For further information, visit www.collegeboard.org.

Editorial inquiries concerning this book should be directed to Guidance Publications, The College Board, 45 Columbus Avenue, New York, NY 10023-6992; or telephone 212-713-8000.

Copies of this book are available from your local bookseller or may be ordered from College Board Publications, P.O. Box 8670, Reston, VA 20195. The book may also be ordered online through the College Board Store at www.collegeboard.org. The price is $31.99.

ISBN: 978-0-87447-973-7

Printed in the United States of America

Distributed by Macmillan

Contents

Dear Friends,

The College Board is dedicated to connecting students to college success and opportunity. We believe in the principles of excellence and equity in education and try to promote them in all that we do. With the College Board's Handbook series, we hope to put an authoritative source of college information at your fingertips as you seek to further your education in the United States.

World events make it ever more evident that a broad knowledge of other cultures is essential for everyone. Through intercultural programs, we hope young people will come to a better understanding of one another and that these programs will foster greater cooperation among the people of the world.

College is a dream worth working hard to achieve. I've been a businessman, a governor and now the president of the College Board, but nothing makes me prouder than to say that I am a college graduate. With perseverance, anyone who desires a college education can attain one. College Board publications can help you get there.

My best wishes on your journey to success.

Gaston Caperton

Gaston Caperton
President
The College Board

Preface

The importance of international educational exchange in promoting understanding across national, cultural, religious and racial borders cannot be underestimated. Hundreds of thousands of students who study overseas each year create a global citizenry that is culturally aware and respectful of people of different backgrounds. These benefits translate into a more understanding and peaceful world society. Individually, students are enriched and draw lifetime benefits from the opportunity to learn a discipline in a different cultural context, acquire or perfect a foreign language, be immersed in and learn from another culture, and teach one's culture to others.

The United States has an unparalleled system of higher education in terms of the number of institutions and the variety and quality of their programs of study. There are more than 3,900 universities offering bachelor's and associate degrees in more than 600 subject areas. The sheer size and diversity of the U.S. higher education system can make the task of finding the institution that is right for you seem daunting. The process of researching, selecting and applying to colleges and universities in the United States is difficult and time-consuming, but it is well worth the investment.

It is important for students to find the institution that will best meet their educational, professional and personal needs. With this in mind, the objective of the *College Board International Student Handbook* is to provide international students with up-to-date, objective and thorough information to help them make informed decisions about their education. The undergraduate institutions described in this book are fully accredited by agencies recognized by the U.S. Department of Education and encourage international student enrollment.

The book is designed to be used in conjunction with the *College Board College Handbook* and the *College Board Book of Majors*, as well as the wide array of resources available on the Internet, in order to find the college or university that best fits a student's needs. Nearly all colleges and universities have websites, which are listed in this publication. The College Board also has a website (www.collegeboard.org) where students can conduct a college search, register for the SAT® and SAT Subject Tests™, and learn about materials to prepare for the exams.

We would like to acknowledge those who worked on the *International Student Handbook*, especially the following nine admissions professionals who provided their expertise.

Peter Briggs, Director, Office for International Students and Scholars, Michigan State University, East Lansing, Mich.

Ken Bus, Director, International Students Program, Glendale Community College, Ariz.

Joseph DeCrosta, Director of International Programs, Duquesne University, Pittsburgh, Pa.

David Dillman, Executive Director of Transfer and International Student Admission, Austin College, Sherman, Texas

Michael Gargano, former Vice Chancellor of Student Affairs, University of Massachusetts, Amherst, Mass.

Ann Gogerty, Senior International Admissions Counselor, Iowa State University, Ames, Iowa

Tatia Granger, former Vice President for Enrollment Services, Bennett College, Greensboro, N.C.

Judith Jurek, Senior Associate Director, Office of Admission, University of Southern California, Los Angeles, Calif.

Mark G. Reid, Executive Director of International Admission, University of Miami, Coral Gables, Fla.

This publication is a culmination of cooperation between the College Board's Office of International Education and College Planning Services department, government agencies involved with international educational exchange, EducationUSA advisers, and international admission officers at U.S. colleges and universities. The college data are based primarily on information supplied by the colleges themselves in response to the College Board's Annual Survey of Colleges 2011, with some data supplied by federal and state agencies. The information was verified by a staff of data editors under the direction of Andy Costello, Roger Harris, Doris Chow and Stan Bernstein, with the assistance of Cathy Serico. Tom Vanderberg and Lauren Reynolds were responsible for the overall editorial direction of this book.

All these professionals share a common belief that the proper placement of and service to international students at U.S. campuses are critical to the development of mutual understanding through the exchange process. As stated by the Bureau of Educational and Cultural Affairs, U.S. Department of State: "The doors of U.S. educational institutions are open to all qualified students from around the world. The United States is proud of an educational system that attracts students and scholars from across the globe."

Office of International Education
The College Board

Part I:
Applying to college in the United States

Planning calendar for U.S. study

Two years before admission...

For admission in August or September, begin two years in advance.

September

- If you have access to the Internet, visit the College Board's website at www.collegeboard.org. It has rich databases of information on colleges, careers and scholarships.

- Find out about sources of U.S. college information in your country — libraries, advising centers, U.S. educational organizations or commissions, and the Internet. The U.S. Department of State sponsors a network of EducationUSA advising centers in more than 150 countries to provide students with free, up-to-date information and help to apply for degree programs at American colleges and universities. A listing of these centers is located in Part III of this book.

- Review the sections in this book on choosing and comparing colleges. Use the College Search on collegeboard.org, where you can find colleges that match the features you want. Once you have a manageable list, use this book to get essential international student information about each of those colleges. College Search also allows you to link directly to any college's website, where you can gather more information.

- If English is not your first language, learn about the English proficiency examination required. Two examples of this type of test are the Test of English as a Foreign Language (TOEFL) and the International English Language Testing System (IELTS). Get the information bulletin and registration materials. See also "Test information" on page 31.

- Be sure you are taking courses that prepare you for college or graduate study at U.S. educational institutions.

- Register for the SAT or SAT Subject Tests if you plan to take the tests in autumn. Information on the SAT is available at sat.collegeboard.org, and on page 31.

October

- Register for the SAT or SAT Subject Tests if you plan to take the tests in winter.

- Discuss your plans with an adviser. Ask your adviser or counselor whether U.S. college representatives will be visiting your country. Note the dates and places, and try to attend at least one meeting.

November

- Register for the SAT or SAT Subject Tests if you plan to take the tests in late winter or early spring.

- Discuss your plans with your teachers, family, people who work in your field of study and, if possible, people who have studied in the United States.

- Contact colleges by visiting their websites, or by airmail or e-mail to request catalogs.

December

- Register for the SAT or SAT Subject Tests if you plan to take the tests in early spring.

January

- Review college information you have collected from guidebooks, college catalogs and online sources. Choose three to six colleges to research more fully.

February

- Develop your financial plan. Consider how you will pay for your education, living expenses and transportation for each year of study in the United States.

- Find out about scholarships and other types of financial aid available in your country. Request the application materials.

March

- Register for the SAT or SAT Subject Tests if you plan to take the tests in spring.

- Schedule an appointment to take the TOEFL, or another English proficiency test.

April

- Register for the SAT or SAT Subject Tests if you plan to take the tests in late spring.

- Write to the colleges you have selected to request a current catalog and application form, or go to their websites to get that material. Be sure to request financial aid and scholarship application forms if you intend to apply for aid.

May

- Identify the teachers, counselors and other adults you will ask for letters of recommendation.

June

- If there is a break in your school schedule, use the time to improve your English skills by reading, writing and speaking in English whenever you can.

July

- Read college application instructions carefully to find out what information is required and when it must reach each college to which you are applying.

One year before admission...

August

- Request information on intensive English language programs in the event you do not meet English proficiency requirements.

- If an essay is required for your applications, begin your first draft.

- If you have not yet taken admission tests, or if you and your adviser think you can improve your scores, register for a test date, preferably no later than November.

September

- Find out the procedures at your school (and any other secondary school or college you have attended) for sending your academic records (transcripts) to the colleges to which you are applying.

- If colleges have provided forms for recommendations, give them to the teachers and other adults you have contacted.

- Register for the SAT or SAT Subject Tests if you plan to take the tests in autumn.

October

- Register for the SAT or SAT Subject Tests if you plan to take the tests in winter.

- Complete the essay for your applications.

- Complete the financial aid application forms.

- Apply early to colleges.

November

- Be sure you request that your scores on all required tests be sent to all the colleges on your list.

- Check to see that the people from whom you requested recommendations have sent them.

- Be sure that your school or college has sent your academic records to all the colleges on your list.

December

- Reply promptly and completely to any requests for additional information you may receive from colleges to which you have applied.

January

- Be sure to keep up the quality of your studies. Your complete academic record can be important in admission decisions.

- If you have not already completed all financial aid application forms, be sure to do so now and mail them as soon as possible.

February

- Review your financial plan for your education. If you think you may need additional help, investigate any sources of financial aid in your country that you may have overlooked.

March

- Some colleges with a rolling admission policy require a response and a deposit soon. Note any reply dates that apply to you.

April

- You will probably hear from colleges this month or next. Review the section in this book on what to do if you are accepted at more than one college.

- Be sure to send your reply and deposit by the acceptance deadline.

- Apply for a passport, if you do not have one already.

May

- Write to colleges from which you have not heard.

- Review predeparture procedures.

- Confirm housing reservations at the college of your choice.

- Apply for a visa appropriate for your student status. Check with the U.S. embassy or consulate to be sure you meet all requirements for entry into the United States.

June

- Investigate predeparture orientation programs in your country. Ask the adviser at the EducationUSA advising center in your country (see Part III).

- Make travel arrangements.

July

- Use this opportunity to continue upgrading your English proficiency.

- If possible, earn money toward your expenses.

August

- Make sure all your predeparture activities are complete.

- Have a wonderful trip!

Why study in the United States?

Although travel of any kind is both exciting and informative, studying outside your home country offers unique possibilities. It allows you to completely immerse yourself in a new environment: in the classroom you gain exposure to new learning techniques and perspectives; outside the classroom you have the opportunity to meet people from different cultures. This can be a life-changing experience, giving you a new understanding of international political, social and economic issues. In addition, study abroad develops self-confidence, cross-cultural awareness and open-mindedness to new ideas and values. Employers worldwide consider these important assets.

Of all the possible places international students choose to study, the largest proportion choose the United States. In fact, today about 20 percent of all international students in the world are studying in the United States. There are a number of features that make U.S. education so popular.

Quality. The U.S. higher education system has an international reputation for quality. There are distinguished programs available at both the undergraduate and graduate levels in almost every field of study. Many universities attract world-renowned faculty and stand at the forefront of research and technological development. State-of-the-art facilities include libraries, laboratories, computers and other resources.

Diversity of institutions and programs available. The range of educational opportunities in the United States is enormous. No matter what college experience you are seeking, you will find it at one or more of the 3,800 higher education institutions throughout the country. Here are just a few of the features you can choose among.

- **Size:** Institutions range from fewer than 1,000 to more than 50,000 students.

- **Student body:** Most colleges are coeducational, but there are 66 for men only and 53 for women only.

- **Selectivity:** College admissions policies range from highly selective to open admission.

- **Setting:** Campuses are located in small and large cities, suburban areas, and rural communities, and in a variety of climates.

- **Field of study:** With more than 600 major fields of study to select from, you are likely to find a program that suits your interests.

- **Type of institution:** Choices range from liberal arts colleges that emphasize broad preparation in academic disciplines to technical schools that provide focused, career-related training. Some offer vocational programs, and a growing number of colleges offer options in distance learning.

Flexibility. One of the hallmarks of U.S. education is flexibility. At the undergraduate level, universities emphasize a broad, well-rounded education. You will be offered a wide range of classes — mathematics, science, the arts, social science, and languages — before finally having to choose a specialization. Even at the graduate level, related courses might be offered outside the department and in interdisciplinary fields. Students are actively involved in designing their course schedules because so many options are available. It is even possible to combine academic classes with work experience that will be recognized as part of the degree program. Most institutions have qualified staff on hand to help you make the best decisions to attain your academic goals. In the classroom, you are encouraged to be an active participant in the learning process. Faculty welcome, and generally expect, student input and encourage you to develop your own ideas and questions, and to express them.

Campus life. A successful college experience involves more than academic work. You will find a wide range of social, cultural and sports activities outside the classroom that will match your interests, such as internships and clubs. These give you a chance to make friends and at the same time develop team and leadership skills that will be useful in your future career.

It is important to understand the differences between the U.S. system of education and your own country's system. Please review the next section on U.S. higher education before continuing.

U.S. higher education

Organization of the U.S. education system

How education systems are organized varies from country to country. Higher education in the United States may be very different from education in your country.

Preuniversity studies in the United States consist of one or more years of preschool, kindergarten and 12 years of elementary and secondary school (also called "high school"). The chart in this section shows that the structure of preuniversity studies varies in how it is organized, but the body of knowledge to be covered is similar across the 50 states, regardless of how the school system is organized. The United States does not have a mandated course for secondary schools or a national examination. However, educators apply a common set of standards for assessing the basic competencies expected of secondary school graduates. The typical student receives a secondary school diploma at age 17 or 18.

The first level of higher (postsecondary) education is called "undergraduate" study and includes two-year and four-year programs. Two-year programs generally lead to an associate degree. An associate degree may be earned at a two-year community or junior college, or at a four-year college or university. There are two types of associate degree programs. Transfer programs provide the first two years of general education for transfer to a four-year program. Terminal programs (sometimes called vocational or technical) prepare students for a career in a specific trade.

Four-year colleges and universities offer programs that lead to a bachelor's degree (sometimes called the baccalaureate). The first two years usually are spent in courses that give you a broad foundation for future specialization. They may include English composition, world history, natural sciences, mathematics, languages and social sciences, plus some courses determined by your chosen field of study. The second two years are devoted to your major

academic subject. Five years of undergraduate study may be required for some fields. A few specialized institutions offer only the last two years of undergraduate study; these are called upper-division institutions.

"Graduate study" follows the completion of undergraduate education at the bachelor's degree level. It leads to the master's and doctoral degrees in academic disciplines or professional degrees such as law (J.D.), medicine (M.D.) and dentistry (D.D.S.). A master's degree generally requires one or two years of full-time study, but three-year master's degree programs exist. Doctoral and professional degrees require at least three years of full-time study and, with some research projects, will take even longer. Admission to graduate programs can be very competitive, and some first-professional degree programs limit admission to applicants who earned their bachelor's degrees at a U.S. college.

Types of institutions

Degree programs are offered at many different types of institutions in the United States. Some institutions are public and some private. Although nearly all institutions receive some financial support from federal and state governments, public institutions rely heavily on public funds, while private institutions depend more on tuition, fees and contributions from foundations and private citizens. There are also some postsecondary schools called "proprietary" schools, which are operated on a for-profit basis by their owners.

Admission Advice

"One advantage of community colleges is pricing. Students can earn two years of credit at a much lower cost to them and their families than at a public or private university. Community colleges also have smaller classes, and there's a lot of support available to international students for improving their English."

— Ken Bus, Glendale Community College, Glendale, Ariz.

"One of the draws of an all-women institution is that families of international students are more comfortable sending their daughters to the U.S. knowing that they're going to an institution that is women-focused and women-centered."

— Tatia Granger, formerly of Bennett College, Greensboro, N.C.

Education in the United States

Postdoctoral study and research

Doctoral or professional degree

Doctoral degree study

Professional school

Master's degree

Master's degree study

Bachelor's degree

Associate degree or certificate

Community or junior college

Technical institute

Undergraduate

High school diploma

Four-year high school

Senior high school

Combined junior-senior high school

Junior high school

(8-4)

(6-3-3)

(6-6)

Elementary or primary school

Kindergarten

Nursery school

7th
6th
5th

Higher education (college, university, professional)

4th
3rd
2nd
1st

12th
11th
10th
9th
8th
7th

Secondary education (academic, vocational, technical)

6th
5th
4th
3rd
2nd
1st

Elementary or primary education

Kindergarten

Nursery school

Degrees offered

Undergraduate degrees

Associate degree programs are offered at two-year colleges, most of which are public *community colleges*, though some are private institutions called *junior colleges*. Associate degrees are also offered at some four-year colleges and universities. If you plan to earn an associate degree and then go on to a four-year bachelor's degree program, after you have enrolled be sure to consult with a transfer adviser to develop a program of study comparable to the first two years of a bachelor's program.

Bachelor's degrees are earned at four-year public or private *colleges* and *universities*. The terms *college* and *university* are used interchangeably in the United States and imply an institution that offers a bachelor's degree. Some *institutes*, such as the California Institute of Technology or the Massachusetts Institute of Technology, also offer bachelor's degrees. Some colleges and institutes, and all universities, also offer graduate degrees. Whether your bachelor's degree is earned at a college, university or institute, it will have the same value as a credential for applying to graduate school, provided that the institution is accredited. (See the accreditation information later in this section.)

Graduate degrees

Graduate degree programs also are offered at several types of higher education institutions. Master's degrees can be earned at some four-year colleges as well as at universities and institutions that offer graduate study only. Master's degree programs generally take one or two years of full-time study to complete, but there are some that require three years of study. Doctoral and professional degree programs are offered at universities and graduate-only institutions. Doctoral degrees usually require a minimum of three years beyond the bachelor's degree.

It is possible to take a professional degree program without first earning a bachelor's degree, but those programs are highly selective and often require a very heavy course load. Professional degrees require a total of at least six years of study, including appropriate undergraduate preparation. An example of this type of program is the six-year medical program.

Academic calendar

The academic year can be divided in a variety of ways. The most common is the semester system, in which the academic year is divided into two 16-week terms in fall and spring, with a long summer vacation and a shorter winter break. In the quarter system, the 12-month academic year is divided into four equal parts; most students take classes for three quarters of the year and take a break in the remaining quarter. There is also a trimester system, which divides the year into three 15-week terms. Under that system, students can attend school year-round and earn the same number of credits in the summer as they do in the fall or spring semesters. Some schools use a modified semester system called 4-1-4; they have a one-month intersession (or "winter term") between the two semesters, during which students take short courses, travel for a short study abroad experience, or do an internship. Regardless of how the calendar is arranged, you will cover approximately the same amount of material in a year of study. If you transfer from a college using the semester system to a university using a quarter system, the university will know how to convert your semester credits to quarter credits, and you will not lose any time.

Accreditation

Accreditation in the United States is managed entirely by the institutions themselves, in cooperation with regional accrediting bodies. Reviews are conducted by committees of educators and other private citizens rather than by the government. Although institutions are not required to seek accreditation, most do because accreditation indicates that an institution meets standards of quality in its faculty and academic programs.

There are six regional accrediting associations that cover the entire country. A college or university that is regionally accredited has the highest type of institutional accreditation granted in the United States. Some institutions are accredited by national agencies that accredit specific types of schools, such as religious or technical schools.

Accreditation by a recognized agency is important for several reasons:

- Credits are more easily transferred from one accredited institution to another.

- Most scholarship, fellowship and grant programs are available only for study in accredited institutions.

- Degrees and diplomas are more generally recognized among accredited institutions within the United States as well as by governments and universities in other countries.

Specific academic or professional programs at a university, such as the engineering department, may also be accredited. Professional associations, concerned about standards of education, offer accreditation reviews to assure that the course offerings, facilities and program administration (such as faculty qualifications and teaching load) meet agreed-upon standards. Two examples of such professional accrediting agencies are the Association to Advance Collegiate Schools of Business and the Accreditation Board for Engineering and Technology, but there are many others. Each institution you consider will be able to tell you the standing of their academic programs with accrediting bodies.

Accreditation alone is not a guarantee of high standards, but the lack of accreditation may be a warning that the degree or credit earned may not be accepted by other institutions or your country's government. All the colleges and universities listed in Part II of this book are accredited by either regional associations or national agencies recognized by the U.S. Department of Education and the Council for Higher Education Accreditation. (A list of these agencies appears on page 14.)

Information on accreditation can be found in the current edition of *Accredited Institutions of Postsecondary Education*, which is available in many libraries and advising centers, or at the Council for Higher Education Accreditation's website (www.chea.org). If a college is not accredited by a regional accrediting association or other nationally recognized agency, you should consult an adviser to find out more about the college before you send any application forms or money.

Credits, grading and evaluation

The "credit" system in the United States is sometimes confusing. Each course is assigned a value, called a credit or unit. The number of credits usually reflects the number of hours the class will meet with the professor during one week. In a three-credit course, the class typically will meet Monday, Wednesday and Friday for one hour of lecture each day. A four-credit course might meet Tuesday and Thursday for two hours of lecture each day, or meet three days a week for lecture and have one hour of discussion or lab. Each professor will give reading or writing assignments, usually weekly, and students should plan to work two to three hours outside of class for every hour inside class. In other words, a three-credit course may produce nine hours of homework a week.

Classroom examinations are given frequently throughout the years of undergraduate education in the United States. While small weekly written tests are common, testing may be limited to two or three large written examinations each semester, often called midterms. Almost all classes conclude with a final examination or large project. Testing gives the instructor or professor a basis for awarding grades and gives students an indication of their academic progress compared with other students in the class. At the graduate level, grades are more likely to be based on research papers in combination with some written or oral examinations.

Grades are determined by a series of evaluations and may include the cumulative assessment of all of the following: weekly quizzes, midterms, final exams, and papers, as well as class attendance and class participation. Each assignment or examination is usually graded, but your permanent record reflects only the final grade earned by the end of the course. If you do not do well on a midterm examination, there are other opportunities during the balance of the term to show the professor that you have improved. Most professors distribute a syllabus outlining the course requirements and grading system to be used. Although there is great variation in grading practices, particularly at the graduate level, most colleges in the United States use some version of the following grading system.

Grade	Represents
A or 4	Consistently high performance
B or 3	Above average
C or 2	Average
D or 1	Minimally passing
E, F or 0	Failure

Grades are recorded in your permanent record at the end of each term by the registrar. Using the points noted above and the credits assigned to each course, a grade point average is determined for each semester and accumulated for the entire time you are in the degree program. Each university has its own grading policies, and that information is usually explained in the university catalog or can be obtained from the office of the registrar.

Regional Accrediting Associations

Middle States Commission on Higher Education
3624 Market Street
Philadelphia, PA 19104-2680
www.msche.org
> Delaware, District of Columbia, Maryland, New Jersey, New York, Pennsylvania, Puerto Rico, Virgin Islands

New England Association of Schools and Colleges
209 Burlington Road, Suite 201
Bedford, MA 01730-1433
www.neasc.org
> Connecticut, Maine, Massachusetts, New Hampshire, Rhode Island, Vermont

North Central Association of Colleges and Schools Higher Learning Commission
230 South LaSalle Street, Suite 7-500
Chicago, IL 60604-1411
www.ncacihe.org
> Arizona, Arkansas, Colorado, Illinois, Indiana, Iowa, Kansas, Michigan, Minnesota, Missouri, Nebraska, New Mexico, North Dakota, Ohio, Oklahoma, South Dakota, West Virginia, Wisconsin, Wyoming

Northwest Accreditation Commission
1510 Robert Street, Suite 103
Boise, ID 83705-5194
www.northwestaccreditation.org
> Alaska, Idaho, Montana, Nevada, Oregon, Utah, Washington

Southern Association of Colleges and Schools
1866 Southern Lane
Decatur, GA 30033-4097
www.sacs.org
> Alabama, Florida, Georgia, Kentucky, Louisiana, Mississippi, North Carolina, South Carolina, Tennessee, Texas, Virginia

Western Association of Schools and Colleges
Accrediting Commission for Senior Colleges
and Universities
985 Atlantic Avenue, Suite 100
Alameda, CA 94501
www.wascsenior.org
Accrediting Commission for Community and Junior
Colleges
10 Commercial Boulevard, Suite 204
Novato, CA 94949
www.accjc.org
> American Samoa, California, Guam, Hawaii, Pacific Basin

National Accrediting Associations

ACICS   **Accrediting Council for Independent Colleges and Schools**
Washington, DC
www.acics.org

ACCSC   **Accrediting Commission of Career Schools and Colleges**
Arlington, VA
www.accsc.org

ABHE   **The Association for Biblical Higher Education**
Orlando, FL
www.abhe.org

AARTS   **Association of Advanced Rabbinical and Talmudic Schools**
11 Broadway, Suite 405
New York, NY 10004

ATS   **Association of Theological Schools in the United States and Canada**
Pittsburgh, PA
www.ats.edu

DETC   **Distance Education and Training Council**
Washington, DC
www.detc.org

TRACS   **Transnational Association of Christian Colleges and Schools**
Forest, VA
www.tracs.org

For specialized program accreditation, see *Accredited Institutions of Postsecondary Education* available from:
American Council on Education
One Dupont Circle NW
Washington, DC 20036
www.ace.edu

Community Colleges in the United States

Judy Irwin
Executive Vice President, Global and College Alliances
Center for Global Advancement of Community Colleges

U.S. community colleges, sometimes called junior or technical colleges, are the "gateway to higher education" for international students. They provide the first two years of a four-year university degree program, at affordable costs, leading to an associate degree. Students with associate degrees can transfer their course credits they earn toward a bachelor's degree at a four-year college or university. Most community colleges have special arrangements with four-year institutions, called articulation agreements, to ensure a seamless transfer process. This process is often called "2+2" in reference to the two years students spend at a community college and the two years at a university.

All U.S. higher education institutions (community colleges, four-year colleges and major universities) are accredited by the same accrediting agencies. Community college programs must meet the same stringent criteria as four-year colleges and universities to attain accreditation status. That's why universities will accept course credits obtained at community colleges.

There are nearly 1,700 two-year, associate-degree granting institutions in the United States, serving more than 11 million students. Forty-six percent of all U.S. undergraduates begin their higher education studies at a community college.

U.S. community colleges are attracting over 14 percent of the international students who study in the United States because of their numerous benefits and opportunities: significantly (approximately 50 percent) lower costs; transfer options to universities; intensive English programs to advance language ability and skills; small class sizes with a focus on individual student success; a wide range of student support services; cutting-edge technologies; hundreds of programs from which to choose; strong ties with the community leading to hands-on access to U.S. culture; and the ability to take one year of optional practice training related to one's degree, upon completion of an associate degree. (Another year of OPT can be undertaken upon completion of a bachelor's degree.)

Community colleges differ widely. Some are large, multicampus institutions located in big cities, while others are much smaller schools located in rural settings and serving smaller student populations. Housing opportunities at community colleges range from living in campus dormitories or nearby apartments, to renting rooms or arranging homestays with host families.

Alumni from community colleges include U.S. government officials, Nobel and Pulitzer Prize recipients, and award-winning producers, actors, and musicians. Some well-known alumni include Arnold Schwarzenegger, governor of California; Eileen Collins, NASA space shuttle commander; George Lucas, producer/director of the "Star Wars" movie series; Tom Hanks and Clint Eastwood, film actors; Walt Disney, founder of Disney studios and Disney World; Calvin Klein, designer; and Craig Ventnor, genome scientist.

Community colleges are a key component of higher education in the United States. They provide academically qualified and motivated international students with an opportunity to obtain high-quality and affordable education in a supportive learning environment as they begin their higher education experience in the United States.

Planning for study in the United States

Applying to college in the United States from another country can be exciting and challenging. The process may be different from the one in your country, but it need not be difficult if you get accurate information and follow the required procedures carefully.

There are over 690,000 students from other countries enrolled in degree programs at nearly 2,000 two-year and four-year colleges and universities in the United States. This represents 3.6 percent of the U.S. higher education enrollment each year. Many of these institutions have more applicants than they can accept in any year. As a result, college admission can be very competitive, especially for applicants from outside the United States.

The key to successful admission lies in careful planning and timely completion of the required steps. Keep in mind the following advice during your college planning.

Consider your own characteristics

- What kind of person are you?
- What makes you happy?
- What are your interests?
- Are you sure you know what you want to study?
- Why do you think studying in another country will be good for you?
- What about studying in another country makes you feel anxious?
- Have you been away from your family for long periods of time before?

Planning Guide

- Begin planning about 24 months before the date you wish to start studying in the United States. Contact universities that interest you at least one year in advance.

- Identify the things that are most important to you when looking for a college in the United States. Make a list of those characteristics to help you compare the colleges that interest you.

- Review and use this book. If you have access to a computer with an Internet browser, link to the College Search on collegeboard.org, where you can find out quickly which colleges have the features you want. College Search also allows you to link directly to college websites, which are a rich source of information about degrees and courses offered, costs, student services and financial aid. Some even provide a virtual campus tour.

- Consult an EducationUSA advising center or the EducationUSA Web site (http://educationusa.state.gov). Locate the center nearest you in the list at the back of this book. You can also e-mail questions in your native language to the Virtual Consulting Office of EducationUSA (www.vco-edusa.net).

- Talk with students in your country who have studied in the United States.

- Start planning your college budget. Be realistic about how you will pay for your education.

- If you plan to apply for scholarships, do so before leaving home. Little financial help is available once the school year starts.

- Be sure that your information is current and correct. Don't rely on hearsay or someone else's experience. Contact universities directly to get information and instructions about admission.

- Complete all the steps in the admission and financial aid process as early as possible. If you do not understand why a college asks for particular information or requires a particular process, ask them for more information about it.

The picture you have of yourself — your academic ability, interests, attitudes and personality — is very useful in choosing colleges and in completing the application forms you will be asked to submit. Colleges will ask you about yourself because they are interested in you and believe that personal factors play an important role in academic success.

Consider your English language skills

One of the main challenges many international students face is their English language proficiency. If your first language is not English and if your previous education was not in English, it is important to take all English language proficiency tests as soon as possible.

You will be expected to read, write, understand and speak English properly and fluently to carry out your studies. Conversational English will not be sufficient.

Colleges and universities require proof of English language proficiency when you apply and measure your skills by asking you to take a standardized test of English. Even with excellent academic qualifications, you may not be admitted if your English language proficiency is too low.

International students often underestimate the stress caused by suddenly changing cultures, education and economic systems, friends, methods of teaching and learning, and living environments. Moving suddenly from speaking and thinking in the language of your country to thinking, listening and speaking in English is very stressful. Get an accurate estimate of your ability in English so that you can enroll in a language school if needed to improve your ability before starting studies in the United States. Be sure to ask the admissions office if the institution offers an intensive course in English as a second language.

Answer the questions below to help you assess your English.

Circle one

1. **I can read textbooks written in English ...**
   A.   easily with the help of a dictionary to check new or difficult words.
   B.   with difficulty and the frequent use of a dictionary.
   C.   with great difficulty, constant use of a dictionary and help from others.
   D.   I have never tried reading a textbook in English.

2. **I can write an essay in English ...**
   A.   easily, using a dictionary to check the spelling and meaning of some words.
   B.   with difficulty and the frequent use of a dictionary and grammar book.
   C.   with great difficulty, translating what I have written in my language into English, with constant use of a dictionary and help from others.
   D.   I have never tried writing an essay in English.

3. **I can understand spoken English about a current news topic...**
   A.   easily except for special words.
   B.   with some difficulty, and only if the information is repeated at least once.
   C.   with difficulty and the use of a dictionary.
   D.   I have not listened to someone speak in English about a current news topic.

4. **I can speak in English ...**
   A.   about any topic, with the occasional use of a dictionary.
   B.   about certain topics with which I am most familiar.
   ▪   if I am asked simple questions.
   ▪   I have not had the opportunity to speak in English.

College cost and paying for your education

College cost

The profiles in Part II of this book give academic-year costs broken down by tuition and fees and living expenses. Remember that college costs are rising and are likely to be higher by the time you enter a program of study. Confirm current costs with the school when you apply.

Just as the types of educational institutions in the United States vary widely, so does the cost of education. Cost may be a major factor in deciding which college to attend. In academic year 2009-10, the average cost for U.S. residents living on campus at four-year undergraduate colleges varied from about $16,140 to $36,993 for nine months. The cost for international students was higher. You must consider living expenses during holidays and the summer and round-trip transportation from your home country. Actual tuition, fees and estimated living expenses for international students are listed in Part II of this book. The estimates do not include expenses for an automobile, unless specified. The cost of going to college in the United States is something you and your family should think about early in your college planning. Cost differs from one institution to another, so you should estimate a budget for the college you are considering. Your total budget should include the following expenses for each year of study.

Tuition and fees

Tuition and fees are generally charged on the basis of a nine-month (September-May) academic year. Some colleges also offer course work in the summer period (June-August); if you plan to take courses in the summer, increase your budget to allow for expenses for a 12-month period. Some universities charge a flat rate for tuition and some calculate tuition by the credit hour. Each course is assigned a number of credits, usually reflecting the number of "contact hours" with the professor per week for one term. A typical course in a U.S. institution is worth three credit hours. Thus, to calculate the additional cost of a summer program, multiply the number of courses you intend to take by three to obtain the total number of credit hours, then multiply that by the tuition per credit hour charge.

Tuition and fees for international students listed in this book are for the 2011-12 academic year unless otherwise stated; the costs tend to increase each year. Be sure to confirm current costs with the college when you apply. To estimate future costs, add an increase for each year. Over the past decade, annual costs have risen 5.6 percent at public four-year institutions.

The items included in fees vary from institution to institution. To compare accurately, ask what is included in the fees. Some typical fees are health insurance, student activity fees, scholarship funds, building funds, lab fees and computer usage fees.

Room and board

Room and board means basic living expenses for food and housing. No matter where you go to college, you will have to consider these expenses. Many colleges have on-campus housing. Some require students to live in a college dormitory, at least for the first year. Others do not, and students commute from housing near the college. Commuting students in general pay somewhat less for housing than students living in college dormitories, but their cost of transportation is higher. Most colleges have housing offices that can help you find local housing in an apartment or a home that you can share with other students.

The room and board cost for colleges with on-campus housing assumes that you will share a room with one student, and have regular meals in the college cafeteria. Find out if the room charges include bedding (sheets, pillows and blankets) and regular linen service.

If you will be attending college during the summer, add an estimate of the cost for housing and meals for three additional months to your budget.

Books and supplies

Colleges estimate the cost for books and supplies for the academic year. If you are planning to study in a field that requires special supplies, such as engineering, art or film, your expenses are likely to be greater than the average. If you attend summer school, add a sum to your budget for books for the summer classes.

Computers

Computers are a common requirement on college campuses today. Most universities have computer labs for student use, but some require students to have their own computers. Ask whether the university you are applying to requires you to have a personal computer. If so, calculate that into your expenses.

Transportation

The living cost figures in this book do not cover trips between the United States and your home country. Be sure to add expenses to your yearly budget for round-trip travel between your home country and college.

If you plan to live off campus and commute to college, you will incur local travel expenses. Commuter colleges have included an estimate of these expenses.

Personal expenses

These expenses include the cost of basic goods such as clothing, services such as laundry and activities such as movies and sports events. Health insurance is required. If you have dependents or if you have special medical needs, substantial additional funds will be needed to meet your living expenses. Most institutions have an estimate of the basic cost.

Sources of funding

Although there are U.S. government-sponsored and institutional financial aid programs, most of those funds are for U.S. citizens or permanent residents. For international students, the cost of higher education in the United States is primarily the student's responsibility. Although many colleges have some financial aid available for students from outside the United States, there is not enough aid to meet the need of all students.

There is more financial aid available for graduate students than for undergraduate students. In 2009–10, 79 percent of international undergraduate students paid for their education with personal or family funds. After personal and family funds, U.S. colleges and universities are the most significant source of funding for international students. In 2009–10, U.S. colleges and universities provided funding for 10.9 percent of all undergraduate students from abroad. In Part II of this book, which lists detailed information about undergraduate institutions, the far right-hand column indicates whether an institution offers financial aid to international students, the number of awards and the average amount of the awards. These lists will give you a realistic idea of your chances of receiving financial assistance from a specific institution.

You are responsible for planning how you will pay for your educational, living and travel expenses. Answer the questions below to begin your financial plan.

- Have you consulted your family, a prospective sponsor or others about your plans for financing your stay in the United States?

- Have they agreed to support you?

- If you are applying for a scholarship, have you submitted all the required documents?

- When will you be notified of the results?

Financial aid

Financial aid to students in the United States includes (1) scholarships or grants, (2) loans, which have to be repaid and (3) jobs, which provide money to help pay college costs. Financial aid may cover all college costs or only a very small fraction. Jobs require a commitment of a specified number of hours per week; teaching and research assistantships for graduate students require up to 20 hours per week.

U.S. sources of financial aid include federal and state governments, private foundations, companies and universities. Financial aid programs usually have specific requirements, such as financial need, citizenship or a particular field and level of study. International students may apply for privately sponsored scholarships where the criteria allow, but should be aware that these scholarships have a very early deadline for applications. If you have Internet access, be sure to use the Scholarship Search on the College Board's website (www.collegeboard.org) to find potential sources of funding.

It is a good idea to investigate sources of financial aid in your own country as well as those in the United States. Keep in mind that the application process for scholarships and other financial aid programs may begin as early as 18 months before your planned date of enrollment. Contact an EducationUSA advising center, the U.S. embassy or consulate in your country, your ministry of education, or other organizations about financial aid as soon as possible.

Part-time work outside of the college or university is sometimes a possible source of additional income once a student is in the United States. Keep in mind, however, that people traveling in the United States on a student visa are not allowed to work off campus until one year of academic study has been completed successfully. Then you have to get permission from the college and the Bureau of Citizenship and Immigration Services before you can work off campus part time. International students can usually work on campus. In either case, your earnings from part-time work will not cover much more than personal expenses. You should not count on employment to pay the major cost of your education.

> *"International students can typically find scholarship information in the college's publications or Web site. Many schools will offer merit scholarship consideration, and that information is pretty easy to find on the Web site, usually in the financial aid or scholarship section."*
>
> — Judith Jurek, University of Southern California, Los Angeles, Calif.

Understanding your U.S. federal income tax obligations

Many students from other countries studying in the United States are not aware that they may incur U.S. federal income tax obligations. According to the U.S. Internal Revenue Service, the international students most likely to incur U.S. tax obligations are those who receive grants or stipends or who earn income as graduate assistants.

According to IRS officials, a large number of international students actually overpay their taxes because they mistakenly believe that the government will automatically withhold the correct amount of taxes and that they therefore do not have to file a return. Seek advice in the personnel office on your campus about your tax withholding, and familiarize yourself with the U.S. tax regulations. Watch for tax seminars on your campus, or ask your international student adviser for advice.

Advice for undergraduate applicants

Choosing a college

Attending college in another country can be a very exciting and rewarding experience. It is important that you select an institution that best matches your interests and needs and offers the academic program you want to study. To find a college that offers what you need, decide what college characteristics are important to you. When you compare your own needs and interests with the characteristics of the college, you will find a good match.

Choosing a college

Make a list of what is important to you when choosing a college. Consider this list and then add other characteristics you seek.

- Does the college offer the degree you are seeking in your desired field of study?

- What type of college is it (for example, two-year community college, four-year university, private or public, urban or rural, religious affiliation)?

- How many students are enrolled? How many of them specialize in the field you're interested in? How many of them are from outside the United States?

- Can you describe the campus environment from what you have read about it?

- Is housing available on campus?

- What is the total cost of tuition, fees, room, and board (meals)? Are scholarships or other forms of financial aid available for international students?

- Is there an orientation program specifically for international students? Are there student services to help you outside the classroom, including an international student advising office? If you need help with your English skills, does the college offer an intensive language learning program?

Admission Advice

"It's all about finding the right fit, or the best fit, for that student. What you need to do is ask questions about yourself first. What kind of environment do I want to be in? What do I want to study? Do I want a preprofessional education or a liberal arts education? Do I want a big city or a small city? Do I want a religiously affiliated institution? Once you ask those questions, you can start plugging your desires and priorities into the schools that fit best."

— Joseph DeCrosta, Duquesne University, Pittsburgh, Pa.

"It's important to decide whether you need an active international student community and how much support you think you will need. If there's an international student organization that you can become a part of, how active is it? If you can, determine whether international students are mainstreamed into the college community or whether they're more of a segregated population. That said, any international student should be sure that the college has an international student adviser."

— David Dillman, Austin College, Sherman, Texas

Finding out more about colleges

Learning as much as you can about the colleges you are considering increases your chances of making a good decision on where to apply. One of the best sources is the Internet. Most U.S. colleges have websites that provide you with complete information about academic programs and course offerings, admission requirements and procedures for applying. Their sites may include photos of the campus and its environment or a virtual campus tour. The College Board's website (www.collegeboard.org) provides detailed resources to plan for, apply to and pay for college. In addition, there are many other sources of information and advising that may be available in your country. The U.S. government, foreign governments and nonprofit organizations support these activities. There is usually no cost to you, although a minimal charge may be requested to cover the expense of printing booklets or the postage if you request information by mail. The U.S. Department of State promotes American higher education through its EducationUSA advising network, located in the following types of centers:

- U.S. embassies, consulates, American centers, American corners and libraries
- Fulbright commissions and foundations
- Binational centers
- Nonprofit exchange organizations, such as the Institute of International Education or AMIDEAST
- University information centers and libraries
- Public libraries

You may also check listings in local telephone books or call or write the U.S. embassy or the ministry of education in your country, stating that (1) you are seeking information and advice about academic study in the United States and (2) you would like to know where to visit or write.

A list of advising centers is provided in Part III of this book. Advice from knowledgeable and experienced advisers can help you make realistic plans and complete the admission process successfully.

Another helpful source of information in your country is people who have studied in the United States. Talk to them, but remember that their experiences will be influenced by how recently they were there and by the location and type of institution they attended. The environment they chose may be different from the one you seek. However, they should be able to give you some ideas about adjusting to college life in the United States. An advising center may offer discussions or workshops with returnees and U.S. college alumni.

Admission Advice

"It's very important for prospective international students to communicate with current students, especially from their home country, even perhaps from their own high school, who may be attending an institution. That way, culturally at least, they can ask the types of questions that are most relevant to them. A student from small-town Iowa and a student calling from Thailand — they might not quite relate on the same level. Speaking with someone from your own culture is probably most helpful. Speaking to parents of current students from your home country is also very helpful."

— Mark G. Reid, Director of International Admission, University of Miami, Fla.

The following sources can provide important facts about U.S. colleges:

The Internet. Most colleges have websites, and their addresses are listed in the alphabetical list of colleges in Part III. When you contact an organization, ask for its website address.

You can also use the Internet to search for colleges with the features you want, using a free service such as the College Board's College Search (www.collegeboard.org/collegesearch).

Other college guidebooks and software. The book you're reading provides current information on international student enrollment, tests required, application deadlines, application fees, tuition and fees, room and board, financial aid, and the availability of international student advisers, orientation and intensive English language programs at U.S. colleges. The *College Board College Handbook* provides in-depth, current information on size, location, degrees and majors offered, admission requirements, cost, student profile, activities, athletics, and special programs and services. The *College Board Book of Majors* provides lists of major fields of study at the undergraduate and graduate degree levels and the colleges that offer each major. It also provides descriptions of the most popular majors.

College catalogs. Colleges produce catalogs and bulletins that give up-to-date information on their admissions requirements, major fields of study, faculty, college costs and other important factors. Most catalogs are available on the Internet and less often in paper form.

College representatives. Some institutions send representatives to other countries to talk about their colleges and to meet students who may be interested in applying. Contact the U.S. embassy, an advising center or the ministry of education to find out whether representatives from colleges will be visiting your country or participating in an online college fair.

Once you have investigated the colleges that you are considering and determined where you wish to study, you are ready to send an application. Since the procedures for applying to college in the United States are likely to be different from those in your own country, here are guidelines to help make this a smooth process.

When to apply

You should begin the application process as soon as you have decided which colleges best meet your needs. This usually should be no later than 12 months before the date you expect to begin study in the United States. Review the planning calendar at the beginning of this book.

Colleges may give a deadline for applications. Usually the deadline is the final date by which they must receive the application. Some colleges will continue to accept applications after the deadline, but they will only process the application if they do not fill their class with applications from students who applied by the deadline. For late applicants, there may be no housing and no financial assistance.

Make a checklist of the admission requirements and deadlines from your college comparison worksheet. Set your own completion dates well ahead of the colleges' stated deadlines, and check off each step as you complete it. Remember to send all required documents and forms as soon as possible. U.S. colleges usually review applications only when *all* the required documents have been received.

Applying to college in the United States

Requesting and filing the application

Most colleges will respond to e-mail requests for information. Whether writing by airmail or using electronic mail, when you first contact a college in the United States, supply enough information so that you will receive correct information in return. Include your intended field of study, your educational background, the term in which you wish to start and information about your source of funds for paying for your education.

The use of computers in the application process and in completing other college procedures is very common. If at all possible, use the electronic application provided by the college. This will accelerate the application process for you and make it easier for the college to process your application.

After you have received an application packet from the colleges of your choice, you should:

- Review the programs offered and the academic preparation required for them.

- Note the important dates, such as deadlines.

- Note which parts of the application will require a contribution by another person. For example, does the college ask for teacher recommendations?

- Pay special attention to the information about tuition, fees and living costs to be sure you understand the financial commitment involved.

You are now ready to file your application for admission. Plan to apply to more than one college in order to increase your opportunities for admission.

Admission Advice

"Some international students will have limited English skills, especially when they are looking at our intensive English program, and may be shy about asking questions because of this. I encourage students to e-mail us anyway."

— Ann Gogerty, Iowa State University, Ames, Iowa

"Before e-mailing a college, look at its Web site to see if your question can be answered with information that's there. Keep the questions short, clear and succinct. The other thing is to be patient. It may take a few days for someone to get to your e-mail."

— Judith Jurek, University of Southern California, Los Angeles

"Don't write chat-room English to college administrators!"

— Ken Bus, Glendale Community College, Glendale, Ariz.

Completing the application form

Many colleges use a preliminary application for an initial review of your background. This preliminary decision may save both you and the university some time and money. Whether you complete a preliminary application or the official application, be sure to read all instructions carefully and answer every question. Many colleges offer an electronic application on the Internet. Be sure to look for it and use it if you have access to appropriate technology.

Application fee

Most colleges charge a nonrefundable application fee. Some colleges waive the fee if you use their electronic application. The fee must be sent in U.S. dollars; follow the instructions provided with the application form.

Writing the essay

As part of the application for admission, most colleges require one or more essays in which you respond to questions provided by the college, write a biographical statement, or describe your academic goals, your previous accomplishments, and reasons why you wish to attend college. Instructions for specific information requested as part of the essays will be included in the application packet. Give each essay a lot of thought because it is given careful consideration by the admissions staff when making a decision about your application. Type the essay or write very clearly.

Admission Advice

"We ask for an essay and give students flexibility on what they write about. It's important for us to see that they can communicate well in English, grammatically and logically."

— David Dillman, Austin College, Sherman, Texas

"I want the essay to come alive. I want to know that person as well as I can on paper. And that's a hard thing, because we want somebody to self-disclose, and that's not necessarily the model in a lot of non-Western cultures."

— Peter Briggs, Michigan State University, East Lansing, Mich.

Important things to remember when completing your application

- Use the same translation of your name on all documents, preferably the one on your passport. If the name is different on some records, enclose an explanation.

- Note the proper dates for filing the application.

- Read and follow the essay instructions carefully.

- Enclose proper financial documentation.

- Include all fees requested.

- If you have an e-mail address and/or fax number, be sure to include it.

- Type the application form and essay, or write clearly.

- Send complete official academic records or certified copies of your academic records along with your application. Have official translations prepared, where necessary, and attach them to the original/official documents.

- Take all required tests in time for your scores to be considered with your application.

Your academic records

The colleges to which you apply will require a complete set of records of your academic performance at previous schools attended. Many colleges will accept unofficial copies for their preliminary evaluation but will require original or official documents to confirm their review. If your original records are not in English, submit an official translation with your academic records. Some EducationUSA advising centers can provide "apostille," or internationally certified, copies or translations of your academic records.

Admission and placement tests

Almost all institutions will require you to take one or more tests as part of the application process. Most colleges and universities require admission tests, such as the SAT and SAT Subject Tests. The tests can be used for admission decisions or for placement — that is, deciding whether you need additional study in some areas or whether you are equal to or ahead of other students being accepted to the college. Tests that are computer-based may be taken any time that is convenient for you. You are advised to register in advance, particularly if you intend to take a test from November through January. Where tests are given on a fixed date, you must register well in advance for a space to take the test. See the test registration schedule on page 32.

Each college will list the required tests in its application instructions. Be sure to take all required tests as early as possible because they will be considered when the college makes a decision about your admission to the university. Check the college application for required tests. See the test information section on page 31 for a description of the various tests.

Undergraduates may also be required to take placement tests in specific subject areas such as English, mathematics or the sciences to assess knowledge in a particular subject. Placement tests are usually taken after arrival on campus, and the information is used in course selection so that students neither repeat things they already know nor are placed in a course for which they do not have the sufficient background.

Letters of recommendation

Some colleges require letters of recommendation from one or more adults who know you well. Letters of recommendation by themselves will not ensure admission, and letters that do not appear to assess the candidate honestly may hinder an applicant's chance. The following guidelines may be useful when requesting letters of recommendation:

- Letters of recommendation should be honest and balanced. A letter that is unrealistically favorable is less useful than one that explains possible areas where you need improvement.

- You should request letters from two or three different people who are familiar with your academic or professional achievement — among them teachers, professors, school counselors and employers. A family member or personal friend is usually not acceptable.

- Letters should focus on your academic abilities more than on your character, but may include information about your community service, volunteer work, employment, service to others and leadership qualities.

- Admission officers reading letters of recommendation find the following information useful:

  Academic record: discussion of your stronger and weaker academic areas; explanation of any gaps in your schooling, such as time off, school closings and so forth.

  Achievements: special accomplishments in school, work or family should be mentioned. Awards you have received should be described so that the admissions officer will understand their significance.

Unusual talents: special skills with languages or in the arts, athletic ability and so on, should be mentioned.

- Give the person writing the letter clear instructions for scanning and e-mailing the letter or for sending the letter airmail to the address the college provides. Ask them to type or print clearly.

Auditions and portfolios

Schools of architecture, film and the arts usually require additional information about you in order to assess your qualifications for admission to their programs. This may include portfolios of your work for art, architecture, and design programs, and auditions for music and theater programs. They will often accept audiotaped or videotaped representations of auditions from applicants who are unable to perform in person.

Interviews

Some colleges require interviews for admission to some or all of their programs. Interviews may be conducted in your home country by alumni, by visiting staff from the colleges, at recruitment fairs or by individuals designated by the college. During the interview, be clear about your education goals and the reasons you want to attend this particular college, and be prepared to ask questions.

Your English skills

Strong English language skills will be very important to your success while studying in the United States. The level of proficiency expected by each college should be identified in the application for admission. Some colleges offer English as a second language (ESL) programs on the campus or nearby to help you improve your English language skills. Be sure to take the English language test required by your chosen college so the college can assess your readiness to study in English. Please refer to the test information on page 34 to find out more about the Test of English as a Foreign Language (TOEFL).

Other Requirements

Health forms and health insurance

Once you are admitted, you may be required to complete forms about your health. If a form is not provided, have a health examination and obtain a certificate written in English.

Most colleges and universities require health insurance while you are enrolled. Refer to the section on health on page 40 for more detailed information.

Financial documentation

A document certifying the amount and sources of income available to you for study in the United States will be required. Most U.S. institutions will send you instructions and a special form to complete. The documentation must show that you have resources to pay for the first year of your college program and a reasonable financial plan for paying for the balance of your education. Once an admissions decision is made, the college will send you the appropriate U.S. government form so you can apply for a student or exchange visitor visa. Refer to the visa information on page 35 for more information regarding financial documentation and procedures for coming to the United States.

Financial aid forms

Many colleges and universities that offer financial aid to international students require applicants to complete a detailed financial aid application form, which is separate from the college application form. Typically, these forms ask the following kinds of questions:

- What is your parents' total annual income?

- What is your annual income?

- What are your annual living expenses?

- What is the value of any assets you and your parents have, such as a house, a car, savings and investments?

- How many family members are in college?

- What plans do you have for locating financial aid from sources other than the college or university?

Most colleges will provide information about the financial aid application process on their Web sites. The forms required may vary by college, and you need to make sure you understand each college's specific financial aid application requirements. Some institutions use their own forms. Others use the CSS/Financial Aid PROFILE®, an online application that allows you to enter information once and electronically submit the data to several institutions.

Complete and submit all the financial aid application materials when you apply for admission. Be sure to answer the questions as completely as possible. Most colleges will ask for documentation of the information you provide on the financial aid application; gather and save those documents as you complete the forms. Be sure to submit any paper financial aid materials by fax or use airmail or courier to the correct address, which may be different from the address you use for the college application.

What happens next

Notice of receipt. Most colleges will send you a notice confirming that they have received your application. If you have not received such a notice within a month to six weeks from the time you submit your application (either by mail or e-mail), you should inquire to be sure it was received and is complete. Be consistent in using the same e-mail address throughout the process.

Evaluating your application. The evaluation of all the admission applications a college receives can take several months. Some colleges send notifications to all students at one time; others respond as soon as an individual admission decision is made. You can eliminate delays in your evaluation by following application instructions carefully and responding to requests for additional information immediately.

Offers of admission. Accompanying your offer of admission will be a packet of information about the college and its programs — things you need to know to get ready to enter the college. It will usually include information about campus housing and orientation programs, and may have forms for you to complete and return. You may be asked to submit a fee to hold a place at the college once you have been offered admission. (See "After colleges decide" on page 35.)

Orientation. Most colleges have orientation programs for new students; many offer special orientation programs for international students. You should try to attend these programs to acquaint yourself with the college environment as well as to obtain program advice.

Other things you should know

Transferring from one U.S. college to another. It is quite common in the United States for students to transfer from one college to another. They may attend a community college for one or two years and then transfer to a four-year college or university; sometimes they transfer from one four-year college to another. If you begin your studies in a community college and want to go on to a four-year college for a bachelor's degree, be sure to plan your studies with an adviser. Without careful course selection, you may extend the time it takes to earn your degree because the college you transfer to may require basic courses other than the ones you have taken.

Transferring academic credits. In the United States, colleges allow the transfer of university-level academic credits from one institution to another and will apply those credits toward your degree at the new institution. This is particularly important when transferring from a two-year to a four-year college. Transferring credits is also possible at the graduate level, though usually only a limited number are allowed. The previous course work must be comparable in content to an equivalent course offered at your new university and must be applicable to the degree you are pursuing. Although there is no guarantee that all previous course work will be accepted, universities make every effort to

apply courses either as general education credit or as fulfillment of a major subject requirement. Your new university will provide you with an evaluation of your credentials as well as documentation of your progress toward your degree. This information will enable you to determine the length of time it may take you to complete your degree.

Comparing colleges and universities

The more information you can gather on colleges and universities, the better your chance of making a good decision about applying to appropriate institutions. Look at the college listings in Part II of this book. If you are interested in undergraduate study, also use the College Search on www.collegeboard.org to identify colleges that have the features you want, read the descriptions in the *College Board College Handbook*, and consult other sources of information that are available to you.

There is no ideal number of colleges and universities to select for application, but advisers often recommend that students identify at least three to six institutions.

The worksheets on the following pages can help you compare institutions on the basis of the characteristics important in choosing and applying to colleges. For each characteristic, write how each college matches (or does not match) your preference. Some of the characteristics you may be comparing are:

- **Degree level.** For which degree do you plan to study at this college or university?

- **Location.** In what city or town, state and region of the country is the college or university located?

- **Type of institution.** Is this a public or private institution? Is it a two-year community college, four-year liberal arts college, university or graduate institution? Does the college admit men only, women only or is it coeducational?

- **Major/field of study.** What field or fields of study that interest you does the institution offer?

- **Religious affiliation.** Was the college or university founded by or is it administered by a religious organization? Does this affect student lifestyle?

- **Enrollment size.** How many students are enrolled in the undergraduate colleges or graduate divisions in which you would be enrolled?

- **International student enrollment.** Does the college enroll many or few students from outside the United States? Are the students from diverse regions?

- **Campus environment.** Is the institution's campus urban, suburban or rural?

- **Housing.** Is on-campus housing available?

- **Academic background of students.** Do most students successfully complete their first year at the college? Do they return as sophomores?

- **Student activities.** Are there groups or organizations on campus to support the cultural, political, social or other activities that interest you?

- **Athletics.** If athletic competition is important to you, does the college offer the sports programs you want?

- **Test requirements.** Is TOEFL required? What is the minimum acceptable score? Is an admission test (e.g., SAT) required?

- **Cost.** What is the estimated international student cost for tuition, fees, room and board for nine months? For 12 months? (Remember, your miscellaneous personal expenses, health insurance and travel expenses will also be part of your total budget.)

- **Financial aid.** Is financial aid available to international students? How many international students receive aid? What is the average amount available for each student who receives aid?

- **English as a second language program.** Is an intensive ESL program available on campus? Is there a writing center for additional help?

- **Conditional admission based on English proficiency.** Will the institution provisionally accept students for academic study who do not meet English proficiency requirements?

- **Deadlines.** When must applications for admission and financial aid be completed and received by the institution?

College comparison worksheet (sample)

Characteristics important to you	College 1 Yoder College	College 2 State University	College 3 Harrison University
Degree level	Bachelor's	Bachelor's	Bachelor's
Location	Baltimore, MD (Mid-Atlantic)	Minneapolis, MN (Midwest)	Boston, MA (New England)
Type of institution	Private college	Public university	Private university
Major	Engineering	Engineering	Engineering
Enrollment size	2,100	10,500 (very large)	6,800
International student enr.	18	113	182
Housing	yes	yes	yes
Academic background	Top half of class, 90% continue after first year	Top half	Most in top third, 45% continue to graduate studies
Test requirements	TOEFL SAT	TOEFL 550 mins.	TOEFL 550 mins. SAT
Cost	$8,030 (9 months) $11,100 (12 months)	$13,400 (9 months) $17,850 (12 months)	$11,950 (9 months) $15,180 (12 months)
Financial aid	yes 12 applied for financial aid, 50% received aid	no	yes 109 applied for aid, 30% received aid
Application deadline	15 February	30 January	1 March
Financial aid deadline	15 March		30 December

College comparison worksheet

Characteristics important to you	College 1	College 2	College 3

Test information

The information tables in this book tell you which tests may be required of international students. Verify which tests are required by the colleges that interest you. Also, familiarize yourself with the format of the test you will be taking. When you register to take a test, ask for the information bulletin and work through the sample questions or sample test in the bulletin.

If you have access to the Internet, go to the websites of the various testing organizations to review the test formats, or take a sample test.

It is important to get up-to-date information about tests that are required by colleges to which you may apply. Although these standardized tests are offered at test centers throughout the world, they are not offered in every country on each test date or in each test format. For example, TOEFL, the test used by most colleges to evaluate English language proficiency, is now most widely offered in an Internet-based format, but is also offered as a paper-based test at designated testing centers. Write or call for information well ahead of time; registration dates often fill up to two months before the test date, particularly between October and February.

College Board tests commonly required or recommended by U.S. institutions are described below.

The SAT®

Overview: The SAT is the most widely used admission test among colleges and universities. The SAT helps colleges get to know students better by giving them insight into how they think, solve problems and communicate. The SAT measures what students have learned in the classroom — basic skills such as reading, writing and mathematics — and how well they apply that knowledge.

Type of test: Undergraduate admission and placement.

Purpose: A student's SAT score combined with his or her high school grades is the best indicator of how well that student will do in college. The SAT gives colleges a more objective way to evaluate what students know and their potential for succeeding in college. It also helps equalize the academic experiences of students from diverse education systems.

Generally required of: Students seeking admission to the first year of undergraduate study.

Format: The SAT includes critical reading, mathematics and writing sections. Each section of the SAT is scored on a scale of 200–800, and the writing section contains two subscores → one for multiple-choice questions and the other for a 25-minute written essay. The SAT is typically taken by high school juniors and seniors. It is also administered widely outside the United States (a calendar of testing dates appears on page 32). The SAT is 3 hours and 45 minutes.

For more information: Visit sat.collegeboard.org, where you can register online. You can also refer to the international edition of the *SAT Registration Guide* or the *SAT Practice Guide*, both of which you can usually obtain from your local EducationUSA advising center at no charge.

SAT Subject Tests™

Overview: SAT Subject Tests are designed to measure students' knowledge and achievement in particular subject areas. The SAT Subject Tests are the only U.S. admission tests that give students the opportunity to demonstrate mastery of content in specific subjects, such as English, history, mathematics, science and various foreign languages.

Type of test: Undergraduate admission and placement.

Purpose: Many colleges use the SAT Subject Tests to make admission decisions, for course placement, and to advise students about course selection. Some colleges specify the SAT Subject Tests they require for admission or placement; others allow applicants to choose which tests to take.

Generally required of: Undergraduates applying for admission as first-year students to selective institutions. One or more Subject Tests may be required. See the list of colleges that require or recommend the Subject Tests in Part III of this book.

Format: One-hour multiple-choice tests in the following subjects: English Literature, U.S. History, World History, Mathematics Level 1 and Level 2 (a calculator is required for some of the questions in the math tests), Biology Ecological/Molecular, Chemistry, Physics, Chinese with Listening, French, French with Listening, German, German with Listening, Modern Hebrew, Italian, Japanese with Listening, Korean with Listening, Latin, Spanish, and Spanish with Listening.

2011–2012 SAT Program Test Calendar						
Test Dates	**Oct. 1***	**Nov. 5**	**Dec. 3**	**Jan. 28***	**May 5***	**June 2**
Registration Deadlines						
Early**	*Aug 23*	*Sept 27*	*Oct 25*	*Dec 20*	*Mar 27*	*Apr 24*
Regular	*Sept 9*	*Oct 7*	*Nov 8*	*Dec 30*	*Apr 6*	*May 22*
SAT	■	■	■	■	■	■
SAT Subject Tests						
Literature	■	■	■	■	■	■
United States (U.S.) History	■	■	■	■	■	■
World History			■			■
Math Level 1	■	■	■	■	■	■
Math Level 2	■	■	■	■	■	■
Biology E/M (Ecological/Molecular)	■	■	■	■	■	■
Chemistry	■	■	■	■	■	■
Physics	■	■	■	■	■	■
Languages: *Reading Only*						
French	■			■	■	■
German						■
Modern Hebrew						■
Italian			■			
Latin			■			■
Spanish	■		■		■	■
Languages: *Reading and Listening*						
Chinese		■				
French		■				
German		■				
Japanese		■				
Korean		■				
Spanish		■				

* *Question-and-Answer Service available.*
** *Applies to closer-to-home testing and registration through SAT International Representatives.*
Note: *Registration deadlines are subject to change. Visit sat.collegeboard.org for updated listings. Sunday test dates follow each Saturday test date for students who cannot test on Saturday because of religious observance.*

AP® Exams

Type of test: Undergraduate credit, advanced placement or both are awarded by almost every university in the United States and Canada, and numerous institutions worldwide. In addition, universities in 60 countries worldwide recognize AP when making credit, advanced placement and/or admission decisions.

Purpose: To measure students' mastery of content within university-level courses taught in secondary schools throughout the world. Universities grant advanced placement, credit or both for successful AP Exam scores. More than 30 exams are administered during a two-week period in May.

Format: Most AP Exams are approximately three hours in length; some are shorter. Except for the three Studio Art exams, which consist of a portfolio assessment, AP Exams include a multiple-choice section and a free-response section. AP Exams in world languages and cultures include a speaking section with recorded student responses.

For more information: Visit the College Board website (www.collegeboard.org/apstudents) or contact:

AP Services
P.O. Box 6671
Princeton, NJ 08541-6671
USA
609-771-7300
888-225-5427 (toll free in the United States and Canada)
e-mail: apexams@info.collegeboard.org

2012 AP Exam Schedule

Week 1	Morning Session 8 a.m.	Afternoon Session 12 Noon	
Monday, May 7	Chemistry Environmental Science	Psychology	
Tuesday, May 8	Computer Science A Spanish Language	Art History	
Wednesday, May 9	Calculus AB Calculus BC	Chinese Language and Culture	
Thursday, May 10	English Literature	Japanese Language and Culture Latin: Vergil	
Friday, May 11	German Language United States History	European History	

Week 2	Morning Session 8 a.m.	Afternoon Session 12 Noon	2 p.m.
Monday, May 14	Biology Music Theory	Physics B Physics C Mechanics	Physics C: E&M
Tuesday, May 15	United States Government & Politics	Comparative Government & Politics French Language	
Wednesday, May 16	English Language	Statistics	
Thursday, May 17	Macroeconomics World History	Microeconomics Italian Language and Culture	
Friday, May 18	Human Geography Spanish Literature		

*Last day for Coordinators to submit digital portfolios and gather 2-D Design and Drawing students for physical portfolio assembly.

†Physics C: Mechanics will be given at 12 noon; Physics C: Electricity & Magnetism will be given at 2 p.m.

Up-to-date information on AP credit policies of U.S. universities may be found at www.collegeboard.org/ap/creditpolicy.

Policies of universities outside the United States may be found at www.collegeboard.org/apintl.

CLEP® (College-Level Examination Program®)

Type of test: Undergraduate credit-by-examination program.

Purpose: To test knowledge of material normally taught in introductory college courses and give students the opportunity to earn undergraduate credit. Knowledge may have been acquired in the classroom or through independent study, academic interests, or on-the-job training. Each college sets its own policy regarding which CLEP exams it will grant credit for and how many credits it will award. There are 33 CLEP exams available in various subject areas, including mathematics, science, social sciences and history, literature, world languages and business.

Who takes CLEP: Adults returning to college, students currently enrolled in college, recent high school graduates and international students who wish to obtain credit from a U.S. university for knowledge acquired at an institution in another country.

Format: The exam is administered on computer at 1,700 colleges and universities in the United States and at some international locations.

For more information: Consult the CLEP website (clep.collegeboard.org), call +011 609 771-7865, or write to:
CLEP
P.O. Box 6600
Princeton, NJ 08541-6600
USA
e-mail: clep@info.collegeboard.org

Other Tests

ACT

The ACT is another admission test. Consult the ACT website for more information.

TOEFL (Test of English as a Foreign Language)

Type of test: English proficiency.

Purpose: To measure the ability of nonnative English speakers to communicate in an academic setting.

Required of: Undergraduates seeking a first degree and graduate students seeking an advanced degree.

Format: There are two versions of the TOEFL test: Internet-based (TOEFL iBT) and paper-based (TOEFL PBT). Results for all versions are valid for two years from the test administration date. It is important to understand where each version will be administered and the differences between them.

Internet-based test (TOEFL iBT): Test-takers have up to four hours to complete the TOEFL iBT test, which has four sections: Reading, Listening, Speaking and Writing. The test is offered on selected dates at authorized ETS test centers. The test emphasizes the use of language for communication by combining, or integrating, the language skills needed to succeed in an academic setting. For more information, consult the TOEFL website (www.ets.org/toefl).

Paper-based test: The TOEFL paper-based test (TOEFL PBT) has three sections: Listening Comprehension, Structure and Written Expression, and Reading Comprehension. There is also a 30-minute essay called the Test of Written English (TWE) that is given at every TOEFL PBT administration. The entire administration takes approximately 3 1/2 hours. The paper-based test will be administered on a limited basis in selected locations on specific dates in countries where TOEFL iBT is not available and to supplement the TOEFL iBT test center network.

After colleges decide

You should receive a reply about two or three months after the college receives all your application documents. If not, write to the admission office and ask about its decision.

If you are accepted. You will be asked to let the college know by a specific date whether you will enroll. Many colleges require a deposit to confirm enrollment, usually $50 to $100, which may not be refundable. This is credited to your tuition when you register. In your admission packet, you will receive a document for use in applying for a visa (SEVIS Form I-20A-B or Form DS-2019 for study in the United States). Be sure to confirm housing reservations with the college and submit the required housing deposits, which average about $200.

If you are accepted by more than one college. If you already know which college you prefer, notify the other colleges that you will not attend, so that admission can be offered to another student. If you are not sure which college you prefer, review your college comparison worksheet to help you decide.

Admission Advice

"International students, given that they can seldom visit campuses, are strongly influenced by family members and others who have been to the institution. Ask around and try to get a feel for each institution. If you're from Malaysia, try to contact a Malaysian student association at the college and ask everything from 'What's it really like there?' to 'Will you pick me up at the airport?'"

— Peter Briggs, Michigan State University, East Lansing, Mich.

If you are not offered the financial aid you need. Some colleges may not be able to offer financial aid, or you may have to choose between one that offers aid and another that offers none or a lesser amount. If you can't meet the college expense budget without additional help, find out if there are any resources in your country from which you can get financial help. Contact an EducationUSA advising center or the ministry of education to see if there are organizations that have helped other students in your country in recent years. However, keep in mind that deadlines for scholarships and financial aid are often earlier than the college application deadlines. Start your financial planning as soon as possible. Your admitting institution may ask you to submit a special form documenting your financial status or to complete the College Board International Student Certification of Finances and/or International Student Financial Aid Application.

Looking ahead

Once you have made your decision, there are many responsibilities to take care of.

Obtaining a passport and visa. You must have a valid passport to apply for a student visa. Your U.S. college or university will send you the documentation necessary to obtain a nonimmigrant student visa from the U.S. embassy or consulate in the country where you are located. The U.S. Department of State maintains consular offices at U.S. embassies and in many major cities around the world. Information on their location and details about the visa application process can be found at www.unitedstatesvisas.gov. Apply for a visa early to avoid any possible delays.

An F-1 student visa is granted to most students who have been accepted for admission to an academic institution in the United States. To obtain an F-1 visa, you must have a SEVIS Form I-20A-B, Certificate of Eligibility for Nonimmigrant (F-1) Student Status, from your U.S. college or university, as well as financial documentation proving that you have the funds to complete an academic program at that college. The documentation may consist of a notarized affidavit from a relative or other person who is supporting you financially, a bank statement showing that you have funds to meet at least your first-year expenses at college, and/or a letter from a government or private agency that is providing funds to support you.

Students entering on an international exchange program or with funding other than their personal funds may have to get a J-1 nonimmigrant Exchange Visitor visa rather than an F-1 visa. This includes students who are being supported by funds from the U.S. government, the government of the student's country, international organizations or a U.S. college or university. If your U.S. college requires a J-1 visa, the college will send you a Form DS-2019, Certificate of Eligibility for Exchange Visitor (J-1) Status. You must take the Form DS-2019, with required financial documentation, to the U.S. embassy or consulate in your country to apply for a J-1 visa.

Students applying for either an F-1 or J-1 visa may have to provide additional documentation. For complete information about U.S. visa issuance requirements, contact the U.S. embassy or consulate. Be sure to read the rules governing the visa status on the form you receive from the university, as it provides different privileges for employment, dependents, practical training and length of stay in the United States. With either visa, you are eligible to enroll as a full-time student and pursue the educational objective for which you entered the United States. You are advised not to enter the United States as a tourist (B-2) or without a visa, because you will not be eligible to enroll in college and pursue full-time studies in the United States.

If you wish to bring a spouse and/or children under age 21 with you, you must prove that you have the funds to support them. The college or university you will be attending will determine the amount of money necessary to support dependents.

Be sure to contact your local EducationUSA advising center for information about the visa application process and tips on preparing for your consular interview.

Upon arrival in the United States. As a guest in the United States, from the time you enter the United States until the time you complete studies and return home, you will be subject to U.S. laws and regulations. These affect your ability to enter the United States, study, work and travel. Although you don't need to know every detail about U.S. immigration law, you should become familiar with the most important regulations that affect your status as a student.

While in the United States, you alone will be responsible for maintaining your status as a student in the United States. The best place to find accurate information about immigration regulations is the international student office on your campus. Although your friends might be willing to share their own experiences and advice with you, every student's situation is different, and the information given by your friends might not be the right information for you.

When you arrive at the U.S. port of entry, usually an airport, you will encounter various representatives of the U.S. government. One will request the Arrival-Departure Record (Form I-94), which you will have received on the airplane, and your passport. The inspector may ask you some questions about your plans and your source of support while in the United States. Such questions are routine, and if you have the proper documents you will be admitted without delay. The I-94 will be stapled into your passport. This card indicates the period of time you have permission to remain in the United States to study. For nonimmigrant students, the notation is "D/S," or "Duration of Status," to signify that you may remain in the United States for the time necessary to complete your program of study.

The inspector will take either your SEVIS Form I-20A-B or DS-2019. After making appropriate notations on the form, part of it will be returned to you — page 3 of Form I-20A-B if you are an F-1 student or a copy of the Form DS-2019 if you are a J-1 Exchange Visitor. It is very important that you check the immigration notations on your documents immediately for possible errors and retain this copy with your passport; it is a record of your stay in the United States, which includes date of entry, employment authorization and expected school graduation date. Keep these documents in a safe place at all times. Also make copies and file them separately.

Upon arrival on your campus. Meet the international student adviser on your campus as soon as possible. Most colleges and universities hold orientation programs for new students, and many have special sessions for new international students. Most of your questions will be answered during these programs, and you will meet other new students before classes begin.

In addition to providing an orientation to your new surroundings and important details about your new community and college, the international adviser can help you with any required modifications to your immigration status, such as getting stay extensions once you are in the United States. Note that your passport must be valid for six months into the future at all times. The international adviser can also give you information on work eligibility and practical training. Students with F-1 or J-1 immigrant status may get permission to work in the United States subject to certain restrictions and the availability of jobs. Be sure not to work without permission, or you will jeopardize your student status.

Important regulations for F-1 and J-1 students

There are some important regulations that apply to international students while studying in the United States. You are responsible for being aware of, and following, these guidelines.

Full course of study

International students are expected to register for a full course of study during each semester or term. For undergraduate students, this means a minimum of 12 credit hours or its equivalent each semester. You are not required to carry a full course of study during your annual vacation or during your final semester of study. The full course of study requirements may vary at colleges that are on the quarter or trimester system. Consult your international student adviser about the requirements for you. Failure to carry a full course of study could result in your losing eligibility for employment and other important benefits. Note that there are limits on online enrollments for international students.

Processing changes in your I-20A-B or DS-2019

If you change your major field of study or your degree objective, transfer from one college to another or need an extension of the expected completion date of the academic program indicated on your I-20A-B or DS-2019, you must process the change officially with a new form or entry in the SEVIS system database. Consult your international student adviser or J-1 sponsor.

Departing and reentering the United States

You must have your I-20A-B or DS-2019 form endorsed each time you leave and reenter the United States. For an endorsement, F-1 students should consult the international student adviser; J-1 students should contact the sponsor.

Many international students make plans to travel during winter, spring or summer breaks. International student offices can be very busy in the weeks leading up to a break, so you should make an appointment to have your I-20 A-B or DS-2019 form endorsed as soon as you have made your travel plans.

Employment in the United States

Many international students are anxious to work in the United States. Employment can be a means of learning about American culture, developing professional skills and earning additional income. However, employment of nonimmigrants in the United States is strictly regulated, and failure to follow U.S. employment law can result in loss of your student or exchange visitor status. Therefore, it is important to understand and follow the rules that govern your prospective employment. Refer to the overview provided below for general information, and consult your international student adviser for details.

You are eligible to apply for and accept employment only if you are in good standing with the immigration authorities. This means that you must carry a full course of study and process all the appropriate forms for change of major, degree objective and school transfer for approval. If you do not maintain your approved status, you may face serious consequences.

Most student employment falls into one of these three categories:

- **Part-time employment on campus:** F-1 students are eligible to accept on-campus employment up to 20 hours per week while school is in session, and full-time (more than 20 hours per week) during holidays, school breaks and vacation periods. Provided that a student is properly maintaining F-1 status, no written authorization is required. J-1 students are also eligible for part-time on-campus employment, but J-1 employment must be authorized in writing on the DS-2019 or in a separate letter from the sponsor.

- **Employment for economic necessity:** Some students experience unexpected financial crises after beginning study in the United States. Examples of such crises could include sudden devaluation of home-country currency, loss of scholarship, or the illness or death of a private sponsor. In such cases, if a student is able to show that off-campus part-time employment could provide a solution to the emergency, he or she may request employment authorization. Check with the international student office for the most current regulations and procedures. Off-campus employment must always be authorized in writing before a student begins work.

- **F-1 Practical Training/J-1 Academic Training:** Employment that applies the concepts learned in the student's academic program is considered practical or curricular training, and may be requested regardless of a student's economic need. Such employment is generally authorized only after the student has had a chance to participate in classroom activities and gain some theoretical background, which she or he would then apply in a practical setting. F-1 students are required to maintain their full-time student status for a minimum of one academic year or nine consecutive months before they become eligible to request practical training. J-1 students, similarly, may not request academic training for

Predeparture checklist

- ❏ Get or renew your passport.
- ❏ Obtain a student or exchange visitor visa.
- ❏ Make airline reservations. Find out about baggage charges or shipping rates. Plan to arrive in time for the orientation program. Try to arrive at the college during regular office hours (8 a.m. to 5 p.m., Monday through Friday).
- ❏ Make hotel reservations if you will be stopping en route. If you have not received a housing assignment or need to find temporary living accommodations, be sure to have sufficient funds to cover these living expenses.
- ❏ Get inoculations and have your doctor complete a World Health Organization yellow immunization card. Have a physical examination and send the report to your college if it is requested. If you wear glasses, get and carry with you a prescription from your doctor. If you take special medication, get a reasonable supply and a new prescription, written in English, from your doctor to take with you.
- ❏ Request information on health insurance and services from your college. Obtain health insurance.
- ❏ If you want on-campus housing, send in your housing reservation form and deposit.
- ❏ Write to the international student adviser to notify him or her of the date and approximate time of your arrival. Ask about airport arrival services.
- ❏ If you would like help on arrival, check with your local EducationUSA adviser, or inquire about the help offered by the YMCA Arrivals Program, c/o International YMCA, 5 West 63rd Street, 2nd floor, New York, NY 10023 USA. Visit its website at www.internationalymca.org.

- ❏ Be sure you understand U.S. currency (bills and coins) and the exchange rate between your country and the United States.
- ❏ Arrange to set up and transfer money to an account at a bank in the United States.
- ❏ Be sure to have funds (in U.S. currency) to cover expenses while traveling to college and for your first month in the United States. A credit card in your name, such as a Visa or MasterCard, will also be extremely helpful.
- ❏ If possible, take about $150 in U.S. currency in small denominations ($1, $5, $10, $20) for use on arrival. Do not keep all the cash in one place.
- ❏ Ask the college or check on its website about the best transportation from the airport to the college. If arriving in a large city, ask how much it should cost to get from the airport to the college. If you take a taxi, be sure to confirm the price of the trip with the driver before leaving the airport. Some colleges offer airport pickup services, particularly if arranged in advance.
- ❏ Arrange in advance to ship belongings that will be over the baggage limit on airlines, unless you are willing to pay the excess baggage charges.
- ❏ Prepare items to be carried on your person or in a carry-on bag (not checked). Be sure to set aside your passport, visa documents, U.S. currency, medication and prescriptions, and the college deposit receipt or registration form to carry with you. Your carry-on bag should contain any items you will need in case your regular baggage is temporarily delayed.
- ❏ Label all of your luggage on the inside and outside with your name and the name and address of the college to which you are going.

a period longer than their length of study in the United States. Both academic training and practical training may be undertaken prior to or following a student's completion of his or her program of studies. The length of authorization for academic or practical training, the type of job, and the employer are all generally regulated for both F-1 and J-1 students. In every case, employment for practical or academic training must be authorized in writing before a student begins work.

Admission Advice

"Many international students will get internships or co-ops. What international students need to keep in mind is that they need to adhere to U.S. immigration regulations, as far as working goes. They need to get involved right away with their international student adviser on campus. They should maintain good standing so that they can get the correct visa and work legally."

— Ann Gogerty, Iowa State University, Ames, Iowa

"Some students want to gain some practical on-the-job training, and they can do that through immigration's OPT program — that's "Optional Practical Training" — which allows them to stay in the United States after earning an associate degree for one year and work in the field for which they were trained."

— Ken Bus, Glendale Community College, Glendale, Ariz.

Accompanying dependents

Students in F-1 and J-1 status may bring eligible dependents (spouse and children), who enter the United States with F-2 or J-2 visas. Additional funds are required for the support of dependents, and these funds must be documented before the dependents can enter the United States. F-2 dependents are not permitted to work under any circumstances. J-2 dependents may request employment authorization but can earn money only to support themselves and other J-2 dependents. If you wish to bring dependents with you when you first come to the United States, notify your university or your J-1 program sponsor so the required dependent information can be included on your I-20A-B or DS-2019 form. If you want your dependents to follow separately after you are settled, consult your international student adviser or sponsor for advice several months before your dependents plan to travel.

SEVIS (Student and Exchange Visitor Information System)

Students planning to study in the United States must be aware of the automated tracking system called "SEVIS." This system is designed to track international students through an electronic network among colleges and universities, U.S. immigration services, and U.S. consular posts overseas. While you are a student in the United States, it will be important to maintain contact with the international student adviser at your institution to report any changes to your status. You can learn more about visa procedures by logging on to the website www.unitedstatesvisas.gov.

Admission Advice

"International students help diversify our campuses and teach us about the rest of the world, as much as we're able to educate them in the academic areas. We encourage students to look at the United States and the educational options they have here."

— Joseph DeCrosta, Duquesne University, Pittsburgh, Pa.

Keeping yourself in good standing with the U.S. government

- Learn the immigration regulations that apply to your student or exchange visitor status in the United States.

- Consult your international student adviser or J-1 program sponsor for current information and answers to your questions. Do not rely on the advice of friends.

- Process all changes of your status (school transfers, change of major or degree objective, extension of stay) promptly, following the advice of your international student adviser or program sponsor.

- Know your responsibilities under SEVIS.

- Answer all questions truthfully when applying for a U.S. visa abroad and when requesting entry into the United States.

- Enroll for a full course of study every academic term during your program of study. Discuss any need to reduce your academic course load with your international student adviser or J-1 program sponsor.

- Learn the rules for various kinds of employment. Work only if you have permission and if you are in good standing with the immigration authorities.

- Remember, all off-campus employment requires written authorization before you begin work.

Consider your health

Your good health is essential for your success as a student. If you have been relatively healthy for most of your life, you may take your good health for granted. But before you leave for the United States, you should take steps to prepare for the big changes ahead.

If you have any unresolved health concerns, take care of them before you leave home. Do you need a new pair of glasses? Have you had a recent dental examination? Have you experienced some unexplained symptoms that need to be checked? Be sure to have these and any similar problems solved before you depart for the United States.

Your U.S. university may request health records from your physician at home, but you should bring copies of your records for yourself. These include your medical history, immunization records, eyeglass prescription, drug prescriptions and a written record of any remedy that you use on a regular basis. These records should be written in English or you should bring translations with you.

Learn as much as you can about health resources on your chosen campus ahead of time so you are prepared when you arrive. These may include a small infirmary or a large hospital, depending on the size of your college. After arriving on campus, find out where you can go for emergency health care if the health center is closed. Do not wait for an emergency to find out where such a facility is located.

Expect changes in your health as you adjust to your new surroundings. Many factors, including your eating habits, sleeping patterns, local climate and level of stress, contribute to your physical health and emotional well-being. When you arrive in a new place and are surrounded by a different culture, these factors change and your health may be affected. Give yourself time to adjust, and if you become uncomfortable or unhappy, consult the international student adviser, student health service or counselors available at your college or university.

Student health insurance

There is no socialized medicine in the United States. Be sure that you have health insurance. If your sponsor provides health coverage, be sure that it covers treatment in the United States and that it covers catastrophic illnesses. Otherwise, purchase medical insurance for yourself and your dependents through your campus health insurance plan or through a U.S. health insurance agent. Medical insurance is absolutely essential to meet health care costs in the United States. Many U.S. universities require medical insurance for international students who enroll, and all J-1 exchange visitor students are required by law to carry medical insurance. But whether your school requires insurance or not, you should buy it as soon as you arrive. Policies differ in the expenses they will pay; find a policy with a reasonable deductible, affordable copayments and limited exclusions. To learn more about how to shop for a health insurance policy, consult with the student health service or international student adviser on your campus.

Glossary

Accelerated program. A college program of study completed in less time than is usually required, most often by attending classes in summer or by taking extra courses during the regular academic terms. Completion of a bachelor's degree program in three years is an example of acceleration.

Accreditation. Recognition by an accrediting organization or agency that a college meets certain acceptable standards in its educational programs, services and facilities. Regional accreditation applies to a college as a whole and not to any particular programs or courses of study. Specialized accreditation of specific types of schools, such as Bible colleges or trade and technical schools, may also be determined by a national organization. Information about the accreditation of specialized programs within a college by organizations, such as the American Chemical Society, American Dietetic Association, etc., is given in *Accredited Institutions of Postsecondary Education*, published for the Commission on Recognition of Postsecondary Accreditation by the American Council on Education.

ACT. A college admission test given at test centers in the United States and other countries on specified dates throughout the year. Please visit the organization's Web site for further information.

Advanced placement. Admission or assignment of a freshman to an advanced course in a certain subject on the basis of evidence that the student has already completed the equivalent of the college's freshman course in that subject.

Advanced Placement Program® (AP®). An academic program of the College Board that provides high school students with the opportunity to study and learn at the college level. AP offers more than 30 courses and exams in a wide variety of subject areas. Most colleges and universities in the United States accept qualifying AP Exam scores for credit, advanced placement or both.

Associate degree. A degree granted by a college or university after the satisfactory completion of a two-year full-time program of study or its part-time equivalent. In general, the associate of arts (A.A.) or associate of science (A.S.) degree is granted after students complete a program of study similar to the first two years of a four-year college curriculum. The associate in applied science (A.A.S.) is awarded by many colleges upon completion of technological or vocational programs of study.

Bachelor's, or baccalaureate, degree. A degree received after the satisfactory completion of a four- or five-year full-time program of study (or its part-time equivalent) at a college or university. The bachelor of arts (B.A.) and bachelor of science (B.S.) are the most common baccalaureates. There is no absolute difference between the degrees, and policies concerning their award vary from college to college.

Calendar. The system by which an institution divides its year into shorter periods for instruction and awarding credit. The most common calendars are those based on the semester, trimester, quarter, and 4-1-4.

Certificate. An award for completing a particular program or course of study, sometimes given by two-year colleges or vocational or technical schools.

College-Level Examination Program® (CLEP®). Thirty-three examinations in the subject areas of composition and literature, world languages, history and social sciences, science and mathematics, and business that provide students the opportunity to earn college credit by achieving a qualifying score. These exams are sponsored by the College Board and administered by 1,700 colleges year-round. More than 2,900 colleges grant credit for passing scores. International students are encouraged to take CLEP exams once they arrive at a U.S. institution to begin their studies.

College-preparatory subjects. A term used to describe subjects required for admission to, or recommended as preparation for, college. It is usually understood to mean subjects from the fields of English, history and social studies, foreign languages, mathematics, science, and the arts.

Combined bachelor's/graduate degree. A program in which students complete a bachelor's degree and a master's degree or first-professional degree in less than the usual amount of time. In most programs, students apply to undergraduate study, and begin the graduate program in their fourth year of college. Successful completion results in the awarding of both bachelor's and graduate degrees. At some colleges, this option is called a joint-degree program.

Common Application. The standard application form distributed by the National Association of Secondary School Principals to private colleges that are subscribers to the Common Application Group.

Community/junior college. A college offering a two-year program rather than a four-year program. A junior college usually offers vocational programs as well as the first two years of a four-year program. The student in the vocational program usually goes directly into a vocation after graduation, while the student in the academic program transfers to a four-year institution.

Comprehensive fee. If the college combines tuition, fees, room and board expenses, that single figure is called a comprehensive fee.

Consortium. When there are several colleges and universities within close geographical proximity, they often join together in a consortium. The advantages of attending a college that is a member of a consortium are that students have the resources of many libraries instead of just one; they have the opportunity to take courses not available at their own college by doing so at a member institution; and they can take advantage of many of the combined cultural and educational opportunities offered when the members of the consortium unite and present panel discussions, special lectures and unusual courses.

Consumer Price Index (CPI). A measure of inflation or deflation at the consumer level, updated monthly by the U.S. Bureau of Labor Statistics.

Cooperative education (co-op). A program that provides for alternative class attendance and employment in business, industry or government. Students are typically paid for their work. Under a cooperative plan, five years are normally required to complete a bachelor's degree, but graduates have the advantage of about a year's practical work experience in addition to their studies.

Credit by examination. Academic credit granted by a college to entering students who have demonstrated proficiency in college-level studies through examinations, such as those administered by the College Board's AP and CLEP programs. This is a means of cutting college costs by reducing the number of courses needed to earn a degree.

Credit hour. A unit of measure representing an hour of instruction over a 15-week period in a semester or trimester system, or a 10-week period in a quarter system. It is applied toward the total number of hours needed for completing the requirements of a degree, diploma, certificate or other formal award.

Credit/no credit grading system. *See* Pass/fail grading system.

Cross-registration. The practice, through agreements between colleges, of permitting students enrolled at one college or university to enroll in courses at another institution without formally applying for admission to the second institution.

Deferred admission. The practice of permitting students to postpone enrollment, usually for one year, after acceptance to college.

Distance learning. An option for earning course credit off campus via cable television, the Internet, satellite classes, videotapes, correspondence courses, or other means.

Double major. Any program in which a student completes the requirements of two majors concurrently.

Exchange student program. Any arrangement that permits a student to study for a semester or more at another college in the United States without extending the amount of time required for a degree.

4-1-4. A variation of the semester calendar system, the 4-1-4 calendar consists of two terms of about 16 weeks each, separated by a one-month intersession used for intensive short courses, independent study, off-campus work or other types of instruction.

Gift aid. Scholarships and grants that do not have to be repaid.

Grade point average or ratio (GPA). A system used by many schools for evaluating the overall scholastic performance of students. Grade points are determined by first multiplying the number of hours given for a course by the numerical value of the grade and then dividing the sum of all grade points by the total number of hours carried. The most common system of numerical values for grades is: A = 4, B = 3, C = 2, D = 1, and E or F = 0. Also called a quality point average ratio.

Graduate study. A program leading to a master's degree or doctoral degree; advanced study generally following a bachelor's degree.

High school. The final three to four years of preuniversity education in the United States. Students usually receive their high school diplomas when they are 17 or 18. Also called "secondary school."

Honors program. A plan designed to encourage superior students to engage in more challenging programs in their areas of concentration than are required. Students who succeed in meeting the stringent requirements of an honors program are usually granted "honor" degrees.

Independent study. Academic work chosen or designed by the student with the approval of the department concerned, under an instructor's supervision. This work is usually undertaken outside of the regular classroom structure.

Interdisciplinary. Refers to programs or courses that use the knowledge from a number of academic disciplines, such as a combination of environmental science and government policy, or of engineering and business.

International Baccalaureate (IB). A high school curriculum offered by some schools in the United States and other countries. Some colleges award credit for completion of this curriculum. For further information, visit the organization's Web site.

Internships. Short-term supervised work experiences, usually related to a student's major field, for which the student earns academic credit. The work can be full time or part time, on or off campus, paid or unpaid. Student teaching and apprenticeships are examples.

Liberal arts. The study of the humanities (literature, the arts and philosophy), history, foreign languages, social sciences, mathematics and natural sciences. Study of the liberal arts and humanities prepares students to develop general knowledge and reasoning ability rather than specific skills.

Major. Short for "major field of concentration," a student's academic field of specialization. In general, most courses in the major are taken at the degree-granting institution during the junior and senior years.

Master's degree. A degree awarded after one or more years of graduate work following the bachelor's degree.

Matriculation. The process whereby a student is accepted, pays fees and enrolls in classes, officially becoming a student at the college. This term is only applied to freshmen or to a transfer student's first enrollment.

Open admission. The college admission policy of admitting high school graduates and other adults generally without regard to conventional academic qualifications, such as high school subjects, high school grades and admission test scores. Virtually all applicants with high school diplomas or their equivalent are accepted.

Optional Practical Training (OPT). This program, sponsored by the U.S. Citizenship and Immigration Services, gives students on F-1 visas the opportunity to work for up to a year in a field related to their program of study.

Pass/fail grading system. Some colleges permit students to take courses where their performance is simply rated as either passing or failing, rather than graded to indicate various levels of passing work. The college's entire grading system may follow this pattern, or it may be an option for individual students in specific courses. It may also be referred to as a credit/no credit grading option.

Prerequisite. A requirement that must be met before a certain course can be taken.

Private institution. An institution of higher education not supported by public taxes. It may be independent or related to a church.

Professional degree. A degree granted upon completion of academic requirements to become licensed in a recognized profession, such as medicine or the law. The programs of study require at least two years of previous college work for entrance, and at least six years of college work for completion.

Public college/university. An institution of higher education supported by public taxes.

Quarter system. An academic calendar period of about 12 weeks. Four quarters make up an academic year, but at colleges using the quarter system, students make normal academic progress by attending three quarters each year. In some colleges, students can accelerate their progress by attending all four quarters in one or more years.

Residency requirements. Most colleges and universities require that a student spend a minimum number of terms taking courses on campus (as opposed to independent study, transfer credits from other colleges or credit by examination) to be eligible for graduation. Also, residency requirements can refer to the minimum amount of time a student is required to have lived in a state to be eligible for in-state tuition at a public (state-controlled) college or university.

Rolling admission. An admission procedure by which the college considers each student's application as soon as all the required credentials, such as school records and test scores, have been received. The college usually notifies an applicant of its decision without delay. At many colleges, rolling admission allows for early notification and works much like nonbinding Early Action programs.

SAT Question-and-Answer Service. A service of the College Board that provides students with a copy of their SAT, their answers and the correct answers, scoring instructions, and information about the questions. The service is only available for certain test dates.

SAT®. A college entrance exam that tests critical reading, writing and mathematics skills is given on specified dates through the year at test centers in the Unites States and other countries. The SAT is required by most colleges and sponsors of financial aid programs.

SAT Subject Tests™. Admission tests in specific subjects are given at test centers in the United States and other countries on specified dates throughout the year. The tests are used by colleges for help in both evaluating applicants for admission and determining course placement and exemption of enrolled first-year students.

Secondary school. *See* High school.

Semester. A period of about 16 weeks. Colleges on a semester system offer two semesters of instruction a year; there may also be an additional summer session.

Student and Exchange Visitor Information System (SEVIS). An automated system created by the U.S. government to track international students.

Terminal program. A program of study in which the student completes his or her studies in a preselected period of time. This type of program is usually directed toward vocational preparation. The amount of time taken to complete the program will vary, but is not usually longer than two years.

Test of English as a Foreign Language (TOEFL). A test generally used by international students to demonstrate their English language proficiency at the advanced level required for study at colleges and universities worldwide. Please visit the organization's website for further information.

Transcript. A copy of a student's official academic record listing all courses taken and grades required.

Transfer program. An educational program in a two-year college (or four-year college that offers associate degrees) primarily for students who plan to continue their studies in a four-year college or university.

Transfer student. A student who has attended another college for any period, which may be defined by various colleges as any time from a single term up to three years. A transfer student may receive credit for all or some of the courses successfully completed before the transfer.

Trimester. An academic calendar period of about 15 weeks. Three trimesters make up one year. Students normally progress by attending two of the trimesters each year and in some colleges can accelerate their progress by attending all three trimesters in one or more years.

Undergraduate study. A program leading to an associate or a bachelor's degree; generally follows high school.

Upper-division college. A college offering bachelor's degree programs that begin with the junior year. Entering students must have completed the freshman and sophomore years at other colleges.

Virtual university. A degree-granting, accredited institution wherein all courses are delivered by distance learning, with no physical campus.

Part II:
Information tables on U.S. colleges and universities

How to use the information tables

The information tables provide detailed information on more than 3,200 undergraduate institutions in the United States. The data were collected directly from the institutions by written questionnaires and telephone follow-up from January through April 2011.

Undergraduate information

The names of the colleges are listed alphabetically by state. Institutions are listed by their full names, which are not always the ones in popular use. For example, UCLA is listed as University of California: Los Angeles. The mailing address, telephone number, website address and fax number (when available) of each college are given in the *College addresses* starting on page 239. The columns in this section include the following information.

Control/degrees. This column shows whether the institution is private (Pr) or public (Pu), and whether the college offers associate degrees (A), bachelor's degrees (B), or both (AB).

Undergraduate enrollment. The first figure is the total number of undergraduate students enrolled in the fall of 2010. The second figure is the number of undergraduate international students enrolled.

Tests required. If the college requires one or more of the following standardized admissions tests, they are indicated in this column: SAT, SAT Subject Test, ACT, or TOEFL.

A slash (/) between two tests means that either test is required; for example, SAT/TOEFL means that applicants must take either the SAT or the TOEFL. A plus (+) between tests means that both are required; for example, SAT + TOEFL means that applicants must take both the SAT and the TOEFL.

TOEFL minimum and average. The minimum score listed is generally acceptable to the college as an indicator of English language proficiency. The average may be significantly higher at some colleges. The scores indicated, which range from 310 to 667, are for the paper-based test. For iBT (Internet-based) scores, which range from 0 to 120, see the concordance table on the TOEFL Web site.

Applications. The deadline is generally the last date by which the college will accept application forms, test scores, transcripts and other documents required for the admission process. Remember that many colleges fill their classes well in advance of this date, so complete your applications as soon as possible before the deadline. The application fee is required at the time you send your application form; the figure here is in U.S. dollars.

Student services. These columns indicate whether the college offers the following services for international students: student adviser, student orientation program or English as a second language (ESL) program on campus.

Housing. These two columns indicate whether the college has housing during the academic year (September-May) and/or summer months (June, July and August) for international students.

Academic year cost. The figure for tuition/fees represents the tuition and general fees the college charges most first-year, full-time international students for the nine-month academic year. For colleges with on-campus housing, the nine-month living cost includes room and board. For colleges that do not offer on-campus housing, the living cost figure includes an estimated expense for room and board. The cost per credit is indicated along with the maximum number of credits the institution allows a student to take during the summer. The cost does not include travel to and from your home country. Cost is for 2011-12, unless otherwise indicated.

Financial aid. The first column indicates whether the institution offers financial aid for undergraduates from other countries. The number of international students who received aid is shown next, followed by the average award (in U.S. dollars). The last column shows the deadline for applying for financial aid. Remember that there is not enough financial aid to meet the needs of all applicants, so complete any financial aid application requirements as soon as possible.

Lists and indexes

International undergraduate student enrollment. Colleges are listed in descending order by enrollment size. If a college did not provide international enrollment information this year, it is not included on the list.

Total financial aid for international undergraduate students. Colleges are listed in descending order by the total dollar amount of financial aid awarded to international students.

Conditional admission based on English language proficiency. Colleges that will admit applicants whose English skills will not permit them to pursue academic course work during their first term are listed here. These colleges require that the student spend time in the first term increasing their English language skills to the required level. English language proficiency is defined differently by different institutions. If you have questions about your English language skills, be sure to check with the colleges of interest to you.

SAT Subject Tests required or recommended. Some colleges require one or more SAT Subject Tests of undergraduate international applicants, and some recommend these tests.

Credit/placement for International Baccalaureate (IB). These colleges offer credit or advanced standing for the IB diploma and/or certificates from individual IB exams. They do not necessarily offer credit for every IB exam, and qualifying scores will vary. Check with the colleges to learn more about their policies.

Credit/placement for Advanced Placement® (AP). These colleges offer credit or advanced placement to students with qualifying scores on certain AP Exams. They do not necessarily offer credit for every AP Exam, and qualifying scores will vary. Check with the colleges, or use the AP Credit Policy Info tool at www.collegeboard.org/ap/creditpolicy, to learn more about the colleges' policies.

ESL programs on campus. Colleges that offer English as a second language programs on campus are listed in alphabetical order by state.

Special housing for international students. Colleges that offer a special on-campus dormitory for international students are listed in alphabetical order by state.

Housing guaranteed for all freshmen. These colleges guarantee that incoming freshmen will be offered on-campus accommodations.

College size (undergraduate enrollment). Colleges are grouped into categories from very small (fewer than 750 undergraduates) to very large (15,000 or more undergraduates).

College type. Colleges are grouped into types that describe the type of courses you'll find at the college, such as liberal arts colleges, business colleges, engineering colleges and military academies. Separate lists show colleges that are affiliated with a religious denomination and colleges that cater to a specific type of student — colleges for women, for example.

Directory of colleges

This listing gives the full name and mailing address for each institution listed in the undergraduate and graduate tables in this section. It includes the school's telephone number and, when available, the website address, fax number, and e-mail address. The office to contact for further information about the institution and for application procedures and forms is also given.

Colleges and universities

Institution	Control/ degrees	Undergraduates		Tests required (Fall 2011)	TOEFL		Application	
		Total	Internat'l		minimum	average	Deadline	Fee
Alabama								
Alabama Agricultural and Mechanical University	Pu/B	4,930		TOEFL	500	650	5/15	20
Alabama State University	Pu/B	4,862	25	TOEFL	500		3/1	25
Athens State University	Pu/B	3,394		TOEFL	500		7/11	30
Auburn University	Pu/B	20,209	135	TOEFL, SAT/ACT	550	560		60
Auburn University at Montgomery	Pu/B	4,714	71	TOEFL, SAT/ACT	500		8/1	25
Birmingham-Southern College	Pr/B	1,521		TOEFL	500		3/1	40
Bishop State Community College	Pu/A			TOEFL	500		7/1	
Calhoun Community College	Pu/A	12,139		TOEFL	500	525		
Chattahoochee Valley Community College	Pu/A	1,734		TOEFL	500		None	
Columbia Southern University	Pr/AB	18,183		TOEFL	500		None	50
Faulkner State Community College	Pu/A			TOEFL	500		7/15	
Faulkner University	Pr/AB	2,334	33	TOEFL	500		None	25
Gadsden State Community College	Pu/A	6,706		TOEFL	500	515	None	
George C. Wallace Community College at Dothan	Pu/A			TOEFL	500			10
Heritage Christian University	Pr/AB						3/30	25
Herzing University	Pr/AB							
Huntingdon College	Pr/B	1,094	7	TOEFL, SAT/ACT	500		5/15	
Huntsville Bible College	Pr/AB							10
Jacksonville State University	Pu/B	7,747		TOEFL	500		None	30
Jefferson State Community College	Pu/A	8,534	76	TOEFL	500		8/15	
Judson College	Pr/B	312	1	TOEFL	500	517	None	35
Lawson State Community College	Pu/A	4,685		TOEFL	500	540	6/1	10
Marion Military Institute	Pu/A	398		TOEFL	500		8/15	30
Miles College	Pr/B			TOEFL	450	550	None	
Oakwood University	Pr/AB			TOEFL	500		6/30	30
Remington College: Mobile	Pr/AB						7/4	50
Samford University	Pr/AB	2,918	16	TOEFL	550		None	35
Selma University	Pr/AB							20
Shelton State Community College	Pu/A			TOEFL	500		None	
Southeastern Bible College	Pr/AB	188		TOEFL	500		None	30
Southern Union State Community College	Pu/A	4,869		TOEFL			None	
Spring Hill College	Pr/B	1,377	8	TOEFL	550		7/1	35
Stillman College	Pr/B			TOEFL, SAT/ACT	500		4/1	25
Talladega College	Pr/B	698		TOEFL	500		None	25
Troy University	Pu/AB	22,043	386	TOEFL	500		3/30	30
Tuskegee University	Pr/B	2,479	24	TOEFL	500		6/15	35
United States Sports Academy	Pr/B	315		TOEFL	550			100
University of Alabama	Pu/B	24,376	280	TOEFL	500		5/1	40
University of Alabama at Birmingham	Pu/B	10,660	190	TOEFL	500		5/1	30
University of Alabama in Huntsville	Pu/B	5,828	162	TOEFL, SAT/ACT	500	547	5/22	30
University of Mobile	Pr/AB	1,478	28	TOEFL, SAT/ACT	500		None	50
University of Montevallo	Pu/B	2,493	54	TOEFL	525		6/1	30
University of North Alabama	Pu/B	5,770	242	TOEFL	500		6/27	25
University of Phoenix: Birmingham	Pr/B							
University of South Alabama	Pu/B	11,536	511	TOEFL	500	580	7/1	35
University of West Alabama	Pu/AB	1,915	5	TOEFL, SAT/ACT	500	530	None	50
Wallace State Community College at Hanceville	Pu/A			TOEFL	500	550	6/1	
Alaska								
Alaska Pacific University	Pr/AB			TOEFL	550		7/1	25
Ilisagvik College	Pu/A	110						
Prince William Sound Community College	Pu/A			TOEFL	450	550	7/31	10
University of Alaska Anchorage	Pu/AB	12,869	81	TOEFL, SAT/ACT	450			50
University of Alaska Fairbanks	Pu/AB	5,631	82	TOEFL, SAT/ACT	550		3/1	50
University of Alaska Southeast	Pu/AB	1,550	6	TOEFL	550		7/1	50

| Student services | | | Housing | | Academic year costs | | Maximum credits/ summer | Credit hour charge | International financial aid | | | |
Adviser	Orien- tation	ESL	Academic year	Summer	Tuition/ fees	Living costs			Avail- able	Number receiving aid	Average award	Deadline
Yes	Yes		Yes	Yes	12,588†	6,260	10	406	Yes	12	$12,084	
Yes	Yes		Yes	Yes	13,476†	4,880	9	526	Yes	10	$21,957	None
Yes					8,970†		19	274	Yes			None
Yes	Yes	Yes	Yes		21,916†	9,739		876				
Yes	Yes	Yes	Yes	Yes	19,090†	3,820	18	618				
Yes	Yes		Yes	Yes	27,890†	10,720	12	1121	Yes			3/1
Yes	Yes		No		5,970†		15	180				
Yes			No		6,120†	4,500	19	180	Yes			None
Yes			No		6,210†		23	180				
			No		6,020†			200				
Yes			Yes		6,060†	4,800		180				
Yes	Yes	Yes	Yes	Yes	14,810†	6,500	12	480				
Yes	Yes	Yes	Yes	Yes	5,970†	3,200	14	180	Yes			None
Yes			No		5,970†		21	180				
Yes	Yes		Yes	Yes	11,670	3,850	15	373				
					12,400†			385				
	Yes		Yes		21,990†	8,700	6	880	Yes			None
					3,980†			130				
Yes			Yes	Yes	13,560†	7,362	18	452	Yes	109	$11,358	None
Yes	Yes		No		6,330†		19	180				
Yes			Yes		14,420‡	8,550	10	450				
Yes			Yes		6,270†	4,000	21	180				
Yes			Yes		14,570†	3,450		400	Yes			None
Yes			Yes		9,896†	6,182		387				
Yes	Yes		Yes		14,250†	9,038						
			No				16					
Yes			Yes	Yes	21,942†	7,024		726	Yes			None
			Yes		5,375†	4,600		175	Yes			6/30
Yes			No		5,970†	4,275	20	180	Yes			None
			Yes		11,600†	2,550		375	Yes	1	$5,750	None
Yes			Yes		5,970†	3,200		180				
Yes			Yes	Yes	28,060	10,760	12	930	Yes			None
			Yes		14,534†	6,524	12	518	Yes			None
Yes			Yes		11,111†	5,885		308	Yes			None
Yes	Yes	Yes	Yes	Yes	13,830†	6,120	21	432				
Yes			Yes		17,720	7,950	9					
					9,750†	6,000		300				
Yes	Yes	Yes	Yes	Yes	20,500†	8,214	12					
Yes	Yes	Yes	Yes	Yes	16,414†	9,470	18	536				
Yes	Yes	Yes	Yes	Yes	17,986†	7,540	18	584	Yes	26	$6,114	7/31
Yes			Yes	Yes	17,130	8,076	18	585	Yes			None
Yes		Yes	Yes	Yes	14,980†	4,924	14	482	Yes	96	$10,736	None
Yes	Yes	Yes	Yes	Yes	12,218†	5,610	12	370	Yes			None
					11,040†							
Yes	Yes	Yes	Yes		13,620†	5,608		454				
Yes			Yes	Yes	11,458†	4,530	18	464		2	$14,286	
Yes			Yes		6,270†	3,150	19	180				
Yes	Yes		Yes		26,360†	9,300	15	1100	Yes			None
			Yes		4,020†	10,650		150				
Yes		Yes	Yes	Yes	4,150†	6,170	15		Yes			
Yes	Yes	Yes	Yes	Yes	15,776†	10,507	15	500	Yes			8/1
Yes	Yes		Yes	Yes	15,906†	6,960	18	500	Yes	50	$12,487	7/1
Yes	Yes		Yes	Yes	15,720†	8,413	12	500	Yes			None

† Tuition and fees are for 2010-11.   ‡ Tuition and fees projected for 2011-12.   * Includes room and board

Institution	Control/ degrees	Undergraduates		Tests required (Fall 2011)	TOEFL		Application	
		Total	Internat'l		minimum	average	Deadline	Fee
Arizona								
Argosy University: Online..................	.Pr/B							50
Argosy University: Phoenix................	.Pr/B							50
Arizona Automotive Institute..............	.Pr/A						None	100
Arizona Christian University...............	.Pr/AB	464		TOEFL	500		4/30	30
Arizona State University..................	.Pu/B	56,232	1,421	TOEFL	500			65
Arizona Western College.................	.Pu/A	7,850	795	TOEFL	500		10/15	25
Art Center Design College...............	.Pr/AB	350		TOEFL	500		None	25
Art Institute of Phoenix..................	.Pr/AB	1,243		TOEFL	500		10/13	50
Art Institute of Tucson..................	.Pr/AB	346					None	35
Brookline College: Phoenix...............	.Pr/AB	1,176						
Brookline College: Tempe................	.Pr/A	476						
Brown Mackie College: Tucson............	.Pr/AB	792		TOEFL				
Bryman School.........................	.Pr/A	643						50
Central Arizona College.................	.Pu/A	5,854					None	
Chamberlain College of Nursing: Phoenix........	.Pr/AB							95
Chandler-Gilbert Community College: Pecos......	.Pu/A	10,219			500		7/15	
Cochise College.......................	.Pu/A	4,739		TOEFL	500		8/1	50
Collins College.......................	.Pr/AB	1,171						50
DeVry University: Phoenix................	.Pr/AB	1,629		TOEFL	500		None	50
Dine College.........................	.Pu/A	1,935		TOEFL	500	520	None	20
Dunlap-Stone University..................	.Pr/B	60		TOEFL				50
Eastern Arizona College.................	.Pu/A	5,120	31	TOEFL	500	540	8/1	25
Embry-Riddle Aeronautical University:								
Prescott Campus.....................	.Pr/B	1,647	73	TOEFL	550	557	6/1	50
Estrella Mountain Community College..........	.Pu/A	5,213		TOEFL	500		8/17	
Everest College: Phoenix.................	.Pr/AB			TOEFL	450		None	
GateWay Community College..............	.Pu/A	7,346		TOEFL	500		2/10	
Glendale Community College...............	.Pu/A	11,572	106	TOEFL	500		7/1	
Golf Academy of America: Phoenix............	.Pr/A	256						50
Grand Canyon University.................	.Pr/B	22,188		TOEFL	500		None	
International Baptist College..............	.Pr/AB	67						35
ITT Technical Institute: Tempe.............	.Pr/AB							
Kaplan College: Phoenix.................	.Pr/A	690						25
Le Cordon Bleu College of Culinary Arts:								
Scottsdale..........................	.Pr/AB	1,522		TOEFL	500	525	None	125
Mesa Community College.................	.Pu/A	26,408		TOEFL	500		7/1	
Mohave Community College...............	.Pu/A	6,051		TOEFL	525		None	
Northcentral University..................	.Pr/B	526		TOEFL			None	75
Northern Arizona University...............	.Pu/B	19,964	771	TOEFL	525	527	3/15	50
Paradise Valley Community College..........	.Pu/A	10,282		TOEFL	500		7/1	
Paralegal Institute.....................	.Pr/A							
Penn Foster College....................	.Pr/AB	32,887		TOEFL	500		None	75
Phoenix College......................	.Pu/A	7,670	43	TOEFL	500		None	
Pima Community College.................	.Pu/A			TOEFL	450		None	25
Prescott College......................	.Pr/B	769	6	TOEFL	550		8/15	25
Rio Salado College....................	.Pu/A	25,266		TOEFL	500		None	
Scottsdale Community College..............	.Pu/A	11,257		TOEFL	500		None	
Sessions College for Professional Design........	.Pr/A							
South Mountain Community College..........	.Pu/A	3,293	25					15
Tohono O'odham Community College..........	.Pu/A							
Universal Technical Institute..............	.Pr/A	2,511					None	
University of Advancing Technology...........	.Pr/AB	978		TOEFL	550		6/12	100
University of Arizona...................	.Pu/B	30,343	1,079	TOEFL	500	595	4/1	50
University of Phoenix: Phoenix-Hohokam........	.Pr/B	4,414		TOEFL	550		None	45
University of Phoenix: Southern Arizona........	.Pr/B	1,757						
Western International University.............	.Pr/AB	2,347	22	TOEFL	500		None	25
Yavapai College......................	.Pu/A			TOEFL	450		4/1	50

Student services			Housing		Academic year costs		Maximum credits/ summer	Credit hour charge	International financial aid			
Adviser	Orientation	ESL	Academic year	Summer	Tuition/ fees	Living costs			Available	Number receiving aid	Average award	Deadline
					6,672 †							
					19,992 †							
			Yes				15					
			Yes		16,074 †	6,780	12	636	Yes			8/31
Yes	Yes	Yes	Yes	Yes	20,596 †	9,706	14	844	Yes	393	$9,664	None
Yes	Yes	Yes	Yes	Yes	6,360 †	5,425	8	212				
Yes			No		21,300 †			710	Yes			None
Yes	Yes		Yes				15					
			Yes				16					
			No		13,000 †	9,000						
			No		13,000 †	9,000						
			No		11,880 †			315				
						19,395						
Yes		Yes	Yes		8,670 †	4,882	6	130	Yes			7/15
					14,820 †							
			Yes									
Yes	Yes	Yes	Yes	Yes	8,770 †	6,826	8	290	Yes			4/15
			No									
Yes					14,826 †							
			Yes	Yes	850 †	3,720	12		Yes			None
					7,440 †			310				
Yes			Yes		8,120 †	4,795	18	140	Yes			
Yes	Yes		Yes	Yes	29,492 ‡	8,900	18	1195	Yes	49	$9,098	None
Yes			No		9,375 ‡		12	312	Yes			
	Yes		No									
Yes	Yes		No		9,375 †		12	312	Yes			None
Yes	Yes	Yes	No		9,375 †	8,388	12	312	Yes			
					15,732 †							
Yes	Yes		Yes	Yes			15		Yes			None
			Yes		10,110 †	5,100						
			No									
Yes						7,876						
Yes	Yes	Yes	No		8,610 †	8,388	9	286	Yes			None
		Yes	No		6,450 †		7	207				
			No		10,470 †	6,500		335	Yes			None
Yes	Yes	Yes	Yes	Yes	20,067 †	12,072	12	807	Yes			None
			No		9,390 †	7,902	6	312				
								150				
			No									
Yes	Yes		No		9,390 †	8,352	12	312				
Yes	Yes	Yes	No		8,225 †	8,050	12	90	Yes			None
					25,275 †	3,810	16		Yes	5	$5,300	None
Yes			No		9,390 ‡	3,996	18	312	Yes			None
Yes	Yes	Yes	No		9,390 †	8,352		312	Yes			None
		Yes	No		9,390 †			286				
						7,622						
Yes			No									
			Yes		19,400	10,926	18		Yes			None
Yes	Yes	Yes	Yes	Yes	24,597 †	9,274	12		Yes	206	$12,573	None
Yes			No		10,440 †							
					10,440 †							
Yes	Yes		No		11,250 †	23,424		375	Yes			None
Yes	Yes		Yes	Yes	8,530 †	5,680	12	340	Yes			None

† Tuition and fees are for 2010-11. ‡ Tuition and fees projected for 2011-12. * Includes room and board

Institution	Control/degrees	Undergraduates		Tests required (Fall 2011)	TOEFL		Application	
		Total	Internat'l		minimum	average	Deadline	Fee
Arkansas								
Arkansas Baptist College.	Pr/AB	1,119						75
Arkansas State University	Pu/AB	9,489	338	TOEFL	500	560	7/15	40
Arkansas State University: Mountain Home	Pu/A	1,236		TOEFL	500		5/1	
Arkansas State University: Newport.	Pu/A			TOEFL, SAT/ACT	500		5/1	
Arkansas Tech University	Pu/AB	8,034	217	TOEFL, SAT/ACT	500		5/1	50
Bryan College: Rogers	Pr/A							
Cossatot Community College of the University of Arkansas	Pu/A	1,512		TOEFL, SAT/ACT	500	507	None	150
Crowley's Ridge College.	Pr/AB			TOEFL, ACT	500	573		
East Arkansas Community College	Pu/A	1,505		TOEFL, ACT	500		2/28	25
Ecclesia College	Pr/AB			TOEFL	500		6/1	35
Harding University.	Pr/B	4,122	257	TOEFL, SAT/ACT	550		None	100
Henderson State University	Pu/AB	3,298	42	TOEFL, SAT/ACT	500		None	30
Hendrix College	Pr/B	1,451	57	TOEFL	550	559	5/1	40
John Brown University.	Pr/AB	1,642	102	TOEFL	500		None	100
Lyon College	Pr/B	634	11	TOEFL, SAT/ACT	550		5/1	50
National Park Community College	Pu/A	3,870		TOEFL	500	540	6/30	
Ouachita Baptist University	Pr/B	1,482	41	TOEFL	550		7/31	
Ouachita Technical College	Pu/A	900	6	TOEFL	500		None	100
Philander Smith College	Pr/B			TOEFL, SAT/ACT	500		4/5	75
Phillips Community College of the University of Arkansas	Pu/A	1,408		TOEFL	500		None	
Pulaski Technical College	Pu/A	10,080		TOEFL, ACT	550		5/15	50
Remington College: Little Rock	Pr/A							50
South Arkansas Community College	Pu/A	1,573		TOEFL			None	
Southeast Arkansas College	Pu/A	1,818					None	100
Southern Arkansas University.	Pu/AB	2,815	88	TOEFL	500	560	7/1	25
Southern Arkansas University Tech.	Pu/A	942	3	TOEFL	500		5/15	
University of Arkansas	Pu/B	16,794	448	TOEFL	550	577	5/31	50
University of Arkansas at Fort Smith.	Pu/AB	6,998	38	TOEFL, SAT/ACT	500		6/1	
University of Arkansas at Little Rock	Pu/AB	9,136	208	TOEFL, SAT/ACT	525		6/1	40
University of Arkansas at Monticello.	Pu/AB	3,638		TOEFL, SAT/ACT	500			30
University of Arkansas at Pine Bluff	Pu/AB	3,265	35	TOEFL, SAT/ACT	525	527	8/1	
University of Central Arkansas.	Pu/AB	9,823		TOEFL	500		7/15	50
University of the Ozarks	Pr/B	615	89	TOEFL	500	540	8/1	30
University of Phoenix: Little Rock	Pr/B							
University of Phoenix: Northwest Arkansas.	Pr/B			TOEFL				
Williams Baptist College.	Pr/AB	564	6	TOEFL	500		None	20
California								
Academy of Art University	Pr/AB	11,728	1,758				None	100
Academy of Couture Art.	Pr/AB							
Allan Hancock College.	Pu/A	15,060		TOEFL	475	500	6/1	
Alliant International University.	Pr/B			TOEFL, SAT, SAT Subject Test(s), or ACT	550		None	45
American Academy of Dramatic Arts: West	Pr/A	165		TOEFL	500		6/25	50
American Jewish University.	Pr/B	129	1	TOEFL	530		5/31	35
American River College	Pu/A	32,448		TOEFL	510	530	7/1	50
Antelope Valley College.	Pu/A	14,554		TOEFL	450		5/1	
Antioch University Los Angeles	Pr/B	204	3				8/1	60
Antioch University Santa Barbara	Pr/B	131	6	TOEFL	550		None	60
Argosy University: Inland Empire.	Pr/B							50
Argosy University: Los Angeles	Pr/B							50
Argosy University: Orange County	Pr/B							50
Argosy University: San Diego	Pr/B							50
Argosy University: San Francisco Bay Area	Pr/B							50
Art Institute of California: Hollywood	Pr/AB	1,327		TOEFL	500		None	50

Student services			Housing		Academic year costs		Maximum credits/ summer	Credit hour charge	International financial aid			
Adviser	Orientation	ESL	Academic year	Summer	Tuition/ fees	Living costs			Available	Number receiving aid	Average award	Deadline
			Yes		7,337†	7,834		275	Yes			5/1
Yes	Yes	Yes	Yes	Yes	12,340†	7,600	12	444	Yes			7/1
Yes			No		4,560†	15,732	6	135				
			No		4,140†		14	131				
Yes	Yes	Yes	Yes	Yes	11,008†	5,372	12	340	Yes	34	$7,397	None
Yes			No		4,900†			150	Yes			None
			Yes		9,860	5,980	12	295	Yes			None
			No		2,850†			87	Yes			7/1
Yes			Yes	Yes	15,240	5,160	11	475	Yes			None
Yes		Yes	Yes	Yes	14,610	6,031	16	472	Yes	106	$10,102	None
Yes	Yes	Yes	Yes	Yes	11,784†	5,084	14	356	Yes			None
Yes	Yes		Yes		34,230	9,714			Yes			None
Yes	Yes	Yes	Yes		20,766	9,062		628	Yes			None
Yes			Yes		22,906	7,340	10	760	Yes			None
Yes			No		6,360†		12	201	Yes			None
Yes	Yes	Yes	Yes	Yes	20,630‡	9,440	15	580	Yes	39	$15,089	6/1
			No		5,892†		12	180	Yes			6/30
Yes	Yes		Yes	Yes	9,450†	7,200	12		Yes			None
			No		3,650†		8	107	Yes			6/30
Yes			No		8,400†		6	267	Yes			5/15
			No		4,595†		14	146	Yes			7/1
			No		5,100‡			156	Yes			None
Yes	Yes		Yes	Yes	9,186†	4,570	12	270	Yes			None
Yes	Yes		Yes	Yes	4,590†	5,500	14	132				
Yes	Yes	Yes	Yes	Yes	16,000†	8,042	12	481	Yes	106	$5,226	None
Yes	Yes	Yes	Yes	Yes	10,888†	7,308	12	318				
Yes	Yes	Yes	Yes		15,590†	3,255	12	473				
			Yes	Yes	9,640†	4,310	12	275	Yes			None
Yes	Yes		Yes	Yes	9,983†	6,368	12	290				
Yes	Yes		Yes	Yes	12,143†	5,030	12	349	Yes			7/1
Yes	Yes		Yes		20,530†	6,300	7	834	Yes			None
					10,200†							
					10,200†							
			Yes	Yes	12,620	6,500		500	Yes	7	$9,243	None
Yes	Yes	Yes	Yes	Yes	22,490†	13,400	9	740				
		Yes	No		6,524†		8	216				
Yes	Yes	Yes	Yes	Yes	16,350†	9,688	18	600	Yes			3/2
Yes			No		29,220†				Yes			None
			Yes		25,688	12,364		1031	Yes	6	$10,000	None
Yes	Yes		No		7,052†	10,872	8	234				
		Yes	No		6,272†	10,872	9	209				
Yes			No		17,979†	5,138	15	580				
Yes	Yes		No		20,685		15	453				
					19,992†							
					19,992†							
					19,992†							
					19,992†							
					19,992†							
Yes	Yes		Yes	Yes	23,360†		15	518				

† Tuition and fees are for 2010-11.   ‡ Tuition/fees projected for 2011-12.   * Includes room and board

Institution	Control/ degrees	Undergraduates Total	Internat'l	Tests required (Fall 2011)	TOEFL minimum	average	Application Deadline	Fee
Art Institute of California: Inland Empire . . . . .Pr/AB		1,939						
Art Institute of California: Los Angeles . . . . .Pr/AB		2,275		TOEFL	480		None	50
Art Institute of California: Orange County . . . . .Pr/AB		2,135		TOEFL	500		None	50
Art Institute of California: Sacramento. . . . . .Pr/AB		1,089						
Art Institute of California: San Diego . . . . .Pr/AB		2,198		TOEFL			None	50
Art Institute of California: San Francisco . . . . .Pr/AB		1,651		TOEFL	500		None	150
Azusa Pacific University. . . . . .Pr/B		5,511	97	TOEFL, SAT/ACT	500	525	6/1	65
Bakersfield College . . . . .Pu/A		18,402		TOEFL	500		3/15	50
Barstow Community College . . . . .Pu/A		4,791		TOEFL	450		None	
Bergin University of Canine Studies . . . . .Pr/AB								
Berkeley City College. .Pu/A		7,263		TOEFL				50
Bethany University . . . . .Pr/B		359		TOEFL	550		6/1	35
Bethesda Christian University. . . . . .Pr/B		210	125	TOEFL	500		9/1	280
Biola University . . . . .Pr/B		4,092	57	TOEFL	600		4/1	45
Brooks Institute. . . . . .Pr/B		862		TOEFL	550		None	100
Bryan College: Los Angeles . . . . .Pr/A		950					None	25
Bryan College: Sacramento . . . . .Pr/A								35
Butte College . . . . .Pu/A		14,361		TOEFL	450	475		100
Cabrillo College . . . . .Pu/A		15,248		TOEFL	450	480	5/30	
California Baptist University . . . . .Pr/B		3,787			500		7/15	45
California Christian College. . . . . .Pr/AB		18						
California Coast University . . . . .Pr/AB								75
California College of the Arts . . . . .Pr/B		1,389	157	TOEFL	550		7/15	60
California College San Diego. . . . . .Pr/AB		1,407						
California Culinary Academy. . . . . .Pr/A		869		TOEFL	500		None	65
California Institute of the Arts . . . . .Pr/B		895	66	TOEFL	550	570	1/5	85
California Institute of Integral Studies . . . . .Pr/B		91	1	TOEFL	550		None	65
California Institute of Technology. . . . . .Pr/B		967	113				1/1	60
California Lutheran University . . . . .Pr/B		2,533		TOEFL	550		3/15	25
California Maritime Academy . . . . .Pu/B		857		TOEFL, SAT/ACT	500		5/1	55
California National University for Advanced Studies. . . . . .Pr/B								100
California Polytechnic State University: San Luis Obispo . . . . .Pu/B		17,275	151	TOEFL	550		11/30	55
California State Polytechnic University: Pomona. . . . . .Pu/B		18,648	827	TOEFL, SAT, SAT Subject Test(s), or ACT	525	544	None	55
California State University: Bakersfield . . . . .Pu/B		6,410		TOEFL	500	530	8/1	55
California State University: Channel Islands . . . . . . .Pu/B		3,589	13	TOEFL	500		4/30	55
California State University: Chico. . . . . .Pu/B		14,758	467	TOEFL	500	530	5/1	55
California State University: Dominguez Hills . . . . . .Pu/B		10,317	209	TOEFL	550		11/30	55
California State University: East Bay. . . . . .Pu/B		9,620	809	TOEFL	530	558	3/31	55
California State University: Fresno . . . . .Pu/B		17,876	239	TOEFL	500		4/1	55
California State University: Fullerton. . . . . .Pu/B		29,876	1,025	TOEFL, SAT/ACT	500	563	11/30	55
California State University: Long Beach. . . . . .Pu/B		27,436	1,314	TOEFL, SAT/ACT	500	547	11/30	55
California State University: Los Angeles . . . . .Pu/B		15,952	800	TOEFL	550			55
California State University: Monterey Bay . . . . .Pu/B		4,422	32	TOEFL	500		1/2	55
California State University: Sacramento . . . . .Pu/B		23,134	290	TOEFL	510			55
California State University: San Bernardino . . . . . . .Pu/B		13,680	471	TOEFL	500	570	None	55
California State University: San Marcos. . . . . .Pu/B		8,797		TOEFL				55
California State University: Stanislaus . . . . .Pu/B		6,963	112	TOEFL	500		11/30	55
California University of Management and Sciences. . . . . .Pr/AB		50		TOEFL	450	500	None	100
Canada College. . . . . .Pu/A		7,354		TOEFL	480	500	4/15	
Carrington College: Antioch. . . . . .Pr/A		685						
Carrington College: Citrus Heights . . . . .Pr/A		739						
Carrington College: Emeryville. . . . . .Pr/AB		423						
Carrington College: Pleasant Hill . . . . .Pr/A		487						
Carrington College: Sacramento . . . . .Pr/A		1,837						
Carrington College: San Jose . . . . .Pr/A		782						

Student services			Housing		Academic year costs		Maximum credits/summer	Credit hour charge	International financial aid			
Adviser	Orientation	ESL	Academic year	Summer	Tuition/fees	Living costs			Available	Number receiving aid	Average award	Deadline
					23,185 †	10,872		518				None
Yes	Yes		Yes	Yes	23,410 †			518	Yes			None
Yes			Yes	Yes	23,510 †	2,997	18	518	Yes			
					23,310 †	6,525		518				
Yes	Yes		Yes		23,310 †			518				
Yes	Yes		Yes		23,360 †	8,370	15	518				
Yes	Yes	Yes	Yes	Yes	29,940	8,488	16	1213	Yes			7/1
Yes	Yes	Yes	No		7,328 †	8,500	7	243				
Yes			No		6,270 †			209				
Yes	Yes	Yes	No		6,964 †		6	231				
Yes			Yes		19,900	7,600	12	764	Yes			None
Yes		Yes			7,160 †	3,200	18	231	Yes			None
Yes	Yes	Yes	Yes	Yes	29,908	13,030		1246	Yes	69	$9,378	None
			No		17,840 †	10,840	12					
			No		12,450							
					12,000 †							
Yes		Yes	No		6,680 †			216				
Yes	Yes	Yes	No		6,452 †		8	213				
Yes	Yes	Yes	Yes	Yes	25,768	8,700	6	923	Yes			None
					9,380	4,150		295				
					4,500 †			150				
Yes	Yes	Yes	Yes		37,310	10,325	6	1540	Yes	29	$7,741	None
Yes			Yes		36,857 †							
Yes	Yes		Yes		38,260	9,626			Yes	32	$9,294	
Yes	Yes		No		15,540	12,000		640	Yes			4/15
Yes	Yes		Yes	Yes	37,704	11,676		324	Yes	30	$42,837	None
Yes	Yes		Yes		32,850	13,570	12	1049	Yes	89	$13,557	None
Yes			Yes	Yes	16,454 †	9,740			Yes			None
					25,920 †			270				
Yes	Yes		Yes		17,640 †	9,992		248	Yes			
Yes	Yes	Yes	Yes	Yes	15,966 †	10,011		248				
Yes		Yes	Yes		16,474 †	7,041		248	Yes			None
Yes			Yes		16,245 †	11,280		372				
Yes	Yes	Yes	Yes	Yes	16,780 †	11,138	12	372				
Yes	Yes	Yes	Yes	Yes	16,009 †	10,085	12	372				
Yes	Yes	Yes	Yes		16,251 †	10,688	22	248				
Yes	Yes	Yes	Yes		16,039 †	11,890		372	Yes	18	$5,299	
Yes	Yes	Yes	Yes		16,046 †	9,632	18	372				
Yes	Yes	Yes	Yes	Yes	15,970 †	11,038	12	372				
Yes	Yes	Yes	Yes	Yes	16,006 †	9,105	12	248				
Yes	Yes		Yes	Yes	15,881 †	9,152		372				
Yes	Yes	Yes	Yes		16,354 †	11,332	12	372				
Yes	Yes	Yes	Yes		16,209 †	9,624		248	Yes			None
Yes	Yes	Yes	Yes		16,284 †	10,494	12	372				
Yes	Yes	Yes	Yes	Yes	16,462 †	8,880	9	372	Yes			None
Yes		Yes			5,565 †			150				
Yes	Yes		No		7,046 †		19	234				
					20,528 †							
			No		14,230 †							
					14,230 †							
					14,230 †							
					14,230 †							
					14,230 †							

† Tuition and fees are for 2010-11.   ‡ Tuition and fees projected for 2011-12.   * Includes room and board

Institution	Control/ degrees	Undergraduates		Tests required (Fall 2011)	TOEFL		Application	
		Total	Internat'l		minimum	average	Deadline	Fee
Carrington College: Stockton	Pr/A							100
Cerritos College	Pu/A	24,521		TOEFL	450		5/1	40
Cerro Coso Community College	Pu/A	6,048		TOEFL	500		None	
Chabot College	Pu/A	14,879	85	TOEFL	500	525	5/15	100
Chaffey College	Pu/A	19,773		TOEFL	450	460	None	35
Chapman University.	Pr/B	4,879	155	TOEFL, SAT/ACT	550	621	3/1	60
Charles Drew University of Medicine and Science	Pr/AB			TOEFL			1/15	35
Citrus College.	Pu/A	11,210		TOEFL	450		6/1	40
City College of San Francisco	Pu/A	31,250		TOEFL	475	500	5/15	50
Claremont McKenna College	Pr/B	1,253	84	TOEFL, SAT/ACT	600	639	1/2	60
Coastline Community College	Pu/A	14,300		TOEFL	500		9/7	30
Cogswell Polytechnical College	Pr/B	233	2	TOEFL	525		3/1	55
Coleman College: San Marcos	Pr/A	120						
Coleman University	Pr/AB	369		TOEFL	500	520	None	100
College of Alameda	Pu/A	7,302		TOEFL	500		1/1	
College of the Canyons.	Pu/A	19,992	94	TOEFL	450		6/15	
College of the Desert	Pu/A	12,026		TOEFL	400	420	7/15	30
College of Marin	Pu/A	7,789		TOEFL	500			50
College of the Redwoods	Pu/A	6,952		TOEFL	500		None	100
College of San Mateo.	Pu/A	11,310		TOEFL	480	520	4/15	
College of the Sequoias	Pu/A	13,502	16	TOEFL	500		4/1	100
College of the Siskiyous	Pu/A	3,045		TOEFL	470	485	6/30	35
Concorde Career College: Garden Grove	Pr/A	675						
Concorde Career College: North Hollywood	Pr/A							
Concorde Career College: San Bernardino	Pr/A	860						
Concordia University	Pr/AB	1,548	38	TOEFL, SAT/ACT	550		6/1	125
Contra Costa College	Pu/A	8,316					5/1	
Copper Mountain College	Pu/A	2,044						
Cosumnes River College.	Pu/A	14,559		TOEFL	510	520		50
Crafton Hills College	Pu/A	5,689	4	TOEFL	500	510	5/1	100
Cuesta College	Pu/A	11,588		TOEFL	500		6/1	
Cuyamaca College.	Pu/A	10,684	40	TOEFL	450		6/1	
Cypress College	Pu/A	15,917		TOEFL	500		7/1	40
De Anza College.	Pu/A	23,523		TOEFL	500	517	6/1	
Deep Springs College.	Pr/A	25					11/15	
Design Institute of San Diego.	Pr/B	390						25
DeVry University: Pomona	Pr/AB			TOEFL	500		None	50
Diablo Valley College	Pu/A	21,103		TOEFL	500		None	50
Dominican University of California.	Pr/B	1,562	25	TOEFL	550		6/1	40
East Los Angeles College	Pu/A	13,152	1,176	TOEFL	450		7/1	35
El Camino College.	Pu/A	23,940		TOEFL	450	480	7/1	50
Epic Bible College.	Pr/AB	258						
Everest College: Ontario Metro	Pr/AB	986						
Evergreen Valley College	Pu/A	11,186		TOEFL	500		4/15	100
Ex'pression College for Digital Arts	Pr/B	891						95
Fashion Careers College	Pr/A	78						125
Fashion Institute of Design and Merchandising: Los Angeles.	Pr/AB	4,424		TOEFL	483		None	325
Fashion Institute of Design and Merchandising: San Diego.	Pr/A	292	5	TOEFL	483		None	325
Fashion Institute of Design and Merchandising: San Francisco.	Pr/AB	960	47	TOEFL	483		None	325
Feather River College.	Pu/A	1,584		TOEFL	500		6/15	
Folsom Lake College	Pu/A	8,669		TOEFL	450			
Foothill College.	Pu/A	18,086		TOEFL	500		6/20	50
Fremont College: Cerritos	Pr/AB	266		TOEFL	500		None	85
Fresno City College.	Pu/A	24,013		TOEFL	500	515	5/1	
Fresno Pacific University	Pr/AB	2,333		TOEFL	500		7/30	40

Student services			Housing		Academic year costs		Maximum credits/summer	Credit hour charge	International financial aid			
Adviser	Orientation	ESL	Academic year	Summer	Tuition/fees	Living costs			Available	Number receiving aid	Average award	Deadline
					12,786†							
Yes		Yes	No		7,462†	11,556		247				
Yes		Yes			7,290†		7	243				
Yes	Yes		No		6,658†	11,556	18	221				
Yes	Yes	Yes	No		7,204†		14	239				
Yes	Yes		Yes		40,234	12,957		1220	Yes	53	$15,623	None
Yes	Yes		No		11,402†							
Yes	Yes	Yes	No		7,442†	11,556	6	246				
Yes	Yes	Yes	No		6,304†	11,160	7	209				
Yes	Yes		Yes		42,240	13,625			Yes			2/1
Yes		Yes	No		6,422†		9	213	Yes			None
Yes	Yes		Yes	Yes	18,924†	7,900	16	781				
					15,143			325				
Yes			No		15,143		12	325				
Yes			No		7,030†		10	231				
Yes	Yes	Yes	No		5,428†	11,160	12	180	Yes			3/2
Yes	Yes	Yes	No	Yes	6,188†	10,980	9	205	Yes			None
Yes		Yes	No		6,756†	13,673		224				
Yes			Yes		7,284†	7,050	12	242				
Yes	Yes	Yes	No		7,056†	11,160	8	234				
Yes		Yes	No		7,651†		8	253				
Yes	Yes	Yes	Yes		6,782†	8,000	12	225				
					21,766							
	Yes		Yes	Yes	27,300	8,590	12	815				
Yes			No		6,482†			216				
			No		6,272†	10,980		209				
Yes		Yes	No		7,052†	11,556	9	234				
Yes		Yes	No		6,598†	11,556	6	219				
Yes	Yes	Yes	No		6,316†	9,900	6	209				
Yes	Yes	Yes	No		6,400†	10,500		212				
Yes	Yes	Yes	No		6,902†			229				
Yes	Yes		No		6,773†	10,872	17	148				
			Yes	Yes					Yes			None
					18,605†							
Yes					14,826†							
Yes	Yes		No		6,480†		9	216	Yes			5/1
Yes	Yes	Yes	Yes		35,540†	13,560	18	1470	Yes	13	$15,366	None
Yes	Yes	Yes	No		6,922†	11,556	6	230				
Yes	Yes	Yes	No		7,205†	12,660	10	239				
					9,930†	10,872		214				
Yes			No		7,546†	11,556	6	250				
					21,080†							
			No		20,425†	10,872						
Yes	Yes		Yes		20,685†		15					
Yes	Yes		Yes		20,685†		15					
Yes	Yes	Yes	No		20,685†		15					
			Yes		7,459†	9,660	19	246	Yes			None
Yes		Yes	No		7,052†	11,556		234				
Yes	Yes	Yes	No		6,702†	11,262	12	148				
			No									
Yes	Yes	Yes	No		7,476†	9,860	11	248				
Yes	Yes	Yes	Yes	Yes	23,904†	7,280	18	845	Yes			

† Tuition and fees are for 2010-11.   ‡ Tuition and fees projected for 2011-12.   * Includes room and board

Institution	Control/ degrees	Undergraduates		Tests required (Fall 2011)	TOEFL		Application	
		Total	Internat'l		minimum	average	Deadline	Fee
Fullerton College. . . . . .Pu/A		22,331		TOEFL	500	510	4/15	25
Glendale Community College. . . . . .Pu/A		12,056	303	TOEFL	430	450		50
Golden Gate University. . . . . .Pr/B		421		TOEFL	525		7/1	110
Golden West College . . . . .Pu/A		13,510		TOEFL	500	515	6/15	30
Golf Academy of America: San Diego. . . . . .Pr/A		236						50
Grossmont College. . . . . .Pu/A		19,838		TOEFL	450	478	6/1	
Hartnell College . . . . .Pu/A		9,694		TOEFL	500	570	None	
Harvey Mudd College. . . . . .Pr/B		771		TOEFL, SAT/ACT, SAT Subject Test(s)	600		1/2	60
Heald College: Concord . . . . .Pr/A		1,350		TOEFL	550		None	
Heald College: Fresno . . . . .Pr/A							11/1	250
Heald College: Hayward . . . . .Pr/A				TOEFL	500			250
Heald College: Rancho Cordova. . . . . .Pr/A		950		TOEFL				250
Heald College: Roseville. . . . . .Pr/A		1,039						250
Heald College: Salinas . . . . .Pr/A				TOEFL	480		None	250
Heald College: San Francisco. . . . . .Pr/A		1,000		TOEFL				250
Heald College: San Jose . . . . .Pr/A				TOEFL	480	520	None	250
Heald College: Stockton . . . . .Pr/A								250
Holy Names University. . . . . .Pr/B		633	14	TOEFL	490		7/1	
Hope International University. . . . . .Pr/AB				TOEFL	500	601	None	50
Horizon College of San Diego . . . . .Pr/AB		50						
Humboldt State University. . . . . .Pu/B		7,155	76	TOEFL	500		6/1	55
Humphreys College . . . . .Pr/AB		710		TOEFL	450	490	3/8	200
Institute of Technology: Clovis. . . . . .Pr/A								
International Academy of Design and Technology: Sacramento . . . . .Pr/AB		599						50
Irvine Valley College . . . . .Pu/A		15,709			470			39
ITT Technical Institute: San Diego . . . . .Pr/AB					500		None	100
John F. Kennedy University. . . . . .Pr/B		216		TOEFL	550		7/1	55
Kaplan College: Palm Springs . . . . .Pr/A								20
Kaplan College: Panorama City . . . . .Pr/A				TOEFL	477		None	100
Kaplan College: Sacramento . . . . .Pr/A		683						25
Kaplan College: Salida . . . . .Pr/A		750						25
Kaplan College: San Diego . . . . .Pr/A		1,402						25
Kaplan College: Vista. . . . . : . . . .Pr/A		850						25
The King's University . . . . .Pr/AB		291		TOEFL	500		7/1	75
LA College International. . . . . .Pr/AB								35
La Sierra University. . . . . .Pr/B		1,138	193	TOEFL	550		None	30
Laguna College of Art and Design . . . . .Pr/B		422		TOEFL	500		6/15	35
Lake Tahoe Community College. . . . . .Pu/A		3,226		TOEFL	500		5/1	100
Laney College. . . . . .Pu/A		13,627		TOEFL	500		None	50
Las Positas College . . . . .Pu/A		8,954		TOEFL	500		None	100
Lassen Community College . . . . .Pu/A		2,250		TOEFL	450	460	8/1	
Le Cordon Bleu College of Culinary Arts: Los Angeles . . . . .Pr/A		2,253		TOEFL	500		None	50
Life Pacific College .Pr/AB		386	2	TOEFL	550	553	5/1	35
Lincoln University. .Pr/AB				TOEFL	500	525	None	75
Loma Linda University. . . . . .Pr/AB		1,031	103	TOEFL	550		6/30	60
Long Beach City College . . . . .Pu/A		26,950		TOEFL	500	535	6/15	40
Los Angeles City College . . . . .Pu/A		19,852					6/15	
Los Angeles Harbor College . . . . .Pu/A		11,109		TOEFL	450		6/20	
Los Angeles Mission College. . . . . .Pu/A		10,792		TOEFL	500	515	8/23	
Los Angeles Pierce College . . . . .Pu/A		21,585		TOEFL	450		6/15	35
Los Angeles Southwest College . . . . .Pu/A		7,866						
Los Angeles Trade and Technical College . . . . .Pu/A		16,243		TOEFL			6/1	
Los Angeles Valley College. . . . . .Pu/A		19,957		TOEFL	450		6/30	35
Los Medanos College. . . . . .Pu/A		10,773		TOEFL			7/1	50
Loyola Marymount University . . . . .Pr/B		5,797	203	TOEFL, SAT/ACT	550	590	1/15	60

Student services			Housing		Academic year costs		Maximum credits/summer	Credit hour charge	International financial aid			
Adviser	Orientation	ESL	Academic year	Summer	Tuition/fees	Living costs			Available	Number receiving aid	Average award	Deadline
Yes	Yes	Yes	No		6,902 †	10,872		229				
Yes	Yes	Yes	No		6,437 †	9,711	7	212				
Yes	Yes	Yes	No		17,100 †			570	Yes			None
Yes	Yes		No		6,422 †		9	213				
					15,732 †							
Yes	Yes	Yes	No		6,390 †	10,500	8	212				
Yes	Yes	Yes	No		6,458 †	10,872		215				
Yes	Yes		Yes		42,410	15,258		1317	Yes	7	$39,196	2/1
Yes			No		9,735 †	10,152	20					
			No		9,735 †	10,152						
					9,735 †	10,152			Yes			None
					9,735 †	10,152			Yes			None
					9,735 †							
					9,735 †	10,872	12		Yes			None
					9,735 †	10,152						
			No		9,735 †	10,152						
			No		9,735 †	8,910						
Yes	Yes	Yes	Yes		30,390	10,260		995	Yes			None
Yes	Yes	Yes	Yes	Yes	24,080	7,900		995	Yes			3/2
					4,800 †			160				
Yes	Yes	Yes	Yes		16,915 †	11,659		372				
Yes			Yes	Yes	10,116 †		16	281	Yes			6/30
					12,800 †			350				
Yes	Yes	Yes	No		7,264 †	10,872	16	241				
			No									
Yes			No		17,232 †			380				
			No									
						8,442						
			No		14,914 †							
					9,375		15	200	Yes			None
					15,330 †	9,153		550				
Yes	Yes	Yes	Yes	Yes	27,240	9,261		726	Yes			None
Yes	Yes		No		22,890 †		4	942				
Yes			No		7,032 †	11,556	9	156				
Yes	Yes				7,030 †		12	231				
Yes	Yes	Yes	No		6,660 †	9,926		221				
Yes	Yes	Yes	Yes		6,773 †	5,700	12	225				
Yes												
Yes			Yes	Yes	12,500	7,000		400	Yes			None
Yes	Yes	Yes	No		9,160		9	365				
Yes	Yes		Yes	Yes	25,845 †	2,520	16	535				
Yes	Yes	Yes	No		7,364 †	11,556		243	Yes			None
Yes		Yes	No		6,922 †	10,872	7	230				
Yes	Yes	Yes	No		6,924 †	11,556	6	230				
Yes		Yes	No		6,922 †	11,556	6	230				
Yes	Yes	Yes	No		6,922 †	11,556	5	230	Yes			None
Yes	Yes	Yes	No		6,922 †	10,872	7	230				
Yes		Yes	No		6,922 †	10,872	6	230				
Yes	Yes	Yes	No		6,924 †	10,872	7	230				
		Yes	No		6,490 †	10,872	6	216				
Yes	Yes		Yes		37,825	13,025		1540	Yes	58	$8,619	5/15

† Tuition and fees are for 2010-11.   ‡ Tuition and fees projected for 2011-12.   * Includes room and board

Institution	Control/degrees	Undergraduates Total	Internat'l	Tests required (Fall 2011)	TOEFL minimum	TOEFL average	Application Deadline	Fee
Marymount College	Pr/AB	793	53				None	40
The Master's College	Pr/B	1,053		TOEFL	550		3/2	40
Menlo College	Pr/B	590	77	TOEFL	500		7/15	40
Merritt College	Pu/A	7,295		TOEFL	500		4/1	50
Mills College	Pr/B	948	20	TOEFL, SAT/ACT	550		3/1	50
MiraCosta College	Pu/A	16,705	522	TOEFL	450		None	
Mission College	Pu/A	11,090		TOEFL	500	525	5/1	
Modesto Junior College	Pu/A	19,431		TOEFL	450	490	5/10	
Monterey Peninsula College	Pu/A	9,578		TOEFL	460	490	None	
Moorpark College	Pu/A	15,013		TOEFL	450		7/1	50
Mount San Antonio College	Pu/A	38,741		TOEFL	450			30
Mount San Jacinto College	Pu/A	17,195		TOEFL	450		5/15	90
Mount St. Mary's College	Pr/AB	2,286		TOEFL, SAT/ACT	550		6/1	40
Mt. Sierra College	Pr/B	535		TOEFL	500		None	50
MTI College	Pr/A							50
Napa Valley College	Pu/A	7,809		TOEFL	480	491	5/1	25
National Hispanic University	Pr/AB	410		TOEFL	450		None	50
National University	Pr/AB	9,455	156	TOEFL	525		None	60
NewSchool of Architecture & Design	Pr/B	647		TOEFL	550	580	None	75
Northwestern Polytechnic University	Pr/B	235		TOEFL, SAT	525		8/2	60
Notre Dame de Namur University	Pr/B	994		TOEFL	500		8/1	50
Occidental College	Pr/B	2,073	40	TOEFL, SAT/ACT	600		1/10	50
Ohlone College	Pu/A	11,799		TOEFL	470		4/10	50
Orange Coast College	Pu/A	23,770	679	TOEFL	500	535	6/30	30
Otis College of Art and Design	Pr/B	1,156	183	TOEFL, SAT/ACT	550	571		50
Oxnard College	Pu/A	7,720		TOEFL	505		7/1	
Pacific College of Oriental Medicine: San Diego	Pr/AB							
Pacific Oaks College	Pr/B	110		TOEFL	550		6/1	55
Pacific States University	Pr/B			TOEFL	450	500	None	100
Pacific Union College	Pr/AB	1,323		TOEFL	525		None	30
Palo Verde College	Pu/A	2,673		TOEFL	450	475	None	
Palomar College	Pu/A	28,327	206	TOEFL	470	472	5/1	25
Pasadena City College	Pu/A	30,366		TOEFL	450	470	5/1	40
Patten University	Pr/AB	1,080		TOEFL, SAT/ACT	550	565	7/31	30
Pepperdine University	Pr/B	3,431	214	TOEFL	550	560	1/15	65
Pitzer College	Pr/B	1,080	36	TOEFL	520		1/1	60
Platt College: Los Angeles	Pr/AB	234		TOEFL	400	425	None	75
Platt College: Ontario	Pr/AB	401		TOEFL	400	425	None	75
Platt College: San Diego	Pr/AB	318					None	
Point Loma Nazarene University	Pr/B	2,401	18	TOEFL	550		3/1	50
Pomona College	Pr/B	1,546	87	TOEFL, SAT, SAT Subject Test(s), or ACT	600		12/15	65
Porterville College	Pu/A	4,571		TOEFL	450	500	None	
Professional Golfers Career College	Pr/A	158		TOEFL	500		None	125
Providence Christian College	Pr/B							
Reedley College	Pu/A	14,762		TOEFL	500	511	None	
Rio Hondo College	Pu/A	31,701		TOEFL	450		None	
Riverside Community College	Pu/A	19,907		TOEFL	450		6/1	50
Sacramento City College	Pu/A	24,631		TOEFL	450	487	7/10	50
Saddleback College	Pu/A	23,260		TOEFL	470		7/15	50
St. Mary's College of California	Pr/AB	2,621		TOEFL	527	550	5/15	55
Salvation Army College for Officer Training at Crestmont	Pr/A							
Samuel Merritt University	Pr/B	584		TOEFL	550		3/1	50
San Bernardino Valley College	Pu/A	14,916		TOEFL	450		5/1	25
San Diego Christian College	Pr/B	471	10	TOEFL	500	510	8/1	100
San Diego City College	Pu/A	17,487		TOEFL	500		6/1	100

Student services			Housing		Academic year costs		Maximum credits/ summer	Credit hour charge	International financial aid			
Adviser	Orientation	ESL	Academic year	Summer	Tuition/ fees	Living costs			Available	Number receiving aid	Average award	Deadline
Yes	Yes	Yes	Yes	Yes	27,846	12,399	9	1050	Yes			None
Yes	Yes		Yes	Yes	26,880‡	9,400	8	1100	Yes			None
Yes	Yes		Yes	Yes	35,100	11,330	12	1438	Yes	71	$12,548	8/1
Yes		Yes	No		6,934†		18	231	Yes			6/30
Yes	Yes		Yes	Yes	37,605†	10,924			Yes	18	$16,755	
Yes	Yes	Yes	No		6,374†		8	211				
Yes		Yes	No		6,808†	11,160	6	225				
Yes	Yes	Yes	No		7,066†	10,980	12	234				
Yes	Yes	Yes	No		6,334†	14,536		209				
Yes			No		6,736†	10,872	7	223				
Yes		Yes	No		7,256†	10,980	14	240				
Yes	Yes		No		6,510†		8	217				
			Yes		31,626	10,125		1218	Yes			
			No		15,715†			347				
			No		12,641†	1,208						
Yes	Yes		No		6,608†	10,980	6	219				
			No		8,690†	10,872		283				
Yes	Yes	Yes	No		11,148†		18	308	Yes			None
Yes		Yes		Yes	22,995	11,400	18	667	Yes			None
Yes	Yes	Yes	Yes	Yes	9,250	6,900	16	300				
Yes	Yes	Yes	Yes	Yes	29,980‡	11,720		955	Yes			None
Yes			Yes		40,835†	11,980	12		Yes	15	$30,340	2/1
Yes	Yes	Yes	No		6,804†		6	225				
Yes	Yes		No		6,421†	11,556	12	213				
Yes	Yes		Yes		32,900†		18	1074	Yes	79	$7,246	None
		Yes	No		6,735†	10,980	10	223				
Yes			No		27,390†		6	911				
Yes	Yes	Yes	Yes	Yes	19,340	12,600	24	315	Yes			None
Yes	Yes		Yes	Yes	25,965	7,275		725	Yes	35	$13,131	None
Yes		Yes	No		6,270†	9,000	6	209	Yes			None
Yes	Yes	Yes	No		6,464†			214				
Yes	Yes		No		7,348†	20,818	8	244				
Yes	Yes	Yes	Yes	Yes	13,440	7,090	12	560	Yes			None
Yes	Yes		Yes	Yes	40,752	11,844	18	1266	Yes	17	$18,025	
Yes	Yes	Yes	Yes	Yes	42,570‡	12,370						
			No									
			No									
Yes	Yes		No		15,310†	14,213		507				
Yes	Yes		Yes	Yes	28,310	8,800	12		Yes			
Yes	Yes		Yes	Yes	39,883	13,227			Yes	31	$40,298	2/1
Yes		Yes	No		7,324†		6	243				
Yes	Yes		No		13,000†							
Yes			Yes		7,474†	5,840	18	248	Yes			None
Yes			No		6,312†		7	209				
Yes	Yes	Yes			7,024†	10,868		233				
Yes	Yes	Yes	No		7,052†	10,872	7	234				
Yes	Yes	Yes	No		7,264†	11,556	9	241				
Yes	Yes	Yes	Yes	Yes	37,150	12,840			Yes	24	$32,469	None
					4,525†							
Yes		Yes		Yes	37,021†			1504				
Yes			No		6,556†			217				
Yes	Yes		Yes		22,692†	8,160	12	874	Yes	8	$18,523	7/15
Yes	Yes		No		6,304†	10,980	12	209				

Institution	Control/ degrees	Undergraduates		Tests required (Fall 2011)	TOEFL		Application	
		Total	Internat'l		minimum	average	Deadline	Fee
San Diego Mesa College....................	Pu/A	24,844		TOEFL	500		6/1	100
San Diego Miramar College.................	Pu/A	11,351		TOEFL	500		6/1	100
San Diego State University	Pu/B	24,590	903	TOEFL	550	570	11/30	55
San Francisco Art Institute	Pr/B	244		TOEFL	550		8/1	75
San Francisco Conservatory of Music	Pr/B	186		TOEFL	500	527	12/1	100
San Francisco State University...............	Pu/B	25,170	1,684	TOEFL	500		5/1	55
San Joaquin Delta College..................	Pu/A	18,217		TOEFL	500		None	50
San Joaquin Valley College.................	Pr/A	452						
San Jose City College......................	Pu/A	12,498		TOEFL	500	505	4/15	35
San Jose State University	Pu/B	23,021	977	TOEFL	500		2/10	55
Santa Ana College.........................	Pu/A	42,268		TOEFL	450	500	7/1	50
Santa Barbara Business College	Pr/A							25
Santa Barbara Business College: Bakersfield.......	Pr/A							25
Santa Barbara Business College: Palm Desert	Pr/A							25
Santa Barbara Business College: Santa Maria	Pr/A							25
Santa Barbara Business College: Ventura	Pr/A							25
Santa Barbara City College	Pu/A	18,876	941				7/1	50
Santa Clara University	Pr/B	5,072	174	TOEFL, SAT/ACT	550		1/7	55
Santa Monica College.....................	Pu/A	33,893	3,098	TOEFL	450	500	6/10	50
Santa Rosa Junior College	Pu/A	30,426		TOEFL	475		6/15	25
Santiago Canyon College	Pu/A	19,131		TOEFL	500		7/1	50
School of Urban Missions: Oakland.............	Pr/AB	226		TOEFL	550		7/31	20
Scripps College...........................	Pr/B	946	32	TOEFL, SAT/ACT	600		1/1	60
Shasta Bible College and Graduate School ...,.....	Pr/AB	73		TOEFL	500		7/1	50
Shasta College	Pu/A	10,578		TOEFL	450		None	
Sierra College.............................	Pu/A	20,312		TOEFL	450		7/1	100
Simpson University	Pr/AB	971	1	TOEFL	500		None	50
Skyline College...........................	Pu/A	10,250		TOEFL	480	495	4/15	
Soka University of America.................	Pr/B	438	185				1/15	45
Solano Community College	Pu/A	11,510		TOEFL	500	520	6/1	
Sonoma State University....................	Pu/B	7,390	71	TOEFL	500	525	5/31	55
South Coast College.....	Pr/A	424						99
Southern California Institute of Architecture	Pr/B	255	44	TOEFL	560		2/15	75
Southern California Institute of Technology	Pr/AB	691		TOEFL	400		None	100
Southern California Seminary................	Pr/AB	75		TOEFL			8/15	126
Southwestern College......................	Pu/A	19,253		TOEFL	460	470	5/1	
Stanbridge College........................	Pr/AB							
Stanford University	Pr/B	6,887	493				1/1	90
Taft College..............................	Pu/A	7,701		TOEFL	450	513	6/10	150
Touro College Los Angeles	Pr/B							
Trident University International	Pr/B	3,568		TOEFL				
University of California: Berkeley.............	Pu/B	25,540	1,844	TOEFL, SAT, SAT Subject Test(s), or ACT	550		11/30	70
University of California: Davis...............	Pu/B	24,497	616	TOEFL, SAT/ACT, SAT Subject Test(s)	550		11/30	70
University of California: Irvine..............	Pu/B	21,976	626	TOEFL, SAT/ACT	550		11/30	70
University of California: Los Angeles	Pu/B	26,162	1,522	TOEFL, SAT/ACT			11/30	70
University of California: Merced..............	Pu/B	4,138	46	TOEFL, SAT/ACT, SAT Subject Test(s)	550		11/30	70
University of California: Riverside	Pu/B	18,236	261	TOEFL, SAT/ACT, SAT Subject Test(s)	550	561	11/30	70
University of California: San Diego...........	Pu/B	23,663		TOEFL, SAT/ACT	550		11/30	70
University of California: Santa Barbara	Pu/B	19,184		TOEFL, SAT/ACT, SAT Subject Test(s)	550		11/30	70
University of California: Santa Cruz	Pu/B	15,666	43	TOEFL, SAT, SAT Subject Test(s), or ACT	550		11/30	70
University of La Verne.....................	Pr/AB	1,869	11	TOEFL	500		4/1	50
University of the Pacific...................	Pr/B	3,740		TOEFL	475		None	60
University of Phoenix: Bay Area	Pr/B							

| Student services | | | Housing | | Academic year costs | | Maximum credits/ summer | Credit hour charge | International financial aid | | | |
Adviser	Orientation	ESL	Academic year	Summer	Tuition/ fees	Living costs			Available	Number receiving aid	Average award	Deadline
Yes	Yes		No		6,304 †		12	209				
Yes	Yes		No		6,304 †	10,980	12	209				
Yes	Yes	Yes	Yes	Yes	16,366 †	12,085		372	Yes	64	$12,750	3/2
Yes	Yes	Yes	Yes		33,294 †	12,810	15	1378	Yes			5/31
Yes	Yes	Yes	Yes		35,430 †	10,800		1540	Yes			None
Yes	Yes	Yes	Yes		16,174 †	12,414	12	372				
Yes	Yes	Yes	No		6,272 †	10,152	9	209				
			No									
Yes		Yes	No		6,784 †	11,567	7	225	Yes			None
Yes	Yes	Yes	Yes		16,530 †	10,438		372	Yes	86	$2,361	6/11
Yes	Yes	Yes	No		6,798 †	10,600	6	226				
Yes	Yes	Yes			6,956 †	10,980	3	229				
Yes	Yes		Yes		39,048	11,997						
Yes	Yes	Yes	No		7,486 †		8	248				
Yes	Yes		No		7,174 †	11,556		238	Yes	15	$500	None
Yes	Yes	Yes	No		6,808 †	10,600	6	226				
			Yes		7,830 †	2,400	6	255	Yes			None
Yes	Yes		Yes		41,950	12,950	8	1304	Yes	9	$23,389	2/1
			Yes		9,620 †	2,400		300				
Yes		Yes	Yes		6,825 †	2,610		225				
Yes	Yes	Yes	Yes	Yes	6,674 †	6,700	18	221				
Yes			Yes	Yes	21,600	8,050		875	Yes			None
Yes	Yes		No		7,082 †	11,160	9	234				
Yes	Yes	Yes	Yes		26,294	10,122			Yes			3/2
		Yes	No		6,523 †	8,082		216				
Yes	Yes	Yes	Yes	Yes	16,668 †	10,522		372				
					9,450 †	10,152						
Yes			No		30,700	11,066			Yes			2/15
Yes	Yes	Yes	No									
Yes			Yes	Yes	12,552	9,100		339				
Yes	Yes	Yes	No		6,524 †	11,556		216				
Yes	Yes		Yes		40,050	12,291			Yes	314	$31,410	None
Yes			Yes		6,450 †	4,186		215				
					9,514 ‡			295				
Yes	Yes		Yes		35,341 †	15,308	10					
Yes	Yes	Yes	Yes	Yes	34,863 †	12,498			Yes	81	$11,091	None
Yes	Yes	Yes	Yes	Yes	34,111 †	11,400				135	$14,906	
Yes	Yes	Yes	Yes	Yes	33,660 †	13,734	18					
			Yes		33,909 †	12,802			Yes			
Yes	Yes		Yes	Yes	33,910 †	11,600	10		Yes			3/2
Yes	Yes	Yes	Yes		33,351 †	11,462			Yes			6/1
Yes	Yes	Yes	Yes		34,591 †	13,109						
Yes	Yes		Yes	Yes	34,384 †	14,172	20					
Yes	Yes	Yes	Yes	Yes	31,300	11,280		890	Yes	4	$10,846	None
Yes	Yes	Yes	Yes	Yes	36,290	11,688	18	1235				
					12,660 †							

† Tuition and fees are for 2010-11.   ‡ Tuition and fees projected for 2011-12.   * Includes room and board

Institution	Control/ degrees	Undergraduates		Tests required (Fall 2011)	TOEFL		Application	
		Total	Internat'l		minimum	average	Deadline	Fee
University of Phoenix: Central Valley	Pr/B							
University of Phoenix: Sacramento Valley	Pr/B							
University of Phoenix: San Diego	Pr/B							
University of Phoenix: Southern California	Pr/B							
University of Redlands	Pr/B	3,020	6	TOEFL	550		2/1	30
University of San Diego	Pr/B	5,299	232	TOEFL	550		1/15	55
University of San Francisco	Pr/B	5,326		TOEFL	550		1/15	55
University of Southern California	Pr/B	17,112	1,833				1/10	65
University of the West	Pr/B	71		TOEFL	500		6/1	100
Vanguard University of Southern California	Pr/B	1,709		TOEFL	550		8/9	45
Ventura College	Pu/A	13,435		TOEFL			None	50
Victor Valley College	Pu/A	13,470		TOEFL	500		5/15	
West Coast University	Pr/AB	2,184					None	75
West Hills College: Coalinga	Pu/A	3,023					7/15	50
West Hills College: Lemoore	Pu/A	4,234					7/15	50
West Los Angeles College	Pu/A	11,866		TOEFL	450	460	6/15	35
West Valley College	Pu/A	11,281		TOEFL	500	520	6/1	
Westmont College	Pr/B	1,367	9	TOEFL, SAT/ACT	560	630	None	25
Westwood College: Anaheim	Pr/AB							50
Westwood College: Los Angeles	Pr/AB	1,116						50
Westwood College: South Bay	Pr/AB	795						50
Whittier College	Pr/B	1,400		TOEFL, SAT/ACT	550	590	None	50
William Jessup University	Pr/AB	673		TOEFL	500		4/1	45
Woodbury University	Pr/B	1,253	158	TOEFL	500	527	None	50
World Mission University	Pr/B	118					None	50
WyoTech: Fremont	Pr/A			TOEFL				
WyoTech: Long Beach	Pr/A	2,166						
WyoTech: Sacramento	Pr/A	737						
Yuba Community College District	Pu/A	7,389		TOEFL	480	490	5/15	25

Colorado

Institution	Control/ degrees	Undergraduates		Tests required (Fall 2011)	TOEFL		Application	
Adams State College	Pu/AB	2,446		TOEFL	550	594	6/1	30
Aims Community College	Pu/A			TOEFL	500		None	
American Sentinel University	Pr/AB			TOEFL	550		None	
Anthem College: Aurora	Pr/A	352					None	50
Arapahoe Community College	Pu/A	7,625	53	TOEFL			None	
Argosy University: Denver	Pr/B							50
Art Institute of Colorado	Pr/AB	2,247		TOEFL	500		None	50
Aspen University	Pr/AB	155		TOEFL	500		None	75
Boulder College of Massage Therapy	Pr/A	149						75
CollegeAmerica: Fort Collins	Pr/AB	440						
Colorado Christian University	Pr/AB	2,275		TOEFL	550		9/1	30
Colorado College	Pr/B	2,040	95			613	1/15	50
Colorado Heights University	Pr/AB	182					None	50
Colorado Mountain College	Pu/A	5,741		TOEFL	500		5/1	
Colorado Northwestern Community College	Pu/A	726	6	TOEFL	500		5/15	
Colorado School of Mines	Pu/B	3,710	201	TOEFL	550	575	5/1	45
Colorado School of Trades	Pr/A	155					None	25
Colorado State University	Pu/B	21,953	444		525	579	5/11	50
Colorado State University: Pueblo	Pu/B	4,853	52	TOEFL	500	540	5/1	30
Colorado Technical University	Pr/AB	2,070		TOEFL	550		10/1	100
Community College of Aurora	Pu/A	5,636		TOEFL	500		None	
Community College of Denver	Pu/A	7,222	336	TOEFL	480		8/1	
Concorde Career College: Aurora	Pr/A	810						
Denver School of Nursing	Pr/AB							50
DeVry University: Westminster	Pr/AB			TOEFL	500		None	50
Everest College: Aurora	Pr/A	355					None	25
Everest College: Colorado Springs	Pr/A	790						
Everest College: Denver	Pr/A	1,021						

Student services			Housing		Academic year costs		Maximum credits/summer	Credit hour charge	International financial aid			
Adviser	Orientation	ESL	Academic year	Summer	Tuition/fees	Living costs			Available	Number receiving aid	Average award	Deadline
					12,660†							
					12,660†							
					11,880†							
					12,660†							
Yes	Yes		Yes		37,302	11,206		1156	Yes	5	$5,666	None
Yes	Yes	Yes	Yes		38,582	11,752		1315	Yes	15	$16,203	
Yes	Yes	Yes	Yes	Yes	37,424	12,250	18	1315	Yes			None
Yes	Yes	Yes	Yes	Yes	41,172†	11,580			Yes	258	$28,372	None
Yes	Yes	Yes	Yes	Yes	10,310	6,290	6	335	Yes			None
			Yes	Yes	26,342†	8,280	9	1098	Yes			3/2
Yes		Yes	No		6,732†	10,872	8	223				
Yes		Yes	No		6,280†		8	209	Yes			None
			No		33,923†	16,530		216				
Yes	Yes	Yes	Yes	Yes	6,480†	8,631		216				
Yes	Yes	Yes		Yes	6,480†	5,576						
Yes	Yes	Yes	No		6,744†	11,556	18	224				
Yes	Yes	Yes	No		6,822†	11,160	6	225				
Yes	Yes		Yes	Yes	34,460†	10,960	9		Yes	11	$21,129	None
					14,317†	7,353						
					14,317†	7,552						
					14,317†							
Yes	Yes		Yes		35,442†	11,526	13	1490	Yes			6/30
			Yes		21,800	8,640		925	Yes	1	$11,000	None
Yes	Yes	Yes	Yes	Yes	28,855†	9,293	18	965				
Yes		Yes	Yes		5,500			180				
			No									
Yes	Yes		No		7,092†		9	236	Yes			3/1
			Yes	Yes	14,931†	7,060	15					
Yes	Yes	Yes	No		12,750†	8,478		405				
			No									
Yes		Yes	No		12,570†	8,478		414				
					552†							
Yes	Yes	Yes	Yes	Yes	22,115†			487	Yes			None
					7,600‡			750				
			No						Yes			None
Yes	Yes		Yes	Yes	22,960	9,840	12		Yes			None
Yes	Yes	Yes	Yes		38,698†	13,300	12	1200				
Yes	Yes	Yes	Yes	Yes					Yes			None
Yes	Yes		Yes		7,880†	7,400		256				
Yes			Yes		5,972†	7,520	12	191				
Yes	Yes		Yes	Yes	27,855†	8,596		866				
Yes	Yes	Yes	Yes	Yes	23,095†	11,880		1068				
Yes	Yes	Yes	Yes	Yes	15,688†	7,650	18		Yes	32	$2,335	None
Yes	Yes		Yes	Yes	13,340†		17					
Yes		Yes	Yes	Yes	12,586†	10,598	15	414				None
Yes		Yes	No		13,045†	8,478		414	Yes			
Yes					14,826†				Yes			None
			No						Yes			None
			No			11,556						

† Tuition and fees are for 2010-11.   ‡ Tuition and fees projected for 2011-12.   * Includes room and board

Institution	Control/ degrees	Undergraduates		Tests required (Fall 2011)	TOEFL		Application	
		Total	Internat'l		minimum	average	Deadline	Fee
Everest College: Thornton.	.Pr/A							
Fort Lewis College	.Pu/B	3,752	22	TOEFL, SAT/ACT	500		6/1	40
Front Range Community College	.Pu/A	15,792	169	TOEFL	475	480	None	
Institute of Business & Medical Careers.	.Pr/A	293						75
IntelliTec College	.Pr/A	503					None	
IntelliTec College: Grand Junction	.Pr/A	435					None	
Johnson & Wales University: Denver.	.Pr/AB	1,532	19	TOEFL	550		None	
Jones International University.	.Pr/AB	1,027		TOEFL	550		None	
Kaplan College: Denver	.Pr/A	321						25
Lamar Community College	.Pu/A	966					6/1	
Mesa State College	.Pu/AB	8,038		TOEFL, SAT/ACT	525	550	5/1	30
Metropolitan State College of Denver	.Pu/B	23,635		TOEFL	500	542	7/19	40
Morgan Community College	.Pu/A			TOEFL	490		None	
Naropa University	.Pr/B	443		TOEFL	550		7/1	50
National American University: Denver.	.Pr/AB	450		TOEFL	500		None	45
Nazarene Bible College.	.Pr/AB	608		TOEFL	500		None	
Northeastern Junior College.	.Pu/A	1,218	10	TOEFL	475		7/15	500
Otero Junior College	.Pu/A	1,660		TOEFL	450		8/1	
Pikes Peak Community College	.Pu/A	14,414		TOEFL	450		None	
Pueblo Community College.	.Pu/A	5,647	1	TOEFL	450	480	4/1	
Red Rocks Community College	.Pu/A	8,251	93				7/15	
Redstone College.	.Pr/A			TOEFL	470		None	100
Regis University	.Pr/B	5,594		TOEFL	550		8/1	40
Remington College: Colorado Springs	.Pr/AB			TOEFL				50
Rocky Mountain College of Art & Design	.Pr/B	679	2	TOEFL	550		None	50
Trinidad State Junior College.	.Pu/A	1,812		TOEFL	450		None	10
University of Colorado at Boulder.	.Pu/B	25,782		TOEFL, SAT/ACT	500		1/15	70
University of Colorado at Colorado Springs	.Pu/B	7,124	36	TOEFL, SAT/ACT	550	560		100
University of Colorado at Denver	.Pu/B	9,768	494	TOEFL	525		7/22	75
University of Denver	.Pr/B	5,004		TOEFL	525		1/15	50
University of Northern Colorado.	.Pu/B	9,975	60	TOEFL	550		5/27	60
University of Phoenix: Denver	.Pr/B	1,426						
University of Phoenix: Southern Colorado	.Pr/B	531						
Western State College of Colorado	.Pu/B	2,083		TOEFL, SAT/ACT	550		6/1	40
Westwood College: Denver North.	.Pr/AB			TOEFL	480	525	None	100
Westwood College: Denver South.	.Pr/AB			TOEFL	475		None	25
Westwood College: Online	.Pr/AB							50
Connecticut								
Albertus Magnus College	.Pr/AB	1,681		TOEFL	550	575	7/1	35
Asnuntuck Community College	.Pu/A			TOEFL			6/2	20
Capital Community College.	.Pu/A	3,942	21	TOEFL	500		5/31	20
Central Connecticut State University	.Pu/B	9,720	98	TOEFL	500		4/1	50
Charter Oak State College.	.Pu/AB	1,957	2					75
Connecticut College.	.Pr/B	1,770	77	TOEFL	600		1/1	60
Eastern Connecticut State University	.Pu/AB	5,035	54	TOEFL	550		None	50
Fairfield University	.Pr/AB	3,689		TOEFL	550	591	1/15	60
Gateway Community College.	.Pu/A	6,341	99	TOEFL	500	530	7/11	20
Goodwin College.	.Pr/AB	2,769		TOEFL			None	50
Holy Apostles College and Seminary.	.Pr/AB	36		TOEFL	510		8/15	50
Housatonic Community College	.Pu/A	6,197		TOEFL	530			20
Lincoln College of New England: Briarwood	.Pr/AB			TOEFL	540		None	30
Lincoln College of New England: Suffield	.Pr/A	114		TOEFL	550		None	30
Lyme Academy College of Fine Arts.	.Pr/B	75		TOEFL, SAT/ACT	520		None	55
Manchester Community College	.Pu/A	6,715		TOEFL	500		3/1	20
Middlesex Community College.	.Pu/A	2,357	2	TOEFL	500		7/1	20
Mitchell College	.Pr/AB	916	11	TOEFL	500	520	7/1	30

Student services			Housing		Academic year costs		Maximum credits/ summer	Credit hour charge	International financial aid			
Adviser	Orientation	ESL	Academic year	Summer	Tuition/fees	Living costs			Available	Number receiving aid	Average award	Deadline
Yes	Yes	Yes	Yes	Yes	17,616†	7,840	18	803	Yes	8	$25,945	None
Yes	Yes	Yes	No		12,698†	8,478	18	414				
			No									
			No			10,362						
Yes	Yes		Yes	Yes	24,429†	9,918		152	Yes			None
Yes			No		11,880‡	2,768		495				
Yes			Yes		6,117†	5,294	18	191				
Yes	Yes		Yes	Yes	16,426†	9,782	12	522	Yes			None
Yes	Yes	Yes	No		14,440†	8,478	12	560				
Yes			No		12,579†	8,478		414				
Yes	Yes		Yes		26,350	5,310	12	850	Yes			None
Yes		Yes	No		13,505†	7,272	20	299				
			No		10,050†		16	315	Yes			None
Yes	Yes	Yes	Yes	Yes	10,519†	5,840	12	331				
Yes	Yes		Yes		5,929†	5,354	10	191				
Yes		Yes			12,677†			414	Yes			7/1
Yes		Yes	No		12,919†	8,478		414				
Yes	Yes	Yes	No		12,705†		9	414				
			Yes									
			Yes		30,598†	9,400	12	919	Yes	21	$19,277	None
			No				12					
Yes			Yes	Yes	26,832†		18	1118	Yes			None
Yes		Yes	Yes	Yes	6,310†	5,118	12	191				
Yes	Yes	Yes	Yes	Yes	29,493†	10,792	15		Yes			None
Yes			Yes	Yes	17,067†	7,698	12			7	$5,428	
Yes	Yes	Yes	Yes		20,011†	8,621	12					
Yes	Yes	Yes	Yes	Yes	37,833	10,440	18	1026	Yes	274	$16,848	3/1
Yes	Yes	Yes	Yes	Yes	16,821†	9,344	15	661	Yes			None
					10,120†							
					8,760†							
Yes			Yes		14,241†	10,770	8	537				
Yes			No		14,227†		21		Yes			None
			No		14,227†	6,594	19					
Yes			Yes		24,374†	10,460		996				
			No		10,178†		18	378				
Yes			No		10,203†			378				
Yes	Yes	Yes	Yes	Yes	18,226†	9,576	12					
			No					275				
Yes	Yes		Yes	Yes	43,990	10,980	8		Yes	67	$46,038	2/1
Yes	Yes		Yes	Yes	18,715†	10,048			Yes	3	$3,664	None
Yes	Yes		Yes	Yes	40,580	12,680	18	595	Yes	34	$39,356	2/15
Yes		Yes	No		10,178†		12	378				
			No		19,364	7,953		587				
		Yes	Yes		9,600†	7,550	9	400				
Yes		Yes	No		10,178†	9,600	12	378				
Yes		Yes	Yes	Yes	19,300†	5,400	18	615	Yes			None
Yes	Yes	Yes	Yes	Yes	19,550†	6,800	18					
					28,252		3	1052				
Yes		Yes	No		10,178†		12	378				
Yes		Yes	No		10,178†		6	378				
Yes			Yes		26,907†	12,127	11	300	Yes	4	$6,000	None

Institution	Control/ degrees	Undergraduates		Tests required (Fall 2011)	TOEFL		Application	
		Total	Internat'l		minimum	average	Deadline	Fee
Naugatuck Valley Community College	.Pu/A	6,503	8	TOEFL	500	575	5/1	20
Norwalk Community College	.Pu/A	6,685					None	20
Paier College of Art	.Pr/AB	190		TOEFL	500		8/15	25
Post University	.Pr/AB	770	25	TOEFL	500	.	None	40
Quinnipiac University	.Pr/AB	6,025	70	TOEFL	550	570	2/1	45
Sacred Heart University	.Pr/AB	4,142	94	TOEFL	570		None	100
Saint Joseph College	.Pr/B	1,037		TOEFL, SAT/ACT			4/1	50
Southern Connecticut State University	.Pu/B	8,776	52	TOEFL	525		6/15	50
Trinity College	.Pr/B	2,240	144	TOEFL, SAT/ACT		563	1/1	60
Tunxis Community College	.Pu/A	3,792		TOEFL	500		7/1	20
University of Bridgeport	.Pr/AB	2,534	230	TOEFL, SAT/ACT	500	544	None	50
University of Connecticut	.Pu/AB	16,970	281	TOEFL, SAT/ACT	550	580	2/1	70
University of New Haven	.Pr/AB	4,159	273	TOEFL	537		None	75
University of Phoenix: Fairfield County	.Pr/B	28						
Wesleyan University	.Pr/B	2,837	193	TOEFL, SAT, SAT Subject Test(s), or ACT	600	628	1/1	55
Yale University	.Pr/B	5,296	520	TOEFL, SAT, SAT Subject Test(s), or ACT	600		12/31	75

Delaware

Delaware College of Art and Design	.Pr/A	224	7	TOEFL	550		None	75
Delaware State University	.Pu/B	3,372	31	TOEFL	550		6/1	25
Delaware Technical and Community College:								
Stanton/Wilmington	.Pu/A	6,873		TOEFL	550		6/15	10
Goldey-Beacom College	.Pr/AB	705	1	TOEFL	500		7/1	
University of Delaware	.Pu/AB	15,887	524	TOEFL	550		1/15	60
Wesley College	.Pr/AB	1,932		TOEFL	550		7/1	25

District of Columbia

American University	.Pr/AB	6,665	471	TOEFL	550	619	1/15	65
Catholic University of America	.Pr/AB	3,519	117	TOEFL, SAT/ACT	550		2/15	55
Corcoran College of Art and Design	.Pr/AB			TOEFL	550		7/31	45
Gallaudet University	.Pr/B	1,064	57	TOEFL, SAT/ACT			1/15	50
George Washington University	.Pr/AB	10,055	670	TOEFL, SAT/ACT	550		1/10	75
Georgetown University	.Pr/B	7,122	526	TOEFL, SAT/ACT			1/10	65
Howard University	.Pr/B			TOEFL, SAT/ACT, SAT Subject Test(s)	550		2/15	45
Potomac College	.Pr/AB			TOEFL	550		None	150
Trinity Washington University	.Pr/AB			TOEFL	550		8/1	40
University of the District of Columbia	.Pu/AB	5,311		TOEFL	550	560	None	100
University of Phoenix: Washington DC	.Pr/B	105						

Florida

Angley College	.Pr/AB	251					None	100
Argosy University: Sarasota	.Pr/B							50
Argosy University: Tampa	.Pr/B							50
Art Institute of Fort Lauderdale	.Pr/AB	2,953	28	TOEFL	480	500	None	50
ATI Career Training Center: Oakland Park	.Pr/A	957						100
ATI College of Health	.Pr/A	1,209						100
Ave Maria University	.Pr/B	692	82	TOEFL, SAT/ACT	550		5/1	
Baptist College of Florida	.Pr/AB	610		TOEFL, SAT/ACT	500		8/1	25
Barry University	.Pr/B	4,838	274	TOEFL	550		None	30
Beacon College	.Pr/AB	134		TOEFL				50
Bethune-Cookman University	.Pr/B	3,299	75	TOEFL, SAT/ACT	550	600	5/30	25
Brevard Community College	.Pu/A	14,305		TOEFL	500		8/1	60
Broward College	.Pu/AB	35,665	1,126		550		6/1	75
Brown Mackie College: Miami	.Pr/AB	1,000		TOEFL			None	
Carlos Albizu University	.Pr/B	340					None	25
Chamberlain College of Nursing: Jacksonville	.Pr/B	174						60

Student services			Housing		Academic year costs		Maximum credits/summer	Credit hour charge	International financial aid			
Adviser	Orientation	ESL	Academic year	Summer	Tuition/fees	Living costs			Available	Number receiving aid	Average award	Deadline
Yes	Yes	Yes	No		10,178†	7,750	6	378				
Yes		Yes	No		10,178†	8,415		378				
Yes					15,960†		8		Yes			None
Yes	Yes	Yes	Yes	Yes	24,950†	9,700	9	800	Yes			None
Yes	Yes		Yes		36,130‡	14,430	12	834	Yes			None
Yes	Yes	Yes	Yes	Yes	32,724	12,776	15	500	Yes	37	$32,112	None
			Yes		30,310	13,200		655				
Yes	Yes		Yes	Yes	18,415†	9,983	12					
Yes	Yes		Yes	Yes	44,070	11,380			Yes	119	$48,998	3/1
Yes		Yes	No		10,178†	6,736	15	378				
Yes	Yes	Yes	Yes	Yes	26,370†	11,400	12	810	Yes			None
Yes	Yes	Yes	Yes	Yes	26,880†	10,782	14	1022				
Yes	Yes		Yes		30,750†	12,960		985	Yes			3/1
					12,600†							
Yes	Yes		Yes	Yes	42,384†	11,592			Yes	125	$43,196	2/15
Yes	Yes	Yes	Yes		40,500	12,200			Yes	305	$50,851	3/1
Yes			Yes		20,270	7,300	18					
Yes		Yes	Yes	Yes	14,310†	9,714	9	562				
Yes	Yes	Yes	No		6,787†			271				
Yes	Yes		Yes	Yes	19,860	5,172	12	652	Yes			None
Yes	Yes	Yes	Yes	Yes	25,408†	10,669	14	1010				
Yes			Yes	Yes	21,565	9,940	12	846	Yes			None
Yes	Yes		Yes	Yes	38,071	13,648	12	1251	Yes			2/15
Yes	Yes	Yes	Yes	Yes	35,460	13,824		1380				
Yes	Yes		Yes		29,180†	12,088			Yes			None
Yes	Yes	Yes	Yes	Yes	23,596‡	10,060	8	1161	Yes	15	$16,384	None
Yes	Yes	Yes	Yes	Yes	44,148‡	10,325	12		Yes	185	$20,376	2/1
Yes	Yes	Yes	Yes	Yes	40,203†	13,388	12	1657	Yes	47	$37,234	2/1
Yes	Yes		Yes	Yes	18,121†	9,500	12		Yes			8/15
Yes			No			6,300						
Yes	Yes	Yes	Yes	Yes	19,910†	11,560	9	625				
Yes	Yes	Yes	No		14,000†	6,600	9	558	Yes			None
					11,880†							
			No		16,750†			350				
					19,992†							
					19,992†							
Yes	Yes	Yes	Yes	Yes	22,730‡		18	504				
			No									
Yes	Yes		Yes	Yes	18,625†	8,350	8		Yes			None
Yes			Yes		8,750†	4,066	10	280	Yes			4/15
Yes	Yes	Yes	Yes	Yes	28,160	9,300	12	845	Yes			None
			Yes		28,460†	8,150		510	Yes			None
Yes	Yes		Yes	Yes	13,990	8,300	9	583	Yes			None
Yes		Yes	No		10,380†		18					
Yes	Yes	Yes	No		9,806†	12,416	18		Yes			None
Yes					13,500†		12	360				
Yes	Yes	Yes	No		14,874†		18					
					14,820†			595				

† Tuition and fees are for 2010-11. ‡ Tuition and fees projected for 2011-12. * Includes room and board

Institution	Control/ degrees	Undergraduates		Tests required (Fall 2011)	TOEFL		Application	
		Total	Internat'l		minimum	average	Deadline	Fee
Chipola College............................	Pu/AB	1,587		TOEFL	525		8/1	100
City College: Casselberry	Pr/A							25
City College: Fort Lauderdale	Pr/AB							40
City College: Gainesville..................	Pr/AB	426						
City College: Miami.......................	Pr/AB	416						25
College of Business and Technology: Flagler	Pr/A	150					None	25
College of Business and Technology: Kendall	Pr/A	110						
College of Central Florida.................	Pu/A	7,845	88				6/15	50
Daytona State College	Pu/AB	14,531	53	TOEFL	500	550	8/5	50
DeVry University: Miramar.................	Pr/AB	1,296		TOEFL	500			50
DeVry University: Orlando	Pr/AB	2,064		TOEFL	500		None	50
Eckerd College	Pr/B	1,819	60	TOEFL, SAT/ACT	550	590	4/15	35
Edison State College	Pu/AB	16,951		TOEFL	550		6/27	50
Edward Waters College....................	Pr/B	769		TOEFL	477		6/30	75
Embry-Riddle Aeronautical University..........	Pr/AB	4,484	619	TOEFL	550	591	7/1	50
Embry-Riddle Aeronautical University:								
Worldwide Campus	Pr/AB	10,785	66	TOEFL	550			50
Everest Institute: Fort Lauderdale	Pr/A							
Everest University: Brandon.................	Pr/AB	9,614		TOEFL	450			25
Everest University: Jacksonville	Pr/AB	1,251						
Everest University: Lakeland	Pr/AB	972						25
Everest University: Largo	Pr/AB	1,073		TOEFL	450	500	None	
Everest University: Melbourne	Pr/AB	865						
Everest University: North Orlando	Pr/AB	1,556		TOEFL	475	500	None	50
Everest University: Orange Park..............	Pr/AB	1,359						
Everest University: Pompano Beach	Pr/AB	1,613		TOEFL	450	490	None	25
Everest University: South Orlando	Pr/AB	7,691						
Everest University: Tampa...................	Pr/AB	1,714		TOEFL	450	500	None	50
Everglades University: Boca Raton	Pr/B	967		TOEFL	500			50
Flagler College	Pr/B	2,747	54	TOEFL, SAT/ACT	550	569	3/1	40
Florida Agricultural and Mechanical University	Pu/AB	11,164	59	TOEFL, SAT/ACT	500		5/15	30
Florida Atlantic University	Pu/AB	22,409	341	TOEFL, SAT/ACT	550		4/1	30
Florida Career College: Boynton Beach	Pr/AB	224						100
Florida Career College: Hialeah	Pr/AB	1,206					None	100
Florida Career College: Jacksonville	Pr/AB	750						100
Florida Career College: Lauderdale Lakes........	Pr/AB	1,329						100
Florida Career College: Miami	Pr/AB	1,496						100
Florida Career College: Pembroke Pines.........	Pr/AB	1,555						100
Florida Career College: Riverview	Pr/AB	913						100
Florida Career College: West Palm Beach........	Pr/AB	1,779						100
Florida Christian College...................	Pr/AB	321		TOEFL, SAT/ACT			5/1	35
Florida College of Natural Health: Bradenton	Pr/A							50
Florida College of Natural Health: Miami.........	Pr/A							
Florida Gateway College....................	Pu/A	2,313	3	TOEFL	500	510		
Florida Gulf Coast University................	Pu/AB	10,302	163	TOEFL, SAT/ACT	550		5/1	30
Florida Institute of Technology...............	Pr/AB	5,371	679	TOEFL	550		7/1	50
Florida International University	Pu/AB	32,967	1,579	TOEFL, SAT/ACT	500		None	30
Florida Keys Community College.............	Pu/A	1,243		TOEFL			7/1	80
Florida Memorial University.................	Pr/B			TOEFL, SAT/ACT	500		5/7	15
Florida National College....................	Pr/AB	2,756	112					150
Florida Southern College....................	Pr/B	1,978	80	TOEFL	550		None	30
Florida State College at Jacksonville	Pu/AB	21,204		TOEFL	460	470	5/31	80
Florida State University	Pu/AB	30,830	132	TOEFL, SAT/ACT	550	580		30
Fortis College: Winter Park.................	Pr/A	500						50
Fortis Institute: Orange Park	Pr/A	514						67
Full Sail University	Pr/AB	7,516		TOEFL	550		None	75
Golf Academy of America: Orlando	Pr/A							
Gulf Coast Community College	Pu/A	5,608	37	TOEFL	550		6/12	20

| Student services | | | Housing | | Academic year costs | | Maximum credits/summer | Credit hour charge | International financial aid | | | |
Adviser	Orientation	ESL	Academic year	Summer	Tuition/fees	Living costs			Available	Number receiving aid	Average award	Deadline
Yes					7,935†		12					
Yes	Yes		No		11,475†			255				
					13,680†			235				
					11,475†			255				
					13,680†							
	Yes	Yes	No		14,280†		12	476	Yes			None
					14,280†			476				
Yes	Yes	Yes	Yes	Yes	10,320†		15					
Yes	Yes	Yes			10,737†	10,000	12					
Yes					14,826†	10,204						
Yes					14,826†	10,204						
Yes	Yes	Yes	Yes	Yes	34,546	9,652	14	1174	Yes			None
Yes		Yes	No		10,737†		15					
Yes			Yes		10,470†	6,474		434	Yes			4/15
Yes	Yes	Yes	Yes	Yes	29,720†	10,320	18	1190	Yes	298	$8,135	None
			No									
			No		17,730†	9,110		390				
					17,730†			390				
Yes		Yes	No		17,730†			390				
			No		17,730†	6,840		390				
Yes	Yes	Yes	Yes	Yes	17,730†		12	390				
					17,730†	9,348		390				
Yes	Yes	Yes	No		17,730†	6,840	16	390				
			Yes		14,510	7,990	9	485	Yes	18	$6,594	None
Yes	Yes		Yes	Yes	16,566†	7,856	12		Yes	27	$8,433	None
Yes	Yes	Yes	Yes	Yes	18,132†	9,690	12		Yes	180	$5,719	None
Yes												
			Yes		11,170†	4,020		350	Yes			7/15
			No		22,133†			334				
					22,133†			334				
					10,333†		12					
Yes	Yes		Yes	Yes	21,308†	8,150	12		Yes	75	$10,559	6/30
Yes	Yes	Yes	Yes	Yes	34,990	11,880	12	995	Yes	337	$12,977	None
Yes	Yes	Yes	Yes	Yes	17,490†	13,345	18		Yes			
Yes		Yes	No		10,152†		15		Yes			None
Yes			Yes	Yes	14,604‡	6,112	12	501	Yes			None
Yes		Yes			17,100†		15	525				
Yes			Yes	Yes	26,112	9,408	18	750	Yes	72	$1,411	7/1
Yes	Yes	Yes	No		10,536†		12		Yes			None
Yes	Yes	Yes	Yes	Yes	19,682†	8,780	15					
Yes	Yes		No									
					15,732†							
Yes			No		9,882†	7,580	12					

† Tuition and fees are for 2010-11.   ‡ Tuition and fees projected for 2011-12.   * Includes room and board

Institution	Control/ degrees	Undergraduates		Tests required (Fall 2011)	TOEFL		Application	
		Total	Internat'l		minimum	average	Deadline	Fee
Herzing University............................	Pr/AB	425		TOEFL	500			
Hillsborough Community College	Pu/A	23,596	955	TOEFL	500		5/10	50
Hodges University............................	Pr/AB	2,307		TOEFL	500		None	20
Indian River State College....................	Pu/AB	17,110			500	550	8/8	
International Academy of Design and Technology: Orlando	Pr/AB	998					None	50
International Academy of Design and Technology: Tampa	Pr/AB			TOEFL	550		None	50
ITT Technical Institute: Lake Mary............	Pr/AB							
Jacksonville University........................	Pr/B	3,158	26	TOEFL, SAT/ACT	540		6/1	30
Johnson & Wales University: North Miami.......	Pr/AB	2,098	166	TOEFL	550		None	
Jones College	Pr/AB	738	3	TOEFL	450	500	None	
Keiser Career College: Greenacres	Pr/A							
Keiser University.............................	Pr/AB	16,524					None	50
Key College	Pr/A	128		TOEFL	400	420	None	35
Lake-Sumter Community College	Pu/A	4,042	17	TOEFL	550		None	70
Le Cordon Bleu College of Culinary Arts: Miami	Pr/A	1,434						
Lynn University	Pr/B	1,620	269	TOEFL, SAT/ACT	500	550	8/1	35
Miami Dade College	Pu/AB	56,894	1,176				5/26	50
Miami International University of Art and Design....................................	Pr/AB	2,251		TOEFL			None	50
New College of Florida.....................	Pu/B	801	1	TOEFL, SAT/ACT	560		4/15	30
North Florida Community College..............	Pu/A	1,251		TOEFL	500		None	20
Northwest Florida State College	Pu/AB	8,424		TOEFL	525		None	
Northwood University: Florida.................	Pr/AB	583	210	TOEFL	500	539	None	25
Nova Southeastern University..................	Pr/AB	6,092	252	TOEFL	550		8/1	50
Palm Beach Atlantic University	Pr/AB	2,426	59	TOEFL	550	600	None	30
Palm Beach State College	Pu/AB	25,490	443	TOEFL	450		8/1	30
Pasco-Hernando Community College...........	Pu/A	9,265		TOEFL	523			25
Pensacola State College	Pu/AB			TOEFL, SAT/ACT	500		None	30
Polk State College...........................	Pu/AB	9,123	70	TOEFL	525	537	5/15	20
Professional Golfers Career College: Orlando	Pr/A	200		TOEFL	473			125
Rasmussen College: Ocala....................	Pr/AB	2,165		TOEFL	500		None	60
Rasmussen College: Pasco County	Pr/AB			TOEFL	500		None	20
Remington College: Tampa	Pr/AB	312					None	50
Ringling College of Art and Design............	Pr/B	1,368	100	TOEFL	500		None	70
Rollins College..............................	Pr/B	1,730	89	TOEFL	550		3/15	40
Saint Leo University	Pr/AB	1,858	116	TOEFL	550	619	6/1	35
St. Petersburg College	Pu/AB	26,755	194				5/28	140
Saint Thomas University......................	Pr/B	1,149	118	TOEFL	525		8/1	40
Sanford-Brown Institute: Jacksonville	Pr/A							25
Santa Fe College.............................	Pu/AB	15,745		TOEFL	400		None	
Schiller International University	Pr/AB	115		TOEFL	500		None	65
Seminole State College of Florida..............	Pu/AB	16,571	401	TOEFL	450		12/1	50
South Florida Community College	Pu/A	2,068	32	TOEFL	500		7/15	
South University: Tampa......................	Pr/AB	608		TOEFL	550			50
South University: West Palm Beach	Pr/AB	887		TOEFL	550			50
Southeastern University.......................	Pr/B	2,368	50	TOEFL, SAT/ACT	500		5/1	40
Southwest Florida College....................	Pr/AB	2,298	1	TOEFL	500		None	25
State College of Florida, Manatee-Sarasota	Pu/AB	10,238		TOEFL, SAT/ACT	500		7/24	75
Stenotype Institute: Jacksonville	Pr/A							100
Stenotype Institute: Orlando..................	Pr/A							
Stetson University	Pr/B	2,124	80	TOEFL	550		3/15	25
Tallahassee Community College	Pu/A			TOEFL	500	550	6/16	
Trinity Baptist College	Pr/AB							30
Trinity College of Florida	Pr/AB	196	2	TOEFL, SAT/ACT	500		None	25
Universidad FLET............................	Pr/AB	265						20
University of Central Florida..................	Pu/AB	47,306	510	TOEFL, SAT/ACT	550		3/1	30

Adviser	Orientation	ESL	Academic year	Summer	Tuition/fees	Living costs	Maximum credits/summer	Credit hour charge	Available	Number receiving aid	Average award	Deadline
Yes			Yes		12,400†			385				
					10,325†	8,725						
		Yes	No		14,330†		16	465				
Yes		Yes	Yes	Yes	10,530†		12					
					17,375†			385				
			No		17,375†			385	Yes			None
Yes	Yes		Yes	Yes	26,600†	9,320	18	883	Yes			None
Yes	Yes	Yes	Yes	Yes	25,407	9,261			Yes			None
Yes			No		9,240		15	305				
			No									
Yes	Yes		No		10,920‡	9,153	16					
Yes			No		10,520†		18		Yes			None
Yes	Yes	Yes	Yes		31,700	11,950	18		Yes	122	$20,827	None
Yes	Yes	Yes	No		10,371†	16,632	12		Yes			6/30
Yes	Yes		Yes	Yes		16,880						
Yes			Yes		27,614†	8,225			Yes			None
Yes			No		9,618†	5,400	12					
Yes			No		10,041†	10,426						
Yes	Yes		Yes	Yes	19,272†	9,076	18	715	Yes			None
Yes	Yes	Yes	Yes	Yes	23,200	9,516	18	755	Yes			None
Yes	Yes		Yes	Yes	24,100	8,400	9		Yes	51	$9,000	8/1
Yes	Yes				9,690†		17		Yes			None
			No		10,014†							
Yes			No		10,266†		6					
Yes		Yes	No		10,443†	3,600	18		Yes			None
Yes												
			No		16,875†				Yes			None
					16,875†			375	Yes			None
			No				15					
Yes	Yes		Yes		34,840	11,750		1505	Yes	31	$26,925	None
Yes	Yes		Yes		37,640†	11,760	8		Yes	49	$25,893	None
Yes	Yes		Yes	Yes	18,570	13,120	12		Yes	113	$11,053	None
Yes	Yes		No		10,249†	10,663	12					
Yes	Yes	Yes	Yes	Yes	23,910	7,715	18	797	Yes	101	$7,578	None
Yes			No		10,182†	7,552	18					
Yes	Yes	Yes	Yes	Yes			10		Yes			4/1
Yes	Yes	Yes	No		10,550†		18		Yes			
Yes	Yes		Yes	Yes	10,432†	5,821	7					
					15,585†							
			No		15,585†							
Yes			Yes	Yes	17,718‡	8,220	12					
		Yes	No		14,850†	6,232		305				
Yes			No		10,737†		12		Yes			7/28
Yes	Yes	Yes	Yes	Yes	35,081	10,255	10	960	Yes	69	$21,598	None
Yes	Yes		No		9,101†		18		Yes			None
					8,050†	5,040						
Yes			Yes		12,154	6,860		473	Yes			9/15
Yes	Yes	Yes	Yes	Yes	20,500†	8,914	15		Yes	55	$970	6/30

† Tuition and fees are for 2010-11. ‡ Tuition/fees projected for 2011-12. * Includes room and board

Institution	Control/ degrees	Undergraduates		Tests required (Fall 2011)	TOEFL		Application	
		Total	Internat'l		minimum	average	Deadline	Fee
University of Florida	Pu/B	32,043	247		550		11/1	30
University of Miami	Pr/B	9,903	912	TOEFL	550		1/15	65
University of North Florida	Pu/AB	14,044		TOEFL, SAT/ACT	500	540	5/1	30
University of Phoenix: Central Florida	Pr/B	1,307						
University of Phoenix: North Florida	Pr/B	1,139						
University of Phoenix: South Florida	Pr/B	1,759						
University of Phoenix: West Florida	Pr/B	802						
University of South Florida	Pu/AB	30,239	398	TOEFL, SAT/ACT	550		3/1	30
University of Tampa	Pr/AB	5,650	544	TOEFL	550	571	None	40
University of West Florida	Pu/AB	9,121	129	TOEFL	525		5/15	30
Valencia College	Pu/A	34,795	580	TOEFL	450		5/9	35
Warner University	Pr/AB	964		TOEFL, SAT/ACT	500	600	5/15	20
Webber International University	Pr/AB	679		TOEFL	500	537	8/1	75

Georgia

Institution	Control/ degrees	Undergraduates		Tests required (Fall 2011)	TOEFL		Application	
		Total	Internat'l		minimum	average	Deadline	Fee
Abraham Baldwin Agricultural College	Pu/AB	3,284		TOEFL	523		8/1	20
Agnes Scott College	Pr/B	830	79	TOEFL			1/1	35
Albany State University	Pu/B	4,154	12	TOEFL	523		5/1	20
Albany Technical College	Pu/A	4,294		TOEFL, SAT/ACT			8/31	15
Altamaha Technical College.	Pu/A	1,629						15
American InterContinental University	Pr/AB	1,964		TOEFL	500		None	50
Andrew College	Pr/A	273	9	TOEFL	500	520	None	20
Argosy University: Atlanta	Pr/B							50
Armstrong Atlantic State University	Pu/AB	6,938	279	TOEFL	523		4/15	25
Art Institute of Atlanta	Pr/AB			TOEFL			None	50
Ashworth College	Pr/AB							
Atlanta Christian College	Pr/AB	1,022	1	TOEFL	550		8/1	25
Atlanta Metropolitan College	Pu/A	3,037		TOEFL	523	525	None	20
Atlanta Technical College	Pu/A	4,575						15
Augusta State University	Pu/AB	5,628	61	TOEFL, SAT/ACT	500		7/15	20
Augusta Technical College	Pu/A	4,679	2	TOEFL	500			15
Bainbridge College	Pu/A	3,513		TOEFL	523		7/30	
Bauder College	Pr/AB			TOEFL	460		None	100
Berry College	Pr/B	1,911	26	TOEFL, SAT/ACT	550	552	2/1	50
Beulah Heights University	Pr/AB	631		TOEFL	500		8/1	35
Brenau University	Pr/AB	795	40	TOEFL	500		None	35
Brewton-Parker College	Pr/AB	624	22				None	25
Carver Bible College	Pr/AB	109						
Central Georgia Technical College	Pu/A	7,699	1					20
Chattahoochee Technical College	Pu/A	12,526	37	TOEFL				15
Clark Atlanta University	Pr/B	3,267	25	TOEFL, SAT/ACT	500	550	5/1	55
Clayton State University	Pu/AB	6,366		TOEFL	550	564	7/1	40
College of Coastal Georgia	Pu/AB		24	TOEFL	523		5/15	20
Columbus State University	Pu/AB	6,890	62	TOEFL	550	653	5/1	30
Columbus Technical College	Pu/A	4,261	3	TOEFL	500			15
Covenant College	Pr/AB	963	16	TOEFL, SAT/ACT	540	590	8/1	35
Darton College	Pu/A	5,879	87	TOEFL	480		7/1	20
DeKalb Technical College	Pu/A	4,742	1					15
DeVry University: Decatur	Pr/AB			TOEFL	500		None	50
East Georgia College	Pu/A	3,063		TOEFL	523		None	20
Emory University	Pr/AB	5,325	747	TOEFL, SAT/ACT		600	1/15	50
Everest College: Atlanta	Pr/AB	1,460						
Fort Valley State University	Pu/AB	3,566	18	TOEFL, SAT/ACT	500		7/15	20
Gainesville State College	Pu/AB			TOEFL	480	560	5/1	25
Georgia College and State University	Pu/B	5,706	83	TOEFL	500		4/1	40
Georgia Gwinnett College	Pu/B	5,178	38					20
Georgia Highlands College	Pu/A	5,226		TOEFL, SAT/ACT	550		7/1	20
Georgia Institute of Technology	Pu/B	13,160	885				1/15	65
Georgia Military College	Pu/A	5,673		TOEFL		460	6/1	40

Student services			Housing		Academic year costs		Maximum credits/ summer	Credit hour charge	International financial aid			
Adviser	Orien-tation	ESL	Academic year	Summer	Tuition/ fees	Living costs			Avail-able	Number receiving aid	Average award	Deadline
Yes	Yes	Yes	Yes		27,322†	8,640	15	911	Yes	144	$22,873	None
Yes	Yes	Yes	Yes	Yes	37,836†	11,062	12	1538	Yes			
Yes	Yes	Yes	Yes	Yes	18,297†	8,293	18					
					10,680†							
					10,680†							
					10,680†							
					11,680†							
Yes	Yes	Yes	Yes	Yes	16,007†	9,000			Yes	241	$8,096	None
Yes	Yes		Yes	Yes	23,976	8,830	16	486	Yes	245	$5,012	None
Yes	Yes	Yes	Yes	Yes	17,675†	7,856	15					
Yes	Yes	Yes	No		10,423†	10,020	19					
			Yes		15,780†	7,758	12		Yes			
Yes	Yes	Yes	Yes	Yes	18,742†	10,700	12	259	Yes			8/1
Yes		Yes	Yes		10,978†	6,540	18	340				
Yes	Yes		Yes	Yes	32,195	11,150	12	1333	Yes	78	$19,973	5/1
Yes	Yes		Yes	Yes	17,048†	6,006						
					8,343†	9,304		180				
					8,343†			180				
Yes					15,465†		18	390				
Yes		Yes	Yes		12,111	7,606	12		Yes			8/1
					19,992†							
Yes	Yes		Yes	Yes	16,966†	8,670		530	Yes			None
Yes	Yes		Yes	Yes	23,535†	9,984		472	Yes			None
			Yes		15,902†	5,670			Yes			8/1
Yes	Yes		No		10,006†		12	310				
	Yes		No		8,346†		21	180				
Yes		Yes	Yes		16,798†		18	530	Yes	22	$5,293	None
Yes			No		8,355†	4,500		180				
Yes			No		9,964†	5,550	17	310				
Yes			Yes		13,866†	8,442			Yes			None
Yes	Yes		Yes	Yes	26,090	9,158	12	863	Yes	24	$24,579	None
Yes	Yes	Yes	Yes	Yes	7,480	7,500	12	240	Yes			
Yes	Yes	Yes	Yes	Yes	21,124	10,666	9	695	Yes			None
Yes	Yes		Yes	Yes	15,845†	6,840	12	455	Yes	7	$12,716	4/15
			Yes		7,420†			230				
			No		5,643†			180				
Yes			No		8,364†			180				
Yes	Yes		Yes	Yes	18,911	8,529	9	754				
Yes	Yes		Yes		17,026†	8,352	12	530	Yes			None
Yes			No		11,136†	8,000	18		Yes			
Yes	Yes	Yes	Yes	Yes	17,872†	7,280	13	553	Yes	11	$6,456	None
			No		8,343†	11,000		180				
Yes			Yes	Yes	27,220	7,740	3	1107	Yes	13	$12,796	None
Yes	Yes	Yes	Yes		10,070†	7,832	15	310	Yes			None
Yes			No		8,391†	9,000	18	180				
Yes					14,826†							
Yes	Yes		No		9,798†	2,600		310	Yes			None
Yes	Yes		Yes	Yes	39,158†	12,198	16	1608	Yes	25	$28,617	3/1
Yes	Yes		Yes	Yes	17,176†	6,646	18	530				
Yes	Yes	Yes	No		10,730†		15	340				
Yes	Yes		Yes	Yes	24,890†	8,414			Yes			None
			Yes		13,320†	8,500		407				
Yes			No		9,910†		17	310				
Yes	Yes	Yes	Yes	Yes	26,926†	8,746	16					
			Yes		5,187†	6,150	15					

† Tuition and fees are for 2010-11.   ‡ Tuition and fees projected for 2011-12.   * Includes room and board

Institution	Control/ degrees	Undergraduates		Tests required (Fall 2011)	TOEFL		Application	
		Total	Internat'l		minimum	average	Deadline	Fee
Georgia Northwestern Technical College	Pu/A	6,513						20
Georgia Perimeter College.	Pu/A	23,301	940	TOEFL	460	495	7/1	20
Georgia Southern University	Pu/B	16,262	192	TOEFL	523		5/1	30
Georgia Southwestern State University.	Pu/B	2,775	77	TOEFL	523		7/1	25
Georgia State University	Pu/B	22,790	408	TOEFL, SAT/ACT	550	593	3/1	60
Gordon College.	Pu/AB	5,009		TOEFL	525		None	20
Gupton Jones College of Funeral Service	Pr/A	246						50
Gwinnett College.	Pr/A							
Herzing University.	Pr/AB			TOEFL	500		None	
ITT Technical Institute: Duluth.	Pr/AB							
ITT Technical Institute: Kennesaw	Pr/AB							
Kennesaw State University	Pu/B	21,363	348	TOEFL, SAT/ACT	527		6/25	40
LaGrange College	Pr/AB	828	13	TOEFL	500		7/1	30
Le Cordon Bleu College of Culinary Arts:								
Atlanta.	Pr/A	1,066						50
Life University	Pr/AB	792		TOEFL	500		8/15	50
Luther Rice University	Pr/B	412						50
Mercer University	Pr/B	2,325	73	TOEFL	550		6/1	50
Middle Georgia College	Pu/AB	3,496		TOEFL	527	530	8/1	20
Middle Georgia Technical College	Pu/A	3,868	1	TOEFL	500			20
Morehouse College	Pr/B			TOEFL, SAT/ACT	500		2/15	45
North Georgia College & State University	Pu/AB	5,353	63	TOEFL, SAT/ACT	550		6/1	30
Oglethorpe University.	Pr/B	1,054	31	TOEFL	550	556	8/1	40
Paine College	Pr/B	918	3	TOEFL, SAT/ACT	500		8/1	40
Piedmont College	Pr/B	1,205	4	TOEFL, SAT/ACT	550		7/1	
Reinhardt University	Pr/AB	1,057	1	TOEFL	500	540	None	25
Savannah College of Art and Design	Pr/B	8,347	776	TOEFL	550	554	None	70
Savannah State University.	Pu/B	3,837		TOEFL, SAT/ACT	523		7/15	20
Savannah Technical College.	Pu/A	5,489	4				None	20
Shorter University	Pr/B	1,524		TOEFL, SAT/ACT	500		8/1	25
South Georgia College	Pu/A			TOEFL	523		None	20
South University: Savannah	Pr/AB	16,288		TOEFL	550		None	50
Southeastern Technical College	Pu/A	1,822		TOEFL	500		3/31	20
Southern Crescent Technical College	Pu/A	6,021	1					20
Southern Polytechnic State University	Pu/AB	4,814	329	TOEFL, SAT/ACT	550		7/1	20
Southwest Georgia Technical College	Pu/A	1,451						15
Spelman College	Pr/B	2,177	12	TOEFL, SAT/ACT	500		12/31	35
Thomas University.	Pr/AB	849		TOEFL	550		None	125
Toccoa Falls College	Pr/AB	758		TOEFL	550		8/1	20
Truett-McConnell College	Pr/AB	486		TOEFL, SAT/ACT	500		8/1	25
University of Georgia.	Pu/B	25,709	179	TOEFL, SAT/ACT	550		1/15	60
University of Phoenix: Atlanta	Pr/B							
University of Phoenix: Augusta	Pr/B							
University of Phoenix: Columbus Georgia	Pr/B							
University of Phoenix: Savannah	Pr/B							
University of West Georgia	Pu/B	9,707	125	TOEFL, SAT/ACT	523		None	30
Valdosta State University	Pu/AB	10,761	194	TOEFL	523		4/1	40
Waycross College	Pu/A			TOEFL, SAT/ACT	523		5/1	20
Wesleyan College	Pr/B	630		TOEFL, SAT/ACT	550	597	5/15	30
Westwood College: Northlake	Pr/AB							50
Wiregrass Georgia Technical College.	Pu/A	5,135						20
Young Harris College.	Pr/AB	818			550	557	4/1	
Hawaii								
Argosy University: Hawaii	Pr/B							50
Brigham Young University-Hawaii	Pr/AB	2,780	955	TOEFL	500	523	2/15	30
Chaminade University of Honolulu	Pr/AB	1,125		TOEFL, SAT/ACT	550			50
Hawaii Pacific University	Pr/AB	6,440		TOEFL	550	569	None	50
Hawaii Tokai International College	Pr/A	57	42	TOEFL	400	450	5/27	50

Student services			Housing		Academic year costs		Maximum credits/summer	Credit hour charge	International financial aid			
Adviser	Orientation	ESL	Academic year	Summer	Tuition/fees	Living costs			Available	Number receiving aid	Average award	Deadline
Yes	Yes	Yes	No		8,343†			180	Yes			6/1
					9,986†			120				
Yes	Yes	Yes	Yes	Yes	18,216†	8,414	12	553	Yes	39	$4,139	
Yes	Yes	Yes	Yes	Yes	16,946†	6,200	18	530				
Yes	Yes	Yes	Yes		26,908†	8,830	18	843	Yes	14	$4,289	11/1
			Yes		10,756†	5,310	18	340				
			No		9,000†			200				
Yes			No		9,475‡							
					12,400†		16	385				
Yes	Yes		Yes		17,918†	8,259	17	553				
Yes	Yes		Yes	Yes	23,212	9,455	17	956	Yes			None
Yes	Yes	Yes	Yes	Yes	8,967		20	182	Yes	5	$2,200	None
					6,830†			209	Yes	5	$2,338	
Yes	Yes		Yes	Yes	31,548	10,408	12	1042	Yes	62	$21,836	None
Yes			Yes	Yes	10,800†	6,980	20		Yes			None
					8,343†			180				
Yes			Yes		23,520	12,184	9	900	Yes	37	$15,426	4/1
Yes	Yes	Yes	Yes	Yes	18,070†	6,206	20	553	Yes			None
Yes	Yes		Yes	Yes	29,150	10,440	16		Yes			None
Yes			Yes		11,794†	5,748	12	454	Yes	1	$17,542	None
Yes			Yes	Yes	19,000	9,200	18	792	Yes	3	$17,600	None
Yes	Yes		Yes	Yes	16,866†	6,598	21	575	Yes			None
Yes	Yes	Yes	Yes	Yes	31,010‡	14,255	15	678	Yes	527	$12,703	None
Yes	Yes		Yes	Yes	17,238†	6,288	9	530	Yes			4/1
Yes	Yes	Yes	No		8,343†		21	180	Yes			None
Yes	Yes		Yes	Yes	17,070†	8,200	19	460	Yes			None
			Yes		10,036†	7,950		310				
Yes			Yes		15,585†				Yes			None
Yes			Yes		8,343†		21	180				
					8,343†	3,400		180				
Yes	Yes	Yes	Yes	Yes	19,294†	9,104	12	604	Yes			None
			No		8,343†	2,700		180				
Yes			Yes		22,010†	10,464			Yes	8	$19,469	None
Yes			Yes	Yes	12,720	4,350	15	500				
Yes			Yes		15,885†	5,950	12	658	Yes			8/1
Yes			Yes		14,540†	6,060	12	468	Yes			None
Yes	Yes		Yes	Yes	26,946†	8,460	9					
					11,880†							
					11,040†							
					11,040†							
					11,040†							
Yes		Yes	Yes	Yes	18,158†	6,754	18	553	Yes			None
Yes	Yes	Yes	Yes	Yes	18,282†	6,520		553				
			No		9,750†	7,578		310				
Yes	Yes		Yes	Yes	18,000†	8,100	12		Yes	65	$15,568	6/3
					14,227†							
					8,376†			180				
Yes			Yes		21,970‡	7,480	6		Yes			None
					20,568†							
Yes	Yes	Yes	Yes	Yes	4,330†	4,756	9		Yes			3/15
Yes			Yes	Yes	18,440	10,890	12	610	Yes			None
Yes	Yes	Yes	Yes	Yes	16,610	12,230	21	345	Yes	195	$5,214	None
Yes	Yes	Yes	Yes	Yes	10,920	7,020	14		Yes			

† Tuition and fees are for 2010-11.   ‡ Tuition and fees projected for 2011-12.   * Includes room and board

Institution	Control/ degrees	Undergraduates		Tests required (Fall 2011)	TOEFL		Application	
		Total	Internat'l		minimum	average	Deadline	Fee
Heald College: Honolulu	Pr/A						None	
Remington College: Honolulu	Pr/AB	615		TOEFL	400		None	50
University of Hawaii at Hilo	Pu/B	3,351	178		500		6/1	25
University of Hawaii at Manoa.	Pu/B	13,599	440	TOEFL, SAT/ACT	500	565	2/1	50
University of Hawaii: Hawaii Community College	Pu/A	3,275		TOEFL	475		8/1	25
University of Hawaii: Honolulu Community College	Pu/A	3,458		TOEFL	500	530	6/15	25
University of Hawaii: Kapiolani Community College	Pu/A	9,102		TOEFL	500	600	7/17	50
University of Hawaii: Kauai Community College	Pu/A	1,428		TOEFL	450		7/1	25
University of Hawaii: Leeward Community College	Pu/A			TOEFL	500		6/30	25
University of Hawaii: Maui College	Pu/AB	4,055		TOEFL	480		7/1	25
University of Hawaii: West Oahu	Pu/B	1,418	41	TOEFL	550		6/15	50
University of Hawaii: Windward Community College	Pu/A			TOEFL	500		6/1	25
University of Phoenix: Hawaii	Pr/B	986						
Idaho								
Boise State University	Pu/AB	16,714	231	TOEFL	500	583	6/1	55
Brigham Young University-Idaho	Pr/AB	14,103		TOEFL			2/1	35
College of Idaho	Pr/B	1,025	87	TOEFL	550		6/1	
College of Southern Idaho.	Pu/A	8,133		TOEFL	450		None	
College of Western Idaho	Pu/A							
Idaho State University	Pu/AB	10,215	157	TOEFL, SAT/ACT	500		6/1	40
ITT Technical Institute: Boise	Pr/AB			TOEFL	500		None	100
Lewis-Clark State College	Pu/AB	3,491	72	TOEFL	500	533	6/1	45
New Saint Andrews College	Pr/AB			TOEFL, SAT/ACT	570		5/1	50
North Idaho College.	Pu/A	5,418		TOEFL	500	550	7/7	15
Northwest Nazarene University.	Pr/B	1,226		TOEFL, SAT/ACT	500	550	None	25
Stevens-Henager College: Boise	Pr/AB	894		TOEFL			None	100
University of Idaho	Pu/B	9,103	169	TOEFL	525	565	5/1	70
University of Phoenix: Idaho	Pr/B	540						
Illinois								
American Academy of Art.	Pr/B	471		TOEFL	500		None	25
Argosy University: Chicago.	Pr/B			TOEFL	500			50
Argosy University: Schaumburg	Pr/B							50
Augustana College.	Pr/B	2,509	25	TOEFL, SAT/ACT	550		4/1	35
Aurora University	Pr/B	2,614	1	TOEFL	550		3/10	25
Benedictine University	Pr/AB	3,582	51	TOEFL	550		7/1	40
Benedictine University at Springfield.	Pr/B	679	17	TOEFL	515		7/15	50
Black Hawk College	Pu/A	4,644	14		550		6/1	
Black Hawk College: East Campus	Pu/A			TOEFL	480			
Blackburn College.	Pr/B	600		TOEFL	515	530	6/1	
Blessing-Rieman College of Nursing	Pr/B	253						
Bradley University.	Pr/B	5,061	34	TOEFL	530		6/1	35
Carl Sandburg College	Pu/A	2,661		TOEFL	600		None	
Chamberlain College of Nursing: Addison	Pr/B	814	3					95
Chamberlain College of Nursing: Chicago	Pr/B	163	2					95
Chicago State University.	Pu/B	5,677		TOEFL	500	525	5/1	30
City Colleges of Chicago: Harold Washington College	Pu/A			TOEFL	450	500	8/15	25
City Colleges of Chicago: Kennedy-King College	Pu/A			TOEFL				
City Colleges of Chicago: Malcolm X College	Pu/A			TOEFL				
City Colleges of Chicago: Olive-Harvey College	Pu/A							

Adviser	Orientation	ESL	Academic year	Summer	Tuition/ fees	Living costs	Maximum credits/ summer	Credit hour charge	Available	Number receiving aid	Average award	Deadline
			No		9,735†				Yes			None
Yes	Yes	Yes	No Yes	Yes	15,904†	7,134	10	650				
Yes	Yes	Yes	Yes	Yes	21,536†	10,355	16	876	Yes	148	$9,963	None
		Yes	Yes		8,564†		10	281				
			No		8,460†		6	281				
Yes	Yes		Yes		8,490†		6	281				
Yes	Yes		No		8,490†		6	281				
Yes	Yes	Yes	No		8,475†			281	Yes			None
Yes	Yes	Yes	Yes	Yes	13,356†		6	441	Yes			None
Yes			No		14,362†		18	598				
			No		8,470† 11,880†			281	Yes			None
Yes	Yes	Yes	Yes	Yes	14,756†	5,314	7	316	Yes	96	$12,102	None
Yes	Yes		Yes	Yes	3,770	7,590	21	145	Yes			None
Yes	Yes	Yes	Yes		22,315‡	9,319		910	Yes	88	$12,982	None
Yes	Yes	Yes	Yes		6,720†	4,870	12	280	Yes			None
Yes	Yes	Yes	Yes No	Yes	15,916†	6,096		423	Yes			None
Yes	Yes	Yes	Yes	Yes	13,906†	5,900	15		Yes	239	$2,083	
			Yes		10,455	4,500		400				
Yes	Yes	Yes	Yes		7,210†	6,000	6	257				
Yes			Yes		24,030	6,260	6	1028	Yes			None
			No		15,432†			419				
Yes	Yes	Yes	Yes	Yes	16,994†	7,194	18	850	Yes	50	$5,040	None
					10,200†							
			No			6,354	17					
Yes	Yes				19,992†							
					19,992†							
Yes	Yes		Yes	Yes	33,363‡	8,866	9		Yes	14	$21,218	None
Yes			Yes	Yes	19,450	8,270	8	570	Yes	1	$10,000	None
Yes	Yes	Yes	Yes	Yes	23,250†	7,360	12	750	Yes			None
Yes			Yes		9,585†	6,900	12	385		3	$2,524	
Yes	Yes	Yes	No		6,075†	6,268	12	193	Yes	17	$2,427	None
			No		6,075†	5,950	6	193				
Yes			Yes		14,996†	4,790	6	496				
			Yes		23,325	8,395		510				
Yes	Yes		Yes	Yes	25,424†	7,950	15					
Yes		Yes	No		6,750† 14,820†			225	Yes			None
						2,748						
Yes	Yes		Yes		17,456†	7,830	6	536	Yes			None
Yes	Yes	Yes	No		8,296†		6	260				
		Yes	No		8,296†			260				
Yes	Yes		No		8,296†		6	260				
			No		8,296†		6	260				

Institution	Control/ degrees	Undergraduates		Tests required (Fall 2011)	TOEFL		Application	
		Total	Internat'l		minimum	average	Deadline	Fee
City Colleges of Chicago: Richard J. Daley College	Pu/A			TOEFL				
City Colleges of Chicago: Wilbur Wright College	Pu/A			TOEFL				
College of DuPage	Pu/A	26,722		TOEFL	550		6/9	20
College of Lake County	Pu/A	13,340			525		7/7	
College of Office Technology	Pr/A							50
Columbia College Chicago	Pr/B	11,135		TOEFL	533		5/1	100
Concordia University Chicago	Pr/B	1,328		TOEFL, SAT/ACT	525		5/5	
Coyne College	Pr/A							
Danville Area Community College	Pu/A	3,311	2	TOEFL	500		7/15	
DePaul University	Pr/B	15,801	232	TOEFL	550		7/1	40
DeVry University: Chicago	Pr/AB			TOEFL	500		None	50
DeVry University: Online	Pr/AB							50
Dominican University	Pr/B	1,789	36	TOEFL	550	560	6/1	100
East-West University	Pr/AB			TOEFL			None	200
Eastern Illinois University	Pu/B	9,826	59	TOEFL	500		5/15	30
Elgin Community College	Pu/A	12,214		TOEFL				50
Elmhurst College	Pr/B	3,032		TOEFL, SAT/ACT	550	600	5/1	
Eureka College	Pr/B			TOEFL	550		6/15	
Governors State University	Pu/B	2,926	1	TOEFL	500	520	None	25
Greenville College	Pr/B	1,329	17	TOEFL	500		8/15	30
Harper College	Pu/A	7,981	44	TOEFL	550		6/12	175
Harrington College of Design	Pr/AB	897		TOEFL	500		None	60
Heartland Community College	Pu/A	5,257		TOEFL	550		6/15	
Hebrew Theological College	Pr/B	481						100
Illinois Central College	Pu/A			TOEFL	500	520	None	
Illinois College	Pr/B	853	19	TOEFL	550	580	None	
Illinois Eastern Community Colleges: Frontier Community College	Pu/A	605		TOEFL	500		None	35
Illinois Eastern Community Colleges: Lincoln Trail College	Pu/A	676		TOEFL	500		None	35
Illinois Eastern Community Colleges: Olney Central College	Pu/A	1,100		TOEFL	500		None	35
Illinois Eastern Community Colleges: Wabash Valley College	Pu/A	961		TOEFL	500		None	35
Illinois Institute of Art: Chicago	Pr/AB	3,024		TOEFL	480		None	50
Illinois Institute of Art: Schaumburg	Pr/AB	1,400		TOEFL				50
Illinois Institute of Technology	Pr/B	2,562	510	TOEFL	550		4/15	
Illinois State University	Pu/B	18,243	76	TOEFL, SAT/ACT	550	594	5/15	40
Illinois Wesleyan University	Pr/B	2,088	78	TOEFL, SAT/ACT	550		3/1	
International Academy of Design and Technology: Chicago	Pr/AB	1,608		TOEFL	500		None	50
ITT Technical Institute: Mount Prospect	Pr/AB			TOEFL	500		None	100
John A. Logan College	Pu/A	6,787		TOEFL	520		None	
John Wood Community College	Pu/A	2,117	9	TOEFL	470		None	
Joliet Junior College	Pu/A			TOEFL	500		None	
Judson University	Pr/B	979	35	TOEFL	550	580	8/1	50
Kankakee Community College	Pu/A	3,588		TOEFL	520		7/1	250
Kaskaskia College	Pu/A	2,839	12	TOEFL	550		6/1	
Kendall College	Pr/AB	2,253	148	TOEFL	525		None	50
Kishwaukee College	Pu/A			TOEFL	485	495	6/1	15
Knox College	Pr/B	1,375	101	TOEFL	550		2/1	40
Lake Forest College	Pr/B	1,404	169	TOEFL, SAT/ACT	550	567	2/15	
Lake Land College	Pu/A	12,212		TOEFL	500	525	None	
Le Cordon Bleu College of Culinary Arts: Chicago	Pr/A	1,051		TOEFL	500		None	50
Lewis University	Pr/AB	4,174	49	TOEFL, SAT/ACT	550		None	40
Lexington College	Pr/AB			TOEFL	547		None	75
Lincoln Christian University	Pr/AB	664		TOEFL	550		3/1	25

Student services			Housing		Academic year costs		Maximum credits/ summer	Credit hour charge	International financial aid			
Adviser	Orien- tation	ESL	Academic year	Summer	Tuition/ fees	Living costs			Avail- able	Number receiving aid	Average award	Deadline
		Yes	No		8,296 †		6	260				
Yes		Yes	No		8,296 †		8	260				
Yes		Yes	No		11,580 †		18					
Yes	Yes	Yes	No		9,128 †	4,732	12	310	Yes			None
					10,368 †							
Yes	Yes	Yes	Yes	Yes	20,730 ‡	12,680	12	638	Yes			None
Yes			Yes	Yes	25,631	8,250	16	779	Yes			None
Yes		Yes	No		5,610 †		9	175	Yes			None
Yes	Yes	Yes	Yes	Yes	28,858 †	10,955	16	490				
Yes		Yes			14,826 †							
					14,826 †							
Yes	Yes	Yes	Yes	Yes	25,810 †	9,800	12	852	Yes	22	$19,686	None
Yes			No		15,795 †	11,100	16					
Yes	Yes		Yes	Yes	25,227 †	8,854		762				
Yes	Yes	Yes	No		13,290 †			443				
Yes	Yes		Yes	Yes	28,600 †	9,266	8	814	Yes			None
Yes	Yes		Yes	Yes	18,045 †	7,760		495	Yes			None
Yes	Yes		No		15,852 †		16		Yes			10/1
			Yes	Yes	22,198	8,338	12	467	Yes			None
Yes	Yes	Yes	No		13,464 †	9,342	9	431				
Yes	Yes		No		18,600 †							
Yes		Yes	No		9,930 †		9	324				
				Yes	18,260 †	9,810		400				
Yes	Yes	Yes	Yes	Yes	6,150 †	5,800	10	203	Yes			None
Yes	Yes		Yes	Yes	24,530	8,200	6	800	Yes	18	$18,483	
Yes	Yes	Yes	No		8,505 †		9	268	Yes			None
Yes	Yes	Yes	No		8,505 †		9	268	Yes			None
Yes	Yes	Yes	No		8,505 †		9	268	Yes			None
Yes	Yes	Yes	No		8,505 †		9	268	Yes			None
Yes			No				9		Yes			None
			Yes		23,184 †	7,470		483				
Yes	Yes	Yes	Yes	Yes	35,125	10,464	9	1056	Yes			None
Yes	Yes	Yes	Yes	Yes	17,617 †	8,436	12	519				
Yes	Yes		Yes	Yes	36,572	8,476		1137	Yes	74	$24,604	None
Yes					18,225 †	14,882	16	405	Yes			None
			No				20					
			No		8,370 †			279				
		Yes	No		7,110 †		10	237				
		Yes	No		10,508 †		9	323	Yes			5/1
Yes	Yes		Yes	Yes	24,780 †	8,500			Yes			5/1
Yes	Yes		No		13,230 ‡	6,000	9	421				
Yes			No		10,530 †		9	340	Yes			None
Yes	Yes		Yes	Yes		9,900		350				
Yes	Yes	Yes	No		10,530 †		9	336				
Yes	Yes		Yes	Yes	34,464	7,788			Yes	93	$18,533	None
Yes	Yes		Yes	Yes	35,525 †	8,327	12		Yes			5/1
Yes	Yes	Yes	No		10,813 †		10	342				
Yes			No			6,904			Yes			None
Yes	Yes	Yes	Yes	Yes	24,770	8,900	8	750	Yes			5/1
Yes					25,200 †				Yes			5/15
Yes				Yes	14,580	6,679	3	478	Yes	4	$7,716	None

† Tuition and fees are for 2010-11.   ‡ Tuition and fees projected for 2011-12.   * Includes room and board

Institution	Control/ degrees	Undergraduates		Tests required (Fall 2011)	TOEFL		Application	
		Total	Internat'l		minimum	average	Deadline	Fee
Lincoln College.............	Pr/AB	1,291	7	TOEFL, SAT/ACT	480	490	7/1	25
Lincoln Land Community College.............	Pu/A	6,512	6	TOEFL	500		None	
Loyola University Chicago	Pr/B	9,386	94	TOEFL, SAT/ACT	550	617		
MacCormac College.............	Pr/A			TOEFL	480		None	20
MacMurray College.............	Pr/AB	528		TOEFL	550	580	None	
McHenry County College.............	Pu/A	6,607		TOEFL	550		None	15
McKendree University.............	Pr/AB			TOEFL, SAT/ACT	520		None	40
Millikin University.............	Pr/B	2,212	17	TOEFL	550		5/1	25
Monmouth College.............	Pr/B	1,328	6	TOEFL	550	585	5/1	
Moody Bible Institute.............	Pr/AB	2,628	158	TOEFL	550		3/1	50
Moraine Valley Community College.............	Pu/A	11,619	237					
Morrison Institute of Technology.............	Pr/A			TOEFL	425		8/1	100
Morton College.............	Pu/A	2,692		TOEFL	500			10
National-Louis University.............	Pr/B	1,437	3	TOEFL	550		None	40
North Central College.............	Pr/B	2,506	25	TOEFL	520		4/15	25
North Park University.............	Pr/B	2,162	85	TOEFL	550		6/1	40
Northern Illinois University.............	Pu/B	17,856	177	TOEFL	550		5/1	40
Northwestern College.............	Pr/A	1,790	1	TOEFL	500		None	100
Northwestern University.............	Pr/B			TOEFL, SAT/ACT	600	637	1/1	65
Oakton Community College.............	Pu/A			TOEFL	520		6/1	25
Olivet Nazarene University.............	Pr/AB	2,930		TOEFL	500		5/1	25
Parkland College.............	Pu/A				500		7/1	40
Prairie State College.............	Pu/A	5,791		TOEFL	570		None	10
Quincy University.............	Pr/AB	1,228	8	TOEFL	550	570	4/1	25
Rasmussen College: Aurora.............	Pr/A							60
Rasmussen College: Rockford.............	Pr/A							60
Rasmussen College: Romeoville/Joliet.............	Pr/AB							60
Resurrection University.............	Pr/B							30
Richland Community College.............	Pu/A	3,807		TOEFL	500	550	None	
Robert Morris University: Chicago.............	Pr/AB	3,999	28	TOEFL	500		None	100
Rock Valley College.............	Pu/A			TOEFL	550		6/15	
Rockford College.............	Pr/B	929	10	TOEFL	550		8/1	50
Roosevelt University.............	Pr/B	3,867	104	TOEFL	525	570	7/1	35
Rush University.............	Pr/B	84	2	TOEFL	550		6/1	40
St. Augustine College.............	Pr/AB							
Saint Xavier University.............	Pr/B	2,947	4	TOEFL	550		7/30	25
Sauk Valley Community College.............	Pu/A	2,152	3	TOEFL	500	530	8/1	
School of the Art Institute of Chicago.............	Pr/B	2,593	422	TOEFL	550		6/1	85
Shimer College.............	Pr/B	112	1	TOEFL				25
Southeastern Illinois College.............	Pu/A	3,265		TOEFL	500		7/15	
Southern Illinois University Carbondale.............	Pu/AB	15,099	298	TOEFL	520		None	30
Southern Illinois University Edwardsville.............	Pu/B	11,251	80	TOEFL, SAT/ACT	550	555	6/1	30
Southwestern Illinois College.............	Pu/A			TOEFL	500		5/21	
Spoon River College.............	Pu/A	2,155		TOEFL	500		None	
Taylor Business Institute.............	Pr/A	308						25
Telshe Yeshiva-Chicago.............	Pr/B							
Trinity Christian College.............	Pr/B	1,273	28	TOEFL	550		None	20
Trinity College of Nursing and Health Sciences.............	Pr/AB	206		TOEFL	550			50
Trinity International University.............	Pr/B			TOEFL	580		5/1	25
Triton College.............	Pu/A	15,253		TOEFL	500	520	7/1	
University of Chicago.............	Pr/B	5,225	467	TOEFL, SAT/ACT	600	615	1/3	75
University of Illinois at Chicago.............	Pu/B	16,697	233	TOEFL, SAT/ACT	550		1/15	50
University of Illinois at Urbana-Champaign.............	Pu/B	30,721		TOEFL, SAT/ACT	550		1/2	50
University of Illinois: Springfield.............	Pu/B	3,086	29	TOEFL, SAT/ACT	500		None	60
University of Phoenix: Chicago.............	Pr/B							
University of St. Francis.............	Pr/B	1,333	12	TOEFL	550		3/15	30
VanderCook College of Music.............	Pr/B	139	7	TOEFL	500		None	35

| Student services | | | Housing | | Academic year costs | | Maximum credits/ summer | Credit hour charge | International financial aid | | | |
Adviser	Orientation	ESL	Academic year	Summer	Tuition/ fees	Living costs			Available	Number receiving aid	Average award	Deadline
Yes			Yes		23,000	9,900	9	260	Yes			6/1
		Yes	No		7,800†	2,475	10	249				
Yes	Yes	Yes	Yes		33,294‡	11,570	12	655				
Yes		Yes	No		12,100†		16	500				
Yes			Yes		20,400	9,650	9	660	Yes			None
		Yes	No		10,478†		9	340				
Yes	Yes		Yes	Yes	25,090	13,830	12		Yes			None
Yes	Yes		Yes	Yes	28,642	9,430	9	931	Yes	8	$8,963	None
Yes	Yes	Yes	Yes		28,650	9,800			Yes			None
Yes	Yes		Yes	Yes	8,004†	5,830	9	250	Yes			None
Yes	Yes	Yes	No		8,676†	6,445	9	284				
			Yes	Yes	14,560†	4,300		579				
Yes		Yes	No		9,332†	8,280	19	271				
Yes		Yes	No		18,435†		21	407				
Yes		Yes	Yes	Yes	29,733	8,610	9	716	Yes	24	$17,540	None
Yes	Yes		Yes	Yes	21,990	12,510	12	730	Yes			8/1
Yes	Yes		Yes		18,305†	9,750	12	589	Yes	21	$2,329	None
Yes			No		19,690†		20	430				
Yes	Yes		Yes		40,223†	12,240			Yes			2/15
Yes	Yes		No		10,552†			348	Yes			
Yes			Yes	Yes	25,590†	7,800	12	1032	Yes	20	$22,617	None
Yes	Yes	Yes	No		11,850†	4,700		395				
Yes			No		10,310†		9	354				
Yes	Yes		Yes	Yes	24,140	9,420	12	565	Yes	5	$8,250	None
					16,875†			375				
					16,875†			375				
					16,875†			375				
		Yes	No		22,616	7,856		747				
Yes			Yes	Yes	15,983†	5,400	6	528				
Yes			No		21,600‡	10,272	16	600	Yes	35	$18,570	None
Yes			No		13,599†	5,500	9	444	Yes			5/1
Yes	Yes	Yes	Yes	Yes	24,750†	8,350	9	675	Yes			None
Yes	Yes	Yes	Yes	Yes	25,000	14,008	12	689				
Yes			Yes		23,828†	9,360	12					
Yes		Yes	No		10,500†							
Yes	Yes		Yes	Yes	27,060	9,040	6	650	Yes			None
Yes		Yes	Yes	Yes	8,970†	6,228	9	289	Yes			None
Yes	Yes	Yes	Yes		35,940†	12,320	9		Yes			None
Yes			Yes	Yes	28,110†	14,526		900	Yes			None
Yes			No		4,320†		12	140	Yes			None
Yes	Yes	Yes	Yes	Yes	21,402†	8,292	12	608	Yes			None
Yes	Yes		Yes	Yes	17,703†	7,821	15	515				
Yes		Yes	No		9,480†		9	313				
Yes		Yes	No		7,860†	7,200	9	250				
					12,000*							
Yes			Yes	Yes	21,733†	8,202		715	Yes			3/1
			No		14,006†			435				
Yes			Yes	Yes	23,370†	7,660	6	957	Yes			None
Yes		Yes	No		8,980†		12	291	Yes			None
Yes		Yes	Yes		41,091†	12,153			Yes	63	$48,435	2/1
Yes	Yes	Yes	Yes		24,446†	9,994	12		Yes	76	$3,627	None
Yes	Yes	Yes	Yes	Yes	27,238†	9,714	9		Yes			None
Yes	Yes	Yes	Yes	Yes	18,965†	9,400	8	575	Yes	6	$7,616	11/15
					11,040†							
Yes			Yes	Yes	24,742†	8,176		790	Yes	9	$20,633	None
			Yes	Yes	23,190	10,464		925	Yes	6	$5,316	

† Tuition and fees are for 2010-11.   ‡ Tuition and fees projected for 2011-12.   * Includes room and board

Institution	Control/ degrees	Undergraduates		Tests required (Fall 2011)	TOEFL		Application	
		Total	Internat'l		minimum	average	Deadline	Fee
Vatterott College: Quincy	.Pr/A							
Western Illinois University	.Pu/B	10,470	126	TOEFL	550	570	3/1	30
Westwood College: Chicago Loop	.Pr/AB							50
Westwood College: DuPage.	.Pr/AB			TOEFL				50
Westwood College: O'Hare Airport.	.Pr/AB			TOEFL	475		8/6	25
Westwood College: River Oaks	.Pr/AB							50
Wheaton College.	.Pr/B	2,406	25	TOEFL	587		1/10	50
Indiana								
Ancilla College.	.Pr/A	599	4	TOEFL	550		None	
Ball State University	.Pu/AB	17,785	367	TOEFL	550	575	5/15	40
Bethel College	.Pr/AB	1,867	40	TOEFL	540		5/1	25
Brown Mackie College: Fort Wayne	.Pr/A	1,679						20
Butler University.	.Pr/AB	3,850	85	TOEFL	550	600	7/1	35
Calumet College of St. Joseph	.Pr/AB	1,069		TOEFL	515		None	
College of Court Reporting	.Pr/A							50
DePauw University	.Pr/B	2,362	225	TOEFL, SAT/ACT	560		2/1	40
Earlham College	.Pr/B	1,152	180	TOEFL	550	600	2/1	
Fortis College: Indianapolis	.Pr/A							
Franklin College	.Pr/B	1,106		TOEFL	550	570	None	30
Goshen College.	.Pr/B	883		TOEFL	550		7/1	25
Hanover College	.Pr/B	1,004	27	TOEFL, SAT/ACT	550		3/1	40
Harrison College: Indianapolis Northwest	.Pr/A	440						50
Holy Cross College	.Pr/AB	455	29	TOEFL	500		8/1	25
Huntington University.	.Pr/AB	1,122	33	TOEFL	525	600	5/1	20
Indiana Institute of Technology	.Pr/AB	4,041	36	TOEFL	523		7/31	.50
Indiana State University	.Pu/AB	9,324	222	TOEFL	500	554	6/15	25
Indiana University Bloomington	.Pu/AB	31,892	2,349					65
Indiana University East.	.Pu/AB	2,628	7				3/13	35
Indiana University Kokomo.	.Pu/AB	2,433	1	TOEFL, SAT/ACT	550		8/3	30
Indiana University Northwest.	.Pu/AB	4,951	9	TOEFL, SAT/ACT	500		2/1	25
Indiana University South Bend.	.Pu/AB	6,450	131	TOEFL	530		None	60
Indiana University Southeast	.Pu/AB	6,061	26	TOEFL, SAT/ACT	530			30
Indiana University-Purdue University Fort Wayne.	.Pu/AB	11,836	156	TOEFL	550		8/1	50
Indiana University-Purdue University Indianapolis	.Pu/AB	21,202	616	TOEFL, SAT/ACT	500		3/1	60
Indiana Wesleyan University	.Pr/AB	3,074	9	TOEFL, SAT/ACT	550		5/1	25
International Business College	.Pr/AB							50
ITT Technical Institute: Newburgh	.Pr/AB							
Ivy Tech Community College: Bloomington	.Pu/A	5,808	1	TOEFL	550		4/15	
Ivy Tech Community College: Central Indiana	.Pu/A	20,335	7	TOEFL	550		4/15	
Ivy Tech Community College: Columbus	.Pu/A	4,368		TOEFL	550		4/15	
Ivy Tech Community College: East Central.	.Pu/A	8,923		TOEFL	550		4/15	
Ivy Tech Community College: Kokomo	.Pu/A	5,265		TOEFL	550		4/15	
Ivy Tech Community College: Lafayette.	.Pu/A	6,932		TOEFL	550		4/15	
Ivy Tech Community College: North Central.	.Pu/A	8,149	1	TOEFL	550		4/15	
Ivy Tech Community College: Northeast	.Pu/A	10,932	2	TOEFL	550		4/15	
Ivy Tech Community College: Northwest	.Pu/A	8,559	1	TOEFL	550		4/15	
Ivy Tech Community College: Richmond.	.Pu/A	3,588		TOEFL	550		4/15	
Ivy Tech Community College: South Central.	.Pu/A	4,719		TOEFL	550		4/15	
Ivy Tech Community College: Southeast	.Pu/A	2,699		TOEFL	550		4/15	
Ivy Tech Community College: Southwest	.Pu/A	5,839	1	TOEFL	550		4/15	
Ivy Tech Community College: Wabash Valley.	.Pu/A	5,610	2	TOEFL	550			
Kaplan College: Hammond	.Pr/A	671						20
Kaplan College: Merrillville.	.Pr/A	370		TOEFL	477		None	100
Manchester College	.Pr/AB	1,247	33	TOEFL	550		5/1	25
Marian University	.Pr/AB	2,005	22	TOEFL	550		7/1	35
Mid-America College of Funeral Service	.Pr/AB	123						50

| Student services | | | Housing | | Academic year costs | | Maximum credits/ summer | Credit hour charge | International financial aid | | | |
Adviser	Orientation	ESL	Academic year	Summer	Tuition/ fees	Living costs			Available	Number receiving aid	Average award	Deadline
Yes	Yes	Yes	Yes	Yes	13,099†	8,138	6	361	Yes			None
					14,227†							
					14,227†	6,973						
Yes					14,227†	6,473	15					
					14,218†							
Yes	Yes		Yes		28,960	11,220	8	1207	Yes	14	$7,026	None
Yes			No		13,880		9	455	Yes			3/1
Yes	Yes	Yes	Yes	Yes	21,666†	8,208	12					
Yes	Yes	Yes	Yes	Yes	23,030	7,070			Yes			3/10
					10,800†	7,274		285				
Yes		Yes	Yes	Yes	31,948	10,600	12	1310	Yes			
Yes					14,780		18	465	Yes			None
					7,925†			325				
Yes	Yes		Yes		34,865†	9,180			Yes			3/1
Yes	Yes	Yes	Yes	Yes	38,284	9,570		1250	Yes	153	$22,041	3/1
Yes	Yes		Yes	Yes	25,865	7,650			Yes	1	$22,211	3/10
Yes	Yes		Yes	Yes	25,700	9,720	8	1070	Yes	39	$18,977	None
Yes	Yes		Yes	Yes	28,850	9,650		785	Yes	10	$19,566	
					12,652†	5,667		340				
Yes		Yes	Yes		22,700‡	8,650			Yes			3/1
Yes		Yes	Yes		23,210	7,680	8		Yes	30	$19,697	None
Yes	Yes	Yes	Yes	Yes	23,430	8,790	9	450	Yes			3/10
Yes	Yes	Yes	Yes	Yes	16,626†	7,752	15	580				
Yes	Yes	Yes	Yes	Yes	27,689†	7,918		837	Yes	415	$7,446	None
			No		16,305†	6,950	18	530	Yes	2	$1,127	None
Yes			No		15,374†	5,982		498	Yes	2	$1,006	3/1
			No		16,381†	9,512	18	531	Yes	2	$1,149	None
Yes	Yes	Yes	Yes	Yes	16,617†	5,382	12	539	Yes	44	$6,032	3/1
Yes	Yes		No		15,428†	6,286	12	498	Yes	5	$800	
Yes	Yes	Yes	Yes	Yes	17,467†	9,957	12	551	Yes	46	$7,857	None
Yes	Yes	Yes	Yes	Yes	24,428†	3,594	12	793	Yes	174	$5,185	None
Yes	Yes		Yes	Yes	21,956	7,648	12	785	Yes	9	$11,223	3/1
			Yes			5,760						
Yes			No		6,761†		18	221	Yes			None
Yes			No		6,761†		18	221	Yes			None
Yes			No		6,761†		18	221	Yes			None
Yes			No		6,761†		18	221	Yes			None
Yes			No		6,761†		18	221	Yes			None
Yes			No		6,761†		18	221	Yes			None
Yes			No		6,761†		18	221	Yes			None
Yes			No		6,761†		18	221	Yes			None
Yes			No		6,761†		18	221	Yes			None
Yes			No		6,761†		18	221	Yes			None
Yes			No		6,761†		18	221	Yes			None
Yes			No		6,761†		18	221	Yes			None
Yes			No		6,761†		18	221	Yes			None
Yes			No		6,761†		18	221	Yes			None
			No			9,610						
Yes	Yes		Yes	Yes	24,920†	11,860		700	Yes			None
Yes			Yes	Yes	24,960†	7,800	9	1090	Yes			
			No		9,000†			200				

† Tuition and fees are for 2010-11. ‡ Tuition and fees projected for 2011-12. * Includes room and board

Institution	Control/ degrees	Undergraduates		Tests required (Fall 2011)	TOEFL		Application	
		Total	Internat'l		minimum	average	Deadline	Fee
National College: Indianapolis	Pr/AB							30
Oakland City University	Pr/AB	1,331	3	TOEFL, SAT/ACT	500	510	None	50
Purdue University	Pu/AB	30,669	3,411	TOEFL	550		3/1	50
Purdue University Calumet	Pu/AB	8,244	350	TOEFL	550	577	5/1	
Purdue University North Central	Pu/AB	3,865	5	TOEFL	550		5/1	30
Rose-Hulman Institute of Technology	Pr/B	1,872	80	TOEFL, SAT/ACT	550		3/1	40
St. Mary-of-the-Woods College	Pr/AB	1,186		TOEFL	500	534	6/30	50
Saint Mary's College	Pr/B	1,536	11	TOEFL	500	550	2/15	30
Taylor University	Pr/AB	1,874	56	TOEFL, SAT/ACT	550		None	25
Trine University	Pr/AB	1,649	44	TOEFL	550		6/1	
University of Evansville	Pr/AB	2,578	139	TOEFL	500		7/1	50
University of Indianapolis	Pr/AB	4,033	204	TOEFL, SAT/ACT	500	555	None	25
University of Notre Dame	Pr/B	8,433	247	TOEFL, SAT/ACT	560		12/31	65
University of Phoenix: Indianapolis	Pr/B							
University of Southern Indiana	Pu/AB	9,641	224	TOEFL	525		5/1	25
University of St. Francis	Pr/AB			TOEFL	500		None	20
Valparaiso University	Pr/AB	2,795	103	TOEFL, SAT/ACT	550		6/1	
Vincennes University	Pu/AB	9,141	55		527		7/1	20
Wabash College	Pr/B	871	55	TOEFL, SAT/ACT			2/1	40
Iowa								
AIB College of Business	Pr/AB	903	1	TOEFL	550		5/1	
Ashford University	Pr/AB	42,977		TOEFL	420		8/15	20
Briar Cliff University	Pr/AB	978	6	TOEFL, SAT	525		7/1	20
Buena Vista University	Pr/B	961	47	TOEFL	475	584	6/1	20
Central College	Pr/B	1,540	8	TOEFL	530	560	None	25
Clarke University	Pr/AB	955	15	TOEFL, SAT/ACT	527		7/1	25
Clinton Community College	Pu/A	1,815		TOEFL	500	530	8/25	
Coe College	Pr/B	1,295	42	TOEFL, SAT/ACT	520	550	3/1	30
Cornell College	Pr/B	1,183	57	TOEFL	550	618	3/1	30
Des Moines Area Community College	Pu/A	16,718	155	TOEFL	500		6/8	100
Divine Word College	Pr/AB	107		TOEFL	550		7/15	25
Drake University	Pr/B	3,523	255	TOEFL, SAT/ACT	530	545	None	25
Ellsworth Community College	Pu/A			TOEFL	500		7/30	
Faith Baptist Bible College and Theological								
Seminary	Pr/AB	314		TOEFL	500		1/1	25
Graceland University	Pr/B	1,334	126	TOEFL	450	504	None	
Grand View University	Pr/AB	2,036	22	TOEFL, SAT/ACT	550		6/15	35
Grinnell College	Pr/B	1,603	192	TOEFL, SAT/ACT			1/2	30
Hamilton Technical College	Pr/AB	267						
Indian Hills Community College	Pu/A	3,469					None	
Iowa Central Community College	Pu/A	6,179		TOEFL	450		None	
Iowa Lakes Community College	Pu/A	2,396		TOEFL	500		7/11	
Iowa State University	Pu/B	22,577	1,525	TOEFL	500	530	7/1	90
Iowa Wesleyan College	Pr/B	771	65	TOEFL	500		6/1	20
Iowa Western Community College	Pu/A	6,799					None	
Kaplan University: Cedar Falls	Pr/AB			TOEFL	477			100
Kaplan University: Cedar Rapids	Pr/AB			TOEFL	525		None	25
Kaplan University: Davenport	Pr/AB			TOEFL	525		None	25
Kaplan University: Des Moines	Pr/AB			TOEFL	477		None	100
Kaplan University: Mason City	Pr/AB			TOEFL	525			20
Kirkwood Community College	Pu/A			TOEFL	500	515	None	
Loras College	Pr/AB	1,506	56	TOEFL	550		None	25
Luther College	Pr/B	2,412	114	TOEFL	550	630	3/1	25
Maharishi University of Management	Pr/B	316	47				8/1	30
Marshalltown Community College	Pu/A			TOEFL	400	500	8/20	100
Morningside College	Pr/B	1,213	26	TOEFL	500		8/15	
Mount Mercy University	Pr/B	1,409		TOEFL, SAT/ACT	550		6/1	

Student services			Housing		Academic year costs		Maximum credits/ summer	Credit hour charge	International financial aid			
Adviser	Orientation	ESL	Academic year	Summer	Tuition/ fees	Living costs			Available	Number receiving aid	Average award	Deadline
					10,840†			239				
Yes	Yes		Yes	Yes	16,200	7,700	15	540	Yes			3/1
Yes	Yes		Yes	Yes	26,622†	9,120	9	868	Yes	92	$4,651	None
Yes	Yes	Yes	Yes	Yes	14,821†	4,900	9	472	Yes	6	$5,111	6/30
Yes			No		15,960†		9	513	Yes			6/30
Yes	Yes		Yes	Yes	37,947	10,455	16	1085	Yes	67	$9,690	None
Yes	Yes		Yes	Yes	27,622	10,684	12	473	Yes	29	$18,970	None
Yes	Yes		Yes	Yes	32,000	10,300	6	1240	Yes	10	$29,572	3/1
Yes	Yes	Yes	Yes		27,438	7,532	12	773	Yes	52	$15,185	3/10
Yes	Yes	Yes	Yes	Yes	26,730	8,800	18	830	Yes	9	$7,611	
Yes	Yes	Yes	Yes	Yes	29,416	9,530	9	800	Yes	99	$15,265	None
Yes	Yes	Yes	Yes	Yes	23,010	8,730		949	Yes			
Yes	Yes		Yes	Yes	41,417	11,388		1705	Yes			2/15
					10,500†							
Yes	Yes	Yes	Yes	Yes	13,386‡	6,920	12	440				
Yes			Yes	Yes	22,810†	6,970	12	695				
Yes	Yes	Yes	Yes	Yes	31,040	10,756	14	1355	Yes	50	$14,225	None
Yes	Yes	Yes	Yes	Yes	10,924†	8,682	12	350	Yes			None
Yes	Yes		Yes	Yes	32,450	8,500			Yes			3/1
			Yes	Yes	13,740‡	4,527	12	250	Yes			None
Yes		Yes	Yes	Yes			6		Yes			None
Yes	Yes		Yes	Yes	23,418†	7,790	10	759	Yes	6	$94,100	None
Yes	Yes	Yes	Yes	Yes	27,226	7,770	12	884	Yes			None
Yes	Yes		Yes	Yes	27,844	9,136	17	952	Yes	7	$5,857	None
Yes	Yes	Yes	Yes	Yes	25,760	9,740	9	630	Yes	6	$15,238	None
Yes		Yes	No		5,310†		12	177				
Yes	Yes	Yes	Yes	Yes	32,380	11,380	2		Yes			None
Yes	Yes	Yes	Yes	Yes	31,050†	8,476		965	Yes	58	$20,786	3/1
Yes	Yes	Yes	Yes		7,500†	5,302		250				
		Yes	Yes		11,700‡	3,150		381	Yes			None
Yes	Yes	Yes	Yes	Yes	28,382	12,220	16		Yes			None
Yes			Yes	Yes	5,730†	5,978	15	165	Yes			4/1
Yes			Yes	Yes	14,478	5,812	8	514	Yes			None
Yes	Yes	Yes	Yes	Yes	21,790	8,930	6	675	Yes			None
Yes	Yes		Yes	Yes	21,088	7,316		495	Yes			None
Yes	Yes		Yes		39,810	9,734		1227	Yes	160	$33,218	2/1
			No						Yes			None
Yes		Yes	Yes	Yes	5,850†	5,805	15					
Yes			Yes	Yes			10		Yes			None
Yes			Yes	Yes	4,907‡	4,800	12	146	Yes			None
Yes	Yes	Yes	Yes	Yes	18,563†	7,397	12	737	Yes	143	$3,546	None
Yes	Yes		Yes		22,050†	7,308	14	550	Yes			None
Yes	Yes	Yes	Yes	Yes	4,110†	9,240	12	124	Yes			7/1
			No		15,372†			405	Yes			None
			No		15,352†	8,190		405	Yes			None
			No		15,352†			402				
			No		15,372†	8,649	16	405				
			No									
Yes	Yes	Yes	No		7,080†	6,939	8	236	Yes			6/30
Yes	Yes	Yes	Yes	Yes	27,258	7,524	9	490	Yes	65	$16,410	None
Yes	Yes		Yes	Yes	34,885	5,850	8	1240	Yes	114	$25,355	None
Yes	Yes		Yes	Yes	24,430‡	7,080		350	Yes			7/30
Yes	Yes	Yes	Yes		5,070†	6,440	12	143				
Yes	Yes	Yes	Yes	Yes	24,050	7,320	8	700	Yes			None
Yes			Yes		23,260†	7,260	16	640	Yes			None

† Tuition and fees are for 2010-11. ‡ Tuition and fees projected for 2011-12. * Includes room and board

Institution	Control/ degrees	Undergraduates Total	Internat'l	Tests required (Fall 2011)	TOEFL minimum	average	Application Deadline	Fee
Muscatine Community College................	Pu/A	1,969		TOEFL	500	530	8/1	
North Iowa Area Community College	Pu/A			TOEFL	500		None	50
Northeast Iowa Community College	Pu/A	3,524	4	TOEFL	500		None	
Northwest Iowa Community College	Pu/A	924		TOEFL	500		None	10
Northwestern College......................	Pr/B	1,192	27	TOEFL	475	520	None	25
St. Ambrose University....................	Pr/B	2,753	5	TOEFL	500	552	6/1	25
St. Luke's College........................	Pr/A	195		TOEFL	500		7/1	50
Scott Community College	Pu/A	5,581		TOEFL	500	530	8/25	
Simpson College..........................	Pr/B	1,897	20	TOEFL	550			
Southeastern Community College: North Campus..................................	Pu/A	3,483	26	TOEFL	525		None	
Southwestern Community College.............	Pu/A			TOEFL	500		None	75
University of Dubuque	Pr/AB	1,542	15	TOEFL	500	525	None	25
University of Iowa........................	Pu/B	20,493	1,172	TOEFL	530		4/1	80
University of Northern Iowa	Pu/B	11,132	254	TOEFL	550		None	50
University of Phoenix: Des Moines...........	Pr/B							
Upper Iowa University	Pr/AB	5,042		TOEFL	500			15
Vatterott College: Des Moines	Pr/A							
Waldorf College	Pr/AB	592	46	TOEFL	500	520	7/15	
Wartburg College	Pr/B	1,746	97	TOEFL	480		None	
Western Iowa Tech Community College.........	Pu/A	3,400		TOEFL	450		None	
William Penn University...................	Pr/AB	1,584		TOEFL, SAT/ACT	500		None	50

Kansas

Institution	Control/ degrees	Undergraduates Total	Internat'l	Tests required (Fall 2011)	TOEFL minimum	average	Application Deadline	Fee
Allen County Community College.............	Pu/A	3,124		TOEFL	520		None	50
Baker University	Pr/B	877	8	TOEFL	525		7/1	
Barclay College..........................	Pr/AB	233	3				None	10
Barton County Community College.............	Pu/A	4,738		TOEFL	500		5/1	150
Benedictine College......................	Pr/AB	1,491	25	TOEFL, SAT/ACT	535		None	25
Bethany College	Pr/B			TOEFL	525		4/15	20
Bethel College	Pr/B	476	8	TOEFL	540	620	None	20
Bryan College: Topeka.....................	Pr/A							50
Butler Community College	Pu/A			TOEFL	500	514	6/15	
Central Christian College of Kansas	Pr/AB	326	5	TOEFL, SAT/ACT	500	525	4/1	20
Cloud County Community College.............	Pu/A	1,199	89	TOEFL	550		None	
Coffeyville Community College..............	Pu/A	1,436		TOEFL		450	None	100
Colby Community College	Pu/A	732	22	TOEFL	500		7/1	150
Cowley County Community College	Pu/A	3,381	61	TOEFL	500		Deadline	
Dodge City Community College..............	Pu/A	1,807		TOEFL	500		7/1	100
Donnelly College.........................	Pr/AB	652	51		525		None	250
Emporia State University...................	Pu/B	3,909	261	TOEFL	520	550	6/1	50
Fort Hays State University..................	Pu/AB	10,317		TOEFL	500		7/1	35
Friends University	Pr/AB	1,951		TOEFL, SAT/ACT	500		8/24	40
Garden City Community College	Pu/A	2,009		TOEFL	500	553	7/1	150
Haskell Indian Nations University.............	Pu/AB							10
Hesston College	Pr/A	448	34	TOEFL	500	510	None	15
Hutchinson Community College..............	Pu/A	4,376	19	TOEFL	500	530	7/1	
Kansas City Kansas Community College	Pu/A	7,137		TOEFL	520		6/1	85
Kansas State University	Pu/AB	18,753	919	TOEFL	550		6/1	55
Kansas Wesleyan University	Pr/AB	825		TOEFL	500		None	30
Labette Community College.................	Pu/A			TOEFL	520		None	40
Manhattan Area Technical College	Pu/A			TOEFL	490		None	40
McPherson College	Pr/B	653	10	TOEFL	550	580	6/1	50
MidAmerica Nazarene University	Pr/AB	1,335		TOEFL, SAT/ACT	550		5/15	25
Neosho County Community College	Pu/A			TOEFL			6/1	50
Newman University.......................	Pr/AB	1,236	56	TOEFL	530		7/15	40
North Central Kansas Technical College.........	Pu/A	570					None	50
Northwest Kansas Technical College...........	Pu/A							25

| Student services | | | Housing | | Academic year costs | | Maximum credits/ summer | Credit hour charge | International financial aid | | | |
Adviser	Orien- tation	ESL	Academic year	Summer	Tuition/ fees	Living costs			Avail- able	Number receiving aid	Average award	Deadline
Yes		Yes	Yes		5,310†	9,100	12	177				
			Yes	Yes	5,657†	4,950		174	Yes			None
		Yes	No		4,890†		9		Yes			None
		Yes	Yes		5,250†	3,695	18	154				
Yes	Yes	Yes	Yes	Yes	23,330†	8,090	8		Yes	34	$15,411	6/30
Yes	Yes		Yes	Yes	23,910†	8,585	18	735	Yes			None
			No		16,220‡		9	425	Yes			None
Yes	Yes	Yes	No		5,310†		12	177				
Yes	Yes		Yes	Yes	28,123	9,963	12	318	Yes	19	$26,162	None
Yes		Yes	Yes		4,080‡	5,420	6	136				
Yes			Yes	Yes	4,635†	5,150	12	143	Yes			7/1
Yes	Yes	Yes	Yes	Yes	22,590	9,960	12	515	Yes			None
Yes	Yes	Yes	Yes	Yes	23,713†	11,101	12	934	Yes	173	$7,142	None
Yes	Yes	Yes	Yes	Yes	15,348†	7,120	12	602	Yes	31	$7,186	None
					11,040†							
Yes	Yes		Yes	Yes	22,350†	6,870	6		Yes			None
			No									
Yes	Yes		Yes	Yes	18,876‡	6,870	17		Yes			None
Yes	Yes		Yes	Yes	30,960	8,150	4	483	Yes	87	$14,902	None
Yes		Yes	Yes	Yes	4,455†	5,477	12	133				
Yes			Yes	Yes	20,234†	7,192	12	450	Yes			None
Yes			Yes		4,560†	5,300	9	134				
Yes	Yes		Yes	Yes	23,310	8,100	14	705	Yes			None
Yes			Yes		13,790‡	6,800	6	250	Yes			7/15
Yes		Yes	Yes	Yes	5,010†	4,600	12	137				
Yes	Yes	Yes	Yes	Yes	21,475	7,705		630	Yes			None
Yes	Yes		Yes	Yes	21,678	7,016	12		Yes			None
Yes	Yes		Yes		21,700‡	11,390	15		Yes	6	$17,327	None
Yes	Yes	Yes	Yes		6,600†	5,150	9	205	Yes			None
Yes	Yes		Yes	Yes	18,400	6,700	6	500	Yes	5	$3,870	None
	Yes		Yes		2,640†	4,900	9	133				
	Yes	Yes	Yes	Yes	4,905†	4,926	9	69				
Yes			Yes	Yes	4,710†	5,840	14	122		1032	$988	
Yes		Yes	Yes		5,280†	4,425	12	104				
Yes		Yes	Yes	Yes	4,680†	4,502	12	116	Yes			None
Yes	Yes	Yes	Yes	Yes	5,888†	2,770	6	196	Yes			
Yes	Yes		Yes	Yes	14,346†	6,320	12	444	Yes	115	$6,913	None
Yes	Yes	Yes	Yes	Yes	12,340†	6,625		381	Yes			None
Yes	Yes		Yes	Yes	21,030	5,966	12	696	Yes	9	$9,512	None
Yes			Yes	Yes	2,640†	4,450	12	65	Yes			None
			Yes									
Yes	Yes	Yes	Yes		21,672‡	7,166	9		Yes	34	$7,647	None
Yes			Yes	Yes	3,953†	5,720	9	115				
Yes		Yes	No		4,800†			147				
Yes	Yes	Yes	Yes	Yes	18,404†	6,954	6	590				
Yes		Yes	Yes		20,200†	6,800	6					
Yes					4,560†		12	119				
					4,130†	5,000		77	Yes			None
Yes			Yes		19,625†	7,325	12		Yes			None
Yes	Yes		Yes	Yes	20,250†	7,078	15	645	Yes			None
Yes	Yes	Yes	Yes	Yes	4,740†	7,700	12	118	Yes			None
Yes	Yes		Yes	Yes	21,666	6,790	12	696	Yes			None
			Yes		4,742†	4,400			Yes			None

† Tuition and fees are for 2010-11.   ‡ Tuition and fees projected for 2011-12.   * Includes room and board

Institution	Control/ degrees	Undergraduates		Tests required (Fall 2011)	TOEFL		Application	
		Total	Internat'l		minimum	average	Deadline	Fee
Ottawa University	Pr/B	568		TOEFL	550		None	25
Pittsburg State University	Pu/AB	5,794		TOEFL	520	541	6/1	50
Pratt Community College	Pu/A			TOEFL	500	515	7/1	
Southwestern College	Pr/B	1,477	27	TOEFL	550		8/1	25
Sterling College	Pr/B	693	6	TOEFL	525		6/1	25
Tabor College	Pr/AB	635		TOEFL	525	530	8/1	30
University of Kansas	Pu/B	19,495	1,037	TOEFL	530		4/1	75
University of Kansas Medical Center	Pu/B	475	15	TOEFL				60
University of Phoenix: Wichita	Pr/B	91						
University of St. Mary	Pr/AB	686	1	TOEFL	500		6/9	25
Washburn University	Pu/AB	5,661		TOEFL	520		6/15	70
Wichita Area Technical College	Pu/A							
Wichita State University	Pu/AB	11,007	574	TOEFL	530	541	6/15	50

Kentucky

Alice Lloyd College	Pr/B			TOEFL	550	575	3/1	
Ashland Community and Technical College	Pu/A			TOEFL, ACT	500		8/20	
Bellarmine University	Pr/B	2,316	29	TOEFL	550		5/1	25
Berea College	Pr/B	1,552	103	TOEFL	500		2/5	
Big Sandy Community and Technical College	Pu/A			TOEFL, ACT	500			
Bluegrass Community and Technical College	Pu/A			TOEFL	500		5/11	
Brescia University	Pr/AB	577	14	TOEFL	550		None	75
Brown Mackie College: North Kentucky	Pr/AB	675						
Campbellsville University	Pr/AB	2,057		TOEFL, SAT/ACT	500	600	7/15	20
Centre College	Pr/B	1,236	25	TOEFL	580		2/1	40
Daymar College: Owensboro	Pr/A	366					None	
Eastern Kentucky University	Pu/AB	13,809		TOEFL, SAT/ACT	500	525	7/15	30
Elizabethtown Community and Technical College	Pu/A	7,889		TOEFL, ACT	500	525	None	
Gateway Community and Technical College	Pu/A	3,094						
Georgetown College	Pr/B	1,252	14	TOEFL	520		6/1	30
Hazard Community and Technical College	Pu/A			TOEFL, SAT/ACT	500		None	
Henderson Community College	Pu/A			TOEFL, ACT	500		None	
Kentucky Christian University	Pr/B			TOEFL	500		None	30
Kentucky Mountain Bible College	Pr/AB	88		TOEFL	500		None	25
Kentucky State University	Pu/AB	2,439	38	TOEFL, SAT/ACT	500	538	None	100
Kentucky Wesleyan College	Pr/B			TOEFL, SAT/ACT	500		7/1	50
Lindsey Wilson College	Pr/AB			TOEFL	500		9/1	
Mid-Continent University	Pr/AB	2,178		TOEFL	500		7/1	100
Midway College	Pr/AB	1,513		TOEFL	530		None	25
Morehead State University	Pu/AB	6,630	37	TOEFL, SAT/ACT	500	535	6/30	30
Murray State University	Pu/AB	7,548	168	TOEFL	525		7/1	30
National College: Danville	Pr/A						None	125
National College: Florence	Pr/A							125
National College: Lexington	Pr/AB						None	125
Northern Kentucky University	Pu/AB	12,658	164	TOEFL	500	537	8/1	25
Owensboro Community and Technical College	Pu/A			TOEFL, ACT	500		None	
Pikeville College	Pr/AB	967	6	TOEFL, SAT/ACT	550		5/1	
St. Catharine College	Pr/AB	679		TOEFL	425	430		15
Somerset Community College	Pu/A	9,262		TOEFL, ACT	500		None	
Southeast Kentucky Community and Technical College	Pu/A	2,334		TOEFL, ACT	500		None	
Spalding University	Pr/AB	1,266	8	TOEFL, SAT/ACT	535		7/1	100
Spencerian College: Lexington	Pr/A	640			500		None	100
Sullivan College of Technology and Design	Pr/AB	703		TOEFL	500	560	None	
Sullivan University	Pr/AB	4,978		TOEFL, SAT/ACT	500		9/1	100
Thomas More College	Pr/AB	1,434	7	TOEFL	515		8/1	25
Transylvania University	Pr/B	1,108	8	TOEFL	550		2/1	30
Union College	Pr/B	832	25	TOEFL, SAT/ACT	520		6/12	20

Student services			Housing		Academic year costs		Maximum credits/ summer	Credit hour charge	International financial aid			
Adviser	Orien- tation	ESL	Academic year	Summer	Tuition/ fees	Living costs			Avail- able	Number receiving aid	Average award	Deadline
Yes	Yes		Yes	Yes	20,800 †	6,312	9	833	Yes			None
Yes	Yes	Yes	Yes	Yes	13,588 †	6,016	12	420				
Yes			Yes	Yes	3,962 †	4,959	8	99	Yes			8/1
Yes	Yes		Yes	Yes	21,680	6,322		897	Yes	19	$12,811	8/15
			Yes		20,050	7,166			Yes			None
Yes			Yes		21,740	7,450			Yes	8	$15,023	None
Yes	Yes	Yes	Yes	Yes	21,538 †	6,982		689	Yes	154	$1,902	None
Yes	Yes	Yes	No		19,316 †			615				
					10,440 †							
Yes	Yes		Yes	Yes	19,960 †	6,350	12	645	Yes			None
Yes	Yes	Yes	Yes	Yes	14,186 †	8,082	9	470	Yes			None
Yes	Yes	Yes	Yes	Yes	13,924 †	6,200		425	Yes	15	$829	None
Yes			Yes		9,500 †	8,150		212	Yes			None
			No		13,350 †	6,952	14	445	Yes			None
Yes	Yes		Yes	Yes	32,140	9,560		730	Yes	29	$23,797	None
Yes	Yes	Yes	Yes	Yes			6		Yes	103	$33,087	5/1
			No		13,350 †	6,952		445	Yes			None
Yes	Yes	Yes	Yes	Yes	13,350 †	7,758		445	Yes			None
Yes	Yes	Yes	Yes	Yes	17,390 †	8,000	9	510	Yes			8/23
					9,000 †	8,700		235				
Yes	Yes	Yes	Yes	Yes	20,740	7,580	12	846	Yes			None
Yes	Yes		Yes	Yes	40,750 *	1,500			Yes	24	$20,548	3/1
Yes			No		14,275 †	9,120	12	290				
Yes	Yes	Yes	Yes	Yes	18,144 †	6,538	12	756	Yes			
			No		13,350 †	6,952	10	445				
					13,350 †			445				
Yes			Yes	Yes	29,300	7,610	14	1210	Yes			3/15
			No		13,350 †		6	445				
			No		13,350 †	6,952	9	445				
Yes			Yes		14,240 †	6,200		468	Yes			None
Yes			Yes	Yes	6,490 †	7,000		195	Yes	3	$6,466	6/30
Yes	Yes	Yes	Yes	Yes	14,904 †	6,480	6	527	Yes	9	$14,245	
Yes			Yes	Yes	19,390	9,120	12	540	Yes			3/15
Yes	Yes		Yes		20,030	8,100	12	825	Yes			None
Yes			Yes	Yes	13,350	9,800	12	403	Yes	34	$10,152	5/30
Yes			Yes	Yes	18,900 †	9,080	12	630	Yes			8/1
Yes	Yes		Yes	Yes	16,236 †	6,582	12	615	Yes			None
Yes	Yes	Yes	Yes	Yes	17,040 †	6,860	15	674	Yes	35	$9,927	None
			No		10,800 †	5,202		239				
			No		10,800 †	5,202		239				
			No		10,800 †	5,202		239				
Yes	Yes	Yes	Yes	Yes	13,896 †	6,280	15	579				
			No		13,350 †		10	445	Yes			None
			Yes		16,250	6,300	12	677	Yes	3	$11,416	None
Yes	Yes		Yes		15,761 †	7,710	9	540				
			No		13,350 †	6,952	10	445	Yes			None
Yes			No		13,350 †	6,952	10	445	Yes			None
Yes	Yes		Yes	Yes	19,350	10,356	6	645	Yes	3	$2,842	None
			Yes		11,523 †	5,355	20	330				
			Yes	Yes		8,325	20		Yes			None
Yes	Yes		Yes			5,355	20		Yes			None
Yes	Yes		Yes	Yes	25,720	7,030	12	560	Yes			None
Yes			Yes	Yes	28,250	8,450	2		Yes	7	$14,035	None
			Yes	Yes	20,004	8,200	15	315	Yes	8	$7,546	None

† Tuition and fees are for 2010-11.   ‡ Tuition and fees projected for 2011-12.   * Includes room and board

Institution	Control/ degrees	Undergraduates		Tests required (Fall 2011)	TOEFL		Application	
		Total	Internat'l		minimum	average	Deadline	Fee
University of the Cumberlands	Pr/B	1,442	70	TOEFL	550	564	6/1	30
University of Kentucky	Pu/B	19,526	328	TOEFL	527	579	2/15	50
University of Louisville	Pu/AB	14,763	166	TOEFL, SAT/ACT	550		5/1	40
University of Phoenix: Louisville	Pr/B							
Western Kentucky University	Pu/AB	16,545	254	TOEFL, SAT/ACT	525		4/1	40
Louisiana								
Baton Rouge Community College	Pu/A	8,325	174	TOEFL	500	520	None	52
Baton Rouge School of Computers	Pr/A	56						25
Blue Cliff College: Metairie	Pr/A	506						
Blue Cliff College: Shreveport	Pr/A	153						25
Bossier Parish Community College	Pu/A	5,801	6	TOEFL	500		6/20	25
Camelot College	Pr/A	188						10
Centenary College of Louisiana	Pr/B	800		TOEFL	550		6/1	30
Delgado Community College	Pu/A	17,585	156		500		7/1	25
Delta College of Arts & Technology	Pr/A	187						100
Dillard University	Pr/B	1,187	12	TOEFL, SAT/ACT	550		6/1	50
Grambling State University	Pu/AB	4,405	396	TOEFL, SAT/ACT	500		None	30
Gretna Career College	Pr/A	131						50
Herzing University	Pr/AB			TOEFL				
ITI Technical College	Pr/A	383					None	
Louisiana College	Pr/AB	1,059		TOEFL, ACT	500	600	None	25
Louisiana State University and Agricultural and Mechanical College	Pu/B	23,170	434	TOEFL, SAT/ACT	550		4/15	40
Louisiana State University at Eunice	Pu/A	3,431		TOEFL, ACT	500	550	5/15	20
Louisiana State University Health Sciences Center	Pu/AB	849						50
Louisiana State University in Shreveport	Pu/B			TOEFL, ACT	500		5/15	20
Louisiana Tech University	Pu/AB	8,978		TOEFL	500		6/1	30
Loyola University New Orleans	Pr/B	2,859	68	TOEFL, SAT/ACT	550		5/1	20
McNeese State University	Pu/AB	7,157	286	TOEFL, SAT/ACT	500		5/15	30
New Orleans Baptist Theological Seminary: Leavell College	Pr/AB	1,005		TOEFL	550		None	25
Nicholls State University	Pu/AB	6,344	106	TOEFL, SAT/ACT	500		7/17	30
Northwestern State University	Pu/AB	7,333	54	TOEFL, SAT/ACT	500		7/6	30
Nunez Community College	Pu/A	1,433						10
Our Lady of Holy Cross College	Pr/AB	963		TOEFL	500		None	15
Remington College: Baton Rouge	Pr/A							50
Remington College: Lafayette	Pr/A						None	50
Remington College: Shreveport	Pr/A							50
St. Joseph Seminary College	Pr/B	74		TOEFL, ACT	520		None	
South Louisiana Community College	Pu/A	3,658	7					5
Southeastern Louisiana University	Pu/AB	12,871	185	TOEFL, ACT	500		6/1	30
Southern University and Agricultural and Mechanical College	Pu/AB	5,920		TOEFL, SAT/ACT	500		5/1	30
Southern University at New Orleans	Pu/AB			TOEFL, SAT/ACT	500		7/1	15
Southern University at Shreveport	Pu/A						6/30	15
Southwest University	Pr/AB							50
Tulane University	Pr/AB	7,754		TOEFL, SAT/ACT	550		1/15	
University of Louisiana at Lafayette	Pu/B	14,715	271	TOEFL	525	546	6/1	30
University of Louisiana at Monroe	Pu/AB	7,507	102	TOEFL, SAT/ACT	500		3/1	30
University of New Orleans	Pu/B	8,164	344	TOEFL	525		6/1	50
University of Phoenix: Louisiana	Pr/B	1,954						
Xavier University of Louisiana	Pr/B	2,686	62	TOEFL, SAT/ACT	550		3/1	25
Maine								
Bates College	Pr/B	1,725	103	TOEFL			1/1	60
Bowdoin College	Pr/B	1,751	60	TOEFL	600		1/1	60

Student services			Housing		Academic year costs		Maximum credits/ summer	Credit hour charge	International financial aid			
Adviser	Orien- tation	ESL	Academic year	Summer	Tuition/ fees	Living costs			Avail- able	Number receiving aid	Average award	Deadline
Yes	Yes	Yes	Yes		18,000	8,326	14	570	Yes	68	$12,065	None
Yes	Yes	Yes	Yes	Yes	17,678 †	9,439	15	697	Yes			2/15
Yes	Yes	Yes	Yes	Yes	20,424 †	6,602	17	851				
					10,200 †							
Yes	Yes	Yes	Yes	Yes	18,840 †	6,543	15	785	Yes	92	$11,521	None
Yes	Yes		No		5,314 †	8,236	9		Yes			6/30
Yes			No		4,746 †				Yes	6	$1,286	7/1
Yes			Yes		25,290	8,730	12	800	Yes			None
Yes	Yes	Yes	No		5,674 †	8,236	9					
						10,392						
Yes	Yes		Yes		13,540 †	8,210	9	542	Yes			5/1
Yes	Yes		Yes	Yes	10,902 †	7,384	14		Yes			6/1
					13,050 †	5,610						
			No		17,425 †			380				
			No									
Yes	Yes		Yes	Yes	13,380	4,820	14	395	Yes			None
Yes	Yes	Yes	Yes		16,549 †	8,210	12		Yes	189	$8,779	None
Yes			No		6,150 †	8,600	10		Yes			None
Yes	Yes	Yes	Yes	Yes	6,747 †	2,187						
			Yes	Yes	9,801 †	11,236	10					
Yes		Yes	Yes		12,387 †	5,160	12		Yes			None
Yes	Yes	Yes	Yes	Yes	33,302	10,990	12	920	Yes	54	$17,786	6/1
Yes		Yes	Yes	Yes	11,629 †	5,882	12		Yes			None
			Yes		5,240 †	2,484	16	170				
Yes	Yes		Yes	Yes	12,784 †	7,208	12		Yes			6/30
Yes			Yes		12,126 †	7,070	12		Yes	28	$4,909	None
			No		4,948 †							
Yes			No		10,862 †	8,236		326	Yes			None
			No									
			No									
		Yes	Yes		14,370	12,440		175				
			No		4,580 †	8,236		97	Yes			None
Yes	Yes	Yes	Yes	Yes	12,499 †	6,590	10		Yes			None
Yes	Yes		Yes	Yes	10,376 †	6,018	10					
Yes	Yes		No		6,920 †	6,480	10					
			No		3,860 †	4,994	10					
			No		5,975			190				
Yes	Yes	Yes	Yes	Yes	43,434	11,450	18	1660	Yes	127	$19,095	2/15
Yes	Yes	Yes	Yes	Yes	13,028 †	4,758	10	357				
Yes	Yes	Yes	Yes	Yes	13,548 †	5,984	6		Yes			None
Yes	Yes	Yes	Yes	Yes	14,399 †	8,127	12	458	Yes	213	$11,613	None
					10,200 †							
Yes			Yes	Yes	17,900	7,400	12	750		19	$8,751	
Yes	Yes		Yes		53,300 *				Yes	79	$45,686	2/1
Yes			Yes	Yes	41,565 †	11,315			Yes	24	$40,962	2/15

† Tuition and fees are for 2010-11.   ‡ Tuition and fees projected for 2011-12.   * Includes room and board

Institution	Control/ degrees	Undergraduates		Tests required (Fall 2011)	TOEFL		Application	
		Total	Internat'l		minimum	average	Deadline	Fee
Central Maine Community College	Pu/A	2,720		TOEFL	500		None	20
Colby College	Pr/B	1,825	100	TOEFL	600		1/1	65
College of the Atlantic	Pr/B	353	57	TOEFL	550		2/15	45
Eastern Maine Community College	Pu/A			TOEFL	500		8/15	20
Husson University	Pr/AB	2,394		TOEFL	500		None	40
Kaplan University: South Portland	Pr/A			TOEFL	477		None	100
Kennebec Valley Community College	Pu/A	1,857		TOEFL				20
Landing School of Boatbuilding and Design	Pr/A							
Maine College of Art	Pr/B	318		TOEFL	550		None	60
Maine Maritime Academy	Pu/AB	921		TOEFL	550		7/1	15
New England School of Communications	Pr/B	509	2	TOEFL	500		None	25
Northern Maine Community College	Pu/A			TOEFL	550		None	20
Saint Joseph's College of Maine	Pr/AB	1,010		TOEFL	500		4/15	50
Southern Maine Community College	Pu/A	6,337		TOEFL	500		None	20
Thomas College	Pr/AB	769	9	TOEFL, SAT/ACT	530	600	None	50
Unity College in Maine	Pr/AB	581		TOEFL	500	530	None	50
University of Maine	Pu/B	8,483	149	TOEFL, SAT/ACT	530	572	3/1	40
University of Maine at Augusta	Pu/AB	4,466	8	TOEFL	500		5/1	40
University of Maine at Farmington	Pu/B	2,166	2	TOEFL	550		None	40
University of Maine at Fort Kent	Pu/AB	741	78	TOEFL	500	525	None	40
University of Maine at Machias	Pu/AB	589	12	TOEFL	500		None	40
University of Maine at Presque Isle	Pu/AB	1,110		TOEFL	550	565	None	40
University of New England	Pr/AB	2,234	20	TOEFL	550		5/1	40
University of Southern Maine	Pu/AB	6,567	39	TOEFL	550	564	None	40
Washington County Community College	Pu/A	412		TOEFL	500		None	20
York County Community College	Pu/A	1,393		TOEFL			None	20
Maryland								
Allegany College of Maryland	Pu/A			TOEFL	550	570	8/15	
Anne Arundel Community College	Pu/A	15,008	163	TOEFL	550		7/1	
Baltimore City Community College	Pu/A	7,160					8/1	10
Baltimore International College	Pr/AB			TOEFL				50
Bowie State University	Pu/B	4,271	27	TOEFL			4/1	40
Capitol College	Pr/AB			TOEFL	450	525	8/15	200
Carroll Community College	Pu/A	4,108		TOEFL	550		6/15	
Chesapeake College	Pu/A	2,558		TOEFL	500		None	
College of Notre Dame of Maryland	Pr/B			TOEFL	500		2/15	45
College of Southern Maryland	Pu/A	7,636	26	TOEFL	500		6/15	
Community College of Baltimore County	Pu/A	23,951		TOEFL	450		6/1	
Coppin State University	Pu/B	3,232	123	TOEFL	500		5/1	35
Frostburg State University	Pu/B	4,759	22	TOEFL, SAT	550		6/1	30
Garrett College	Pu/A	860	10	TOEFL	550		None	
Goucher College	Pr/B	1,456	27	TOEFL	550	609	2/1	55
Griggs University	Pr/AB	1,102		TOEFL	250			50
Harford Community College	Pu/A	6,079	38	TOEFL	500		6/1	
Hood College	Pr/B	1,422	26	TOEFL, SAT/ACT	550		2/15	35
Howard Community College	Pu/A	8,809	453	TOEFL	537		6/1	50
ITT Technical Institute: Owings Mills	Pr/AB							
Johns Hopkins University	Pr/B	4,980	394	TOEFL, SAT/ACT	600	624	1/1	70
Johns Hopkins University: Peabody Conservatory of Music	Pr/B	322	56	TOEFL	550		4/1	100
Kaplan University: Hagerstown	Pr/AB	995						20
Loyola University Maryland	Pr/B	3,777	21	TOEFL	550		1/15	50
Maryland Institute College of Art	Pr/B	1,732	80	TOEFL	550		2/15	60
McDaniel College	Pr/B	1,600	3	TOEFL	550		2/1	50
Morgan State University	Pu/B	6,551	239	TOEFL, SAT/ACT	550		11/1	35
Mount St. Mary's University	Pr/B	1,604	15	TOEFL, SAT/ACT	550		3/1	35
National Labor College	Pr/B	473					None	60

Adviser	Orientation	ESL	Academic year	Summer	Tuition/fees	Living costs	Maximum credits/summer	Credit hour charge	Available	Number receiving aid	Average award	Deadline
		Yes	Yes		5,784†	7,976		168				
Yes	Yes	Yes	Yes		53,800*				Yes			2/1
Yes	Yes		Yes		36,063	12,223		1184	Yes	57	$40,520	2/15
			Yes	Yes	5,979†	6,490	12	168				
Yes			Yes	Yes	13,450†	7,239	12	438	Yes	2	$3,250	None
						8,649	18		Yes			None
Yes			No		5,634†		9	168	Yes			None
			Yes		29,130†	9,995		1165	Yes			None
Yes			Yes	Yes	19,245†	8,870	12		Yes			None
Yes			Yes	Yes	12,310‡	7,500	15	400	Yes			None
			Yes		5,728†	5,960		168				
			Yes		27,345†	13,650		875	Yes			None
Yes			Yes	Yes	5,789†	8,226	12	168				
Yes			Yes		22,770	9,170		924	Yes			None
Yes			Yes		23,240	8,380			Yes			None
Yes	Yes	Yes	Yes	Yes	25,172†	10,044	9	768	Yes	74	$10,818	5/1
Yes			No		16,005†		12	504	Yes	5	$11,641	None
Yes	Yes		Yes	Yes	17,498†	8,409	16	524	Yes			
Yes		Yes	Yes		16,763†	8,200	9	531	Yes			2/1
Yes			Yes		18,390†	7,282		587	Yes			None
Yes	Yes		Yes	Yes	16,600†	6,894	12	531	Yes			None
			Yes		30,500	12,020		1040	Yes			None
Yes	Yes	Yes	Yes	Yes	20,898†	9,384		654	Yes			None
			Yes		5,654†	3,450		168				
			No		5,622†	6,000		168	Yes			None
Yes		Yes	Yes	Yes	7,046†		8	228	Yes			None
Yes	Yes	Yes	No		9,340†	9,241	7	299				
Yes		Yes	No		6,722†		12	168	Yes			None
			Yes	Yes	27,390†	8,542						
Yes	Yes		Yes	Yes	16,678†	7,940	12	629	Yes			3/1
Yes		Yes	Yes	Yes	20,610†	4,770	12	638	Yes			None
		Yes	No		7,368†	5,000		246				
		Yes	No		7,924†			244				
Yes	Yes	Yes	Yes	Yes	28,350†	9,500	9		Yes			None
Yes	Yes		No		8,745†		6	237	Yes			None
Yes	Yes	Yes	No		8,982†			286	Yes			3/1
Yes	Yes		Yes		14,582†	7,871	9	441				
Yes	Yes		Yes	Yes	16,950†	7,378	12	427				
			Yes		8,280†	5,590	6	255	Yes			3/1
Yes	Yes		Yes		36,553	10,569		1200	Yes	11	$21,793	2/1
					9,830†			325	Yes			None
Yes	Yes		No		7,680†		6	246	Yes			None
Yes	Yes		Yes	Yes	31,060	11,390		885	Yes	24	$21,960	None
Yes	Yes	Yes	No		7,903†		12					
Yes	Yes		Yes	Yes	42,780	12,962		1410	Yes			3/1
Yes	Yes		Yes		38,125	12,200		1055	Yes			2/1
			Yes									
Yes	Yes		Yes	Yes	39,350†	10,650	12	615				
Yes	Yes		Yes	Yes	37,470	12,770	9	1506	Yes			2/15
Yes	Yes		Yes		34,780	7,380	12	1087	Yes			None
Yes			Yes		15,870‡	8,380	6	536				
Yes			Yes	Yes	31,536	10,544	12	1030	Yes	9	$27,648	3/1

† Tuition and fees are for 2010-11.   ‡ Tuition and fees projected for 2011-12.   * Includes room and board

Institution	Control/ degrees	Undergraduates		Tests required (Fall 2011)	TOEFL		Application	
		Total	Internat'l		minimum	average	Deadline	Fee
Prince George's Community College	Pu/A	13,685		TOEFL	450		5/1	25
St. John's College	Pr/B	463	34	TOEFL, SAT/ACT	600		None	
St. Mary's College of Maryland	Pu/B	1,943	31	TOEFL, SAT/ACT			1/1	50
Salisbury University.	Pu/B	7,527	40	TOEFL	550	565	3/1	45
Sojourner-Douglass College.	Pr/B	1,335		TOEFL	500		None	25
Stevenson University	Pr/B	3,529	19	TOEFL	550		8/1	40
TESST College of Technology: Beltsville.	Pr/A	744						
Towson University.	Pu/B	17,076	485	TOEFL	500	533	6/1	30
United States Naval Academy	Pu/B	4,603	50	TOEFL, SAT/ACT			12/1	
University of Baltimore.	Pu/B	3,207	36	TOEFL, SAT/ACT	550		2/15	30
University of Maryland: Baltimore	Pu/B	768	26	TOEFL	550		4/1	50
University of Maryland: Baltimore County	Pu/B	10,075	391	TOEFL	550		11/1	50
University of Maryland: College Park	Pu/B	26,194	588	TOEFL	575		11/1	55
University of Maryland: Eastern Shore.	Pu/B	3,882	118	TOEFL	500	550	7/15	25
University of Maryland: University College	Pu/AB	24,771	362	TOEFL	550		None	50
University of Phoenix: Maryland	Pr/B	570						
Washington Adventist University	Pr/AB	1,125		TOEFL			6/1	25
Washington Bible College.	Pr/AB			TOEFL	550		None	35
Washington College.	Pr/B	1,385	21	TOEFL	550	580	2/15	55
Massachusetts								
American International College.	Pr/AB	1,755		TOEFL, SAT/ACT	550		8/1	25
Amherst College	Pr/B	1,795	163	TOEFL, SAT, SAT Subject Test(s), or ACT	600	633	1/1	60
Anna Maria College.	Pr/AB	1,089	1	TOEFL	550		None	40
Art Institute of Boston at Lesley University	Pr/B	530		TOEFL, SAT/ACT	500	550	None	40
Assumption College.	Pr/B	2,024	15	TOEFL	550		2/15	50
Atlantic Union College.	Pr/AB	480		TOEFL	525	550	7/1	25
Babson College.	Pr/B	1,956	479	TOEFL, SAT/ACT	600		1/1	75
Bard College at Simon's Rock	Pr/AB	371	12	TOEFL	600		5/31	50
Bay Path College.	Pr/AB	1,563		TOEFL, SAT/ACT	500		7/1	25
Bay State College	Pr/AB	1,214	58	TOEFL	550		8/15	25
Becker College	Pr/AB	1,751		TOEFL	500		None	30
Benjamin Franklin Institute of Technology	Pr/AB	540		TOEFL	500			50
Bentley University.	Pr/AB	4,196	457	TOEFL, SAT/ACT	550		1/15	75
Berklee College of Music	Pr/B	3,644	796	TOEFL	500		1/15	150
Berkshire Community College	Pu/A	2,172	27	TOEFL	500		None	35
Boston Baptist College	Pr/AB							50
Boston College	Pr/B	9,099	286	TOEFL, SAT, SAT Subject Test(s), or ACT	600	630	1/1	70
Boston Conservatory	Pr/B	520	50	TOEFL	550		12/1	110
Boston University	Pr/B	16,624	1,562	TOEFL, SAT, SAT Subject Test(s), or ACT	550		1/1	75
Brandeis University.	Pr/B	3,325	383	TOEFL	600		1/15	55
Bridgewater State University	Pu/B	9,179	58	TOEFL	500	520	2/15	25
Bristol Community College	Pu/A	8,893					8/1	35
Bunker Hill Community College.	Pu/A	10,429	336	TOEFL	423	521	7/15	35
Cambridge College	Pr/B	1,062	100	TOEFL	550		None	30
Cape Cod Community College	Pu/A	4,657		TOEFL	520		5/1	
Clark University	Pr/B	2,252	167	TOEFL, SAT/ACT	550	605	1/15	55
College of the Holy Cross	Pr/B	2,862	33	TOEFL	550		1/15	60
Curry College.	Pr/B	2,578	30	TOEFL, SAT/ACT	500	550	4/1	50
Dean College	Pr/AB	1,021		TOEFL	500	518	7/31	35
Eastern Nazarene College	Pr/AB	839		TOEFL, SAT/ACT	500		None	25
Elms College	Pr/AB	1,134		TOEFL	450	520	6/15	30
Emerson College.	Pr/B	3,450	110	TOEFL	550		1/5	65
Emmanuel College.	Pr/B	2,198	24	TOEFL, SAT/ACT	550		3/1	40
Endicott College	Pr/AB	2,390	50	TOEFL	550	603	2/15	50
Fisher College.	Pr/AB	1,486	123	TOEFL	500	510	None	50

Student services			Housing		Academic year costs		Maximum credits/summer	Credit hour charge	International financial aid			
Adviser	Orientation	ESL	Academic year	Summer	Tuition/fees	Living costs			Available	Number receiving aid	Average award	Deadline
Yes		Yes	No		8,690†	6,893	12	255				
Yes	Yes		Yes		43,656	11,334			Yes			None
Yes	Yes		Yes		25,023†	10,235	8		Yes	18	$6,116	2/28
Yes	Yes	Yes	Yes		15,404†	8,112	7	559	Yes	1	$2,500	5/31
Yes			No		8,850	7,000		519				
Yes			Yes		23,636	11,278		557				
Yes	Yes	Yes	Yes	Yes	19,114†	9,768	15	641	Yes	102	$8,842	2/10
Yes	Yes		Yes	Yes								
Yes	Yes		No		16,846†	13,100	6	784	Yes			None
Yes	Yes		Yes		26,400†	19,350		639	Yes			None
Yes	Yes	Yes	Yes	Yes	19,108†	9,620	12	691	Yes	61	$5,819	None
Yes	Yes	Yes	Yes	Yes	24,831†	9,599	16	966				
Yes	Yes		Yes	Yes	13,746†	8,983	6	430	Yes			4/1
Yes			No		12,366†	17,820	18	499				
Yes		Yes	Yes	Yes	11,880† 20,180†	7,530	6	760	Yes			3/31
Yes			Yes	Yes	13,230†	6,770	9	420	Yes			3/1
Yes	Yes		Yes		36,738†	7,834			Yes	18	$13,611	None
Yes	Yes	Yes	Yes	Yes	26,700†	10,930	12	550	Yes			None
Yes	Yes		Yes		40,860†	11,460			Yes			
	Yes		Yes		28,159†	10,202	18	1068	Yes			None
Yes	Yes		Yes		28,750	13,250	9		Yes			None
Yes			Yes	Yes	32,545	10,485	12	1073	Yes			2/15
Yes		Yes	Yes	Yes	17,890‡	7,875	16		Yes			9/16
Yes	Yes		Yes	Yes	39,040†	12,876	8		Yes			2/15
Yes			Yes		41,160†	13,950	10		Yes			None
Yes	Yes	Yes	Yes		27,045	12,220	6	475	Yes			None
Yes	Yes	Yes	Yes	Yes	22,355	13,300		731	Yes			None
Yes	Yes		Yes	Yes	26,880†	10,020	12	1075				
Yes		Yes	Yes		15,950‡	11,000	17	665				
Yes	Yes		Yes	Yes	38,328	12,520	15		Yes	46	$19,033	2/1
Yes	Yes	Yes	Yes	Yes	35,505†	15,830	16	1110				
Yes		Yes	No		12,552†	9,151		280	Yes			None
					12,449†	7,486						
Yes	Yes		Yes		42,204	14,525	12					
Yes	Yes	Yes	Yes	Yes	35,485†	17,765	6	1400	Yes	44	$27,097	None
Yes	Yes	Yes	Yes	Yes	41,420	14,327	16	1276	Yes	110	$36,401	2/15
Yes	Yes	Yes	Yes		40,274†	11,214	12		Yes	110	$28,322	None
Yes	Yes	Yes	Yes	Yes	13,193†	9,882	6	294				
		Yes	No		10,634†		15	230				
Yes	Yes	Yes	No		10,110†		12	230	Yes			None
Yes	Yes		No									
			No		10,710†	6,300	6	230				
Yes	Yes	Yes	Yes	Yes	37,350	7,100	8	1156	Yes	134	$22,350	2/1
Yes	Yes		Yes		39,892†	10,940						
Yes	Yes		Yes		30,815†	12,170	12					
Yes	Yes	Yes	Yes	Yes	29,140†	12,442						
Yes			Yes		23,772†	8,000		901	Yes			8/1
Yes	Yes	Yes	Yes		27,045†	10,010		524				
Yes	Yes		Yes	Yes	31,272†	12,881	16	961	Yes			None
Yes	Yes		Yes		32,300	12,750	4		Yes			None
Yes	Yes		Yes	Yes	27,230	12,760		820	Yes	26	$13,016	None
Yes	Yes	Yes	Yes	Yes	25,778‡	13,786	12	788	Yes			None

† Tuition and fees are for 2010-11. ‡ Tuition and fees projected for 2011-12. * Includes room and board

Institution	Control/ degrees	Undergraduates		Tests required (Fall 2011)	TOEFL		Application	
		Total	Internat'l		minimum	average	Deadline	Fee
Fitchburg State University	Pu/B	4,026	14	TOEFL, SAT/ACT	550		3/1	25
Framingham State University	Pu/B	3,528	32	TOEFL, SAT/ACT	550	560	2/15	60
Franklin W. Olin College of Engineering	Pr/B	338	21				1/1	100
Gordon College.	Pr/B	1,496	57	TOEFL			4/1	50
Greenfield Community College.	Pu/A	2,583		TOEFL	550		None	35
Hampshire College.	Pr/B	1,505	70	TOEFL	577	591	1/1	60
Harvard College	Pr/B	6,641	675				1/1	75
Hellenic College/Holy Cross	Pr/B	81	5	TOEFL	500		None	50
ITT Technical Institute: Wilmington	Pr/AB							
Lasell College.	Pr/B	1,613	25	TOEFL	525		8/15	40
Lesley University.	Pr/AB	1,451	27	TOEFL, SAT/ACT	550	578	3/1	50
Marian Court College.	Pr/A	230		TOEFL	500		None	75
Massachusetts Bay Community College	Pu/A	4,184		TOEFL	500		None	20
Massachusetts College of Art and Design	Pu/B	1,825	40	TOEFL	550		3/1	65
Massachusetts College of Liberal Arts	Pu/B	1,677	1	TOEFL, SAT/ACT	550		4/1	35
Massachusetts College of Pharmacy and Health Sciences.	Pr/B	1,549		TOEFL, SAT/ACT	550		2/1	
Massachusetts Institute of Technology	Pr/B	4,285	398		577	632	1/1	75
Massachusetts Maritime Academy.	Pu/B	1,188		TOEFL	500		5/1	50
Massasoit Community College	Pu/A	6,099	27	TOEFL	500		6/1	
Merrimack College	Pr/AB	2,020	30	TOEFL	550	590	2/1	
Middlesex Community College.	Pu/A	8,865	88	TOEFL	500		None	
Montserrat College of Art	Pr/B	357	3	TOEFL	520		5/1	50
Mount Holyoke College	Pr/B	2,287	487	TOEFL		611	1/15	60
Mount Ida College.	Pr/AB	1,447	55	TOEFL	525		None	45
Mount Wachusett Community College	Pu/A	4,363	41	TOEFL	550		5/15	10
New England College of Business and Finance	Pr/AB	601		TOEFL	500			50
New England Conservatory of Music.	Pr/B	413	114	TOEFL	500		12/1	105
New England Institute of Art	Pr/AB			TOEFL			None	150
Newbury College.	Pr/AB	1,007		TOEFL	500		None	25
Nichols College.	Pr/AB	1,267	10	TOEFL	550		None	25
North Shore Community College	Pu/A	7,985		TOEFL	500		8/11	
Northeastern University.	Pr/B	15,905	1,548	TOEFL	563	598	1/15	70
Northern Essex Community College	Pu/A	6,503		TOEFL	500		8/1	25
Pine Manor College	Pr/AB	165		TOEFL	500	528	None	25
Quincy College.	Pu/A			TOEFL	463		8/1	30
Quinsigamond Community College	Pu/A	7,533	38				7/1	50
Regis College.	Pr/AB	1,101	12	TOEFL	550	590	6/1	50
Roxbury Community College.	Pu/A	2,749					None	135
Salem State University	Pu/B	7,296	223	TOEFL, SAT/ACT	500		3/1	75
School of the Museum of Fine Arts.	Pr/B	528	41	TOEFL	550	600	2/1	65
Simmons College.	Pr/B	1,876	56	TOEFL, SAT/ACT	560	597	2/1	55
Smith College.	Pr/B	2,588	230	TOEFL	600		1/15	60
Springfield College.	Pr/B	3,703		TOEFL, SAT	525		4/1	50
Springfield Technical Community College	Pu/A	5,985	59	TOEFL	525		6/1	35
Stonehill College.	Pr/B	2,573	12	TOEFL	550	596	1/15	60
Suffolk University	Pr/AB	5,583	667	TOEFL, SAT/ACT	550		7/1	50
Tufts University	Pr/B	5,187	328	TOEFL, SAT, SAT Subject Test(s), or ACT	600		1/1	70
University of Massachusetts Amherst.	Pu/AB	20,791	229	TOEFL, SAT/ACT	550		1/15	70
University of Massachusetts Boston.	Pu/B	10,745	433	TOEFL	550		4/1	100
University of Massachusetts Dartmouth	Pu/B	7,586	25	TOEFL, SAT/ACT	520	568	6/15	60
University of Massachusetts Lowell.	Pu/AB	10,417	63	TOEFL, SAT/ACT	550		7/1	60
University of Phoenix: Boston	Pr/B	212						
Wellesley College	Pr/B	2,296	236	TOEFL		657	1/15	50
Wentworth Institute of Technology	Pr/AB	3,698	143	TOEFL	525		None	50
Western New England College.	Pr/AB	2,709	8	TOEFL	500		None	40
Westfield State University	Pu/B	5,098	13	TOEFL, SAT/ACT	550		2/1	50

Adviser	Orien-tation	ESL	Academic year	Summer	Tuition/fees	Living costs	Maximum credits/summer	Credit hour charge	Avail-able	Number receiving aid	Average award	Deadline
Yes	Yes		Yes		13,880†	8,106		294				
Yes		Yes	Yes		13,145†	8,600	16	294				
Yes			Yes		38,425†	13,500		1267	Yes	21	$33,476	2/15
Yes	Yes		Yes	Yes	30,606	10,434			Yes	50	$20,832	
Yes	Yes	Yes	No		13,007†		18	281				
Yes	Yes		Yes		42,880	11,180			Yes	53	$36,146	2/1
Yes	Yes		Yes		38,416†	12,308			Yes	523	$45,486	2/1
Yes			Yes	Yes	19,600†	12,250	6	797	Yes			4/1
Yes	Yes	Yes	Yes		26,000†	11,800		825				
Yes	Yes		Yes	Yes	30,420	13,250	9	495	Yes			None
			No		15,400†							
Yes	Yes	Yes	No		10,710†	8,478	19	230				
Yes	Yes		Yes	Yes	25,400†	11,750						
			Yes	Yes	16,695†	8,246		416				
Yes	Yes	Yes	Yes	Yes	26,460	12,850	12	945				
Yes	Yes		Yes	Yes	39,212†	11,234		605	Yes	326	$44,650	2/15
Yes			Yes		20,259†	9,202			Yes			None
		Yes	No		10,830†		12	230	Yes			None
Yes	Yes	Yes	Yes	Yes	31,380†	10,700	16	1100	Yes	15	$10,533	2/1
Yes	Yes		No		10,980†			366				
			Yes		24,790†	7,370		993	Yes	1	$7,036	None
Yes	Yes		Yes	Yes	41,456	12,140	8	1290	Yes	472	$35,895	3/1
Yes	Yes	Yes	Yes	Yes	25,915	12,500		700	Yes			None
Yes	Yes	Yes	No		11,700†	7,200	12	230				
			No		11,075†		6	366				
Yes	Yes	Yes	Yes		36,700	12,100	8	1155	Yes			12/1
Yes	Yes		Yes		23,190†		15	773	Yes			None
Yes	Yes		Yes		25,100†	13,250	18		Yes			5/1
Yes			Yes		28,870†	9,330		952	Yes	3	$11,000	6/1
Yes	Yes		No		11,610†		12	257				
Yes	Yes	Yes	Yes	Yes	36,792†	12,760	16		Yes	250	$16,386	
Yes		Yes	No		11,460†		12	266				
Yes	Yes	Yes	Yes	Yes	21,400†	12,254	8	650	Yes			None
Yes	Yes		No		6,300†		12					
Yes		Yes	No		11,430†	7,978	12	230				
Yes	Yes	Yes	Yes	Yes	31,785	12,800	12		Yes	9	$13,403	None
Yes	Yes	Yes	No		11,940†		9	247	Yes			5/1
Yes	Yes	Yes	Yes	Yes	13,310†	9,546	18	294				
Yes	Yes		Yes	Yes	31,585†	19,400			Yes			3/15
Yes	Yes		Yes	Yes	32,230†	12,470		978	Yes	31	$8,541	3/1
Yes	Yes		Yes	Yes	40,070	13,390	12	1245	Yes	132	$42,197	2/15
Yes	Yes	Yes	Yes	Yes	28,585†	11,520		850				
Yes		Yes	No		10,896†		12	242				
Yes	Yes		Yes	Yes	33,920	12,860		1131				
Yes	Yes	Yes	Yes	Yes	29,894	14,624	12	730	Yes	110	$9,664	2/15
Yes	Yes	Yes	Yes	Yes	41,598†	11,268			Yes	81	$38,832	2/15
Yes	Yes	Yes	Yes	Yes	23,813†	10,239	12					
Yes	Yes	Yes	No		23,188†		12	406				
Yes	Yes		Yes	Yes	20,420†	9,883						
Yes	Yes		Yes	Yes	22,945†	9,347		357				
					12,600†							
Yes	Yes		Yes	Yes	40,660	12,590			Yes	107	$46,739	
Yes	Yes		Yes	Yes	24,000	11,300	20		Yes	77	$6,366	None
Yes	Yes		Yes		30,844	11,732		541	Yes			4/15
Yes	Yes		Yes		13,511†	8,521		95				

† Tuition and fees are for 2010-11.   ‡ Tuition and fees projected for 2011-12.   * Includes room and board

Institution	Control/ degrees	Undergraduates		Tests required (Fall 2011)	TOEFL		Application	
		Total	Internat'l		minimum	average	Deadline	Fee
Wheaton College	Pr/B	1,635	99	TOEFL	580	595	1/15	55
Wheelock College	Pr/B	828	5	TOEFL, SAT/ACT	500	550	3/1	15
Williams College	Pr/B	1,994	142	TOEFL, SAT, SAT Subject Test(s), or ACT			1/1	60
Worcester Polytechnic Institute	Pr/B	3,537	351	TOEFL	550	598	2/1	60
Worcester State University	Pu/B	4,395	43	TOEFL, SAT/ACT	550	567	3/1	40
Zion Bible College	Pr/B	280		TOEFL	500		8/1	75
Michigan								
Adrian College	Pr/AB	1,688		TOEFL	500		3/15	
Albion College	Pr/B	1,587	49	TOEFL	550	597	4/1	40
Alma College	Pr/B	1,401		TOEFL	525		7/1	25
Andrews University	Pr/AB	1,819	211	TOEFL	550		None	30
Aquinas College	Pr/AB	1,920	4	TOEFL, SAT/ACT	550	600	5/1	
Art Institute of Michigan	Pr/AB	930						50
Baker College of Allen Park	Pr/AB	3,926						20
Baker College of Auburn Hills	Pr/AB	4,179		TOEFL	500			20
Baker College of Cadillac	Pr/AB	2,094		TOEFL	550		9/20	20
Baker College of Jackson	Pr/AB	2,917		TOEFL	550		None	20
Baker College of Muskegon	Pr/AB	5,810		TOEFL	500		9/22	20
Baker College of Owosso	Pr/AB	3,532		TOEFL	500		None	20
Baker College of Port Huron	Pr/AB	1,776		TOEFL	550		None	20
Bay de Noc Community College	Pu/A	2,600		TOEFL	550	575	5/1	
Calvin College	Pr/B	3,839	320	TOEFL	550		4/1	35
Central Michigan University	Pu/B	21,055	248	TOEFL, ACT	550	555	6/1	35
Cleary University	Pr/AB	617	2	TOEFL	550		None	25
College for Creative Studies	Pr/B	1,318	87	TOEFL	527		7/1	35
Cornerstone University	Pr/AB	2,091	16	TOEFL	500		6/1	25
Davenport University	Pr/AB	9,560		TOEFL	500		None	125
Delta College	Pu/A	9,673	78	TOEFL	500	550	5/20	20
Eastern Michigan University	Pu/B	18,131	322	TOEFL	500		3/1	30
Ferris State University	Pu/AB	12,646	118	TOEFL	500		None	30
Finlandia University	Pr/AB			TOEFL	500		None	30
Glen Oaks Community College	Pu/A	1,650		TOEFL	500			
Gogebic Community College	Pu/A			TOEFL	500		6/1	100
Grand Rapids Community College	Pu/A	16,945		TOEFL	525	608	6/1	40
Grand Valley State University	Pu/B	20,818	200	TOEFL	598		6/1	30
Henry Ford Community College	Pu/A	17,137		TOEFL	550		6/1	30
Hillsdale College	Pr/B	1,402		TOEFL	560	570	2/15	35
Hope College	Pr/B	3,139	39	TOEFL, SAT/ACT	550		2/1	50
ITT Technical Institute: Canton	Pr/AB							
Kalamazoo College	Pr/B	1,341	78	TOEFL, SAT/ACT	550	600	2/1	40
Kalamazoo Valley Community College	Pu/A	11,210	49	TOEFL	500			
Kellogg Community College	Pu/A			TOEFL	500	550	6/1	
Kettering University	Pr/B	1,789	52	TOEFL	550		None	35
Kirtland Community College	Pu/A	1,808	4	TOEFL	550		None	
Kuyper College	Pr/AB			TOEFL	550	560	None	25
Lake Michigan College	Pu/A	4,064			500		None	
Lake Superior State University	Pu/AB	2,448	219	TOEFL	550		7/15	35
Lansing Community College	Pu/A	20,440	389	TOEFL	500	540	6/15	
Lawrence Technological University	Pr/AB	2,032	155	TOEFL, SAT/ACT	550		6/15	30
Macomb Community College	Pu/A	14,918	130	TOEFL	550		7/21	
Madonna University	Pr/AB	2,950	127	TOEFL	540		7/1	55
Marygrove College	Pr/AB	983		TOEFL	520		3/15	25
Michigan Jewish Institute	Pr/AB			TOEFL	550		None	50
Michigan State University	Pu/B	35,765	2,796	TOEFL, SAT/ACT	550			50
Michigan Technological University	Pu/AB	5,620	427	TOEFL	550		5/1	
Montcalm Community College	Pu/A	1,851	7	TOEFL	500		5/1	

Adviser	Orientation	ESL	Academic year	Summer	Tuition/fees	Living costs	Maximum credits/summer	Credit hour charge	Available	Number receiving aid	Average award	Deadline
Yes	Yes		Yes		41,894	10,670			Yes	65	$26,378	2/1
			Yes		30,055	12,370		910	Yes	2	$29,000	None
Yes	Yes		Yes		41,434 †	10,906			Yes	128	$47,673	2/1
Yes	Yes	Yes	Yes	Yes	39,860 ‡	12,650	15		Yes	276	$21,311	2/1
Yes	Yes	Yes	Yes	Yes	13,235 †	9,658	12	294				
Yes			Yes		9,225 †	6,780		280	Yes			None
	Yes	Yes	Yes		25,900 †	7,900	12		Yes			
Yes	Yes		Yes	Yes	32,662	9,260		1365	Yes	43	$15,664	None
Yes			Yes		29,230	11,840		1000	Yes			None
Yes	Yes	Yes	Yes	Yes	23,428	7,374		945	Yes			None
Yes	Yes		Yes	Yes	24,286	7,438	12	732	Yes	2	$6,375	None
					21,735 †			483				
					9,225 †			205				
Yes			No		9,225 †	7,200	16	205				
Yes			No		9,225 †		16	205				
Yes					9,225 †	7,200	16	205				
			Yes	Yes	9,225 †	2,925	16	205				
Yes			Yes		9,225 †	2,800	16	205				
Yes			No		9,225 †		16	205				
Yes			Yes	Yes	6,030 †	2,800	8	190				
Yes	Yes		Yes	Yes	25,565	8,760	13	610	Yes	306	$14,126	None
Yes	Yes	Yes	Yes	Yes	25,361 †	9,092	12	845	Yes	66	$8,532	
Yes			No		16,560 †	3,834	12	345	Yes			None
Yes	Yes		Yes	Yes	32,785	8,500	6	1048	Yes			None
Yes			Yes		22,388	9,114	8	836	Yes	15	$14,636	None
Yes	Yes	Yes	Yes	Yes	15,560	8,412		504	Yes			None
Yes	Yes		No		5,787 ‡	3,990						
Yes	Yes	Yes	Yes	Yes	22,283 †	7,785		702	Yes			None
Yes	Yes		Yes	Yes	15,900 †	9,180	15	530	Yes			None
Yes	Yes	Yes	Yes		18,974 †	6,154	12	616	Yes			
Yes			No		3,230 †	4,876	18		Yes			None
Yes			Yes	Yes	7,463 †	4,004	12	230				
Yes	Yes		No		8,870 †		12	293				
Yes	Yes	Yes	Yes	Yes	13,402 †	7,478	16	571	Yes	117	$8,537	None
Yes			No		4,552 †			135				
Yes			Yes		21,310 ‡	9,300	8	790	Yes			3/15
Yes	Yes	Yes	Yes	Yes	27,010	8,260	12		Yes			None
Yes	Yes	Yes	Yes		34,417 †	8,693			Yes			
Yes		Yes	No		5,100 †	4,073		170				
Yes	Yes		No		5,535 †		12					
Yes	Yes		Yes	Yes	29,290 †	7,272	20	896	Yes	48	$8,326	None
			No		6,885 †		9	221	Yes	2	$5,673	None
Yes	Yes		Yes	Yes	17,486	6,720			Yes			None
Yes			No		5,850 †		18	163	Yes			None
Yes			Yes	Yes	17,328 †	8,081		722	Yes			None
Yes	Yes	Yes	No		6,530 ‡			216				
Yes	Yes	Yes	Yes	Yes	26,278	8,306	30	370	Yes	20	$5,412	
Yes		Yes	No		4,870 †	5,877	12	159				
Yes	Yes	Yes	Yes	Yes	18,345	9,730	18	608	Yes			None
Yes	Yes		Yes		17,180 †	7,600	7	595				
Yes		Yes	No		10,500 †			350				
Yes	Yes	Yes	Yes	Yes	29,108 †	7,820	6	970	Yes	154	$9,243	None
Yes	Yes	Yes	Yes	Yes	24,527 †	8,462	18	789	Yes	296	$6,068	None
Yes			No		6,780 †		8	217				

† Tuition and fees are for 2010-11. ‡ Tuition and fees projected for 2011-12. * Includes room and board

Institution	Control/ degrees	Undergraduates		Tests required (Fall 2011)	TOEFL		Application	
		Total	Internat'l		minimum	average	Deadline	Fee
Mott Community College	Pu/A	8,034		TOEFL	500		None	
Muskegon Community College.	Pu/A	3,994		TOEFL	500	600	None	
North Central Michigan College	Pu/A			TOEFL	550		6/1	
Northern Michigan University	Pu/AB	8,427	79	TOEFL	500		6/1	30
Northwestern Michigan College	Pu/A			TOEFL	550	570	7/15	25
Northwood University: Michigan	Pr/AB	1,677	185	TOEFL	500	550	None	25
Oakland Community College	Pu/A	16,873	825	TOEFL	350		6/1	
Oakland University	Pu/B	15,037	129	TOEFL	550		5/30	
Olivet College.	Pr/B	1,072		TOEFL	500	520	7/15	25
Robert B. Miller College.	Pr/B	290						
Rochester College	Pr/AB			TOEFL, ACT	500		None	25
Sacred Heart Major Seminary.	Pr/AB	88	2	TOEFL			8/1	30
Saginaw Chippewa Tribal College.	Pu/A							25
Saginaw Valley State University.	Pu/B	8,944	245	TOEFL	525		None	25
St. Clair County Community College.	Pu/A			TOEFL	500	550	7/1	10
Siena Heights University.	Pr/AB	2,027		TOEFL	500		8/1	50
Southwestern Michigan College	Pu/A	2,874	35	TOEFL	550		6/1	
Spring Arbor University	Pr/AB	2,848		TOEFL	525		4/1	30
University of Detroit Mercy.	Pr/B	3,065					4/1	50
University of Michigan.	Pu/B	26,830	1,578	TOEFL, SAT/ACT	570		2/1	75
University of Michigan: Dearborn.	Pu/B	6,760	50	TOEFL, SAT/ACT	550	570	8/15	75
University of Michigan: Flint.	Pu/B	6,615	121	TOEFL	500		None	30
University of Phoenix: Metro Detroit.	Pr/B							
University of Phoenix: West Michigan.	Pr/B							
Walsh College of Accountancy and Business Administration.	Pr/B	1,051	24	TOEFL	550		None	25
Washtenaw Community College	Pu/A	14,202		TOEFL	500		None	15
Wayne County Community College.	Pu/A	20,793	36	TOEFL				
Wayne State University.	Pu/B	19,797	469	TOEFL	550		5/1	50
Western Michigan University.	Pu/B	19,698	533	TOEFL	550		4/1	100

Minnesota

Institution	Control/ degrees	Undergraduates		Tests required (Fall 2011)	TOEFL		Application	
		Total	Internat'l		minimum	average	Deadline	Fee
Academy College	Pr/AB							40
Alexandria Technical College.	Pu/A	2,347		TOEFL	500		6/1	20
Anthem College: Minneapolis	Pr/A							50
Argosy University: Twin Cities	Pr/AB							50
Art Institutes International Minnesota.	Pr/AB	2,017		TOEFL	480		None	50
Augsburg College	Pr/B	3,000	46	TOEFL	550		7/15	25
Bemidji State University.	Pu/AB	4,519	133	TOEFL	500		None	20
Bethany Lutheran College	Pr/B	591	9	TOEFL	550		7/1	250
Bethel University.	Pr/AB	3,287	10	TOEFL	525		4/15	
Brown College: Brooklyn Center	Pr/AB							
Brown College: Mendota Heights	Pr/AB			TOEFL	500	550	None	25
Capella University.	Pr/B	8,345			550		None	100
Carleton College	Pr/B	1,991	151	TOEFL, SAT/ACT	600		1/15	30
Central Lakes College.	Pu/A	4,378		TOEFL	500		8/1	20
Century College	Pu/A	9,965	133	TOEFL	500	525	5/1	20
College of St. Benedict.	Pr/B	2,082	121	TOEFL	500		4/1	
College of St. Scholastica	Pr/B	2,814	104	TOEFL	550		6/1	50
College of Visual Arts	Pr/B	205		TOEFL	500		None	40
Concordia College: Moorhead	Pr/B	2,705	82	TOEFL	533		None	20
Concordia University St. Paul	Pr/AB	1,493	3	TOEFL	500		8/1	30
Crown College	Pr/AB	1,011		TOEFL, SAT/ACT	500		6/15	20
Dakota County Technical College.	Pu/A	3,287		TOEFL	500		6/1	20
Dunwoody College of Technology	Pr/AB	1,229		TOEFL	475	500	8/15	50
Fond du Lac Tribal and Community College.	Pu/A			TOEFL	500		None	20
Globe University.	Pr/AB	940					None	50
Gustavus Adolphus College.	Pr/B	2,412		TOEFL	550	593	3/1	

| Student services | | | Housing | | Academic year costs | | Maximum credits/summer | Credit hour charge | International financial aid | | | |
Adviser	Orientation	ESL	Academic year	Summer	Tuition/fees	Living costs			Available	Number receiving aid	Average award	Deadline
Yes			No		6,281†		8	197				
Yes			No		5,860†	5,300		185				
Yes			Yes		5,145†	6,150	6	153	Yes			4/1
Yes	Yes	Yes	Yes	Yes	12,505‡	8,026	16	486	Yes	21	$1,933	None
Yes		Yes	Yes	Yes	6,213†	8,598	18	195	Yes			None
Yes	Yes		Yes	Yes	20,140‡	8,350	15	745	Yes			None
Yes	Yes	Yes	No		4,822†	6,680	16	158	Yes			None
Yes	Yes	Yes	Yes	Yes	21,675†	11,380			Yes			None
Yes	Yes	Yes	Yes	Yes	21,092	7,000			Yes			None
Yes	Yes		Yes	Yes	18,056†	6,046		533				
Yes		Yes			16,027	8,681	4	373	Yes	2	$19,055	None
			No		2,550†			60				
Yes	Yes	Yes	Yes	Yes	17,157†	7,550	12	557	Yes			None
Yes			No		7,700†	5,040		247	Yes			None
Yes	Yes	Yes	Yes	Yes	19,790†	7,170	6		Yes			8/15
Yes		Yes	Yes	Yes	5,970†	7,353	12	167				
Yes	Yes	Yes	Yes	Yes	20,536†	7,254	8	504	Yes	41	$9,387	None
Yes	Yes	Yes	Yes	Yes	30,660†	8,740		780	Yes			
Yes	Yes	Yes	Yes	Yes	36,001†	9,962		1463				
Yes	Yes		No		20,659†			800				
Yes	Yes	Yes	Yes	Yes	16,399†	7,080		646	Yes	26	$1,712	None
					11,880†							
					11,880†							
Yes			No		11,895‡	18,066		320	Yes			None
Yes		Yes	No		5,430†	6,568	12	181				
Yes	Yes		No		4,270†	4,715	9	130	Yes			None
Yes	Yes	Yes	Yes	Yes	19,225†	7,650	18					
Yes	Yes	Yes	Yes	Yes	20,894†	8,095		694				
Yes			No			7,200						
Yes			No		4,904†	5,200			Yes			None
			No		19,992†							
Yes			Yes		23,088†		16	481				
Yes	Yes	Yes	Yes	Yes	30,418	8,072	3	900	Yes			8/1
Yes	Yes	Yes	Yes	Yes	7,497†	6,480						
Yes	Yes		Yes	Yes	20,950†	8,700		870	Yes			None
Yes	Yes		Yes	Yes	29,460	9,030	8	1225	Yes			None
			Yes		17,496†		20					
			No		13,725†			305				
Yes	Yes		Yes	Yes	42,942	11,238			Yes	93	$32,465	2/15
Yes		Yes	No		4,927†		16		Yes			None
Yes	Yes	Yes	No		5,024†	12,000	18		Yes			None
Yes	Yes	Yes	Yes	Yes	34,308	8,956		1394	Yes	106	$20,211	None
Yes	Yes		Yes	Yes	29,506	9,716		916	Yes			None
Yes			No		24,810‡	5,300	6	1175	Yes			
Yes	Yes		Yes	Yes	29,360	8,620	12	1145	Yes	70	$14,153	None
Yes			Yes	Yes	28,500	7,500		600	Yes			None
Yes	Yes		Yes	Yes	20,870†	7,180	12	870	Yes	2	$18,525	8/1
	Yes	Yes	No		5,298†			156				
Yes			No		16,828†			212				
Yes			Yes		9,075†	3,536	9	287	Yes			None
Yes	Yes		No		24,075†		12	535				
Yes	Yes		Yes	Yes	35,897	8,700			Yes			4/15

† Tuition and fees are for 2010-11.   ‡ Tuition and fees projected for 2011-12.   * Includes room and board

Institution	Control/ degrees	Undergraduates		Tests required (Fall 2011)	TOEFL		Application	
		Total	Internat'l		minimum	average	Deadline	Fee
Hamline University	Pr/B	1,866	63	TOEFL	550		6/15	100
Hennepin Technical College	Pu/A	6,218		TOEFL	500		6/1	20
Herzing University	Pr/AB			TOEFL	500			
Hibbing Community College	Pu/A	1,629		TOEFL	500		7/1	20
Institute of Production and Recording	Pr/A							
Inver Hills Community College	Pu/A	5,400	30	TOEFL	500		6/1	20
Itasca Community College	Pu/A			TOEFL	500		8/1	20
ITT Technical Institute: Eden Prairie	Pr/AB			TOEFL				
Lake Superior College	Pu/A	3,823	4	TOEFL	513		7/16	20
Le Cordon Bleu College of Culinary Arts: Minneapolis-St. Paul	Pr/A	800						50
Macalester College	Pr/B	2,005	226	TOEFL, SAT/ACT	590	638	1/15	40
Mesabi Range Community and Technical College	Pu/A	1,417		TOEFL	500		None	20
Minneapolis Business College	Pr/A	370					None	50
Minneapolis Community and Technical College	Pu/A	10,548		TOEFL	310		None	20
Minnesota School of Business	Pr/AB						None	50
Minnesota School of Business: Blaine	Pr/AB							50
Minnesota School of Business: Plymouth	Pr/AB							50
Minnesota School of Business: Rochester	Pr/AB							50
Minnesota School of Business: Shakopee	Pr/AB							50
Minnesota State College - Southeast Technical	Pu/A	2,324	9	TOEFL	500		None	20
Minnesota State Community and Technical College	Pu/A	6,925		TOEFL	550		7/1	20
Minnesota State University Mankato	Pu/AB	12,629	422	TOEFL	500	530	4/1	20
Minnesota State University Moorhead	Pu/AB	6,582	334	TOEFL	500		6/1	20
Minnesota West Community and Technical College	Pu/A	2,863		TOEFL	500		6/10	20
Normandale Community College	Pu/A	10,030		TOEFL	500	520	7/15	20
North Central University	Pr/AB			TOEFL, SAT/ACT	500		3/1	25
North Hennepin Community College	Pu/A	6,850	87	TOEFL	500		7/1	20
Northland Community & Technical College	Pu/A	4,135		TOEFL	500		None	20
Northwest Technical College	Pu/A	992	2	TOEFL	500		None	20
Northwest Technical Institute	Pr/A	120		TOEFL			None	25
Northwestern College	Pr/AB	1,807	16	TOEFL, SAT/ACT	530	542	6/1	30
Northwestern Health Sciences University	Pr/B							50
Pine Technical College	Pu/A	1,022		TOEFL	500		None	20
Rainy River Community College	Pu/A	342		TOEFL	550		None	20
Rasmussen College: Bloomington	Pr/AB			TOEFL	500		None	60
Rasmussen College: Brooklyn Park	Pr/AB			TOEFL	500		None	60
Rasmussen College: Eagan	Pr/AB			TOEFL	500		None	60
Rasmussen College: Lake Elmo/Woodbury	Pr/AB							60
Rasmussen College: Mankato	Pr/AB			TOEFL	500		None	60
Rasmussen College: St. Cloud	Pr/AB			TOEFL	500		None	60
Ridgewater College	Pu/A	4,052			500			20
Riverland Community College	Pu/A			TOEFL	500	520	6/1	20
Rochester Community and Technical College	Pu/A	6,235	67	TOEFL	450		8/9	20
St. Catherine University	Pr/AB	3,736	38	TOEFL	500	575	6/30	20
Saint Cloud State University	Pu/AB	13,861	773	TOEFL	500		4/1	20
St. Cloud Technical and Community College	Pu/A	4,443		TOEFL	500		7/1	20
St. John's University	Pr/B	1,932	133	TOEFL	500		4/1	
St. Mary's University of Minnesota	Pr/B	2,040	47	TOEFL	495	550	None	40
St. Olaf College	Pr/B	3,114	86	TOEFL, SAT/ACT	550	601	1/15	40
South Central College	Pu/A			TOEFL	500		3/1	20
Southwest Minnesota State University	Pu/AB	2,578	172	TOEFL, SAT, SAT Subject Test(s), or ACT	500		6/15	20
University of Minnesota: Crookston	Pu/B	1,462	101	TOEFL	520	540	6/30	30
University of Minnesota: Duluth	Pu/B	9,659	137	TOEFL, SAT/ACT	550	560	8/1	50

Student services			Housing		Academic year costs		Maximum credits/summer	Credit hour charge	International financial aid			
Adviser	Orientation	ESL	Academic year	Summer	Tuition/fees	Living costs			Available	Number receiving aid	Average award	Deadline
Yes	Yes		Yes	Yes	31,802	8,504	8	990	Yes	50	$13,681	None
Yes	Yes		No		4,624†	11,609	12					
					12,400†			385				
Yes			Yes		6,029†	2,900	12	182				
Yes		Yes	No		4,965†							
Yes			Yes	Yes	6,037†	4,560	6	182				
Yes		Yes	No		8,793†		19	272				
Yes			No									
Yes	Yes		Yes	Yes	42,021	10,046		1306	Yes	204	$33,520	3/1
Yes			Yes	Yes	6,029†	5,764	9	182				
			Yes		13,760†	6,700						
Yes	Yes	Yes	No		4,974†				Yes			None
			No		24,075†		16	535				
					24,075†			535				
					24,075†			535				
					24,075†	7,092		535				
					24,075†			535				
Yes			Yes		4,986†							
Yes		Yes	Yes	Yes	5,033†	2,750	20		Yes			None
Yes	Yes	Yes	Yes	Yes	13,478†	6,300	12	505	Yes			
Yes	Yes		Yes	Yes	6,923†	6,968	12		Yes			None
Yes		Yes	No		5,151†	1,800	20					
		Yes	No		5,125†		13		Yes			None
Yes	Yes		Yes	Yes	17,440	5,410	15	559	Yes			None
Yes	Yes	Yes	No		4,963†	9,015	10		Yes			None
Yes			No		5,060†	4,500						
Yes			Yes	Yes	5,079†	6,024						
			No		16,975†			529				
Yes	Yes		Yes		24,570†	7,720	12	1040	Yes	9	$13,135	8/1
	Yes		No		9,006†		9	284				
Yes			Yes	Yes	6,059†	3,600		182	Yes			None
			No		18,900†	7,011		420	Yes			None
			No		18,900†	7,011		420	Yes			None
			No		18,900†	7,011		420	Yes			None
					18,900†	7,011		420				
			No		18,900†	7,011		420	Yes			None
			No		18,900†	7,011		420	Yes			None
			No		4,950†		12					
Yes	Yes	Yes	Yes	Yes	5,063†	4,150	6		Yes			None
Yes	Yes		No		5,243†	7,200						
Yes	Yes		Yes	Yes	29,780	11,132		980	Yes			None
Yes	Yes	Yes	Yes	Yes	13,733†	6,306	9	431				
Yes	Yes	Yes	No		4,922†				Yes			
Yes	Yes	Yes	Yes	Yes	33,606	8,344		1376	Yes	125	$20,832	
Yes	Yes	Yes	Yes	Yes	27,250‡	7,150	18	895	Yes	36	$13,768	None
Yes	Yes		Yes		38,150	8,800	4	1195	Yes	84	$30,005	3/1
Yes	Yes		No		4,910†	6,500			Yes			None
Yes	Yes		Yes	Yes	7,244†	7,782	20		Yes			None
Yes	Yes	Yes	Yes	Yes	10,627†	6,568	9		Yes	38	$2,364	None
Yes	Yes		Yes	Yes	13,807†	6,422	12	442	Yes			None

† Tuition and fees are for 2010-11.   ‡ Tuition and fees projected for 2011-12.   * Includes room and board

Institution	Control/ degrees	Undergraduates		Tests required (Fall 2011)	TOEFL		Application	
		Total	Internat'l		minimum	average	Deadline	Fee
University of Minnesota: Morris	Pu/B	1,811		TOEFL, SAT/ACT	550		3/15	75
University of Minnesota: Rochester	Pu/B	141		TOEFL			8/1	50
University of Minnesota: Twin Cities	Pu/B	30,519	1,868	TOEFL	475		None	45
University of Phoenix: Minneapolis-St. Paul	Pr/B			TOEFL				
University of St. Thomas	Pr/B	6,115	104	TOEFL	550		None	
Walden University	Pr/B	9,245	919	TOEFL	550	598	None	50
White Earth Tribal and Community College	Pr/A	105						
Winona State University	Pu/AB	7,862	173	TOEFL	550		3/4	20
Mississippi								
Alcorn State University	Pu/AB	2,980	38	TOEFL, SAT/ACT	525		None	
Antonelli College: Jackson	Pr/A							50
Belhaven University	Pr/AB	2,443		TOEFL	500	513	None	25
Blue Cliff College: Gulfport	Pr/A	260						
Blue Mountain College	Pr/B	528	2	TOEFL, SAT/ACT	500			10
Coahoma Community College	Pu/A	2,565		TOEFL, SAT/ACT		500		
Delta State University	Pu/B	2,948	50	TOEFL, SAT/ACT	525	530	8/1	25
Hinds Community College	Pu/A			TOEFL	500		8/17	
Jackson State University	Pu/B	6,592		TOEFL	525	560	8/15	
Jones County Junior College	Pu/A	5,573						
Meridian Community College	Pu/A				500	535	None	
Millsaps College	Pr/B	948	24	TOEFL, SAT/ACT	550		2/1	
Mississippi College	Pr/B			TOEFL			8/15	
Mississippi Delta Community College	Pu/A							
Mississippi Gulf Coast Community College	Pu/A	10,002		TOEFL	525	540	7/1	
Mississippi State University	Pu/B	14,673		TOEFL, SAT/ACT	525	587	None	40
Mississippi University for Women	Pu/AB	2,394		TOEFL	525			25
Mississippi Valley State University	Pu/B			TOEFL, SAT/ACT	525	560	6/15	
Northeast Mississippi Community College	Pu/A			TOEFL	525		None	
Rust College	Pr/AB			TOEFL	540	570	7/15	10
Southeastern Baptist College	Pr/AB						7/1	15
Tougaloo College	Pr/AB	912	8	TOEFL	500		4/30	25
University of Mississippi	Pu/B	13,983	150	TOEFL	550	565	6/15	50
University of Southern Mississippi	Pu/B	12,814	67	TOEFL, SAT/ACT	525	540	6/1	35
Virginia College at Jackson	Pr/A							100
Virginia College Gulf Coast	Pr/A							
William Carey University	Pr/B	2,287		TOEFL, SAT/ACT	523		7/15	30
Missouri								
Anthem College: Kansas City	Pr/A							
Avila University	Pr/B	1,161	48	TOEFL	500	573	None	25
Bolivar Technical College	Pr/A	117						45
Brown Mackie College: St. Louis	Pr/AB							
Calvary Bible College and Theological Seminary	Pr/AB	282		TOEFL, SAT/ACT	525		7/15	30
Central Methodist University	Pr/AB			TOEFL	500		6/1	20
College of the Ozarks	Pr/B	1,367	19	TOEFL	550		2/15	
Colorado Technical University: North Kansas City	Pr/AB	984						
Columbia College	Pr/AB	992	95	TOEFL	500	540	7/25	35
Concorde Career College: Kansas City	Pr/A							100
Cottey College	Pr/A	309		TOEFL	500	547	None	20
Cox College	Pr/AB	515		TOEFL	500		4/1	100
Crowder College	Pu/A	4,121	16	TOEFL	500		None	25
Culver-Stockton College	Pr/B	758	18	TOEFL	550		7/1	
DeVry University: Kansas City	Pr/AB			TOEFL	500		None	50
Drury University	Pr/AB	1,621		TOEFL	530		None	25
East Central College	Pu/A	3,322		TOEFL	550		7/15	

	Student services		Housing		Academic year costs		Maximum credits/summer	Credit hour charge	International financial aid			
Adviser	Orientation	ESL	Academic year	Summer	Tuition/fees	Living costs			Available	Number receiving aid	Average award	Deadline
Yes	Yes	Yes	Yes	Yes	11,532†	7,050	20					
Yes	Yes		Yes	Yes	11,102†				Yes			
Yes	Yes	Yes	Yes	Yes	16,503†	7,576		542	Yes			None
					11,880†							
Yes	Yes	Yes	Yes	Yes	30,493‡	8,320	16	936	Yes	42	$21,934	None
					11,805†	8,400		260				
					3,375†			101				
Yes	Yes	Yes	Yes	Yes	13,279†	7,330	12	381				
Yes			Yes	Yes	11,952†	6,174	12	399	Yes	4	$7,769	None
			No			8,610						
Yes	Yes	Yes	Yes		18,420	6,630	15	375	Yes			None
			No									
			Yes		9,020†	3,900	14	265	Yes			7/31
			Yes		5,000†	3,714	12	100				
Yes	Yes		Yes	Yes	12,558†	6,002	12	419	Yes			None
Yes			Yes	Yes	4,680†	3,510	12	200				
Yes	Yes	Yes	Yes	Yes	12,380†	6,342	12	413				
			Yes		4,320†	3,432	14	195				
Yes	Yes	Yes	Yes	Yes	4,000†	3,300	12	177	Yes			None
Yes	Yes		Yes	Yes	29,482	10,312	12	856	Yes			None
Yes	Yes	Yes	Yes		13,550†	6,150	12	405	Yes			None
			Yes		3,828†	2,540						
Yes			Yes		4,438†	5,810		192				
Yes	Yes	Yes	Yes	Yes	13,801†	7,729		460				
Yes	Yes		Yes	Yes	12,654†	5,562		422	Yes			None
Yes			Yes	Yes	11,923†	5,537	12	397				
Yes		Yes	Yes		4,260†	3,060	12	235				
Yes			Yes		7,610†	3,320	6	330	Yes			5/1
Yes			Yes		6,100†	1,300	12	200				
Yes			Yes		9,710†	6,597	12	385				
			Yes		13,894†	6,508	12	463	Yes	140	$11,887	None
Yes	Yes	Yes	Yes	Yes	13,408†	6,688	19	447	Yes	244	$12,562	None
Yes	Yes		Yes	Yes	10,350†	3,945	12	325	Yes			9/1
Yes	Yes	Yes	Yes	Yes	23,100	6,550	12	565	Yes			4/1
			No		11,940†			340				
Yes			Yes	Yes	10,048‡	4,400		290	Yes			4/1
			Yes	Yes	20,130	6,480	9	185	Yes			None
Yes	Yes		Yes	Yes		5,600			Yes	19	$16,900	None
Yes	Yes	Yes	Yes	Yes	16,532	6,254	8		Yes			None
						9,024						
Yes	Yes		Yes		15,100†	6,500		150	Yes			None
			Yes		11,340†							
Yes	Yes	Yes	Yes		4,050†	4,000	9	123	Yes			None
Yes			Yes		22,550	8,600	9	515	Yes	17	$14,441	6/1
Yes					14,826†							
Yes	Yes	Yes	Yes	Yes	21,043	9,000	13	685	Yes	74	$1,844	3/1
Yes			No		4,530†		9	141	Yes			None

† Tuition and fees are for 2010-11.   ‡ Tuition and fees projected for 2011-12.   * Includes room and board

Institution	Control/ degrees	Undergraduates		Tests required (Fall 2011)	TOEFL		Application	
		Total	Internat'l		minimum	average	Deadline	Fee
Evangel University............................	Pr/AB	1,770	11	TOEFL	490	604	6/1	25
Everest College: Springfield...................	Pr/AB							
Fontbonne University........................	Pr/B	1,629	42	TOEFL	500		8/1	25
Global University	Pr/AB						None	40
Goldfarb School of Nursing at Barnes-Jewish College	Pr/B	524	1	TOEFL	575		None	50
Grantham University	Pr/AB	6,776		TOEFL	500		None	
Hannibal-LaGrange University	Pr/AB	929	93	TOEFL	520		None	150
Harris-Stowe State University................	Pu/B	1,648		TOEFL	500		6/1	15
ITT Technical Institute: Kansas City	Pr/AB							
Jefferson College...........................	Pu/A	5,870	15	TOEFL	475	534	6/1	25
Kansas City Art Institute....................	Pr/B	733		TOEFL	550	558	8/1	35
L'Ecole Culinaire	Pr/A							
Lincoln University..........................	Pu/AB	2,692	63	TOEFL, SAT/ACT	500		12/1	20
Lindenwood University.......................	Pr/B	7,170	738	TOEFL	500		None	100
Linn State Technical College	Pu/A	1,118		TOEFL, SAT/ACT	500		None	
Maryville University of Saint Louis............	Pr/B	2,864	34	TOEFL	500		7/1	30
Metro Business College: Rolla	Pr/A							
Metropolitan Community College: Blue River ...	Pu/A	2,852		TOEFL	550		7/1	50
Metropolitan Community College: Business & Technology...............................	Pu/A	681		TOEFL	550		7/1	50
Metropolitan Community College: Longview......	Pu/A	5,080		TOEFL	550		7/1	50
Metropolitan Community College: Maple Woods..................................	Pu/A	4,101		TOEFL	550		7/1	50
Metropolitan Community College: Penn Valley	Pu/A	4,214		TOEFL	500		7/1	50
Midwest University	Pr/B							100
Missouri Baptist University	Pr/AB	1,648	37	TOEFL	500		None	30
Missouri College...........................	Pr/AB							35
Missouri Southern State University	Pu/AB	5,360		TOEFL	535	545	7/1	50
Missouri State University	Pu/B	15,210	603	TOEFL	500	520	4/15	50
Missouri Technical School...................	Pr/AB			TOEFL	500		None	95
Missouri University of Science and Technology...............................	Pu/B	5,458	260	TOEFL	550		6/1	45
Missouri Valley College	Pr/AB	1,476		TOEFL	500		5/1	75
Moberly Area Community College	Pu/A			TOEFL	450	487	None	
National American University: Kansas City........	Pr/AB			TOEFL	490			45
National American University: Lee's Summit	Pr/AB							
North Central Missouri College	Pu/A	1,832		TOEFL	500	518	7/15	15
Northwest Missouri State University	Pu/AB	5,798	121	TOEFL	500	520	7/1	50
Ozarks Technical Community College	Pu/A	13,907		TOEFL			None	50
Park University............................	Pr/AB	10,645	335	TOEFL, SAT/ACT	500	510	7/1	25
Pinnacle Career Institute: Kansas City	Pr/A	1,242						
Research College of Nursing	Pr/B	339		TOEFL, SAT/ACT	550		5/1	50
Rockhurst University	Pr/B	1,534	17	TOEFL, SAT/ACT	550		None	50
St. Louis Community College at Florissant Valley	Pu/A			TOEFL	500		4/20	
Saint Louis University	Pr/B	8,208	708	TOEFL	550		6/1	25
Sanford-Brown College......................	Pr/AB	1,044			500		None	25
Sanford-Brown College: Hazelwood	Pr/A	929						25
Sanford-Brown College: St. Peters	Pr/AB							25
Southeast Missouri Hospital College of Nursing and Health Sciences	Pr/A	188						40
Southeast Missouri State University...........	Pu/AB	9,184	297	TOEFL	500		6/1	40
Southwest Baptist University	Pr/AB	2,598	27	TOEFL, SAT/ACT	550		4/1	100
State Fair Community College	Pu/A	4,383		TOEFL	450	475	7/1	25
Stephens College...........................	Pr/AB	821	2	TOEFL	550		5/30	25
Stevens Institute of Business & Arts	Pr/AB						None	15
Texas County Technical Institute	Pr/A	117						45
Three Rivers Community College..............	Pu/A	3,028		TOEFL	550		None	

| Student services | | | Housing | | Academic year costs | | Maximum credits/ summer | Credit hour charge | International financial aid | | | |
Adviser	Orien- tation	ESL	Academic year	Summer	Tuition/ fees	Living costs			Avail- able	Number receiving aid	Average award	Deadline
Yes			Yes		17,900	6,310	12		Yes	8	$10,822	None
Yes	Yes	Yes	Yes	Yes	21,220	7,916	15	558	Yes	25	$5,190	4/1
			No		3,300†		6	110				
Yes			No		16,005‡		22	575				
			No						Yes			None
Yes	Yes	Yes	Yes	Yes	16,890	6,200	17	539	Yes			None
Yes			Yes		10,092†	8,080	9	323	Yes			None
Yes	Yes	Yes	Yes	Yes	5,100‡	6,894	9		Yes	10	$9,366	None
Yes		Yes	Yes		30,792	9,372	6	1280	Yes	3	$15,000	4/1
Yes	Yes		Yes	Yes	11,405‡	5,146	9	364	Yes	56	$3,159	None
Yes	Yes		Yes	Yes	14,360	7,000	12	395	Yes			None
Yes			Yes		9,330†	4,980		292	Yes			None
Yes	Yes	Yes	Yes	Yes	22,882	8,892	16	658	Yes	23	$4,321	None
					9,375†							
Yes		Yes	No		5,850†	5,574		195				
Yes		Yes			5,850†	5,574		195				
Yes		Yes	No		5,850†	5,574		195				
					5,850†	5,574		195				
Yes	Yes	Yes	No		5,850†	5,574		195				
Yes	Yes		Yes	Yes	18,700†	7,440	21		Yes			None
			No									
Yes	Yes	Yes	Yes	Yes	9,190†	5,500	8	286	Yes	16	$7,808	None
Yes	Yes	Yes	Yes	Yes	11,856†	9,194	10	372	Yes	90	$9,419	None
Yes			Yes	Yes		6,320	18		Yes			None
Yes	Yes	Yes	Yes	Yes	20,543†	8,290	9	646				
Yes	Yes	Yes	Yes		17,720	6,700	12	350	Yes			None
Yes	Yes		Yes		4,560†	4,000	12	141	Yes			None
					13,505†		16	299	Yes			None
			Yes	Yes	4,650†	5,243	12	135	Yes			
Yes	Yes	ESL	Yes	Yes	12,398†	7,290	18	413	Yes	70	$6,192	None
		Yes	No		4,905†		6	147				
Yes	Yes	Yes	Yes	Yes	9,950	7,325	6	330	Yes			8/1
			No		13,350‡	6,624						
Yes	Yes		Yes	Yes	27,190†	7,890	12	882				
			Yes	Yes	28,510	9,320	18	925	Yes	9	$28,934	None
					5,040†		9	168				
Yes	Yes	Yes	Yes	Yes	33,986	9,432		1170	Yes	149	$9,708	None
			No		10,755†			352				
					9,255†	6,316		349				
			No		9,345†			370				
			No		13,000‡	6,300		300				
Yes	Yes	Yes	Yes	Yes	11,190†	6,510	15	349	Yes	145	$4,649	None
	Yes		Yes	Yes	18,200	6,050	12		Yes	26	$14,955	None
Yes		Yes	Yes	Yes	5,820†	4,350	9	180	Yes			None
Yes			Yes		25,400†	8,070	18	700	Yes			None
	Yes				10,125		18	225				
			No		14,440‡	3,700		345				
			Yes		4,425†	3,324	12	134				

† Tuition and fees are for 2010-11.   ‡ Tuition and fees projected for 2011-12.   * Includes room and board

Institution	Control/degrees	Total	Internat'l	Tests required (Fall 2011)	TOEFL minimum	TOEFL average	Deadline	Fee
Truman State University	Pu/B	5,501	268	TOEFL	550	579	6/1	
University of Central Missouri	Pu/AB	8,596		TOEFL, SAT/ACT	500	527	5/1	50
University of Missouri: Columbia	Pu/B	24,603	467	TOEFL, SAT, SAT Subject Test(s), or ACT	500			60
University of Missouri: Kansas City	Pu/B	8,187	236	TOEFL	500	599	7/1	50
University of Missouri: St. Louis	Pu/B	9,072	289	TOEFL	500	537	5/1	40
University of Phoenix: Kansas City	Pr/B							
University of Phoenix: Springfield	Pr/B							
University of Phoenix: St. Louis	Pr/B							
Vatterott College: Berkeley	Pr/AB							25
Vatterott College: Joplin	Pr/A	400						
Vatterott College: Kansas City	Pr/A							
Vatterott College: O'Fallon	Pr/A							
Vatterott College: Sunset Hills	Pr/AB							
Washington University in St. Louis	Pr/B	6,542	421	TOEFL, SAT/ACT			1/15	55
Webster University	Pr/B	3,249	55	TOEFL, SAT/ACT	550	560	3/1	35
Wentworth Military Junior College	Pr/A						None	100
Westminster College	Pr/B	1,124	133	TOEFL	550	603	5/1	25
William Jewell College	Pr/B	1,060	28	TOEFL	550		7/15	25
William Woods University	Pr/AB	1,107	1	TOEFL, SAT/ACT	525	550	None	25
Montana								
Carroll College	Pr/AB	1,353	9	TOEFL	550		None	35
Dawson Community College	Pu/A	527		TOEFL	500		5/1	30
Flathead Valley Community College	Pu/A	2,138	1	TOEFL	500		None	15
Little Big Horn College	Pr/A							
Montana State University: Billings	Pu/AB	4,644	7	TOEFL	500		None	30
Montana State University: Bozeman	Pu/B	11,468	299	TOEFL	525	565	5/15	30
Montana State University: Northern	Pu/AB	1,076		TOEFL, SAT/ACT	475		8/1	30
Montana Tech of the University of Montana	Pu/AB	2,484	221	TOEFL	525		7/1	30
Rocky Mountain College	Pr/AB	906	38	TOEFL, SAT/ACT	525		None	40
University of Great Falls	Pr/AB	883		TOEFL	500		6/1	35
University of Montana	Pu/AB	15,642		TOEFL	500	525	7/1	30
University of Montana: Western	Pu/AB	1,365	2	TOEFL	500	550	5/1	30
Nebraska								
Bellevue University	Pr/B	6,652	210	TOEFL	500	513	None	75
BryanLGH College of Health Sciences	Pr/AB	466						40
Chadron State College	Pu/B			TOEFL	550		6/1	15
College of Saint Mary	Pr/AB	778		TOEFL	550		None	30
Concordia University	Pr/B	1,150	12	TOEFL, SAT/ACT	500	525	6/15	
Creighton University	Pr/AB	4,206	70	TOEFL	550		5/1	40
Doane College	Pr/B	1,044	9	TOEFL	525		8/15	15
Grace University	Pr/AB	379		TOEFL, SAT/ACT	550		8/1	35
Kaplan University: Lincoln	Pr/AB			TOEFL	560		None	25
Metropolitan Community College	Pu/A	8,225	169	TOEFL	480		6/12	
Mid-Plains Community College Area	Pu/A	1,383		TOEFL	500		2/15	
Nebraska Christian College	Pr/AB	138		TOEFL			6/1	100
Nebraska College of Technical Agriculture	Pu/A	265		TOEFL, ACT	550		None	25
Nebraska Indian Community College	Pu/A	130					None	50
Nebraska Wesleyan University	Pr/B	1,848		TOEFL	525		5/1	30
Northeast Community College	Pu/A	2,906	32	TOEFL	500			
Peru State College	Pu/B			TOEFL	550	570	8/1	10
Union College	Pr/AB	725		TOEFL, ACT	550		None	
University of Nebraska - Kearney	Pu/B	4,881	254	TOEFL	500		5/1	45
University of Nebraska - Lincoln	Pu/AB	19,383	721	TOEFL	523	568	5/1	45
University of Nebraska - Omaha	Pu/B	11,574	307	TOEFL	500		6/1	45
University of Phoenix: Omaha	Pr/B							

| Student services | | | Housing | | Academic year costs | | Maximum credits/summer | Credit hour charge | International financial aid | | | |
Adviser	Orien-tation	ESL	Academic year	Summer	Tuition/fees	Living costs			Avail-able	Number receiving aid	Average award	Deadline
Yes	Yes	Yes	Yes	Yes	12,090 †	7,097	9		Yes	308	$4,343	None
Yes	Yes	Yes	Yes	Yes	12,444 †	6,320		391	Yes			None
Yes	Yes	Yes	Yes	Yes	20,516 †	8,607		646	Yes			None
Yes	Yes	Yes	Yes		20,191 †	9,038	6	632				
Yes	Yes	Yes	Yes	Yes	20,220 †	8,620	9	632	Yes	130	$6,880	None
					11,100 †							
					10,200 †							
					11,100 †							
Yes	Yes	Yes	Yes	Yes	41,992	13,119	14		Yes			2/15
Yes	Yes	Yes	Yes	Yes	21,688 †	9,290	9	570	Yes			None
Yes	Yes	Yes	Yes	Yes	19,000 †	6,800			Yes			4/30
Yes	Yes	Yes	Yes	Yes	20,570	8,925	3	750	Yes			None
Yes	Yes		Yes	Yes	29,600	9,260	8	850	Yes	25	$19,492	None
			Yes		19,050	9,050	18		Yes			None
Yes	Yes	Yes	Yes	Yes	25,198	7,750	13	1027	Yes			None
Yes			Yes		8,619 ‡	3,300	12	244				
Yes		Yes			10,724 †		12					
			No		3,180			75				
Yes	Yes	Yes	Yes	Yes	15,235 †	5,620	18		Yes			None
Yes	Yes	Yes	Yes	Yes	18,204 †	7,900		703		50	$4,449	
Yes			Yes	Yes	15,122 †	6,461	18	380	Yes	3	$1,146	None
Yes	Yes		Yes	Yes	16,497 †	6,924	12		Yes			None
Yes	Yes	Yes	Yes	Yes	22,134	7,546	12	904	Yes	37	$17,199	None
Yes	Yes		Yes	Yes	19,580	6,712	12	586	Yes	14	$18,283	None
Yes	Yes	Yes	Yes	Yes	19,172 †	6,860	18		Yes			None
Yes			Yes	Yes	13,064 †	6,195	12	435	Yes	4	$4,716	None
Yes	Yes	Yes	No		7,650 †		15	250	Yes			None
			No		12,915 ‡	1,800		430	Yes			5/1
Yes			Yes		8,855 †	4,900	18	258	Yes			None
			Yes	Yes	24,830	6,700	11	785	Yes	17	$27,295	None
Yes	Yes		Yes	Yes	23,060	6,410	12	715	Yes			None
Yes	Yes	Yes	Yes	Yes	31,894	9,238	15	952	Yes	38	$15,111	None
Yes	Yes	Yes	Yes	Yes	23,590	6,650	12	770	Yes	7	$16,557	None
			Yes	Yes	16,616 ‡	5,712	6		Yes			4/1
			No		15,352 †			405	Yes			None
Yes	Yes		Yes	Yes	3,443 †	3,555		72				
Yes	Yes		Yes		3,150 †	5,960	9	90	Yes			None
Yes	Yes		Yes	Yes	11,200 †	5,800		335	Yes			None
Yes	Yes	Yes	Yes	Yes	7,092 †	4,309	6	213				
			No			6,400			Yes			None
Yes	Yes		Yes	Yes	24,656	6,672	12	913	Yes	1	$11,000	None
Yes		Yes	Yes	Yes	3,053 †	5,812		88				
Yes			Yes	Yes	4,966 †	5,568	6		Yes			None
Yes	Yes	Yes	Yes	Yes	18,150 †	5,900		735	Yes			4/1
Yes	Yes	Yes	Yes	Yes	11,006 †	7,706	15	329	Yes			None
Yes	Yes	Yes	Yes	Yes	18,924 †	8,098	15	588	Yes			None
Yes	Yes	Yes	Yes	Yes	17,186 †	7,750	12	533	Yes	34	$11,180	None
					9,440 †							

† Tuition and fees are for 2010-11. ‡ Tuition and fees projected for 2011-12. * Includes room and board

Institution	Control/ degrees	Undergraduates		Tests required (Fall 2011)	TOEFL		Application	
		Total	Internat'l		minimum	average	Deadline	Fee
Wayne State College	Pu/B	2,928	15	TOEFL	550			30
Western Nebraska Community College	Pu/A	1,837	54	TOEFL	500		8/1	
York College	Pr/AB	479		TOEFL, SAT/ACT	500		7/1	100
Nevada								
Art Institute of Las Vegas	Pr/AB	1,346		TOEFL	500		None	150
Career College of Northern Nevada.	Pr/A	500		TOEFL	500		None	25
Carrington College: Reno	Pr/A							
College of Southern Nevada	Pu/AB	44,088		TOEFL	450		None	50
Everest College: Las Vegas	Pr/A	1,050		TOEFL			None	
Great Basin College.	Pu/AB	2,434	8	TOEFL	500		None	10
International Academy of Design and Technology: Henderson.	Pr/AB	699		TOEFL	550			50
Morrison University.	Pr/AB	252		TOEFL	500		None	125
Sierra Nevada College	Pr/B	458	5	TOEFL	500		None	
Truckee Meadows Community College	Pu/A			TOEFL	500	520	None	10
University of Nevada: Las Vegas	Pu/B	21,867	810	TOEFL	500		7/1	95
University of Nevada: Reno.	Pu/AB	13,660	206	TOEFL	500	558	3/1	95
University of Phoenix: Las Vegas	Pr/B							
University of Phoenix: Northern Nevada	Pr/B							
University of Southern Nevada.	Pr/B	200	6	TOEFL	550		6/15	100
Western Nevada College.	Pu/AB	4,132		TOEFL	500		3/12	15
New Hampshire								
Chester College of New England	Pr/B			TOEFL	550		7/31	35
Colby-Sawyer College	Pr/AB	1,155	66	TOEFL	500		7/1	45
Daniel Webster College	Pr/AB	790		TOEFL	520	525	7/8	35
Dartmouth College.	Pr/B	4,135	302	TOEFL, SAT/ACT, SAT Subject Test(s)			1/1	70
Franklin Pierce University.	Pr/AB	1,769	45	TOEFL	500		None	40
Granite State College	Pu/AB	1,393		TOEFL	550		None	45
Hesser College	Pr/AB			TOEFL	450	475	None	10
Lakes Region Community College	Pu/A			TOEFL	500		6/1	10
Lebanon College.	Pr/A	135	10					40
Magdalen College	Pr/AB						5/1	35
Manchester Community College	Pu/A			TOEFL	500		None	10
Nashua Community College.	Pu/A	2,235		TOEFL	500		None	20
New England College.	Pr/AB	972	60				None	30
NHTI-Concord's Community College	Pu/A			TOEFL	500	550	None	10
Plymouth State University.	Pu/B	4,346		TOEFL	520	560	4/1	45
River Valley Community College	Pu/A			TOEFL	500		8/1	20
Rivier College.	Pr/AB	1,394		TOEFL	500		7/1	25
Saint Anselm College.	Pr/B	1,866	7	TOEFL, SAT/ACT	550	600	2/15	55
Southern New Hampshire University.	Pr/AB			TOEFL	530		None	50
Thomas More College of Liberal Arts	Pr/B			TOEFL			8/20	
University of New Hampshire	Pu/AB	12,183	71	TOEFL, SAT/ACT	550		2/1	65
University of New Hampshire at Manchester.	Pu/AB	883	1	TOEFL	550		4/1	60
White Mountains Community College	Pu/A	843		TOEFL			None	20
New Jersey								
Atlantic Cape Community College	Pu/A	7,168			480		5/1	100
Berkeley College.	Pr/AB	3,712	48	TOEFL	500		None	50
Bloomfield College	Pr/B	2,159	47	TOEFL	550		4/30	40
Brookdale Community College.	Pu/A	14,243	106	TOEFL	430		7/1	25
Burlington County College	Pu/A	9,693		TOEFL	450		None	100
Caldwell College.	Pr/B	1,657		TOEFL	550		None	40
Centenary College	Pr/AB	1,993	26	TOEFL	550		7/1	50
The College of New Jersey	Pu/B	6,410	27	TOEFL, SAT/ACT	550	600	1/15	75
College of St. Elizabeth	Pr/B	1,188	65	TOEFL	500	527	8/15	35

	Student services		Housing		Academic year costs		Maximum credits/ summer	Credit hour charge	Avail-able	International financial aid		
Adviser	Orien-tation	ESL	Academic year	Summer	Tuition/fees	Living costs				Number receiving aid	Average award	Deadline
Yes			Yes	Yes	8,933 †	5,540		258	Yes			None
Yes		Yes	Yes		2,970 †	6,150	12	84	Yes	20	$5,307	None
Yes			Yes		14,998 †	8,280	9	400	Yes			None
Yes			Yes	Yes	21,565 †		16	467	Yes			None
			No					205	Yes			5/30
Yes	Yes	Yes	No		8,590 †		12					
			No		17,640 †	7,056		387				
Yes		Yes	Yes		8,590 †	2,299	6		Yes			None
					18,425 †			405				
Yes					9,950 †	17,840	16	220				
Yes		Yes	Yes		25,370	11,530	15		Yes			None
Yes	Yes		No		6,512 †		9	139				
Yes	Yes	Yes	Yes	Yes	18,755 †	10,756	18		Yes	88	$17,373	None
Yes	Yes	Yes	Yes	Yes	18,851 †	12,159	15		Yes			None
					10,500 †							
					10,500 †							
			No		31,568	17,820		543				
Yes			No		8,590 †		12		Yes			None
Yes			Yes		18,525 †	8,360	12		Yes			None
Yes	Yes	Yes	Yes		32,640 †	11,200		1080	Yes			3/1
Yes			Yes	Yes	14,225 †	9,990	12		Yes			None
Yes	Yes		Yes	Yes	42,996	12,369	4		Yes	259	$45,199	2/1
Yes	Yes	Yes	Yes	Yes	28,800 †	12,800	16	923	Yes	25	$9,600	3/1
Yes			No		8,445 †	6,579		275				
Yes	Yes		Yes	Yes	15,040 †	9,094	15	585				
			No		13,500 †	8,100		445				
		Yes	No		6,615 †			175	Yes	1	$300	None
			Yes		16,000 †	7,000			Yes			6/30
Yes		Yes	No		13,530 †	13,160		445				
			No		13,830 †	10,644		445				
Yes	Yes	Yes	Yes		30,400	11,954	18	1440	Yes	52	$13,954	None
Yes		Yes	Yes	Yes	13,950 †	8,002		445				
Yes	Yes	Yes	Yes	Yes	18,076 †	8,840	9	660	Yes			None
			No		13,500 †	6,000	18	445				
Yes			Yes		25,020 †	10,222	12	814	Yes			None
Yes	Yes		Yes	Yes	31,575 †	11,630	9		Yes			3/15
Yes	Yes	Yes	Yes	Yes	26,442 †	10,926	12		Yes			None
			Yes		16,100 †	9,100			Yes			None
Yes	Yes	Yes	Yes	Yes	27,642 †	10,452	12	1029	Yes			3/1
		Yes	No		25,276 †		8	1029	Yes			3/1
			No		13,890 †			445				
Yes		Yes	No		12,003 †			379	Yes			None
Yes	Yes		Yes	Yes	20,700 †	10,812	18	465	Yes			None
Yes	Yes	Yes	Yes	Yes	23,700	10,600	16		Yes	41	$17,556	6/1
			No		8,713 †	9,287		262				
Yes		Yes	No		6,045 †	9,900		173	Yes			None
Yes	Yes	Yes	Yes	Yes	26,890	10,500	12	712	Yes			None
Yes	Yes	Yes	Yes	Yes	28,054 †	9,434	18	520	Yes			6/1
Yes	Yes		Yes		22,679 †	10,358	12	663				
Yes	Yes	Yes	Yes	Yes	26,885 †	13,340	9		Yes			10/1

† Tuition and fees are for 2010-11. ‡ Tuition and fees projected for 2011-12. * Includes room and board

Institution	Control/ degrees	Undergraduates		Tests required (Fall 2011)	TOEFL		Application	
		Total	Internat'l		minimum	average	Deadline	Fee
County College of Morris	Pu/A	7,540		TOEFL	400		7/1	30
Cumberland County College	Pu/A	4,014		TOEFL			None	25
DeVry University: North Brunswick	Pr/AB	1,738		TOEFL	500		None	50
Drew University	Pr/B	1,715	34	TOEFL	550		2/15	50
Eastern International College	Pr/A							
Essex County College.	Pu/A	13,314					7/10	25
Fairleigh Dickinson University: College at Florham	Pr/B	2,397	21	TOEFL	550		7/1	40
Fairleigh Dickinson University: Metropolitan Campus	Pr/AB	3,962	264	TOEFL	550		7/1	40
Felician College	Pr/AB	1,778	10	TOEFL	500	550	None	30
Georgian Court University.	Pr/B	1,666	7	TOEFL	550		3/1	40
Gloucester County College	Pu/A	6,609		TOEFL	500		9/1	20
Hudson County Community College	Pu/A							15
Kean University	Pu/B	12,671	194				5/31	150
Mercer County Community College.	Pu/A	8,805	364	TOEFL	400	500	None	50
Middlesex County College.	Pu/A	11,528					6/15	25
Monmouth University.	Pr/AB	4,603	24	TOEFL	550		6/1	50
Montclair State University.	Pu/B	14,040	266	TOEFL, SAT/ACT	550		3/1	60
New Jersey City University	Pu/B	6,552	56	TOEFL, SAT	500	520	4/1	35
New Jersey Institute of Technology.	Pu/B	5,737	1,063	TOEFL, SAT/ACT	550	589	4/1	70
Ocean County College	Pu/A	10,367		TOEFL	500		7/15	
Passaic County Community College	Pu/A	9,004					None	
Princeton University.	Pr/B	5,142	542				1/1	65
Rabbinical College of America.	Pr/B							150
Ramapo College of New Jersey	Pu/B	5,536	53	TOEFL	550		3/1	75
Raritan Valley Community College	Pu/A	7,218	175	TOEFL	500		6/1	225
Richard Stockton College of New Jersey	Pu/B	6,964	13	TOEFL	550		3/15	50
Rider University	Pr/AB	4,592	172	TOEFL, SAT/ACT	550		3/15	50
Rowan University	Pu/B	9,599	94	TOEFL	500	525	3/1	65
Rutgers, The State University of New Jersey: Camden Regional Campus.	Pu/B	4,453	22	TOEFL, SAT/ACT	550		4/15	65
Rutgers, The State University of New Jersey: New Brunswick/Piscataway Campus	Pu/B	30,038	581	TOEFL, SAT/ACT	550		4/15	65
Rutgers, The State University of New Jersey: Newark Regional Campus	Pu/B	6,829	137	TOEFL, SAT/ACT	550		4/15	65
Saint Peter's College	Pr/AB	2,313	78	TOEFL	550		4/1	40
Salem Community College	Pu/A	1,499		TOEFL	520		7/1	27
Seton Hall University.	Pr/B	5,051	95	TOEFL	550		None	55
Stevens Institute of Technology	Pr/B	2,369		TOEFL, SAT/ACT	550	587	7/1	55
Sussex County Community College.	Pu/A	4,122					None	15
Thomas Edison State College.	Pu/AB	17,722	249	TOEFL	500		None	75
Union County College	Pu/A	11,729	272				7/1	35
University of Medicine and Dentistry of New Jersey: School of Nursing	Pu/B	490		TOEFL			3/10	50
University of Medicine and Dentistry of New Jersey: School of Health Related Professions	Pu/AB	560		TOEFL	550		3/12	75
University of Phoenix: Jersey City	Pr/B	585						
William Paterson University of New Jersey.	Pu/B	9,759	71	TOEFL, SAT/ACT	550		5/1	50
New Mexico								
Brookline College: Albuquerque	Pr/A	490						
Dona Ana Community College of New Mexico State University	Pu/A			TOEFL	500		None	15
Eastern New Mexico University	Pu/AB	3,618	92	TOEFL, SAT/ACT	500	525	6/15	
Eastern New Mexico University: Roswell.	Pu/A	2,640	37	TOEFL	500		None	
Institute of American Indian Arts	Pu/AB	300		TOEFL	500		4/1	5
Luna Community College	Pu/A	1,791						
Mesalands Community College.	Pu/A			TOEFL	540			
Navajo Technical College	Pu/AB	911						

Student services			Housing		Academic year costs		Maximum credits/summer	Credit hour charge	International financial aid			
Adviser	Orien-tation	ESL	Academic year	Summer	Tuition/fees	Living costs			Avail-able	Number receiving aid	Average award	Deadline
Yes		Yes	No		10,458	2,350	11	326	Yes			None
		Yes	No		12,750†		12	396				
Yes			No		14,826†	11,878						
Yes	Yes	Yes	Yes	Yes	39,875†	10,772	20	1615	Yes	20	$23,662	2/15
Yes	Yes	Yes	No		7,305†							
Yes	Yes	Yes	Yes	Yes	33,410†	11,578	9	866	Yes			None
Yes	Yes	Yes	Yes	Yes	31,060†	12,018	9	866				
Yes	Yes	Yes	Yes	Yes	27,925	10,750	9	865	Yes	24	$18,829	None
Yes		Yes	Yes	Yes	27,984	10,250	9	611	Yes	7	$31,209	None
Yes			No		6,390†	5,771	16	190	Yes			None
	Yes	Yes	No		10,296†	9,000	6	304				
Yes	Yes	Yes	Yes	Yes	15,404†	12,950	12	400	Yes	21	$4,546	
Yes	Yes	Yes	No		7,635†	7,340	18	230	Yes			5/1
Yes	Yes	Yes	No		6,945†	5,935	12	198				
Yes	Yes		Yes	Yes	28,000	11,239	12	793	Yes			None
Yes	Yes	Yes	Yes	Yes	18,445†	10,912	8	522	Yes			None
Yes	Yes	Yes	Yes	Yes	16,917†	9,364	12	479				
Yes	Yes	Yes	Yes		23,922†	10,562		932	Yes			5/15
Yes		Yes	No		7,070‡		18	206	Yes			None
Yes		Yes	No		6,630†	10,800	12	194				
Yes	Yes		Yes	Yes	36,640†	11,940			Yes	405	$40,680	None
			Yes		10,200	6,800						
Yes	Yes		Yes	Yes	19,679†	11,730	12	488	Yes	57	$22,156	None
Yes	Yes	Yes	No		4,650†	8,100	12	126	Yes			None
Yes			Yes	Yes	17,304†	10,380	24	474	Yes	1	$11,000	None
Yes	Yes		Yes	Yes	31,930	11,810		930	Yes	25	$13,390	None
		Yes	Yes		19,034†	10,348	12	607				
Yes			Yes		23,423†	10,362	12	380	Yes			None
Yes	Yes	Yes	Yes	Yes	24,044†	11,216	12	693	Yes			None
Yes	Yes	Yes	Yes		23,531†	11,653	12	693	Yes			None
Yes	Yes		Yes	Yes	28,332†	13,010	12	873	Yes			None
Yes			No		4,434†	5,400	12	115				
Yes	Yes	Yes	Yes	Yes	33,490	12,412		958	Yes			None
Yes	Yes		Yes	Yes	40,465†	12,500	18	1280	Yes			None
		Yes	No		7,140†			214				
Yes			No		7,190†							
Yes	Yes	Yes	No		7,020†			200				
Yes			Yes		18,428†		15	510				
Yes			Yes				12					
					10,500†							
Yes	Yes	Yes	Yes	Yes	18,262†	9,760	12	449	Yes			
			No		13,750†	9,000						
Yes	Yes	Yes	Yes	Yes	4,056†	6,526	14	169				
	Yes		Yes	Yes	9,432†	5,612	9	342	Yes	7	$1,723	None
Yes			Yes		4,212†	7,951	12	170				
Yes			Yes		3,450†	5,516			Yes			None
					1,942†							
			No		2,775†			81				
			Yes									

† Tuition and fees are for 2010-11. ‡ Tuition and fees projected for 2011-12. * Includes room and board

Institution	Control/ degrees	Undergraduates		Tests required (Fall 2011)	TOEFL		Application	
		Total	Internat'l		minimum	average	Deadline	Fee
New Mexico Highlands University	Pu/AB	2,099		TOEFL	500	540	4/1	15
New Mexico Institute of Mining and Technology.	Pu/AB	1,262	11	TOEFL	540	556	6/1	50
New Mexico Junior College.	Pu/A			TOEFL	500	550	5/1	
New Mexico Military Institute	Pu/A			TOEFL, SAT/ACT	500		7/30	85
New Mexico State University.	Pu/AB	14,628	366	TOEFL	500		3/1	50
New Mexico State University at Alamogordo	Pu/A	3,946	53	TOEFL	500		None	50
New Mexico State University at Carlsbad.	Pu/A	1,484		TOEFL	500		None	20
New Mexico State University at Grants	Pu/A	1,478		TOEFL	450		None	15
Northern New Mexico College.	Pu/AB			TOEFL			5/1	
St. John's College	Pr/B	409	36	TOEFL, SAT/ACT	550		None	
San Juan College.	Pu/A	6,139	15	TOEFL	550	580	5/29	10
Santa Fe Community College.	Pu/A	3,497	24	TOEFL	517		7/1	
University of New Mexico	Pu/AB			TOEFL, SAT/ACT	520		5/1	50
University of Phoenix: New Mexico	Pr/B							
University of the Southwest.	Pr/B	309		TOEFL, SAT/ACT	550		None	25
New York								
Adelphi University.	Pr/AB	4,917	123	TOEFL	550		None	50
Adirondack Community College.	Pu/A	3,447	5	TOEFL	500			50
Albany College of Pharmacy and Health Sciences.	Pr/B	1,128	90	TOEFL, SAT/ACT	600		None	75
Alfred University.	Pr/B	1,868		TOEFL, SAT/ACT	550		3/15	50
American Academy of Dramatic Arts	Pr/A	211	59	TOEFL, SAT/ACT	500		8/1	50
Art Institute of New York City.	Pr/A	1,531			500			50
ASA Institute of Business and Computer Technology.	Pr/A	5,797	320				9/1	25
Bard College	Pr/B	1,928	237	TOEFL	600	620	1/15	50
Barnard College	Pr/B	2,456	123	TOEFL, SAT, SAT Subject Test(s), or ACT	600	620	1/1	55
Beis Medrash Heichal Dovid	Pr/B	116						100
Berkeley College.	Pr/AB	758	38	TOEFL	500		None	50
Berkeley College of New York City	Pr/AB	4,377	588	TOEFL	500		None	50
Beth Hamedrash Shaarei Yosher Institute	Pr/B	33						
Beth Hatalmud Rabbinical College	Pr/B	70						
Bramson ORT College	Pr/A	841					9/12	50
Briarcliffe College.	Pr/AB	1,922		TOEFL	500		None	35
Broome Community College	Pu/A	6,735		TOEFL	527		None	
Bryant & Stratton College: Albany	Pr/A	844		TOEFL	500			
Bryant & Stratton College: Buffalo	Pr/AB	956					None	35
Bryant & Stratton College: Rochester	Pr/A	935					None	25
Bryant & Stratton College: Syracuse North	Pr/A	624					9/20	
Business Informatics Center.	Pr/A	151					None	50
Canisius College	Pr/AB	3,078	134	TOEFL	500		7/15	40
Cayuga Community College	Pu/A	4,005		TOEFL	500		None	
Cazenovia College.	Pr/AB	1,067		TOEFL	550		None	30
Central Yeshiva Tomchei Tmimim-Lubavitch	Pr/B	606						
City University of New York: Baruch College.	Pu/B	12,802	1,544	TOEFL	620	650	2/1	65
City University of New York: Borough of Manhattan Community College.	Pu/A	22,026	1,617	TOEFL	450	550		65
City University of New York: Bronx Community College	Pu/A	10,347		TOEFL	500		8/15	60
City University of New York: Brooklyn College	Pu/B	11,740	580	TOEFL	500		None	65
City University of New York: City College.	Pu/B	11,786	1,120	TOEFL	500	558	3/15	65
City University of New York: College of Staten Island.	Pu/AB	12,454	350	TOEFL	450		2/1	65
City University of New York: CUNY Online	Pu/B	860			580		6/1	70
City University of New York: Hostos Community College	Pu/A	5,720	393				7/15	65

Student services			Housing		Academic year costs		Maximum credits/ summer	Credit hour charge	International financial aid			
Adviser	Orien- tation	ESL	Academic year	Summer	Tuition/ fees	Living costs			Avail- able	Number receiving aid	Average award	Deadline
Yes	Yes		Yes	Yes	6,192 †	5,968	9		Yes			5/1
Yes	Yes		Yes	Yes	14,620 †	7,574	6	582	Yes			None
Yes			Yes	Yes	1,794 †	5,050	14	56	Yes			None
Yes			Yes		9,082 †	3,830	2		Yes			None
Yes	Yes	Yes	Yes	Yes	16,680 †	6,526	12	695				
Yes	Yes	Yes	No		4,488 †		10	181				
Yes			No		2,812 †	8,038	14	113				
		Yes	No		3,072 †	7,526	9	127				
Yes			Yes		2,855 †	6,432	9	102				
Yes			Yes	Yes	43,656	10,334			Yes	20	$44,939	None
Yes			No		8,730 †		12	91				
Yes		Yes	No		2,694 ‡		7	85	Yes			None
Yes	Yes	Yes	Yes	Yes	18,691 †	7,948	9	779	Yes			None
Yes			Yes		10,120 † 13,633 ‡	10,590	12	486	Yes			6/1
Yes	Yes	Yes	Yes	Yes	28,460	11,420	24	835	Yes	88	$14,348	None
			No		7,044 †		12	284				
Yes			Yes		26,930	9,560		855	Yes	14	$9,587	5/1
Yes	Yes	Yes	Yes		25,976 †	12,864	16	814	Yes			3/15
Yes	Yes		No		30,500				Yes			None
Yes	Yes		No		24,705 †	17,501		546				
Yes		Yes	Yes		12,099 †	12,580	18	495	Yes			None
Yes		Yes	Yes	Yes	41,670 †	11,810		1277	Yes	223	$39,375	2/15
Yes			Yes	Yes	40,546 †	12,950		1295	Yes	10	$35,669	2/1
					8,450 †	4,500						
Yes	Yes		Yes	Yes	21,750	8,400	18		Yes			None
Yes	Yes	Yes			21,750 ‡	12,500	18		Yes			None
			Yes		6,200 †							
		Yes	No		10,560 †		12					
			Yes		18,592			683				
Yes	Yes	Yes	No		7,264 †	3,929		290				
Yes			No		15,570 ‡		18					
			No		15,120 †		21					
			No		15,120 †	4,865						
					15,570 ‡		18		Yes			None
			No		12,500 †		15					
Yes	Yes		Yes	Yes	30,657	11,360	9	845	Yes	134	$22,025	
Yes			No		7,496 †		15	280				
			Yes		25,482 †	10,824	12		Yes	3	$10,000	None
					5,700 †	2,300						
Yes	Yes		Yes		13,730 ‡		12	445	Yes			4/30
Yes	Yes	Yes	No		6,618 †		6	210				
Yes			No		6,654 †	10,201		210				
Yes	Yes	Yes	No		13,504 ‡		6	435	Yes			None
Yes	Yes	Yes	Yes		12,779 †	11,660	6	415				
Yes	Yes	Yes	No		12,828 †		8	415	Yes			None
					4,980 †		12					
Yes	Yes	Yes	No		6,655 †		6	210				

† Tuition and fees are for 2010-11.   ‡ Tuition and fees projected for 2011-12.   * Includes room and board

Institution	Control/ degrees	Undergraduates		Tests required (Fall 2011)	TOEFL		Application	
		Total	Internat'l		minimum	average	Deadline	Fee
City University of New York: Hunter College	.Pu/B	14,609	1,219	TOEFL	500		11/15	65
City University of New York: John Jay College of Criminal Justice	.Pu/AB	12,821	352	TOEFL	500		1/16	65
City University of New York: Kingsborough Community College	.Pu/A	15,058		TOEFL	475		9/1	65
City University of New York: LaGuardia Community College	.Pu/A	15,507	1,258	TOEFL	450		3/15	65
City University of New York: Lehman College	.Pu/B	8,810	306	TOEFL	500			65
City University of New York: Medgar Evers College	.Pu/AB	6,514		TOEFL	475	480	None	65
City University of New York: Queens College	.Pu/B	15,337	780	TOEFL	500		10/15	80
City University of New York: Queensborough Community College	.Pu/A	15,316		TOEFL	475		None	65
City University of New York: York College	.Pu/B	7,022		TOEFL	500		2/1	65
Clarkson University	.Pr/B	2,800	93	TOEFL, SAT/ACT	550		1/15	50
Clinton Community College	.Pu/A	2,352		TOEFL	425		7/1	
Colgate University	.Pr/B	2,868	174	TOEFL, SAT/ACT			1/15	60
College of Mount St. Vincent	.Pr/AB	1,463		TOEFL, SAT/ACT	550	600	7/1	35
College of New Rochelle	.Pr/B	881		TOEFL	550	605	None	20
College of Saint Rose	.Pr/B	2,990	39	TOEFL	500		5/1	40
Columbia University	.Pr/B	5,888	664	TOEFL, SAT/ACT, SAT Subject Test(s)	600		1/1	80
Columbia University: School of General Studies	.Pr/B	1,464	222	TOEFL	600		4/1	75
Columbia-Greene Community College	.Pu/A	2,031		TOEFL	575		None	40
Concordia College	.Pr/AB	721	79	TOEFL	550	553	7/1	100
Cooper Union for the Advancement of Science and Art	.Pr/B	891	139	TOEFL, SAT/ACT	600	650	1/1	65
Cornell University	.Pr/B	13,885	1,208	TOEFL, SAT/ACT	600			70
Corning Community College	.Pu/A	3,636	9	TOEFL	550		5/1	25
Culinary Institute of America	.Pr/AB	2,673		TOEFL		534	None	50
Daemen College	.Pr/B	1,797	19		500		None	25
Davis College	.Pr/AB	340		TOEFL, SAT/ACT	525		None	45
DeVry College of New York	.Pr/AB			TOEFL	500		None	50
Dominican College of Blauvelt	.Pr/AB	1,648		TOEFL	550		None	35
Dowling College	.Pr/B	2,554	90		550		None	35
Dutchess Community College	.Pu/A	10,319		TOEFL	500	520	6/15	
D'Youville College	.Pr/B	1,902	140	TOEFL	500	515	5/1	25
Eastman School of Music of the University of Rochester	.Pr/B	521		TOEFL			12/1	100
Elmira College	.Pr/AB	1,445	32	TOEFL	500	550	None	50
Erie Community College	.Pu/A	15,176		TOEFL	460	470	5/31	25
Eugene Lang College The New School for Liberal Arts	.Pr/B	1,511	75	TOEFL	600		1/5	50
Excelsior College	.Pr/AB	28,536		TOEFL	525		None	75
Fashion Institute of Technology	.Pu/AB	8,077	1,014	TOEFL	550		1/1	50
Five Towns College	.Pr/AB	1,183		TOEFL	520		None	35
Fordham University	.Pr/B	8,106	268	TOEFL	550	575	2/1	50
Fulton-Montgomery Community College	.Pu/A	2,255	114	TOEFL	500		8/1	
Genesee Community College	.Pu/A	4,481	103	TOEFL	460	500		
Globe Institute of Technology	.Pr/AB						None	250
Hamilton College	.Pr/B	1,843	85	TOEFL	600	631	1/1	60
Hartwick College	.Pr/B	1,516	45	TOEFL	550		2/15	35
Herkimer County Community College	.Pu/A	3,067		TOEFL	500	525	None	
Hilbert College	.Pr/AB	1,057		TOEFL	500		6/1	20
Hobart and William Smith Colleges	.Pr/B	2,138	83	TOEFL	550	600	2/1	45
Hofstra University	.Pr/B	7,262	133	TOEFL	550		6/1	75
Houghton College	.Pr/AB	1,223	57	TOEFL	550		3/1	40
Hudson Valley Community College	.Pu/A	13,798		TOEFL	450		None	30
Institute of Design and Construction	.Pr/A	145	2				None	30

Student services			Housing		Academic year costs		Maximum credits/ summer	Credit hour charge	International financial aid			
Adviser	Orientation	ESL	Academic year	Summer	Tuition/ fees	Living costs			Available	Number receiving aid	Average award	Deadline
Yes		Yes	Yes		12,849†	3,930	7	415	Yes			None
Yes	Yes	Yes	No		12,779†		6	415	Yes			None
Yes		Yes	No		6,650†		8	210				
Yes	Yes	Yes	No		6,642†	10,382	6	210	Yes			
Yes	Yes	Yes	No		12,828†		8	415	Yes			None
Yes		Yes	No		13,352‡	7,425	9	435				
Yes	Yes	Yes	Yes		12,927†	8,920	11	415				
Yes	Yes	Yes	No		6,640†			210				
Yes	Yes	Yes	No		12,816†	10,200	12	415	Yes	6	$250	None
Yes	Yes	Yes	Yes	Yes	36,780	12,050	12	1198	Yes	62	$12,827	3/1
Yes		Yes	Yes	Yes	8,928†		12	350				
Yes	Yes		Yes	Yes	42,920	10,650			Yes	110	$45,051	1/15
	Yes		Yes		26,910†	10,380	9	760	Yes			None
Yes		Yes	Yes	Yes	28,010†	10,176	6	861	Yes			None
Yes	Yes		Yes	Yes	25,464	10,534	12	819	Yes	4	$22,516	None
Yes	Yes	Yes	Yes	Yes	43,304†	10,570			Yes	202	$44,654	3/1
Yes	Yes		Yes		41,822†	12,960	15	1330	Yes	167	$10,086	
Yes			No		7,232†	7,000	15	288				
Yes	Yes	Yes	Yes	Yes	25,570†	11,480			Yes			None
Yes	Yes		Yes		39,150‡	15,550	6		Yes	139	$35,000	6/1
Yes	Yes	Yes	Yes	Yes	41,541	13,154			Yes	213	$37,622	1/2
			No		7,630†		12	306				
Yes			Yes		26,180‡	8,240			Yes	81	$3,256	None
Yes	Yes	Yes	Yes		21,420†	10,350	9	695				
			Yes	Yes	13,910‡	6,300		420				
Yes					14,826†							
			Yes		22,940	10,980		670	Yes	25	$11,976	None
Yes	Yes	Yes	Yes	Yes	24,890†	10,770	15	767	Yes	50	$17,732	None
Yes			No		6,220†		12		Yes			None
Yes	Yes		Yes	Yes	21,760	10,800		660	Yes			None
Yes	Yes	Yes	Yes	Yes	40,542†	12,900	6	1150	Yes			2/28
Yes	Yes	Yes	Yes	Yes	35,900†	14,650	9		Yes			None
Yes	Yes	Yes	No		6,990†	5,800		276				
Yes	Yes	Yes	Yes	Yes	37,810	15,260		1255	Yes	47	$13,767	None
Yes			No						Yes			None
Yes		Yes	Yes	Yes	11,592†	11,700		464				
Yes			Yes		18,750†	12,760	12	765				2/1
Yes	Yes	Yes	Yes	Yes	38,602†	14,491	12	757	Yes			
Yes	Yes	Yes	No		6,932†	6,240	12	266				
Yes	Yes	Yes	Yes	Yes	4,320†		12	160				
Yes	Yes	Yes	Yes	Yes	12,738†		19	456				None
Yes	Yes	Yes	Yes	Yes	42,640	10,830			Yes	70	$44,889	2/8
Yes	Yes		Yes		36,440	9,625		1115	Yes			None
Yes	Yes	Yes	Yes		6,140†	7,300	15	233				
			Yes		18,580†	7,690	12	430	Yes			None
Yes	Yes	Yes	Yes	Yes	42,915	10,852			Yes	58	$24,053	2/15
Yes	Yes	Yes	Yes	Yes	31,800†	11,710	15	940	Yes	79	$18,981	None
Yes	Yes		Yes		26,094	7,550		1092	Yes	57	$16,361	None
Yes			No		10,778†	6,300	12	426				
Yes			No		9,130	6,000		300				

† Tuition and fees are for 2010-11.   ‡ Tuition and fees projected for 2011-12.   * Includes room and board

Institution	Control/ degrees	Undergraduates		Tests required (Fall 2011)	TOEFL		Application	
		Total	Internat'l		minimum	average	Deadline	Fee
Iona College............................	Pr/B	3,228	38	TOEFL, SAT/ACT	550	561	2/15	50
Island Drafting and Technical Institute., ...	Pr/A	133		TOEFL				25
Ithaca College...........................	Pr/B	6,382	106	TOEFL, SAT/ACT	550		2/1	60
Jamestown Community College	Pu/A	3,911	9	TOEFL	500		6/1	
Jewish Theological Seminary of America	Pr/B	176	3	TOEFL, SAT/ACT			2/15	65
Juilliard School..........................	Pr/B	510	110	TOEFL			12/1	100
Kehilath Yakov Rabbinical Seminary...........	Pr/B	108						
Keuka College	Pr/B	1,627	30		500		None	50
The King's College	Pr/B	381	8	TOEFL, SAT/ACT	580		3/1	30
Le Moyne College.........................	Pr/B	2,569	14	TOEFL	550		2/1	35
LIM College.............................	Pr/AB			TOEFL	550		None	40
Long Island Business Institute	Pr/A	571	13				None	55
Long Island University: Brooklyn Campus	Pr/AB	4,987	58	TOEFL	550			30
Long Island University: C. W. Post Campus	Pr/AB	4,518	344	TOEFL	527	567	6/1	30
Machzikei Hadath Rabbinical College	Pr/B	117						150
Manhattan College........................	Pr/B	3,002	60	TOEFL	550		5/1	60
Manhattan School of Music	Pr/B	402	129	TOEFL	550		12/1	100
Manhattanville College.....................	Pr/B	1,692	206	TOEFL, SAT/ACT	550	595	None	75
Mannes College The New School for Music	Pr/B	190	75	TOEFL				100
Marist College	Pr/B	4,811	18	TOEFL	550	580	2/15	50
Marymount Manhattan College................	Pr/AB	2,039	58	TOEFL	550	600	None	60
Medaille College	Pr/AB	1,820	23	TOEFL, SAT/ACT	550	553	None	25
Medaille College: Amherst	Pr/AB	241						25
Medaille College: Rochester.................	Pr/AB	100						25
Mercy College	Pr/AB	6,380		TOEFL	550		8/1	40
Mesivta Torah Vodaath Seminary	Pr/B	131						200
Metropolitan College of New York	Pr/AB	807		TOEFL	550		7/1	30
Mildred Elley...........................	Pr/A	502					None	50
Mirrer Yeshiva Central Institute	Pr/B	248						
Mohawk Valley Community College............	Pu/A	5,933	86				None	
Molloy College..........................	Pr/AB	3,117	14	TOEFL	500		None	30
Monroe College..........................	Pr/AB	6,528		TOEFL	450		4/25	35
Monroe Community College	Pu/A	18,995		TOEFL	500		6/1	20
Mount Saint Mary College	Pr/B	2,254	3	TOEFL, SAT/ACT	500		8/1	45
Nassau Community College..................	Pu/A	21,476	551				8/1	40
Nazareth College.........................	Pr/B	2,175	29	TOEFL	550	630	2/15	40
New York Career Institute..................	Pr/A	805					None	50
New York Institute of Technology	Pr/AB	4,901	612	TOEFL, SAT/ACT	550	568	7/15	50
New York School of Interior Design	Pr/AB	536	6	TOEFL	550		None	100
New York University	Pr/AB	21,646	2,003	TOEFL, SAT, SAT Subject Test(s), or ACT	600		1/1	75
Niagara County Community College	Pu/A	5,955		TOEFL	500		8/1	
Niagara University........................	Pr/AB	3,267	325	TOEFL	500		4/15	30
North Country Community College	Pu/A	2,273		TOEFL	500	520	None	
Nyack College	Pr/AB	2,109	100	TOEFL	550		None	25
Ohr Somayach Tanenbaum Education Center	Pr/B	75						75
Onondaga Community College................	Pu/A	8,706	44	TOEFL	500		6/15	
Pace University..........................	Pr/AB	7,604	354	TOEFL	570		7/15	50
Parsons The New School for Design	Pr/AB	4,191	1,437	TOEFL	580			50
Paul Smith's College	Pr/AB	1,005	2	TOEFL	500	570	None	30
Phillips Beth Israel School of Nursing	Pr/A	251		TOEFL	550	580	4/1	50
Polytechnic Institute of New York University	Pr/B	1,616	183	TOEFL, SAT	550	605	None	50
Pratt Institute	Pr/AB	2,980	441	TOEFL	530	543	1/5	90
Professional Business College	Pr/A	732						
Rabbinical Academy Mesivta Rabbi Chaim Berlin	Pr/B	222						
Rabbinical College Beth Shraga	Pr/B	35						
Rabbinical College Bobover Yeshiva B'nei Zion	Pr/B	199						

| Student services | | | Housing | | Academic year costs | | Maximum credits/ summer | Credit hour charge | International financial aid | | | |
Adviser	Orientation	ESL	Academic year	Summer	Tuition/ fees	Living costs			Available	Number receiving aid	Average award	Deadline
Yes	Yes		Yes		30,192	12,154	12	937	Yes	37	$24,389	4/15
					15,200†			495				
Yes	Yes		Yes	Yes	33,630†	12,314	15	1121	Yes	95	$25,493	None
Yes			Yes	Yes	7,885†	8,640	12	281				
		Yes	Yes	Yes	15,940†	10,200		850	Yes			3/1
Yes	Yes	Yes	Yes	Yes	32,180†	12,280			Yes	103	$25,184	3/1
					5,800†	2,200						
Yes			Yes		25,110	9,880	15	810	Yes	20	$12,345	None
Yes			Yes		29,240	11,050		1204	Yes	7	$12,663	None
Yes	Yes		Yes	Yes	28,380	10,890	12	574	Yes	22	$23,902	None
Yes			Yes		21,475†	19,875	9	695	Yes			None
Yes		Yes	No		13,899‡		18		Yes	21	$400	None
Yes	Yes	Yes	Yes		28,370†	10,860		896	Yes			5/1
Yes	Yes	Yes	Yes		30,210†	11,400		896				
			Yes		7,350†			720				
Yes	Yes	Yes	Yes	Yes	29,765‡	11,420	12					
Yes	Yes	Yes	Yes	Yes	32,815†	11,480		1300	Yes	53	$18,690	3/1
Yes	Yes	Yes	Yes	Yes	34,350†	13,920	12	765	Yes			3/1
Yes	Yes	Yes	Yes		36,780	15,260		1175	Yes	43	$18,620	None
Yes	Yes		Yes	Yes	27,750†	11,676	9	634	Yes			5/1
Yes	Yes		Yes		24,708	14,030	6	785	Yes	12	$9,285	None
			Yes		20,580†	9,750	6	725	Yes	11	$13,000	None
					20,580†			725				
					20,580†			725				
Yes	Yes	Yes	Yes	Yes	17,010†	11,140	12	692	Yes			None
					7,500†	4,500						
Yes		Yes	No		16,750†		16		Yes			None
Yes			No		11,100†	5,722		354	Yes			None
					4,700†	4,000						
Yes	Yes	Yes	Yes	Yes	7,270†	10,260	22	240	Yes			None
Yes		Yes	No		22,130†	7,312		700	Yes	18	$8,645	5/1
Yes			Yes		12,200†	8,150	15	475	Yes			3/31
Yes			Yes		6,378†	5,895	12	250				
Yes			Yes		24,410	12,320	12	782				
Yes	Yes	Yes	No		7,744†		15	312	Yes			None
Yes	Yes		Yes		28,332	11,144	12	621	Yes	5	$12,260	
			No		12,000†							
Yes	Yes		Yes	Yes	27,290	14,570		895	Yes			None
Yes	Yes		Yes	Yes	23,856		6	796	Yes	3	$5,133	None
Yes	Yes	Yes	Yes	Yes	40,082†	13,507	16	1116				
Yes			Yes		7,280†	6,500	12	290				
Yes	Yes	Yes	Yes	Yes	26,400	11,000	12	845	Yes	79	$10,140	None
Yes			Yes		10,300†	7,900	12	390				
Yes		Yes	Yes		21,500	8,250		855	Yes	78	$4,034	None
Yes		Yes	Yes	Yes	7,000†	7,000	12		Yes			None
Yes	Yes	Yes	Yes		8,028†		12	302				
Yes	Yes	Yes	Yes	Yes	33,812†	13,800	12	937	Yes	207	$11,033	None
Yes	Yes	Yes	Yes	Yes	39,350	15,260	18	1310	Yes	1041	$7,258	None
Yes			Yes		21,505	11,670		580	Yes			None
Yes			No		18,190†	12,000	7	380	Yes			6/1
Yes	Yes		Yes		37,864	10,080	12	1116	Yes	164	$18,009	None
Yes	Yes	Yes	Yes	Yes	39,310	10,300		1210	Yes			2/1
			No		9,310†							
					10,850†	3,000						
					9,550†	4,200						
					7,560†	4,500						

† Tuition and fees are for 2010-11.   ‡ Tuition and fees projected for 2011-12.   * Includes room and board

Institution	Control/ degrees	Undergraduates		Tests required (Fall 2011)	TOEFL		Application	
		Total	Internat'l		minimum	average	Deadline	Fee
Rabbinical College Ch'san Sofer of New York	Pr/B	40						
Rabbinical College of Long Island	Pr/B	118						
Rabbinical College of Ohr Shimon Yisroel	Pr/B	176						
Rabbinical Seminary of America.	Pr/B	300						
Rensselaer Polytechnic Institute	Pr/B	5,348	170	TOEFL, SAT/ACT	570	584	1/15	70
Roberts Wesleyan College.	Pr/AB	1,332	31	TOEFL	550		2/1	35
Rochester Institute of Technology	Pr/AB	13,511	609	TOEFL	550	600	6/1	50
Rockland Community College	Pu/A	6,908	106				7/15	30
Russell Sage College	Pr/B	712	1	TOEFL	550		7/1	30
Sage College of Albany	Pr/AB	874	1	TOEFL	550			30
Saint Bonaventure University.	Pr/B	1,936	32	TOEFL	550		4/15	30
St. Elizabeth College of Nursing.	Pr/A	236	5	TOEFL	500		None	30
St. Francis College.	Pr/AB	2,562		TOEFL	500	515	None	35
St. John Fisher College.	Pr/B	2,864	7	TOEFL, SAT/ACT	550		2/15	30
St. John's University	Pr/AB	12,067	538	TOEFL	600		5/1	50
St. Joseph's College	Pr/B	1,228	1	TOEFL, SAT	550	580	3/1	25
St. Joseph's College: Suffolk Campus	Pr/B	3,813		TOEFL	550		4/1	25
St. Lawrence University	Pr/B	2,295	134	TOEFL	600		2/1	60
St. Thomas Aquinas College	Pr/AB	1,360		TOEFL	500	520	3/1	30
Sarah Lawrence College	Pr/B	1,244	62	TOEFL	600		1/1	60
Schenectady County Community College	Pu/A	6,358		TOEFL	550		3/1	
School of Visual Arts.	Pr/B	3,417	648	TOEFL		567	None	80
Shor Yoshuv Rabbinical College.	Pr/B	197						460
Siena College	Pr/B	3,307	25	TOEFL, SAT/ACT	550		2/15	50
Skidmore College	Pr/B	2,703	88	TOEFL, SAT/ACT	590	611	1/15	60
Suffolk County Community College	Pu/A	25,246		TOEFL	500		7/15	35
Sullivan County Community College.	Pu/A	1,749		TOEFL	550		5/1	25
SUNY College at Brockport	Pu/B	7,277		TOEFL	530	620	7/1	50
SUNY College at Buffalo	Pu/B	9,788		TOEFL, SAT, SAT Subject Test(s), or ACT	500			40
SUNY College at Cortland	Pu/B	6,462		TOEFL	550		6/1	40
SUNY College at Fredonia	Pu/B	5,331	75	TOEFL	500	510	None	50
SUNY College at Geneseo	Pu/B	5,448	134	TOEFL	525		6/1	40
SUNY College at New Paltz	Pu/B	6,401	188	TOEFL	550		3/1	40
SUNY College at Old Westbury.	Pu/B	4,039	57	TOEFL	513		None	50
SUNY College at Oneonta.	Pu/B	5,785		TOEFL	500	550	5/15	50
SUNY College at Oswego.	Pu/B	7,342	69	TOEFL	550	570	4/15	50
SUNY College at Plattsburgh.	Pu/B	5,746		TOEFL	540	560	None	50
SUNY College at Potsdam	Pu/B	3,863		TOEFL	550	573	7/3	50
SUNY College at Purchase	Pu/B	3,817	67	TOEFL, SAT/ACT	550		1/1	40
SUNY College of Agriculture and Technology at Cobleskill	Pu/AB			TOEFL	500		None	40
SUNY College of Agriculture and Technology at Morrisville	Pu/AB	3,448		TOEFL	500	550		40
SUNY College of Environmental Science and Forestry.	Pu/AB	1,629	16	TOEFL	550		None	50
SUNY College of Technology at Alfred.	Pu/AB	3,637		TOEFL	500	530	None	40
SUNY College of Technology at Canton	Pu/AB	3,294		TOEFL	550		5/1	40
SUNY College of Technology at Delhi	Pu/AB	3,095	33	TOEFL	475		7/15	40
SUNY College of Technology at Farmingdale. . . .	Pu/AB	6,228	60	TOEFL	500		6/1	40
SUNY Empire State College	Pu/AB	10,099		TOEFL	550		None	
SUNY Institute of Technology at Utica/Rome	Pu/B	1,939	13	TOEFL, SAT/ACT	550		6/1	50
SUNY Maritime College. . . . . . :	Pu/AB	1,645	101	TOEFL, SAT/ACT	550		5/1	40
SUNY University at Albany	Pu/B	12,623	394	TOEFL	550		3/1	50
SUNY University at Binghamton	Pu/B	11,745	1,194	TOEFL	550	580	3/15	50
SUNY University at Buffalo	Pu/B	19,199	2,839	TOEFL	550	584	None	50
SUNY University at Stony Brook.	Pu/B	16,045	1,126	TOEFL			3/1	50
SUNY Upstate Medical University	Pu/B	328		TOEFL	550	575	None	50
Swedish Institute.	Pr/A			TOEFL				45

Student services			Housing		Academic year costs		Maximum credits/summer	Credit hour charge	International financial aid			
Adviser	Orien-tation	ESL	Academic year	Summer	Tuition/fees	Living costs			Avail-able	Number receiving aid	Average award	Deadline
			Yes		7,500 †							
					6,600 †							
			Yes		7,000 †	6,000						
Yes	Yes	Yes	Yes	Yes	42,704	11,975	16	1733				
Yes		Yes	Yes	Yes	24,707 †	8,826	12	978	Yes			None
Yes	Yes	Yes	Yes	Yes	32,037	10,963	18	714	Yes	150	$8,000	None
Yes	Yes	Yes	No		7,323 †	7,200	15	292				
Yes			Yes		28,000	10,675		900	Yes			None
Yes			Yes		28,000	10,675		900	Yes			None
Yes	Yes		Yes	Yes	27,890	11,840	12	805	Yes	32	$10,670	None
					13,750			375	Yes			None
Yes	Yes				17,280 †		12		Yes			None
Yes			Yes		26,260	10,510	14	700	Yes	5	$9,530	None
Yes	Yes	Yes	Yes		31,980 †	14,500	18	1042	Yes	368	$19,498	None
Yes			Yes		18,415		9	593	Yes	14	$7,098	None
Yes			No		18,415	4,810	9	593	Yes			None
Yes	Yes		Yes		42,735	11,355	12		Yes	133	$41,380	2/1
Yes	Yes	Yes	Yes	Yes	22,410 †	11,800	12	705	Yes			None
Yes			Yes		45,212	13,958		1474	Yes	35	$37,219	2/1
Yes			No		6,813 †	6,975	6	283				
Yes	Yes	Yes	Yes	Yes	28,140 †	12,950	18	940	Yes	166	$6,988	3/1
					9,460 †	6,000						
Yes	Yes		Yes	Yes	28,985	11,434			Yes			5/1
Yes	Yes		Yes	Yes	41,184 †	10,986		1345	Yes	56	$51,402	2/1
Yes	Yes	Yes	No		7,972 †	6,080	12	316	Yes			6/1
Yes			No		8,266 †	6,800	10	200	Yes			None
Yes	Yes		Yes		14,586 †	11,293	16	558	Yes			None
Yes	Yes	Yes	Yes	Yes	14,463 †	11,026	16	558				
Yes	Yes		Yes		14,630 †	10,490	12	558	Yes			None
Yes	Yes		Yes	Yes	14,743 †	10,110	12	558	Yes	26	$5,000	5/15
Yes	Yes	Yes	Yes	Yes	14,811 †	10,042		558	Yes	104	$3,566	2/15
Yes	Yes	Yes	Yes	Yes	14,545 †	9,786	12	558				
Yes	Yes		Yes	Yes	14,376 †	10,160	16	558				
Yes	Yes	Yes	Yes	Yes	14,660 †	10,384	12	558				
Yes	Yes	Yes	Yes	Yes	14,596 †	13,810	12	558	Yes			None
Yes	Yes	ESL	Yes	Yes	14,553 †	9,000	12	558	Yes	372	$5,331	None
Yes	Yes		Yes	Yes	14,593 †	9,630	18	558	Yes	111	$9,180	5/1
Yes	Yes	Yes	Yes	Yes	14,924 †	10,696	8	558	Yes			None
Yes	Yes	Yes	Yes	Yes	10,516 †	9,926	6	379	Yes			2/15
Yes	Yes	Yes	Yes		10,265 †	10,058	12	379				
Yes	Yes	Yes	Yes	Yes	14,351 †			558	Yes			None
Yes	Yes	Yes	Yes		10,348 †	10,519		379	Yes	11	$4,332	None
Yes	Yes		Yes	Yes	10,427 †	10,210	6	379	Yes			
Yes	Yes	Yes	Yes		10,575 †	9,720		379				
Yes	Yes		Yes	Yes	14,503 †	15,280	12	558	Yes			None
Yes			No		13,605 †			558				
Yes	Yes		Yes	Yes	14,524 †	9,190	8	558	Yes			None
Yes	Yes		Yes		14,567 †	10,090	9	558	Yes			7/15
Yes	Yes	Yes	Yes	Yes	15,240 †	10,633		558				
Yes	Yes	Yes	Yes	Yes	15,291 †	12,553	16	558	Yes	49	$17,297	None
Yes	Yes	Yes	Yes	Yes	15,546 †	10,028	19	558	Yes	23	$7,576	None
Yes	Yes	Yes	Yes	Yes	14,990 †	10,142	16	558	Yes	140	$11,734	None
Yes			Yes	Yes	13,945 †	8,024		558				
					11,450 †							

† Tuition and fees are for 2010-11. ‡ Tuition and fees projected for 2011-12. * Includes room and board

Institution	Control/ degrees	Undergraduates		Tests required (Fall 2011)	TOEFL		Application	
		Total	Internat'l		minimum	average	Deadline	Fee
Syracuse University	Pr/AB	13,753	901	TOEFL, SAT/ACT			1/1	70
Talmudical Institute of Upstate New York	Pr/B	27					9/1	
Talmudical Seminary Oholei Torah	Pr/B	297					None	
Technical Career Institutes	Pr/A						None	
Tompkins Cortland Community College	Pu/A	3,551	72	TOEFL	450	480	6/1	15
Torah Temimah Talmudical Seminary	Pr/B	176						
Touro College	Pr/AB	8,632		TOEFL	500	525	4/15	30
Trocaire College	Pr/A			TOEFL	550		None	25
U.T.A. Mesivta-Kiryas Jocl	Pr/B	1,273						
Ulster County Community College	Pu/A	3,696		TOEFL	500	550	8/1	25
Union College	Pr/B	2,159	85	TOEFL	600		1/15	50
United States Merchant Marine Academy	Pu/B	1,081		TOEFL, SAT/ACT	533	614	2/1	
United Talmudical Seminary	Pr/B	1,566						
University of Rochester	Pr/B	5,416	507	TOEFL, SAT/ACT	600	619	1/1	60
University of Rochester School of Nursing	Pr/B							
Utica College	Pr/B	2,616	35	TOEFL	525		None	40
Utica School of Commerce	Pr/A	532					None	20
Vassar College	Pr/B	2,408	143	TOEFL, SAT, SAT Subject Test(s), or ACT	600	640	1/1	60
Vaughn College of Aeronautics and Technology	Pr/AB	1,523	35	TOEFL	580	640	None	40
Villa Maria College of Buffalo	Pr/AB	493		TOEFL	450		None	
Wagner College	Pr/B	1,825	23	TOEFL	550		2/15	75
Wells College	Pr/B	551	7	TOEFL	550		3/1	40
Westchester Community College	Pu/A	11,906		TOEFL	500		None	25
Wood Tobe-Coburn School	Pr/A	421						50
Yeshiva and Kolel Bais Medrash Elyon	Pr/B	9						
Yeshiva and Kollel Harbotzas Torah	Pr/B	16						
Yeshiva Derech Chaim	Pr/B	110						
Yeshiva D'Monsey Rabbinical College	Pr/B	74						
Yeshiva Gedolah Imrei Yosef D'Spinka	Pr/B	121						
Yeshiva Gedolah Zichron Moshe	Pr/B	180						
Yeshiva Karlin Stolin	Pr/B	96						
Yeshiva of Nitra	Pr/B	214						
Yeshiva of the Telshe Alumni	Pr/B	57						50
Yeshiva Shaar Hatorah	Pr/B	92						100
Yeshiva Shaarei Torah of Rockland	Pr/B	22						250
Yeshivas Novominsk	Pr/B	126						100
Yeshivat Mikdash Melech	Pr/B	48	2				None	400
Yeshivath Viznitz	Pr/B	340						

North Carolina

Institution	Control/ degrees	Undergraduates		Tests required (Fall 2011)	TOEFL		Application	
		Total	Internat'l		minimum	average	Deadline	Fee
Apex School of Theology	Pr/AB	362						25
Appalachian State University	Pu/B	14,969	80	TOEFL	500		None	50
Art Institute of Charlotte	Pr/AB	1,118		TOEFL	500		None	150
Asheville-Buncombe Technical Community College	Pu/A	7,542		TOEFL	550		7/15	
Barton College	Pr/B	1,131	17	TOEFL	525		None	50
Belmont Abbey College	Pr/B	1,719	44	TOEFL	550	590	7/15	35
Bennett College for Women	Pr/B	714	4	TOEFL	500		None	35
Bladen Community College	Pu/A	1,857						
Brevard College	Pr/B	634	16	TOEFL	550		5/1	30
Cabarrus College of Health Sciences	Pr/AB	426						50
Campbell University	Pr/AB	4,421	113	TOEFL	500	570	None	35
Carteret Community College	Pu/A	1,707		TOEFL, SAT	550		None	
Catawba College	Pr/B	1,247	28	TOEFL	525		None	25
Central Piedmont Community College	Pu/A	17,351		TOEFL	500		6/1	35
Chowan University	Pr/AB	1,173		TOEFL, SAT/ACT	475	500	8/1	20
College of the Albemarle	Pu/A	2,599	4	TOEFL	500		None	

Student services			Housing		Academic year costs		Maximum credits/ summer	Credit hour charge	International financial aid			
Adviser	Orien- tation	ESL	Academic year	Summer	Tuition/ fees	Living costs			Avail- able	Number receiving aid	Average award	Deadline
Yes	Yes	Yes	Yes	Yes	37,667	17,754		1580				
			Yes		5,500†	4,000						
			Yes		6,600†	3,200						
Yes		Yes	No		12,285†			496	Yes			
Yes	Yes	Yes	Yes	Yes	8,471†		12	288				
					9,250†	3,000						
Yes			Yes		11,900†	7,000	6	490	Yes			6/1
			No		13,010†		12	513				
					6,500†	4,000						
			No		8,228†	4,250	24	280	Yes			None
Yes	Yes		Yes	Yes	54,273*		1		Yes	76	$33,173	2/1
Yes			Yes									
Yes	Yes	Yes	Yes	Yes	41,802	12,120	16	1284	Yes	253	$14,035	2/1
Yes	Yes		Yes	Yes	30,516	11,650	12	950	Yes			None
			No		12,100†	6,500	15	487				
Yes			Yes		44,705	10,430		1491	Yes	122	$47,622	2/1
Yes	Yes		Yes	Yes	18,520‡	16,400	12	605	Yes	35	$2,877	None
			Yes		16,325	7,536	12	530				
Yes	Yes		Yes	Yes	35,820	10,680	4		Yes	3	$6,700	None
Yes	Yes		Yes		32,180‡	12,000			Yes			None
Yes	Yes	Yes	No		9,989†			403				
			No		16,640†				Yes			None
					7,900†							
					6,050†							
			Yes		9,400†	3,600						
					4,350†	3,600						
					7,000†							
					10,100†	3,000						
					6,500†	3,200						
					7,000†	3,300						
					7,900†	4,600						
			Yes		15,250*							
					10,500†	3,000						
					8,500†	3,500						
			Yes	Yes	7,000	4,000			Yes			None
					5,700†	1,650						
					6,200‡	14,498		200				
Yes	Yes	Yes	Yes		16,487†	7,475						
Yes			Yes	Yes	21,335†	5,100	16	473				
		Yes	No		7,525†		18	249				
Yes			Yes		22,982	7,632	12	898	Yes			None
Yes	Yes		Yes		24,584†	12,594	6	819	Yes	42	$7,334	None
Yes			Yes		16,794	9,628	7	609	Yes	694	$1,491	4/15
			No		7,475†	5,112		249				
			Yes		22,700	8,650		450	Yes			None
			No		10,145†	7,680		310				
Yes	Yes		Yes	Yes	22,520†	7,800	12	360	Yes			None
Yes			No		7,515†			249	Yes			None
			Yes		25,160	8,700	6	655	Yes			None
Yes	Yes	Yes	No		7,543†	7,026	15	249	Yes			6/1
Yes			Yes	Yes	20,070†	8,160	9	335	Yes			None
Yes		Yes	No		7,521†	8,325	12	249	Yes			None

† Tuition and fees are for 2010-11.   ‡ Tuition and fees projected for 2011-12.   * Includes room and board

Institution	Control/ degrees	Undergraduates		Tests required (Fall 2011)	TOEFL		Application	
		Total	Internat'l		minimum	average	Deadline	Fee
Craven Community College..................	.Pu/A	3,521						
Davidson College	.Pr/B	1,738	67	TOEFL, SAT/ACT	600		1/2	50
Duke University	.Pr/B	6,510	475	TOEFL, SAT, SAT Subject Test(s), or ACT			1/2	75
Durham Technical Community College	.Pu/A	5,642						
East Carolina University	.Pu/B	20,811	106	TOEFL, SAT/ACT	550		4/15	60
Elizabeth City State University..............	.Pu/B	2,930	14	TOEFL, SAT/ACT	500		None	30
Elon University.......................	.Pr/B	5,032	118	TOEFL, SAT/ACT	550		6/1	50
Fayetteville State University...............	.Pu/B	4,868	16	TOEFL, SAT/ACT	550		7/1	35
Fayetteville Technical Community College	.Pu/A	8,681		TOEFL	550		3/1	
Gardner-Webb University	.Pr/AB	2,792	9	TOEFL, SAT/ACT	500	515	None	40
Greensboro College	.Pr/B	1,101	3	TOEFL, SAT/ACT	550		7/15	35
Guilford College......................	.Pr/B	2,658	23	TOEFL	550	600	2/15	25
Guilford Technical Community College	.Pu/A	14,211		TOEFL	486		None	
Halifax Community College.................	.Pu/A	1,641					None	
High Point University....................	.Pr/B	3,727	50	TOEFL	500	530	6/2	40
Johnson & Wales University: Charlotte	.Pr/AB	2,587	44	TOEFL	550			
Johnson C. Smith University................	.Pr/B	1,331	31	TOEFL, SAT/ACT	300		3/15	25
Johnston Community College................	.Pu/A	3,765		TOEFL	550			
Laurel University......................	.Pr/AB	134		TOEFL	500		5/6	35
Lees-McRae College	.Pr/B	894		TOEFL	500		None	
Lenoir-Rhyne University..................	.Pr/B	1,571		TOEFL	550		6/1	35
Livingstone College.....................	.Pr/B	1,156		TOEFL	500		7/1	25
Louisburg College.....................	.Pr/A	670		TOEFL	500	590	7/1	25
Mars Hill College	.Pr/B	1,153		TOEFL	500		None	25
Martin Community College	.Pu/A	696						
Mayland Community College................	.Pu/A	1,466		TOEFL	500		6/8	
McDowell Technical Community College.........	.Pu/A	1,519		TOEFL	450			
Meredith College......................	.Pr/B	1,774	45	TOEFL	500		2/15	40
Methodist University	.Pr/AB	2,217		TOEFL	500	575	None	25
Mid-Atlantic Christian University	.Pr/AB	169		TOEFL	500		5/23	50
Miller-Motte College: Fayetteville............	.Pr/A							
Miller-Motte Technical College: Cary	.Pr/A	525						35
Montreat College......................	.Pr/AB	811	9	TOEFL	500		5/1	30
Mount Olive College	.Pr/AB	3,463		TOEFL	500		8/15	20
Nash Community College	.Pu/A	5,310		TOEFL	550		6/1	
North Carolina Central University.............	.Pu/B			TOEFL, SAT/ACT	500		5/1	30
North Carolina State University	.Pu/AB	23,500	335	TOEFL	550		2/1	70
North Carolina Wesleyan College	.Pr/B	1,408		TOEFL, SAT/ACT	500	550	5/1	25
Pamlico Community College	.Pu/A	401						
Peace College........................	.Pr/B	730		TOEFL, SAT/ACT	550		None	25
Pfeiffer University.....................	.Pr/B	1,041	29	TOEFL, SAT/ACT	500		8/1	35
Piedmont Baptist College and Graduate School	.Pr/AB	300		TOEFL, ACT	500		None	50
Piedmont Community College	.Pu/A	2,489		TOEFL	550			
Queens University of Charlotte..............	.Pr/AB	1,975	68	TOEFL	550		7/1	40
Roanoke-Chowan Community College..........	.Pu/A	886		TOEFL	500		6/1	
Robeson Community College................	.Pu/A							
Rockingham Community College	.Pu/A	2,301	3	TOEFL			None	
St. Andrews Presbyterian College	.Pr/B			TOEFL	500	550	5/1	30
St. Augustine's College...................	.Pr/B	1,508	22	TOEFL, SAT/ACT	500		7/1	25
Salem College........................	.Pr/B	840		TOEFL, SAT/ACT	550		5/1	30
Sandhills Community College	.Pu/A			TOEFL	550		3/1	
Shaw University	.Pr/AB	2,550	22	TOEFL, SAT/ACT			7/30	40
Shepherds Theological Seminary..............	.Pr/A	8		TOEFL				30
Southeastern Baptist Theological Seminary	.Pr/AB							30
Southeastern Community College	.Pu/A	1,933		TOEFL			None	
Southwestern Community College.............	.Pu/A			TOEFL	500		None	
Tri-County Community College	.Pu/A	1,475						
University of North Carolina at Asheville........	.Pu/B	3,418	26	TOEFL	550		4/1	50

Adviser	Orientation	ESL	Housing Academic year	Housing Summer	Tuition/fees	Living costs	Maximum credits/summer	Credit hour charge	Available	Number receiving aid	Average award	Deadline
			No		7,515†	10,656		249				
Yes	Yes		Yes	Yes	38,866	10,857			Yes			2/15
Yes	Yes	Yes	Yes	Yes	41,938	11,967	16	1271	Yes			3/1
Yes		Yes	No		7,535†			249	Yes			
Yes	Yes		Yes	Yes	17,831†	9,350	14	712	Yes	106	$16,987	None
Yes			Yes		13,276†	5,639	9		Yes	2	$6,500	6/1
Yes	Yes	Yes	Yes	Yes	26,827†	8,648	8	831				
Yes			Yes		14,220†	5,501	18					
		Yes	No		7,545†	6,750		249	Yes			7/15
Yes	Yes		Yes	Yes	23,510	7,570	16	372	Yes			None
Yes	Yes		Yes	Yes	23,350†	8,720	16	635	Yes			None
Yes	Yes	Yes	Yes	Yes	30,430	8,270	16	923	Yes	10	$15,416	None
Yes	Yes	Yes	No		7,522†	7,722	12	249				None
			No		7,545†	5,400		249	Yes			None
Yes	Yes	Yes	Yes	Yes	37,800*	3,500	12	750				
			Yes		25,107	10,314			Yes			None
Yes	Yes		Yes	Yes	17,368	6,762	9	398	Yes			None
			No		7,550†		9	249				
			Yes	Yes	10,730†	5,269	12	375	Yes			None
Yes	Yes	Yes	Yes		22,164†	9,800	12	615	Yes			None
Yes			Yes	Yes	26,524	9,370	12	1100	Yes			None
Yes			Yes		14,358†	6,342			Yes			6/30
Yes			Yes		14,336†	9,752	15		Yes			None
Yes	Yes	Yes	Yes	Yes	23,318	9,182	18	775	Yes			None
			No		7,493†			249				
Yes		Yes	No		7,551†	8,945		249	Yes			None
Yes			No		7,507†		18	249	Yes			None
Yes	Yes		Yes	Yes	26,200†	7,500	12	650	Yes			None
Yes	Yes	Yes	Yes	Yes	24,220†	8,899	18		Yes			7/1
			Yes		10,500	9,000		350	Yes			
					12,672‡			264				
Yes			Yes		23,164	10,346		600	Yes			None
Yes			Yes		15,500	6,200	12	380	Yes	52	$7,353	None
		Yes	No		7,575†			249				
Yes		Yes	Yes		15,052†	6,754			Yes			None
Yes	Yes	Yes	Yes	Yes	19,064†	8,154	15		Yes	79	$13,669	None
Yes			Yes		23,000†	7,890	14	330	Yes			None
			No		7,490†	4,800		249				
Yes			Yes		26,011	8,880	15	670	Yes	3	$15,666	None
Yes	Yes		Yes	Yes	20,577†	8,266	14	460	Yes			None
			Yes	Yes	11,170†	5,760	18	346	Yes			None
			No		7,498†		12	249				
Yes	Yes		Yes	Yes	23,752†	8,608	12	395	Yes	45	$8,527	None
Yes			No		7,552†	6,000	9	249	Yes			None
			No		7,523†			249	Yes			None
Yes			No		7,551†	7,600		249				
Yes	Yes		Yes		21,614†	13,438	6	450	Yes			None
Yes	Yes		Yes	Yes	17,160	7,340	12	515	Yes			3/15
Yes	Yes		Yes		21,948†	11,520	16		Yes			None
Yes		Yes	No		7,552†	8,891		249	Yes			6/1
Yes	Yes		Yes	Yes	12,580†	7,560	9	410	Yes			6/30
			No		4,350			235				
				Yes	7,200†			229				
Yes			No		7,567†			249				
			No		7,489†			249	Yes			6/30
			No		7,514†			249	Yes			
Yes	Yes		Yes	Yes	17,544†	7,040						

† Tuition and fees are for 2010-11.   ‡ Tuition and fees projected for 2011-12.   * Includes room and board

Institution	Control/ degrees	Undergraduates		Tests required (Fall 2011)	TOEFL		Application	
		Total	Internat'l		minimum	average	Deadline	Fee
University of North Carolina at Chapel Hill	.Pu/B	17,943	392	TOEFL, SAT/ACT	600		1/15	70
University of North Carolina at Charlotte	.Pu/B	19,662	512	TOEFL	507		5/1	50
University of North Carolina at Greensboro	.Pu/B	14,590	170	TOEFL	550		3/1	45
University of North Carolina at Pembroke	.Pu/B	5,871		TOEFL	500			40
University of North Carolina at Wilmington	.Pu/B	11,343	61	TOEFL	525	544	2/1	60
University of North Carolina School of the Arts.	.Pu/B	740		TOEFL	550		3/1	100
University of Phoenix: Charlotte.	.Pr/B							
University of Phoenix: Raleigh.	.Pr/B							
Vance-Granville Community College.	.Pu/A	4,352		TOEFL			6/1	
Wake Forest University.	.Pr/B	4,642	82	TOEFL	600		1/15	50
Wake Technical Community College.	.Pu/A	17,351			540		5/1	30
Warren Wilson College.	.Pr/B	924		TOEFL	550	560	3/15	15
Western Carolina University	.Pu/B	7,251	124	TOEFL, SAT/ACT	550		4/1	45
Wilkes Community College.	.Pu/A							
Wilson Community College.	.Pu/A	1,777		TOEFL	550			
Wingate University	.Pr/B	1,607	59	TOEFL	550	575	6/1	30
Winston-Salem State University	.Pu/B			TOEFL	550		None	40
North Dakota								
Bismarck State College.	.Pu/AB			TOEFL	525		6/15	35
Dakota College at Bottineau	.Pu/A	863		TOEFL, ACT			None	35
Dickinson State University	.Pu/AB	2,767		TOEFL	525	540	None	35
Fort Berthold Community College.	.Pu/A	323						
Jamestown College	.Pr/B	902	37	TOEFL	525		6/1	35
Lake Region State College	.Pu/A	765	14	TOEFL	510		None	35
Mayville State University	.Pu/AB	982	34	TOEFL	520	550	None	35
Minot State University	.Pu/AB	3,551		TOEFL, ACT	525	553	None	35
North Dakota State College of Science.	.Pu/A	2,833			400		8/1	35
North Dakota State University	.Pu/B	11,977		TOEFL	525		5/1	35
Rasmussen College: Bismarck	.Pr/AB			TOEFL	500		None	60
Rasmussen College: Fargo.	.Pr/AB	765		TOEFL	500		None	60
United Tribes Technical College.	.Pr/A			TOEFL	500			
University of Mary	.Pr/B	2,036	25	TOEFL	500		8/1	25
University of North Dakota	.Pu/B	11,139	657	TOEFL	525	560	4/1	35
Valley City State University	.Pu/B	940	29	TOEFL	525		5/1	35
Williston State College.	.Pu/A	464	22	TOEFL	525		None	35
Ohio								
Academy of Court Reporting and Technology	.Pr/A	420						100
Akron Institute of Herzing University	.Pr/AB							
Allegheny Wesleyan College	.Pr/B							
Antonelli College: Cincinnati.	.Pr/A	445		TOEFL	500			100
Art Academy of Cincinnati	.Pr/AB			TOEFL, SAT/ACT	550		6/30	
Art Institute of Cincinnati	.Pr/A	48					None	100
Art Institute of Ohio: Cincinnati.	.Pr/A			TOEFL	500		None	50
Ashland University	.Pr/AB	3,145		TOEFL, SAT/ACT	500		7/1	50
Baldwin-Wallace College	.Pr/B	3,560	45	TOEFL	500	574	7/1	25
Belmont Technical College	.Pu/A	2,180		TOEFL			None	
Bluffton University	.Pr/B	848		TOEFL	500	600	6/1	20
Bowling Green State University	.Pu/B	14,522	251	TOEFL	500		5/1	40
Bowling Green State University: Firelands College	.Pu/AB	2,515		TOEFL				40
Bryant & Stratton College: Parma.	.Pr/AB	856	1	TOEFL	500	525	9/8	35
Capital University	.Pr/B	2,611	37	TOEFL	500	550	None	25
Case Western Reserve University	.Pr/B	4,125	259	TOEFL	550		1/15	
Cedarville University	.Pr/B	3,045	42	TOEFL	550		None	30
Central Ohio Technical College	.Pu/A	4,232		TOEFL	550		6/1	20

Student services			Housing		Academic year costs		Maximum credits/summer	Credit hour charge	International financial aid			
Adviser	Orientation	ESL	Academic year	Summer	Tuition/fees	Living costs			Available	Number receiving aid	Average award	Deadline
Yes	Yes		Yes	Yes	24,736†	9,306	12					
Yes	Yes	Yes	Yes	Yes	16,185†	7,260	6		Yes	29	$16,964	None
Yes	Yes		Yes	Yes	16,281†	6,655	6	1819	Yes			None
Yes	Yes	Yes	Yes	Yes	13,347†	7,510	17		Yes			None
Yes	Yes	Yes	Yes	Yes	16,515†	7,608	12		Yes	29	$9,952	None
Yes			Yes		18,811†	7,546			Yes			None
					11,040†							
					11,040†							
			No		7,517†			249				
Yes	Yes		Yes	Yes	41,576	11,410		1704	Yes			3/1
Yes	Yes	Yes	No		7,535†		14	249	Yes			None
Yes	Yes		Yes	Yes	25,626†	8,028		1056	Yes			None
Yes	Yes		Yes	Yes	14,721†	6,178	12					
			No		7,575†			249				
		Yes	No		7,552†			249	Yes			None
Yes			Yes		22,180	9,370	12	700				
Yes			Yes		13,234†	7,106	12		Yes			None
			Yes		9,647†	5,043	10	299	Yes			None
Yes			Yes		5,417†	4,456		195	Yes			None
Yes		Yes	Yes	Yes	12,585†	4,718	7	479	Yes			None
			No				18					
			Yes	Yes	17,270	5,700	12	415	Yes			None
Yes	Yes	Yes	Yes	Yes	8,506†	4,900	12	319	Yes			None
Yes	Yes		Yes	Yes	13,065†	5,319	10	475	Yes	25	$4,518	None
Yes	Yes		Yes	Yes	5,637†	4,856	18	187	Yes	150	$2,961	None
Yes			Yes	Yes	9,533†	5,026	12	300	Yes	9	$9,033	None
Yes	Yes	Yes	Yes	Yes	16,147†	9,298	15	627	Yes	156	$5,348	
			No		16,875†	7,011		375	Yes			None
			No		16,875†	7,011		375	Yes			None
Yes			Yes	Yes	3,650†	3,400	7	95				
Yes	Yes		Yes		13,545	5,340	12	435	Yes	28	$5,181	None
Yes	Yes	Yes	Yes	Yes	16,373†	5,950	12	628	Yes			None
	Yes		Yes	Yes	13,478†	5,422	9	394	Yes	34	$6,838	None
			Yes	Yes	3,378†	6,057		101	Yes	24	$4,373	None
			No									
			Yes		5,550†	3,300		185				
Yes												
			Yes		23,530	6,000	18	965				
			No			6,750						
			Yes			8,700	20					
Yes	Yes	Yes	Yes	Yes	28,582	9,352	12		Yes			None
Yes	Yes	Yes	Yes	Yes	26,396	7,346	20	820	Yes	18	$12,060	9/1
			No		6,799†		21	128				
Yes	Yes		Yes	Yes	26,154	8,756	17	1071	Yes	14	$21,650	10/1
Yes	Yes	Yes	Yes	Yes	17,012†	7,800			Yes			None
Yes	Yes		No		11,836†				Yes			None
					15,120†		18					
Yes	Yes	Yes	Yes	Yes	30,450	8,180	18	1015	Yes	19	$14,933	None
Yes	Yes	Yes	Yes	Yes	39,120	11,938	9	1615				
Yes	Yes		Yes		24,400	5,242	12					
Yes			Yes		6,552†		19	158	Yes			None

† Tuition and fees are for 2010-11. ‡ Tuition and fees projected for 2011-12. * Includes room and board

Institution	Control/ degrees	Undergraduates		Tests required (Fall 2011)	TOEFL		Application	
		Total	Internat'l		minimum	average	Deadline	Fee
Central State University	.Pu/B	2,197	3	TOEFL, SAT/ACT	500	520	None	20
Chamberlain College of Nursing: Columbus	.Pr/AB	718	1					95
Cincinnati Christian University.	.Pr/AB	753	11	TOEFL	550		2/15	40
Cincinnati State Technical and Community College	.Pu/A	10,103	127	TOEFL	500	525	None	
Clark State Community College	.Pu/A	4,211	1	TOEFL	500		None	15
Cleveland Institute of Art	.Pr/B	525	14	TOEFL	525		5/1	30
Cleveland Institute of Electronics	.Pr/A	1,731					None	
Cleveland Institute of Music	.Pr/B	244		TOEFL	550		12/1	100
Cleveland State University. . . . :	.Pu/B	10,676	275	TOEFL	525	530	5/15	30
College of Mount St. Joseph	.Pr/AB	1,962	1	TOEFL	510		None	25
College of Wooster	.Pr/B	1,958	108	TOEFL, SAT/ACT	550	600	2/15	40
Columbus College of Art and Design.	.Pr/B	1,354	56	TOEFL	500	550	None	30
Columbus State Community College	.Pu/A			TOEFL	480		6/15	
Cuyahoga Community College: Metropolitan.	.Pu/A	15,131	198				None	
Defiance College.	.Pr/AB	983	4	TOEFL	550		7/1	25
Denison University	.Pr/B	2,259	132	TOEFL	550		1/15	40
DeVry University: Columbus	.Pr/AB	3,369		TOEFL	500		None	50
Edison State Community College	.Pu/A	3,019	5	TOEFL	500		None	20
ETI Technical College of Niles	.Pr/A	270						50
Fortis College: Cuyahoga	.Pr/A							55
Franciscan University of Steubenville	.Pr/AB			TOEFL	550	653	5/1	20
Franklin University	.Pr/AB	6,962	145	TOEFL	450		7/12	40
Gallipolis Career College	.Pr/A	164						50
God's Bible School and College	.Pr/AB			TOEFL, SAT	450		8/1	50
Heidelberg University.	.Pr/B	1,223	20	TOEFL	550		6/1	25
Hiram College	.Pr/B	1,349	83	TOEFL, SAT/ACT	550	598	3/15	35
Hocking College	.Pu/A						None	50
Hondros College	.Pr/A	880						25
International College of Broadcasting.	.Pr/A							100
ITT Technical Institute: Hilliard	.Pr/AB							
James A. Rhodes State College	.Pu/A	3,969		TOEFL	550		None	25
John Carroll University.	.Pr/B	2,935		TOEFL	550		2/1	
Kaplan College: Dayton	.Pr/A	656		TOEFL	477		None	20
Kent State University	.Pu/B	20,577	604	TOEFL	525		None	30
Kent State University: Geauga	.Pu/A	2,054	7	TOEFL, SAT/ACT	525		3/15	30
Kenyon College.	.Pr/B	1,618	62	TOEFL, SAT/ACT	600		1/15	50
Kettering College of Medical Arts.	.Pr/AB			TOEFL	550		1/31	25
Lake Erie College	.Pr/B	1,000		TOEFL	550		None	50
Lakeland Community College	.Pu/A	9,866		TOEFL	500		8/1	15
Lorain County Community College	.Pu/A			TOEFL	500		None	
Lourdes College	.Pr/AB	1,992	1	TOEFL	500		8/1	25
Malone University	.Pr/B	1,996	28	TOEFL	550		7/1	20
Marietta College	.Pr/AB	1,438	166	TOEFL	550		5/1	50
Miami University: Hamilton	.Pu/AB			TOEFL	530		None	35
Miami University: Middletown.	.Pu/AB	2,804						35
Miami University: Oxford	.Pu/AB	14,741		TOEFL, SAT/ACT	533		2/1	70
Mount Vernon Nazarene University.	.Pr/AB	1,835	8	TOEFL, SAT/ACT		550	5/1	25
Muskingum University	.Pr/B	1,679	41	TOEFL	550		6/1	
National College: Cincinnati	.Pr/A							30
National College: Columbus	.Pr/A							30
National College: Dayton	.Pr/A							30
National College: Stow	.Pr/A							30
National College: Youngstown	.Pr/A							30
North Central State College	.Pu/A			TOEFL	500		None	
Notre Dame College.	.Pr/AB			TOEFL	550	600	7/1	30
Oberlin College.	.Pr/B	2,948	177	TOEFL, SAT/ACT	600	630	1/15	35
Ohio College of Massotherapy	.Pr/A	121						25
Ohio Dominican University	.Pr/AB	1,781	16	TOEFL	550		6/1	25

Student services			Housing		Academic year costs		Maximum credits/ summer	Credit hour charge	International financial aid			
Adviser	Orien-tation	ESL	Academic year	Summer	Tuition/ fees	Living costs			Avail-able	Number receiving aid	Average award	Deadline
Yes		Yes	Yes	Yes	12,220†	8,198	18		Yes			None
					14,820†							
Yes	Yes		Yes	Yes	13,780†	6,710	9	425	Yes	9	$11,756	None
Yes		Yes	No		8,514‡		18	172				
Yes			No		6,930†	5,000	17	142				
Yes	Yes		Yes		33,882‡	11,366		1325	Yes	9	$7,611	None
			No		3,770‡							
Yes		Yes	Yes		38,901†	11,104		1500	Yes	42	$20,941	None
Yes	Yes	Yes	Yes	Yes	11,437†	10,250	18	426	Yes	53	$12,965	None
Yes			Yes	Yes	24,400	7,632	9	485	Yes			None
Yes	Yes		Yes	Yes	38,290	9,310			Yes			None
Yes	Yes		Yes		26,112	7,746	18	1088	Yes	56	$10,298	3/1
Yes	Yes	Yes	No		9,500†	7,690	18	210	Yes			None
Yes	Yes	Yes			6,869†	2,276	16	221	Yes	48	$6,531	None
Yes	Yes		Yes	Yes	24,320†	8,120	12	360	Yes			None
Yes	Yes		Yes		40,200	9,960		1230	Yes			None
Yes					14,826†							
Yes			No		6,900†		6	230				
					8,038†			258				
Yes	Yes		Yes	Yes	20,320†	7,500	15	665	Yes			None
Yes	Yes	Yes			9,900‡		18	330	Yes			None
			No		9,650†			200				
Yes			Yes	Yes	6,560	3,650		210	Yes			None
Yes	Yes		Yes	Yes	22,780†	9,636	16		Yes			None
Yes	Yes	Yes	Yes	Yes	28,950	9,460	12		Yes			None
Yes	Yes	Yes	Yes	Yes	7,590†	6,915	18	172	Yes			None
			No		10,881†			210				
Yes					8,627†		21	192				
Yes	Yes		Yes	Yes	31,710	9,150	21	935	Yes			3/15
			No				12					
Yes	Yes	Yes	Yes	Yes	16,990†	8,416	12	773	Yes	81	$17,310	None
			No		13,070†	3,840	12	595				
Yes	Yes		Yes	Yes	42,630	10,020			Yes	61	$35,836	2/15
Yes			Yes	Yes	11,460	5,938	13	382	Yes			None
Yes	Yes		Yes		25,674†	10,192	6		Yes			None
Yes	Yes				7,598†	6,911	12	241	Yes			3/1
Yes		Yes	No		6,251†	3,450	18	235	Yes			None
Yes			Yes		16,470	7,800		484				
Yes			Yes	Yes	23,420‡	8,088	18	425	Yes	27	$19,710	7/31
Yes	Yes	Yes	Yes	Yes	28,340†	8,440	11		Yes	109	$6,645	4/15
Yes		Yes			16,992†							
			No		16,992†				Yes			None
Yes	Yes		Yes	Yes	27,576†	9,786	12		Yes	274	$6,329	None
Yes			Yes	Yes	22,280‡	6,630	8	787	Yes	7	$20,790	None
Yes	Yes	Yes	Yes		20,946†	8,660	12	425	Yes			8/1
					10,800†			239				
					10,800†			239				
					10,800†			239				
					10,800†			239				
					10,800†			239				
			No		7,785†	4,758	18	159	Yes			None
Yes			Yes		23,630†	7,820	12	475	Yes			5/1
Yes	Yes		Yes		41,577†	11,010		1710	Yes	161	$30,269	2/1
Yes	Yes		Yes	Yes	25,280†	8,322	16	501	Yes			None

† Tuition and fees are for 2010-11.   ‡ Tuition/fees projected for 2011-12.   * Includes room and board

Institution	Control/ degrees	Undergraduates Total	Internat'l	Tests required (Fall 2011)	TOEFL minimum	average	Application Deadline	Fee
Ohio Northern University	Pr/B	2,313	57	TOEFL	550		7/15	30
Ohio State University: Columbus Campus.........	Pu/AB	40,851	2,114	TOEFL, SAT/ACT	527		2/1	50
Ohio Technical College...................	Pr/A	1,350						100
Ohio University.........................	Pu/AB	20,298	740		550		2/1	45
Ohio University: Eastern Campus	Pu/AB	960		TOEFL				20
Ohio University: Southern Campus at Ironton	Pu/AB	2,528		TOEFL, SAT/ACT				20
Ohio University: Zanesville Campus	Pu/AB	1,877	3					20
Ohio Wesleyan University..................	Pr/B	1,911	176	TOEFL, SAT/ACT	550	608	3/1	35
Otterbein University	Pr/B			TOEFL	523	530	7/1	30
Owens Community College: Toledo	Pu/A	14,608		TOEFL	500		None	
PowerSport Institute.....................	Pr/A							
Remington College: Cleveland	Pr/A	461					None	50
Shawnee State University	Pu/AB	4,297	33	TOEFL	500	525	6/30	65
Sinclair Community College	Pu/A	21,514	96	TOEFL	520		7/12	20
Southwestern College: Tri-County............	Pr/A							100
Stark State College of Technology	Pu/A	14,834		TOEFL	500	505	6/1	65
Temple Baptist College...................	Pr/B							25
Tiffin University	Pr/AB	3,651	88	TOEFL	550		None	20
Tri-State Bible College...................	Pr/AB	60						25
Union Institute & University	Pr/B	968		TOEFL			None	
University of Akron......................	Pu/AB	21,043	231	TOEFL	500		5/1	50
University of Akron: Wayne College...........	Pu/A	2,061						30
University of Cincinnati	Pu/AB	22,007	478	TOEFL	515		8/11	50
University of Cincinnati: Clermont College......	Pu/A	3,559	12	TOEFL	515		None	50
University of Cincinnati: Raymond Walters College	Pu/AB	5,084		TOEFL	515		None	35
University of Dayton	Pr/B	7,465	117	TOEFL	523		5/1	50
University of Findlay	Pr/AB	3,027	178	TOEFL	500		None	
University of Mount Union	Pr/B	2,185	50	TOEFL		550	None	
University of Northwestern Ohio	Pr/AB			TOEFL	500	550	None	50
University of Phoenix: Cincinnati	Pr/B	95						
University of Phoenix: Cleveland	Pr/B	515						
University of Phoenix: Columbus Ohio	Pr/B	172						
University of Rio Grande	Pr/AB	1,546	18	TOEFL	400	600	None	25
University of Toledo	Pu/AB	17,626	585	TOEFL	500		7/1	40
Urbana University	Pr/AB			TOEFL	500	525	6/15	100
Ursuline College	Pr/B	1,017	7	TOEFL	500		6/1	25
Walsh University........................	Pr/AB	2,221	20	TOEFL	500		None	25
Wilberforce University	Pr/B			TOEFL	500		6/1	20
Wilmington College......................	Pr/B	1,345	15	TOEFL	500		6/1	25
Wittenberg University....................	Pr/B	1,703		TOEFL	550	580	4/15	40
Wright State University...................	Pu/AB	13,874	154	TOEFL, SAT/ACT	500	530	5/10	30
Wright State University: Lake Campus..........	Pu/AB	988	1	TOEFL	500	530	5/10	30
Xavier University	Pr/AB	4,186	42	TOEFL, SAT/ACT	530	673	2/15	35
Youngstown State University................	Pu/AB	13,536	78	TOEFL	500		3/1	30
Oklahoma								
Bacone College.........................	Pr/AB			TOEFL, SAT/ACT	500	550	None	25
Cameron University......................	Pu/AB	5,523	297	TOEFL	500	594	6/15	35
Carl Albert State College	Pu/A			TOEFL, ACT	500		None	
East Central University...................	Pu/B	3,952	140	TOEFL, SAT/ACT	500		7/15	50
Eastern Oklahoma State College..............	Pu/A	2,084		TOEFL, ACT	500	510	None	25
Family of Faith College	Pr/B	24						25
Hillsdale Free Will Baptist College	Pr/AB							20
ITT Technical Institute: Tulsa	Pr/AB							
Langston University......................	Pu/AB	2,203	47	TOEFL, ACT	500		7/1	25
Northeastern Oklahoma Agricultural and Mechanical College	Pu/A	2,134		TOEFL	500		6/20	
Northeastern State University...............	Pu/B	8,362	196	TOEFL	500		8/1	25

Student services			Housing		Academic year costs		Maximum credits/summer	Credit hour charge	International financial aid			
Adviser	Orientation	ESL	Academic year	Summer	Tuition/fees	Living costs			Available	Number receiving aid	Average award	Deadline
Yes	Yes	Yes	Yes	Yes	34,380‡	9,476	16		Yes			None
Yes	Yes	Yes	Yes	Yes	23,604†	9,180			Yes	517	$6,731	None
Yes	Yes	Yes	Yes	Yes	18,567†	9,621		599	Yes	135	$2,744	4/1
					5,781†		20	172	Yes			None
Yes			No		5,781†			174	Yes			None
			No		8,985†		20	292				
Yes	Yes		Yes	Yes	37,820	13,404	2		Yes			5/1
Yes	Yes		Yes	Yes	28,413†	7,887	15		Yes			None
Yes	Yes	Yes	No		5,860†			255	Yes			
			No									
Yes	Yes	Yes	Yes	Yes	11,190†	8,416	20	424	Yes			None
Yes		Yes	No		7,030†	5,385	19	153	Yes			8/1
Yes					6,323†	8,494		211				
Yes	Yes		Yes	Yes	19,124‡	9,000	9	637	Yes	88	$8,078	None
					5,710†							
Yes			No		14,310			473	Yes			None
Yes	Yes	Yes	Yes	Yes	16,903†	9,160		641	Yes	24	$6,956	None
					11,939†		9	491	Yes			3/15
Yes	Yes	Yes	Yes	Yes	24,588†	9,702	19		Yes			None
Yes			No		11,715†	2,981		305	Yes			None
Yes			No		13,833†	9,240		364				
Yes	Yes	Yes	Yes	Yes	31,640	9,950	18	1011	Yes	82	$11,641	None
Yes	Yes	Yes	Yes	Yes	28,104	9,074	9	605	Yes			9/1
Yes	Yes	Yes	Yes	Yes	25,700	8,150	12	1065	Yes			None
Yes			Yes	Yes			19		Yes			None
					11,880†							
					11,880†							
					11,800†							
Yes	Yes		Yes	Yes	18,808†	7,828	15		Yes			None
Yes	Yes	Yes	Yes	Yes	17,749†	8,814	21	684	Yes	419	$10,979	None
			Yes		21,725‡	8,120	18	445	Yes			4/15
			Yes	Yes	23,940†	7,970	12	790	Yes	4	$10,507	None
Yes	Yes	Yes	Yes	Yes	23,550	8,640	12	745	Yes	20	$16,843	None
Yes			Yes		12,470†	9,130		469	Yes			6/1
Yes			Yes	Yes	25,714†	8,520	18		Yes			6/1
Yes	Yes		Yes	Yes	36,434	10,794	15	1196	Yes	28	$24,393	None
Yes	Yes	Yes	Yes	Yes	15,213†	8,020		459				
Yes	Yes		No		12,549†		18	382				
Yes	Yes	Yes	Yes	Yes	31,160	10,130	12	590	Yes	29	$12,434	
Yes	Yes	Yes	Yes	Yes	12,872†	7,600			Yes			None
	Yes		Yes	Yes	12,300†	7,700	9	450	Yes			None
Yes	Yes		Yes	Yes	10,552†	3,668	9	306				
Yes			Yes		5,370†	3,722	9	152				
Yes	Yes		Yes	Yes	10,798†	4,480	10	318	Yes			3/1
			Yes		6,608†	4,268	9	194				
			Yes		5,310†	1,600		165				
			Yes		10,020†	5,500						
Yes			Yes		9,833†	7,190		288				
Yes	Yes		Yes	Yes	6,812†	4,494	9	196	Yes			None
Yes	Yes	Yes	Yes	Yes	10,747†*	5,194	12	323	Yes	63	$2,851	None

† Tuition and fees are for 2010-11. ‡ Tuition and fees projected for 2011-12. * Includes room and board

Institution	Control/ degrees	Undergraduates		Tests required (Fall 2011)	TOEFL		Application	
		Total	Internat'l		minimum	average	Deadline	Fee
Northern Oklahoma College.................	Pu/A	5,228		TOEFL	500	520	None	25
Northwestern Oklahoma State University	Pu/B	2,008	44	TOEFL	500		6/10	15
Oklahoma Baptist University	Pr/AB	1,498	48	TOEFL	500	525	4/15	
Oklahoma Christian University................	Pr/B	1,899	145	TOEFL	500	510	8/1	25
Oklahoma City Community College	Pu/A	14,146		TOEFL	500	515	7/19	25
Oklahoma City University....................	Pr/B	2,314	394	TOEFL	550		None	70
Oklahoma Panhandle State University	Pu/AB	1,286	40	TOEFL, SAT, SAT Subject Test(s), or ACT	500	571	None	
Oklahoma State University	Pu/B	17,985	457	TOEFL	500	538	5/15	75
Oklahoma State University Institute of Technology: Okmulgee	Pu/AB	3,360		TOEFL	500		None	15
Oklahoma State University: Oklahoma City	Pu/AB			TOEFL	500	510	None	15
Oklahoma Wesleyan University	Pr/AB	1,034		TOEFL, SAT/ACT	500	550	None	25
Oral Roberts University	Pr/B	2,645		TOEFL, SAT/ACT	500	521	7/1	35
Platt College: Moore	Pr/A							
Platt College: Oklahoma City Central	Pr/A	250						100
Platt College: Tulsa	Pr/AB	435						100
Redlands Community College	Pu/A	2,319		TOEFL	500		None	25
Rogers State University.....................	Pu/AB	4,337	33	TOEFL			None	
Rose State College........................	Pu/A	8,346	7	TOEFL	500		None	
St. Gregory's University	Pr/AB	692		TOEFL	500	540	None	40
Southeastern Oklahoma State University.........	Pu/B	3,748	87	TOEFL	500	538	6/15	55
Southern Nazarene University	Pr/AB	1,625		TOEFL	500	510	7/1	25
Southwestern Christian University.............	Pr/AB			TOEFL	500		None	200
Southwestern Oklahoma State University	Pu/AB	4,566		TOEFL, SAT/ACT	500	515	8/8	15
Spartan College of Aeronautics and Technology.........................	Pr/AB	1,033		TOEFL	500	515	None	100
Tulsa Community College....................	Pu/A	15,502		TOEFL	500	520	None	15
Tulsa Welding School......................	Pr/A	1,862					None	
University of Central Oklahoma...............	Pu/AB	15,049	816	TOEFL, SAT/ACT	500		6/1	25
University of Oklahoma	Pu/B	20,498	492	TOEFL	550		4/1	90
University of Phoenix: Oklahoma City..........	Pr/B	777						
University of Phoenix: Tulsa	Pr/B	703						
University of Science and Arts of Oklahoma......	Pu/B	998	50	TOEFL, SAT	500	505	9/1	25
University of Tulsa	Pr/B	3,059	480	TOEFL	500	568	7/15	35
Vatterott College: Oklahoma City	Pr/A	410						
Vatterott College: Tulsa	Pr/A	325						
Western Oklahoma State College	Pu/A	3,820		TOEFL	500		None	15

Oregon

Institution	Control/ degrees	Total	Internat'l	Tests required (Fall 2011)	minimum	average	Deadline	Fee
Art Institute of Portland	Pr/AB	1,925		TOEFL	500		None	50
Chemeketa Community College	Pu/A	9,973		TOEFL				
Clackamas Community College	Pu/A	11,164					8/26	50
Clatsop Community College	Pu/A	2,836		TOEFL	520		8/1	150
Concordia University	Pr/AB	1,220	7	TOEFL	525		7/1	50
Corban College..........................	Pr/AB	874	8	TOEFL, SAT, SAT Subject Test(s), or ACT	500		6/1	35
Eastern Oregon University...................	Pu/AB	3,377	38	TOEFL	520		8/15	50
Everest College: Portland	Pr/A	737						
George Fox University	Pr/B	2,107	134	TOEFL	550		7/1	40
Gutenberg College........................	Pr/B	26						40
Heald College: Portland	Pr/A	430						
ITT Technical Institute: Portland..............	Pr/AB			TOEFL	500			100
Lane Community College	Pu/A	12,691		TOEFL	480	490	8/1	
Lewis & Clark College.....................	Pr/B	1,917	115	TOEFL	575		8/1	50
Linfield College	Pr/B	1,684	63	TOEFL	550		None	
Linn-Benton Community College	Pu/A	6,771	23	TOEFL	500		8/5	100
Marylhurst University......................	Pr/B	869	15	TOEFL	550		None	50
Mount Angel Seminary.....................	Pr/B	100		TOEFL	475		6/15	27

Student services			Housing		Academic year costs		Maximum credits/ summer	Credit hour charge	International financial aid			
Adviser	Orientation	ESL	Academic year	Summer	Tuition/ fees	Living costs			Available	Number receiving aid	Average award	Deadline
Yes			Yes	Yes	6,133†	4,120	10	181	Yes			None
Yes			Yes	Yes	10,141†	3,800		317	Yes			None
Yes	Yes	Yes	Yes	Yes	19,756	7,000	12		Yes			None
Yes	Yes	Yes	Yes	Yes	18,456	6,825	12	692	Yes	115	$10,188	8/31
Yes	Yes	Yes	No		7,087†	8,258	12	213	Yes			None
Yes	Yes	Yes	Yes	Yes	28,190	9,170	12	840	Yes			6/30
Yes		Yes	Yes	Yes	11,463†	3,502	9	280	Yes			None
Yes	Yes	Yes	Yes	Yes	17,912†	6,627		498	Yes	70	$5,329	None
Yes			Yes	Yes	9,105†	5,376	21	272				
Yes			No		8,113†		9	249	Yes			None
Yes			Yes		19,200†	6,546	12	755	Yes	920	$4,280	None
Yes	Yes	Yes	Yes	Yes	20,044†	8,304	16	810	Yes			None
			No		15,100†							
			No		15,100†							
Yes			Yes		5,280†	5,870	6	176				
Yes			Yes	Yes	10,270†	7,095	9	288				
Yes			No		7,984†	5,626	9	246				
Yes	Yes	Yes	Yes	Yes	17,516†	6,780	12	548	Yes			None
			Yes		11,379†	4,900	12	353	Yes	44	$7,653	None
Yes			Yes		19,794‡	7,900	9		Yes			None
Yes			Yes		10,700†	4,800	6	350				
Yes			Yes	Yes	10,050†	4,500	10	304				
Yes			Yes		15,000‡	3,510						
Yes			No		7,741†	8,798	9	230	Yes			None
									Yes			None
Yes			Yes		11,242†	6,301	12	357				
Yes	Yes	Yes	Yes	Yes	18,295†	7,826		470	Yes	8	$3,949	
					10,200†							
					10,200†							
Yes	Yes		Yes	Yes	11,155†	5,140	20	332	Yes	48	$9,654	None
Yes	Yes	Yes	Yes	Yes	31,126	9,464	12		Yes	127	$4,990	None
			No									
			Yes	Yes	6,431†	3,750	12	180	Yes			None
Yes	Yes		Yes		21,695†	9,519	18	481	Yes			None
Yes	Yes	Yes	No		10,980†			235				
Yes	Yes	Yes	No		10,080†		18	219	Yes			None
			No		11,790†			256				
Yes	Yes	Yes	Yes	Yes	24,400†	7,100	12	750				
Yes			Yes	Yes	25,405	7,980		1040	Yes			None
Yes	Yes		Yes	Yes	6,639†	8,227			Yes	11	$1,009	None
Yes	Yes	Yes	Yes		29,380	9,050		880	Yes	132	$8,950	None
			Yes		11,853†							
					9,735†	10,152						
			No									
Yes	Yes	Yes	No		10,066†		18	213	Yes			2/15
Yes	Yes	Yes	Yes	Yes	36,632†	9,648	20	1832	Yes	86	$25,597	None
Yes	Yes	Yes	Yes	Yes	32,416	9,090	20	1000	Yes			None
Yes	Yes	Yes	No		10,350†	8,367	20	230				
Yes	Yes	Yes	No		17,730†	12,900	15	394				
		Yes	Yes		14,562‡	10,148		463				

† Tuition and fees are for 2010-11.   ‡ Tuition and fees projected for 2011-12.   * Includes room and board

Institution	Control/ degrees	Undergraduates		Tests required (Fall 2011)	TOEFL		Application	
		Total	Internat'l		minimum	average	Deadline	Fee
Mt. Hood Community College	Pu/A			TOEFL	500		8/1	25
Northwest Christian University.	Pr/AB	475		TOEFL	500		6/1	
Oregon College of Art & Craft.	Pr/B	127		TOEFL	550		None	35
Oregon Health & Science University	Pu/B	736	7	TOEFL	560		1/15	120
Oregon Institute of Technology	Pu/AB	3,758		TOEFL, SAT/ACT	520		None	50
Oregon State University	Pu/B	18,466	564	TOEFL, SAT/ACT	527		6/15	50
Pacific Northwest College of Art	Pr/B	582	2	TOEFL	550		7/1	35
Pacific University	Pr/B	1,605	51	TOEFL	550	570	7/15	40
Portland Community College	Pu/A	32,056					7/15	50
Portland State University.	Pu/B	19,531	995	TOEFL	525	550	3/1	50
Reed College	Pr/B	1,418	76	TOEFL, SAT Subject Test(s)	600		1/15	50
Rogue Community College	Pu/A	4,648	1	TOEFL	490		8/20	
Southern Oregon University.	Pu/B	4,492	84	TOEFL	520	553	None	50
Southwestern Oregon Community College	Pu/A			TOEFL	450	480	None	30
Treasure Valley Community College	Pu/A	2,500		TOEFL	500		7/30	
Umpqua Community College	Pu/A	2,418		TOEFL	500	505	None	50
University of Oregon	Pu/B	19,219	1,344	TOEFL	500	507	2/15	50
University of Phoenix: Oregon	Pr/B	1,013						
University of Portland.	Pr/B	3,259	83	TOEFL	525		3/1	50
Warner Pacific College.	Pr/AB	1,359		TOEFL	525			50
Western Oregon University	Pu/AB	5,154	268	TOEFL	500	520	None	50
Willamette University.	Pr/B	1,800	16	TOEFL	560	590	2/1	50

Pennsylvania

Institution	Control/ degrees	Undergraduates		Tests required (Fall 2011)	TOEFL		Application	
		Total	Internat'l		minimum	average	Deadline	Fee
Albright College	Pr/B	2,309	101	TOEFL	520	572	6/1	25
Allegheny College.	Pr/B	2,123	31	TOEFL, SAT/ACT	550		2/15	35
Alvernia University	Pr/AB	2,052	5	TOEFL			None	25
Arcadia University.	Pr/B	2,160	23	TOEFL	530		3/1	30
Art Institute of Pittsburgh	Pr/AB	2,765		TOEFL	490		None	50
Baptist Bible College of Pennsylvania	Pr/AB	609		TOEFL, SAT/ACT	500		2/28	30
Bidwell Training Center	Pr/A							
Bloomsburg University of Pennsylvania	Pu/B	8,877	79	TOEFL	500	550	3/1	60
Bryn Mawr College	Pr/B	1,287	159	TOEFL, SAT, SAT Subject Test(s), or ACT	600	634	1/15	50
Bucknell University	Pr/B	3,487	144	TOEFL, SAT/ACT	550	607	1/15	60
Bucks County Community College	Pu/A			TOEFL	550		5/1	30
Cabrini College.	Pr/B	1,390	4	TOEFL	550		None	35
California University of Pennsylvania	Pu/AB	7,419		TOEFL	450	510	6/1	35
Cambria-Rowe Business College: Indiana	Pr/A	122					9/1	15
Carlow University	Pr/B	1,429	4	TOEFL	500		None	20
Carnegie Mellon University.	Pr/B	6,020	940	TOEFL, SAT/ACT	600		1/1	70
Cedar Crest College.	Pr/B	1,444	6	TOEFL	500		None	
Central Pennsylvania College.	Pr/AB	1,433	1	TOEFL	550		None	20
Chatham University	Pr/B	751	59	TOEFL	580		None	35
Chestnut Hill College.	Pr/AB	1,574	49	TOEFL	550		7/15	35
Cheyney University of Pennsylvania	Pu/B	1,519		TOEFL, SAT	500		6/15	20
Clarion University of Pennsylvania	Pu/AB	6,160	31	TOEFL	500		7/15	30
Community College of Allegheny County.	Pu/A	19,466					6/1	
Community College of Beaver County.	Pu/A	2,779		TOEFL	450		6/15	
Community College of Philadelphia.	Pu/A	19,506						20
Curtis Institute of Music	Pr/B	122	47	TOEFL, SAT	550		12/12	150
Delaware County Community College	Pu/A	12,705					None	25
DeSales University.	Pr/B	2,366		TOEFL	550	600	5/1	30
DeVry University: Fort Washington.	Pr/AB			TOEFL	500			50
Dickinson College	Pr/B	2,368	164	TOEFL	600		2/1	65
Douglas Education Center	Pr/A			TOEFL	400			50
Drexel University	Pr/AB	13,652	1,038		550		3/1	75
Duquesne University	Pr/B	5,705	135		575		None	50

Student services			Housing		Academic year costs		Maximum credits/ summer	Credit hour charge	International financial aid			
Adviser	Orien- tation	ESL	Academic year	Summer	Tuition/ fees	Living costs			Avail- able	Number receiving aid	Average award	Deadline
Yes			No		11,269 †	6,966	16	241	Yes			None
Yes			Yes	Yes	23,600	7,400		787	Yes			None
			Yes		22,782 †							
Yes	Yes		No		30,606 †	9,900		547	Yes	2	$16,500	None
Yes	Yes		Yes	Yes	20,400 †	8,145	18		Yes			None
Yes	Yes	Yes	Yes	Yes	20,435 †	10,311	19		Yes	13	$951	5/1
Yes	Yes		Yes	Yes	26,926 †		6	1079	Yes			None
Yes	Yes	Yes	Yes		33,612	9,208	9	1368	Yes	36	$8,102	None
Yes	Yes	Yes	No		9,516 †		9	204	Yes			None
Yes	Yes	Yes	Yes	Yes	21,642 †	9,300	21		Yes	70	$4,037	None
Yes	Yes		Yes	Yes	42,800	11,950		1813	Yes	49	$45,234	2/1
Yes		Yes	No		11,625 †	7,164	15	251				
Yes	Yes		Yes	Yes	20,430 †	9,336	18		Yes			None
Yes	Yes	Yes	Yes	Yes	11,040 †	5,735	18		Yes			3/1
Yes			Yes	Yes	6,660 ‡	6,680		134				
Yes			No		9,075 †			191				
Yes	Yes	Yes	Yes	Yes	25,830 †	9,429		546	Yes	163	$7,343	None
					11,040 †							
Yes	Yes	Yes	Yes	Yes	33,780	9,965	9	1055	Yes	48	$22,212	None
Yes	Yes		Yes	Yes	17,604 †	6,980			Yes	2	$6,125	8/30
Yes	Yes	Yes	Yes	Yes	18,981 †	8,370	12		Yes			None
Yes	Yes		Yes		39,012	9,350			Yes	8	$14,187	None
Yes	Yes	Yes	Yes	Yes	33,990	9,200	8	1038	Yes			None
Yes	Yes		Yes	Yes	36,190	9,160		1494	Yes	31	$17,128	None
			Yes		25,480 †	9,420	12	690	Yes			None
Yes	Yes		Yes		34,150 ‡	13,040	16	560	Yes			None
Yes	Yes		Yes	Yes	22,015 †	9,407	15	487	Yes			None
			Yes		18,240	6,650	6	598	Yes			5/1
			No									
Yes		Yes	Yes	Yes	16,162 †	6,890	12	605	Yes	43	$8,017	None
Yes	Yes		Yes	Yes	40,824	12,890	8		Yes	111	$32,694	3/1
Yes	Yes		Yes	Yes	43,866	11,947	8	1198	Yes	24	$39,547	1/15
Yes	Yes	Yes	No		10,304 †		12	315				
Yes	Yes		Yes	Yes	32,084 †	12,400	12		Yes	1	$32,084	4/1
Yes	Yes		Yes	Yes	17,018 †	9,826	12	387	Yes			None
			No		10,725 †			270				
Yes	Yes		Yes		23,504	9,256	18	738	Yes			None
Yes	Yes		Yes	Yes	43,812	11,110		599				
Yes	Yes		Yes	Yes	28,967 †	9,540	12	952	Yes	1	$5,000	
			Yes	Yes	17,820 †	6,480		380	Yes			None
Yes	Yes	Yes	Yes	Yes	30,312	9,318	12	709	Yes			None
Yes	Yes	Yes	Yes	Yes	29,200	9,340	12	620	Yes	18	$22,069	None
Yes			Yes		16,542 †	8,038		605	Yes			None
Yes	Yes		Yes	Yes	16,427 †	6,666	19	605	Yes			4/15
Yes	Yes	Yes	No		7,486 †	6,293		256	Yes			None
			No		9,045 †		15	278				
Yes	Yes	Yes	No		12,480 †		12	384				
Yes	Yes	Yes				14,940			Yes			3/1
Yes	Yes		Yes	Yes	8,790 †							
Yes			Yes		29,000	10,520	15	1170				
Yes					14,826 †							
Yes	Yes	Yes	Yes		43,085	10,800	8	1333	Yes	143	$33,018	2/1
Yes			Yes									
Yes	Yes	Yes	Yes	Yes	34,405	13,395		890	Yes			3/1
Yes	Yes	Yes	Yes	Yes	28,671	12,806	12	861	Yes	66	$15,176	5/1

† Tuition and fees are for 2010-11.   ‡ Tuition and fees projected for 2011-12.   * Includes room and board

Institution	Control/ degrees	Undergraduates Total	Internat'l	Tests required (Fall 2011)	TOEFL minimum	TOEFL average	Application Deadline	Fee
East Stroudsburg University of Pennsylvania	Pu/AB	6,274	51	TOEFL	550		3/1	50
Eastern University	Pr/AB	2,688	51	TOEFL	500		None	25
Edinboro University of Pennsylvania	Pu/AB	6,587	54	TOEFL	500		7/1	30
Elizabethtown College	Pr/AB	2,295	48	TOEFL	525	565	5/1	30
Erie Business Center	Pr/A							25
Erie Business Center South	Pr/A							25
Everest Institute: Pittsburgh	Pr/A	762						
Franklin & Marshall College	Pr/B	2,285	197	TOEFL, SAT/ACT	600		2/1	60
Gannon University	Pr/AB	2,586	87	TOEFL			6/1	25
Geneva College	Pr/AB	1,445		TOEFL	550		None	40
Gettysburg College	Pr/B	2,472		TOEFL, SAT/ACT	570		2/1	55
Gratz College	Pr/B			TOEFL	450	500	None	50
Grove City College	Pr/B	2,482	14	TOEFL, SAT/ACT	550	600	2/1	50
Gwynedd-Mercy College	Pr/AB	2,187	7	TOEFL, SAT/ACT	525		7/9	50
Harcum College	Pr/A			TOEFL	500		8/1	25
Harrisburg Area Community College	Pu/A	14,376	256				6/15	35
Haverford College	Pr/B	1,177	31	TOEFL, SAT, SAT Subject Test(s), or ACT	600		1/15	60
Holy Family University	Pr/AB	2,054	12	TOEFL, SAT	550	582	7/1	25
Immaculata University	Pr/AB	2,931	23	TOEFL, SAT/ACT	550		8/15	35
Indiana University of Pennsylvania	Pu/AB	12,433	165	TOEFL	500		6/15	35
ITT Technical Institute: Bensalem	Pr/A			TOEFL				
ITT Technical Institute: King of Prussia	Pr/A			TOEFL				
JNA Institute of Culinary Arts	Pr/A	80					None	
Johnson College	Pr/A	467		TOEFL			8/1	30
Juniata College	Pr/B	1,475	70	TOEFL	550		3/15	30
Keystone College	Pr/AB	1,685	9	TOEFL	550		6/1	30
Keystone Technical Institute	Pr/A						None	20
King's College	Pr/AB	2,073	6	TOEFL	530	550	6/1	30
Kutztown University of Pennsylvania	Pu/B	9,325	65	TOEFL	550		None	35
La Roche College	Pr/AB	1,230	131				None	50
La Salle University	Pr/AB	4,246	36	TOEFL	500	550	4/15	35
Lackawanna College	Pr/A	1,381		TOEFL	450		6/30	30
Lafayette College	Pr/B	2,375	141	TOEFL, SAT/ACT	550	625	1/1	65
Lansdale School of Business	Pr/A	575						30
Laurel Business Institute	Pr/A	300					None	55
Laurel Technical Institute	Pr/A	293					None	50
Lebanon Valley College	Pr/AB	1,680	2	TOEFL	550		3/15	30
Lehigh University	Pr/B	4,766	215	TOEFL, SAT/ACT	570		1/1	70
Lincoln University	Pu/B	1,796	37	TOEFL, SAT/ACT	550		6/1	20
Lock Haven University of Pennsylvania	Pu/AB	4,973	36	TOEFL	550		3/1	100
Lycoming College	Pr/B	1,288	21	TOEFL, SAT/ACT	500	570	4/1	35
Manor College	Pr/A	751		TOEFL	480	530	8/15	25
Mansfield University of Pennsylvania	Pu/AB	2,887	27	TOEFL	550		6/15	25
Marywood University	Pr/B	2,203	15	TOEFL	530		6/1	35
McCann School of Business and Technology: Dickson City	Pr/A							40
McCann School of Business and Technology: Pottsville	Pr/A							40
McCann School of Business and Technology: Sunbury	Pr/A							40
Mercyhurst College	Pr/AB	3,901	178	TOEFL	550	560	7/1	30
Messiah College	Pr/B	2,757	80	TOEFL, SAT/ACT	550		6/10	30
Metropolitan Career Center Computer Technology Institute	Pr/A							50
Millersville University of Pennsylvania	Pu/AB	7,498	25	TOEFL	500	579	None	50
Misericordia University	Pr/B	2,342		TOEFL	550		None	25
Montgomery County Community College	Pu/A	13,919	292				7/1	25
Moore College of Art and Design	Pr/B	499	15	TOEFL, SAT/ACT	527		None	60

	Student services			Housing		Academic year costs		Maximum credits/ summer	Credit hour charge	International financial aid			
Adviser	Orien- tation	ESL	Academic year	Summer	Tuition/ fees	Living costs			Avail- able	Number receiving aid	Average award	Deadline
Yes	Yes		Yes	Yes	16,484 †	6,658	15	605	Yes			3/1
Yes	Yes		Yes	Yes	25,850	11,330	12	540	Yes			None
Yes	Yes		Yes	Yes	10,632 †	7,820	12	363	Yes	49	$4,680	5/1
Yes	Yes	Yes	Yes	Yes	34,830	9,299	9	845	Yes			None
					11,680 †			353				
			No		6,540 †			199				
Yes	Yes		Yes	Yes	42,610	11,500	16		Yes	150	$35,924	2/15
Yes	Yes	Yes	Yes	Yes	25,522	10,230	12	775	Yes	52	$18,909	None
Yes	Yes	Yes	Yes	Yes	22,236 †	8,000		745	Yes			None
Yes	Yes		Yes	Yes	42,610	10,180			Yes	43	$48,908	2/15
Yes			No		14,920 †	10,750	12					
Yes	Yes		Yes		13,598	7,410			Yes	8	$6,867	4/15
			Yes		26,810 ‡	10,515	12					
Yes	Yes	Yes	Yes	Yes	19,820	8,400	12	630	Yes			5/1
Yes		Yes	No		8,925 †		12					
Yes	Yes		Yes	Yes	42,208	12,842			Yes	13	$41,876	2/1
Yes			Yes		23,520 †	10,400	12	490	Yes			None
Yes	Yes	Yes	Yes	Yes	28,850	11,460	12	455	Yes			4/15
Yes	Yes	Yes	Yes	Yes	16,277 †	9,300	12	605	Yes			None
			No									
			Yes		15,772 †	5,233						
Yes	Yes	Yes	Yes	Yes	34,090	9,330	8	1385	Yes	63	$15,645	3/1
Yes			Yes	Yes	19,620	9,200	12	400	Yes	4	$8,500	5/1
			No		14,780 †	15,250		328				
Yes		Yes	Yes	Yes	27,680	10,470	12	509	Yes			None
Yes	Yes	Yes	Yes	Yes	16,438 †	8,094	18	605	Yes	56	$9,036	None
Yes	Yes	Yes	Yes	Yes	23,160	9,182	15	575	Yes	66	$9,712	5/1
Yes	Yes	Yes	Yes	Yes	35,240	11,680	12		Yes	26	$21,668	None
Yes			Yes	Yes	11,770	7,400	6	395	Yes	1	$3,000	None
Yes	Yes		Yes	Yes	41,358	12,362	16	1075	Yes			3/1
			No									
			No		8,500 †	2,152	18	250				
			No			4,255	15					
Yes	Yes		Yes	Yes	31,620 †	8,365	15	510	Yes	2	$10,303	None
Yes	Yes	Yes	Yes	Yes	40,960	10,840	16	1695	Yes	58	$43,375	2/15
Yes	Yes		Yes		13,222 †	8,004	12	431	Yes			5/1
Yes		Yes	Yes	Yes	16,246 †	7,024		605	Yes			3/15
Yes	Yes		Yes	Yes	31,818	10,970	12	974	Yes	13	$18,615	None
Yes	Yes		Yes	Yes	13,816	5,972	18	299	Yes	2	$500	None
Yes		Yes	Yes	Yes	16,764 †	6,970	12	605	Yes			None
Yes	Yes	Yes	Yes	Yes	28,175	12,520	12	600	Yes			None
			No									
Yes	Yes		Yes	Yes	26,346 †	11,195	6	822	Yes			None
Yes	Yes		Yes	Yes	28,356	8,420	8	1147	Yes	55	$20,149	None
Yes	Yes		Yes	Yes	16,406 †	8,298	15	605	Yes			3/15
Yes			Yes	Yes	25,990	10,760	12	495	Yes			5/1
Yes	Yes	Yes	No		9,870 †		12	288				
Yes			Yes		31,626	11,823	18	1270	Yes			5/1

† Tuition and fees are for 2010-11. ‡ Tuition and fees projected for 2011-12. * Includes room and board

Institution	Control/ degrees	Undergraduates Total	Undergraduates Internat'l	Tests required (Fall 2011)	TOEFL minimum	TOEFL average	Application Deadline	Application Fee
Moravian College	Pr/B	1,599	11	TOEFL, SAT/ACT	550	553	3/1	40
Mount Aloysius College	Pr/AB	1,535	10	TOEFL, SAT/ACT	500		None	30
Muhlenberg College	Pr/AB	2,406	7	TOEFL	550	580	2/15	50
Neumann University	Pr/AB	2,524		TOEFL	550		None	35
Northampton Community College	Pu/A	11,081	104				7/1	25
Oakbridge Academy of Arts	Pr/A	63						50
Orleans Technical Institute	Pr/A	641						125
Pace Institute	Pr/A							10
Peirce College	Pr/AB	2,131	24				None	50
Penn State Abington	Pu/AB	3,007	39	TOEFL	550		2/1	50
Penn State Altoona	Pu/AB	4,000	47	TOEFL	550		2/1	50
Penn State Beaver	Pu/AB	716	2	TOEFL	550		2/1	50
Penn State Berks	Pu/AB	2,567	29	TOEFL	550		2/1	50
Penn State Brandywine	Pu/AB	1,407	4	TOEFL	550		2/1	50
Penn State DuBois	Pu/AB	757	2	TOEFL	550		2/1	50
Penn State Erie, The Behrend College	Pu/AB	4,056	69	TOEFL	550		2/1	50
Penn State Fayette, The Eberly Campus	Pu/AB	913	8	TOEFL	550		2/1	50
Penn State Greater Allegheny	Pu/AB	677	15	TOEFL	550		2/1	50
Penn State Harrisburg	Pu/AB	2,829	95	TOEFL	550		2/1	50
Penn State Hazleton	Pu/AB	1,254	10	TOEFL	550		2/1	50
Penn State Lehigh Valley	Pu/AB	759	1	TOEFL	550		2/1	50
Penn State Mont Alto	Pu/AB	1,125	5	TOEFL	550		2/1	50
Penn State New Kensington	Pu/AB	743	1	TOEFL	550		2/1	50
Penn State Schuylkill	Pu/AB	963	5	TOEFL	550		2/1	50
Penn State Shenango	Pu/AB	592	1	TOEFL	550		2/1	50
Penn State University Park	Pu/AB	37,830	2,038	TOEFL	550		2/1	50
Penn State Wilkes-Barre	Pu/AB	627	1	TOEFL	550		2/1	50
Penn State Worthington Scranton	Pu/AB	1,244	2	TOEFL	550		2/1	50
Penn State York	Pu/AB	1,131	45	TOEFL	550		2/1	50
Pennsylvania Academy of the Fine Arts	Pr/B							
Pennsylvania College of Technology	Pu/AB	6,201		TOEFL	520		6/1	50
Pennsylvania Highlands Community College	Pu/A	1,500		TOEFL				
Philadelphia Biblical University	Pr/B	997		TOEFL	520		5/31	25
Philadelphia University	Pr/AB	2,987	48	TOEFL, SAT/ACT	500		None	40
Pittsburgh Institute of Aeronautics	Pr/A	210	1	TOEFL	500	520	None	150
Pittsburgh Institute of Mortuary Science	Pr/A			TOEFL			None	40
Point Park University	Pr/AB	3,418	32	TOEFL	500	520	6/1	40
Reading Area Community College	Pu/A	4,461		TOEFL	450		6/1	
Restaurant School at Walnut Hill College	Pr/AB			TOEFL	500	550	None	200
Robert Morris University	Pr/B	3,718	113	TOEFL	500		7/1	30
Rosemont College	Pr/B	497	6	TOEFL	500	530	None	35
St. Charles Borromeo Seminary - Overbrook	Pr/B	68	1	TOEFL	400		7/15	
St. Francis University	Pr/AB	1,806	57	TOEFL	550		7/30	30
Saint Joseph's University	Pr/AB	5,278	65	TOEFL	550		2/1	65
St. Vincent College	Pr/B	1,613	12		550		2/15	25
Sanford-Brown Institute: Monroeville	Pr/A	550						25
Seton Hill University	Pr/B	1,594		TOEFL	600		8/1	35
Shippensburg University of Pennsylvania	Pu/B	7,047	16	TOEFL, SAT/ACT	600		None	30
Slippery Rock University of Pennsylvania	Pu/B	7,891	67	TOEFL	500	550	5/1	30
Susquehanna University	Pr/B	2,222	16	TOEFL	550		3/1	35
Swarthmore College	Pr/B	1,509	110			611	1/1	60
Temple University	Pu/AB	27,075	675	TOEFL	550	555	3/1	50
Thiel College	Pr/AB	1,019	34	TOEFL	503		None	35
Triangle Tech: Bethlehem	Pr/A	134						
Triangle Tech: Greensburg	Pr/A	276						
University of the Arts	Pr/B			TOEFL	550		None	60
University of Pennsylvania	Pr/AB	9,865	1,071	TOEFL, SAT, SAT Subject Test(s), or ACT			1/1	75
University of Phoenix: Harrisburg	Pr/B			TOEFL				

| Student services | | | Housing | | Academic year costs | | Maximum credits/ summer | Credit hour charge | International financial aid | | | |
Adviser	Orientation	ESL	Academic year	Summer	Tuition/ fees	Living costs			Available	Number receiving aid	Average award	Deadline
Yes	Yes		Yes	Yes	33,446	11,423		951	Yes			3/15
Yes			Yes	Yes	18,750	8,120	12	560	Yes			None
Yes			Yes		39,915	9,040	8	1165				
Yes			Yes	Yes	22,256 †	10,162	6	490	Yes			None
Yes	Yes	Yes	Yes	Yes	10,650 †	7,066	12	237				
			No		11,475 †				Yes			5/1
			No		13,650 †	6,102		259				
Yes	Yes		No		15,900			495	Yes	1	$1,000	
Yes	Yes	Yes	No		18,986 †			756				
Yes	Yes	Yes	Yes		19,828 †	9,030		791				
			Yes		18,986 †	9,030		756				
Yes	Yes		Yes	Yes	19,828 †	9,820		791				
			No		18,986 †			756				
			No		18,852 †			756				
Yes	Yes		Yes	Yes	19,828 †	9,030		791				
			No		18,872 †			756				
Yes		Yes	Yes	Yes	18,986 †	9,030		756				
Yes	Yes		Yes	Yes	19,818 †	10,240		791				
			Yes		18,934 †	9,030		756				
			No		18,976 †			756				
			Yes	Yes	18,986 †	9,030		756				
Yes	Yes		No		18,934 †			756				
			Yes	Yes	18,882 †			756				
			No		18,778 †			756				
Yes	Yes	Yes	Yes	Yes	27,114 †	9,030		1095				
			No		18,872 †			756				
Yes	Yes		No		18,852 †			756				
		Yes	No		18,852 †			756				
Yes	Yes	Yes	Yes	Yes	16,380 †	9,500		478				
					9,450 †	3,600		270				
Yes	Yes		Yes	Yes	21,088	8,275	6	613	Yes	16	$8,696	None
Yes	Yes	Yes	Yes	Yes	30,446	9,834	12	530	Yes	36	$6,001	4/15
Yes			No		14,715							
			No		16,730	11,532	20	250				
Yes	Yes	Yes	Yes	Yes	22,500 †	9,480	12	602	Yes			None
Yes	Yes	Yes	No		8,910 †	10,800	15	249				
			Yes		21,975 †	6,120						
Yes	Yes		Yes	Yes	23,038	11,030	15	745	Yes	95	$20,505	None
Yes	Yes		Yes	Yes	29,050	11,440	12	1070	Yes	3	$24,126	None
		Yes	Yes	Yes	18,228 †	11,472	6					
Yes	Yes		Yes		26,534 †	11,066	16	795	Yes	28	$21,390	None
Yes	Yes	Yes	Yes		36,640	12,206	12		Yes			
Yes	Yes		Yes	Yes	28,370	9,248	12	860	Yes			5/1
			No		9,125 †							
Yes	Yes	Yes	Yes	Yes	27,654	10,326	12	742	Yes	29	$20,095	None
Yes	Yes		Yes	Yes	16,762 †	7,400	15	605	Yes	13	$11,040	None
Yes	Yes		Yes	Yes	10,568 †	8,884	18	484	Yes	59	$5,258	
Yes	Yes		Yes		34,070 †	11,355	8	1065	Yes	12	$22,600	5/1
Yes	Yes		Yes	Yes	41,150	12,100			Yes	58	$45,909	2/15
Yes	Yes	Yes	Yes	Yes	22,252 †	9,550	12	771	Yes	116	$3,490	3/1
	Yes		Yes	Yes	25,156	11,152	16	770	Yes			None
					14,834 †			404	Yes			None
			No		14,866 †			404	Yes			None
Yes	Yes	Yes	Yes		32,200 †	9,465		1329	Yes			None
Yes	Yes	Yes	Yes	Yes	42,098	11,878	12	1201	Yes			None
					12,600 †							

Institution	Control/ degrees	Undergraduates		Tests required (Fall 2011)	TOEFL		Application	
		Total	Internat'l		minimum	average	Deadline	Fee
University of Phoenix: Philadelphia.	.Pr/B			TOEFL				
University of Phoenix: Pittsburgh	.Pr/B							
University of Pittsburgh	.Pu/B	17,994	358	TOEFL, SAT/ACT	550		4/1	45
University of Pittsburgh at Bradford	.Pu/AB	1,579	12	TOEFL	550		4/15	45
University of Pittsburgh at Greensburg.	.Pu/B	1,798	6	TOEFL	550		5/1	45
University of Pittsburgh at Johnstown	.Pu/AB	2,969	23	TOEFL	550		3/1	45
University of Pittsburgh at Titusville	.Pu/A	510		TOEFL	550		2/1	45
University of the Sciences in Philadelphia.	.Pr/B	2,517	44	TOEFL, SAT/ACT	550	590	4/15	45
University of Scranton	.Pr/AB	3,999	63	TOEFL	550		3/15	
Ursinus College.	.Pr/B	1,779	6	TOEFL, SAT/ACT	500	580	2/15	50
Valley Forge Christian College.	.Pr/AB	893	1	TOEFL	500		3/1	25
Valley Forge Military Academy and College.	.Pr/A			TOEFL	550	570	8/1	25
Vet Tech Institute	.Pr/A							50
Villanova University	.Pr/AB	6,878	209	TOEFL, SAT/ACT	550	631	1/7	75
Washington & Jefferson College.	.Pr/B	1,425	3	TOEFL, SAT/ACT	563		3/1	25
Waynesburg University.	.Pr/AB	1,671	2	TOEFL	500		3/1	20
West Chester University of Pennsylvania	.Pu/B	11,873	34	TOEFL	550		4/1	35
Widener University	.Pr/AB	3,162	74	TOEFL	500	550	7/7	35
Wilson College.	.Pr/AB	515		TOEFL	500	551	5/1	35
WyoTech: Blairsville	.Pr/A							
York College of Pennsylvania	.Pr/AB	5,158	20	TOEFL	530	600	5/31	30
YTI Career Institute: Altoona.	.Pr/A							
YTI Career Institute: Capital Region	.Pr/A							
YTI Career Institute: Lancaster.	.Pr/A	875						50
Puerto Rico								
American University of Puerto Rico	.Pr/AB						None	25
Bayamon Central University	.Pr/AB	1,727					None	25
Caribbean University	.Pr/AB	3,628						25
Colegio de las Ciencias Artes y Television	.Pr/A	657					9/3	25
Columbia Centro Universitario: Yauco.	.Pr/AB	1,105						50
Conservatory of Music of Puerto Rico.	.Pu/B	406	39				12/20	35
EDIC College	.Pr/A	1,174						25
Escuela de Artes Plasticas de Puerto Rico.	.Pu/B	522					6/10	25
Huertas Junior College	.Pr/A	1,980						25
Humacao Community College	.Pr/AB	610					None	17
ICPR Junior College	.Pr/A	764					None	25
Inter American University of Puerto Rico: Aguadilla Campus	.Pr/AB	4,299						
Inter American University of Puerto Rico: Arecibo Campus	.Pr/AB						5/1	
Inter American University of Puerto Rico: Barranquitas Campus	.Pr/AB	2,247					None	
Inter American University of Puerto Rico: Bayamon Campus	.Pr/AB	4,971					5/15	
Inter American University of Puerto Rico: Fajardo Campus.	.Pr/AB	2,222						
Inter American University of Puerto Rico: Guayama Campus	.Pr/AB	2,260					None	
Inter American University of Puerto Rico: Metropolitan Campus	.Pr/AB	6,787					5/15	
Inter American University of Puerto Rico: Ponce Campus.	.Pr/AB	5,989						
Inter American University of Puerto Rico: San German Campus	.Pr/AB	4,497					5/15	
National University College: Arecibo.	.Pr/AB	1,786					None	25
National University College: Bayamon.	.Pr/AB						None	25
National University College: Ponce.	.Pr/AB							
Ponce Paramedical College	.Pr/A							25
Pontifical Catholic University of Puerto Rico	.Pr/AB	5,642					7/15	15

144

| | Student services | | Housing | | Academic year costs | | Maximum credits/summer | Credit hour charge | International financial aid | | | |
Adviser	Orientation	ESL	Academic year	Summer	Tuition/fees	Living costs			Available	Number receiving aid	Average award	Deadline
					12,600†							
Yes	Yes	Yes	Yes	Yes	12,600† 24,592†	9,230		988				
			Yes	Yes	21,846†	7,650	18	878	Yes	6	$3,923	None
Yes	Yes		Yes	Yes	21,976†	8,110	15	878	Yes			
			Yes		21,878†	7,826		878	Yes	14	$4,662	
			Yes		19,558†	8,666	15	782				
Yes		Yes	Yes		30,794†	12,034	12	1220	Yes			3/15
Yes	Yes		Yes		34,626†	11,862	12	882	Yes			None
			Yes	Yes	41,650	11,500		1302	Yes	4	$11,250	5/1
Yes			Yes		17,302	7,236			Yes	1	$1,460	None
Yes	Yes	Yes	Yes		31,160 13,680†	11,060			Yes			5/1
Yes	Yes	Yes	Yes	Yes	41,260	10,940	12	1690	Yes	73	$35,011	2/7
Yes	Yes		Yes		36,420	9,756	12	902.5	Yes			None
Yes	Yes		Yes		19,090	7,930	12	790	Yes	2	$6,000	None
Yes		Yes	Yes		16,386†	7,372	12	605	Yes			None
Yes	Yes	Yes	Yes	Yes	34,762	11,896	12	1138	Yes	13	$15,075	None
Yes	Yes	Yes	Yes	Yes	29,340	9,710	4	2875	Yes			None
Yes	Yes		Yes		15,880	8,920	15	445	Yes	5	$500	None
			No									
			No			4,200						
Yes	Yes	Yes	No		8,230†	4,068	12	150				
			No		5,570†	4,280		160	Yes			
						1,200						
					6,100†				Yes			
Yes	Yes		No		2,750†				Yes			None
			No		6,621†	5,920		180	Yes			5/23
					9,600†	4,800			Yes			None
			No		6,340†							
			No		6,116†							
			No		5,578†			170				
		Yes	No		5,616†		12	170	Yes			5/15
			No		5,578†		6	170	Yes			4/30
			Yes		5,616†	9,511	18	170	Yes			
	Yes		No		5,616†	9,261	6	170				
Yes	Yes		No		5,578†		18	170				
Yes			No		5,616†		12	170	Yes			4/30
					5,616†			170				
Yes		Yes	Yes	Yes	5,616†	4,500	6	170				
			No		7,440†			165				
			No		7,440†			165				
Yes			Yes	Yes	5,468†	1,300	12	165	Yes			5/30

† Tuition and fees are for 2010-11. ‡ Tuition and fees projected for 2011-12. * Includes room and board

Institution	Control/ degrees	Undergraduates		Tests required (Fall 2011)	TOEFL		Application	
		Total	Internat'l		minimum	average	Deadline	Fee
Turabo University	.Pr/AB	13,105					None	15
Universidad Adventista de las Antillas	.Pr/AB	1,111					None	20
Universidad del Este	.Pr/AB	12,630					None	15
Universidad Metropolitana.	.Pr/AB	10,523						15
Universidad Pentecostal Mizpa.	.Pr/AB	288					None	45
Universidad Politecnica de Puerto Rico	.Pr/B	4,436					7/28	100
University College of San Juan.	.Pu/AB	1,692					8/15	15
University of Phoenix: Puerto Rico	.Pr/B							
University of Puerto Rico: Aguadilla	.Pu/AB	2,842					12/15	20
University of Puerto Rico: Arecibo	.Pu/AB						11/30	20
University of Puerto Rico: Bayamon University College	.Pu/AB	4,992					12/10	15
University of Puerto Rico: Carolina Regional College	.Pu/AB	3,907					1/31	20
University of Puerto Rico: Cayey University College	.Pu/B						12/1	20
University of Puerto Rico: Humacao	.Pu/AB	4,183					1/31	20
University of Puerto Rico: Mayaguez.	.Pu/B	11,993	16					20
University of Puerto Rico: Medical Sciences	.Pu/AB	530						20
University of Puerto Rico: Ponce	.Pu/AB	3,233					12/11	20
University of Puerto Rico: Rio Piedras.	.Pu/B	14,065					12/15	20
University of Puerto Rico: Utuado	.Pu/AB	1,390					5/31	20
Rhode Island								
Brown University	.Pr/B	6,102	586	TOEFL, SAT, SAT Subject Test(s), or ACT	600		1/1	75
Bryant University	.Pr/B	3,332	190	TOEFL, SAT/ACT	550		5/1	50
Community College of Rhode Island	.Pu/A	16,625		TOEFL			3/31	20
Johnson & Wales University: Providence	.Pr/AB	9,703	872	TOEFL	550		None	
New England Institute of Technology	.Pr/AB	3,258	96	TOEFL	550		None	25
Providence College	.Pr/AB	3,892	55	TOEFL	550	600	1/15	55
Rhode Island College	.Pu/B	7,394	14	TOEFL	550		3/15	50
Rhode Island School of Design.	.Pr/B			TOEFL, SAT/ACT	580		2/15	60
Roger Williams University	.Pr/B	4,310			500		None	50
Salve Regina University	.Pr/AB	2,022		TOEFL	500	520	None	50
University of Rhode Island	.Pu/B	12,818	41	TOEFL, SAT/ACT	550		2/1	65
South Carolina								
Aiken Technical College.	.Pu/A	3,108	2	TOEFL	500		None	
Allen University	.Pr/B	848			450		1/31	
Anderson University.	.Pr/B	2,330		TOEFL	550	575	7/1	25
Benedict College	.Pr/B	3,154		TOEFL	500		None	60
Bob Jones University	.Pr/AB	3,288		TOEFL, ACT	500		8/1	
Central Carolina Technical College	.Pu/A	4,075						
Charleston Southern University.	.Pr/B	2,765	13	TOEFL, SAT/ACT	550		7/11	40
The Citadel	.Pu/B	2,384		TOEFL, SAT/ACT	550		6/1	40
Claflin University	.Pr/B	1,775	37	TOEFL, SAT	550		5/1	21
Clemson University	.Pu/B			TOEFL, SAT/ACT	550		5/1	60
Clinton Junior College	.Pr/A							25
Coastal Carolina University	.Pu/B	7,974	83	TOEFL	550	563	6/1	45
Coker College.	.Pr/B	674	17	TOEFL	500	525	None	15
College of Charleston	.Pu/B	9,771	57	TOEFL	550		4/1	50
Columbia College	.Pr/B	1,161		TOEFL, SAT/ACT	550	562	6/1	25
Columbia International University.	.Pr/AB	542	19	TOEFL	525		5/30	45
Converse College.	.Pr/B			TOEFL	550		3/15	
Denmark Technical College.	.Pu/A	1,200					None	10
Erskine College.	.Pr/B	548	20	TOEFL, SAT/ACT	550			25
Florence-Darlington Technical College.	.Pu/A	5,549		TOEFL	500		5/15	15
Forrest Junior College.	.Pr/A	97					None	250
Francis Marion University	.Pu/B	3,462	35	TOEFL, SAT/ACT	500		7/1	30

	Student services			Housing		Academic year costs		Maximum credits/ summer	Credit hour charge	International financial aid			
Adviser	Orien- tation	ESL	Academic year	Summer	Tuition/ fees	Living costs				Avail- able	Number receiving aid	Average award	Deadline
			No		4,924 †				171	Yes			
Yes		Yes	Yes	Yes				12		Yes			None
Yes			No		4,924 †	8,118		21	171				
					4,924 †	7,382		12	171				
Yes			Yes		3,840 †	3,320		12	115				
						11,704		12		Yes			6/30
			No		3,150 †	7,350		9					
					6,360 †								
Yes			No		5,003 †	8,280		6		Yes			5/6
			No		5,003 †								
		Yes	No		5,003 †	8,180		6					
					5,003 †								
			No		5,003 †			7		Yes			6/30
			No		5,003 †			7		Yes			6/30
Yes		Yes	No		5,003 †			6					
			No		5,003 †								
			No		5,003 †			6					
Yes			Yes	Yes	5,003 †	8,280		10		Yes			4/1
					5,003 †	8,280		9					
Yes	Yes		Yes		40,820 †	10,540				Yes	188	$40,414	2/1
Yes	Yes	Yes	Yes	Yes	34,624	12,829		6		Yes	77	$19,599	2/15
Yes			No		9,792 †	8,415		12	454				
Yes	Yes	Yes	Yes	Yes	24,429 †	8,904		18	152	Yes			None
Yes	Yes	Yes	No		18,815 †	7,492			430				
Yes			Yes		40,975	12,140		6	1338	Yes	48	$39,361	2/1
Yes			Yes		16,878 †	9,256		14	604				
Yes	Yes		Yes		39,777	11,652			1315				
	Yes	Yes	Yes	Yes	29,718 †	12,710		12	1160	Yes			2/1
Yes	Yes	Yes	Yes		32,800	12,600		12	1083	Yes	9	$25,538	
Yes	Yes		Yes	Yes	27,182 †	10,854			1072				
Yes			No		10,130 †	4,050		15		Yes			6/1
Yes			Yes		11,540	5,560			960	Yes			7/20
Yes	Yes		Yes	Yes	20,910	7,725				Yes	1934	$7,266	6/30
Yes			Yes		17,190	7,906			515				
Yes		Yes	Yes		12,730			14	576	Yes	21	$8,738	
			No		5,872 †	9,830							
Yes			Yes		20,600 ‡	8,000		12	450	Yes			None
Yes		Yes	Yes		24,800 †	7,138		12	640	Yes	8	$29,635	None
Yes			Yes		12,868 †	7,078		9	460	Yes	9	$12,868	None
Yes	Yes		Yes	Yes	27,420 †	8,046		14	1171				
Yes					4,185	7,253							
Yes			Yes		20,270 †	7,350		15	830	Yes	48	$15,077	None
Yes		Yes	Yes	Yes	20,928 †	7,640			965	Yes			6/1
Yes	Yes		Yes	Yes	23,172 †	9,843		15	965				
Yes	Yes		Yes		24,060 †	7,574		16	635	Yes	1122	$8,227	None
Yes	Yes		Yes		17,395 †	6,410			695				
		Yes	Yes		26,138 †	8,032		15	800	Yes			3/15
			Yes		4,870 †	3,666		9		Yes			None
Yes			Yes		26,475 †	8,775		14	917	Yes			None
Yes			No		7,614 †			25		Yes			None
			No		12,050 †	8,054		18	245	Yes			4/1
Yes			Yes	Yes	16,625 †	6,380		15	815	Yes			None

† Tuition and fees are for 2010-11.   ‡ Tuition and fees projected for 2011-12.   * Includes room and board

Institution	Control/ degrees	Undergraduates		Tests required (Fall 2011)	TOEFL		Application	
		Total	Internat'l		minimum	average	Deadline	Fee
Furman University.	.Pr/B	2,728	36	TOEFL	570		1/15	50
Golf Academy of America: The Carolinas	.Pr/A							250
Greenville Technical College.	.Pu/A	13,695			500		5/1	35
Horry-Georgetown Technical College	.Pu/A			TOEFL			None	40
Lander University	.Pu/B			TOEFL, SAT/ACT	550		None	35
Limestone College.	.Pr/AB	857	56	TOEFL, SAT/ACT	500		9/1	25
Midlands Technical College.	.Pu/A	11,719	6	TOEFL	500	510	6/10	35
Miller-Motte Technical College	.Pr/A	864						35
Miller-Motte Technical College: Conway	.Pr/A							
Morris College	.Pr/B	1,048		TOEFL	500		3/31	20
Newberry College	.Pr/B	1,148	24	TOEFL, SAT/ACT	525		5/1	30
North Greenville University.	.Pr/AB	2,006	16	TOEFL, SAT/ACT	500		4/30	35
Northeastern Technical College	.Pu/A	1,219						25
Orangeburg-Calhoun Technical College	.Pu/A			TOEFL	500			50
Piedmont Technical College.	.Pu/A	4,957		TOEFL, SAT	500		None	
Presbyterian College.	.Pr/B	1,147	12	TOEFL	550		4/1	40
South Carolina State University	.Pu/B	3,716	3	TOEFL, SAT/ACT	500		5/30	25
South University: Columbia.	.Pr/AB	1,173		TOEFL			None	50
Southern Wesleyan University	.Pr/AB	1,444	11	TOEFL, SAT/ACT	500		6/1	25
Spartanburg Community College.	.Pu/A	5,871		TOEFL	450		None	15
Spartanburg Methodist College.	.Pr/A	780	1	TOEFL, SAT/ACT	525	570	6/30	20
Tri-County Technical College.	.Pu/A	6,758		TOEFL	500		5/15	30
Trident Technical College	.Pu/A	14,445		TOEFL				30
University of Phoenix: Columbia	.Pr/B							
University of South Carolina: Aiken	.Pu/B	2,948	43	TOEFL, SAT/ACT	550		6/1	45
University of South Carolina: Beaufort.	.Pu/AB	1,754		TOEFL, SAT/ACT	550		None	40
University of South Carolina: Columbia	.Pu/AB	21,031	300	TOEFL	550		12/1	50
University of South Carolina: Lancaster	.Pu/A			TOEFL, SAT/ACT		500	None	40
University of South Carolina: Sumter.	.Pu/A	828		TOEFL	550		None	40
University of South Carolina: Union	.Pu/AB	525		TOEFL	550		None	40
University of South Carolina: Upstate	.Pu/B	5,143	59	TOEFL, SAT/ACT	500	530	7/15	40
Voorhees College	.Pr/B			TOEFL, SAT, SAT Subject Test(s)	500	550	5/1	25
Winthrop University.	.Pu/B	4,642	134	TOEFL, SAT/ACT	520		None	60
Wofford College	.Pr/B	1,479	14	TOEFL	550	596	2/1	35

South Dakota

Institution	Control/ degrees	Total	Internat'l	Tests required	minimum	average	Deadline	Fee
Augustana College.	.Pr/B	1,717	52	TOEFL	550	590	8/1	
Black Hills State University.	.Pu/AB			TOEFL	500	535	7/1	108
Dakota State University	.Pu/AB	1,631	42	TOEFL	550		7/15	20
Dakota Wesleyan University	.Pr/AB	717	6	TOEFL	500	550	5/30	25
Lake Area Technical Institute.	.Pu/A			TOEFL	500			20
Mitchell Technical Institute	.Pu/A	973		TOEFL	500			
Mount Marty College.	.Pr/AB	876		TOEFL	500	550	8/1	35
National American University: Rapid City	.Pr/AB	1,685		TOEFL	500		None	45
Northern State University	.Pu/AB	1,765	35	TOEFL	500		6/15	20
Oglala Lakota College	.Pu/AB	1,727					None	
Presentation College.	.Pr/AB	700		TOEFL, ACT	500		5/1	25
Sinte Gleska University.	.Pu/AB	799		TOEFL	500			
Sisseton Wahpeton College	.Pu/A	261						
South Dakota School of Mines and Technology.	.Pu/AB	1,758	55	TOEFL	530	576	None	20
South Dakota State University	.Pu/AB	10,079	129	TOEFL	500		4/15	20
University of Sioux Falls.	.Pr/AB	1,125		TOEFL, SAT/ACT	500	610	None	25
University of South Dakota	.Pu/AB	6,103	34	TOEFL	550		None	20

Tennessee

Institution	Control/ degrees	Total	Internat'l	Tests required	minimum	average	Deadline	Fee
American Baptist College	.Pr/AB			TOEFL			7/1	35

	Student services			Housing		Academic year costs		Maximum credits/ summer	Credit hour charge	International financial aid			
Adviser	Orientation	ESL	Academic year	Summer	Tuition/ fees	Living costs			Available	Number receiving aid	Average award	Deadline
Yes	Yes		Yes	Yes	39,560	13,442	12		Yes	35	$38,768	1/15
					15,732†							
Yes			Yes	Yes	7,372†		12					
Yes			No		5,424†							
	Yes		Yes		17,304†	10,216	17	721	Yes			None
Yes	Yes		Yes		20,000	7,500	14	835	Yes	52	$12,989	None
Yes	Yes	Yes	No		10,760†		18					
Yes			Yes		10,290†	4,497	14	417				
Yes	Yes		Yes	Yes	22,518†	8,150	12	525	Yes			
Yes		Yes	Yes	Yes	13,396	7,850	12	230	Yes			6/30
			No		5,886†							
Yes			No		6,238†	2,737	18					
Yes			No		5,064†	6,728						
Yes	Yes		Yes		31,130	8,670	12	1200	Yes	12	$29,995	6/30
Yes			Yes		17,470†	8,718		728	Yes			5/1
			No		15,585†				Yes			None
Yes			Yes		20,550‡	8,410		825	Yes	6	$15,069	6/30
Yes			No		7,338†	5,790	18		Yes			5/1
Yes	Yes	Yes	Yes	Yes	14,058	7,918	14	375	Yes			8/22
Yes			No		7,944†	6,556	18		Yes			8/2
		Yes	No		6,682†	6,488			Yes			None
					10,200†							
Yes			Yes	Yes	16,592†	6,450	6	706	Yes	27	$2,547	None
			Yes		16,572†	8,200	6	676	Yes			None
Yes	Yes	Yes	Yes	Yes	25,362†	7,670	12	1050	Yes	87	$9,061	None
		Yes	No		14,144†	6,279	12	573	Yes			None
			No		14,214†		12	573				
			No		14,174†	6,279	6	573				
Yes	Yes	Yes	Yes		18,404†	6,600	12	759	Yes	53	$18,585	7/15
Yes			Yes		10,780†	10,246	10		Yes			None
Yes	Yes		Yes	Yes	22,942†	6,712		954	Yes			None
Yes			Yes		34,270	9,375	12		Yes			3/15
Yes	Yes		Yes	Yes	26,590	7,900		400	Yes	51	$10,396	None
Yes		Yes	Yes		8,013†	5,729	12	150				
Yes	Yes	Yes	Yes	Yes	8,668†	5,782	12	150	Yes	5	$5,579	None
Yes	Yes		Yes	Yes	20,810	8,700	12	450	Yes			None
Yes		Yes	No				12					
			No		4,900†		12					
Yes			Yes	Yes	20,656	5,918	18		Yes			None
Yes	Yes	Yes	Yes	Yes		7,272			Yes			None
Yes		Yes	Yes	Yes	7,848†	5,576	14	150	Yes			None
		Yes	Yes		2,900†	5,400						
			Yes	Yes	14,960†	5,650	12		Yes			None
			No		3,590†			110				
			No		3,790†	3,000						
Yes	Yes	Yes	Yes	Yes	8,799†	5,601		150	Yes			None
Yes	Yes		Yes	Yes	7,941†	9,493	18	150	Yes	18	$9,061	None
Yes	Yes		Yes	Yes	21,895†	9,330	12	280	Yes			None
Yes	Yes	Yes	Yes	Yes	8,259†	6,233	12	150				
			Yes	Yes	7,634†	2,000	12	240				

† Tuition and fees are for 2010-11.   ‡ Tuition and fees projected for 2011-12.   * Includes room and board

Institution	Control/ degrees	Undergraduates		Tests required (Fall 2011)	TOEFL		Application	
		Total	Internat'l		minimum	average	Deadline	Fee
Aquinas College	.Pr/AB	717		TOEFL	525	545	None	25
Argosy University: Nashville	.Pr/B							50
Austin Peay State University	.Pu/AB	9,644	46	TOEFL	500		7/28	15
Belmont University	.Pr/B	4,554	40	TOEFL, SAT/ACT	500	540	None	50
Bethel University.	.Pr/B	2,691		TOEFL	513		None	30
Bryan College.	.Pr/AB	1,080	15	TOEFL, SAT/ACT	533		5/1	30
Carson-Newman College.	.Pr/B	1,731	42	TOEFL, SAT/ACT	550	570	5/1	50
Christian Brothers University	.Pr/B	1,341		TOEFL	500		None	25
Cleveland State Community College	.Pu/A	2,452		TOEFL, SAT/ACT	500		7/15	10
Cumberland University	.Pr/AB	1,062		TOEFL, SAT/ACT	500	527	5/1	50
Daymar Institute: Nashville	.Pr/A				500		None	75
Dyersburg State Community College	.Pu/A	2,870		TOEFL	450	475	7/1	10
East Tennessee State University	.Pu/B	11,809	145	TOEFL, SAT/ACT	500	513	7/1	25
Fisk University	.Pr/B	501	40	TOEFL, SAT/ACT	500		3/1	75
Free Will Baptist Bible College	.Pr/AB	250	2	TOEFL, SAT/ACT	550		5/1	35
Freed-Hardeman University	.Pr/B	1,457	37	TOEFL	500		None	
International Academy of Design and Technology: Nashville.	.Pr/AB							50
ITT Technical Institute: Knoxville.	.Pr/AB			TOEFL	500			
ITT Technical Institute: Nashville.	.Pr/AB			TOEFL	500			
Jackson State Community College.	.Pu/A	5,361		TOEFL, SAT/ACT	500		None	10
Johnson Bible College	.Pr/AB	680	14	TOEFL	500		7/1	35
King College	.Pr/B	1,534	27	TOEFL	523		None	50
Lambuth University	.Pr/B	654		TOEFL, SAT/ACT	500		7/1	175
Lane College	.Pr/B	2,222	3	TOEFL			6/15	
Lee University	.Pr/B	3,714	206	TOEFL	450	520	8/1	25
LeMoyne-Owen College	.Pr/B	987	8	TOEFL		475	3/15	25
Lincoln Memorial University	.Pr/AB	1,685	50	TOEFL, SAT/ACT	450		6/1	25
Lipscomb University	.Pr/B	2,590	51	TOEFL	550		None	25
Maryville College	.Pr/B	1,080	41				None	25
Memphis College of Art	.Pr/B	372	13	TOEFL	500	550	8/1	25
Middle Tennessee State University	.Pu/B	23,217		TOEFL, SAT/ACT	500		7/31	30
Miller-Motte Technical College: Clarksville	.Pr/A			TOEFL	500		None	
Milligan College	.Pr/B	885	18	TOEFL	550	578	6/1	30
Motlow State Community College.	.Pu/A	5,053		TOEFL, SAT/ACT	500	530	7/31	25
Nashville State Community College.	.Pu/A	9,853		TOEFL	500		7/8	20
National College: Bartlett	.Pr/A							30
National College: Knoxville.	.Pr/A							30
National College: Madison	.Pr/A							30
National College: Memphis	.Pr/A							30
Nossi College of Art	.Pr/AB			TOEFL			None	100
O'More College of Design	.Pr/B	204		TOEFL	500		None	50
Pellissippi State Community College	.Pu/A			TOEFL	450	520	8/1	10
Remington College: Memphis	.Pr/AB							50
Remington College: Nashville	.Pr/A	332						50
Rhodes College.	.Pr/B	1,693	58	TOEFL, SAT/ACT	550	618	2/1	40
Roane State Community College.	.Pu/A	5,465	19	TOEFL	500			10
South College.	.Pr/AB	886		TOEFL	525		9/1	50
Southwest Tennessee Community College.	.Pu/A	12,416	130	TOEFL, SAT/ACT	500		None	30
Tennessee State University	.Pu/AB	6,694	22	TOEFL, SAT/ACT	500	550	6/1	25
Tennessee Technological University	.Pu/B	9,192		TOEFL, SAT/ACT	500		5/1	30
Tennessee Wesleyan College	.Pr/B	1,101	31	TOEFL	500		7/1	25
Trevecca Nazarene University	.Pr/AB	1,254	15	TOEFL, SAT/ACT	500			25
Tusculum College	.Pr/B	2,019	29	TOEFL, SAT/ACT	550	560	None	
Union University.	.Pr/AB	2,493	32	TOEFL, SAT/ACT	500	582	5/1	50
University of Memphis.	.Pu/B	16,746	215	TOEFL, SAT/ACT	500		5/1	50
University of Phoenix: Chattanooga.	.Pr/B	530						
University of Phoenix: Memphis.	.Pr/B							
University of Phoenix: Nashville.	.Pr/B							

| Student services | | | Housing | | Academic year costs | | Maximum credits/ summer | Credit hour charge | International financial aid | | | |
Adviser	Orien- tation	ESL	Academic year	Summer	Tuition/ fees	Living costs			Avail- able	Number receiving aid	Average award	Deadline
					19,050		12	615	Yes			None
					19,596†							
Yes		Yes	Yes	Yes	19,224†	6,450	14	723				
Yes	Yes		Yes	Yes	24,960	9,390	12	910	Yes	22	$19,486	None
Yes			Yes	Yes	13,552	7,782		413	Yes			6/30
Yes			Yes	Yes	19,550	5,720		840	Yes			None
Yes	Yes	Yes	Yes	Yes	21,774‡	7,247	14	865	Yes			None
Yes	Yes		Yes	Yes	26,110	6,490	14	895	Yes	27	$19,280	None
Yes			No		12,395†	6,009		487				
Yes	Yes		Yes	Yes	19,200‡	7,600	18	758	Yes			None
			No		12,960†							
Yes					12,397†		14	487	Yes			None
Yes	Yes	Yes	Yes	Yes	18,999†	6,382	17	723				
Yes	Yes		Yes	Yes	18,358†	8,586	12	702	Yes	32	$8,705	7/1
Yes			Yes		14,306†	6,042	6	447	Yes			None
Yes			Yes	Yes	15,922†	7,216	17	428	Yes			None
					15,950†	7,012		350				
			No									
			No									
			No		12,379†	11,144	18	487				
Yes			Yes	Yes	9,100†	5,400	6		Yes			8/1
Yes	Yes		Yes		22,908†	7,790	6		Yes	25	$8,910	None
Yes	Yes	Yes	Yes	Yes	19,500†	8,500	12	786	Yes			None
Yes			Yes		8,220	7,800	8		Yes			None
Yes	Yes	Yes	Yes	Yes	12,680	6,010	18	506	Yes	161	$6,777	None
Yes			Yes	Yes	10,318‡	4,852		421	Yes			None
Yes	Yes	Yes	Yes	Yes	17,720	6,220		730	Yes	49	$14,465	None
Yes	Yes		Yes	Yes	23,494	9,790	12	915	Yes			None
Yes	Yes	Yes	Yes	Yes	29,924	13,234	14		Yes			None
Yes	Yes		Yes	Yes	22,950†	9,000	12	1012	Yes			None
Yes	Yes		Yes	Yes	19,474†	7,415		723				
						6,300	12					
	Yes		Yes		25,260	5,650	12		Yes	17	$20,275	
					12,399†		12	487				
Yes		Yes			11,913†		12	487				
					10,800†			239				
					10,800†			239				
					10,800†			239				
					10,800†			239				
Yes	Yes					5,400	12					
					21,584†	9,600			Yes			None
Yes	Yes	Yes			12,423†		12	487				
Yes	Yes		Yes	Yes	36,464	8,976	12		Yes			3/1
Yes			No		12,408†	5,175	21	487	Yes			None
Yes			No			11,500	18					
Yes	Yes	Yes			12,411†			487	Yes			None
Yes	Yes		Yes	Yes	18,850†	5,760	12	723				
Yes	Yes	Yes	Yes	Yes	18,386†	7,382	16	723				
Yes			Yes		19,100†	6,350	18		Yes	28	$11,073	None
			Yes		20,590	7,488			Yes	19	$12,496	8/1
Yes			Yes		19,920†	8,000	12		Yes			2/15
Yes	Yes		Yes	Yes	24,030	9,090	14	735	Yes			3/1
Yes	Yes	Yes	Yes	Yes	20,856†	6,190	16	789	Yes	74	$15,281	8/1
					10,500†							
					10,500†							
					10,680†							

† Tuition and fees are for 2010-11.   ‡ Tuition and fees projected for 2011-12.   * Includes room and board

Institution	Control/degrees	Undergraduates		Tests required (Fall 2011)	TOEFL		Application	
		Total	Internat'l		minimum	average	Deadline	Fee
University of the South.................	Pr/B	1,431	30	TOEFL	550	650	2/1	45
University of Tennessee Health Science Center	Pu/B	89	3	TOEFL	550		6/15	75
University of Tennessee: Chattanooga	Pu/B	9,167		TOEFL	500		6/15	30
University of Tennessee: Knoxville............	Pu/B	21,142	250	TOEFL	523		4/1	30
University of Tennessee: Martin	Pu/B	6,786	143	TOEFL	500	520	None	130
Vanderbilt University.....................	Pr/B	6,836	323	TOEFL, SAT/ACT	570		1/3	50
Victory University......................	Pr/AB	691	4	TOEFL, SAT/ACT	500		7/15	25
Visible School - Music and Worship Arts College	Pr/B			TOEFL, SAT/ACT				30
Volunteer State Community College	Pu/A	7,501	34	TOEFL, ACT	500		6/1	10
Walters State Community College..............	Pu/A	5,697	12	TOEFL, SAT/ACT	550		6/15	10
Watkins College of Art, Design & Film..........	Pr/B	396		TOEFL, SAT/ACT	550		7/15	50
West Tennessee Business College	Pr/A	395						50
Williamson Christian College.................	Pr/AB	150		TOEFL, SAT/ACT	500		None	25
Texas								
Abilene Christian University	Pr/AB	3,756		TOEFL	525		2/15	50
Amarillo College........................	Pu/A	9,445		TOEFL	550		7/15	
Angelo State University	Pu/AB	6,074	51	TOEFL, SAT/ACT	550		6/11	50
Argosy University: Dallas	Pr/B							50
Arlington Baptist College	Pr/B	208	6	TOEFL	550		6/5	15
Art Institute of Dallas....................	Pr/AB	2,040		TOEFL				50
Austin College	Pr/B	1,289	25	TOEFL, SAT/ACT	550	597	3/1	
Austin Community College	Pu/A	44,100		TOEFL	530		6/1	100
Baptist University of the Americas	Pr/AB	200						25
Baylor University	Pr/B	12,376	269	TOEFL, SAT/ACT	540		2/1	50
Blinn College	Pu/A	17,559		TOEFL	500		7/15	200
Brazosport College.......................	Pu/AB	4,174		TOEFL	550		8/15	
Brookhaven College......................	Pu/A	10,747	73	TOEFL	525		None	
Cedar Valley College	Pu/A			TOEFL	530		None	
Central Texas College.....................	Pu/A	18,742	63	TOEFL	520		4/1	400
Clarendon College.......................	Pu/A	1,584		TOEFL	525		6/1	200
Coastal Bend College.....................	Pu/A	4,348		TOEFL	500		5/1	10
Collin County Community College District........	Pu/A	26,846	1,036	TOEFL	525		None	
Commonwealth Institute of Funeral Service	Pr/A						None	50
Concordia University Texas.................	Pr/AB	1,299	1	TOEFL	550	600	5/1	50
Criswell College	Pr/AB			TOEFL	550		6/30	30
Culinary Institute Alain & Marie LeNotre.........	Pr/A							50
Dallas Baptist University...................	Pr/AB	3,523	265	TOEFL	525		None	25
Del Mar College	Pu/A	12,236					None	
DeVry University: Houston	Pr/AB							50
DeVry University: Irving...................	Pr/AB			TOEFL	500		None	50
East Texas Baptist University................	Pr/B	1,090	12	TOEFL	500		6/1	50
Eastfield College........................	Pu/A	10,196	17	TOEFL	530		7/15	
El Centro College	Pu/A	7,808	10	TOEFL	530	550	7/15	
Everest College: Arlington..................	Pr/A	783						25
Everest College: Dallas....................	Pr/A	1,261						
Everest College: Fort Worth	Pr/A							
Frank Phillips College	Pu/A	776	3	TOEFL	500		None	
Galveston College.......................	Pu/A	2,322		TOEFL	500		7/7	
Grayson County College...................	Pu/A	4,551		TOEFL	450			
Hallmark College of Aeronautics	Pr/A	227		TOEFL	450		None	187
Hallmark College of Technology	Pr/AB	536		TOEFL	450		None	187
Hardin-Simmons University.................	Pr/B	1,854	25	TOEFL	550		4/1	50
Hill College	Pu/A	4,442		TOEFL			None	50
Houston Baptist University	Pr/AB	2,188	92	TOEFL	550		7/1	
Houston Community College System...........	Pu/A	46,713	5,041				7/15	75
Howard Payne University	Pr/AB	1,154	11	TOEFL	550		6/1	50

Student services			Housing		Academic year costs		Maximum credits/ summer	Credit hour charge	International financial aid			
Adviser	Orien- tation	ESL	Academic year	Summer	Tuition/ fees	Living costs			Avail- able	Number receiving aid	Average award	Deadline
Yes	Yes		Yes	Yes	32,292	9,226	9	1162	Yes	23	$39,775	None
			Yes		21,187†				Yes			None
Yes	Yes	Yes	Yes	Yes	18,376†	8,210	16	718	Yes	156	$922	None
Yes	Yes	Yes	Yes	Yes	22,420†	9,800	12	897	Yes	78	$10,845	None
Yes	Yes	Yes	Yes	Yes	18,600†	5,104	18	732				
Yes	Yes	Yes	Yes	Yes	39,932†	13,058		1623	Yes	30	$35,969	None
			No		10,620†	9,666	12	335				
					17,400†	3,400						
		Yes	No		11,957‡		18	487				
Yes		Yes	No		12,395†	3,600	21	487	Yes			None
			Yes	Yes	20,460	6,200	9	630				
			No									
		Yes	No		9,830		12	320	Yes			None
Yes	Yes	Yes	Yes	Yes	25,270	8,316	14	787	Yes	114	$4,809	None
		Yes	Yes		3,743†							
Yes	Yes	Yes	Yes	Yes	15,991†	7,768	12	462	Yes			None
					19,992†							
Yes			Yes	Yes	7,340†	4,200	12	220	Yes			7/15
									Yes			None
Yes			Yes		31,270	10,078		1106	Yes	23	$20,317	None
	Yes	Yes	No		9,120†	9,172	12	288	Yes			4/1
					5,700†	2,000		170				
Yes	Yes		Yes		31,658	9,650	18	1197	Yes	226	$13,456	
Yes	Yes	Yes	Yes	Yes	5,220†	5,150	14	144	Yes			None
Yes			No		3,822†	8,174	14	112	Yes			None
Yes	Yes	Yes	No		3,630†	7,154	6	121				
Yes			No		3,630†	7,154	14	121				
Yes	Yes	Yes	Yes	Yes	4,500†	3,630	12	150				
		Yes	Yes		3,990†	3,956	12		Yes			None
Yes			Yes		4,220†	4,598	14					
Yes	Yes	Yes			3,510†	6,106	14					
			No		10,220†		20					
Yes			Yes		23,020	8,460	15	760	Yes	1	$13,500	None
Yes			No		6,934†		9	261	Yes			4/15
			No									
Yes	Yes	Yes	Yes	Yes	19,800	6,120	17	660	Yes	135	$4,262	5/1
		Yes	No		5,050†		18	130				
					14,826†							
Yes					14,826†							
Yes	Yes		Yes	Yes	20,500	5,666	21	656	Yes	17	$6,579	
Yes			No		3,960‡	7,154	14	132	Yes			None
Yes	Yes	Yes	No		3,630†	7,408	14	121	Yes			None
						8,751						
Yes			Yes		3,398†	4,545						
Yes			No		2,314†	5,754	16	60				
Yes	Yes	Yes	Yes		3,690†	4,042		210	Yes			None
Yes	Yes		No		29,872†							
Yes	Yes		No		12,600†							
Yes			Yes	Yes	22,460	7,804	15	715	Yes	25	$7,974	None
Yes			Yes		2,920†	3,350	12		Yes			7/1
Yes			Yes	Yes	25,395	6,975	14		Yes			4/15
Yes	Yes	Yes	No		4,254†	10,160						
			Yes		21,700	6,144	14		Yes	1	$2,000	None

† Tuition and fees are for 2010-11.   ‡ Tuition and fees projected for 2011-12.   * Includes room and board

Institution	Control/ degrees	Undergraduates		Tests required (Fall 2011)	TOEFL		Application	
		Total	Internat'l		minimum	average	Deadline	Fee
Huston-Tillotson University	Pr/B	889	29	TOEFL	500		7/1	75
ITT Technical Institute: Arlington	Pr/AB			TOEFL	500			100
ITT Technical Institute: Houston	Pr/AB			TOEFL	500		None	100
ITT Technical Institute: San Antonio	Pr/AB			TOEFL	500			
Jacksonville College	Pr/A	402		TOEFL	450	500	None	100
Kilgore College	Pu/A	6,691	90				6/1	
Lamar Institute of Technology	Pu/A	3,243		TOEFL	500			
Lamar State College at Orange	Pu/A	2,649		TOEFL	500			
Lamar State College at Port Arthur	Pu/A	2,473		TOEFL	500		None	
Lamar University	Pu/AB	9,258	56	TOEFL, SAT/ACT	500	541	5/15	75
Laredo Community College	Pu/A	9,347		TOEFL	450		None	
Le Cordon Bleu College of Culinary Arts:								
Austin	Pr/A	1,183						50
Lee College	Pu/A	6,092		TOEFL	500		None	25
LeTourneau University	Pr/AB	2,759	50	TOEFL, SAT/ACT	500		None	25
Lon Morris College	Pr/A			TOEFL	450		None	300
Lone Star College System	Pu/A	69,339					None	
Lubbock Christian University	Pr/AB	1,629	26	TOEFL, SAT/ACT	525		6/1	25
McLennan Community College	Pu/A	7,959		TOEFL	500		7/1	50
McMurry University	Pr/B	1,327	5	TOEFL, SAT/ACT	550		3/1	50
Midland College	Pu/AB	3,828		TOEFL	530	535	None	20
Midwestern State University	Pu/AB	5,691	421	TOEFL, SAT/ACT			3/31	50
Mountain View College	Pu/A	8,463	23	TOEFL	530	540	7/31	
National American University: Austin	Pr/AB							
Navarro College	Pu/A	10,166		TOEFL	450		None	60
North Central Texas College	Pu/A	3,938		TOEFL	550		8/1	
North Lake College	Pu/A	10,432		TOEFL	530	540	7/1	
Northeast Texas Community College	Pu/A	2,722		TOEFL	550		None	
Northwest Vista College	Pu/A	13,924						
Northwood University: Texas	Pr/B	422	26	TOEFL	500	538	None	25
Odessa College	Pu/A	3,773	11	TOEFL	525		6/1	50
Our Lady of the Lake University of San								
Antonio	Pr/B	1,554	16	TOEFL	525		7/1	50
Panola College	Pu/A	2,303	28	TOEFL	525		5/1	
Paris Junior College	Pu/A	6,197		TOEFL		475	8/15	
Platt College: Dallas	Pr/A							
Prairie View A&M University	Pu/B	6,973	75	TOEFL, SAT/ACT	500		6/1	50
Ranger College	Pu/A	1,111		TOEFL	550		7/15	100
Remington College: Dallas	Pr/A							50
Remington College: Fort Worth	Pr/A						None	50
Remington College: Houston	Pr/A							50
Remington College: North Houston	Pr/A							50
Rice University	Pr/B			TOEFL, SAT, SAT Subject Test(s), or ACT	600		1/2	70
Richland College	Pu/A	15,775		TOEFL	530	535	7/1	
St. Edward's University	Pr/B	4,437	145	TOEFL	500		5/1	50
St. Mary's University	Pr/B	2,426	55	TOEFL	550			30
St. Philip's College	Pu/A	9,029	20	TOEFL	500			100
Sam Houston State University	Pu/B	14,689	151	TOEFL	550		8/1	40
San Antonio College	Pu/A	23,710					5/15	15
San Jacinto College	Pu/A	26,954	602	TOEFL	525		None	
Sanford-Brown College: Houston	Pr/A							
Schreiner University	Pr/AB	1,036	5	TOEFL, SAT/ACT	550		7/15	25
South Plains College	Pu/A	7,936		TOEFL	550	560	7/31	20
South Texas College	Pu/AB			TOEFL	500		None	
Southern Methodist University	Pr/B	6,116	395	TOEFL, SAT/ACT	550		None	60
Southwest Texas Junior College	Pu/A							
Southwestern Adventist University	Pr/AB	718		TOEFL	520		7/1	

Student services			Housing		Academic year costs		Maximum credits/summer	Credit hour charge	International financial aid			
Adviser	Orientation	ESL	Academic year	Summer	Tuition/fees	Living costs			Available	Number receiving aid	Average award	Deadline
Yes			Yes		12,430†	6,946	9	347	Yes	10	$11,432	None
			No									
			No									
			No									
Yes			Yes		6,920	3,258	20	210				
Yes	Yes	Yes	Yes	Yes	4,260†	3,980	14	120	Yes			7/15
Yes		Yes	Yes		13,358†			400				
			No		12,970†	3,306	18	363				
Yes		Yes			13,537†							
Yes	Yes	Yes	Yes	Yes	16,245†	8,706	12	468	Yes	15	$2,870	None
Yes		Yes	Yes		5,016†		14					
					38,625†	7,096						
Yes			No		3,102†	8,894		85	Yes			None
Yes			Yes		21,980†	8,390	16	858	Yes			None
Yes		Yes	Yes	Yes	13,500†	6,330	18		Yes			None
Yes	Yes	Yes	No		4,032†	7,450	12	123	Yes	96	$932	None
Yes			Yes		16,870	5,200	12	517	Yes	7	$7,244	None
Yes	Yes		Yes		4,923‡	6,395	14	144				
			Yes	Yes	21,870	7,225	14	657	Yes	5	$11,534	None
Yes		Yes	Yes		3,600†	4,100	14		Yes			6/1
Yes	Yes	Yes	Yes	Yes	16,020†	5,820	18	360	Yes	295	$1,835	None
Yes		Yes	No		3,630†			121	Yes			
Yes	Yes		Yes	Yes	3,732‡	4,705	14					
Yes			Yes	Yes	3,750†	3,040	12	115				
Yes	Yes	Yes	No		3,630†	7,154	14	121	Yes			5/1
			Yes		4,486†	4,600	14	113	Yes			None
			No		6,704†			214	Yes			None
Yes	Yes		Yes	Yes	20,140	8,437	18	745	Yes	16	$11,250	None
Yes			Yes	Yes	3,690†	6,111	16	112	Yes			None
Yes	Yes		Yes	Yes	22,784	7,326		718	Yes			None
Yes			Yes		3,690†	4,453	12	123	Yes			None
Yes	Yes		Yes	Yes	3,570†	4,500		269				
Yes	Yes		Yes		16,156†	7,064	14		Yes			3/15
Yes			Yes		2,830†	3,698	14	73	Yes			7/24
			No									
Yes	Yes	Yes	Yes		33,771†	11,750	12		Yes	61	$20,923	
Yes	Yes	Yes	No		3,630†	7,154	15	121	Yes			None
Yes	Yes		Yes		28,700	14,144	15	944	Yes	39	$19,884	5/1
Yes	Yes	Yes	Yes	Yes	22,576†	7,550	12	660	Yes			None
Yes			No		9,284†		14	300				
Yes		Yes	Yes		16,300†	7,022		473	Yes			None
Yes	Yes	Yes	No		6,704†		18	214	Yes			None
Yes	Yes	Yes	No		3,886‡		14	113	Yes			None
Yes			Yes	Yes	20,354	9,675*	6	843	Yes	3	$9,711	None
Yes		Yes	Yes	Yes	3,152†	3,100	18					
Yes			No		7,150†	4,620						
Yes	Yes	Yes	Yes	Yes	39,430	13,215	12	1462	Yes	178	$21,889	None
Yes			Yes		3,491†	3,600		95	Yes			None
Yes	Yes	Yes	Yes	Yes	16,456†	7,242	12	669	Yes			None

† Tuition and fees are for 2010-11.   ‡ Tuition and fees projected for 2011-12.   * Includes room and board

Institution	Control/ degrees	Undergraduates		Tests required (Fall 2011)	TOEFL		Application	
		Total	Internat'l		minimum	average	Deadline	Fee
Southwestern Assemblies of God University	Pr/AB	2,064		TOEFL	450		7/1	30
Southwestern Baptist Theological Seminary	Pr/B	338						
Southwestern Christian College	Pr/AB	224	19	TOEFL	500		7/31	20
Southwestern University	Pr/B	1,359	4	TOEFL, SAT/ACT	570		2/15	40
Stephen F. Austin State University	Pu/B	11,269	107	TOEFL	550		6/1	50
Sul Ross State University	Pu/AB	2,237	12	TOEFL, SAT/ACT	520		None	50
Tarleton State University.	Pu/AB	7,824	52	TOEFL, SAT/ACT	520		5/31	130
Tarrant County College.	Pu/A	49,142			550		7/15	
Texas A&M International University	Pu/B	5,798	129	TOEFL	550		6/1	
Texas A&M University.	Pu/B	39,027	556	TOEFL	550	601	1/15	75
Texas A&M University-Commerce	Pu/B	6,143		TOEFL, SAT/ACT	500	530	8/1	50
Texas A&M University-Corpus Christi.	Pu/B	8,054	268	TOEFL, SAT/ACT	550	570	6/1	30
Texas A&M University-Galveston.	Pu/B	1,805	12	TOEFL, SAT/ACT	550		3/1	75
Texas A&M University-Kingsville	Pu/B	5,252	94	TOEFL	550		6/1	50
Texas A&M University-Texarkana	Pu/B	1,301		TOEFL, SAT/ACT	550			
Texas Christian University.	Pr/B	7,804	384	TOEFL	550		3/1	50
Texas College.	Pr/AB	891	4	TOEFL, SAT/ACT	500	537	None	20
Texas Lutheran University.	Pr/B	1,299	18	TOEFL	550	560	5/1	40
Texas Southern University.	Pu/B	6,964	215	TOEFL, SAT/ACT	500		4/30	78
Texas State Technical College: Harlingen.	Pu/A	2,547		TOEFL	450			
Texas State Technical College: Marshall	Pu/A	708						
Texas State Technical College: Waco	Pu/A			TOEFL			7/30	
Texas State Technical College: West Texas.	Pu/A	1,094		TOEFL	550		None	
Texas State University: San Marcos.	Pu/B	27,448	85	TOEFL, SAT/ACT	550		5/1	75
Texas Tech University	Pu/B	25,409	717	TOEFL	550		5/1	75
Texas Tech University Health Sciences Center.	Pu/B	972	1					40
Texas Wesleyan University	Pr/B	1,578	30	TOEFL	520		None	25
Texas Woman's University	Pu/B	8,335	122	TOEFL, SAT/ACT	550	590	6/1	75
Trinity University	Pr/B	2,416	181	TOEFL, SAT/ACT	600		2/1	50
Trinity Valley Community College	Pu/A	6,157		TOEFL	450		None	80
University of Dallas.	Pr/B	1,333	33	TOEFL, SAT/ACT	550		3/1	40
University of Houston.	Pu/B	29,378	1,243	TOEFL	550	587	5/1	75
University of Houston-Clear Lake.	Pu/B	4,483		TOEFL	550		6/1	75
University of Houston-Downtown	Pu/B	12,616	606	TOEFL	550		5/1	60
University of Houston-Victoria.	Pu/B	2,268	33	TOEFL	550		6/1	
University of the Incarnate Word	Pr/AB	5,445	166	TOEFL	560		6/1	20
University of Mary Hardin-Baylor.	Pr/B	2,653	27		550		7/1	135
University of North Texas.	Pu/B	28,283	705	TOEFL	550	592	3/15	85
University of Phoenix: Austin	Pr/B	418						
University of Phoenix: Dallas Fort Worth.	Pr/B	1,071						
University of Phoenix: Houston Westside	Pr/B	2,644						
University of Phoenix: San Antonio.	Pr/B	803						
University of St. Thomas	Pr/B	1,552	86	TOEFL	550		6/1	25
University of Texas at Arlington.	Pu/B	23,835	1,300	TOEFL, SAT	550		None	50
University of Texas at Austin.	Pu/B	37,689	1,712	TOEFL, SAT/ACT	550		12/1	90
University of Texas at Brownsville - Texas Southmost College.	Pu/AB	13,680		TOEFL				
University of Texas at Dallas.	Pu/B	10,330	394	TOEFL, SAT/ACT	550	593	5/1	100
University of Texas at El Paso.	Pu/B	18,051	1,127	TOEFL	500		5/1	65
University of Texas at San Antonio.	Pu/B	25,492	623	TOEFL, SAT/ACT	500		6/1	40
University of Texas at Tyler	Pu/B	5,051	49	TOEFL, SAT/ACT	550	579	5/30	50
University of Texas Health Science Center at Houston.	Pu/B	574		TOEFL	565		None	10
University of Texas Health Science Center at San Antonio	Pu/B	906	12	TOEFL	550			45
University of Texas Medical Branch at Galveston.	Pu/B	546	3	TOEFL				50
University of Texas of the Permian Basin.	Pu/B	2,688	11	TOEFL, SAT/ACT	550		7/15	

Adviser	Orientation	ESL	Academic year	Summer	Tuition/fees	Living costs	Maximum credits/summer	Credit hour charge	Available	Number receiving aid	Average award	Deadline
Yes			Yes	Yes	14,830†	5,490	12	465	Yes			None
					6,948†							
Yes			Yes		6,438†	4,388		240	Yes	6	$8,787	6/1
Yes	Yes		Yes	Yes	31,360	9,230	12	1320	Yes			
Yes		Yes	Yes	Yes	16,298†	7,670	12	480	Yes	156	$939	None
			Yes	Yes	14,816†	6,600	14	438	Yes	6	$3,141	4/1
Yes	Yes		Yes		15,499†	7,338	12	454				
Yes	Yes		No		4,950†		14	165	Yes			
Yes	Yes	Yes	Yes	Yes	15,393†	10,906	12	449	Yes			None
Yes	Yes	Yes	Yes	Yes	22,817†	9,088	12	658	Yes			None
Yes	Yes	Yes	Yes	Yes	15,298†	6,836	14					
Yes			Yes	Yes	15,759†	9,500	12	465	Yes	187	$1,070	
Yes		Yes	Yes	Yes	16,458†	6,276		492				
Yes	Yes	Yes	Yes	Yes	15,646†	5,130			Yes			None
			No		14,246†							
Yes	Yes	Yes	Yes	Yes	32,490	10,410	15		Yes	238	$23,889	5/1
Yes			Yes		9,482†	6,600	6	333	Yes	2	$7,956	
Yes	Yes		Yes	Yes	23,930	9,610	14	790	Yes			None
Yes	Yes	Yes	Yes	Yes	15,772†	9,112	12		Yes			None
Yes			Yes	Yes	7,575†	3,160	12					
					7,575†	2,390						
			Yes	Yes	7,575†	5,970	15					
Yes			Yes	Yes	7,575†	4,450						
Yes	Yes	Yes	Yes	Yes	17,138†	6,810	12	501	Yes	63	$7,536	None
Yes	Yes	Yes	Yes	Yes	17,560†	7,800	16	489	Yes			
			No		14,946†	6,861			Yes			None
Yes	Yes		Yes	Yes	19,760	7,180	12	605	Yes			None
Yes	Yes		Yes	Yes	16,260†	7,190	16	405	Yes			None
Yes	Yes		Yes		31,356	10,966		1299	Yes			4/1
Yes	Yes	Yes	Yes	Yes	3,000†	4,000	12	68	Yes			None
Yes	Yes		Yes		29,325	9,326	12	1150				
Yes	Yes	Yes	Yes	Yes	18,300†	7,300	9	519	Yes	153	$1,736	None
Yes	Yes	Yes			16,508†	10,340	12		Yes	27	$7,309	None
Yes	Yes	Yes	No		14,792†	8,600	12	458	Yes	44	$2,789	None
Yes			Yes		14,904†			459	Yes			None
Yes	Yes	Yes	Yes	Yes	22,790	9,658		725	Yes	114	$9,622	None
Yes	Yes	Yes	Yes	Yes	23,050	7,221	12	690	Yes			
Yes	Yes	Yes	Yes	Yes	17,260‡	6,716						
					11,640†							
					11,640†							
					11,640†							
					11,640†							
Yes	Yes	Yes	Yes	Yes	23,500†	7,900	12	772	Yes	42	$8,583	None
Yes	Yes	Yes	Yes	Yes	17,800†	6,097	14		Yes	561	$3,904	None
Yes	Yes	Yes	Yes	Yes	31,266†	10,112	14		Yes			None
Yes		Yes	Yes		15,015†	9,021		451	Yes			8/15
Yes	Yes		Yes		25,866†	8,210	12	862	Yes	200	$6,438	4/12
Yes	Yes		Yes	Yes	15,837†	4,635	9	479	Yes			3/15
Yes	Yes	Yes	Yes	Yes	18,183‡	9,100	15	522	Yes	32	$2,567	None
Yes	Yes		Yes	Yes	15,622†	8,106	15	360	Yes	31	$2,730	None
Yes	Yes		Yes		21,935†							
			No		16,800†	14,818	9	552	Yes			None
Yes			Yes	Yes	15,397‡	3,195		480				
Yes		Yes	Yes	Yes	15,321†		12	460	Yes	11	$3,230	None

† Tuition and fees are for 2010-11.   ‡ Tuition and fees projected for 2011-12.   * Includes room and board

Institution	Control/ degrees	Undergraduates		Tests required (Fall 2011)	TOEFL		Application	
		Total	Internat'l		minimum	average	Deadline	Fee
University of Texas Southwestern Medical Center at Dallas . . . . .Pu/B		65	2	TOEFL	550			10
University of Texas: Pan American . . . . .Pu/B		15,978	324	TOEFL, SAT/ACT	500		2/1	
Victoria College . . . . .Pu/A		4,335	29	TOEFL	500		None	
Wade College . . . . .Pr/AB		264		TOEFL			None	25
Wayland Baptist University . . . . .Pr/AB		973	27	TOEFL, SAT/ACT	500		8/1	35
Weatherford College. . . . . .Pu/A		5,372	43	TOEFL	525	565	6/1	50
West Texas A&M University . . . . .Pu/B		6,410	78	TOEFL, SAT/ACT	525		5/1	75
Western Technical College . . . . .Pr/A								100
Western Technical College: Diana Drive . . . . .Pr/A								100
Western Texas College .Pu/A		2,309		TOEFL	500		8/12	25
Westwood College: Dallas. . . . . .Pr/AB								50
Westwood College: Houston South . . . . .Pr/AB				TOEFL				50
Wharton County Junior College . . . . .Pu/A		6,922	1	TOEFL	525		7/15	
Wiley College. . . . . .Pr/AB		1,351		TOEFL	500		7/1	25
Utah								
Argosy University: Salt Lake City. . . . . .Pr/B								50
Brigham Young University . . . . .Pr/B		30,409		TOEFL, SAT/ACT	550		2/15	30
Broadview University: Orem . . . . .Pr/AB								
Careers Unlimited . . . . .Pr/B		119						50
College of Eastern Utah . . . . .Pu/A		1,950		TOEFL	500		8/15	50
Dixie State College . . . . .Pu/AB		7,555	43	TOEFL	500		7/15	50
Eagle Gate College: Layton . . . . .Pr/AB		442						40
Eagle Gate College: Murray. . . . . .Pr/AB								40
Everest College: Salt Lake City . . . . .Pr/AB		500						
Independence University . . . . .Pr/AB							None	35
Neumont University . . . . .Pr/B		272		TOEFL	550		None	125
Provo College . . . . .Pr/A		487						40
Salt Lake Community College . . . . .Pu/A		25,770	341	TOEFL	450	500	6/1	65
Snow College . . . . .Pu/A		4,386		TOEFL	500	550	None	50
Southern Utah University . . . . .Pu/AB		5,847	149	TOEFL	500		7/1	25
Stevens-Henager College: Logan. . . . . .Pr/AB		275						
Stevens-Henager College: Orem . . . . .Pr/AB		900		TOEFL, SAT/ACT	475	500	None	50
University of Phoenix: Utah. . . . . .Pr/B		1,492						
University of Utah . . . . .Pu/B		22,260	743	TOEFL, SAT/ACT	500	543	4/1	55
Utah State University .Pu/AB		14,573	467	TOEFL	500		None	40
Utah Valley University . . . . .Pu/AB		26,267	356	TOEFL	500		None	100
Vista College . . . . .Pr/A								
Weber State University. . . . . .Pu/AB		18,226	277				None	65
Westminster College . . . . .Pr/B		2,308	73	TOEFL, SAT/ACT	550		None	50
Vermont								
Bennington College . . . . .Pr/B		668	45	TOEFL	577		1/3	60
Burlington College. . . . . .Pr/AB		186	1	TOEFL	550		None	50
Castleton State College . . . . .Pu/AB		2,037	18	TOEFL	500		None	40
Champlain College. . . . . .Pr/B		2,067	2	TOEFL	500	580	None	50
College of St. Joseph in Vermont . . . . .Pr/AB		214		TOEFL, SAT/ACT	550		8/1	25
Community College of Vermont . . . . .Pu/A		7,303		TOEFL	550		None	
Goddard College . . . . .Pr/B				TOEFL	550		None	20
Green Mountain College . . . . .Pr/B		692	6	TOEFL	500	560	6/1	30
Johnson State College. . . . . .Pu/AB		1,673	1	TOEFL	500		None	40
Landmark College . . . . .Pr/A		487	14	TOEFL	550		None	75
Lyndon State College .Pu/AB		1,323	5	TOEFL	500		None	40
Marlboro College. . . . . .Pr/B		278	2	TOEFL	550	575	3/1	50
Middlebury College . . . . .Pr/B		2,502	243	TOEFL, SAT, SAT Subject Test(s), or ACT			1/1	65
New England Culinary Institute . . . . .Pr/AB				TOEFL	550		None	25

Student services			Housing		Academic year costs		Maximum credits/ summer	Credit hour charge	International financial aid			
Adviser	Orientation	ESL	Academic year	Summer	Tuition/ fees	Living costs			Available	Number receiving aid	Average award	Deadline
Yes			No		13,918†			435				
Yes	Yes	Yes	Yes		14,999†	5,510	12	466	Yes	279	$6,704	
Yes			No		4,110†	6,060	14					
Yes			Yes		11,250†	4,400						
Yes			Yes	Yes	13,940	6,076	12	435	Yes	27	$13,357	None
Yes	Yes		Yes	Yes	4,410†	7,380	12					
Yes	Yes	Yes	Yes	Yes	15,582†	6,134	12	456	Yes	58	$2,967	None
									Yes			None
Yes		Yes	Yes	Yes	3,400‡ 13,825†	8,100	10	91				
					13,825†							
Yes			Yes		3,180†	3,200	14	64				
Yes			Yes		11,050†	6,136	7	299	Yes			None
					19,992†							
Yes	Yes	Yes	Yes	Yes	4,560	7,228		234	Yes	761	$3,871	None
			No									
Yes	Yes	Yes	Yes	Yes	4,940†	3,500						
Yes	Yes	Yes	Yes	Yes	12,136†	4,100	12	482				
					13,977†							
		Yes			13,977†							
Yes			No									
Yes			Yes	Yes	23,100‡	4,044 5,700		495				
Yes	Yes	Yes	No		9,172†		18					
Yes	Yes	Yes	Yes	Yes	8,984†	2,600	18		Yes			7/15
Yes		Yes	Yes		14,386†	5,486		660	Yes			None
Yes	Yes		Yes	Yes		7,688			Yes			None
					10,680†							
Yes	Yes	Yes	Yes	Yes	19,841†	6,473		524	Yes	1	$1,000	None
Yes	Yes	Yes	Yes	Yes	14,797†	5,070	18					
Yes	Yes	Yes	No		12,246†				Yes	23	$6,281	None
Yes	Yes	Yes	Yes	Yes	11,902†	4,050			Yes			None
Yes	Yes	Yes	Yes	Yes	27,182	7,584		1113	Yes	69	$17,088	None
Yes	Yes		Yes		42,800	12,160		1390	Yes	37	$36,525	2/15
Yes			Yes	Yes	21,340†	6,750	15					
			Yes		19,656†	8,120	18	783	Yes			None
Yes	Yes		Yes	Yes	28,490	13,520	12	1180	Yes			3/1
			Yes		18,300†	8,600	15	250				
			No		12,400†		15	410	Yes			None
			Yes						Yes			None
Yes	Yes	Yes	Yes		27,948†	11,142		898	Yes			None
Yes		Yes	Yes		19,055†	8,120			Yes			None
Yes			Yes		48,710	8,620	12		Yes			None
Yes		Yes	Yes	Yes	18,624†	8,120	9					
Yes			Yes		36,560	12,140		1175	Yes			3/1
Yes	Yes				53,800*				Yes	183	$44,736	2/1
Yes			Yes	Yes	26,300†	6,776			Yes			None

† Tuition and fees are for 2010-11.   ‡ Tuition and fees projected for 2011-12.   * Includes room and board

Institution	Control/ degrees	Undergraduates		Tests required (Fall 2011)	TOEFL		Application	
		Total	Internat'l		minimum	average	Deadline	Fee
Norwich University	Pr/B	2,212		TOEFL, SAT/ACT	500		None	35
St. Michael's College	Pr/B	1,859	38	TOEFL	550		2/1	50
Southern Vermont College.	Pr/AB	485		TOEFL, SAT/ACT	500	520	7/30	30
Sterling College.	Pr/B	98		TOEFL	500		None	35
University of Vermont	Pu/B	10,461	110	TOEFL, SAT/ACT	550	600	1/15	55
Virginia								
Argosy University: Washington D.C.	Pr/B							50
Art Institute of Washington	Pr/AB	2,151		TOEFL	500		None	50
Averett University	Pr/AB	838	79	TOEFL	500	585	6/1	35
Aviation Institute of Maintenance: Virginia Beach	Pr/A	247						25
Blue Ridge Community College	Pu/A	4,983		TOEFL			None	
Bluefield College.	Pr/B	675	1	TOEFL	500		8/4	30
Bridgewater College.	Pr/B	1,673	5	TOEFL, SAT/ACT	500		6/1	30
Bryant & Stratton College: Virginia Beach	Pr/AB	838		TOEFL	500		None	35
Catholic Distance University	Pr/AB	161		TOEFL	500			100
Central Virginia Community College	Pu/A	5,420		TOEFL	500	525	None	
Centura College: Chesapeake	Pr/A	210						25
Centura College: Newport News	Pr/A							25
Centura College: Norfolk	Pr/A	380						25
Centura College: Richmond	Pr/A	285						25
Christendom College	Pr/AB	409		TOEFL, SAT/ACT			3/1	25
Christopher Newport University	Pu/B	4,768	23	TOEFL, SAT/ACT	530	560	3/1	50
College of William and Mary.	Pu/B	5,862	160	TOEFL, SAT/ACT	600		1/1	60
Danville Community College	Pu/A	4,534		TOEFL	560		4/30	
DeVry University: Arlington	Pr/AB	747		TOEFL	500			50
Eastern Mennonite University.	Pr/AB	1,036	31	TOEFL	550		6/1	25
ECPI College of Technology: Virginia Beach	Pr/AB	12,670		TOEFL			None	45
Emory & Henry College	Pr/B	884	1	TOEFL, SAT/ACT	550		3/1	30
Everest College: Arlington.	Pr/A	783						
Everest College: Tysons Corner	Pr/A	408						
Ferrum College	Pr/B	1,484	7	TOEFL	550		None	25
George Mason University	Pu/B	19,623	623	TOEFL, SAT/ACT	570		1/15	75
Germanna Community College	Pu/A	7,582		TOEFL			None	
Hampden-Sydney College	Pr/B	1,058	21	TOEFL, SAT/ACT	570	590	3/1	30
Hampton University	Pr/AB	4,175		TOEFL, SAT/ACT	550	575	3/1	35
Hollins University	Pr/B	759	30	TOEFL	550	576	2/15	40
ITT Technical Institute: Chantilly	Pr/AB							
ITT Technical Institute: Springfield	Pr/AB							
J. Sargeant Reynolds Community College.	Pu/A	12,619		TOEFL	550		None	
James Madison University	Pu/B	17,306	227	TOEFL	550		4/1	50
Jefferson College of Health Sciences	Pr/AB	825		TOEFL	550			250
Liberty University	Pr/AB	33,693	926	TOEFL	500	573	None	40
Longwood University	Pu/B	4,074	14	TOEFL, SAT/ACT	550		3/1	50
Lynchburg College.	Pr/B	2,166	5	TOEFL	525		3/15	30
Mary Baldwin College	Pr/B	1,338	17	TOEFL	500	550	None	35
Marymount University	Pr/B	2,262	232	TOEFL, SAT/ACT	550		7/1	40
National College: Harrisonburg.	Pr/AB						None	125
National College: Roanoke Valley.	Pr/AB						None	125
Norfolk State University	Pu/AB	6,075	31	TOEFL	500	525	None	25
Northern Virginia Community College	Pu/A	48,996		TOEFL	500		7/1	
Old Dominion University	Pu/B	18,506	269	TOEFL	550		4/15	50
Patrick Henry College.	Pr/B	301						40
Patrick Henry Community College	Pu/A	2,688		TOEFL	500		5/31	
Paul D. Camp Community College	Pu/A	1,579		TOEFL	450	500	None	
Piedmont Virginia Community College	Pu/A			TOEFL	500			
Potomac College	Pr/AB	23		TOEFL	550		None	15
Radford University.	Pu/B	7,921	58	TOEFL	520	560	4/1	50

| Student services | | | Housing | | Academic year costs | | Maximum credits/ summer | Credit hour charge | International financial aid | | | |
Adviser	Orien-tation	ESL	Academic year	Summer	Tuition/ fees	Living costs			Avail-able	Number receiving aid	Average award	Deadline
Yes	Yes		Yes		30,194	10,454	20	839	Yes			None
Yes	Yes	Yes	Yes	Yes	36,240	9,030	12	1200	Yes	33	$15,696	2/15
Yes			Yes	Yes	19,955†	9,200	15		Yes			None
			Yes		27,152	8,590			Yes	1	$25,396	None
	Yes		Yes	Yes	32,630†	9,352		1281	Yes			None
					19,992†							
Yes	Yes		Yes	Yes	23,328†	10,144	16					
Yes			Yes	Yes	22,956†	8,138	12	375	Yes	51	$9,371	None
			Yes		10,800†							
			No		8,976†			279				
			Yes	Yes	19,980‡	7,800	21		Yes	6	$14,249	None
Yes			Yes	Yes	26,750	10,350	11	895	Yes	5	$21,000	None
			No		15,120†	4,820			Yes			None
								270				
Yes			No		8,653†			279				
					13,500†			450				
					13,500†			450				
					13,500†			450				
					13,500†			450				
			Yes		19,668†	7,506	18		Yes			6/1
Yes			Yes		17,992†	9,340	18	749				
Yes	Yes		Yes		33,212†	8,564	16	920				
			No		8,613†			279				
Yes					14,826†	11,878						
Yes	Yes	Yes	Yes	Yes	26,400	8,520	7	1100	Yes			None
			No		13,550†				Yes			None
Yes			Yes		27,040	9,064	12	1082	Yes			None
Yes			Yes		26,375	8,530		545	Yes			None
Yes	Yes	Yes	Yes		25,448†	8,020		954				
			No		8,651†	6,350		279				
Yes			Yes		34,219	10,632	6		Yes			5/1
Yes	Yes		Yes	Yes	18,074†	7,724	12	390	Yes	6	$22,521	None
Yes	Yes		Yes		30,795	10,670			Yes	22	$23,703	None
Yes	Yes	Yes	No		8,823†		18	279				
Yes	Yes	Yes	Yes	Yes	21,738	8,340	15		Yes	79	$16,226	
		Yes	Yes	Yes	19,750	5,200	15	575	Yes			None
Yes	Yes	Yes	Yes		19,720‡	7,247	9	594	Yes			3/1
Yes	Yes		Yes		20,085†	12,114	20	520	Yes			None
Yes	Yes		Yes	Yes	30,805	8,380	12	415	Yes	4	$12,662	None
Yes	Yes	Yes	Yes		26,960	7,790		415	Yes			None
Yes	Yes		Yes		23,972	10,580		770	Yes			None
Yes	Yes		No		10,840†	5,463		239				
Yes	Yes		Yes	Yes	10,840†			239				
Yes	Yes		Yes		19,280†	7,622	9	711	Yes			None
Yes		Yes	No		9,276†	5,810		297				
Yes	Yes	Yes	Yes	Yes	21,148†	8,322		697	Yes	32	$9,375	3/15
			Yes		22,758	9,128						
			No		8,638†		18	280	Yes			None
Yes			No		8,613†	7,900		280				
Yes			No		8,678†	6,920	12	280	Yes			None
			No									
Yes	Yes		Yes	Yes	18,018†	7,198		639	Yes			None

† Tuition and fees are for 2010-11.   ‡ Tuition and fees projected for 2011-12.   * Includes room and board

Institution	Control/ degrees	Undergraduates		Tests required (Fall 2011)	TOEFL		Application	
		Total	Internat'l		minimum	average	Deadline	Fee
Randolph College	Pr/B	500	65	TOEFL	550		4/1	50
Randolph-Macon College	Pr/B	1,199	23	TOEFL	550	580	3/1	30
Rappahannock Community College	Pu/A	3,756		TOEFL	500		8/20	
Regent University	Pr/AB	2,145	9	TOEFL	577		3/1	50
Richard Bland College	Pu/A	1,587		TOEFL	500		8/15	20
Roanoke College	Pr/B	2,039	25	TOEFL	520	572	3/1	30
St. Paul's College	Pr/B	555		TOEFL			None	20
Shenandoah University	Pr/B	1,851	56	TOEFL	527		None	30
Southern Virginia University	Pr/B	736	10	TOEFL, SAT/ACT	550		None	290
Southwest Virginia Community College	Pu/A	3,755		TOEFL	500			
Stratford University: Falls Church	Pr/AB			TOEFL				50
Stratford University: Woodbridge	Pr/AB	518		TOEFL			None	50
Sweet Briar College	Pr/B			TOEFL, SAT	550		2/1	40
Thomas Nelson Community College	Pu/A						None	
Tidewater Community College	Pu/A	31,308		TOEFL	500		None	
University of Management and Technology	Pr/AB				550			30
University of Mary Washington	Pu/A	4,271	20	TOEFL	570		2/1	50
University of Phoenix: Northern Virginia	Pr/B	549						
University of Phoenix: Richmond	Pr/B							
University of Richmond	Pr/B	2,945	185	TOEFL, SAT/ACT	550		1/15	50
University of Virginia	Pu/B	14,232	774	TOEFL, SAT/ACT			1/1	60
University of Virginia's College at Wise	Pu/B	1,680	3	TOEFL, SAT/ACT	550	570	4/1	25
Virginia Commonwealth University	Pu/B	21,835	630	TOEFL	550	579	None	40
Virginia Intermont College	Pr/AB	547	8	TOEFL	500	550	7/1	25
Virginia Military Institute	Pu/B	1,569	27	TOEFL	500	572		40
Virginia Polytechnic Institute and State University	Pu/AB	23,600	455	TOEFL, SAT/ACT	520	594	2/1	70
Virginia State University	Pu/AB	4,950		TOEFL	500		5/1	25
Virginia Union University	Pr/B	1,303		TOEFL, SAT, SAT Subject Test(s)	500	520	6/15	25
Virginia University of Lynchburg	Pr/AB						None	25
Virginia Wesleyan College	Pr/B	1,241	3	TOEFL	550		6/1	40
Washington and Lee University	Pr/B	1,757	75	TOEFL, SAT/ACT, SAT Subject Test(s)	600		1/15	50
Westwood College: Annandale	Pr/AB							
Westwood College: Arlington Ballston	Pr/AB							50
World College	Pr/B	489						
Washington								
Argosy University: Seattle	Pr/B							50
Art Institute of Seattle	Pr/AB	2,245		TOEFL	480	500	None	50
Bastyr University	Pr/B	199		TOEFL	550		4/15	60
Bates Technical College	Pu/A	11,180		TOEFL			None	62
Bellingham Technical College	Pu/A			TOEFL	470		None	35
Big Bend Community College	Pu/A	1,481	1	TOEFL	450		7/25	30
Cascadia Community College	Pu/A	1,938	22					50
Central Washington University	Pu/B	11,052		TOEFL	525		4/1	55
Centralia College	Pu/A	4,492			400	490	8/1	35
Clark College	Pu/A	7,309	47		520		7/24	35
Clover Park Technical College	Pu/A	7,356					8/30	50
Columbia Basin College	Pu/AB	6,978		TOEFL	500			29
Cornish College of the Arts	Pr/B	850		TOEFL	530		None	35
DeVry University: Federal Way	Pr/AB			TOEFL	500			50
DigiPen Institute of Technology	Pr/B	867		TOEFL	550		None	35
Eastern Washington University	Pu/B	10,214	197	TOEFL	525		5/15	50
Everest College: Vancouver	Pr/A	453						
Everett Community College	Pu/A	4,526	91				7/1	40
Evergreen State College	Pu/B	4,314	19	TOEFL, SAT/ACT	550		3/1	50
Faith Evangelical Seminary	Pr/B							40

Adviser	Orientation	ESL	Academic year	Summer	Tuition/ fees	Living costs	Maximum credits/ summer	Credit hour charge	Available	Number receiving aid	Average award	Deadline
Yes	Yes		Yes		30,376	10,986		1245	Yes			None
Yes	Yes		Yes	Yes	32,265	10,575	8		Yes	22	$21,579	2/15
			No		8,649 †		18	280	Yes			None
Yes	Yes		Yes	Yes	15,308 ‡	7,900			Yes			None
			Yes		12,394 †	8,750	15	515				
Yes	Yes	Yes	Yes	Yes	32,900	12,522	16		Yes			None
Yes			Yes		13,210 †	6,640	12	495	Yes			None
Yes	Yes	Yes	Yes	Yes	27,820	9,120	12	774	Yes	44	$12,372	None
			Yes	Yes	18,300	7,400		650	Yes	17	$5,464	None
Yes			No		8,578 †		15	279	Yes			None
Yes					16,650 †			370				
Yes	Yes	Yes			16,650 †		18	370				
Yes	Yes		Yes		30,195 †	10,780	18	760	Yes			
		Yes			8,624 †			280				
Yes		Yes	No		9,374 †		18	280				
			No									
Yes	Yes		Yes	Yes	19,590 †	9,528	12	768				
					11,880 †							
					11,880 †							
Yes	Yes	Yes	Yes	Yes	43,170	9,250	9		Yes	107	$44,622	2/15
Yes	Yes	Yes	Yes		32,902 †	8,652	12	1022				
Yes			Yes	Yes	19,784 †	8,351	14	699	Yes			
Yes	Yes	Yes	Yes	Yes	21,536 †	8,526		821	Yes			None
Yes	Yes		Yes		24,542 ‡	7,690	8	231	Yes	8	$22,072	6/1
			Yes		30,320 †	8,632		675				
Yes	Yes	Yes	Yes	Yes	22,648 †	6,290	14	854				
Yes			Yes	Yes	15,136 †	8,152	10	500	Yes			5/1
Yes			Yes		14,630 †	6,830	6					
			Yes	Yes	5,300 †	5,400		167				
Yes	Yes		Yes	Yes	28,556 †	7,680	12	1169	Yes	2	$10,250	None
Yes	Yes		Yes		41,927	10,687		1464	Yes	57	$43,772	2/15
					3,770 †							
					19,992 †							
Yes	Yes		Yes	Yes	21,825 †	13,656	18	485				
	Yes		Yes		19,995 †	4,100		528	Yes	5	$1,000	None
Yes		Yes							Yes			None
Yes			No		3,925 †				Yes			4/1
Yes	Yes		Yes		9,200 ‡	2,700	15	285				
Yes	Yes	Yes	No		8,505 †							
Yes	Yes	Yes	Yes	Yes	17,754 †	8,901	12		Yes			None
Yes	Yes	Yes	No		8,662 †	10,052	12	259	Yes			9/1
Yes	Yes	Yes	No		4,008 †	8,460	18	103				
Yes	Yes	Yes	No		7,977 †			168	Yes			8/25
Yes	Yes	Yes	No		8,531 †	7,140	18					
Yes			No		29,150 †	8,300	16	1200	Yes			None
Yes					14,826 †							
Yes	Yes		No		20,602	8,460		757	Yes			None
Yes	Yes	Yes	Yes	Yes	15,323 †	7,350	18					
Yes	Yes	Yes	No		8,475 †		18	259				
Yes	Yes		Yes	Yes	17,806 †	8,460	20	575	Yes	6	$9,448	None
					6,585 †			140				

† Tuition and fees are for 2010-11.   ‡ Tuition and fees projected for 2011-12.   * Includes room and board

Institution	Control/ degrees	Undergraduates Total	Undergraduates Internat'l	Tests required (Fall 2011)	TOEFL minimum	TOEFL average	Application Deadline	Fee
Gonzaga University	Pr/B	4,735	84	TOEFL	550	596	8/1	50
Green River Community College	Pu/A			TOEFL	500		8/25	50
Highline Community College	Pu/A	4,802		TOEFL	480		None	50
ITT Technical Institute: Seattle	Pr/AB						None	100
ITT Technical Institute: Spokane	Pr/AB			TOEFL	500		None	100
Lake Washington Technical College	Pu/AB				480		None	50
Lower Columbia College	Pu/A	1,998		TOEFL	460	500	None	66
North Seattle Community College	Pu/A	2,177	4		520		7/31	35
Northwest Aviation College	Pr/A			TOEFL	500		None	200
Northwest College of Art	Pr/B	99		TOEFL	500		9/1	100
Northwest School of Wooden Boatbuilding	Pr/A						8/7	100
Northwest University	Pr/AB	1,050	22	TOEFL	500	575	6/1	30
Olympic College	Pu/AB	8,533			480		None	35
Pacific Lutheran University	Pr/B	3,196	149	TOEFL	550		7/1	40
Peninsula College	Pu/AB			TOEFL	500	510	None	35
Pierce College	Pu/A			TOEFL	480	501	8/1	30
Renton Technical College	Pu/A			TOEFL	500		None	25
Saint Martin's University	Pr/B	1,363	58	TOEFL	525		7/1	35
Seattle Central Community College	Pu/A	12,789		TOEFL	490	538	7/15	35
Seattle Pacific University	Pr/B	3,129	30	TOEFL	550	653	11/15	50
Seattle University	Pr/B	4,530	395	TOEFL	520	592	6/1	45
Shoreline Community College	Pu/A	7,769					None	50
Skagit Valley College	Pu/A	6,250					None	25
South Puget Sound Community College	Pu/A	5,617		TOEFL	450	500	8/21	40
South Seattle Community College	Pu/AB	9,996			580		None	50
Spokane Community College	Pu/A	7,445		TOEFL	500		None	40
Tacoma Community College	Pu/A	6,825					8/15	
Trinity Lutheran College	Pr/AB	156		TOEFL	500		None	30
University of Phoenix: Western Washington	Pr/B			TOEFL				
University of Puget Sound	Pr/B	2,577	14	TOEFL, SAT/ACT	550	595	1/15	50
University of Washington	Pu/B	27,647	2,024	TOEFL	540		12/15	75
University of Washington Bothell	Pu/B	2,726	86	TOEFL, SAT/ACT	580		None	75
University of Washington Tacoma	Pu/B	2,733	22	TOEFL	580		1/15	75
Walla Walla Community College	Pu/A	5,438		TOEFL	500	510	None	
Walla Walla University	Pr/AB	1,549		TOEFL			None	30
Washington State University	Pu/B	21,374	785	TOEFL	520		1/31	50
Western Washington University	Pu/B	13,653	145	TOEFL	550		3/1	50
Whatcom Community College	Pu/A				480	500	8/18	35
Whitman College	Pr/B	1,535	44	TOEFL, SAT/ACT	560		1/15	50
Whitworth University	Pr/B	2,667	33	TOEFL, SAT/ACT	550		None	
Yakima Valley Community College	Pu/A	4,940		TOEFL	480		None	25

West Virginia

Institution	Control/ degrees	Undergraduates Total	Undergraduates Internat'l	Tests required (Fall 2011)	TOEFL minimum	TOEFL average	Application Deadline	Fee
Alderson-Broaddus College	Pr/AB	546	13	TOEFL, ACT	500		8/1	25
Appalachian Bible College	Pr/AB	300		TOEFL	500		8/10	20
Bethany College	Pr/B	872	6	TOEFL	500	574	None	
Bluefield State College	Pu/AB	1,876		TOEFL	500			
Bridgemont Community and Technical College	Pu/A	921						
Concord University	Pu/AB			TOEFL, SAT/ACT	500		7/15	
Davis and Elkins College	Pr/AB	681	31	TOEFL	500		5/30	
Everest Institute: Cross Lanes	Pr/A	550						
Fairmont State University	Pu/AB	4,301	68	TOEFL, SAT/ACT	500	550	7/15	
Glenville State College	Pu/AB	1,639		TOEFL, SAT/ACT	530		None	25
Kanawha Valley Community and Technical College	Pu/A	2,226		TOEFL, SAT/ACT	500			
Marshall University	Pu/AB	9,418	120	TOEFL, SAT/ACT	500		7/15	30
Mountain State College	Pr/A							115
Mountain State University	Pr/AB	4,756	254	TOEFL	500	544	7/15	50
New River Community and Technical College	Pu/A	2,154						

Student services			Housing		Academic year costs		Maximum credits/ summer	Credit hour charge	International financial aid			
Adviser	Orientation	ESL	Academic year	Summer	Tuition/ fees	Living costs			Available	Number receiving aid	Average award	Deadline
Yes	Yes	Yes	Yes	Yes	30,915†	8,300	14	850	Yes			6/30
Yes	Yes	Yes	Yes	Yes	9,117†		20					
Yes	Yes	Yes	No		8,445†		18	259				
			No				18					
			No									
Yes	Yes	Yes		Yes	8,730†							
Yes	Yes	Yes	No		8,640†	7,017	18	259				
Yes	Yes	Yes	No		9,277‡	9,000	18		Yes			7/31
Yes							15					
					18,815	9,000	15	800	Yes			6/1
			No									
Yes	Yes	Yes	Yes	Yes	23,400	6,724	10	960	Yes	17	$12,883	8/1
Yes	Yes	Yes	No		8,571†		18	259	Yes			None
Yes	Yes	Yes	Yes	Yes	30,950	9,350	12	970	Yes	135	$9,083	None
Yes	Yes	Yes	*		8,457†	8,495		262	Yes			4/1
Yes	Yes	Yes			8,711†	8,052	18	259				
Yes		Yes	No		7,121†	8,952						
Yes	Yes	Yes	Yes	Yes	27,622	8,960	12	910	Yes	4	$7,125	None
Yes	Yes	Yes	No		8,535†		18	259	Yes			4/30
Yes	Yes	Yes	Yes	Yes	30,339	9,081	20	833	Yes	18	$13,800	None
Yes	Yes	Yes	Yes	Yes	30,825†	9,315	18	685	Yes	112	$12,345	None
Yes	Yes	Yes	No		8,628†		15					
Yes	Yes	Yes	Yes	Yes	8,580†	5,640	18	260				
Yes	Yes	Yes		Yes	8,450†	8,460	18	258				
Yes	Yes	Yes	No		8,718†	8,460	20					
Yes	Yes	Yes	No		8,556†		15	259				
Yes	Yes	Yes	No		8,573†							
Yes	Yes		Yes	Yes	20,870†	6,900		830	Yes			None
					11,880†							
Yes	Yes		Yes		38,720	13,670	12	1215	Yes	6	$20,333	None
Yes	Yes	Yes	Yes	Yes	25,601†	8,169						
Yes	Yes		Yes	Yes	26,324†							
			Yes	Yes	25,317†	9,399						
Yes	Yes				8,625†		15					
Yes	Yes		Yes	Yes	23,454†	8,088	12	607	Yes	43	$5,777	None
Yes	Yes	Yes	Yes	Yes	20,531†	9,664			Yes	298	$3,387	None
Yes	Yes	Yes	Yes	Yes	17,205†	8,749	18		Yes	27	$2,382	None
Yes	Yes	Yes	No		8,550†	8,064	20	265				
Yes	Yes		Yes	Yes	40,496	10,160		1674	Yes	6	$258,346	2/15
Yes	Yes	Yes	Yes	Yes	32,144	8,918	12	1326	Yes			None
	Yes	Yes	Yes	Yes	8,678†		18	259				
Yes	Yes		Yes	Yes	22,204†	7,222	6	733	Yes			None
Yes			Yes		11,258†	5,790		391	Yes			6/15
Yes	Yes		Yes		23,854	9,546	4	650	Yes			None
Yes	Yes		No		9,288†	7,400	12	387				
					11,846†	7,310		494				
Yes	Yes	Yes	Yes		11,050†	6,962		460	Yes			4/15
Yes	Yes	Yes	Yes	Yes	22,320	7,950	12	700	Yes			None
Yes	Yes	Yes	Yes	Yes	10,904†	7,236	12	454	Yes			3/1
		Yes	Yes		12,000†	7,350	9	500	Yes			None
Yes						5,513						
Yes	Yes	Yes	Yes	Yes	12,896†	7,858	24	537				
			No		8,215†	5,850			Yes			None
Yes	Yes	Yes	Yes	Yes	9,000†	6,366	12	215				
					7,240‡	6,000		302				

† Tuition and fees are for 2010-11. ‡ Tuition and fees projected for 2011-12. * Includes room and board

Institution	Control/ degrees	Undergraduates		Tests required (Fall 2011)	TOEFL		Application	
		Total	Internat'l		minimum	average	Deadline	Fee
Ohio Valley University	Pr/AB	439	23	TOEFL, SAT/ACT	500		None	20
Potomac State College of West Virginia University	Pu/AB	1,524	4	TOEFL, SAT/ACT	550		None	
Salem International University	Pr/AB	477					None	20
Shepherd University	Pu/B	3,703	8	TOEFL, SAT/ACT	550	600	7/1	45
University of Charleston	Pr/AB	1,119	137	TOEFL	500		None	25
West Liberty University	Pu/AB	2,487		TOEFL	500	510	7/1	
West Virginia Junior College: Bridgeport	Pr/A	300					None	
West Virginia Northern Community College	Pu/A	2,758		TOEFL	500		None	
West Virginia State University	Pu/B	2,784		TOEFL	500		None	
West Virginia University	Pu/B	22,303	488	TOEFL	500		4/1	60
West Virginia University at Parkersburg	Pu/AB	4,450		TOEFL			4/1	
West Virginia University Institute of Technology	Pu/B	1,209		TOEFL, SAT/ACT	500	510	8/1	100
West Virginia Wesleyan College	Pr/B	1,347	54	TOEFL, SAT/ACT	500		3/1	35
Wheeling Jesuit University	Pr/B	988	38	TOEFL	550		None	25
Wisconsin								
Alverno College	Pr/AB	2,263	13	TOEFL	520		5/15	20
Bellin College	Pr/B	274		TOEFL, ACT			5/1	30
Beloit College	Pr/B	1,308	112	TOEFL	525	650	1/15	35
Cardinal Stritch University	Pr/AB			TOEFL	550		4/1	25
Carroll University	Pr/B	2,990	54	TOEFL	550	578	None	
Carthage College	Pr/B			TOEFL	500		None	30
Chippewa Valley Technical College	Pu/A	6,062		TOEFL	500		None	30
Concordia University Wisconsin	Pr/AB	4,043	32	TOEFL	500	509	7/1	125
Edgewood College	Pr/AB	1,843	37	TOEFL	525		5/1	25
Fox Valley Technical College	Pu/A	7,749	21	TOEFL, ACT			None	30
Gateway Technical College	Pu/A	7,856		TOEFL	500		None	30
Globe University: Green Bay	Pr/AB						None	
Herzing University	Pr/AB	1,027		TOEFL	500		None	
ITT Technical Institute: Green Bay	Pr/AB							
Lakeland College	Pr/AB			TOEFL	500		None	20
Lakeshore Technical College	Pu/A	2,573		TOEFL	550		None	30
Lawrence University	Pr/B	1,520	132	TOEFL	577	605	2/15	40
Madison Area Technical College	Pu/A			TOEFL	550			30
Maranatha Baptist Bible College	Pr/AB	795	6	TOEFL, SAT/ACT	450		12/31	50
Marian University	Pr/B	1,966	23	TOEFL	525		5/1	25
Marquette University	Pr/B	7,912	149		525	560	None	40
Milwaukee Area Technical College	Pu/A	20,215		TOEFL	500	510	8/2	30
Milwaukee Institute of Art & Design	Pr/B	695	5	TOEFL	550		None	25
Milwaukee School of Engineering	Pr/B	2,393	74	TOEFL	550	580	8/1	25
Moraine Park Technical College	Pu/A	4,156		TOEFL	500		None	30
Mount Mary College	Pr/B	1,250		TOEFL	500	550	None	75
Northeast Wisconsin Technical College	Pu/A			TOEFL	550		8/31	30
Northland College	Pr/B	536	17	TOEFL	525	600	6/1	
Rasmussen College: Green Bay	Pr/A							60
Rasmussen College: Wausau	Pr/AB	769						60
St. Norbert College	Pr/B	2,127	117	TOEFL	550	555	None	50
Silver Lake College	Pr/AB	316	4	TOEFL, SAT/ACT	550		6/1	50
Southwest Wisconsin Technical College	Pu/A	3,421		TOEFL	450		None	30
University of Phoenix: Madison	Pr/B	191						
University of Phoenix: Milwaukee	Pr/B	543						
University of Wisconsin-Baraboo/Sauk County	Pu/A			TOEFL	500		6/1	35
University of Wisconsin-Barron County	Pu/A			TOEFL	500		None	35
University of Wisconsin-Eau Claire	Pu/AB	10,505	187	TOEFL	550		6/1	44
University of Wisconsin-Fox Valley	Pu/A			TOEFL	500		7/15	44
University of Wisconsin-Green Bay	Pu/AB	6,085	59	TOEFL	550		None	44
University of Wisconsin-La Crosse	Pu/AB	8,680	233	TOEFL	550		6/15	94

Student services			Housing		Academic year costs		Maximum credits/summer	Credit hour charge	International financial aid			
Adviser	Orientation	ESL	Academic year	Summer	Tuition/fees	Living costs			Available	Number receiving aid	Average award	Deadline
Yes		Yes	Yes	Yes	16,960†	6,886	12	475	Yes			None
			Yes		8,746†	7,208	14	366				
Yes	Yes	Yes	Yes	Yes	14,100†	6,600	20	425	Yes			None
Yes	Yes		Yes	Yes	14,046†	7,720	12	581	Yes	8	$1,904	None
Yes	Yes	Yes	Yes	Yes	25,000	10,000	12	900	Yes			None
Yes			Yes		12,750†	8,510	18	531	Yes			None
			No									
Yes			No		6,670†		12					
Yes			Yes		10,904†	6,225	9	454	Yes			6/15
Yes	Yes	Yes	Yes		17,002†	8,120		708				
Yes			No		7,346†	5,000	12	306	Yes			None
Yes	Yes		Yes		13,264†	10,482	12	553				
Yes		Yes	Yes	Yes	23,980†	7,140	12		Yes			None
Yes	Yes	Yes	Yes	Yes	25,640	9,028	12	675	Yes	30	$13,200	None
Yes	Yes	Yes	Yes	Yes	21,063	6,966	18	856	Yes	13	$7,962	None
			No		19,639†			934				
Yes	Yes	Yes	Yes	Yes	36,674	7,802		1139	Yes	103	$22,197	3/1
Yes	Yes		Yes	Yes	22,750‡	6,780		710	Yes			None
Yes	Yes		Yes	Yes	24,065†	7,371	20	298	Yes	25	$18,791	None
Yes			Yes	Yes	29,750†	8,150	16	400	Yes			None
Yes		Yes	No		4,975†		9	159				
Yes		Yes	Yes	Yes	23,140	8,700	10		Yes	14	$4,455	None
Yes	Yes		Yes	Yes	22,850	8,113	6	719	Yes	21	$6,535	None
Yes		Yes	No		5,085†	6,145	12	159				
Yes			No		5,024†			159				
Yes			No		12,400†			385	Yes			None
Yes	Yes	Yes	Yes	Yes	19,640†	6,820	12		Yes			7/1
Yes			No		4,945†	6,137		159				
Yes	Yes		Yes	Yes	38,481	9,390			Yes	131	$18,966	None
		Yes	No		4,977†		6	159				
Yes			Yes		12,260	6,290	6	465	Yes			None
Yes	Yes		Yes	Yes	21,490†	7,230	15	350	Yes	21	$8,118	None
Yes	Yes	Yes	Yes	Yes	31,822	10,340	16	915	Yes			None
Yes	Yes	Yes	No		5,200†	6,841	12	159	Yes			None
Yes			Yes		28,654	8,416		900	Yes			None
Yes	Yes	Yes	Yes	Yes	30,990‡	7,794	19	538	Yes	25	$11,289	None
Yes		Yes	No		4,944†	6,137	9	159	Yes			None
Yes	Yes		Yes	Yes	23,000	7,550	10	675	Yes			None
Yes	Yes	Yes	No		4,973†		6	159				
Yes			Yes	Yes	26,566	8,210		500	Yes			None
					16,875†	7,011		375				
					16,875†			375				
Yes	Yes	Yes	Yes	Yes	29,398	7,513	12	904	Yes	83	$16,078	None
Yes		Yes	Yes	Yes	21,820	9,500	18	720	Yes	1	$20,950	None
		Yes	Yes	Yes	4,945†		6	159	Yes			None
					11,040†							
					11,880†							
Yes			No		11,644†		12	469				
Yes		Yes	No		11,732†	5,170	9	469				
Yes	Yes	Yes	Yes	Yes	14,933†	5,770	11	571	Yes	73	$4,591	None
Yes			No		11,516†	6,710	6	469	Yes			None
Yes	Yes		Yes	Yes	14,546†	5,450		551	Yes	45	$8,693	None
Yes	Yes	Yes	Yes	Yes	15,484†	5,630		599	Yes			None

† Tuition and fees are for 2010-11.   ‡ Tuition and fees projected for 2011-12.   * Includes room and board

Institution	Control/ degrees	Undergraduates		Tests required (Fall 2011)	TOEFL		Application	
		Total	Internat'l		minimum	average	Deadline	Fee
University of Wisconsin-Madison	.Pu/B	28,897	1,673	TOEFL, SAT/ACT	550		12/15	44
University of Wisconsin-Marathon County	.Pu/A			TOEFL, SAT/ACT	500	540	7/1	35
University of Wisconsin-Marinette	.Pu/A			TOEFL, SAT/ACT	500		6/1	44
University of Wisconsin-Marshfield/Wood County.	.Pu/A			TOEFL	500		6/1	35
University of Wisconsin-Milwaukee	.Pu/B	23,636	327	TOEFL	520		3/1	84
University of Wisconsin-Oshkosh	.Pu/B	10,806	90	TOEFL	550		5/15	44
University of Wisconsin-Parkside	.Pu/B	4,749	53	TOEFL	525		6/1	60
University of Wisconsin-Platteville	.Pu/AB	7,064	35	TOEFL	500	580	5/15	44
University of Wisconsin-Richland	.Pu/A	455		TOEFL	500		5/31	44
University of Wisconsin-River Falls	.Pu/B	6,159	43	TOEFL		550	2/1	44
University of Wisconsin-Rock County	.Pu/A			TOEFL	500		6/1	35
University of Wisconsin-Sheboygan.	.Pu/A			TOEFL	500		None	45
University of Wisconsin-Stevens Point	.Pu/AB	8,921	178	TOEFL			7/11	100
University of Wisconsin-Stout	.Pu/B	8,213	70	TOEFL	500	550	None	44
University of Wisconsin-Superior	.Pu/AB	2,566	176	TOEFL	500	535	7/1	44
University of Wisconsin-Washington County.	.Pu/A	1,117		TOEFL	500		6/1	44
University of Wisconsin-Waukesha	.Pu/A	1,886		TOEFL	500		6/1	44
University of Wisconsin-Whitewater	.Pu/AB			TOEFL	500		5/1	44
Viterbo University	.Pr/AB	2,153	30	TOEFL	525		6/1	25
Western Technical College	.Pu/A						None	30
Wisconsin Indianhead Technical College	.Pu/A	3,474		TOEFL	500		None	30
Wisconsin Lutheran College.	.Pr/B			TOEFL	550		None	35
Wyoming								
Casper College	.Pu/A	3,166	38	TOEFL, SAT/ACT	500		None	
Central Wyoming College	.Pu/A	1,408	14	TOEFL	500		None	
Eastern Wyoming College	.Pu/A	737	5	TOEFL	520		None	
Laramie County Community College	.Pu/A	3,678	60	TOEFL	500		None	20
Northwest College	.Pu/A	1,876	101	TOEFL	500		6/15	50
Sheridan College	.Pu/A	2,059	27	TOEFL	500	525	5/10	
University of Phoenix: Cheyenne	.Pr/B							
University of Wyoming.	.Pu/B	9,893	331	TOEFL	525		6/1	40
Western Wyoming Community College	.Pu/A			TOEFL	500		6/15	100
WyoTech: Laramie	.Pr/A	1,227					None	

Student services			Housing		Academic year costs		Maximum credits/summer	Credit hour charge	International financial aid			
Adviser	Orien-tation	ESL	Academic year	Summer	Tuition/fees	Living costs			Avail-able	Number receiving aid	Average award	Deadline
Yes	Yes	Yes	Yes	Yes	24,233 †	7,435		966				
Yes			Yes	Yes	11,528 †		6	469				
Yes		Yes	No		11,544 †		12	469				
					11,595 †		9	469				
Yes	Yes	Yes	Yes	Yes	17,880 †	7,018		708				
Yes	Yes		Yes	Yes	14,253 †	6,576	9	556				
Yes	Yes		Yes	Yes	14,192 †	6,624		551	Yes			None
Yes	Yes		Yes	Yes	14,345 †	5,208	9	556	Yes			None
Yes	Yes		Yes		11,739 †		9	469				
Yes	Yes	Yes	Yes	Yes	14,467 †	5,530	8	554				
					11,559 †		9	469				
Yes			No		11,560 †		9	469	Yes			None
Yes	Yes	Yes	Yes	Yes	14,418 †	5,760	6	551	Yes	90	$5,641	5/1
Yes	Yes	Yes	Yes	Yes	14,869 †	5,560	10	468	Yes	46	$7,759	None
Yes	Yes	Yes	Yes	Yes	14,739 †	5,330		560	Yes	171	$6,436	None
Yes			No		11,579 †		9	469				
Yes			No		11,556 †		6	483	Yes			None
Yes	Yes		Yes	Yes	14,409 †	5,402	12	560	Yes			6/30
Yes	Yes		Yes	Yes	20,850 †	9,470	12	600	Yes			None
Yes		Yes	Yes	Yes	4,996 †	5,110	12	159				
			No		4,997 †			159	Yes			
Yes	Yes	Yes	Yes	Yes	21,960 †	9,880		660	Yes			None
Yes	Yes		Yes		5,112 †	4,650		204	Yes			None
Yes	Yes		Yes	Yes	5,400 †	4,085		204	Yes			None
Yes		Yes	Yes		5,408 †	3,806		204	Yes			None
Yes		Yes	Yes		5,736 †	6,482		204		25	$7,578	
Yes	Yes	Yes	Yes	Yes	5,496 †	4,202		204				
Yes		Yes	Yes	Yes	5,629 †	4,600	8	204	Yes			None
					10,200 †							
Yes	Yes		Yes	Yes	12,237 †	8,360	12	376	Yes	212	$5,848	None
Yes	Yes	Yes	Yes	Yes	5,258 †	4,530	12	204	Yes			None
			Yes									

Part III:
Lists and indexes

International undergraduate student enrollment

International undergraduate student enrollment

Total financial aid for international undergraduate students

Harvard College (MA) 23,789,521
Mount Holyoke
    College (MA) 16,942,487
Princeton University (NJ).... 16,475,530
Yale University (CT) 15,509,771
Massachusetts Institute of
    Technology (MA) 14,556,198
Anderson University (SC)... 14,053,122
Newberry College (SC)....... 13,163,631
Dartmouth College (NH).... 11,706,712
Stanford University (CA)...... 9,862,995
Columbia College (SC) 9,231,473
Columbia University (NY)..... 9,020,265
Bard College (NY) 8,780,810
Middlebury College (VT)...... 8,186,710
Cornell University (NY)....... 8,013,493
Brown University (RI)......... 7,597,965
Parsons The New School
    for Design (NY)................ 7,556,278
University of Southern
    California (CA)................ 7,320,155
St. John's University (NY).... 7,175,405
Macalester College (MN)...... 6,838,080
Savannah College of Art
    and Design (GA) 6,694,506
Williams College (MA)......... 6,102,206
Worcester Polytechnic
    Institute (MA) ..,............. 5,881,856
Trinity College (CT)............ 5,830,825
Vassar College (NY)............. 5,809,964
Texas Christian
    University (TX) 5,685,736
Smith College (MA).............. 5,570,077
St. Lawrence
    University (NY) 5,503,540
Wesleyan University (CT)..... 5,399,622
Franklin & Marshall
    College (PA) 5,388,730
Grinnell College (IA).......... 5,315,013
Wellesley College (MA)........ 5,001,152
Colgate University (NY) 4,955,703
Oberlin College (OH)........... 4,873,456
Cooper Union for the
    Advancement of Science
    and Art (NY) 4,865,000
University of
    Richmond (VA)................ 4,774,630
Dickinson College (PA)......... 4,721,691
University of Denver (CO) ... 4,616,438
University of Toledo (OH).... 4,600,238
Washington University in
    St. Louis (MO) 4,458,938
Florida Institute of
    Technology (FL) 4,373,350
Calvin College (MI) 4,322,633
Northeastern
    University (MA) 4,096,533
Boston University (MA)........ 4,004,131
Oklahoma Wesleyan
    University (OK)................ 3,938,091
Southern Methodist
    University (TX) 3,896,275
Arizona State
    University (AZ) 3,798,241
George Washington
    University (DC) 3,769,710
Bryn Mawr College (PA) 3,629,133

Bates College (ME)............... 3,609,253
University of
    Rochester (NY).................. 3,551,038
Ohio State University:
    Columbus Campus (OH)... 3,480,180
Berea College (KY)............... 3,407,968
Earlham College (IN)............ 3,372,289
University of Miami (FL) 3,293,794
Tufts University (MA)........... 3,145,400
Hamilton College (NY).......... 3,142,288
Brandeis University (MA)..... 3,115,452
Indiana University
    Bloomington (IN)............ 3,090,315
Connecticut College (CT) 3,084,547
University of Southern
    Mississippi (MS)............... 3,065,348
University of Chicago (IL)..... 3,051,450
Baylor University (TX) 3,041,081
Carleton College (MN)......... 3,019,268
Clark University (MA) 2,994,996
Polytechnic Institute of
    New York
    University (NY) 2,953,616
Canisius College (NY) 2,951,385
Brigham Young
    University (UT) 2,946,540
Luther College (IA)............... 2,890,526
Skidmore College (NY)........ 2,878,535
Swarthmore College (PA)...... 2,662,728
St. John's University (MN).... 2,604,004
Juilliard School (NY) 2,594,005
University of Arizona (AZ)... 2,590,203
Villanova University (PA) 2,555,818
Lynn University (FL)............. 2,540,966
Union College (NY) 2,521,221
St. Olaf College (MN).......... 2,520,490
Lehigh University (PA) 2,515,800
Washington and Lee
    University (VA).................. 2,495,054
Lawrence University (WI)..... 2,484,576
University of New
    Orleans (LA)..................... 2,473,602
Tulane University (LA) 2,425,137
Embry-Riddle Aeronautical
    University (FL).................. 2,424,501
Ithaca College (NY) 2,421,892
College of the
    Atlantic (ME)................... 2,309,664
Beloit College (WI) 2,286,381
Pace University (NY) 2,283,928
Reed College (OR)............... 2,216,467
Lewis & Clark
    College (OR)..................... 2,201,382
University of Texas at
    Arlington (TX)................. 2,190,204
Kenyon College (OH) 2,186,017
College of St.
    Benedict (MN)................. 2,142,455
Gettysburg College (PA) 2,103,050
University of California:
    Irvine (CA)....................... 2,012,363
SUNY College at
    Plattsburgh (NY)............... 1,983,137
University of South
    Florida (FL) 1,951,314
Robert Morris
    University (PA)................. 1,948,064

Hampshire College (MA)...... 1,915,785
Providence College (RI)........ 1,889,334
University of Texas: Pan
    American (TX)................... 1,870,417
Illinois Wesleyan
    University (IL)................. 1,820,725
East Carolina
    University (NC)................ 1,800,625
Michigan Technological
    University (MI)................. 1,796,356
Georgetown
    University (DC) 1,750,000
Miami University:
    Oxford (OH) 1,734,387
Knox College (IL) 1,723,641
Wheaton College (MA) 1,714,610
Columbia University:
    School of General
    Studies (NY) 1,684,367
University of
    Mississippi (MS)............... 1,664,319
Louisiana State University
    and Agricultural and
    Mechanical College (LA).. 1,659,299
SUNY University at Stony
    Brook (NY)....................... 1,642,802
Agnes Scott College (GA) 1,557,918
Whitman College (WA)......... 1,550,076
University of Nevada: Las
    Vegas (NV) 1,528,876
University of
    Evansville (IN)................. 1,511,247
Bryant University (RI)........... 1,509,176
Hofstra University (NY)......... 1,499,564
Stetson University (FL)......... 1,490,286
University of Hawaii at
    Manoa (HI) 1,474,613
Saint Louis
    University (MO) 1,446,543
Michigan State
    University (MI)................. 1,423,445
Elizabethtown College (PA).. 1,406,750
Kent State University (OH).. 1,402,110
University of New
    Hampshire (NH) 1,397,979
Hobart and William Smith
    Colleges (NY).................... 1,395,111
Seattle University (WA) 1,382,671
Furman University (SC)........ 1,356,909
Mercer University (GA) 1,353,836
Bennington College (VT)...... 1,351,450
Fairfield University (CT)........ 1,338,122
Truman State
    University (MO) 1,337,944
St. Norbert College (WI)....... 1,334,493
Randolph College (VA) 1,317,565
Sarah Lawrence
    College (NY) 1,302,683
Wartburg College (IA)........... 1,296,559
Hendrix College (AR) 1,295,493
University of Texas at
    Dallas (TX) 1,287,706
California Institute of
    Technology (CA) 1,285,127
James Madison
    University (VA)................. 1,281,895
Rice University (TX)............. 1,276,309
Rollins College (FL)............. 1,268,770
Ramapo College of New
    Jersey (NJ) 1,262,913
Adelphi University (NY)....... 1,262,660
Pomona College (CA) 1,249,261
Saint Leo University (FL)..... 1,249,045
University of
    Wyoming (WY) 1,239,946
Jacksonville State
    University (AL) 1,238,110
University of Iowa (IA)........ 1,235,666
University of Tampa (FL) 1,228,000
Pacific Lutheran
    University (WA)................ 1,226,232
California Lutheran
    University (CA) 1,206,640
Cornell College (IA).............. 1,205,635

Rochester Institute of
    Technology (NY)............... 1,200,000
University of Oregon (OR) ... 1,197,001
Boston Conservatory (MA) ... 1,192,291
Sacred Heart
    University (CT).................. 1,188,146
George Fox
    University (OR) 1,181,529
Westminster College (UT)..... 1,179,109
Oklahoma Christian
    University (OK)................ 1,171,723
Boise State University (ID)... 1,161,792
School of Visual Arts (NY) .. 1,160,011
College of Idaho (ID)............ 1,142,456
University of
    Memphis (TN) 1,130,865
Messiah College (PA)........... 1,108,237
University of Wisconsin-
    Superior (WI).................... 1,100,634
University of the Incarnate
    Word (TX)......................... 1,096,926
Lee University (TN).............. 1,091,097
North Carolina State
    University (NC)................. 1,079,914
Vanderbilt University (TN) ... 1,079,094
Harding University (AR)....... 1,070,904
Loras College (IA)................ 1,066,711
University of Portland (OR).. 1,066,214
Suffolk University (MA)........ 1,063,061
Western Kentucky
    University (KY)................. 1,060,002
Gordon College (MA) 1,041,635
Bennett College for
    Women (NC) 1,034,982
University of
    Montevallo (AL).............. 1,030,656
Florida Atlantic
    University (FL).................. 1,029,557
Coe College (IA) 1,020,132
Colby Community
    College (KS) 1,020,131
SUNY College at
    Potsdam (NY) 1,019,040
Hawaii Pacific
    University (HI).................. 1,016,866
Wesleyan College (GA)........ 1,011,941
Washington State
    University (WA)............... 1,009,425
Duquesne University (PA)..... 1,001,632
Grand Valley State
    University (MI) 998,831
Concordia College:
    Moorhead (MN).................. 990,758
Manhattan School of
    Music (NY) 990,592
Juniata College (PA).............. 985,665
University of South
    Carolina: Upstate (SC) 985,037
Gannon University (PA)........... 983,276
Bowdoin College (ME) 983,095
Loyola University New
    Orleans (LA)....................... 960,494
University of Dayton (OH) 954,562
Bucknell University (PA) 949,128
Houghton College (NY) 932,620
University of St.
    Thomas (MN) 921,234
University of the
    South (TN) 914,829
Iona College (NY) 902,426
Indiana University-Purdue
    University
    Indianapolis (IN)................. 902,275
Towson University (MD)......... 901,926
St. John's College (NM).......... 898,783
University of California:
    Davis (CA)........................... 898,418
University of Missouri: St.
    Louis (MO) 894,482
Menlo College (CA)................ 890,925
Dowling College (NY)............ 886,600
Cleveland Institute of
    Music (OH).......................... 879,560
Bentley University (MA)......... 875,525

Missouri State University (MO) 847,781
SUNY University at Binghamton (NY) 847,580
University of Tennessee: Knoxville (TN) 845,933
Ringling College of Art and Design (FL)........................ 834,689
North Dakota State University (ND) 834,437
Chapman University (CA) 828,019
University of the Cumberlands (KY)............... 820,429
San Diego State University (CA) 816,000
Utica College (NY) 805,242
Niagara University (NY) 801,087
Mannes College The New School for Music (NY) 800,670
University of Maine (ME) 800,537
Clarkson University (NY) 795,331
Emporia State University (KS)...................... 795,005
Florida Gulf Coast University (FL) 791,951
Taylor University (IN) 789,658
University of South Carolina: Columbia (SC) 788,356
St. Mary's College of California (CA) 779,257
St. Edward's University (TX) 775,476
Saint Thomas University (FL) 765,403
Goshen College (IN) 740,127
New England College (NH) 725,617
Marietta College (OH) 724,326
Coastal Carolina University (SC) 723,732
Bloomfield College (NJ) 719,796
Emory University (GA) 715,440
Valparaiso University (IN) 711,286
Tiffin University (OH)............. 710,915
Lincoln Memorial University (TN) 708,827
Franklin W. Olin College of Engineering (MA)................ 703,000
Bellarmine University (KY)..... 690,124
Cleveland State University (OH) 687,182
Hamline University (MN) 684,096
Wittenberg University (OH) 683,020
Limestone College (SC) 675,447
Southeast Missouri State University (MO) 674,179
Albion College (MI) 673,593
Newman University (KS) 670,322
Robert Morris University: Chicago (IL)......................... 649,959
Rose-Hulman Institute of Technology (IN)................. 649,267
Biola University (CA) 647,121
Eugene Lang College The New School for Liberal Arts (NY) 647,068
La Roche College (PA) 641,000
St. Catherine University (MN) 640,950
Rocky Mountain College (MT) 636,366
Radford University (VA) 636,347
University of Tulsa (OK) 633,801
Roanoke College (VA) 633,466
University of Alaska Fairbanks (AK) 624,379
St. Francis University (PA) 598,938
Huntington University (IN) 590,920
Berry College (GA) 589,901
Ouachita Baptist University (AR) 588,509
Seton Hill University (PA) 582,757
Columbus College of Art and Design (OH) 576,728
Dallas Baptist University (TX) 575,465

Creighton University (NE) 574,218
Otis College of Art and Design (CA)......................... 572,500
Morehouse College (GA) 570,783
Wofford College (SC)............... 566,141
Briar Cliff University (IA) 564,600
La Salle University (PA) 563,380
Central Michigan University (MI)..................... 563,129
University of Arkansas (AR) 554,015
St. Mary-of-the-Woods College (IN)........................ 550,146
Abilene Christian University (TX) 548,332
Shenandoah University (VA)..................... 544,400
Haverford College (PA)............ 544,399
Green Mountain College (VT) 541,759
Midwestern State University (TX) 541,354
Malone University (OH) 532,178
Allegheny College (PA)............ 530,996
Augustana College (SD) 530,196
Hood College (MD)................. 527,040
Le Moyne College (NY) 525,844
Northwestern College (IA)........ 523,989
Hollins University (VA) 521,485
Christian Brothers University (TN) 520,570
St. Michael's College (VT) 517,997
University of Wisconsin- Stevens Point (WI) 507,701
Iowa State University (IA) 507,092
Kutztown University of Pennsylvania (PA)................. 506,059
Loyola Marymount University (CA) 499,917
Lewis-Clark State College (ID) 498,049
Simpson College (IA).............. 497,092
St. Mary's University of Minnesota (MN) 495,663
Centre College (KY) 493,160
University of North Carolina at Greensboro (NC) 491,966
Wentworth Institute of Technology (MA) 490,250
William Jewell College (MO)..................... 487,307
Averett University (VA)............ 477,967
McDaniel College (MD) 476,211
Texas State University: San Marcos (TX) 474,824
Randolph-Macon College (VA) 474,745
Drew University (NJ) 473,249
Carroll University (WI) 469,786
Austin College (TX) 467,308
College of Saint Mary (NE)...... 464,019
University of Science and Arts of Oklahoma (OK) 463,406
Pacific Union College (CA)..... 459,600
Palm Beach Atlantic University (FL).................... 459,000
Occidental College (CA) 455,101
Olivet Nazarene University (IL)..................... 452,340
Felician College (NJ).............. 451,900
Embry-Riddle Aeronautical University: Prescott Campus (AZ) 445,819
Minot State University (ND) 444,299
Northwest Missouri State University (MO) 433,474
Dominican University (IL)....... 433,106
Belmont University (TN) 428,700
Montreat College (NC) 428,348
Purdue University (IN)............. 427,922
North Central College (IL)....... 420,974
Temple University (PA)........... 404,939
Regis University (CO)............. 404,825

Kettering University (MI) 399,663
Chestnut Hill College (PA) 397,250
Wheeling Jesuit University (WV) 396,000
Marist College (NY)................. 393,520
University of Wisconsin- Green Bay (WI) 391,196
Southwest Baptist University (MO) 388,842
Spring Arbor University (MI) 384,881
Queens University of Charlotte (NC) 383,736
Mount Olive College (NC) 382,366
University of Nebraska - Omaha (NE)........................ 380,134
Northland College (WI) 374,000
Oklahoma State University (OK) 373,089
Jamestown College (ND) 372,056
SUNY College at Geneseo (NY) 370,925
Ohio University (OH) 370,500
Indiana University-Purdue University Fort Wayne (IN) 361,461
Wayland Baptist University (TX) 360,639
Xavier University (OH)............ 360,595
University of St. Thomas (TX) 360,487
Presbyterian College (SC) 359,949
University of Wisconsin- Stout (WI) 356,936
Barnard College (NY) 356,691
University of Maryland: Baltimore County (MD) 355,017
Murray State University (KY) 347,471
Mid-Continent University (KY) 345,171
Bloomsburg University of Pennsylvania (PA)................. 344,762
Milligan College (TN) 344,680
Lipscomb University (TN) 342,870
Saint Bonaventure University (NY) 341,452
Endicott College (MA) 338,427
Walsh University (OH)............. 336,870
Southeastern Oklahoma State University (OK).......... 336,759
University of Wisconsin- Eau Claire (WI) 335,148
Rider University (NJ) 334,763
Illinois College (IL)................. 332,711
Arcadia University (PA)........... 324,160
College of the Ozarks (MO) 321,100
Nyack College (NY)................. 314,700
Cuyahoga Community College: Metropolitan (OH) 313,492
Slippery Rock University of Pennsylvania (PA)................. 310,226
Tennessee Wesleyan College (TN)........................ 310,060
Belmont Abbey College (NC)........................ 308,059
Pepperdine University (CA).... 306,434
Bluffton University (OH) 303,110
Mills College (CA) 301,590
Old Dominion University (VA)................... 300,000
Dominican College of Blauvelt (NY) 299,400
California Institute of the Arts (CA) 297,431
Augustana College (IL)............ 297,062
Saint Mary's College (IN) 295,720
University of Kansas (KS) 292,980
Pacific University (OR)............ 291,673
University of North Carolina at Wilmington (NC) 288,616
Capital University (OH) 283,740

Portland State University (OR) 282,619
Milwaukee School of Engineering (WI)................. 282,245
Fisk University (TN) 278,580
University of Illinois at Chicago (IL)...................... 275,654
Harvey Mudd College (CA)..... 274,375
Susquehanna University (PA).................... 271,200
University of Houston (TX)..... 265,692
Indiana University South Bend (IN)........................ 265,418
Simmons College (MA) 264,790
Culinary Institute of America (NY) 263,800
Rockhurst University (MO)...... 260,409
Hesston College (KS) 260,000
University of Great Falls (MT) 255,974
University of Idaho (ID) 252,000
Arkansas Tech University (AR) 251,512
Mount St. Mary's University (MD) 248,834
Walla Walla University (WA)................... 248,453
Seattle Pacific University (WA)................... 248,417
Keuka College (NY) 246,900
Gallaudet University (DC) 245,774
Culver-Stockton College (MO)..................... 245,500
Washington College (MD)........ 245,000
Southwestern College (KS) 243,426
University of San Diego (CA) 243,055
Lycoming College (PA) 242,000
Franklin Pierce University (NH) 240,000
Goucher College (MD) 239,726
Trevecca Nazarene University (TN) 237,433
The Citadel (SC) 237,087
Lyon College (AR) 236,298
Valley City State University (ND) 232,509
Westmont College (CA) 232,420
Salve Regina University (RI) 229,850
Trinity Christian College (IL) 229,481
Edinboro University of Pennsylvania (PA)................. 229,351
Florida Agricultural and Mechanical University (FL) 227,693
California College of the Arts (CA) 224,500
University of Northern Iowa (IA) 222,767
King College (TN).................... 222,761
Montana State University: Bozeman (MT).................... 222,463
Alabama State University (AL) 219,576
Cornerstone University (MI) 219,553
Northwest University (WA)...... 219,012
Georgian Court University (NJ) 218,463
Baldwin-Wallace College (OH) 217,081
Philadelphia University (PA) 216,044
Scripps College (CA) 210,505
Fort Lewis College (CO).......... 207,561
Moravian College (PA) 205,094
San Jose State University (CA) 203,092
Texas A&M University- Corpus Christi (TX)............. 200,250
Dominican University of California (CA)................... 199,770

Total financial aid for international undergraduate students

Hardin-Simmons
   University (TX) 199,368
University of Houston-
   Clear Lake (TX) 197,359
Widener University (PA) 195,983
Hanover College (IN) 195,667
Laramie County
   Community
   College (WY) 189,450
University of St.
   Francis (IL) 185,703
Bob Jones University (SC) 183,502
Northwood University:
   Texas (TX) 180,000
Northeastern State
   University (OK) 179,634
Lincoln University (MO) 176,918
Virginia Intermont
   College (VA) 176,580
Baker University (KS) 174,886
SUNY University at
   Buffalo (NY) 174,257
West Texas A&M
   University (TX) 172,131
Marian University (WI) 170,481
University of Akron (OH) 166,954
Covenant College (GA) 166,360
Xavier University of
   Louisiana (LA) 166,282
South Dakota State
   University (SD) 163,114
Georgia Southern
   University (GA) 161,429
University of Alabama in
   Huntsville (AL) 158,980
Merrimack College (MA) 158,000
Spelman College (GA) 155,756
Molloy College (NY) 155,625
Guilford College (NC) 154,162
San Diego Christian
   College (CA) 148,191
Stephen F. Austin State
   University (TX) 146,532
Mount Vernon Nazarene
   University (OH) 145,532
University of Mary (ND) 145,077
Alabama Agricultural and
   Mechanical
   University (AL) 145,015
Utah Valley
   University (UT) 144,476
University of Tennessee:
   Chattanooga (TN) 143,912
Shippensburg University of
   Pennsylvania (PA) 143,526
Medaille College (NY) 143,000
Philadelphia Biblical
   University (PA) 139,150
Northwestern State
   University (LA) 137,472
Edgewood College (WI) 137,242
Drury University (MO) 136,500
Hampton University (VA) 135,128
Albany College of
   Pharmacy and Health
   Sciences (NY) 134,230
SUNY College at
   Fredonia (NY) 130,000
Fontbonne University (MO) 129,750
Kentucky State
   University (KY) 128,212
Missouri Southern State
   University (MO) 124,940
University of Houston-
   Downtown (TX) 122,750
University of Puget
   Sound (WA) 122,000
Lake Region State
   College (ND) 120,644
Regis College (MA) 120,634
Tabor College (KS) 120,190
Flagler College (FL) 118,705
Northwestern College (MN) 118,220
Augusta State
   University (GA) 116,447

Doane College (NE) 115,900
Claflin University (SC) 115,812
Huston-Tillotson
   University (TX) 114,320
Willamette University (OR) 113,500
Mayville State
   University (ND) 112,956
Washington & Jefferson
   College (PA) 112,780
East Texas Baptist
   University (TX) 111,858
Marymount Manhattan
   College (NY) 111,423
St. Mary's College of
   Maryland (MD) 110,100
Lawrence Technological
   University (MI) 108,250
Western Nebraska
   Community College (NE) 106,141
Cincinnati Christian
   University (OH) 105,805
Bridgewater College (VA) 105,000
Williston State
   College (ND) 104,975
Bethel College (KS) 103,964
Alverno College (WI) 103,515
Florida Southern
   College (FL) 101,661
Indiana Wesleyan
   University (IN) 101,011
Vaughn College of
   Aeronautics and
   Technology (NY) 100,698
Maryville University of
   Saint Louis (MO) 99,400
St. Joseph's College (NY) 99,384
Wheaton College (IL) 98,372
Transylvania
   University (KY) 98,250
Kean University (NJ) 95,482
California State University:
   Fresno (CA) 95,399
Jefferson College (MO) 93,660
Southern Virginia
   University (VA) 92,899
Clarke University (IA) 91,430
Southern Wesleyan
   University (SC) 90,415
College of Saint Rose (NY) 90,064
University of Minnesota:
   Crookston (MN) 89,862
Lone Star College
   System (TX) 89,521
Brewton-Parker
   College (GA) 89,013
The King's College (NY) 88,644
Evangel University (MO) 86,580
Friends University (KS) 85,610
Bluefield College (VA) 85,495
University of Texas at
   Tyler (TX) 84,631
Huntingdon College (AL) 83,289
University of Texas at San
   Antonio (TX) 82,145
North Dakota State College
   of Science (ND) 81,302
Colorado State University:
   Pueblo (CO) 74,750
Rosemont College (PA) 72,378
Millikin University (IL) 71,708
Columbus State
   University (GA) 71,025
University of South
   Carolina: Aiken (SC) 68,795
Cleveland Institute of
   Art (OH) 68,500
Trine University (IN) 68,500
University of Pittsburgh at
   Johnstown (PA) 65,280
Williams Baptist
   College (AR) 64,707
Western Washington
   University (WA) 64,320
Concordia University
   Wisconsin (WI) 62,380

Nazareth College (NY) 61,300
Union College (KY) 60,369
Georgia State
   University (GA) 60,048
American Jewish
   University (CA) 60,000
University of Maine at
   Augusta (ME) 58,205
Wheelock College (MA) 58,000
McMurry University (TX) 57,672
Evergreen State
   College (WA) 56,689
Simpson University (CA) 55,807
Grove City College (PA) 54,938
University of Central
   Florida (FL) 53,350
Piedmont College (GA) 52,800
Southwestern Christian
   College (TX) 52,724
Benedictine College (KS) 52,475
Lubbock Christian
   University (TX) 50,710
Lynchburg College (VA) 50,650
Thomas College (ME) 50,000
Northern Illinois
   University (IL) 48,917
SUNY College of
   Technology at
   Alfred (NY) 47,658
St. John Fisher
   College (NY) 47,650
Peace College (NC) 47,000
University of Illinois:
   Springfield (IL) 45,700
Kansas City Art
   Institute (MO) 45,000
Ursinus College (PA) 45,000
University of Michigan:
   Flint (MI) 44,512
University of La
   Verne (CA) 43,385
Lamar University (TX) 43,050
Ursuline College (OH) 42,029
Black Hawk College (IL) 41,259
Quincy University (IL) 41,250
Central College (IA) 41,000
Northern Michigan
   University (MI) 40,600
Sacred Heart Major
   Seminary (MI) 38,110
University of Colorado at
   Colorado Springs (CO) 37,996
Crown College (MN) 37,050
University of Texas of the
   Permian Basin (TX) 35,539
Pikeville College (KY) 34,250
Keystone College (PA) 34,000
Nichols College (MA) 33,000
Oregon Health & Science
   University (OR) 33,000
Cabrini College (PA) 32,084
VanderCook College of
   Music (IL) 31,900
University of
   Oklahoma (OK) 31,595
Alcorn State
   University (MS) 31,078
Lincoln Christian
   University (IL) 30,867
Purdue University
   Calumet (IN) 30,671
Cazenovia College (NY) 30,000
Schreiner University (TX) 29,133
University of West
   Alabama (AL) 28,572
Saint Martin's
   University (WA) 28,500
University of
   Redlands (CA) 28,330
Dakota State
   University (SD) 27,895
Prescott College (AZ) 26,500
Sterling College (VT) 25,396
Mitchell College (CT) 24,000

University of Pittsburgh at
   Bradford (PA) 23,541
Franklin College (IN) 22,211
Silver Lake College (WI) 20,950
Lebanon Valley
   College (PA) 20,606
Virginia Wesleyan
   College (VA) 20,500
Wagner College (NY) 20,100
Kentucky Mountain Bible
   College (KY) 19,400
Central Christian College of
   Kansas (KS) 19,350
University of Montana:
   Western (MT) 18,865
Sul Ross State
   University (TX) 18,847
Paine College (GA) 17,542
Texas College (TX) 15,912
New York School of
   Interior Design (NY) 15,400
Shepherd University (WV) 15,232
Concordia University
   Texas (TX) 13,500
Elizabeth City State
   University (NC) 13,000
Aquinas College (MI) 12,750
Wichita State
   University (KS) 12,449
Oregon State
   University (OR) 12,375
Warner Pacific
   College (OR) 12,250
Eastern New Mexico
   University (NM) 12,064
Waynesburg
   University (PA) 12,000
Luther Rice
   University (GA) 11,694
Kirtland Community
   College (MI) 11,347
Eastern Oregon
   University (OR) 11,100
Life University (GA) 11,000
Nebraska Wesleyan
   University (NE) 11,000
Richard Stockton College
   of New Jersey (NJ) 11,000
William Jessup
   University (CA) 11,000
Eastern Connecticut State
   University (CT) 10,992
Aurora University (IL) 10,000
Spalding University (KY) 8,526
Long Island Business
   Institute (NY) 8,400
Bossier Parish Community
   College (LA) 7,716
Benedictine University at
   Springfield (IL) 7,572
Santa Rosa Junior
   College (CA) 7,500
Montserrat College of
   Art (MA) 7,036
Husson University (ME) 6,500
Southeastern Bible
   College (AL) 5,750
Bastyr University (WA) 5,000
Cedar Crest College (PA) 5,000
Indiana University
   Southeast (IN) 4,000
Montana State University:
   Northern (MT) 3,440
Lackawanna College (PA) 3,000
Salisbury University (MD) 2,500
York College of
   Pennsylvania (PA) 2,500
Indiana University
   Northwest (IN) 2,298
Indiana University
   East (IN) 2,254
Indiana University
   Kokomo (IN) 2,012
Howard Payne
   University (TX) 2,000

City University of New
  York: York College (NY) 1,500
Valley Forge Christian
  College (PA) 1,460
Manor College (PA) 1,000
Peirce College (PA) 1,000
University of Utah (UT) 1,000
Lebanon College (NH) 300

Conditional admission based on English-language proficiency

Alabama

Alabama Agricultural and Mechanical University
Auburn University
Bishop State Community College
Chattahoochee Valley Community College
Faulkner State Community College
Faulkner University
Gadsden State Community College
Jacksonville State University
Miles College
Samford University
Spring Hill College
United States Sports Academy
University of Alabama
University of Alabama at Birmingham
University of Alabama in Huntsville
University of Mobile
University of North Alabama
University of South Alabama

Alaska

Alaska Pacific University
Prince William Sound Community College
University of Alaska Anchorage

Arizona

Arizona State University
Arizona Western College
Art Center Design College
Cochise College
Dine College
Dunlap-Stone University
Everest College: Phoenix
Glendale Community College
Northern Arizona University
Pima Community College
Prescott College
Rio Salado College
Scottsdale Community College
University of Advancing Technology
University of Arizona
Western International University

Arkansas

Arkansas State University: Newport
Arkansas Tech University
Cossatot Community College of the University of Arkansas
Crowley's Ridge College
Ecclesia College
Harding University
John Brown University
National Park Community College
Ouachita Baptist University

Phillips Community College of the University of Arkansas
University of Arkansas
University of Arkansas at Little Rock
University of Central Arkansas

California

Academy of Art University
Allan Hancock College
Alliant International University
Art Institute of California: San Diego
Art Institute of California: San Francisco
Azusa Pacific University
Bethesda Christian University
Biola University
Bryan College: Los Angeles
California Baptist University
California College of the Arts
California Institute of the Arts
California Lutheran University
California State University: Chico
California State University: Fresno
California State University: Long Beach
California State University: Los Angeles
California State University: Monterey Bay
California State University: Stanislaus
California University of Management and Sciences
Canada College
Chaffey College
Charles Drew University of Medicine and Science
Citrus College
City College of San Francisco
Coastline Community College
Coleman University
College of the Desert
College of the Sequoias
College of the Siskiyous
Contra Costa College
East Los Angeles College
El Camino College
Fashion Institute of Design and Merchandising: San Francisco
Feather River College
Foothill College
Fremont College: Cerritos
Fresno Pacific University
Glendale Community College
Golden Gate University
Holy Names University
Hope International University
Humboldt State University
Humphreys College
Kaplan College: Panorama City
The King's University
La Sierra University
Laguna College of Art and Design
Las Positas College
Lincoln University

Long Beach City College
Los Angeles City College
Los Angeles Pierce College
Marymount College
The Master's College
Menlo College
Merritt College
Mills College
MiraCosta College
Mission College
Monterey Peninsula College
Napa Valley College
National University
NewSchool of Architecture & Design
Northwestern Polytechnic University
Notre Dame de Namur University
Ohlone College
Otis College of Art and Design
Oxnard College
Pacific States University
Pacific Union College
Palomar College
Patten University
Pepperdine University
Pitzer College
Platt College: San Diego
Point Loma Nazarene University
Sacramento City College
Saddleback College
St. Mary's College of California
San Diego Christian College
San Diego Mesa College
San Diego State University
San Francisco Art Institute
San Francisco Conservatory of Music
San Joaquin Delta College
San Jose City College
Santa Ana College
Santa Barbara City College
Santa Monica College
Santiago Canyon College
School of Urban Missions: Oakland
Scripps College
Shasta College
Sierra College
Soka University of America
Solano Community College
Southern California Institute of Architecture
Southern California Institute of Technology
Southern California Seminary
Taft College
University of California: Santa Barbara
University of La Verne
University of Redlands
University of San Diego
University of San Francisco
University of Southern California
Ventura College
West Hills College: Coalinga
West Los Angeles College
Whittier College
World Mission University
Yuba Community College District

Colorado

Aims Community College
Arapahoe Community College
Art Institute of Colorado
Boulder College of Massage Therapy
Colorado Christian University
Colorado Heights University
Colorado Mountain College
Colorado Northwestern Community College
Colorado State University
Colorado State University: Pueblo
IntelliTec College
IntelliTec College: Grand Junction
Johnson & Wales University: Denver
Mesa State College

Northeastern Junior College
Pikes Peak Community College
Red Rocks Community College
Rocky Mountain College of Art & Design
Trinidad State Junior College
University of Denver
University of Northern Colorado
Westwood College: Denver North

Connecticut

Asnuntuck Community College
Central Connecticut State University
Gateway Community College
Housatonic Community College
Lincoln College of New England: Briarwood
Lincoln College of New England: Suffield
Mitchell College
Naugatuck Valley Community College
Post University
Quinnipiac University
Sacred Heart University
Tunxis Community College
University of Bridgeport
University of Connecticut
University of New Haven

Delaware

Delaware College of Art and Design
Delaware Technical and Community College: Stanton/Wilmington
University of Delaware
Wesley College

District of Columbia

American University
Catholic University of America
Gallaudet University
George Washington University
Georgetown University
Howard University
Potomac College
Trinity Washington University
University of the District of Columbia

Florida

Ave Maria University
Barry University
Carlos Albizu University
City College: Fort Lauderdale
College of Business and Technology: Flagler
Eckerd College
Edison State College
Embry-Riddle Aeronautical University
Everest University: Largo
Florida Institute of Technology
Florida Memorial University
Florida National College
Florida Southern College
Florida State College at Jacksonville
Fortis College: Winter Park
Full Sail University
Johnson & Wales University: North Miami
Key College
Lynn University
Miami Dade College
Northwood University: Florida
Palm Beach State College
Pensacola State College
Polk State College

Remington College: Tampa
Ringling College of Art and Design
Saint Leo University
Saint Thomas University
Schiller International University
Seminole State College of Florida
Southwest Florida College
University of Miami
University of South Florida
University of Tampa
Valencia College
Warner University
Webber International University

Georgia

Abraham Baldwin Agricultural College
American InterContinental University
Andrew College
Armstrong Atlantic State University
Art Institute of Atlanta
Augusta Technical College
Bauder College
Columbus State University
Darton College
DeKalb Technical College
Fort Valley State University
Gainesville State College
Georgia Highlands College
Georgia Southern University
Georgia Southwestern State University
Georgia State University
Life University
Mercer University
Middle Georgia College
North Georgia College & State
   University
Piedmont College
Savannah College of Art and Design
Savannah Technical College
Thomas University
University of Georgia

Hawaii

Brigham Young University-Hawaii
Chaminade University of Honolulu
Hawaii Pacific University
Hawaii Tokai International College
University of Hawaii: Honolulu
   Community College
University of Hawaii: Kapiolani
   Community College
University of Hawaii: Leeward
   Community College
University of Hawaii: Windward
   Community College

Idaho

Boise State University
College of Idaho
Idaho State University
Lewis-Clark State College
North Idaho College
Stevens-Henager College: Boise
University of Idaho

Illinois

Benedictine University
Black Hawk College
Carl Sandburg College
City Colleges of Chicago: Harold
   Washington College
City Colleges of Chicago: Wilbur
   Wright College
College of DuPage

College of Lake County
Columbia College Chicago
Concordia University Chicago
Danville Area Community College
DePaul University
Dominican University
East-West University
Elgin Community College
Harper College
Illinois Central College
Illinois Eastern Community Colleges:
   Frontier Community College
Illinois Eastern Community Colleges:
   Lincoln Trail College
Illinois Eastern Community Colleges:
   Olney Central College
Illinois Eastern Community Colleges:
   Wabash Valley College
Kendall College
Kishwaukee College
Lake Land College
Lewis University
Lexington College
Lincoln College
Loyola University Chicago
MacCormac College
McKendree University
Moraine Valley Community College
Morrison Institute of Technology
National-Louis University
North Central College
North Park University
Northwestern College
Parkland College
Resurrection University
Richland Community College
Rockford College
Roosevelt University
Sauk Valley Community College
School of the Art Institute of Chicago
Southern Illinois University Carbondale
Southern Illinois University
   Edwardsville
Southwestern Illinois College
Trinity Christian College
Triton College
Western Illinois University

Indiana

Ancilla College
Ball State University
Butler University
Earlham College
Franklin College
Goshen College
Huntington University
Indiana Institute of Technology
Indiana State University
Indiana University Bloomington
Indiana University East
Indiana University-Purdue University
   Fort Wayne
Indiana University-Purdue University
   Indianapolis
Ivy Tech Community College:
   Bloomington
Ivy Tech Community College: Central
   Indiana
Ivy Tech Community College:
   Columbus
Ivy Tech Community College: East
   Central
Ivy Tech Community College: Kokomo
Ivy Tech Community College:
   Lafayette
Ivy Tech Community College: North
   Central
Ivy Tech Community College:
   Northeast
Ivy Tech Community College:
   Northwest

Ivy Tech Community College:
   Richmond
Ivy Tech Community College: South
   Central
Ivy Tech Community College:
   Southeast
Ivy Tech Community College:
   Southwest
Ivy Tech Community College: Wabash
   Valley
Marian University
Oakland City University
Taylor University
Trine University
University of Evansville
University of Indianapolis
University of Southern Indiana
Vincennes University

Iowa

Ashford University
Buena Vista University
Central College
Clarke University
Coe College
Des Moines Area Community College
Drake University
Ellsworth Community College
Graceland University
Iowa State University
Iowa Wesleyan College
Iowa Western Community College
Kaplan University: Des Moines
Kirkwood Community College
Loras College
Maharishi University of Management
Marshalltown Community College
Northwestern College
Scott Community College
University of Dubuque
University of Iowa
University of Northern Iowa
Upper Iowa University
Waldorf College
Wartburg College
Western Iowa Tech Community
   College
William Penn University

Kansas

Barclay College
Barton County Community College
Benedictine College
Cloud County Community College
Colby Community College
Dodge City Community College
Donnelly College
Emporia State University
Fort Hays State University
Hesston College
Kansas City Kansas Community
   College
Kansas State University
McPherson College
Neosho County Community College
Ottawa University
Pittsburg State University
Pratt Community College
Southwestern College
University of Kansas
University of Kansas Medical Center
University of St. Mary
Washburn University
Wichita State University

Kentucky

Bluegrass Community and Technical
   College

Brescia University
Campbellsville University
Daymar College: Owensboro
Henderson Community College
Kentucky Mountain Bible College
Kentucky State University
Lindsey Wilson College
Mid-Continent University
Morehead State University
Murray State University
Northern Kentucky University
Owensboro Community and Technical
   College
Somerset Community College
Southeast Kentucky Community and
   Technical College
Sullivan College of Technology and
   Design
Thomas More College
Transylvania University
University of the Cumberlands
University of Kentucky
University of Louisville
Western Kentucky University

Louisiana

Bossier Parish Community College
Delgado Community College
Herzing University
Louisiana College
Louisiana State University at Eunice
Louisiana Tech University
McNeese State University
Nunez Community College
St. Joseph Seminary College
Tulane University
University of Louisiana at Lafayette
University of Louisiana at Monroe
University of New Orleans

Maine

Central Maine Community College
Colby College
Husson University
Maine Maritime Academy
Southern Maine Community College
Unity College in Maine
University of Maine
University of Maine at Fort Kent
University of Maine at Presque Isle
University of New England
University of Southern Maine
Washington County Community
   College

Maryland

Anne Arundel Community College
Baltimore City Community College
Baltimore International College
Capitol College
Carroll Community College
Chesapeake College
Community College of Baltimore
   County
Griggs University
Harford Community College
Hood College
Howard Community College
Johns Hopkins University: Peabody
   Conservatory of Music
Maryland Institute College of Art
Prince George's Community College
Salisbury University
Stevenson University
Towson University
University of Maryland: Baltimore
   County

Conditional admission based on English-language proficiency

University of Maryland: College Park
University of Maryland: Eastern Shore
University of Maryland: University
  College
Washington Adventist University

Massachusetts

American International College
Atlantic Union College
Bay Path College
Bay State College
Benjamin Franklin Institute of
  Technology
Berklee College of Music
Berkshire Community College
Boston Conservatory
Boston University
Bristol Community College
Bunker Hill Community College
Clark University
Dean College
Eastern Nazarene College
Elms College
Fisher College
Gordon College
Hellenic College/Holy Cross
Massachusetts Bay Community College
Massachusetts College of Pharmacy
  and Health Sciences
Merrimack College
Middlesex Community College
Montserrat College of Art
Mount Ida College
Mount Wachusett Community College
New England Conservatory of Music
Nichols College
Northeastern University
Northern Essex Community College
Pine Manor College
Quincy College
Regis College
School of the Museum of Fine Arts
Springfield College
Suffolk University
University of Massachusetts Boston
Wentworth Institute of Technology
Wheaton College
Worcester Polytechnic Institute

Michigan

Albion College
Alma College
Andrews University
Baker College of Auburn Hills
Baker College of Cadillac
Baker College of Jackson
Baker College of Muskegon
Baker College of Port Huron
Calvin College
Central Michigan University
Cornerstone University
Davenport University
Eastern Michigan University
Finlandia University
Kettering University
Kuyper College
Lawrence Technological University
Macomb Community College
Madonna University
Michigan Jewish Institute
Michigan State University
Michigan Technological University
Muskegon Community College
Northern Michigan University
Northwood University: Michigan
Oakland Community College
Oakland University
Olivet College
Rochester College
Saginaw Valley State University

Siena Heights University
Southwestern Michigan College
Spring Arbor University
University of Detroit Mercy
University of Michigan: Dearborn
University of Michigan: Flint
Wayne State University
Western Michigan University

Minnesota

Art Institutes International Minnesota
Augsburg College
Bemidji State University
Bethel University
College of St. Benedict
College of St. Scholastica
Concordia University St. Paul
Crown College
Dakota County Technical College
Globe University
Hamline University
Hibbing Community College
Itasca Community College
Lake Superior College
Minnesota State Community and
  Technical College
Minnesota West Community and
  Technical College
North Central University
North Hennepin Community College
Northwest Technical College
Pine Technical College
Rainy River Community College
Rochester Community and Technical
  College
St. Catherine University
Saint Cloud State University
St. Cloud Technical and Community
  College
St. John's University
St. Mary's University of Minnesota
University of Minnesota: Crookston
University of St. Thomas
Winona State University

Mississippi

Belhaven University
Hinds Community College
Meridian Community College
Mississippi College
Mississippi State University
Northeast Mississippi Community
  College
Southeastern Baptist College
University of Mississippi
University of Southern Mississippi
William Carey University

Missouri

Avila University
Crowder College
Culver-Stockton College
Drury University
Fontbonne University
Grantham University
Jefferson College
Kansas City Art Institute
Maryville University of Saint Louis
Metropolitan Community College:
  Penn Valley
Missouri Baptist University
Missouri Southern State University
Missouri State University
Missouri Technical School
Missouri University of Science and
  Technology
Missouri Valley College

National American University: Kansas
  City
Northwest Missouri State University
Rockhurst University
Saint Louis University
Southeast Missouri State University
Southwest Baptist University
State Fair Community College
Stephens College
Truman State University
University of Central Missouri
University of Missouri: Columbia
University of Missouri: Kansas City
University of Missouri: St. Louis
Washington University in St. Louis
Webster University
Westminster College
William Woods University

Montana

Carroll College
Montana State University: Billings
Montana State University: Bozeman
Montana Tech of the University of
  Montana
University of Great Falls
University of Montana
University of Montana: Western

Nebraska

Creighton University
Doane College
Metropolitan Community College
Nebraska Christian College
Nebraska Wesleyan University
Northeast Community College
Union College
University of Nebraska - Kearney
University of Nebraska - Lincoln
University of Nebraska - Omaha
Western Nebraska Community College
York College

Nevada

Career College of Northern Nevada
College of Southern Nevada
Great Basin College
Morrison University
Sierra Nevada College
University of Nevada: Las Vegas
University of Nevada: Reno
Western Nevada College

New Hampshire

Chester College of New England
Colby-Sawyer College
Daniel Webster College
Franklin Pierce University
Hesser College
Magdalen College
Manchester Community College
New England College
NHTI-Concord's Community College
Rivier College
Southern New Hampshire University
University of New Hampshire at
  Manchester

New Jersey

Atlantic Cape Community College
Bloomfield College

Brookdale Community College
Burlington County College
Caldwell College
Centenary College
College of St. Elizabeth
County College of Morris
Cumberland County College
Fairleigh Dickinson University:
  College at Florham
Fairleigh Dickinson University:
  Metropolitan Campus
Felician College
Hudson County Community College
Mercer County Community College
Middlesex County College
Monmouth University
Montclair State University
New Jersey City University
New Jersey Institute of Technology
Seton Hall University
Stevens Institute of Technology
Sussex County Community College

New Mexico

Eastern New Mexico University
Institute of American Indian Arts
New Mexico Institute of Mining and
  Technology
New Mexico Military Institute
New Mexico State University
New Mexico State University at
  Alamogordo
Santa Fe Community College
University of New Mexico
University of the Southwest

New York

Adelphi University
Bramson ORT College
Briarcliffe College
Broome Community College
Bryant & Stratton College: Albany
Bryant & Stratton College: Rochester
Bryant & Stratton College: Syracuse
  North
Canisius College
City University of New York: Baruch
  College
City University of New York: Borough
  of Manhattan Community College
City University of New York: Bronx
  Community College
City University of New York:
  Brooklyn College
City University of New York: City
  College
City University of New York: College
  of Staten Island
City University of New York:
  LaGuardia Community College
City University of New York: Queens
  College
City University of New York: York
  College
Clinton Community College
College of Mount St. Vincent
Columbia University: School of
  General Studies
Columbia-Greene Community College
Concordia College
Daemen College
Dowling College
Dutchess Community College
Eastman School of Music of the
  University of Rochester
Elmira College
Eugene Lang College The New School
  for Liberal Arts
Excelsior College
Five Towns College

Fordham University
Fulton-Montgomery Community College
Globe Institute of Technology
Herkimer County Community College
Institute of Design and Construction
Ithaca College
Long Island University: C. W. Post Campus
Manhattan College
Manhattan School of Music
Manhattanville College
Mannes College The New School for Music
Medaille College
Mercy College
Mildred Elley
Mohawk Valley Community College
Molloy College
Nazareth College
New York Institute of Technology
New York University
Niagara County Community College
North Country Community College
Nyack College
Ohr Somayach Tanenbaum Education Center
Onondaga Community College
Pace University
Parsons The New School for Design
Polytechnic Institute of New York University
Pratt Institute
Rensselaer Polytechnic Institute
Roberts Wesleyan College
Rochester Institute of Technology
Rockland Community College
Saint Bonaventure University
St. Francis College
St. John's University
St. Thomas Aquinas College
School of Visual Arts
Siena College
Suffolk County Community College
SUNY College at New Paltz
SUNY College at Plattsburgh
SUNY College of Agriculture and Technology at Morrisville
SUNY College of Technology at Alfred
SUNY College of Technology at Canton
SUNY College of Technology at Delhi
SUNY University at Albany
SUNY University at Buffalo
SUNY University at Stony Brook
Syracuse University
Technical Career Institutes
Tompkins Cortland Community College
Touro College
University of Rochester
Utica College
Vaughn College of Aeronautics and Technology
Wagner College
Yeshivat Mikdash Melech

North Carolina

Appalachian State University
Belmont Abbey College
Brevard College
Central Piedmont Community College
Chowan University
College of the Albemarle
Elizabeth City State University
Elon University
Guilford College
High Point University
Laurel University
Mayland Community College

McDowell Technical Community College
Methodist University
Mount Olive College
Pfeiffer University
Piedmont Baptist College and Graduate School
Piedmont Community College
Southeastern Community College
University of North Carolina at Charlotte
University of North Carolina at Pembroke
University of North Carolina at Wilmington
University of North Carolina School of the Arts
Vance-Granville Community College
Warren Wilson College
Wilson Community College
Wingate University

North Dakota

Bismarck State College
Dickinson State University
Lake Region State College
North Dakota State College of Science
North Dakota State University
United Tribes Technical College
University of Mary

Ohio

Antonelli College: Cincinnati
Art Institute of Ohio: Cincinnati
Ashland University
Baldwin-Wallace College
Capital University
Central Ohio Technical College
Central State University
Cincinnati State Technical and Community College
Cleveland State University
Columbus College of Art and Design
Columbus State Community College
Cuyahoga Community College: Metropolitan
Defiance College
Franklin University
Heidelberg University
Hiram College
Hocking College
Kent State University
Lake Erie College
Lorain County Community College
Miami University: Middletown
Miami University: Oxford
Muskingum University
Oberlin College
Ohio Dominican University
Ohio Northern University
Ohio State University: Columbus Campus
Ohio University
Otterbein University
Shawnee State University
Tiffin University
Union Institute & University
University of Akron
University of Dayton
University of Findlay
University of Mount Union
University of Northwestern Ohio
University of Rio Grande
University of Toledo
Urbana University
Walsh University
Wilmington College
Wittenberg University
Xavier University
Youngstown State University

Oklahoma

Bacone College
Eastern Oklahoma State College
Northeastern Oklahoma Agricultural and Mechanical College
Northeastern State University
Oklahoma Baptist University
Oklahoma Christian University
Oklahoma City Community College
Oklahoma City University
Oklahoma State University
Oklahoma State University: Oklahoma City
Oklahoma Wesleyan University
Oral Roberts University
St. Gregory's University
Southern Nazarene University
Southwestern Christian University
Southwestern Oklahoma State University
University of Oklahoma
University of Tulsa

Oregon

Chemeketa Community College
Concordia University
George Fox University
Lewis & Clark College
Linfield College
Marylhurst University
Mount Angel Seminary
Mt. Hood Community College
Oregon Institute of Technology
Oregon State University
Pacific University
Portland Community College
Portland State University
Southwestern Oregon Community College
Treasure Valley Community College
University of Oregon
University of Portland
Western Oregon University

Pennsylvania

Albright College
Arcadia University
Art Institute of Pittsburgh
Baptist Bible College of Pennsylvania
Bloomsburg University of Pennsylvania
Cabrini College
Carlow University
Chatham University
Curtis Institute of Music
Douglas Education Center
Drexel University
Duquesne University
Geneva College
Gratz College
Gwynedd-Mercy College
Harcum College
Harrisburg Area Community College
Immaculata University
Juniata College
Keystone College
Keystone Technical Institute
King's College
Kutztown University of Pennsylvania
La Roche College
Laurel Business Institute
Laurel Technical Institute
Lehigh University
Lock Haven University of Pennsylvania
Lycoming College
Manor College
Mansfield University of Pennsylvania

Marywood University
Mercyhurst College
Misericordia University
Moore College of Art and Design
Oakbridge Academy of Arts
Penn State Abington
Penn State Altoona
Penn State Beaver
Penn State Berks
Penn State Brandywine
Penn State DuBois
Penn State Erie, The Behrend College
Penn State Fayette, The Eberly Campus
Penn State Greater Allegheny
Penn State Harrisburg
Penn State Hazleton
Penn State Lehigh Valley
Penn State Mont Alto
Penn State New Kensington
Penn State Schuylkill
Penn State Shenango
Penn State University Park
Penn State Wilkes-Barre
Penn State Worthington Scranton
Penn State York
Pittsburgh Institute of Aeronautics
Pittsburgh Institute of Mortuary Science
Point Park University
Robert Morris University
Rosemont College
St. Charles Borromeo Seminary - Overbrook
St. Francis University
Saint Joseph's University
St. Vincent College
Seton Hill University
Thiel College
University of the Arts
University of Scranton
Valley Forge Christian College
Valley Forge Military Academy and College
Villanova University
Widener University

Puerto Rico

ICPR Junior College
Inter American University of Puerto Rico: San German Campus
University of Puerto Rico: Mayaguez

Rhode Island

Bryant University
Johnson & Wales University: Providence
New England Institute of Technology
Roger Williams University

South Carolina

Anderson University
Bob Jones University
Charleston Southern University
The Citadel
Coker College
Forrest Junior College
Greenville Technical College
Horry-Georgetown Technical College
Morris College
Newberry College
North Greenville University
Southern Wesleyan University
Spartanburg Community College
Spartanburg Methodist College
Tri-County Technical College
University of South Carolina: Aiken

Conditional admission based on English-language proficiency

University of South Carolina: Beaufort
University of South Carolina: Sumter
University of South Carolina: Upstate
Winthrop University

South Dakota

Dakota State University
Lake Area Technical Institute
National American University: Rapid
  City
Presentation College
South Dakota School of Mines and
  Technology
South Dakota State University
University of South Dakota

Tennessee

Bethel University
Carson-Newman College
East Tennessee State University
King College
Lane College
Lincoln Memorial University
Lipscomb University
Maryville College
Nossi College of Art
O'More College of Design
Pellissippi State Community College
Tennessee Wesleyan College
University of Memphis
University of Tennessee: Knoxville
University of Tennessee: Martin
Victory University
Volunteer State Community College
Williamson Christian College

Texas

Abilene Christian University
Arlington Baptist College
Blinn College
Cedar Valley College
Central Texas College
Concordia University Texas
Dallas Baptist University
East Texas Baptist University
El Centro College
Frank Phillips College
Galveston College
Grayson County College
Hallmark College of Aeronautics
Hallmark College of Technology
Hill College
Houston Community College System
Huston-Tillotson University
Kilgore College
Lamar State College at Port Arthur
LeTourneau University
Lon Morris College
Midland College
Midwestern State University
Mountain View College
Northwood University: Texas
Our Lady of the Lake University of
  San Antonio
Richland College
St. Mary's University
Schreiner University
South Plains College
Southwestern Adventist University
Texas A&M University
Texas A&M University-Galveston
Texas Christian University
Texas Southern University
Texas State Technical College:
  Harlingen
Texas State University: San Marcos
Texas Tech University

Texas Woman's University
Trinity Valley Community College
University of Dallas
University of the Incarnate Word
University of Mary Hardin-Baylor
University of North Texas
University of Texas at Arlington
University of Texas at El Paso
University of Texas at San Antonio
University of Texas of the Permian
  Basin
Wade College
Wayland Baptist University
Weatherford College
West Texas A&M University
Wiley College

Utah

Brigham Young University
College of Eastern Utah
Dixie State College
Independence University
Salt Lake Community College
Snow College
Southern Utah University
University of Utah
Utah State University
Weber State University
Westminster College

Vermont

Burlington College
Community College of Vermont
Green Mountain College
Johnson State College
Lyndon State College
St. Michael's College

Virginia

Bryant & Stratton College: Virginia
  Beach
Christendom College
Eastern Mennonite University
ECPI College of Technology: Virginia
  Beach
George Mason University
J. Sargeant Reynolds Community
  College
James Madison University
Jefferson College of Health Sciences
Liberty University
Old Dominion University
Patrick Henry Community College
Paul D. Camp Community College
St. Paul's College
Shenandoah University
Stratford University: Falls Church
Stratford University: Woodbridge
Thomas Nelson Community College
Tidewater Community College
University of Mary Washington
University of Richmond
University of Virginia's College at
  Wise
Virginia Commonwealth University
Virginia Union University
Virginia Wesleyan College

Washington

Art Institute of Seattle
Bates Technical College
Cascadia Community College
Central Washington University
Centralia College

Clark College
Clover Park Technical College
Eastern Washington University
Everett Community College
Gonzaga University
Highline Community College
Lake Washington Technical College
Lower Columbia College
North Seattle Community College
Olympic College
Pacific Lutheran University
Peninsula College
Pierce College
Saint Martin's University
Seattle Central Community College
Seattle Pacific University
Seattle University
Skagit Valley College
South Puget Sound Community
  College
South Seattle Community College
Spokane Community College
Trinity Lutheran College
Walla Walla Community College
Walla Walla University
Washington State University
Western Washington University
Whatcom Community College
Whitworth University
Yakima Valley Community College

West Virginia

Alderson-Broaddus College
Appalachian Bible College
Bluefield State College
Concord University
Davis and Elkins College
Glenville State College
Marshall University
Mountain State University
Ohio Valley University
Salem International University
University of Charleston
West Virginia Junior College:
  Bridgeport
West Virginia Northern Community
  College
West Virginia State University
West Virginia University
West Virginia University Institute of
  Technology
West Virginia Wesleyan College
Wheeling Jesuit University

Wisconsin

Beloit College
Carroll University
Concordia University Wisconsin
Edgewood College
Fox Valley Technical College
Lakeland College
Lakeshore Technical College
Marquette University
Milwaukee School of Engineering
Northland College
St. Norbert College
Silver Lake College
Southwest Wisconsin Technical
  College
University of Wisconsin-Baraboo/Sauk
  County
University of Wisconsin-Eau Claire
University of Wisconsin-La Crosse
University of Wisconsin-Marshfield/
  Wood County
University of Wisconsin-Milwaukee
University of Wisconsin-Platteville
University of Wisconsin-Richland
University of Wisconsin-Rock County
University of Wisconsin-Sheboygan

University of Wisconsin-Stevens Point
University of Wisconsin-Stout
University of Wisconsin-Superior
Viterbo University
Western Technical College
Wisconsin Lutheran College

Wyoming

Central Wyoming College
Northwest College
Western Wyoming Community College

SAT Subject Tests required or recommended

Alabama

University of Mobile*

Arkansas

John Brown University*

California

California Institute of Technology
Harvey Mudd College
Mills College*
Occidental College*
Stanford University*
University of California: Berkeley
University of California: Davis
University of California: Irvine*
University of California: Merced
University of California: Riverside
University of California: Santa Barbara
University of the Pacific*
University of Southern California*

Connecticut

Yale University*

District of Columbia

Catholic University of America*
Georgetown University*
Howard University

Florida

Florida International University*

Georgia

Emory University*
Morehouse College*

Illinois

Northwestern University*

Louisiana

Loyola University New Orleans*

Maryland

Hood College*

Massachusetts

Babson College*
Boston College
Eastern Nazarene College*
Franklin W. Olin College of
  Engineering
Gordon College*
Harvard College
Massachusetts Institute of Technology
Smith College*

Michigan

Hillsdale College*

Minnesota

Carleton College*

Montana

University of Great Falls*

New Hampshire

Dartmouth College

New Jersey

Princeton University
Stevens Institute of Technology*

New York

Columbia University
Mercy College*
Polytechnic Institute of New York
  University*
Skidmore College*
University of Rochester*

North Carolina

North Carolina State University*

Ohio

Columbus College of Art and Design*
Ohio Wesleyan University*

Oregon

Reed College

Pennsylvania

Immaculata University*
Susquehanna University*

Puerto Rico

Inter American University of Puerto
  Rico: Barranquitas Campus
University of Puerto Rico: Aguadilla
University of Puerto Rico: Carolina
  Regional College
University of Puerto Rico: Cayey
  University College
University of Puerto Rico: Humacao
University of Puerto Rico: Mayaguez
University of Puerto Rico: Utuado

South Carolina

Voorhees College

Tennessee

Cumberland University*

Texas

Hill College*

Vermont

Bennington College*
Green Mountain College*

Virginia

Hampden-Sydney College*
University of Richmond*
University of Virginia*
Virginia Union University
Washington and Lee University

Colleges that recommend SAT Subject Tests are noted with an asterisk   189

Credit/placement for International Baccalaureate (IB)

Alabama

Auburn University at Montgomery
Birmingham-Southern College
Faulkner University
Huntingdon College
Jefferson State Community College
Judson College
Samford University
Shelton State Community College
Southeastern Bible College
Spring Hill College
University of Alabama
University of Alabama at Birmingham
University of Alabama in Huntsville
University of Mobile
University of Montevallo

Alaska

Alaska Pacific University
Prince William Sound Community
    College
University of Alaska Anchorage
University of Alaska Fairbanks

Arizona

Arizona State University
Arizona Western College
Art Center Design College
Art Institute of Phoenix
Chandler-Gilbert Community College:
    Pecos
Dunlap-Stone University
Eastern Arizona College
Embry-Riddle Aeronautical University:
    Prescott Campus
Estrella Mountain Community College
GateWay Community College
Glendale Community College
Grand Canyon University
Mesa Community College
Mohave Community College
Northcentral University
Northern Arizona University
Phoenix College
Pima Community College
Prescott College
South Mountain Community College
University of Advancing Technology
University of Arizona
University of Phoenix: Phoenix-
    Hohokam
Western International University
Yavapai College

Arkansas

Arkansas Tech University
Harding University

Hendrix College
John Brown University
Lyon College
Ouachita Baptist University
South Arkansas Community College
University of Arkansas
University of Arkansas at Little Rock
University of Arkansas at Monticello
University of Arkansas at Pine Bluff
University of Central Arkansas
Williams Baptist College

California

Academy of Art University
Alliant International University
American Jewish University
American River College
Antioch University Santa Barbara
Art Institute of California: Orange
    County
Art Institute of California: San
    Francisco
Azusa Pacific University
Bethany University
Bethesda Christian University
Biola University
California Baptist University
California College of the Arts
California Institute of the Arts
California Lutheran University
California Polytechnic State University:
    San Luis Obispo
California State University: Chico
California State University: Dominguez
    Hills
California State University: East Bay
California State University: Fresno
California State University: Fullerton
California State University: Long
    Beach
California State University: Monterey
    Bay
California State University: Sacramento
California State University: San
    Bernardino
California State University: San
    Marcos
California State University: Stanislaus
Canada College
Chapman University
Charles Drew University of Medicine
    and Science
Citrus College
Claremont McKenna College
Cogswell Polytechnical College
College of San Mateo
Concordia University
Dominican University of California
El Camino College
Fashion Institute of Design and
    Merchandising: Los Angeles
Fashion Institute of Design and
    Merchandising: San Diego

Fashion Institute of Design and
    Merchandising: San Francisco
Fresno Pacific University
Golden Gate University
Holy Names University
Hope International University
Humboldt State University
Humphreys College
The King's University
La Sierra University
Long Beach City College
Los Angeles Harbor College
Los Angeles Valley College
Loyola Marymount University
Marymount College
The Master's College
Menlo College
Mills College
MiraCosta College
Mount St. Mary's College
Mt. Sierra College
National Hispanic University
Northwestern Polytechnic University
Notre Dame de Namur University
Occidental College
Ohlone College
Otis College of Art and Design
Pacific States University
Pacific Union College
Pepperdine University
Pitzer College
Point Loma Nazarene University
Pomona College
St. Mary's College of California
San Diego Christian College
San Diego State University
San Francisco Art Institute
San Francisco State University
San Joaquin Delta College
San Jose City College
Santa Barbara City College
Santa Clara University
Santa Rosa Junior College
Scripps College
Southwestern College
Stanford University
University of California: Irvine
University of California: Merced
University of California: Riverside
University of California: San Diego
University of California: Santa Cruz
University of the Pacific
University of Redlands
University of San Diego
University of San Francisco
University of Southern California
Vanguard University of Southern
    California
Westmont College
Whittier College
William Jessup University
Woodbury University
World Mission University

Colorado

Adams State College
Arapahoe Community College
Art Institute of Colorado
Colorado Christian University
Colorado College
Colorado Heights University
Colorado Mountain College
Colorado School of Mines
Colorado State University
Colorado State University: Pueblo
Community College of Aurora
Fort Lewis College
Mesa State College
Metropolitan State College of Denver
Naropa University
Northeastern Junior College
Pikes Peak Community College

Red Rocks Community College
Regis University
Rocky Mountain College of Art &
    Design
University of Colorado at Boulder
University of Colorado at Colorado
    Springs
University of Colorado at Denver
University of Denver
University of Northern Colorado
Western State College of Colorado

Connecticut

Central Connecticut State University
Connecticut College
Fairfield University
Norwalk Community College
Paier College of Art
Post University
Quinnipiac University
Sacred Heart University
Trinity College
University of Bridgeport
University of Connecticut
University of New Haven
Wesleyan University
Yale University

Delaware

University of Delaware

District of Columbia

American University
Catholic University of America
Corcoran College of Art and Design
George Washington University
Georgetown University
Howard University
University of the District of Columbia

Florida

Art Institute of Fort Lauderdale
Ave Maria University
Baptist College of Florida
Barry University
Bethune-Cookman University
Brevard Community College
Broward College
Carlos Albizu University
Chipola College
City College: Fort Lauderdale
College of Central Florida
Daytona State College
Eckerd College
Edison State College
Embry-Riddle Aeronautical University
Flagler College
Florida Agricultural and Mechanical
    University
Florida Atlantic University
Florida Christian College
Florida Gateway College
Florida Gulf Coast University
Florida Institute of Technology
Florida International University
Florida Keys Community College
Florida Southern College
Florida State University
Gulf Coast Community College
Herzing University
Hillsborough Community College
Hodges University
Indian River State College

International Academy of Design and
 Technology: Tampa
Jacksonville University
Lynn University
Miami Dade College
Miami International University of Art
 and Design
North Florida Community College
Northwood University: Florida
Nova Southeastern University
Palm Beach Atlantic University
Palm Beach State College
Pasco-Hernando Community College
Pensacola State College
Polk State College
Rasmussen College: Ocala
Rasmussen College: Pasco County
Ringling College of Art and Design
Rollins College
Saint Leo University
St. Petersburg College
Santa Fe College
Schiller International University
Seminole State College of Florida
South Florida Community College
Southeastern University
Stetson University
Tallahassee Community College
University of Central Florida
University of Florida
University of Miami
University of North Florida
University of South Florida
University of Tampa
University of West Florida
Valencia College
Warner University
Webber International University

Georgia

Agnes Scott College
American InterContinental University
Armstrong Atlantic State University
Art Institute of Atlanta
Atlanta Christian College
Atlanta Technical College
Augusta State University
Berry College
Brenau University
Chattahoochee Technical College
Clark Atlanta University
Clayton State University
College of Coastal Georgia
Columbus State University
Covenant College
Darton College
East Georgia College
Emory University
Georgia College and State University
Georgia Gwinnett College
Georgia Highlands College
Georgia Institute of Technology
Georgia Perimeter College
Georgia Southern University
Georgia Southwestern State University
Georgia State University
Gordon College
Herzing University
Kennesaw State University
LaGrange College
Mercer University
Oglethorpe University
Savannah College of Art and Design
Shorter University
South Georgia College
South University: Savannah
Southern Polytechnic State University
Spelman College
University of Georgia
University of West Georgia
Valdosta State University

Wesleyan College
Young Harris College

Hawaii

Brigham Young University-Hawaii
Chaminade University of Honolulu
Hawaii Pacific University
University of Hawaii at Hilo
University of Hawaii at Manoa
University of Hawaii: Leeward
 Community College
University of Hawaii: West Oahu

Idaho

Brigham Young University-Idaho
College of Idaho
Idaho State University
Lewis-Clark State College
Northwest Nazarene University
University of Idaho

Illinois

Augustana College
Blessing-Rieman College of Nursing
Bradley University
City Colleges of Chicago: Wilbur
 Wright College
Columbia College Chicago
Concordia University Chicago
Danville Area Community College
DePaul University
Dominican University
Eastern Illinois University
Elmhurst College
Greenville College
Illinois College
Illinois Institute of Technology
Illinois Wesleyan University
International Academy of Design and
 Technology: Chicago
Judson University
Kendall College
Knox College
Lake Forest College
Lewis University
Loyola University Chicago
MacCormac College
MacMurray College
McKendree University
Millikin University
Monmouth College
Moody Bible Institute
Morrison Institute of Technology
Morton College
North Central College
North Park University
Northwestern University
Olivet Nazarene University
Quincy University
St. Augustine College
School of the Art Institute of Chicago
Southern Illinois University Carbondale
Spoon River College
Trinity Christian College
Trinity International University
University of Chicago
University of Illinois at Chicago
University of Illinois at Urbana-
 Champaign
University of Illinois: Springfield
University of St. Francis
VanderCook College of Music
Western Illinois University
Wheaton College

Indiana

Ball State University
Bethel College
Butler University
DePauw University
Earlham College
Goshen College
Hanover College
Holy Cross College
Indiana Institute of Technology
Indiana University Bloomington
Indiana University South Bend
Indiana University Southeast
Indiana University-Purdue University
 Fort Wayne
Indiana University-Purdue University
 Indianapolis
Manchester College
Marian University
Oakland City University
Purdue University
Rose-Hulman Institute of Technology
St. Mary-of-the-Woods College
Saint Mary's College
Taylor University
Trine University
University of Evansville
University of Indianapolis
University of Notre Dame
Valparaiso University
Vincennes University

Iowa

Briar Cliff University
Buena Vista University
Central College
Clarke University
Coe College
Cornell College
Drake University
Graceland University
Grand View University
Grinnell College
Iowa State University
Iowa Wesleyan College
Kirkwood Community College
Loras College
Luther College
Maharishi University of Management
Morningside College
Mount Mercy University
Northwestern College
St. Ambrose University
Simpson College
University of Dubuque
University of Iowa
University of Northern Iowa
Upper Iowa University
Waldorf College
William Penn University

Kansas

Baker University
Barclay College
Barton County Community College
Benedictine College
Bethany College
Bethel College
Central Christian College of Kansas
Emporia State University
Friends University
Hesston College
Kansas City Kansas Community
 College
Kansas State University
McPherson College
MidAmerica Nazarene University
Newman University

Ottawa University
Pittsburg State University
Pratt Community College
Sterling College
Tabor College
University of Kansas
University of St. Mary
Wichita State University

Kentucky

Alice Lloyd College
Bellarmine University
Brescia University
Centre College
Georgetown College
Kentucky Christian University
Kentucky State University
Kentucky Wesleyan College
Midway College
Morehead State University
Northern Kentucky University
Spencerian College: Lexington
Sullivan University
Thomas More College
Transylvania University
University of the Cumberlands
University of Kentucky
University of Louisville
Western Kentucky University

Louisiana

Centenary College of Louisiana
Dillard University
Herzing University
Louisiana State University and
 Agricultural and Mechanical College
Loyola University New Orleans
St. Joseph Seminary College
South Louisiana Community College
Tulane University
University of New Orleans

Maine

Bates College
Bowdoin College
Central Maine Community College
Colby College
College of the Atlantic
Husson University
Unity College in Maine
University of Maine
University of Maine at Farmington
University of Maine at Fort Kent
University of Maine at Presque Isle
University of New England
University of Southern Maine
Washington County Community
 College

Maryland

Anne Arundel Community College
Baltimore City Community College
College of Notre Dame of Maryland
Coppin State University
Frostburg State University
Goucher College
Griggs University
Harford Community College
Hood College
Howard Community College
Johns Hopkins University
Johns Hopkins University: Peabody
 Conservatory of Music
Loyola University Maryland

Maryland Institute College of Art
McDaniel College
Mount St. Mary's University
St. Mary's College of Maryland
Salisbury University
Stevenson University
Towson University
United States Naval Academy
University of Baltimore
University of Maryland: Baltimore County
University of Maryland: College Park
University of Maryland: Eastern Shore
University of Maryland: University College
Washington College

Massachusetts

American International College
Amherst College
Assumption College
Atlantic Union College
Babson College
Bay Path College
Bay State College
Becker College
Benjamin Franklin Institute of Technology
Bentley University
Berkshire Community College
Boston College
Boston University
Brandeis University
Bridgewater State University
Clark University
College of the Holy Cross
Curry College
Dean College
Eastern Nazarene College
Elms College
Emerson College
Emmanuel College
Endicott College
Fisher College
Framingham State University
Gordon College
Harvard College
Hellenic College/Holy Cross
Lasell College
Lesley University
Massachusetts Bay Community College
Massachusetts College of Art and Design
Massachusetts College of Liberal Arts
Massachusetts College of Pharmacy and Health Sciences
Massachusetts Institute of Technology
Massachusetts Maritime Academy
Merrimack College
Montserrat College of Art
Mount Holyoke College
Mount Ida College
Mount Wachusett Community College
New England College of Business and Finance
New England Conservatory of Music
Newbury College
Northeastern University
Pine Manor College
Quinsigamond Community College
Regis College
Simmons College
Smith College
Springfield College
Stonehill College
Suffolk University
Tufts University
University of Massachusetts Amherst
University of Massachusetts Dartmouth
Wellesley College
Wentworth Institute of Technology
Western New England College

Wheaton College
Williams College
Worcester Polytechnic Institute
Worcester State University

Michigan

Adrian College
Albion College
Alma College
Andrews University
Baker College of Auburn Hills
Baker College of Cadillac
Baker College of Jackson
Baker College of Muskegon
Baker College of Owosso
Baker College of Port Huron
Calvin College
Central Michigan University
College for Creative Studies
Cornerstone University
Davenport University
Delta College
Eastern Michigan University
Finlandia University
Grand Valley State University
Hillsdale College
Hope College
Kalamazoo College
Kellogg Community College
Kettering University
Lake Superior State University
Lansing Community College
Lawrence Technological University
Madonna University
Michigan Jewish Institute
Michigan State University
Michigan Technological University
North Central Michigan College
Northern Michigan University
Northwood University: Michigan
Oakland University
Rochester College
Saginaw Valley State University
Spring Arbor University
University of Michigan
Walsh College of Accountancy and Business Administration
Wayne State University
Western Michigan University

Minnesota

Alexandria Technical College
Augsburg College
Bemidji State University
Bethany Lutheran College
Bethel University
Capella University
Carleton College
Central Lakes College
Century College
College of St. Benedict
College of St. Scholastica
Concordia College: Moorhead
Concordia University St. Paul
Crown College
Dakota County Technical College
Dunwoody College of Technology
Fond du Lac Tribal and Community College
Gustavus Adolphus College
Hamline University
Hennepin Technical College
Inver Hills Community College
Itasca Community College
Macalester College
Minnesota State College - Southeast Technical
Minnesota State Community and Technical College
Minnesota State University Mankato

Minnesota West Community and Technical College
Normandale Community College
North Hennepin Community College
Northland Community & Technical College
Northwest Technical College
Northwestern College
Rainy River Community College
Rasmussen College: Mankato
Riverland Community College
St. Catherine University
Saint Cloud State University
St. John's University
St. Mary's University of Minnesota
St. Olaf College
South Central College
University of Minnesota: Crookston
University of Minnesota: Duluth
University of Minnesota: Morris
University of Minnesota: Rochester
University of Minnesota: Twin Cities
University of St. Thomas
Walden University
Winona State University

Mississippi

Belhaven University
Blue Mountain College
Millsaps College
Mississippi College
Mississippi State University
Tougaloo College
University of Mississippi
William Carey University

Missouri

Avila University
Calvary Bible College and Theological Seminary
Central Methodist University
College of the Ozarks
Columbia College
Cottey College
Culver-Stockton College
Drury University
Evangel University
Fontbonne University
Goldfarb School of Nursing at Barnes-Jewish College
Grantham University
Jefferson College
Kansas City Art Institute
Lindenwood University
Maryville University of Saint Louis
Missouri Southern State University
Missouri State University
Missouri Technical School
Missouri University of Science and Technology
Moberly Area Community College
Northwest Missouri State University
Ozarks Technical Community College
Research College of Nursing
Rockhurst University
Saint Louis University
Southwest Baptist University
Stephens College
Truman State University
University of Central Missouri
University of Missouri: Columbia
University of Missouri: Kansas City
University of Missouri: St. Louis
Washington University in St. Louis
Webster University
Westminster College
William Jewell College
William Woods University

Montana

Carroll College
Flathead Valley Community College
Montana State University: Bozeman
Montana State University: Northern
Montana Tech of the University of Montana
Rocky Mountain College
University of Great Falls
University of Montana: Western

Nebraska

Bellevue University
College of Saint Mary
Concordia University
Creighton University
Doane College
Nebraska Wesleyan University
Peru State College
Union College
University of Nebraska - Lincoln
Western Nebraska Community College
York College

Nevada

Art Institute of Las Vegas
Morrison University
Sierra Nevada College
Truckee Meadows Community College
University of Nevada: Las Vegas
University of Nevada: Reno

New Hampshire

Colby-Sawyer College
Daniel Webster College
Dartmouth College
Franklin Pierce University
Hesser College
Lakes Region Community College
New England College
NHTI-Concord's Community College
Rivier College
Saint Anselm College
Southern New Hampshire University
University of New Hampshire
University of New Hampshire at Manchester

New Jersey

Caldwell College
Centenary College
The College of New Jersey
College of St. Elizabeth
Drew University
Felician College
Hudson County Community College
Kean University
Monmouth University
Montclair State University
New Jersey City University
Princeton University
Ramapo College of New Jersey
Richard Stockton College of New Jersey
Rider University
Rowan University
Rutgers, The State University of New Jersey: Camden Regional Campus
Rutgers, The State University of New Jersey: New Brunswick/Piscataway Campus

Rutgers, The State University of New Jersey: Newark Regional Campus
Saint Peter's College
Seton Hall University
Stevens Institute of Technology
Sussex County Community College
University of Medicine and Dentistry of New Jersey: School of Health Related Professions

New Mexico

Eastern New Mexico University: Roswell
Northern New Mexico College
University of New Mexico
University of the Southwest

New York

Adelphi University
Adirondack Community College
Alfred University
Bard College
Barnard College
Canisius College
Cazenovia College
City University of New York: Baruch College
City University of New York: Bronx Community College
City University of New York: Brooklyn College
City University of New York: City College
City University of New York: College of Staten Island
City University of New York: CUNY Online
City University of New York: Hunter College
City University of New York: John Jay College of Criminal Justice
City University of New York: Lehman College
City University of New York: Medgar Evers College
City University of New York: Queens College
City University of New York: York College
Clarkson University
Clinton Community College
Colgate University
College of Mount St. Vincent
College of Saint Rose
Columbia University
Concordia College
Cornell University
Daemen College
Dominican College of Blauvelt
Dowling College
D'Youville College
Elmira College
Eugene Lang College The New School for Liberal Arts
Excelsior College
Fashion Institute of Technology
Fordham University
Genesee Community College
Hamilton College
Hartwick College
Hilbert College
Hobart and William Smith Colleges
Hofstra University
Houghton College
Iona College
Ithaca College
The King's College
Le Moyne College
Long Island University: Brooklyn Campus

Long Island University: C. W. Post Campus
Manhattan College
Manhattanville College
Marist College
Marymount Manhattan College
Medaille College
Medaille College: Amherst
Metropolitan College of New York
Molloy College
Monroe College
Mount Saint Mary College
Nassau Community College
Nazareth College
New York Institute of Technology
New York School of Interior Design
New York University
Niagara County Community College
Onondaga Community College
Pace University
Parsons The New School for Design
Paul Smith's College
Polytechnic Institute of New York University
Rensselaer Polytechnic Institute
Roberts Wesleyan College
Rochester Institute of Technology
Rockland Community College
Russell Sage College
Sage College of Albany
Saint Bonaventure University
St. Francis College
St. John Fisher College
St. John's University
St. Joseph's College: Suffolk Campus
St. Lawrence University
St. Thomas Aquinas College
Sarah Lawrence College
School of Visual Arts
Siena College
Skidmore College
Suffolk County Community College
SUNY College at Brockport
SUNY College at Buffalo
SUNY College at Cortland
SUNY College at Fredonia
SUNY College at Geneseo
SUNY College at New Paltz
SUNY College at Old Westbury
SUNY College at Oneonta
SUNY College at Oswego
SUNY College at Plattsburgh
SUNY College at Potsdam
SUNY College of Environmental Science and Forestry
SUNY College of Technology at Alfred
SUNY College of Technology at Canton
SUNY College of Technology at Delhi
SUNY Empire State College
SUNY Institute of Technology at Utica/Rome
SUNY Maritime College
SUNY University at Albany
SUNY University at Binghamton
SUNY University at Buffalo
SUNY University at Stony Brook
Syracuse University
Tompkins Cortland Community College
Union College
University of Rochester
Utica College
Vassar College
Vaughn College of Aeronautics and Technology
Wagner College
Wells College
Westchester Community College

North Carolina

Appalachian State University
Barton College

Belmont Abbey College
Brevard College
Campbell University
Catawba College
Chowan University
Davidson College
Duke University
East Carolina University
Elizabeth City State University
Elon University
Fayetteville Technical Community College
Gardner-Webb University
Greensboro College
Guilford College
Guilford Technical Community College
High Point University
Johnston Community College
Laurel University
Lees-McRae College
Lenoir-Rhyne University
Mars Hill College
Meredith College
Methodist University
Montreat College
Nash Community College
North Carolina State University
Peace College
Pfeiffer University
Queens University of Charlotte
Robeson Community College
St. Andrews Presbyterian College
St. Augustine's College
Salem College
University of North Carolina at Asheville
University of North Carolina at Chapel Hill
University of North Carolina at Charlotte
University of North Carolina at Greensboro
University of North Carolina at Wilmington
Wake Forest University
Wake Technical Community College
Western Carolina University
Wilkes Community College
Wingate University
Winston-Salem State University

North Dakota

Jamestown College
Mayville State University
North Dakota State University
Rasmussen College: Fargo
University of Mary
University of North Dakota

Ohio

Ashland University
Baldwin-Wallace College
Bowling Green State University
Bryant & Stratton College: Parma
Capital University
Case Western Reserve University
Cedarville University
Central Ohio Technical College
Cincinnati Christian University
Cincinnati State Technical and Community College
Cleveland Institute of Art
Cleveland Institute of Music
Cleveland State University
College of Mount St. Joseph
College of Wooster
Columbus College of Art and Design
Columbus State Community College
Defiance College
Denison University

Franciscan University of Steubenville
Franklin University
Heidelberg University
Hiram College
John Carroll University
Kent State University
Kenyon College
Lake Erie College
Marietta College
Miami University: Hamilton
Miami University: Middletown
Miami University: Oxford
Mount Vernon Nazarene University
Muskingum University
Oberlin College
Ohio Dominican University
Ohio Northern University
Ohio State University: Columbus Campus
Ohio University
Ohio Wesleyan University
Otterbein University
Sinclair Community College
Tiffin University
Union Institute & University
University of Akron
University of Cincinnati: Clermont College
University of Cincinnati: Raymond Walters College
University of Dayton
University of Mount Union
Wilmington College
Wittenberg University
Wright State University: Lake Campus
Xavier University
Youngstown State University

Oklahoma

Cameron University
Northeastern State University
Oklahoma Baptist University
Oklahoma Christian University
Oklahoma City Community College
Oklahoma City University
Oklahoma State University
Rogers State University
Rose State College
St. Gregory's University
Southeastern Oklahoma State University
Southern Nazarene University
Southwestern Oklahoma State University
University of Oklahoma
University of Tulsa
Western Oklahoma State College

Oregon

Art Institute of Portland
Chemeketa Community College
Clackamas Community College
Corban College
Eastern Oregon University
George Fox University
Lewis & Clark College
Linfield College
Marylhurst University
Mt. Hood Community College
Northwest Christian University
Oregon College of Art & Craft
Oregon State University
Pacific University
Reed College
Southern Oregon University
University of Oregon
University of Portland
Western Oregon University
Willamette University

Pennsylvania

Albright College
Allegheny College
Alvernia University
Arcadia University
Baptist Bible College of Pennsylvania
Bryn Mawr College
Bucknell University
Cabrini College
California University of Pennsylvania
Carlow University
Carnegie Mellon University
Cedar Crest College
Central Pennsylvania College
Chatham University
Chestnut Hill College
Clarion University of Pennsylvania
Dickinson College
Drexel University
Duquesne University
Eastern University
Elizabethtown College
Franklin & Marshall College
Gannon University
Gettysburg College
Grove City College
Harrisburg Area Community College
Haverford College
Immaculata University
Indiana University of Pennsylvania
Juniata College
Keystone College
King's College
Kutztown University of Pennsylvania
La Roche College
Lafayette College
Lebanon Valley College
Lincoln University
Lock Haven University of
　Pennsylvania
Lycoming College
Mansfield University of Pennsylvania
Marywood University
Mercyhurst College
Messiah College
Millersville University of Pennsylvania
Misericordia University
Moore College of Art and Design
Moravian College
Muhlenberg College
Peirce College
Penn State Abington
Penn State Altoona
Penn State Beaver
Penn State Berks
Penn State Brandywine
Penn State DuBois
Penn State Erie, The Behrend College
Penn State Fayette, The Eberly
　Campus
Penn State Greater Allegheny
Penn State Harrisburg
Penn State Hazleton
Penn State Lehigh Valley
Penn State Mont Alto
Penn State New Kensington
Penn State Schuylkill
Penn State Shenango
Penn State University Park
Penn State Wilkes-Barre
Penn State Worthington Scranton
Penn State York
Philadelphia Biblical University
Point Park University
Rosemont College
St. Francis University
Saint Joseph's University
St. Vincent College
Seton Hill University
Shippensburg University of
　Pennsylvania
Slippery Rock University of
　Pennsylvania

Susquehanna University
Swarthmore College
Temple University
Thiel College
University of the Arts
University of Pennsylvania
University of Pittsburgh
University of Pittsburgh at Bradford
University of Pittsburgh at Johnstown
University of the Sciences in
　Philadelphia
University of Scranton
Ursinus College
Valley Forge Christian College
Villanova University
Washington & Jefferson College
West Chester University of
　Pennsylvania
Widener University
Wilson College
York College of Pennsylvania

Puerto Rico

Conservatory of Music of Puerto Rico
University of Puerto Rico: Arecibo

Rhode Island

Bryant University
Providence College
Rhode Island School of Design
Roger Williams University
Salve Regina University
University of Rhode Island

South Carolina

Anderson University
Central Carolina Technical College
Charleston Southern University
Clemson University
Coastal Carolina University
Coker College
College of Charleston
Columbia College
Columbia International University
Converse College
Erskine College
Florence-Darlington Technical College
Furman University
Greenville Technical College
Lander University
Newberry College
North Greenville University
Northeastern Technical College
Piedmont Technical College
Presbyterian College
Southern Wesleyan University
Spartanburg Community College
Tri-County Technical College
Trident Technical College
University of South Carolina: Aiken
University of South Carolina:
　Columbia
University of South Carolina:
　Lancaster
University of South Carolina: Upstate
Voorhees College
Winthrop University
Wofford College

South Dakota

Augustana College
Dakota State University
Dakota Wesleyan University
Mount Marty College

National American University: Rapid
　City
Northern State University
South Dakota School of Mines and
　Technology
South Dakota State University
University of Sioux Falls

Tennessee

Belmont University
Bryan College
Christian Brothers University
East Tennessee State University
Fisk University
Free Will Baptist Bible College
Freed-Hardeman University
Lambuth University
Lee University
LeMoyne-Owen College
Lincoln Memorial University
Lipscomb University
Maryville College
Middle Tennessee State University
Milligan College
Pellissippi State Community College
Rhodes College
Tennessee Technological University
Tennessee Wesleyan College
Trevecca Nazarene University
Union University
University of Memphis
University of the South
University of Tennessee: Knoxville
Vanderbilt University
Victory University
Watkins College of Art, Design & Film

Texas

Abilene Christian University
Austin College
Austin Community College
Baylor University
Blinn College
Brookhaven College
Central Texas College
Concordia University Texas
Dallas Baptist University
Del Mar College
East Texas Baptist University
Eastfield College
El Centro College
Frank Phillips College
Houston Baptist University
Houston Community College System
Howard Payne University
Lamar Institute of Technology
LeTourneau University
Lon Morris College
Lone Star College System
Lubbock Christian University
McMurry University
Midland College
Midwestern State University
Mountain View College
Northwood University: Texas
Our Lady of the Lake University of
　San Antonio
Rice University
St. Edward's University
Sam Houston State University
San Antonio College
Schreiner University
Southern Methodist University
Southwestern Adventist University
Southwestern University
Stephen F. Austin State University
Texas A&M International University
Texas A&M University
Texas A&M University-Commerce
Texas A&M University-Corpus Christi

Texas A&M University-Galveston
Texas A&M University-Texarkana
Texas Christian University
Texas Lutheran University
Texas State Technical College: Waco
Texas State University: San Marcos
Texas Tech University
Trinity University
University of Dallas
University of Houston
University of Houston-Downtown
University of Mary Hardin-Baylor
University of North Texas
University of St. Thomas
University of Texas at Arlington
University of Texas at Austin
University of Texas at Brownsville -
　Texas Southmost College
University of Texas at Dallas
University of Texas at El Paso
University of Texas at Tyler
University of Texas Medical Branch at
　Galveston
University of Texas: Pan American
Victoria College
Wade College
Wayland Baptist University
West Texas A&M University

Utah

Brigham Young University
Salt Lake Community College
Stevens-Henager College: Orem
University of Utah
Utah State University
Utah Valley University
Weber State University
Westminster College

Vermont

Bennington College
Burlington College
Champlain College
College of St. Joseph in Vermont
Community College of Vermont
Goddard College
Green Mountain College
Johnson State College
Lyndon State College
Marlboro College
Middlebury College
New England Culinary Institute
Norwich University
St. Michael's College
Sterling College
University of Vermont

Virginia

Art Institute of Washington
Blue Ridge Community College
Bluefield College
Bridgewater College
Central Virginia Community College
Christopher Newport University
College of William and Mary
Eastern Mennonite University
Emory & Henry College
Ferrum College
George Mason University
Hampden-Sydney College
Hampton University
Hollins University
J. Sargeant Reynolds Community
　College
James Madison University
Jefferson College of Health Sciences
Liberty University

Longwood University
Lynchburg College
Mary Baldwin College
Marymount University
Northern Virginia Community College
Old Dominion University
Patrick Henry College
Radford University
Randolph College
Randolph-Macon College
Regent University
Roanoke College
Shenandoah University
Southern Virginia University
Sweet Briar College
University of Mary Washington
University of Richmond
University of Virginia
University of Virginia's College at
  Wise
Virginia Commonwealth University
Virginia Intermont College
Virginia Military Institute
Virginia Polytechnic Institute and State
  University
Virginia Union University
Virginia University of Lynchburg
Virginia Wesleyan College
Washington and Lee University

Washington

Art Institute of Seattle
Bates Technical College
Cascadia Community College
Central Washington University
Centralia College
Clark College
Columbia Basin College
DigiPen Institute of Technology
Eastern Washington University
Everett Community College
Evergreen State College
Gonzaga University
Lake Washington Technical College
North Seattle Community College
Northwest University
Olympic College
Pacific Lutheran University
Saint Martin's University
Seattle Pacific University
Seattle University
Shoreline Community College
Skagit Valley College
South Puget Sound Community
  College
South Seattle Community College
Tacoma Community College
Trinity Lutheran College
University of Puget Sound
University of Washington
University of Washington Bothell
University of Washington Tacoma
Walla Walla University
Washington State University
Western Washington University
Whatcom Community College
Whitman College
Whitworth University
Yakima Valley Community College

West Virginia

Bethany College
Bluefield State College
Davis and Elkins College
Fairmont State University
Marshall University
Mountain State University
Ohio Valley University
Salem International University
Shepherd University

University of Charleston
West Virginia State University
West Virginia University
West Virginia University at
  Parkersburg
West Virginia Wesleyan College
Wheeling Jesuit University

Wisconsin

Alverno College
Beloit College
Cardinal Stritch University
Carroll University
Carthage College
Concordia University Wisconsin
Edgewood College
Lakeland College
Lawrence University
Marian University
Marquette University
Milwaukee School of Engineering
Mount Mary College
Northland College
St. Norbert College
Silver Lake College
University of Wisconsin-Baraboo/Sauk
  County
University of Wisconsin-Eau Claire
University of Wisconsin-Green Bay
University of Wisconsin-La Crosse
University of Wisconsin-Madison
University of Wisconsin-Marathon
  County
University of Wisconsin-Oshkosh
University of Wisconsin-Parkside
University of Wisconsin-Richland
University of Wisconsin-River Falls
University of Wisconsin-Sheboygan
University of Wisconsin-Stevens Point
University of Wisconsin-Stout
University of Wisconsin-Superior
University of Wisconsin-Washington
  County
University of Wisconsin-Whitewater
Viterbo University

Wyoming

Casper College
Eastern Wyoming College
Laramie County Community College
University of Wyoming
Western Wyoming Community College

Credit/placement for Advanced Placement (AP)

Alabama

Alabama Agricultural and Mechanical University
Alabama State University
Athens State University
Auburn University
Auburn University at Montgomery
Birmingham-Southern College
Calhoun Community College
Faulkner University
Gadsden State Community College
George C. Wallace Community College at Dothan
Heritage Christian University
Huntingdon College
Jacksonville State University
Jefferson State Community College
Judson College
Lawson State Community College
Marion Military Institute
Oakwood University
Samford University
Shelton State Community College
Southeastern Bible College
Spring Hill College
Talladega College
Troy University
Tuskegee University
University of Alabama
University of Alabama at Birmingham
University of Alabama in Huntsville
University of Mobile
University of North Alabama
University of South Alabama
University of West Alabama
Wallace State Community College at Hanceville

Alaska

University of Alaska Anchorage
University of Alaska Fairbanks
University of Alaska Southeast

Arizona

Arizona Christian University
Arizona State University
Arizona Western College
Art Center Design College
Art Institute of Phoenix
Art Institute of Tucson
Chandler-Gilbert Community College: Pecos
Cochise College
Everest College: Phoenix
GateWay Community College
Glendale Community College
Grand Canyon University
Northcentral University
Northern Arizona University
Paradise Valley Community College
Phoenix College
Pima Community College
Prescott College
Rio Salado College

Scottsdale Community College
University of Advancing Technology
University of Arizona
University of Phoenix: Phoenix-Hohokam
Western International University
Yavapai College

Arkansas

Arkansas State University: Mountain Home
Arkansas State University: Newport
Arkansas Tech University
Cossatot Community College of the University of Arkansas
East Arkansas Community College
Harding University
Henderson State University
Hendrix College
John Brown University
Lyon College
National Park Community College
Ouachita Baptist University
Ouachita Technical College
Philander Smith College
Pulaski Technical College
Remington College: Little Rock
South Arkansas Community College
Southeast Arkansas College
Southern Arkansas University
Southern Arkansas University Tech
University of Arkansas
University of Arkansas at Fort Smith
University of Arkansas at Little Rock
University of Arkansas at Monticello
University of Central Arkansas
University of the Ozarks
Williams Baptist College

California

Academy of Art University
Allan Hancock College
Alliant International University
American Academy of Dramatic Arts: West
American River College
Antelope Valley College
Antioch University Los Angeles
Art Institute of California: Hollywood
Art Institute of California: San Diego
Art Institute of California: San Francisco
Azusa Pacific University
Barstow Community College
Bethany University
Biola University
Cabrillo College
California Baptist University
California College of the Arts
California Institute of the Arts
California Institute of Integral Studies
California Lutheran University
California Polytechnic State University: San Luis Obispo
California State Polytechnic University: Pomona

California State University: Bakersfield
California State University: Channel Islands
California State University: Chico
California State University: Dominguez Hills
California State University: East Bay
California State University: Fresno
California State University: Fullerton
California State University: Long Beach
California State University: Los Angeles
California State University: Monterey Bay
California State University: Sacramento
California State University: San Bernardino
California State University: San Marcos
California State University: Stanislaus
California University of Management and Sciences
Canada College
Cerro Coso Community College
Chapman University
Charles Drew University of Medicine and Science
Citrus College
City College of San Francisco
Claremont McKenna College
Coastline Community College
Cogswell Polytechnical College
Coleman University
College of the Canyons
College of San Mateo
College of the Siskiyous
Concordia University
Copper Mountain College
Crafton Hills College
Cuyamaca College
De Anza College
Diablo Valley College
Dominican University of California
East Los Angeles College
El Camino College
Evergreen Valley College
Fashion Institute of Design and Merchandising: Los Angeles
Fashion Institute of Design and Merchandising: San Diego
Fashion Institute of Design and Merchandising: San Francisco
Feather River College
Folsom Lake College
Foothill College
Fresno Pacific University
Glendale Community College
Golden Gate University
Grossmont College
Holy Names University
Hope International University
Humboldt State University
Humphreys College
John F. Kennedy University
Kaplan College: Panorama City
Kaplan College: San Diego
The King's University
La Sierra University
Lassen Community College
Le Cordon Bleu College of Culinary Arts: Los Angeles
Life Pacific College
Loma Linda University
Long Beach City College
Los Angeles Harbor College
Los Angeles Valley College
Loyola Marymount University
Marymount College
The Master's College
Menlo College
Mills College
MiraCosta College
Modesto Junior College
Moorpark College

Mount San Jacinto College
Mt. Sierra College
Northwestern Polytechnic University
Notre Dame de Namur University
Occidental College
Ohlone College
Orange Coast College
Otis College of Art and Design
Oxnard College
Pacific Union College
Palo Verde College
Palomar College
Patten University
Pepperdine University
Pitzer College
Platt College: San Diego
Point Loma Nazarene University
Pomona College
Reedley College
Saddleback College
St. Mary's College of California
San Bernardino Valley College
San Diego Christian College
San Diego City College
San Diego Mesa College
San Diego State University
San Francisco Art Institute
San Francisco State University
San Joaquin Delta College
San Jose State University
Santa Ana College
Santa Barbara City College
Santa Clara University
Santa Monica College
Santa Rosa Junior College
School of Urban Missions: Oakland
Scripps College
Shasta Bible College and Graduate School
Shasta College
Sierra College
Simpson University
Skyline College
Soka University of America
Solano Community College
Sonoma State University
Southwestern College
Stanford University
Taft College
Trident University International
University of California: Berkeley
University of California: Davis
University of California: Irvine
University of California: Los Angeles
University of California: Merced
University of California: Riverside
University of California: San Diego
University of California: Santa Barbara
University of California: Santa Cruz
University of La Verne
University of the Pacific
University of Redlands
University of San Diego
University of San Francisco
University of Southern California
Vanguard University of Southern California
Ventura College
West Hills College: Coalinga
West Hills College: Lemoore
Westmont College
Westwood College: Anaheim
Whittier College
William Jessup University
Woodbury University
Yuba Community College District

Colorado

Adams State College
Aims Community College
American Sentinel University
Arapahoe Community College

Colorado Christian University
Colorado College
Colorado Mountain College
Colorado Northwestern Community
    College
Colorado School of Mines
Colorado State University
Colorado State University: Pueblo
Community College of Denver
Everest College: Colorado Springs
Fort Lewis College
Front Range Community College
Institute of Business & Medical
    Careers
IntelliTec College
Jones International University
Mesa State College
Metropolitan State College of Denver
Morgan Community College
Naropa University
National American University: Denver
Nazarene Bible College
Northeastern Junior College
Otero Junior College
Pueblo Community College
Red Rocks Community College
Regis University
Remington College: Colorado Springs
Rocky Mountain College of Art &
    Design
Trinidad State Junior College
University of Colorado at Boulder
University of Colorado at Colorado
    Springs
University of Colorado at Denver
University of Denver
University of Northern Colorado
Western State College of Colorado

Connecticut

Albertus Magnus College
Capital Community College
Central Connecticut State University
Charter Oak State College
Connecticut College
Fairfield University
Gateway Community College
Goodwin College
Holy Apostles College and Seminary
Lincoln College of New England:
    Briarwood
Lincoln College of New England:
    Suffield
Lyme Academy College of Fine Arts
Manchester Community College
Mitchell College
Naugatuck Valley Community College
Norwalk Community College
Paier College of Art
Post University
Quinnipiac University
Sacred Heart University
Saint Joseph College
Southern Connecticut State University
Trinity College
University of Bridgeport
University of Connecticut
University of New Haven
Wesleyan University
Yale University

Delaware

Delaware College of Art and Design
Delaware State University
Delaware Technical and Community
    College: Stanton/Wilmington
Goldey-Beacom College
University of Delaware
Wesley College

District of Columbia

American University
Catholic University of America
Corcoran College of Art and Design
Gallaudet University
George Washington University
Georgetown University
Howard University
Trinity Washington University

Florida

Angley College
Ave Maria University
Baptist College of Florida
Barry University
Beacon College
Bethune-Cookman University
Brevard Community College
Broward College
Chipola College
College of Central Florida
Daytona State College
Eckerd College
Edison State College
Edward Waters College
Embry-Riddle Aeronautical University
Embry-Riddle Aeronautical University:
    Worldwide Campus
Everest University: Brandon
Flagler College
Florida Agricultural and Mechanical
    University
Florida Atlantic University
Florida Christian College
Florida Gateway College
Florida Gulf Coast University
Florida Institute of Technology
Florida International University
Florida Memorial University
Florida National College
Florida Southern College
Florida State College at Jacksonville
Florida State University
Gulf Coast Community College
Herzing University
Hillsborough Community College
Hodges University
Indian River State College
International Academy of Design and
    Technology: Orlando
International Academy of Design and
    Technology: Tampa
ITT Technical Institute: Lake Mary
Jacksonville University
Jones College
Key College
Lake-Sumter Community College
Lynn University
Miami Dade College
Miami International University of Art
    and Design
New College of Florida
North Florida Community College
Northwest Florida State College
Northwood University: Florida
Nova Southeastern University
Palm Beach Atlantic University
Palm Beach State College
Pensacola State College
Polk State College
Rasmussen College: Ocala
Rasmussen College: Pasco County
Ringling College of Art and Design
Rollins College
Saint Leo University
St. Petersburg College
Saint Thomas University
Santa Fe College
Schiller International University
Seminole State College of Florida
South Florida Community College

Southeastern University
Southwest Florida College
Stetson University
Tallahassee Community College
Trinity College of Florida
University of Central Florida
University of Florida
University of Miami
University of North Florida
University of South Florida
University of Tampa
University of West Florida
Valencia College
Warner University
Webber International University

Georgia

Abraham Baldwin Agricultural College
Agnes Scott College
Albany State University
Andrew College
Armstrong Atlantic State University
Atlanta Christian College
Atlanta Metropolitan College
Augusta State University
Bainbridge College
Bauder College
Berry College
Brenau University
Brewton-Parker College
Chattahoochee Technical College
Clark Atlanta University
Clayton State University
College of Coastal Georgia
Columbus State University
Columbus Technical College
Covenant College
Darton College
DeKalb Technical College
Emory University
Gainesville State College
Georgia College and State University
Georgia Gwinnett College
Georgia Institute of Technology
Georgia Military College
Georgia Perimeter College
Georgia Southern University
Georgia Southwestern State University
Georgia State University
Gordon College
ITT Technical Institute: Duluth
LaGrange College
Le Cordon Bleu College of Culinary
    Arts: Atlanta
Life University
Mercer University
Middle Georgia College
Middle Georgia Technical College
Morehouse College
North Georgia College & State
    University
Paine College
Piedmont College
Reinhardt University
Savannah College of Art and Design
Savannah State University
Savannah Technical College
Shorter University
South Georgia College
Southern Polytechnic State University
Spelman College
Thomas University
Toccoa Falls College
Truett-McConnell College
University of Georgia
University of West Georgia
Valdosta State University
Wesleyan College
Young Harris College

Hawaii

Brigham Young University-Hawaii
Chaminade University of Honolulu
Hawaii Pacific University
Hawaii Tokai International College
University of Hawaii at Manoa
University of Hawaii: Honolulu
    Community College
University of Hawaii: Kauai
    Community College
University of Hawaii: West Oahu

Idaho

Boise State University
Brigham Young University-Idaho
College of Idaho
College of Southern Idaho
Idaho State University
ITT Technical Institute: Boise
Lewis-Clark State College
Northwest Nazarene University
Stevens-Henager College: Boise
University of Idaho

Illinois

Augustana College
Aurora University
Benedictine University
Benedictine University at Springfield
Black Hawk College
Blackburn College
Bradley University
Carl Sandburg College
Chicago State University
City Colleges of Chicago: Harold
    Washington College
City Colleges of Chicago: Wilbur
    Wright College
College of DuPage
College of Lake County
College of Office Technology
Columbia College Chicago
Concordia University Chicago
Danville Area Community College
DePaul University
Dominican University
Eastern Illinois University
Elgin Community College
Elmhurst College
Eureka College
Governors State University
Greenville College
Harrington College of Design
Heartland Community College
Hebrew Theological College
Illinois Central College
Illinois College
Illinois Eastern Community Colleges:
    Frontier Community College
Illinois Eastern Community Colleges:
    Lincoln Trail College
Illinois Eastern Community Colleges:
    Olney Central College
Illinois Eastern Community Colleges:
    Wabash Valley College
Illinois Institute of Technology
Illinois State University
Illinois Wesleyan University
International Academy of Design and
    Technology: Chicago
ITT Technical Institute: Mount
    Prospect
John Wood Community College
Joliet Junior College
Judson University
Kankakee Community College
Kendall College
Kishwaukee College

Knox College
Lake Forest College
Lake Land College
Le Cordon Bleu College of Culinary
   Arts: Chicago
Lewis University
Lexington College
Lincoln Christian University
Lincoln College
Lincoln Land Community College
Loyola University Chicago
MacMurray College
McHenry County College
McKendree University
Millikin University
Monmouth College
Moody Bible Institute
Moraine Valley Community College
Morrison Institute of Technology
Morton College
National-Louis University
North Central College
North Park University
Northern Illinois University
Northwestern College
Northwestern University
Oakton Community College
Olivet Nazarene University
Parkland College
Quincy University
Richland Community College
Robert Morris University: Chicago
Rock Valley College
Rockford College
Roosevelt University
Saint Xavier University
Sauk Valley Community College
School of the Art Institute of Chicago
Southeastern Illinois College
Southern Illinois University Carbondale
Southern Illinois University
   Edwardsville
Southwestern Illinois College
Spoon River College
Trinity Christian College
Trinity College of Nursing and Health
   Sciences
Trinity International University
Triton College
University of Chicago
University of Illinois at Chicago
University of Illinois at Urbana-
   Champaign
University of Illinois: Springfield
VanderCook College of Music
Western Illinois University
Westwood College: O'Hare Airport
Wheaton College

Indiana

Ancilla College
Ball State University
Bethel College
Butler University
Calumet College of St. Joseph
DePauw University
Franklin College
Goshen College
Hanover College
Holy Cross College
Huntington University
Indiana Institute of Technology
Indiana State University
Indiana University Bloomington
Indiana University East
Indiana University Kokomo
Indiana University Northwest
Indiana University South Bend
Indiana University Southeast
Indiana University-Purdue University
   Fort Wayne

Indiana University-Purdue University
   Indianapolis
Indiana Wesleyan University
Ivy Tech Community College:
   Bloomington
Ivy Tech Community College: Central
   Indiana
Ivy Tech Community College:
   Columbus
Ivy Tech Community College: East
   Central
Ivy Tech Community College: Kokomo
Ivy Tech Community College:
   Lafayette
Ivy Tech Community College: North
   Central
Ivy Tech Community College:
   Northeast
Ivy Tech Community College:
   Northwest
Ivy Tech Community College:
   Richmond
Ivy Tech Community College: South
   Central
Ivy Tech Community College:
   Southeast
Ivy Tech Community College:
   Southwest
Ivy Tech Community College: Wabash
   Valley
Manchester College
Marian University
Oakland City University
Purdue University
Purdue University Calumet
Purdue University North Central
Rose-Hulman Institute of Technology
St. Mary-of-the-Woods College
Saint Mary's College
Taylor University
Trine University
University of Evansville
University of Indianapolis
University of Notre Dame
University of Southern Indiana
University of St. Francis
Valparaiso University
Wabash College

Iowa

AIB College of Business
Ashford University
Briar Cliff University
Buena Vista University
Central College
Clarke University
Clinton Community College
Coe College
Cornell College
Des Moines Area Community College
Divine Word College
Drake University
Ellsworth Community College
Faith Baptist Bible College and
   Theological Seminary
Graceland University
Grand View University
Grinnell College
Indian Hills Community College
Iowa Central Community College
Iowa State University
Iowa Wesleyan College
Kaplan University: Cedar Falls
Kaplan University: Cedar Rapids
Kaplan University: Des Moines
Loras College
Luther College
Marshalltown Community College
Morningside College
Mount Mercy University
Muscatine Community College
North Iowa Area Community College

Northwest Iowa Community College
Northwestern College
St. Ambrose University
St. Luke's College
Scott Community College
Simpson College
Southeastern Community College:
   North Campus
Southwestern Community College
University of Dubuque
University of Iowa
University of Northern Iowa
Upper Iowa University
Waldorf College
Wartburg College
Western Iowa Tech Community
   College
William Penn University

Kansas

Allen County Community College
Baker University
Barclay College
Barton County Community College
Benedictine College
Bethany College
Bethel College
Central Christian College of Kansas
Cloud County Community College
Coffeyville Community College
Cowley County Community College
Emporia State University
Friends University
Garden City Community College
Hesston College
Hutchinson Community College
Kansas City Kansas Community
   College
Kansas State University
Kansas Wesleyan University
Labette Community College
Manhattan Area Technical College
McPherson College
MidAmerica Nazarene University
Newman University
Pittsburg State University
Southwestern College
Sterling College
University of Kansas
University of St. Mary
Washburn University
Wichita State University

Kentucky

Alice Lloyd College
Ashland Community and Technical
   College
Bellarmine University
Berea College
Big Sandy Community and Technical
   College
Bluegrass Community and Technical
   College
Brescia University
Campbellsville University
Centre College
Daymar College: Owensboro
Eastern Kentucky University
Elizabethtown Community and
   Technical College
Georgetown College
Henderson Community College
Kentucky Christian University
Kentucky Mountain Bible College
Kentucky State University
Kentucky Wesleyan College
Lindsey Wilson College
Mid-Continent University
Midway College
Morehead State University

Murray State University
Northern Kentucky University
Owensboro Community and Technical
   College
Pikeville College
St. Catharine College
Somerset Community College
Southeast Kentucky Community and
   Technical College
Spalding University
Sullivan College of Technology and
   Design
Thomas More College
Transylvania University
Union College
University of the Cumberlands
University of Kentucky
University of Louisville

Louisiana

Bossier Parish Community College
Centenary College of Louisiana
Delgado Community College
Dillard University
Grambling State University
Louisiana College
Louisiana State University and
   Agricultural and Mechanical College
Louisiana State University at Eunice
Louisiana State University in
   Shreveport
Louisiana Tech University
Loyola University New Orleans
Nicholls State University
Northwestern State University
Nunez Community College
Our Lady of Holy Cross College
St. Joseph Seminary College
Southeastern Louisiana University
Southern University and Agricultural
   and Mechanical College
Tulane University
University of Louisiana at Lafayette
University of Louisiana at Monroe
University of New Orleans
Xavier University of Louisiana

Maine

Bates College
Bowdoin College
Central Maine Community College
Colby College
College of the Atlantic
Husson University
Kennebec Valley Community College
Maine Maritime Academy
New England School of
   Communications
Saint Joseph's College of Maine
Southern Maine Community College
Thomas College
Unity College in Maine
University of Maine
University of Maine at Augusta
University of Maine at Farmington
University of Maine at Fort Kent
University of Maine at Machias
University of Maine at Presque Isle
University of New England
University of Southern Maine
Washington County Community
   College

Maryland

Allegany College of Maryland
Anne Arundel Community College
Baltimore International College

Bowie State University
Capitol College
Carroll Community College
College of Notre Dame of Maryland
College of Southern Maryland
Community College of Baltimore
County
Coppin State University
Frostburg State University
Garrett College
Goucher College
Griggs University
Harford Community College
Hood College
Howard Community College
Johns Hopkins University
Johns Hopkins University: Peabody
Conservatory of Music
Kaplan University: Hagerstown
Loyola University Maryland
McDaniel College
Morgan State University
Mount St. Mary's University
Prince George's Community College
St. Mary's College of Maryland
Salisbury University
Stevenson University
Towson University
University of Baltimore
University of Maryland: Baltimore
County
University of Maryland: College Park
University of Maryland: Eastern Shore
University of Maryland: University
College
Washington Bible College
Washington College

Massachusetts

American International College
Amherst College
Anna Maria College
Art Institute of Boston at Lesley
University
Assumption College
Atlantic Union College
Babson College
Bay State College
Becker College
Bentley University
Berklee College of Music
Boston College
Boston Conservatory
Boston University
Brandeis University
Bristol Community College
Bunker Hill Community College
Cape Cod Community College
Clark University
College of the Holy Cross
Curry College
Dean College
Elms College
Emerson College
Emmanuel College
Endicott College
Fitchburg State University
Framingham State University
Gordon College
Greenfield Community College
Hampshire College
Harvard College
Hellenic College/Holy Cross
Lasell College
Lesley University
Massachusetts Bay Community College
Massachusetts College of Art and
Design
Massachusetts College of Liberal Arts
Massachusetts College of Pharmacy
and Health Sciences
Massachusetts Institute of Technology

Massachusetts Maritime Academy
Merrimack College
Middlesex Community College
Montserrat College of Art
Mount Holyoke College
Mount Ida College
Mount Wachusett Community College
New England Conservatory of Music
New England Institute of Art
Newbury College
Nichols College
North Shore Community College
Northeastern University
Northern Essex Community College
Pine Manor College
Quinsigamond Community College
Regis College
Salem State University
Simmons College
Smith College
Springfield College
Springfield Technical Community
College
Stonehill College
Suffolk University
Tufts University
University of Massachusetts Amherst
University of Massachusetts Boston
University of Massachusetts Dartmouth
University of Massachusetts Lowell
Wellesley College
Wentworth Institute of Technology
Western New England College
Westfield State University
Wheaton College
Wheelock College
Williams College
Worcester Polytechnic Institute
Worcester State University
Zion Bible College

Michigan

Adrian College
Albion College
Alma College
Andrews University
Aquinas College
Baker College of Auburn Hills
Baker College of Cadillac
Baker College of Jackson
Baker College of Muskegon
Baker College of Owosso
Baker College of Port Huron
Bay de Noc Community College
Calvin College
Central Michigan University
College for Creative Studies
Cornerstone University
Davenport University
Delta College
Eastern Michigan University
Ferris State University
Finlandia University
Glen Oaks Community College
Gogebic Community College
Grand Rapids Community College
Grand Valley State University
Hillsdale College
Hope College
Kalamazoo College
Kellogg Community College
Kettering University
Kirtland Community College
Kuyper College
Lake Michigan College
Lansing Community College
Lawrence Technological University
Macomb Community College
Madonna University
Marygrove College
Michigan Jewish Institute
Michigan State University

Michigan Technological University
Montcalm Community College
Mott Community College
Muskegon Community College
North Central Michigan College
Northern Michigan University
Northwestern Michigan College
Northwood University: Michigan
Oakland Community College
Oakland University
Olivet College
Rochester College
Sacred Heart Major Seminary
Saginaw Valley State University
St. Clair County Community College
Siena Heights University
Southwestern Michigan College
Spring Arbor University
University of Detroit Mercy
University of Michigan
University of Michigan: Dearborn
University of Michigan: Flint
Washtenaw Community College
Wayne State University
Western Michigan University

Minnesota

Academy College
Alexandria Technical College
Art Institutes International Minnesota
Augsburg College
Bemidji State University
Bethany Lutheran College
Bethel University
Brown College: Mendota Heights
Carleton College
Central Lakes College
Century College
College of St. Benedict
College of St. Scholastica
College of Visual Arts
Concordia College: Moorhead
Concordia University St. Paul
Crown College
Dakota County Technical College
Globe University
Gustavus Adolphus College
Hamline University
Hennepin Technical College
Inver Hills Community College
Itasca Community College
Lake Superior College
Macalester College
Minneapolis Community and Technical
College
Minnesota State College - Southeast
Technical
Minnesota State Community and
Technical College
Minnesota State University Mankato
Minnesota State University Moorhead
Minnesota West Community and
Technical College
Normandale Community College
North Hennepin Community College
Northland Community & Technical
College
Northwest Technical College
Northwest Technical Institute
Northwestern College
Pine Technical College
Rainy River Community College
Rasmussen College: Bloomington
Rasmussen College: Brooklyn Park
Rasmussen College: Eagan
Rasmussen College: Mankato
Rasmussen College: St. Cloud
Ridgewater College
Riverland Community College
Rochester Community and Technical
College
St. Catherine University

Saint Cloud State University
St. Cloud Technical and Community
College
St. John's University
St. Mary's University of Minnesota
St. Olaf College
South Central College
Southwest Minnesota State University
University of Minnesota: Crookston
University of Minnesota: Duluth
University of Minnesota: Morris
University of Minnesota: Rochester
University of Minnesota: Twin Cities
University of St. Thomas
Walden University
Winona State University

Mississippi

Alcorn State University
Belhaven University
Blue Mountain College
Delta State University
Jackson State University
Meridian Community College
Millsaps College
Mississippi College
Mississippi State University
Mississippi University for Women
Mississippi Valley State University
Northeast Mississippi Community
College
Rust College
Tougaloo College
University of Mississippi
University of Southern Mississippi
William Carey University

Missouri

Avila University
Central Methodist University
College of the Ozarks
Columbia College
Cottey College
Crowder College
Culver-Stockton College
Drury University
East Central College
Evangel University
Fontbonne University
Goldfarb School of Nursing at Barnes-
Jewish College
Hannibal-LaGrange University
Harris-Stowe State University
Jefferson College
Kansas City Art Institute
Lincoln University
Lindenwood University
Maryville University of Saint Louis
Metropolitan Community College: Blue
River
Metropolitan Community College:
Longview
Metropolitan Community College:
Maple Woods
Metropolitan Community College:
Penn Valley
Missouri Baptist University
Missouri Southern State University
Missouri State University
Missouri University of Science and
Technology
Missouri Valley College
Moberly Area Community College
North Central Missouri College
Northwest Missouri State University
Park University
Research College of Nursing
Rockhurst University
Saint Louis University

Southeast Missouri Hospital College of
Nursing and Health Sciences
Southeast Missouri State University
Southwest Baptist University
Stephens College
Stevens Institute of Business & Arts
Three Rivers Community College
Truman State University
University of Central Missouri
University of Missouri: Columbia
University of Missouri: Kansas City
University of Missouri: St. Louis
Webster University
Westminster College
William Jewell College
William Woods University

Montana

Carroll College
Flathead Valley Community College
Montana State University: Billings
Montana State University: Bozeman
Montana State University: Northern
Montana Tech of the University of
Montana
Rocky Mountain College
University of Great Falls
University of Montana: Western

Nebraska

Bellevue University
BryanLGH College of Health Sciences
Chadron State College
College of Saint Mary
Concordia University
Creighton University
Doane College
Grace University
Metropolitan Community College
Mid-Plains Community College Area
Nebraska Christian College
Nebraska College of Technical
Agriculture
Nebraska Wesleyan University
Northeast Community College
Peru State College
Union College
University of Nebraska - Lincoln
University of Nebraska - Omaha
Wayne State College
Western Nebraska Community College
York College

Nevada

College of Southern Nevada
Great Basin College
International Academy of Design and
Technology: Henderson
Sierra Nevada College
Truckee Meadows Community College
University of Nevada: Las Vegas
University of Nevada: Reno
Western Nevada College

New Hampshire

Chester College of New England
Colby-Sawyer College
Daniel Webster College
Dartmouth College
Franklin Pierce University
Granite State College
Hesser College
Lakes Region Community College
Nashua Community College

New England College
NHTI-Concord's Community College
Plymouth State University
Rivier College
Saint Anselm College
Southern New Hampshire University
University of New Hampshire
University of New Hampshire at
Manchester

New Jersey

Atlantic Cape Community College
Berkeley College
Bloomfield College
Brookdale Community College
Burlington County College
Caldwell College
Centenary College
The College of New Jersey
College of St. Elizabeth
County College of Morris
Drew University
Essex County College
Felician College
Hudson County Community College
Kean University
Mercer County Community College
Monmouth University
Montclair State University
New Jersey City University
New Jersey Institute of Technology
Ocean County College
Passaic County Community College
Princeton University
Ramapo College of New Jersey
Raritan Valley Community College
Richard Stockton College of New
Jersey
Rowan University
Rutgers, The State University of New
Jersey: Camden Regional Campus
Rutgers, The State University of New
Jersey: New Brunswick/Piscataway
Campus
Rutgers, The State University of New
Jersey: Newark Regional Campus
Saint Peter's College
Salem Community College
Seton Hall University
Stevens Institute of Technology
Thomas Edison State College
Union County College
William Paterson University of New
Jersey

New Mexico

Eastern New Mexico University
Mesalands Community College
New Mexico Highlands University
New Mexico Institute of Mining and
Technology
New Mexico Junior College
New Mexico State University at
Alamogordo
New Mexico State University at
Carlsbad
Santa Fe Community College
University of New Mexico
University of the Southwest

New York

Adelphi University
Adirondack Community College
Albany College of Pharmacy and
Health Sciences
Alfred University

ASA Institute of Business and
Computer Technology
Bard College
Barnard College
Berkeley College
Berkeley College of New York City
Briarcliffe College
Broome Community College
Bryant & Stratton College: Buffalo
Bryant & Stratton College: Syracuse
North
Business Informatics Center
Canisius College
Cayuga Community College
Cazenovia College
City University of New York: Baruch
College
City University of New York: Borough
of Manhattan Community College
City University of New York: Bronx
Community College
City University of New York:
Brooklyn College
City University of New York: City
College
City University of New York: College
of Staten Island
City University of New York: CUNY
Online
City University of New York: Hunter
College
City University of New York: John Jay
College of Criminal Justice
City University of New York:
Kingsborough Community College
City University of New York:
LaGuardia Community College
City University of New York: Medgar
Evers College
City University of New York: Queens
College
City University of New York:
Queensborough Community College
City University of New York: York
College
Clarkson University
Clinton Community College
Colgate University
College of Mount St. Vincent
College of New Rochelle
Columbia University
Columbia University: School of
General Studies
Columbia-Greene Community College
Concordia College
Cooper Union for the Advancement of
Science and Art
Cornell University
Corning Community College
Daemen College
Davis College
Dominican College of Blauvelt
Dowling College
Dutchess Community College
Eastman School of Music of the
University of Rochester
Elmira College
Excelsior College
Five Towns College
Fordham University
Fulton-Montgomery Community
College
Genesee Community College
Globe Institute of Technology
Hamilton College
Hartwick College
Herkimer County Community College
Hilbert College
Hobart and William Smith Colleges
Hofstra University
Houghton College
Iona College
Ithaca College
Jamestown Community College

Jewish Theological Seminary of
America
Juilliard School
Keuka College
The King's College
Le Moyne College
LIM College
Long Island University: Brooklyn
Campus
Long Island University: C. W. Post
Campus
Manhattan College
Manhattanville College
Marist College
Marymount Manhattan College
Medaille College
Medaille College: Amherst
Medaille College: Rochester
Mildred Elley
Mohawk Valley Community College
Molloy College
Monroe College
Monroe Community College
Mount Saint Mary College
Nassau Community College
Nazareth College
New York Career Institute
New York Institute of Technology
New York School of Interior Design
New York University
Niagara County Community College
Niagara University
North Country Community College
Nyack College
Onondaga Community College
Pace University
Paul Smith's College
Phillips Beth Israel School of Nursing
Polytechnic Institute of New York
University
Pratt Institute
Rensselaer Polytechnic Institute
Roberts Wesleyan College
Rochester Institute of Technology
Rockland Community College
Russell Sage College
Sage College of Albany
Saint Bonaventure University
St. Francis College
St. John Fisher College
St. John's University
St. Joseph's College
St. Joseph's College: Suffolk Campus
St. Lawrence University
St. Thomas Aquinas College
Sarah Lawrence College
Schenectady County Community
College
School of Visual Arts
Siena College
Skidmore College
Suffolk County Community College
Sullivan County Community College
SUNY College at Brockport
SUNY College at Buffalo
SUNY College at Cortland
SUNY College at Fredonia
SUNY College at Geneseo
SUNY College at New Paltz
SUNY College at Old Westbury
SUNY College at Oneonta
SUNY College at Oswego
SUNY College at Plattsburgh
SUNY College at Potsdam
SUNY College at Purchase
SUNY College of Agriculture and
Technology at Cobleskill
SUNY College of Environmental
Science and Forestry
SUNY College of Technology at
Alfred
SUNY College of Technology at Delhi
SUNY College of Technology at
Farmingdale
SUNY Empire State College

SUNY Institute of Technology at Utica/Rome
SUNY Maritime College
SUNY University at Albany
SUNY University at Binghamton
SUNY University at Buffalo
SUNY Upstate Medical University
Syracuse University
Tompkins Cortland Community College
Touro College
Union College
University of Rochester
Utica College
Vassar College
Vaughn College of Aeronautics and Technology
Wagner College
Wells College
Westchester Community College

North Carolina

Appalachian State University
Barton College
Belmont Abbey College
Bennett College for Women
Brevard College
Cabarrus College of Health Sciences
Campbell University
Carteret Community College
Catawba College
Central Piedmont Community College
College of the Albemarle
Davidson College
Duke University
Durham Technical Community College
East Carolina University
Elizabeth City State University
Elon University
Fayetteville State University
Fayetteville Technical Community College
Gardner-Webb University
Greensboro College
Guilford College
Guilford Technical Community College
High Point University
Johnson C. Smith University
Johnston Community College
Laurel University
Lees-McRae College
Lenoir-Rhyne University
Louisburg College
Mars Hill College
Martin Community College
Mayland Community College
Meredith College
Methodist University
Mid-Atlantic Christian University
Montreat College
Nash Community College
North Carolina Central University
North Carolina State University
North Carolina Wesleyan College
Peace College
Pfeiffer University
Piedmont Baptist College and Graduate School
Queens University of Charlotte
Roanoke-Chowan Community College
St. Andrews Presbyterian College
Salem College
Sandhills Community College
Tri-County Community College
University of North Carolina at Asheville
University of North Carolina at Chapel Hill
University of North Carolina at Charlotte
University of North Carolina at Greensboro

University of North Carolina at Pembroke
University of North Carolina at Wilmington
University of North Carolina School of the Arts
Wake Forest University
Wake Technical Community College
Warren Wilson College
Wilkes Community College
Wilson Community College
Wingate University
Winston-Salem State University

North Dakota

Bismarck State College
Jamestown College
Lake Region State College
Mayville State University
Minot State University
North Dakota State University
Rasmussen College: Bismarck
Rasmussen College: Fargo
University of Mary
University of North Dakota
Valley City State University
Williston State College

Ohio

Allegheny Wesleyan College
Art Academy of Cincinnati
Art Institute of Ohio: Cincinnati
Ashland University
Baldwin-Wallace College
Belmont Technical College
Bluffton University
Bowling Green State University
Bowling Green State University: Firelands College
Bryant & Stratton College: Parma
Capital University
Case Western Reserve University
Cedarville University
Central State University
Cincinnati Christian University
Cincinnati State Technical and Community College
Clark State Community College
Cleveland Institute of Art
Cleveland Institute of Music
Cleveland State University
College of Mount St. Joseph
College of Wooster
Columbus College of Art and Design
Columbus State Community College
Defiance College
Denison University
Edison State Community College
Franciscan University of Steubenville
Franklin University
Heidelberg University
Hiram College
Hocking College
James A. Rhodes State College
John Carroll University
Kaplan College: Dayton
Kent State University
Kent State University: Geauga
Kenyon College
Kettering College of Medical Arts
Lake Erie College
Lakeland Community College
Lorain County Community College
Lourdes College
Malone University
Marietta College
Miami University: Hamilton
Miami University: Middletown
Miami University: Oxford
Mount Vernon Nazarene University

Muskingum University
Oberlin College
Ohio Dominican University
Ohio Northern University
Ohio State University: Columbus Campus
Ohio University
Ohio University: Zanesville Campus
Ohio Wesleyan University
Otterbein University
Owens Community College: Toledo
Shawnee State University
Sinclair Community College
Tiffin University
University of Akron
University of Akron: Wayne College
University of Cincinnati
University of Cincinnati: Clermont College
University of Cincinnati: Raymond Walters College
University of Dayton
University of Findlay
University of Mount Union
University of Northwestern Ohio
University of Rio Grande
University of Toledo
Urbana University
Ursuline College
Walsh University
Wilberforce University
Wilmington College
Wittenberg University
Wright State University
Xavier University
Youngstown State University

Oklahoma

Bacone College
Cameron University
Carl Albert State College
East Central University
Eastern Oklahoma State College
Langston University
Northeastern Oklahoma Agricultural and Mechanical College
Northeastern State University
Northwestern Oklahoma State University
Oklahoma Baptist University
Oklahoma Christian University
Oklahoma City Community College
Oklahoma City University
Oklahoma Panhandle State University
Oklahoma State University
Oklahoma State University Institute of Technology: Okmulgee
Oklahoma Wesleyan University
Oral Roberts University
Redlands Community College
Rogers State University
Rose State College
St. Gregory's University
Southeastern Oklahoma State University
Southern Nazarene University
Southwestern Christian University
Southwestern Oklahoma State University
Tulsa Community College
University of Central Oklahoma
University of Oklahoma
University of Science and Arts of Oklahoma
University of Tulsa
Western Oklahoma State College

Oregon

Art Institute of Portland
Chemeketa Community College

Clackamas Community College
Concordia University
Corban College
Eastern Oregon University
George Fox University
Lewis & Clark College
Linfield College
Linn-Benton Community College
Marylhurst University
Northwest Christian University
Oregon College of Art & Craft
Oregon State University
Pacific Northwest College of Art
Pacific University
Portland Community College
Portland State University
Reed College
Rogue Community College
Southern Oregon University
Southwestern Oregon Community College
Treasure Valley Community College
Umpqua Community College
University of Oregon
University of Portland
Warner Pacific College
Western Oregon University
Willamette University

Pennsylvania

Albright College
Allegheny College
Alvernia University
Art Institute of Pittsburgh
Baptist Bible College of Pennsylvania
Bloomsburg University of Pennsylvania
Bryn Mawr College
Bucknell University
Bucks County Community College
Cabrini College
California University of Pennsylvania
Cambria-Rowe Business College: Indiana
Carlow University
Carnegie Mellon University
Cedar Crest College
Central Pennsylvania College
Chatham University
Chestnut Hill College
Cheyney University of Pennsylvania
Clarion University of Pennsylvania
Community College of Allegheny County
Community College of Beaver County
Community College of Philadelphia
Curtis Institute of Music
Delaware County Community College
DeSales University
Dickinson College
Drexel University
Duquesne University
East Stroudsburg University of Pennsylvania
Eastern University
Edinboro University of Pennsylvania
Elizabethtown College
Franklin & Marshall College
Gannon University
Geneva College
Gettysburg College
Grove City College
Gwynedd-Mercy College
Harcum College
Harrisburg Area Community College
Haverford College
Holy Family University
Immaculata University
Indiana University of Pennsylvania
ITT Technical Institute: Bensalem
JNA Institute of Culinary Arts
Johnson College

Juniata College
Keystone College
Keystone Technical Institute
King's College
Kutztown University of Pennsylvania
La Roche College
La Salle University
Lafayette College
Laurel Business Institute
Lebanon Valley College
Lehigh University
Lincoln University
Lock Haven University of
Pennsylvania
Lycoming College
Manor College
Mansfield University of Pennsylvania
Marywood University
Mercyhurst College
Messiah College
Millersville University of Pennsylvania
Misericordia University
Moore College of Art and Design
Moravian College
Mount Aloysius College
Muhlenberg College
Neumann University
Northampton Community College
Oakbridge Academy of Arts
Penn State Abington
Penn State Altoona
Penn State Beaver
Penn State Berks
Penn State Brandywine
Penn State DuBois
Penn State Erie, The Behrend College
Penn State Fayette, The Eberly
Campus
Penn State Greater Allegheny
Penn State Harrisburg
Penn State Hazleton
Penn State Lehigh Valley
Penn State Mont Alto
Penn State New Kensington
Penn State Schuylkill
Penn State Shenango
Penn State University Park
Penn State Wilkes-Barre
Penn State Worthington Scranton
Penn State York
Pennsylvania College of Technology
Philadelphia Biblical University
Philadelphia University
Pittsburgh Institute of Aeronautics
Point Park University
Reading Area Community College
Robert Morris University
Rosemont College
St. Charles Borromeo Seminary -
Overbrook
St. Francis University
Saint Joseph's University
St. Vincent College
Seton Hill University
Shippensburg University of
Pennsylvania
Slippery Rock University of
Pennsylvania
Susquehanna University
Swarthmore College
Temple University
Thiel College
Triangle Tech: Greensburg
University of the Arts
University of Pennsylvania
University of Pittsburgh
University of Pittsburgh at Bradford
University of Pittsburgh at Greensburg
University of Pittsburgh at Johnstown
University of Pittsburgh at Titusville
University of the Sciences in
Philadelphia
University of Scranton
Ursinus College
Valley Forge Christian College

Valley Forge Military Academy and
College
Vet Tech Institute
Villanova University
Washington & Jefferson College
Waynesburg University
West Chester University of
Pennsylvania
Widener University
York College of Pennsylvania

Puerto Rico

American University of Puerto Rico
Bayamon Central University
Conservatory of Music of Puerto Rico
Escuela de Artes Plasticas de Puerto
Rico
Humacao Community College
Inter American University of Puerto
Rico: Aguadilla Campus
Inter American University of Puerto
Rico: Arecibo Campus
Inter American University of Puerto
Rico: Bayamon Campus
Inter American University of Puerto
Rico: Metropolitan Campus
Inter American University of Puerto
Rico: San German Campus
National University College: Arecibo
National University College: Bayamon
Pontifical Catholic University of Puerto
Rico
Universidad Adventista de las Antillas
Universidad del Este
Universidad Politecnica de Puerto Rico
University College of San Juan
University of Puerto Rico: Arecibo
University of Puerto Rico: Bayamon
University College
University of Puerto Rico: Carolina
Regional College
University of Puerto Rico: Cayey
University College
University of Puerto Rico: Humacao
University of Puerto Rico: Mayaguez
University of Puerto Rico: Rio Piedras
University of Puerto Rico: Utuado

Rhode Island

Brown University
Bryant University
Community College of Rhode Island
New England Institute of Technology
Providence College
Rhode Island School of Design
Roger Williams University
Salve Regina University
University of Rhode Island

South Carolina

Aiken Technical College
Anderson University
Benedict College
Central Carolina Technical College
Charleston Southern University
The Citadel
Claflin University
Clemson University
Coastal Carolina University
Coker College
College of Charleston
Columbia College
Columbia International University
Converse College
Denmark Technical College
Erskine College
Florence-Darlington Technical College

Forrest Junior College
Francis Marion University
Furman University
Greenville Technical College
Lander University
Limestone College
Morris College
Newberry College
North Greenville University
Northeastern Technical College
Presbyterian College
South Carolina State University
South University: Columbia
Southern Wesleyan University
Spartanburg Community College
Tri-County Technical College
Trident Technical College
University of South Carolina: Aiken
University of South Carolina: Beaufort
University of South Carolina:
Columbia
University of South Carolina:
Lancaster
University of South Carolina: Sumter
University of South Carolina: Union
University of South Carolina: Upstate
Voorhees College
Winthrop University
Wofford College

South Dakota

Augustana College
Black Hills State University
Dakota Wesleyan University
Mitchell Technical Institute
Mount Marty College
National American University: Rapid
City
Northern State University
South Dakota State University
University of Sioux Falls
University of South Dakota

Tennessee

Aquinas College
Austin Peay State University
Belmont University
Bethel University
Bryan College
Carson-Newman College
Christian Brothers University
Cleveland State Community College
Cumberland University
Dyersburg State Community College
East Tennessee State University
Fisk University
Free Will Baptist Bible College
Freed-Hardeman University
ITT Technical Institute: Knoxville
ITT Technical Institute: Nashville
Jackson State Community College
King College
Lee University
LeMoyne-Owen College
Lipscomb University
Maryville College
Memphis College of Art
Middle Tennessee State University
Milligan College
Motlow State Community College
Nashville State Community College
O'More College of Design
Pellissippi State Community College
Rhodes College
Roane State Community College
Southwest Tennessee Community
College
Tennessee State University
Tennessee Technological University
Tennessee Wesleyan College

Trevecca Nazarene University
Tusculum College
Union University
University of Memphis
University of the South
University of Tennessee: Chattanooga
University of Tennessee: Knoxville
University of Tennessee: Martin
Vanderbilt University
Victory University
Volunteer State Community College
Walters State Community College
Watkins College of Art, Design & Film
Williamson Christian College

Texas

Abilene Christian University
Arlington Baptist College
Austin College
Austin Community College
Baylor University
Blinn College
Central Texas College
Collin County Community College
District
Concordia University Texas
Dallas Baptist University
Del Mar College
East Texas Baptist University
Eastfield College
El Centro College
Frank Phillips College
Grayson County College
Hallmark College of Aeronautics
Hallmark College of Technology
Hardin-Simmons University
Hill College
Houston Baptist University
Houston Community College System
Howard Payne University
Huston-Tillotson University
ITT Technical Institute: Arlington
ITT Technical Institute: Houston
Jacksonville College
Kilgore College
Lamar University
Laredo Community College
LeTourneau University
Lon Morris College
Lone Star College System
Lubbock Christian University
Midland College
Midwestern State University
Mountain View College
North Central Texas College
North Lake College
Northwood University: Texas
Odessa College
Panola College
Prairie View A&M University
Rice University
Richland College
St. Edward's University
St. Mary's University
St. Philip's College
Sam Houston State University
San Antonio College
San Jacinto College
Schreiner University
South Plains College
South Texas College
Southern Methodist University
Southwestern Adventist University
Southwestern Assemblies of God
University
Southwestern Christian College
Southwestern University
Stephen F. Austin State University
Sul Ross State University
Tarleton State University
Tarrant County College
Texas A&M International University

Texas A&M University
Texas A&M University-Commerce
Texas A&M University-Galveston
Texas A&M University-Kingsville
Texas A&M University-Texarkana
Texas Christian University
Texas College
Texas Lutheran University
Texas Southern University
Texas State Technical College: Harlingen
Texas State Technical College: Waco
Texas State Technical College: West Texas
Texas State University: San Marcos
Texas Tech University
Texas Wesleyan University
Texas Woman's University
Trinity University
University of Dallas
University of Houston-Clear Lake
University of Houston-Downtown
University of the Incarnate Word
University of Mary Hardin-Baylor
University of North Texas
University of St. Thomas
University of Texas at Arlington
University of Texas at Austin
University of Texas at Brownsville - Texas Southmost College
University of Texas at Dallas
University of Texas at El Paso
University of Texas at San Antonio
University of Texas at Tyler
University of Texas Health Science Center at Houston
University of Texas: Pan American
Victoria College
Wade College
Weatherford College
West Texas A&M University
Western Texas College
Westwood College: Houston South
Wharton County Junior College
Wiley College

Utah

Brigham Young University
College of Eastern Utah
Dixie State College
Neumont University
Salt Lake Community College
Snow College
Southern Utah University
Stevens-Henager College: Orem
University of Utah
Utah State University
Utah Valley University
Weber State University
Westminster College

Vermont

Bennington College
Burlington College
Castleton State College
Champlain College
College of St. Joseph in Vermont
Community College of Vermont
Goddard College
Green Mountain College
Johnson State College
Landmark College
Lyndon State College
Marlboro College
Middlebury College
New England Culinary Institute
Norwich University
St. Michael's College
Sterling College

Virginia

Art Institute of Washington
Averett University
Bluefield College
Bridgewater College
Bryant & Stratton College: Virginia Beach
Christendom College
Christopher Newport University
College of William and Mary
Danville Community College
Eastern Mennonite University
ECPI College of Technology: Virginia Beach
Emory & Henry College
Ferrum College
George Mason University
Germanna Community College
Hampden-Sydney College
Hampton University
Hollins University
ITT Technical Institute: Chantilly
J. Sargeant Reynolds Community College
James Madison University
Jefferson College of Health Sciences
Liberty University
Longwood University
Lynchburg College
Mary Baldwin College
Marymount University
Northern Virginia Community College
Old Dominion University
Patrick Henry College
Patrick Henry Community College
Paul D. Camp Community College
Piedmont Virginia Community College
Radford University
Randolph College
Randolph-Macon College
Rappahannock Community College
Regent University
Richard Bland College
Roanoke College
St. Paul's College
Shenandoah University
Southern Virginia University
Southwest Virginia Community College
Sweet Briar College
Thomas Nelson Community College
University of Mary Washington
University of Richmond
University of Virginia
University of Virginia's College at Wise
Virginia Commonwealth University
Virginia Intermont College
Virginia Military Institute
Virginia Polytechnic Institute and State University
Virginia State University
Virginia Union University
Virginia University of Lynchburg
Virginia Wesleyan College
Washington and Lee University

Washington

Art Institute of Seattle
Bastyr University
Big Bend Community College
Cascadia Community College
Central Washington University
Centralia College
Clark College
Cornish College of the Arts
DigiPen Institute of Technology
Eastern Washington University
Everett Community College
Evergreen State College
Gonzaga University

Green River Community College
ITT Technical Institute: Spokane
Lower Columbia College
North Seattle Community College
Northwest College of Art
Northwest School of Wooden Boatbuilding
Northwest University
Olympic College
Pacific Lutheran University
Peninsula College
Pierce College
Saint Martin's University
Seattle Pacific University
Seattle University
South Puget Sound Community College
Spokane Community College
Tacoma Community College
Trinity Lutheran College
University of Puget Sound
University of Washington
University of Washington Bothell
University of Washington Tacoma
Walla Walla Community College
Walla Walla University
Washington State University
Western Washington University
Whatcom Community College
Whitman College
Whitworth University
Yakima Valley Community College

West Virginia

Alderson-Broaddus College
Appalachian Bible College
Bethany College
Bluefield State College
Concord University
Davis and Elkins College
Fairmont State University
Glenville State College
Marshall University
Mountain State University
Ohio Valley University
Potomac State College of West Virginia University
Salem International University
Shepherd University
University of Charleston
West Liberty University
West Virginia Northern Community College
West Virginia University
West Virginia University at Parkersburg
West Virginia University Institute of Technology
Wheeling Jesuit University

Wisconsin

Alverno College
Bellin College
Beloit College
Cardinal Stritch University
Carroll University
Carthage College
Chippewa Valley Technical College
Concordia University Wisconsin
Edgewood College
Fox Valley Technical College
Gateway Technical College
Herzing University
ITT Technical Institute: Green Bay
Lakeland College
Lawrence University
Maranatha Baptist Bible College
Marian University
Marquette University
Milwaukee Area Technical College

Milwaukee Institute of Art & Design
Milwaukee School of Engineering
Moraine Park Technical College
Mount Mary College
Northeast Wisconsin Technical College
Northland College
St. Norbert College
Silver Lake College
University of Wisconsin-Baraboo/Sauk County
University of Wisconsin-Barron County
University of Wisconsin-Fox Valley
University of Wisconsin-La Crosse
University of Wisconsin-Madison
University of Wisconsin-Marathon County
University of Wisconsin-Marinette
University of Wisconsin-Marshfield/Wood County
University of Wisconsin-Milwaukee
University of Wisconsin-Parkside
University of Wisconsin-Richland
University of Wisconsin-River Falls
University of Wisconsin-Rock County
University of Wisconsin-Sheboygan
University of Wisconsin-Stevens Point
University of Wisconsin-Stout
University of Wisconsin-Superior
University of Wisconsin-Washington County
University of Wisconsin-Waukesha
University of Wisconsin-Whitewater
Viterbo University
Western Technical College
Wisconsin Lutheran College

Wyoming

Casper College
Central Wyoming College
Eastern Wyoming College
Laramie County Community College
Northwest College
Sheridan College
University of Wyoming
Western Wyoming Community College

ESL programs on campus

Alabama

Auburn University
Auburn University at Montgomery
Faulkner University
Gadsden State Community College
Troy University
University of Alabama
University of Alabama at Birmingham
University of Alabama in Huntsville
University of Montevallo
University of North Alabama
University of South Alabama

Alaska

Prince William Sound Community
  College
University of Alaska Anchorage

Arizona

Arizona State University
Arizona Western College
Central Arizona College
Cochise College
Glendale Community College
Mesa Community College
Mohave Community College
Northern Arizona University
Pima Community College
Scottsdale Community College
South Mountain Community College
University of Arizona

Arkansas

Arkansas State University
Arkansas Tech University
Harding University
Henderson State University
John Brown University
Ouachita Baptist University
University of Arkansas
University of Arkansas at Fort Smith
University of Arkansas at Little Rock
University of Central Arkansas

California

Academy of Art University
Allan Hancock College
Alliant International University
Antelope Valley College
Azusa Pacific University
Bakersfield College
Berkeley City College
Bethesda Christian University
Biola University
Butte College
Cabrillo College
California Baptist University
California College of the Arts

California State Polytechnic University:
  Pomona
California State University: Bakersfield
California State University: Chico
California State University: Dominguez
  Hills
California State University: East Bay
California State University: Fresno
California State University: Fullerton
California State University: Long
  Beach
California State University: Los
  Angeles
California State University: Sacramento
California State University: San
  Bernardino
California State University: San
  Marcos
California State University: Stanislaus
California University of Management
  and Sciences
Cerritos College
Cerro Coso Community College
Chaffey College
Citrus College
City College of San Francisco
Coastline Community College
College of the Canyons
College of the Desert
College of Marin
College of San Mateo
College of the Sequoias
College of the Siskiyous
Cosumnes River College
Crafton Hills College
Cuesta College
Cuyamaca College
Cypress College
Dominican University of California
East Los Angeles College
El Camino College
Fashion Institute of Design and
  Merchandising: San Francisco
Folsom Lake College
Foothill College
Fresno City College
Fresno Pacific University
Fullerton College
Glendale Community College
Golden Gate University
Grossmont College
Hartnell College
Holy Names University
Hope International University
Humboldt State University
Irvine Valley College
La Sierra University
Las Positas College
Lassen Community College
Lincoln University
Long Beach City College
Los Angeles City College
Los Angeles Harbor College
Los Angeles Mission College
Los Angeles Pierce College
Los Angeles Southwest College
Los Angeles Trade and Technical
  College
Los Angeles Valley College
Los Medanos College
Marymount College
Merritt College

MiraCosta College
Mission College
Modesto Junior College
Monterey Peninsula College
Mount San Antonio College
National University
NewSchool of Architecture & Design
Northwestern Polytechnic University
Notre Dame de Namur University
Ohlone College
Oxnard College
Pacific States University
Palo Verde College
Palomar College
Patten University
Pitzer College
Porterville College
Riverside Community College
Sacramento City College
Saddleback College
St. Mary's College of California
Samuel Merritt University
San Diego State University
San Francisco Art Institute
San Francisco Conservatory of Music
San Francisco State University
San Joaquin Delta College
San Jose City College
San Jose State University
Santa Ana College
Santa Barbara City College
Santa Mónica College
Santiago Canyon College
Shasta College
Sierra College
Soka University of America
Solano Community College
Sonoma State University
Southern California Institute of
  Technology
Southwestern College
University of California: Davis
University of California: Irvine
University of California: Los Angeles
University of California: San Diego
University of California: Santa Barbara
University of La Verne
University of the Pacific
University of San Diego
University of San Francisco
University of Southern California
University of the West
Ventura College
Victor Valley College
West Hills College: Coalinga
West Hills College: Lemoore
West Los Angeles College
West Valley College
Woodbury University
World Mission University

Colorado

Aims Community College
Arapahoe Community College
Art Institute of Colorado
Colorado College
Colorado Heights University
Colorado State University
Colorado State University: Pueblo
Community College of Aurora
Community College of Denver
Fort Lewis College
Front Range Community College
Metropolitan State College of Denver
National American University: Denver
Northeastern Junior College
Pikes Peak Community College
Pueblo Community College
Red Rocks Community College
Trinidad State Junior College
University of Colorado at Boulder
University of Colorado at Denver

University of Denver
University of Northern Colorado

Connecticut

Central Connecticut State University
Gateway Community College
Holy Apostles College and Seminary
Housatonic Community College
Lincoln College of New England:
  Briarwood
Lincoln College of New England:
  Suffield
Manchester Community College
Middlesex Community College
Naugatuck Valley Community College
Norwalk Community College
Post University
Sacred Heart University
Tunxis Community College
University of Bridgeport
University of Connecticut
Yale University

Delaware

Delaware State University
Delaware Technical and Community
  College: Stanton/Wilmington
University of Delaware

District of Columbia

Catholic University of America
Gallaudet University
George Washington University
Georgetown University
Trinity Washington University
University of the District of Columbia

Florida

Art Institute of Fort Lauderdale
Barry University
Brevard Community College
Broward College
Carlos Albizu University
College of Business and Technology:
  Flagler
College of Central Florida
Daytona State College
Eckerd College
Edison State College
Embry-Riddle Aeronautical University
Everest University: Largo
Everest University: Pompano Beach
Everest University: Tampa
Florida Atlantic University
Florida Institute of Technology
Florida International University
Florida Keys Community College
Florida National College
Florida State College at Jacksonville
Florida State University
Hodges University
Indian River State College
Johnson & Wales University: North
  Miami
Lynn University
Miami Dade College
Nova Southeastern University
Palm Beach State College
Polk State College
St. Petersburg College
Saint Thomas University
Santa Fe College
Schiller International University
Seminole State College of Florida

Southwest Florida College
Stetson University
University of Central Florida
University of Florida
University of Miami
University of North Florida
University of South Florida
University of West Florida
Valencia College
Webber International University

Georgia

Abraham Baldwin Agricultural College
Andrew College
Augusta State University
Beulah Heights University
Brenau University
Columbus State University
Darton College
Gainesville State College
Georgia Institute of Technology
Georgia Perimeter College
Georgia Southern University
Georgia Southwestern State University
Georgia State University
Gordon College
Life University
North Georgia College & State
  University
Savannah College of Art and Design
Savannah Technical College
Southern Polytechnic State University
University of West Georgia
Valdosta State University

Hawaii

Brigham Young University-Hawaii
Hawaii Pacific University
Hawaii Tokai International College
University of Hawaii at Hilo
University of Hawaii at Manoa
University of Hawaii: Hawaii
  Community College
University of Hawaii: Leeward
  Community College
University of Hawaii: Maui College

Idaho

Boise State University
College of Idaho
College of Southern Idaho
Idaho State University
Lewis-Clark State College
North Idaho College
University of Idaho

Illinois

Benedictine University
Black Hawk College
Carl Sandburg College
City Colleges of Chicago: Harold
  Washington College
City Colleges of Chicago: Kennedy-
  King College
City Colleges of Chicago: Malcolm X
  College
City Colleges of Chicago: Richard J.
  Daley College
City Colleges of Chicago: Wilbur
  Wright College
College of DuPage
College of Lake County
Columbia College Chicago
Danville Area Community College

DePaul University
DeVry University: Chicago
Dominican University
Elgin Community College
Harper College
Heartland Community College
Illinois Central College
Illinois Eastern Community Colleges:
  Frontier Community College
Illinois Eastern Community Colleges:
  Lincoln Trail College
Illinois Eastern Community Colleges:
  Olney Central College
Illinois Eastern Community Colleges:
  Wabash Valley College
Illinois Institute of Technology
Illinois State University
John Wood Community College
Joliet Junior College
Kishwaukee College
Lake Land College
Lewis University
Lincoln Land Community College
Loyola University Chicago
MacCormac College
McHenry County College
Monmouth College
Moraine Valley Community College
Morton College
National-Louis University
North Central College
North Park University
Parkland College
Richland Community College
Rockford College
Roosevelt University
St. Augustine College
Sauk Valley Community College
School of the Art Institute of Chicago
Southern Illinois University Carbondale
Southwestern Illinois College
Spoon River College
Triton College
University of Chicago
University of Illinois at Chicago
University of Illinois at Urbana-
  Champaign
University of Illinois: Springfield
Western Illinois University

Indiana

Ball State University
Bethel College
Butler University
Earlham College
Holy Cross College
Huntington University
Indiana Institute of Technology
Indiana State University
Indiana University Bloomington
Indiana University South Bend
Indiana University-Purdue University
  Fort Wayne
Indiana University-Purdue University
  Indianapolis
Purdue University Calumet
Taylor University
Trine University
University of Evansville
University of Indianapolis
University of Southern Indiana
Valparaiso University
Vincennes University

Iowa

Ashford University
Buena Vista University
Clarke University
Clinton Community College
Coe College

Cornell College
Des Moines Area Community College
Divine Word College
Drake University
Graceland University
Indian Hills Community College
Iowa State University
Iowa Western Community College
Kirkwood Community College
Loras College
Marshalltown Community College
Morningside College
Muscatine Community College
Northeast Iowa Community College
Northwest Iowa Community College
Northwestern College
Scott Community College
Southeastern Community College:
  North Campus
University of Dubuque
University of Iowa
University of Northern Iowa
Western Iowa Tech Community
  College

Kansas

Barton County Community College
Benedictine College
Butler Community College
Cloud County Community College
Coffeyville Community College
Cowley County Community College
Dodge City Community College
Donnelly College
Fort Hays State University
Hesston College
Kansas City Kansas Community
  College
Kansas State University
Kansas Wesleyan University
Neosho County Community College
Pittsburg State University
University of Kansas
University of Kansas Medical Center
Washburn University
Wichita State University

Kentucky

Berea College
Bluegrass Community and Technical
  College
Brescia University
Campbellsville University
Eastern Kentucky University
Kentucky State University
Murray State University
Northern Kentucky University
University of the Cumberlands
University of Kentucky
University of Louisville
Western Kentucky University

Louisiana

Delgado Community College
Louisiana State University and
  Agricultural and Mechanical College
Louisiana State University Health
  Sciences Center
Louisiana Tech University
Loyola University New Orleans
McNeese State University
St. Joseph Seminary College
Southeastern Louisiana University
Tulane University
University of Louisiana at Lafayette
University of Louisiana at Monroe
University of New Orleans

Maine

Central Maine Community College
Colby College
University of Maine
University of Maine at Fort Kent
University of Southern Maine

Maryland

Allegany College of Maryland
Anne Arundel Community College
Baltimore City Community College
Capitol College
Carroll Community College
Chesapeake College
College of Notre Dame of Maryland
Community College of Baltimore
  County
Howard Community College
Prince George's Community College
Salisbury University
Towson University
University of Maryland: Baltimore
  County
University of Maryland: College Park
Washington Adventist University

Massachusetts

American International College
Atlantic Union College
Bay Path College
Bay State College
Benjamin Franklin Institute of
  Technology
Berklee College of Music
Berkshire Community College
Boston Conservatory
Boston University
Brandeis University
Bridgewater State University
Bristol Community College
Bunker Hill Community College
Clark University
Dean College
Elms College
Fisher College
Framingham State University
Greenfield Community College
Lasell College
Massachusetts Bay Community College
Massachusetts College of Pharmacy
  and Health Sciences
Massasoit Community College
Merrimack College
Mount Ida College
Mount Wachusett Community College
New England Conservatory of Music
Northeastern University
Northern Essex Community College
Pine Manor College
Quinsigamond Community College
Regis College
Roxbury Community College
Salem State University
Springfield College
Springfield Technical Community
  College
Suffolk University
Tufts University
University of Massachusetts Amherst
University of Massachusetts Boston
Worcester Polytechnic Institute
Worcester State University

Michigan

Adrian College
Andrews University

ESL programs on campus

Central Michigan University
Davenport University
Eastern Michigan University
Finlandia University
Grand Valley State University
Hope College
Kalamazoo College
Kalamazoo Valley Community College
Lansing Community College
Lawrence Technological University
Macomb Community College
Madonna University
Michigan Jewish Institute
Michigan State University
Michigan Technological University
Northern Michigan University
Northwestern Michigan College
Oakland Community College
Oakland University
Olivet College
Sacred Heart Major Seminary
Saginaw Valley State University
Siena Heights University
Southwestern Michigan College
Spring Arbor University
University of Detroit Mercy
University of Michigan
University of Michigan: Flint
Washtenaw Community College
Wayne State University
Western Michigan University

Minnesota

Augsburg College
Bemidji State University
Central Lakes College
Century College
College of St. Benedict
Crown College
Dakota County Technical College
Inver Hills Community College
Lake Superior College
Minneapolis Community and Technical
College
Minnesota State Community and
Technical College
Minnesota State University Mankato
Minnesota West Community and
Technical College
Normandale Community College
North Hennepin Community College
Riverland Community College
Saint Cloud State University
St. Cloud Technical and Community
College
St. John's University
St. Mary's University of Minnesota
University of Minnesota: Crookston
University of Minnesota: Morris
University of Minnesota: Twin Cities
University of St. Thomas
Winona State University

Mississippi

Belhaven University
Jackson State University
Meridian Community College
Mississippi College
Mississippi State University
Northeast Mississippi Community
College
University of Southern Mississippi

Missouri

Avila University
Columbia College
Crowder College

Drury University
Fontbonne University
Hannibal-LaGrange University
Jefferson College
Kansas City Art Institute
Maryville University of Saint Louis
Metropolitan Community College: Blue
River
Metropolitan Community College:
Business & Technology
Metropolitan Community College:
Longview
Metropolitan Community College:
Penn Valley
Missouri Southern State University
Missouri State University
Missouri University of Science and
Technology
Missouri Valley College
Northwest Missouri State University
Ozarks Technical Community College
Park University
Saint Louis University
Southeast Missouri State University
State Fair Community College
Truman State University
University of Central Missouri
University of Missouri: Columbia
University of Missouri: Kansas City
University of Missouri: St. Louis
Washington University in St. Louis
Webster University
Wentworth Military Junior College
Westminster College

Montana

Carroll College
Flathead Valley Community College
Montana State University: Billings
Montana State University: Bozeman
Rocky Mountain College
University of Montana

Nebraska

Bellevue University
Creighton University
Doane College
Metropolitan Community College
Nebraska College of Technical
Agriculture
Northeast Community College
Union College
University of Nebraska - Kearney
University of Nebraska - Lincoln
University of Nebraska - Omaha
Western Nebraska Community College

Nevada

College of Southern Nevada
Great Basin College
Sierra Nevada College
University of Nevada: Las Vegas
University of Nevada: Reno

New Hampshire

Colby-Sawyer College
Franklin Pierce University
Lebanon College
Manchester Community College
New England College
NHTI-Concord's Community College
Plymouth State University
Southern New Hampshire University
University of New Hampshire

University of New Hampshire at
Manchester

New Jersey

Atlantic Cape Community College
Bloomfield College
Burlington County College
Caldwell College
Centenary College
College of St. Elizabeth
County College of Morris
Cumberland County College
Drew University
Essex County College
Fairleigh Dickinson University:
College at Florham
Fairleigh Dickinson University:
Metropolitan Campus
Felician College
Georgian Court University
Hudson County Community College
Kean University
Mercer County Community College
Middlesex County College
Montclair State University
New Jersey City University
New Jersey Institute of Technology
Ocean County College
Passaic County Community College
Raritan Valley Community College
Rowan University
Rutgers, The State University of New
Jersey: New Brunswick/Piscataway
Campus
Rutgers, The State University of New
Jersey: Newark Regional Campus
Seton Hall University
Sussex County Community College
Union County College
William Paterson University of New
Jersey

New Mexico

Dona Ana Community College of New
Mexico State University
New Mexico State University
New Mexico State University at
Alamogordo
New Mexico State University at Grants
Santa Fe Community College
University of New Mexico

New York

Adelphi University
Alfred University
ASA Institute of Business and
Computer Technology
Bard College
Berkeley College of New York City
Bramson ORT College
Broome Community College
City University of New York: Borough
of Manhattan Community College
City University of New York:
Brooklyn College
City University of New York: City
College
City University of New York: College
of Staten Island
City University of New York: Hostos
Community College
City University of New York: Hunter
College
City University of New York: John Jay
College of Criminal Justice
City University of New York:
Kingsborough Community College

City University of New York:
LaGuardia Community College
City University of New York: Lehman
College
City University of New York: Medgar
Evers College
City University of New York: Queens
College
City University of New York:
Queensborough Community College
City University of New York: York
College
Clarkson University
Clinton Community College
College of New Rochelle
Columbia University
Columbia University: School of
General Studies
Concordia College
Cornell University
Daemen College
Dowling College
Eastman School of Music of the
University of Rochester
Elmira College
Erie Community College
Eugene Lang College The New School
for Liberal Arts
Fashion Institute of Technology
Fordham University
Fulton-Montgomery Community
College
Genesee Community College
Globe Institute of Technology
Hamilton College
Herkimer County Community College
Hobart and William Smith Colleges
Hofstra University
Jewish Theological Seminary of
America
Juilliard School
Long Island Business Institute
Long Island University: Brooklyn
Campus
Long Island University: C. W. Post
Campus
Manhattan College
Manhattan School of Music
Manhattanville College
Mannes College The New School for
Music
Mercy College
Metropolitan College of New York
Mohawk Valley Community College
Molloy College
Nassau Community College
New York Institute of Technology
New York University
Niagara University
Nyack College
Ohr Somayach Tanenbaum Education
Center
Onondaga Community College
Pace University
Parsons The New School for Design
Pratt Institute
Rensselaer Polytechnic Institute
Roberts Wesleyan College
Rochester Institute of Technology
Rockland Community College
St. John's University
St. Thomas Aquinas College
School of Visual Arts
Suffolk County Community College
SUNY College at Buffalo
SUNY College at Geneseo
SUNY College at New Paltz
SUNY College at Oneonta
SUNY College at Oswego
SUNY College at Plattsburgh
SUNY College at Purchase
SUNY College of Agriculture and
Technology at Cobleskill
SUNY College of Agriculture and
Technology at Morrisville

SUNY College of Environmental
 Science and Forestry
SUNY College of Technology at
 Alfred
SUNY College of Technology at Delhi
SUNY University at Albany
SUNY University at Binghamton
SUNY University at Buffalo
SUNY University at Stony Brook
Syracuse University
Technical Career Institutes
Tompkins Cortland Community
 College
University of Rochester
Westchester Community College

North Carolina

Appalachian State University
Asheville-Buncombe Technical
 Community College
Central Piedmont Community College
College of the Albemarle
Duke University
Durham Technical Community College
Elon University
Fayetteville Technical Community
 College
Guilford College
Guilford Technical Community College
High Point University
Lees-McRae College
Mars Hill College
Mayland Community College
Methodist University
Nash Community College
North Carolina Central University
North Carolina State University
Sandhills Community College
University of North Carolina at
 Charlotte
University of North Carolina at
 Pembroke
University of North Carolina at
 Wilmington
Wake Technical Community College
Wilson Community College

North Dakota

Dickinson State University
Lake Region State College
North Dakota State University
University of North Dakota

Ohio

Ashland University
Baldwin-Wallace College
Bowling Green State University
Capital University
Case Western Reserve University
Central State University
Cincinnati State Technical and
 Community College
Cleveland Institute of Music
Cleveland State University
Columbus State Community College
Cuyahoga Community College:
 Metropolitan
Franklin University
Hiram College
Hocking College
Kent State University
Lorain County Community College
Marietta College
Miami University: Hamilton
Muskingum University
Ohio Northern University

Ohio State University: Columbus
 Campus
Ohio University
Owens Community College: Toledo
Shawnee State University
Sinclair Community College
University of Akron
University of Cincinnati
University of Dayton
University of Findlay
University of Mount Union
University of Toledo
Walsh University
Wright State University
Xavier University
Youngstown State University

Oklahoma

Northeastern State University
Oklahoma Baptist University
Oklahoma Christian University
Oklahoma City Community College
Oklahoma City University
Oklahoma Panhandle State University
Oklahoma State University
Oral Roberts University
St. Gregory's University
Tulsa Community College
University of Oklahoma
University of Tulsa

Oregon

Chemeketa Community College
Clackamas Community College
Concordia University
George Fox University
Lane Community College
Lewis & Clark College
Linfield College
Linn-Benton Community College
Marylhurst University
Mount Angel Seminary
Oregon State University
Pacific University
Portland Community College
Portland State University
Rogue Community College
Southern Oregon University
Southwestern Oregon Community
 College
University of Oregon
University of Portland
Western Oregon University

Pennsylvania

Albright College
Bloomsburg University of
 Pennsylvania
Bucks County Community College
Chatham University
Chestnut Hill College
Community College of Allegheny
 County
Community College of Philadelphia
Curtis Institute of Music
Delaware County Community College
Dickinson College
Drexel University
Duquesne University
Elizabethtown College
Gannon University
Geneva College
Harcum College
Harrisburg Area Community College
Immaculata University
Indiana University of Pennsylvania
Juniata College

King's College
Kutztown University of Pennsylvania
La Roche College
La Salle University
Lehigh University
Lock Haven University of
 Pennsylvania
Mansfield University of Pennsylvania
Marywood University
Montgomery County Community
 College
Northampton Community College
Penn State Abington
Penn State Altoona
Penn State Greater Allegheny
Penn State University Park
Penn State York
Pennsylvania College of Technology
Philadelphia University
Point Park University
Reading Area Community College
St. Charles Borromeo Seminary -
 Overbrook
Saint Joseph's University
Seton Hill University
Temple University
University of the Arts
University of Pennsylvania
University of Pittsburgh
University of the Sciences in
 Philadelphia
Ursinus College
Valley Forge Christian College
Valley Forge Military Academy and
 College
Villanova University
West Chester University of
 Pennsylvania
Widener University
Wilson College

Puerto Rico

Bayamon Central University
Inter American University of Puerto
 Rico: Arecibo Campus
Inter American University of Puerto
 Rico: San German Campus
Universidad Adventista de las Antillas
University of Puerto Rico: Bayamon
 University College
University of Puerto Rico: Mayaguez

Rhode Island

Bryant University
Johnson & Wales University:
 Providence
New England Institute of Technology
Roger Williams University
Salve Regina University

South Carolina

Bob Jones University
The Citadel
Coker College
Converse College
Midlands Technical College
North Greenville University
Spartanburg Methodist College
Trident Technical College
University of South Carolina:
 Columbia
University of South Carolina: Upstate

South Dakota

Black Hills State University
Dakota State University
Lake Area Technical Institute
National American University: Rapid
 City
Northern State University
Oglala Lakota College
South Dakota School of Mines and
 Technology
University of South Dakota

Tennessee

Austin Peay State University
Carson-Newman College
East Tennessee State University
Lambuth University
Lee University
Lincoln Memorial University
Maryville College
Nashville State Community College
Pellissippi State Community College
Southwest Tennessee Community
 College
Tennessee Technological University
University of Memphis
University of Tennessee: Chattanooga
University of Tennessee: Knoxville
University of Tennessee: Martin
Vanderbilt University
Volunteer State Community College
Walters State Community College
Williamson Christian College

Texas

Abilene Christian University
Amarillo College
Angelo State University
Austin Community College
Blinn College
Brookhaven College
Central Texas College
Clarendon College
Collin County Community College
 District
Dallas Baptist University
Del Mar College
El Centro College
Grayson County College
Houston Community College System
Kilgore College
Lamar Institute of Technology
Lamar State College at Port Arthur
Lamar University
Laredo Community College
Lon Morris College
Lone Star College System
Midland College
Midwestern State University
Mountain View College
North Lake College
Rice University
Richland College
St. Mary's University
Sam Houston State University
San Antonio College
San Jacinto College
South Plains College
Southern Methodist University
Southwestern Adventist University
Stephen F. Austin State University
Texas A&M International University
Texas A&M University
Texas A&M University-Commerce
Texas A&M University-Galveston
Texas A&M University-Kingsville
Texas Christian University
Texas Southern University

Texas State Technical College: Harlingen
Texas State University: San Marcos
Texas Tech University
Trinity Valley Community College
University of Houston
University of Houston-Clear Lake
University of Houston-Downtown
University of the Incarnate Word
University of Mary Hardin-Baylor
University of North Texas
University of St. Thomas
University of Texas at Arlington
University of Texas at Austin
University of Texas at Brownsville - Texas Southmost College
University of Texas at El Paso
University of Texas at San Antonio
University of Texas of the Permian Basin
University of Texas: Pan American
West Texas A&M University
Western Texas College

Utah

Brigham Young University
College of Eastern Utah
Dixie State College
Everest College: Salt Lake City
Salt Lake Community College
Snow College
Southern Utah University
University of Utah
Utah State University
Utah Valley University
Weber State University
Westminster College

Vermont

Green Mountain College
Johnson State College
Lyndon State College
St. Michael's College

Virginia

Eastern Mennonite University
George Mason University
J. Sargeant Reynolds Community College
James Madison University
Jefferson College of Health Sciences
Liberty University
Mary Baldwin College
Northern Virginia Community College
Old Dominion University
Roanoke College
Shenandoah University
Stratford University: Woodbridge
Thomas Nelson Community College
Tidewater Community College
University of Richmond
University of Virginia
Virginia Commonwealth University
Virginia Polytechnic Institute and State University

Washington

Bates Technical College
Cascadia Community College
Central Washington University
Centralia College
Clark College
Clover Park Technical College
Columbia Basin College

Eastern Washington University
Everett Community College
Gonzaga University
Green River Community College
Highline Community College
Lake Washington Technical College
Lower Columbia College
North Seattle Community College
Northwest University
Olympic College
Pacific Lutheran University
Peninsula College
Pierce College
Renton Technical College
Saint Martin's University
Seattle Central Community College
Seattle Pacific University
Seattle University
Shoreline Community College
Skagit Valley College
South Puget Sound Community College
South Seattle Community College
Spokane Community College
Tacoma Community College
University of Washington
Washington State University
Western Washington University
Whatcom Community College
Whitworth University
Yakima Valley Community College

West Virginia

Concord University
Davis and Elkins College
Fairmont State University
Glenville State College
Marshall University
Mountain State University
Ohio Valley University
Salem International University
University of Charleston
West Virginia University
West Virginia Wesleyan College
Wheeling Jesuit University

Wisconsin

Alverno College
Beloit College
Chippewa Valley Technical College
Concordia University Wisconsin
Fox Valley Technical College
Lakeland College
Madison Area Technical College
Marquette University
Milwaukee Area Technical College
Milwaukee School of Engineering
Moraine Park Technical College
Northeast Wisconsin Technical College
St. Norbert College
Silver Lake College
Southwest Wisconsin Technical College
University of Wisconsin-Barron County
University of Wisconsin-Eau Claire
University of Wisconsin-La Crosse
University of Wisconsin-Madison
University of Wisconsin-Marinette
University of Wisconsin-Milwaukee
University of Wisconsin-River Falls
University of Wisconsin-Stevens Point
University of Wisconsin-Stout
University of Wisconsin-Superior
Western Technical College
Wisconsin Lutheran College

Wyoming

Eastern Wyoming College
Laramie County Community College
Northwest College
Sheridan College
Western Wyoming Community College

Special housing for international students

Alabama

Alabama State University
Birmingham-Southern College
Faulkner University
Jacksonville State University
Samford University
Troy University
University of Alabama
University of North Alabama

Alaska

University of Alaska Anchorage

Arizona

Northern Arizona University
University of Arizona

Arkansas

Henderson State University
University of Central Arkansas

California

California Polytechnic State University:
  San Luis Obispo
California State University: Chico
California State University: Long
  Beach
California State University: Los
  Angeles
California State University: Monterey
  Bay
California State University: San
  Marcos
Loyola Marymount University
The Master's College
San Diego State University
San Francisco State University
San Jose State University
Simpson University
Sonoma State University
University of California: Berkeley
University of California: Irvine
University of California: Riverside
University of California: San Diego
University of California: Santa Cruz
University of La Verne
University of Southern California
Whittier College

Colorado

Art Institute of Colorado
Colorado Heights University

Connecticut

University of Connecticut

Delaware

Delaware State University

District of Columbia

American University

Florida

Lynn University
Nova Southeastern University
University of Florida
University of South Florida

Georgia

Carver Bible College
Columbus State University
Fort Valley State University
Georgia College and State University
Georgia Southern University
Georgia Southwestern State University
Mercer University
Southern Polytechnic State University
Toccoa Falls College
University of Georgia
Valdosta State University

Idaho

Brigham Young University-Idaho
University of Idaho

Illinois

Illinois State University
Illinois Wesleyan University
Knox College
Millikin University
Monmouth College
University of Illinois at Chicago
University of Illinois at Urbana-
  Champaign
University of Illinois: Springfield
Western Illinois University

Indiana

Ball State University
DePauw University
Earlham College
Indiana University Bloomington
Indiana University South Bend

Indiana University-Purdue University
  Indianapolis

Iowa

Iowa State University
University of Iowa

Kansas

Emporia State University

Kentucky

Centre College
Eastern Kentucky University
Morehead State University
University of Kentucky
Western Kentucky University

Louisiana

Louisiana Tech University
McNeese State University
Nicholls State University

Maine

University of Maine at Farmington

Maryland

Frostburg State University
Maryland Institute College of Art
Towson University
University of Maryland: College Park
Washington College

Massachusetts

Bridgewater State University
Endicott College
Hampshire College
Merrimack College
Northeastern University
University of Massachusetts Amherst
Westfield State University
Wheaton College
Worcester Polytechnic Institute

Michigan

Central Michigan University
Eastern Michigan University
Ferris State University
Hope College
Michigan State University
Michigan Technological University
Oakland University
Olivet College
Siena Heights University
Spring Arbor University
University of Michigan
Western Michigan University

Minnesota

College of St. Scholastica
Gustavus Adolphus College

Northwest Technical College
Saint Cloud State University
University of Minnesota: Twin Cities
University of St. Thomas

Missouri

Columbia College
Fontbonne University
Missouri State University
University of Central Missouri
University of Missouri: St. Louis
Webster University
William Woods University

Montana

University of Montana

Nebraska

University of Nebraska - Lincoln

Nevada

University of Nevada: Las Vegas

New Hampshire

Dartmouth College
University of New Hampshire

New Jersey

The College of New Jersey
Montclair State University
Ramapo College of New Jersey
Rowan University

New Mexico

Dona Ana Community College of New
  Mexico State University

New York

Canisius College
Clarkson University
Columbia University: School of
  General Studies
Cornell University
Genesee Community College
Globe Institute of Technology
Herkimer County Community College
Houghton College
Mohawk Valley Community College
New York Institute of Technology
Pratt Institute
Rochester Institute of Technology
St. Lawrence University
Siena College
Skidmore College
SUNY College at Brockport
SUNY College at Buffalo
SUNY College at Cortland
SUNY College at Geneseo
SUNY College at New Paltz
SUNY College at Potsdam
SUNY College at Purchase

SUNY College of Agriculture and
Technology at Cobleskill
SUNY College of Technology at
Alfred
SUNY University at Albany
SUNY University at Buffalo
Tompkins Cortland Community
College
University of Rochester
Vassar College

North Carolina

Appalachian State University
East Carolina University
Elon University
Livingstone College
North Carolina State University
Pfeiffer University
University of North Carolina at Chapel
Hill
University of North Carolina at
Charlotte
University of North Carolina at
Greensboro
University of North Carolina at
Wilmington

North Dakota

Minot State University
North Dakota State University

Ohio

Baldwin-Wallace College
Capital University
Cincinnati Christian University
John Carroll University
Kent State University
Kenyon College
Miami University: Oxford
Ohio Northern University
Ohio State University: Columbus
Campus
Ohio University
Ohio Wesleyan University
Tiffin University
University of Akron
University of Dayton
University of Findlay
University of Mount Union
University of Toledo
Walsh University
Wittenberg University

Oklahoma

Northeastern Oklahoma Agricultural
and Mechanical College
University of Oklahoma

Oregon

Oregon State University
Portland State University
Southern Oregon University
Western Oregon University

Pennsylvania

Bucknell University
Chatham University
Delaware County Community College

Drexel University
Elizabethtown College
Franklin & Marshall College
Juniata College
Lehigh University
Lycoming College
Messiah College
Moravian College
Muhlenberg College
Penn State University Park
Philadelphia Biblical University
St. Francis University
Susquehanna University
Ursinus College
West Chester University of
Pennsylvania

Rhode Island

University of Rhode Island

South Carolina

Furman University
Presbyterian College
University of South Carolina:
Columbia

South Dakota

Northern State University

Tennessee

Belmont University
Middle Tennessee State University
Tennessee Technological University
University of the South
University of Tennessee: Martin
Vanderbilt University

Texas

Baylor University
Houston Baptist University
Kilgore College
McLennan Community College
Texas A&M University-Commerce
Texas Woman's University
Western Texas College

Utah

Southern Utah University
University of Utah
Utah State University

Vermont

Champlain College
St. Michael's College

Virginia

Aviation Institute of Maintenance:
Virginia Beach
College of William and Mary
Ferrum College
Hampden-Sydney College
Hampton University

Longwood University
Lynchburg College
Mary Baldwin College
Old Dominion University
Radford University
Randolph-Macon College
University of Mary Washington
University of Virginia
Virginia Polytechnic Institute and State
University
Washington and Lee University

Washington

Central Washington University
Evergreen State College
Gonzaga University
Green River Community College
Washington State University

West Virginia

Concord University
West Virginia University
Wheeling Jesuit University

Wisconsin

Marquette University
St. Norbert College
University of Wisconsin-La Crosse
University of Wisconsin-Madison
University of Wisconsin-Oshkosh
University of Wisconsin-Parkside
University of Wisconsin-Stevens Point
University of Wisconsin-Whitewater

Housing guaranteed for all freshmen

Alabama

Faulkner University
Heritage Christian University
Samford University
Stillman College
Talladega College
University of Alabama
University of Alabama in Huntsville
University of Mobile
University of Montevallo

Alaska

Alaska Pacific University

Arizona

Arizona State University
Embry-Riddle Aeronautical University:
 Prescott Campus
Northern Arizona University
University of Advancing Technology

Arkansas

Arkansas Tech University
Harding University
Henderson State University
Hendrix College
John Brown University
University of Central Arkansas
University of the Ozarks

California

Academy of Art University
Biola University
California Baptist University
Chapman University
College of the Siskiyous
Concordia University
Harvey Mudd College
Hope International University
Life Pacific College
Loyola Marymount University
Menlo College
Mount St. Mary's College
Notre Dame de Namur University
Occidental College
Pacific Union College
Pepperdine University
Pitzer College
Point Loma Nazarene University
St. Mary's College of California
Santa Clara University
Scripps College
Sonoma State University
University of California: Berkeley
University of California: Davis
University of California: Irvine
University of California: Los Angeles
University of California: Merced
University of California: Riverside
University of California: San Diego
University of California: Santa Barbara
University of California: Santa Cruz
University of the Pacific
University of Redlands
University of San Diego
University of San Francisco
University of Southern California
University of the West
Whittier College
William Jessup University

Colorado

Adams State College
Colorado Christian University
Colorado Mountain College
Colorado Northwestern Community
 College
Colorado School of Mines
Colorado State University
Community College of Aurora
Lamar Community College
Naropa University
Northeastern Junior College
Regis University
University of Colorado at Boulder
University of Denver
University of Northern Colorado
Western State College of Colorado

Connecticut

Lincoln College of New England:
 Suffield
Post University
Quinnipiac University
Trinity College
University of New Haven
Yale University

Delaware

Delaware State University

District of Columbia

American University
Catholic University of America
Corcoran College of Art and Design
Gallaudet University
George Washington University
Georgetown University
Howard University

Florida

Bethune-Cookman University
Eckerd College
Edward Waters College
Embry-Riddle Aeronautical University
Flagler College
Florida Agricultural and Mechanical
 University
Florida Atlantic University
Florida Institute of Technology
Florida Memorial University
Jacksonville University
Johnson & Wales University: North
 Miami
New College of Florida
Northwood University: Florida
Nova Southeastern University
Palm Beach Atlantic University
Rollins College
Southeastern University
University of Miami
Webber International University

Georgia

Atlanta Christian College
Berry College
Brewton-Parker College
Clark Atlanta University
Covenant College
Emory University
Georgia College and State University
Georgia Institute of Technology
Georgia Southern University
Georgia Southwestern State University
Mercer University
Morehouse College
Oglethorpe University
Reinhardt University
Shorter University
Spelman College
Thomas University
Toccoa Falls College
University of Georgia
University of West Georgia

Hawaii

Brigham Young University-Hawaii
Chaminade University of Honolulu
University of Hawaii at Manoa

Idaho

College of Idaho
University of Idaho

Illinois

Bradley University
Concordia University Chicago
Dominican University
Eastern Illinois University
Illinois State University
Illinois Wesleyan University
Knox College
Lake Forest College
Loyola University Chicago
Millikin University
Northern Illinois University
Northwestern University
Saint Xavier University
Shimer College
Southern Illinois University Carbondale
Trinity Christian College
Trinity International University
University of Illinois at Urbana-
 Champaign
University of Illinois: Springfield
University of St. Francis
Wheaton College

Indiana

Ball State University
Bethel College
Indiana Institute of Technology
Indiana State University
Indiana University Bloomington
Manchester College
Marian University
Rose-Hulman Institute of Technology
Taylor University
University of Evansville
University of Notre Dame
University of St. Francis

Iowa

Briar Cliff University
Clarke University
Cornell College
Drake University
Ellsworth Community College
Faith Baptist Bible College and
 Theological Seminary
Loras College
Morningside College
Mount Mercy University
St. Ambrose University
University of Dubuque
Wartburg College
William Penn University

Kansas

Baker University
Barclay College
Barton County Community College
Benedictine College
Dodge City Community College
Emporia State University
Fort Hays State University
Kansas Wesleyan University
McPherson College
MidAmerica Nazarene University
Neosho County Community College
Newman University
Ottawa University
Pittsburg State University
Southwestern College
Tabor College
University of St. Mary
Wichita State University

Kentucky

Bellarmine University
Brescia University
Eastern Kentucky University
Kentucky State University
Kentucky Wesleyan College
Murray State University
Spalding University
Spencerian College: Lexington
Transylvania University
Union College

Louisiana

Dillard University
Louisiana Tech University
Loyola University New Orleans
Southern University and Agricultural
 and Mechanical College
Tulane University

Maine

Bowdoin College
College of the Atlantic
New England School of
  Communications
Thomas College
Unity College in Maine
University of Maine
University of Maine at Farmington
University of Maine at Presque Isle
University of New England

Maryland

Goucher College
Johns Hopkins University
Johns Hopkins University: Peabody
  Conservatory of Music
Loyola University Maryland
Maryland Institute College of Art
McDaniel College
St. John's College
Towson University
University of Maryland: Baltimore
  County
University of Maryland: College Park
Washington Adventist University
Washington Bible College
Washington College

Massachusetts

Anna Maria College
Bard College at Simon's Rock
Becker College
Boston College
Brandeis University
Clark University
Endicott College
Hampshire College
Hellenic College/Holy Cross
Massachusetts College of Pharmacy
  and Health Sciences
Massachusetts Institute of Technology
Merrimack College
Mount Ida College
New England Conservatory of Music
Newbury College
Northeastern University
Pine Manor College
Tufts University
University of Massachusetts Amherst
University of Massachusetts Lowell
Western New England College
Wheelock College
Worcester Polytechnic Institute

Michigan

Aquinas College
Baker College of Owosso
Calvin College
Central Michigan University
Gogebic Community College
Grand Valley State University
Kettering University
Kuyper College
Lake Superior State University
Michigan State University
Michigan Technological University
Northwestern Michigan College
Northwood University: Michigan
Oakland University
Rochester College
Spring Arbor University
University of Michigan

Minnesota

Augsburg College
Bethel University
College of St. Benedict
College of St. Scholastica
Concordia College: Moorhead
Concordia University St. Paul
Hamline University
Macalester College
North Central University
Northwestern College
St. Catherine University
St. John's University
University of Minnesota: Twin Cities
Winona State University

Mississippi

Millsaps College
Mississippi State University
University of Mississippi
William Carey University

Missouri

Avila University
Columbia College
Drury University
Evangel University
Kansas City Art Institute
Lincoln University
Missouri Southern State University
Missouri State University
Missouri University of Science and
  Technology
Northwest Missouri State University
Park University
Research College of Nursing
Saint Louis University
Southwest Baptist University
Truman State University
University of Missouri: Columbia
Washington University in St. Louis
Webster University
Westminster College
William Woods University

Montana

Carroll College
Montana State University: Bozeman
Montana Tech of the University of
  Montana
Rocky Mountain College
University of Great Falls
University of Montana
University of Montana: Western

Nebraska

Chadron State College
College of Saint Mary
Creighton University
Doane College
Grace University
Nebraska Christian College
Nebraska College of Technical
  Agriculture
Peru State College
University of Nebraska - Kearney
University of Nebraska - Lincoln
Wayne State College

Nevada

Sierra Nevada College
University of Nevada: Las Vegas

New Hampshire

Daniel Webster College
Dartmouth College
Hesser College
University of New Hampshire

New Jersey

Caldwell College
The College of New Jersey
Fairleigh Dickinson University:
  College at Florham
Felician College
Monmouth University
New Jersey Institute of Technology
Ramapo College of New Jersey
Richard Stockton College of New
  Jersey
Rider University
Rowan University
Rutgers, The State University of New
  Jersey: New Brunswick/Piscataway
  Campus

New Mexico

Eastern New Mexico University
Institute of American Indian Arts
New Mexico Highlands University
St. John's College
University of the Southwest

New York

Albany College of Pharmacy and
  Health Sciences
Alfred University
Bard College
Cazenovia College
Clarkson University
Clinton Community College
Cornell University
Culinary Institute of America
Daemen College
Davis College
D'Youville College
Eastman School of Music of the
  University of Rochester
Hartwick College
Houghton College
Juilliard School
Long Island University: C. W. Post
  Campus
Manhattan School of Music
Marist College
Polytechnic Institute of New York
  University
Pratt Institute
Rensselaer Polytechnic Institute
Roberts Wesleyan College
Rochester Institute of Technology
Sage College of Albany
St. John Fisher College
St. Thomas Aquinas College
Siena College
SUNY College at Brockport
SUNY College at Cortland
SUNY College at New Paltz
SUNY College at Oneonta
SUNY College of Agriculture and
  Technology at Cobleskill

SUNY College of Environmental
  Science and Forestry
SUNY College of Technology at
  Canton
SUNY College of Technology at Delhi
SUNY Institute of Technology at
  Utica/Rome
SUNY University at Albany
SUNY University at Binghamton
Syracuse University
Union College
University of Rochester
Utica College
Yeshivat Mikdash Melech

North Carolina

Appalachian State University
Barton College
Campbell University
Davidson College
Duke University
East Carolina University
Elizabeth City State University
Elon University
Guilford College
High Point University
Johnson C. Smith University
Lees-McRae College
Meredith College
Mount Olive College
North Carolina Wesleyan College
Peace College
Piedmont Baptist College and Graduate
  School
Queens University of Charlotte
St. Augustine's College
Salem College
University of North Carolina at
  Asheville
University of North Carolina at Chapel
  Hill
University of North Carolina School of
  the Arts
Western Carolina University

North Dakota

Minot State University
North Dakota State College of Science
North Dakota State University
University of Mary
University of North Dakota
Valley City State University

Ohio

Baldwin-Wallace College
Bowling Green State University
Capital University
Case Western Reserve University
Central State University
College of Mount St. Joseph
Columbus College of Art and Design
Defiance College
Franciscan University of Steubenville
God's Bible School and College
Kent State University
Lake Erie College
Lourdes College
Marietta College
Miami University: Oxford
Mount Vernon Nazarene University
Muskingum University
Ohio Northern University
Ohio State University: Columbus
  Campus
Ohio University
Otterbein University
Tiffin University

University of Cincinnati
University of Dayton
University of Findlay
Urbana University
Wilberforce University
Xavier University

Oklahoma

Northeastern State University
Oklahoma Panhandle State University
Oklahoma State University
St. Gregory's University
Southern Nazarene University
University of Oklahoma
University of Science and Arts of Oklahoma
University of Tulsa

Oregon

Concordia University
Corban College
Eastern Oregon University
Lewis & Clark College
Northwest Christian University
Pacific University
Reed College
Southern Oregon University
Southwestern Oregon Community College
University of Portland
Warner Pacific College
Western Oregon University
Willamette University

Pennsylvania

Alvernia University
Bloomsburg University of Pennsylvania
Carnegie Mellon University
Central Pennsylvania College
Cheyney University of Pennsylvania
Clarion University of Pennsylvania
Drexel University
Duquesne University
East Stroudsburg University of Pennsylvania
Edinboro University of Pennsylvania
Franklin & Marshall College
Gannon University
Holy Family University
Indiana University of Pennsylvania
Keystone College
Kutztown University of Pennsylvania
Lackawanna College
Lehigh University
Lincoln University
Lock Haven University of Pennsylvania
Marywood University
Millersville University of Pennsylvania
Moore College of Art and Design
Philadelphia Biblical University
Philadelphia University
Saint Joseph's University
St. Vincent College
Shippensburg University of Pennsylvania
Slippery Rock University of Pennsylvania
Temple University
University of Pennsylvania
University of Pittsburgh
University of Pittsburgh at Bradford
University of the Sciences in Philadelphia
Villanova University

Widener University
York College of Pennsylvania

Puerto Rico

Universidad Adventista de las Antillas

Rhode Island

Bryant University
Johnson & Wales University: Providence
Providence College
Rhode Island School of Design
Roger Williams University
Salve Regina University
University of Rhode Island

South Carolina

Allen University
Anderson University
Benedict College
Charleston Southern University
Claflin University
Coker College
Columbia College
Furman University
Limestone College
Newberry College
South Carolina State University
University of South Carolina: Columbia
Winthrop University

South Dakota

Augustana College
Black Hills State University
Dakota State University
Dakota Wesleyan University
Mount Marty College
South Dakota School of Mines and Technology
South Dakota State University
University of South Dakota

Tennessee

Belmont University
Bethel University
Carson-Newman College
Christian Brothers University
Freed-Hardeman University
Johnson Bible College
Lambuth University
Lee University
Rhodes College
Tennessee Technological University
Tennessee Wesleyan College
Tusculum College
University of the South
University of Tennessee: Chattanooga
University of Tennessee: Knoxville
University of Tennessee: Martin
Vanderbilt University
Watkins College of Art, Design & Film

Texas

Abilene Christian University
Arlington Baptist College
Austin College
Baylor University

Clarendon College
Concordia University Texas
Hardin-Simmons University
Houston Baptist University
Howard Payne University
Lamar University
Lubbock Christian University
Midwestern State University
Northwood University: Texas
Our Lady of the Lake University of San Antonio
Prairie View A&M University
Rice University
St. Edward's University
St. Mary's University
Sam Houston State University
Southern Methodist University
Southwestern Assemblies of God University
Southwestern University
Stephen F. Austin State University
Sul Ross State University
Tarleton State University
Texas A&M University-Corpus Christi
Texas A&M University-Kingsville
Texas Christian University
Texas College
Texas Lutheran University
Texas Southern University
Texas State University: San Marcos
Texas Tech University
Trinity University
University of Dallas
University of Mary Hardin-Baylor
University of North Texas
Wayland Baptist University

Utah

Westminster College

Vermont

Castleton State College
Champlain College
Johnson State College
Lyndon State College
Marlboro College
Norwich University
Southern Vermont College
University of Vermont

Virginia

Christopher Newport University
College of William and Mary
Eastern Mennonite University
George Mason University
Hampton University
James Madison University
Longwood University
Marymount University
Patrick Henry College
Radford University
Roanoke College
Shenandoah University
Southern Virginia University
University of Mary Washington
University of Richmond
University of Virginia
Virginia Polytechnic Institute and State University
Virginia State University
Virginia Wesleyan College
Washington and Lee University

Washington

Central Washington University
Evergreen State College
Gonzaga University
Saint Martin's University
Seattle University
University of Puget Sound
Washington State University
Whitman College
Whitworth University

West Virginia

Concord University
Fairmont State University
Glenville State College
Marshall University
Mountain State University
University of Charleston
West Virginia State University
West Virginia University

Wisconsin

Carroll University
Carthage College
Lakeland College
Marquette University
Mount Mary College
Northland College
University of Wisconsin-Eau Claire
University of Wisconsin-Oshkosh
University of Wisconsin-Platteville
University of Wisconsin-River Falls
University of Wisconsin-Stout
University of Wisconsin-Superior
University of Wisconsin-Whitewater
Viterbo University

Wyoming

Northwest College

College size (undergraduate enrollment)

Four-year

Alabama
Judson College
Southeastern Bible College
Talladega College
United States Sports Academy

Arizona
Arizona Christian University
Art Center Design College
Art Institute of Tucson
Dunlap-Stone University
International Baptist College
Northcentral University

Arkansas
Lyon College
University of the Ozarks
Williams Baptist College

California
American Jewish University
Antioch University
    Los Angeles
    Santa Barbara
Bethany University
Bethesda Christian University
California Christian College
California Institute of Integral Studies
California University of Management
    and Sciences
Carrington College
    Emeryville
Cogswell Polytechnical College
Coleman University
Design Institute of San Diego
Golden Gate University
Holy Names University
Horizon College of San Diego
Humphreys College
International Academy of Design and
    Technology
    Sacramento
John F. Kennedy University
The King's University
Laguna College of Art and Design
Life Pacific College
Menlo College
Mt. Sierra College
National Hispanic University
NewSchool of Architecture & Design
Northwestern Polytechnic University
Pacific Oaks College
Platt College
    Ontario
    San Diego
Samuel Merritt University
San Diego Christian College
San Francisco Art Institute
San Francisco Conservatory of Music
School of Urban Missions: Oakland
Shasta Bible College and Graduate
    School
Soka University of America

Southern California Institute of
    Architecture
Southern California Institute of
    Technology
Southern California Seminary
University of the West
William Jessup University
World Mission University

Colorado
Aspen University
CollegeAmerica
    Fort Collins
Colorado Heights University
Naropa University
National American University
    Denver
Nazarene Bible College
Rocky Mountain College of Art &
    Design
University of Phoenix
    Southern Colorado

Connecticut
Holy Apostles College and Seminary
Lyme Academy College of Fine Arts
Paier College of Art
University of Phoenix
    Fairfield County

Delaware
Goldey-Beacom College

District of Columbia
University of Phoenix
    Washington DC

Florida
Ave Maria University
Baptist College of Florida
Beacon College
Carlos Albizu University
Chamberlain College of Nursing
    Jacksonville
Florida Career College: Boynton Beach
Florida Christian College
Jones College
Northwood University
    Florida
Remington College
    Tampa
Schiller International University
South University: Tampa
Trinity College of Florida
Universidad FLET
Webber International University

Georgia
Beulah Heights University
Brewton-Parker College
Carver Bible College
Luther Rice University
Truett-McConnell College
Wesleyan College

Idaho
University of Phoenix
    Idaho

Illinois
American Academy of Art
Blackburn College
Blessing-Rieman College of Nursing
Chamberlain College of Nursing
    Chicago
Hebrew Theological College
Lincoln Christian University
MacMurray College
Rush University
Shimer College
Trinity College of Nursing and Health
    Sciences
VanderCook College of Music

Indiana
Holy Cross College

Iowa
Divine Word College
Faith Baptist Bible College and
    Theological Seminary
Hamilton Technical College
Maharishi University of Management
Waldorf College

Kansas
Barclay College
Bethel College
Central Christian College of Kansas
McPherson College
Ottawa University
Sterling College
Tabor College
University of Kansas Medical Center
University of Phoenix
    Wichita
University of St. Mary

Kentucky
Brescia University
Kentucky Mountain Bible College
St. Catharine College

Louisiana
St. Joseph Seminary College

Maine
College of the Atlantic
Maine College of Art
New England School of
    Communications
Unity College in Maine
University of Maine
    Fort Kent
    Machias

Maryland
Johns Hopkins University: Peabody
    Conservatory of Music
National Labor College
St. John's College
University of Phoenix
    Maryland

Massachusetts
Art Institute of Boston at Lesley
    University
Atlantic Union College
Bard College at Simon's Rock
Boston Conservatory
Franklin W. Olin College of
    Engineering
Hellenic College/Holy Cross
Montserrat College of Art
New England Conservatory of Music
Pine Manor College
School of the Museum of Fine Arts
University of Phoenix
    Boston
Zion Bible College

Michigan
Cleary University
Robert B. Miller College
Sacred Heart Major Seminary

Minnesota
Bethany Lutheran College
College of Visual Arts
University of Minnesota
    Rochester

Mississippi
Blue Mountain College

Missouri
Calvary Bible College and Theological
    Seminary
Cox College
Goldfarb School of Nursing at Barnes-
    Jewish College
Kansas City Art Institute
Research College of Nursing

Nebraska
BryanLGH College of Health Sciences
Grace University
Nebraska Christian College
Union College
York College

Nevada
International Academy of Design and
    Technology
    Henderson
Morrison University
Sierra Nevada College
University of Southern Nevada

New Jersey
University of Medicine and Dentistry
    of New Jersey
        School of Health Related
            Professions
        School of Nursing
University of Phoenix
    Jersey City

New Mexico
Institute of American Indian Arts
St. John's College
University of the Southwest

New York
Beis Medrash Heichal Dovid
Beth Hamedrash Shaarei Yosher
    Institute
Beth Hatalmud Rabbinical College
Central Yeshiva Tomchei Tmimim-
    Lubavitch
Concordia College
Davis College
Eastman School of Music of the
    University of Rochester
Jewish Theological Seminary of
    America
Juilliard School
Kehilath Yakov Rabbinical Seminary
The King's College
Machzikei Hadath Rabbinical College
Manhattan School of Music
Mannes College The New School for
    Music
Medaille College: Amherst
Medaille College: Rochester
Mesivta Torah Vodaath Seminary
Mirrer Yeshiva Central Institute
New York School of Interior Design
Ohr Somayach Tanenbaum Education
    Center
Rabbinical Academy Mesivta Rabbi
    Chaim Berlin
Rabbinical College Beth Shraga
Rabbinical College Bobover Yeshiva
    B'nei Zion
Rabbinical College Ch'san Sofer of
    New York
Rabbinical College of Long Island
Rabbinical College of Ohr Shimon
    Yisroel
Rabbinical Seminary of America
Russell Sage College
Shor Yoshuv Rabbinical College

SUNY
Upstate Medical University
Talmudical Institute of Upstate New
York
Talmudical Seminary Oholei Torah
Torah Temimah Talmudical Seminary
Wells College
Yeshiva and Kolel Bais Medrash Elyon
Yeshiva and Kolel Harbotzas Torah
Yeshiva D'Monsey Rabbinical College
Yeshiva Derech Chaim
Yeshiva Gedolah Imrei Yosef D'Spinka
Yeshiva Gedolah Zichron Moshe
Yeshiva Karlin Stolin
Yeshiva of Nitra
Yeshiva of the Telshe Alumni
Yeshiva Shaar Hatorah
Yeshiva Shaarei Torah of Rockland
Yeshivas Novominsk
Yeshivat Mikdash Melech
Yeshivath Viznitz

North Carolina

Apex School of Theology
Bennett College for Women
Brevard College
Cabarrus College of Health Sciences
Laurel University
Mid-Atlantic Christian University
Peace College
Piedmont Baptist College and Graduate
School
University of North Carolina
School of the Arts

Ohio

Chamberlain College of Nursing
Columbus
Cleveland Institute of Art
Cleveland Institute of Music
Tri-State Bible College
University of Phoenix
Cincinnati
Cleveland
Columbus Ohio

Oklahoma

Family of Faith College
St. Gregory's University
University of Phoenix
Tulsa

Oregon

Gutenberg College
Mount Angel Seminary
Northwest Christian University
Oregon College of Art & Craft
Oregon Health & Science University
Pacific Northwest College of Art

Pennsylvania

Baptist Bible College of Pennsylvania
Curtis Institute of Music
Moore College of Art and Design
Penn State
Beaver
Greater Allegheny
New Kensington
Shenango
Wilkes-Barre
Rosemont College
St. Charles Borromeo Seminary -
Overbrook
Wilson College

Puerto Rico

Conservatory of Music of Puerto Rico
Escuela de Artes Plasticas de Puerto
Rico
Universidad Pentecostal Mizpa
University of Puerto Rico
Medical Sciences

South Carolina

Coker College
Columbia International University
Erskine College

South Dakota

Dakota Wesleyan University
Presentation College

Tennessee

Aquinas College
Fisk University
Free Will Baptist Bible College
Johnson Bible College
Lambuth University
Memphis College of Art
O'More College of Design
University of Phoenix
Chattanooga
University of Tennessee
Health Science Center
Victory University
Watkins College of Art, Design & Film
Williamson Christian College

Texas

Arlington Baptist College
Baptist University of the Americas
Northwood University
Texas
Southwestern Adventist University
Southwestern Baptist Theological
Seminary
Southwestern Christian College
University of Phoenix
Austin
University of Texas
Health Science Center at Houston
Medical Branch at Galveston
Southwestern Medical Center at
Dallas

Utah

Neumont University
Stevens-Henager College
Logan

Vermont

Bennington College
Burlington College
College of St. Joseph in Vermont
Green Mountain College
Marlboro College
Southern Vermont College
Sterling College

Virginia

Bluefield College
Catholic Distance University
Christendom College
DeVry University
Arlington
Patrick Henry College
Potomac College
Randolph College
St. Paul's College
Southern Virginia University
Stratford University: Woodbridge
University of Phoenix
Northern Virginia
Virginia Intermont College
World College

Washington

Bastyr University
Northwest College of Art
Trinity Lutheran College

West Virginia

Alderson-Broaddus College
Appalachian Bible College
Davis and Elkins College
Ohio Valley University
Salem International University

Wisconsin

Bellin College
Milwaukee Institute of Art & Design
Northland College
Silver Lake College
University of Phoenix
Madison
Milwaukee

Two-year

Alabama

Marion Military Institute

Alaska

Ilisagvik College

Arizona

Brookline College
Tempe
Bryman School
Golf Academy of America: Phoenix
Kaplan College: Phoenix

California

American Academy of Dramatic Arts:
West
Carrington College
Antioch
Citrus Heights
Pleasant Hill
Coleman College: San Marcos
Concorde Career College
Garden Grove
Deep Springs College
Epic Bible College
Fashion Careers College
Fashion Institute of Design and
Merchandising
San Diego
Fremont College: Cerritos
Golf Academy of America: San Diego
Kaplan College: Sacramento
Platt College
Los Angeles
Professional Golfers Career College
San Joaquin Valley College
South Coast College
WyoTech: Sacramento

Colorado

Anthem College
Aurora
Boulder College of Massage Therapy
Colorado Northwestern Community
College
Colorado School of Trades
Everest College
Aurora
Institute of Business & Medical
Careers
IntelliTec College
IntelliTec College: Grand Junction
Kaplan College: Denver

Connecticut

Lincoln College of New England:
Suffield

Delaware

Delaware College of Art and Design

Florida

Angley College
City College
Gainesville
Miami
College of Business and Technology:
Flagler
College of Business and Technology:
Kendall
Fortis College: Winter Park
Fortis Institute: Orange Park
Herzing University
Key College
Professional Golfers Career College:
Orlando

Georgia

Andrew College
Gupton Jones College of Funeral
Service

Hawaii

Hawaii Tokai International College
Remington College
Honolulu

Illinois

Benedictine University at Springfield
Illinois Eastern Community Colleges
Frontier Community College
Lincoln Trail College
Taylor Business Institute

Indiana

Ancilla College
Harrison College
Indianapolis Northwest
Kaplan College: Hammond
Kaplan College: Merrillville
Mid-America College of Funeral
Service

Iowa

St. Luke's College

Kansas

Colby Community College
Donnelly College
Hesston College
North Central Kansas Technical
College

Kentucky

Brown Mackie College
North Kentucky
Daymar College
Owensboro
Spencerian College: Lexington
Sullivan College of Technology and
Design

Louisiana

Baton Rouge School of Computers
Blue Cliff College
Metairie
Shreveport
Camelot College
Delta College of Arts & Technology
Gretna Career College
ITI Technical College

Maine

Washington County Community
College

Maryland

TESST College of Technology
Beltsville

Massachusetts

Benjamin Franklin Institute of
Technology
Marian Court College
New England College of Business and
Finance

Minnesota

Minneapolis Business College
Northwest Technical Institute
Rainy River Community College
White Earth Tribal and Community
College

Mississippi

Blue Cliff College
Gulfport

Missouri

Bolivar Technical College
Cottey College
Metropolitan Community College:
Business & Technology
Southeast Missouri Hospital College of
Nursing and Health Sciences
Texas County Technical Institute
Vatterott College
Joplin

Montana

Dawson Community College

Nebraska

Nebraska College of Technical
Agriculture
Nebraska Indian Community College

Very small (fewer than 750)

Nevada
Career College of Northern Nevada

New Hampshire
Lebanon College

New Mexico
Brookline College
    Albuquerque

New York
American Academy of Dramatic Arts
Bryant & Stratton College
    Syracuse North
Business Informatics Center
Institute of Design and Construction
Island Drafting and Technical Institute
Long Island Business Institute
Mildred Elley
Phillips Beth Israel School of Nursing
Professional Business College
St. Elizabeth College of Nursing
Utica School of Commerce
Villa Maria College of Buffalo
Wood Tobe-Coburn School

North Carolina
Louisburg College
Martin Community College
Miller-Motte Technical College: Cary
Pamlico Community College
Shepherds Theological Seminary

North Dakota
Fort Berthold Community College
Williston State College

Ohio
Academy of Court Reporting and
    Technology
Antonelli College
    Cincinnati
Art Institute of Cincinnati
ETI Technical College of Niles
Gallipolis Career College
Kaplan College: Dayton
Ohio College of Massotherapy
Remington College
    Cleveland

Oklahoma
Platt College
    Oklahoma City Central
    Tulsa
Vatterott College
    Oklahoma City
    Tulsa

Oregon
Everest College
    Portland
Heald College
    Portland

Pennsylvania
Cambria-Rowe Business College:
    Indiana
JNA Institute of Culinary Arts
Johnson College
Lansdale School of Business
Laurel Business Institute
Laurel Technical Institute
Oakbridge Academy of Arts
Orleans Technical Institute
Pittsburgh Institute of Aeronautics
Sanford-Brown Institute
    Monroeville
Triangle Tech
    Bethlehem
    Greensburg
University of Pittsburgh
    Titusville

Puerto Rico
Colegio de las Ciencias Artes y
    Television
Humacao Community College

South Carolina
Forrest Junior College
University of South Carolina
    Union

South Dakota
Sisseton Wahpeton College

Tennessee
Remington College
    Nashville
West Tennessee Business College

Texas
Hallmark College of Aeronautics
Hallmark College of Technology
Jacksonville College
Texas State Technical College
    Marshall
Wade College

Utah
Careers Unlimited
Eagle Gate College: Layton
Everest College
    Salt Lake City
Provo College

Vermont
Landmark College

Virginia
Aviation Institute of Maintenance:
    Virginia Beach
Centura College: Chesapeake
Centura College: Norfolk
Centura College: Richmond
Everest College
    Tysons Corner

Washington
Everest College
    Vancouver

West Virginia
Everest Institute: Cross Lanes
West Virginia Junior College:
    Bridgeport

Wisconsin
University of Wisconsin
    Richland

Wyoming
Eastern Wyoming College

Small (750-1,999)

Four-year

Alabama
Birmingham-Southern College
Huntingdon College
Spring Hill College
University of Mobile
University of West Alabama

Alaska
University of Alaska
    Southeast

Arizona
Art Institute of Phoenix
Brown Mackie College
    Tucson
Collins College
DeVry University
    Phoenix
Embry-Riddle Aeronautical University:
    Prescott Campus
Prescott College
University of Advancing Technology
University of Phoenix
    Southern Arizona

Arkansas
Arkansas Baptist College
Hendrix College

John Brown University
Ouachita Baptist University

California
Art Institute of California: Hollywood
Art Institute of California: Inland
    Empire
Art Institute of California: Sacramento
Art Institute of California: San
    Francisco
Brooks Institute
California College of the Arts
California College San Diego
California Institute of Technology
California Institute of the Arts
California Maritime Academy
Claremont McKenna College
Concordia University
Dominican University of California
Everest College
    Ontario Metro
Ex'pression College for Digital Arts
Harvey Mudd College
La Sierra University
Loma Linda University
The Master's College
Mills College
Notre Dame de Namur University
Otis College of Art and Design
Pacific Union College
Patten University
Pitzer College
Pomona College
Scripps College
Simpson University
University of La Verne
Vanguard University of Southern
    California
Westmont College
Westwood College
    South Bay
Whittier College
Woodbury University

Colorado
Johnson & Wales University: Denver
Jones International University
University of Phoenix
    Denver

Connecticut
Albertus Magnus College
Charter Oak State College
Connecticut College
Mitchell College
Post University
Saint Joseph College

Delaware
Wesley College

District of Columbia
Gallaudet University

Florida
Chipola College
DeVry University
    Miramar
Eckerd College
Edward Waters College
Everest University
    Jacksonville
    Lakeland
    Largo
    Melbourne
    North Orlando
    Orange Park
    Pompano Beach
    Tampa
Everglades University
    Boca Raton
Florida Career College: Jacksonville
Florida Career College: Lauderdale
    Lakes
Florida Career College: Riverview
Florida Southern College

International Academy of Design and
    Technology
    Orlando
Lynn University
New College of Florida
Ringling College of Art and Design
Rollins College
Saint Leo University
Saint Thomas University
South University: West Palm Beach
University of Phoenix
    Central Florida
    North Florida
    South Florida
    West Florida
Warner University

Georgia
Agnes Scott College
American InterContinental University
Atlanta Christian College
Berry College
Brenau University
Covenant College
LaGrange College
Life University
Oglethorpe University
Paine College
Piedmont College
Reinhardt University
Shorter University
Thomas University
Toccoa Falls College

Hawaii
Chaminade University of Honolulu
University of Hawaii
    West Oahu
University of Phoenix
    Hawaii

Idaho
College of Idaho
Northwest Nazarene University

Illinois
Chamberlain College of Nursing
    Addison
Concordia University Chicago
Dominican University
Greenville College
Harrington College of Design
Illinois College
Illinois Institute of Art: Schaumburg
International Academy of Design and
    Technology
    Chicago
Judson University
Knox College
Lake Forest College
Monmouth College
National-Louis University
Quincy University
Rockford College
Trinity Christian College
University of St. Francis

Indiana
Bethel College
Calumet College of St. Joseph
Earlham College
Franklin College
Goshen College
Hanover College
Huntington University
Manchester College
Oakland City University
Rose-Hulman Institute of Technology
Saint Mary's College
St. Mary-of-the-Woods College
Taylor University
Trine University
Wabash College

Iowa
Briar Cliff University
Buena Vista University
Central College

Clarke University
Coe College
Cornell College
Graceland University
Grinnell College
Iowa Wesleyan College
Loras College
Morningside College
Mount Mercy University
Northwestern College
Simpson College
University of Dubuque
Wartburg College
William Penn University

Kansas

Baker University
Benedictine College
Friends University
Kansas Wesleyan University
MidAmerica Nazarene University
Newman University
Southwestern College

Kentucky

Berea College
Centre College
Georgetown College
Midway College
Pikeville College
Spalding University
Thomas More College
Transylvania University
Union College
University of the Cumberlands

Louisiana

Centenary College of Louisiana
Dillard University
Louisiana College
Louisiana State University
    Health Sciences Center
New Orleans Baptist Theological
    Seminary: Leavell College
Our Lady of Holy Cross College
University of Phoenix
    Louisiana

Maine

Bates College
Bowdoin College
Colby College
Maine Maritime Academy
Saint Joseph's College of Maine
Thomas College
University of Maine
    Presque Isle

Maryland

Goucher College
Griggs University
Hood College
Maryland Institute College of Art
McDaniel College
Mount St. Mary's University
St. Mary's College of Maryland
Sojourner-Douglass College
University of Maryland
    Baltimore
Washington Adventist University
Washington College

Massachusetts

American International College
Amherst College
Anna Maria College
Babson College
Bay Path College
Becker College
Cambridge College
Eastern Nazarene College
Elms College
Gordon College
Hampshire College
Lasell College
Lesley University
Massachusetts College of Art and
    Design

Massachusetts College of Liberal Arts
Massachusetts College of Pharmacy
    and Health Sciences
Massachusetts Maritime Academy
Mount Ida College
Newbury College
Nichols College
Regis College
Simmons College
Wheaton College
Wheelock College
Williams College

Michigan

Adrian College
Albion College
Alma College
Andrews University
Aquinas College
Art Institute of Michigan
Baker College
    of Port Huron
College for Creative Studies
Hillsdale College
Kalamazoo College
Kettering University
Marygrove College
Northwood University
    Michigan
Olivet College
Walsh College of Accountancy and
    Business Administration

Minnesota

Carleton College
Concordia University St. Paul
Crown College
Globe University
Hamline University
Northwestern College
St. John's University
University of Minnesota
    Crookston
    Morris

Mississippi

Millsaps College
Tougaloo College

Missouri

Avila University
College of the Ozarks
Columbia College
Culver-Stockton College
Drury University
Evangel University
Fontbonne University
Hannibal-LaGrange University
Harris-Stowe State University
Missouri Baptist University
Missouri Valley College
Rockhurst University
Stephens College
Westminster College
William Jewell College
William Woods University

Montana

Carroll College
Montana State University
    Northern
Rocky Mountain College
University of Great Falls
University of Montana: Western

Nebraska

College of Saint Mary
Concordia University
Doane College
Nebraska Wesleyan University

Nevada

Art Institute of Las Vegas

New Hampshire

Colby-Sawyer College
Daniel Webster College
Franklin Pierce University

Granite State College
New England College
Rivier College
Saint Anselm College
University of New Hampshire at
    Manchester

New Jersey

Caldwell College
Centenary College
College of St. Elizabeth
DeVry University
    North Brunswick
Drew University
Felician College
Georgian Court University

New Mexico

New Mexico Institute of Mining and
    Technology

New York

Albany College of Pharmacy and
    Health Sciences
Alfred University
Bard College
Berkeley College
Briarcliffe College
Cazenovia College
City University of New York
    CUNY Online
College of Mount St. Vincent
College of New Rochelle
Columbia University
    School of General Studies
Cooper Union for the Advancement of
    Science and Art
D'Youville College
Daemen College
Dominican College of Blauvelt
Elmira College
Eugene Lang College The New School
    for Liberal Arts
Five Towns College
Hamilton College
Hartwick College
Hilbert College
Houghton College
Keuka College
Manhattanville College
Medaille College
Metropolitan College of New York
Paul Smith's College
Polytechnic Institute of New York
    University
Roberts Wesleyan College
Sage College of Albany
Saint Bonaventure University
St. Joseph's College
St. Thomas Aquinas College
Sarah Lawrence College
SUNY
    College of Environmental Science
        and Forestry
    Institute of Technology at Utica/
        Rome
    Maritime College
U.T.A. Mesivta-Kiryas Jocl
United States Merchant Marine
    Academy
United Talmudical Seminary
Vaughn College of Aeronautics and
    Technology
Wagner College

North Carolina

Art Institute of Charlotte
Barton College
Belmont Abbey College
Catawba College
Chowan University
Davidson College
Greensboro College
Johnson C. Smith University
Lees-McRae College
Lenoir-Rhyne University
Livingstone College

Mars Hill College
Meredith College
Montreat College
North Carolina Wesleyan College
Pfeiffer University
Queens University of Charlotte
St. Augustine's College
Salem College
Warren Wilson College
Wingate University

North Dakota

Jamestown College
Mayville State University
Rasmussen College
    Fargo
Valley City State University

Ohio

Bluffton University
Bryant & Stratton College
    Parma
Cincinnati Christian University
College of Mount St. Joseph
College of Wooster
Columbus College of Art and Design
Defiance College
Heidelberg University
Hiram College
Kenyon College
Lake Erie College
Lourdes College
Malone University
Marietta College
Mount Vernon Nazarene University
Muskingum University
Ohio Dominican University
Ohio University
    Eastern Campus
    Zanesville Campus
Ohio Wesleyan University
Union Institute & University
University of Rio Grande
Ursuline College
Wilmington College
Wittenberg University

Oklahoma

Oklahoma Baptist University
Oklahoma Christian University
Oklahoma Panhandle State University
Oklahoma Wesleyan University
Southern Nazarene University
Spartan College of Aeronautics and
    Technology
University of Phoenix
    Oklahoma City
University of Science and Arts of
    Oklahoma

Oregon

Art Institute of Portland
Concordia University
Corban College
Lewis & Clark College
Linfield College
Marylhurst University
Pacific University
Reed College
University of Phoenix
    Oregon
Warner Pacific College
Willamette University

Pennsylvania

Bryn Mawr College
Cabrini College
Carlow University
Cedar Crest College
Central Pennsylvania College
Chatham University
Chestnut Hill College
Cheyney University of Pennsylvania
Geneva College
Haverford College
Juniata College
Keystone College

Small (750-1,999)

La Roche College
Lebanon Valley College
Lincoln University
Lycoming College
Moravian College
Mount Aloysius College
Penn State
  Brandywine
  DuBois
  Fayette, The Eberly Campus
  Hazleton
  Lehigh Valley
  Mont Alto
  Schuylkill
  Worthington Scranton
  York
Philadelphia Biblical University
St. Francis University
St. Vincent College
Seton Hill University
Swarthmore College
Thiel College
University of Pittsburgh
  Bradford
  Greensburg
Ursinus College
Valley Forge Christian College
Washington & Jefferson College
Waynesburg University

Puerto Rico
Bayamon Central University
National University College: Arecibo
Universidad Adventista de las Antillas
University College of San Juan
University of Puerto Rico
  Utuado

South Carolina
Allen University
Claflin University
Columbia College
Limestone College
Morris College
Newberry College
Presbyterian College
South University: Columbia
Southern Wesleyan University
University of South Carolina
  Beaufort
Wofford College

South Dakota
Augustana College
Dakota State University
Mount Marty College
National American University
  Rapid City
Northern State University
Oglala Lakota College
Sinte Gleska University
South Dakota School of Mines and
  Technology
University of Sioux Falls

Tennessee
Bryan College
Carson-Newman College
Christian Brothers University
Cumberland University
Freed-Hardeman University
King College
LeMoyne-Owen College
Lincoln Memorial University
Maryville College
Milligan College
Rhodes College
South College
Tennessee Wesleyan College
Trevecca Nazarene University
University of the South

Texas
Austin College
Concordia University Texas
East Texas Baptist University
Hardin-Simmons University

Howard Payne University
Huston-Tillotson University
Lubbock Christian University
McMurry University
Our Lady of the Lake University of
  San Antonio
Schreiner University
Southwestern University
Texas A&M University
  Galveston
  Texarkana
Texas College
Texas Lutheran University
Texas Tech University Health Sciences
  Center
Texas Wesleyan University
University of Dallas
University of Phoenix
  Dallas Fort Worth
  San Antonio
University of St. Thomas
University of Texas
  Health Science Center at San
  Antonio
Wayland Baptist University
Wiley College

Utah
Stevens-Henager College
  Orem
University of Phoenix
  Utah

Vermont
Johnson State College
Lyndon State College
St. Michael's College

Virginia
Averett University
Bridgewater College
Eastern Mennonite University
Emory & Henry College
Ferrum College
Hampden-Sydney College
Hollins University
Jefferson College of Health Sciences
Mary Baldwin College
Randolph-Macon College
Shenandoah University
University of Virginia's College at
  Wise
Virginia Military Institute
Virginia Union University
Virginia Wesleyan College
Washington and Lee University

Washington
Cornish College of the Arts
DigiPen Institute of Technology
Northwest University
Saint Martin's University
Walla Walla University
Whitman College

West Virginia
Bethany College
Bluefield State College
Glenville State College
University of Charleston
West Virginia University Institute of
  Technology
West Virginia Wesleyan College
Wheeling Jesuit University

Wisconsin
Beloit College
Edgewood College
Herzing University
Lawrence University
Maranatha Baptist Bible College
Marian University
Mount Mary College

Two-year

Alabama
Chattahoochee Valley Community
  College

Arizona
Brookline College
  Phoenix
Dine College
Le Cordon Bleu College of Culinary
  Arts
  Scottsdale

Arkansas
Arkansas State University
  Mountain Home
Cossatot Community College of the
  University of Arkansas
East Arkansas Community College
Ouachita Technical College
Phillips Community College of the
  University of Arkansas
South Arkansas Community College
Southeast Arkansas College
Southern Arkansas University Tech

California
Bryan College
  Los Angeles
California Culinary Academy
Carrington College
  Sacramento
  San Jose
Concorde Career College
  San Bernardino
Fashion Institute of Design and
  Merchandising
  San Francisco
Feather River College
Heald College
  Concord
  Rancho Cordova
  Roseville
  San Francisco
Kaplan College: Salida
Kaplan College: San Diego
Kaplan College: Vista
Marymount College
Westwood College
  Los Angeles

Colorado
Concorde Career College
  Aurora
Everest College
  Colorado Springs
  Denver
Lamar Community College
Northeastern Junior College
Otero Junior College
Trinidad State Junior College

Florida
ATI Career Training Center
  Oakland Park
ATI College of Health
Brown Mackie College
  Miami
Florida Career College: Hialeah
Florida Career College: Miami
Florida Career College: Pembroke
  Pines
Florida Career College: West Palm
  Beach
Florida Keys Community College
Le Cordon Bleu College of Culinary
  Arts
  Miami
North Florida Community College

Georgia
Altamaha Technical College
Everest College
  Atlanta
Le Cordon Bleu College of Culinary
  Arts
  Atlanta
Southeastern Technical College
Southwest Georgia Technical College
Young Harris College

Hawaii
University of Hawaii
  Kauai Community College

Idaho
Stevens-Henager College
  Boise

Illinois
Illinois Eastern Community Colleges
  Olney Central College
  Wabash Valley College
Le Cordon Bleu College of Culinary
  Arts
  Chicago
Lincoln College
Northwestern College

Indiana
Brown Mackie College
  Fort Wayne

Iowa
AIB College of Business
Clinton Community College
Muscatine Community College
Northwest Iowa Community College

Kansas
Cloud County Community College
Coffeyville Community College
Dodge City Community College

Louisiana
Nunez Community College

Maine
Kennebec Valley Community College
York County Community College

Maryland
Garrett College
Kaplan University
  Hagerstown

Massachusetts
Bay State College
Dean College
Fisher College

Michigan
Glen Oaks Community College
Kirtland Community College
Montcalm Community College

Minnesota
Dunwoody College of Technology
Hibbing Community College
Le Cordon Bleu College of Culinary
  Arts
  Minneapolis-St. Paul
Mesabi Range Community and
  Technical College
Northwest Technical College
Pine Technical College

Missouri
Colorado Technical University
  North Kansas City
Linn State Technical College
North Central Missouri College
Pinnacle Career Institute: Kansas City
Sanford-Brown College
  Hazelwood

Nebraska
Mid-Plains Community College Area
Western Nebraska Community College

Nevada
Everest College
  Las Vegas

New Hampshire
White Mountains Community College

New Jersey
Salem Community College

New Mexico
Luna Community College
Navajo Technical College

New Mexico State University
 Carlsbad
 Grants

New York
Art Institute of New York City
Bramson ORT College
Bryant & Stratton College
 Albany
 Buffalo
 Rochester
New York Career Institute
Sullivan County Community College

North Carolina
Bladen Community College
Carteret Community College
Halifax Community College
Mayland Community College
McDowell Technical Community
 College
Roanoke-Chowan Community College
Southeastern Community College
Tri-County Community College
Wilson Community College

North Dakota
Dakota College at Bottineau
Lake Region State College

Ohio
Cleveland Institute of Electronics
Hondros College
Ohio Technical College
Wright State University: Lake Campus

Oklahoma
Tulsa Welding School

Pennsylvania
Everest Institute: Pittsburgh
Lackawanna College
Manor College
Pennsylvania Highlands Community
 College
YTI Career Institute
 Lancaster

Puerto Rico
Columbia Centro Universitario: Yauco
EDIC College
Huertas Junior College
ICPR Junior College

South Carolina
Denmark Technical College
Miller-Motte Technical College
Northeastern Technical College
Spartanburg Methodist College
University of South Carolina
 Sumter

South Dakota
Mitchell Technical Institute

Texas
Clarendon College
Everest College
 Arlington
 Dallas
Frank Phillips College
Le Cordon Bleu College of Culinary
 Arts
 Austin
Ranger College
Texas State Technical College
 West Texas

Utah
College of Eastern Utah

Virginia
Bryant & Stratton College
 Virginia Beach
Everest College
 Arlington
Paul D. Camp Community College
Richard Bland College

Washington
Big Bend Community College
Cascadia Community College
Lower Columbia College

West Virginia
Bridgemont Community and Technical
 College
Potomac State College of West
 Virginia University

Wisconsin
Rasmussen College
 Wausau
University of Wisconsin
 Washington County
 Waukesha

Wyoming
Central Wyoming College
Northwest College
WyoTech: Laramie

Medium to large (2,000-7,499)

Four-year

Alabama
Alabama Agricultural and Mechanical
 University
Alabama State University
Athens State University
Auburn University at Montgomery
Faulkner University
Samford University
Tuskegee University
University of Alabama
 Huntsville
University of Montevallo
University of North Alabama

Alaska
University of Alaska
 Fairbanks

Arizona
University of Phoenix
 Phoenix-Hohokam
Western International University

Arkansas
Harding University
Henderson State University
Southern Arkansas University
University of Arkansas
 Fort Smith
 Monticello
 Pine Bluff

California
Art Institute of California: Orange
 County
Art Institute of California: San Diego
Azusa Pacific University
Biola University
California Baptist University
California Lutheran University
California State University
 Bakersfield
 Channel Islands
 Monterey Bay
 Stanislaus
Chapman University
Fresno Pacific University
Humboldt State University
Loyola Marymount University
Mount St. Mary's College
Occidental College
Pepperdine University
Point Loma Nazarene University
St. Mary's College of California
Santa Clara University
Sonoma State University
Stanford University
Trident University International

University of California
 Merced
University of Redlands
University of San Diego
University of San Francisco
University of the Pacific
West Coast University

Colorado
Adams State College
Art Institute of Colorado
Colorado Christian University
Colorado College
Colorado School of Mines
Colorado State University
 Pueblo
Colorado Technical University
Fort Lewis College
Regis University
University of Colorado
 Colorado Springs
University of Denver
Western State College of Colorado

Connecticut
Eastern Connecticut State University
Fairfield University
Quinnipiac University
Sacred Heart University
Trinity College
University of Bridgeport
University of New Haven
Wesleyan University
Yale University

Delaware
Delaware State University

District of Columbia
American University
Catholic University of America
Georgetown University
University of the District of Columbia

Florida
Art Institute of Fort Lauderdale
Barry University
Bethune-Cookman University
DeVry University
 Orlando
Embry-Riddle Aeronautical University
Flagler College
Florida Institute of Technology
Hodges University
Jacksonville University
Johnson & Wales University: North
 Miami
Miami International University of Art
 and Design
Nova Southeastern University
Palm Beach Atlantic University
Rasmussen College
 Ocala
Southeastern University
Stetson University
University of Tampa

Georgia
Albany State University
Armstrong Atlantic State University
Augusta State University
Clark Atlanta University
Clayton State University
Columbus State University
Emory University
Fort Valley State University
Georgia College and State University
Georgia Gwinnett College
Georgia Southwestern State University
Mercer University
North Georgia College & State
 University
Savannah State University
Southern Polytechnic State University
Spelman College

Hawaii
Brigham Young University-Hawaii
Hawaii Pacific University
University of Hawaii
 Hilo

Idaho
Lewis-Clark State College

Illinois
Augustana College
Aurora University
Benedictine University
Bradley University
Chicago State University
Elmhurst College
Governors State University
Illinois Institute of Art: Chicago
Illinois Institute of Technology
Illinois Wesleyan University
Kendall College
Lewis University
Millikin University
Moody Bible Institute
North Central College
North Park University
Olivet Nazarene University
Robert Morris University: Chicago
Roosevelt University
Saint Xavier University
School of the Art Institute of Chicago
University of Chicago
University of Illinois
 Springfield
Wheaton College

Indiana
Butler University
DePauw University
Indiana Institute of Technology
Indiana University
 East
 Kokomo
 Northwest
 South Bend
 Southeast
Indiana Wesleyan University
Marian University
Purdue University
 North Central
University of Evansville
University of Indianapolis
Valparaiso University

Iowa
Drake University
Grand View University
Luther College
St. Ambrose University
Upper Iowa University

Kansas
Emporia State University
Pittsburg State University
Washburn University

Kentucky
Bellarmine University
Campbellsville University
Kentucky State University
Mid-Continent University
Morehead State University
Sullivan University

Louisiana
Grambling State University
Loyola University New Orleans
McNeese State University
Nicholls State University
Northwestern State University
Southern University and Agricultural
 and Mechanical College
Xavier University of Louisiana

Maine
Husson University
University of Maine
 Augusta

Farmington
University of New England
University of Southern Maine

Maryland

Bowie State University
Coppin State University
Frostburg State University
Johns Hopkins University
Loyola University Maryland
Morgan State University
Stevenson University
United States Naval Academy
University of Baltimore
University of Maryland
   Eastern Shore

Massachusetts

Assumption College
Bentley University
Berklee College of Music
Brandeis University
Clark University
College of the Holy Cross
Curry College
Emerson College
Emmanuel College
Endicott College
Fitchburg State University
Framingham State University
Harvard University
Massachusetts Institute of Technology
Merrimack College
Mount Holyoke College
Salem State University
Smith College
Springfield College
Stonehill College
Suffolk University
Tufts University
Wellesley College
Wentworth Institute of Technology
Western New England College
Westfield State University
Worcester Polytechnic Institute
Worcester State University

Michigan

Baker College
   of Allen Park
   of Auburn Hills
   of Cadillac
   of Jackson
   of Muskegon
   of Owosso
Calvin College
Cornerstone University
Hope College
Lake Superior State University
Lawrence Technological University
Madonna University
Michigan Technological University
Siena Heights University
Spring Arbor University
University of Detroit Mercy
University of Michigan
   Dearborn
   Flint

Minnesota

Art Institutes International Minnesota
Augsburg College
Bemidji State University
Bethel University
College of St. Benedict
College of St. Scholastica
Concordia College: Moorhead
Gustavus Adolphus College
Macalester College
Minnesota State University
   Moorhead
St. Catherine University
St. Mary's University of Minnesota
St. Olaf College
Southwest Minnesota State University
University of St. Thomas

Mississippi

Alcorn State University
Belhaven University
Delta State University
Jackson State University
Mississippi University for Women
William Carey University

Missouri

Grantham University
Lincoln University
Lindenwood University
Maryville University of Saint Louis
Missouri Southern State University
Missouri University of Science and
   Technology
Northwest Missouri State University
Southwest Baptist University
Truman State University
Washington University in St. Louis
Webster University

Montana

Montana State University
   Billings
Montana Tech of the University of
   Montana

Nebraska

Bellevue University
Creighton University
University of Nebraska
   Kearney
Wayne State College

Nevada

Great Basin College

New Hampshire

Dartmouth College
Plymouth State University

New Jersey

Berkeley College
Bloomfield College
The College of New Jersey
Fairleigh Dickinson University
   College at Florham
   Metropolitan Campus
Monmouth University
New Jersey City University
New Jersey Institute of Technology
Princeton University
Ramapo College of New Jersey
Richard Stockton College of New
   Jersey
Rider University
Rutgers, The State University of New
   Jersey
   Camden Regional Campus
   Newark Regional Campus
Saint Peter's College
Seton Hall University
Stevens Institute of Technology

New Mexico

Eastern New Mexico University
New Mexico Highlands University

New York

Adelphi University
Barnard College
Berkeley College of New York City
Canisius College
City University of New York
   Medgar Evers College
   York College
Clarkson University
Colgate University
College of Saint Rose
Columbia University
Culinary Institute of America
Dowling College
Hobart and William Smith Colleges
Hofstra University
Iona College
Ithaca College
Le Moyne College

Long Island University
   Brooklyn Campus
   C. W. Post Campus
Manhattan College
Marist College
Marymount Manhattan College
Mercy College
Molloy College
Monroe College
Mount Saint Mary College
Nazareth College
New York Institute of Technology
Niagara University
Nyack College
Parsons The New School for Design
Pratt Institute
Rensselaer Polytechnic Institute
St. Francis College
St. John Fisher College
St. Joseph's College: Suffolk Campus
St. Lawrence University
School of Visual Arts
Siena College
Skidmore College
SUNY
   College at Brockport
   College at Cortland
   College at Fredonia
   College at Geneseo
   College at New Paltz
   College at Old Westbury
   College at Oneonta
   College at Oswego
   College at Plattsburgh
   College at Potsdam
   College at Purchase
   College of Technology at
      Farmingdale
Union College
University of Rochester
Utica College
Vassar College

North Carolina

Campbell University
Duke University
Elizabeth City State University
Elon University
Fayetteville State University
Gardner-Webb University
Guilford College
High Point University
Johnson & Wales University: Charlotte
Methodist University
Mount Olive College
Shaw University
University of North Carolina
   Asheville
   Pembroke
Wake Forest University
Western Carolina University

North Dakota

Dickinson State University
Minot State University
University of Mary

Ohio

Ashland University
Baldwin-Wallace College
Capital University
Case Western Reserve University
Cedarville University
Central State University
Denison University
DeVry University
   Columbus
Franklin University
John Carroll University
Oberlin College
Ohio Northern University
Ohio University
   Southern Campus at Ironton
Shawnee State University
Tiffin University
University of Dayton

University of Findlay
University of Mount Union
Walsh University
Xavier University

Oklahoma

Cameron University
East Central University
Langston University
Northwestern Oklahoma State
   University
Oklahoma City University
Oral Roberts University
Rogers State University
Southeastern Oklahoma State
   University
Southwestern Oklahoma State
   University
University of Tulsa

Oregon

Eastern Oregon University
George Fox University
Oregon Institute of Technology
Southern Oregon University
University of Portland
Western Oregon University

Pennsylvania

Albright College
Allegheny College
Alvernia University
Arcadia University
Art Institute of Pittsburgh
Bucknell University
California University of Pennsylvania
Carnegie Mellon University
Clarion University of Pennsylvania
DeSales University
Dickinson College
Duquesne University
East Stroudsburg University of
   Pennsylvania
Eastern University
Edinboro University of Pennsylvania
Elizabethtown College
Franklin & Marshall College
Gannon University
Gettysburg College
Grove City College
Gwynedd-Mercy College
Holy Family University
Immaculata University
King's College
La Salle University
Lafayette College
Lehigh University
Lock Haven University of
   Pennsylvania
Mansfield University of Pennsylvania
Marywood University
Mercyhurst College
Messiah College
Millersville University of Pennsylvania
Misericordia University
Muhlenberg College
Neumann University
Peirce College
Penn State
   Abington
   Altoona
   Berks
   Erie, The Behrend College
   Harrisburg
Pennsylvania College of Technology
Philadelphia University
Point Park University
Robert Morris University
Saint Joseph's University
Shippensburg University of
   Pennsylvania
Susquehanna University
University of Pittsburgh
   Johnstown
University of Scranton

University of the Sciences in
  Philadelphia
Villanova University
Widener University
York College of Pennsylvania

Puerto Rico

Caribbean University
Inter American University of Puerto
  Rico
    Aguadilla Campus
    Barranquitas Campus
    Bayamon Campus
    Fajardo Campus
    Guayama Campus
    Metropolitan Campus
    Ponce Campus
    San German Campus
Pontifical Catholic University of Puerto
  Rico
Universidad Politecnica de Puerto Rico
University of Puerto Rico
    Aguadilla
    Bayamon University College
    Carolina Regional College
    Humacao
    Ponce

Rhode Island

Brown University
Bryant University
New England Institute of Technology
Providence College
Rhode Island College
Roger Williams University
Salve Regina University

South Carolina

Anderson University
Benedict College
Bob Jones University
Charleston Southern University
The Citadel
Francis Marion University
Furman University
North Greenville University
South Carolina State University
University of South Carolina
    Aiken
    Upstate
Winthrop University

South Dakota

University of South Dakota

Tennessee

Belmont University
Bethel University
Lane College
Lee University
Lipscomb University
Tennessee State University
Tusculum College
Union University
University of Tennessee
    Martin
Vanderbilt University

Texas

Abilene Christian University
Angelo State University
Art Institute of Dallas
Dallas Baptist University
Houston Baptist University
LeTourneau University
Midwestern State University
Prairie View A&M University
St. Edward's University
St. Mary's University
Southern Methodist University
Southwestern Assemblies of God
  University
Sul Ross State University
Texas A&M International University
Texas A&M University
    Commerce
    Kingsville
Texas Southern University

Trinity University
University of Houston
    Clear Lake
    Victoria
University of Mary Hardin-Baylor
University of Phoenix
    Houston Westside
University of Texas
    Tyler
    of the Permian Basin
University of the Incarnate Word
West Texas A&M University

Utah

Southern Utah University
Westminster College

Vermont

Castleton State College
Champlain College
Middlebury College
Norwich University

Virginia

Art Institute of Washington
Christopher Newport University
College of William and Mary
Hampton University
Longwood University
Lynchburg College
Marymount University
Norfolk State University
Regent University
Roanoke College
University of Mary Washington
University of Richmond
Virginia State University

Washington

Art Institute of Seattle
Evergreen State College
Gonzaga University
Pacific Lutheran University
Seattle Pacific University
Seattle University
University of Puget Sound
University of Washington Bothell
University of Washington Tacoma
Whitworth University

West Virginia

Fairmont State University
Mountain State University
Shepherd University
West Liberty University
West Virginia State University
West Virginia University at
    Parkersburg

Wisconsin

Alverno College
Carroll University
Concordia University Wisconsin
Milwaukee School of Engineering
St. Norbert College
University of Wisconsin
    Green Bay
    Parkside
    Platteville
    River Falls
    Superior
Viterbo University

Two-year

Alabama

Gadsden State Community College
Lawson State Community College
Southern Union State Community
  College

Arizona

Central Arizona College
Cochise College
Eastern Arizona College
Estrella Mountain Community College
GateWay Community College
Mohave Community College

South Mountain Community College
Universal Technical Institute

Arkansas

National Park Community College

California

Art Institute of California: Los Angeles
Barstow Community College
Berkeley City College
Canada College
Cerro Coso Community College
College of Alameda
College of the Redwoods
College of the Siskiyous
Copper Mountain College
Crafton Hills College
Fashion Institute of Design and
  Merchandising
    Los Angeles
Lake Tahoe Community College
Lassen Community College
Le Cordon Bleu College of Culinary
  Arts
    Los Angeles
Merritt College
Palo Verde College
Porterville College
West Hills College: Coalinga
West Hills College: Lemoore
WyoTech: Long Beach
Yuba Community College District

Colorado

Colorado Mountain College
Community College of Aurora
Community College of Denver
Pueblo Community College

Connecticut

Capital Community College
Gateway Community College
Goodwin College
Housatonic Community College
Manchester Community College
Middlesex Community College
Naugatuck Valley Community College
Norwalk Community College
Tunxis Community College

Delaware

Delaware Technical and Community
  College
    Stanton/Wilmington

Florida

Florida Gateway College
Florida National College
Gulf Coast Community College
Lake-Sumter Community College
South Florida Community College
Southwest Florida College

Georgia

Abraham Baldwin Agricultural College
Albany Technical College
Atlanta Metropolitan College
Atlanta Technical College
Augusta Technical College
Bainbridge College
Columbus Technical College
Darton College
DeKalb Technical College
East Georgia College
Georgia Highlands College
Georgia Military College
Georgia Northwestern Technical
  College
Gordon College
Middle Georgia College
Middle Georgia Technical College
Savannah Technical College
Southern Crescent Technical College
Wiregrass Georgia Technical College

Hawaii

University of Hawaii
    Hawaii Community College

Honolulu Community College
Maui College

Idaho

North Idaho College

Illinois

Black Hawk College
Carl Sandburg College
Danville Area Community College
Heartland Community College
John A. Logan College
John Wood Community College
Kankakee Community College
Kaskaskia College
Lincoln Land Community College
McHenry County College
Morton College
Prairie State College
Richland Community College
Sauk Valley Community College
Southeastern Illinois College
Spoon River College

Indiana

Ivy Tech Community College
    Bloomington
    Columbus
    Kokomo
    Lafayette
    Richmond
    South Central
    Southeast
    Southwest
    Wabash Valley

Iowa

Indian Hills Community College
Iowa Central Community College
Iowa Lakes Community College
Iowa Western Community College
Northeast Iowa Community College
Scott Community College
Southeastern Community College
    North Campus
Western Iowa Tech Community
  College

Kansas

Allen County Community College
Barton County Community College
Cowley County Community College
Garden City Community College
Hutchinson Community College
Kansas City Kansas Community
  College

Kentucky

Gateway Community and Technical
  College
Southeast Kentucky Community and
  Technical College

Louisiana

Bossier Parish Community College
Louisiana State University
    Eunice
South Louisiana Community College

Maine

Central Maine Community College
Southern Maine Community College

Maryland

Baltimore City Community College
Carroll Community College
Chesapeake College
Harford Community College

Massachusetts

Berkshire Community College
Cape Cod Community College
Greenfield Community College
Massachusetts Bay Community College
Massasoit Community College
Mount Wachusett Community College
Northern Essex Community College
Roxbury Community College

Medium to large (2,000-7,499)

Springfield Technical Community
College

Michigan
Bay de Noc Community College
Lake Michigan College
Muskegon Community College
Southwestern Michigan College

Minnesota
Alexandria Technical College
Central Lakes College
Dakota County Technical College
Hennepin Technical College
Inver Hills Community College
Lake Superior College
Minnesota State College - Southeast
Technical
Minnesota State Community and
Technical College
Minnesota West Community and
Technical College
North Hennepin Community College
Northland Community & Technical
College
Ridgewater College
Rochester Community and Technical
College
St. Cloud Technical and Community
College

Mississippi
Coahoma Community College
Jones County Junior College

Missouri
Crowder College
East Central College
Jefferson College
Metropolitan Community College: Blue
River
Metropolitan Community College:
Longview
Metropolitan Community College:
Maple Woods
Metropolitan Community College:
Penn Valley
State Fair Community College
Three Rivers Community College

Montana
Flathead Valley Community College

Nebraska
Northeast Community College

Nevada
Western Nevada College

New Hampshire
Nashua Community College

New Jersey
Atlantic Cape Community College
Cumberland County College
Gloucester County College
Raritan Valley Community College
Sussex County Community College

New Mexico
Eastern New Mexico University:
Roswell
New Mexico State University
Alamogordo
San Juan College
Santa Fe Community College

New York
Adirondack Community College
ASA Institute of Business and
Computer Technology
Broome Community College
Cayuga Community College
City University of New York
Hostos Community College
Clinton Community College
Columbia-Greene Community College
Corning Community College

Fulton-Montgomery Community
College
Genesee Community College
Herkimer County Community College
Jamestown Community College
Mohawk Valley Community College
Niagara County Community College
North Country Community College
Rockland Community College
Schenectady County Community
College
SUNY
College of Agriculture and
Technology at Morrisville
College of Technology at Alfred
College of Technology at Canton
College of Technology at Delhi
Tompkins Cortland Community
College
Ulster County Community College

North Carolina
College of the Albemarle
Craven Community College
Durham Technical Community College
Johnston Community College
Nash Community College
Piedmont Community College
Rockingham Community College
Vance-Granville Community College

North Dakota
North Dakota State College of Science

Ohio
Belmont Technical College
Bowling Green State University:
Firelands College
Central Ohio Technical College
Clark State Community College
Edison State Community College
James A. Rhodes State College
Kent State University
Geauga
Miami University
Middletown
University of Akron: Wayne College
University of Cincinnati
Clermont College
Raymond Walters College

Oklahoma
Eastern Oklahoma State College
Northeastern Oklahoma Agricultural
and Mechanical College
Northern Oklahoma College
Oklahoma State University
Institute of Technology: Okmulgee
Redlands Community College
Western Oklahoma State College

Oregon
Clatsop Community College
Linn-Benton Community College
Rogue Community College
Treasure Valley Community College
Umpqua Community College

Pennsylvania
Community College of Beaver County
Reading Area Community College

South Carolina
Aiken Technical College
Central Carolina Technical College
Florence-Darlington Technical College
Piedmont Technical College
Spartanburg Community College
Tri-County Technical College

Tennessee
Cleveland State Community College
Dyersburg State Community College
Jackson State Community College
Motlow State Community College
Roane State Community College
Walters State Community College

Texas
Brazosport College
Coastal Bend College
Galveston College
Grayson County College
Hill College
Kilgore College
Lamar Institute of Technology
Lamar State College at Orange
Lamar State College at Port Arthur
Lee College
Midland College
North Central Texas College
Northeast Texas Community College
Odessa College
Panola College
Paris Junior College
Texas State Technical College
Harlingen
Trinity Valley Community College
Victoria College
Weatherford College
Western Texas College
Wharton County Junior College

Utah
Snow College

Vermont
Community College of Vermont

Virginia
Blue Ridge Community College
Central Virginia Community College
Danville Community College
Patrick Henry Community College
Rappahannock Community College
Southwest Virginia Community
College

Washington
Centralia College
Clark College
Clover Park Technical College
Columbia Basin College
Everett Community College
Highline Community College
North Seattle Community College
Skagit Valley College
South Puget Sound Community
College
Spokane Community College
Tacoma Community College
Walla Walla Community College
Yakima Valley Community College

West Virginia
Kanawha Valley Community and
Technical College
New River Community and Technical
College
West Virginia Northern Community
College

Wisconsin
Chippewa Valley Technical College
Lakeshore Technical College
Moraine Park Technical College
Southwest Wisconsin Technical
College
Wisconsin Indianhead Technical
College

Wyoming
Casper College
Laramie County Community College
Sheridan College

Large (7,500-14,499)

Four-year

Alabama
Jacksonville State University
University of Alabama
Birmingham
University of South Alabama

Alaska
University of Alaska
Anchorage

Arkansas
Arkansas State University
Arkansas Tech University
University of Arkansas
Little Rock
University of Central Arkansas

California
Academy of Art University
California State University
Chico
Dominguez Hills
East Bay
San Bernardino
San Marcos
National University

Colorado
Mesa State College
University of Colorado
Denver
University of Northern Colorado

Connecticut
Central Connecticut State University
Southern Connecticut State University

District of Columbia
George Washington University

Florida
Embry-Riddle Aeronautical University:
Worldwide Campus
Everest University
Brandon
South Orlando
Florida Agricultural and Mechanical
University
Florida Gulf Coast University
Full Sail University
Northwest Florida State College
State College of Florida, Manatee-
Sarasota
University of Miami
University of North Florida
University of West Florida

Georgia
Georgia Institute of Technology
Savannah College of Art and Design
University of West Georgia
Valdosta State University

Hawaii
University of Hawaii
Manoa

Idaho
Brigham Young University-Idaho
Idaho State University
University of Idaho

Illinois
Columbia College Chicago
Eastern Illinois University
Loyola University Chicago
Southern Illinois University
Edwardsville
Western Illinois University

Indiana
Indiana State University
Indiana University-Purdue University
Fort Wayne
Purdue University
Calumet
University of Notre Dame
University of Southern Indiana

Iowa
University of Northern Iowa

Kansas
Fort Hays State University
Wichita State University

Kentucky
Eastern Kentucky University
Murray State University
Northern Kentucky University
University of Louisville

Louisiana
Louisiana Tech University
Southeastern Louisiana University
Tulane University
University of Louisiana at Lafayette
University of Louisiana at Monroe
University of New Orleans

Maine
University of Maine

Maryland
Salisbury University
University of Maryland
    Baltimore County

Massachusetts
Boston College
Bridgewater State University
University of Massachusetts
    Boston
    Dartmouth
    Lowell

Michigan
Davenport University
Ferris State University
Northern Michigan University
Saginaw Valley State University

Minnesota
Capella University
Minnesota State University
    Mankato
Saint Cloud State University
University of Minnesota
    Duluth
Walden University
Winona State University

Mississippi
Mississippi State University
University of Mississippi
University of Southern Mississippi

Missouri
Park University
Saint Louis University
Southeast Missouri State University
University of Central Missouri
University of Missouri
    Kansas City
    St. Louis

Montana
Montana State University
    Bozeman

Nebraska
University of Nebraska
    Omaha

Nevada
University of Nevada
    Reno

New Hampshire
University of New Hampshire

New Jersey
Kean University
Montclair State University
Rowan University
William Paterson University of New
    Jersey

New Mexico
New Mexico State University

New York
City University of New York
    Baruch College
    Brooklyn College
    City College
    College of Staten Island

Hunter College
John Jay College of Criminal
    Justice
Lehman College
Cornell University
Fashion Institute of Technology
Fordham University
Pace University
Rochester Institute of Technology
St. John's University
SUNY
    College at Buffalo
    Empire State College
    University at Albany
    University at Binghamton
Syracuse University
Touro College

North Carolina
Appalachian State University
University of North Carolina
    Greensboro
    Wilmington

North Dakota
North Dakota State University
University of North Dakota

Ohio
Bowling Green State University
Cleveland State University
Miami University
    Oxford
Wright State University
Youngstown State University

Oklahoma
Northeastern State University

Pennsylvania
Bloomsburg University of
    Pennsylvania
Drexel University
Indiana University of Pennsylvania
Kutztown University of Pennsylvania
Slippery Rock University of
    Pennsylvania
University of Pennsylvania
West Chester University of
    Pennsylvania

Puerto Rico
Turabo University
Universidad del Este
Universidad Metropolitana
University of Puerto Rico
    Mayaguez
    Rio Piedras

Rhode Island
Johnson & Wales University:
    Providence
University of Rhode Island

South Carolina
Coastal Carolina University
College of Charleston

South Dakota
South Dakota State University

Tennessee
Austin Peay State University
East Tennessee State University
Tennessee Technological University
University of Tennessee
    Chattanooga

Texas
Baylor University
Lamar University
Sam Houston State University
Stephen F. Austin State University
Tarleton State University
Texas A&M University
    Corpus Christi
Texas Christian University
Texas Woman's University

University of Houston
    Downtown
University of Texas
    Brownsville - Texas Southmost
        College
    Dallas

Utah
Dixie State College
Utah State University

Vermont
University of Vermont

Virginia
ECPI College of Technology: Virginia
    Beach
Radford University
University of Virginia

Washington
Central Washington University
Eastern Washington University
Western Washington University

West Virginia
Marshall University

Wisconsin
Marquette University
University of Wisconsin
    Eau Claire
    La Crosse
    Oshkosh
    Stevens Point
    Stout

Wyoming
University of Wyoming

Two-year

Alabama
Calhoun Community College
Jefferson State Community College

Arizona
Arizona Western College
Chandler-Gilbert Community College
    Pecos
Glendale Community College
Paradise Valley Community College
Phoenix College
Scottsdale Community College

Arkansas
Pulaski Technical College

California
Antelope Valley College
Butte College
Chabot College
Citrus College
Coastline Community College
College of Marin
College of San Mateo
College of the Desert
College of the Sequoias
Contra Costa College
Cosumnes River College
Cuesta College
Cuyamaca College
East Los Angeles College
Evergreen Valley College
Folsom Lake College
Glendale Community College
Golden West College
Hartnell College
Laney College
Las Positas College
Los Angeles Harbor College
Los Angeles Mission College
Los Angeles Southwest College
Los Medanos College
Mission College
Monterey Peninsula College
Napa Valley College
Ohlone College
Oxnard College

Reedley College
San Bernardino Valley College
San Diego Miramar College
San Jose City College
Shasta College
Skyline College
Solano Community College
Taft College
Ventura College
Victor Valley College
West Los Angeles College
West Valley College

Colorado
Arapahoe Community College
Pikes Peak Community College
Red Rocks Community College

Florida
Brevard Community College
College of Central Florida
Daytona State College
Pasco-Hernando Community College
Polk State College

Georgia
Central Georgia Technical College
Chattahoochee Technical College

Hawaii
University of Hawaii
    Kapiolani Community College

Idaho
College of Southern Idaho

Illinois
College of Lake County
Elgin Community College
Harper College
Lake Land College
Moraine Valley Community College

Indiana
Ivy Tech Community College
    East Central
    North Central
    Northeast
    Northwest
Vincennes University

Kentucky
Elizabethtown Community and
    Technical College
Somerset Community College

Louisiana
Baton Rouge Community College

Maryland
College of Southern Maryland
Howard Community College
Prince George's Community College

Massachusetts
Bristol Community College
Bunker Hill Community College
Middlesex Community College
North Shore Community College
Quinsigamond Community College

Michigan
Delta College
Kalamazoo Valley Community College
Macomb Community College
Mott Community College
Washtenaw Community College

Minnesota
Century College
Minneapolis Community and Technical
    College
Normandale Community College

Mississippi
Mississippi Gulf Coast Community
    College

Missouri
Ozarks Technical Community College

Large (7,500-14,499)

Nebraska
Metropolitan Community College

New Jersey
Brookdale Community College
Burlington County College
County College of Morris
Essex County College
Mercer County Community College
Middlesex County College
Ocean County College
Passaic County Community College
Union County College

New York
City University of New York
   Bronx Community College
Dutchess Community College
Hudson Valley Community College
Onondaga Community College
Westchester Community College

North Carolina
Asheville-Buncombe Technical
   Community College
Fayetteville Technical Community
   College
Guilford Technical Community College

Ohio
Cincinnati State Technical and
   Community College
Lakeland Community College
Owens Community College
   Toledo
Stark State College of Technology

Oklahoma
Oklahoma City Community College
Rose State College

Oregon
Chemeketa Community College
Clackamas Community College
Lane Community College

Pennsylvania
Delaware County Community College
Harrisburg Area Community College
Montgomery County Community
   College
Northampton Community College

South Carolina
Greenville Technical College
Midlands Technical College
Trident Technical College

Tennessee
Nashville State Community College
Southwest Tennessee Community
   College
Volunteer State Community College

Texas
Amarillo College
Brookhaven College
Del Mar College
Eastfield College
El Centro College
Laredo Community College
McLennan Community College
Mountain View College
Navarro College
North Lake College
Northwest Vista College
St. Philip's College
South Plains College

Virginia
Germanna Community College
J. Sargeant Reynolds Community
   College

Washington
Bates Technical College
Olympic College
Seattle Central Community College
Shoreline Community College
South Seattle Community College

Wisconsin
Fox Valley Technical College
Gateway Technical College

Very large (15,000 or more)

Four-year

Alabama
Auburn University
Columbia Southern University
Troy University
University of Alabama

Arizona
Arizona State University
Grand Canyon University
Northern Arizona University
University of Arizona

Arkansas
University of Arkansas

California
California Polytechnic State University:
   San Luis Obispo
California State Polytechnic University:
   Pomona
California State University
   Fresno
   Fullerton
   Long Beach
   Los Angeles
   Sacramento
San Diego State University
San Francisco State University
San Jose State University
University of California
   Berkeley
   Davis
   Irvine
   Los Angeles
   Riverside
   San Diego
   Santa Barbara
   Santa Cruz
University of Southern California

Colorado
Colorado State University
Metropolitan State College of Denver
University of Colorado
   Boulder

Connecticut
University of Connecticut

Delaware
University of Delaware

Florida
Edison State College
Florida Atlantic University
Florida International University
Florida State University
University of Central Florida
University of Florida
University of South Florida

Georgia
Georgia Southern University
Georgia State University
Kennesaw State University
South University: Savannah
University of Georgia

Idaho
Boise State University

Illinois
DePaul University
Illinois State University
Northern Illinois University
Southern Illinois University Carbondale
University of Illinois
   Chicago
   Urbana-Champaign

Indiana
Ball State University
Indiana University
   Bloomington
Indiana University-Purdue University
   Indianapolis
Purdue University

Iowa
Ashford University
Iowa State University
University of Iowa

Kansas
Kansas State University
University of Kansas

Kentucky
University of Kentucky
Western Kentucky University

Louisiana
Louisiana State University and
   Agricultural and Mechanical College

Maryland
Towson University
University of Maryland
   College Park
   University College

Massachusetts
Boston University
Northeastern University
University of Massachusetts
   Amherst

Michigan
Central Michigan University
Eastern Michigan University
Grand Valley State University
Michigan State University
Oakland University
University of Michigan
Wayne State University
Western Michigan University

Minnesota
University of Minnesota
   Twin Cities

Missouri
Missouri State University
University of Missouri
   Columbia

Montana
University of Montana

Nebraska
University of Nebraska
   Lincoln

Nevada
University of Nevada
   Las Vegas

New Jersey
Rutgers, The State University of New
   Jersey
   New Brunswick/Piscataway
      Campus
Thomas Edison State College

New York
City University of New York
   Queens College
Excelsior College
New York University
SUNY
   University at Buffalo
   University at Stony Brook

North Carolina
East Carolina University
North Carolina State University
University of North Carolina
   Chapel Hill
   Charlotte

Ohio
Kent State University
Ohio State University
   Columbus Campus
Ohio University
University of Akron
University of Cincinnati
University of Toledo

Oklahoma
Oklahoma State University
University of Central Oklahoma
University of Oklahoma

Oregon
Oregon State University
Portland State University
University of Oregon

Pennsylvania
Penn State
   University Park
Temple University
University of Pittsburgh

South Carolina
University of South Carolina
   Columbia

Tennessee
Middle Tennessee State University
University of Memphis
University of Tennessee
   Knoxville

Texas
Texas A&M University
Texas State University: San Marcos
Texas Tech University
University of Houston
University of North Texas
University of Texas
   Arlington
   Austin
   El Paso
   Pan American
   San Antonio

Utah
Brigham Young University
University of Utah
Utah Valley University
Weber State University

Virginia
George Mason University
James Madison University
Liberty University
Old Dominion University
Virginia Commonwealth University
Virginia Polytechnic Institute and State
   University

Washington
University of Washington
Washington State University

West Virginia
West Virginia University

Wisconsin
University of Wisconsin
   Madison
   Milwaukee

Two-year

Arizona
Mesa Community College
Penn Foster College
Rio Salado College

California
Allan Hancock College
American River College
Bakersfield College
Cabrillo College
Cerritos College
Chaffey College
City College of San Francisco

College of the Canyons
Cypress College
De Anza College
Diablo Valley College
El Camino College
Foothill College
Fresno City College
Fullerton College
Grossmont College
Irvine Valley College
Long Beach City College
Los Angeles City College
Los Angeles Pierce College
Los Angeles Trade and Technical
    College
Los Angeles Valley College
MiraCosta College
Modesto Junior College
Moorpark College
Mount San Antonio College
Mount San Jacinto College
Orange Coast College
Palomar College
Pasadena City College
Rio Hondo College
Riverside Community College
Sacramento City College
Saddleback College
San Diego City College
San Diego Mesa College
San Joaquin Delta College
Santa Ana College
Santa Barbara City College
Santa Monica College
Santa Rosa Junior College
Santiago Canyon College
Sierra College
Southwestern College

Colorado
Front Range Community College

Florida
Broward College
Florida State College at Jacksonville
Hillsborough Community College
Indian River State College
Keiser University
Miami Dade College
Palm Beach State College
St. Petersburg College
Santa Fe College
Seminole State College of Florida
Valencia College

Georgia
Georgia Perimeter College

Illinois
College of DuPage
Triton College

Indiana
Ivy Tech Community College
    Central Indiana

Iowa
Des Moines Area Community College

Louisiana
Delgado Community College

Maryland
Anne Arundel Community College
Community College of Baltimore
    County

Michigan
Grand Rapids Community College
Henry Ford Community College
Lansing Community College
Oakland Community College
Wayne County Community College

Nevada
College of Southern Nevada

New York
City University of New York
    Borough of Manhattan
        Community College
    Kingsborough Community College
    LaGuardia Community College
    Queensborough Community
        College
Erie Community College
Monroe Community College
Nassau Community College
Suffolk County Community College

North Carolina
Central Piedmont Community College
Wake Technical Community College

Ohio
Cuyahoga Community College
    Metropolitan
Sinclair Community College

Oklahoma
Tulsa Community College

Oregon
Portland Community College

Pennsylvania
Community College of Allegheny
    County
Community College of Philadelphia

Rhode Island
Community College of Rhode Island

Texas
Austin Community College
Blinn College
Central Texas College
Collin County Community College
    District
Houston Community College System
Lone Star College System
Richland College
San Antonio College
San Jacinto College
Tarrant County College

Utah
Salt Lake Community College

Virginia
Northern Virginia Community College
Tidewater Community College

Wisconsin
Milwaukee Area Technical College

College type

Liberal arts colleges

Four-year

Alabama
Athens State University
Birmingham-Southern College
Faulkner University
Huntingdon College
Judson College
Miles College
Oakwood University
Spring Hill College
Stillman College
Talladega College
University of Mobile
University of Montevallo

Alaska
Alaska Pacific University
University of Alaska
Southeast

Arizona
Arizona Christian University
Prescott College

Arkansas
Arkansas Baptist College
Arkansas Tech University
Ecclesia College
Henderson State University
Hendrix College
John Brown University
Lyon College
Ouachita Baptist University
Philander Smith College
University of the Ozarks
Williams Baptist College

California
American Jewish University
Antioch University
Los Angeles
Santa Barbara
Bethany University
California Institute of Integral Studies
California Lutheran University
California State University
Bakersfield
Chico
Monterey Bay
San Bernardino
Stanislaus
Chapman University
Claremont McKenna College
Concordia University
Dominican University of California
Fresno Pacific University
Harvey Mudd College
Hope International University
Horizon College of San Diego
Humboldt State University
Humphreys College
International Academy of Design and
Technology
Sacramento
La Sierra University
The Master's College
Menlo College
Mills College
Mount St. Mary's College
NewSchool of Architecture & Design
Notre Dame de Namur University
Occidental College
Pacific Union College
Patten University

Pepperdine University
Pitzer College
Point Loma Nazarene University
Pomona College
Providence Christian College
St. Mary's College of California
San Diego Christian College
San Jose State University
Scripps College
Simpson University
Soka University of America
Sonoma State University
Stanford University
Touro College Los Angeles
University of La Verne
University of Redlands
University of the West
Vanguard University of Southern
California
Westmont College
Whittier College
William Jessup University

Colorado
Adams State College
Colorado Christian University
Colorado College
Colorado Heights University
Fort Lewis College
Mesa State College
Metropolitan State College of Denver
Naropa University
Regis University
Western State College of Colorado

Connecticut
Albertus Magnus College
Charter Oak State College
Connecticut College
Eastern Connecticut State University
Holy Apostles College and Seminary
Mitchell College
Sacred Heart University
Saint Joseph College
Trinity College
Wesleyan University

Delaware
Wesley College

District of Columbia
Gallaudet University
Trinity Washington University
University of the District of Columbia

Florida
Ave Maria University
Beacon College
Bethune-Cookman University
Eckerd College
Edison State College
Edward Waters College
Flagler College
Florida Memorial University
Florida Southern College
Jacksonville University
New College of Florida
Palm Beach Atlantic University
Rollins College
Southeastern University
University of Tampa
Warner University

Georgia
Agnes Scott College
Albany State University
Atlanta Christian College
Augusta State University
Berry College

Brenau University
Brewton-Parker College
Clayton State University
Columbus State University
Covenant College
Fort Valley State University
Georgia College and State University
Georgia Gwinnett College
Georgia Southwestern State University
LaGrange College
Morehouse College
Oglethorpe University
Paine College
Piedmont College
Savannah State University
Shorter University
Spelman College
Thomas University
Toccoa Falls College
Truett-McConnell College
Wesleyan College

Hawaii
Brigham Young University-Hawaii
Hawaii Pacific University
University of Hawaii
Hilo
West Oahu

Idaho
College of Idaho
Lewis-Clark State College
New Saint Andrews College

Illinois
Augustana College
Benedictine University
Blackburn College
Columbia College Chicago
Dominican University
Elmhurst College
Eureka College
Greenville College
Hebrew Theological College
Illinois College
Illinois Wesleyan University
Judson University
Knox College
Lake Forest College
MacMurray College
McKendree University
Monmouth College
North Central College
North Park University
Olivet Nazarene University
Quincy University
Rockford College
St. Augustine College
Shimer College
Trinity Christian College
Trinity International University
University of Chicago
University of Illinois
Springfield
University of St. Francis
Wheaton College

Indiana
Bethel College
Calumet College of St. Joseph
DePauw University
Earlham College
Franklin College
Goshen College
Hanover College
Holy Cross College
Huntington University
Indiana Wesleyan University
Manchester College
Marian University
Oakland City University
Saint Mary's College
St. Mary-of-the-Woods College
Taylor University
University of Evansville
University of Indianapolis
University of St. Francis

University of Southern Indiana
Wabash College

Iowa
Briar Cliff University
Buena Vista University
Central College
Clarke University
Coe College
Cornell College
Divine Word College
Graceland University
Grand View University
Grinnell College
Iowa Wesleyan College
Loras College
Luther College
Maharishi University of Management
Morningside College
Mount Mercy University
Northwestern College
St. Ambrose University
Simpson College
Waldorf College
Wartburg College
William Penn University

Kansas
Baker University
Benedictine College
Bethany College
Bethel College
Central Christian College of Kansas
Friends University
Kansas Wesleyan University
McPherson College
MidAmerica Nazarene University
Newman University
Ottawa University
Southwestern College
Sterling College
Tabor College

Kentucky
Alice Lloyd College
Bellarmine University
Berea College
Brescia University
Centre College
Georgetown College
Kentucky Christian University
Kentucky State University
Kentucky Wesleyan College
Lindsey Wilson College
Mid-Continent University
Midway College
Pikeville College
St. Catharine College
Thomas More College
Transylvania University
Union College
University of the Cumberlands

Louisiana
Centenary College of Louisiana
Dillard University
Louisiana College
Louisiana State University
Shreveport
Loyola University New Orleans
Our Lady of Holy Cross College
St. Joseph Seminary College

Maine
Bates College
Bowdoin College
Colby College
College of the Atlantic
Saint Joseph's College of Maine
Thomas College
Unity College in Maine
University of Maine
Farmington
Machias
University of Southern Maine

Maryland

College of Notre Dame of Maryland
Coppin State University
Goucher College
Griggs University
Hood College
Loyola University Maryland
McDaniel College
Morgan State University
Mount St. Mary's University
National Labor College
St. John's College
St. Mary's College of Maryland
Salisbury University
Sojourner-Douglass College
University of Baltimore
Washington Adventist University
Washington College

Massachusetts

American International College
Amherst College
Anna Maria College
Assumption College
Atlantic Union College
Bard College at Simon's Rock
Bay Path College
Becker College
Bridgewater State University
Cambridge College
Clark University
College of the Holy Cross
Curry College
Eastern Nazarene College
Elms College
Emmanuel College
Endicott College
Fitchburg State University
Framingham State University
Gordon College
Hampshire College
Harvard College
Hellenic College/Holy Cross
Lasell College
Lesley University
Massachusetts College of Liberal Arts
Merrimack College
Mount Holyoke College
Mount Ida College
Newbury College
Nichols College
Pine Manor College
Regis College
Simmons College
Smith College
Springfield College
Stonehill College
Wellesley College
Wheaton College
Wheelock College
Williams College
Worcester State University

Michigan

Adrian College
Albion College
Alma College
Aquinas College
Calvin College
Cornerstone University
Finlandia University
Hillsdale College
Hope College
Kalamazoo College
Kuyper College
Madonna University
Marygrove College
Michigan Jewish Institute
Olivet College
Robert B. Miller College
Rochester College
Siena Heights University
Spring Arbor University

Minnesota

Augsburg College
Bethany Lutheran College
Bethel University
Brown College: Mendota Heights
Carleton College
College of St. Benedict
College of St. Scholastica
Concordia College: Moorhead
Crown College
Gustavus Adolphus College
Hamline University
Macalester College
Northwestern College
St. Catherine University
St. John's University
St. Olaf College
Southwest Minnesota State University
University of Minnesota
    Morris
University of St. Thomas

Mississippi

Belhaven University
Blue Mountain College
Millsaps College
Mississippi University for Women
Mississippi Valley State University
Rust College
Tougaloo College
William Carey University

Missouri

Avila University
Central Methodist University
College of the Ozarks
Columbia College
Culver-Stockton College
Drury University
Evangel University
Fontbonne University
Hannibal-LaGrange University
Lincoln University
Lindenwood University
Missouri Baptist University
Missouri Southern State University
Missouri Valley College
Rockhurst University
Stephens College
Truman State University
Westminster College
William Jewell College
William Woods University

Montana

Carroll College
Rocky Mountain College
University of Great Falls
University of Montana
University of Montana: Western

Nebraska

Chadron State College
College of Saint Mary
Doane College
Nebraska Wesleyan University
Peru State College
Union College
Wayne State College
York College

Nevada

Sierra Nevada College

New Hampshire

Chester College of New England
Colby-Sawyer College
Daniel Webster College
Dartmouth College
Franklin Pierce University
Granite State College
Magdalen College
New England College
Rivier College
Saint Anselm College
Thomas More College of Liberal Arts

University of New Hampshire at
    Manchester

New Jersey

Bloomfield College
Caldwell College
Centenary College
The College of New Jersey
College of St. Elizabeth
Drew University
Felician College
Georgian Court University
Kean University
Ramapo College of New Jersey
Richard Stockton College of New
    Jersey
Saint Peter's College
Thomas Edison State College
William Paterson University of New
    Jersey

New Mexico

Institute of American Indian Arts
New Mexico Institute of Mining and
    Technology
St. John's College
University of the Southwest

New York

Bard College
Barnard College
Canisius College
Cazenovia College
City University of New York
    Baruch College
    Brooklyn College
    College of Staten Island
    Hunter College
    Lehman College
    Medgar Evers College
    Queens College
    York College
Colgate University
College of Mount St. Vincent
College of New Rochelle
College of Saint Rose
Columbia University
    School of General Studies
Concordia College
D'Youville College
Daemen College
Dowling College
Elmira College
Eugene Lang College The New School
    for Liberal Arts
Excelsior College
Five Towns College
Hamilton College
Hartwick College
Hilbert College
Hobart and William Smith Colleges
Houghton College
Iona College
Ithaca College
Keuka College
The King's College
Le Moyne College
Long Island University
    Brooklyn Campus
    C. W. Post Campus
Manhattan College
Manhattanville College
Marist College
Marymount Manhattan College
Medaille College
Medaille College: Amherst
Medaille College: Rochester
Mercy College
Metropolitan College of New York
Molloy College
Mount Saint Mary College
Nazareth College
Nyack College
Paul Smith's College
Roberts Wesleyan College
Russell Sage College

Sage College of Albany
St. Francis College
St. John Fisher College
St. Joseph's College
St. Joseph's College: Suffolk Campus
St. Lawrence University
St. Thomas Aquinas College
Sarah Lawrence College
Siena College
Skidmore College
SUNY
    College at Brockport
    College at Buffalo
    College at Cortland
    College at Fredonia
    College at Geneseo
    College at New Paltz
    College at Old Westbury
    College at Oneonta
    College at Plattsburgh
    College at Potsdam
    Empire State College
    Institute of Technology at Utica/
        Rome
Touro College
Union College
Utica College
Vassar College
Wagner College
Wells College

North Carolina

Barton College
Belmont Abbey College
Bennett College for Women
Brevard College
Campbell University
Catawba College
Chowan University
Davidson College
Elizabeth City State University
Elon University
Gardner-Webb University
Greensboro College
Guilford College
High Point University
Johnson C. Smith University
Lees-McRae College
Lenoir-Rhyne University
Livingstone College
Mars Hill College
Meredith College
Methodist University
Montreat College
Mount Olive College
North Carolina Wesleyan College
Peace College
Pfeiffer University
St. Andrews Presbyterian College
St. Augustine's College
Salem College
Shaw University
University of North Carolina
    Asheville
    Pembroke
Warren Wilson College

North Dakota

Jamestown College
Minot State University
Valley City State University

Ohio

Ashland University
Baldwin-Wallace College
Bluffton University
Cedarville University
Central State University
College of Mount St. Joseph
College of Wooster
Defiance College
Denison University
Heidelberg University
Hiram College
Kenyon College
Lake Erie College

Lourdes College
Marietta College
Muskingum University
Notre Dame College
Oberlin College
Ohio Dominican University
Ohio Wesleyan University
Otterbein University
Temple Baptist College
Tiffin University
University of Rio Grande
Urbana University
Ursuline College
Walsh University
Wilberforce University
Wilmington College
Wittenberg University

Oklahoma
Bacone College
Hillsdale Free Will Baptist College
Langston University
Oklahoma Baptist University
Oklahoma Christian University
Oklahoma City University
Oklahoma Panhandle State University
Oklahoma Wesleyan University
Oral Roberts University
St. Gregory's University
Southeastern Oklahoma State
    University
Southern Nazarene University
Southwestern Christian University
University of Science and Arts of
    Oklahoma

Oregon
Art Institute of Portland
Concordia University
Corban College
Eastern Oregon University
Gutenberg College
Lewis & Clark College
Linfield College
Marylhurst University
Reed College
Southern Oregon University
Warner Pacific College
Western Oregon University
Willamette University

Pennsylvania
Albright College
Allegheny College
Alvernia University
Bloomsburg University of
    Pennsylvania
Bryn Mawr College
Cabrini College
Carlow University
Cedar Crest College
Chatham University
Chestnut Hill College
Dickinson College
Elizabethtown College
Franklin & Marshall College
Geneva College
Gettysburg College
Gratz College
Grove City College
Gwynedd-Mercy College
Haverford College
Immaculata University
Juniata College
Keystone College
King's College
La Roche College
La Salle University
Lafayette College
Lebanon Valley College
Lincoln University
Lock Haven University of
    Pennsylvania
Lycoming College
Mercyhurst College
Messiah College

Millersville University of Pennsylvania
Misericordia University
Moravian College
Mount Aloysius College
Muhlenberg College
Rosemont College
St. Francis University
St. Vincent College
Seton Hill University
Susquehanna University
Swarthmore College
Thiel College
University of Pittsburgh
    Greensburg
    Johnstown
University of Scranton
Ursinus College
Valley Forge Christian College
Washington & Jefferson College
Waynesburg University
Wilson College
York College of Pennsylvania

Puerto Rico
Inter American University of Puerto
    Rico
        Aguadilla Campus
        Arecibo Campus
Universidad Adventista de las Antillas
Universidad del Este
Universidad Metropolitana
University of Puerto Rico
    Aguadilla
    Cayey University College
    Humacao

Rhode Island
Brown University
Bryant University
Providence College
Rhode Island College
Roger Williams University
Salve Regina University

South Carolina
Allen University
Benedict College
Bob Jones University
Charleston Southern University
Claflin University
Coker College
College of Charleston
Columbia College
Converse College
Erskine College
Francis Marion University
Furman University
Lander University
Limestone College
Morris College
Newberry College
North Greenville University
Presbyterian College
Southern Wesleyan University
University of South Carolina
    Aiken
    Beaufort
Voorhees College
Wofford College

South Dakota
Augustana College
Black Hills State University
Dakota Wesleyan University
Mount Marty College
Northern State University
Oglala Lakota College
Sinte Gleska University
University of Sioux Falls

Tennessee
Aquinas College
Austin Peay State University
Bethel University
Bryan College
Carson-Newman College
Cumberland University

Fisk University
Freed-Hardeman University
King College
Lambuth University
Lane College
Lee University
LeMoyne-Owen College
Lincoln Memorial University
Lipscomb University
Maryville College
Milligan College
Rhodes College
South College
Tennessee Wesleyan College
Trevecca Nazarene University
Tusculum College
Union University
Victory University
Williamson Christian College

Texas
Austin College
Concordia University Texas
East Texas Baptist University
Houston Baptist University
Howard Payne University
Huston-Tillotson University
Lubbock Christian University
McMurry University
Midwestern State University
St. Edward's University
Schreiner University
Southwestern Adventist University
Southwestern Christian College
Southwestern University
Texas College
Texas Lutheran University
Trinity University
University of Dallas
University of St. Thomas
University of the Incarnate Word
Wayland Baptist University
Wiley College

Utah
Dixie State College
Westminster College

Vermont
Bennington College
Burlington College
Castleton State College
Champlain College
College of St. Joseph in Vermont
Goddard College
Green Mountain College
Johnson State College
Lyndon State College
Marlboro College
Middlebury College
St. Michael's College
Southern Vermont College
Sterling College

Virginia
Averett University
Bluefield College
Bridgewater College
Christendom College
Christopher Newport University
Eastern Mennonite University
Emory & Henry College
Ferrum College
Hampden-Sydney College
Hollins University
Lynchburg College
Mary Baldwin College
Patrick Henry College
Randolph College
Randolph-Macon College
Roanoke College
St. Paul's College
Southern Virginia University
Sweet Briar College
University of Mary Washington
University of Richmond

University of Virginia's College at
    Wise
Virginia Intermont College
Virginia Military Institute
Virginia Union University
Virginia University of Lynchburg
Virginia Wesleyan College
Washington and Lee University

Washington
Evergreen State College
Gonzaga University
Northwest University
Trinity Lutheran College
University of Puget Sound
Walla Walla University
Whitman College
Whitworth University

West Virginia
Alderson-Broaddus College
Bethany College
Bluefield State College
Concord University
Davis and Elkins College
Glenville State College
Ohio Valley University
Salem International University
University of Charleston
West Virginia State University
West Virginia University Institute of
    Technology
West Virginia Wesleyan College
Wheeling Jesuit University

Wisconsin
Alverno College
Beloit College
Carroll University
Carthage College
Concordia University Wisconsin
Edgewood College
Lakeland College
Lawrence University
Marian University
Mount Mary College
Northland College
St. Norbert College
Silver Lake College
University of Wisconsin
    Green Bay
    River Falls
    Superior
Viterbo University
Wisconsin Lutheran College

Two-year

Arkansas
Arkansas State University
    Newport
National Park Community College

California
Deep Springs College
Feather River College
Fresno City College
Marymount College

Colorado
Colorado Mountain College

Georgia
Andrew College
College of Coastal Georgia
Georgia Highlands College
Georgia Perimeter College
Waycross College
Young Harris College

Hawaii
Hawaii Tokai International College

Illinois
Lincoln College

Indiana
Ancilla College

Iowa
Kaplan University
    Cedar Rapids

Kansas
Donnelly College

Massachusetts
Dean College
Fisher College

Michigan
Montcalm Community College
Wayne County Community College

Minnesota
Itasca Community College

Missouri
Cottey College
Crowder College
Stevens Institute of Business & Arts

New Jersey
Gloucester County College

New York
SUNY
    College of Technology at Alfred
    College of Technology at Delhi
Villa Maria College of Buffalo

Pennsylvania
University of Pittsburgh
    Titusville

Puerto Rico
Colegio de las Ciencias Artes y
    Television

South Carolina
Clinton Junior College
Spartanburg Methodist College
University of South Carolina
    Union

Texas
Eastfield College
Everest College
    Fort Worth
Jacksonville College
Lamar State College at Orange
Lon Morris College
North Lake College

Vermont
Community College of Vermont
Landmark College

Virginia
Richard Bland College

Washington
Olympic College

Wisconsin
University of Wisconsin
    Baraboo/Sauk County
    Fox Valley
    Marathon County
    Marinette
    Richland
    Rock County
    Washington County

Upper-division colleges

Alabama
Athens State University
United States Sports Academy

California
Alliant International University
Antioch University
    Los Angeles
    Santa Barbara
California Institute of Integral Studies
John F. Kennedy University

Pacific Oaks College
Samuel Merritt University

Illinois
Governors State University
Resurrection University
Rush University

Kansas
University of Kansas Medical Center

Louisiana
Louisiana State University
    Health Sciences Center

Maryland
University of Maryland
    Baltimore

Michigan
Walsh College of Accountancy and
    Business Administration

Minnesota
Northwestern Health Sciences
    University

Missouri
Goldfarb School of Nursing at Barnes-
    Jewish College
Midwest University

Nevada
University of Southern Nevada

New Jersey
University of Medicine and Dentistry
    of New Jersey
        School of Health Related
            Professions

New York
SUNY
    Upstate Medical University

Tennessee
University of Tennessee
    Health Science Center

Texas
Texas A&M University
    Texarkana
Texas Tech University Health Sciences
    Center
University of Houston
    Clear Lake
University of Texas
    Health Science Center at Houston
    Health Science Center at San
        Antonio
    Medical Branch at Galveston
    Southwestern Medical Center at
        Dallas

Virginia
Catholic Distance University

Washington
Bastyr University

Agricultural and technical colleges

Four-year

Alabama Agricultural and Mechanical
    University, AL
Alcorn State University, MS
Art Institute of Fort Lauderdale, FL
Art Institute of Seattle, WA
Baker College
    of Auburn Hills, MI
    of Jackson, MI
    of Muskegon, MI
    of Owosso, MI
    of Port Huron, MI
Bergin University of Canine Studies,
    CA
Bluefield State College, WV

Briarcliffe College, NY
Carrington College
    Emeryville, CA
Central Pennsylvania College, PA
City College
    Fort Lauderdale, FL
Clayton State University, GA
Coleman University, CA
CollegeAmerica
    Fort Collins, CO
Collins College, AZ
Colorado Technical University, CO
Design Institute of San Diego, CA
DeVry College of New York, NY
ECPI College of Technology: Virginia
    Beach, VA
Everest College
    Springfield, MO
Ex'pression College for Digital Arts,
    CA
Florida Career College: Boynton
    Beach, FL
Florida Career College: Jacksonville,
    FL
Florida Career College: Lauderdale
    Lakes, FL
Florida Career College: Riverview, FL
Hamilton Technical College, IA
Herzing University, LA
Herzing University, AL
Herzing University, GA
International Academy of Design and
    Technology
        Chicago, IL
        Henderson, NV
        Sacramento, CA
International Academy of Design and
    Technology: Tampa, FL
ITT Technical Institute
    Boise, ID
    Chantilly, VA
    Duluth, GA
    Green Bay, WI
    Knoxville, TN
    Lake Mary, FL
    Mount Prospect, IL
    Nashville, TN
    Owings Mills, MD
    Portland, OR
    San Diego, CA
    Seattle, WA
    Spokane, WA
    Springfield, VA
    Tempe, AZ
    Tulsa, OK
LA College International, CA
Lewis-Clark State College, ID
Louisiana State University and
    Agricultural and Mechanical
    College, LA
Minnesota School of Business, MN
Minnesota School of Business:
    Plymouth, MN
Minnesota School of Business:
    Shakopee, MN
Mississippi State University, MS
Missouri Technical School, MO
Montana State University
    Billings, MT
Montana Tech of the University of
    Montana, MT
National American University
    Rapid City, SD
National University College: Arecibo,
    PR
National University College: Bayamon,
    PR
Neumont University, UT
New England Institute of Art, MA
New England Institute of Technology,
    RI
Peirce College, PA
Pennsylvania College of Technology,
    PA

Platt College
    Ontario, CA
    San Diego, CA
Rasmussen College
    Lake Elmo/Woodbury, MN
Remington College
    Tampa, FL
Spartan College of Aeronautics and
    Technology, OK
Stanbridge College, CA
Stevens-Henager College
    Logan, UT
SUNY
    College of Technology at
        Farmingdale, NY
University College of San Juan, PR
University of Arkansas
    Monticello, AR
University of Puerto Rico
    Aguadilla, PR
    Bayamon University College, PR
    Utuado, PR
Utah Valley University, UT
Wentworth Institute of Technology,
    MA
Westwood College
    Anaheim, CA
    Chicago Loop, IL
    Denver North, CO
    Denver South, CO
    DuPage, IL
    Northlake, GA
    O'Hare Airport, IL
    South Bay, CA
World College, VA

Two-year

Abraham Baldwin Agricultural
    College, GA
Academy of Court Reporting and
    Technology, OH
Aiken Technical College, SC
Albany Technical College, GA
Alexandria Technical College, MN
Altamaha Technical College, GA
Angley College, FL
Anthem College
    Aurora, CO
    Kansas City, MO
    Minneapolis, MN
Antonelli College
    Cincinnati, OH
    Jackson, MS
Arizona Automotive Institute, AZ
Arkansas State University
    Mountain Home, AR
Art Institute of New York City, NY
Asheville-Buncombe Technical
    Community College, NC
Asnuntuck Community College, CT
ATI Career Training Center
    Oakland Park, FL
ATI College of Health, FL
Atlanta Technical College, GA
Augusta Technical College, GA
Aviation Institute of Maintenance:
    Virginia Beach, VA
Bainbridge College, GA
Bates Technical College, WA
Baton Rouge School of Computers, LA
Bellingham Technical College, WA
Belmont Technical College, OH
Benjamin Franklin Institute of
    Technology, MA
Big Sandy Community and Technical
    College, KY
Blue Cliff College
    Metairie, LA
    Shreveport, LA
Bluegrass Community and Technical
    College, KY
Bolivar Technical College, MO
Bramson ORT College, NY
Bridgemont Community and Technical
    College, WV

Bryan College
   Sacramento, CA
   Topeka, KS
Cambria-Rowe Business College:
   Indiana, PA
Camelot College, LA
Capital Community College, CT
Carrington College
   Antioch, CA
   Citrus Heights, CA
   Pleasant Hill, CA
   Sacramento, CA
   San Jose, CA
   Stockton, CA
Carteret Community College, NC
Central Carolina Technical College, SC
Central Georgia Technical College, GA
Central Lakes College, MN
Central Maine Community College,
   ME
Central Ohio Technical College, OH
Central Texas College, TX
Centura College: Newport News, VA
Centura College: Richmond, VA
Century College, MN
Chattahoochee Technical College, GA
Chippewa Valley Technical College,
   WI
Cincinnati State Technical and
   Community College, OH
Cleveland Institute of Electronics, OH
Clover Park Technical College, WA
Coffeyville Community College, KS
Colegio de las Ciencias Artes y
   Television, PR
Coleman College: San Marcos, CA
College of Business and Technology:
   Flagler, FL
College of Business and Technology:
   Kendall, FL
College of Court Reporting, IN
College of Western Idaho, ID
Colorado School of Trades, CO
Colorado Technical University
   North Kansas City, MO
Columbus State Community College,
   OH
Columbus Technical College, GA
Concorde Career College
   Garden Grove, CA
   San Bernardino, CA
Cowley County Community College,
   KS
Coyne College, IL
Dakota County Technical College, MN
Daytona State College, FL
DeKalb Technical College, GA
Delaware Technical and Community
   College
   Stanton/Wilmington, DE
Delta College of Arts & Technology,
   LA
Denmark Technical College, SC
Dodge City Community College, KS
Dunwoody College of Technology, MN
Durham Technical Community College,
   NC
Eagle Gate College: Murray, UT
Eastern Maine Community College,
   ME
EDIC College, PR
Elizabethtown Community and
   Technical College, KY
ETI Technical College of Niles, OH
Everest College
   Arlington, TX
   Aurora, CO
   Dallas, TX
   Phoenix, AZ
   Portland, OR
Everest Institute: Cross Lanes, WV
Fayetteville Technical Community
   College, NC
Florence-Darlington Technical College,
   SC

Florida Career College: Hialeah, FL
Florida Career College: Miami, FL
Florida Career College: Pembroke
   Pines, FL
Florida Career College: West Palm
   Beach, FL
Fortis College: Cuyahoga, OH
Fortis College: Winter Park, FL
Fox Valley Technical College, WI
Fullerton College, CA
Gadsden State Community College, AL
Gallipolis Career College, OH
Gateway Community and Technical
   College, KY
GateWay Community College, AZ
Gateway Technical College, WI
Georgia Northwestern Technical
   College, GA
Grayson County College, TX
Greenville Technical College, SC
Gretna Career College, LA
Gupton Jones College of Funeral
   Service, GA
Hallmark College of Aeronautics, TX
Hallmark College of Technology, TX
Hazard Community and Technical
   College, KY
Heald College
   Concord, CA
   Fresno, CA
   Hayward, CA
   Honolulu, HI
   Portland, OR
   Rancho Cordova, CA
Hennepin Technical College, MN
Herzing University, MN
Hibbing Community College, MN
Hocking College, OH
Horry-Georgetown Technical College,
   SC
Huertas Junior College, PR
Indian Hills Community College, IA
Institute of Business & Medical
   Careers, CO
Institute of Design and Construction,
   NY
IntelliTec College, CO
IntelliTec College: Grand Junction, CO
International College of Broadcasting,
   OH
Iowa Western Community College, IA
Island Drafting and Technical Institute,
   NY
ITI Technical College, LA
ITT Technical Institute
   Arlington, TX
   Bensalem, PA
   Canton, MI
   Eden Prairie, MN
   Hilliard, OH
   Houston, TX
   Kansas City, MO
   Kennesaw, GA
   King of Prussia, PA
   Newburgh, IN
   San Antonio, TX
   Wilmington, MA
James A. Rhodes State College, OH
Jefferson College, MO
JNA Institute of Culinary Arts, PA
Johnson College, PA
Johnston Community College, NC
Kanawha Valley Community and
   Technical College, WV
Kaplan College: Dayton, OH
Kaplan College: Denver, CO
Kaplan College: Hammond, IN
Kaplan College: Merrillville, IN
Kaplan College: Palm Springs, CA
Kaplan College: Panorama City, CA
Kaplan College: Phoenix, AZ
Kaplan College: Sacramento, CA
Kaplan College: Salida, CA
Kaplan College: Vista, CA

Kennebec Valley Community College,
   ME
Key College, FL
Keystone Technical Institute, PA
Lake Area Technical Institute, SD
Lake Region State College, ND
Lake Superior College, MN
Lake Washington Technical College,
   WA
Lakes Region Community College, NH
Lakeshore Technical College, WI
Lamar Institute of Technology, TX
Lamar State College at Port Arthur, TX
Laurel Business Institute, PA
Laurel Technical Institute, PA
Le Cordon Bleu College of Culinary
   Arts
   Atlanta, GA
   Scottsdale, AZ
Linn State Technical College, MO
Los Angeles Trade and Technical
   College, CA
Luna Community College, NM
Madison Area Technical College, WI
Manchester Community College, NH
Manhattan Area Technical College, KS
Martin Community College, NC
McCann School of Business and
   Technology
   Dickson City, PA
   Pottsville, PA
   Sunbury, PA
McDowell Technical Community
   College, NC
Mesabi Range Community and
   Technical College, MN
Mesalands Community College, NM
Metropolitan Career Center Computer
   Technology Institute, PA
Metropolitan Community College, NE
Metropolitan Community College:
   Business & Technology, MO
Mid-Plains Community College Area,
   NE
Middle Georgia Technical College, GA
Midlands Technical College, SC
Miller-Motte College: Fayetteville, NC
Miller-Motte Technical College, SC
Miller-Motte Technical College: Cary,
   NC
Milwaukee Area Technical College, WI
Minneapolis Business College, MN
Minneapolis Community and Technical
   College, MN
Minnesota State College - Southeast
   Technical, MN
Minnesota State Community and
   Technical College, MN
Minnesota West Community and
   Technical College, MN
Missouri College, MO
Mitchell Technical Institute, SD
Moraine Park Technical College, WI
Morrison Institute of Technology, IL
MTI College, CA
Nashua Community College, NH
Nashville State Community College,
   TN
National College
   Dayton, OH
   Knoxville, TN
National Park Community College, AR
Naugatuck Valley Community College,
   CT
Navajo Technical College, NM
Nebraska College of Technical
   Agriculture, NE
New Mexico Junior College, NM
New River Community and Technical
   College, WV
NHTI-Concord's Community College,
   NH
North Central Kansas Technical
   College, KS
North Central State College, OH

North Dakota State College of Science,
   ND
Northeast Wisconsin Technical
   College, WI
Northeastern Technical College, SC
Northern Maine Community College,
   ME
Northland Community & Technical
   College, MN
Northwest Aviation College, WA
Northwest Kansas Technical College,
   KS
Northwest School of Wooden
   Boatbuilding, WA
Northwest Technical College, MN
Northwest Technical Institute, MN
Northwestern College, IL
Norwalk Community College, CT
Nossi College of Art, TN
Nunez Community College, LA
Ohio Technical College, OH
Oklahoma State University
   Institute of Technology:
      Okmulgee, OK
   Oklahoma City, OK
Orangeburg-Calhoun Technical
   College, SC
Orleans Technical Institute, PA
Ouachita Technical College, AR
Owensboro Community and Technical
   College, KY
Ozarks Technical Community College,
   MO
Pellissippi State Community College,
   TN
Piedmont Technical College, SC
Pima Community College, AZ
Pine Technical College, MN
Pinnacle Career Institute: Kansas City,
   MO
Pittsburgh Institute of Aeronautics, PA
Pittsburgh Institute of Mortuary
   Science, PA
Platt College
   Los Angeles, CA
PowerSport Institute, OH
Pratt Community College, KS
Pulaski Technical College, AR
Rainy River Community College, MN
Rasmussen College
   Aurora, IL
   Green Bay, WI
   Rockford, IL
Redstone College, CO
Remington College
   Baton Rouge, LA
   Cleveland, OH
   Colorado Springs, CO
   Dallas, TX
   Fort Worth, TX
   Houston, TX
   Little Rock, AR
   Memphis, TN
   Nashville, TN
   North Houston, TX
   Shreveport, LA
Renton Technical College, WA
Ridgewater College, MN
Riverland Community College, MN
Rochester Community and Technical
   College, MN
Salt Lake Community College, UT
San Jacinto College, TX
Sanford-Brown College
   Hazelwood, MO
Savannah Technical College, GA
Shelton State Community College, AL
Sisseton Wahpeton College, SD
Somerset Community College, KY
South Central College, MN
South Florida Community College, FL
South Texas College, TX
Southeast Arkansas College, AR
Southeast Kentucky Community and
   Technical College, KY

Southeastern Technical College, GA
Southern Arkansas University Tech, AR
Southern Crescent Technical College, GA
Southern Maine Community College, ME
Southern Union State Community College, AL
Southwest Georgia Technical College, GA
Southwest Wisconsin Technical College, WI
Spartanburg Community College, SC
Spencerian College: Lexington, KY
Springfield Technical Community College, MA
Stark State College of Technology, OH
Stenotype Institute: Orlando, FL
Stevens-Henager College
   Boise, ID
Sullivan College of Technology and Design, KY
SUNY
   College of Agriculture and Technology at Cobleskill, NY
   College of Agriculture and Technology at Morrisville, NY
   College of Technology at Alfred, NY
   College of Technology at Canton, NY
   College of Technology at Delhi, NY
Technical Career Institutes, NY
TESST College of Technology
   Beltsville, MD
Texas County Technical Institute, MO
Texas State Technical College
   Harlingen, TX
   Marshall, TX
   Waco, TX
   West Texas, TX
Tri-County Technical College, SC
Triangle Tech
   Bethlehem, PA
   Greensburg, PA
Trident Technical College, SC
Truckee Meadows Community College, NV
Tulsa Welding School, OK
United Tribes Technical College, ND
Universal Technical Institute, AZ
University of Hawaii
   Honolulu Community College, HI
University of Northwestern Ohio, OH
Vatterott College
   Berkeley, MO
   Des Moines, IA
   Joplin, MO
   Kansas City, MO
   O'Fallon, MO
   Oklahoma City, OK
   Quincy, IL
   Sunset Hills, MO
   Tulsa, OK
Vet Tech Institute, PA
Wake Technical Community College, NC
Walla Walla Community College, WA
Washington County Community College, ME
West Virginia Northern Community College, WV
Western Technical College, TX
Western Technical College, WI
Western Technical College: Diana Drive, TX
Westwood College
   Dallas, TX
   Houston South, TX
   Los Angeles, CA
Wichita Area Technical College, KS
Wiregrass Georgia Technical College, GA

Wisconsin Indianhead Technical College, WI
WyoTech: Blairsville, PA
WyoTech: Fremont, CA
WyoTech: Laramie, WY
WyoTech: Long Beach, CA
WyoTech: Sacramento, CA
York County Community College, ME
YTI Career Institute
   Altoona, PA
   Lancaster, PA

Arts/music colleges

Four-year

Academy of Art University, CA
American Academy of Art, IL
Art Academy of Cincinnati, OH
Art Center Design College, AZ
Art Institute of Atlanta, GA
Art Institute of Boston at Lesley University, MA
Art Institute of California: Hollywood, CA
Art Institute of California: Inland Empire, CA
Art Institute of California: Orange County, CA
Art Institute of California: Sacramento, CA
Art Institute of California: San Diego, CA
Art Institute of California: San Francisco, CA
Art Institute of Charlotte, NC
Art Institute of Colorado, CO
Art Institute of Dallas, TX
Art Institute of Fort Lauderdale, FL
Art Institute of Las Vegas, NV
Art Institute of Michigan, MI
Art Institute of Phoenix, AZ
Art Institute of Pittsburgh, PA
Art Institute of Portland, OR
Art Institute of Seattle, WA
Art Institute of Tucson, AZ
Art Institute of Washington, VA
Art Institutes International Minnesota, MN
Berklee College of Music, MA
Boston Conservatory, MA
Brooks Institute, CA
Burlington College, VT
California College of the Arts, CA
California Institute of the Arts, CA
Chester College of New England, NH
Cleveland Institute of Art, OH
Cleveland Institute of Music, OH
Cogswell Polytechnical College, CA
College for Creative Studies, MI
College of Visual Arts, MN
Collins College, AZ
Columbia College Chicago, IL
Columbus College of Art and Design, OH
Conservatory of Music of Puerto Rico, PR
Cooper Union for the Advancement of Science and Art, NY
Corcoran College of Art and Design, DC
Cornish College of the Arts, WA
Curtis Institute of Music, PA
DePauw University, IN
DigiPen Institute of Technology, WA
Eastman School of Music of the University of Rochester, NY
Escuela de Artes Plasticas de Puerto Rico, PR
Ex'pression College for Digital Arts, CA
Fashion Institute of Technology, NY
Five Towns College, NY
Full Sail University, FL

Harrington College of Design, IL
Illinois Institute of Art: Chicago, IL
Illinois Institute of Art: Schaumburg, IL
Institute of American Indian Arts, NM
International Academy of Design and Technology
   Chicago, IL
   Henderson, NV
   Nashville, TN
International Academy of Design and Technology: Tampa, FL
Johns Hopkins University: Peabody Conservatory of Music, MD
Juilliard School, NY
Kansas City Art Institute, MO
Laguna College of Art and Design, CA
Lawrence University, WI
Lyme Academy College of Fine Arts, CT
Maine College of Art, ME
Manhattan School of Music, NY
Mannes College The New School for Music, NY
Maryland Institute College of Art, MD
Massachusetts College of Art and Design, MA
Memphis College of Art, TN
Miami International University of Art and Design, FL
Milwaukee Institute of Art & Design, WI
Montserrat College of Art, MA
Moore College of Art and Design, PA
Mt. Sierra College, CA
New England Conservatory of Music, MA
New England Institute of Art, MA
New York School of Interior Design, NY
NewSchool of Architecture & Design, CA
Northwest College of Art, WA
O'More College of Design, TN
Oberlin College, OH
Oregon College of Art & Craft, OR
Otis College of Art and Design, CA
Pacific Northwest College of Art, OR
Paier College of Art, CT
Parsons The New School for Design, NY
Pennsylvania Academy of the Fine Arts, PA
Platt College
   San Diego, CA
Pratt Institute, NY
Rhode Island School of Design, RI
Ringling College of Art and Design, FL
Rocky Mountain College of Art & Design, CO
San Francisco Art Institute, CA
San Francisco Conservatory of Music, CA
Savannah College of Art and Design, GA
School of the Art Institute of Chicago, IL
School of the Museum of Fine Arts, MA
School of Visual Arts, NY
Southern California Institute of Architecture, CA
University of North Carolina School of the Arts, NC
University of the Arts, PA
VanderCook College of Music, IL
Visible School - Music and Worship Arts College, TN
Watkins College of Art, Design & Film, TN
Westwood College
   Northlake, GA

Two-year

American Academy of Dramatic Arts, NY
American Academy of Dramatic Arts: West, CA
Antonelli College
   Cincinnati, OH
Art Institute of California: Los Angeles, CA
Art Institute of Cincinnati, OH
Art Institute of Ohio: Cincinnati, OH
Delaware College of Art and Design, DE
Delta College of Arts & Technology, LA
Douglas Education Center, PA
Fashion Institute of Design and Merchandising
   Los Angeles, CA
   San Diego, CA
   San Francisco, CA
ITT Technical Institute
   King of Prussia, PA
Nossi College of Art, TN
Oakbridge Academy of Arts, PA
Platt College
   Los Angeles, CA
Sessions College for Professional Design, AZ
Villa Maria College of Buffalo, NY

Bible colleges

Four-year

Allegheny Wesleyan College, OH
American Baptist College, TN
Apex School of Theology, NC
Appalachian Bible College, WV
Arlington Baptist College, TX
Atlanta Christian College, GA
Baptist Bible College of Pennsylvania, PA
Baptist College of Florida, FL
Baptist University of the Americas, TX
Barclay College, KS
Bethany University, CA
Beulah Heights University, GA
Biola University, CA
Bob Jones University, SC
Boston Baptist College, MA
California Christian College, CA
Calvary Bible College and Theological Seminary, MO
Carver Bible College, GA
Columbia International University, SC
Criswell College, TX
Davis College, NY
Ecclesia College, AR
Faith Baptist Bible College and Theological Seminary, IA
Family of Faith College, OK
Florida Christian College, FL
Free Will Baptist Bible College, TN
Global University, MO
God's Bible School and College, OH
Grace University, NE
Heritage Christian University, AL
Huntsville Bible College, AL
International Baptist College, AZ
Johnson Bible College, TN
Kentucky Christian University, KY
Kentucky Mountain Bible College, KY
The King's University, CA
Laurel University, NC
Life Pacific College, CA
Lincoln Christian University, IL
Maranatha Baptist Bible College, WI
Mid-Atlantic Christian University, NC
Mid-Continent University, KY
Moody Bible Institute, IL
Nazarene Bible College, CO
Nebraska Christian College, NE

New Orleans Baptist Theological
    Seminary: Leavell College, LA
North Central University, MN
Philadelphia Biblical University, PA
Piedmont Baptist College and Graduate
    School, NC
School of Urban Missions: Oakland,
    CA
Shasta Bible College and Graduate
    School, CA
Southeastern Baptist College, MS
Southeastern Baptist Theological
    Seminary, NC
Southeastern Bible College, AL
Southern California Seminary, CA
Southwestern Assemblies of God
    University, TX
Southwestern Baptist Theological
    Seminary, TX
Southwestern Christian College, TX
Toccoa Falls College, GA
Tri-State Bible College, OH
Trinity Baptist College, FL
Trinity College of Florida, FL
Trinity Lutheran College, WA
Universidad FLET, FL
Universidad Pentecostal Mizpa, PR
Visible School - Music and Worship
    Arts College, TN
Washington Bible College, MD
William Jessup University, CA
World Mission University, CA
Zion Bible College, MA

Two-year

Epic Bible College, CA

Business colleges

Four-year

American University of Puerto Rico,
    PR
Babson College, MA
Baker College
    of Allen Park, MI
    of Auburn Hills, MI
    of Cadillac, MI
    of Jackson, MI
    of Muskegon, MI
    of Owosso, MI
    of Port Huron, MI
Baltimore International College, MD
Bellevue University, NE
Bentley University, MA
Berkeley College, NY
Berkeley College, NJ
Berkeley College of New York City,
    NY
Briarcliffe College, NY
Brown College: Mendota Heights, MN
Bryant University, RI
California College San Diego, CA
California State University
    Stanislaus, CA
Capitol College, MD
Chadron State College, NE
City College
    Fort Lauderdale, FL
City University of New York
    Baruch College, NY
Clarion University of Pennsylvania, PA
Cleary University, MI
Colorado Heights University, CO
Columbia Southern University, AL
Daniel Webster College, NH
Davenport University, MI
DeVry College of New York, NY
Dowling College, NY
Everest College
    Ontario Metro, CA
Everest University
    Brandon, FL

Jacksonville, FL
    Largo, FL
    Melbourne, FL
    North Orlando, FL
    Orange Park, FL
    Pompano Beach, FL
    South Orlando, FL
    Tampa, FL
Fashion Institute of Technology, NY
Franklin University, OH
Globe Institute of Technology, NY
Globe University, MN
Goldey-Beacom College, DE
Herzing University, AL
Herzing University, GA
Herzing University, WI
Hesser College, NH
Hodges University, FL
Humphreys College, CA
Husson University, ME
Huston-Tillotson University, TX
Indiana Institute of Technology, IN
International Business College, IN
Iona College, NY
ITT Technical Institute
    Owings Mills, MD
    Tulsa, OK
Jones College, FL
King's College, PA
LA College International, CA
Lincoln University, CA
Loyola University Maryland, MD
Mayville State University, ND
Menlo College, CA
Metropolitan College of New York,
    NY
Michigan Jewish Institute, MI
Millsaps College, MS
Minnesota School of Business, MN
Minnesota School of Business: Blaine,
    MN
Minnesota School of Business:
    Plymouth, MN
Minnesota School of Business:
    Shakopee, MN
Monroe College, NY
Morrison University, NV
Mount Ida College, MA
Mt. Sierra College, CA
National American University
    Rapid City, SD
National College
    Roanoke Valley, VA
Newbury College, MA
Nichols College, MA
Northwest Florida State College, FL
Northwestern Polytechnic University,
    CA
Northwood University
    Florida, FL
    Michigan, MI
    Texas, TX
Peirce College, PA
Post University, CT
Potomac College, VA
Potomac College, DC
Presentation College, SD
Reinhardt University, GA
Restaurant School at Walnut Hill
    College, PA
Rockhurst University, MO
Sage College of Albany, NY
Savannah State University, GA
Silver Lake College, WI
Southern California Institute of
    Technology, CA
Stevens-Henager College
    Logan, UT
SUNY
    College at Old Westbury, NY
    Institute of Technology at Utica/
    Rome, NY
Thomas College, ME
University of Management and
    Technology, VA

University of Phoenix
    Indianapolis, IN
    West Michigan, MI
University of the West, CA
Walsh College of Accountancy and
    Business Administration, MI
Webber International University, FL
Western International University, AZ

Two-year

AIB College of Business, IA
Bidwell Training Center, PA
Brown Mackie College
    Fort Wayne, IN
    Miami, FL
    North Kentucky, KY
Bryant & Stratton College
    Albany, NY
    Buffalo, NY
    Rochester, NY
    Virginia Beach, VA
Business Informatics Center, NY
Cambria-Rowe Business College:
    Indiana, PA
Centura College: Chesapeake, VA
Centura College: Newport News, VA
City College
    Gainesville, FL
    Miami, FL
College of Court Reporting, IN
Columbia Centro Universitario: Yauco,
    PR
Concorde Career College
    Kansas City, MO
Daymar College
    Owensboro, KY
Douglas Education Center, PA
Eagle Gate College: Murray, UT
Erie Business Center, PA
Erie Business Center South, PA
Everest College
    Arlington, TX
    Arlington, VA
    Colorado Springs, CO
    Dallas, TX
    Las Vegas, NV
    Portland, OR
    Salt Lake City, UT
    Vancouver, WA
Everest Institute: Pittsburgh, PA
Fashion Careers College, CA
Fashion Institute of Design and
    Merchandising
    Los Angeles, CA
    San Diego, CA
    San Francisco, CA
Fisher College, MA
Florida Career College: Miami, FL
Florida Career College: Pembroke
    Pines, FL
Forrest Junior College, SC
Fortis Institute: Orange Park, FL
Gallipolis Career College, OH
Heald College
    Concord, CA
    Fresno, CA
    Portland, OR
    Salinas, CA
    San Francisco, CA
    San Jose, CA
Herzing University, FL
Humacao Community College, PR
ICPR Junior College, PR
ITT Technical Institute
    Canton, MI
    Hilliard, OH
    Kansas City, MO
    Kennesaw, GA
    Newburgh, IN
Kaplan College: Hammond, IN
Kaplan College: Sacramento, CA
Kaplan College: San Diego, CA
Kaplan University
    Hagerstown, MD
    South Portland, ME

Keiser Career College: Greenacres, FL
Keiser University, FL
Key College, FL
Laurel Technical Institute, PA
Lincoln College of New England:
    Suffield, CT
Long Island Business Institute, NY
McCann School of Business and
    Technology
    Dickson City, PA
Metro Business College
    Rolla, MO
Miller-Motte Technical College:
    Clarksville, TN
Minneapolis Business College, MN
MTI College, CA
National College
    Danville, KY
    Dayton, OH
    Florence, KY
    Harrisonburg, VA
    Knoxville, TN
    Lexington, KY
New England College of Business and
    Finance, MA
Professional Business College, NY
Remington College
    Memphis, TN
Sanford-Brown College, MO
South Coast College, CA
Stenotype Institute: Jacksonville, FL
Stevens Institute of Business & Arts,
    MO
Taylor Business Institute, IL
University of Northwestern Ohio, OH
Utica School of Commerce, NY
Virginia College Gulf Coast, MS

Culinary schools

Four-year

Art Institute of Atlanta, GA
Art Institute of California: Hollywood,
    CA
Art Institute of California: Inland
    Empire, CA
Art Institute of California: Orange
    County, CA
Art Institute of California: Sacramento,
    CA
Art Institute of California: San
    Francisco, CA
Art Institute of Colorado, CO
Art Institute of Las Vegas, NV
Art Institute of Phoenix, AZ
Art Institute of Pittsburgh, PA
Art Institute of Tucson, AZ
Art Institute of Washington, VA
Art Institutes International Minnesota,
    MN
Baltimore International College, MD
Culinary Institute of America, NY
Kendall College, IL
Restaurant School at Walnut Hill
    College, PA

Two-year

Art Institute of New York City, NY
Art Institute of Ohio: Cincinnati, OH
Atlantic Cape Community College, NJ
California Culinary Academy, CA
Culinary Institute Alain & Marie
    LeNotre, TX
Institute of Technology: Clovis, CA
L'Ecole Culinaire, MO
Le Cordon Bleu College of Culinary
    Arts
    Austin, TX
    Chicago, IL
    Los Angeles, CA
    Miami, FL
    Minneapolis-St. Paul, MN

Scottsdale, AZ
Lincoln College of New England:
Suffield, CT
Mitchell Technical Institute, SD
New England Culinary Institute, VT
Platt College
Moore, OK
Tulsa, OK
Southwestern Oregon Community
College, OR
Walters State Community College, TN

Engineering colleges

Four-year

Capitol College, MD
Clemson University, SC
Cogswell Polytechnical College, CA
Colorado School of Mines, CO
Cooper Union for the Advancement of
Science and Art, NY
DigiPen Institute of Technology, WA
Franklin W. Olin College of
Engineering, MA
Harvey Mudd College, CA
Illinois Institute of Technology, IL
Indiana Institute of Technology, IN
Inter American University of Puerto
Rico
Bayamon Campus, PR
Kettering University, MI
Lafayette College, PA
Lake Superior State University, MI
Manhattan College, NY
Missouri Technical School, MO
Montana Tech of the University of
Montana, MT
Neumont University, UT
New Mexico Institute of Mining and
Technology, NM
Northwestern Polytechnic University,
CA
Rose-Hulman Institute of Technology,
IN
Southern California Institute of
Technology, CA
Southern Polytechnic State University,
GA
Stevens Institute of Technology, NJ
Trine University, IN
Union College, NY
Universidad Politecnica de Puerto
Rico, PR
University of Management and
Technology, VA
University of Pittsburgh
Johnstown, PA
University of Puerto Rico
Mayaguez, PR
Vaughn College of Aeronautics and
Technology, NY
Wentworth Institute of Technology,
MA
West Virginia University Institute of
Technology, WV

Maritime colleges

Four-year

California Maritime Academy, CA
Maine Maritime Academy, ME
Massachusetts Maritime Academy, MA
SUNY
Maritime College, NY
United States Merchant Marine
Academy, NY

Two-year

Northwest School of Wooden
Boatbuilding, WA
Northwestern Michigan College, MI

Military colleges

Four-year

The Citadel, SC
North Georgia College & State
University, GA
Norwich University, VT
United States Merchant Marine
Academy, NY
United States Naval Academy, MD
Virginia Military Institute, VA

Two-year

Georgia Military College, GA
Marion Military Institute, AL
New Mexico Military Institute, NM
Valley Forge Military Academy and
College, PA
Wentworth Military Junior College,
MO

Nursing and health science colleges

Four-year

Albany College of Pharmacy and
Health Sciences, NY
Aquinas College, TN
Baker College
of Allen Park, MI
of Cadillac, MI
Bastyr University, WA
Bellin College, WI
Blessing-Rieman College of Nursing,
IL
Bloomfield College, NJ
BryanLGH College of Health Sciences,
NE
Bryant & Stratton College
Parma, OH
Cabarrus College of Health Sciences,
NC
California College San Diego, CA
Chamberlain College of Nursing
Addison, IL
Columbus, OH
Jacksonville, FL
Phoenix, AZ
Charles Drew University of Medicine
and Science, CA
Coe College, IA
College of New Rochelle, NY
CollegeAmerica
Fort Collins, CO
Cox College, MO
Curry College, MA
D'Youville College, NY
Denver School of Nursing, CO
ECPI College of Technology: Virginia
Beach, VA
Globe University, MN
Goldfarb School of Nursing at Barnes-
Jewish College, MO
Gwynedd-Mercy College, PA
Husson University, ME
Independence University, UT
Ithaca College, NY
Jefferson College of Health Sciences,
VA
Kettering College of Medical Arts, OH
King College, TN
Loma Linda University, CA
Louisiana State University
Health Sciences Center, LA

Massachusetts College of Pharmacy
and Health Sciences, MA
Misericordia University, PA
Monroe College, NY
Mount Marty College, SD
Mountain State University, WV
National University College: Ponce, PR
New York Institute of Technology, NY
Northwestern Health Sciences
University, MN
Oregon Health & Science University,
OR
Presentation College, SD
Regis College, MA
Research College of Nursing, MO
Resurrection University, IL
Rivier College, NH
Rush University, IL
Russell Sage College, NY
Saint Anselm College, NH
St. Catharine College, KY
St. Catherine University, MN
Samuel Merritt University, CA
Simmons College, MA
Springfield College, MA
State College of Florida, Manatee-
Sarasota, FL
Stevens-Henager College
Orem, UT
SUNY
Upstate Medical University, NY
Trinity College of Nursing and Health
Sciences, IL
University of Findlay, OH
University of Kansas Medical Center,
KS
University of Maryland
Baltimore, MD
University of Medicine and Dentistry
of New Jersey
School of Health Related
Professions, NJ
School of Nursing, NJ
University of Minnesota
Rochester, MN
University of Phoenix
Central Florida, FL
North Florida, FL
West Florida, FL
University of Tennessee
Health Science Center, TN
University of Texas
Health Science Center at Houston,
TX
Health Science Center at San
Antonio, TX
Medical Branch at Galveston, TX
Southwestern Medical Center at
Dallas, TX
University of the Sciences in
Philadelphia, PA
West Coast University, CA
Winston-Salem State University, NC

Two-year

ATI College of Health, FL
Bidwell Training Center, PA
Boulder College of Massage Therapy,
CO
Brown Mackie College
North Kentucky, KY
Bryman School, AZ
Camelot College, LA
Careers Unlimited, UT
Carrington College
Citrus Heights, CA
Pleasant Hill, CA
Reno, NV
Sacramento, CA
Centura College: Chesapeake, VA
City College
Gainesville, FL
Miami, FL
Colorado Technical University
North Kansas City, MO

Columbia Centro Universitario: Yauco,
PR
Concorde Career College
Aurora, CO
Garden Grove, CA
Kansas City, MO
North Hollywood, CA
Dakota College at Bottineau, ND
Eastern International College, NJ
EDIC College, PR
Everest College
Atlanta, GA
Las Vegas, NV
Florida College of Natural Health
Bradenton, FL
Florida Keys Community College, FL
Fortis College: Cuyahoga, OH
Fortis Institute: Orange Park, FL
Fremont College: Cerritos, CA
Goodwin College, CT
Harrison College
Indianapolis Northwest, IN
Herzing University, FL
Hondros College, OH
Kaplan College: Palm Springs, CA
Kaplan College: Salida, CA
Kaplan College: San Diego, CA
Keiser Career College: Greenacres, FL
Keiser University, FL
Keystone Technical Institute, PA
Lebanon College, NH
Miller-Motte Technical College:
Clarksville, TN
Miller-Motte Technical College:
Conway, SC
Ohio College of Massotherapy, OH
Pacific College of Oriental Medicine:
San Diego, CA
Phillips Beth Israel School of Nursing,
NY
Platt College
Moore, OK
Tulsa, OK
Ponce Paramedical College, PR
Remington College
North Houston, TX
St. Elizabeth College of Nursing, NY
St. Luke's College, IA
Sanford-Brown College, MO
Houston, TX
Sanford-Brown Institute
Jacksonville, FL
Monroeville, PA
Southeast Missouri Hospital College of
Nursing and Health Sciences, MO
Swedish Institute, NY
Texas County Technical Institute, MO
University of Rochester School of
Nursing, NY
Vatterott College
Des Moines, IA
Vet Tech Institute, PA
Virginia College Gulf Coast, MS
Wallace State Community College at
Hanceville, AL
West Virginia Junior College:
Bridgeport, WV
WyoTech: Long Beach, CA

Schools of mortuary science

Two-year

Commonwealth Institute of Funeral
Service, TX
Mid-America College of Funeral
Service, IN

Seminary/rabbinical colleges

Four-year

Baptist Bible College of Pennsylvania, PA
Beis Medrash Heichal Dovid, NY
Beth Hamedrash Shaarei Yosher Institute, NY
Beth Hatalmud Rabbinical College, NY
Calvary Bible College and Theological Seminary, MO
Central Yeshiva Tomchei Tmimim-Lubavitch, NY
Criswell College, TX
Divine Word College, IA
Earlham College, IN
Erskine College, SC
Faith Baptist Bible College and Theological Seminary, IA
Faith Evangelical Seminary, WA
George Fox University, OR
Global University, MO
Hebrew Theological College, IL
Hellenic College/Holy Cross, MA
Holy Apostles College and Seminary, CT
International Baptist College, AZ
Jewish Theological Seminary of America, NY
Kehilath Yakov Rabbinical Seminary, NY
The King's University, CA
Luther Rice University, GA
Machzikei Hadath Rabbinical College, NY
The Master's College, CA
Mesivta Torah Vodaath Seminary, NY
Midwest University, MO
Mirrer Yeshiva Central Institute, NY
Moody Bible Institute, IL
Mount Angel Seminary, OR
New Orleans Baptist Theological Seminary: Leavell College, LA
Ohr Somayach Tanenbaum Education Center, NY
Piedmont Baptist College and Graduate School, NC
Rabbinical Academy Mesivta Rabbi Chaim Berlin, NY
Rabbinical College Beth Shraga, NY
Rabbinical College Bobover Yeshiva B'nei Zion, NY
Rabbinical College Ch'san Sofer of New York, NY
Rabbinical College of America, NJ
Rabbinical College of Long Island, NY
Rabbinical College of Ohr Shimon Yisroel, NY
Rabbinical Seminary of America, NY
Sacred Heart Major Seminary, MI
St. Charles Borrómeo Seminary - Overbrook, PA
St. Joseph Seminary College, LA
Shor Yoshuv Rabbinical College, NY
Southeastern Baptist Theological Seminary, NC
Southern California Seminary, CA
Southwestern Baptist Theological Seminary, TX
Talmudical Institute of Upstate New York, NY
Talmudical Seminary Oholei Torah, NY
Telshe Yeshiva-Chicago, IL
Torah Temimah Talmudical Seminary, NY
U.T.A. Mesivta-Kiryas Jocl, NY
United Talmudical Seminary, NY
University of Dubuque, IA
Virginia University of Lynchburg, VA
Washington Bible College, MD
World Mission University, CA

Yeshiva and Kolel Bais Medrash Elyon, NY
Yeshiva and Kollel Harbotzas Torah, NY
Yeshiva D'Monsey Rabbinical College, NY
Yeshiva Derech Chaim, NY
Yeshiva Gedolah Imrei Yosef D'Spinka, NY
Yeshiva Gedolah Zichron Moshe, NY
Yeshiva Karlin Stolin, NY
Yeshiva of Nitra, NY
Yeshiva of the Telshe Alumni, NY
Yeshiva Shaar Hatorah, NY
Yeshiva Shaarei Torah of Rockland, NY
Yeshivas Novominsk, NY
Yeshivat Mikdash Melech, NY
Yeshivath Viznitz, NY

Two-year

Salvation Army College for Officer Training at Crestmont, CA
Shepherds Theological Seminary, NC

Teacher's colleges

Four-year

Arlington Baptist College, TX
Athens State University, AL
Augusta State University, GA
Austin College, TX
Baker University, KS
Baptist College of Florida, FL
Black Hills State University, SD
Bluefield College, VA
Bridgewater State University, MA
California State University Monterey Bay, CA
Cambridge College, MA
Canisius College, NY
Clarion University of Pennsylvania, PA
College of St. Joseph in Vermont, VT
College of Saint Rose, NY
Concordia University, OR
Concordia University Chicago, IL
Eastern Illinois University, IL
Fitchburg State University, MA
Florida Christian College, FL
Fort Valley State University, GA
Framingham State University, MA
Free Will Baptist Bible College, TN
Frostburg State University, MD
Glenville State College, WV
Great Basin College, NV
Howard Payne University, TX
Jones College, FL
Kendall College, IL
Lander University, SC
Lesley University, MA
Lyndon State College, VT
Manhattanville College, NY
Mayville State University, ND
National-Louis University, IL
New England College, NH
Northwestern Oklahoma State University, OK
Oglala Lakota College, SD
Pacific Oaks College, CA
Peru State College, NE
Piedmont College, GA
Plymouth State University, NH
Rabbinical College of Long Island, NY
Reinhardt University, GA
St. Joseph's College, NY
Southeastern Oklahoma State University, OK
Southeastern University, FL
SUNY
   College at Buffalo, NY
   College at Cortland, NY
   College at Plattsburgh, NY

College at Potsdam, NY
Tennessee Wesleyan College, TN
Trinity Baptist College, FL
Union College, KY
University of Hawaii West Oahu, HI
University of Maine Farmington, ME
University of Montana: Western, MT
University of the Southwest, NM
Valley City State University, ND
VanderCook College of Music, IL
Virginia Intermont College, VA
Wayne State College, NE
West Virginia State University, WV
Western Oregon University, OR
Westfield State University, MA
Wheelock College, MA
Worcester State University, MA
York College, NE

Two-year

Gordon College, GA

Colleges for men

Four-year

Beis Medrash Heichal Dovid, NY
Beth Hamedrash Shaarei Yosher Institute, NY
Beth Hatalmud Rabbinical College, NY
Central Yeshiva Tomchei Tmimim-Lubavitch, NY
Divine Word College, IA
Hampden-Sydney College, VA
Kehilath Yakov Rabbinical Seminary, NY
Machzikei Hadath Rabbinical College, NY
Mesivta Torah Vodaath Seminary, NY
Mirrer Yeshiva Central Institute, NY
Morehouse College, GA
Mount Angel Seminary, OR
Ohr Somayach Tanenbaum Education Center, NY
Rabbinical Academy Mesivta Rabbi Chaim Berlin, NY
Rabbinical College Beth Shraga, NY
Rabbinical College Bobover Yeshiva B'nei Zion, NY
Rabbinical College Ch'san Sofer of New York, NY
Rabbinical College of America, NJ
Rabbinical College of Long Island, NY
Rabbinical College of Ohr Shimon Yisroel, NY
Rabbinical Seminary of America, NY
St. Charles Borromeo Seminary - Overbrook, PA
St. John's University, MN
St. Joseph Seminary College, LA
Shor Yoshuv Rabbinical College, NY
Talmudical Institute of Upstate New York, NY
Talmudical Seminary Oholei Torah, NY
Telshe Yeshiva-Chicago, IL
Torah Temimah Talmudical Seminary, NY
U.T.A. Mesivta-Kiryas Jocl, NY
United Talmudical Seminary, NY
Wabash College, IN
Yeshiva and Kolel Bais Medrash Elyon, NY
Yeshiva and Kollel Harbotzas Torah, NY
Yeshiva D'Monsey Rabbinical College, NY
Yeshiva Derech Chaim, NY
Yeshiva Gedolah Imrei Yosef D'Spinka, NY
Yeshiva Gedolah Zichron Moshe, NY

Yeshiva Karlin Stolin, NY
Yeshiva of Nitra, NY
Yeshiva of the Telshe Alumni, NY
Yeshiva Shaar Hatorah, NY
Yeshiva Shaarei Torah of Rockland, NY
Yeshivas Novominsk, NY
Yeshivat Mikdash Melech, NY
Yeshivath Viznitz, NY

Two-year

Deep Springs College, CA

Colleges for women

Four-year

Agnes Scott College, GA
Alverno College, WI
Barnard College, NY
Bay Path College, MA
Bennett College for Women, NC
Brenau University, GA
Bryn Mawr College, PA
Cedar Crest College, PA
Chatham University, PA
College of New Rochelle, NY
College of Notre Dame of Maryland, MD
College of St. Benedict, MN
College of St. Elizabeth, NJ
College of Saint Mary, NE
Columbia College, SC
Converse College, SC
Georgian Court University, NJ
Hollins University, VA
Judson College, AL
Lexington College, IL
Mary Baldwin College, VA
Meredith College, NC
Midway College, KY
Mills College, CA
Moore College of Art and Design, PA
Mount Holyoke College, MA
Mount Mary College, WI
Mount St. Mary's College, CA
Peace College, NC
Pine Manor College, MA
Russell Sage College, NY
St. Catherine University, MN
Saint Joseph College, CT
Saint Mary's College, IN
St. Mary-of-the-Woods College, IN
Salem College, NC
Scripps College, CA
Simmons College, MA
Smith College, MA
Spelman College, GA
Stephens College, MO
Sweet Briar College, VA
Ursuline College, OH
Wellesley College, MA
Wesleyan College, GA
Wilson College, PA

Two-year

Cottey College, MO

Affiliated with a religion

African Methodist Episcopal Church

Four-year

Allen University, SC
Edward Waters College, FL
Wilberforce University, OH

African Methodist Episcopal Zion Church

Four-year

Livingstone College, NC

American Baptist Churches in the USA

Four-year

Alderson-Broaddus College, WV
Arkansas Baptist College, AR
Bacone College, OK
Benedict College, SC
Eastern University, PA
Florida Memorial University, FL
Franklin College, IN
Judson University, IL
Keuka College, NY
Linfield College, OR
Ottawa University, KS
University of Sioux Falls, SD

Assemblies of God

Four-year

Bethany University, CA
Evangel University, MO
Global University, MO
North Central University, MN
Northwest University, WA
School of Urban Missions: Oakland, CA
Southeastern University, FL
Southwestern Assemblies of God University, TX
Valley Forge Christian College, PA
Vanguard University of Southern California, CA
Zion Bible College, MA

Baptist faith

Four-year

American Baptist College, TN
Arizona Christian University, AZ
Arlington Baptist College, TX
Baptist Bible College of Pennsylvania, PA
Baptist University of the Americas, TX
Baylor University, TX
Bluefield College, VA
Boston Baptist College, MA
Campbellsville University, KY
Cedarville University, OH
Corban College, OR
Dallas Baptist University, TX
East Texas Baptist University, TX
Georgetown College, KY
Hardin-Simmons University, TX
Houston Baptist University, TX
Howard Payne University, TX
International Baptist College, AZ
Judson College, AL
Liberty University, VA
Maranatha Baptist Bible College, WI
Mars Hill College, NC
Mercer University, GA
Missouri Baptist University, MO
Morris College, SC
Piedmont Baptist College and Graduate School, NC
Selma University, AL
Shasta Bible College and Graduate School, CA
Shaw University, NC
Southeastern Baptist College, MS
University of Mary Hardin-Baylor, TX
University of Mobile, AL
University of the Cumberlands, KY
Virginia Intermont College, VA
Virginia Union University, VA
William Carey University, MS
Wingate University, NC

Two-year

Jacksonville College, TX

Baptist General Conference

Four-year

Bethel University, MN
Oakland City University, IN

Brethren Church

Four-year

Ashland University, OH

Christian and Missionary Alliance

Four-year

Crown College, MN
Nyack College, NY
Simpson University, CA
Toccoa Falls College, GA

Christian Church

Four-year

Atlanta Christian College, GA
Bethesda Christian University, CA
Johnson Bible College, TN
Visible School - Music and Worship Arts College, TN

Christian Church (Disciples of Christ)

Four-year

Barton College, NC
Bethany College, WV
Chapman University, CA
Columbia College, MO
Culver-Stockton College, MO
Eureka College, IL
Hiram College, OH
Lynchburg College, VA
Midway College, KY
Northwest Christian University, OR
Texas Christian University, TX
Transylvania University, KY
William Woods University, MO

Christian Methodist Episcopal Church

Four-year

Lane College, TN
Miles College, AL
Texas College, TX

Christian Reformed Church

Four-year

Calvin College, MI
Kuyper College, MI

Church of Christ

Four-year

Abilene Christian University, TX
Cincinnati Christian University, OH
Faulkner University, AL
Florida Christian College, FL
Freed-Hardeman University, TN
Harding University, AR
Heritage Christian University, AL
Kentucky Christian University, KY
Lincoln Christian University, IL
Lipscomb University, TN
Lubbock Christian University, TX
Mid-Atlantic Christian University, NC
Milligan College, TN
Nebraska Christian College, NE
Ohio Valley University, WV
Oklahoma Christian University, OK
Pepperdine University, CA
Rochester College, MI
Southwestern Christian College, TX
York College, NE

Two-year

Crowley's Ridge College, AR

Church of God

Four-year

Lee University, TN
University of Findlay, OH
Warner Pacific College, OR
Warner University, FL

Church of Jesus Christ of Latter-day Saints

Four-year

Brigham Young University, UT
Brigham Young University-Hawaii, HI
Brigham Young University-Idaho, ID
Southern Virginia University, VA

Church of the Brethren

Four-year

Bridgewater College, VA
Elizabethtown College, PA
Manchester College, IN
McPherson College, KS

Church of the Nazarene

Four-year

Eastern Nazarene College, MA
MidAmerica Nazarene University, KS
Mount Vernon Nazarene University, OH
Nazarene Bible College, CO
Northwest Nazarene University, ID
Olivet Nazarene University, IL
Point Loma Nazarene University, CA
Southern Nazarene University, OK
Trevecca Nazarene University, TN

Cumberland Presbyterian Church

Four-year

Bethel University, TN

Episcopal Church

Four-year

Bard College, NY
St. Augustine College, IL
St. Augustine's College, NC
St. Paul's College, VA
University of the South, TN
Voorhees College, SC

Evangelical Covenant Church of America

Four-year

North Park University, IL

Evangelical Free Church of America

Four-year

Trinity International University, IL

Evangelical Lutheran Church in America

Four-year

Augsburg College, MN
Augustana College, IL
Augustana College, SD
Bethany College, KS
California Lutheran University, CA
Capital University, OH
Carthage College, WI
Concordia College: Moorhead, MN
Finlandia University, MI
Gettysburg College, PA
Grand View University, IA
Gustavus Adolphus College, MN
Lenoir-Rhyne University, NC
Luther College, IA
Muhlenberg College, PA
Newberry College, SC
Pacific Lutheran University, WA
Roanoke College, VA

St. Olaf College, MN
Susquehanna University, PA
Texas Lutheran University, TX
Thiel College, PA
Waldorf College, IA
Wartburg College, IA
Wittenberg University, OH

Evangelical Lutheran Synod

Four-year

Bethany Lutheran College, MN

Free Methodist Church of North America

Four-year

Central Christian College of Kansas, KS
Greenville College, IL
Roberts Wesleyan College, NY
Seattle Pacific University, WA
Spring Arbor University, MI

Free Will Baptists

Four-year

California Christian College, CA
Free Will Baptist Bible College, TN
Mount Olive College, NC

General Association of Regular Baptist Churches

Four-year

Faith Baptist Bible College and Theological Seminary, IA

interdenominational tradition

Four-year

Azusa Pacific University, CA
Belmont University, TN
Beulah Heights University, GA
Biola University, CA
Bryan College, TN
College of the Ozarks, MO
Cornerstone University, MI
Ecclesia College, AR
God's Bible School and College, OH
Grace University, NE
John Brown University, AR
Laurel University, NC
Messiah College, PA
Moody Bible Institute, IL
Patten University, CA
Regent University, VA
Taylor University, IN
Trinity College of Florida, FL
Williamson Christian College, TN

Jewish faith

Four-year

American Jewish University, CA
Beis Medrash Heichal Dovid, NY
Beth Hamedrash Shaarei Yosher Institute, NY
Beth Hatalmud Rabbinical College, NY
Central Yeshiva Tomchei Tmimim-Lubavitch, NY
Gratz College, PA
Hebrew Theological College, IL
Jewish Theological Seminary of America, NY
Kehilath Yakov Rabbinical Seminary, NY
Machzikei Hadath Rabbinical College, NY
Mesivta Torah Vodaath Seminary, NY
Michigan Jewish Institute, MI
Mirrer Yeshiva Central Institute, NY
Ohr Somayach Tanenbaum Education Center, NY
Rabbinical Academy Mesivta Rabbi Chaim Berlin, NY
Rabbinical College Beth Shraga, NY

Affiliated with a religion

Rabbinical College Bobover Yeshiva
  B'nei Zion, NY
Rabbinical College Ch'san Sofer of
  New York, NY
Rabbinical College of America, NJ
Rabbinical College of Long Island, NY
Rabbinical Seminary of America, NY
Shor Yoshuv Rabbinical College, NY
Talmudical Institute of Upstate New
  York, NY
Talmudical Seminary Oholei Torah,
  NY
Telshe Yeshiva-Chicago, IL
Torah Temimah Talmudical Seminary,
  NY
U.T.A. Mesivta-Kiryas Jocl, NY
United Talmudical Seminary, NY
Yeshiva and Kolel Bais Medrash
  Elyon, NY
Yeshiva and Kollel Harbotzas Torah,
  NY
Yeshiva D'Monsey Rabbinical College,
  NY
Yeshiva Derech Chaim, NY
Yeshiva Gedolah Imrei Yosef
  D'Spinka, NY
Yeshiva Gedolah Zichron Moshe, NY
Yeshiva Karlin Stolin, NY
Yeshiva of Nitra, NY
Yeshiva of the Telshe Alumni, NY
Yeshiva Shaar Hatorah, NY
Yeshiva Shaarei Torah of Rockland,
  NY
Yeshivas Novominsk, NY
Yeshivat Mikdash Melech, NY

Two-year

Bramson ORT College, NY

Lutheran Church

Four-year

Trinity Lutheran College, WA
Valparaiso University, IN

Lutheran Church - Missouri Synod

Four-year

Concordia College, NY
Concordia University, CA
Concordia University, OR
Concordia University, NE
Concordia University Chicago, IL
Concordia University St. Paul, MN
Concordia University Texas, TX
Concordia University Wisconsin, WI

Lutheran Church in America

Four-year

Wagner College, NY

Mennonite Brethren Church

Four-year

Fresno Pacific University, CA
Tabor College, KS

Mennonite Church

Four-year

Bethel College, KS
Bluffton University, OH
Eastern Mennonite University, VA
Goshen College, IN

Two-year

Hesston College, KS

Missionary Church

Four-year

Bethel College, IN

Moravian Church in America

Four-year

Moravian College, PA
Salem College, NC

nondenominational tradition

Four-year

Appalachian Bible College, WV
Bob Jones University, SC
Calvary Bible College and Theological
  Seminary, MO
Colorado Christian University, CO
Davis College, NY
Friends University, KS
Gordon College, MA
Horizon College of San Diego, CA
Kenyon College, OH
The King's College, NY
The King's University, CA
LeTourneau University, TX
Northwestern College, MN
Occidental College, CA
Oral Roberts University, OK
Palm Beach Atlantic University, FL
San Diego Christian College, CA
Southeastern Bible College, AL
Victory University, TN
Washington Bible College, MD
Westmont College, CA
Wheaton College, IL
William Jessup University, CA
World Mission University, CA

Pentecostal Holiness Church

Four-year

Southwestern Christian University, OK
Universidad Pentecostal Mizpa, PR

Presbyterian Church (USA)

Four-year

Agnes Scott College, GA
Alma College, MI
Arcadia University, PA
Austin College, TX
Belhaven University, MS
Blackburn College, IL
Bloomfield College, NJ
Buena Vista University, IA
Carroll University, WI
Centre College, KY
Coe College, IA
Davidson College, NC
Davis and Elkins College, WV
Eckerd College, FL
Grove City College, PA
Hampden-Sydney College, VA
Hanover College, IN
Illinois College, IL
Jamestown College, ND
King College, TN
Lafayette College, PA
Lees-McRae College, NC
Lindenwood University, MO
Lyon College, AR
Macalester College, MN
Mary Baldwin College, VA
Maryville College, TN
Millikin University, IL
Missouri Valley College, MO
Monmouth College, IL
Muskingum University, OH
Peace College, NC
Pikeville College, KY
Presbyterian College, SC
Queens University of Charlotte, NC
Rhodes College, TN
Rocky Mountain College, MT
St. Andrews Presbyterian College, NC
Schreiner University, TX
Sterling College, KS
Stillman College, AL
Trinity University, TX
Tusculum College, TN

University of Dubuque, IA
University of the Ozarks, AR
University of Tulsa, OK
Warren Wilson College, NC
Waynesburg University, PA
Westminster College, MO
Whitworth University, WA
Wilson College, PA

Reformed Church in America

Four-year

Central College, IA
Hope College, MI
Northwestern College, IA

Reformed Presbyterian Church of North America

Four-year

Geneva College, PA

Roman Catholic Church

Four-year

Albertus Magnus College, CT
Alvernia University, PA
Alverno College, WI
Anna Maria College, MA
Aquinas College, MI
Aquinas College, TN
Assumption College, MA
Ave Maria University, FL
Avila University, MO
Barry University, FL
Bayamon Central University, PR
Bellarmine University, KY
Belmont Abbey College, NC
Benedictine College, KS
Benedictine University, IL
Boston College, MA
Brescia University, KY
Briar Cliff University, IA
Cabrini College, PA
Caldwell College, NJ
Calumet College of St. Joseph, IN
Canisius College, NY
Cardinal Stritch University, WI
Carlow University, PA
Carroll College, MT
Catholic Distance University, VA
Catholic University of America, DC
Chaminade University of Honolulu, HI
Chestnut Hill College, PA
Christendom College, VA
Christian Brothers University, TN
Clarke University, IA
College of Mount St. Joseph, OH
College of Mount St. Vincent, NY
College of New Rochelle, NY
College of Notre Dame of Maryland,
  MD
College of St. Benedict, MN
College of St. Elizabeth, NJ
College of St. Joseph in Vermont, VT
College of Saint Mary, NE
College of St. Scholastica, MN
College of the Holy Cross, MA
Creighton University, NE
DePaul University, IL
DeSales University, PA
Divine Word College, IA
Dominican University, IL
Duquesne University, PA
Edgewood College, WI
Elms College, MA
Emmanuel College, MA
Fairfield University, CT
Felician College, NJ
Fontbonne University, MO
Fordham University, NY
Franciscan University of Steubenville,
  OH
Gannon University, PA
Georgetown University, DC
Georgian Court University, NJ

Gonzaga University, WA
Gwynedd-Mercy College, PA
Hilbert College, NY
Holy Apostles College and Seminary,
  CT
Holy Cross College, IN
Holy Family University, PA
Holy Names University, CA
Immaculata University, PA
Iona College, NY
John Carroll University, OH
King's College, PA
La Roche College, PA
La Salle University, PA
Le Moyne College, NY
Lewis University, IL
Lexington College, IL
Loras College, IA
Lourdes College, OH
Loyola Marymount University, CA
Loyola University Chicago, IL
Loyola University Maryland, MD
Loyola University New Orleans, LA
Madonna University, MI
Magdalen College, NH
Manhattan College, NY
Marian University, IN
Marian University, WI
Marquette University, WI
Marygrove College, MI
Marylhurst University, OR
Marymount University, VA
Marywood University, PA
Mercyhurst College, PA
Merrimack College, MA
Misericordia University, PA
Molloy College, NY
Mount Aloysius College, PA
Mount Angel Seminary, OR
Mount Marty College, SD
Mount Mary College, WI
Mount Mercy University, IA
Mount Saint Mary College, NY
Mount St. Mary's College, CA
Mount St. Mary's University, MD
Neumann University, PA
Newman University, KS
Niagara University, NY
Notre Dame College, OH
Notre Dame de Namur University, CA
Ohio Dominican University, OH
Our Lady of Holy Cross College, LA
Our Lady of the Lake University of
  San Antonio, TX
Pontifical Catholic University of Puerto
  Rico, PR
Presentation College, SD
Providence College, RI
Quincy University, IL
Regis College, MA
Regis University, CO
Resurrection University, IL
Rivier College, NH
Rockhurst University, MO
Rosemont College, PA
Sacred Heart Major Seminary, MI
Sacred Heart University, CT
St. Ambrose University, IA
Saint Anselm College, NH
Saint Bonaventure University, NY
St. Catharine College, KY
St. Catherine University, MN
St. Charles Borromeo Seminary -
  Overbrook, PA
St. Edward's University, TX
St. Francis College, NY
St. Francis University, PA
St. Gregory's University, OK
St. John Fisher College, NY
St. John's University, NY
St. John's University, MN
Saint Joseph College, CT
St. Joseph Seminary College, LA
Saint Joseph's College of Maine, ME
Saint Joseph's University, PA

Saint Leo University, FL
Saint Louis University, MO
Saint Martin's University, WA
Saint Mary's College, IN
St. Mary's College of California, CA
St. Mary's University, TX
St. Mary's University of Minnesota, MN
St. Mary-of-the-Woods College, IN
St. Michael's College, VT
St. Norbert College, WI
Saint Peter's College, NJ
Saint Thomas University, FL
St. Vincent College, PA
Saint Xavier University, IL
Salve Regina University, RI
Santa Clara University, CA
Seattle University, WA
Seton Hall University, NJ
Seton Hill University, PA
Siena College, NY
Siena Heights University, MI
Silver Lake College, WI
Spalding University, KY
Spring Hill College, AL
Stonehill College, MA
Thomas More College, KY
Thomas More College of Liberal Arts, NH
Trinity Washington University, DC
University of Dallas, TX
University of Dayton, OH
University of Detroit Mercy, MI
University of Great Falls, MT
University of Mary, ND
University of Notre Dame, IN
University of Portland, OR
University of St. Francis, IN
University of St. Francis, IL
University of St. Mary, KS
University of St. Thomas, TX
University of St. Thomas, MN
University of San Diego, CA
University of San Francisco, CA
University of Scranton, PA
University of the Incarnate Word, TX
Ursuline College, OH
Villanova University, PA
Viterbo University, WI
Walsh University, OH
Wheeling Jesuit University, WV
Xavier University, OH
Xavier University of Louisiana, LA

Two-year
Ancilla College, IN
Benedictine University at Springfield, IL
Donnelly College, KS
Marian Court College, MA
Marymount College, CA
St. Elizabeth College of Nursing, NY
Trocaire College, NY
Villa Maria College of Buffalo, NY

Seventh-day Adventists
Four-year
Andrews University, MI
Atlantic Union College, MA
Griggs University, MD
Kettering College of Medical Arts, OH
La Sierra University, CA
Loma Linda University, CA
Oakwood University, AL
Pacific Union College, CA
Southwestern Adventist University, TX
Union College, NE
Universidad Adventista de las Antillas, PR
Walla Walla University, WA
Washington Adventist University, MD

Society of Friends (Quaker)
Four-year
Earlham College, IN
George Fox University, OR

Guilford College, NC
William Penn University, IA
Wilmington College, OH

Southern Baptist Convention
Four-year
Anderson University, SC
Baptist College of Florida, FL
Blue Mountain College, MS
Brewton-Parker College, GA
California Baptist University, CA
Carson-Newman College, TN
Charleston Southern University, SC
Chowan University, NC
Criswell College, TX
Gardner-Webb University, NC
Hannibal-LaGrange University, MO
Louisiana College, LA
Mid-Continent University, KY
Mississippi College, MS
New Orleans Baptist Theological Seminary: Leavell College, LA
North Greenville University, SC
Oklahoma Baptist University, OK
Ouachita Baptist University, AR
Samford University, AL
Shorter University, GA
Southeastern Baptist Theological Seminary, NC
Southwest Baptist University, MO
Truett-McConnell College, GA
Union University, TN
Wayland Baptist University, TX
Williams Baptist College, AR

Ukrainian Catholic Church
Two-year
Manor College, PA

United Brethren in Christ
Four-year
Huntington University, IN

United Church of Christ
Four-year
Catawba College, NC
Defiance College, OH
Doane College, NE
Elmhurst College, IL
Elon University, NC
Fisk University, TN
Heidelberg University, OH
Lakeland College, WI
LeMoyne-Owen College, TN
Northland College, WI
Olivet College, MI
Pacific University, OR
Piedmont College, GA
Talladega College, AL

United Methodist Church
Four-year
Adrian College, MI
Alaska Pacific University, AK
Albion College, MI
Albright College, PA
Allegheny College, PA
American University, DC
Baker University, KS
Baldwin-Wallace College, OH
Bennett College for Women, NC
Bethune-Cookman University, FL
Birmingham-Southern College, AL
Brevard College, NC
BryanLGH College of Health Sciences, NE
Centenary College, NJ
Centenary College of Louisiana, LA
Central Methodist University, MO
Claflin University, SC
Clark Atlanta University, GA
Columbia College, SC

Cornell College, IA
Dakota Wesleyan University, SD
DePauw University, IN
Drew University, NJ
Duke University, NC
Emory & Henry College, VA
Emory University, GA
Ferrum College, VA
Florida Southern College, FL
Green Mountain College, VT
Greensboro College, NC
Hamline University, MN
Hendrix College, AR
High Point University, NC
Huntingdon College, AL
Huston-Tillotson University, TX
Iowa Wesleyan College, IA
Kansas Wesleyan University, KS
Kentucky Wesleyan College, KY
LaGrange College, GA
Lambuth University, TN
Lebanon Valley College, PA
Lindsey Wilson College, KY
Lycoming College, PA
MacMurray College, IL
McKendree University, IL
McMurry University, TX
Methodist University, NC
Millsaps College, MS
Morningside College, IA
Nebraska Wesleyan University, NE
North Carolina Wesleyan College, NC
North Central College, IL
Ohio Northern University, OH
Ohio Wesleyan University, OH
Oklahoma City University, OK
Otterbein University, OH
Paine College, GA
Pfeiffer University, NC
Philander Smith College, AR
Randolph College, VA
Randolph-Macon College, VA
Reinhardt University, GA
Rust College, MS
Shenandoah University, VA
Simpson College, IA
Southern Methodist University, TX
Southwestern College, KS
Southwestern University, TX
Tennessee Wesleyan College, TN
Texas Wesleyan University, TX
Union College, KY
University of Evansville, IN
University of Indianapolis, IN
University of Mount Union, OH
Virginia Wesleyan College, VA
Wesley College, DE
Wesleyan College, GA
West Virginia Wesleyan College, WV
Wiley College, TX
Willamette University, OR
Wofford College, SC

Two-year
Andrew College, GA
Lon Morris College, TX
Louisburg College, NC
Spartanburg Methodist College, SC
Young Harris College, GA

Wesleyan Church
Four-year
Houghton College, NY
Indiana Wesleyan University, IN
Oklahoma Wesleyan University, OK
Southern Wesleyan University, SC

Wisconsin Evangelical Lutheran Synod
Four-year
Wisconsin Lutheran College, WI

Historically Black colleges

Four-year
Alabama Agricultural and Mechanical University, AL
Alabama State University, AL
Albany State University, GA
Alcorn State University, MS
Allen University, SC
Arkansas Baptist College, AR
Benedict College, SC
Bennett College for Women, NC
Bluefield State College, WV
Bowie State University, MD
Central State University, OH
Cheyney University of Pennsylvania, PA
Claflin University, SC
Clark Atlanta University, GA
Coppin State University, MD
Delaware State University, DE
Dillard University, LA
Edward Waters College, FL
Elizabeth City State University, NC
Fisk University, TN
Florida Agricultural and Mechanical University, FL
Florida Memorial University, FL
Fort Valley State University, GA
Grambling State University, LA
Hampton University, VA
Harris-Stowe State University, MO
Howard University, DC
Huston-Tillotson University, TX
Jackson State University, MS
Johnson C. Smith University, NC
Kentucky State University, KY
Lane College, TN
Langston University, OK
LeMoyne-Owen College, TN
Lincoln University, MO
Lincoln University, PA
Livingstone College, NC
Miles College, AL
Mississippi Valley State University, MS
Morehouse College, GA
Morgan State University, MD
Morris College, SC
Norfolk State University, VA
North Carolina Central University, NC
Oakwood University, AL
Paine College, GA
Philander Smith College, AR
Prairie View A&M University, TX
Rust College, MS
St. Augustine's College, NC
St. Paul's College, VA
Savannah State University, GA
Selma University, AL
Shaw University, NC
South Carolina State University, SC
Southern University New Orleans, LA
Southern University and Agricultural and Mechanical College, LA
Southwestern Christian College, TX
Spelman College, GA
Stillman College, AL
Talladega College, AL
Tennessee State University, TN
Texas College, TX
Texas Southern University, TX
Tougaloo College, MS
Tuskegee University, AL
University of Arkansas Pine Bluff, AR
University of Maryland Eastern Shore, MD
University of the District of Columbia, DC
Virginia State University, VA
Voorhees College, SC
West Virginia State University, WV
Wilberforce University, OH

Wiley College, TX
Winston-Salem State University, NC
Xavier University of Louisiana, LA

Two-year

Bishop State Community College, AL
Coahoma Community College, MS
Denmark Technical College, SC
Hinds Community College, MS
Lawson State Community College, AL
St. Philip's College, TX
Southern University
    Shreveport, LA

Hispanic serving colleges

Four-year

Adams State College, CO
American University of Puerto Rico, PR
Barry University, FL
Bayamon Central University, PR
California State University
    Bakersfield, CA
    Dominguez Hills, CA
    Fresno, CA
    Los Angeles, CA
    Monterey Bay, CA
    San Bernardino, CA
    Stanislaus, CA
Caribbean University, PR
Carlos Albizu University, FL
City University of New York
    City College, NY
    John Jay College of Criminal Justice, NY
    Lehman College, NY
Conservatory of Music of Puerto Rico, PR
Escuela de Artes Plasticas de Puerto Rico, PR
Florida International University, FL
Inter American University of Puerto Rico
    Aguadilla Campus, PR
    Arecibo Campus, PR
    Barranquitas Campus, PR
    Bayamon Campus, PR
    Fajardo Campus, PR
    Guayama Campus, PR
    Metropolitan Campus, PR
    Ponce Campus, PR
    San German Campus, PR
Lexington College, IL
Mercy College, NY
Mount Angel Seminary, OR
Mount St. Mary's College, CA
New Jersey City University, NJ
New Mexico State University, NM
Occidental College, CA
Our Lady of the Lake University of San Antonio, TX
Pontifical Catholic University of Puerto Rico, PR
Robert Morris University: Chicago, IL
St. Augustine College, IL
St. Edward's University, TX
St. Mary's University, TX
Saint Peter's College, NJ
Saint Thomas University, FL
San Diego State University, CA
Sul Ross State University, TX
Texas A&M International University, TX
Texas A&M University
    Corpus Christi, TX
    Kingsville, TX
Turabo University, PR
Universidad Adventista de las Antillas, PR
Universidad del Este, PR
Universidad Metropolitana, PR

Universidad Politecnica de Puerto Rico, PR
University College of San Juan, PR
University of Houston
    Downtown, TX
University of La Verne, CA
University of Miami, FL
University of New Mexico, NM
University of Puerto Rico
    Aguadilla, PR
    Arecibo, PR
    Bayamon University College, PR
    Carolina Regional College, PR
    Cayey University College, PR
    Humacao, PR
    Mayaguez, PR
    Medical Sciences, PR
    Ponce, PR
    Rio Piedras, PR
    Utuado, PR
University of Texas
    Brownsville - Texas Southmost College, TX
    El Paso, TX
    Health Science Center at San Antonio, TX
    Pan American, TX
    San Antonio, TX
    of the Permian Basin, TX
University of the Incarnate Word, TX
Vaughn College of Aeronautics and Technology, NY
Whittier College, CA
Woodbury University, CA

Two-year

Allan Hancock College, CA
Arizona Western College, AZ
Bakersfield College, CA
Central Arizona College, AZ
Cerritos College, CA
Chaffey College, CA
Citrus College, CA
City Colleges of Chicago
    Malcolm X College, IL
    Richard J. Daley College, IL
    Wilbur Wright College, IL
City University of New York
    Borough of Manhattan Community College, NY
    Bronx Community College, NY
    Hostos Community College, NY
    LaGuardia Community College, NY
Coastal Bend College, TX
Cochise College, AZ
College of the Desert, CA
College of the Sequoias, CA
Community College of Denver, CO
Del Mar College, TX
Dodge City Community College, KS
Dona Ana Community College of New Mexico State University, NM
East Los Angeles College, CA
Eastern New Mexico University: Roswell, NM
El Camino College, CA
Evergreen Valley College, CA
Fresno City College, CA
Fullerton College, CA
Hartnell College, CA
Heald College
    Fresno, CA
    Salinas, CA
    San Jose, CA
    Stockton, CA
Hudson County Community College, NJ
Humacao Community College, PR
Laredo Community College, TX
Long Beach City College, CA
Los Angeles City College, CA
Los Angeles Harbor College, CA
Los Angeles Mission College, CA

Los Angeles Trade and Technical College, CA
Los Angeles Valley College, CA
MacCormac College, IL
Miami Dade College, FL
Morton College, IL
Mount San Antonio College, CA
Mountain View College, TX
New Mexico Junior College, NM
New Mexico State University
    Carlsbad, NM
    Grants, NM
Northern New Mexico College, NM
Odessa College, TX
Otero Junior College, CO
Oxnard College, CA
Palo Verde College, CA
Pasadena City College, CA
Passaic County Community College, NJ
Phoenix College, AZ
Pima Community College, AZ
Porterville College, CA
Pueblo Community College, CO
Reedley College, CA
Rio Hondo College, CA
Riverside Community College, CA
St. Philip's College, TX
San Antonio College, TX
San Bernardino Valley College, CA
San Jose City College, CA
Santa Ana College, CA
Santa Fe Community College, NM
South Mountain Community College, AZ
South Plains College, TX
Southwest Texas Junior College, TX
Southwestern College, CA
Texas State Technical College
    Harlingen, TX
Trinidad State Junior College, CO
Ventura College, CA
Victoria College, TX
West Hills College: Coalinga, CA

College addresses

Abilene Christian University
www.acu.edu
Center for International & Intercultural
Education
ACU Box 29000
Abilene, TX 79699
Fax: (325) 674-2966
E-mail: kehlk@acu.edu
Phone: (325) 674-2710

Abraham Baldwin Agricultural College
www.abac.edu
Admissions
ABAC 4, 2802 Moore Highway
Tifton, GA 31793-2601
Fax: (229) 391-5002
E-mail: admissions@abac.edu
Phone: (229) 391-5004

Academy College
www.academycollege.edu
Admissions
1101 East 78th Street
Bloomington, MN 55420
Fax: (952) 851-0094
E-mail: sbrustad@academycollege.edu
Phone: (952) 851-0066

Academy of Art University
www.academyart.edu
International Admissions Office
79 New Montgomery Street
San Francisco, CA 94105-3410
Fax: (415) 618-6278
E-mail: intladmissions@academyart.edu
Phone: (415) 274-2208

Academy of Court Reporting and Technology
www.acr.edu
2044 Euclid Avenue
Cleveland, OH 44115
Fax: (216) 861-4517
Phone: (216) 861-3222

Academy of Couture Art
www.academyofcoutureart.com
PDC, 8687 Melrose Avenue
West Hollywood, CA 90069
E-mail: info@academycoutureart.edu
Phone: (310) 360-8888

Adams State College
www.adams.edu
Assistant Vice President of Enrollment
Management
208 Edgemont Boulevard
Alamosa, CO 81102
Fax: (719) 587-7522
E-mail: ascadmit@adams.edu
Phone: (719) 587-7712

Adelphi University
www.adelphi.edu
Office of International Admissions
One South Avenue, Levermore 110
PO Box 701
Garden City, NY 11530-0701
Fax: (516) 877-3039
E-mail: intladmissions@adelphi.edu
Phone: (516) 877-3020

Adirondack Community College
www.sunyacc.edu
Enrollment Management
640 Bay Road
Queensbury, NY 12804
Fax: (518) 743-2317
E-mail: linehans@sunyacc.edu
Phone: (518) 743-2264

Adrian College
www.adrian.edu
Admissions
110 South Madison Street
Adrian, MI 49221-2575
Fax: (517) 264-3878
E-mail: admissions@adrian.edu
Phone: (800) 877-2246

Agnes Scott College
www.agnesscott.edu
Office of Admission
141 East College Avenue
Decatur, GA 30030-3797
Fax: (404) 471-6414
E-mail: mhammond@agnesscott.edu
Phone: (404) 471-6485

AIB College of Business
www.aib.edu
Admissions
2500 Fleur Drive
Des Moines, IA 50321-1799
Fax: (515) 244-6773
E-mail: krouchs@aib.edu
Phone: (515) 246-5359

Aiken Technical College
www.atc.edu
Director of Admissions and Records
PO Drawer 696
Aiken, SC 29802
Fax: (803) 593-6526
E-mail: buttsd@atc.edu
Phone: (803) 593-9954 ext. 1400

Aims Community College
www.aims.edu
International Student Office
5401 West 20th Street
PO Box 69
Greeley, CO 80632
Fax: (970) 506-6947
E-mail: alan.hendrickson@aims.edu
Phone: (970) 339-6675

Akron Institute of Herzing University
www.akroninstitute.com
1600 South Arlington Street, Suite 100
Akron, OH 44306
Fax: (330) 724-9688
E-mail: info@akr.herzing.edu
Phone: (330) 724-1600

Alabama Agricultural and Mechanical University
www.aamu.edu
Admissions Office
Box 908
Normal, AL 35762
Fax: (256) 372-5249
E-mail: venita.king@aamu.edu
Phone: (256) 372-5245

Alabama State University
www.alasu.edu
Minority/International Student Affairs
PO Box 271
Montgomery, AL 36101-0271
Fax: (334) 229-4984
E-mail: dcrump@alasu.edu
Phone: (334) 229-6588

Alaska Pacific University
www.alaskapacific.edu
Admissions
4101 University Drive
Anchorage, AK 99508-3051
Fax: (907) 564-8317
E-mail: sidney-andoa@alaskapacific.edu
Phone: (907) 563-8338

Albany College of Pharmacy and Health Sciences
www.acphs.edu
Admissions
106 New Scotland Avenue
Albany, NY 12208-3492
Fax: (518) 694-7322
E-mail: admissions@acphs.edu
Phone: (518) 694-7221

Albany State University
www.asurams.edu/
Office of Recruitment and Admissions
504 College Drive
Albany, GA 31705-2796
Fax: (229) 430-4105
E-mail: fred.suttles@asurams.edu
Phone: (229) 430-7862

Albany Technical College
www.albanytech.edu
Admissions Office
1704 South Slappy Boulevard
Albany, GA 31701-3514
Fax: (229) 430-6180
Phone: (229) 430-3520

Albertus Magnus College
www.albertus.edu
Office of Admission
700 Prospect Street
New Haven, CT 06511-1189
Fax: (203) 773-5248
E-mail: nperez@albertus.edu
Phone: (203) 773-8526

Albion College
www.albion.edu
Associate Director for International Student
Recruitment
611 East Porter Street
Albion, MI 49224-1831
Fax: (517) 629-0569
E-mail: lcardenas@albion.edu
Phone: (517) 629-0321

Albright College
www.albright.edu
Admission Office
13th & Bern Streets
PO Box 15234
Reading, PA 19612-5234
Fax: (610) 921-7729
E-mail: nchristie@alb.edu
Phone: (610) 921-7700

Alcorn State University
www.alcorn.edu
Admissions
1000 ASU Drive #300
Alcorn State, MS 39096-7500
Fax: (601) 877-6347
E-mail: ebarnes@alcorn.edu
Phone: (601) 877-6146

Alderson-Broaddus College
www.ab.edu
Admissions
101 College Hill Drive
Campus Box 2003
Philippi, WV 26416
Fax: (304) 457-6239
E-mail: dionnemi@ab.edu
Phone: (304) 457-6326

Alexandria Technical College
www.alextech.edu
Counseling & Assessment Center
1601 Jefferson Street
Alexandria, MN 56308-3799
Fax: (320) 762-4603
E-mail: international@alextech.edu
Phone: (320) 762-4588

Alfred University
www.alfred.edu
Office of Admissions
Alumni Hall
One Saxon Drive
Alfred, NY 14802-1205
Fax: (607) 871-2198
E-mail: unis@alfred.edu
Phone: (607) 871-2115

Alice Lloyd College
www.alc.edu
Admissions
100 Purpose Road
Pippa Passes, KY 41844
Fax: (606) 368-6215
E-mail: admissions@alc.edu
Phone: (606) 368-6036

Allan Hancock College
www.hancockcollege.edu
Admissions and Records
800 South College Drive
Santa Maria, CA 93454-6399
Fax: (805) 922-3477
E-mail: pwood@hancockcollege.edu
Phone: (805) 922-6366 ext. 3281

Allegany College of Maryland
www.allegany.edu
Admissions Office
12401 Willowbrook Road, SE
Cumberland, MD 21502
Fax: (301) 784-5027
E-mail: ckauffman@allegany.edu
Phone: (301) 784-5199

Allegheny College
www.allegheny.edu
Admissions
Box 5, 520 North Main Street
Meadville, PA 16335
Fax: (814) 337-0431
E-mail: admissions@allegheny.edu
Phone: (814) 332-6234

Allegheny Wesleyan College
www.awc.edu
2161 Woodside Road
Salem, OH 44460-9598
Fax: (330) 337-6255
E-mail: college@awc.edu
Phone: (330) 337-6403

Allen County Community College
www.allencc.edu
Foreign Student Adviser
1801 North Cottonwood
Iola, KS 66749
Fax: (785) 654-2336
E-mail: jsteel@allencc.edu
Phone: (785) 654-2416

Allen University
www.allenuniversity.edu
Admissions
1530 Harden Street
Columbia, SC 29204
Fax: (803) 376-5731
E-mail: tparker@allenuniversity.edu
Phone: (803) 775-82702

Alliant International University
www.alliant.edu
10455 Pomerado Road
San Diego, CA 92131-1799
Fax: (858) 635-4739
E-mail: admissions3@alliant.edu
Phone: (866) 825-5426

Alma College
www.alma.edu
Admissions
614 West Superior Street
Alma, MI 48801-1599
Fax: (989) 463-7057
E-mail: admissions@alma.edu
Phone: (989) 463-7139

Altamaha Technical College
www.altamahatech.edu
1777 West Cherry Street
Jesup, GA 31545
Fax: (912) 427-1901
E-mail: atcadmissions@altamahatech.edu
Phone: (912) 427-1958

Alvernia University
www.alvernia.edu
Admissions
400 St. Bernardine Street
Reading, PA 19607-1799
Fax: (610) 796-2873
E-mail: stephanie.garcia@alvernia.edu
Phone: (610) 568-1473

Alverno College
www.alverno.edu
International and Intercultural Center
3400 South 43rd Street
PO Box 343922
Milwaukee, WI 53234-3922
Fax: (414) 382-6354
E-mail: maryellen.spicuzza@alverno.edu
Phone: (414) 382-6099

Amarillo College
www.actx.edu
Office of Admissions
Box 447
Amarillo, TX 79178
Fax: (806) 371-5066
E-mail: AskAC@actx.edu
Phone: (806) 371-5030

American Academy of Art
www.aaart.edu
Office of the Registrar
332 South Michigan Avenue, Suite 300
Chicago, IL 60604-4302
Fax: (312) 294-9570
E-mail: info@aaart.edu
Phone: (312) 461-0600 ext. 134

American Academy of Dramatic Arts
www.aada.org
120 Madison Avenue
New York, NY 10016
Fax: (212) 686-1284
E-mail: admissions-ny@aada.org
Phone: (212) 686-0620

American Academy of Dramatic Arts: West
www.aada.org
1336 N. La Brea Avenue
Los Angeles, CA 90028
Fax: (323) 464-1250
E-mail: hnelson@ca.aada.org
Phone: (323) 464-2777 ext. 108

American Baptist College
www.abcnash.edu
1800 Baptist World Center Drive
Nashville, TN 37207
Fax: (615) 226-7855
E-mail: rjweems@abcnash.edu
Phone: (615) 687-6896

American InterContinental University
www.buckhead.aiuniv.edu/
Admission
6600 Peachtree Dunwoody Road, 500
Embassy Row
Atlanta, GA 30328
Fax: (404) 955-5701
E-mail: tina.rowe@buckhead.aiuniv.edu
Phone: (404) 965-5700 ext. 5797

American International College
www.aic.edu
Admissions
1000 State Street
Springfield, MA 01109
Fax: (413) 205-3051
E-mail: pauline.mortenson@aic.edu
Phone: (800) 242-3142

American Jewish University
www.ajula.edu
Director of Admissions
Office of Undergraduate Admissions
Familian Campus, 15600 Mulholland Drive
Los Angeles, CA 90077
Fax: (310) 471-3657
E-mail: mspooner@ajula.edu
Phone: (310) 476-9777 ext. 250

American River College
www.arc.losrios.edu
Enrollment Services
4700 College Oak Drive
Sacramento, CA 95841
Fax: (916) 484-8864
E-mail: recadmis@arc.losrios.edu
Phone: (916) 484-8172

American Sentinel University
www.americansentinel.edu
Birmingham Office
500 Century Park South, Suite 202
Birmingham, AL 35226
Fax: (866) 505-2450
E-mail: natalie.nixon@americansentinel.edu
Phone: (866) 922-5690

American University
www.american.edu
Office of Admissions
4400 Massachusetts Avenue NW
Washington, DC 20016-8001
Fax: (202) 885-1025
E-mail: intadm@american.edu
Phone: (202) 885-6000

American University of Puerto Rico
www.aupr.edu
PO Box 2037
Bayamon, PR 00960-2037
Fax: (787) 785-7377
E-mail: oficinaadmisiones@aupr.edu
Phone: (787) 620-2040 ext. 2020

Amherst College
www.amherst.edu
Admission Office
PO Box 5000
Amherst, MA 01002-5000
Fax: (413) 542-2040
E-mail: admission@amherst.edu
Phone: (413) 542-2328

Ancilla College
www.ancilla.edu
Admissions
9001 Union Road
PO Box 1
Donaldson, IN 46513
Fax: (574) 935-1773
E-mail: sarah.lawrence@ancilla.edu
Phone: (574) 936-8898 ext. 396

Anderson University
www.andersonuniversity.edu
Coordinator of International and Multicultural
Recruitment
316 Boulevard
Anderson, SC 29621-4002
Fax: (864) 231-2033
E-mail: ljohnson@andersonuniversity.edu
Phone: (800) 542-3594

Andrew College
www.andrewcollege.edu
Office of Admission
501 College Street
Cuthbert, GA 39840-1395
Fax: (229) 732-2176
E-mail: admissions@andrewcollege.edu
Phone: (229) 732-2171

Andrews University
www.andrews.edu
100 US Highway 31
Berrien Springs, MI 49104
Fax: (269) 471-3228
E-mail: enroll@andrews.edu
Phone: (800) 253-2874

Angelo State University
www.angelo.edu
Center for International Studies
ASU Station #11014
San Angelo, TX 76909-1014
Fax: (325) 942-2084
E-mail: meghan.pace@angelo.edu
Phone: (325) 942-2083

Angley College
www.angley.edu
Corporate Office
1700 Woodland Boulevard
Deland, FL 32720-4289
Fax: (407) 327-9303
E-mail: dray@angley.edu
Phone: (407) 327-8600 ext. 404

Anna Maria College
www.annamaria.edu
Admissions
50 Sunset Lane, Box O
Paxton, MA 01612-1198
Fax: (508) 849-3362
E-mail: mmcdonough@annamaria.edu
Phone: (508) 849-3362

Anne Arundel Community College
www.aacc.edu
Admissions and Enrollment Development
101 College Parkway
Arnold, MD 21012-1895
Fax: (410) 777-4246
E-mail: admissions@aacc.edu
Phone: (410) 777-2152

Antelope Valley College
www.avc.edu
Admissions and Records
3041 West Avenue K
Lancaster, CA 93536-5426
Fax: (661) 722-6531
E-mail: hahlgreen@avc.edu
Phone: (661) 722-6332

Anthem College: Aurora
www.cambridgecollege.com
350 Blackhawk Street
Aurora, CO 80011
Fax: (303) 338-9701
Phone: (720) 859-7900

Anthem College: Kansas City
www.hightechinstitute.edu
9001 State Line Road
Kansas City, MO 64114
Phone: (816) 444-4300

Anthem College: Minneapolis
www.anthem.edu
5100 Gamble Drive
St. Louis Park, MN 55416
Phone: (952) 417-2200

Antioch University Los Angeles
www.antiochla.edu
Admissions Counselor
400 Corporate Pointe
Culver City, CA 90230-7615
Fax: (310) 822-4824
E-mail: MHall@antioch.edu
Phone: (800) 726-8462

Antioch University Santa Barbara
www.antiochsb.edu
Admissions
801 Garden Street, Suite 101
Santa Barbara, CA 93101-1581
Fax: (805) 962-4786
E-mail: sweir@antioch.edu
Phone: (805) 962-8179 ext. 152

Antonelli College: Cincinnati
www.antonellicollege.edu
124 East Seventh Street
Cincinnati, OH 45202
Fax: (513) 241-9396
Phone: (513) 241-4338

Antonelli College: Jackson
www.antonellicollege.edu
2323 Lakeland Drive
Jackson, MS 39232
Phone: (601) 362-9991

Apex School of Theology
www.apexsot.edu
2945 South Miami Boulevard, Suite 114
Durham, NC 27703
E-mail: registrar@apexsot.edu
Phone: (919) 572-1625 ext. 7025

Appalachian Bible College
www.abc.edu
Admissions
Director of Admissions
161 College Drive
Mount hope, WV 25880
Fax: (304) 877-5082
E-mail: scott.ross@abc.edu
Phone: (304) 877-6428

Appalachian State University
www.appstate.edu
Admissions
ASU Box 32004
Boone, NC 28608
Fax: (828) 262-4037
E-mail: molljs@appstate.edu
Phone: (828) 262-2120

Aquinas College
www.aquinas.edu
Admissions Representative
1607 Robinson Road Southeast
Grand Rapids, MI 49506-1799
Fax: (616) 732-4469
E-mail: marzang@aquinas.edu
Phone: (616) 632-2858

Aquinas College
www.aquinascollege.edu
Admissions
4210 Harding Road
Nashville, TN 37205-2086
Fax: (615) 279-3893
E-mail: hansomc@aquinascollege.edu
Phone: (615) 297-7545 ext. 411

Arapahoe Community College
www.arapahoe.edu
Advising
PO Box 9002
5900 South Santa Fe Drive
Littleton, CO 80160-9002
Fax: (303) 797-5970
E-mail: janet.ludwig@arapahoe.edu
Phone: (303) 797-5652

Arcadia University
www.arcadia.edu
Enrollment Management
450 South Easton Road
Glenside, PA 19038-3295
Fax: (215) 572-4049
E-mail: international@arcadia.edu
Phone: (215) 572-2910

Argosy University: Atlanta
www.argosy.edu/atlanta
980 Hammond Drive, Suite 100
Atlanta, GA 30328
E-mail: auaadmissions@argosy.edu
Phone: (770) 671-1200

Argosy University: Chicago
www.argosy.edu/chicago
Student Services
225 North Michigan Avenue, Suite 1300
Chicago, IL 60601
E-mail: jlanderson@argosy.edu
Phone: (312) 777-7622

Argosy University: Dallas
www.argosy.edu/dallas
5001 Lyndon B. Johnson Freeway, Heritage
Square
Farmers Branch, TX 75244
E-mail: audadmis@argosy.edu
Phone: (214) 459-2237

Argosy University: Denver
www.argosy.edu/denver
1200 Lincoln Street
Denver, CO 80203
Phone: (303) 248-2700

Argosy University: Hawaii
www.argosy.edu/hawaii
400 ASB Tower, 1001 Bishop Street
Honolulu, HI 96813
E-mail: auhonadmissions@argosy.edu
Phone: (808) 791-5214

Argosy University: Inland Empire
www.argosy.edu/inlandempire
636 East Brier Drive, Suite 120
San Bernardino, CA 92408
Phone: (909) 915-3800

Argosy University: Los Angeles
www.argosy.edu/losangeles
5230 Pacific Concourse, Suite 200
Los Angeles, CA 90045
E-mail: ausmadms@argosy.edu

Argosy University: Nashville
www.argosy.edu/nashville
100 Centerview Drive, Suite 225
Nashville, TN 37214
Phone: (615) 525-2800

Argosy University: Online
www.online.argosy.edu
2233 West Dunlap Avenue
Phoenix, AZ 85021
Phone: (866) 427-4679

Argosy University: Orange County
www.argosy.edu/orangecounty
601 South Lewis Street
Orange, CA 92868
Phone: (714) 620-3715

Argosy University: Phoenix
www.argosy.edu/phoenix
2233 West Dunlap Avenue
Phoenix, AZ 85021
Phone: (602) 216-2600

Argosy University: Salt Lake City
www.argosy.edu/saltlakecity
121 Election Road, Suite 300
Draper, UT 84020
Phone: (601) 601-5000

Argosy University: San Diego
www.argosy.edu/sandiego
1615 Murray Canyon Road
San Diego, CA 92108
E-mail: ausdadmissions@argosy.edu

Argosy University: San Francisco Bay Area
www.argosy.edu/sanfrancisco
1005 Atlantic Avenue
Alameda, CA 94501
E-mail: ausfadmissions@argosy.edu
Phone: (510) 217-4777

Argosy University: Sarasota
www.argosy.edu/sarasota
5250 17th Street
Sarasota, FL 34235
E-mail: ausradmissions@argosy.edu
Phone: (877) 331-4480

Argosy University: Schaumburg
www.argosy.edu/schaumburg
999 North Plaza Drive, Suite 111
Schaumburg, IL 60173-5403
Phone: (847) 969-4910

Argosy University: Seattle
www.argosy.edu/seattle
2601-A Elliott Avenue
Seattle, WA 98121
E-mail: ausadmissions@argosy.edu
Phone: (206) 393-3516

Argosy University: Tampa
www.argosy.edu/tampa
1403 North Howard Avenue
Tampa, FL 33607
E-mail: autaadmis@argosy.edu
Phone: (866) 357-4426

Argosy University: Twin Cities
www.argosy.edu/twincities
1515 Central Parkway
Eagan, MN 55121
E-mail: autcadmissions@argosy.edu
Phone: (651) 846-3300

Argosy University: Washington D.C.
www.argosy.edu/washingtondc
1550 Wilson Boulevard, Suite 600
Arlington, VA 22209
E-mail: auwadmissions@argosy.edu
Phone: (703) 526-5800

Arizona Automotive Institute
www.aai.edu
6829 North 46th Avenue
Glendale, AZ 85301
Fax: (623) 930-4948
E-mail: info@azautoinst.com
Phone: (623) 934-7273

Arizona Christian University
www.arizonachristian.edu
Admissions
2625 East Cactus Road
Phoenix, AZ 85032-7042
Fax: (602) 404-2159
E-mail: admissions@arizonachristian.edu
Phone: (602) 489-5500 ext. 136

Arizona State University
www.asu.edu
Director of International Undergraduate
Admissions
Box 870112
Tempe, AZ 85287-0112
Fax: (480) 727-6453
E-mail: ISSO@asu.edu
Phone: (480) 965-2688

Arizona Western College
www.azwestern.edu
International Students Office
PO Box 929
Yuma, AZ 85366-0929
Fax: (928) 344-7710
E-mail: ken.kuntzelman@azwestern.edu
Phone: (928) 344-7699

Arkansas Baptist College
www.arkansasbaptist.edu
Admissions and Recruitment
1621 Dr. Martin Luther King Drive
Little Rock, AR 72202
Fax: (501) 372-0321
E-mail: admissions@arkansasbaptist.edu
Phone: (501) 244-5186

Arkansas State University
www.astate.edu
Office of International Programs
PO Box 1630
State University, AR 72467-1630
Fax: (870) 972-3288
E-mail: chandni@astate.edu
Phone: (870) 972-2329

Arkansas State University: Mountain Home
www.asumh.edu
Assistant Vice Chancellor for Enrollment
1600 South College Street
Attention: Admissions
Mountain Home, AR 72653
Fax: (870) 508-6287
E-mail: rblagg@asumh.edu
Phone: (870) 508-6104

Arkansas State University: Newport
www.asun.edu
Registrar
7648 Victory Boulevard
Newport, AR 72112
Fax: (870) 512-7825
E-mail: rsummers@asun.edu
Phone: (870) 512-7716

Arkansas Tech University
www.atu.edu
International and Multicultural Student
Services
1605 Coliseum Drive, Suite 141
Russellville, AR 72801-2222
Fax: (479) 880-2039
E-mail: apennington@atu.edu
Phone: (479) 964-0832

Arlington Baptist College
www.abconline.edu
Academic Dean
3001 West Division
Arlington, TX 76012
Fax: (817) 274-1138
E-mail: hsullivan@abconline.org
Phone: (817) 461-8741 ext. 103

Armstrong Atlantic State University
www.armstrong.edu
Admissions Office
11935 Abercorn Street
Savannah, GA 31419-1997
Fax: (912) 344-3417
E-mail: jessica.tuttle@armstrong.edu
Phone: (912) 344-3237

Art Academy of Cincinnati
www.artacademy.edu
Admissions
1212 Jackson Street
Cincinnati, OH 45202
Fax: (513) 562-8778
E-mail: admissions@artacademy.edu
Phone: (513) 562-8740

Art Center Design College
www.theartcenter.edu
Admissions Office
2525 North Country Club Road
Tucson, AZ 85716
Fax: (520) 325-5535
E-mail: inquire@theartcenter.edu
Phone: (520) 325-0123

Art Institute of Atlanta
www.artinstitutes.edu/atlanta/
Admissions
6600 Peachtree Dunwoody Road, NE
100 Embassy Row
Atlanta, GA 30328
Fax: (770) 394-0008
E-mail: darrieta@aii.edu
Phone: (770) 689-4755

Art Institute of Boston at Lesley University
www.aiboston.edu
Student Affairs
700 Beacon Street
Boston, MA 02215-2598
Fax: (617) 349-8558
E-mail: jbess@lesley.edu
Phone: (617) 349-8542

Art Institute of California: Hollywood
www.artinstitutes.edu/hollywood
International Student Advisor
5250 Lankershim Boulevard
North Hollywood, CA 91601
Fax: (818) 299-5151
E-mail: cgrice@aii.edu
Phone: (818) 299-5626

Art Institute of California: Inland Empire
www.artinstitutes.edu/inland-empire/
674 East Brier Drive
San Bernardino, CA 92408-2800

Art Institute of California: Los Angeles
www.artinstitutes.edu/losangeles
Admissions
2900 31st Street
Santa Monica, CA 90405-3035
Fax: (310) 752-4708
E-mail: wilkinso@aii.edu
Phone: (310) 752-4700

Art Institute of California: Orange County
www.artinstitutes.edu/orangecounty
Admissions
3601 West Sunflower Avenue
Santa Ana, CA 92704-7931
Fax: (714) 556-1923
E-mail: tkotler@aii.edu
Phone: (714) 830-0200

Art Institute of California: Sacramento
www.artinstitutes.edu/sacramento
2850 Gateway Oaks Drive, Suite 100
Sacramento, CA 95833
Phone: (800) 477-1957

Art Institute of California: San Diego
www.artinstitutes.edu/sandiego
7650 Mission Valley Road
San Diego, CA 92108-4423
E-mail: aicaadmin@aii.edu
Phone: (866) 275-2422

Art Institute of California: San Francisco
www.artinstitutes.edu/sanfrancisco
1170 Market Street
San Francisco, CA 94102
Fax: (415) 863-6344
E-mail: aisfadm@aii.edu
Phone: (415) 865-0198

Art Institute of Charlotte
www.artinstitutes.edu/charlotte
Admissions
Three LakePointe Plaza
2110 Water Ridge Parkway
Charlotte, NC 28217-4536
Fax: (704) 357-1133
E-mail: aichadmin@aii.edu
Phone: (704) 357-8020 ext. 5872

Art Institute of Cincinnati
www.aic-arts.edu
Admissions/Marketing
1171 East Kemper Road
Cincinnati, OH 45246
Fax: (513) 751-1209
E-mail: admissions@aic-arts.edu
Phone: (513) 751-1206

Art Institute of Colorado
www.artinstitutes.edu/denver
International Admissions
1200 Lincoln Street
Denver, CO 80203-2172
Fax: (303) 860-8520
E-mail: sljohnson@aii.edu
Phone: (303) 837-0825

Art Institute of Dallas
www.aid.edu
Two North Park, 8080 Park Lane
Suite 100
Dallas, TX 75231
E-mail: cwilliams@aii.edu
Phone: (214) 692-8080

Art Institute of Fort Lauderdale
www.aifl.edu
Admissions
1799 SE 17th Street
Fort Lauderdale, FL 33316
Fax: (954) 728-8637
E-mail: byusty@aii.edu
Phone: (800) 275-7603 ext. 2159

Art Institute of Las Vegas
www.artinstitutes.edu/lasvegas/
Admissions
2350 Corporate Circle
Henderson, NV 89074-7737
Fax: (702) 992-8458
Phone: (800) 833-2678 ext. 8408

Art Institute of Michigan
www.artinstitutes.edu/detroit
28125 Cabot Drive, Suite 120
Novi, MI 48377
Phone: (248) 675-3800

Art Institute of New York City
www.ainyc.artinstitutes.edu
Admissions
11 Beach Street
New York, NY 10013-1917
Fax: (212) 625-6055
E-mail: ajarmillo@edmc.edu
Phone: (212) 226-5500 ext. 6749

Art Institute of Ohio: Cincinnati
www.artinstitutes.edu/cincinnati
8845 Governor's Hill Drive
Cincinnati, OH 45249-3317
Fax: (513) 833-2411
E-mail: amyerly@aii.edu

Art Institute of Phoenix
www.artinstitutes.edu/phoenix
International Admissions
2233 West Dunlap Avenue
Phoenix, AZ 85021-2859
Fax: (602) 331-5301
E-mail: mdomblisky@aii.edu
Phone: (602) 331-7500

Art Institute of Pittsburgh
www.artinstitutes.edu/pittsburgh
Assistant Director of Admissions
420 Boulevard of the Allies
Pittsburgh, PA 15219-1328
Fax: (412) 263-6667
E-mail: aipadm@aii.edu
Phone: (412) 263-6600

Art Institute of Portland
www.aipd.artinstitutes.edu
Admissions
1122 Northwest Davis Street
Portland, OR 97209-2911
Fax: (503) 227-1945
E-mail: bkline@aii.edu
Phone: (503) 228-6528

Art Institute of Seattle
www.ais.edu
Admissions
2323 Elliott Avenue
Seattle, WA 98121-1622
Fax: (206) 269-0275
E-mail: bcicero@aii.edu
Phone: (206) 448-6600

Art Institute of Tucson
www.artinstitutes.edu/tucson
5099 East Grant Road, #100
Tucson, AZ 85712
Fax: (520) 881-4234
Phone: (520) 881-2900

Art Institute of Washington
www.aiw.artinstitutes.edu
Office of Admissions
1820 North Fort Myer Drive
Arlington, VA 22209-1802
Fax: (703) 358-9759
E-mail: aiwadm@aii.edu
Phone: (703) 358-9550

Art Institutes International Minnesota
www.artinstitutes.edu/minneapolis
Dean of Student Affairs
15 South Ninth Street
Minneapolis, MN 55402
Fax: (612) 332-3934
E-mail: pboersig@aii.edu
Phone: (612) 332-3361 ext. 6865

ASA Institute of Business and Computer Technology
www.asa.edu
International Student Services
81 Willoughby Street
Brooklyn, NY 11201
Fax: (718) 532-1432
E-mail: gtrahanis@asa.edu
Phone: (718) 522-9073 ext. 2120

Asheville-Buncombe Technical Community College
www.abtech.edu
Academic Advisor, College Transfer Advisor, Student Services
340 Victoria Road
Asheville, NC 28801-4897
Fax: (828) 251-6718
E-mail: rhowell@abtech.edu
Phone: (828) 254-1921 ext. 441

Ashford University
www.ashford.edu
400 North Bluff Boulevard
Box 2967
Clinton, IA 52733-2967
Fax: (563) 243-6102
E-mail: admissions@ashford.edu
Phone: (563) 242-4153

Ashland Community and Technical College
www.ashland.kctcs.edu
Student Affairs/Admissions
1400 College Drive
Ashland, KY 41101-3683
Fax: (606) 326-2912
E-mail: willie.mccullough@kctcs.net
Phone: (606) 326-2193

Ashland University
www.ashland.edu
International Student Services
401 College Avenue
Ashland, OH 44805-9981
Fax: (419) 289-5629
E-mail: srosa@ashland.edu
Phone: (419) 289-5068

Ashworth College
www.ashworthcollege.edu
430 Technology Parkway
Norcross, GA 30092-3406
Fax: (770) 729-9389
E-mail: info@ashworthcollege.edu
Phone: (770) 729-8400

Asnuntuck Community College
www.acc.commnet.edu
Admissions Office
170 Elm Street
Enfield, CT 06082
Fax: (860) 253-3014
E-mail: tstjames@commnet.edu
Phone: (860) 253-3000 ext. 3087

Aspen University
www.aspen.edu
720 South Colorado Boulevard, Suite 1150N
Denver, CO 80246
Fax: (303) 336-1144
E-mail: admissions@aspen.edu
Phone: (303) 333-4224

Assumption College
www.assumption.edu
Office of Student Affairs
500 Salisbury Street
Worcester, MA 01609-1296
Fax: (508) 799-4412
E-mail: rravanel@assumption.edu
Phone: (508) 767-7325

Athens State University
www.athens.edu
300 North Beaty Street
Athens, AL 35611
Fax: (256) 233-8128
E-mail: larry.keenum@athens.edu
Phone: (256) 233-8141

ATI Career Training Center: Oakland Park
www.aticareertraining.edu
3501 NW 9th Avenue
Oakland Park, FL 33309
Fax: (954) 568-0874
E-mail: lead130@atienterprises.edu
Phone: (954) 563-5899

ATI College of Health
www.aticareertraining.edu
1395 NW 167th Street
Miami, FL 33169-5745
Fax: (305) 628-1461
E-mail: ekranidis@atienterprises.edu
Phone: (305) 628-1000

Atlanta Christian College
www.acc.edu
Admission Office
2605 Ben Hill Road
East Point, GA 30344
Fax: (404) 460-2451
E-mail: mhall@acc.edu
Phone: (404) 761-8861

Atlanta Metropolitan College
www.atlm.edu
Admissions
1630 Metropolitan Parkway, SW
Atlanta, GA 30310-4498
Fax: (404) 756-4407
E-mail: areid@atlm.edu
Phone: (404) 756-4004

Atlanta Technical College
www.atlantatech.edu
Student Affairs
1560 Metropolitan Parkway, SW
Atlanta, GA 30310-4446
Fax: (404) 225-4451
E-mail: sbryant@atlantatech.edu
Phone: (404) ext. 4474

Atlantic Cape Community College
www.atlantic.edu
Admissions
5100 Black Horse Pike
Mays Landing, NJ 08330-2699
Fax: (609) 343-4921
E-mail: kfletche@atlantic.edu
Phone: (609) 343-4916

Atlantic Union College
www.auc.edu
Student Accounts Office
Main Street
Box 1000
South Lancaster, MA 01561
Fax: (978) 368-2567
E-mail: bordes.henry-saturne@auc.edu
Phone: (978) 368-2275

Auburn University
www.auburn.edu
Office of International Student Life & Admissions
Quad Center
Auburn, AL 36849-5111
Fax: (334) 844-6754
E-mail: orgenny@auburn.edu
Phone: (334) 844-2401

Auburn University at Montgomery
www.aum.edu
International Education Services
7400 East Drive, Room 139 Taylor Center
Box 244023
Montgomery, AL 36124-4023
Fax: (334) 244-3795
E-mail: rblaesin@aum.edu
Phone: (334) 244-3758

Augsburg College
www.augsburg.edu
2211 Riverside Avenue
Minneapolis, MN 55454
Fax: (612) 330-1590
E-mail: admissions@augsburg.edu
Phone: (612) 330-1001

Augusta State University
www.aug.edu
Admissions
2500 Walton Way
Augusta, GA 30904-2200
Fax: (706) 667-4355
E-mail: cgiardin@aug.edu
Phone: (706) 737-1632

Augusta Technical College
www.augustatech.edu
Admissions
3200 Augusta Tech Drive
Augusta, GA 30906
Fax: (706) 771-4034
E-mail: broberts@augustatech.edu
Phone: (706) 771-4150

Augustana College
www.augustana.edu
Admissions
639 38th Street
Rock Island, IL 61201-2296
Fax: (309) 794-7422
E-mail: aaodc@augustana.edu
Phone: (309) 794-7314

Augustana College
www.augie.edu
Office of International Programs
2001 South Summit Avenue
Sioux Falls, SD 57197-9990
Fax: (605) 274-5518
E-mail: donn.grinager@augie.edu
Phone: (605) 274-4498

Aurora University
www.aurora.edu
Office of Admission
347 South Gladstone Avenue
Aurora, IL 60506-4892
Fax: (630) 844-5535
E-mail: admission@aurora.edu
Phone: (630) 844-5533

Austin College
www.austincollege.edu
Admission, Transfer and International
Students
900 North Grand Avenue, Suite 6N
Sherman, TX 75090-4400
Fax: (903) 813-3198
E-mail: admission@austincollege.edu
Phone: (903) 813-2380

Austin Community College
www.austincc.edu
International Student Office
PO Box 15306
Austin, TX 78761-5306
Fax: (512) 223-6239
E-mail: intadm@austincc.edu
Phone: (512) 223-6241

Austin Peay State University
www.apsu.edu
Office of Admissions
PO Box 4548
Clarksville, TN 37044
Fax: (931) 221-6168
E-mail: rousselott@apsu.edu
Phone: (931) 221-6851

Ave Maria University
www.avemaria.edu
Director of Admissions
5050 Ave Maria Boulevard
Ave Maria, FL 34142-9505
Fax: (239) 280-2566
E-mail: jason.fabaz@avemaria.edu
Phone: (239) 280-2480

Averett University
www.averett.edu
Admissions
420 West Main Street
Danville, VA 24541
Fax: (434) 797-2784
E-mail: stephanie.mullins@averett.edu
Phone: (434) 791-5666

**Aviation Institute of Maintenance: Virginia
Beach**
www.aviationmaintenance.edu
2211 South Military Highway
Chesapeake, VA 23320
E-mail:
Admdiramn@AviationMaintenance.edu
Phone: (757) 363-2121

Avila University
www.avila.edu
International Language & Cultural Program
11901 Wornall Road
Kansas City, MO 64145-1007
Fax: (816) 501-2461
E-mail: bruce.inwards@avila.edu
Phone: (816) 501-3772

Azusa Pacific University
www.apu.edu
International Admissions
901 East Alosta Avenue
Box 7000
Azusa, CA 91702-7000
Fax: (626) 815-3801
E-mail: mgrams@apu.edu
Phone: (626) 815-6000 ext. 3055

Babson College
www.babson.edu
Undergraduate Admission Office
231 Forest Street
Babson Park, MA 02457-0310
Fax: (781) 239-4006
E-mail: aramsey@babson.edu
Phone: (781) 239-5522

Bacone College
www.bacone.edu
Admissions
2299 Old Bacone Road
Muskogee, OK 74403
Fax: (918) 781-7416
E-mail: admissions@bacone.edu
Phone: (918) 683-4581

Bainbridge College
www.bainbridge.edu
Admissions/Records
2500 East Shotwell Street
PO Box 990
Bainbridge, GA 39818-0990
Fax: (229) 248-2623
E-mail: csnyder@bainbridge.edu
Phone: (229) 248-2504

Baker College of Allen Park
www.baker.edu
Admissions
4500 Enterprise Drive
Allen Park, MI 48101
Phone: (313) 425-3700

Baker College of Auburn Hills
www.baker.edu
Academic Office
1500 University Drive
Auburn Hills, MI 48326
Fax: (248) 340-0608
Phone: (248) 276-8229

Baker College of Cadillac
www.baker.edu
Admissions
9600 East 13th Street
Cadillac, MI 49601
Fax: (231) 775-8505
E-mail: mike.tisdal@baker.edu
Phone: (231) 876-3100

Baker College of Jackson
www.baker.edu
2800 Springport Road
Jackson, MI 49202
Fax: (517) 789-7331
E-mail: adm-jk@baker.edu
Phone: (517) 788-7800

Baker College of Muskegon
www.baker.edu
Admissions
1903 Marquette Avenue
Muskegon, MI 49442
Fax: (231) 777-5201
E-mail: kathy.jacobson@baker.edu
Phone: (231) 777-5200

Baker College of Owosso
www.baker.edu
Admissions
1020 South Washington Street
Owosso, MI 48867
Fax: (989) 729-3359
E-mail: michael.konopacke@baker.edu
Phone: (989) 729-3350

Baker College of Port Huron
www.baker.edu
Admissions Office
3403 Lapeer Road
Port Huron, MI 48060-2597
Fax: (810) 985-7066
E-mail: daniel.kenny@baker.edu
Phone: (810) 985-7000

Baker University
www.bakeru.edu
Office of Admissions
618 Eighth Street
PO Box 65
Baldwin City, KS 66006-0065
Fax: (785) 594-8353
E-mail: kevin.kropf@bakeru.edu
Phone: (785) 594-8307

Bakersfield College
www.bakersfieldcollege.edu
Admissions and Records Office
1801 Panorama Drive
Bakersfield, CA 93305
Fax: (661) 395-4500
E-mail: lallday@bakersfieldcollege.edu
Phone: (661) 395-4332

Baldwin-Wallace College
www.bw.edu
Office of Undergraduate Admission
275 Eastland Road
Berea, OH 44017-2088
Fax: (440) 826-3830
E-mail: admission@bw.edu
Phone: (440) 826-2222

Ball State University
www.bsu.edu
Rinker Center for International Programs
2000 West University Avenue
Muncie, IN 47306-1022
Fax: (765) 285-3710
E-mail: kdontamsetti@bsu.edu
Phone: (765) 285-5422

Baltimore City Community College
www.bccc.edu
International Student Services
2901 Liberty Heights Avenue
Baltimore, MD 21215-7893
Fax: (410) 462-8345
E-mail: ddangerfield@bccc.edu
Phone: (410) 462-8311

Baltimore International College
www.bic.edu
Admissions
17 Commerce Street
Baltimore, MD 21202-3230
Fax: (410) 752-3730
E-mail: admissions@bic.edu
Phone: (410) 752-4710 ext. 226

Baptist Bible College of Pennsylvania
www.bbc.edu
Admissions - Michelle Hammaker
538 Venard Road
Clarks Summit, PA 18411-1297
Fax: (570) 585-9299
E-mail: admissions@bbc.edu
Phone: (570) 585-9385

Baptist College of Florida
www.baptistcollege.edu
Admissions
5400 College Drive
Graceville, FL 32440-3306
Fax: (850) 263-9026
E-mail: admissions@baptistcollege.edu
Phone: (800) 328-2660 ext. 460

Baptist University of the Americas
www.bua.edu
8019 South Pan Am Expressway
San Antonio, TX 78224
E-mail: mranjel@bua.edu
Phone: (210) 924-4338

Barclay College
www.barclaycollege.edu
Director of Admissions
607 North Kingman
Haviland, KS 67059
Fax: (620) 862-5403
E-mail: admissions@barclaycollege.edu
Phone: (620) 862-5252 ext. 43

Bard College
www.bard.edu
Admissions
30 Campus Road
PO Box 5000
Annandale-on-Hudson, NY 12504-5000
Fax: (845) 758-5208
E-mail: admission@bard.edu
Phone: (845) 758-7472

Bard College at Simon's Rock
www.simons-rock.edu
Office of Admission
Office of Admission
84 Alford Road
Great Barrington, MA 01230-1990
Fax: (413) 528-7334
E-mail: admit@simons-rock.edu
Phone: (413) 528-7355

Barnard College
www.barnard.edu
Admissions
3009 Broadway
New York, NY 10027-6598
Fax: (212) 854-6220
E-mail: jfishbein@barnard.edu
Phone: (212) 854-2506

Barry University
www.barry.edu
Division of Enrollment Management
11300 NE Second Avenue
Miami Shores, FL 33161-6695
Fax: (305) 899-2971
E-mail: ascott@mail.barry.edu
Phone: (305) 899-3666

Barstow Community College
www.barstow.edu
Admissions, Records and Financial Aid
Manager
2700 Barstow Road
Barstow, CA 92311-9984
Fax: (760) 252-6754
E-mail: hcaldon@barstow.edu
Phone: (760) 252-2411 ext. 7236

Barton College
www.barton.edu
International Student Adviser
Box 5000
Wilson, NC 27893-7000
Fax: (252) 399-6572
E-mail: mgakins@barton.edu
Phone: (252) 399-6609

Barton County Community College
www.bartonccc.edu
Admissions
245 North East 30th Road
Great Bend, KS 67530-9283
Fax: (620) 786-1160
E-mail: mooret@bartonccc.edu
Phone: (620) 792-9241

Bastyr University
www.bastyr.edu
Admissions
14500 Juanita Drive, NE
Kenmore, WA 98028
Fax: (425) 602-3090
E-mail: tolsen@bastyr.edu
Phone: (425) 602-3330

Bates College
www.bates.edu
International Admissions Office
23 Campus Avenue, Lindholm House
Lewiston, ME 04240-9917
Fax: (207) 786-6025
E-mail: kcrosby@bates.edu
Phone: (207) 786-6000

Bates Technical College
www.bates.ctc.edu
Career Specialist
1101 South Yakima Avenue
Tacoma, WA 98405
E-mail: larnold@bates.ctc.edu
Phone: (253) 680-7007

Baton Rouge Community College
www.mybrcc.edu
International Student Adviser
201 Community College Drive
Baton Rouge, LA 70806
Fax: (225) 216-8010
E-mail: clayn@mybrcc.edu
Phone: (225) 216-8703

Baton Rouge School of Computers
www.brsc.net
10425 Plaza Americana
Baton Rouge, LA 70816
Fax: (225) 923-2979
Phone: (225) 923-2525

Bauder College
www.bauder.edu
Admissions (International)
384 Northyards Boulevard NW, Ste 190
Atlanta, GA 30313
Fax: (404) 237-1619
E-mail: llanier@bauder.edu
Phone: (404) 237-7573 ext. 1795

Bay de Noc Community College
www.baycollege.edu
Executive Dean of Student Services
2001 North Lincoln Road
Escanaba, MI 49829-2511
Fax: (906) 217-1649
E-mail: soucym@baycollege.edu
Phone: (906) 217-4068

Bay Path College
www.baypath.edu
Director of Admissions
588 Longmeadow Street
Longmeadow, MA 01106
Fax: (413) 565-1105
E-mail: admiss@baypath.edu
Phone: (413) 565-1331

Bay State College
www.baystate.edu
Admissions
122 Commonwealth Avenue
Boston, MA 02116
Fax: (617) 249-0400
E-mail: cregan@baystate.edu
Phone: (617) 217-9000

Bayamon Central University
www.ucb.edu.pr
Admissions
PO Box 1725
Bayamon, PR 00960-1725
Fax: (787) 740-2200
E-mail: chernandez@ucb.edu.pr
Phone: (787) 786-3030 ext. 2100

Baylor University
www.baylor.edu
International Programs
One Bear Place #97056
Waco, TX 76798-7056
Fax: (254) 710-1468
E-mail: alexine_burke@baylor.edu
Phone: (254) 710-1461

Beacon College
www.beaconcollege.edu
Admissions
105 East Main Street
Leesburg, FL 34748
Fax: (352) 787-0721
E-mail: admissions@beaconcollege.edu
Phone: (352) 787-7249

Becker College
www.becker.edu
Director of Admissions
61 Sever Street
Worcester, MA 01609
Fax: (508) 890-1500
E-mail: admissions@beckercollege.edu
Phone: (774) 354-0460

Beis Medrash Heichal Dovid
211 Beach 17th Street
Far Rockaway, NY 11691
Fax: (718) 406-8359
Phone: (718) 868-2300 ext. 360

Belhaven University
www.belhaven.edu
Institutional Advancement
1500 Peachtree Street
Box 153
Jackson, MS 39202
Fax: (601) 968-8946
E-mail: admission@belhaven.edu
Phone: (800) 960-5940

Bellarmine University
www.bellarmine.edu
Admission
2001 Newburg Road
Louisville, KY 40205
Fax: (502) 272-8002
E-mail: dkline@bellarmine.edu
Phone: (502) 272-8131

Bellevue University
www.bellevue.edu
International Programs
1000 Galvin Road South
Bellevue, NE 68005-3098
Fax: (402) 557-5423
E-mail: curtis.freerking@bellevue.edu
Phone: (402) 557-7283

Bellin College
www.bellincollege.edu
Admissions Office
3201 Eaton Road
Green Bay, WI
Fax: (920) 433-7416
E-mail: carol.rafferty@bcon.edu
Phone: (920) 433-5805

Bellingham Technical College
www.btc.ctc.edu
Admissions Office
3028 Lindbergh Avenue
Bellingham, WA 98225-1599
Fax: (360) 676-2798
E-mail: erunestr@btc.ctc.edu
Phone: (360) 752-8324

Belmont Abbey College
www.belmontabbeycollege.edu
Admissions Office
100 Belmont - Mt. Holly Road
Belmont, NC 28012-2795
Fax: (704) 825-6220
E-mail: rogerljones@bac.edu
Phone: (888) 222-0110

Belmont Technical College
www.btc.edu
120 Fox Shannon Place
St. Clairsville, OH 43950
Fax: (740) 699-3049
E-mail: thouston@btc.edu
Phone: (740) 695-9500 ext. 1563

Belmont University
www.belmont.edu
International Education
1900 Belmont Boulevard
Nashville, TN 37212-3757
Fax: (615) 460-5539
E-mail: kathy.skinner@belmont.edu
Phone: (615) 460-5500

Beloit College
www.beloit.edu
Coordinator of International Admission
700 College Street
Beloit, WI 53511-5595
Fax: (608) 363-2075
E-mail: intadmis@beloit.edu
Phone: (608) 363-2500

Bemidji State University
www.bemidjistate.edu
International Program Center
1500 Birchmont Drive NE, #13
Bemidji, MN 56601
Fax: (218) 755-2074
E-mail: lritchie@bemidjistate.edu
Phone: (218) 755-4096

Benedict College
www.benedict.edu
Student Records
1600 Harden Street
Columbia, SC 29204
Fax: (803) 253-5085
E-mail: scottkinney@benedict.edu
Phone: (803) 705-4680

Benedictine College
www.benedictine.edu
Director of International Admission and
Retention
1020 North Second Street
Atchison, KS 66002-1499
Fax: (913) 360-7970
E-mail: sfox@benedictine.edu
Phone: (800) 367-5340

Benedictine University
www.ben.edu
International Programs
5700 College Road
Lisle, IL 60532
Fax: (630) 829-6301
E-mail: admissions@ben.edu
Phone: (630) 829-6355

Benedictine University at Springfield
www.sci.edu
Enrollment Services
1500 North Fifth Street
Springfield, IL 62702-2694
Fax: (217) 525-1497
E-mail: dbryant@sci.edu
Phone: (217) 525-1420 ext. 210

Benjamin Franklin Institute of Technology
www.bfit.edu
Admissions Office
41 Berkeley Street
Boston, MA 02116
Fax: (617) 482-3706
E-mail: mchen@bfit.edu
Phone: (617) 423-4630 ext. 121

Bennett College for Women
www.bennett.edu
Admissions
900 East Washington Street
Greensboro, NC 27401-3239
Fax: (336) 517-2166
E-mail: admiss@bennett.edu
Phone: (336) 370-8624

Bennington College
www.bennington.edu
Office of Admissions
One College Drive
Bennington, VT 05201-6003
Fax: (802) 440-4320
E-mail: ldietrich@bennington.edu
Phone: (802) 440-4596

Bentley University
www.bentley.edu
Undergraduate Admissions
175 Forest Street
Waltham, MA 02452-4713
Fax: (781) 891-3414
E-mail: ugadmission@bentley.edu
Phone: (781) 891-2244

Berea College
www.berea.edu
Admissions
CPO 2220
Berea, KY 40404
Fax: (859) 985-3512
E-mail: admissions@berea.edu
Phone: (800) 326-5948

Bergin University of Canine Studies
www.berginu.edu
1215 Sebastopol Road
Santa Rosa, CA 95407
E-mail: info@berginu.edu
Phone: (707) 545-3647 ext. 21

Berkeley City College
www.berkeleycitycollege.edu
International Specialist, International Affairs
& Distance Education
2050 Center Street
Berkeley, CA 94704
Fax: (510) 465-3257
E-mail: dgephart@Peralta.edu
Phone: (510) 587-7834

Berkeley College
www.berkeleycollege.edu
International Division
44 Rifle Camp Road
Woodland Park, NJ 07424-0440
Fax: (212) 986-7827
E-mail: international@berkeleycollege.edu
Phone: (212) 687-3730

Berkeley College
www.berkeleycollege.edu
International Division
99 Church Street
White Plains, NY 10601
Fax: (212) 986-7827
E-mail: naj@berkeleycollege.edu
Phone: (212) 687-3730

Berkeley College of New York City
www.berkeleycollege.edu
Berkeley College, International Division
3 East 43rd Street
New York, NY 10017
Fax: (212) 986-7827
E-mail: international@berkeleycollege.edu
Phone: (212) 687-3730

Berklee College of Music
www.berklee.edu
Office of Admissions
1140 Boylston Street
Boston, MA 02215
Fax: (617) 747-2047
E-mail: admissions@berklee.edu
Phone: (617) 747-2222

Berkshire Community College
www.berkshirecc.edu
Multicultural Admissions Counselor
1350 West Street
Pittsfield, MA 01201-5786
Fax: (413) 499-4576
E-mail: evelez@berkshirecc.edu
Phone: (413) 236-1601

Berry College
www.berry.edu
Admissions
PO Box 490159
2277 Martha Berry Highway NW
Mount Berry, GA 30149-0159
Fax: (706) 290-2178
E-mail: admissions@berry.edu
Phone: (706) 236-2215

Beth Hamedrash Shaarei Yosher Institute
4102-10 16th Avenue
Brooklyn, NY 11204
Phone: (718) 854-2290

Beth Hatalmud Rabbinical College
2127 82nd Street
Brooklyn, NY 11214
Phone: (718) 259-2525

Bethany College
www.bethanylb.edu
Admissions
335 East Swensson
Lindsborg, KS 67456-1897
Fax: (785) 227-8993
E-mail: admissions@bethanylb.edu
Phone: (800) 826-2281

Bethany College
www.bethanywv.edu
Office of Admission
Office of Admission
Bethany, WV 26032-0428
Fax: (304) 829-7142
E-mail: rzitzelberger@bethanywv.edu
Phone: (304) 829-7514

Bethany Lutheran College
www.blc.edu
700 Luther Drive
Mankato, MN 56001-4490
Fax: (507) 344-7376
E-mail: lloge@blc.edu
Phone: (507) 344-7000 ext. 322

Bethany University
www.bethany.edu
Admissions
800 Bethany Drive
Scotts Valley, CA 95066-2898
Fax: (831) 461-1621
E-mail: info@fc.bethany.edu
Phone: (831) 438-3800 ext. 3900

Bethel College
www.BethelCollege.edu
Admission Office
1001 Bethel Circle
Mishawaka, IN 46545-5591
Fax: (574) 807-7650
E-mail: admissions@BethelCollege.edu
Phone: (574) 807-7600

Bethel College
www.bethelks.edu
Admissions
300 E 27th Street
North Newton, KS 67117-8061
Fax: (316) 284-5870
E-mail: admissions@bethelks.edu
Phone: (800) 522-1887 ext. 230

Bethel University
www.bethel.edu
Office of Admissions
3900 Bethel Dr.
Saint Paul, MN 55112
Fax: (651) 635-1490
E-mail: c-vang@bethel.edu
Phone: (800) 255-8706 ext. 6242

Bethel University
www.bethelu.edu
International Student Affairs
325 Cherry Avenue
Attention: Admissions
McKenzie, TN 38201
Fax: (731) 352-4069
E-mail: campbellj@bethel-college.edu
Phone: (731) 352-4024

Bethesda Christian University
www.bcu.edu
Admissions
730 North Euclid Street
Anaheim, CA 92801
Fax: (714) 517-1948
E-mail: admission@bcu.edu
Phone: (714) 517-1945

Bethune-Cookman University
www.cookman.edu
Admissions
Dr. Mary McLeod Bethune Boulevard
Daytona Beach, FL 32114-3099
Fax: (386) 481-2601
E-mail: admissions@cookman.edu
Phone: (386) 481-2600

Beulah Heights University
www.beulah.org
Admissions
892 Berne Street SE
PO Box 18145
Atlanta, GA 30316
Fax: (404) 627-0702
E-mail: john.dreher@beulah.org
Phone: (404) 627-2681 ext. 117

Bidwell Training Center
www.bidwell-training.org
1815 Metropolitan Street
Pittsburgh, PA 15233
Fax: (412) 321-2120
E-mail: dfarah@mcg-btc.org
Phone: (412) 323-4000 ext. 156

Big Bend Community College
www.bigbend.edu
Admissions/Registration
7662 Chanute Street
Moses Lake, WA 98837-3299
Fax: (509) 762-6243
E-mail: ruthc@bigbend.edu
Phone: (509) 793-2065

Big Sandy Community and Technical College
www.bigsandy.kctcs.edu
One Bert T. Combs Drive
Prestonsburg, KY 41653
Fax: (606) 886-6943
E-mail: jimmy.wright@kctcs.edu
Phone: (606) 886-3863 ext. 67366

Biola University
www.biola.edu
Admissions
13800 Biola Avenue
La Mirada, CA 90639-0001
Fax: (562) 903-4709
E-mail: fitsum.mulat@biola.edu
Phone: (562) 903-4752

Birmingham-Southern College
www.bsc.edu
Office of International Programs
900 Arkadelphia Road
Box 549008
Birmingham, AL 35254
Fax: (205) 226-4805
E-mail: aledvina@bsc.edu
Phone: (205) 226-7722

Bishop State Community College
www.bishop.edu
Student Development Services
351 North Broad Street
Mobile, AL 36603-5898
Fax: (251) 690-6998
E-mail: mvodom@bishop.edu
Phone: (251) 405-7065

Bismarck State College
www.bismarckstate.edu
Admissions
PO Box 5587
Bismarck, ND 58506-5587
Fax: (701) 224-5643
E-mail: gregory.sturm@bsc.nodak.edu
Phone: (701) 224-5426

Black Hawk College
www.bhc.edu
International Student Office/ESL
6600-34th Avenue
Moline, IL 61265-5899
Fax: (309) 796-5124
E-mail: bollatia@bhc.edu
Phone: (309) 796-5183

Black Hawk College: East Campus
www.bhc.edu
26230 Black Hawk Road
Galva, IL 61434-9476
Fax: (309) 856-6005
E-mail: riced@bhc.edu
Phone: (309) 854-1703

Black Hills State University
www.bhsu.edu
International Student Office
1200 University Street Box 9502
Spearfish, SD 57799-9502
Fax: (605) 642-6022
E-mail: jamesfleming@bhsu.edu
Phone: (605) 642-6058

Blackburn College
www.blackburn.edu
Admissions Office
700 College Avenue
Carlinville, IL 62626
Fax: (217) 854-3713
E-mail: jmali@blackburn.edu
Phone: (217) 854-3231 ext. 4252

Bladen Community College
www.bladencc.edu
Post Office Box 266
Dublin, NC 28332-0266
Fax: (910) 879-5564
E-mail: ywilloughby@bladencc.edu
Phone: (910) 879-5593

Blessing-Rieman College of Nursing
www.brcn.edu
PO Box 7005
Quincy, IL 62305-7005
Fax: (217) 223-4661
E-mail: admissions@brcn.edu
Phone: (217) 228-5520 ext. 6949

Blinn College
www.blinn.edu
Student Services
902 College Avenue
Brenham, TX 77833
Fax: (979) 830-4110
E-mail: jharris@blinn.edu
Phone: (979) 830-4140

Bloomfield College
www.bloomfield.edu
Office of Enrollment Management and
Admission
One Park Place
Bloomfield, NJ 07003
Fax: (973) 748-0916
E-mail: admission@bloomfield.edu
Phone: (800) 848-4555 ext. 127

Bloomsburg University of Pennsylvania
www.bloomu.edu
Office of Admissions
104 Student Service Center
400 East Second Street
Bloomsburg, PA 17815
Fax: (570) 389-4741
E-mail: buadmiss@bloomu.edu
Phone: (570) 389-4316

Blue Cliff College: Gulfport
www.bluecliffcollege.com
12251 Bernard Parkway
Gulfport, MS 39503
Fax: (228) 896-8659
E-mail: AlbertF@BlueCliffCollege.com
Phone: (288) 896-9727

Blue Cliff College: Metairie
www.bluecliffcollege.com
3200 Cleary Avenue
Metairie, LA 70002
Fax: (504) 456-7849
E-mail: pattyr@bluecliffcollege.com
Phone: (504) 456-3141

Blue Cliff College: Shreveport
www.bluecliffcollege.com
8731 Park Plaza Drive
Shreveport, LA 71105-5682
Phone: (318) 425-7941

Blue Mountain College
www.bmc.edu
Office of Admissions
201 West Main Street, PO Box 160
Blue Mountain, MS 38610-0160
Fax: (662) 685-4776
E-mail: jherrington@bmc.edu
Phone: (662) 685-4771 ext. 158

Blue Ridge Community College
www.brcc.edu
Admissions and Records
Box 80
Weyers Cave, VA 24486-9989
Fax: (540) 453-2437
E-mail: mathiasc@brcc.edu
Phone: (540) 453-2360

Bluefield College
www.bluefield.edu
Office of Enrollment Management
3000 College Drive
Bluefield, VA 24605
Fax: (276) 326-4602
E-mail: admissions@bluefield.edu
Phone: (800) 872-0175

Bluefield State College
www.bluefieldstate.edu
Enrollment Management
219 Rock Street
Bluefield, WV 24701
Fax: (304) 325-7747
E-mail: bscadmit@bluefield.wvnet.edu
Phone: (304) 327-4567

Bluegrass Community and Technical College
www.bluegrass.kctcs.edu
Admissions
200 Oswald Building, Cooper Drive
Lexington, KY 40506-0235
Fax: (859) 246-4666
E-mail: nathan.congleton@kctcs.edu
Phone: (859) 246-4647

Bluffton University
www.bluffton.edu
Director of Admissions
1 University Drive
Bluffton, OH 45817-2104
Fax: (419) 358-3081
E-mail: jebsenc@bluffton.edu
Phone: (419) 358-3257

Bob Jones University
www.bju.edu
Office of Admission
1700 Wade Hampton Boulevard
Greenville, SC 29614
Fax: (864) 770-1323
E-mail: bboudrea@bju.edu
Phone: (864) 242-5100 ext. 2092

Boise State University
www.boisestate.edu
Undergraduate Admissions
1910 University Drive
Boise, ID 83725
Fax: (208) 426-3765
E-mail: nikicallison@boisestate.edu
Phone: (208) 426-2715

Bolivar Technical College
www.bolivarcollege.org
PO Box 592
2001 West Broadway
Bolivar, MO 65613
Fax: (417) 777-8908
E-mail: info@bolivarcollege.org
Phone: (417) 777-5062

Bossier Parish Community College
www.bpcc.edu
Registrar's Office
6220 East Texas Street
Bossier City, LA 71111-6922
Fax: (318) 678-6390
E-mail: pstewart@bpcc.edu
Phone: (318) 678-6034

Boston Baptist College
www.boston.edu/
950 Metropolitan Avenue
Boston, MA 02136
E-mail: admissions@boston.edu
Phone: (617) 364-3510 ext. 217

Boston College
www.bc.edu
Office of Undergraduate Admissions
140 Commonwealth Avenue, Devlin Hall 208
Chestnut Hill, MA 02467-3809
Fax: (617) 552-0798
Phone: (617) 552-3100

Boston Conservatory
www.bostonconservatory.edu
Admissions
8 The Fenway
Boston, MA 02215
Fax: (857) 207-3116
E-mail: admissions@bostonconservatory.edu
Phone: (617) 912-9116

Boston University
www.bu.edu
Office of International Admissions
121 Bay State Road
Boston, MA 02215
Fax: (617) 353-5334
E-mail: mduschan@bu.edu
Phone: (617) 353-4492

Boulder College of Massage Therapy
www.bcmt.org
Admissions Office
6255 Longbow Drive
Boulder, CO 80301
Fax: (303) 530-2204
E-mail: jwolfe@bcmt.org
Phone: (303) 530-2100

Bowdoin College
www.bowdoin.edu
Admissions Office
5000 College Station
Brunswick, ME 04011-8441
Fax: (207) 725-3101
E-mail: jthursto@bowdoin.edu
Phone: (207) 725-3232

Bowie State University
www.bowiestate.edu
Career Co-Op and International Services
14000 Jericho Park Road
Attn: Admissions Office
Bowie, MD 20715
Fax: (301) 860-3824
E-mail: rbatton@bowiestate.edu
Phone: (301) 860-3830

Bowling Green State University
www.bgsu.edu
Center for International Programs
110 McFall Center
Bowling Green State University
Bowling Green, OH 43403-0085
Fax: (419) 372-2429
E-mail: cip@bgsu.edu
Phone: (419) 372-2247

Bowling Green State University: Firelands College
www.firelands.bgsu.edu
Center for International Programs
One University Drive
Huron, OH 44839
Fax: (419) 372-0604
E-mail: phofman@bgsu.edu
Phone: (419) 372-2248

Bradley University
www.bradley.edu
Undergraduate Admissions
1501 West Bradley Avenue
Peoria, IL 61625
Fax: (309) 677-2799
E-mail: intlam@bradley.edu
Phone: (309) 677-1000

Bramson ORT College
www.bramsonort.edu
6930 Austin Street
Forest Hills, NY 11375
Fax: (718) 575-5118
Phone: (718) 261-5800

Brandeis University
www.brandeis.edu
Undergraduate Admissions
Box 549110
Waltham, MA 02454-9110
Fax: (781) 736-3536
E-mail: kwest@brandeis.edu
Phone: (781) 736-3531

Brazosport College
www.brazosport.edu
Admissions
500 College Drive
Lake Jackson, TX 77566
Fax: (979) 230-3376
E-mail: wade.wilson@brazosport.edu
Phone: (979) 230-3216

Brenau University
www.brenau.edu
Women's College Admission Office
500 Washington Street SE
Gainesville, GA 30501
Fax: (770) 538-4306
E-mail: mswitzer@brenau.edu
Phone: (770) 531-3178

Brescia University
www.brescia.edu
717 Frederica Street
Owensboro, KY 42301-3023
Fax: (270) 686-4314
E-mail: admissions@brescia.edu
Phone: (270) 686-4241

Brevard College
www.brevard.edu
Admissions Counselor
One Brevard College Drive
Brevard, NC 28712
Fax: (828) 884-3790
E-mail: atkinsk@brevard.edu
Phone: (828) 884-8378

Brevard Community College
www.brevardcc.edu
Global Education and Exchange
1519 Clearlake Road
Cocoa, FL 32922-9987
Fax: (321) 433-7357
E-mail: gopakumars@brevardcc.edu
Phone: (321) 433-7342

Brewton-Parker College
www.bpc.edu
International Student Services Office
Brewton-Parker College # 2011
201 David-Eliza Fountain Circle
Mount Vernon, GA 30445
Fax: (912) 583-4498
E-mail: sclay@bpc.edu
Phone: (912) 583-3247

Briar Cliff University
www.briarcliff.edu
Admissions
3303 Rebecca Street
PO Box 2100
Sioux City, IA 51104-0100
Fax: (712) 279-1632
E-mail: admissions@briarcliff.edu
Phone: (712) 279-5200

Briarcliffe College
www.briarcliffe.edu
1055 Stewart Avenue
Bethpage, NY 11714
Fax: (516) 470-6020
E-mail: spescador@bcl.edu
Phone: (516) 918-3600

Bridgemont Community and Technical College
www.bridgemont.edu
619 Second Avenue
Montgomery, WV 25136
E-mail: joyce.surbaugh@bridgemont.edu
Phone: (304) 734-6603

Bridgewater College
www.bridgewater.edu
Admissions Office
402 East College Street
Bridgewater, VA 22812-1599
Fax: (540) 828-5481
E-mail: admissions@bridgewater.edu
Phone: (540) 828-5375

Bridgewater State University
www.bridgew.edu
Admissions
Gates House
Bridgewater, MA 02325
Fax: (508) 531-1746
E-mail: gmeyer@bridgew.edu
Phone: (508) 531-1237

Brigham Young University
www.byu.edu
International Admissions
A-41ASB, BYU
Provo, UT 84602
Fax: (801) 422-0973
E-mail: intladm@byu.edu
Phone: (801) 422-2500

Brigham Young University-Hawaii
www.byuh.edu
Admissions
55-220 Kulanui Street, #1973
Laie, HI 96762-1294
Fax: (808) 675-3741
E-mail: sudlowm@byuh.edu
Phone: (808) 675-3535

Brigham Young University-Idaho
www.byui.edu
International Services
120 Kimball Building
Rexburg, ID 83460-1615
Fax: (208) 496-5648
E-mail: international@byui.edu
Phone: (208) 496-1320

Bristol Community College
www.bristolcc.edu
Office of Admissions
777 Elsbree Street
Fall River, MA 02720-7395
Fax: (508) 730-3265
E-mail: admission@bristolcc.edu
Phone: (508) 678-2811 ext. 2947

Broadview University: Orem
www.broadviewuniversity.edu
898 North 1200 West
Orem, UT 84057
E-mail: mmoon@broadviewuniversity.edu
Phone: (801) 822-5800

Brookdale Community College
www.brookdalecc.edu
Director/International Education Center
765 Newman Springs Road
Lincroft, NJ 07738
Fax: (732) 224-2271
E-mail: jthomas@brookdalecc.edu
Phone: (732) 224-2375

Brookhaven College
www.brookhavencollege.edu
Multi-Cultural Center
3939 Valley View Lane
Farmers Branch, TX 75244-4997
Fax: (972) 860-4886
E-mail: bhcmulticulturalcenter@dcccd.edu
Phone: (972) 860-4936

Brookline College: Albuquerque
www.brooklinecollege.edu
4201 Central Avenue NW, Suite J
Albuquerque, NM 87105-1649
Fax: (505) 352-0199
E-mail: awebb@brooklinecollege.edu
Phone: (505) 880-2877

Brookline College: Phoenix
www.brooklinecollege.edu
2445 West Dunlap Avenue, Suite 100
Phoenix, AZ 85021-5820
Fax: (602) 973-2572
E-mail: madkins@brooklinecollege.edu
Phone: (602) 242-6265

Brookline College: Tempe
www.brooklinecollege.edu
1140-1150 South Priest Drive
Tempe, AZ 85281-5240
Fax: (480) 926-1371
E-mail: ckindred@brooklinecollege.edu
Phone: (480) 545-8755

Brooks Institute
www.brooks.edu
27 East Cota Street
Santa Barbara, CA 93101
Fax: (805) 565-1386
E-mail: admissions@brooks.edu
Phone: (888) 304-3456

Broome Community College
www.sunybroome.edu
Admissions Office
Box 1017
Binghamton, NY 13902
Fax: (607) 778-5310
E-mail: carra_m@sunybroome.edu
Phone: (607) 778-5001

Broward College
www.broward.edu
College Registrar's Office
225 East Las Olas Boulevard
Fort Lauderdale, FL 33301
Fax: (954) 201-7086
E-mail: sgreive@broward.edu
Phone: (954) 201-7468

Brown College: Brooklyn Center
www.browncollege.edu
6860 Shingle Creek Parkway
Brooklyn Center, MN 55430
E-mail: jhuston@browncollege.edu
Phone: (763) 279-2549

Brown College: Mendota Heights
www.browncollege.edu
Admissions
1440 Northland Drive
Mendota Heights, MN 55120
Fax: (651) 905-3540
E-mail: info@browncollege.edu
Phone: (651) 905-3400

Brown Mackie College: Fort Wayne
www.brownmackie.com
3000 Coliseum Boulevard, Suite 100
Fort Wayne, IN 46805
Fax: (260) 484-2678
E-mail: ktaboh@brownmackie.edu
Phone: (260) 484-4400

Brown Mackie College: Miami
www.brownmackie.edu
Academic Affairs
One Herald Plaza
Miami, FL 33132
Fax: (305) 373-8814
E-mail: psitton@brownmackie.edu
Phone: (305) 341-6619

Brown Mackie College: North Kentucky
www.brownmackie.edu
309 Buttermilk Pike
Fort Mitchell, KY 41017
Fax: (859) 341-6483
Phone: (859) 341-5627

Brown Mackie College: St. Louis
www.brownmackie.edu
#2 Soccer Park Road
Fenton, MO 63026

Brown Mackie College: Tucson
www.brownmackie.edu
4585 East Speedway Boulevard
Tucson, AZ 85712
Fax: (520) 319-3495
E-mail: kowens@brownmackie.edu
Phone: (520) 391-3300

Brown University
www.brown.edu
International Admission
45 Prospect Street
PO Box 1876
Providence, RI 02912
Fax: (401) 863-9300
E-mail: Panetha_Ott@brown.edu
Phone: (401) 863-2378

Bryan College
www.bryan.edu
Admissions
PO Box 7000
Dayton, TN 37321-7000
Fax: (423) 775-7199
E-mail: admissions@bryan.edu
Phone: (423) 775-7204

Bryan College: Los Angeles
www.bryancollege.edu
Admissions
3580 Wilshire Boulevard, Suite 400
Los Angeles, CA 90010
Fax: (213) 483-3936
E-mail: info@bryancollege.edu
Phone: (213) 484-8850

Bryan College: Rogers
www.bryancolleges.edu
3704 West Walnut Street
Rogers, AR 72756
Phone: (479) 899-6644

Bryan College: Sacramento
www.bryancollege.edu
2317 Gold Meadow Way
Gold River, CA 95670
Fax: (916) 641-8649
E-mail: admissions@bryancollege.com
Phone: (916) 649-2400

Bryan College: Topeka
www.bryancolleges.com
1527 SW Fairlawn Road
Topeka, KS 66604
E-mail: csollars@bryancc.com
Phone: (785) 272-0889

BryanLGH College of Health Sciences
www.bryanlghcollege.edu
5035 Everett Street
Lincoln, NE 68506
Fax: (402) 481-8621
E-mail: admissions@bryanlghcollege.edu
Phone: (402) 481-8697

Bryant & Stratton College: Albany
www.bryantstratton.edu
Admissions
1259 Central Avenue
Albany, NY 12205
Fax: (518) 437-1049
Phone: (518) 437-1802

Bryant & Stratton College: Buffalo
www.bryantstratton.edu
465 Main Street, Suite 400
Buffalo, NY 14203
Fax: (716) 884-0091
E-mail: mbrobinson@bryantstratton.edu
Phone: (716) 884-9120

Bryant & Stratton College: Parma
www.bryantstratton.edu
Admissions Department
12955 Snow Road
Parma, OH 44130-1013
Fax: (216) 265-0325
E-mail: atinman@bryantstratton.edu
Phone: (216) 265-3151 ext. 229

Bryant & Stratton College: Rochester
www.bryantstratton.edu
1225 Jefferson Road
Rochester, NY 14623
Phone: (585) 292-5627

Bryant & Stratton College: Syracuse North
www.bryantstratton.edu
8687 Carling Road
Liverpool, NY 13090
Phone: (315) 652-6500

Bryant & Stratton College: Virginia Beach
www.bryantstratton.edu
Admissions
301 Centre Pointe Drive
Virginia Beach, VA 23462-4417
Fax: (757) 499-9977
E-mail: dmsoutherland@bryantstratton.edu
Phone: (757) 499-7900

Bryant University
www.bryant.edu
Office of Admission
1150 Douglas Pike
Smithfield, RI 02917-1291
Fax: (401) 232-6741
E-mail: admission@bryant.edu
Phone: (401) 232-6107

Bryman School
www.brymanschool.edu
2250 West Peoria Avenue
Phoenix, AZ 85029-4919
Phone: (602) 274-4300

Bryn Mawr College
www.brynmawr.edu
Office of Admissions
101 North Merion Avenue
Bryn Mawr, PA 19010-2899
Fax: (610) 526-7471
E-mail: jrussell@brynmawr.edu
Phone: (610) 526-5152

Bucknell University
www.bucknell.edu
Admissions Office
Freas Hall
Bucknell University
Lewisburg, PA 17837-9988
Fax: (570) 577-3538
E-mail: admissions@bucknell.edu
Phone: (570) 577-1101

Bucks County Community College
www.bucks.edu
Adult and Multicultural Student Services
275 Swamp Road
Office of Admissions
Newtown, PA 18940
Fax: (215) 968-8110
E-mail: barlowm@bucks.edu
Phone: (215) 968-8137

Buena Vista University
www.bvu.edu
International Programs Coordinator
610 West Fourth Street
Storm Lake, IA 50588
Fax: (712) 749-2037
E-mail: admissions@bvu.edu
Phone: (712) 749-2073

Bunker Hill Community College
www.bhcc.mass.edu
Executive Director of International Center
250 New Rutherford Avenue
Boston, MA 02129-2925
Fax: (617) 228-2442
E-mail: international@bhcc.mass.edu
Phone: (617) 228-2460

Burlington College
www.burlington.edu
Admissions
95 North Avenue
Burlington, VT 05401
Fax: (802) 660-4331
E-mail: admissions@burlington.edu
Phone: (802) 862-9616 ext. 104

Burlington County College
www.bcc.edu
International Program Specialist
601 Pemberton-Browns Mills Road
Pemberton, NJ 08068-1599
Fax: (856) 439-1205
E-mail: cghiran@bcc.edu
Phone: (609) 894-9311 ext. 1350

Business Informatics Center
www.thecollegeforbusiness.com
Admissions
134 South Central Avenue
Valley Stream, NY 11580-5431
Fax: (516) 561-0074
Phone: (516) 561-0050 ext. 101

Butler Community College
www.butlercc.edu
International Specialist
901 South Haverhill Road
El Dorado, KS 67042-3280
Fax: (316) 322-6852
E-mail: mdugger@butlercc.edu
Phone: (316) 322-3255

Butler University
www.butler.edu
International Admissions
4600 Sunset Avenue
Indianapolis, IN 46208
Fax: (317) 940-8150
E-mail: intadmission@butler.edu
Phone: (888) 940-8100

Butte College
www.butte.edu
3536 Butte Campus Drive
Oroville, CA 95965
Fax: (530) 895-2411
E-mail: admissions@butte.edu
Phone: (530) 895-2361

Cabarrus College of Health Sciences
www.cabarruscollege.edu
401 Medical Park Drive
Concord, NC 28025-2405
Fax: (704) 403-2077
E-mail: admissions@cabarruscollege.edu
Phone: (704) 403-1556

Cabrillo College
www.cabrillo.edu
International Student Advisor/Counselor
6500 Soquel Drive
Aptos, CA 95003
Fax: (831) 479-5769
E-mail: anna.zagorska@cabrillo.edu
Phone: (831) 477-3375

Cabrini College
www.cabrini.edu
Admissions Office
610 King of Prussia Road
Radnor, PA 19087-3698
Fax: (610) 902-8508
E-mail: charles.spencer@cabrini.edu
Phone: (610) 902-8556

Caldwell College
www.caldwell.edu
International Student Advisor
120 Bloomfield Avenue
Caldwell, NJ 07006-6195
Fax: (973) 618-3600
E-mail: heatondwyer@caldwell.edu
Phone: (973) 618-3519

Calhoun Community College
www.calhoun.edu
Admissions and Records
Box 2216
Decatur, AL 35609-2216
Fax: (256) 306-2941
E-mail: bjt@calhoun.edu
Phone: (256) 306-2599

California Baptist University
www.calbaptist.edu
Undergraduate International Admissions
Counselor
8432 Magnolia Avenue
Riverside, CA 92504-3297
Fax: (951) 343-4728
E-mail: dbutler@calbaptist.edu
Phone: (951) 343-4947

California Christian College
www.calchristiancollege.org
4881 East University Avenue
Fresno, CA 93703
Fax: (559) 251-4231
E-mail: cccadmissions@sbcglobal.net
Phone: (559) 455-5571

California Coast University
www.calcoast.edu
925 North Spurgeon Street
Santa Ana, CA 92701
E-mail: admissions@calcoast.edu
Phone: (714) 547-9625

California College of the Arts
www.cca.edu
Enrollment Services
1111 Eighth Street
San Francisco, CA 94107-2247
Fax: (415) 703-9539
E-mail: schavan@cca.edu
Phone: (415) 703-9520

California College San Diego
www.cc-sd.edu
2820 Camino del Rio South 300
San Diego, CA 92108
Fax: (619) 295-5762
Phone: (619) 680-4430

California Culinary Academy
www.chefs.edu/San-Francisco
Admissions Office
350 Rhode Island Street
San Francisco, CA 94103
Fax: (415) 771-2194
E-mail: admissions@baychef.com
Phone: (415) 771-3500

California Institute of the Arts
www.calarts.edu
Admissions
24700 McBean Parkway
Valencia, CA 91355
Fax: (661) 253-7710
E-mail: mryan@calarts.edu
Phone: (661) 255-1050

California Institute of Integral Studies
www.ciis.edu
Student Affairs Office
1453 Mission Street
San Francisco, CA 94103
Fax: (415) 575-6158
E-mail: joconnor@ciis.edu
Phone: (415) 575-6157

California Institute of Technology
www.caltech.edu
Office of Admissions
383 South Hill Avenue, Mail Code 10-90
Pasadena, CA 91125
Fax: (626) 683-3026
E-mail: ugadmissions@caltech.edu
Phone: (626) 395-6341

California Lutheran University
www.callutheran.edu
Admission
60 West Olsen Road #1350
Thousand Oaks, CA 91360-2787
Fax: (805) 493-3114
E-mail: admissions@callutheran.edu
Phone: (805) 493-3135

California Maritime Academy
www.csum.edu
Director of Admission
200 Maritime Academy Drive
Vallejo, CA 94590
Fax: (707) 654-1336
E-mail: mmcgee@csum.edu
Phone: (707) 654-1330

California National University for Advanced Studies
www.cnuas.edu
8550 Balboa Boulevard, Suite 210
Northridge, CA 91325
Fax: (818) 830-2418
E-mail: cnuadms@mail.cnuas.edu
Phone: (818) 830-2411

California Polytechnic State University: San Luis Obispo
www.calpoly.edu
Admissions
Admissions Office, Cal Poly
San Luis Obispo, CA 93407-0031
Fax: (805) 756-5400
E-mail: ccjones@calpoly.edu
Phone: (805) 756-2311

California State Polytechnic University: Pomona
www.csupomona.edu
Coordinator of International Admissions
3801 West Temple Avenue
Pomona, CA 91768-4019
Fax: (909) 869-5858
E-mail: kevinmartin@csupomona.edu
Phone: (909) 869-2107

California State University: Bakersfield
www.csub.edu
Admission Office
9001 Stockdale Highway
Bakersfield, CA 93311-1099
Fax: (661) 654-3389
E-mail: jmimms@csub.edu
Phone: (661) 654-3036

California State University: Channel Islands
www.csuci.edu
One University Drive
Camarillo, CA 93012
E-mail: international@csuci.edu
Phone: (805) 437-3107

California State University: Chico
www.csuchico.edu
International Undergraduate Admissions
400 West First Street
Chico, CA 95929-0722
Fax: (530) 898-4790
E-mail: iuga@csuchico.edu
Phone: (530) 898-4895

California State University: Dominguez Hills
www.csudh.edu
Admissions Office
1000 East Victoria Street
Carson, CA 90747
Fax: (310) 516-4573
E-mail: mtaylor@csudh.edu
Phone: (310) 243-3645

California State University: East Bay
www.csueastbay.edu
Director, International Admissions
25800 Carlos Bee Boulevard
Hayward, CA 94542-3095
Fax: (510) 885-3816
E-mail: admissions@csueastbay.edu
Phone: (510) 885-4038

California State University: Fresno
www.csufresno.edu
Director of International Student Services and Programs
5150 North Maple Avenue, M/S JA 57
Fresno, CA 93740-8026
Fax: (559) 278-4812
E-mail: lhammar@csufresno.edu
Phone: (559) 278-2409

California State University: Fullerton
www.fullerton.edu
Admissions and Records
800 North State College Boulevard, Langsdorf Hall-114
Fullerton, CA 92831-6900
Fax: (657) 278-2356
E-mail: admissions@fullerton.edu
Phone: (657) 278-2371

California State University: Long Beach
www.csulb.edu
Center for International Education
1250 Bellflower Boulevard
Long Beach, CA 90840-0106
Fax: (562) 985-4973
E-mail: eslb@csulb.edu
Phone: (562) 985-5476

California State University: Los Angeles
www.calstatela.edu
International Programs and Services
5151 State University Drive SA101
Los Angeles, CA 90032
Fax: (323) 343-6478
E-mail: admission@calstatela.edu
Phone: (323) 343-3170

California State University: Monterey Bay
www.csumb.edu
Admissions
100 Campus Center, Student Services Building
Building 47
Seaside, CA 93955-8001
Fax: (831) 582-3783
E-mail: pcarter@csumb.edu
Phone: (831) 582-3738

California State University: Sacramento
www.csus.edu
Coordinator of International Admissions
6000 J Street
Lassen Hall, Lobby
Sacramento, CA 95819-6048
Fax: (916) 278-7471
E-mail: mlima.wells@csus.edu
Phone: (916) 278-7772

California State University: San Bernardino
www.csusb.edu
Admissions (Foreign Evaluations)
5500 University Parkway
San Bernardino, CA 92407-2397
Fax: (909) 537-7020
E-mail: pamaya@csusb.edu
Phone: (909) 537-3208

California State University: San Marcos
www.csusm.edu
Office of Global Education
333 South Twin Oaks Valley Road
San Marcos, CA 92096-0001
Fax: (760) 750-3284
E-mail: apply@csusm.edu
Phone: (760) 750-4090

California State University: Stanislaus
www.csustan.edu
Office of International Education
One University Circle
Turlock, CA 95382-0256
Fax: (209) 667-3791
E-mail: intlstudent@csustan.edu
Phone: (209) 667-3117

California University of Management and Sciences
www.calums.edu
Admissions
721 North Euclid Streeet
Anaheim, CA 92801
Fax: (714) 533-7778
E-mail: lisa@calums.edu
Phone: (714) 533-3946

California University of Pennsylvania
www.calu.edu
250 University Avenue
California, PA 15419-1394
Fax: (724) 938-4564
E-mail: inquiry@calu.edu
Phone: (724) 938-4404

Calumet College of St. Joseph
www.ccsj.edu
Admissions
2400 New York Avenue
Whiting, IN 46394-2195
Fax: (219) 473-4259
E-mail: gpirtle@ccsj.edu
Phone: (877) 700-9100 ext. 215

Calvary Bible College and Theological Seminary
www.calvary.edu
Admissions
15800 Calvary Road
Kansas City, MO 64147-1341
Fax: (816) 331-4474
E-mail: admissions@calvary.edu
Phone: (816) 322-63960

Calvin College
www.calvin.edu
Admissions
3201 Burton Street Southeast
Grand Rapids, MI 49546
Fax: (616) 526-6777
E-mail: intladm@calvin.edu
Phone: (616) 526-6106

Cambria-Rowe Business College: Indiana
www.crbc.net
422 South 13th Street
Indiana, PA 15701
E-mail: sbell-leger@crbc.net
Phone: (724) 463-0222

Cambridge College
www.cambridgecollege.edu
International Students Office
1000 Massachusetts Avenue
Cambridge, MA 02138-5304
Fax: (617) 868-2675
E-mail: anna.shanley@cambridgecollege.edu
Phone: (617) 873-0169

Camelot College
www.camelotcollege.com
2618 Wooddale Boulevard, Suite A
Baton Rouge, LA 70805
Fax: (225) 927-3794
E-mail: home@camelotcollege.com
Phone: (225) 928-3005

Cameron University
www.cameron.edu
Admissions
2800 West Gore Boulevard
Lawton, OK 73505-6377
Fax: (580) 581-5416
E-mail: international@cameron.edu
Phone: (888) 454-7600

Campbell University
www.campbell.edu
International Admissions
PO Box 546
Buies Creek, NC 27506
Fax: (910) 893-1288
E-mail: intl@email.campbell.edu
Phone: (800) 334-4111 ext. 1417

Campbellsville University
www.campbellsville.edu
International Admissions Counselor
One University Drive
Campbellsville, KY 42718-2799
Fax: (270) 789-55071
E-mail: admissions@campbellsville.edu
Phone: (800) 264-6014 ext. 5367

Canada College
www.canadacollege.edu
Admissions & Records Office
4200 Farm Hill Boulevard
Redwood City, CA 94061
Fax: (650) 306-3113
E-mail: sohrabi@smccd.net
Phone: (650) 306-3494

Canisius College
www.canisius.edu
Admissions Office
2001 Main Street
Buffalo, NY 14208-1098
Fax: (716) 888-3116
E-mail: shaffner@canisius.edu
Phone: (716) 888-2502

Cape Cod Community College
www.capecod.edu
Admissions
2240 Iyannough Road
West Barnstable, MA 02668-1599
Fax: (508) 375-4089
E-mail: sklinesy@capecod.edu
Phone: (508) 362-2131 ext. 4311

Capella University
www.capella.edu
Enrollment Services
225 South Sixth Street, Capella Tower
Minneapolis, MN 55402
Fax: (612) 977-5060
E-mail: info@capella.edu
Phone: (888) 227-2736

Capital Community College
www.ccc.commnet.edu
Admissions
950 Main Street
Hartford, CT 06103-1207
E-mail: mball-davis@ccc.commnet.edu
Phone: (860) 906-5127

Capital University
www.capital.edu
Office of International Education
1 College and Main
Columbus, OH 43209-2394
Fax: (614) 236-6171
E-mail: international@capital.edu
Phone: (614) 236-7102

Capitol College
www.capitol-college.edu
11301 Springfield Road
Laurel, MD 20708
Fax: (301) 953-1442
E-mail: agmiller@capitol-college.edu
Phone: (301) 369-2800

Cardinal Stritch University
www.stritch.edu
Associate Director of Admission
6801 North Yates Road, Box 516
Milwaukee, WI 53217-7516
Fax: (414) 410-4058
E-mail: kndiener@stritch.edu
Phone: (414) 410-4055

Career College of Northern Nevada
www.ccnn.edu
1421 Pullman Drive
Sparks, NV 89434
E-mail: mbuendia@ccnn4u.com
Phone: (775) 856-2266

Careers Unlimited
www.ucdh.edu/
1176 South 1480 West
Orem, UT 84058
Fax: (801) 224-5437
E-mail: admissions@ucdh.edu
Phone: (801) 426-8234

Caribbean University
www.caribbean.edu
Office of Admissions
PO Box 493
Bayamon, PR 00960-0493
Fax: (787) 785-0101
E-mail: ialvarado@caribbean.edu
Phone: (787) 780-0070 ext. 1110

Carl Albert State College
www.carlalbert.edu
Admissions
1507 South McKenna
Poteau, OK 74953-5208
Fax: (918) 647-1306
E-mail: asutter@carlalbert.edu
Phone: (918) 647-1301

Carl Sandburg College
www.sandburg.edu
2400 Tom L. Wilson Boulevard
Galesburg, IL 61401
Fax: (309) 344-3291
E-mail: ckreider@csc.cc.il.us
Phone: (309) 344-2518

Carleton College
www.carleton.edu
Admissions
100 South College Street
Northfield, MN 55057
Fax: (507) 222-4526
E-mail: admissionsglobal@carleton.edu
Phone: (507) 222-4190

Carlos Albizu University
www.albizu.edu
Student Affairs
2173 NW 99th Avenue
Miami, FL 33172
Fax: (305) 593-1854
E-mail: prubio@albizu.edu
Phone: (305) 593-1223 ext. 208

Carlow University
www.carlow.edu
International Student Center
3333 Fifth Avenue
Pittsburgh, PA 15213-3165
Fax: (412) 578-8722
E-mail: nesgodajl@carlow.edu
Phone: (412) 578-6010

Carnegie Mellon University
www.cmu.edu
Admissions Office
5000 Forbes Avenue
Pittsburgh, PA 15213-3890
Fax: (412) 268-7838
E-mail: undergraduate-
admissions@andrew.cmu.edu
Phone: (412) 268-2082

Carrington College: Antioch
www.westerncollege.edu
2157 Country Hills Drive
Antioch, CA 94531
Phone: (925) 522-7777

Carrington College: Citrus Heights
www.westerncollege.edu
7301 Greenback Lane, Suite A
Citrus Heights, CA 95621

Carrington College: Emeryville
www.westerncollege.edu
6001 Shellmound, #145
Emeryville, CA 94608
Phone: (510) 601-0133

Carrington College: Pleasant Hill
www.westerncollege.com
380 Civic Drive, Suite 300
Pleasant Hill, CA 94523
Fax: (925) 609-6666
Phone: (925) 609-6650

Carrington College: Reno
www.carrington.edu/nevada/reno/home
5580 Kietzke Lane
Reno, NV 89511
E-mail: brossini@carrington.edu
Phone: (775) 335-2900

Carrington College: Sacramento
www.westerncollege.edu
7801 Folsom Blvd #210
Sacramento, CA 95826
E-mail: info@westerncollege.edu
Phone: (800) 321-2386

Carrington College: San Jose
www.svcollege.com
6201 San Ignacio Avenue
San Jose, CA 95119
Fax: (408) 360-0848
Phone: (408) 360-0840

Carrington College: Stockton
www.carrington.edu
1313 West Robinhood Drive, Suite B
Stockton, CA 95207

Carroll College
www.carroll.edu
International Programs
1601 North Benton Avenue
Helena, MT 59625
Fax: (406) 447-5461
E-mail: intl@carroll.edu
Phone: (406) 447-5406

Carroll Community College
www.carrollcc.edu
Office of Admissions
1601 Washington Road
Westminster, MD 21157
Fax: (410) 386-8446
E-mail: cedwards@carrollcc.edu
Phone: (410) 386-8435

Carroll University
www.carrollu.edu
International Study Abroad Advisor
100 North East Avenue
Waukesha, WI 53186-9988
Fax: (262) 524-7139
E-mail: kcizausk@carrollu.edu
Phone: (262) 951-3137

Carson-Newman College
www.cn.edu
Office of Admissions
1646 Russell Avenue
Jefferson City, TN 37760
Fax: (865) 471-3502
E-mail: rtrantham@cn.edu
Phone: (865) 471-4826

Carteret Community College
www.carteret.edu
Admissions Office
3505 Arendell Street
Morehead City, NC 28557-2989
Fax: (252) 222-6265
E-mail: admissions@carteret.edu
Phone: (252) 222-6155

Carthage College
www.carthage.edu
Admissions
2001 Alford Park Drive
Kenosha, WI 53140-1994
Fax: (262) 551-5762
E-mail: admissions@carthage.edu
Phone: (262) 551-6000

Carver Bible College
www.carver.edu
3837 Cascade Road, SW
Atlanta, GA 30313
Fax: (404) 527-4524
Phone: (404) 527-4520

Cascadia Community College
www.cascadia.edu
International Programs
18345 Campus Way, NE
Bothell, WA 98011
Fax: (425) 352-8304
E-mail: International@cascadia.edu
Phone: (425) 352-8276

Case Western Reserve University
www.case.edu
Undergraduate Admission
Wolstein Hall
11318 Bellflower Road
Cleveland, OH 44106-7055
Fax: (216) 368-5111
E-mail: mariya.chetyrkina@case.edu
Phone: (216) 368-4450

Casper College
www.caspercollege.edu
Office of Admissions
125 College Drive
Casper, WY 82601
Fax: (307) 268-2611
E-mail: amcnulty@caspercollege.edu
Phone: (307) 268-3123

Castleton State College
www.castleton.edu
Admissions Office
Seminary Street
Castleton, VT 05735
Fax: (802) 468-1476
E-mail: erica.terault@castleton.edu
Phone: (802) 468-1213

Catawba College
www.catawba.edu
Director of Admissions Operations
2300 West Innes Street
Salisbury, NC 28144-2488
Fax: (704) 637-4222
E-mail: dasnook@catawba.edu
Phone: (704) 637-4402

Catholic Distance University
www.cdu.edu
Admissions
120 East Colonial Highway
Hamilton, VA 20158-9012
Fax: (540) 338-4788
E-mail: admissions@cdu.edu
Phone: (888) 254-4238 ext. 700

Catholic University of America
www.cua.edu
Dean, University Admissions
102 McMahon Hall
620 Michigan Avenue, NE
Washington, DC 20064
Fax: (202) 319-6533
E-mail: mica@cua.edu
Phone: (202) 319-5305

Cayuga Community College
www.cayuga-cc.edu
Admissions Office
197 Franklin Street
Auburn, NY 13021-3099
Fax: (315) 255-2117
E-mail: blodgett@cayuga-cc.edu
Phone: (315) 255-1743

Cazenovia College
www.cazenovia.edu
Admissions and Financial Aid
3 Sullivan Street
Cazenovia, NY 13035
Fax: (315) 655-4860
E-mail: jaustin@cazenovia.edu
Phone: (315) 655-7208

Cedar Crest College
www.cedarcrest.edu
Office of Admissions
100 College Drive
Allentown, PA 18104-6196
Fax: (610) 606-4647
E-mail: Katrina.Xander@cedarcrest.edu
Phone: (610) 740-3780

Cedar Valley College
www.cedarvalleycollege.edu
Admissions
3030 North Dallas Avenue
Lancaster, TX 75134
Fax: (972) 860-8207
E-mail: cdw3310@dccd.edu
Phone: (972) 860-8203

Cedarville University
www.cedarville.edu
Academic Program Development
251 North Main Street
Cedarville, OH 45314-0601
Fax: (937) 766-4129
E-mail: tbetcher@cedarville.edu
Phone: (937) 766-7681

Centenary College
www.centenarycollege.edu
International Department
400 Jefferson Street
Hackettstown, NJ 07840-9989
Fax: (908) 852-3454
E-mail:
internationalstudies@centenarycollege.edu
Phone: (908) 852-1400 ext. 2217

Centenary College of Louisiana
www.centenary.edu
Admissions Office
Box 41188
Shreveport, LA 71134-1188
Fax: (318) 869-5005
E-mail: admissions@centenary.edu
Phone: (318) 869-5131

Central Arizona College
www.centralaz.edu
Director of Admission and Records
Admissions Office
8470 North Overfield Road
Coolidge, AZ 85128-9030
Fax: (520) 494-5083
E-mail: james.moore7@centralaz.edu
Phone: (520) 494-5261

Central Carolina Technical College
www.cctech.edu
506 North Guignard Drive
Sumter, SC 29150-2499
Fax: (803) 778-6696
Phone: (803) 778-6605

Central Christian College of Kansas
www.centralchristian.edu
Admissions
1200 South Main
Box 1403
McPherson, KS 67460-5740
Fax: (620) 241-6032
E-mail: admissions@centralchristian.edu
Phone: (620) 241-0723 ext. 380

Central College
www.central.edu
Admission Office, Central College
812 University Street
Pella, IA 50219-1999
Fax: (641) 628-7637
E-mail: freiburgerc@central.edu
Phone: (877) 462-3687

Central Connecticut State University
www.ccsu.edu
Recruitment and Admissions
1615 Stanley Street
New Britain, CT 06050
Fax: (860) 832-2295
E-mail: admissions@ccsu.edu
Phone: (860) 832-2278

Central Georgia Technical College
www.centralgatech.edu
3300 Macon Tech Drive
Macon, GA 31206
Fax: (478) 757-3454
E-mail: tcarter@centralgatech.edu
Phone: (478) 757-3408

Central Lakes College
www.clcmn.edu
Admissions
501 West College Drive
Brainerd, MN 56401
Fax: (218) 855-8230
E-mail: cdaniels@clcmn.edu
Phone: (218) 855-8000

Central Maine Community College
www.cmcc.edu
Admissions
1250 Turner Street
Auburn, ME 04210
Fax: (207) 755-5493
E-mail: enroll@cmcc.edu
Phone: (207) 755-5334

Central Methodist University
www.centralmethodist.edu
Admissions
411 Central Methodist Square
Fayette, MO 65248-1198
Fax: (660) 248-1872
E-mail: admissions@centralmethodist.edu
Phone: (660) 248-6626

Central Michigan University
www.cmich.edu
Office of International Affairs
Admissions Office
Warriner Hall
Mount Pleasant, MI 48859
Fax: (989) 774-3690
E-mail: intlapp@cmich.edu
Phone: (989) 774-4308

Central Ohio Technical College
www.cotc.edu
Minority/Disadvantaged Recruiter-Admissions
1179 University Drive
Newark, OH 43055
Fax: (740) 366-5047
E-mail: mlabutis@cotc.edu
Phone: (740) 366-9392

Central Pennsylvania College
www.centralpenn.edu
Admissions
College Hill & Valley Roads
Summerdale, PA 17093-0309
Fax: (717) 732-5254
E-mail: stacyscott@centralpenn.edu
Phone: (800) 759-2727 ext. 2214

Central Piedmont Community College
www.cpcc.edu
International Student Adviser
Box 35009
Charlotte, NC 28235-5009
Fax: (704) 330-6130
E-mail: dotty.holley@cpcc.edu
Phone: (704) 330-6456

Central State University
www.centralstate.edu
Admissions
PO Box 1004
Wilberforce, OH 45384-1004
Fax: (937) 376-6530
E-mail: admissions@centralstate.edu
Phone: (937) 376-6582

Central Texas College
www.ctcd.edu
International Student Services
Box 1800
Killeen, TX 76540
Fax: (254) 526-1481
E-mail: ctc.international@ctcd.edu
Phone: (254) 526-1107

Central Virginia Community College
www.cvcc.va.us
Counseling
3506 Wards Road
Lynchburg, VA 24502-2498
Fax: (434) 386-4681
Phone: (434) 832-7800

Central Washington University
www.cwu.edu
Office of Admissions
400 East University Way
Ellensburg, WA 98926-7463
Fax: (509) 963-3022
E-mail: cwuadmis@cwu.edu
Phone: (509) 963-1211

Central Wyoming College
www.cwc.edu
Admissions
2660 Peck Avenue
Riverton, WY 82501
Fax: (307) 855-2093
E-mail: jason@cwc.edu
Phone: (307) 855-2270

Central Yeshiva Tomchei Tmimim-Lubavitch
841-853 Ocean Parkway
Brooklyn, NY 11230
E-mail: uofiop@juno.com
Phone: (718) 859-7600

Centralia College
www.centralia.edu
International Programs
600 Centralia College Boulevard
Centralia, WA 98531
Fax: (360) 736-9391
E-mail: intl@centralia.edu
Phone: (360) 736-9391 ext. 492

Centre College
www.centre.edu
Admission
600 West Walnut Street
Danville, KY 40422-1394
Fax: (859) 238-5373
E-mail: ned.frazier@centre.edu
Phone: (859) 238-5350

Centura College: Chesapeake
www.centuracollege.edu
932 Ventures Way
Chesapeake, VA 23320-2882
Fax: (757) 548-1196

Centura College: Newport News
www.centuracollege.edu
616 Denbigh Boulevard
Newport News, VA 23608
Fax: (757) 874-3857
E-mail: admdirttp@tidewatertech.edu
Phone: (757) 874-2121

Centura College: Norfolk
www.centuracollege.edu
7020 North Military Highway
Norfolk, VA 23518-4202
Fax: (757) 852-9017
E-mail: admdirttn@tidetech.com
Phone: (757) 853-2121

Centura College: Richmond
www.centuracollege.edu
7914 Midlothian Turnpike
Richmond, VA 23608
E-mail: admdirbtr@betatech.edu
Phone: (804) 330-0111

Century College
www.century.edu
Multicultural Center
3300 Century Avenue North
White Bear Lake, MN 55110
Fax: (651) 747-4053
E-mail: tom.black@century.edu
Phone: (651) 779-5754

Cerritos College
www.cerritos.edu
11110 Alondra Boulevard
Norwalk, CA 90650
Fax: (562) 860-9680
Phone: (562) 860-2451 ext. 2211

Cerro Coso Community College
www.cerrocoso.edu
Vice President
3000 College Heights Boulevard
Ridgecrest, CA 93555-7777
Fax: (760) 384-6377
E-mail: jboard@cerrocoso.edu
Phone: (760) 384-6354

Chabot College
www.chabotcollege.edu
Office of Special Admissions, Room 168,
Chabot College
25555 Hesperian Boulevard
Hayward, CA 94545
Fax: (510) 723-7510
E-mail: dbalangitao@chabotcollege.edu
Phone: (510) 723-6715

Chadron State College
www.csc.edu
1000 Main Street
Chadron, NE 69337
Fax: (308) 432-6229
E-mail: ccousin@csc.edu
Phone: (308) 432-6496

Chaffey College
www.chaffey.edu
International Student Admissions
5885 Haven Avenue
Rancho Cucamonga, CA 91701-3002
Fax: (909) 652-6006
E-mail: donna.colondres@chaffey.edu
Phone: (909) 652-6226

Chamberlain College of Nursing: Addison
www.chamberlain.edu
1221 North Swift Road
Addison, IL 60101-6106

Chamberlain College of Nursing: Chicago
www.chamberlain.edu/Locations/Chicago.aspx
3300 North Campbell Avenue
Chicago, IL 60618

Chamberlain College of Nursing: Columbus
www.chamberlain.edu
1350 Alum Creek Drive
Columbus, OH 43209

Chamberlain College of Nursing: Jacksonville
www.chamberlan.edu
5200 Belfort Road
Jacksonville, FL 32256

Chamberlain College of Nursing: Phoenix
www.chamberlain.edu
2149 West Dunlap Avenue
Phoenix
Phoenix, AZ 85021

Chaminade University of Honolulu
www.chaminade.edu
Admissions Office
3140 Waialae Avenue
Honolulu, HI 96816
Fax: (808) 739-4647
E-mail: admissions@chaminade.edu
Phone: (808) 735-4735

Champlain College
www.champlain.edu
Office of Admission
163 South Willard Street
PO Box 670
Burlington, VT 05402-0670
Fax: (802) 860-2767
E-mail: kamato@champlain.edu
Phone: (802) 860-2727

Chandler-Gilbert Community College: Pecos
www.cgc.maricopa.edu
International Education Programs
2626 East Pecos Road
Chandler, AZ 85225
Fax: (480) 866-8242
E-mail: iss@cgcmail.maricopa.edu
Phone: (480) 732-7391

Chapman University
www.chapman.edu
Associate Director of Admission/International
Admission Officer
One University Drive
Orange, CA 92866
Fax: (714) 997-6713
E-mail: konowicz@chapman.edu
Phone: (714) 997-6711

Charles Drew University of Medicine and Science
www.cdrewu.edu
Office of Admissions
1731 East 120th Street
Los Angeles, CA 90059
Fax: (323) 569-0597
E-mail: makaylahall@cdrewu.edu
Phone: (323) 563-5886

Charleston Southern University
www.csuniv.edu
Assistant Director of Admissions
9200 University Boulevard
Box 118087
Charleston, SC 29423-8087
Fax: (843) 863-7070
E-mail: psmith@csuniv.edu
Phone: (843) 863-7050

Charter Oak State College
www.charteroak.edu
Admission
55 Paul Manafort Drive
New Britain, CT 06053-2150
Fax: (860) 832-3999
E-mail: info@charteroak.edu
Phone: (860) 832-3858

Chatham University
www.chatham.edu
Office of Admissions
Woodland Road
Pittsburgh, PA 15232
Fax: (412) 365-1609
E-mail: TViti@Chatham.edu
Phone: (412) 365-1618

Chattahoochee Technical College
www.chattahoocheetech.edu
International
980 South Cobb Drive, SE
Marietta, GA 30060-3300
Fax: (770) 528-5818
E-mail: gmoor@chattahoocheetech.edu
Phone: (770) 528-4528

Chattahoochee Valley Community College
www.cv.edu
Admissions
2602 College Drive
Phenix City, AL 36869
Fax: (334) 291-4994
E-mail: admissions@cv.edu
Phone: (334) 291-4929

Chemeketa Community College
www.chemeketa.edu
International Student Admissions
Admissions Office
PO Box 14007
Salem, OR 97309-7070
Fax: (503) 365-4768
E-mail: ngodfrey@chemeketa.edu
Phone: (503) 399-2527

Chesapeake College
www.chesapeake.edu
Registrar
Box 8
1000 College Circle
Wye Mills, MD 21679-0008
Fax: (410) 827-9466
E-mail: cjewell@chesapeake.edu
Phone: (410) 822-5400 ext. 420

Chester College of New England
www.chestercollege.edu
Admissions
40 Chester Street
Chester, NH 03036
Fax: (603) 887-1777
E-mail: sarah.vogell@chestercollege.edu
Phone: (603) 887-7400

Chestnut Hill College
www.chc.edu
Admissions
9601 Germantown Avenue
Philadelphia, PA 19118-2693
Fax: (215) 248-7155
E-mail: mclaughlinja@chc.edu
Phone: (215) 242-7989

Cheyney University of Pennsylvania
www.cheyney.edu
Admissions Office
1837 University Circle
PO Box 200
Cheyney, PA 19319-0019
Fax: (610) 399-2099
E-mail: abrown@cheyney.edu
Phone: (610) 399-2275

Chicago State University
www.csu.edu
Office of Admissions
9501 South King Drive
Chicago, IL 60628
Fax: (773) 995-3820
E-mail: ug-admissions@csu.edu
Phone: (773) 995-2513

Chipola College
www.chipola.edu
Vice President Student Affairs
3094 Indian Circle
Marianna, FL 32446
Fax: (850) 718-2255
E-mail: robertsj@chipola.edu
Phone: (850) 718-2209

Chippewa Valley Technical College
www.cvtc.edu
620 West Clairemont Avenue
Eau Claire, WI 54701-6162
Fax: (715) 833-6470
E-mail: jmoldenhauer@cvtc.edu
Phone: (715) 833-6247

Chowan University
www.chowan.edu
Office of Admissions
One University Place
Murfreesboro, NC 27855-9901
Fax: (252) 398-1190
E-mail: holtc@chowan.edu
Phone: (252) 398-6298

Christendom College
www.christendom.edu
134 Christendom Drive
Front Royal, VA 22630
Fax: (540) 636-1655
E-mail: admissions@christendom.edu
Phone: (540) 636-2900

Christian Brothers University
www.cbu.edu
Admissions
650 East Parkway South
Memphis, TN 38104-5519
Fax: (901) 321-3202
E-mail: akenwort@cbu.edu
Phone: (901) 321-3205

Christopher Newport University
www.cnu.edu
Associate Director of Admissions
1 University Place
Newport News, VA 23606-2998
Fax: (757) 594-7333
E-mail: admit@cnu.edu
Phone: (757) 594-7015

Cincinnati Christian University
www.ccuniversity.edu
Director Undergraduate Admissions
2700 Glenway Avenue
Cincinnati, OH 45204-3200
Fax: (513) 244-8453
E-mail: cbcadmission@ccuniversity.edu
Phone: (513) 244-8170

Cincinnati State Technical and Community College
www.cincinnatistate.edu
3520 Central Parkway
Cincinnati, OH 45223-2690
Fax: (513) 569-1498
E-mail: yolanda.lawrence@cincinnatistate.edu
Phone: (513) 569-1543

The Citadel
www.citadel.edu
Associate Director of Admissions
171 Moultrie Street
Charleston, SC 29409
Fax: (843) 953-7036
E-mail: nimmichd@citadel.edu
Phone: (843) 953-5200

Citrus College
www.citruscollege.edu
International Student Office
1000 West Foothill Boulevard
Glendora, CA 91741-1899
Fax: (626) 963-4854
E-mail: clamoureux@citruscollege.edu
Phone: (626) 914-8549

City College of San Francisco
www.ccsf.edu
Director of Foreign Student Admissions
Office of Admissions and Records E-107
50 Phelan Avenue
San Francisco, CA 94112
Fax: (415) 239-3936
E-mail: jlow@ccsf.edu
Phone: (415) 239-3837

City College: Casselberry
www.citycollege.edu
853 Semoran Boulevard 436
Casselberry, FL 32707-5353
Fax: (407) 831-1147
Phone: (407) 831-8466

City College: Fort Lauderdale
www.citycollege.edu
Admissions
2000 West Commercial Boulevard
Fort Lauderdale, FL 33309
Fax: (954) 491-1965
E-mail: jhernandez@citycollege.edu
Phone: (954) 492-5353

City College: Gainesville
www.citycollege.edu
7001 NW 4th Boulevard
Gainesville, FL 32607
Fax: (352) 335-4303
E-mail: kbowden@citycollege.edu
Phone: (352) 335-4000 ext. 410

City College: Miami
www.citycollege.edu
9300 South Dadeland Boulevard
Miami, FL 33156
Fax: (305) 666-9243
E-mail: dgivens@citycollege.edu
Phone: (305) 666-9242

**City Colleges of Chicago: Harold
Washington College**
www.ccc.edu
Admissions Office
30 East Lake Street
Chicago, IL 60601
Fax: (312) 553-6084
E-mail: ytownsend@ccc.edu
Phone: (312) 553-6004

**City Colleges of Chicago: Kennedy-King
College**
www.ccc.edu
6301 South Halsted Street
Chicago, IL 60621
Fax: (773) 602-5247
Phone: (773) 602-5273

**City Colleges of Chicago: Malcolm X
College**
www.ccc.edu
1900 West Van Buren Street
Chicago, IL 60612
Fax: (312) 850-7092
Phone: (312) 850-7126

**City Colleges of Chicago: Olive-Harvey
College**
www.ccc.edu
10001 South Woodlawn Avenue
Chicago, IL 60628
Fax: (773) 291-6185
Phone: (773) 291-6384

**City Colleges of Chicago: Richard J. Daley
College**
www.ccc.edu
7500 South Pulaski Road
Chicago, IL 60652
Fax: (773) 838-7605
Phone: (773) 838-7606

**City Colleges of Chicago: Wilbur Wright
College**
www.ccc.edu
4300 North Narragansett Avenue
Chicago, IL 60634-4276
Fax: (773) 481-8053
Phone: (773) 481-8259

**City University of New York: Baruch
College**
www.baruch.cuny.edu
Office of Undergraduate Admissions
One Bernard Baruch Way, Box H-0720
New York, NY 10010-5585
Fax: (646) 312-1363
E-mail: admissions@baruch.cuny.edu
Phone: (646) 312-1400

**City University of New York: Borough of
Manhattan Community College**
www.bmcc.cuny.edu
Office of Admissions
199 Chambers Street
New York, NY 10007-1097
Fax: (212) 220-2366
E-mail: lyielkin@bmcc.cuny.edu
Phone: (212) 220-1270

**City University of New York: Bronx
Community College**
www.bcc.cuny.edu/
2155 University Avenue
Bronx, NY 10453
Fax: (718) 289-6352
E-mail: alba.cancetty@bcc.cuny.edu
Phone: (718) 289-5888

**City University of New York: Brooklyn
College**
www.brooklyn.cuny.edu
CUNY Office of Admissions Services
2900 Bedford Avenue
Brooklyn, NY 11210
Fax: (718) 951-4506
E-mail: adminqry@brooklyn.cuny.edu
Phone: (212) 947-4800

City University of New York: City College
www.ccny.cuny.edu
Admissions
160 Convent Avenue, A100
New York, NY 10031
Fax: (212) 650-417
E-mail: asabal@ccny.cuny.edu
Phone: (212) 650-6444

**City University of New York: College of
Staten Island**
www.csi.cuny.edu
Recruitment & Admissions
2800 Victory Boulevard 2A-104
Staten Island, NY 10314
Fax: (718) 982-2500
E-mail: michelle.buonocore@csi.cuny.edu
Phone: (718) 982-2010

City University of New York: CUNY Online
www.online.sps.cuny.edu/
Admissions
101 West 31st Street, 7th Floor
New York, NY 10001-3507
Fax: (212) 652-2887
E-mail: jennifer.lee@mail.cuny.edu
Phone: (212) 652-2070

**City University of New York: Hostos
Community College**
www.hostos.cuny.edu
Office of Admissions
500 Grand Concourse
Bronx, NY 10451
Fax: (718) 518-4256
E-mail: rvelez@hostos.cuny.edu
Phone: (718) 518-4406

**City University of New York: Hunter
College**
www.hunter.cuny.edu/
International Student Office
695 Park Avenue
New York, NY 10065
E-mail:
internationalstudent.ser@hunter.cuny.edu
Phone: (212) 772-4864

City University of New York: John Jay College of Criminal Justice
www.jjay.cuny.edu/
Admissions
445 West 59th Street
New York, NY 10019
Fax: (212) 484-1185
E-mail: svavasis@jjay.cuny.edu
Phone: (212) 237-8777

City University of New York: Kingsborough Community College
www.kbcc.cuny.edu
Office of International Student Affairs
2001 Oriental Boulevard
Brooklyn, NY 11235
Fax: (718) 368-4535
E-mail: isa@kbcc.cuny.edu
Phone: (718) 368-6800

City University of New York: LaGuardia Community College
www.lagcc.cuny.edu
Foreign Student Office
31-10 Thomson Avenue
Long Island City, NY 11101
Fax: (718) 609-2013
E-mail: pnicolov@lagcc.cuny.edu
Phone: (718) 482-5143

City University of New York: Lehman College
www.lehman.edu
Office for International Students
250 Bedford Park Boulevard West
Bronx, NY 10468
Fax: (718) 960-8712
E-mail: enroll@lehman.cuny.edu
Phone: (718) 960-7274

City University of New York: Medgar Evers College
www.mec.cuny.edu
Admissions
1665 Bedford Avenue
Brooklyn, NY 11225-2201
Fax: (718) 270-6411
E-mail: jaugustin@mec.cuny.edu
Phone: (718) 270-6021

City University of New York: Queens College
www.qc.cuny.edu
Admissions
6530 Kissena Boulevard, Jefferson 117
Flushing, NY 11367-1597
Fax: (718) 997-5617
E-mail: admissions@qc.cuny.edu
Phone: (718) 997-5600

City University of New York: Queensborough Community College
www.qcc.cuny.edu
Admissions Services CUNY, 101 West 31 Street, NY 1001-3503
Springfield Boulevard & 56th Avenue
Bayside, NY 11364-1497
Fax: (718) 281-5189
Phone: (718) 631-6611

City University of New York: York College
www.york.cuny.edu
Admission Services
94-20 Guy R. Brewer Boulevard
Jamaica, NY 11451-9989
Fax: (718) 262-2601
E-mail: admissions@york.cuny.edu
Phone: (718) 262-2165

Clackamas Community College
www.clackamas.edu
Admissions Specialist
19600 Molalla Avenue
Oregon City, OR 97045
Fax: (503) 722-5864
E-mail: pattyw@clackamas.edu
Phone: (503) 594-3379

Claflin University
www.claflin.edu
Admissions
400 Magnolia Street
Orangeburg, SC 29115
Fax: (803) 535-5385
E-mail: admissions@claflin.edu
Phone: (803) 535-5340

Claremont McKenna College
www.claremontmckenna.edu
Office of Admission
890 Columbia Avenue
Claremont, CA 91711-6425
Fax: (909) 621-8516
E-mail: admission@claremontmckenna.edu
Phone: (909) 621-8088

Clarendon College
www.clarendoncollege.edu
Office of Admissions
PO Box 968
Clarendon, TX 79226
Fax: (806) 874-5080
E-mail: martha.smith@clarendoncollege.edu
Phone: (806) 874-3571 ext. 106

Clarion University of Pennsylvania
www.clarion.edu
Office of International Programs
840 Wood Street
Clarion, PA 16214
Fax: (814) 393-2341
E-mail: lheineman@clarion.edu
Phone: (814) 393-2340

Clark Atlanta University
www.cau.edu
Admissions
223 James P. Brawley Drive, SW
101 Trevor Arnett Hall
Atlanta, GA 30314-4391
Fax: (404) 880-6174
E-mail: mdavis@cau.edu
Phone: (404) 880-6605

Clark College
www.clark.edu
International Education
1933 Fort Vancouver Way
Vancouver, WA 98663
Fax: (360) 992-2868
E-mail: sktaylor@clark.edu
Phone: (360) 992-2495

Clark State Community College
www.clarkstate.edu
DIirector Retention Services & Student Life
Box 570
Springfield, OH 45501-0570
Fax: (937) 328-6097
E-mail: wileyn@clarkstate.edu
Phone: (937) 328-7936

Clark University
www.clarku.edu
950 Main Street
Worcester, MA 01610-1477
Fax: (508) 793-8821
E-mail: intadmissions@clarku.edu
Phone: (508) 793-7431

Clarke University
www.clarke.edu
Senior Admissions Representative
1550 Clarke Drive
Dubuque, IA 52001-3198
Fax: (563) 588-6789
E-mail: alicia.flores@clarke.edu
Phone: (563) 588-6373

Clarkson University
www.clarkson.edu
Associate Dean of International Admission and New Student Financial Aid
Holcroft House
PO Box 5605
Potsdam, NY 13699
Fax: (315) 268-7647
E-mail: pperrier@clarkson.edu
Phone: (315) 268-3716

Clatsop Community College
www.clatsopcollege.com
Admissions Office
1653 Jerome Avenue
Astoria, OR 97103
Fax: (503) 325-5738
E-mail: jswenson@clatsop.cc.or.us
Phone: (503) 338-2325

Clayton State University
www.clayton.edu
Office of the Registrar
2000 Clayton State Boulevard
Morrow, GA 30260-0285
Fax: (678) 466-4169
E-mail: jeanmyers@mail.clayton.edu
Phone: (678) 466-4145

Cleary University
www.cleary.edu
Admissions
3750 Cleary Drive
Howell, MI 48843
Fax: (517) 338-3336
E-mail: rosemsmith@cleary.edu
Phone: (517) 338-3330

Clemson University
www.clemson.edu
Office of Admissions
105 Sikes Hall
Box 345124
Clemson, SC 29634-5124
Fax: (864) 656-2464
E-mail: cuadmissions@clemson.edu
Phone: (864) 656-2287

Cleveland Institute of Art
www.cia.edu
Admissions
11141 East Boulevard
Cleveland, OH 44106-1710
Fax: (216) 754-3634
E-mail: admiss@cia.edu
Phone: (216) 421-7418

Cleveland Institute of Electronics
www.cie-wc.edu
1776 East 17th Street
Cleveland, OH 44114-3679
Fax: (216) 781-0331
E-mail: instruct@cie-wc.edu
Phone: (216) 781-9400

Cleveland Institute of Music
www.cim.edu
Admission Office
11021 East Boulevard
Cleveland, OH 44106
E-mail: admission@cim.edu
Phone: (216) 795-3107

Cleveland State Community College
www.clevelandstatecc.edu
Office of Admissions
3535 Adkisson Drive
P. O. Box 3570
Cleveland, TN 37320-3570
Fax: (423) 478-6255
E-mail: mburnette@clevelandstatecc.edu
Phone: (423) 472-7141 ext. 212

Cleveland State University
www.csuohio.edu
Associate Director, International Admissions
2121 Euclid Avenue
RW 204
Cleveland, OH 44115-2214
E-mail: b.turner@csuohio.edu
Phone: (216) 687-4823

Clinton Community College
www.eicc.edu
Admissions Officer
1000 Lincoln Boulevard
Clinton, IA 52732
Fax: (563) 244-7107
E-mail: scarmody@eicc.edu
Phone: (563) 244-7007

Clinton Community College
www.clinton.edu
Student Services
136 Clinton Point Drive
Plattsburgh, NY 12901-4297
Fax: (518) 562-4141
E-mail: kathaleen.alexander@clinton.edu
Phone: (518) 562-4120

Clinton Junior College
www.clintonjuniorcollege.edu
Admissions Office
1029 Crawford Road
Rock Hill, SC 29730
E-mail: rcopeland@clintonjuniorcollege.edu
Phone: (803) 327-7402 ext. 242

Cloud County Community College
www.cloud.edu
Office of Admissions
2221 Campus Drive
Box 1002
Concordia, KS 66901-1002
Fax: (785) 243-9380
E-mail: kreynolds@cloud.edu
Phone: (785) 243-1435 ext. 212

Clover Park Technical College
www.cptc.edu
International Programs
4500 Steilacoom Boulevard, SW
Lakewood, WA 98499-4098
Fax: (253) 589-6054
E-mail: international@cptc.edu
Phone: (253) 589-6089

Coahoma Community College
www.coahomacc.edu
Admissions and Records
3240 Friars Point Road
Clarksdale, MS 38614-9799
Fax: (800) 844-1222
E-mail: wholmes@coahomacc.edu
Phone: (662) 621-4205

Coastal Bend College
www.coastalbend.edu
3800 Charco Road
Beeville, TX 78102
Fax: (361) 354-2254
E-mail: register@coastalbend.edu
Phone: (361) 354-2245

Coastal Carolina University
www.coastal.edu
Director of Enrollment Planning
PO Box 261954
Conway, SC 29528-6054
Fax: (843) 349-2252
E-mail: tim@coastal.edu
Phone: (843) 349-2054

Coastline Community College
www.coastline.edu
11460 Warner Avenue
Fountain Valley, CA 92708
Fax: (714) 241-6288
E-mail: jmcdonald@cccd.edu
Phone: (714) 241-6165

Cochise College
www.cochise.edu
International Student Office
901 North Colombo Avenue
Sierra Vista, AZ 85635
Fax: (520) 417-4192
E-mail: international@cochise.edu
Phone: (520) 417-4038

Coe College
www.coe.edu
Admission Office
1220 First Avenue NE
Cedar Rapids, IA 52402
Fax: (319) 399-8816
E-mail: pcook@coe.edu
Phone: (319) 399-8500

Coffeyville Community College
www.coffeyville.edu
International
400 West 11th Street
Coffeyville, KS 67337-5064
Fax: (620) 252-7098
E-mail: marlal@coffeyville.edu
Phone: (620) 251-7700 ext. 2086

Cogswell Polytechnical College
www.cogswell.edu
Admissions
1175 Bordeaux Drive
Sunnyvale, CA 94089-1299
Fax: (408) 747-0764
E-mail: jdonohoe@cogswell.edu
Phone: (800) 264-7955

Coker College
www.coker.edu
Admissions
300 East College Avenue
Hartsville, SC 29550
Fax: (843) 383-8048
E-mail: dsmall@pascal.coker.edu
Phone: (800) 950-1908

Colby College
www.colby.edu
Admissions
4800 Mayflower Hill
Waterville, ME 04901-8848
Fax: (207) 859-4828
E-mail: admissions@colby.edu
Phone: (207) 859-4818

Colby Community College
www.colbycc.edu
Admissions
1255 South Range Avenue
Colby, KS 67701
Fax: (785) 460-4691
E-mail: doug.johnson@colbycc.edu
Phone: (785) 460-5498

Colby-Sawyer College
www.colby-sawyer.edu
Office of Admissions
541 Main Street
New London, NH 03257-7835
Fax: (603) 526-3452
E-mail: admissions@colby-sawyer.edu
Phone: (603) 526-3701

Colegio de las Ciencias Artes y Television
www.ccat.edu
PO Box 10774
San Juan, PR 00922
Fax: (787) 995-2525
E-mail: admissions@ccat.edu
Phone: (787) 779-2500

Coleman College: San Marcos
www.coleman.edu
1284 West San Marcos Boulevard, Suite 110
San Marcos, CA 92069
Phone: (760) 747-3990

Coleman University
www.coleman.edu
Office of International Admissions
8888 Balboa Avenue
San Diego, CA 92123
Fax: (619) 463-0162
E-mail: ateeple@coleman.edu
Phone: (619) 465-3990

Colgate University
www.colgate.edu
13 Oak Drive
Hamilton, NY 13346-1383
Fax: (315) 228-7544
E-mail: ksryan@mail.colgate.edu
Phone: (315) 228-7401

College for Creative Studies
www.collegeforcreativestudies.edu
International Student Services
201 East Kirby
Detroit, MI 48202-4034
Fax: (313) 872-2739
E-mail: jdickey@collegeforcreativestudies.edu
Phone: (313) 664-7428

College of Alameda
www.alameda.peralta.edu
International Specialist, International Affairs
& Distance Education
555 Ralph Appezzato Memorial Parkway
Alameda, CA 94501
Fax: (510) 748-5227
E-mail: dgephart@Peralta.edu
Phone: (510) 587-7834

College of the Albemarle
www.albemarle.cc.nc.us
Admissions
1208 North Road Street
PO Box 2327
Elizabeth City, NC 27906-2327
Fax: (252) 335-2011
E-mail: kkrentz@albemarle.cc.nc.us
Phone: (252) 335-0821 ext. 2220

College of the Atlantic
www.coa.edu
Admission
105 Eden Street
Bar Harbor, ME 04609
Fax: (207) 288-4126
E-mail: mmadigan@coa.edu
Phone: (207) 801-5643

College of Business and Technology: Flagler
www.cbt.edu
International Students
8230 West Flagler Street
Miami, FL 33144
Fax: (305) 485-4411
E-mail: ivis@cbt.edu
Phone: (305) 273-4499 ext. 2-204

College of Business and Technology: Kendall
www.cbt.edu
8991 SW 107 Avenue
Suite 200
Miami, FL 33176
E-mail: admissions@cbt.edu
Phone: (305) 273-4499

College of the Canyons
www.canyons.edu
International Students Programs
26455 Rockwell Canyon Road
Santa Clarita, CA 91355
Fax: (661) 259-8302
E-mail: isp@canyons.edu
Phone: (661) 362-3580

College of Central Florida
www.cf.edu
International Students Admissions and
Advising
3001 SW College Road
Ocala, FL 34474-4415
Fax: (352) 873-5882
E-mail: shores@cf.edu
Phone: (352) 854-2322 ext. 1386

College of Charleston
www.cofc.edu
Admissions
Office of Admissions and Adult Student
Services
66 George Street
Charleston, SC 29424-0001
Fax: (843) 953-6322
E-mail: admissions@cofc.edu
Phone: (843) 953-5670

College of Coastal Georgia
www.ccga.edu
Admissions
3700 Altama Avenue
Brunswick, GA 31520
Fax: (912) 262-3072
E-mail: cltoler@ccga.edu
Phone: (912) 279-5735

College of Court Reporting
www.ccr.edu
111 West 10th Street, Suite 111
Hobart, IN 46342
Fax: (219) 942-1631
E-mail: information@ccr.edu
Phone: (219) 942-1459

College of the Desert
www.collegeofthedesert.edu
International Education Program
43500 Monterey Avenue
Palm Desert, CA 92260
Fax: (760) 862-1361
E-mail: cdelgado@collegeofthedesert.edu
Phone: (760) 776-7205

College of DuPage
www.cod.edu
Admissions
425 Fawell Boulevard
Glen Ellyn, IL 60137-6599
Fax: (630) 790-2686
E-mail: carrma@cod.edu
Phone: (630) 942-2979

College of Eastern Utah
www.ceu.edu
International Student Affairs
451 East 400 North
Price, UT 84501
Fax: (435) 637-5418
E-mail: jane.johnson@ceu.edu
Phone: (435) 613-5333

College of the Holy Cross
www.holycross.edu
Admissions
One College Street
Fenwick 105
Worcester, MA 01610-2395
Fax: (508) 793-3888
E-mail: admissions@holycross.edu
Phone: (508) 793-2443

College of Idaho
www.collegeofidaho.edu
Admission
2112 Cleveland Boulevard
Caldwell, ID 83605-4432
Fax: (208) 459-5757
E-mail: admission@collegeofidaho.edu
Phone: (800) 224-3246 ext. 5896

College of Lake County
www.clcillinois.edu
International Education
19351 West Washington Street
Grayslake, IL 60030-1198
Fax; (847) 543-3733
E-mail: ssmith2@clcillinois.edu
Phone: (847) 543-2733

College of Marin
www.marin.edu
835 College Avenue
Kentfield, CA 94904
Phone: (415) 457-8811 ext. 7719

College of Mount St. Joseph
www.msj.edu
International Programs
5701 Delhi Road
Cincinnati, OH 45233-1670
Fax: (513) 244-4211
E-mail: international@mail.msj.edu
Phone: (513) 244-4241

College of Mount St. Vincent
www.mountsaintvincent.edu
Office of Admission
6301 Riverdale Avenue
Riverdale, NY 10471-1093
Fax: (718) 549-7945
E-mail: tim.nash@mountsaintvincent.edu
Phone: (718) 405-3268

The College of New Jersey
www.tcnj.edu
Admissions
2000 Pennington Road Box 7718
Paul Loser Hall 228
Ewing, NJ 08628-0718
Fax: (609) 637-5174
E-mail: fay2@tcnj.edu
Phone: (609) 771-2131

College of New Rochelle
www.cnr.edu
Admissions
29 Castle Place
New Rochelle, NY 10805-2339
Fax: (914) 654-5464
E-mail: nnickerson@cnr.edu
Phone: (914) 654-5011

College of Notre Dame of Maryland
www.ndm.edu
Admissions Office
4701 North Charles Street
Baltimore, MD 21210
Fax: (410) 532-6287
E-mail: admiss@ndm.edu
Phone: (800) 435-0200

College of Office Technology
www.cot.edu
1520 West Division Street
Chicago, IL 60642-3312
Fax: (773) 278-0143
E-mail: info@cotedu.com
Phone: (773) 278-0042

College of the Ozarks
www.cofo.edu
Admissions
PO Box 17
Point Lookout, MO 65726-0017
Fax: (417) 690-2635
E-mail: admiss4@cofo.edu
Phone: (417) 690-2636

College of the Redwoods
www.redwoods.edu
Enrollment Services
7351 Tompkins Hill Road
Eureka, CA 95501-9300
Fax: (707) 476-4406
E-mail: admissions@redwoods.edu
Phone: (707) 476-4200

College of Saint Mary
www.csm.edu
International Admissions Counselor
7000 Mercy Road
Omaha, NE 68106
Fax: (402) 399-2412
E-mail: kbuscher@csm.edu
Phone: (402) 399-2410

College of Saint Rose
www.strose.edu
Undergraduate Admissions Office
432 Western Avenue
Albany, NY 12203
Fax: (518) 454-2013
E-mail: admit@mail.strose.edu
Phone: (518) 454-5150

College of San Mateo
www.collegeofsanmateo.edu
International Student Center
1700 West Hillsdale Boulevard
San Mateo, CA 94402-3784
Fax: (650) 574-6506
E-mail: villarealh@smccd.net
Phone: (415) 574-6525

College of the Sequoias
www.cos.edu
915 South Mooney Boulevard
Visalia, CA 93277
Fax: (559) 730-4820
E-mail: tamarar@cos.edu
Phone: (559) 737-4844

College of the Siskiyous
www.siskiyous.edu
Student Services
800 College Avenue
Weed, CA 96094-2899
Fax: (530) 938-5367
E-mail: info@siskiyous.edu
Phone: (530) 938-5374

College of Southern Idaho
www.csi.edu
Box 1238
Twin Falls, ID 83303-1238
Fax: (208) 736-3014
E-mail: kprestwich@csi.edu
Phone: (208) 732-6293

College of Southern Maryland
www.csmd.edu
Admissions Department
College of Southern Maryland-AOD
8730 Mitchell Road, POB 910
La Plata, MD 20646-0910
Fax: (301) 934-7698
E-mail: info@csmd.edu
Phone: (301) 934-7853

College of Southern Nevada
www.csn.edu
International Student Center
6375 West Charleston Boulevard
Las Vegas, NV 89146-1164
Fax: (702) 651-5821
E-mail: Tammy.Silver@csn.edu
Phone: (702) 651-5820

College of St. Benedict
www.csbsju.edu
Admissions
College of St Benedict/St John's University
PO Box 7155
Collegeville, MN 56321-7155
Fax: (320) 363-3206
E-mail: ryoung@csbsju.edu
Phone: (320) 363-2190

College of St. Elizabeth
www.cse.edu
2 Convent Road
Morristown, NJ 07960-6989
Fax: (973) 290-4710
E-mail: apply@cse.edu
Phone: (973) 290-4700

College of St. Joseph in Vermont
www.csj.edu
Admissions Counselor
71 Clement Road
Rutland, VT 05701-3899
Fax: (802) 776-5310
E-mail: vvaldez@csj.edu
Phone: (802) 776-5231

College of St. Scholastica
www.css.edu
Office of Admissions
1200 Kenwood Avenue
Duluth, MN 55811-4199
Fax: (218) 723-6394
E-mail: omeyer@css.edu
Phone: (218) 723-6045

College of Visual Arts
www.cva.edu
Senior Associate Director of Admissions
344 Summit Avenue
Saint Paul, MN 55102-2199
Fax: (651) 757-4010
E-mail: epaz@cva.edu
Phone: (651) 757-4041

College of Western Idaho
www.cwidaho.cc
Mail Stop 1000, PO Box 3010
Nampa, ID 83653
Fax: (888) 562-3216
E-mail: onestop@cwidaho.cc
Phone: (208) 562-3000

College of William and Mary
www.wm.edu
Associate Dean of Admission
PO Box 8795
Williamsburg, VA 23187-8795
Fax: (757) 221-1242
E-mail: dlbask@wm.edu
Phone: (757) 221-1837

College of Wooster
www.wooster.edu
Director of International Recruitment
Gault Admissions Center
847 College Avenue
Wooster, OH 44691-2363
Fax: (330) 263-2322
E-mail: batkins@wooster.edu
Phone: (330) 263-2322

CollegeAmerica: Fort Collins
www.collegeamerica.edu
4601 South Mason Street
Fort Collins, CO 80525
Phone: (970) 223-6060

Collin County Community College District
www.collin.edu
Admissions & Records Office
2800 East Spring Creek Parkway
Plano, TX 75074
Fax: (972) 881-5175
E-mail: smeinhardt@collin.edu
Phone: (972) 881-5710

Collins College
www.collinscollege.edu
4750 South 44th Place
Phoenix, AZ 85040
Fax: (480) 902-0663
Phone: (480) 966-3000

Colorado Christian University
www.ccu.edu
Undergraduate Admission Office
8787 West Alameda Avenue
Lakewood, CO 80226
Fax: (303) 963-3201
E-mail: admission@ccu.edu
Phone: (303) 963-3000

Colorado College
www.coloradocollege.edu
Admission Office
14 East Cache La Poudre Street
Colorado Springs, CO 80903-9854
Fax: (719) 389-6816
E-mail: mbonser@coloradocollege.edu
Phone: (719) 389-6344

Colorado Heights University
www.chu.edu
Office of Admissions
3001 South Federal Boulevard
Denver, CO 80236
Fax: (303) 937-4224
E-mail: jjohnson@chu.edu
Phone: (303) 937-4221

Colorado Mountain College
www.coloradomtn.edu
Enrollment Services
831 Grand Avenue
Glenwood Springs, CO 81601
Fax: (970) 947-8324
E-mail: bsommers@coloradomtn.edu
Phone: (800) 621-8559 ext. 8328

Colorado Northwestern Community College
www.cncc.edu
500 Kennedy Drive
Rangely, CO 81648
Fax: (970) 675-3343
E-mail: tresa.england@cncc.edu
Phone: (970) 675-2261 ext. 285

Colorado School of Mines
www.mines.edu
Office for International Student & Scholar
Services
Undergraduate Admissions
CSM Student Center - 1600 Maple Street
Golden, CO 80401-6114
Fax: (303) 273-3509
E-mail: admit@mines.edu
Phone: (303) 273-3210

Colorado School of Trades
www.schooloftrades.com
Admissions
1575 Hoyt Street
Lakewood, CO 80215-2945
Fax: (303) 233-4723
Phone: (303) 233-4697 ext. 16

Colorado State University
www.colostate.edu
Admissions
Office of Admissions/Colorado State
University
1062 Campus Delivery
Fort Collins, CO 80523-1062
Fax: (970) 491-7799
E-mail: admissions@colostate.edu
Phone: (970) 491-6909

Colorado State University: Pueblo
www.colostate-pueblo.edu
International Programs
2200 Bonforte Boulevard
Pueblo, CO 81001-4901
Fax: (719) 549-2221
E-mail: intprog@colostate-pueblo.edu
Phone: (719) 549-2329

Colorado Technical University
www.coloradotech.edu
Admissions
4435 North Chestnut Street
Colorado Springs, CO 80907
Fax: (719) 598-3740
E-mail: cosadmissions@coloradotech.edu
Phone: (719) 598-0200

Colorado Technical University: North Kansas City
www.ctukansascity.com
520 East 19th Avenue
North Kansas City, MO 64116
Phone: (816) 472-7400

Columbia Basin College
www.columbiabasin.edu
Admissions
2600 North 20th Avenue
Pasco, WA 99301
Fax: (509) 546-0401
E-mail: pmcgarry@columbiabasin.edu
Phone: (509) 542-5500

Columbia Centro Universitario: Yauco
www.columbiaco.edu
Box 3062
Calle Betances#3
Yauco, PR 00698-3062
Fax: (787) 856-0945
E-mail: rpadilla@columbiaco.edu
Phone: (787) 856-0930

Columbia College
www.ccis.edu
Admissions
1001 Rogers Street
Columbia, MO 65216
Fax: (573) 875-7506
E-mail: pjlobczowski@ccis.edu
Phone: (573) 875-7736

Columbia College
www.columbiasc.edu
Admission
1301 Columbia College Drive
Columbia, SC 29203
Fax: (803) 786-3674
E-mail: admissions@columbiasc.edu
Phone: (803) 786-3871

Columbia College Chicago
www.colum.edu
International Student Admissions
600 South Michigan Avenue
Room 301
Chicago, IL 60605-1996
Fax: (312) 369-8024
E-mail: gposejpal@colum.edu
Phone: (312) 369-7458

Columbia International University
www.ciu.edu
Admissions Office
PO Box 3122
Columbia, SC 29230-3122
Fax: (803) 786-4209
E-mail: yesciu@ciu.edu
Phone: (800) 777-2227 ext. 5345

Columbia Southern University
www.columbiasouthern.edu
Admissions
21982 University Lane
PO Box 3110
Orange Beach, AL 36561
Fax: (251) 981-3815
E-mail: admissions@columbiasouthern.edu
Phone: (251) 981-3771 ext. 521

Columbia University
www.columbia.edu
Undergraduate Admissions
1130 Amsterdam Avenue
212 Hamilton Hall, MC 2807
New York, NY 10027
Fax: (212) 854-1209
E-mail: ugrad-ask@columbia.edu
Phone: (212) 854-2522

Columbia University: School of General Studies
www.gs.columbia.edu
Admissions
408 Lewisohn Hall, Mail Code 4101
2970 Broadway
New York, NY 10027
Fax: (212) 854-6316
E-mail: gsdegree@columbia.edu
Phone: (212) 854-2772

Columbia-Greene Community College
www.sunycgcc.edu
Admissions
4400 Route 23
Hudson, NY 12534
Fax: (518) 822-2015
E-mail: pepitone@sunycgcc.edu
Phone: (518) 828-4181 ext. 5513

Columbus College of Art and Design
www.ccad.edu
Admissions Office
60 Cleveland Avenue
Columbus, OH 43215-3875
Fax: (614) 232-8344
E-mail: jneeley@ccad.edu
Phone: (614) 224-9101 ext. 3265

Columbus State Community College
www.cscc.edu
International Enrollment Services
550 East Spring Street
Box 1609
Columbus, OH 43216-1609
Fax: (614) 287-6019
E-mail: istudent@cscc.edu
Phone: (614) 287-2074

Columbus State University
www.colstate.edu
Admissions Office
4225 University Avenue
Columbus, GA 31907-5645
Fax: (706) 568-5091
E-mail: lovell_susan@colstate.edu
Phone: (706) 507-8800

Columbus Technical College
www.columbustech.org
Student Services
928 Manchester Expressway
Columbus, GA 31904-6572
Fax: (404) 649-1885
E-mail: admissions@columbustech.edu
Phone: (706) 649-1800

Commonwealth Institute of Funeral Service
www.commonwealthinst.org
415 Barren Springs Drive
Houston, TX 77090-5913
Fax: (281) 873-5232
Phone: (281) 873-0262

Community College of Allegheny County
www.ccac.edu
International Student Services Office
808 Ridge Avenue
Pittsburgh, PA 15212
Fax: (412) 237-4581
Phone: (412) 237-2629

Community College of Aurora
www.ccaurora.edu
Advising
16000 East CentreTech Parkway
Aurora, CO 80011-9036
Fax: (303) 361-7401
E-mail: dino.madariaga@cca.cccoes.edu
Phone: (303) 360-4797

Community College of Baltimore County
www.ccbcmd.edu
International Student Services
800 South Rolling Road
Baltimore, MD 21228
Fax: (443) 840-5046
E-mail: kmckenney@ccbcmd.edu
Phone: (443) 840-4533

Community College of Beaver County
www.ccbc.edu
Registrar
One Campus Drive
Monaca, PA 15061-2588
Fax: (724) 728-7599
E-mail: dan.slater@ccbc.edu
Phone: (724) 775-8561 ext. 254

Community College of Denver
www.ccd.edu
Dean of Students
Campus Box 201, PO Box 173363
Denver, CO 80217-3363
Fax: (303) 556-2431
E-mail: enrollment_services@ccd.edu
Phone: (303) 556-2430

Community College of Philadelphia
www.ccp.edu
1700 Spring Garden Street
Philadelphia, PA 19130-3991
Fax: (215) 972-6324
E-mail: internationaladmissions@ccp.edu
Phone: (215) 751-8835

Community College of Rhode Island
www.ccri.edu
Enrollment Services
400 East Avenue
Warwick, RI 02886-1807
Fax: (401) 825-2394
E-mail: tkless@ccri.edu
Phone: (401) 825-2278

Community College of Vermont
www.ccv.edu
CCV St. Albans
PO Box 489
Montpelier, VT 05601
Fax: (802) 828-2947
E-mail: maryellen.lowe@ccv.edu
Phone: (802) 524-6541

Concord University
www.concord.edu
Admissions Office
PO Box 1000
Athens, WV 24712-1000
Fax: (304) 384-9044
E-mail: tabora@concord.edu
Phone: (304) 384-5248

Concorde Career College: Aurora
www.concorde.edu/denver
111 North Havana Street
Aurora, CO 80010
Phone: (303) 861-1151

Concorde Career College: Garden Grove
www.concorde.edu
12951 Euclid Street, #101
Garden Grove, CA 92840
E-mail: agueco@concorde.edu
Phone: (714) 703-1900

Concorde Career College: Kansas City
www.concorde.edu/kansas
3239 Broadway
Kansas City, MO 64111
Fax: (816) 756-3231
E-mail: dcrow@concorde.edu
Phone: (816) 531-5223

Concorde Career College: North Hollywood
www.concorde.edu
12412 Victory Boulevard
North Hollywood, CA 91606
Fax: (818) 766-1587
Phone: (818) 766-8151

Concorde Career College: San Bernardino
www.concorde.edu
201 East Airport Dr.
San Bernardino, CA 92408

Concordia College
www.concordia-ny.edu
Admission
171 White Plains Road
Bronxville, NY 10708-1923
Fax: (914) 395-4636
E-mail: jcj@concordia-ny.edu
Phone: (914) 337-9300 ext. 2152

Concordia College: Moorhead
www.concordiacollege.edu
Admissions Office
901 Eighth Street South
Moorhead, MN 56562
Fax: (218) 299-4720
E-mail: buegel@cord.edu
Phone: (218) 299-3004

Concordia University
www.cui.edu
Admissions
1530 Concordia West
Irvine, CA 92612-3203
Fax: (949) 854-6894
E-mail: admission@cui.edu
Phone: (949) 214-3016

Concordia University
www.cune.edu
Office of Admission
800 North Columbia Avenue
Seward, NE 68434-1556
Fax: (402) 643-4073
E-mail: admiss@cune.edu
Phone: (800) 535-5494 ext. 7233

Concordia University
www.cu-portland.edu
Admissions
2811 Northeast Holman Street
Portland, OR 97211-6099
Fax: (503) 280-8531
E-mail: daferguson@cu-portland.edu
Phone: (503) 493-6437

Concordia University Chicago
www.cuchicago.edu
Undergraduate Admission
7400 Augusta Street
River Forest, IL 60305-1499
Fax: (708) 209-3473
E-mail: crfadmis@cuchicago.edu
Phone: (708) 209-3100

Concordia University St. Paul
www.csp.edu
Director of Undergraduate Admission
275 Syndicate Street North
St. Paul, MN 55104-5494
Fax: (651) 603-6320
E-mail: admission@csp.edu
Phone: (651) 641-8230

Concordia University Texas
www.concordia.edu
Office of Admissions
11400 Concordia University Drive
Austin, TX 78726
Fax: (512) 313-1632
E-mail: Nicole.Lapeyrolerie@concordia.edu
Phone: (512) 313-4632

Concordia University Wisconsin
www.cuw.edu
Admissions
12800 North Lake Shore Drive
Mequon, WI 53097
Fax: (262) 243-4545
E-mail: ken.gaschk@cuw.edu
Phone: (262) 243-4305

Connecticut College
www.connecticutcollege.edu
270 Mohegan Avenue
New London, CT 06320-4196
Fax: (860) 439-4301
E-mail: admit@conncoll.edu
Phone: (860) 439-2200

Conservatory of Music of Puerto Rico
www.cmpr.edu
Counselor
951 Ave. Ponce de Leon
San Juan, PR 00907-3373
Fax: (787) 763-3886
E-mail: pruibal@cmpr.gobierno.pr
Phone: (787) 751-0160 ext. 251

Contra Costa College
www.contracosta.edu
International Student Office
2600 Mission Bell Drive
San Pablo, CA 94806
Fax: (510) 236-6768
E-mail: AIllich@contracosta.edu
Phone: (510) 235-7800 ext. 4211

Converse College
www.converse.edu
Admissions
580 East Main Street
Spartanburg, SC 29302-0006
Fax: (864) 596-9225
E-mail: april.lewis@converse.edu
Phone: (864) 596-9746

Cooper Union for the Advancement of Science and Art
www.cooper.edu
Admissions and Records
30 Cooper Square, Suite 300
New York, NY 10003-7183
Fax: (212) 353-4342
E-mail: falls@cooper.edu
Phone: (212) 353-4120

Copper Mountain College
www.cmccd.edu
6162 Rotary Way
PO Box 1398
Joshua Tree, CA 92252
Fax: (760) 366-5257
E-mail: lburns@cmccd.edu
Phone: (760) 366-3791 ext. 4232

Coppin State University
www.coppin.edu
Office of Admissions
2500 West North Avenue
Baltimore, MD 21216
Fax: (410) 523-7351
E-mail: mgross@coppin.edu
Phone: (410) 951-3600

Corban College
www.corban.edu
Admissions
5000 Deer Park Drive SE
Salem, OR 97317-9392
Fax: (503) 585-4316
E-mail: admissions@corban.edu
Phone: (800) 845-3005

Corcoran College of Art and Design
www.corcoran.edu
Office of Admissions
500 17th Street, NW
Washington, DC 20006-4804
Fax: (202) 639-1830
E-mail: admissions@corcoran.org
Phone: (202) 639-1814

Cornell College
www.cornellcollege.edu
Admissions
600 First Street SW
Mount Vernon, IA 52314-1098
Fax: (319) 895-4451
E-mail: international@cornellcollege.edu
Phone: (319) 895-4215

Cornell University
www.cornell.edu
Undergraduate Admissions
410 Thurston Avenue
Ithaca, NY 14850-2488
Fax: (607) 255-0659
E-mail: admissions@cornell.edu
Phone: (607) 255-5241

Cornerstone University
www.cornerstone.edu
Assistant Director of Admissions
1001 East Beltline NE
Grand Rapids, MI 49525-5897
Fax: (616) 222-1418
E-mail: david.emerson@cornerstone.edu
Phone: (616) 949-5300

Corning Community College
www.corning-cc.edu
Admissions
One Academic Drive
Corning, NY 14830
Fax: (607) 962-9582
E-mail: kbrown7@corning-cc.edu
Phone: (607) 962-9299

Cornish College of the Arts
www.cornish.edu
Admissions
1000 Lenora Street
Seattle, WA 98121
Fax: (206) 720-1011
E-mail: admissions@cornish.edu
Phone: (206) 726-5016

Cossatot Community College of the University of Arkansas
www.cccua.edu
Student Serivces
183 Highway 399
PO Box 960
De Queen, AR 71832
Fax: (870) 642-3320
E-mail: ncowling@cccua.edu
Phone: (870) 584-4471

Cosumnes River College
www.crc.losrios.edu
8401 Center Parkway
Sacramento, CA 95823
Fax: (916) 691-7467
E-mail: kimuraj@exi.crc.losrios.cc.ca.us
Phone: (916) 691-7469

Cottey College
www.cottey.edu
Office of Enrollment Management
1000 West Austin Boulevard
Nevada, MO 64772
Fax: (417) 667-1025
E-mail: reber@cottey.edu
Phone: (417) 667-8181 ext. 2238

County College of Morris
www.ccm.edu
Admissions
214 Center Grove Road
Randolph, NJ 07869-2086
Fax: (973) 328-5199
E-mail: julmer@ccm.edu
Phone: (973) 328-5097

Covenant College
www.covenant.edu
Admissions
14049 Scenic Highway
Lookout Mountain, GA 30750
Fax: (706) 820-0893
E-mail: amy.smith@covenant.edu
Phone: (706) 419-1657

Cowley County Community College
www.cowley.edu
Executive Director of Enrollment and Outreach Services
PO Box 1147
Arkansas City, KS 67005-1147
Fax: (620) 441-5350
E-mail: schears@cowley.edu
Phone: (620) 442-0430

Cox College
www.coxcollege.edu
Admissions
1423 North Jefferson Avenue
Springfield, MO 65802
Fax: (417) 269-3586
E-mail: admissions@coxcollege.edu
Phone: (417) 269-3038

Coyne College
www.coynecollege.edu
330 North Green Street
Chicago, IL 60607
Fax: (312) 226-3818
E-mail: ppauletti@coynecollege.edu
Phone: (773) 577-8102

Crafton Hills College
www.craftonhills.edu
Counseling
11711 Sand Canyon Road
Yucaipa, CA 92399-1799
Fax: (909) 794-3863
E-mail: gmolino@craftonhills.edu
Phone: (909) 389-3366

Craven Community College
www.cravencc.edu
800 College Court
New Bern, NC 28562
Fax: (252) 638-4649
Phone: (252) 638-7200

Creighton University
www.creighton.edu
International Programs
2500 California Plaza
Omaha, NE 68178-0001
Fax: (402) 280-2211
E-mail: mkrane@creighton.edu
Phone: (402) 280-2059

Criswell College
www.criswell.edu
4010 Gaston Avenue
Dallas, TX 75246-1537
Fax: (214) 818-1310
E-mail: tccsa@criswell.edu
Phone: (214) 818-1305

Crowder College
www.crowder.edu
Coordinator of International Studies
601 LaClede Avenue
Neosho, MO 64850
Fax: (417) 455-5731
E-mail: suzannehurt@crowder.edu
Phone: (417) 455-5550

Crowley's Ridge College
www.crc.edu
Registrar
100 College Drive
Paragould, AR 72450
Fax: (870) 236-7748
E-mail: pmcfadden@crowleysridgecollege.edu
Phone: (870) 236-6901

Crown College
www.crown.edu
Admissions
8700 College View Drive
St. Bonifacius, MN 55375-9001
Fax: (952) 446-4149
E-mail: info@crown.edu
Phone: (952) 446-4321

Cuesta College
www.cuesta.org
Box 8106
San Luis Obispo, CA 93403
Fax: (805) 546-3975
E-mail: admit@bass.cuesta.cc.ca.us
Phone: (805) 546-3140

Culinary Institute Alain & Marie LeNotre
www.culinaryinstitute.edu
7070 Allensby Street
Houston, TX 77022
Fax: (713) 692-7399
E-mail: admission@culinaryinstitute.edu
Phone: (713) 692-0077

Culinary Institute of America
www.ciachef.edu
Admissions Office
1946 Campus Drive
Hyde Park, NY 12538-1499
Fax: (845) 451-1068
E-mail: v_reilly@culinary.edu
Phone: (845) 451-1531

Culver-Stockton College
www.culver.edu
International Admissions Coordinator
One College Hill
Canton, MO 63435-1299
Fax: (573) 288-6618
E-mail: admissions@culver.edu
Phone: (573) 288-6331

Cumberland County College
www.cccnj.edu
PO Box 1500
3322 College Drive
Vineland, NJ 08362-9912
Fax: (609) 691-6157
Phone: (856) 691-8600

Cumberland University
www.cumberland.edu
Admissions
One Cumberland Square
Lebanon, TN 37087
Fax: (615) 444-2569
E-mail: ppope@cumberland.edu
Phone: (615) 444-2562 ext. 1224

Curry College
www.curry.edu
Admission
1071 Blue Hill Avenue
Milton, MA 02186-9984
Fax: (617) 333-2114
E-mail: lmarsen0109@curry.edu
Phone: (617) 333-2210

Curtis Institute of Music
www.curtis.edu
1726 Locust Street
Philadelphia, PA 19103-6187
Fax: (215) 893-9065
E-mail: admissions@curtis.edu
Phone: (215) 717-3117

**Cuyahoga Community College:
Metropolitan**
www.tri-c.edu
Admissions
2900 Community College Avenue
Cleveland, OH 44115-2878
Fax: (216) 696-2567
E-mail: george.koussa@tri-c.edu
Phone: (216) 987-4167

Cuyamaca College
www.cuyamaca.edu
Admissions and Records
900 Rancho San Diego Parkway
El Cajon, CA 92019-4304
Fax: (619) 660-4575
E-mail: vanessa.saenz@gcccd.edu
Phone: (619) 660-4565

Cypress College
www.cypresscollege.edu
International Students
9200 Valley View Street
Cypress, CA 90630
Fax: (714) 484-7446
E-mail: yhan@cypresscollege.edu
Phone: (714) 484-7050

Daemen College
www.daemen.edu
Admissions
4380 Main Street
Amherst, NY 14226-3592
Fax: (716) 839-8229
E-mail: admissions@daemen.edu
Phone: (716) 839-8225

Dakota College at Bottineau
www.dakotacollege.edu
Student Services
105 Simrall Boulevard
Bottineau, ND 58318-1198
Fax: (701) 228-5488
E-mail: paula.berg@dakotacollege.edu
Phone: (800) 542-6866

Dakota County Technical College
www.dctc.edu
Office of Admissions
1300 145th Street East
Rosemount, MN 55068
Fax: (651) 423-8775
E-mail: patrick.lair@dctc.edu
Phone: (651) 423-8399

Dakota State University
www.dsu.edu
International Program Office
820 North Washington Avenue
Admissions Office
Madison, SD 57042
Fax: (605) 256-5095
E-mail: international@dsu.edu
Phone: (605) 256-5267

Dakota Wesleyan University
www.dwu.edu
Admissions
1200 West University Avenue
Mitchell, SD 57301-4398
Fax: (605) 995-2699
E-mail: mementzel@dwu.edu
Phone: (605) 995-2665

Dallas Baptist University
www.dbu.edu
International Office
3000 Mountain Creek Parkway
Dallas, TX 75211-9299
Fax: (214) 333-5409
E-mail: globalinfo@dbu.edu
Phone: (214) 333-5426

Daniel Webster College
www.dwc.edu
Admissions
20 University Drive
Nashua, NH 03063
Fax: (603) 577-6001
E-mail: admissions@dwc.edu
Phone: (603) 577-6600

Danville Area Community College
www.dacc.edu
Admissions and Records
2000 East Main Street
Danville, IL 61832
Fax: (217) 443-8337
E-mail: stacy@dacc.edu
Phone: (217) 443-8803

Danville Community College
www.dcc.vccs.edu
Admissions
1008 South Main Street
Danville, VA 24541
Fax: (434) 797-8451
E-mail: hgraves@dcc.vccs.edu
Phone: (434) 797-8420

Dartmouth College
www.dartmouth.edu
International Admissions
6016 McNutt Hall
Hanover, NH 03755
Fax: (603) 646-1216
E-mail: Katrina.Davis@Dartmouth.edu
Phone: (603) 646-3369

Darton College
www.darton.edu
Student Affairs
2400 Gillionville Road
Albany, GA 31707-3098
Fax: (229) 317-6614
E-mail: diana.garner@darton.edu
Phone: (229) 317-6924

Davenport University
www.davenport.edu
Senior Advisor for Study Abroad and
International Students
6191 Kraft Avenue SE
Grand Rapids, MI 49512-5926
Fax: (616) 554-5239
E-mail: alex.akulli@davenport.edu
Phone: (616) 698-7111

Davidson College
www.davidson.edu
Admissions Office
Box 7156
Davidson, NC 28035-7156
Fax: (704) 894-2016
E-mail: admission@davidson.edu
Phone: (704) 894-2230

Davis and Elkins College
www.dewv.edu
Admissions
100 Campus Drive
Elkins, WV 26241-3996
Fax: (304) 637-1800
E-mail: hinklen@dewv.edu
Phone: (304) 637-1328

Davis College
www.davisny.edu
Enrollment Management
400 Riverside Drive
Johnson City, NY 13790
Fax: (607) 798-7754
E-mail: cgodfroy@davisny.edu
Phone: (607) 729-1581 ext. 341

Dawson Community College
www.dawson.edu
300 College Drive
Box 421
Glendive, MT 59330
Fax: (406) 377-8132
E-mail: lholte@dawson.edu
Phone: (406) 377-3396 ext. 404

Daymar College: Owensboro
www.daymarcollege.edu
Admissions
3361 Buckland Square
Owensboro, KY 42301
Fax: (304) 685-4090
E-mail: vmcdougal@daymarcollege.edu
Phone: (270) 926-4040

Daymar Institute: Nashville
www.daymarinstitute.edu
Admissions
340 & 283 Plus Park at Pavilion Boulevard
Nashville, TN 37217
Fax: (615) 367-2736
E-mail: admissions@daymarinstitute.edu
Phone: (615) 361-7555

Daytona State College
www.daytonastate.edu
Admissions Office
Daytona State College Admissions Office
1200 W International Speedway Boulevard
PO Box 2811
Daytona Beach, FL 32114-2811
Fax: (386) 506-3940
E-mail: admissions@daytonastate.edu
Phone: (386) 506-3059 ext. 3059

De Anza College
www.deanza.edu
Foreign Student Adviser
21250 Stevens Creek Boulevard
Cupertino, CA 95014
Fax: (408) 864-5638
E-mail: webreg@fhda.edu
Phone: (408) 864-8813

Dean College
www.dean.edu
Admissions
99 Main Street
Franklin, MA 02038-1994
Fax: (508) 541-8726
E-mail: dshapiro@dean.edu
Phone: (508) 541-1512

Deep Springs College
www.deepsprings.edu
Applications Committee
Applications Committee
HC 72 Box 45001
Dyer, NV 89010-9803
Fax: (760) 874-7077
E-mail: apcom@deepsprings.edu
Phone: (760) 872-2000

Defiance College
www.defiance.edu
Admissions
701 North Clinton Street
Defiance, OH 43512-1695
Fax: (419) 783-2468
E-mail: bharsha@defiance.edu
Phone: (419) 783-2365

DeKalb Technical College
www.dekalbtech.edu
Admissions, International Student Advisors
495 North Indian Creek Drive
Clarkston, GA 30021-2397
Fax: (404) 294-3424
E-mail: petersl@dekalbtech.edu
Phone: (404) 297-9522 ext. 1154

Del Mar College
www.delmar.edu
Admissions and Registrar's Office
101 Baldwin Boulevard
Corpus Christi, TX 78404-3897
Fax: (361) 698-1595
E-mail: bthomps@delmar.edu
Phone: (361) 698-1255

Delaware College of Art and Design
www.dcad.edu
Admissions Office
600 North Market Street
Wilmington, DE 19801
Fax: (302) 622-8870
E-mail: egatti@dcad.edu
Phone: (302) 622-8867 ext. 123

Delaware County Community College
www.dccc.edu
Admissions
901 South Media Line Road
Media, PA 19063
Fax: (610) 723-1530
E-mail: admiss@dccc.edu
Phone: (610) 359-5050

Delaware State University
www.desu.edu
1200 North DuPont Highway
Dover, DE 19901
Fax: (302) 857-6352
E-mail: ehill@desu.edu
Phone: (302) 857-6351

Delaware Technical and Community College: Stanton/Wilmington
www.dtcc.edu
400 Stanton-Christiana Road
Newark, DE 19713
Fax: (302) 453-3084
E-mail: s-admissions@dtcc.edu
Phone: (302) 571-5343

Delgado Community College
www.dcc.edu
Office of Admissions and Enrollment Services
615 City Park Avenue
New Orleans, LA 70119
Fax: (504) 483-1895
E-mail: gboutt@dcc.edu
Phone: (504) 671-5099

Delta College
www.delta.edu
Admissions
1961 Delta Road D101
University Center, MI 48710
Fax: (989) 667-2202
E-mail: danielsegura@delta.edu
Phone: (989) 686-9507

Delta College of Arts & Technology
www.deltacollege.com
7380 Exchange Place
Baton Rouge, LA 70806
Fax: (225) 927-9096
E-mail: admissions@deltacollege.com
Phone: (225) 928-7770

Delta State University
www.deltastate.edu
International Students Office
117 Kent Wyatt Hall
Cleveland, MS 38733
Fax: (662) 846-4684
E-mail: ppetrova@deltastate.edu
Phone: (662) 846-4730

Denison University
www.denison.edu
Coordinator of International Admissions
100 West College PO Box B
Granville, OH 43023
Fax: (740) 587-6306
E-mail: leavell@denison.edu
Phone: (740) 587-6789

Denmark Technical College
www.denmarktech.edu
1126 Solomon Blatt Boulevard
PO Box 327
Denmark, SC 29042
Fax: (803) 793-5942
E-mail: thomast@denmarktech.edu
Phone: (803) 793-5176

Denver School of Nursing
www.denverschoolofnursing.edu
1401 19th Street
Denver, CO 80202
E-mail: j.johnson@denverschoolofnursing.edu
Phone: (303) 292-0015

DePaul University
www.depaul.edu
Director of International Admission
One East Jackson Boulevard
DePaul Center, Suite 9000
Chicago, IL 60604-2287
Fax: (312) 362-8521
E-mail: dpruccol@depaul.edu
Phone: (312) 362-5620

DePauw University
www.depauw.edu
Admission
101 East Seminary Street
Greencastle, IN 46135-1611
Fax: (765) 658-4007
E-mail: admission@depauw.edu
Phone: (765) 658-4006

Des Moines Area Community College
www.dmacc.edu
International Student Advisor
2006 South Ankeny Boulevard
Ankeny, IA 50023-3993
Fax: (515) 964-6391
E-mail: khuang@dmacc.edu
Phone: (515) 964-6471

DeSales University
www.desales.edu
Enrollment Services
2755 Station Avenue
Center Valley, PA 18034-9568
Fax: (610) 282-0131
E-mail: brian.macdonald@desales.edu
Phone: (610) 282-4443

Design Institute of San Diego
www.disd.edu
8555 Commerce Avenue
San Diego, CA 92121
Fax: (858) 566-2711
Phone: (858) 566-1200

DeVry College of New York
www.devry.edu
180 Madison Avenue, Suite 900
New York, NY 10016
Fax: (630) 571-0317
Phone: (630) 571-7700 ext. 3150

DeVry University: Arlington
www.devry.edu
2450 Crystal Drive
Arlington, VA 22202
Fax: (630) 571-0317
E-mail: admissions@crys.devry.edu
Phone: (630) 571-7700 ext. 4006

DeVry University: Chicago
www.devry.edu
International Student Coordinator
3300 North Campbell Avenue
Chicago, IL 60618-5994
Fax: (630) 571-0317
E-mail: admissions2@devry.edu
Phone: (630) 571-7700 ext. 3150

DeVry University: Columbus
www.devry.edu
International Student Coordinator
1350 Alum Creek Drive
Columbus, OH 43209-2705
Fax: (630) 571-0317
E-mail: admissions@devry.edu
Phone: (630) 571-7700 ext. 3150

DeVry University: Decatur
www.devry.edu
International Student Coordinator
One West Court Square, Suite 100
Decatur, GA 30030-2556
Fax: (630) 571-0317
E-mail: dsilva@admin.atl.devry.edu
Phone: (630) 571-7700 ext. 3150

DeVry University: Federal Way
www.devry.edu
3600 South 344th Way
Federal Way, WA 98001-9558
Fax: (630) 571-0317
E-mail: admissions@sea.devry.edu
Phone: (630) 571-7700 ext. 4006

DeVry University: Fort Washington
www.devry.edu
International Student Coordinator
1140 Virginia Drive
Fort Washington, PA 19034-3204
Fax: (630) 571-0317
E-mail: admissions@phi.devry.edu
Phone: (630) 571-7700 ext. 3150

DeVry University: Houston
www.devry.edu
11125 Equity Drive
Houston, TX 77041-8217
Fax: (713) 896-7650
Phone: (713) 973-3000

DeVry University: Irving
www.devry.edu
International Student Coordinator
4800 Regent Boulevard
Dallas, TX 75063-2439
Fax: (630) 571-0317
Phone: (630) 571-7700 ext. 3150

DeVry University: Kansas City
www.devry.edu
International Student Coordinator
11224 Holmes Street
Kansas City, MO 64131-3626
Fax: (630) 571-0317
E-mail: ssmeed@kc.devry.edu
Phone: (630) 571-7700 ext. 3150

DeVry University: Miramar
www.devry.edu
International Student Coordinator
2300 SW 145th Avenue
Miramar, FL 33027
Fax: (630) 571-0317
E-mail: openhouse@mir.devry.edu
Phone: (630) 571-7700 ext. 3150

DeVry University: North Brunswick
www.devry.edu
International Student Coordinator
630 US Highway One
North Brunswick, NJ 08902-3362
Fax: (630) 571-0317
E-mail: admissions@devry.edu
Phone: (630) 571-7700 ext. 3150

DeVry University: Online
www.devry.edu
One Tower Lane
Oakbrook Terrace, IL 60181

DeVry University: Orlando
www.devry.edu
4000 Millennia Boulevard
Orlando, FL 32839-2426
Fax: (630) 571-0317
Phone: (630) 571-7700 ext. 3150

DeVry University: Phoenix
www.devry.edu
International Student Coordinator
2149 West Dunlap Avenue
Phoenix, AZ 85021-2995
Fax: (630) 571-0317
E-mail: admissions@phx.devry.edu
Phone: (630) 571-7700 ext. 3150

DeVry University: Pomona
www.devry.edu
901 Corporate Center Drive
Pomona, CA 91768-2642
Fax: (630) 517-0317
Phone: (630) 571-7700 ext. 3150

DeVry University: Westminster
www.devry.edu
1870 West 122 Avenue
Westminster, CO 80234-2010
Fax: (630) 571-0317
E-mail: denver-admissions@den.devry.edu
Phone: (630) 571-7700 ext. 3150

Diablo Valley College
www.dvc.edu
International Student Admissions and Services
321 Golf Club Road
Pleasant Hill, CA 94523-1529
Fax: (925) 691-9503
E-mail: gzarabozo@dvc.edu
Phone: (925) 685-1230 ext. 2075

Dickinson College
www.dickinson.edu
PO Box 1773
Carlisle, PA 17013-2896
Fax: (717) 245-1442
E-mail: studyusa@dickinson.edu
Phone: (800) 644-1773

Dickinson State University
www.dsu.nodak.edu
Center for Multicultural Affairs
291 Campus Drive
Campus Box 169
Dickinson, ND 58601-4896
Fax: (701) 483-2831
E-mail: thy.yang@dickinsonstate.edu
Phone: (701) 483-2598

DigiPen Institute of Technology
www.digipen.edu
Admissions Office
9931 Willows Road NE
Redmond, WA 98052
Fax: (425) 558-0378
E-mail: admissions@digipen.edu
Phone: (425) 558-0299

Dillard University
www.dillard.edu
Admissions
2601 Gentilly Boulevard
New Orleans, LA 70122-3097
Fax: (504) 816-4332
E-mail: mreed@dillard.edu
Phone: (800) 216-6637

Dine College
www.dinecollege.edu
Registrar
Box 67
Tsaile, AZ 86556
Fax: (928) 724-3349
E-mail: louise@dinecollege.edu
Phone: (928) 724-6630

Divine Word College
www.dwci.edu
102 Jacoby Drive SW
PO Box 380
Epworth, IA 52045
Fax: (563) 876-5515
E-mail: svdvocations@dwci.edu
Phone: (563) 876-3332

Dixie State College
www.dixie.edu/
International Student Admissions Office
225 South 700 East
St. George, UT 84770-3876
Fax: (435) 656-4070
E-mail: mpthompson@dixie.edu
Phone: (435) 652-7689

Doane College
www.doane.edu
Midwest Institute
1014 Boswell Avenue
Crete, NE 68333
Fax: (402) 826-8592
E-mail: mfranklin@doane.edu
Phone: (402) 826-8215

Dodge City Community College
www.dc3.edu
2501 North 14th Avenue
Dodge City, KS 67801-2399
Fax: (620) 227-9277
E-mail: tamtabor@dc3.edu
Phone: (620) 227-9217

Dominican College of Blauvelt
www.dc.edu
Admissions
470 Western Highway
Orangeburg, NY 10962-1210
Fax: (845) 365-3150
E-mail: joyce.elbe@dc.edu
Phone: (845) 848-7901

Dominican University
www.dom.edu
Undergraduate Office of Admissions
7900 West Division Street
River Forest, IL 60305-1099
Fax: (708) 524-5990
E-mail: domadmis@dom.edu
Phone: (708) 524-6800

Dominican University of California
www.dominican.edu
Admissions Office
50 Acacia Avenue
San Rafael, CA 94901-2298
Fax: (415) 485-3214
E-mail: nichelle.passanisi@dominican.edu
Phone: (415) 485-3206

Dona Ana Community College of New Mexico State University
www.dacc.nmsu.edu
International Programs, New Mexico State University
MSC-3DA
PO Box 30001
Las Cruces, NM 88003-8001
Fax: (575) 646-1517
E-mail: marjaspe@ad.nmsu.edu
Phone: (575) 646-2017

Donnelly College
www.donnelly.edu
International Student Admissions
608 North 18th Street
Kansas City, KS 66102-4210
Fax: (913) 621-8719
E-mail: cshadfar@donnelly.edu
Phone: (913) 621-8720

Douglas Education Center
www.dec.edu
Admissions
130 Seventh Street
Monessen, PA 15062
E-mail: swalters@dec.edu
Phone: (800) 413-6013 ext. 120

Dowling College
www.dowling.edu
International Student Services
150 Idle Hour Boulevard
Oakdale, NY 11769-1999
Fax: (631) 244-5097
E-mail: International@dowling.edu
Phone: (631) 244-3124

Drake University
www.drake.edu
Office of Admission
2507 University Avenue
Des Moines, IA 50311-4505
Fax: (515) 271-2831
E-mail: international@drake.edu
Phone: (515) 271-3181 ext. 2086

Drew University
www.drew.edu
Office of Admissions
36 Madison Avenue
Madison, NJ 07940-4063
Fax: (973) 408-3068
E-mail: pfairwea@drew.edu
Phone: (973) 408-3523

Drexel University
www.drexel.edu
International Admissions
3141 Chestnut Street
Philadelphia, PA 19104-2876
Fax: (215) 895-5939
E-mail: enroll@drexel.edu
Phone: (215) 895-2400

Drury University
www.drury.edu
International and IEP Admission
900 North Benton Avenue
Springfield, MO 65802-3712
Fax: (417) 866-3873
E-mail: iadmissions@drury.edu
Phone: (417) 873-7506

Duke University
www.duke.edu
2138 Campus Drive
Box 90586
Durham, NC 27708
Fax: (919) 684-8128
E-mail: anne.sjostrom@duke.edu
Phone: (919) 684-3214

Dunlap-Stone University
www.dunlap-stone.edu
Registrar
11225 North 28th Drive Suite B201
Phoenix, AZ 85029
Fax: (62) 648-5755
E-mail: tandrews@expandglobal.com
Phone: (602) 648-5750

Dunwoody College of Technology
www.dunwoody.edu
Admissions Manager
818 Dunwoody Boulevard
attn: Admissions
Minneapolis, MN 55403-1192
Fax: (612) 374-4128
E-mail: bbielen@dunwoody.edu
Phone: (612) 374-5800 ext. 8110

Duquesne University
www.duq.edu
Office of International Programs
600 Forbes Avenue, Administration Building
Pittsburgh, PA 15282-0201
Fax: (412) 396-5178
E-mail: oip@duq.edu
Phone: (412) 396-6113

Durham Technical Community College
www.durhamtech.edu
International Student Adviser
1637 Lawson Street
Durham, NC 27703
Fax: (919) 686-3669
E-mail: newhousem@durhamtech.edu
Phone: (919) 686-3305

Dutchess Community College
www.sunydutchess.edu
Student Services
53 Pendell Road
Poughkeepsie, NY 12601-1595
Fax: (845) 431-8997
E-mail: holst@sunydutchess.edu
Phone: (845) 431-8974

Dyersburg State Community College
www.dscc.edu
Admissions and Records
1510 Lake Road
Dyersburg, TN 38024
Fax: (731) 286-3325
E-mail: enroll@dscc.edu
Phone: (731) 286-3330

D'Youville College
www.dyc.edu
International Admissions
320 Porter Avenue
Buffalo, NY 14201-1084
Fax: (716) 829-7788
E-mail: dannecrh@dyc.edu
Phone: (716) 829-8119

Eagle Gate College: Layton
www.eaglegatecollege.edu
915 North 400 West Layton
Layton, UT 84041
Fax: (801) 593-6654
E-mail: admissions@eaglegatecollege.edu
Phone: (801) 546-7500 ext. 7512

Eagle Gate College: Murray
www.eaglegatecollege.edu
5588 South Green Street
Murray, UT 84123
Phone: (801) 281-7700

Earlham College
www.earlham.edu
International Student Admissions
801 National Road West
Richmond, IN 47374-4095
Fax: (765) 983-1560
E-mail: admissions@earlham.edu
Phone: (765) 983-1600

East Arkansas Community College
www.eacc.edu
Admissions and Records
1700 Newcastle Road
Forrest City, AR 72335-9598
Fax: (870) 633-3840
E-mail: scollier@eacc.edu
Phone: (870) 633-4480 ext. 300

East Carolina University
www.ecu.edu
Assistant Director for International Student Recruitment
Office of Undergraduate Admissions
106 Whichard Building
Greenville, NC 27858-4353
Fax: (252) 328-4813
E-mail: intlprgm@ecu.edu
Phone: (252) 328-6769

East Central College
www.eastcentral.edu
Academic Advising & Counseling
1964 Prairie Dell Road
Union, MO 63084-0529
Fax: (636) 583-1011
E-mail: weinhota@eastcentral.edu
Phone: (636) 584-6577

East Central University
www.ecok.edu
International Program and Services
PMBJ8, 1100 East 14th Street
Ada, OK 74820
Fax: (580) 559-5755
E-mail: jstudbkr@ecok.edu
Phone: (580) 559-5675

East Georgia College
www.ega.edu
Admissions
131 College Circle
Swainsboro, GA 30401-2699
Fax: (478) 289-2140
E-mail: kjones@ega.edu
Phone: (478) 289-2219

East Los Angeles College
www.elac.edu
International Student Program
1301 Avenida Cesar Chavez
Monterey Park, CA 91754-6099
Fax: (323) 260-8192
E-mail: elac_iso@elac.edu
Phone: (323) 265-8796

East Stroudsburg University of Pennsylvania
www4.esu.edu
Undergraduate Admissions
200 Prospect Street
East Stroudsburg, PA 18301-2999
Fax: (570) 422-3933
E-mail: undergrads@po-box.esu.edu
Phone: (570) 422-3577

East Tennessee State University
www.etsu.edu
Admissions Office
ETSU Box 70731
Johnson City, TN 37614
Fax: (423) 439-4630
E-mail: go2etsu@etsu.edu
Phone: (423) 439-4213

East Texas Baptist University
www.etbu.edu
Admissions
1209 North Grove
Marshall, TX 75670-1498
Fax: (903) 923-2001
E-mail: admissions@etbu.edu
Phone: (903) 923-2000

East-West University
www.eastwest.edu
Admission
816 South Michigan Avenue
Chicago, IL 60605
Fax: (312) 939-0111
E-mail: agniezka@eastwest.edu
Phone: (312) 939-0111 ext. 1825

Eastern Arizona College
www.eac.edu
Records and Registration
615 North Stadium Avenue
Thatcher, AZ 85552-0769
Fax: (928) 428-2446
E-mail: admissions@eac.edu
Phone: (928) 428-8252

Eastern Connecticut State University
www.easternct.edu
Admissions
83 Windham Street
Willimantic, CT 06226-2295
Fax: (860) 465-5544
E-mail: satsukd@easternct.edu
Phone: (860) 465-5286

Eastern Illinois University
www.eiu.edu
Office of International Students & Scholars
600 Lincoln Avenue
Charleston, IL 61920-3011
Fax: (217) 581-7207
E-mail: international@eiu.edu
Phone: (217) 581-2321

Eastern International College
www.eicollege.edu
3000 JF Kennedy Boulevard
Jersey City, NJ 07306
E-mail: eicollege@verizon.net
Phone: (201) 216-9901

Eastern Kentucky University
www.eku.edu
Admissions Director
SSB CPO 54, 521 Lancaster Avenue
Richmond, KY 40475-3102
Fax: (859) 622-1552
E-mail: stephen.byrn@eku.edu
Phone: (859) 622-1478

Eastern Maine Community College
www.emcc.edu
354 Hogan Road
Bangor, ME 04401
Fax: (207) 974-4608
E-mail: gswett@emcc.edu
Phone: (207) 974-4604

Eastern Mennonite University
www.emu.edu
Admissions Office
1200 Park Road
Harrisonburg, VA 22802-2462
Fax: (540) 432-4444
E-mail: kratzj@emu.edu
Phone: (540) 432-4118

Eastern Michigan University
www.emich.edu
Admissions
400 Pierce Hall
Ypsilanti, MI 48197
Fax: (734) 487-6559
E-mail: international.admissions@emich.edu
Phone: (734) 487-3060

Eastern Nazarene College
www.enc.edu
Office of Admissions
23 East Elm Avenue
Quincy, MA 02170
Fax: (617) 745-3992
E-mail: admissions@enc.edu
Phone: (617) 745-3711

Eastern New Mexico University
www.enmu.edu
International Student Advising
1500 South Avenue K
Station 7
Portales, NM 88130
Fax: (575) 562-2118
E-mail: tracy.henderson@enmu.edu
Phone: (575) 562-4698

Eastern New Mexico University: Roswell
www.roswell.enmu.edu
Admissions
Box 6000
Roswell, NM 88202-6000
Fax: (505) 624-7144
E-mail: lily.quezada@roswell.enmu.edu
Phone: (575) 624-7142

Eastern Oklahoma State College
www.eosc.edu
Director of Recruitment, Admissions, and Financial Aid
1301 West Main Street
Wilburton, OK 74578-4999
Fax: (918) 465-2431
E-mail: lmiller@eosc.edu
Phone: (918) 465-2361 ext. 240

Eastern Oregon University
www.eou.edu
Admissions
One University Boulevard
Inlow Hall, Room 115
La Grande, OR 97850
Fax: (541) 962-3418
E-mail: admissions@eou.edu
Phone: (541) 962-3406

Eastern University
www.eastern.edu
Admissions
1300 Eagle Road
St. Davids, PA 19087-3696
Fax: (610) 341-1723
E-mail: mdziedzi@eastern.edu
Phone: (610) 341-1376

Eastern Washington University
www.ewu.edu
International Student Programs
101 Sutton Hall
Cheney, WA 99004-2447
Fax: (509) 359-7869
E-mail: isp@mail.ewu.edu
Phone: (509) 359-2331

Eastern Wyoming College
www.ewc.wy.edu
Admissions
3200 West C Street
Torrington, WY 82240
Fax: (307) 532-8222
E-mail: rex.cogdill@ewc.wy.edu
Phone: (800) 658-3195

Eastfield College
www.efc.dcccd.edu
Admissions Office
3737 Motley Drive
Mesquite, TX 75150
Fax: (972) 860-8306
E-mail: efc@dcccd.edu
Phone: (972) 860-7059

Eastman School of Music of the University of Rochester
www.esm.rochester.edu
Admissions
26 Gibbs Street
Rochester, NY 14604-2599
Fax: (585) 232-8601
E-mail: admissions@esm.rochester.edu
Phone: (585) 274-1060

Ecclesia College
www.ecollege.edu
International Student Office
9653 Nations Drive
Springdale, AR 72762
Fax: (479) 248-1455
E-mail: abriggs@ecollege.edu
Phone: (479) 248-7236 ext. 225

Eckerd College
www.eckerd.edu
Assistant Director of Admissions
4200 54th Avenue South
St. Petersburg, FL 33711-4700
Fax: (727) 866-2304
E-mail: crabtram@eckerd.edu
Phone: (727) 864-8331

ECPI College of Technology: Virginia Beach
www.ecpi.edu
Academic Support Services
5555 Greenwich Road, Suite 300
Virginia Beach, VA 23462-6542
Fax: (757) 671-8661
E-mail: rmckain@ecpi.edu
Phone: (757) 490-9090

Edgewood College
www.edgewood.edu
International Admissions
1000 Edgewood College Drive
Madison, WI 53711-1997
Fax: (608) 663-2214
E-mail: admissions@edgewood.edu
Phone: (608) 663-2294

EDIC College
www.ediccollege.com
Box 9120
Caguas, PR 00726-9120
Fax: (787) 258-6300
E-mail: admisiones@ediccollege.edu
Phone: (787) 744-8519 ext. 229

Edinboro University of Pennsylvania
www.edinboro.edu
International Student Services
200 East Normal Street
Academy Hall
Edinboro, PA 16444
Fax: (814) 732-2443
E-mail: international@edinboro.edu
Phone: (814) 732-2770

Edison State College
www.edison.edu
District Office of Information and Recruitment
Box 60210
Fort Myers, FL 33906-6210
Fax: (239) 489-9094
E-mail: bsilva@edison.edu
Phone: (239) 489-9362

Edison State Community College
www.edisonohio.edu
Admissions
1973 Edison Drive
Piqua, OH 45356-9253
Fax: (937) 778-1920
E-mail: vbogart@edisonohio.edu
Phone: (937) 778-7854

Edward Waters College
www.ewc.edu
Admissions Office
1658 Kings Road
Jacksonville, FL 32209
Fax: (904) 470-8048
E-mail: edward.alexander@ewc.edu
Phone: (904) 470-8201

El Camino College
www.elcamino.edu
International Student Program Office
16007 Crenshaw Boulevard
Torrance, CA 90506
Fax: (310) 660-3818
E-mail: lrachman@elcamino.edu
Phone: (310) 660-3431

El Centro College
www.elcentrocollege.edu
International Office Director
801 Main Street
Dallas, TX 75202
Fax: (214) 860-2022
E-mail: rreyes@dcccd.edu
Phone: (214) 860-2664

Elgin Community College
www.elgin.edu
International Student Services
1700 Spartan Drive
Elgin, IL 60123-7193
Fax: (847) 214-7484
E-mail: LNehlsen@elgin.edu
Phone: (847) 214-7809

Elizabeth City State University
www.ecsu.edu
Director of Admissions
1704 Weeksville Road, Campus Box 901
Elizabeth City, NC 27909
Fax: (252) 335-3537
E-mail: tllee@mail.ecsu.edu
Phone: (252) 335-3970

Elizabethtown College
www.etown.edu
Admission
One Alpha Drive
Elizabethtown, PA 17022-2298
Fax: (717) 361-1365
E-mail: admissions@etown.edu
Phone: (717) 361-1400

Elizabethtown Community and Technical College
www.elizabethtown.kctcs.edu
Coordinator of Admissions
600 College Street Road
Elizabethtown, KY 42701
Fax: (270) 769-1618
E-mail: bryan.smith@kctcs.edu
Phone: (270) 769-2371 ext. 68616

Ellsworth Community College
www.iavalley.cc.ia.us/ecc
Counseling Office
1100 College Avenue
Iowa Falls, IA 50126
Fax: (641) 648-3128
E-mail: nwalters@iavalley.cc.ia.us
Phone: (641) 648-4611 ext. 424

Elmhurst College
www.elmhurst.edu
Admission
190 South Prospect Avenue
Elmhurst, IL 60126-3296
Fax: (630) 617-5501
E-mail: admit@elmhurst.edu
Phone: (630) 617-3400

Elmira College
www.elmira.edu
Office of Admissions
One Park Place
Elmira, NY 14901
Fax: (607) 735-1718
E-mail: bmoore@elmira.edu
Phone: (607) 735-1724

Elms College
www.elms.edu
Director of Admission
291 Springfield Street
Chicopee, MA 01013-2839
Fax: (413) 594-2781
E-mail: wagnerj@elms.edu
Phone: (413) 592-3189

Elon University
www.elon.edu
Director of International Admissions/Associate
Director of Admissions
2700 Campus Box
100 Campus Drive
Elon, NC 27244-2010
Fax: (336) 278-7699
E-mail: cborden2@elon.edu
Phone: (800) 334-8448

Embry-Riddle Aeronautical University
www.embryriddle.edu
International Recruitment
600 South Clyde Morris Boulevard
Daytona Beach, FL 32114-3900
Fax: (386) 226-7070
E-mail: keith.deaton@erau.edu
Phone: (386) 226-6103

**Embry-Riddle Aeronautical University:
Prescott Campus**
www.embryriddle.edu
3700 Willow Creek Road
Prescott, AZ 86301-3720
Fax: (928) 777-6606
E-mail: frahera@erau.edu
Phone: (928) 777-3774

**Embry-Riddle Aeronautical University:
Worldwide Campus**
www.embryriddle.edu
Enrollment Management
600 South Clyde Morris Boulevard
Daytona Beach, FL 32114-3900
Fax: (386) 226-6984
E-mail: wwem@erau.edu
Phone: (866) 509-0743

Emerson College
www.emerson.edu
Office of Undergraduate Admission
120 Boylston Street
Boston, MA 02116-4624
Fax: (617) 824-8609
E-mail: admission@emerson.edu
Phone: (617) 824-8600

Emmanuel College
www.emmanuel.edu
International Student Coordinator
400 The Fenway
Boston, MA 02115
Fax: (617) 735-9801
E-mail: enroll@emmanuel.edu
Phone: (617) 735-9715

Emory & Henry College
www.ehc.edu
Admissions Office
Box 10
Emory, VA 24327
Fax: (276) 944-6935
E-mail: ehadmiss@ehc.edu
Phone: (276) 944-6133

Emory University
www.emory.edu
Office of Admissions
1390 Oxford Road NE, 3rd Floor
Atlanta, GA 30322
Fax: (404) 727-4303
E-mail: admiss@emory.edu
Phone: (404) 727-6036

Emporia State University
www.emporia.edu
Office of International Education
1200 Commercial, Campus Box 4034
Emporia, KS 66801-5087
Fax: (620) 341-5918
E-mail: gbruce@emporia.edu
Phone: (620) 341-5374

Endicott College
www.endicott.edu
Admission
376 Hale Street
Beverly, MA 01915-9985
Fax: (978) 232-2520
E-mail: tredman@endicott.edu
Phone: (978) 921-1000

Epic Bible College
www.tlbc.edu
5225 Hillsdale Boulevard
Sacramento, CA 95842
Phone: (916) 348-4689

Erie Business Center
www.eriebc.edu
246 West Ninth Street
Erie, PA 16501
Fax: (814) 459-3701
E-mail: admissions@eriebc.edu
Phone: (814) 456-7504 ext. 102

Erie Business Center South
www.eriebc.edu/newcastle
170 Cascade Galleria
New Castle, PA 16101
Fax: (724) 658-3083
E-mail: musolinok@eriebcs.com
Phone: (724) 658-9066

Erie Community College
www.ecc.edu
Foreign Student Adviser
121 Ellicott Street
Buffalo, NY 14203-2698
Fax: (716) 851-1429
E-mail: danna@ecc.edu
Phone: (716) 851-1359

Erskine College
www.erskine.edu
Admissions
PO Box 176
Due West, SC 29639-0176
Fax: (864) 379-2167
E-mail: ggambrel@erskine.edu
Phone: (864) 379-8721

Escuela de Artes Plasticas de Puerto Rico
www.eap.edu
Admissions
PO Box 9021112
San Juan, PR 00902-1112
Fax: (787) 721-3798
E-mail: llayer@eap.edu
Phone: (787) 725-8120 ext. 319

Essex County College
www.essex.edu
Admissions
303 University Avenue
Newark, NJ 07102
Fax: (973) 623-6449
E-mail: dizdarev@essex.edu
Phone: (973) 877-3154

Estrella Mountain Community College
www.estrellamountain.edu
Admission and Records
3000 North Dysart Road
Avondale, AZ 85392
Fax: (623) 935-8848
E-mail: elaine.trask@emcmail.maricopa.edu
Phone: (623) 935-8881

ETI Technical College of Niles
www.eticollege.edu
2076 Youngstown Warren Road
Niles, OH 44446-4398
Fax: (330) 652-4399
E-mail: etiadmissionsdir@hotmail.com
Phone: (330) 652-9919

Eugene Lang College The New School for Liberal Arts
www.newschool.edu/lang/
Admissions
72 Fifth Avenue
2nd Floor
New York, NY 10011
Fax: (212) 229-5355
E-mail: lang@newschool.edu
Phone: (212) 229-5665 ext. 2300

Eureka College
www.eureka.edu
Admissions
300 East College Avenue
Box 280
Eureka, IL 61530-1500
Fax: (309) 467-6576
E-mail: admissions@eureka.edu
Phone: (309) 467-6530

Evangel University
www.evangel.edu
Admissions
1111 North Glenstone
Springfield, MO 65802
Fax: (417) 865-9599
E-mail: Pochinga@evangel.edu
Phone: (417) 865-2811 ext. 7450

Everest College: Arlington
www.everest.edu/campus/arlington_mid_cities_
300 Six Flags Drive, Suite 100
Arlington, TX 76011
Fax: (817) 649-6033
E-mail: tevans@cci.edu
Phone: (817) 652-7790

Everest College: Arlington
801 North Quincy Street
Arlington, VA 22207
E-mail: elubin@cci.edu
Phone: (703) 248-8887

Everest College: Atlanta
www.georgia-med.com
1706 Northeast Expressway
Atlanta, GA 30329
Phone: (404) 327-8787

Everest College: Aurora
www.cci.edu
Director of Admissions
14280 East Jewell Suite 100
Aurora, CO 80012
Fax: (303) 745-6245
E-mail: mthibault@cci.edu
Phone: (303) 745-6244

Everest College: Colorado Springs
www.cci.edu
1815 Jet Wing Drive
Colorado Springs, CO 80916
Fax: (719) 638-6818
E-mail: mcollins@cci.edu
Phone: (719) 638-6580

Everest College: Dallas
www.everest.edu
6060 North Central Expressway, Suite 101
Dallas, TX 75206
Fax: (214) 696-6208
E-mail: zbelyea@cci.edu
Phone: (214) 234-4850

Everest College: Denver
www.everest.edu
9065 Grant Street
Thornton, CO 80229
Fax: (303) 457-4030
Phone: (303) 457-2757

Everest College: Fort Worth
www.everest-college.com
5237 North Riverside Drive, Suite 100
Forth Worth, TX 76137
Phone: (817) 838-3000

Everest College: Las Vegas
www.lasvegas-college.com
170 North Stephanie Street
Henderson, NV 89074
E-mail: spetty@cci.edu
Phone: (702) 567-1920

Everest College: Ontario Metro
www.everest.edu/campus/ontario_metro
9616 Archibald Avenue, Suite 100
Rancho Cucamonga, CA 91730-8525
Fax: (909) 484-1162
Phone: (909) 484-4311

Everest College: Phoenix
www.everestcollegephoenix.edu
Admissions
10400 North 25th Avenue Suite 190
Phoenix, AZ 85021
Fax: (602) 943-0960
E-mail: smilgram@cci.edu
Phone: (602) 942-4141 ext. 2704

Everest College: Portland
www.everest.edu
425 SW Washington Street
Portland, OR 97204
Fax: (503) 228-6926
Phone: (503) 222-3225 ext. 102

Everest College: Salt Lake City
www.cci.edu
Admissions
3280 West 3500 Street
West Valley City, UT 84119-2668
Fax: (801) 969-0828
Phone: (801) 840-4800

Everest College: Springfield
www.everest.edu
1010 West Sunshine
Springfield, MO 65807
Fax: (417) 864-5697
E-mail: mexter@cci.edu
Phone: (417) 864-7220

Everest College: Thornton
www.everest.edu/campus/thornton
9065 Grant Street
Thornton, CO 80229
E-mail: jhedrick@cci.edu
Phone: (303) 457-2757

Everest College: Tysons Corner
www.parks-college.com
1430 Spring Hill Road, Suite 200
McLean, VA 22102
Fax: (703) 288-3757
E-mail: dbrent@cci.edu
Phone: (703) 288-3131

Everest College: Vancouver
www.everest.edu
120 NE 136th Avenue, Suite 130
Vancouver, WA 98684
Fax: (360) 254-3035
E-mail: All-548-WebRequests@cci.edu
Phone: (360) 254-3282

Everest Institute: Cross Lanes
www.everest.edu
Admissions
5514 Big Tyler Road
Cross Lanes, WV 25313
Fax: (304) 776-6262
Phone: (304) 776-6290

Everest Institute: Fort Lauderdale
www.everest.edu
1040 Bayview Drive
Fort Lauderdale, FL 33304
E-mail: cshea@cci.edu
Phone: (954) 630-0066

Everest Institute: Pittsburgh
www.everest.edu
100 Forbes Avenue, Suite 1200
Pittsburgh, PA 15222
Fax: (412) 261-4546
Phone: (412) 261-4520

Everest University: Brandon
www.everest.edu
3924 Coconut Palm Drive
Tampa, FL 33619
Fax: (813) 628-0919
E-mail: spointer@cci.edu
Phone: (813) 621-0041 ext. 106

Everest University: Jacksonville
www.fmu.edu
8226 Phillips Highway
Jacksonville, FL 32256
Phone: (904) 731-4949

Everest University: Lakeland
www.everest.edu
995 East Memorial Boulevard, Suite 110
Lakeland, FL 33801-1919
Phone: (863) 686-1444

Everest University: Largo
www.everest.edu
Admissions
1199 East Bay Drive Largo
Largo, FL 33770
Fax: (727) 796-3722
Phone: (800) 353-3687

Everest University: Melbourne
www.cci.edu
Admissions
2401 North Harbor City Boulevard
Melbourne, FL 32935
Fax: (321) 255-2071
E-mail: tkumar@cci.edu
Phone: (321) 253-2929

Everest University: North Orlando
www.everest.edu
5421 Diplomat Circle
Orlando, FL 32810
Fax: (407) 628-1344
E-mail: jdweber@cci.edu
Phone: (407) 628-5870 ext. 108

Everest University: Orange Park
www.everest.edu
805 Wells Road
Orange Park, FL 32073
Phone: (904) 264-9122

Everest University: Pompano Beach
www.everest.edu
225 North Federal Highway
Pompano Beach, FL 33062
Phone: (954) 783-7339

Everest University: South Orlando
www.everest.edu
9200 Southpark Center Loop
Orlando, FL 32819
Phone: (407) 851-2525

Everest University: Tampa
www.everest.edu
3319 West Hillsborough Avenue
Tampa, FL 33614
Fax: (813) 871-2483
Phone: (813) 879-6000

Everett Community College
www.everettcc.edu
International Education
2000 Tower Street
Everett, WA 98201-1352
Fax: (425) 388-9173
E-mail: jfitzpatrick@everettcc.edu
Phone: (425) 388-9220

Everglades University: Boca Raton
www.EvergladesUniversity.edu
Admissions Office
5002 T-REX Avenue, Suite 100
Boca Raton, FL 33431
Fax: (561) 912-1191
E-mail: admissions-
boca@evergladesuniversity.edu
Phone: (561) 912-1211

Evergreen State College
www.evergreen.edu
Admissions
2700 Evergreen Parkway NW
Olympia, WA 98505
Fax: (360) 867-5114
E-mail: admissions@evergreen.edu
Phone: (360) 867-6176

Evergreen Valley College
www.evc.edu
International Student Coordinator
3095 Yerba Buena Road
San Jose, CA 95135
Fax: (408) 223-9351
E-mail: beverly.lynch@evc.edu
Phone: (408) 274-7900 ext. 6638

Excelsior College
www.excelsior.edu
Admissions
7 Columbia Circle
Albany, NY 12203-5159
Fax: (518) 464-8833
E-mail: international@excelsior.edu
Phone: (888) 647-2388

Ex'pression College for Digital Arts
www.expression.edu
6601 Shellmound Street
Emeryville, CA 94608
Phone: (510) 654-2934

Fairfield University
www.fairfield.edu
Undergraduate Admission
1073 North Benson Road
Fairfield, CT 06824-5195
Fax: (203) 254-4199
E-mail: international@fairfield.edu
Phone: (203) 254-4100

Fairleigh Dickinson University: College at Florham
www.fdu.edu
Office of International and Graduate Student Admissions
285 Madison Avenue
Madison, NJ 07940
Fax: (201) 692-2560
E-mail: global@fdu.edu
Phone: (201) 692-2205

Fairleigh Dickinson University: Metropolitan Campus
www.fdu.edu
Office of International and Graduate Student Admissions
1000 River Road, H-DH3-10
Teaneck, NJ 07666-1996
Fax: (201) 692-2560
E-mail: global@fdu.edu
Phone: (201) 692-2205

Fairmont State University
www.fairmontstate.edu
International Student Adviser
Office of Admissions
1201 Locust Avenue
Fairmont, WV 26554-2470
Fax: (304) 367-4995
E-mail: ghines@fairmontstate.edu
Phone: (304) 367-4490

Faith Baptist Bible College and Theological Seminary
www.faith.edu
Admissions
1900 NW Fourth Street
Ankeny, IA 50023
Fax: (515) 964-1638
E-mail: admissions@faith.edu
Phone: (515) 964-0601

Faith Evangelical Seminary
www.faithseminary.edu
3504 North Pearl Street
Tacoma, WA 98407
E-mail: admissions@faithseminary.edu
Phone: (888) 777-7675 ext. 21

Family of Faith College
www.familyoffaithcollege.edu
PO Box 1805
Shawnee, OK 74802-1805
Fax: (405) 273-8535
E-mail: info@familyoffaithcollege.edu
Phone: (405) 273-5331

Fashion Careers College
www.fashioncareerscollege.com
1923 Morena Boulevard
San Diego, CA 92110
Fax: (619) 275-0635
E-mail: info@fashioncareerscollege.com
Phone: (619) 275-4700

Fashion Institute of Design and Merchandising: Los Angeles
www.fidm.edu
Director of Admissions
919 South Grand Avenue
Los Angeles, CA 90015-1421
Fax: (213) 624-4799
E-mail: laronoff@fidm.edu
Phone: (213) 624-1201 ext. 5425

Fashion Institute of Design and Merchandising: San Diego
www.fidm.edu
Director of Admissions
350 Tenth Avenue, Third Floor
San Diego, CA 92101
Fax: (213) 624-4799
E-mail: laronoff@fidm.edu
Phone: (213) 624-1201 ext. 5425

Fashion Institute of Design and Merchandising: San Francisco
www.fidm.edu
Admissions Advisor
55 Stockton Street
San Francisco, CA 94108-5805
Fax: (415) 296-7299
E-mail: tsmiles@fidm.com
Phone: (415) 675-5200

Fashion Institute of Technology
www.fitnyc.edu
Admissions
Seventh Avenue at 27th Street
Marvin Feldman Building Room C139
New York, NY 10001-5992
Fax: (212) 217-3761
E-mail: fitinfo@fitnyc.edu
Phone: (212) 217-3760

Faulkner State Community College
www.faulknerstate.edu
Admissions
1900 Highway 31 South
Bay Minette, AL 36507
Fax: (334) 580-2186
E-mail: pduck@faulknerstate.edu
Phone: (334) 580-2111

Faulkner University
www.faulkner.edu
International Students
5345 Atlanta Highway
Montgomery, AL 36109-3398
Fax: (334) 386-7137
E-mail: ehicks@faulkner.edu
Phone: (334) 386-7309

Fayetteville State University
www.uncfsu.edu
Admissions
1200 Murchison Road
Fayetteville, NC 28301-4298
Fax: (910) 672-1414
E-mail: ubowles@uncfsu.edu
Phone: (910) 672-1371

Fayetteville Technical Community College
www.faytechcc.edu
Admissions
PO Box 35236
2201 Hull Road
Fayetteville, NC 28303-0236
Fax: (910) 678-8407
E-mail: jonesma@faytechcc.edu
Phone: (910) 678-8286

Feather River College
www.frc.edu
Admissions
570 Golden Eagle Avenue
Quincy, CA 95971
Fax: (530) 283-9961
E-mail: Lmikesell@frc.edu
Phone: (530) 283-0202 ext. 285

Felician College
www.felician.edu
Director of International Student Services
262 South Main Street
Lodi, NJ 07644-2198
Fax: (201) 559-6188
E-mail: Kunyczkac@felician.edu
Phone: (201) 559-6047

Ferris State University
www.ferris.edu
Coordinator of International Student
Recruiting
1201 South State Street, CSS 201
Big Rapids, MI 49307-2714
Fax: (231) 591-2423
E-mail: tartaril@ferris.edu
Phone: (231) 591-5444

Ferrum College
www.ferrum.edu
Spilman-Daniel House, 40 Stratton Lane
PO Box 1000
Ferrum, VA 24088
Fax: (540) 365-4266
E-mail: admissions@ferrum.edu
Phone: (540) 365-4290

Finlandia University
www.finlandia.edu
International Enrollment Officer
601 Quincy Street
Hancock, MI 49930-1882
Fax: (906) 487-7383
E-mail: kitti.loukus@finlandia.edu
Phone: (906) 487-7208

Fisher College
www.fisher.edu
Senior Assistant Director of International
Recruitment
Office of Admissions
118 Beacon Street
Boston, MA 02116
Fax: (617) 236-5473
E-mail: aschumacher@fisher.edu
Phone: (617) 236-8819

Fisk University
www.fisk.edu
Office of Admissions
1000 17th Avenue North
Nashville, TN 37208-3051
Fax: (615) 329-8774
E-mail: kchandler@fisk.edu
Phone: (615) 329-8819

Fitchburg State University
www.fitchburgstate.edu
Admissions
160 Pearl Street
Fitchburg, MA 01420-2697
Fax: (978) 665-4540
E-mail: admissions@fitchburgstate.edu
Phone: (978) 665-3144

Five Towns College
www.ftc.edu
Admissions Office
305 North Service Road
Dix Hills, NY 11746-6055
Fax: (631) 656-3199
E-mail: edgar.avagyan@ftc.edu
Phone: (631) 424-7000 ext. 3113

Flagler College
www.flagler.edu
Admissions Office
74 King Street
St. Augustine, FL 32084
Fax: (904) 819-6466
E-mail: runger@flagler.edu
Phone: (800) 304-4208

Flathead Valley Community College
www.fvcc.edu
777 Grandview Drive
Kalispell, MT 59901
Fax: (406) 756-3965
E-mail: gshryock@fvcc.edu
Phone: (406) 756-3886

Florence-Darlington Technical College
www.fdtc.edu
Admissions
PO Box 100548
Florence, SC 29501-0548
Fax: (843) 661-8041
E-mail: delores.dingel@fdtc.edu
Phone: (843) 661-8324

Florida Agricultural and Mechanical University
www.famu.edu
Office of Admissions
FHAC, G-9
1700 Lee Hall Drive
Tallahassee, FL 32307-3200
Fax: (850) 599-3069
E-mail: barbara.cox@famu.edu
Phone: (850) 599-3796

Florida Atlantic University
www.fau.edu
International Students and Scholars
777 Glades Road
Box 3091
Boca Raton, FL 33431
Fax: (561) 297-2446
E-mail: isss@fau.edu
Phone: (561) 297-3049

Florida Career College: Boynton Beach
www.careercollege.edu
1749 North Congress Avenue
Boynton Beach, FL 33426

Florida Career College: Hialeah
www.careercollege.edu
3750 West 18th Avenue
Hialeah, FL 33012
Fax: (305) 825-3436
E-mail: pbrum@careercollege.edu
Phone: (954) 547-6989

Florida Career College: Jacksonville
www.careercollege.edu
6600 Youngerman Circle
Jacksonville, FL 32244

Florida Career College: Lauderdale Lakes
www.careercollege.edu
3383 North State Road 7
Lauderdale Lakes, FL 33319
Phone: (954) 535-8700

Florida Career College: Miami
www.careercollege.edu
1321 SW 107 Avenue, Suite 201B
Miami, FL 3317-521
Phone: (305) 553-6065

Florida Career College: Pembroke Pines
www.careercollege.edu
7891 Pines Boulevard
Pembroke Pines, FL 33024
Fax: (954) 983-2707
E-mail: info@careercollege.edu
Phone: (954) 965-7272

Florida Career College: Riverview
www.careercollege.edu
2662 South Falkenburg Road
Riverview, FL 33578

Florida Career College: West Palm Beach
www.careercollege.edu
6058 Okeechobee Boulevard
West Palm Beach, FL 33417
Fax: (561) 689-0739
Phone: (561) 689-0550

Florida Christian College
www.fcc.edu
Registrar's Office
1011 Bill Beck Boulevard
Kissimmee, FL 34744-4402
Fax: (321) 206-2007
E-mail: brian.smith@fcc.edu
Phone: (407) 569-1336

Florida College of Natural Health: Bradenton
www.fcnh.com
Admissions
616 67th Street Circle East
Bradenton, FL 34208
Fax: (941) 744-1242
E-mail: sarasota@fcnh.com
Phone: (941) 744-1244

Florida College of Natural Health: Miami
www.fcnh.com
7925 Northwest 12th Street, Suite 201
Miami, FL 33126
Fax: (305) 597-9110
E-mail: miami@fcnh.com
Phone: (305) 597-9599

Florida Gateway College
www.fgc.edu
Admissions
149 SE College Place
Lake City, FL 32025-2007
Fax: (386) 754-4736
E-mail: Bonnie.Gootee@fgc.edu
Phone: (386) 754-4236

Florida Gulf Coast University
www.fgcu.edu
International Admissions Coordinator
10501 FGCU Boulevard South
Ft. Myers, FL 33965-6565
Fax: (239) 590-7894
E-mail: sbannwor@fgcu.edu
Phone: (239) 590-7882

Florida Institute of Technology
www.fit.edu
International Admissions
150 West University Boulevard
Melbourne, FL 32901-6975
Fax: (321) 674-8004
E-mail: admission@fit.edu
Phone: (321) 674-8030

Florida International University
www.fiu.edu
Undergraduate Admissions
University Park Campus, PC 140
Miami, FL 33199
Fax: (305) 348-3648
E-mail: admiss@fiu.edu
Phone: (305) 348-2363

Florida Keys Community College
www.fkcc.edu
Office of Enrollment Services
5901 College Road
Key West, FL 33040
Fax: (305) 292-5155
E-mail: carol.anderson@fkcc.edu
Phone: (305) 809-3278

Florida Memorial University
www.fmuniv.edu
15800 NW 42nd Avenue
Miami Gardens, FL 33054
Fax: (305) 623-1462
E-mail: admit@fmuniv.edu
Phone: (305) 626-3750

Florida National College
www.fnc.edu
Office of International Students
4425 West 20th Avenue
Hialeah, FL 33012
Fax: (305) 362-0595
E-mail: jsanchez@mm.fnc.edu
Phone: (305) 821-333 ext. 1059

Florida Southern College
www.flsouthern.edu
Admissions Advisor
111 Lake Hollingsworth Drive
Lakeland, FL 33801-5698
Fax: (863) 680-4120
E-mail: adale@flsouthern.edu
Phone: (863) 680-3902

Florida State College at Jacksonville
www.fscj.edu
Office of Admissions
501 West State Street
Jacksonville, FL 32202
Fax: (904) 632-5105
E-mail: rdexter@fscj.edu
Phone: (904) 632-3375

Florida State University
www.fsu.edu
Admissions
PO Box 3062400
282 Champions Way
Tallahassee, FL 32306-2400
Fax: (850) 644-0197
E-mail: hferguson@admin.fsu.edu
Phone: (850) 644-6200

Folsom Lake College
www.flc.losrios.edu
Admissions and Records
10 College Parkway
Folsom, CA 95630
Fax: (916) 608-6569
E-mail: rettere@flc.losrios.edu
Phone: (916) 608-5000

**Fond du Lac Tribal and Community
College**
www.fdltcc.edu
2101 14th Street
Cloquet, MN 55720
Fax: (218) 879-0814
E-mail: admissions@fdltcc.edu
Phone: (218) 879-0808

Fontbonne University
www.fontbonne.edu
Office of International Students
6800 Wydown Boulevard
St. Louis, MO 63105
Fax: (314) 889-1451
E-mail: rbahan@fontbonne.edu
Phone: (314) 889-4509

Foothill College
www.foothill.edu
International Student Admissions
12345 El Monte Road
Los Altos Hills, CA 94022
Fax: (650) 949-7048
E-mail: beersgeorge@foothill.edu
Phone: (650) 949-7293

Fordham University
www.fordham.edu
Office of Undergraduate Admissions
441 East Fordham Road
Bronx, NY 10458-9993
Fax: (718) 367-9404
E-mail: messer@fordham.edu
Phone: (718) 817-4000

Forrest Junior College
www.forrestcollege.edu
Admissions
601 East River Street
Anderson, SC 29624
Fax: (864) 261-7471
E-mail: janieturmon@forrestcollege.edu
Phone: (864) 225-7653 ext. 210

Fort Berthold Community College
www.fortbertholdcc.edu
Box 490
220 8th Avenue N
New Town, ND 58763
Fax: (701) 627-4790
E-mail: taulau@fbcc.bia.edu
Phone: (701) 627-4738 ext. 286

Fort Hays State University
www.fhsu.edu
600 Park Street
Hays, KS 67601
Fax: (785) 628-4085
E-mail: jmaxwell@fhsu.edu
Phone: (785) 628-4222

Fort Lewis College
www.fortlewis.edu
Admissions
1000 Rim Drive
Durango, CO 81301-3999
Fax: (970) 247-7179
E-mail: martin_b@fortlewis.edu
Phone: (970) 247-7187

Fort Valley State University
www.fvsu.edu
1005 State University Drive
Fort Valley, GA 31030-4313
Fax: (478) 825-6169
E-mail: admissap@fvsu.edu
Phone: (478) 825-6307

Fortis College: Cuyahoga
www.nationalinstituteoftechnology.edu
2545 Bailey Road
Cuyahoga Falls, OH 44221
Fax: (330) 923-0886
E-mail: LNelly@edaff.com
Phone: (330) 923-9959 ext. 4660

Fortis College: Indianapolis
www.fortiscollege.edu
9001 North Wesleyan Road, Suite 101
Indianapolis, IN 46268
Phone: (317) 808-4800

Fortis College: Winter Park
www.centralfloridacollege.edu
Admissions
1573 West Fairbanks Avenue
Winter Park, FL 32789
Fax: (407) 843-9828
E-mail: admissions@centralfloridacollege.edu
Phone: (407) 843-3984

Fortis Institute: Orange Park
www.fortis.edu
560 Wells Road
Orange Park, FL 32073
Phone: (904) 269-7086

Fox Valley Technical College
www.fvtc.edu
International Studies
1825 North Bluemound Drive
PO Box 2277
Appleton, WI 54912-2277
Fax: (920) 735-2538
E-mail: martinm@fvtc.edu
Phone: (920) 735-5677

Framingham State University
www.framingham.edu
Undergraduate Admissions
PO Box 9101
Framingham, MA 01701-9101
Fax: (508) 626-4017
E-mail: sbailey2@framingham.edu
Phone: (508) 626-4500

Francis Marion University
www.fmarion.edu
Admissions Office
PO Box 100547
Florence, SC 29502-0547
Fax: (843) 661-4635
E-mail: pwilson@fmarion.edu
Phone: (843) 661-1231

Franciscan University of Steubenville
www.franciscan.edu
Student Life Office
1235 University Boulevard
Steubenville, OH 43952-1763
Fax: (740) 284-7225
E-mail: korbon@franciscan.edu
Phone: (740) 283-6470

Frank Phillips College
www.fpctx.edu
Student Services
Box 5118
Borger, TX 79008-5118
Fax: (806) 457-4224
E-mail: bgreen@fpctx.edu
Phone: (806) 457-4200 ext. 720

Franklin & Marshall College
www.fandm.edu
Admissions
PO Box 3003
Lancaster, PA 17604-3003
Fax: (717) 291-4389
E-mail: Penny.Johnston@fandm.edu
Phone: (717) 291-3953

Franklin College
www.franklincollege.edu
Admissions
101 Branigin Boulevard
Franklin, IN 46131-2623
Fax: (317) 738-8274
E-mail: jacosta@franklincollege.edu
Phone: (317) 738-8062

Franklin Pierce University
www.franklinpierce.edu
Admissions
40 University Drive
Rindge, NH 03461-0060
Fax: (603) 899-4372
E-mail: oehlscs@fpc.edu
Phone: (603) 899-4397

Franklin University
www.franklin.edu
International Services and Program
201 South Grant Avenue
Columbus, OH 43215-5399
Fax: (614) 255-9515
E-mail: waltersk@franklin.edu
Phone: (614) 947-6752

Franklin W. Olin College of Engineering
www.olin.edu
Office of Admission
Olin Way
Needham, MA 02492-1245
Fax: (781) 292-2210
E-mail: charles.nolan@olin.edu
Phone: (781) 292-2201

Free Will Baptist Bible College
www.fwbbc.edu
Provost
3606 West End Avenue
Nashville, TN 37205-2403
Fax: (615) 269-6028
E-mail: jketteman@fwbbc.edu
Phone: (615) 844-5214

Freed-Hardeman University
www.fhu.edu
International Admissions
158 East Main Street
Henderson, TN 38340
Fax: (731) 989-6047
E-mail: wscott@fhu.edu
Phone: (731) 989-6790

Fremont College: Cerritos
www.fremont.edu
Admissions
18000 Studebaker Road, 900A
Cerritos, CA 90703-5342
Fax: (562) 809-7100
E-mail: doa@fremont.edu
Phone: (562) 809-5100

Fresno City College
www.fresnocitycollege.edu
International Students
1101 East University Avenue
Fresno, CA 93741
Fax: (559) 237-4232
E-mail: fccintad@fresnocitycollege.edu
Phone: (559) 442-8224

Fresno Pacific University
www.fresno.edu
Director of International Programs and
Services
1717 South Chestnut Avenue
Fresno, CA 93702-4709
Fax: (559) 453-7147
E-mail: apprieb@fresno.edu
Phone: (559) 453-2128

Friends University
www.friends.edu
Admissions
2100 West University Avenue
Wichita, KS 67213
Fax: (316) 295-5101
E-mail: quinn_bowman@friends.edu
Phone: (316) 295-5816

Front Range Community College
www.frontrange.edu
Office of Admissions and Records
3645 West 112th Avenue
Westminster, CO 80031
Fax: (303) 404-5150
E-mail: nancy.meisinger@frontrange.edu
Phone: (303) 404-5471

Frostburg State University
www.frostburg.edu
Center for International Education
101 Braddock Road
Frostburg, MD 21532-1099
Fax: (301) 687-1069
E-mail: fsuadmissions@frostburg.edu
Phone: (301) 687-4714

Full Sail University
www.fullsail.edu
International Liaison
3300 University Boulevard
Winter Park, FL 32792-7429
E-mail: admissions@fullsail.com
Phone: (407) 679-0100

Fullerton College
www.fullcoll.edu
321 East Chapman Avenue
Fullerton, CA 92832-2095
Fax: (714) 870-7751
E-mail: admissions@fullcoll.edu
Phone: (714) 992-7580

Fulton-Montgomery Community College
www.fmcc.suny.edu
Director, International Students and ESL
Programs
2805 State Highway 67
Johnstown, NY 12095
Fax: (518) 762-6518
E-mail: intl@fmcc.suny.edu
Phone: (518) 762-4651 ext. 4750

Furman University
www.furman.edu
Admissions
3300 Poinsett Highway
Greenville, SC 29613
Fax: (864) 294-2018
E-mail: admissions@furman.edu
Phone: (864) 294-2034

Gadsden State Community College
www.gadsdenstate.edu
International Student Office
1001 George Wallace Drive
PO Box 227
Gadsden, AL 35902-0227
Fax: (256) 549-8344
E-mail: pross@gadsdenstate.edu
Phone: (256) 549-8324

Gainesville State College
www.gsc.edu
Admissions Office
PO Box 1358
Gainesville, GA 30503
Fax: (678) 717-3643
E-mail: admissions@gsc.edu
Phone: (678) 717-3941

Gallaudet University
www.gallaudet.edu
Admissions Office
800 Florida Avenue, NE
Washington, DC 20002
Fax: (202) 651-5774
E-mail: melba.goodwin@gallaudet.edu
Phone: (202) 651-5750

Gallipolis Career College
www.gallipoliscareercollege.com
1176 Jackson Pike, Suite 312
Gallipolis, OH 45631
Fax: (740) 446-4124
Phone: (740) 446-4367 ext. 12

Galveston College
www.gc.edu
Admissions Office
4015 Avenue Q
Galveston, TX 77550-7447
Fax: (409) 944-1501
E-mail: nmontoya@gc.edu
Phone: (409) 944-1232

Gannon University
www.gannon.edu
Admissions
109 University Square
Erie, PA 16541-0001
Fax: (814) 871-5803
E-mail: international@gannon.edu
Phone: (814) 871-7480

Garden City Community College
www.gcccks.edu
Office of Admissions
801 Campus Drive
Garden City, KS 67846-6333
Fax: (620) 276-9650
E-mail: nikki.geier@gcccks.edu
Phone: (620) 276-9531

Gardner-Webb University
www.gardner-webb.edu
Undergraduate Admissions
PO Box 817
Boiling Springs, NC 28017
Fax: (704) 406-4488
E-mail: cforbes@gardner-webb.edu
Phone: (704) 406-4495

Garrett College
www.garrettcollege.edu
Admissions Recruiter
687 Mosser Road
McHenry, MD 21541
Fax: (301) 387-3038
E-mail: globaled@garrettcollege.edu
Phone: (301) 387-3010

Gateway Community and Technical College
www.gateway.kctcs.edu
790 Thomas More Parkway
Edgewood, KY 41017
Fax: (859) 442-1107
Phone: (859) 442-1134

GateWay Community College
www.gatewaycc.edu
Admissions and Records
108 North 40th Street
Phoenix, AZ 85034
Fax: (602) 286-8159
E-mail: nunez@gatewaycc.edu
Phone: (602) 286-8063

Gateway Community College
www.gwcc.commnet.edu
Admissions
60 Sargent Drive
New Haven, CT 06511-5970
Fax: (203) 285-2018
E-mail: csurface@gwcc.commnet.edu
Phone: (203) 285-2028

Gateway Technical College
www.gtc.edu
Admissions
3520 30th Avenue
Kenosha, WI 53144-1690
Fax: (262) 741-8115
E-mail: admissionsgroup@gtc.edu
Phone: (262) 741-8168

Genesee Community College
www.genesee.edu
Admissions
One College Road
Batavia, NY 14020-9704
Fax: (585) 345-6810
E-mail: tmlanemartin@genesee.edu
Phone: (585) 345-6800

Geneva College
www.geneva.edu
Admissions Office
3200 College Avenue
Beaver Falls, PA 15010
Fax: (724) 847-6776
E-mail: akmodro@geneva.edu
Phone: (724) 847-6517

George C. Wallace Community College at Dothan
www.wallace.edu
Admissions
1141 Wallace Drive
Dothan, AL 36303-0943
Fax: (334) 983-6066
E-mail: sjacobs@wallace.edu
Phone: (334) 556-2472

George Fox University
www.georgefox.edu
Office of International Recruitment
414 North Meridian Street #6089
Newberg, OR 97132-2697
Fax: (503) 554-3894
E-mail: tpeng@georgefox.edu
Phone: (503) 554-2614

George Mason University
www.gmu.edu
Associate Director, International Admissions
4400 University Drive, MSN 3A4
Fairfax, VA 22030-4444
Fax: (703) 993-4622
E-mail: world@gmu.edu
Phone: (703) 993-2400

George Washington University
www.gwu.edu/explore/
2121 I Street NW, Suite 201
Washington, DC 20052
Fax: (202) 994-7266
E-mail: siskmn@gwunix2.gwu.edu
Phone: (202) 994-4940

Georgetown College
www.georgetowncollege.edu
Admissions
400 East College Street
Georgetown, KY 40324
Fax: (502) 868-7733
E-mail: julie_sams@georgetowncollege.edu
Phone: (502) 863-8013

Georgetown University
www.georgetown.edu
Undergraduate Admissions
103 White-Gravenor
Box 571002
Washington, DC 20057-1002
Fax: (202) 687-5084
E-mail: guadmiss@georgetown.edu
Phone: (202) 687-3600

Georgia College and State University
www.gcsu.edu
International Education
Campus Box 23
Milledgeville, GA 31061-0490
Fax: (478) 445-2623
E-mail: jason.wynn@gcsu.edu
Phone: (478) 445-1245

Georgia Gwinnett College
www.ggc.edu
1000 University Center Lane
Lawrenceville, GA 30043
Fax: (678) 407-5747
E-mail: ggcadmissions@ggc.edu
Phone: (678) 407-5313

Georgia Highlands College
www.highlands.edu
Admissions
3175 Cedartown Highway
Rome, GA 30161
Fax: (706) 295-6341
E-mail: cgraham@highlands.edu
Phone: (706) 295-6339

Georgia Institute of Technology
www.gatech.edu
Office of Undergraduate Admissions
Atlanta, GA 30332-0320
Fax: (404) 894-9511
E-mail:
brandon.phillips@admission.gatech.edu
Phone: (404) 894-4154

Georgia Military College
www.gmc.cc.ga.us
Admissions Office
201 East Greene Street
Milledgeville, GA 31061
Fax: (478) 445-6520
E-mail: admission@gmc.cc.ga.us
Phone: (478) 387-4948

Georgia Northwestern Technical College
www.gntc.edu
One Maurice Culberson Drive
Rome, GA 30161
E-mail: dmcburnett@gntc.edu
Phone: (706) 295-6933

Georgia Perimeter College
www.gpc.edu
International Student Admissions and Advising
555 North Indian Creek Drive
Clarkston, GA 30021-2361
Fax: (678) 891-3280
E-mail: veronique.barnes@gpc.edu
Phone: (678) 891-3235

Georgia Southern University
www.georgiasouthern.edu
Admissions
PO Box 8024
Statesboro, GA 30460
Fax: (912) 478-7240
E-mail: intladmissions@georgiasouthern.edu
Phone: (912) 478-5391

Georgia Southwestern State University
www.gsw.edu
Admissions Office
800 Georgia Southwestern State University
Drive
Americus, GA 31709-9957
Fax: (229) 931-9283
E-mail: gswapps@canes.gsw.edu
Phone: (229) 928-1273

Georgia State University
www.gsu.edu
Admissions
Box 4009
Atlanta, GA 30302-4009
Fax: (404) 413-2002
E-mail: admissions@gsu.edu
Phone: (404) 413-2500

Georgian Court University
www.georgian.edu
Admissions
900 Lakewood Avenue
Lakewood, NJ 08701-2697
Fax: (732) 987-2000
E-mail: admissions@georgian.edu
Phone: (732) 987-2379

Germanna Community College
www.germanna.edu
Admissions and Records
2130 Germanna Highway
Locust Grove, VA 22508-2102
Fax: (540) 423-9158
Phone: (540) 423-9131

Gettysburg College
www.gettysburg.edu
Admissions Office
300 North Washington Street
Gettysburg, PA 17325-1400
Fax: (717) 337-6145
E-mail: intladmiss@gettysburg.edu
Phone: (717) 337-6100

Glen Oaks Community College
www.glenoaks.edu
Counseling Office-International Student
Adviser
62249 Shimmel Road
Centreville, MI 49032-9719
Fax: (269) 467-9068
E-mail: chayden@glenoaks.edu
Phone: (269) 294-4242

Glendale Community College
www.gccaz.edu
International Student Center
6000 West Olive Avenue
Glendale, AZ 85302
Fax: (623) 845-3060
E-mail: ken.bus@gcmail.maricopa.edu
Phone: (623) 845-3136

Glendale Community College
www.glendale.edu
International Students Admission
1500 North Verdugo Road
Glendale, CA 91208-2809
Fax: (818) 549-9436
E-mail: pkamarak@glendale.edu
Phone: (818) 240-1000 ext. 5440

Glenville State College
www.glenville.edu
Office of Enrollment Services
200 High Street
Glenville, WV 26351-1292
Fax: (304) 462-8619
E-mail: Rebecca.Radcliff@glenville.edu
Phone: (304) 462-4128 ext. 6132

Global University
www.globaluniversity.edu
International Student Services Director
1211 South Glenstone Avenue
Springfield, MO 65804
Fax: (417) 862-0863
E-mail: info@globaluniversity.edu
Phone: (417) 862-9533

Globe Institute of Technology
www.globe.edu
Admissions
500 Seventh Avenue, 2nd Floor
New York, NY 10018
Fax: (212) 302-9242
E-mail: admissions@globe.edu
Phone: (212) 349-4330

Globe University
www.globeuniversity.edu
8089 Globe Drive
Woodbury, MN 55125
Fax: (877) 455-3697
E-mail: admissions@globecollege.com
Phone: (612) 455-3025

Globe University: Green Bay
www.globeuniversity.edu
2620 Development Drive
Green Bay, WI 54311
E-mail: cheltsley@globeuniversity.edu
Phone: (920) 264-1600

Gloucester County College
www.gccnj.edu
Admissions
1400 Tanyard Road
Sewell, NJ 08080
Fax: (856) 468-8498
E-mail: kmomballou@gccnj.edu
Phone: (856) 415-2260

Goddard College
www.goddard.edu
Admissions
123 Pitkin Road
Plainfield, VT 05667
Fax: (802) 454-1029
E-mail: josh.castle@goddard.edu
Phone: (802) 454-8311 ext. 288

God's Bible School and College
www.gbs.edu
Office of the Registrar
1810 Young Street
Cincinnati, OH 45202-6838
Fax: (513) 721-1357
E-mail: clambeth@gbs.edu
Phone: (513) 721-7944 ext. 210

Gogebic Community College
www.gogebic.edu
Admissions
E4946 Jackson Road
Ironwood, MI 49938
Fax: (906) 932-2339
E-mail: jeanneg@gogebic.edu
Phone: (906) 932-4231 ext. 306

Golden Gate University
www.ggu.edu
International Admissions Office
536 Mission Street
San Francisco, CA 94105-2968
Fax: (415) 442-7807
E-mail: iss@ggu.edu
Phone: (415) 442-7290

Golden West College
www.goldenwestcollege.edu
International Students Office
15744 Golden West Street, Box 2748
Huntington Beach, CA 92647-2748
Fax: (714) 895-8960
E-mail: jleighton@gwc.cccd.edu
Phone: (714) 895-8146

Goldey-Beacom College
www.gbc.edu
International Admissions
4701 Limestone Road
Wilmington, DE 19808
Fax: (302) 996-5408
E-mail: taylorl@gbc.edu
Phone: (302) 225-6383

Goldfarb School of Nursing at Barnes-Jewish College
www.barnesjewishcollege.edu
Office of Student Services
4483 Duncan Avenue
St. Louis, MO 63110-1091
Fax: (314) 362-9250
E-mail: MJaime@bjc.org
Phone: (314) 454-8686

Golf Academy of America: The Carolinas
www.golfacademy.edu
7373 North Scottsdale Road, Suite B-100
Scottsdale, AZ 82253
Fax: (480) 905-8705
E-mail: sdga@sdgagolf.com
Phone: (480) 905-9288

Golf Academy of America: Orlando
www.golfacademy.edu
7373 North Scottsdale Road, Suite B-100
Scottsdale, AZ 85253
Fax: (480) 905-8705
E-mail: sdga@sdgagolf.com
Phone: (480) 905-9288

Golf Academy of America: Phoenix
www.golfacademy.edu
2031 North Arizona Avenue, Suite 2
Chandler, AZ 85225
Fax: (480) 905-8705
E-mail: phoenix.info@golfacademy.edu
Phone: (480) 905-9288

Golf Academy of America: San Diego
www.golfacademy.edu
1950 Camino Vida Roble, Suite 125
Carlsbad, CA 92008
E-mail: sdga@sdgagolf.com
Phone: (760) 734-1208

Gonzaga University
www.gonzaga.edu
International Student Programs
502 East Boone Avenue
Spokane, WA 99258-0001
Fax: (509) 323-5814
E-mail: fadeley@gonzaga.edu
Phone: (509) 323-6562

Goodwin College
www.goodwin.edu
Admissions
One Riverside Drive
East Hartford, CT 06118-9980
Fax: (860) 291-9550
E-mail: dnoonan@goodwin.edu
Phone: (860) 528-4111

Gordon College
www.gdn.edu
Admissions
419 College Drive
Barnesville, GA 30204
Fax: (770) 358-5080
E-mail: lisas@gdn.edu
Phone: (678) 359-5021

Gordon College
www.gordon.edu
Admissions Office
255 Grapevine Road
Wenham, MA 01984-0198
Fax: (978) 867-4682
E-mail: admissions@gordon.edu
Phone: (978) 867-4218

Goshen College
www.goshen.edu
Admissions
1700 South Main Street
Goshen, IN 46526-4724
Fax: (574) 535-7609
E-mail: admission@goshen.edu
Phone: (574) 535-7535

Goucher College
www.goucher.edu
Admissions
1021 Dulaney Valley Road
Baltimore, MD 21204-2753
Fax: (410) 337-6354
E-mail: jheitsen@goucher.edu
Phone: (410) 337-6100

Governors State University
www.govst.edu
Office of International Programs
One University Parkway
University Park, IL 60484
Fax: (708) 534-1640
E-mail: v-mendoza@govst.edu
Phone: (708) 534-3087

Grace University
www.graceuniversity.edu
Admissions Office
1311 South Ninth Street
Omaha, NE 68108-3629
Fax: (402) 449-2999
E-mail: admissions@graceuniversity.edu
Phone: (402) 449-2831

Graceland University
www.graceland.edu
Admissions
One University Place
Lamoni, IA 50140
Fax: (641) 784-5480
E-mail: gsanchez@graceland.edu
Phone: (641) 784-5423

Grambling State University
www.gram.edu
Center for International Affairs & Programs
403 Main Street, GSU Box 4200
100 Founder Street- Grambling Hall, Suite 51
Grambling, LA 71245
Fax: (318) 274-3256
E-mail: lamadaniem@gram.edu
Phone: (318) 274-7798

Grand Canyon University
www.gcu.edu/clgbrd
3300 West Camelback Road
Phoenix, AZ 85017-8562
Fax: (602) 589-2017
E-mail: admissionsonline@gcu.edu
Phone: (888) 261-2393

Grand Rapids Community College
www.grcc.edu
Office of Admissions
143 Bostwick Avenue NE
Grand Rapids, MI 49503-3295
Fax: (616) 234-4107
E-mail: mnicolet@grcc.edu
Phone: (616) 234-3567

Grand Valley State University
www.gvsu.edu
Office of Admssions
1 Campus Drive
Allendale, MI 49401-9403
Fax: (616) 331-2000
E-mail: go2gvsu@gvsu.edu
Phone: (800) 748-0246

Grand View University
www.grandview.edu
Admissions
1200 Grandview Avenue
Des Moines, IA 50316-1599
Fax: (515) 263-2974
E-mail: cthompson@grandview.edu
Phone: (515) 263-2810

Granite State College
www.granite.edu
Conway Campus
8 Old Suncook Road
Concord, NH 03301-7317
Fax: (603) 447-2740
E-mail: janice.hodges@granite.edu
Phone: (603) 447-3970

Grantham University
www.grantham.edu
Admissions
7200 NW 86th Street
Kansas City, MO 64153
Fax: (816) 595-5757
E-mail: admissions@grantham.edu
Phone: (800) 955-2527

Gratz College
www.gratz.edu
7605 Old York Road
Melrose Park, PA 19027
Fax: (215) 635-7320
E-mail: rsandberg@gratz.edu
Phone: (215) 635-7300 ext. 168

Grayson County College
www.grayson.edu
International Office
6101 Grayson Drive
Denison, TX 75020
Fax: (903) 463-8758
E-mail: mcclennyb@grayson.edu
Phone: (903) 463-8749

Great Basin College
www.gbcnv.edu
Admissions and Records
1500 College Parkway
Elko, NV 89801
Fax: (755) 753-2311
E-mail: bjulie@gbcnv.edu
Phone: (755) 753-2361

Green Mountain College
www.greenmtn.edu
Assistant Director of Admissions for
International Programs
One Brennan Circle
Poultney, VT 05764
Fax: (802) 287-8099
E-mail: hoagk@greenmtn.edu
Phone: (802) 287-8000

Green River Community College
www.greenriver.edu
International Programs
12401 SE 320th Street
Auburn, WA 98092
Fax: (253) 931-6346
E-mail: EnrollmentServices@greenriver.edu
Phone: (253) 288-3300

Greenfield Community College
www.gcc.mass.edu
Student Affairs
One College Drive
Greenfield, MA 01301
Fax: (413) 773-5129
E-mail: hentz@gcc.mass.edu
Phone: (413) 775-1809

Greensboro College
www.greensborocollege.edu
Admissions Counselor
815 West Market Street
Greensboro, NC 27401-1875
Fax: (336) 378-0154
E-mail: mblanton@greensborocollege.edu
Phone: (336) 272-7102 ext. 211

Greenville College
www.greenville.edu
Admissions
315 East College Avenue
Greenville, IL 62246-0159
Fax: (618) 664-9841
E-mail: ginny.smith@greenville.edu
Phone: (618) 664-7103

Greenville Technical College
www.gvltec.edu
Admissions
P.O. Box 5616
Greenville, SC 29606-5616
Fax: (864) 250-8534
E-mail: greenvilletech@gvltec.edu
Phone: (864) 250-8109

Gretna Career College
www.gccla.edu/
1415 Whitney Avenue
Gretna, LA 70037
E-mail: admissions@gretnacareercollege.edu
Phone: (504) 366-5409 ext. 23

Griggs University
www.griggs.edu
Admissions
12501 Old Columbia Pike
Silver Spring, MD 20904-6600
Phone: (301) 680-6570

Grinnell College
www.grinnell.edu
Admission
1103 Park Street
Grinnell, IA 50112-1690
Fax: (641) 269-4800
E-mail: askgrin@grinnell.edu
Phone: (641) 269-3600

Grossmont College
www.grossmont.edu
Admissions Office
8800 Grossmont College Drive
El Cajon, CA 92020
Fax: (619) 644-7083
E-mail: mika.miller@gcccd.edu
Phone: (619) 644-7182

Grove City College
www.gcc.edu
100 Campus Drive
Grove City, PA 16127-2104
Fax: (724) 458-3395
E-mail: admissions@gcc.edu
Phone: (724) 458-2100

Guilford College
www.guilford.edu
Admissions/Enrollment
Admissions, New Garden Hall
5800 West Friendly Avenue
Greensboro, NC 27410-4108
Fax: (336) 316-2443
E-mail: madenyikatb@guilford.edu
Phone: (800) 992-7759

Guilford Technical Community College
www.gtcc.edu
Foreign Student Adviser/Counselor
PO Box 309
Jamestown, NC 27282
Fax: (336) 819-2022
E-mail: mncarmon@gtcc.edu
Phone: (336) 334-4822 ext. 2356

Gulf Coast Community College
www.gulfcoast.edu
International Student Representative
5230 West US Highway 98
Panama City, FL 32401
Fax: (850) 913-3308
E-mail: awalls@gulfcoast.edu
Phone: (850) 769-1551 ext. 3282

Gupton Jones College of Funeral Service
www.gupton-jones.edu
5141 Snapfinger Woods Drive
Decatur, GA 30035
Fax: (770) 593-1891
E-mail: jahinz@yahoo.com
Phone: (770) 593-2257

Gustavus Adolphus College
www.gustavus.edu
Center for International and Cultural
Education
800 West College Avenue
St. Peter, MN 56082
Fax: (507) 933-7900
E-mail: jeffa@gustavus.edu
Phone: (507) 933-7493

Gutenberg College
www.gutenberg.edu
1883 University Street
Eugene, OR 97403
E-mail: admissions@gutenberg.edu
Phone: (541) 683-5141

Gwinnett College
www.gwinnettcollege.edu
Director of Admissions
4230 Highway 29
Suite 11
Lilburn, GA 30047
Fax: (770) 381-0454
E-mail: admissions@gwinnettcollege.com
Phone: (770) 381-7200

Gwynedd-Mercy College
www.gmc.edu
Admissions Office
1325 Sumneytown Pike
PO Box 901
Gwynedd Valley, PA 19437-0901
Fax: (215) 641-5556
E-mail: admissions@gmc.edu
Phone: (800) 342-5462

Halifax Community College
www.halifaxcc.edu/
100 College Drive, Drawer 809
Weldon, NC 27890
Fax: (252) 538-4311
E-mail: washingtonj@halifaxcc.edu
Phone: (252) 536-7220

Hallmark College of Aeronautics
www.hallmarkcollege.edu
Director of Admissions
8901 Wetmore Road
San Antonio, TX 78230-4229
Fax: (210) 826-3707
E-mail: slross@hallmarkcollege.com
Phone: (210) 826-1000 ext. 106

Hallmark College of Technology
www.hallmarkcollege.edu
Admissions Office
Hallmark College
10401 IH-10 West
San Antonio, TX 78230-1737
Fax: (210) 697-8225
E-mail: sross@hallmarkcollege.edu
Phone: (210) 690-9000 ext. 212

Hamilton College
www.hamilton.edu
International Student Admissions
198 College Hill Road
Office of Admission
Clinton, NY 13323-1293
Fax: (315) 859-4457
E-mail: dcrawfor@hamilton.edu
Phone: (315) 859-4421

Hamilton Technical College
www.hamiltontechcollege.com
1011 East 53rd Street
Davenport, IA 52807
Fax: (563) 386-6756
E-mail: mchristy@hamiltontechcollege.com
Phone: (563) 386-3570

Hamline University
www.hamline.edu
Office of Admission
1536 Hewitt Avenue
MS-C1930
St. Paul, MN 55104-1284
Fax: (651) 523-2458
E-mail: admission@hamline.edu
Phone: (651) 523-2207

Hampden-Sydney College
www.hsc.edu
Admissions
Box 667
Hampden-Sydney, VA 23943
Fax: (434) 223-6346
E-mail: jferguson@hsc.edu
Phone: (434) 223-6120

Hampshire College
www.hampshire.edu
Senior Assistant Director of Admissions
893 West Street
Amherst, MA 01002-9988
Fax: (413) 559-5631
E-mail: wemmanuel@hampshire.edu
Phone: (413) 559-5471

Hampton University
www.hamptonu.edu
Admissions
Office of Admissions
Hampton University
Hampton, VA 23668
Fax: (757) 727-5095
E-mail: admissions@hamptonu.edu
Phone: (757) 727-5328

Hannibal-LaGrange University
www.hlg.edu
International Student Center
2800 Palmyra Road
Hannibal, MO 63401
Fax: (573) 221-6594
E-mail: sgonzalez@hlg.edu
Phone: (573) 629-3031

Hanover College
www.hanover.edu
Admission
PO Box 108
Hanover, IN 47243-0108
Fax: (812) 866-7098
E-mail: gage@hanover.edu
Phone: (800) 213-2178

Harcum College
www.harcum.edu
Center for International Programs or
Admissions
750 Montgomery Avenue
Bryn Mawr, PA 19010-3476
Fax: (610) 526-6191
E-mail: elaharcum@harcum.edu
Phone: (610) 526-6116

Hardin-Simmons University
www.hsutx.edu
PO Box 16050
Abilene, TX 79698-0001
Fax: (325) 670-1564
E-mail: maim@hsutx.edu
Phone: (325) 670-1299

Harding University
www.harding.edu
International student advisor
915 East Market Avenue
HU 12255
Searcy, AR 72149-2255
Fax: (501) 279-4122
E-mail: nboyd@harding.edu
Phone: (501) 279-4023

Harford Community College
www.harford.edu
Admissions
401 Thomas Run Road
Bel Air, MD 21015
Fax: (443) 443-2169
E-mail: jlares@harford.edu
Phone: (443) 412-2423

Harper College
www.harpercollege.edu
International Students Office
1200 West Algonquin Road
Palatine, IL 60067-7398
Fax: (847) 925-6048
E-mail: jizumika@harpercollege.edu
Phone: (847) 925-6227

Harrington College of Design
www.harringtoncollege.com
Director of Admissions
200 West Madison Avenue
Chicago, IL 60606
Fax: (312) 697-8111
E-mail: rhacker@harringtoncollege.com
Phone: (312) 939-4975 ext. 1122

Harris-Stowe State University
www.hssu.edu
Office of Admissions
3026 Laclede Avenue
St. Louis, MO 63103-2199
Fax: (314) 340-3555
E-mail: admissions@hssu.edu
Phone: (314) 340-3300

Harrisburg Area Community College
www.hacc.edu
International Admissions Coordinator
One HACC Drive, Cooper 206
Harrisburg, PA 17110-2999
Fax: (717) 231-7674
E-mail: jlmatoly@hacc.edu
Phone: (717) 780-2403

Harrison College: Indianapolis Northwest
www.harrison.edu
6300 Technology Center Drive
Indianapolis, IN 46278
Phone: (317) 873-6500

Hartnell College
www.hartnell.edu
International Student Services
411 Central Avenue
Salinas, CA 93901
Fax: (831) 755-6751
Phone: (831) 755-6829

Hartwick College
www.hartwick.edu
Admissions
Box 4022
Oneonta, NY 13820-4022
Fax: (607) 431-4102
E-mail: admissions@hartwick.edu
Phone: (607) 431-4150

Harvard College
www.college.harvard.edu
86 Brattle Street
Cambridge, MA 02138
Fax: (617) 495-8821
E-mail: college@fas.harvard.edu
Phone: (617) 495-1551

Harvey Mudd College
www.hmc.edu
Admission
301 Platt Boulevard
Claremont, CA 91711-5901
Fax: (909) 607-7046
E-mail: Raissa.diamante@hmc.edu
Phone: (909) 621-8011

Haskell Indian Nations University
www.haskell.edu
155 Indian Avenue #5031
Lawrence, KS 66046-4800
Fax: (913) 749-8429
E-mail: pgrantorosco@haskell.edu
Phone: (785) 749-8454

Haverford College
www.haverford.edu
Admission
370 Lancaster Avenue
Haverford, PA 19041-1392
Fax: (610) 896-1338
E-mail: epandian@haverford.edu
Phone: (610) 896-1350

Hawaii Pacific University
www.hpu.edu
Office of International Recruitment
1164 Bishop Street, Suite 200
Honolulu, HI 96813
Fax: (808) 543-8065
E-mail: international@hpu.edu
Phone: (808) 543-8076

Hawaii Tokai International College
www.hawaiitokai.edu
Student Services
2241 Kapiolani Boulevard
Honolulu, HI 96826
Fax: (808) 983-4173
E-mail: admissions@tokai.edu
Phone: (808) 983-4121

Hazard Community and Technical College
www.hazard.kctcs.edu
Director of Admissions
One Community College Drive
Hazard, KY 41701
Fax: (606) 672-6805
E-mail: hallie.bowling@kctcs.edu
Phone: (800) 246-7521 ext. 73486

Heald College: Concord
www.heald.edu
5130 Commercial Circle
Concord, CA 94520
Fax: (925) 288-5896
E-mail: info@heald.edu
Phone: (925) 288-5800

Heald College: Fresno
www.heald.edu
Dean
255 West Bullard Avenue
Fresno, CA 93704-1706
Fax: (559) 438-6368
E-mail: info@heald.edu
Phone: (559) 438-4222

Heald College: Hayward
www.heald.edu
Registrar
25500 Industrial Boulevard
Hayward, CA 94545
Fax: (510) 783-3287
E-mail: sandi_galan@heald.edu
Phone: (510) 783-2100

Heald College: Honolulu
www.heald.edu
Admissions
1500 Kapiolani Boulevard
Honolulu, HI 96814-3715
Fax: (808) 955-6964
E-mail: paul_billington@heald.edu
Phone: (808) 955-1500 ext. 554

Heald College: Portland
www.heald.edu
6035 NE 78th Court
Portland, OR 97218
Phone: (503) 229-0492

Heald College: Rancho Cordova
www.heald.edu
2910 Prospect Park Drive
Rancho Cordova, CA 95670
Fax: (916) 414-2675
E-mail: info@heald.edu
Phone: (916) 414-2700

Heald College: Roseville
www.heald.edu
7 Sierra Gate Plaza
Roseville, CA 95678
Fax: (916) 789-8616
E-mail: rosevilleinfo@heald.edu
Phone: (916) 789-8600

Heald College: Salinas
www.heald.edu
1450 North Main Street
Salinas, CA 93906
Fax: (831) 444-4600
Phone: (831) 443-1700

Heald College: San Francisco
www.heald.edu
350 Mission Street
San Francisco, CA 94105
Fax: (418) 808-3005
Phone: (415) 808-3000

Heald College: San Jose
www.heald.edu
341 Great Mall Parkway
Milpitas, CA 95035
Fax: (415) 934-7777
E-mail: sanjoseinfo@heald.edu
Phone: (408) 934-4900

Heald College: Stockton
www.heald.edu
Registrar's Office
1605 East March Lane
Stockton, CA 95210
Fax: (209) 477-2739
Phone: (209) 473-5200

Heartland Community College
www.heartland.edu
Student Services
1500 West Raab Road
Normal, IL 61761
Fax: (309) 268-7992
E-mail: chris.riley@heartland.edu
Phone: (309) 268-8033

Hebrew Theological College
www.htc.edu
7135 North Carpenter Road
Skokie, IL 60077
Fax: (847) 674-6381
E-mail: admissions@htt.edu
Phone: (847) 982-2500

Heidelberg University
www.heidelberg.edu
Office of Admission
310 East Market Street
Tiffin, OH 44883-2462
Fax: (419) 448-2334
E-mail: adminfo@heidelberg.edu
Phone: (419) 448-2330

Hellenic College/Holy Cross
www.hchc.edu
Admissions
50 Goddard Avenue
Brookline, MA 02445
Fax: (617) 850-1460
E-mail: admissions@hchc.edu
Phone: (617) 850-1260

Henderson Community College
www.hencc.kctcs.edu
Student Services
2660 South Green Street
Henderson, KY 42420
Fax: (270) 826-8391
E-mail: pattymitchell@kctcs.net
Phone: (270) 827-1867

Henderson State University
www.getreddie.com
Director of International Student Program
1100 Henderson Street
Box 7560
Arkadelphia, AR 71999-0001
Fax: (870) 230-5419
E-mail: smithc@hsu.edu
Phone: (870) 230-5265

Hendrix College
www.hendrix.edu
Office of Admission
1600 Washington Avenue
Conway, AR 72032-3080
Fax: (501) 450-3843
E-mail: gororo@hendrix.edu
Phone: (501) 450-1362

Hennepin Technical College
www.hennepintech.edu
9000 Brooklyn Boulevard
Brooklyn Park, MN 55455
Fax: (952) 952-1391
E-mail: rob.mestas@hennepintech.edu
Phone: (952) 995-1440

Henry Ford Community College
www.hfcc.edu
5101 Evergreen Road
Dearborn, MI 48128
Fax: (313) 845-9891
E-mail: pdwebb1@hfcc.edu
Phone: (313) 317-6519

Heritage Christian University
www.hcu.edu
Office of Admissions
3625 Helton Drive
PO Box HCU
Florence, AL 35630
Fax: (256) 766-9289
E-mail: hcu@hcu.edu
Phone: (256) 766-6610

Herkimer County Community College
www.herkimer.edu
International Programs
100 Reservoir Road
Herkimer, NY 13350-1598
Fax: (315) 866-0062
E-mail: simt@hcce.suny.edu
Phone: (315) 866-0300 ext. 8318

Herzing University
www.herzing.edu
280 West Valley Avenue
Birmingham, AL 35209
Fax: (205) 916-2807
E-mail: admiss@bhm.herzing.edu
Phone: (205) 916-2800

Herzing University
www.herzing.edu
1865 SR 436
Winter Park, FL 32792
Fax: (401) 418-0501
E-mail: info@orl.herzing.edu
Phone: (407) 478-0500

Herzing University
www.herzing.edu
Admissions
3393 Peachtree Road NE, Suite 1003
Atlanta, GA 30326
Fax: (404) 816-5576
E-mail: rhinton@atl.herzing.edu
Phone: (404) 816-4533

Herzing University
www.herzing.edu
2500 Williams Boulevard
Kenner, LA 70062
Fax: (504) 733-0020
E-mail: info@nor.herzing.edu
Phone: (504) 733-0074

Herzing University
www.herzing.edu
5700 West Broadway
Minneapolis, MN 55428
E-mail: info@mpls.herzing.edu
Phone: (763) 535-3000

Herzing University
www.herzing.edu/madison
Admissions Advisor
5218 East Terrace Drive
Madison, WI 53718
Fax: (608) 249-8593
E-mail: info@msn.herzing.edu
Phone: (608) 249-6611

Hesser College
www.hesser.edu
Director of Admissions
3 Sundial Avenue
Manchester, NH 03103
Fax: (603) 666-4722
E-mail: kwilkinson@hesser.edu
Phone: (603) 668-6660

Hesston College
www.hesston.edu
Director of International Admissions
Box 3000
Hesston, KS 67062-2093
Fax: (620) 327-8300
E-mail: admissions@hesston.edu
Phone: (620) 327-8133

Hibbing Community College
www.hibbing.edu
Student Services
1515 East 25th Street
Hibbing, MN 55746
Fax: (218) 263-2992
E-mail: heidikippenhan@hibbing.edu
Phone: (218) 312-9800

High Point University
www.highpoint.edu
Admissions
833 Montlieu Avenue
PO Box 3188
High Point, NC 27262-3598
Fax: (336) 888-6382
E-mail: agalbrai@highpoint.edu
Phone: (336) 841-9148

Highline Community College
www.highline.edu
International Student Programs
2400 South 240th Street
PO Box 98000
Des Moines, WA 98198-9800
Fax: (206) 870-3782
E-mail: lwesterg@highline.edu
Phone: (206) 878-3710 ext. 3725

Hilbert College
www.hilbert.edu
Admissions
5200 South Park Avenue
Hamburg, NY 14075-1597
Fax: (716) 649-1152
E-mail: tlee@hilbert.edu
Phone: (716) 649-7900 ext. 244

Hill College
www.hillcollege.edu
Admissions
112 Lamar Drive
Hillsboro, TX 76645
Fax: (254) 582-7591
E-mail: rballew@hillcollege.edu
Phone: (254) 582-2555 ext. 288

Hillsborough Community College
www.hccfl.edu
International Education
Box 31127
Tampa, FL 33631-3127
Fax: (813) 253-7070
E-mail: acarlson6@hccfl.edu
Phone: (813) 253-7397

Hillsdale College
www.hillsdale.edu
Admissions
33 East College Street
Hillsdale, MI 49242
Fax: (517) 607-2223
E-mail: jbrewer@hillsdale.edu
Phone: (517) 607-2324

Hillsdale Free Will Baptist College
www.hc.edu
PO Box 7208
Moore, OK 73153
E-mail: recruitment@hc.edu
Phone: (415) 912-9011

Hinds Community College
www.hindscc.edu
Foreign Student Counseling Office
505 East Main Street
P.O. Box 1100
Raymond, MS 39154-1100
Fax: (601) 857-3539
E-mail: records@hindscc.edu
Phone: (601) 857-3219

Hiram College
www.hiram.edu
Center for International Studies
Teachout Price Hall
Box 96
Hiram, OH 44234
Fax: (330) 569-5944
E-mail: mcgillsk@hiram.edu
Phone: (330) 569-5159

Hobart and William Smith Colleges
www.hws.edu
Admissions
629 South Main Street
Geneva, NY 14456
Fax: (315) 781-3914
E-mail: admissions@hws.edu
Phone: (315) 781-3622

Hocking College
www.hocking.edu
International Admissions
3301 Hocking Parkway
Nelsonville, OH 45764-9704
Fax: (740) 753-7065
E-mail: springer_r@hocking.edu
Phone: (740) 753-7080

Hodges University
www.hodges.edu
Admissions
2655 Northbrooke Drive
Naples, FL 34119
Fax: (239) 513-9071
E-mail: rlampus@hodges.edu
Phone: (239) 513-1122

Hofstra University
www.hofstra.edu
Multicultural and International Student Office
Admissions Center, 100 Hofstra University
Hempstead, NY 11549
Fax: (516) 463-5328
E-mail: admission@hofstra.edu
Phone: (516) 463-6627

Hollins University
www.hollins.edu
Admissions Office
PO Box 9707
8060 Quadrangle Lane
Roanoke, VA 24020-1707
Fax: (540) 362-6218
E-mail: huadm@hollins.edu
Phone: (800) 456-9595

Holy Apostles College and Seminary
www.holyapostles.edu
Admissions
33 Prospect Hill Road
Cromwell, CT 06416-2005
Fax: (860) 632-3030
E-mail: admissions@holyapostles.edu
Phone: (860) 632-3012

Holy Cross College
www.hcc-nd.edu
Admissions
54515 State Road 933 North
PO Box 308
Notre Dame, IN 46556-0308
Fax: (574) 233-7427
E-mail: vduke@hcc-nd.edu
Phone: (574) 239-8407

Holy Family University
www.holyfamily.edu
Admissions
9801 Frankford Avenue
Philadelphia, PA 19114-2009
Fax: (215) 281-1022
E-mail: lcampbell@holyfamily.edu
Phone: (215) 637-3050

Holy Names University
www.hnu.edu
Undergraduate Admission Counselor
3500 Mountain Boulevard
Oakland, CA 94619-1699
Fax: (510) 436-1325
E-mail: admission@hnu.edu
Phone: (800) 430-1321

Hondros College
www.nursing.hondros.edu
4140 Executive Parkway
Westerville, OH 43081-3855
Fax: (614) 508-7280
E-mail: admissions@hondros.edu
Phone: (888) 466-3767

Hood College
www.hood.edu
Admissions
401 Rosemont Avenue
Frederick, MD 21701-8575
Fax: (301) 696-3819
E-mail: international@hood.edu
Phone: (301) 696-3813

Hope College
www.hope.edu
Admissions
69 East 10th Street
Box 9000
Holland, MI 49422-9000
Fax: (616) 395-7130
E-mail: admissions@hope.edu
Phone: (616) 395-7850

Hope International University
www.hiu.edu
Admissions
2500 East Nutwood Avenue
Fullerton, CA 92831-3199
Fax: (714) 681-7423
E-mail: rfbarnes@hiu.edu
Phone: (714) 879-3901 ext. 2234

Horizon College of San Diego
www.horizoncollege.org
10625 Scripps Ranch Boulevard, Suite F
San Diego, CA 92131
Fax: (858) 695-9527
E-mail: info@horizoncollege.org
Phone: (858) 695-8587

Horry-Georgetown Technical College
www.hgtc.edu
PO Box 261966
2050 Highway 501 East
Conway, SC 29528-6066
Fax: (843) 349-7501
E-mail: admissions@hgtc.edu
Phone: (843) 349-5277 ext. 5277

Houghton College
www.houghton.edu
Office of Admission
1 Willard Avenue/PO Box 128
Houghton, NY 14744-0128
Fax: (585) 567-9522
E-mail: admission@houghton.edu
Phone: (585) 567-9353

Housatonic Community College
www.hcc.commnet.edu
Dean of Learning
900 Lafayette Boulevard
Bridgeport, CT 06604-4704
Fax: (203) 332-5123
E-mail: HO-WAdmissions@hcc.commnet.edu
Phone: (203) 332-5100

Houston Baptist University
www.hbu.edu
Vice President of Enrollment Management
7502 Fondren Road
Houston, TX 77074-3298
Fax: (281) 649-3217
E-mail: jsteen@hbu.edu
Phone: (281) 649-3000 ext. 3208

Houston Community College System
www.hccs.edu
Director, Student Support
3100 Main
PO Box 667517
Houston, TX 77266-7517
Fax: (713) 718-2111
E-mail: dona.fields@hccs.edu
Phone: (713) 718-8536

Howard Community College
www.howardcc.edu
Admissions and Advising
10901 Little Patuxent Parkway
Columbia, MD 21044-3197
Fax: (443) 518-4589
E-mail: intlstudent@howardcc.edu
Phone: (443) 518-4420

Howard Payne University
www.hputx.edu
Admission Office
1000 Fisk Street
Brownwood, TX 76801-2794
Fax: (325) 649-8901
E-mail: cmangrum@hputx.edu
Phone: (325) 649-8027

Howard University
www.howard.edu
International Admission Counselor
2400 Sixth Street NW
Washington, DC 20059
Fax: (202) 806-9194
E-mail: gansah-birikorang@howard.edu
Phone: (202) 806-7517

Hudson County Community College
www.hccc.edu
Enrollment Services
70 Sip Avenue, 1st Floor
Jersey City, NJ 07306
Fax: (201) 714-2136
E-mail: rsosa@hccc.edu
Phone: (201) 360-4136

Hudson Valley Community College
www.hvcc.edu
International Student Office
80 Vandenburgh Avenue
Troy, NY 12180
Fax: (518) 629-4576
E-mail: j.deitchman@hvcc.edu
Phone: (518) 629-7567

Huertas Junior College
www.huertas.edu
PO Box 8429
Caguas, PR 00726
Fax: (787) 743-0203
E-mail: admisiones@huertas.edu
Phone: (787) 743-1242

Humacao Community College
www.humacaocommunitycollege.com
Admissions
PO Box 9139
Georgetti St. #69
Humacao, PR 00792-9139
Fax: (787) 850-1577
E-mail: admisiones_hcc@yahoo.com
Phone: (787) 852-1430 ext. 31

Humboldt State University
www.humboldt.edu
International Center
One Harpst Street
Arcata, CA 95521-8299
Fax: (707) 826-3939
E-mail: karynn@humboldt.edu
Phone: (707) 826-4142

Humphreys College
www.humphreys.edu
Enrollment Management
6650 Inglewood Avenue
Stockton, CA 95207-3896
Fax: (209) 478-8721
E-mail: salopez@humphreys.edu
Phone: (209) 478-0800 ext. 202

Huntingdon College
www.huntingdon.edu
Office of Admission
1500 East Fairview Avenue
Montgomery, AL 36106-2148
Fax: (334) 833-4347
E-mail: admiss@huntingdon.edu
Phone: (334) 833-4497

Huntington University
www.huntington.edu
Admissions
2303 College Avenue
Huntington, IN 46750-1237
Fax: (260) 358-3699
E-mail: admissions@huntington.edu
Phone: (260) 359-4016

Huntsville Bible College
www.hbc1.edu
904 Oakwood Avenue
Huntsville, AL 35811
Fax: (256) 539-0854
E-mail: students@hbc1.edu
Phone: (256) 539-0834

Husson University
www.husson.edu
Director of Admissions
One College Circle
Bangor, ME 04401-2999
Fax: (207) 941-7935
E-mail: beanc@husson.edu
Phone: (207) 941-7067

Huston-Tillotson University
www.htu.edu
Enrollment Management
900 Chicon Street
Austin, TX 78702-2795
Fax: (512) 505-3190
E-mail: slstinson@htu.edu
Phone: (512) 505-3027

Hutchinson Community College
www.hutchcc.edu
Guidance and Counseling
1300 North Plum
Hutchinson, KS 67501
Fax: (620) 728-8155
E-mail: wintersd@hutchcc.edu
Phone: (620) 728-8163

ICPR Junior College
www.icprjc.edu
PO Box 190304
San Juan, PR 00919-0304
Fax: (787) 763-7249
E-mail: itapia@icprjc.edu
Phone: (787) 763-1010

Idaho State University
www.isu.edu
International Undergraduate Admissions
921 South 8th Stop 8270
Pocatello, ID 83209-8270
Fax: (208) 282-2924
E-mail: ipomail@isu.edu
Phone: (208) 282-4320

Ilisagvik College
www.ilisagvik.edu
100 Stevenson Road
PO Box 749
Barrow, AK 99723
Fax: (907) 852-1784
E-mail: dararath.cahoon@ilisagvik.cc
Phone: (907) 852-1763

Illinois Central College
www.icc.edu
International Education Coordinator
One College Drive
East Peoria, IL 61635-0001
Fax: (309) 694-8461
E-mail: enroll@icc.edu
Phone: (309) 694-8817

Illinois College
www.ic.edu
Admission
1101 West College Avenue
Jacksonville, IL 62650
Fax: (217) 245-3034
E-mail: rlbystry@ic.edu
Phone: (217) 245-3030

Illinois Eastern Community Colleges:
Frontier Community College
www.iecc.edu/fcc
Program Director of International Students
Two Frontier Drive
Fairfield, IL 62837-9801
Fax: (618) 392-3293
E-mail: swansonp@iecc.edu
Phone: (618) 395-7777

Illinois Eastern Community Colleges:
Lincoln Trail College
www.iecc.edu/ltc
Program Director of International Students
11220 State Highway 1
Robinson, IL 62454-5707
Fax: (618) 392-3293
E-mail: swansonp@iecc.edu
Phone: (618) 395-7777

Illinois Eastern Community Colleges: Olney
Central College
www.iecc.edu/occ
Program Director of International Students
305 North West Street
Olney, IL 62450
Fax: (618) 392-3293
E-mail: swansonp@iecc.edu
Phone: (618) 395-7777

Illinois Eastern Community Colleges:
Wabash Valley College
www.iecc.edu/wvc
Program Director of International Students
2200 College Drive
Mount Carmel, IL 62863-2657
Fax: (618) 392-3293
E-mail: swansonp@iecc.edu
Phone: (618) 395-7777

Illinois Institute of Art: Chicago
www.ilic.artinstitutes.edu
350 North Orleans Street
Chicago, IL 60654
E-mail: antonj@aii.edu
Phone: (312) 280-3500

Illinois Institute of Art: Schaumburg
www.artinstitutes.edu/schaumburg
1000 North Plaza Drive
Suite 100
Schaumburg, IL 60173
Fax: (847) 619-3064
E-mail: ilisadmissions@aii.edu
Phone: (847) 619-3450

Illinois Institute of Technology
www.iit.edu
Office of Undergraduate Admission
10 West 33rd Street
Perlstein Hall 101
Chicago, IL 60616
Fax: (312) 567-6939
E-mail: schoen@iit.edu
Phone: (312) 567-6940

Illinois State University
www.ilstu.edu
Office of International Studies
Campus Box 2200
Normal, IL 61790-2200
Fax: (309) 438-3987
E-mail: oisp@ilstu.edu
Phone: (309) 438-5365

Illinois Wesleyan University
www.iwu.edu
Admissions Office
PO Box 2900
Bloomington, IL 61702-2900
Fax: (309) 556-3820
E-mail: pschley@iwu.edu
Phone: (309) 556-3031

Immaculata University
www.immaculata.edu
Admission
1145 King Road
Immaculata, PA 19345
Fax: (610) 640-0836
E-mail: admiss@immaculata.edu
Phone: (610) 647-4400 ext. 3046

Independence University
www.independence.edu
Admissions
5295 South Commerce Drive Suite G-50
Murray, UT 84107
Fax: (619) 477-4360
E-mail: gfairley@cchs.edu
Phone: (619) 477-4800 ext. 355

Indian Hills Community College
www.indianhills.edu
Enrollment Services
623 Indian Hills Drive, Building 12
Ottumwa, IA 52501
Fax: (641) 683-4277
E-mail: enrollment_services@ihcc.cc
Phone: (641) 683-5167

Indian River State College
www.irsc.edu
3209 Virginia Avenue
Fort Pierce, FL 34981-5596
Fax: (772) 462-4699
E-mail: tspivey@ircc.edu
Phone: (772) 462-4327

Indiana Institute of Technology
www.indianatech.edu
International Admissions Counselor
1600 East Washington Boulevard
Fort Wayne, IN 46803-1297
Fax: (260) 422-7696
E-mail: srrodriguez@indianatech.edu
Phone: (260) 422-5561 ext. 2251

Indiana State University
www.indstate.edu
International Programs and Services
Office of Admissions, Erickson 114
218 North 6th Street
Terre Haute, IN 47809-9989
Fax: (812) 237-4316
E-mail: isu-ips@indstate.edu
Phone: (812) 237-2440

Indiana University Bloomington
www.iub.edu
300 North Jordan Avenue
Bloomington, IN 47405-1106
Fax: (812) 856-5378
E-mail: intladm@indiana.edu
Phone: (812) 855-4306

Indiana University East
www.iue.edu
Admissions
2325 Chester Boulevard
Box WZ116
Richmond, IN 47374-1289
Fax: (765) 973-8288
E-mail: eaadmit@indiana.edu
Phone: (765) 973-8208

Indiana University Kokomo
www.iuk.edu
International Admissions
Box 9003, KC 230A
Kokomo, IN 46904-9003
Fax: (765) 455-9537
E-mail: iuadmis@iuk.edu
Phone: (812) 855-4306

Indiana University Northwest
www.iun.edu
3400 Broadway
Hawthorn 100
Gary, IN 46408
Fax: (219) 981-4219
E-mail: admit@iun.edu
Phone: (219) 980-6764

Indiana University of Pennsylvania
www.iup.edu
Office of International Affairs
117 John Sutton Hall, 1011 South Drive
Indiana, PA 15705-1088
Fax: (724) 357-2514
E-mail: intl-affairs@iup.edu
Phone: (724) 357-2295

Indiana University South Bend
www.iusb.edu
Director, International Programs
1700 Mishawaka Avenue
Box 7111
South Bend, IN 46634-7111
Fax: (574) 520-4590
E-mail: grobinso@iusb.edu
Phone: (574) 520-4419

Indiana University Southeast
www.ius.edu
Admissions
4201 Grant Line Road
Box UC-100
New Albany, IN 47150-6405
Fax: (812) 941-2595
E-mail: admissions@ius.edu
Phone: (812) 941-2212

Indiana University-Purdue University Fort Wayne
www.ipfw.edu
International Student Services
2101 East Coliseum Boulevard
Fort Wayne, IN 46805-1499
Fax: (260) 481-6674
E-mail: iss@ipfw.edu
Phone: (260) 481-6034

Indiana University-Purdue University Indianapolis
www.iupui.edu
International Admissions
420 North University Boulevard, Cavanaugh Hall R129
Indianapolis, IN 46202-5143
Fax: (317) 278-2213
E-mail: nroof@iupui.edu
Phone: (317) 278-1290

Indiana Wesleyan University
www.indwes.edu
Admissions
4201 South Washington Street
Marion, IN 46953-4999
Fax: (765) 677-2140
E-mail: tony.stevens@indwes.edu
Phone: (765) 677-2254

Institute of American Indian Arts
www.iaia.edu
Director, Admissions
83 Avan Nu Po Road
Santa Fe, NM 87508-1300
Fax: (505) 424-4500
E-mail: nanaya@iaia.edu
Phone: (505) 424-2331

Institute of Business & Medical Careers
www.ibmc.edu
3842 South Mason Street
Fort Collins, CO 80525
E-mail: info@ibmc.edu
Phone: (970) 223-2669

Institute of Design and Construction
www.idc.edu
Administrative Office
141 Willoughby Street
Brooklyn, NY 11201-5380
Fax: (718) 852-5889
E-mail: rdavis@idc.edu
Phone: (718) 855-3661

Institute of Production and Recording
www.ipr.edu
312 Washington Avenue North
Minneapolis, MN 55401
E-mail: sferkingstad@ipr.edu
Phone: (612) 375-1900

Institute of Technology: Clovis
www.it-colleges.edu
564 West Herndon Avenue
Clovis, CA 93612
E-mail: rgardner@it-email.com
Phone: (559) 297-4500

IntelliTec College
www.intelliteccollege.com
Financial Aid
2315 East Pikes Peak Avenue
Colorado Springs, CO 80909
Fax: (719) 632-7451
E-mail: twright@intelliteccollege.com
Phone: (719) 632-7626

IntelliTec College: Grand Junction
www.intelliteccollege.edu
772 Horizon Drive
Grand Junction, CO 81506
Fax: (970) 243-8074
E-mail: frontdeskGJ@intellitec.edu
Phone: (970) 245-8101

Inter American University of Puerto Rico: Aguadilla Campus
www.aguadilla.inter.edu
Box 20000
Aguadilla, PR 00605
Fax: (787) 882-3020
Phone: (787) 891-0925 ext. 2101

Inter American University of Puerto Rico: Arecibo Campus
www.arecibo.inter.edu
Admission Office
PO Box 4050
Arecibo, PR 00614-4050
Fax: (787) 880-1624
E-mail: pmontalvo@arecibo.inter.edu
Phone: (787) 878-5475 ext. 2268

Inter American University of Puerto Rico: Barranquitas Campus
www.br.inter.edu
Admission Office
PO Box 517
Barranquitas, PR 00794
Fax: (787) 857-2244
E-mail: mdiaz@br.inter.edu
Phone: (787) 857-3600 ext. 2011

Inter American University of Puerto Rico: Bayamon Campus
www.bc.inter.edu
Admissions
500 Dr. John Will Harris Road
Bayamon, PR 00957
Fax: (787) 279-2205
E-mail: calicea@bc.inter.edu
Phone: (787) 279-1912 ext. 2017

Inter American University of Puerto Rico: Fajardo Campus
www.fajardo.inter.edu
Admissions Office
Call Box 70003
Fajardo, PR 00738-7003
Fax: (787) 863-3470
E-mail: ada.caraballo@fajardo.inter.edu
Phone: (787) 863-2390 ext. 2210

Inter American University of Puerto Rico: Guayama Campus
www.guayama.inter.edu
PO Box 10004
Guayama, PR 00785
Fax: (787) 864-8232
E-mail: lferrer@inter.edu
Phone: (787) 864-7059

Inter American University of Puerto Rico: Metropolitan Campus
www.metro.inter.edu
International Relations Office
Box 191293
San Juan, PR 00919-1293
Fax: (787) 250-0742
E-mail: ori@metro.inter.edu
Phone: (787) 250-1912 ext. 2305

Inter American University of Puerto Rico: Ponce Campus
www.ponce.inter.edu
104 Turpo Industrial Park Road #1
Mercedita, PR 00715-1602
Fax: (787) 841-0103
E-mail: fldiaz@poce.inter.edu
Phone: (787) 841-0110

Inter American University of Puerto Rico: San German Campus
www.sg.inter.edu
Director of International Studies
Box 5100
San German, PR 00683-9801
Fax: (787) 892-6350
E-mail: rlopesm@sg.inter.edu
Phone: (787) 264-1912 ext. 7280

International Academy of Design and Technology: Chicago
www.iadtchicago.edu
Registrar's Office
One North State Street, Suite 500
Chicago, IL 60602
Fax: (312) 980-4829
E-mail: ttimmons@iadtchicago.com
Phone: (312) 980-9200

International Academy of Design and Technology: Henderson
www.iadtvegas.com
2495 Village View Drive
Henderson, NV 89074
Fax: (702) 990-0161
E-mail: vegas_web@iadtvegas.com
Phone: (702) 990-0150

International Academy of Design and Technology: Nashville
www.iadtnashville.com
1 Bridgestone Park
Nashville, TN 37214
E-mail: admissions@iadtnashville.com
Phone: (866) 302-4238

International Academy of Design and Technology: Orlando
www.iadt.edu
Admissions
6039 S Rio Grande Avenue
Orlando, FL 32809
E-mail: trobinson@iadt.edu
Phone: (407) 857-2300

International Academy of Design and Technology: Sacramento
www.iadtsacramento.com
2450 Del Paso Road
Sacramento, CA 95834
Fax: (916) 285-6986
E-mail: aepperson@iadtsacramento.com
Phone: (916) 285-9468

International Academy of Design and Technology: Tampa
www.academy.edu
Vice President of Admissions and Marketing
5104 Eisenhower Boulevard
Tampa, FL 33634
Fax: (813) 881-0008
E-mail: bpassey@academy.edu
Phone: (813) 881-0007

International Baptist College
www.ibconline.edu
2211 West Germann Road
Chandler, AZ 85286
Fax: (480) 245-7908
E-mail: info@ibconline.edu
Phone: (480) 245-7903

International Business College
www.ibcfortwayne.edu
5699 Coventry Lane
Fort Wayne, IN 46804
Fax: (260) 436-1896
Phone: (260) 459-4500

International College of Broadcasting
www.icbcollege.com
6 South Smithville Road
Dayton, OH 45431
Fax: (937) 258-8714
E-mail: zenaicb@aol.com
Phone: (937) 258-8251 ext. 202

Inver Hills Community College
www.inverhills.edu
Admissions Office
2500 80th Street East
Inver Grove Heights, MN 55076-3224
Fax: (651) 450-3677
E-mail: solson@inverhills.edu
Phone: (651) 450-3594

Iona College
www.iona.edu
Admissions
715 North Avenue
New Rochelle, NY 10801-1890
Fax: (914) 637-2778
E-mail: snastlkova@iona.edu
Phone: (914) 633-2249

Iowa Central Community College
www.iowacentral.edu
One Triton Circle
Fort Dodge, IA 50501
Fax: (515) 576-7724
Phone: (515) 576-0099 ext. 1175

Iowa Lakes Community College
www.iowalakes.edu
Admissions
300 South 18th Street
Estherville, IA 51334-2725
Fax: (712) 852-2152
E-mail: astansbury@iowalakes.edu
Phone: (800) 346-6018

Iowa State University
www.iastate.edu
Admissions
100 Enrollment Services Center
Ames, IA 50011-2011
Fax: (515) 294-2592
E-mail: admissions@iastate.edu
Phone: (515) 294-5836

Iowa Wesleyan College
www.iwc.edu
Admissions Office
601 North Main Street
Mount Pleasant, IA 52641-1398
Fax: (319) 385-6240
E-mail: admit@iwc.edu
Phone: (319) 385-6231

Iowa Western Community College
www.iwcc.edu
Coordinator of International/Intercultural Programs
2700 College Road
Box 4-C
Council Bluffs, IA 51502-3004
Fax: (712) 388-6803
E-mail: mlusajo@iwcc.edu
Phone: (712) 325-3419

Irvine Valley College
www.ivc.edu
International Student Office
5500 Irvine Center Drive
Irvine, CA 92618-4399
Fax: (949) 451-5466
E-mail: gvendley@ivc.edu
Phone: (949) 451-5624

Island Drafting and Technical Institute
www.idti.edu
Admissions
128 Broadway
Amityville, NY 11701-2704
Fax: (631) 691-8738
E-mail: info@idti.edu
Phone: (631) 691-8733

Itasca Community College
www.itascacc.edu
Enrollment Management Office
1851 Highway 169 East
Grand Rapids, MN 55744
Fax: (218) 322-2332
E-mail: cperry@itascacc.edu
Phone: (218) 322-2340

Ithaca College
www.ithaca.edu
Admission
953 Danby Road
Ithaca, NY 14850-7002
Fax: (607) 274-1900
E-mail: neversley@ithaca.edu
Phone: (800) 429-4274

ITI Technical College
www.iticollege.edu
Director of Admissions
13944 Airline Highway
Baton Rouge, LA 70817
Fax: (225) 756-0903
E-mail: mstevens@iticollege.edu
Phone: (225) 752-4233 ext. 233

ITT Technical Institute: Arlington
www.itt-tech.edu
International Admissions
551 Ryan Plaza Drive
Arlington, TX 76011
Fax: (817) 275-8446
Phone: (800) 388-3368

ITT Technical Institute: Bensalem
www.itt-tech.edu
3330 Tillman Drive
Bensalem, PA 19020
Fax: (215) 244-8872
Phone: (215) 244-8871

ITT Technical Institute: Boise
www.itt-tech.edu
International Admissions
12302 West Explorer Drive
Boise, ID 83713-1529
Fax: (208) 322-0173
Phone: (800) 388-3368

ITT Technical Institute: Canton
www.itt-tech.edu
1905 South Haggerty Road
Canton, MI 48188

ITT Technical Institute: Chantilly
www.itt-tech.edu
14420 Albemarle Point Place
Chantilly, VA 20151
Fax: (703) 263-0846
Phone: (703) 263-2541

ITT Technical Institute: Duluth
www.itt-tech.edu
10700 Abbotts Bridge Road
Duluth, GA 30097
Phone: (866) 489-8818

ITT Technical Institute: Eden Prairie
www.itt-tech.edu/campus/school.cfm?lloc_
numlm=27
8911 Columbine Road
Eden Prairie, MN 55347
Phone: (952) 914-5300

ITT Technical Institute: Green Bay
www.itt-tech.edu
470 Security Boulevard
Green Bay, WI 54313
Fax: (920) 662-9384
Phone: (920) 662-9000

ITT Technical Institute: Hilliard
www.itt-tech.edu
3781 Park Mill Run Drive, Suite 1
Hilliard, OH 43026

ITT Technical Institute: Houston
www.itt-tech.edu
International Admissions
2950 South Gessner
Houston, TX 77063-3751
Fax: (713) 952-2393
Phone: (800) 388-3368

ITT Technical Institute: Kansas City
www.itt-tech.edu
9150 East 41st Terrace
Kansas City, MO 64133

ITT Technical Institute: Kennesaw
www.itt-tech.edu
2065 ITT Tech Way N.W.
Kennesaw, GA 30144

ITT Technical Institute: King of Prussia
www.itt-tech.edu
760 Moore Road, Suite 150
King of Prussia, PA 19406-1212

ITT Technical Institute: Knoxville
www.itt-tech.edu
International Admissions
10208 Technology Drive
Knoxville, TN 37932
Fax: (865) 671-2811
Phone: (800) 388-3368

ITT Technical Institute: Lake Mary
www.itt-tech.edu
1400 International Parkway South
Lake Mary, FL 32746
Fax: (407) 660-2566
Phone: (407) 660-2900

ITT Technical Institute: Mount Prospect
www.itt-tech.edu
Office of International Admissions
1401 Feehanville Drive
Mount Prospect, IL 60056
Fax: (317) 706-3042
Phone: (800) 388-3368

ITT Technical Institute: Nashville
www.itt-tech.edu
International Admissions
2845 Elm Hill Pike
Nashville, TN 37214
Fax: (615) 872-7209
Phone: (800) 388-3368

ITT Technical Institute: Newburgh
www.itt-tech.edu
10999 Stahl Road
Newburgh, IN 47630

ITT Technical Institute: Owings Mills
www.itt-tech.edu
11301 Red Run Boulevard
Owings Mills, MD 21117

ITT Technical Institute: Portland
www.itt-tech.edu
International Admissions
9500 NE Cascades Parkway
Portland, OR 97220
Fax: (503) 255-6500
Phone: (800) 388-3368

ITT Technical Institute: San Antonio
www.itt-tech.edu
International Admissions
5700 Northwest Parkway
San Antonio, TX 78249-3303
Fax: (210) 694-4651
Phone: (800) 388-3368

ITT Technical Institute: San Diego
www.itt-tech.edu
International Admissions
9680 Granite Ridge Drive
San Diego, CA 92123
Phone: (800) 388-3368

ITT Technical Institute: Seattle
www.itt-tech.edu
12720 Gateway Drive, Suite 100
Seattle, WA 98168
Fax: (206) 246-7635
Phone: (206) 244-3300

ITT Technical Institute: Spokane
www.itt-tech.edu
International Admissions
13518 East Indiana Avenue
Spokane Valley, WA 99216
Fax: (509) 926-2908
Phone: (800) 388-3368

ITT Technical Institute: Springfield
www.itt-tech.edu
7300 Boston Boulevard
Springfield, VA 22153
Fax: (703) 440-9561
Phone: (703) 440-9535

ITT Technical Institute: Tempe
www.itt-tech.edu
5005 South Wendler Drive
Tempe, AZ 85282
Fax: (602) 267-8727
Phone: (602) 437-7500

ITT Technical Institute: Tulsa
www.itt-tech.edu
8421 East 61st Street, Suite U
Tulsa, OK 74133

ITT Technical Institute: Wilmington
www.itt-tech.edu
200 Ballardvale Street, Building 1 Suite 200
Wilmington, MA 01887

Ivy Tech Community College: Bloomington
www.ivytech.edu
Registrar
200 Daniels Way
Bloomington, IN 47404-1511
Fax: (812) 332-8147
E-mail: askeens@ivytech.edu
Phone: (812) 330-6016

Ivy Tech Community College: Central Indiana
www.ivytech.edu
Assistant Director of International Student Relations
50 West Fall Creek Parkway North Drive
Indianapolis, IN 46208-5752
Fax: (317) 917-5919
E-mail: tywebb@ivytech.edu
Phone: (317) 921-4613

Ivy Tech Community College: Columbus
www.ivytech.edu
Assistant Director of Admissions
4475 Central Avenue
Columbus, IN 47203-1868
Fax: (812) 372-0311
E-mail: kbaker17@ivytech.edu
Phone: (812) 374-5255

Ivy Tech Community College: East Central
www.ivytech.edu
Dean of Student Affairs
4301 South Cowan Road
Box 3100
Muncie, IN 47302-9448
Fax: (765) 289-2292
E-mail: mlewelle@ivytech.edu
Phone: (765) 289-2291 ext. 1391

Ivy Tech Community College: Kokomo
www.ivytech.edu
Director of Admissions
1815 East Morgan Street
Kokomo, IN 46903-1373
Fax: (765) 454-5111
E-mail: mfedersp@ivytech.edu
Phone: (765) 459-0561 ext. 233

Ivy Tech Community College: Lafayette
www.ivytech.edu
Director of Admissions
3101 South Creasy Lane
Lafayette, IN 47905-6299
Fax: (765) 722-9293
E-mail: ihernand@ivytech.edu
Phone: (765) 269-5253

Ivy Tech Community College: North Central
www.ivytech.edu
Assistant Director of Admissions
220 Dean Johnson Boulevard
South Bend, IN 46601-3415
Fax: (574) 236-7177
E-mail: tteat@ivytech.edu
Phone: (574) 289-7001

Ivy Tech Community College: Northeast
www.ivytech.edu
Assistant Director of Diversity Affairs
3800 North Anthony Boulevard
Fort Wayne, IN 46805-1489
Fax: (260) 480-2053
E-mail: djackson@ivytech.edu
Phone: (260) 480-4115

Ivy Tech Community College: Northwest
www.ivytech.edu
Associate Dean of Student Affairs
1440 East 35th Avenue
Gary, IN 46409-1499
Fax: (219) 981-4415
E-mail: tlewis@ivytech.edu
Phone: (219) 980-7708

Ivy Tech Community College: Richmond
www.ivytech.edu
Assistant Director of Admissions
2357 Chester Boulevard
Richmond, IN 47374-1298
Fax: (765) 962-8174
E-mail: lprzybys@ivytech.edu
Phone: (765) 966-2656 ext. 1214

Ivy Tech Community College: South Central
www.ivytech.edu
Assistant Director of Admissions
8204 Highway 311
Sellersburg, IN 47172-1897
Fax: (812) 246-9905
E-mail: jgoodman17@ivytech.edu
Phone: (812) 246-3301 ext. 4315

Ivy Tech Community College: Southeast
www.ivytech.edu
Vice Chancellor
590 Ivy Tech Drive
Madison, IN 47250-1881
Fax: (812) 265-4028
E-mail: dheiderm@ivytech.edu
Phone: (812) 265-2580

Ivy Tech Community College: Southwest
www.ivytech.edu
Director of Admissions
3501 First Avenue
Evansville, IN 47710-3398
Fax: (812) 429-9878
E-mail: ajohnson@ivytech.edu
Phone: (812) 429-1430

Ivy Tech Community College: Wabash Valley
www.ivytech.edu
International Student Coordinator
8000 South Education Drive
Terre Haute, IN 47802-4898
Fax: (812) 299-5723
E-mail: bcandler@ivytech.edu
Phone: (812) 298-2286

J. Sargeant Reynolds Community College
www.reynolds.edu
Admissions and Records
Box 85622
Richmond, VA 23285-5622
Fax: (804) 371-3650
E-mail: lmunson@reynolds.edu
Phone: (804) 523-5029

Jackson State Community College
www.jscc.edu
Admissions Office
2046 North Parkway
Jackson, TN 38301-3797
Fax: (731) 425-9559
E-mail: awinchester@jscc.edu
Phone: (731) 425-8844 ext. 484

Jackson State University
www.jsums.edu
Office of International Programs
1400 John R. Lynch Street
Box 17330
Jackson, MS 39217
Fax: (601) 973-3388
E-mail: ksims@jsums.edu
Phone: (601) 979-3794

Jacksonville College
www.gotojbc.com
International Student Adviser
105 B.J. Albritton Drive
Jacksonville, TX 75766-4759
Fax: (903) 586-0743
E-mail: acadean@jacksonville-college.edu
Phone: (903) 586-2518 ext. 7108

Jacksonville State University
www.jsu.edu
Director of Admission
700 Pelham Road North
Jacksonville, AL 36265-1602
Fax: (256) 782-5291
E-mail: green@jsu.edu
Phone: (256) 782-5400

Jacksonville University
www.ju.edu
Admissions Office
2800 University Boulevard North
Jacksonville, FL 32211-3394
Fax: (904) 256-7012
E-mail: ymartel@ju.edu
Phone: (800) 225-2027 ext. 7006

James A. Rhodes State College
www.rhodesstate.edu
Student Affairs Division
4240 Campus Drive, PS 148
Lima, OH 45804-3597
Fax: (419) 995-8098
E-mail: admissions@rhodesstate.edu
Phone: (419) 995-8304

James Madison University
www.jmu.edu
Office of Admissions
Sonner Hall, MSC 0101
Harrisonburg, VA 22807
Fax: (540) 568-3332
E-mail: mooneyms@jmu.edu
Phone: (540) 568-3453

Jamestown College
www.jc.edu
Admissions
6081 College Lane
Jamestown, ND 58405
Fax: (701) 253-4318
E-mail: jhager@jc.edu
Phone: (701) 252-3467 ext. 5548

Jamestown Community College
www.sunyjcc.edu
Admissions
525 Falconer Street
PO Box 20
Jamestown, NY 14702-0020
Fax: (716) 338-1450
E-mail: wendypresent@mail.sunyjcc.edu
Phone: (716) 338-1000 ext. 1070

Jefferson College
www.jeffco.edu
Admissions
1000 Viking Drive
Hillsboro, MO 63050-2441
Fax: (636) 789-5103
E-mail: sdean1@jeffco.edu
Phone: (636) 797-3000 ext. 216

Jefferson College of Health Sciences
www.jchs.edu
Office of Admissions
Box 13186
Roanoke, VA 24031-3186
Fax: (540) 224-6703
E-mail: jomckeon@jchs.edu
Phone: (540) 985-9773

Jefferson State Community College
www.jeffstateonline.com
International Student Office
2601 Carson Road
Birmingham, AL 35215-3098
Fax: (205) 856-6070
E-mail: keubanks@jeffstateonline.com
Phone: (205) 856-7920

Jewish Theological Seminary of America
www.jtsa.edu
Office of Admissions
3080 Broadway
New York, NY 10027
Fax: (212) 280-6022
E-mail: lcadmissions@jtsa.edu
Phone: (212) 678-8832

JNA Institute of Culinary Arts
www.culinaryarts.edu
1212 South Broad Street
Philadelphia, PA 19146
E-mail: admissions@culinaryarts.edu
Phone: (215) 468-8800

John A. Logan College
www.jalc.edu
Admissions
700 Logan College Road
Carterville, IL 62918
Fax: (618) 985-4433
E-mail: terry.crain@jal.cc.il.us
Phone: (618) 985-3741

John Brown University
www.jbu.edu
Admissions
2000 West University Street
Siloam Springs, AR 72761-2121
Fax: (479) 524-4196
E-mail: jbuinfo@jbu.edu
Phone: (479) 524-7262

John Carroll University
www.jcu.edu
Director of Transfer and International
Admission
Office of Admission
20700 North Park Boulevard
University Heights, OH 44118-4581
Fax: (216) 397-4981
E-mail: rdinnen@jcu.edu
Phone: (216) 397-4294

John F. Kennedy University
www.jfku.edu
International Student Advisor
100 Ellinwood Way
Pleasant Hill, CA 94523-4817
Fax: (925) 969-3331
E-mail: ssermeno@jfku.edu
Phone: (925) 969-3339

John Wood Community College
www.jwcc.edu
Admissions
1301 South 48th Street
Quincy, IL 62305-8736
Fax: (217) 224-4208
E-mail: admissions@jwcc.edu
Phone: (217) 641-4314

Johns Hopkins University
www.jhu.edu
Office of Undergraduate Admissions
3400 North Charles Street, Mason Hall
Baltimore, MD 21218
Fax: (410) 516-6025
E-mail: cowan@jhu.edu
Phone: (410) 516-8124

**Johns Hopkins University: Peabody
Conservatory of Music**
www.peabody.jhu.edu
One East Mount Vernon Place
Baltimore, MD 21202
Fax: (410) 659-8102
E-mail: admissions@peabody.jhu.edu
Phone: (410) 659-8100 ext. 3075

Johnson & Wales University: Charlotte
www.jwu.edu
Admissions Office
801 West Trade Street
Charlotte, NC 28202
Fax: (980) 598-1111
E-mail: KMoniz@jwu.edu
Phone: (980) 598-1100

Johnson & Wales University: Denver
www.jwu.edu
Academic Services Associate
7150 Montview Boulevard
Denver, CO 80220
Fax: (303) 256-9389
E-mail: cabrahamson@jwu.edu
Phone: (303) 256-9557

Johnson & Wales University: North Miami
www.jwu.edu
International Admissions
1701 Northeast 127th Street
North Miami, FL 33181
Fax: (305) 892-7020
E-mail: mia@admissions.jwu.edu
Phone: (305) 892-7005

Johnson & Wales University: Providence
www.jwu.edu
International Admissions
8 Abbott Park Place
Providence, RI 02903-3703
Fax: (401) 598-4773
E-mail: admissons.pvd@jwu.edu
Phone: (401) 598-1074

Johnson Bible College
www.jbc.edu
Admissions
7900 Johnson Drive
Knoxville, TN 37998-0001
Fax: (865) 251-2336
E-mail: twingfield@jbc.edu
Phone: (865) 251-2233

Johnson C. Smith University
www.jcsu.edu
Admissions
100 Beatties Ford Road
Charlotte, NC 28216-5398
Fax: (704) 378-1242
E-mail: admissions@jcsu.edu
Phone: (704) 378-1010

Johnson College
www.johnson.edu
Admissions
3427 North Main Avenue
Scranton, PA 18508
Fax: (570) 348-2181
E-mail: admit@epix.net
Phone: (570) 342-6404 ext. 125

Johnson State College
www.jsc.edu
Admissions
337 College Hill
Johnson, VT 05656
Fax: (802) 635-1230
E-mail: jscadmissions@jsc.edu
Phone: (802) 635-1219

Johnston Community College
www.johnstoncc.edu
Director of Admissions and Counseling
PO Box 2350
Smithfield, NC 27577
Fax: (919) 989-7862
E-mail: jsmclendon@johnstoncc.edu
Phone: (919) 209-2079

Joliet Junior College
www.jjc.edu
Admissions and Records
1215 Houbolt Road
Joliet, IL 60431-8938
Fax: (815) 744-5507
E-mail: awalsh@jjc.edu
Phone: ext. 2247

Jones College
www.jones.edu
Director International Student Support
5353 Arlington Expressway
Jacksonville, FL 32211
Fax: (904) 743-4446
E-mail: mbarber@jones.edu
Phone: (904) 743-1122 ext. 282

Jones County Junior College
www.jcjc.edu
900 South Court Street
Ellisville, MS 39437
Fax: (601) 477-4017
E-mail: admissions@jcjc.edu
Phone: (601) 477-4025

Jones International University
www.jiu.edu
Enrollment Center
9697 East Mineral Avenue
Centennial, CO 80112
Fax: (303) 799-0966
E-mail: registrar@jonesinternational.edu
Phone: (800) 811-5663

Judson College
www.judson.edu
Admissions Office
302 Bibb Street
Marion, AL 36756
Fax: (334) 683-5282
E-mail: admissions@judson.edu
Phone: (334) 683-5110

Judson University
www.judsonu.edu
Admissions
1151 North State Street
Elgin, IL 60123-1404
Fax: (847) 628-2526
E-mail: admissions@judsonu.edu
Phone: (847) 628-1572

Juilliard School
www.juilliard.edu
Admissions Office
60 Lincoln Center Plaza
New York, NY 10023-6588
Fax: (212) 724-0263
E-mail: admissions@juilliard.edu
Phone: (212) 799-5000 ext. 223

Juniata College
www.juniata.edu
Enrollment Office
1700 Moore Street
Huntingdon, PA 16652-2196
Fax: (814) 641-3100
E-mail: basomb@juniata.edu
Phone: (814) 641-3427

Kalamazoo College
www.kzoo.edu
1200 Academy Street
Kalamazoo, MI 49006
Fax: (269) 337-7390
E-mail: roderick.malcolm@kzoo.edu
Phone: (269) 337-7166

Kalamazoo Valley Community College
www.kvcc.edu
6767 West O Avenue
PO Box 4070
Kalamazoo, MI 49003-4070
Fax: (269) 488-4161
E-mail: mmccall@kvcc.edu
Phone: (269) 488-4207

Kanawha Valley Community and Technical College
www.kvctc.edu
Admissions
PO Box 1000
106 Ferrell Hall
Institute, WV 25112-1000
Fax: (304) 766-4104
E-mail: admission@wvstateu.edu
Phone: (304) 766-3221

Kankakee Community College
www.kcc.edu
Admissions
100 College Drive
Kankakee, IL 60901-6505
Fax: (815) 802-8521
E-mail: mdriscoll@kcc.edu
Phone: (815) 802-8524

Kansas City Art Institute
www.kcai.edu
Admissions
4415 Warwick Boulevard
Kansas City, MO 64111
Fax: (816) 802-3309
E-mail: admiss@kcai.edu
Phone: (800) 522-5224

Kansas City Kansas Community College
www.kckcc.edu
English as a Second Language Office
7250 State Avenue
Kansas City, KS 66112
Fax: (913) 288-7648
E-mail: sneff@kckcc.edu
Phone: (913) 288-7201

Kansas State University
www.k-state.edu
International Student Center
119 Anderson Hall
Manhattan, KS 66506
Fax: (785) 532-6550
E-mail: intlpreadmit@ksu.edu
Phone: (785) 532-7277

Kansas Wesleyan University
www.kwu.edu
Director of Admissions
100 East Claflin Avenue
Salina, KS 67401-6196
Fax: (785) 827-0927
E-mail: jallen@kwu.edu
Phone: (785) 827-5541

Kaplan College: Dayton
www.kaplancollege.com
Admissions Office
2800 East River Road
Dayton, OH 45439
Fax: (937) 294-2259
E-mail: ckirby@kaplan.edu
Phone: (937) 294-6155

Kaplan College: Denver
www.kaplancollege.com
500 East 84th Avenue, Suite W-200
Thornton, CO 80229
Fax: (303) 295-0102
Phone: (303) 295-0550

Kaplan College: Hammond
www.kaplan.com
7833 Indianapolis Boulevard
Hammond, IN 46324
Fax: (219) 844-0105
Phone: (219) 844-0100

Kaplan College: Merrillville
www.sawyercollege.edu
3803 East Lincoln Highway
Merrillville, IN 46410
Fax: (219) 942-3762
E-mail: cartim@kaplan.edu
Phone: (219) 947-8400

Kaplan College: Palm Springs
www.kc-palmsprings.com
2475 East Tahquitz Canyon Way
Palm Springs, CA 92262
Phone: (760) 327-4562

Kaplan College: Panorama City
www.panorama-city.kaplancollege.com/
Admissions
14355 Roscoe Boulevard
Panorama City, CA 91402
Fax: (818) 672-8919
E-mail: enalvarez@kaplan.edu
Phone: (818) 672-3000 ext. 3005

Kaplan College: Phoenix
www.kc-phoenix.com
13610 North Black Canyon Highway, Suite 104
Phoenix, AZ 85029
Fax: (602) 548-1956
E-mail: mcrance@kaplan.edu
Phone: (602) 548-1955 ext. 1366

Kaplan College: Sacramento
www.mariccollege.edu
4330 Watt Avenue, Suite 400
Sacramento, CA 95821
E-mail: admissions@mariccollege.edu
Phone: (916) 649-8168

Kaplan College: Salida
www.mariccollege.edu
5172 Kiernan Court
Salida, CA 95368
E-mail: wtriplett@mariccollege.edu
Phone: (209) 543-7000

Kaplan College: San Diego
www.mariccollege.edu
9055 Balboa Avenue
San Diego, CA 92123
Fax: (858) 279-4885
Phone: (858) 279-4500

Kaplan College: Vista
www.mariccollege.edu
2022 University Drive
Vista, CA 92083
Fax: (760) 630-1656
Phone: (760) 630-1555

Kaplan University: Cedar Falls
www.kucampus.edu
7009 Nordic Drive
Cedar Falls, IA 50613
Fax: (319) 243-2961
Phone: (319) 277-0220

Kaplan University: Cedar Rapids
www.kucampus.edu
Admissions
3165 Edgewood Parkway, SW
Cedar Rapids, IA 52404
Fax: (319) 363-3812
E-mail: druddy@kaplan.edu
Phone: (319) 363-0481

Kaplan University: Davenport
www.kucampus.edu
Director of Admissions
1801 East Kimberly Road, Suite 1
Davenport, IA 52807-2095
Fax: (563) 355-1320
E-mail: rhoffmann@kucampus.edu
Phone: (563) 441-2496

Kaplan University: Des Moines
www.kucampus.edu
Admissions Office
4655 121st Street
Urbandale, IA 50323
Fax: (515) 727-2115
E-mail: erogan_dm@hamiltonia.edu
Phone: (515) 727-2100

Kaplan University: Hagerstown
www.Hagerstown.KaplanUniversity.edu
18618 Crestwood Drive
Hagerstown, MD 21742
Fax: (301) 791-7661
E-mail: info@ku-hagerstown.edu
Phone: (301) 739-2670

Kaplan University: Lincoln
www.kucampus.edu
Admissions
1821 K Street
Lincoln, NE 68508
Fax: (402) 474-5302
E-mail: kfrette@kaplan.edu
Phone: (402) 474-5315

Kaplan University: Mason City
www.ku-masoncity.edu
Plaza West 2570 Fourth Street, SW
Mason City, IA 50401
Fax: (641) 423-7512
E-mail: mklacik@kaplan.edu
Phone: (641) 423-2530

Kaplan University: South Portland
www.kaplanuniversity.edu
265 Western Avenue
South Portland, ME 04106
Fax: (207) 774-1715
E-mail: enroll@andovercollege.edu
Phone: (207) 774-6126 ext. 8701

Kaskaskia College
www.kaskaskia.edu
Admissions and Records
27210 College Road
Centralia, IL 62801
Fax: (618) 532-1990
E-mail: jripperda@kaskaskia.edu
Phone: (618) 545-3041

Kean University
www.kean.edu
Admissions Office
1000 Morris Avenue
PO Box 411
Union, NJ 07083-0411
Fax: (908) 737-7105
E-mail: admitme@kean.edu
Phone: (908) 737-7109

Kehilath Yakov Rabbinical Seminary
206 Wilson Street
Brooklyn, NY 11211
Fax: (718) 387-8586
Phone: (718) 963-3940

Keiser Career College: Greenacres
www.keisercareer.edu
6812 Forest Hill Boulevard
Greenacres, FL 33413
Phone: (561) 433-2330

Keiser University
www.keiseruniversity.edu
1500 Northwest 49th Street
Fort Lauderdale, FL 33309
Fax: (954) 771-4894
E-mail: admissions-ftl@keisercollege.edu
Phone: (954) 776-4456

Kellogg Community College
www.kellogg.edu
Enrollment Services
450 North Avenue
Battle Creek, MI 49017-3397
Fax: (269) 966-4089
E-mail: admissions@kellogg.edu
Phone: (269) 965-4153

Kendall College
www.kendall.edu
International Director of Admissions
900 N. North Branch Street
Chicago, IL 60642-4278
Fax: (312) 752-2021
E-mail: tfitzgibbon@kendall.edu
Phone: (312) 752-2160

Kennebec Valley Community College
www.kvcc.me.edu
Director of Admissions
92 Western Avenue
Fairfield, ME 04937-1367
Fax: (207) 453-5011
E-mail: jbourgoin@kvcc.me.edu
Phone: (207) 453-5035

Kennesaw State University
www.kennesaw.edu
International Student Admissions
1000 Chastain Road
Campus Box 0115
Kennesaw, GA 30144-5591
Fax: (678) 797-2573
E-mail: jespana@kennesaw.edu
Phone: (770) 423-6336

Kent State University
www.kent.edu
International Admissions
PO Box 5190
Kent, OH 44242-0001
Fax: (330) 672-2499
E-mail: intladm@kent.edu
Phone: (330) 672-7980

Kent State University: Geauga
www.geauga.kent.edu
International Admissions
Office of Admissions
14111 Claridon-Troy Road
Burton, OH 44021
E-mail: intladm@kent.edu
Phone: (330) 672-7980

Kentucky Christian University
www.kcu.edu
Enrollment Services
100 Academic Parkway
Box 2021
Grayson, KY 41143-2205
Fax: (606) 474-3155
E-mail: knights@kcu.edu
Phone: (606) 474-3281

Kentucky Mountain Bible College
www.kmbc.edu
Office of Recruiting
Box 10
Vancleve, KY 41385-0010
Fax: (606) 693-4884
E-mail: kmbc@kmbc.edu
Phone: (606) 693-5000 ext. 138

Kentucky State University
www.kysu.edu
Admissions
400 East Main Street, ASB 312
Frankfort, KY 40601
Fax: (502) 597-5978
E-mail: james.burrell@kysu.edu
Phone: (502) 597-6813

Kentucky Wesleyan College
www.kwc.edu
Admissions Office
3000 Frederica Street
Owensboro, KY 42301
Fax: (270) 926-3196
E-mail: llee@kwc.edu
Phone: (270) 852-3120

Kenyon College
www.kenyon.edu
Admissions
Ransom Hall-Admissions
106 College-Park Street
Gambier, OH 43022-9623
Fax: (740) 427-5770
E-mail: morse@kenyon.edu
Phone: (800) 848-2468

Kettering College of Medical Arts
www.kcma.edu
3737 Southern Boulevard
Kettering, OH 45429-1299
Fax: (937) 395-8338
E-mail: studentadmissions@kcma.edu
Phone: (800) 422-5262

Kettering University
www.kettering.edu
Admissions
1700 University Avenue
Flint, MI 48504-6214
Fax: (810) 762-9837
E-mail:
InternationalAdmissions@kettering.edu
Phone: (810) 762-9568

Keuka College
www.keuka.edu
Admissions
141 Central Avenue
Keuka Park, NY 14478-0098
Fax: (315) 279-5386
E-mail: admissions@mail.keuka.edu
Phone: (800) 335-3852

Key College
www.keycollege.edu
Financial Services
225 East Dania Beach Boulevard
Dania Beach, FL 33004-3046
Fax: (954) 923-9226
E-mail: financialaid@keycollege.edu
Phone: (954) 923-4440

Keystone College
www.keystone.edu
Office of Admissions
One College Green
PO Box 50
La Plume, PA 18440-1099
Fax: (570) 945-7916
E-mail: jonathan.summers@keystone.edu
Phone: (570) 945-8120

Keystone Technical Institute
www.kti.edu
2301 Academy Drive
Harrisburg, PA 17112-1012
Fax: (717) 901-9090
E-mail: info@kti.edu
Phone: (717) 545-4747

Kilgore College
www.kilgore.edu
1100 Broadway
Kilgore, TX 75662-3299
Fax: (903) 983-8607
E-mail: bthornhill@kilgore.edu
Phone: (903) 983-8204

King College
www.king.edu
Admission Office
1350 King College Road
Bristol, TN 37620-2699
Fax: (423) 652-4861
E-mail: eabrowne@king.edu
Phone: (423) 652-4769

The King's College
www.tkc.edu
Office of Admissions
350 Fifth Avenue, Lower Lobby
New York, NY 10118
Fax: (212) 659-3611
E-mail: mosborne@tkc.edu
Phone: (212) 659-3610

King's College
www.kings.edu
Admissions
133 North River Street
Wilkes-Barre, PA 18711
Fax: (570) 208-5971
E-mail: jamesanderson@kings.edu
Phone: (570) 208-5858

The King's University
www.kingsuniversity.edu
Office of Admission
14800 Sherman Way
Van Nuys, CA 91405-2233
Fax: (818) 779-8429
E-mail: admissions@kingsuniversity.edu
Phone: (818) 779-8040

Kirkwood Community College
www.kirkwood.edu
International Student Adviser Office
6301 Kirkwood Boulevard SW
PO Box 2068
Cedar Rapids, IA 52406
Fax: (319) 398-1244
E-mail: gglick@kirkwood.edu
Phone: (319) 398-5411 ext. 5579

Kirtland Community College
www.kirtland.edu
Student Services
10775 North Saint Helen Road
Roscommon, MI 48653
Fax: (989) 275-6727
E-mail: kochk@kirtland.edu
Phone: (989) 275-5000 ext. 253

Kishwaukee College
www.kishwaukeecollege.edu
Vice President of Student Services
21193 Malta Road
Malta, IL 60150-9699
Fax: (815) 825-2306
E-mail: apperson@kishwaukeecollege.edu
Phone: (815) 825-2086 ext. 249

Knox College
www.knox.edu
Admission Office
2 East South Street K-148
Galesburg, IL 61401-4999
Fax: (309) 341-7070
E-mail: jferchau@knox.edu
Phone: (309) 341-7136

Kutztown University of Pennsylvania
www.kutztown.edu
International Programs
Admissions Office
PO Box 730
Kutztown, PA 19530-0730
Fax: (610) 683-1356
E-mail: wade@kutztown.edu
Phone: (484) 646-4256

Kuyper College
www.kuyper.edu
Academic Office
3333 East Beltline Avenue Northeast
Grand Rapids, MI 49525-9749
Fax: (616) 988-3608
E-mail: mvandermeer@kuyper.edu
Phone: (616) 222-3000

LA College International
www.lac.edu
3200 Wilshire Boulevard, Suite 400
Los Angeles, CA 90010-1308
Fax: (213) 383-9369
Phone: (213) 381-3333

La Roche College
www.laroche.edu
Admissions
9000 Babcock Boulevard
Pittsburgh, PA 15237
Fax: (412) 536-1048
E-mail: david.mcfarland@laroche.edu
Phone: (412) 536-1276

La Salle University
www.lasalle.edu
Admission and Financial Aid
1900 West Olney Avenue
Philadelphia, PA 19141-1199
Fax: (215) 951-1656
E-mail: arcangel@lasalle.edu
Phone: (215) 951-1500

La Sierra University
www.lasierra.edu
4500 Riverwalk Parkway
Riverside, CA 92515-8247
Fax: (951) 785-2477
E-mail: admissions@lasierra.edu
Phone: (951) 785-2176

Labette Community College
www.labette.edu
Admissions
200 South 14th Street
Parsons, KS 67357
Fax: (620) 421-2309
E-mail: tammyf@labette.edu
Phone: (620) 421-6700 ext. 1228

Lackawanna College
www.lackawanna.edu
Admissions Office
501 Vine Street
Scranton, PA 18509
Fax: (570) 961-7843
E-mail: tantallam@lackawanna.edu
Phone: (570) 504-8094

Lafayette College
www.lafayette.edu
Admissions
118 Markle Hall
Easton, PA 18042
Fax: (610) 330-5355
E-mail: internatl@lafayette.edu
Phone: (610) 330-5100

LaGrange College
www.lagrange.edu
Office of Admission
601 Broad Street
LaGrange, GA 30240-2999
Fax: (706) 880-8010
E-mail: kpirrman@lagrange.edu
Phone: (706) 880-8005

Laguna College of Art and Design
www.lagunacollege.edu
2222 Laguna Canyon Road
Laguna Beach, CA 92651-1136
Fax: (949) 376-6009
E-mail: admissions@lagunacollege.edu
Phone: (949) 376-6000

Lake Area Technical Institute
www.lakeareatech.edu
Registrar
PO Box 730
Watertown, SD 57201
Fax: (605) 882-6299
Phone: (605) 882-5284

Lake Erie College
www.lec.edu
Admissions
391 West Washington Street
Painesville, OH 44077-3389
Fax: (440) 375-7005
E-mail: evalyko@lec.edu
Phone: (440) 375-7050

Lake Forest College
www.lakeforest.edu
Admission Office
555 North Sheridan Road
Lake Forest, IL 60045-2338
Fax: (847) 735-6271
E-mail: international@lakeforest.edu
Phone: (847) 735-5000

Lake Land College
www.lakelandcollege.edu
Admissions
5001 Lake Land Boulevard
Mattoon, IL 61938-9366
Fax: (217) 234-5390
E-mail: admissions@lakeland.cc.il.us
Phone: (217) 234-5382

Lake Michigan College
www.lakemichigancollege.edu
International and Veteran Affairs Office
2755 East Napier Avenue
Benton Harbor, MI 49022-1899
Fax: (269) 927-6718
E-mail: pliml@lakemichigancollege.edu
Phone: (269) 927-6181

Lake Region State College
www.lrsc.edu
Student Services
1801 College Drive North
Devils Lake, ND 58301-1598
Fax: (701) 662-1581
E-mail: Nicole.M.Walford@lrsc.edu
Phone: (701) 662-1568

Lake Superior College
www.lsc.edu
Intercultural Services Coordinator
2101 Trinity Road
Duluth, MN 55811
Fax: (218) 733-5945
E-mail: c.crawford@lsc.edu
Phone: (218) 733-7617

Lake Superior State University
www.lssu.edu
Admissions
650 West Easterday Avenue
Sault Ste. Marie, MI 49783-1699
Fax: (906) 635-6696
E-mail: acase@lssu.edu
Phone: (906) 635-2231

Lake Tahoe Community College
www.ltcc.edu
Admissions & Records
One College Drive
South Lake Tahoe, CA 96150-4524
Fax: (530) 542-1781
E-mail: admissions@ltcc.edu
Phone: (530) 541-4660 ext. 211

Lake Washington Technical College
www.lwtc.edu
International Programs Office
11605 132nd Avenue, NE
Kirkland, WA 98034
Fax: (425) 739-8148
E-mail: international.students@lwtc.edu
Phone: (425) 739-8145

Lake-Sumter Community College
www.lscc.edu
Senior Progam Specialist
9501 U.S. Highway 441
Leesburg, FL 34788-8751
Fax: (352) 365-3553
E-mail: MurphyD@lscc.edu
Phone: (352) 323-3686

Lakeland College
www.lakeland.edu
International Student Advisor
Box 359
Sheboygan, WI 53082-0359
Fax: (920) 565-1556
E-mail: international@lakeland.edu
Phone: (920) 565-1337

Lakeland Community College
www.lakelandcc.edu
Admissions
7700 Clocktower Drive
Kirtland, OH 44094-5198
Fax: (440) 525-7651
E-mail: tcooper@lakelandcc.edu
Phone: (440) 525-7230

Lakes Region Community College
www.lrcc.edu
Admission
379 Belmont Road
Laconia, NH 03246-9204
Fax: (603) 524-8084
E-mail: wfraser@ccsnh.edu
Phone: (603) 524-3207

Lakeshore Technical College
www.gotoltc.edu
1290 North Avenue
Cleveland, WI 53015-9761
Fax: (920) 693-3561
E-mail: scott.lieburn@gotoltc.edu
Phone: (920) 693-1378

Lamar Community College
www.lamarcc.edu
Admissions
2401 South Main Street
Lamar, CO 81052-3999
E-mail: amy.thompson@lamarcc.edu
Phone: (719) 336-1626

Lamar Institute of Technology
www.lit.edu
International Admissions Office
PO Box 10043
Beaumont, TX 77705
Fax: (409) 880-8414
Phone: (409) 880-8356

Lamar State College at Orange
www.lsco.edu
410 Front Street
Orange, TX 77630
Fax: (409) 882-3374
Phone: (409) 883-7750

Lamar State College at Port Arthur
www.lamarpa.edu
Vice President for Student Services
Box 310
Port Arthur, TX 77641-0310
Fax: (409) 984-6025
E-mail: Tom.Neal@lamarpa.edu
Phone: (409) 984-6156

Lamar University
www.lamar.edu
International Student Services
Box 10009
Beaumont, TX 77705
Fax: (409) 880-8414
E-mail: intladm@hal.lamar.edu
Phone: (409) 880-8356

Lambuth University
www.lambuth.edu
Senior Associate Director of Admissions
705 Lambuth Boulevard
Jackson, TN 38301-5296
Fax: (731) 988-4600
E-mail: torres@lambuth.edu
Phone: (800) 526-2884

Lander University
www.lander.edu
Office of Admissions
Stanley Avenue
Box 6007
Greenwood, SC 29649-2099
Fax: (864) 388-8125
E-mail: jmathis@lander.edu
Phone: (864) 388-8307

Landing School of Boatbuilding and Design
www.landingschool.edu
P.O. Box 1490
Kennebunkport, ME 04046
E-mail: info@landingschool.edu
Phone: (207) 985-7976 ext. 406

Landmark College
www.landmark.edu
Admissions
River Road South
PO Box 820
Putney, VT 05346
Fax: (802) 387-6868
E-mail: admissions@landmark.edu
Phone: (802) 387-6718

Lane College
www.lanecollege.edu
Admissions
545 Lane Avenue
Jackson, TN 38301-4598
Fax: (731) 426-7559
E-mail: ebrown@lanecollege.edu
Phone: (731) 426-7533

Lane Community College
www.lanecc.edu
International/Multi-Cultural Services
4000 East 30th Avenue
Eugene, OR 97405
Fax: (541) 463-3991
E-mail: Sheldonc@lanecc.edu
Phone: (541) 463-5165

Laney College
www.laney.peralta.edu
International Specialist, International Affairs
& Distance Education
900 Fallon Street
Oakland, CA 94607
Fax: (510) 465-3257
E-mail: dgephart@Peralta.edu
Phone: (510) 587-7834

Langston University
www.lunet.edu
Box 728
Langston, OK 73050
Fax: (405) 466-3391
E-mail: gtrobertson@lunet.edu
Phone: (405) 466-3428

Lansdale School of Business
www.lsb.edu
290 Wissahickon Avenue
North Wales, PA 19454-4114
Fax: (215) 699-8770
E-mail: mjohnson@lsb.edu
Phone: (215) 699-5700

Lansing Community College
www.lansing.cc.mi.us
Admissions
422 North Washington Square
Lansing, MI 48901
Fax: (517) 483-9668
E-mail: Admissions@lcc.edu
Phone: (517) 483-1200

Laramie County Community College
www.lccc.wy.edu
1400 East College Drive
Cheyenne, WY 82007-3299
Fax: (307) 778-1350
E-mail: hallison@lccc.wy.edu
Phone: (307) 778-1117

Laredo Community College
www.laredo.edu
International Student and Veteran Office
West End Washington Street
Laredo, TX 78040-4395
Fax: (956) 721-5493
E-mail: vghernandez@laredo.edu
Phone: (956) 764-5768

Las Positas College
www.laspositascollege.edu
Admissions and Records
3033 Collier Canyon Road
Livermore, CA 94551
Fax: (925) 606-6437
E-mail: sdupree@clpccd.cc.ca.us
Phone: (925) 373-5815

Lasell College
www.lasell.edu
Associate Director of International and Multi-
Cultural Admission
1844 Commonwealth Avenue
Newton, MA 02466-2709
Fax: (617) 243-2380
E-mail: internationaladmiss@lasell.edu
Phone: (617) 243-2203

Lassen Community College
www.lassencollege.edu
Box 3000
Susanville, CA 96130
Fax: (530) 257-8964
Phone: (530) 251-8808

Laurel Business Institute
www.laurel.edu
11 East Penn Street
PO Box 877
Uniontown, PA 15401
Fax: (724) 439-3607
E-mail: ddecker@laurel.edu
Phone: (724) 439-4900

Laurel Technical Institute
www.laurel.edu
Admissions Officer
200 Sterling Avenue
Sharon, PA 16146
Fax: (724) 983-8355
E-mail: info@laurel.edu
Phone: (724) 983-0700

Laurel University
www.johnwesley.edu
Admissions
2314 North Centennial
High Point, NC 27265-3197
Fax: (336) 889-2261
E-mail: jreese@johnwesley.edu
Phone: (336) 889-2262 ext. 127

Lawrence Technological University
www.ltu.edu
Director of Admissions
21000 West Ten Mile Road
Southfield, MI 48075-1058
Fax: (248) 204-2228
E-mail: international@ltu.edu
Phone: (248) 204-3160

Lawrence University
www.lawrence.edu
Admissions
711 East Boldt Way
Appleton, WI 54912-0599
Fax: (920) 832-6782
E-mail: excelinternational@lawrence.edu
Phone: (920) 832-6500 ext. 7067

Lawson State Community College
www.lawsonstate.edu
Admissions and Records
3060 Wilson Road SW
Birmingham, AL 35221-1717
Fax: (205) 923-7106
E-mail: jshelley@lawsonstate.edu
Phone: (205) 929-6361

**Le Cordon Bleu College of Culinary Arts:
Atlanta**
www.atlantaculinary.com
1927 Lakeside Parkway
Tucker, GA 30084
Fax: (773) 938-4571
Phone: (770) 938-4711

**Le Cordon Bleu College of Culinary Arts:
Austin**
www.chefs.edu/austin
Admissions
3110 Esperanza Crossing, Suite 100
Austin, TX 78758-3641
E-mail: info@austin.chefs.edu
Phone: (888) 553-2433

**Le Cordon Bleu College of Culinary Arts:
Chicago**
www.chefs.edu
Admissions
361 West Chestnut
Chicago, IL 60610-3050
Fax: (312) 798-2922
E-mail: mcalafiore@chicnet.org
Phone: (312) 873-2018

**Le Cordon Bleu College of Culinary Arts:
Los Angeles**
www.chefs.edu/los-angeles
530 East Colorado Boulevard
Pasadena, CA 91101
Fax: (626) 585-0486
E-mail: imarschikr@csca.edu
Phone: (626) 229-1300

**Le Cordon Bleu College of Culinary Arts:
Miami**
www.miamiculinary.com
3221 Enterprise Way
Miramar, FL 33025
Phone: (954) 438-8882

**Le Cordon Bleu College of Culinary Arts:
Minneapolis-St. Paul**
www.chefs.edu/Minneapolis-St-Paul
1315 Mendota Heights Road
Mendota Heights, MN 55120
Fax: (651) 452-5282
E-mail: info@msp.chefs.edu
Phone: (651) 675-4700

Le Cordon Bleu College of Culinary Arts: Scottsdale
www.scichefs.com
8100 East Camelback Road, Suite 1001
Scottsdale, AZ 85251
Fax: (480) 990-0351
E-mail: sciadmissions@scichefs.com
Phone: (480) 990-3773

Le Moyne College
www.lemoyne.edu
Admission Office
1419 Salt Springs Road
Syracuse, NY 13214-1301
Fax: (315) 445-4711
E-mail: admission@lemoyne.edu
Phone: (315) 445-4300

Lebanon College
www.lebanoncollege.edu
Admissions Office
15 Hanover Street
Lebanon, NH 03766
Fax: (603) 448-2491
E-mail: pbuskey@lebanoncollege.edu
Phone: (603) 448-2445 ext. 103

Lebanon Valley College
www.lvc.edu
Admission Office
101 North College Avenue
Annville, PA 17003-1400
Fax: (717) 867-6026
E-mail: kounlavo@lvc.edu
Phone: (717) 867-6181

L'Ecole Culinaire
www.lecoleculinaire.com
9811 South Outer Forty Drive
St. Louis, MO 63124

Lee College
www.lee.edu
Registrar
Box 818
Baytown, TX 77522
Fax: (281) 425-6831
E-mail: bgriffith@lee.edu
Phone: (281) 467-5611

Lee University
www.leeuniversity.edu
Office of Admissions
1120 North Ocoee Street
PO Box 3450
Cleveland, TN 37320-3450
Fax: (423) 614-8533
E-mail: admissions@leeuniversity.edu
Phone: (423) 614-8500

Lees-McRae College
www.lmc.edu
Admissions
Box 128
Banner Elk, NC 28604
Fax: (828) 898-8707
E-mail: weedm@lmc.edu
Phone: (828) 898-3432

Lehigh University
www.lehigh.edu
Admissions
27 Memorial Drive West
Bethlehem, PA 18015-3094
Fax: (610) 758-4361
E-mail: admissions@lehigh.edu
Phone: (610) 758-3100

LeMoyne-Owen College
www.loc.edu
Admissions
807 Walker Avenue
Memphis, TN 38126
Fax: (901) 435-1524
E-mail: june_chinn-jointer@loc.edu
Phone: (901) 435-1500

Lenoir-Rhyne University
www.lr.edu
Office of Enrollment Management
PO Box 7227
Hickory, NC 28603
Fax: (828) 328-7378
E-mail: admission@lr.edu
Phone: (800) 277-5721

Lesley University
www.lesley.edu
Director of Admissions
29 Everett Street
Cambridge, MA 02140-2790
Fax: (617) 349-8810
E-mail: dkocar@lesley.edu
Phone: (617) 349-8800

LeTourneau University
www.letu.edu
Admissions
PO Box 7001
Longview, TX 75607-7001
Fax: (903) 233-4301
E-mail: admissions@letu.edu
Phone: (800) 759-8811

Lewis & Clark College
www.lclark.edu
International Students Office
0615 SW Palatine Hill Road
Portland, OR 97219-7899
Fax: (503) 768-7301
E-mail: caldwell@lclark.edu
Phone: (503) 768-7304

Lewis University
www.lewisu.edu
International Student Services
One University Parkway
Unit #297
Romeoville, IL 60446-2200
Fax: (815) 836-5002
E-mail: maloneycl@lewisu.edu
Phone: (815) 838-0500

Lewis-Clark State College
www.lcsc.edu
International Admissions
500 Eighth Avenue
Lewiston, ID 83501-2698
Fax: (208) 792-2824
E-mail: ssdecker@lcsc.edu
Phone: (208) 792-2177

Lexington College
www.lexingtoncollege.edu
Director of Advising
310 South Peoria Street, Suite 512
Chicago, IL 60607-3534
Fax: (312) 226-6405
E-mail: ckustner@lexingtoncollege.edu
Phone: (312) 226-6294

Liberty University
www.liberty.edu
Office of International Admissions
1971 University Boulevard
Lynchburg, VA 24502
Fax: (434) 582-2424
E-mail: ejshin2@liberty.edu
Phone: (434) 592-4118

Life Pacific College
www.lifepacific.edu
Admissions
Attn: Admissions
1100 West Covina Boulevard
San Dimas, CA 91773
Fax: (909) 599-6690
E-mail: admissions@lifepacific.edu
Phone: (909) 599-5433 ext. 314

Life University
www.life.edu
New Student Development - International
1269 Barclay Circle
Marietta, GA 30060
Fax: (770) 426-2895
E-mail: wononvah@life.edu
Phone: (770) 426-2847

LIM College
www.limcollege.edu
Admissions Office
12 East 53rd Street
New York, NY 10022
Fax: (212) 421-4341
E-mail: aurmey@limcollege.edu
Phone: (800) 677-1323

Limestone College
www.limestone.edu
Admissions
1115 College Drive
Gaffney, SC 29340-3799
Fax: (864) 487-8706
E-mail: cphenicie@limestone.edu
Phone: (800) 795-7151 ext. 4554

Lincoln Christian University
www.lincolnchristian.edu
Admissions Office Manager
100 Campus View Drive
Lincoln, IL 62656-2111
Fax: (217) 732-4199
E-mail: admissions@lincolnchristian.edu
Phone: (217) 732-3168 ext. 2251

Lincoln College
www.lincolncollege.edu
Admissions
300 Keokuk Street
Lincoln, IL 62656
Fax: (217) 732-7715
E-mail: gbree@lincolncollege.edu
Phone: (800) 569-0556

**Lincoln College of New England:
Briarwood**
www.lincolncollegene.edu
Admissions
2279 Mount Vernon Road
Southington, CT 06489-1057
Fax: (860) 628-6444
E-mail: vbrennan@lincolncollegene.edu
Phone: (860) 628-4751 ext. 214

Lincoln College of New England: Suffield
www.lincolncollegene.edu
Admissions
1760 Mapleton Avenue
Suffield, CT 06078
Fax: (860) 668-7369
E-mail: areich@lincolncollegene.edu
Phone: (860) 668-3515 ext. 228

Lincoln Land Community College
www.llcc.edu
Special Admissions
5250 Shepherd Road
Box 19256
Springfield, IL 62794-9256
Fax: (217) 786-2492
E-mail: ron.gregoire@llcc.cc.il.us
Phone: (217) 786-2296

Lincoln Memorial University
www.lmunet.edu
6965 Cumberland Gap Parkway
Harrogate, TN 37752-1901
Fax: (423) 869-6444
E-mail: admissions@lmunet.edu
Phone: (423) 869-6280

Lincoln University
www.lincolnuca.edu
Admissions
401 15th Street
Oakland, CA 94612
Fax: (510) 628-8012
E-mail: peggyau@lincolnuca.edu
Phone: (510) 628-8010

Lincoln University
www.lincolnu.edu
Admissions
820 Chestnut Street, B7 Young Hall
Jefferson City, MO 65102-0029
Fax: (573) 681-5889
E-mail: kosherm@lincolnu.edu
Phone: (573) 681-5599

Lincoln University
www.lincoln.edu
International Programs and Services
1570 Baltimore Pike
PO Box 179
Lincoln University, PA 19352-0999
Fax: (484) 365-7822
E-mail: clundy@lincoln.edu
Phone: (484) 365-7785

Lindenwood University
www.lindenwood.edu/
International Admissions
209 South Kingshighway
St. Charles, MO 63301
Fax: (636) 949-4108
E-mail: international@lindenwood.edu
Phone: (636) 949-4982

Lindsey Wilson College
www.lindsey.edu
Office Manager/Admissions Counselor
210 Lindsey Wilson Street
Columbia, KY 42728
Fax: (270) 384-8060
E-mail: talleyd@lindsey.edu
Phone: (270) 384-8236

Linfield College
www.linfield.edu
Admission Office
900 Southeast Baker Street
McMinnville, OR 97128-3725
Fax: (503) 883-2472
E-mail: admission@linfield.edu
Phone: (503) 883-2213

Linn State Technical College
www.linnstate.edu
Office of Admissions
One Technology Drive
Linn, MO 65051
Fax: (573) 897-5026
E-mail: becca.mehmert@linnstate.edu
Phone: (573) 897-5153

Linn-Benton Community College
www.linnbenton.edu
Admissions
6500 SW Pacific Boulevard
Albany, OR 97321-3779
Fax: (541) 917-4868
E-mail: admissions@linnbenton.edu
Phone: (541) 917-4811

Lipscomb University
www.lipscomb.edu
Office of Transfer and International Students
One University Park Drive
Nashville, TN 37204-3951
Fax: (615) 966-1804
E-mail: sylvia.braden@lipscomb.edu
Phone: (615) 966-6151

Little Big Horn College
www.lbhc.edu
Box 370
Crow Agency, MT 59022
Fax: (406) 638-3169
E-mail: tina@lbhc.cc.mt.us
Phone: (406) 638-3116

Livingstone College
www.livingstone.edu
Admissions
701 West Monroe Street
Salisbury, NC 28144-5213
Fax: (704) 216-6215
E-mail: admissions@livingstone.edu
Phone: (704) 216-6001

Lock Haven University of Pennsylvania
www.lhup.edu
Admissions
LHU Office of Admissions
Lock Haven, PA 17745
Fax: (570) 484-2201
E-mail: admissions@lhup.edu
Phone: (570) 484-2027

Loma Linda University
www.llu.edu
International Student and Scholar Services
Admissions Processing
Loma Linda University
Loma Linda, CA 92350
Fax: (909) 558-4879
E-mail: intlstdsrv@llu.edu
Phone: (909) 558-4955

Lon Morris College
www.lonmorris.edu
Admission
800 College Avenue
Jacksonville, TX 75766
Fax: (903) 589-4033
E-mail: jchiles@lonmorris.edu
Phone: (903) 589-4063

Lone Star College System
www.lonestar.edu/
Admissions Office
5000 Research Forest Drive
The Woodlands, TX 77381-4356
Phone: (832) 813-6500

Long Beach City College
www.lbcc.edu
International Student Program
4901 East Carson Street
Mail Code R6
Long Beach, CA 90808
Fax: (562) 938-4747
E-mail: international_staff@lbcc.edu
Phone: (562) 938-4745

Long Island Business Institute
www.libi.edu
Admissions
136-18 39th Avenue, 5th Floor
Flushing, NY 11354
Fax: (718) 939-9235
E-mail: wchong@libi.edu
Phone: (718) 939-5100

Long Island University: Brooklyn Campus
www.liu.edu
Office of Admissions
1 University Plaza
Office of Admissions
Brooklyn, NY 11201-8423
Fax: (718) 797-2399
E-mail: admissions@brooklyn.liu.edu
Phone: (718) 488-1011

Long Island University: C. W. Post Campus
www.liu.edu
Admissions
720 Northern Boulevard
Brookville, NY 11548-1300
Fax: (516) 299-2137
E-mail: enroll@cwpost.liu.edu
Phone: (516) 299-2637

Longwood University
www.longwood.edu
Admissions Office
201 High Street
Farmville, VA 23909-1898
Fax: (434) 395-2332
E-mail: admissions@longwood.edu
Phone: (434) 395-2060

Lorain County Community College
www.lorainccc.edu
International Recruitment and Support
Services
1005 Abbe Road North
Elyria, OH 44035-1691
Fax: (440) 366-4167
E-mail: darredon@lorainccc.edu
Phone: (440) 366-4794

Loras College
www.loras.edu
Admissions Office
1450 Alta Vista Street
Dubuque, IA 52004-0178
Fax: (563) 588-7119
E-mail: barb.harrington@loras.edu
Phone: (563) 588-4915

Los Angeles City College
www.lacitycollege.edu
International Student Center
855 North Vermont Avenue
Los Angeles, CA 90029-3589
Fax: (323) 953-4013
E-mail: bradyr@lacitycollege.edu
Phone: (323) 953-4000 ext. 2470

Los Angeles Harbor College
www.lahc.edu
International Student Office
1111 Figueroa Place
Wilmington, CA 90744-2397
Fax: (310) 233-4223
E-mail: gradyp@lahc.edu
Phone: (310) 233-4112

Los Angeles Mission College
www.lamission.edu
Counseling Office
13356 Eldridge Avenue
Sylmar, CA 91342-3245
Fax: (818) 365-3623
Phone: (818) 364-7600

Los Angeles Pierce College
www.piercecollege.edu
Evaluation Tech/DSO, International
Admissions
6201 Winnetka Avenue
Woodland Hills, CA 91371
Fax: (818) 347-8704
E-mail: intlstu@piercecollege.edu
Phone: (818) 710-2511

Los Angeles Southwest College
www.lasc.edu
1600 West Imperial Highway
Los Angeles, CA 90047-4899
Phone: (323) 241-5321

Los Angeles Trade and Technical College
www.lattc.edu
International Students Program Coordinator/
DSO
400 West Washington Boulevard
Los Angeles, CA 90015-4181
Fax: (213) 286-5386
E-mail: SandicAC@lattc.edu
Phone: (213) 763-5327

Los Angeles Valley College
www.lavc.edu
International Students Coordinator
5800 Fulton Avenue
Valley Glen, CA 91401-4096
Fax: (818) 778-5519
E-mail: dunnae@lavc.edu
Phone: (818) 778-5518

Los Medanos College
www.losmedanos.edu
International Students Admissions
2700 East Leland Road
Pittsburg, CA 94565
Fax: (925) 427-6351
E-mail: mherste@losmedanos.edu
Phone: (925) 439-2181

Louisburg College
www.louisburg.edu
Admissions
501 North Main Street
Louisburg, NC 27549
Fax: (919) 496-1788
E-mail: stolbert@louisburg.edu
Phone: (919) 497-3244

Louisiana College
www.lacollege.edu
Admissions
LC Box 566
Pineville, LA 71359
Fax: (318) 487-7550
E-mail: admissions@lacollege.edu
Phone: (318) 487-7259

Louisiana State University and Agricultural and Mechanical College
www.lsu.edu
Undergraduate Admissions
1146 Pleasant Halll
Baton Rouge, LA 70803-2750
Fax: (225) 578-4433
E-mail: admissions@lsu.edu
Phone: (225) 578-1175

Louisiana State University at Eunice
www.lsue.edu
Registrar
Box 1129
Eunice, LA 70535
Fax: (337) 550-1306
E-mail: bwilliam@lsue.edu
Phone: (337) 550-1302

Louisiana State University Health Sciences Center
www.lsuhsc.edu
433 Bolivar Street
New Orleans, LA 70112-2223
Phone: (504) 568-4808

Louisiana State University in Shreveport
www.lsus.edu
Data Management Coordinator
One University Place
Shreveport, LA 71115-2399
Fax: (318) 797-5286
E-mail: darlena.atkins@lsus.edu
Phone: (318) 797-5063

Louisiana Tech University
www.latech.edu
Office of Admissions
Box 3178
Ruston, LA 71272
Fax: (318) 257-2499
E-mail: usjba@vm.cc.latech.edu
Phone: (318) 257-3036

Lourdes College
www.lourdes.edu
Admissions
6832 Convent Boulevard
Sylvania, OH 43560-2898
Fax: (419) 824-3916
E-mail: AdmissionsLCAdmits@lourdes.edu
Phone: (419) 824-3677

Lower Columbia College
www.lowercolumbia.edu
International Student Admissions Office
1600 Maple Street
Box 3010
Longview, WA 98632-0310
Fax: (360) 442-2379
E-mail: sstonge@lowercolumbia.edu
Phone: (360) 442-2300

Loyola Marymount University
www.lmu.edu
Director of International Outreach
Admissions, One LMU Drive
Xavier Hall 100
Los Angeles, CA 90045-8350
Fax: (310) 338-2797
E-mail: csamay@lmu.edu
Phone: (310) 258-5478

Loyola University Chicago
www.luc.edu
Office of Undergraduate Admission
820 North Michigan Avenue
Chicago, IL 60611-9810
Fax: (773) 508-8926
E-mail: mdevilliers@luc.edu
Phone: (773) 508-7349

Loyola University Maryland
www.loyola.edu
Admissions
4501 North Charles Street
Baltimore, MD 21210-2699
Fax: (410) 617-2176
E-mail: alfollensbee@loyola.edu
Phone: (800) 221-9107 ext. 2569

Loyola University New Orleans
www.loyno.edu/
Director of Undergraduate Admissions
6363 St. Charles Avenue
Campus Box 18
New Orleans, LA 70118-6195
Fax: (504) 865-3383
E-mail: admit@loyno.edu
Phone: (504) 865-3240

Lubbock Christian University
www.lcu.edu
Admissions Office
5601 19th Street
Lubbock, TX 79407-2099
Fax: (806) 720-7162
E-mail: shelley.parnell@lcu.edu
Phone: (806) 720-7160

Luna Community College
www.luna.edu
366 Luna Drive
Las Vegas, NM 87701
E-mail: tmares@luna.edu
Phone: (505) 454-2550

Luther College
www.luther.edu
Director of International Recruiting
700 College Drive
Decorah, IA 52101-1042
Fax: (563) 387-2159
E-mail: lundjon@luther.edu
Phone: (563) 387-1428

Luther Rice University
www.lru.edu
3038 Evans Mill Road
Lithonia, GA 30038
E-mail: admissions@lru.edu

Lycoming College
www.lycoming.edu
Admissions Office
700 College Place
Williamsport, PA 17701
Fax: (570) 321-4317
E-mail: admissions@lycoming.edu
Phone: (570) 321-4026

Lyme Academy College of Fine Arts
www.lymeacademy.edu
Assistant Dean of Admissions
84 Lyme Street
Old Lyme, CT 06371
Fax: (860) 434-8725
E-mail: Schurchill@lymeacademy.edu
Phone: (860) 434-3571 ext. 120

Lynchburg College
www.lynchburg.edu
Admissions
1501 Lakeside Drive
Lynchburg, VA 24501-3199
Fax: (434) 544-8653
E-mail: admissions@lynchburg.edu
Phone: (800) 426-8101 ext. 8300

Lyndon State College
www.lyndonstate.edu
Office of Admissions
1001 College Road
PO Box 919
Lyndonville, VT 05851
Fax: (802) 626-4848
E-mail: trevor.barski@lyndonstate.edu
Phone: (800) 225-1998

Lynn University
www.lynn.edu
Admissions
3601 North Military Trail
Boca Raton, FL 33431-5598
Fax: (561) 237-7100
E-mail: admission@lynn.edu
Phone: (561) 237-7900

Lyon College
www.lyon.edu
Enrollment Services
PO Box 2317
Batesville, AR 72503-2317
Fax: (870) 307-7250
E-mail: admissions@lyon.edu
Phone: (800) 423-2542

Macalester College
www.macalester.edu
Admissions
1600 Grand Avenue
St. Paul, MN 55105-1899
Fax: (651) 696-6724
E-mail: admissions@macalester.edu
Phone: (651) 696-6357

MacCormac College
www.maccormac.edu
Registrar's Office
29 East Madison Street
Chicago, IL 60602
Fax: (312) 922-4286
E-mail: msilva@maccormac.edu
Phone: (312) 922-1884 ext. 203

Machzikei Hadath Rabbinical College
5407 16th Avenue
Brooklyn, NY 11204
Fax: (718) 851-1265
Phone: (718) 854-8777 ext. 23

MacMurray College
www.mac.edu
Admissions
447 East College Avenue
Jacksonville, IL 62650-2590
Fax: (217) 291-0702
E-mail: admissions@mac.edu
Phone: (217) 479-7056

Macomb Community College
www.macomb.edu
South Campus - G301
14500 East Twelve Mile Road
Warren, MI 48088-3896
Fax: (586) 445-7140
E-mail: hughesr@macomb.cc.mi.us
Phone: (586) 445-7183

Madison Area Technical College
www.matcmadison.edu
3350 Anderson Street
Madison, WI 53704-2599
Fax: (608) 258-2329
Phone: (608) 246-6205

Madonna University
www.madonna.edu
International Students Office
36600 Schoolcraft Road
Livonia, MI 48150-1176
Fax: (734) 432-5393
E-mail: gphilson@madonna.edu
Phone: (734) 432-5791

Magdalen College
www.magdalen.edu
Admissions
511 Kearsarge Mountain Road
Warner, NH 03278
Fax: (603) 456-2660
E-mail: admissions@magdalen.edu
Phone: (603) 456-2656

Maharishi University of Management
www.mum.edu
Office for International Student Admissions
Office of Admissions
1000 North Fourth Street
Fairfield, IA 52557
Fax: (641) 472-1179
E-mail: intadmiss@mum.edu
Phone: (641) 472-1110

Maine College of Art
www.meca.edu
Admissions
522 Congress Street
Portland, ME 04101
Fax: (207) 699-5080
E-mail: scote@meca.edu
Phone: (207) 699-5023

Maine Maritime Academy
www.mainemaritime.edu
Admissions Office
Pleasant Street
Castine, ME 04420
Fax: (207) 326-2515
E-mail: admissions@mma.edu
Phone: (207) 326-2206

Malone University
www.malone.edu
Admissions
2600 Cleveland Avenue NW
Canton, OH 44709-3897
Fax: (330) 471-8149
E-mail: rsampsel@malone.edu
Phone: (330) 471-8100 ext. 8355

Manchester College
www.manchester.edu
Success Center
604 East College Avenue
North Manchester, IN 46962-0365
Fax: (260) 982-5408
E-mail: SKBendsen@manchester.edu
Phone: (260) 982-5888

Manchester Community College
www.mcc.commnet.edu
Great Path PO Box 1046, MS 12
Manchester, CT 06040-1046
Fax: (860) 512-3221
E-mail: jmesquita@mcc.commnet.edu
Phone: (860) 512-3205

Manchester Community College
www.manchestercommunitycollege.edu
Admissions Department
1066 Front Street
Manchester, NH 03102-8518
Fax: (603) 668-5354
E-mail: lbaia@ccsnh.edu
Phone: (603) 668-6706 ext. 208

Manhattan Area Technical College
www.matc.net
Director of Admissions
3136 Dickens Avenue
Manhattan, KS 66503-2499
Fax: (785) 587-28l04
E-mail: rsmith@matc.net
Phone: (785) 587-2800 ext. 104

Manhattan College
www.manhattan.edu
International Student Advisor
4513 Manhattan College Parkway
Riverdale, NY 10471
Fax: (718) 862-8019
E-mail: admit@manhattan.edu
Phone: (718) 862-7200

Manhattan School of Music
www.msmnyc.edu
Admission and Financial Aid
120 Claremont Avenue
New York, NY 10027-4698
Fax: (212) 749-3025
E-mail: admission@msmnyc.edu
Phone: (212) 749-2802 ext. 4501

Manhattanville College
www.manhattanville.edu
Admissions
2900 Purchase Street
Purchase, NY 10577
Fax: (914) 694-1732
E-mail: admissions@mville.edu
Phone: (914) 323-5464

Mannes College The New School for Music
www.mannes.edu
Admissions
150 West 85th Street
New York, NY 10024
Fax: (212) 580-1738
E-mail: mannesadmissions@newschool.edu
Phone: (212) 580-0210 ext. 4862

Manor College
www.manor.edu
Full-Time Admissions
700 Fox Chase Road
Jenkintown, PA 19046-3319
Fax: (215) 576-6564
E-mail: ftadmiss@mail.manor.edu
Phone: (215) 884-2216 ext. 206

Mansfield University of Pennsylvania
www.mansfield.edu
Admissions Office
South Hall
Mansfield, PA 16933
Fax: (570) 662-4121
E-mail: tsoderbe@mansfield.edu
Phone: (570) 662-4243

Maranatha Baptist Bible College
www.mbbc.edu
Admissions Office
745 West Main Street
Watertown, WI 53094
Fax: (920) 261-9109
E-mail: admissions@mbbc.edu
Phone: (920) 261-9300

Marian Court College
www.mariancourt.edu
Admissions
35 Little's Point Road
Swampscott, MA 01907-2896
Fax: (781) 309-5286
E-mail: bboppert@mariancourt.edu
Phone: (781) 309-5200

Marian University
www.marian.edu
Office of Admission
3200 Cold Spring Road
Indianapolis, IN 46222-1997
Fax: (317) 955-6401
E-mail: cstoughton@marian.edu
Phone: (317) 955-6326

Marian University
www.marianuniversity.edu
Admissions
45 South National Avenue
Fond du Lac, WI 54935-4699
Fax: (920) 923-8755
E-mail: jhartzell@marianuniversity.edu
Phone: (920) 923-8117

Marietta College
www.marietta.edu
Office of Admission
215 Fifth Street
Marietta, OH 45750-4005
Fax: (740) 376-8888
E-mail: tara.hildt@marietta.edu
Phone: (800) 331-7896

Marion Military Institute
www.marionmilitary.edu
Admissions
1101 Washington Street
Marion, AL 36756-0420
Fax: (334) 683-2383
E-mail: divey@marionmilitary.edu
Phone: (800) 664-1842

Marist College
www.marist.edu
Undergraduate Admission
3399 North Road
Poughkeepsie, NY 12601-1387
Fax: (845) 575-3215
E-mail: admission@marist.edu
Phone: (845) 575-3226

Marlboro College
www.marlboro.edu
Admissions
PO Box A
2582 South Road
Marlboro, VT 05344-0300
Fax: (802) 451-7555
E-mail: admissions@marlboro.edu
Phone: (800) 343-0049

Marquette University
www.marquette.edu
Office of International Education
PO Box 1881
Milwaukee, WI 53201-1881
Fax: (414) 288-3701
E-mail: ellen.blauw@marquette.edu
Phone: (414) 288-7289

Mars Hill College
www.mhc.edu
Admissions
Blackwell Hall, Box 370
Mars Hill, NC 28754
Fax: (828) 689-1473
E-mail: kvance@mhc.edu
Phone: (828) 689-1353

Marshall University
www.marshall.edu
Graduate/International Admissions
One John Marshall Drive
Huntington, WV 25755
Fax: (304) 696-3135
E-mail: admissions@marshall.edu
Phone: (304) 696-7250

Marshalltown Community College
www.iavalley.edu/mcc/
Carole Permar
3700 South Center Street
Marshalltown, IA 50158
Fax: (641) 752-8149
Phone: (641) 752-7106

Martin Community College
www.martincc.edu
1161 Kehukee Park Road
Williamston, NC 27892-9988
Fax: (252) 792-0826
E-mail: jbussell@martincc.edu
Phone: (252) 792-1521 ext. 268

Mary Baldwin College
www.mbc.edu
Spencer Center Civic & Global Engagement
Office of Admissions
Box 1500
Staunton, VA 24401
Fax: (540) 887-7185
E-mail: hward@mbc.edu
Phone: (540) 887-7113

Marygrove College
www.marygrove.edu
Office of Undergraduate Admissions
8425 West McNichols Road
Detroit, MI 48221
Fax: (313) 927-1399
E-mail: info@marygrove.edu
Phone: (313) 927-1240

Maryland Institute College of Art
www.mica.edu
International Admissions
1300 Mount Royal Avenue
Baltimore, MD 21217-4134
Fax: (410) 225-2337
E-mail: mlynn@mica.edu
Phone: (410) 225-2222

Marylhurst University
www.marylhurst.edu
Admissions Office
PO Box 261
Marylhurst, OR 97036-0261
Fax: (503) 636-9526
E-mail: bjones@marylhurst.edu
Phone: (800) 634-9982 ext. 3321

Marymount College
www.marymountpv.edu
Office of Admission
30800 Palos Verdes Drive East
Rancho Palos Verdes, CA 90275-6299
Fax: (310) 265-0962
E-mail: admissions@marymountpv.edu
Phone: (310) 377-5501 ext. 211

Marymount Manhattan College
www.mmm.edu
Admissions Office
221 East 71st Street
New York, NY 10021-4597
Fax: (212) 517-0541
E-mail: odakaj@mmm.edu
Phone: (212) 517-0436

Marymount University
www.marymount.edu
Office of Admissions
2807 North Glebe Road
Arlington, VA 22207-4299
Fax: (703) 522-0349
E-mail:
international.admissions@marymount.edu
Phone: (703) 284-1500

Maryville College
www.maryvillecollege.edu
International Services
502 East Lamar Alexander Parkway
Maryville, TN 37804-5907
Fax: (865) 981-8010
E-mail: micki.pruitt@maryvillecollege.edu
Phone: (865) 981-8186

Maryville University of Saint Louis
www.maryville.edu
Office of Admissions
650 Maryville University Drive
St. Louis, MO 63141-7299
Fax: (314) 529-9927
E-mail:
internationaladmissions@maryville.edu
Phone: (314) 529-9350 ext. 6857

Marywood University
www.marywood.edu
Office of University Admissions
2300 Adams Avenue
Scranton, PA 18509-1598
Fax: (570) 961-4763
E-mail: digregorio@marywood.edu
Phone: (570) 348-6234 ext. 2434

Massachusetts Bay Community College
www.massbay.edu
Admissions
50 Oakland Street
Wellesley Hills, MA 02481
Fax: (781) 239-2525
E-mail: info@massbay.edu
Phone: (781) 239-2500

Massachusetts College of Art and Design
www.massart.edu
Admissions
621 Huntington Avenue
Boston, MA 02115-5882
Fax: (617) 879-7250
E-mail: admissions@massart.edu
Phone: (617) 879-7222

Massachusetts College of Liberal Arts
www.mcla.edu
Office of Admission
375 Church Street
North Adams, MA 01247
Fax: (413) 662-5179
E-mail: admissions@mcla.edu
Phone: (413) 662-5410

**Massachusetts College of Pharmacy and
Health Sciences**
www.mcphs.edu
Director of Undergraduate and International
Recruitment
179 Longwood Avenue
Boston, MA 02115-5896
Fax: (617) 732-2118
E-mail: Rene.cabrera@mcphs.edu
Phone: (617) 879-5974

Massachusetts Institute of Technology
web.mit.edu
Undergraduate Admissions
77 Massachusetts Avenue, Room 3-108
Cambridge, MA 02139-4307
Fax: (617) 258-8304
E-mail: mitintl@mit.edu
Phone: (617) 253-3400

Massachusetts Maritime Academy
www.maritime.edu
101 Academy Drive
Blinn Hall
Buzzards Bay, MA 02532-1803
Fax: (508) 830-5077
E-mail: admissions@maritime.edu
Phone: (800) 544-3400

Massasoit Community College
www.massasoit.mass.edu
Admissions Counselor
One Massasoit Boulevard
Brockton, MA 02302-3996
Fax: (508) 427-1255
E-mail: edesatnick@massasoit.mass.edu
Phone: (508) 588-9100 ext. 1422

The Master's College
www.masters.edu
International Student Office
21726 Placerita Canyon Road
Santa Clarita, CA 91321-1200
Fax: (661) 254-6232
E-mail: jmelcon@masters.edu
Phone: (661) 259-3540 ext. 3375

Mayland Community College
www.mayland.edu
Registrar's Office
Box 547
Spruce Pine, NC 28777
Fax: (828) 765-0728
Phone: (828) 765-7351

Mayville State University
www.mayvillestate.edu
Admissions and Extended Learning
330 Third Street, NE
Mayville, ND 58257-1299
Fax: (701) 788-4748
E-mail: misti.wuori@mayvillestate.edu
Phone: (701) 788-4631

**McCann School of Business and
Technology: Dickson City**
www.mccann.edu
2227 Scranton Carbondale Highway
Dickson City, PA 18519
Phone: (570) 307-2000

**McCann School of Business and
Technology: Pottsville**
www.mccann.edu
2650 Woodglen Road
Pottsville, PA 17901
Fax: (570) 622-7770
Phone: (570) 622-7622

**McCann School of Business and
Technology: Sunbury**
www.mccann.edu
1147 North 4th Street
Sunbury, PA 17801
E-mail: lisa.davis@mccann.edu
Phone: (570) 286-3058

McDaniel College
www.mcdaniel.edu
Office of Admissions
Two College Hill
Westminster, MD 21157-4390
Fax: (410) 857-2757
E-mail: sdesantis@mcdaniel.edu
Phone: (410) 857-2230

McDowell Technical Community College
www.mcdowelltech.edu
Admissions
54 College Drive
Marion, NC 28752
Fax: (828) 652-1014
E-mail: rickw@mcdowelltech.edu
Phone: (828) 652-0632

McHenry County College
www.mchenry.edu
New Student Enrollment
8900 US Highway 14
Crystal Lake, IL 60012-2738
Fax: (815) 455-3766
E-mail: akarman@mchenry.edu
Phone: (815) 479-7782

McKendree University
www.mckendree.edu
Admission
701 College Road
Lebanon, IL 62254
Fax: (618) 537-6496
E-mail: jlblasdel@mckendree.edu
Phone: (618) 537-6836

McLennan Community College
www.mclennan.edu
1400 College Drive
Waco, TX 76708
Fax: (254) 299-8694
Phone: (254) 299-8628

McMurry University
www.mcm.edu
Admission
South 14th and Sayles Boulevard
McMurry Station, Box 278
Abilene, TX 79697-0001
Fax: (325) 793-4701
E-mail: admissions@mcm.edu
Phone: (325) 793-4700

McNeese State University
www.mcneese.edu
International Student Affairs
MSU Box 91740
Lake Charles, LA 70609-1740
Fax: (337) 562-4238
E-mail: intinfo@mcneese.edu
Phone: (337) 475-5962

McPherson College
www.mcpherson.edu
Admissions
1600 East Euclid Street
Box 1402
McPherson, KS 67460-1402
Fax: (620) 241-8443
E-mail: admiss@mcpherson.edu
Phone: (620) 242-0400

Medaille College
www.medaille.edu
Admissions
18 Agassiz Circle
Buffalo, NY 14214
Fax: (716) 632-1811
E-mail: jmatheny@medaille.edu
Phone: (716) 631-1061 ext. 2541

Medaille College: Amherst
www.medaille.edu
30 Wilson Road
Centerpointe Corporate Park
Williamsville, NY 14221
E-mail: sageadmissions@medaille.edu
Phone: (716) 631-1061

Medaille College: Rochester
www.medaille.edu
1880 South Winton Road
Rochester, NY 14618
E-mail: sageadmissions@medaille.edu
Phone: (585) 272-0030

Memphis College of Art
www.mca.edu
Admissions
1930 Poplar Avenue
Overton Park
Memphis, TN 38104-2764
Fax: (901) 272-5158
E-mail: info@mca.edu
Phone: (901) 272-5151

Menlo College
www.menlo.edu
Office of Admissions
1000 El Camino Real
Atherton, CA 94027
Fax: (650) 543-4496
E-mail: bwilms@menlo.edu
Phone: (650) 543-3812

Mercer County Community College
www.mccc.edu
International Students Coordinator
Box B
Trenton, NJ 08690-1099
Fax: (609) 570-3861
E-mail: bambhrol@mccc.edu
Phone: (609) 570-3438

Mercer University
www.mercer.edu
Admissions
1400 Coleman Avenue
Macon, GA 31207-0001
Fax: (478) 301-2828
E-mail: tatum_cr@mercer.edu
Phone: (478) 301-2653

Mercy College
www.mercy.edu
International Student Office
555 Broadway
Dobbs Ferry, NY 10522
Fax: (914) 693-9455
E-mail: jkondratowicz@mercy.edu
Phone: (914) 674-7588

Mercyhurst College
www.mercyhurst.edu
International House
501 East 38th Street
Erie, PA 16546-0001
Fax: (814) 824-2071
E-mail: eevans@mercyhurst.edu
Phone: (814) 824-2478

Meredith College
www.meredith.edu
Office of Admissions
3800 Hillsborough Street
Raleigh, NC 27607-5298
Fax: (919) 760-2348
E-mail: admissions@meredith.edu
Phone: (919) 760-8581

Meridian Community College
www.meridiancc.edu
Admissions
910 Highway 19 North
Meridian, MS 39307-5890
Fax: (601) 484-8838
E-mail: apayne@meridiancc.edu
Phone: (601) 481-1357

Merrimack College
www.merrimack.edu
Admissions
315 Turnpike Street
North Andover, MA 01845
Fax: (978) 837-5133
E-mail: admission@merrimack.edu
Phone: (978) 837-5000 ext. 5100

Merritt College
www.merritt.edu
International Specialist, International Affairs
& Distance Education
12500 Campus Drive
Oakland, CA 94619
Fax: (510) 436-2512
E-mail: dgephart@Peralta.edu
Phone: (510) 587-7834

Mesa Community College
www.mesacc.edu
International Education
1833 West Southern Avenue
Mesa, AZ 85202
Fax: (480) 461-7805
E-mail: shereen.lerner@mcmail.maricopa.edu
Phone: (480) 461-7306

Mesa State College
www.mesastate.edu
Director of Admissions
1100 North Avenue
Grand Junction, CO 81501
Fax: (970) 248-1973
E-mail: intladmissions@mesastate.edu
Phone: (970) 248-1613

Mesabi Range Community and Technical College
www.mesabirange.edu
Enrollment Services
1001 Chestnut Street West
Virginia, MN 55792-3448
Fax: (218) 749-0318
E-mail: s.twaddle@mr.mnscu.edu
Phone: (218) 749-0313

Mesalands Community College
www.mesalands.edu
911 South Tenth Street
Tucumcari, NM 88401
Phone: (575) 461-4413

Mesivta Torah Vodaath Seminary
425 East Ninth Street
Brooklyn, NY 11218
Phone: (718) 941-8000

Messiah College
www.messiah.edu
Admissions
PO Box 3005
One College Avenue
Grantham, PA 17027-0800
Fax: (717) 691-2307
E-mail: cblount@messiah.edu
Phone: (717) 691-6000

Methodist University
www.methodist.edu
Director of International Programs
5400 Ramsey Street
Fayetteville, NC 28311-1498
Fax: (910) 630-7672
E-mail: bvamasiri@methodist.edu
Phone: (910) 630-7225

Metro Business College: Rolla
www.metrobusinesscollege.edu
1202 East Highway 72
Rolla, MO 65401
Fax: (573) 364-8077
E-mail: dana@metrobusinesscollege.edu
Phone: (573) 364-8464

Metropolitan Career Center Computer Technology Institute
www.careersinit.org
100 South Broad Street, Suite 830
Philadelphia, PA 19110
Fax: (215) 568-3511
E-mail: jmannino@mccworks.org
Phone: (215) 568-9215

Metropolitan College of New York
www.metropolitan.edu
431 Canal Street
New York, NY 10013-1919
Fax: (212) 343-8470
E-mail: pramos@mcny.edu
Phone: (212) 343-1234 ext. 2705

Metropolitan Community College
www.mccneb.edu
Associate Vice President for Student Affairs
Box 3777
Omaha, NE 68103-0777
Fax: (402) 457-2238
E-mail: plewisrodriguez@mccneb.edu
Phone: (402) 457-2430

Metropolitan Community College: Blue River
www.mcckc.edu
Associate Dean of Students
3200 Broadway Boulevard
Kansas City, MO 64111-2429
Fax: (816) 759-4478
E-mail: carroll.oneal@mcckc.edu
Phone: (816) 604-4101

Metropolitan Community College: Business & Technology
www.mcckc.edu
Associate Dean of Students
1775 Universal Avenue
Kansas City, MO 64120-2429
Fax: (816) 759-4478
E-mail: carroll.oneal@mcckc.edu
Phone: (816) 604-4101

Metropolitan Community College: Longview
www.mcckc.edu
Associate Dean of Students
500 Longview Road
Lee's Summit, MO 64081-2105
Fax: (816) 672-2040
E-mail: carroll.oneal@mcckc.edu
Phone: (816) 604-2249

Metropolitan Community College: Maple Woods
www.mcckc.edu
Associate Dean of Students
2601 NE Barry Road
Kansas City, MO 64156-1299
Fax: (816) 759-4103
E-mail: carroll.oneal@kcmetro.edu
Phone: (816) 759-4339

Metropolitan Community College: Penn Valley
www.mcckc.edu
Office of Student Services
3201 Southwest Trafficway
Kansas City, MO 64111-2429
Fax: (816) 759-4478
E-mail: Bobbie.Gustin@mcckc.edu
Phone: (816) 604-4339

Metropolitan State College of Denver
www.mscd.edu
Admission
Campus Box 16
Box 173362
Denver, CO 80217
Fax: (303) 556-6345
E-mail: gomezr@mscd.edu
Phone: (303) 556-3066

Miami Dade College
www.mdc.edu/main
International Student Services
11011 SW 104th Street
Miami, FL 33176-3393
Fax: (305) 237-2586
E-mail: fgiol@mdc.edu
Phone: (305) 237-2363

Miami International University of Art and Design
www.mymiu.edu
Senior Director of Admissions
1501 Biscayne Boulevard, Suite 100
Miami, FL 33132-1418
Fax: (305) 374-7946
E-mail: kryan@aii.edu
Phone: (305) 428-5600

Miami University: Hamilton
www.ham.muohio.edu
Office of Admission
1601 University Boulevard
Hamilton, OH 45011-3399
Fax: (513) 785-1807
E-mail: leeje1@muohio.edu
Phone: (513) 785-3111

Miami University: Middletown
www.mid.muohio.edu
4200 East University Boulevard
Middletown, OH 45042
Fax: (513) 727-3223
E-mail: mlflynn@muohio.edu
Phone: (513) 727-3216

Miami University: Oxford
www.muohio.edu
Assistant Director of Admission for International Recruitment
301 South Campus Avenue
Oxford, OH 45056
Fax: (513) 529-1550
E-mail: ann.rahmat@muohio.edu
Phone: (513) 529-2288

Michigan Jewish Institute
www.mji.edu
Student Affairs
6890 West Maple Road
West Bloomfield, MI 48322
Fax: (248) 414-6907
E-mail: plevine@mji.edu
Phone: (248) 414-6900 ext. 106

Michigan State University
www.msu.edu
International Students and Scholars
250 Administration Building
East Lansing, MI 48824
Fax: (517) 355-4657
E-mail: inhadms@msu.edu
Phone: (517) 353-1720

Michigan Technological University
www.mtu.edu
International Programs and Services
1400 Townsend Drive
Houghton, MI 49931-1295
Fax: (906) 487-1891
E-mail: rhyy@mtu.edu
Phone: (906) 487-2160

Mid-America College of Funeral Service
www.mid-america.edu
3111 Hamburg Pike
Jeffersonville, IN 47130
Fax: (812) 288-5942
E-mail: macfs@mindspring.com
Phone: (812) 288-8878

Mid-Atlantic Christian University
www.macuniversity.edu
Registrar
715 North Poindexter Street
Elizabeth City, NC 27909
Fax: (252) 334-2071
E-mail: joan.sawyer@macuniversity.edu
Phone: (252) 334-2012

Mid-Continent University
www.midcontinent.edu
Associate Dean for Student Life/Admissions/Orientation
99 Powell Road East
Mayfield, KY 42066-9007
Fax: (270) 247-3115
E-mail: khatton@midcontinent.edu
Phone: (270) 247-8521 ext. 312

Mid-Plains Community College Area
www.mpcc.edu
Student Advising
1101 Halligan Drive
North Platte, NE 69101
Fax: (308) 535-3710
E-mail: mihels@mpcc.edu
Phone: (800) 658-4308 ext. 3710

MidAmerica Nazarene University
www.mnu.edu
Admissions Office
2030 East College Way
Olathe, KS 66062-1899
Fax: (913) 971-3410
E-mail: dmiller@mnu.edu
Phone: (913) 971-3785

Middle Georgia College
www.mgc.edu
Admissions
1100 Second Street SE
Cochran, GA 31014
Fax: (478) 934-3403
E-mail: ltravis@mgc.edu
Phone: (478) 934-3136

Middle Georgia Technical College
www.middlegatech.edu
Admissions
80 Cohen Walker Drive
Warner Robins, GA 31088
Fax: (478) 988-6947
E-mail: dwebb@middlegatech.edu
Phone: (478) 988-6800 ext. 4023

Middle Tennessee State University
www.mtsu.edu
International Programs and Services Office
1301 East Main Street
Cope Administration Building 208
Murfreesboro, TN 37132
Fax: (615) 898-5178
E-mail: twubneh@mtsu.edu
Phone: (615) 898-2238

Middlebury College
www.middlebury.edu
The Emma Willard House
Middlebury, VT 05753-6002
Fax: (802) 443-2056
E-mail: admissions@middlebury.edu
Phone: (802) 443-3000

Middlesex Community College
www.mxcc.commnet.edu
Admissions
100 Training Hill Road
Middletown, CT 06457-4889
Fax: (860) 344-7488
E-mail: mshabazz@mxcc.commnet.edu
Phone: (860) 343-5719

Middlesex Community College
www.middlesex.mass.edu
International Student Office
33 Kearney Square
Lowell, MA 01852-1987
Fax: (978) 656-3322
E-mail: admissions@middlesex.mass.edu
Phone: (978) 656-3207

Middlesex County College
www.middlesexcc.edu
Admissions
2600 Woodbridge Avenue
Box 3050
Edison, NJ 08818-3050
Fax: (732) 906-7728
E-mail: admssions@middlesex.cc.nj.us
Phone: (732) 406-2510 ext. 3510

Midland College
www.midland.edu
Director of Counseling
3600 North Garfield
Midland, TX 79705
Fax: (432) 685-4623
E-mail: sgrinnan@midland.edu
Phone: (432) 685-4505

Midlands Technical College
www.midlandstech.edu
International Admissions
PO Box 2408
Columbia, SC 29202
Fax: (803) 790-7584
E-mail: grossmanr@midlandstech.edu
Phone: (803) 738-7811

Midway College
www.midway.edu
Director of Admissions
512 East Stephens Street
Midway, KY 40347-1120
Fax: (859) 846-5787
E-mail: admissions@midway.edu
Phone: (859) 846-5347

Midwest University
www.midwest.edu
851 Parr Road
Wentzville, MO 63385
E-mail: usa@midwest.edu
Phone: (636) 327-4645

Midwestern State University
www.mwsu.edu
International Student Service
3410 Taft Boulevard
Wichita Falls, TX 76308-2099
Fax: (940) 397-4087
E-mail: kerrie.cale@mwsu.edu
Phone: (940) 397-4344

Mildred Elley
www.mildred-elley.edu
Admissions
855 Central Avenue
Albany, NY 12206-1513
Fax: (518) 786-0011
E-mail: admissions@mildred-elley.edu
Phone: (518) 786-3171

Miles College
www.miles.edu
Office of the Dean of Students
5500 Myron-Massey Boulevard
Fairfield, AL 35064
Fax: (205) 923-9292
E-mail: carolyn@miles.edu
Phone: (205) 929-1655

Miller-Motte College: Fayetteville
www.miller-motte.edu
3725 Ramsey Street, Suite 103A
Fayetteville, NC 28311

Miller-Motte Technical College
www.miller-motte.net
8085 Rivers Avenue, Suite E
North Charleston, SC 29406
Fax: (843) 329-4992
Phone: (843) 574-0101

Miller-Motte Technical College: Cary
www.mmccary.net
2205 Walnut Street
Cary, NC 27518

Miller-Motte Technical College: Clarksville
www.miller-motte.com
Admissions
1820 Business Park Drive
Clarksville, TN 37040
Fax: (931) 552-2916
E-mail: rgmmb@usit.net
Phone: (931) 553-0071

Miller-Motte Technical College: Conway
www.miller-motte.edu
2451 Highway 501 East
Conway, SC 29526
E-mail: jill.miskelly@miller-motte.edu
Phone: (843) 591-1102

Millersville University of Pennsylvania
www.millersville.edu
Admissions
PO Box 1002
Lyle Hall
Millersville, PA 17551-0302
Fax: (717) 871-2147
E-mail: Susan.Kastner@millersville.edu
Phone: (717) 872-3371

Milligan College
www.milligan.edu
Admissions
Box 210
Milligan College, TN 37682
Fax: (423) 461-8982
E-mail: tnbrinn@milligan.edu
Phone: (423) 461-8730

Millikin University
www.millikin.edu
Admission Office
1184 West Main Street
Decatur, IL 62522-2084
Fax: (217) 425-4669
E-mail: admis@millikin.edu
Phone: (217) 424-6210

Mills College
www.mills.edu
Admission Office
5000 MacArthur Boulevard
Oakland, CA 94613
Fax: (510) 430-3298
E-mail: admission@mills.edu
Phone: (510) 430-2135

Millsaps College
www.millsaps.edu
Office of Admissions
1701 North State Street
Jackson, MS 39210-0001
Fax: (601) 974-1059
E-mail: admissions@millsaps.edu
Phone: (601) 974-1051

Milwaukee Area Technical College
www.matc.edu
Admissions
700 West State Street
Milwaukee, WI 53233-1443
Fax: (414) 297-7800
E-mail: zollicoc@matc.edu
Phone: (414) 297-7087

Milwaukee Institute of Art & Design
www.miad.edu
Admissions
273 East Erie Street
Milwaukee, WI 53202
Fax: (414) 291-8077
E-mail: staceysteinberg@miad.edu
Phone: (414) 847-3255

Milwaukee School of Engineering
www.msoe.edu
Director of Admissions
1025 North Broadway
Milwaukee, WI 53202-3109
Fax: (414) 277-7475
E-mail: black@msoe.edu
Phone: (414) 277-6765

Minneapolis Business College
www.mplsbusinesscollege.com
1711 West County Road B
Roseville, MN 55113
Fax: (651) 636-8185
Phone: (651) 636-7406

Minneapolis Community and Technical College
www.minneapolis.edu
International Students Counselor
1501 Hennepin Avenue
Minneapolis, MN 55403-1779
Fax: (612) 659-6210
E-mail: kevin.kujawa@minneapolis.edu
Phone: (612) 659-6000

Minnesota School of Business
www.msbcollege.edu
1401 West 76 Street, Suite 500
Richfield, MN 55423
Fax: (612) 861-5548
E-mail: pmurray@msbcollege.edu
Phone: (612) 861-2000

Minnesota School of Business: Blaine
www.msbcollege.edu
3680 Pheasant Ridge Dr. NE
Blaine, MN 55449
E-mail: kswanson@msbcollege.edu

Minnesota School of Business: Plymouth
www.msbcollege.edu
1455 County Road 101 North
Plymouth, MN 55447
Fax: (736) 476-1000
Phone: (866) 476-2121

Minnesota School of Business: Rochester
www.msbcollege.edu
2521 Pennington Drive NW
Rochester, MN 55901
Phone: (507) 536-9500

Minnesota School of Business: Shakopee
www.msbcollege.edu
1200 Shakopee Town Square
Shakopee, MN 55379
Phone: (866) 776-1200

Minnesota State College - Southeast Technical
www.southeastmn.edu
Admissions
1250 Homer Road
PO Box 409
Winona, MN 55987-0409
Fax: (507) 453-2715
E-mail: glanning@southeastmn.edu
Phone: (877) 853-8324

Minnesota State Community and Technical College
www.minnesota.edu
Student Services
1414 College Way
Fergus Falls, MN 56537-1000
Fax: (218) 736-1510
E-mail: carrie.brimhall@minnesota.edu
Phone: (218) 736-1528

Minnesota State University Mankato
www.mnsu.edu
Admissions Office
122 Taylor Center
Mankato, MN 56001
Fax: (507) 389-1511
E-mail: diane.berge@mnsu.edu
Phone: (507) 389-1822

Minnesota State University Moorhead
www.mnstate.edu
Office of International Programs
Owens Hall
1104 7th Ave S
Moorhead, MN 56563
Fax: (218) 299-5928
E-mail: intladms@mnstate.edu
Phone: (218) 477-2956

Minnesota West Community and Technical College
www.mnwest.edu
Student Services
1314 North Hiawatha Avenue
Pipestone, MN 56164
Fax: (501) 372-5801
E-mail: beth.bents@mnwest.edu
Phone: (507) 372-3418

Minot State University
www.minotstateu.edu
Admissions Counselor
500 University Avenue West
Minot, ND 58707-5002
Fax: (701) 858-3386
E-mail: Lynda.Opp@minotstateu.edu
Phone: (701) 858-3348

MiraCosta College
www.miracosta.edu
Institute for International Perspectives
One Barnard Drive
Oceanside, CA 92056-3899
Fax: (760) 757-8209
E-mail: iip@miracosta.edu
Phone: (760) 795-6897

Mirrer Yeshiva Central Institute
1795 Ocean Parkway
Brooklyn, NY 11223
Phone: (718) 645-0536

Misericordia University
www.misericordia.edu
Admissions
301 Lake Street
Dallas, PA 18612-1098
Fax: (570) 675-2441
E-mail: jdessoye@misericordia.edu
Phone: (570) 674-6168

Mission College
www.missioncollege.org
International Students
3000 Mission College Boulevard
Santa Clara, CA 95054-1897
Fax: (408) 980-8980
E-mail: carol_qazi@wvm.edu
Phone: (408) 855-5110

Mississippi College
www.mc.edu
International Center
PO Box 4026
200 South Capitol Street
Clinton, MS 39058
Fax: (601) 925-7704
E-mail: brackenr@mc.edu
Phone: (601) 925-7635

Mississippi Delta Community College
www.msdelta.edu
Box 668
Moorhead, MS 38761
Fax: (662) 246-6321
E-mail: admissions@msdelta.edu
Phone: (662) 246-6306

Mississippi Gulf Coast Community College
www.mgccc.edu
Admissions
PO Box 548
Perkinston, MS 39573
Fax: (601) 928-6345
E-mail: nichol.armstrong@mgccc.edu
Phone: (601) 928-6264

Mississippi State University
www.msstate.edu
Office of Admission and Scholarships
Box 6334
Mississippi State, MS 39762
Fax: (662) 325-1678
E-mail: international@msstate.edu
Phone: (662) 325-1562

Mississippi University for Women
www.muw.edu
Admissions
1100 College St. MUW-1613
Columbus, MS 39701
Fax: (662) 329-7106
E-mail: smcnees@admissions.muw.edu
Phone: (662) 329-7106

Mississippi Valley State University
www.mvsu.edu
Admissions and Recruitment
14000 Highway 82 West
Box 7222
Itta Bena, MS 38941-1400
Fax: (662) 254-3759
E-mail: nbtaylor@mvsu.edu
Phone: (662) 254-3347

Missouri Baptist University
www.mobap.edu
Admissions Office
One College Park Drive
St. Louis, MO 63141-8660
Fax: (314) 392-2232
E-mail: saundersk@mobap.edu
Phone: (314) 744-5301

Missouri College
www.missouricollege.com
1405 South Hanley Road
Brentwood, MO 63144
E-mail: kjefferson@missouricollege.com
Phone: (314) 821-7700

Missouri Southern State University
www.mssu.edu
International Student Exchange Program
3950 East Newman Road
Joplin, MO 64801-1595
Fax: (417) 659-4445
E-mail: parker-1@mssu.edu
Phone: (417) 625-3109

Missouri State University
www.missouristate.edu
Office of International Student Services
901 South National Avenue
Springfield, MO 65897
Fax: (417) 836-7656
E-mail:
internationalstudentservices@missouristate.edu
Phone: (417) 836-6618

Missouri Technical School
www.motech.edu
Student Affairs
1690 Country Club Plaza Drive
St. Charles, MO 63303
Fax: (314) 569-1167
E-mail: bob@motech.edu
Phone: (314) 569-3600

Missouri University of Science and Technology
www.mst.edu
Admissions
106 Parker Hall
300 West 13th Street
Rolla, MO 65409-1060
Fax: (573) 341-4082
E-mail: admissions@mst.edu
Phone: (573) 341-4164

Missouri Valley College
www.moval.edu
Admissions
500 East College Street
Marshall, MO 65340
Fax: (660) 831-4129
E-mail: simicm@moval.edu
Phone: (660) 831-4129

Mitchell College
www.mitchell.edu
Enrollment Management
437 Pequot Avenue
New London, CT 06320-4498
Fax: (860) 444-1209
E-mail: boehm_g@mitchell.edu
Phone: (800) 443-2811

Mitchell Technical Institute
www.mitchelltech.edu
821 North Capital Street
Mitchell, SD 57301
Fax: (605) 996-3299
E-mail: questions@mitchelltech.edu
Phone: (605) 995-3025

Moberly Area Community College
www.macc.edu
Student Services Office
101 College Avenue
Moberly, MO 65270-1304
Fax: (660) 263-2406
E-mail: jamesg@macc.edu
Phone: (660) 263-4110 ext. 235

Modesto Junior College
www.mjc.edu
Counseling Office
435 College Avenue
Modesto, CA 95350-5800
Fax: (209) 575-6720
E-mail: sturbainb@yosemite.cc.ca.us
Phone: (209) 575-6012

Mohave Community College
www.mohave.edu
Registrar
1971 Jagerson Avenue
Kingman, AZ 86409
Fax: (928) 757-0808
E-mail: johwil@mohave.edu
Phone: (928) 757-0809

Mohawk Valley Community College
www.mvcc.edu
Office of Services for International Students
1101 Sherman Drive
Utica, NY 13501-5394
Fax: (315) 792-5527
E-mail: international.admissions@mvcc.edu
Phone: (315) 792-5350

Molloy College
www.molloy.edu
Admissions
PO Box 5002
Rockville Centre, NY 11570
Fax: (516) 256-2247
E-mail: mlane@molloy.edu
Phone: (516) 678-5000 ext. 6230

Monmouth College
www.monm.edu
Admission
700 East Broadway
Monmouth, IL 61462-1998
Fax: (309) 457-2141
E-mail: ocorrea@monm.edu
Phone: (309) 457-2131

Monmouth University
www.monmouth.edu
Undergraduate Admission
400 Cedar Avenue
West Long Branch, NJ 07764-1898
Fax: (732) 263-5166
E-mail: lvento@monmouth.edu
Phone: (732) 571-3456

Monroe College
www.monroecollege.edu
International Admissions
Monroe College Way
Bronx, NY 10468
Fax: (718) 364-3552
E-mail: glopez@monroecollege.edu
Phone: (914) 632-5400

Monroe Community College
www.monroecc.edu
Admission Office
Office of Admissions-Monroe Community
College
Box 92808
Rochester, NY 14692-8908
Fax: (585) 292-3860
Phone: (585) 292-2200

Montana State University: Billings
www.msubillings.edu
International Studies
1500 University Drive
Billings, MT 59101-0298
Fax: (406) 657-2254
E-mail: klacy@msubillings.edu
Phone: (406) 247-5785

Montana State University: Bozeman
www.montana.edu
International Programs
PO Box 172190
Bozeman, MT 59717-2190
Fax: (406) 994-1619
E-mail: ddebode@montana.edu
Phone: (406) 994-4031

Montana State University: Northern
www.msun.edu
Admissions/Multicultural Coordinator
Box 7751
Havre, MT 59501
Fax: (406) 265-3792
E-mail: gonsalez@msun.edu
Phone: (800) 662-6132 ext. 3704

**Montana Tech of the University of
Montana**
www.mtech.edu
Office of Enrollment Services
1300 West Park Street
Butte, MT 59701-8997
Fax: (406) 496-4710
E-mail: tcampeau@mtech.edu
Phone: (406) 496-4632

Montcalm Community College
www.montcalm.edu
Associate Dean of Student Services
2800 College Drive
Sidney, MI 48885
Fax: (989) 328-2950
E-mail: debraj@montcalm.edu
Phone: (989) 328-1276

Montclair State University
www.montclair.edu
Undergraduate Admissions Office
One Normal Avenue
Upper Montclair, NJ 07043-1624
Fax: (973) 655-7700
E-mail: kasperl@mail.montclair.edu
Phone: (973) 655-5116

Monterey Peninsula College
www.mpc.edu
International Student Programs
980 Fremont Street
Monterey, CA 93940-4799
Fax: (831) 645-1390
E-mail: international_center@mpc.cc.ca.us
Phone: (831) 645-1357

Montgomery County Community College
www.mc3.edu
Office of Admissions
340 DeKalb Pike
PO Box 400
Blue Bell, PA 19422
Fax: (215) 619-7188
E-mail: dbarrera@mc3.edu
Phone: (215) 641-6676

Montreat College
www.montreat.edu
Admissions
College Box 865, P.O. Box 1267
Montreat, NC 28757-1267
Fax: (828) 669-0120
E-mail: sgardner@montreat.edu
Phone: (828) 669-8012 ext. 3783

Montserrat College of Art
www.montserrat.edu
Admissions
23 Essex Street
Beverly, MA 01915
Fax: (978) 921-4241
E-mail: jnewell@montserrat.edu
Phone: (978) 921-4242 ext. 1152

Moody Bible Institute
www.moody.edu
Dean of Admissions
820 N LaSalle Boulevard
Chicago, IL 60610
Fax: (312) 329-8987
E-mail: charles.dresser@moody.edu
Phone: (312) 329-4267

Moore College of Art and Design
www.moore.edu
Admissions Office
The Parkway at 20th Street
Philadelphia, PA 19103-1179
Fax: (215) 568-3547
E-mail: admiss@moore.edu
Phone: (215) 965-4014

Moorpark College
www.moorparkcollege.edu
International Student
7075 Campus Road
Moorpark, CA 93021
Fax: (805) 378-1499
E-mail: international@vcccd.net
Phone: (805) 378-1414

Moraine Park Technical College
www.morainepark.edu
Student Services
235 North National Avenue
Box 1940
Fond du Lac, WI 54935-1940
Fax: (920) 924-3421
E-mail: lholte@morainepark.edu
Phone: (920) 924-6378

Moraine Valley Community College
www.morainevalley.edu
Office of International Student Affairs
9000 West College Parkway
Palos Hills, IL 60465-0937
Fax: (708) 974-0561
E-mail: viverito@morainevalley.edu
Phone: (708) 974-5334

Moravian College
www.moravian.edu
Admissions Office
1200 Main Street
Bethlehem, PA 18018
Fax: (610) 625-7930
E-mail: admissions@moravian.edu
Phone: (610) 861-1320

Morehead State University
www.moreheadstate.edu
Senior ES (Enrollment Services) Counselor
for International Recruitment
100 Admissions Center
Morehead, KY 40351
Fax: (606) 783-5038
E-mail: w.sun@moreheadstate.edu
Phone: (606) 783-9431

Morehouse College
www.morehouse.edu
International Studies
830 Westview Drive SW
Atlanta, GA 30314
Fax: (404) 524-5635
E-mail: gwade@morehouse.edu
Phone: (404) 681-2800 ext. 2690

Morgan Community College
www.morgancc.edu
Student Services
920 Barlow Road
Fort Morgan, CO 80701
Fax: (970) 867-6608
Phone: (970) 867-3081

Morgan State University
www.morgan.edu
Admission/ Recruiting
1700 East Cold Spring Lane
Baltimore, MD 21251
Fax: (443) 885-8200
E-mail: admissions@morgan.edu
Phone: (443) 885-3000

Morningside College
www.morningside.edu
Admissions
1501 Morningside Avenue
Sioux City, IA 51106
Fax: (712) 274-5101
E-mail: curryte@morningside.edu
Phone: (712) 274-5511

Morris College
www.morris.edu
Admissions and Records
100 West College Street
Sumter, SC 29150-3599
Fax: (803) 773-8241
E-mail: dcalhoun@morris.edu
Phone: (803) 934-3225

Morrison Institute of Technology
www.morrisontech.edu
Admissions
701 Portland Avenue
Morrison, IL 61270-2959
Fax: (815) 772-7584
E-mail: admissions@morrison.tec.il.us
Phone: (815) 772-7218

Morrison University
www.morrisonuniversity.com
Office of Admissions
10315 Professional Circle, #201
Reno, NV 89521
Fax: (775) 850-0711
E-mail: jdecker@morrison.anthem.edu
Phone: (775) 335-3900

Morton College
www.morton.edu
Director of Student Development
3801 South Central Avenue
Cicero, IL 60804-4398
Fax: (708) 656-9592
E-mail: Victor.Sanchez@morton.edu
Phone: (708) 656-8000 ext. 401

Motlow State Community College
www.mscc.edu
Admissions and Records
Box 8500
Lynchburg, TN 37352-8500
Fax: (931) 393-1971
E-mail: galsup@mscc.edu
Phone: (931) 393-1529 ext. 1529

Mott Community College
www.mcc.edu
Executive Dean, Student Services
1401 East Court Street
Flint, MI 48503-2089
Fax: (810) 232-9503
E-mail: delores.deen@mcc.edu
Phone: (810) 762-0243

Mount Aloysius College
www.mtaloy.edu
Admissions
7373 Admiral Peary Highway
Cresson, PA 16630
Fax: (814) 886-6441
E-mail: admissions@mtaloy.edu
Phone: (814) 886-6383

Mount Angel Seminary
www.mountangelabbey.org
Director of Immigration Services
One Abbey Drive
St. Benedict, OR 97373
Fax: (503) 845-3128
E-mail: tamara.swanson@mtangel.edu
Phone: (503) 845-3951 ext. 3549

Mount Holyoke College
www.mtholyoke.edu
Office of Admission
Newhall Center
50 College Street
South Hadley, MA 01075-1488
Fax: (413) 538-2409
E-mail: admission@mtholyoke.edu
Phone: (413) 538-2773

Mount Ida College
www.mountida.edu
Admissions Office
777 Dedham Street
Newton, MA 02459
Fax: (617) 928-4507
E-mail: admissions@mountida.edu
Phone: (617) 928-4553

Mount Marty College
www.mtmc.edu
Admission
1105 West Eighth Street
Yankton, SD 57078
Fax: (605) 668-1508
E-mail: mmcadmit@mtmc.edu
Phone: (800) 658-4552

Mount Mary College
www.mtmary.edu
Admission
2900 North Menomonee River Parkway
Milwaukee, WI 53222-4597
Fax: (414) 256-0180
E-mail: admiss@mtmary.edu
Phone: (414) 256-1219

Mount Mercy University
www.mtmercy.edu
Admissions
1330 Elmhurst Drive NE
Cedar Rapids, IA 52402-4797
Fax: (319) 363-5270
E-mail: jnewnum@mtmercy.edu
Phone: (319) 368-6460

Mount Olive College
www.moc.edu
Vice President Student Development
634 Henderson Street
Mount Olive, NC 28365
Fax: (919) 658-9816
E-mail: dfried@moc.edu
Phone: (919) 658-2502

Mount Saint Mary College
www.msmc.edu
Admissions
330 Powell Avenue
Newburgh, NY 12550
Fax: (845) 562-3438
E-mail: admissions@msmc.edu
Phone: (845) 569-3248

Mount San Antonio College
www.mtsac.edu
1100 North Grand Avenue
Walnut, CA 91789
Fax: (909) 468-4068
Phone: (909) 594-5611 ext. 4415

Mount San Jacinto College
www.msjc.edu
Student Services
1499 North State Street
San Jacinto, CA 92583
Fax: (951) 654-6738
E-mail: jpadilla@msjc.edu
Phone: (951) 487-3211

Mount St. Mary's College
www.msmc.la.edu
Admissions
12001 Chalon Road
Los Angeles, CA 90049
Fax: (310) 954-4259
E-mail: tlaw@msmc.la.edu
Phone: (800) 999-9893

Mount St. Mary's University
www.msmary.edu
Admissions Office
16300 Old Emmitsburg Road
Emmitsburg, MD 21727
Fax: (301) 447-5860
E-mail: thomas@msmary.edu
Phone: (301) 447-5214

Mount Vernon Nazarene University
www.mvnu.edu
Admissions
800 Martinsburg Road
Mount Vernon, OH 43050
Fax: (740) 393-0511
E-mail: admissions@mvnu.edu
Phone: (866) 462-6868 ext. 4510

Mount Wachusett Community College
www.mwcc.edu
Admissions
444 Green Street
Gardner, MA 01440-1000
Fax: (978) 630-9554
E-mail: j_walsh@mwcc.mass.edu
Phone: (978) 630-9110

Mountain State College
www.msc.edu
1508 Spring Street
Parkersburg, WV 26101-3993
Fax: (304) 485-3524
E-mail: adm@msc.edu
Phone: (304) 485-5487

Mountain State University
www.mountainstate.edu
Director of International Student Services
609 South Kanawha Street
PO Box 9003
Beckley, WV 25802-9003
Fax: (304) 252-2896
E-mail: clowry@mountainstate.edu
Phone: (304) 929-1744

Mountain View College
www.mvc.dcccd.edu
Office of Enrollment Management
4849 West Illinois Avenue
Dallas, TX 75211-6599
Fax: (214) 860-3074
E-mail: ghall@dcccd.edu
Phone: (214) 860-8600

Mt. Hood Community College
www.mhcc.cc.or.us
Admissions
26000 SE Stark Street
Gresham, OR 97030
Fax: (503) 491-7388
E-mail: peggy.maas@mhcc.edu
Phone: (503) 491-7384

Mt. Sierra College
www.mtsierra.edu
Admissions
101 East Huntington Drive
Monrovia, CA 91016
Fax: (626) 359-1378
E-mail: pazadian@mtsierra.edu
Phone: (626) 873-2100

MTI College
www.mticollege.edu
Admissions
5221 Madison Avenue
Sacramento, CA 95841
Fax: (916) 339-0305
E-mail: epatterson@mticollege.edu
Phone: (916) 339-1500

Muhlenberg College
www.muhlenberg.edu
Office of Admissions
2400 Chew Street
Allentown, PA 18104
Fax: (484) 664-3234
E-mail: admissions@muhlenberg.edu
Phone: (484) 664-3245

Murray State University
www.murraystate.edu
102 Curris Center Murray State University
Murray, KY 42071
Fax: (270) 809-3211
E-mail: Mark.galloway@murraystate.edu
Phone: (270) 809-3229

Muscatine Community College
www.eicc.edu
Admissions
152 Colorado Street
Muscatine, IA 52761-5396
Fax: (563) 288-6104
E-mail: kwatson@eicc.edu
Phone: (563) 288-6012

Muskegon Community College
www.muskegoncc.edu
Special Services / Enrollment Services
221 South Quarterline Road
Muskegon, MI 49442
Fax: (231) 777-0443
E-mail: donella.cooper@muskegoncc.edu
Phone: (231) 777-0404

Muskingum University
www.muskingum.edu
Director of International Admission and
Immigration Services Operations
163 Stormont Street
New Concord, OH 43762-1199
Fax: (740) 826-8100
E-mail: memerson@muskingum.edu
Phone: (740) 826-8127

Napa Valley College
www.napavalley.edu
2277 Napa-Vallejo Highway
Napa, CA 94558
Fax: (707) 253-3064
E-mail: snelson@napavalley.edu
Phone: (707) 253-3000

Naropa University
www.naropa.edu
Admissions
2130 Arapahoe Avenue
Boulder, CO 80302-6697
Fax: (303) 546-3583
E-mail: jhinton@naropa.edu
Phone: (303) 245-4657

Nash Community College
www.nashcc.edu
Admissions
Box 7488
Rocky Mount, NC 27804-0488
Fax: (252) 451-8401
E-mail: dgardner@nashcc.edu
Phone: (252) 451-8300

Nashua Community College
www.nashuacc.edu
Admissions
505 Amherst Street
Nashua, NH 03063-1026
Fax: (603) 882-6923
E-mail: jcurtis@ccsnh.edu
Phone: (603) 882-6923 ext. 1547

Nashville State Community College
www.nscc.edu
Adriane Gordon
120 White Bridge Road
Nashville, TN 37209-4515
Fax: (615) 353-3243
E-mail: adriane.gordon@nscc.edu
Phone: (615) 353-3219

Nassau Community College
www.ncc.edu
Admissions
One Education Drive
Garden City, NY 11530
Fax: (516) 572-9743
E-mail: Rosemary.Ortlieb@ncc.edu
Phone: (516) 572-7053

National American University: Austin
www.national.edu
13801 Burnet Road, Suite 300
Austin, TX 78727
E-mail: sljones@national.edu
Phone: (512) 651-4700

National American University: Denver
www.national.edu
Admissions
1325 South Colorado Boulevard, Suite 100
Denver, CO 80222-3308
Fax: (303) 876-7105
E-mail: sthompson@national.edu
Phone: (303) 876-7100

National American University: Kansas City
www.national.edu
Admissions
3620 Arrowhead Avenue
Independence, MO 64057
Fax: (816) 412-7705
Phone: (816) 412-7715

National American University: Lee's Summit
www.national.edu
401 NW Murray Road
Lee's Summit, MO 64081
E-mail: lsadmissions@national.edu
Phone: (816) 600-3900

National American University: Rapid City
www.national.edu
International Admissions
321 Kansas City Street
Rapid City, SD 57701
Fax: (605) 394-4900
E-mail: patfox@national.edu
Phone: (605) 394-4800

National College: Bartlett
www.national-college.edu
5760 Stage Road
Bartlett, TN 38134
Phone: (901) 213-1681

National College: Cincinnati
www.national-college.edu
6871 Steger Drive
Cincinnati, OH 45237
Phone: (513) 761-1291

National College: Columbus
www.ncbt.edu
5665 Forest Hills Boulevard
Columbus, OH 43231

National College: Danville
www.ncbt.edu
PO Box 6400
Roanoke, VA 24017
Fax: (859) 236-1063
E-mail: market@educorp.edu
Phone: (859) 236-6991

National College: Dayton
www.national-college.edu
1837 Woodman Center Drive
Kettering, OH 45420
Phone: (937) 299-9450

National College: Florence
www.ncbt.edu
PO Box 6400
Roanoke, VA 24017
Fax: (606) 525-8961
E-mail: market@educorp.edu
Phone: (606) 525-6510

National College: Harrisonburg
www.national-college.edu
PO Box 6400
Roanoke, VA 24017
Fax: (540) 432-1133
E-mail: market@national-college.edu
Phone: (800) 664-1886

National College: Indianapolis
www.national-college.edu
6060 Castleway Drive West
Indianapolis, IN 46250
Phone: (317) 578-7353

National College: Knoxville
www.ncbt.edu
8415 Kingston Pike
Knoxville, TN 37919
Phone: (865) 539-2011

National College: Lexington
www.ncbt.edu
PO Box 6400
Roanoke, VA 24017
Fax: (859) 233-3054
E-mail: market@educorp.edu
Phone: (859) 253-0621

National College: Madison
www.national-college.edu
900 Madison Square
Madison, TN 37115
Phone: (615) 612-3015

National College: Memphis
www.national-college.edu
3545 Lamar Avenue, Suite 1
Memphis, TN 38118
Phone: (901) 363-9046

National College: Roanoke Valley
www.national-college.edu
PO Box 6400
Roanoke, VA 24017-0400
Fax: (540) 444-4198
Phone: (540) 986-1800

National College: Stow
www.national-college.edu
3855 Fishercreek Road
Stow, OH 44224

National College: Youngstown
www.national-college.edu
3487 Belmont Avenue
Youngstown, OH 44505

National Hispanic University
www.nhu.edu
Admissions/Registrar
14271 Story Road
San Jose, CA 95127-3823
Fax: (408) 254-1369
E-mail: pbustil@nhu.edu
Phone: (408) 273-2696

National Labor College
www.nlc.edu
10000 New Hampshire Avenue
Silver Spring, MD 20903
Fax: (301) 628-0160
E-mail: registration@nlc.edu
Phone: (301) 431-6400

National Park Community College
www.npcc.edu
Vice President of Student Affairs
101 College Drive
Hot Springs, AR 71913
Fax: (501) 760-4100
E-mail: mpicking@gccc.edu
Phone: (501) 760-4222

National University
www.nu.edu
International Programs Office
11255 North Torrey Pines Road
La Jolla, CA 92037-1011
Fax: (858) 541-7995
E-mail: ipo@nu.edu
Phone: (858) 541-7960

National University College: Arecibo
www.nuc.edu
Admissions and Marketing Director
PO Box 4035, MSC 452
Arecibo, PR 00614
Fax: (787) 879-5047
E-mail: mpagan@nuc.edu
Phone: (787) 879-5044 ext. 5203

National University College: Bayamon
www.nuc.edu
Special Assistant to the President
PO Box 2036
Bayamon, PR 00960
Fax: (787) 779-4909
E-mail: aaviles@nuc.edu
Phone: (787) 780-5134 ext. 4133

National University College: Ponce
www.nuc.edu
PO Box 801243
Coto Laurel, PR 00780-1243
E-mail: mbermudez@nuc.edu
Phone: (787) 840-4474 ext. 7000

National-Louis University
www.nl.edu
Student Affairs
122 South Michigan Avenue
Chicago, IL 60603
Fax: (847) 465-5730
E-mail: brouzan@nl.edu
Phone: (312) 261-3461

Naugatuck Valley Community College
www.nvcc.commnet.edu
Admissions
750 Chase Parkway
Waterbury, CT 06708-3089
Fax: (203) 596-8766
E-mail: lstango@nvcc.commnet.edu
Phone: (203) 575-8054

Navajo Technical College
www.navajotech.edu
PO Box 849
Crownpoint, NM 87313
Fax: (505) 786-5644
E-mail: rdamon@navajotech.edu
Phone: (505) 786-4326

Navarro College
www.navarrocollege.edu
3200 West Seventh Avenue
Corsicana, TX 75110
Fax: (903) 875-7353
E-mail: justin.ball@navarrocollege.edu
Phone: (903) 875-7370

Nazarene Bible College
www.nbc.edu
Campus Academic Services
1111 Academy Park Loop
Colorado Springs, CO 80910-3704
Fax: (719) 884-5199
E-mail: campusadmissions@nbc.edu
Phone: (719) 884-5091

Nazareth College
www.naz.edu
Undergraduate Admissions
4245 East Avenue
Rochester, NY 14618-3790
Fax: (585) 389-2826
E-mail: dshrest2@naz.edu
Phone: (585) 389-2825

Nebraska Christian College
www.nechristian.edu
Director of Admissions
12550 South 114th Street
Papillion, NE 68046
Fax: (402) 935-9500
E-mail: admissions@nechristian.edu
Phone: (402) 935-9400

Nebraska College of Technical Agriculture
www.ncta.unl.edu
404 East 7th Street
Curtis, NE 69025-0069
Fax: (308) 367-5203
E-mail: vluke1@unl.edu
Phone: (308) 367-5200

Nebraska Indian Community College
www.thenicc.edu
PO Box 428
Macy, NE 68039
Fax: (402) 837-4183
E-mail: sscahayes@thenicc.edu
Phone: (402) 494-2311 ext. 2569

Nebraska Wesleyan University
www.nebrwesleyan.edu
Admissions Office
5000 St. Paul Avenue
Lincoln, NE 68504
Fax: (402) 465-2177
E-mail: admissions@nebrwesleyan.edu
Phone: (402) 465-2218

Neosho County Community College
www.neosho.edu
Coordinator for International Services
800 West 14th Street
Chanute, KS 66720
Fax: (620) 431-0082
E-mail: aneff@neosho.edu
Phone: (620) 431-2820 ext. 240

Neumann University
www.neumann.edu
Admissions
One Neumann Drive
Aston, PA 19014-1298
Fax: (610) 558-5652
E-mail: neumann@neumann.edu
Phone: (610) 558-5616

Neumont University
www.neumont.edu
10701 South River Front Parkway, Suite 300
South Jordan, UT 84095
Fax: (801) 302-2880
E-mail: admissions@neumont.edu
Phone: (801) 302-2879

New College of Florida
www.ncf.edu
Office of Admissions
5800 Bay Shore Road
Sarasota, FL 34243-2109
Fax: (941) 487-5010
E-mail: admissions@ncf.edu
Phone: (941) 487-5000

New England College
www.nec.edu
Admissions
102 Bridge Street
Henniker, NH 03242
Fax: (603) 428-7230
E-mail: jmerrill@nec.edu
Phone: (603) 428-2392

New England College of Business and Finance
www.necb.edu
Admissions
10 High Street, Suite 204
Boston, MA 02110
Fax: (617) 951-2533
E-mail: pamela.dellaporta@necb.edu
Phone: (617) 603-6914

New England Conservatory of Music
www.necmusic.edu
Admissions
290 Huntington Avenue
Boston, MA 02115
Fax: (617) 585-1115
E-mail: admission@necmusic.edu
Phone: (617) 585-1101

New England Culinary Institute
www.neci.edu
Admissions
56 College Street
Montpelier, VT 05602
Fax: (802) 225-3280
E-mail: admissions@neci.edu
Phone: (877) 223-6324

New England Institute of Art
www.artinstitutes.edu/boston
Admissions
10 Brookline Place West
Brookline, MA 02445-7295
Fax: (617) 582-4680
E-mail: asanford@aii.edu
Phone: (800) 903-4425

New England Institute of Technology
www.neit.edu
Admissions Office
2500 Post Road
Warwick, RI 02886-2286
Fax: (401) 738-5122
E-mail: mseltzer@neit.edu
Phone: (401) 780-4199 ext. 3489

New England School of Communications
www.nescom.edu
Admissions
One College Circle
Bangor, ME 04401
Fax: (207) 947-3987
E-mail: grantl@nescom.edu
Phone: (207) 941-7176

New Jersey City University
www.njcu.edu
2039 Kennedy Boulevard
Jersey City, NJ 07305-1597
E-mail: admissions@njcu.edu
Phone: (201) 200-3234

New Jersey Institute of Technology
www.njit.edu
Office of International Students and Faculty
University Heights
Newark, NJ 07102
Fax: (973) 596-5450
E-mail: grundy@njit.edu
Phone: (973) 596-2451

New Mexico Highlands University
www.nmhu.edu
International Education Center
Box 9000
Las Vegas, NM 87701
Fax: (505) 454-3511
E-mail: eclayton@nmhu.edu
Phone: (505) 454-3058

New Mexico Institute of Mining and Technology
www.nmt.edu
International & Exchange Programs
801 Leroy Place
Socorro, NM 87801
Fax: (575) 835-5959
E-mail: cbuffington@admin.nmt.edu
Phone: (575) 835-5022

New Mexico Junior College
www.nmjc.edu
Office of Admission
5317 Lovington Highway
Hobbs, NM 88240
Fax: (575) 392-0322
E-mail: jmcdonald@nmjc.edu
Phone: (575) 392-5112

New Mexico Military Institute
www.nmmi.edu
Student Assistance Center
101 West College Boulevard
Roswell, NM 88201-5173
Fax: (505) 624-8058
E-mail: admissions@nmmi.edu
Phone: (505) 624-8360

New Mexico State University
www.nmsu.edu
International Programs, MSC 3567
Box 30001, MSC 3A
Las Cruces, NM 88003-8001
Fax: (575) 646-2558
E-mail: marjaspe@ad.nmsu.edu
Phone: (575) 646-2017

New Mexico State University at Alamogordo
www.nmsua.edu/
Graduate and International Student Services
2400 North Scenic Drive
Alamogordo, NM 88310
E-mail: marjaspe@ad.nmsu.edu
Phone: (575) 646-2017

New Mexico State University at Carlsbad
www.cavern.nmsu.edu
International Student Services Office
1500 University Drive
Carlsbad, NM 88220
Fax: (575) 646-2558
E-mail: marjaspe@ad.nmsu.edu
Phone: (575) 646-2017

New Mexico State University at Grants
www.grants.nmsu.edu
Graduate and International Student Services
1500 North Third Street
Grants, NM 87020
Fax: (575) 646-2558
E-mail: marjaspe@ad.nmsu.edu
Phone: (575) 646-2017

New Orleans Baptist Theological Seminary: Leavell College
www.nobts.edu
3939 Gentilly Boulevard
New Orleans, LA 70126-4858
E-mail: leavelladmission@nobts.edu
Phone: (504) 282-4455

New River Community and Technical College
www.newriver.edu
167 Dye Drive
Beckley, WV 25801
Fax: (304) 255-5889
Phone: (304) 255-5812

New Saint Andrews College
www.nsa.edu
PO Box 9025
Moscow, ID 83843
Fax: (208) 882-4293
E-mail: admissions@nsa.edu
Phone: (208) 882-1566 ext. 113

New York Career Institute
www.nyci.edu
11 Park Place
New York, NY 10007
Fax: (212) 385-7574
E-mail: lstieglitz@nyci.edu
Phone: (212) 962-0002 ext. 100

New York Institute of Technology
www.nyit.edu
Admissions
Box 8000
Old Westbury, NY 11568
Fax: (516) 686-7613
E-mail: adelcid@nyit.edu
Phone: (516) 686-7859

New York School of Interior Design
www.nysid.edu
International Student Adviser
170 East 70th Street
New York, NY 10021-5110
Fax: (212) 472-1867
E-mail: ddavee@nysid.edu
Phone: (212) 472-1500 ext. 203

New York University
www.nyu.edu
Undergraduate Admissions
665 Broadway, 11th floor
New York, NY 10012-2339
Fax: (212) 995-4902
E-mail: admissions@nyu.edu
Phone: (212) 998-4500

Newberry College
www.newberry.edu
Admissions
2100 College Street
Newberry, SC 29108
Fax: (803) 321-5138
E-mail: admissions@newberry.edu
Phone: (803) 321-5131

Newbury College
www.newbury.edu
Office of Admission
129 Fisher Avenue
Office of Admission
Brookline, MA 02445
Fax: (617) 731-9618
E-mail: info@newbury.edu
Phone: (617) 730-7007

Newman University
www.newmanu.edu
Admissions
3100 McCormick
Wichita, KS 67213-2097
Fax: (316) 942-4483
E-mail: dakajo@newmanu.edu
Phone: (316) 942-4291 ext. 2233

NewSchool of Architecture & Design
www.newschoolarch.edu
1249 F Street
San Diego, CA 92101
Fax: (619) 235-4651
E-mail: admissions@newschoolarch.edu
Phone: (619) 684-8841

NHTI-Concord's Community College
www.nhti.edu
Admissions
31 College Drive
Concord, NH 03301
Fax: (603) 271-7139
E-mail: nhtiadm@nhctc.edu
Phone: (603) 271-7130

Niagara County Community College
www.niagaracc.suny.edu
Admissions Office
3111 Saunders Settlement Road
Sanborn, NY 14132-9460
Fax: (716) 614-6820
E-mail: ryanl@niagaracc.suny.edu
Phone: (716) 614-6282

Niagara University
www.niagara.edu
Student Life
Niagara University, NY 14109
Fax: (716) 286-8477
E-mail: deb@niagara.edu
Phone: (716) 286-8405

Nicholls State University
www.nicholls.edu
Office of Admissions
PO Box 2004-NSU
Thibodaux, LA 70310
Fax: (985) 448-4929
E-mail: marilyn.gonzales@nicholls.edu
Phone: (985) 449-7038

Nichols College
www.nichols.edu
Admissions
PO Box 5000
Dudley, MA 01571-5000
Fax: (508) 943-9885
E-mail: emily.reardon@nichols.edu
Phone: (508) 213-2275

Norfolk State University
www.nsu.edu
Admissions
700 Park Avenue
Norfolk, VA 23504
Fax: (757) 823-2078
E-mail: internationaladmissions@nsu.edu
Phone: (757) 823-8396

Normandale Community College
www.normandale.edu
Admissions
9700 France Avenue South
Bloomington, MN 55431
Fax: (952) 487-8230
E-mail: antoinette.bowling-
harris@normandale.edu
Phone: (952) 487-8207

North Carolina Central University
www.nccu.edu
Student Affairs
PO Box 19717
Durham, NC 27707
Fax: (919) 530-7645
E-mail: emosby@nccu.edu
Phone: (919) 530-7492

North Carolina State University
www.ncsu.edu
Assistant Director of Admissions
203 Peele Hall, Box 7103
Raleigh, NC 27695-7103
Fax: (919) 515-5039
E-mail: dana_troutman@ncsu.edu
Phone: (919) 515-2434

North Carolina Wesleyan College
www.ncwc.edu
Office of Admissions
3400 North Wesleyan Boulevard
Rocky Mount, NC 27804
Fax: (252) 985-5319
E-mail: adm@ncwc.edu
Phone: (800) 488-6292

North Central College
www.northcentralcollege.edu
Office of Admissions
PO Box 3063
Naperville, IL 60566-7063
Fax: (630) 637-5819
E-mail: msotermat@noctrl.edu
Phone: (630) 637-5800

North Central Kansas Technical College
www.ncktc.edu
PO Box 507
3033 US Hwy 24
Beloit, KS 67420
Fax: (785) 738-2903
E-mail: dhughes@ncktc.edu
Phone: (800) 658-4655

North Central Michigan College
www.ncmich.edu
Student Services
1515 Howard Street
Petoskey, MI 49770
Fax: (231) 348-6672
E-mail: pwelmers@ncmich.edu
Phone: (888) 298-6605

North Central Missouri College
www.ncmissouri.edu
Admissions Office
1301 Main Street
Trenton, MO 64683
Fax: (660) 359-2211
E-mail: kmccollum@mail.ncmissouri.edu
Phone: (660) 359-3948 ext. 1401

North Central State College
www.ncstatecollege.edu
Office of Admissions
2441 Kenwood Circle, PO Box 698
Mansfield, OH 44901-0698
Fax: (419) 775-4757
E-mail: mmonnes@ncstatecollege.edu
Phone: (419) 775-4824

North Central Texas College
www.nctc.edu
1525 West California Street
Gainesville, TX 76240
Fax: (940) 668-6049
E-mail: admissions@nctc.edu
Phone: (940) 668-4404

North Central University
www.northcentral.edu
Admissions
910 Elliot Avenue
Minneapolis, MN 55404
Fax: (612) 343-4146
E-mail: spshawa@northcentral.edu
Phone: (612) 343-4466

North Country Community College
www.nccc.edu
Enrollment Management
23 Santanoni Avenue
PO Box 89
Saranac Lake, NY 12983
Fax: (518) 891-0898
E-mail: admissions@nccc.edu
Phone: (888) 879-6222 ext. 233

North Dakota State College of Science
www.ndscs.edu
Admissions Office
800 North 6th Street
Wahpeton, ND 58076-0001
Fax: (701) 671-2201
E-mail: admissions@kitten.nodak.edu
Phone: (800) 342-4325 ext. 32202

North Dakota State University
www.ndsu.edu
Office of International Programs
Ceres Hall 114
Dept 5320 PO Box 6050
Fargo, ND 58108-6050
Fax: (701) 231-1014
E-mail: ndsu.international@ndsu.nedu
Phone: (701) 231-7895

North Florida Community College
www.nfcc.edu
Admissions
325 NW Turner Davis Drive
Madison, FL 32340
Fax: (850) 973-1697
E-mail: wallerd@nfcc.edu
Phone: (850) 973-1622

North Georgia College & State University
www.northgeorgia.edu
Admissions
82 College Circle
Dahlonega, GA 30597
Fax: (706) 864-1478
E-mail: jchadwick@northgeorgia.edu
Phone: (706) 864-1800

North Greenville University
www.ngu.edu
Admissions
PO Box 1892
7801 North Tigerville Road
Tigerville, SC 29688-1892
Fax: (864) 977-7177
E-mail: ewall@ngc.edu
Phone: (864) 977-7001

North Hennepin Community College
www.nhcc.edu
Admissions
7411 85th Avenue North
Brooklyn Park, MN 55445
Fax: (763) 493-0563
E-mail: lkirkeby@nhcc.edu
Phone: (763) 424-0722

North Idaho College
www.nic.edu
Office of Admissions
1000 West Garden Avenue
Coeur d'Alene, ID 83814-2199
Fax: (208) 769-3399
E-mail: cahanhi@nic.edu
Phone: (208) 769-3311

North Iowa Area Community College
www.niacc.edu
Student Services
500 College Drive
Mason City, IA 50401
Fax: (641) 422-4385
E-mail: pierskar@niacc.edu
Phone: (641) 422-4245

North Lake College
www.northlakecollege.edu
International Center
5001 North MacArthur Boulevard
Irving, TX 75038-3899
Fax: (972) 273-3138
E-mail: nlcintl@dcccd.edu
Phone: (972) 273-3155

North Park University
www.northpark.edu
Admission
3225 West Foster Avenue Box 19
Chicago, IL 60625-4895
Fax: (773) 279-7952
E-mail: internationals@northpark.edu
Phone: (773) 244-5510

North Seattle Community College
www.northseattle.edu
International Student Programs
9600 College Way North
Seattle, WA 98103-3599
Fax: (206) 527-3794
E-mail: international@sccd.ctc.edu
Phone: (206) 527-3672

North Shore Community College
www.northshore.edu
Enrollment Services
One Ferncroft Road
Box 3340
Danvers, MA 01923-0840
Fax: (781) 477-2143
E-mail: lbarrett@northshore.edu
Phone: (978) 762-4000 ext. 6225

Northampton Community College
www.northampton.edu
Admissions
3835 Green Pond Road
Bethlehem, PA 18020-7599
Fax: (610) 861-4560
E-mail: pboulous@northampton.edu
Phone: (610) 861-5500

Northcentral University
www.ncu.edu
Director of Admissions
10000 East University Drive
Prescott Valley, AZ 86314
Fax: (928) 541-7817
E-mail: klustig@ncu.edu
Phone: (928) 541-7777 ext. 8085

Northeast Community College
www.northeast.edu
Admissions
801 East Benjamin Avenue
Box 469
Norfolk, NE 68702-0469
Fax: (402) 844-7400
E-mail: shelley@northeast.edu
Phone: (402) 844-7282

Northeast Iowa Community College
www.nicc.edu
Admissions
Box 400
Calmar, IA 52132
Fax: (563) 562-4369
E-mail: mcconnellb@nicc.edu
Phone: (800) 728-2256 ext. 307

Northeast Mississippi Community College
www.nemcc.edu
Admissions
101 Cunningham Boulevard
Booneville, MS 38829
Fax: (662) 720-7405
E-mail: admitme@nemcc.edu
Phone: (662) 720-7239

Northeast Texas Community College
www.ntcc.edu
Director of Admissions
PO Box 1307
Mount Pleasant, TX 75456-1307
Fax: (903) 572-6712
E-mail: swoods@ntcc.edu
Phone: (903) 434-8354

Northeast Wisconsin Technical College
www.nwtc.edu
2740 West Mason Street
Box 19042
Green Bay, WI 54307-9042
Fax: (920) 498-6882
E-mail: mark.franks@nwtc.edu
Phone: (920) 498-6269

Northeastern Junior College
www.njc.edu
Admissions
100 College Avenue
Sterling, CO 80751
Fax: (970) 521-6715
E-mail: andy.long@njc.edu
Phone: (970) 521-6652

Northeastern Oklahoma Agricultural and Mechanical College
www.neo.edu
International Student Office
200 I Street Northeast
Box 3843
Miami, OK 74354-6497
Fax: (918) 542-7065
E-mail: scbrown@neo.edu
Phone: (918) 540-6393

Northeastern State University
www.nsuok.edu
International Programs
600 North Grand Avenue
Tahlequah, OK 74464-2399
Fax: (918) 458-2056
E-mail: international@nsuok.edu
Phone: (918) 444-2050

Northeastern Technical College
www.netc.edu
Drawer 1007
Cheraw, SC 29520
Fax: (843) 921-1476
E-mail: mpace@netc.edu
Phone: (843) 921-6900

Northeastern University
www.northeastern.edu
International Admissions
360 Huntington Avenue, 150 Richards Hall
Boston, MA 02115
Fax: (617) 373-8780
E-mail: internationaladmissions@neu.edu
Phone: (617) 373-2200

Northern Arizona University
www.nau.edu
Director, International Admissions &
Recruitment
PO Box 4084
Flagstaff, AZ 86011-4084
Fax: (928) 523-9489
E-mail: Mandy.Hansen@nau.edu
Phone: (928) 523-2409

Northern Essex Community College
www.necc.mass.edu
100 Elliott Street
Haverhill, MA 01830-2399
E-mail: admissions@necc.mass.edu
Phone: (978) 556-3600

Northern Illinois University
www.niu.edu
International Student Office
DeKalb, IL 60115-2854
Fax: (815) 753-1488
E-mail: admission-info@niu.edu
Phone: (815) 753-8276

Northern Kentucky University
www.nku.edu
International Students and Scholars
Administrative Center 401, Northern
Kentucky University
Nunn Drive
Highland Heights, KY 41099
Fax: (859) 572-6178
E-mail: leibache1@nku.edu
Phone: (859) 572-5223

Northern Maine Community College
www.nmcc.edu
Admissions
33 Edgemont Drive
Presque Isle, ME 04769
Fax: (207) 768-2848
E-mail: admission@nmcc.edu
Phone: (207) 768-2785

Northern Michigan University
www.nmu.edu
International Studies
1401 Presque Isle Avenue
Marquette, MI 49855
Fax: (906) 227-2204
E-mail: ipo@nmu.edu
Phone: (906) 227-2510

Northern New Mexico College
www.nnmc.edu
Director of Recruitment & Admissions
921 Paseo de Onate
Espanola, NM 87532
Fax: (505) 747-2191
E-mail: forona@nnmc.edu
Phone: (505) 747-2161

Northern Oklahoma College
www.north-ok.edu
Registrar's Office
Box 310
1220 East Grand
Tonkawa, OK 74653-0310
Fax: (580) 628-6371
E-mail: rick.edgington@north-ok.edu
Phone: (580) 628-6221

Northern State University
www.northern.edu
1200 South Jay Street
Aberdeen, SD 57401-7198
Fax: (605) 626-2587
E-mail: admissions2@northern.edu
Phone: (800) 678-5330

Northern Virginia Community College
www.nvcc.edu
4001 Wakefield Chapel Road
Annandale, VA 22003-3796
Phone: (703) 323-3000

Northland College
www.northland.edu
Admission Office
1411 Ellis Avenue
Ashland, WI 54806-3999
Fax: (715) 682-1258
E-mail: admit@northland.edu
Phone: (715) 682-1224

Northland Community & Technical College
www.northlandcollege.edu
Admissions
1101 Highway One East
Thief River Falls, MN 56701
Fax: (218) 681-0774
E-mail: eugene.klinke@northlandcollege.edu
Phone: (218) 681-0701

Northwest Aviation College
www.NorthwestAviationCollege.edu
506 23rd Street, NE
Auburn, WA 98002
Fax: (253) 931-0768
E-mail: Shawn@NACstaff.com
Phone: (253) 854-4960

Northwest Christian University
www.nwcu.edu
Admissions
828 East 11th Avenue
Eugene, OR 97401-3745
Fax: (541) 684-7317
E-mail: admissions@northwestchristian.edu
Phone: (541) 684-7201

Northwest College
www.northwestcollege.edu
Multicultural Program Office
231 West 6th Street
Powell, WY 82435
Fax: (307) 754-6249
E-mail: mary.baumann@northwestcollege.edu
Phone: (307) 754-6138

Northwest College of Art
www.nca.edu
Admissions
16301 Creative Drive NE
Poulsbo, WA 98370-8651
Fax: (360) 779-9933
E-mail: admissions@nca.edu
Phone: (360) 779-9993

Northwest Florida State College
www.nwfsc.edu
Counseling
100 College Boulevard
Niceville, FL 32578-1295
Fax: (850) 729-5215
E-mail: registrar@nwfsc.edu
Phone: (850) 729-5372

Northwest Iowa Community College
www.nwicc.edu
603 West Park Street
Sheldon, IA 51201
Fax: (712) 324-4136
E-mail: lstory@nwicc.edu
Phone: (712) 324-5061 ext. 115

Northwest Kansas Technical College
www.nwktc.edu
1209 Harrison
Goodland, KS 67735
Phone: (785) 890-3641

Northwest Missouri State University
www.nwmissouri.edu
Admissions
800 University Drive
248 Admission Building
Maryville, MO 64468-6001
Fax: (660) 562-1821
E-mail: aheng@nwmissouri.edu
Phone: (660) 562-1149

Northwest Nazarene University
www.nnu.edu
Student Development
623 S. University Boulevard
Nampa, ID 83686-5897
Fax: (208) 467-8468
E-mail: plrogers@nnu.edu
Phone: (208) 467-8768

Northwest School of Wooden Boatbuilding
www.nwboatschool.org
42 North Water Street
Port Hadlock, WA 98339
Fax: (360) 385-5089
E-mail: info@nwboatschool.org
Phone: (360) 385-4948

Northwest Technical College
www.ntcmn.edu
Admissions Office
905 Grant Avenue Southeast
Bemidji, MN 56601-4907
Fax: (218) 333-6697
E-mail: sue.ludwig@ntcmn.edu
Phone: (218) 333-6647

Northwest Technical Institute
www.nti.edu
950 Blue Gentian Road
Eagan, MN 55121
Fax: (952) 944-9274
E-mail: info@nti.edu
Phone: (952) 944-0080

Northwest University
www.northwestu.edu
Director of Traditional Admissions
5520 108th Avenue, NE
Box 579
Kirkland, WA 98083-0579
Fax: (425) 889-5224
E-mail: jessica.velasco@northwestu.edu
Phone: (425) 889-5212

Northwest Vista College
www.alamo.edu/nvc
3535 North Ellison Drive
San Antonio, TX 78251-4217
Fax: (210) 486-4170
E-mail: nvc-admissions@mail.accd.edu
Phone: (210) 486-4700

Northwestern College
www.northwesternbc.edu
4839 North Milwaukee Avenue
Chicago, IL 60630
Fax: (773) 777-2861
Phone: (773) 481-3730

Northwestern College
www.nwciowa.edu
Director of International and Multicultural
Affairs
101 Seventh Street, SW
Orange City, IA 51041
Fax: (712) 707-7164
E-mail: kmcmahan@nwciowa.edu
Phone: (712) 707-7016

Northwestern College
www.nwc.edu
Admissions Office
3003 Snelling Avenue North
Saint Paul, MN 55113-1598
Fax: (651) 631-5680
E-mail: admissions@nwc.edu
Phone: (651) 631-5209

Northwestern Health Sciences University
www.nwhealth.edu
2501 West 84th Street
Bloomington, MN 55431
E-mail: admit@nwhealth.edu
Phone: (952) 888-4777 ext. 409

Northwestern Michigan College
www.nmc.edu
Admissions Office
1701 East Front Street
Traverse City, MI 49686
Fax: (231) 995-1339
E-mail: jbensley@nmc.edu
Phone: (231) 995-1034

Northwestern Oklahoma State University
www.nwosu.edu
International Student Advisor
709 Oklahoma Boulevard
Alva, OK 73717-2799
Fax: (580) 327-8413
E-mail: jabarraza@nwosu.edu
Phone: (580) 327-8435

Northwestern Polytechnic University
www.npu.edu
Director of Admissions
47671 Westinghouse Drive
Fremont, CA 94539
Fax: (510) 657-8975
E-mail: judyweng@npu.edu
Phone: (510) 592-9688 ext. 21

Northwestern State University
www.nsula.edu
Admissions Office
South Hall, 444 Caspari Street
Northwestern State University
Natchitoches, LA 71497
Fax: (318) 357-4660
E-mail: admissions@nsula.edu
Phone: (318) 357-4078

Northwestern University
www.northwestern.edu
Office of Undergraduate Admission
1801 Hinman Avenue
PO Box 3060
Evanston, IL 60204-3060
Fax: (847) 467-2331
E-mail: fss@northwestern.edu
Phone: (847) 491-7271

Northwood University: Florida
www.northwood.edu
Admissions
2600 North Military Trail
West Palm Beach, FL 33409-2911
Fax: (561) 640-3328
E-mail: fladmit@northwood.edu
Phone: (561) 478-5500

Northwood University: Michigan
www.northwood.edu
Admissions
4000 Whiting Drive
Midland, MI 48640
Fax: (989) 837-4490
E-mail: miadmit@northwood.edu
Phone: (989) 837-4273

Northwood University: Texas
www.northwood.edu
Admissions
1114 West FM 1382
Cedar Hill, TX 75104
Fax: (972) 291-3824
E-mail: txadmit@northwood.edu
Phone: (800) 927-9663

Norwalk Community College
www.ncc.commnet.edu
International Student Office
188 Richards Avenue
Norwalk, CT 06854-1655
Fax: (203) 857-6948
E-mail: dbogusky@ncc.commnet.edu
Phone: (203) 857-7289

Norwich University
www.norwich.edu
158 Harmon Drive
Northfield, VT 05663
Fax: (802) 485-2032
E-mail: nuadm@norwich.edu
Phone: (802) 485-2002

Nossi College of Art
www.nossi.com
Admissions
907 Rivergate Parkway, Building E-6
Goodlettsville, TN 37072
Fax: (615) 851-1087
E-mail: admissions@nossi.com
Phone: (615) 851-1088

Notre Dame College
www.notredamecollege.edu
Admissions
4545 College Road
Cleveland, OH 44121-4293
Fax: (216) 381-3802
E-mail: cnolan@ndc.edu
Phone: (216) 381-1680 ext. 5355

Notre Dame de Namur University
www.ndnu.edu
Admission Office
1500 Ralston Avenue
Belmont, CA 94002-1908
Fax: (650) 508-3426
E-mail: admiss@ndnu.edu
Phone: (650) 508-3600

Nova Southeastern University
www.nova.edu
Individual Program Offices
3301 College Avenue
Fort Lauderdale, FL 33314
Fax: (954) 262-3846
E-mail: intl@nsu.nova.edu
Phone: (954) 262-7240

Nunez Community College
www.nunez.edu
Admissions Office
3710 Paris Road
Chalmette, LA 70043
Fax: (504) 278-6487
E-mail: bmaillet@nunez.edu
Phone: (504) 278-6467

Nyack College
www.nyack.edu
Admissions
1 South Boulevard
Nyack, NY 10960-3698
Fax: (845) 358-3047
E-mail: admissions@nyack.edu
Phone: (845) 675-4401

Oakbridge Academy of Arts
www.oaa.edu
Admissions
1250 Greensburg Road
Lower Burrell, PA 15068
Fax: (724) 335-3367
E-mail: admissions@oaa.edu
Phone: (724) 335-5336

Oakland City University
www.oak.edu
Admissions
138 North Lucretia Street
Oakland City, IN 47660
Fax: (812) 749-1433
E-mail: ocuadmit@oak.edu
Phone: (800) 737-5125

Oakland Community College
www.oaklandcc.edu
International Student Advisor
2480 Opdyke Road
Bloomfield Hills, MI 48304-2266
Fax: (248) 232-4441
E-mail: ddschack@oaklandcc.edu
Phone: (248) 232-4440

Oakland University
www.oakland.edu
Senior Recruitment Advisor
101 North Foundation Hall
Oakland University
Rochester, MI 48309-4401
Fax: (248) 370-4462
E-mail: rosebroc@oakland.edu
Phone: (248) 370-3310

Oakton Community College
www.oakton.edu
Enrollment Services
1600 East Golf Road
Des Plaines, IL 60016
Fax: (847) 635-1706
E-mail: lynn@oakton.edu
Phone: (847) 635-1713

Oakwood University
www.oakwood.edu
Enrollment Management
7000 Adventist Boulevard, NW
Huntsville, AL 35896
Fax: (256) 726-7154
E-mail: jbartholomew@oakwood.edu
Phone: (256) 726-7423

Oberlin College
www.oberlin.edu
Coordinator for International Admissions
Carnegie Building, 101 North Professor Street
Oberlin, OH 44074-1075
Fax: (440) 775-6905
E-mail: joel.presti@oberlin.edu
Phone: (440) 775-8411

Occidental College
www.oxy.edu
Assistant Dean of Admissions
1600 Campus Road
Los Angeles, CA 90041
Fax: (323) 341-4875
E-mail: tokuza@oxy.edu
Phone: (323) 259-2700

Ocean County College
www.ocean.edu
Admissions/Records
College Drive
Box 2001
Toms River, NJ 08754-2001
Fax: (732) 255-0444
E-mail: mmehlmann@ocean.edu
Phone: (732) 255-0400 ext. 2969

Odessa College
www.odessa.edu
Admissions
201 West University
Odessa, TX 79764-7127
Fax: (432) 335-6636
E-mail: thilliard@odessa.edu
Phone: (432) 335-6432

Oglala Lakota College
www.olc.edu
Registrar
Box 490
Kyle, SD 57752-0490
Fax: (605) 455-2787
Phone: (605) 455-6033

Oglethorpe University
www.oglethorpe.edu
Office of Admission
4484 Peachtree Road NE
Atlanta, GA 30319-2797
Fax: (404) 364-8491
E-mail: admission@oglethorpe.edu
Phone: (404) 364-8307

Ohio College of Massotherapy
www.ocm.edu
225 Heritage Woods Drive
Akron, OH 44321
Fax: (330) 665-5021
E-mail: admissions@ocm.edu
Phone: (330) 665-1084

Ohio Dominican University
www.ohiodominican.edu
International Office
1216 Sunbury Road
Columbus, OH 43219
Fax: (614) 251-4639
E-mail: ochelm@ohiodominican.edu
Phone: (614) 251-4645

Ohio Northern University
www.onu.edu
Director of International Admissions
525 South Main Street
Ada, OH 45810
Fax: (419) 772-2484
E-mail: d-shine@onu.edu
Phone: (419) 772-2483

Ohio State University: Columbus Campus
www.osu.edu
Undergraduate Admissions and First Year
Experience
110 Enarson Hall
154 West 12th Avenue
Columbus, OH 43210
Fax: (614) 292-4818
E-mail: askabuckeye@osu.edu
Phone: (614) 292-3980

Ohio Technical College
www.ohiotechnicalcollege.com
1374 East 51st Street
Cleveland, OH 44103-1269
Fax: (216) 881-9145
E-mail: info@ohiotechnicalcollege.com
Phone: (216) 881-1700

Ohio University
www.ohio.edu
Office of Undergraduate Admissions
120 Chubb Hall
Athens, OH 45701-2979
Fax: (740) 593-0560
E-mail: admissions.international@ohio.edu
Phone: (740) 593-4100

Ohio University: Eastern Campus
www.eastern.ohiou.edu
45425 National Road West
St. Clairsville, OH 43950-9724
Fax: (740) 695-7077
E-mail: admissions@ohio.edu
Phone: (740) 695-1720

Ohio University: Southern Campus at Ironton
www.southern.ohiou.edu
Student Services
1804 Liberty Avenue
Ironton, OH 45638
Fax: (740) 533-4632
E-mail: queenn@ohio.edu
Phone: (740) 533-4600

Ohio University: Zanesville Campus
www.zanesville.ohiou.edu
1425 Newark Road
Zanesville, OH 43701
Fax: (740) 588-1444
E-mail: ouzservices@ohio.edu
Phone: (740) 588-1439

Ohio Valley University
www.ovu.edu
Admissions Office
One Campus View Drive
Vienna, WV 26105
Fax: (304) 865-6175
E-mail: gerald.cole@ovu.edu
Phone: (304) 865-6205

Ohio Wesleyan University
www.owu.edu
International Recruitment
75 South Sandusky Street
Delaware, OH 43015-2398
Fax: (740) 368-3314
E-mail: owuintl@owu.edu
Phone: (740) 368-3020

Ohlone College
www.ohlone.edu
International Programs and Services
43600 Mission Boulevard
Fremont, CA 94539-0390
Fax: (510) 659-7321
E-mail: ewest@ohlone.edu
Phone: (510) 659-6100

Ohr Somayach Tanenbaum Education Center
www.os.edu
244 Route 306
Box 334
Monsey, NY 10952
Fax: (845) 425-8865
E-mail: ohr@os.edu
Phone: (845) 425-1370

Oklahoma Baptist University
www.okbu.edu
Office of Admissions
500 West University
OBU Box 61174
Shawnee, OK 74804
Fax: (405) 878-2068
E-mail: admissions@mail.okbu.edu
Phone: (405) 878-2033

Oklahoma Christian University
www.oc.edu
Office of International Programs
Box 11000
Oklahoma City, OK 73136-1100
Fax: (405) 425-5477
E-mail: greg.gillham@oc.edu
Phone: (405) 425-5475

Oklahoma City Community College
www.occc.edu
Coordinator of International Student Services
7777 South May Avenue
Oklahoma City, OK 73159
Fax: (405) 682-7521
E-mail: sgarner@occc.edu
Phone: (405) 682-7884

Oklahoma City University
www.okcu.edu
International Admission Services
2501 North Blackwelder Avenue
Oklahoma City, OK 73106-1493
Fax: (405) 208-5946
E-mail: iso@okcu.edu
Phone: (405) 208-5130

Oklahoma Panhandle State University
www.opsu.edu
International Students Office
OPSU Admissions
Box 430
Goodwell, OK 73939-0430
Fax: (580) 349-2302
E-mail: international@opsu.edu
Phone: (580) 349-1314

Oklahoma State University
www.okstate.edu
International Students and Scholars
219 Student Union
Stillwater, OK 74078
Fax: (405) 744-8120
E-mail: admissions-iss@okstate.edu
Phone: (405) 744-5459

Oklahoma State University Institute of Technology: Okmulgee
www.osuit.edu
International and Multicultural Coordinator
1801 East Fourth Street
Okmulgee, OK 74447-3901
Fax: (918) 293-4633
E-mail: thomas.kiipkirgat@okstate.edu
Phone: (918) 293-5071

Oklahoma State University: Oklahoma City
www.osuokc.edu
International Student Adviser
900 North Portland
Oklahoma City, OK 73107-6195
Fax: (405) 945-3277
E-mail: drarche@osuokc.edu
Phone: (405) 945-3324

Oklahoma Wesleyan University
www.okwu.edu
Admissions Office
2201 Silver Lake Road
Bartlesville, OK 74006
Fax: (918) 335-6229
E-mail: admissions@okwu.edu
Phone: (918) 335-6219

Old Dominion University
www.odu.edu
Office of International Admissions
108 Rollins Hall, 5215 Hampton Boulevard
Norfolk, VA 23529
Fax: (757) 683-3651
E-mail: intladm@odu.edu
Phone: (757) 683-3701

Olivet College
www.olivetcollege.edu
Admissions
320 South Main Street
Olivet, MI 49076
Fax: (269) 749-6617
E-mail: mcasarez@olivetcollege.edu
Phone: (269) 749-7635

Olivet Nazarene University
www.olivet.edu
International Student Admissions Counselor
One University Avenue
Bourbonnais, IL 60914
Fax: (815) 935-4998
E-mail: jfish1@olivet.edu
Phone: (815) 939-5011

Olympic College
www.olympic.edu
International Student Programs
1600 Chester Avenue
Bremerton, WA 98337-1699
Fax: (360) 475-7202
E-mail: abates@olympic.edu
Phone: (360) 475-7718

O'More College of Design
www.omorecollege.edu
Admissions Office
423 South Margin Street
Franklin, TN 37064-0908
Fax: (615) 790-1662
E-mail: clee@omorecollege.edu
Phone: (615) 794-4254 ext. 232

Onondaga Community College
www.sunyocc.edu
Office of Recruitment & Admission
4585 West Seneca Turnpike
Syracuse, NY 13215-4585
Fax: (315) 498-2107
E-mail: international@sunyocc.edu
Phone: (315) 498-7266

Oral Roberts University
www.oru.edu
International Admissions
7777 South Lewis Avenue
Tulsa, OK 74171
Fax: (918) 495-6788
E-mail: thannon@oru.edu
Phone: (918) 495-6488

Orange Coast College
www.orangecoastcollege.edu
International Center
2701 Fairview Road
Box 5005
Costa Mesa, CA 92628-5005
Fax: (714) 432-5191
E-mail: mniroumand@occ.cccd.edu
Phone: (714) 432-5940

Orangeburg-Calhoun Technical College
www.octech.edu
Admissions
3250 St. Matthews Road
Orangeburg, SC 29118-8222
Fax: (803) 535-1388
E-mail: felderb@octech.edu
Phone: (803) 536-0311

Oregon College of Art & Craft
www.ocac.edu
Assistant Director of Admissions
8245 SW Barnes Road
Portland, OR 97225-6349
Fax: (503) 297-9651
E-mail: dsimpson@ocac.edu
Phone: (971) 255-4141

Oregon Health & Science University
www.ohsu.edu
Admissions Office for Desired Program
3181 SW Sam Jackson Park Road
Mail Code L109
Portland, OR 97239-3098
Fax: (503) 494-4629
E-mail: proginfo@ohsu.edu
Phone: (503) 494-8311

Oregon Institute of Technology
www.oit.edu
Admissions Director
3201 Campus Drive
Klamath Falls, OR 97601
Fax: (541) 885-1115
E-mail: oit@oit.edu
Phone: (541) 885-1150

Oregon State University
www.oregonstate.edu
International Programs
104 Kerr Administration Building
Corvallis, OR 97331-2130
Fax: (541) 737-6482
E-mail: julie.g.walkin@oregonstate.edu
Phone: (541) 737-2697

Orleans Technical Institute
www.orleanstech.edu
2770 Red Lion Road
Philadelphia, PA 19114
Fax: (215) 745-1689
E-mail: debbie.bello@jevs.org
Phone: (215) 728-4426

Otero Junior College
www.ojc.edu
1802 Colorado Avenue
La Junta, CO 81050
Fax: (719) 384-6933
E-mail: brad.smith@ojc.cccoes.edu
Phone: (719) 384-6869

Otis College of Art and Design
www.otis.edu
Office of Admissions
9045 Lincoln Boulevard
Los Angeles, CA 90045-9785
Fax: (310) 665-6821
E-mail: admissions@otis.edu
Phone: (310) 665-6820

Ottawa University
www.ottawa.edu
Foreign Student Advisor
1001 South Cedar Street, #17
Ottawa, KS 66067-3399
Fax: (785) 229-1007
E-mail: murle.mordy@ottawa.edu
Phone: (785) 229-1072

Otterbein University
www.otterbein.edu
Office of Admission
One Otterbein College
Westerville, OH 43081
Fax: (614) 823-1200
E-mail: kmessenheimer@otterbein.edu
Phone: (614) 823-1500

Ouachita Baptist University
www.obu.edu
International Programs
OBU Box 3776
Arkadelphia, AR 71998-0001
Fax: (870) 245-5312
E-mail: zimnyr@obu.edu
Phone: (870) 245-5224

Ouachita Technical College
www.otcweb.edu
Registrar
One College Circle
Malvern, AR 72104
Fax: (501) 337-9382
E-mail: ljohnson@otcweb.edu
Phone: (501) 337-5000 ext. 1133

Our Lady of Holy Cross College
www.olhcc.edu
Enrollment Services
4123 Woodland Drive
New Orleans, LA 70131-7399
Fax: (504) 391-2421
E-mail: kkopecky@olhcc.edu
Phone: (504) 394-7744 ext. 175

Our Lady of the Lake University of San Antonio
www.ollusa.edu
Office of International Admissions
411 Southwest 24th Street
San Antonio, TX 78207-4689
Fax: (210) 431-4036
E-mail: international@ollusa.edu
Phone: (210) 431-3978

Owens Community College: Toledo
www.owens.edu
International Student Services
30335 Oregon Road
PO Box 10000
Toledo, OH 43699-1947
Fax: (567) 661-2046
E-mail: deborah_gavlik@owens.edu
Phone: (567) 661-7510

Owensboro Community and Technical College
www.octc.kctcs.edu
4800 New Hartford Road
Owensboro, KY 42303-1899
Fax: (270) 686-4648
E-mail: barbara.tipmore@kctcs.net
Phone: (270) 686-4530

Oxnard College
www.oxnardcollege.edu
Admissions & Records
4000 South Rose Avenue
Oxnard, CA 93033
Fax: (805) 986-5943
E-mail: ocadmissions@vcccd.edu
Phone: (805) 986-5810

Ozarks Technical Community College
www.otc.edu
1001 East Chestnut Expressway
Springfield, MO 65802
Fax: (417) 447-6906
E-mail: lundstrl@otc.edu
Phone: (417) 447-8197

Pace Institute
www.paceinstitute.com
606 Court Street
Reading, PA 19601
E-mail: pace4u2@aol.com
Phone: (610) 375-1212

Pace University
www.pace.edu
International Programs & Services
1 Pace Plaza
New York, NY 10038-1598
Fax: (212) 346-1116
E-mail: wfontana@pace.edu
Phone: (212) 346-1064

Pacific College of Oriental Medicine: San Diego
www.pacificcollege.edu
7445 Mission Valley Road, Suite 105
San Diego, CA 92108
E-mail: admissions-sd@pacificcollege.edu
Phone: (619) 574-6909

Pacific Lutheran University
www.plu.edu
Office of Admission
1010 South 122nd Street
Tacoma, WA 98447-0003
Fax: (235) 536-5136
E-mail: kuriwha@plu.edu
Phone: (800) 274-6758

Pacific Northwest College of Art
www.pnca.edu
Admissions
1241 NW Johnson Street
Portland, OR 97209
Fax: (503) 821-8978
E-mail: csweet@pnca.edu
Phone: (503) 821-8972

Pacific Oaks College
www.pacificoaks.edu
Admissions Office
5 Westmoreland Place
Pasadena, CA 91103
Fax: (626) 666-1220
E-mail: apickens@pacificoaks.edu
Phone: (626) 397-1349

Pacific States University
www.psuca.edu
Associate Director of Admission
1516 South Western Avenue
Los Angeles, CA 90006
Fax: (323) 731-7276
E-mail: admissions@psuca.edu
Phone: (323) 731-2383 ext. 17

Pacific Union College
www.puc.edu
Enrollment Services
One Angwin Avenue
Angwin, CA 94508-9707
Fax: (707) 965-6432
E-mail: enroll@puc.edu
Phone: (707) 965-6336

Pacific University
www.pacificu.edu
Office of International Admissions
2043 College Way
Forest Grove, OR 97116-1797
Fax: (503) 352-2970
E-mail: JohnHarn@pacificu.edu
Phone: (503) 352-2851

Paier College of Art
www.paiercollegeofart.edu
Registrar
20 Gorham Avenue
Hamden, CT 06514-3902
Fax: (203) 287-3021
E-mail: paier.admin@snet.net
Phone: (203) 287-3032

Paine College
www.paine.edu
Office of Admissions
1235 15th Street
Augusta, GA 30901-3182
Fax: (706) 821-8648
E-mail: jtinsley@paine.edu
Phone: (706) 821-8320

Palm Beach Atlantic University
www.pba.edu
Undergraduate Admissions
PO Box 24708
West Palm Beach, FL 33416-4708
Fax: (561) 803-2115
E-mail: rod_sullivan@pba.edu
Phone: (561) 803-2000

Palm Beach State College
www.palmbeachstate.edu
International Student Admissions Office
4200 Congress Avenue
Lake Worth, FL 33461
Fax: (561) 868-3605
E-mail: labordef@palmbeachstate.edu
Phone: (561) 868-3031

Palo Verde College
www.paloverde.edu
Admissions & Records
One College Drive
Blythe, CA 92225
Fax: (760) 921-3608
E-mail: shamilton@paloverde.edu
Phone: (760) 921-5483

Palomar College
www.palomar.edu
International Edcuation Office
1140 West Mission Road
San Marcos, CA 92069-1487
Fax: (760) 761-3592
E-mail: yoneill@palomar.edu
Phone: (760) 744-1150 ext. 2167

Pamlico Community College
www.pamlicocc.edu
PO Box 185
Grantsboro, NC 28529
Fax: (252) 249-2377
E-mail: jgibbs@pamlicocc.edu
Phone: (252) 249-1851

Panola College
www.panola.edu
Testing Coordinator/Advisor/International
Student Coordinator
1109 West Panola Street
Carthage, TX 75633
Fax: (903) 693-2031
E-mail: sgee@panola.edu
Phone: (903) 693-2046

Paradise Valley Community College
www.pvc.maricopa.edu
18401 North 32nd Street
Phoenix, AZ 85032
Fax: (602) 787-6625
Phone: (602) 787-7020

Paralegal Institute
www.theparalegalinstitute.edu
18275 North 59th Avenue, Suite 186 Building N
Glendale, AZ 85308
Fax: (602) 212-0502
E-mail: kscheib@theparalegalinstitute.edu
Phone: (800) 354-1254

Paris Junior College
www.parisjc.edu
International Student Adviser
2400 Clarksville Street
Paris, TX 75460
Fax: (903) 784-9370
E-mail: bthomas@parisjc.edu
Phone: (214) 784-9434

Park University
www.park.edu
International Student Office
8700 NW River Park Drive
Parkville, MO 64152
Fax: (816) 505-5443
E-mail: admissions@park.edu
Phone: (816) 584-6379

Parkland College
www.parkland.edu
International Education
2400 West Bradley Avenue
Champaign, IL 61821-1899
Fax: (217) 353-2640
E-mail: intlinfo@parkland.edu
Phone: (217) 351-2890

Parsons The New School for Design
www.parsons.edu
Office of Admissions
72 Fifth Avenue
2nd Floor
New York, NY 10011
Fax: (212) 229-8975
E-mail: norrisdm@newschool.edu
Phone: (212) 229-8989

Pasadena City College
www.pasadena.edu
International Students Office
1570 East Colorado Boulevard
Pasadena, CA 91106
Fax: (626) 585-7912
Phone: (818) 585-7391

Pasco-Hernando Community College
www.phcc.edu
Admissions and Student Records
10230 Ridge Road
New Port Richey, FL 34654-5199
Fax: (727) 816-3389
E-mail: bullard@phcc.edu
Phone: (727) 816-3261

Passaic County Community College
www.pccc.edu
Admissions Office
One College Boulevard
Paterson, NJ 07505-1179
Fax: (973) 684-6778
E-mail: mdavila@pccc.edu
Phone: (973) 684-6307

Patrick Henry College
www.phc.edu
Ten Patrick Henry Circle
Purcellville, VA 20132-3197
Fax: (540) 441-8119
E-mail: admissions@phc.edu
Phone: (540) 441-8110

Patrick Henry Community College
www.ph.vccs.edu
Admissions Office
645 Patriot Avenue
Martinsville, VA 24115-5311
Fax: (276) 656-0352
E-mail: ttisdale@ph.vccs.edu
Phone: (276) 656-0311

Patten University
www.patten.edu
Admissions
2433 Coolidge Avenue
Oakland, CA 94601-2699
Fax: (510) 534-4344
E-mail: bailey@patten.edu
Phone: (510) 261-8500 ext. 7764

Paul D. Camp Community College
www.pc.vccs.edu
Admissions and Records
100 North College Drive
PO Box 737
Franklin, VA 23851-0737
Fax: (757) 569-6795
E-mail: mwilliams@pc.cc.va.us
Phone: (757) 569-6700

Paul Smith's College
www.paulsmiths.edu
Admissions
PO Box 265, Routes 30 & 86
Paul Smiths, NY 12970-0265
Fax: (518) 327-6016
E-mail: admissions@paulsmiths.edu
Phone: (800) 421-2605

Peace College
www.peace.edu
Admissions
15 East Peace Street
Raleigh, NC 27604-1194
Fax: (919) 508-2306
E-mail: cjdegroot@peace.edu
Phone: (919) 508-2000 ext. 2020

Peirce College
www.peirce.edu
Admissions
1420 Pine Street
Philadelphia, PA 19102-4699
Fax: (215) 670-9366
E-mail: info@peirce.edu
Phone: (888) 467-3472 ext. 9214

Pellissippi State Community College
www.pstcc.edu
International Admissions and Records
Box 22990
Knoxville, TN 37933-0990
Fax: (865) 539-7217
E-mail: latouzeau@pstcc.edu
Phone: (865) 539-7013

Peninsula College
www.pencol.edu
International Coordinator Students
1502 East Lauridsen Boulevard
Port Angeles, WA 98362
Fax: (360) 417-6482
E-mail: gyl@pcadmin.ctc.edu
Phone: (360) 417-6491

Penn Foster College
www.pennfostercollege.edu
Manager, DP Services
14300 North Northsight Boulevard, Suite 120
Scottsdale, AZ 85260
E-mail: info@pennfoster.edu
Phone: (570) 342-7701

Penn State Abington
www.abington.psu.edu
Admissions
106 Sutherland
1600 Woodland Road
Abingdon, PA 19001-3990
Fax: (814) 863-7590
E-mail: admissions@psu.edu
Phone: (814) 865-5471

Penn State Altoona
www.aa.psu.edu
Admissions
E108 Smith Building
Altoona, PA 16801-3760
Fax: (814) 863-7590
E-mail: admissions@psu.edu
Phone: (814) 865-5471

Penn State Beaver
www.br.psu.edu
Admissions
100 University Drive
113 Student Union
Monaca, PA 15061-2799
Fax: (814) 863-7590
E-mail: admissions@psu.edu
Phone: (814) 865-5471

Penn State Berks
www.bk.psu.edu
Admissions
Tulpehocken Road
PO Box 7009
Reading, PA 19610-6009
Fax: (814) 863-7590
E-mail: admissions@psu.edu
Phone: (814) 865-5471

Penn State Brandywine
www.brandywine.psu.edu
Admissions
25 Yearsley Mill Road
Media, PA 19063-5596
Fax: (814) 863-7590
E-mail: admissions@psu.edu
Phone: (814) 865-5471

Penn State DuBois
www.ds.psu.edu
Admissions
Enrollment Services House
DuBois, PA 15801-3199
Fax: (814) 863-7590
E-mail: admissions@psu.edu
Phone: (814) 865-5471

Penn State Erie, The Behrend College
www.erie.psu.edu
Executive Director for Undergraduate
Admissions
4701 College Drive
Erie, PA 16563-0105
Fax: (814) 898-6044
E-mail: admissions@psu.edu
Phone: (814) 865-5471

Penn State Fayette, The Eberly Campus
www.fe.psu.edu
Admissions
PO Box 519, Route 119 North
108 Williams Building
Uniontown, PA 15401-0519
Fax: (814) 863-7590
E-mail: admissions@psu.edu
Phone: (814) 865-5471

Penn State Greater Allegheny
www.ga.psu.edu
Admissions
101 Frable Building
4000 University Drive
McKeesport, PA 15132-7698
Fax: (814) 863-7590
E-mail: admissions@psu.edu
Phone: (814) 865-5471.

Penn State Harrisburg
www.hbg.psu.edu
Admissions
Swatara Building
777 West Harrisburg Pike
Middletown, PA 17057-4898
Fax: (814) 863-7590
E-mail: admissions@psu.edu
Phone: (814) 865-5471

Penn State Hazleton
www.hn.psu.edu
Admissions
110 Administration Building
76 University Drive
University Park, PA 18202-1291
Fax: (814) 863-7590
E-mail: admissions@psu.edu
Phone: (814) 865-5471

Penn State Lehigh Valley
www.lv.psu.edu
Admissions
2809 Saucon Valley Road
Center Vally, PA 18034-8447
Fax: (814) 863-7590
E-mail: admissions@psu.edu
Phone: (814) 865-5471

Penn State Mont Alto
www.ma.psu.edu
Executive Director for Undergraduate
Admissions
1 Campus Drive
Mont Alto, PA 17237-9703
Fax: (814) 863-7590
E-mail: admissions@psu.edu
Phone: (814) 865-5471

Penn State New Kensington
www.nk.psu.edu
Admissions
3550 Seventh Street Road, Route 780
New Kensington, PA 15068-1765
Fax: (814) 863-7590
E-mail: admissions@psu.edu
Phone: (814) 865-5471

Penn State Schuylkill
www.sl.psu.edu
Admissions
200 University Drive
A-102 Administration Building
Schuylkill Haven, PA 17972-2208
Fax: (814) 863-7590
E-mail: admissions@psu.edu
Phone: (814) 865-5471

Penn State Shenango
www.shenango.psu.edu
Admissions
147 Shenango Avenue, Room 206
Sharon Hall
Sharon, PA 16146-1597
Fax: (814) 863-7590
E-mail: admissions@psu.edu
Phone: (814) 865-5471

Penn State University Park
www.psu.edu
Admissions
201 Shields Building
Box 3000
University Park, PA 16804-3000
Fax: (814) 863-7590
E-mail: admissions@psu.edu
Phone: (814) 865-5471

Penn State Wilkes-Barre
www.wb.psu.edu
Admissions
Hayfield House 101
Lehman, PA 18627-0217
Fax: (814) 863-7590
E-mail: admissions@psu.edu
Phone: (814) 865-5471

Penn State Worthington Scranton
www.sn.psu.edu
Admissions
120 Ridge View Drive
Dunmore, PA 18512-1602
Fax: (814) 863-7590
E-mail: admissions@psu.edu
Phone: (814) 865-5471

Penn State York
www.yk.psu.edu
Admissions
1031 Edgecomb Avenue
York, PA 17403-3398
Fax: (814) 863-7590
E-mail: admissions@psu.edu
Phone: (814) 865-5471

Pennsylvania Academy of the Fine Arts
www.pafa.edu
128 North Broad Street
Philadelphia, PA 19102
E-mail: admissions@pafa.edu

Pennsylvania College of Technology
www.pct.edu
Associate Dean for Admissions and Financial
Aid
One College Avenue
DIF #119
Williamsport, PA 17701-5799
Fax: (570) 321-5551
E-mail: dcorrell@pct.edu
Phone: (570) 327-4761

Pennsylvania Highlands Community College
www.pennhighlands.edu
Director of Admissions
101 Community College Way
Johnstown, PA 15904
Fax: (814) 262-6420
E-mail: jmaul@pennhighlands.edu
Phone: (814) 262-6431

Pensacola State College
www.pensacolastate.edu
Director Admissions and Registrar
1000 College Boulevard
Pensacola, FL 32504-8998
Fax: (850) 484-1829
E-mail: mcaughey@pjc.edu
Phone: (850) 484-1623

Pepperdine University
www.pepperdine.edu
International Student Services
24255 Pacific Coast Highway
Malibu, CA 90263-4392
Fax: (310) 506-7403
E-mail: oiss@pepperdine.edu
Phone: (310) 506-4246

Peru State College
www.peru.edu
Admissions
Box 10
Peru, NE 68421-0010
Fax: (402) 872-2296
E-mail: admissions@peru.edu
Phone: (402) 872-2221

Pfeiffer University
www.pfeiffer.edu
Associate Director of Admissions
Box 960
Misenheimer, NC 28109
Fax: (704) 463-1363
E-mail: diane.martin@fsmail.pfeiffer.edu
Phone: (704) 463-3052

Philadelphia Biblical University
www.pbu.edu
Admissions
200 Manor Avenue
Langhorne, PA 19047-2990
Fax: (215) 702-4248
E-mail: admissions@pbu.edu
Phone: (215) 702-4241

Philadelphia University
www.philau.edu
Admissions Office
School House Lane and Henry Avenue
Philadelphia, PA 19144-5497
Fax: (215) 951-2907
E-mail: Regerj@philau.edu
Phone: (215) 951-2800

Philander Smith College
www.philander.edu
Admissions
900 Daisy Bates Drive
Little Rock, AR 72202-3718
Fax: (501) 370-5225
E-mail: bevrich@philander.edu
Phone: (501) 370-5221

Phillips Beth Israel School of Nursing
www.futurenursebi.org
Admissions
776 Sixth Avenue, Fourth Floor
New York, NY 10001
Fax: (212) 614-6109
E-mail: bstern@chpnet.org
Phone: (212) 614-6176

**Phillips Community College of the
University of Arkansas**
www.pccua.edu
Admissions and Records
1000 Campus Drive
PO Box 785
Helena, AR 72342
Fax: (870) 338-7542
E-mail: lboone@pccua.edu
Phone: (870) 338-6474 ext. 1235

Phoenix College
www.pc.maricopa.edu
International Student Office
1202 West Thomas Road
Phoenix, AZ 85013
Fax: (602) 285-7813
E-mail: annette.duran@pcmail.maricopa.edu
Phone: (602) 285-7424

**Piedmont Baptist College and Graduate
School**
www.pbc.edu
Admissions
420 South Boad Street
Winston-Salem, NC 27101-5133
Fax: (336) 725-5522
E-mail: holritzk@pbc.edu
Phone: (336) 725-8344 ext. 7927

Piedmont College
www.piedmont.edu
Admissions
165 Central Avenue
PO Box 10
Demorest, GA 30535-0010
Fax: (706) 776-0103
E-mail: jkelly@piedmont.edu
Phone: (800) 277-7020

Piedmont Community College
www.piedmontcc.edu
Admissions
1715 College Drive
PO Box 1197
Roxboro, NC 27573-1197
Fax: (336) 598-9283
Phone: (336) 599-1181 ext. 219

Piedmont Technical College
www.ptc.edu
Admissions
PO Box 1467
Greenwood, SC 29648
Fax: (864) 941-8555
E-mail: omundson.a@ptc.edu
Phone: (864) 941-8357

Piedmont Virginia Community College
www.pvcc.edu
Office of Admissions
501 College Drive
Charlottesville, VA 22902-7589
Fax: (434) 961-5425
E-mail: mwalsh@pvcc.edu
Phone: (434) 961-6540

Pierce College
www.pierce.ctc.edu
International Education
9401 Farwest Drive SW
Lakewood, WA 98498-1999
Fax: (253) 964-6256
E-mail: intledu@pierce.ctc.edu
Phone: (253) 964-7327

Pikes Peak Community College
www.ppcc.edu
Admissions
5675 South Academy Boulevard
Colorado Springs, CO 80906-5498
Fax: (719) 502-2609
E-mail: vicki.furaus@ppcc.edu
Phone: (719) 502-2035

Pikeville College
www.pc.edu
Undergraduate Admissions
147 Sycamore Street
Pikeville, KY 41501-1194
Fax: (606) 218-5255
E-mail: abranham@pc.edu
Phone: (606) 218-5251

Pima Community College
www.pima.edu
International Student Admissions Office
4905B East Broadway
Tucson, AZ 85709-1120
Fax: (520) 206-3265
E-mail: intadmit@pima.edu
Phone: (520) 206-6732

Pine Manor College
www.pmc.edu
Director of International Recruitment
400 Heath Street
Chestnut Hill, MA 02467
Fax: (617) 731-7102
E-mail: SpinazoJ@pmc.edu
Phone: (617) 731-7104

Pine Technical College
www.pinetech.edu
Admissions Office
900 Fourth Street, SE
Pine City, MN 55063
Fax: (320) 629-5101
E-mail: machn@pinetech.edu
Phone: (320) 629-5100

Pinnacle Career Institute: Kansas City
www.pcitraining.edu
1001 East 101st Terrace, Suite 325
Kansas City, MO 64131-3367
Fax: (816) 331-2026
E-mail: bricks@pcitraining.edu
Phone: (816) 331-5700

Pittsburg State University
www.pittstate.edu
International Admission Coordinator
1701 South Broadway
Pittsburg, KS 66762
Fax: (620) 235-4962
E-mail: ahurt@pittstate.edu
Phone: (620) 235-4093

Pittsburgh Institute of Aeronautics
www.pia.edu
Admissions
Box 10897
Pittsburgh, PA 15236-0897
Fax: (412) 466-0513
E-mail: ssabold@pia.edu
Phone: (412) 346-2100

Pittsburgh Institute of Mortuary Science
www.pims.edu
5808 Baum Boulevard
Pittsburgh, PA 15206-3706
Fax: (412) 362-1684
E-mail: pims5808@aol.com
Phone: (412) 362-8500

Pitzer College
www.pitzer.edu
International Programs Office
1050 North Mills Avenue
Claremont, CA 91711-6101
Fax: (909) 621-0518
E-mail: todd_sasaki@pitzer.edu
Phone: (909) 621-8308

Platt College: Dallas
www.plattcolleges.edu
2974 LBJ Freeway, Suite 300
Dallas, TX 75234

Platt College: Los Angeles
www.plattcollege.edu
Admissions
1000 South Fremont Avenue A9W
Alhambra, CA 91803
Fax: (626) 300-3978
E-mail: jboylan@plattcollege.edu
Phone: (626) 300-5444

Platt College: Moore
www.plattcolleges.org
201 North Eastern
Moore, OK 73160
Phone: (405) 912-3260

Platt College: Oklahoma City Central
www.plattcollege.org
309 South Ann Arbor
Oklahoma City, OK 73128
Fax: (405) 943-2150
E-mail: klamb@plattcollege.org
Phone: (405) 946-7799

Platt College: Ontario
www.plattcollege.edu
Admissions
3700 Inland Empire Boulevard
Ontario, CA 91764
Fax: (909) 941-9660
E-mail: cconceicao@plattcollege.edu
Phone: (909) 941-9410

Platt College: San Diego
www.platt.edu
6250 El Cajon Boulevard
San Diego, CA 92115
Fax: (619) 308-0570
E-mail: info@platt.edu
Phone: (619) 265-0107 ext. 23

Platt College: Tulsa
www.plattcollege.org
3801 South Sheridan
Tulsa, OK 74145-1132
Fax: (918) 622-1240
E-mail: stephanieh@plattcollege.org
Phone: (918) 663-9000

Plymouth State University
www.plymouth.edu
Admission Office
17 High Street MSC 52
Plymouth, NH 03264-1595
Fax: (603) 535-2714
E-mail: plymouthadmit@plymouth.edu
Phone: (800) 842-6900

Point Loma Nazarene University
www.pointloma.edu
Admissions
3900 Lomaland Drive
Admissions
San Diego, CA 92106-2899
Fax: (619) 849-2601
E-mail: admissions@pointloma.edu
Phone: (619) 849-2273

Point Park University
www.pointpark.edu
International Student Services and Enrollment
201 Wood Street
Pittsburgh, PA 15222-1984
Fax: (412) 392-4792
E-mail: iss@pointpark.edu
Phone: (412) 392-4775

Polk State College
www.polk.edu
Enrollment Management, Winter Haven
Campus
999 Avenue H NE
Winter Haven, FL 33881-4299
Fax: (863) 297-1060
E-mail: mwestgate@polk.edu
Phone: (863) 297-1010 ext. 5201

Polytechnic Institute of New York University
www.poly.edu
Polytechnic Admissions
6 Metrotech Center
Brooklyn, NY 11201-2999
Fax: (718) 260-3446
E-mail: mgendel@poly.edu
Phone: (800) 765-9832

Pomona College
www.pomona.edu
Admissions Office
333 North College Way
Claremont, CA 91711-6312
Fax: (909) 621-8952
E-mail: admissions@pomona.edu
Phone: (909) 621-8134

Ponce Paramedical College
www.popac.edu
Calle Acacia 1213, Urb. Villa Flores
PO Box 800106
Ponce, PR 00780-0106
E-mail: admisiones@popac.edu
Phone: (787) 848-1589 ext. 413

Pontifical Catholic University of Puerto Rico
www.pucpr.edu
Admissions
2250 Las Americas Avenue, Suite 284
Ponce, PR 00717-9777
Fax: (787) 651-2044
E-mail: admisiones@pucpr.edu
Phone: (787) 841-2000 ext. 1000

Porterville College
www.portervillecollege.edu
Admissions and Records Office
100 East College Avenue
Porterville, CA 93257
Fax: (209) 791-2349
Phone: (209) 791-2222

Portland Community College
www.pcc.edu
International Student Education
Box 19000
Portland, OR 97280-0990
Fax: (971) 722-7170
E-mail: jeandarc.campbell@pcc.edu
Phone: (503) 614-7148

Portland State University
www.pdx.edu
International Admissions
PO Box 751-ADM
Portland, OR 97207-0751
Fax: (503) 725-5525
E-mail: intladm@pdx.edu
Phone: (503) 725-5503

Post University
www.post.edu
International Admissions
800 Country Club Road
PO Box 2540
Waterbury, CT 06723-2540
Fax: (203) 596-4579
E-mail: jwallace@post.edu
Phone: (203) 596-4512

Potomac College
www.potomac.edu
Admissions
4000 Chesapeake Street NW
Washington, DC 20016
Fax: (202) 686-0818
E-mail: joseph.mure@potomac.edu
Phone: (202) 686-0876

Potomac College
www.potomac.edu
1029 Herndon Parkway
Herndon, VA 20170
Fax: (703) 709-8972
Phone: (703) 709-5875

Potomac State College of West Virginia University
www.potomacstatecollege.edu
Enrollment Services
75 Arnold Street
Keyser, WV 26726
Fax: (304) 788-6939
E-mail: BELittle@mail.wvu.edu
Phone: (304) 788-6820

PowerSport Institute
www.psi-now.com
21210 Emery Road
North Randall, OH 44128
E-mail: admissions@ohiotechnicalcollege.com

Prairie State College
www.prairiestate.edu
Career and Transfer Center
202 South Halsted Street
Chicago Heights, IL 60411
Fax: (708) 755-2587
Phone: (708) 709-3512

Prairie View A&M University
www.pvamu.edu
Office of Admissions
PO Box 519, MS 1009
Prairie View, TX 77446-0519
Fax: (936) 261-1079
E-mail: ntwoods@pvamu.edu
Phone: (936) 261-1067

Pratt Community College
www.prattcc.edu
Director of Admissions
348 Northeast State Road 61
Pratt, KS 67124-8317
Fax: (620) 672-5288
E-mail: lynnp@prattcc.edu
Phone: (620) 450-2222

Pratt Institute
www.pratt.edu
International Admissions Office
200 Willoughby Avenue
Brooklyn, NY 11205-3817
Fax: (718) 399-4242
E-mail: admissions@pratt.edu
Phone: (718) 636-3683

Presbyterian College
www.presby.edu
Dean of Admissions
503 South Broad Street
Clinton, SC 29325-2865
Fax: (864) 833-8195
E-mail: admissions@presby.edu
Phone: (864) 833-8258

Prescott College
www.prescott.edu
Admissions
220 Grove Avenue
Prescott, AZ 86301
Fax: (928) 776-5242
E-mail: admissions@prescott.edu
Phone: (877) 350-1201

Presentation College
www.presentation.edu
Vice President for Student Enrollment
1500 North Main Street
Aberdeen, SD 57401
Fax: (605) 229-8332
E-mail: joellen.lindner@presentation.edu
Phone: (605) 229-8424

Prince George's Community College
www.pgcc.edu
Admissions and Records
301 Largo Road
Largo, MD 20774
Fax: (301) 322-0119
E-mail: enrollmentservices@pgcc.edu
Phone: (301) 322-0863

Prince William Sound Community College
www.pwscc.edu
Student Services
Box 97
Valdez, AK 99686
Fax: (907) 834-1691
E-mail: bpainter@pwscc.edu
Phone: (907) 834-1631

Princeton University
www.princeton.edu
Box 430
Princeton, NJ 08542-0430
Fax: (609) 258-6743
E-mail: uaoffice@princeton.edu
Phone: (609) 258-3060

Professional Business College
www.pbcny.edu
125 Canal Street
New York, NY 10002
E-mail: dwang@pbcny.edu

Professional Golfers Career College
www.golfcollege.edu
26109 Ynez Road
Temecula, CA 92591
Fax: (951) 719-1643
E-mail: patti.paulsen@golfcollege.edu
Phone: (800) 877-4380

Professional Golfers Career College: Orlando
www.golfcollege.edu
Temecula
PO Box 892319
Temecula, CA 92589-2319
Fax: (951) 719-1643
E-mail: patti.paulsen@golfcollege.edu
Phone: (800) 877-4380

Providence Christian College
www.providencecc.net
1539 East Howard Street
Pasadena, CA 91104
E-mail: admissions@providencecc.net
Phone: (626) 696-4000

Providence College
www.providence.edu
Admissions
Harkins Hall 222, One Cunningham Square
Providence, RI 02918-0001
Fax: (401) 865-2826
E-mail: rfonts@providence.edu
Phone: (401) 865-2754

Provo College
www.provocollege.edu
1450 West 820 North
Provo, UT 84601
Fax: (801) 375-9728
Phone: (801) 375-1861

Pueblo Community College
www.pueblocc.edu
Admissions
900 West Orman Avenue
Pueblo, CO 81004-1499
Fax: (719) 549-3012
E-mail: laura.lucero@pueblocc.edu
Phone: (719) 549-3015

Pulaski Technical College
www.pulaskitech.edu
Student Services
3000 West Scenic Drive
North Little Rock, AR 72118-3347
Fax: (501) 812-2316
E-mail: catkins@pulaskitech.edu
Phone: (501) 812-2734

Purdue University
www.purdue.edu
Office of International Students and Scholars
475 Stadium Mall Drive
West Lafayette, IN 47907-2050
Fax: (765) 494-6340
E-mail: iss@purdue.edu
Phone: (765) 494-5770

Purdue University Calumet
www.calumet.purdue.edu
International Student Mentoring Center
2200 169th Street
Hammond, IN 46323-2094
Fax: (219) 989-2581
E-mail: grad@calumet.purdue.edu
Phone: (219) 989-2559

Purdue University North Central
www.pnc.edu
Director of School Partnerships
1401 South US Highway 421
Westville, IN 46391-9542
Fax: (219) 785-5538
E-mail: swilson@pnc.edu
Phone: (219) 785-5236

Queens University of Charlotte
www.queens.edu
Traditional Undergradute Office of
Admissions
1900 Selwyn Ave
Harris Welcome Center - MSC 1428
Charlotte, NC 28274-0001
Fax: (704) 337-2403
E-mail: kammerds@queens.edu
Phone: (704) 337-2212 ext. 2425

Quincy College
www.quincycollege.edu
International Student Office
24 Saville Avenue
Quincy, MA 02169
Fax: (617) 984-1794
E-mail: jfoley@quincycollege.edu
Phone: (617) 984-1665

Quincy University
www.quincy.edu
Admissions Office
1800 College Avenue
Quincy, IL 62301-2699
Fax: (217) 228-5479
E-mail: admissions@quincy.edu
Phone: (217) 228-5210

Quinnipiac University
www.quinnipiac.edu
Undergraduate or Graduate Admissions
275 Mount Carmel Avenue
Hamden, CT 06518-1908
Fax: (582) 582-8906
E-mail: admissions@quinnipiac.edu
Phone: (582) 582-8600

Quinsigamond Community College
www.qcc.edu
Admissions
670 West Boylston Street
Worcester, MA 01606
Fax: (508) 854-7525
E-mail: admissions@qcc.mass.edu
Phone: (508) 854-4262

**Rabbinical Academy Mesivta Rabbi Chaim
Berlin**
1605 Coney Island Avenue
Brooklyn, NY 11230
Phone: (718) 377-0777

Rabbinical College Beth Shraga
PO Box 412
Monsey, NY 10952
Phone: (845) 356-1980

**Rabbinical College Bobover Yeshiva B'nei
Zion**
1577 48th Street
Brooklyn, NY 11219
Phone: (718) 438-2018

**Rabbinical College Ch'san Sofer of New
York**
1876 50th Street
Brooklyn, NY 11204
Phone: (718) 236-1171

Rabbinical College of America
226 Sussex Avenue, CN 1996
Morristown, NJ 07962-1996
Fax: (973) 267-5208
Phone: (973) 267-9404

Rabbinical College of Long Island
205 West Beech Street
Long Beach, NY 11561
Phone: (516) 431-7414

Rabbinical College of Ohr Shimon Yisroel
215-217 Hewes Street
Brooklyn, NY 11211
Phone: (718) 855-4092

Rabbinical Seminary of America
76-01 147th Street
Flushing, NY 11367
Fax: (718) 268-4684
E-mail: registrar@rabbinical.org
Phone: (718) 268-4700

Radford University
www.radford.edu
Admissions Office
115 Martin Hall
PO Box 6903
Radford, VA 24142
Fax: (540) 831-5038
E-mail: admissions@radford.edu
Phone: (540) 831-5371

Rainy River Community College
www.rrcc.mnscu.edu
Admissions
1501 Highway 71
International Falls, MN 56649
Fax: (218) 285-2314
E-mail: bhagen@rrcc.mnscu.edu
Phone: (218) 285-2207

Ramapo College of New Jersey
www.ramapo.edu
Admissions
505 Ramapo Valley Road
Admissions- McBride Building
Mahwah, NJ 07430-1680
Fax: (201) 684-7964
E-mail: mdibarto@ramapo.edu
Phone: (201) 684-7302

Randolph College
www.randolphcollege.edu
Admissions Office
2500 Rivermont Avenue
Lynchburg, VA 24503-1555
Fax: (434) 947-8996
E-mail: admissions@randolphcollege.edu
Phone: (434) 947-8100

Randolph-Macon College
www.rmc.edu
Admissions
PO Box 5005
Ashland, VA 23005-5505
Fax: (804) 752-4707
E-mail: admissions@rmc.edu
Phone: (804) 752-7305

Ranger College
www.rangercollege.edu
Registrar
1100 College Circle
Ranger, TX 76470
Fax: (254) 647-3739
E-mail: rstephens@rangercollege.edu
Phone: (254) 647-3234

Rappahannock Community College
www.rappahannock.edu
Registra
12745 College Drive
Glenns, VA 23149-2616
Fax: (804) 758-3852
E-mail: fpackett@rappahannock.edu
Phone: (804) 333-6741

Raritan Valley Community College
www.raritanval.edu
Advising and Counseling
PO Box 3300
Office of Admissions - College Center
Somerville, NJ 08876-1265
Fax: (908) 253-6691
E-mail: iss@raritanval.edu
Phone: (908) 526-1200 ext. 8452

Rasmussen College: Aurora
www.rasmussen.edu
2363 Sequoia Drive, Suite 131
Aurora, IL 60506
Phone: (630) 888-3500

Rasmussen College: Bismarck
www.rasmussen.edu
Admissions
1701 East Century Avenue
Bismarck, ND 58503
Fax: (701) 530-9604
E-mail: mike.heitkamp@rasmussen.edu
Phone: (701) 530-9600

Rasmussen College: Bloomington
www.rasmussen.edu
Admissions
4400 West 78th Street
Eden Prairie, MN 55435
E-mail: jeff.lust@rasmussen.edu
Phone: (952) 545-2000

Rasmussen College: Brooklyn Park
www.rasmussen.edu
Admissions
8301 93rd Avenue North
Brooklyn Park, MN 55445
E-mail: lori.kaiser@rasmussen.edu
Phone: (763) 493-4500

Rasmussen College: Eagan
www.rasmussen.edu
Admissions
3500 Federal Drive
Eagan, MN 55122
Fax: (651) 687-0507
E-mail: jon.peterson@rasmussen.edu
Phone: (651) 687-9000

Rasmussen College: Fargo
www.rasmussen.edu
Admissions
4012 19th Avenue SW
Fargo, ND 58103
Fax: (701) 277-5604
E-mail: peter.limvere@rasmussen.edu
Phone: (701) 277-3889

Rasmussen College: Green Bay
www.rasmussen.edu
904 South Taylor Street, Suite 100
Green Bay, WI 54303-2349
Phone: (920) 593-8400

Rasmussen College: Lake Elmo/Woodbury
www.rasmussen.edu
8565 Eagle Point Circle
Lake Elmo, MN 55042-8637
E-mail: patrick.green@rasmussen.edu
Phone: (651) 259-6600

Rasmussen College: Mankato
www.rasmussen.edu
Admissions
130 Saint Andrews Drive
Mankato, MN 56001
Fax: (507) 625-6557
E-mail: kathy.clifford@rasmussen.edu
Phone: (507) 625-6556

Rasmussen College: Ocala
www.rasmussen.edu
Admissions
2221 Southwest 19th Avenue Road
Ocala, FL 34471
Fax: (352) 629-0926
E-mail: miguel.ramos@rasmussen.edu
Phone: (352) 629-1941

Rasmussen College: Pasco County
www.rasmussen.edu
Financial Aid
2127 Grand Boulevard
Holiday, FL 34690
Fax: (727) 938-5709
E-mail: tina.fisher@rasmussen.edu
Phone: (727) 942-0069

Rasmussen College: Rockford
www.rasmussen.edu
6000 East State Street, Fourth Floor
Rockford, IL 61108-2513
Phone: (815) 316-4800

Rasmussen College: Romeoville/Joliet
www.rasmussen.edu
400 West Normantown Road
Romeoville, IL 60446

Rasmussen College: St. Cloud
www.rasmussen.edu
Admissions
226 Park Avenue South
St. Cloud, MN 56301-3713
Fax: (320) 251-3702
E-mail: andrea.peters@rasmussen.edu
Phone: (320) 251-5600

Rasmussen College: Wausau
www.rasmussen.edu
1101 Westwood Drive
Wausau, WI 54401

Reading Area Community College
www.racc.edu
Enrollment Services Office
10 South Second Street
PO Box 1706
Reading, PA 19603-1706
Fax: (610) 607-6257
E-mail: jmelones@racc.edu
Phone: (610) 607-6224

Red Rocks Community College
www.rrcc.edu
Office of English Language/Intercultural
Services
13300 West Sixth Avenue
Box 5
Lakewood, CO 80228-1255
Fax: (303) 314-6716
E-mail: international@rrcc.edu
Phone: (303) 914-6416

Redlands Community College
www.redlandscc.edu
Student Services
1300 South Country Club Road
El Reno, OK 73036
Fax: (405) 422-1239
E-mail: duel@redlandscc.edu
Phone: (405) 262-2552 ext. 1427

Redstone College
www.redstonecollege.com
10851 West 120th Avenue
Broomfield, CO 80021-3401
Fax: (303) 469-3797
Phone: (303) 466-1714

Reed College
www.reed.edu
Admission
3203 SE Woodstock Boulevard
Portland, OR 97202-8199
Fax: (503) 777-7553
E-mail: ktodd@reed.edu
Phone: (503) 777-7511

Reedley College
www.reedleycollege.edu
Admissions and Records
995 North Reed Avenue
Reedley, CA 93654
Fax: (559) 638-5040
E-mail: leticia.alvarez@reedleycollege.edu
Phone: (559) 638-0323

Regent University
www.regent.edu
Undergrad Admissions
1000 Regent University Drive
LIB 102
Virginia Beach, VA 23464-9800
Fax: (757) 352-4509
E-mail: kbaker@regent.edu
Phone: (757) 352-4845

Regis College
www.regiscollege.edu
Admission
235 Wellesley Street
Weston, MA 02493-1571
Fax: (781) 768-7071
E-mail: wanda.suriel@regiscollege.edu
Phone: (781) 768-7100

Regis University
www.regis.edu
Office of Admissions
3333 Regis Boulevard, Mail Code B20
Denver, CO 80221-1099
Fax: (303) 964-5534
E-mail: regisadm@regis.edu
Phone: (303) 458-4900

Reinhardt University
www.reinhardt.edu
Admissions
7300 Reinhardt Circle
Waleska, GA 30183-2981
Fax: (770) 720-5899
E-mail: jcf@reinhardt.edu
Phone: (770) 720-5527

Remington College: Baton Rouge
www.remingtoncollege.edu
10551 Coursey Boulevard
Baton Rouge, LA 70816
Fax: (225) 922-6569
Phone: (225) 922-3990

Remington College: Cleveland
www.remingtoncollege.edu
Director of Recruitment
14445 Broadway Avenue
Cleveland, OH 44125
Fax: (216) 475-6055
E-mail: jeri.prochaska@remingtoncollege.edu
Phone: (216) 475-7520

Remington College: Colorado Springs
www.remingtoncollege.edu
Recruiting
6050 Erin Park Drive
Colorado Springs, CO 80918
Fax: (719) 264-1234
E-mail:
danielle.webster@remingtoncollege.edu
Phone: (719) 532-1234

Remington College: Dallas
www.remingtoncollege.edu
1800 Eastgate Drive
Garland, TX 75041
E-mail: swhisenhunt@edamerica.com
Phone: (972) 686-7878

Remington College: Fort Worth
www.remingtoncollege.edu
300 East Loop 820
Fort Worth, TX 76112
Fax: (817) 496-1257
E-mail: marcia.kline@remingtoncollege.edu
Phone: (817) 451-0017

Remington College: Honolulu
www.remingtoncollege.edu
Admissions Office
1111 Bishop Street, Suite 400
Honolulu, HI 96813-2811
Fax: (808) 533-3064
E-mail: ken.heinemann@remingtoncollege.edu
Phone: (808) 942-1000

Remington College: Houston
www.remingtoncollege.edu
Admissions
3110 Hayes Road, Suite 380
Houston, TX 77082
Fax: (281) 597-8466
E-mail:
kevin.wilkinson@remingtoncollege.edu
Phone: (281) 899-1240

Remington College: Lafayette
www.remingtoncollege.edu
Director of Admissions
303 Rue Louis XIV
Lafayette, LA 70508
Fax: (337) 983-7130
E-mail: admissions@remingtoncollege.edu
Phone: (337) 981-4010

Remington College: Little Rock
www.remingtoncollege.edu
19 Remington Drive
Little Rock, AR 72204
Fax: (501) 225-3819
Phone: (501) 312-0007

Remington College: Memphis
www.remingtoncollege.edu
2710 Nonconnah Boulevard
Memphis, TN 38132
Fax: (901) 396-8310
Phone: (901) 345-1000

Remington College: Mobile
www.remingtoncollege.edu
Registrar
828 Downtowner Loop West
Mobile, AL 36609-5404
Fax: (251) 343-0577
Phone: (251) 343-8200

Remington College: Nashville
www.remingtoncollege.edu
441 Donelson Pike, Suite 150
Nashville, TN 37214
Phone: (615) 493-9329

Remington College: North Houston
www.remingtoncollege.edu
11310 Greens Crossing, Suite 200
Houston, TX 77067
Phone: (281) 885-4450

Remington College: Shreveport
www.remingtoncollege.edu
2106 Bert Kouns Industrial Loop
Shreveport, LA 71118

Remington College: Tampa
www.remingtoncollege.edu
International Department
6302 East Dr. Martin Luther King, Jr.,
Boulevard
Tampa, FL 33619
Fax: (813) 935-7415
E-mail: gary.schwartz@remingtoncollege.edu
Phone: (813) 935-5700

Rensselaer Polytechnic Institute
www.rpi.edu
Admissions Office
110 Eighth Street
Troy, NY 12180-3590
Fax: (518) 276-4072
E-mail: rosatn@rpi.edu
Phone: (518) 276-6216

Renton Technical College
www.RTC.edu
3000 NE Fourth Street
Renton, WA 98056-4195
Fax: (425) 235-7832
E-mail: briverman@rtc.edu
Phone: (425) 235-5840

Research College of Nursing
www.researchcollege.edu
Student Development
2525 East Meyer Boulevard
Kansas City, MO 64132-1199
Fax: (816) 995-2813
Phone: (816) 501-4000

Restaurant School at Walnut Hill College
www.walnuthillcollege.edu
Admissions
4207 Walnut Street
Philadelphia, PA 19104
Fax: (215) 222-2811
E-mail: info@walnuthillcollege.edu
Phone: (215) 222-4200

Resurrection University
www.wscn.edu
Three Erie Court
Oak Park, IL 60302
Fax: (708) 763-1531
E-mail: admissions@wscn.edu
Phone: (708) 763-6530

Rhode Island College
www.ric.edu
Admissions Office
600 Mount Pleasant Avenue
Forman Center
Providence, RI 02908
Fax: (401) 456-8817
E-mail: admissions@ric.edu
Phone: (401) 456-8234

Rhode Island School of Design
www.risd.edu
Admissions
Two College Street
Providence, RI 02903-2791
Fax: (401) 454-6309
E-mail: admissions@risd.edu
Phone: (401) 454-6300

Rhodes College
www.rhodes.edu
Associate Director of Admissions
2000 North Parkway
Memphis, TN 38112
Fax: (901) 843-3631
E-mail: SEFTONL@rhodes.edu
Phone: (901) 843-3700

Rice University
www.rice.edu
Admission Office
6100 Main Street
Office of Admission MS-17 PO Box 1892
Houston, TX 77251-1892
Fax: (713) 348-5323
E-mail: admission@rice.edu
Phone: (713) 348-7423

Richard Bland College
www.rbc.edu
Division of Student Affairs
11301 Johnson Road
Petersburg, VA 23805
Fax: (804) 862-6490
E-mail: admit@rbc.edu
Phone: (804) 862-6249

Richard Stockton College of New Jersey
www.stockton.edu
Admissions Office
Jim Leeds Road
PO Box 195
Pomona, NJ 08240-0195
Fax: (609) 748-5541
E-mail: admissions@stockton.edu
Phone: (609) 652-4261

Richland College
www.rlc.dcccd.edu
Multicultural Center
12800 Abrams Road
Dallas, TX 75243-2199
Fax: (972) 682-6165
E-mail: tadams@dcccd.edu
Phone: (972) 238-6903

Richland Community College
www.richland.edu
Registrar
One College Park
Decatur, IL 62521
Fax: (217) 875-7783
E-mail: jwirey@richland.edu
Phone: (217) 875-7200 ext. 284

Rider University
www.rider.edu
Undergraduate Admissions
2083 Lawrenceville Road
Box 3001
Lawrenceville, NJ 08648-3099
Fax: (609) 895-6645
E-mail: wlarrousse@rider.edu
Phone: (609) 896-5000 ext. 5194

Ridgewater College
www.ridgewater.edu
Admissions Office
2101 15th Avenue Northwest
Box 1097
Willmar, MN 56201
Fax: (320) 222-5216
E-mail: sally.kerfeld@ridgewater.edu
Phone: (320) 222-5977

Ringling College of Art and Design
www.ringling.edu
Admissions
2700 North Tamiami Trail
Sarasota, FL 34234-5895
Fax: (941) 359-7517
E-mail: afischer@ringling.edu
Phone: (941) 351-5100

Rio Hondo College
www.riohondo.edu
3600 Workman Mill Road
Whittier, CA 90601-1699
Fax: (562) 692-8318
Phone: (562) 692-0921 ext. 3134

Rio Salado College
www.riosalado.edu
Registration and Records
2323 West 14th Street
Tempe, AZ 85281
Fax: (480) 377-4689
E-mail: admissions@email.rio.maricopa.edu
Phone: (480) 517-8152

River Valley Community College
www.rivervalley.edu
Admissions
One College Drive
Claremont, NH 03743-9707
Fax: (603) 543-1844
E-mail: ckusselow@ccsnh.edu
Phone: (603) 542-7744

Riverland Community College
www.riverland.edu
1900 Eighth Avenue, NW
Austin, MN 55912-1407
Fax: (507) 433-0515
E-mail: mmorem@river.cc.mn.us
Phone: (507) 433-0600

Riverside Community College
www.rcc.edu
Center for International Students and
Programs
4800 Magnolia Avenue
Riverside, CA 92506
Fax: (951) 222-8376
E-mail: internationalcenter@rcc.edu
Phone: (951) 222-8160

Rivier College
www.rivier.edu
Director of Admissions
420 South Main Street
Nashua, NH 03060-5086
Fax: (603) 891-1799
E-mail: dboisvert@rivier.edu
Phone: (603) 897-8507

Roane State Community College
www.roanestate.edu
Recruitment Office
276 Patton Lane
Harriman, TN 37748
Fax: (865) 882-4585
E-mail: gonzalesmr@roanestate.edu
Phone: (865) 882-4628

Roanoke College
www.roanoke.edu
Admissions
221 College Lane
Salem, VA 24153-3794
Fax: (540) 375-2267
E-mail: admissions@roanoke.edu
Phone: (540) 375-2270

Roanoke-Chowan Community College
www.roanokechowan.edu
Student Services
109 Community College Road
Ahoskie, NC 27910-9522
Fax: (252) 862-1355
E-mail: sandrac@roanokehowan.edu
Phone: (252) 862-1200

Robert B. Miller College
www.millercollege.edu
450 North Avenue
Battle Creek, MI 49017
Phone: (269) 660-8021

Robert Morris University
www.rmu.edu
Office of Enrollment Management
6001 University Boulevard
Moon Township, PA 15108-1189
Fax: (412) 397-2425
E-mail: admissionsoffice@rmu.edu
Phone: (800) 762-0097

Robert Morris University: Chicago
www.robertmorris.edu
Student Information
401South State Street
Chicago, IL 60605
Fax: (312) 935-4177
E-mail: studentrecords@robertmorris.edu
Phone: (312) 935-4180

Roberts Wesleyan College
www.roberts.edu
Vice President for Admissions and Marketing
2301 Westside Drive
Rochester, NY 14624-1997
Fax: (585) 594-6371
E-mail: admissions@roberts.edu
Phone: (585) 594-6400

Robeson Community College
www.robeson.edu
PO Box 1420
5160 Fayetteville Road
Lumberton, NC 28359
Fax: (910) 618-5686
E-mail: jrevels@robeson.cc.nc.us
Phone: (910) 272-3700 ext. 3347

Rochester College
www.rc.edu
Enrollment Services
800 West Avon Road
Rochester Hills, MI 48307
Fax: (248) 218-2035
E-mail: admissions@rc.edu
Phone: (248) 218-2031

Rochester Community and Technical College
www.roch.edu
International Admissions Office
851 30th Avenue SE
Rochester, MN 55904-4999
Fax: (507) 285-7496
E-mail: glen.saponari@roch.edu
Phone: (507) 280-5511

Rochester Institute of Technology
www.rit.edu
Undergraduate Admissions Office
60 Lomb Memorial Drive
Rochester, NY 14623-5604
Fax: (585) 475-7424
E-mail: admissions@rit.edu
Phone: (585) 475-6631

Rock Valley College
www.rockvalleycollege.edu
3301 North Mulford Road
Rockford, IL 61114-5699
Fax: (815) 921-4269
E-mail: m.foreman@rvc.cc.il.us
Phone: (815) 921-4251

Rockford College
www.rockford.edu
Office of Undergraduate Admission
5050 East State Street
Rockford, IL 61108-2311
Fax: (818) 226-2822
E-mail: rcadmissions@rockford.edu
Phone: (815) 226-4050

Rockhurst University
www.rockhurst.edu
Admission
1100 Rockhurst Road
Kansas City, MO 64110-2561
Fax: (816) 501-4142
E-mail: mitch.nelson@rockhurst.edu
Phone: (816) 501-4538

Rockingham Community College
www.rockinghamcc.edu
Box 38
Wentworth, NC 27375-0038
Fax: (336) 342-1809
E-mail: bouldinc@rockinghamcc.edu
Phone: (336) 342-4261 ext. 2333

Rockland Community College
www.sunyrockland.edu
International Student Services
145 College Road
Suffern, NY 10901-3699
Fax: (845) 574-4433
E-mail: info@sunyrockland.edu
Phone: (914) 574-4263

Rocky Mountain College
www.rocky.edu
International Programs
1511 Poly Drive
Billings, MT 59102-1796
Fax: (406) 259-9751
E-mail: michael.west@rocky.edu
Phone: (406) 657-1107

Rocky Mountain College of Art & Design
www.rmcad.edu
Admissions
1600 Pierce Street
Denver, CO 80214
Fax: (303) 759-4970
E-mail: jmeurer@rmcad.edu
Phone: (303) 225-8567

Roger Williams University
www.rwu.edu
Office of Admission
1 Old Ferry Road
Bristol, RI 02809-2921
Fax: (401) 254-3557
E-mail: admit@rwu.edu
Phone: (401) 254-3500

Rogers State University
www.rsu.edu
Office of Admissions
1701 West Will Rogers Boulevard
Office of Admissions
Claremore, OK 74017
Fax: (918) 343-7550
E-mail: astevens@rsu.edu
Phone: (918) 343-7548

Rogue Community College
www.roguecc.edu
Enrollment Services
3345 Redwood Highway
Grants Pass, OR 97527
E-mail: csullivan@roguecc.edu
Phone: (541) 956-7176

Rollins College
www.rollins.edu
Admissions
1000 Holt Avenue, Campus Box 2720
Winter Park, FL 32789
Fax: (407) 646-1502
E-mail: admission@rollins.edu
Phone: (407) 646-2161

Roosevelt University
www.roosevelt.edu
Office of International Porgrams
430 South Michigan Avenue
Room 104
Chicago, IL 60605-1394
Fax: (312) 341-6377
E-mail: dhougland@roosevelt.edu
Phone: (312) 341-6464

Rose State College
www.rose.edu
Admissions
6420 SE 15th Street
Midwest City, OK 73110-2799
Fax: (405) 736-0309
E-mail: dsorrell@rose.edu
Phone: (405) 736-0203

Rose-Hulman Institute of Technology
www.rose-hulman.edu
Assistant Director of Admissions
Office of Admissions
5500 Wabash Avenue, CM 1
Terre Haute, IN 47803-3999
Fax: (812) 877-8941
E-mail: Goulding@rose-hulman.edu
Phone: (800) 248-7448

Rosemont College
www.rosemont.edu
Undergraduate College Admissions
1400 Montgomery Avenue
Rosemont, PA 19010-1699
Fax: (610) 520-4399
E-mail: kfoster@rosemont.edu
Phone: (610) 527-0200 ext. 2608

Rowan University
www.rowan.edu
International Center
Savitz Hall, 201 Mullica Hill Road
Glassboro, NJ 08028
Fax: (856) 256-5676
E-mail: smithe@rowan.edu
Phone: (856) 256-4105

Roxbury Community College
www.rcc.mass.edu
Admissions
1234 Columbus Avenue
Roxbury Crossing, MA 02120-3400
Fax: (617) 541-5316
E-mail: msamuels@rcc.mass.edu
Phone: (617) 541-5310

Rush University
www.rushu.rush.edu
International Affairs
College Admissions
600 South Paulina Street, Suite 440
Chicago, IL 60612
Fax: (312) 942-7773
E-mail: helen_lavelle@rush.edu
Phone: (312) 942-2030

Russell Sage College
www.sage.edu/rsc
Admission
65 1st Street
Troy, NY 12180-4115
Fax: (518) 244-6880
E-mail: collip3@sage.edu
Phone: (518) 244-2217

Rust College
www.rustcollege.edu
150 Rust Avenue
Holly Springs, MS 38635-2328
Fax: (662) 252-2258
E-mail: csmith@rustcollege.edu
Phone: (662) 252-8000 ext. 4056

Rutgers, The State University of New Jersey: Camden Regional Campus
www.rutgers.edu
Assistant Dean, International Students
406 Penn Street
Camden, NJ 08102
Fax: (856) 225-6579
E-mail: atkins1@camden.rutgers.edu
Phone: (856) 225-2521

Rutgers, The State University of New Jersey: New Brunswick/Piscataway Campus
www.rutgers.edu
65 Davidson Road, Room 202
Piscataway, NJ 08854-8097
Fax: (732) 445-0237
E-mail: sjenkins@rci.rutgers.edu
Phone: (732) 445-6464

Rutgers, The State University of New Jersey: Newark Regional Campus
www.rutgers.edu
249 University Avenue
Newark, NJ 07102-1896
Fax: (732) 445-0237
E-mail: sjenkins@rci.rutgers.edu
Phone: (732) 445-6464

Sacramento City College
www.scc.losrios.edu
International Student Office
3835 Freeport Boulevard
Sacramento, CA 95822
Fax: (916) 558-2490
E-mail: sccaeinfo@scc.losrios.edu
Phone: (916) 558-2486

Sacred Heart Major Seminary
www.shms.edu
Office of the Vice Rector
2701 Chicago Boulevard
Detroit, MI 48206-1799
Fax: (313) 883-8659
E-mail: Forrester.Linda@shms.edu
Phone: (313) 883-8563

Sacred Heart University
www.sacredheart.edu
Office of Undergraduate Admission
5151 Park Avenue
Fairfield, CT 06825
Fax: (203) 365-7607
E-mail: neversc@sacredheart.edu
Phone: (203) 371-7880

Saddleback College
www.saddleback.edu
International Education Office
28000 Marguerite Parkway
Mission Viejo, CA 92692
Fax: (949) 582-4800
E-mail: intnled@saddleback.cc.ca.us
Phone: (949) 582-4635

Sage College of Albany
www.sage.edu
Admission
140 New Scotland Avenue
Albany, NY 12208
Fax: (518) 292-1912
E-mail: collip3@sage.edu
Phone: (518) 292-1730

Saginaw Chippewa Tribal College
www.sagchip.edu
2274 Enterprise Drive
Mount Pleasant, MI 48858
Fax: (989) 775-4528
E-mail: reed.tracy@sagchip.edu
Phone: (989) 775-4123

Saginaw Valley State University
www.svsu.edu
International Programs
7400 Bay Road
University Center, MI 48710
Fax: (989) 964-6066
E-mail: oip@svsu.edu
Phone: (989) 964-4473

St. Ambrose University
www.sau.edu
Center for International Education
518 West Locust Street
Davenport, IA 52803-2898
Fax: (563) 333-6243
E-mail: global@sau.edu
Phone: (563) 333-6389

St. Andrews Presbyterian College
www.sapc.edu
Director of Admissions
1700 Dogwood Mile
Laurinburg, NC 28352
Fax: (910) 277-5087
E-mail: simmonskm@sapc.edu
Phone: (910) 277-5555 ext. 3943

Saint Anselm College
www.anselm.edu
Admission
100 Saint Anselm Drive
Manchester, NH 03102-1310
Fax: (603) 641-7550
E-mail: admission@anselm.edu
Phone: (603) 641-7500

St. Augustine College
www.staugustine.edu
1345 West Argyle
Chicago, IL 60640-3501
Fax: (773) 878-0937
Phone: (773) 878-8756

St. Augustine's College
www.st-aug.edu
Admissions
1315 Oakwood Avenue
Raleigh, NC 27610-2298
Fax: (919) 516-4415
E-mail: admissions@st-aug.edu
Phone: (919) 516-4085

Saint Bonaventure University
www.sbu.edu
Office of Foreign Studies
Route 417
Box D
St. Bonaventure, NY 14778-2284
Fax: (716) 375-7882
E-mail: asayegh@sbu.edu
Phone: (716) 375-4009

St. Catharine College
www.sccky.edu
Admissions
2735 Bardstown Road
St. Catharine, KY 40061
Fax: (859) 336-5031
E-mail: twiley@sccky.edu
Phone: (859) 336-5082 ext. 1240

St. Catherine University
www.stkate.edu
Assistant Director International Admission
2004 Randolph Avenue #4-02
St. Paul, MN 55105
Fax: (651) 690-8824
E-mail: aethostenson@stkate.edu
Phone: (651) 690-6029

St. Charles Borromeo Seminary - Overbrook
www.scs.edu
Vice Rector
100 East Wynnewood Road
Wynnewood, PA 19096
Fax: (610) 617-9267
E-mail: frdd@adphila.org
Phone: (610) 785-6271

St. Clair County Community College
www.sc4.edu
Dean of Student Services
323 Erie Street
Box 5015
Port Huron, MI 48061-5015
Fax: (810) 984-4730
E-mail: jmorris@sc4.edu
Phone: (810) 989-5560

Saint Cloud State University
www.stcloudstate.edu
Center for International Studies
720 Fourth Avenue South, AS 115
St. Cloud, MN 56301
Fax: (320) 308-4223
E-mail: international@stcloudstate.edu
Phone: (320) 308-4287

St. Cloud Technical and Community College
www.sctcc.edu
Admissions
1540 Northway Drive
St. Cloud, MN 56303
Fax: (320) 308-5087
E-mail: jelness@sctc.edu
Phone: (800) 222-1009

St. Edward's University
www.gotostedwards.com
Undergraduate Admission
3001 South Congress Avenue
Austin, TX 78704-6489
Fax: (512) 464-8841
E-mail: davidbe@stedwards.edu
Phone: (800) 555-0164

St. Elizabeth College of Nursing
www.secon.edu
Registrar's Office
2215 Genesee Street
Utica, NY 13501
Fax: (315) 798-8271
E-mail: dseymour@stemc.org
Phone: (315) 798-8253

St. Francis College
www.stfranciscollege.edu
Admissions
180 Remsen Street
Brooklyn Heights, NY 11201-9902
Fax: (718) 802-0453
E-mail: admissions@stfranciscollege.edu
Phone: (718) 489-5200

St. Francis University
www.francis.edu
Office of International Admissions and
Student Services
Box 600
117 Evergreen Drive
Loretto, PA 15940
Fax: (814) 472-3335
E-mail: intl@francis.edu
Phone: (800) 472-3100

St. Gregory's University
www.stgregorys.edu
International Office
1900 West MacArthur Drive
Shawnee, OK 74804
Fax: (405) 878-5198
E-mail: int-admissions@stgregorys.edu
Phone: (405) 878-5177

St. John Fisher College
www.sjfc.edu
Office of Freshman Admissions
3690 East Avenue
Rochester, NY 14618-3597
Fax: (585) 385-8386
E-mail: apytlak@sjfc.edu
Phone: (585) 385-8064

St. John's College
www.stjohnscollege.edu
Admissions
PO Box 2800
Annapolis, MD 21404
Fax: (410) 269-7916
E-mail: admissions@sjca.edu
Phone: (410) 626-2522

St. John's College
www.sjcsf.edu
Admissions Office, Undergraduate
1160 Camino Cruz Blanca
Santa Fe, NM 87505
Fax: (505) 984-6162
E-mail: admissions@sjcsf.edu
Phone: (505) 984-6060

St. John's University
www.csbsju.edu/
Admissions
College of St Benedict/St John's University
PO Box 7155
Collegeville, MN 56321-7155
Fax: (320) 363-3206
E-mail: ryoung@csbsju.edu
Phone: (320) 363-2190

St. John's University
www.stjohns.edu
Office of Admission
8000 Utopia Parkway
Queens, NY 11439
Fax: (718) 990-8220
E-mail: intladm@stjohns.edu
Phone: (718) 990-8034

Saint Joseph College
www.sjc.edu
Admissions
1678 Asylum Avenue
West Hartford, CT 06117
E-mail: admissions@sjc.edu
Phone: (860) 231-5303

St. Joseph Seminary College
www.sjasc.edu
Registrar
75376 River Road
St. Benedict, LA 70457-9990
Fax: (985) 327-1085
E-mail: registrat@sjasc.edu
Phone: (985) 867-2273

St. Joseph's College
www.sjcny.edu
International Student Admissions
245 Clinton Avenue
Brooklyn, NY 11205-3688
Fax: (718) 636-8303
E-mail: asilva@sjcny.edu
Phone: (718) 940-5800

Saint Joseph's College of Maine
www.sjcme.edu
Admissions Office
278 Whites Bridge Road
Standish, ME 04084-5236
Fax: (207) 893-7862
E-mail: jgronros@sjcme.edu
Phone: (207) 893-7746

St. Joseph's College: Suffolk Campus
www.sjcny.edu
Admissions Office
155 West Roe Boulevard
Patchogue, NY 11772-2603
Fax: (631) 447-3601
E-mail: glamens@sjcny.edu
Phone: (631) 447-3219

Saint Joseph's University
www.sju.edu
Undergraduate Admissions
5600 City Avenue
Philadelphia, PA 19131
Fax: (610) 660-1314
E-mail: rachel.johnson@sju.edu
Phone: (610) 660-1300

St. Lawrence University
www.stlawu.edu
Admissions
Payson Hall
Canton, NY 13617
Fax: (315) 229-5818
E-mail: admissions@stlawu.edu
Phone: (315) 229-5261

Saint Leo University
www.saintleo.edu
Office of Admission
Box 6665 MC2008
Saint Leo, FL 33574-6665
Fax: (352) 588-8257
E-mail: admission@saintleo.edu
Phone: (352) 588-8283

St. Louis Community College at Florissant Valley
www.stlcc.edu
3400 Pershall Road
St. Louis, MO 63135
Fax: (314) 513-4724
Phone: (314) 513-4244

Saint Louis University
www.slu.edu
Division of Enrollment Management
One Grand Boulevard
DuBourg Hall, Room 100
St. Louis, MO 63103
Fax: (314) 977-3412
E-mail: icadmit@slu.edu
Phone: (314) 977-2318

St. Luke's College
www.stlukescollege.edu
Student Services
2720 Stone Park Boulevard
Box 2000
Sioux City, IA 51104
Fax: (712) 233-8017
E-mail: johanndd@stlukescollege.edu
Phone: (712) 279-3377

Saint Martin's University
www.stmartin.edu
Office of International Programs and Development
5300 Pacific Avenue SE
Lacey, WA 98503-7500
Fax: (360) 438-4359
E-mail: jyung@stmartin.edu
Phone: (360) 438-4504

St. Mary-of-the-Woods College
www.smwc.edu
Office of Admission
Rooney Library, SMWC
1 Saint Mary of the Woods
St. Mary of the Woods, IN 47876
Fax: (812) 535-5010
E-mail: smwcadms@smwc.edu
Phone: (812) 535-5106

Saint Mary's College
www.saintmarys.edu
Admission Office
122 Le Mans Hall
Notre Dame, IN 46556-5001
Fax: (574) 284-4716
E-mail: tcerrone@saintmarys.edu
Phone: (574) 284-4587

St. Mary's College of California
www.stmarys-ca.edu
Dean of Admissions
Box 4800
Moraga, CA 94575-4800
Fax: (925) 376-7193
E-mail: international@stmarys-ca.edu
Phone: (925) 631-4552

St. Mary's College of Maryland
www.smcm.edu
Office of Admissions
18952 East Fisher Road
St. Mary's City, MD 20686-3001
Fax: (240) 895-5001
E-mail: rjedgar@smcm.edu
Phone: (240) 895-5000

St. Mary's University
www.stmarytx.edu
Office of Undergraduate Admission
One Camino Santa Maria
San Antonio, TX 78228-8503
Fax: (210) 431-6742
E-mail: ndelgado@stmarytx.edu
Phone: (210) 436-3126

St. Mary's University of Minnesota
www.smumn.edu
Center for International Students
700 Terrace Heights #2
Winona, MN 55987-1399
Fax: (507) 457-6917
E-mail: mgarza@smumn.edu
Phone: (507) 457-1483

St. Michael's College
www.smcvt.edu
Office of Admission
One Winooski Park
Box 7
Colchester, VT 05439
Fax: (802) 654-2906
E-mail: admission@smcvt.edu
Phone: (802) 654-3000

St. Norbert College
www.snc.edu
Admissions
100 Grant Street
De Pere, WI 54115-2099
Fax: (920) 403-4072
E-mail: admit@snc.edu
Phone: (920) 403-3005

St. Olaf College
www.stolaf.edu
Admissions
1520 St. Olaf Avenue
Northfield, MN 55057
Fax: (507) 786-3832
E-mail: howensti@stolaf.edu
Phone: (507) 786-3813

St. Paul's College
www.saintpauls.edu
Office of Admissions
115 College Drive
Lawrenceville, VA 23868
Fax: (434) 848-1846
E-mail: rlewis@saintpauls.edu
Phone: (434) 848-1856

Saint Peter's College
www.spc.edu
Associate Director of Admissions
2641 Kennedy Boulevard
Jersey City, NJ 07306
Fax: (201) 761-7105
E-mail: ktillotson@spc.edu
Phone: (201) 761-7100

St. Petersburg College
www.spcollege.edu
Director of International Programs
Box 13489
St. Petersburg, FL 33733-3489
Fax: (727) 341-3510
E-mail: sweet.violetta@spcollege.edu
Phone: (727) 341-4735

St. Philip's College
www.alamo.edu/spc
International Student Services
1801 Martin Luther King Drive
San Antonio, TX 78203
Fax: (210) 486-2604
E-mail: pballard4@alamo.edu
Phone: (210) 486-2876

St. Thomas Aquinas College
www.stac.edu
Admissions Office
125 Route 340
Sparkill, NY 10976
Fax: (845) 398-4372
E-mail: frodrigu@stac.edu
Phone: (845) 398-4103

Saint Thomas University
www.stu.edu
Admissions
16401 Northwest 37th Avenue
Miami Gardens, FL 33054-6459
Fax: (305) 628-6510
E-mail: signup@stu.edu
Phone: (305) 628-6546

St. Vincent College
www.stvincent.edu
Admission
300 Fraser Purchase Road
Latrobe, PA 15650-2690
Fax: (724) 537-5069
E-mail: admission@stvincent.edu
Phone: (724) 805-2500

Saint Xavier University
www.sxu.edu
Recruitment & Admission Enrollment
3700 West 103rd Street
Chicago, IL 60655
Fax: (773) 298-3076
E-mail: admission@sxu.edu
Phone: (773) 298-3059

Salem College
www.salem.edu
Admissions Counselor
601 South Church Street
Winston-Salem, NC 27108
Fax: (336) 917-5972
E-mail: tricia.rybak@salem.edu
Phone: (336) 917-5567

Salem Community College
www.salemcc.edu
Admissions
460 Hollywood Avenue
Carneys Point, NJ 08069-2799
Fax: (856) 299-9193
E-mail: akellen@salemcc.edu
Phone: (856) 351-2919

Salem International University
www.salemu.edu
Admissions
223 West Main Street
Box 500
Salem, WV 26426
Fax: (304) 326-1592
E-mail: lningi@salemu.edu
Phone: (304) 326-1518

Salem State University
www.salemstate.edu/
Assistant Dean of Undergraduate Admissions
352 Lafayette Street
Salem, MA 01970-5353
Fax: (978) 542-6893
E-mail: admissions@salemstate.edu
Phone: (978) 542-6200

Salisbury University
www.salisbury.edu
Center for International Education
1200 Camden Avenue
Salisbury, MD 21801-6862
Fax: (410) 219-2853
E-mail: axliszkowska@salisbury.edu
Phone: (410) 334-3495

Salt Lake Community College
www.slcc.edu
International Students Office
4600 South Redwood Road
Box 30808
Salt Lake City, UT 84130-0808
Fax: (801) 957-4432
E-mail: nancy.fillat@slcc.edu
Phone: (801) 957-4528

Salvation Army College for Officer Training at Crestmont
www.crestmont.edu
30840 Hawthorne Boulevard
Rancho Palos Verdes, CA 90275
Phone: (310) 377-0481

Salve Regina University
www.salve.edu
Admissions Office
100 Ochre Point Avenue
Newport, RI 02840-4192
Fax: (401) 848-2823
E-mail: sruadmis@salve.edu
Phone: (401) 341-2412

Sam Houston State University
www.shsu.edu
Office of International Programs
Box 2418
Huntsville, TX 77341-2418
Fax: (936) 294-4620
E-mail: oip@shsu.edu
Phone: (936) 294-3892

Samford University
www.samford.edu
International Studies
800 Lakeshore Drive
Birmingham, AL 35229
Fax: (205) 726-2171
E-mail: dsshiple@samford.edu
Phone: (205) 726-2064

Samuel Merritt University
www.samuelmerritt.edu
Office of Admission
370 Hawthorne Avenue
Oakland, CA 94609-9954
Fax: (510) 869-6610
E-mail: admission@samuelmerritt.edu
Phone: (510) 869-6610

San Antonio College
www.accd.edu/sac
International Students Office
1300 San Pedro Avenue
San Antonio, TX 78212-4299
Fax: (210) 733-2030
E-mail: scecconi@accd.edu
Phone: (210) 733-2306

San Bernardino Valley College
www.valleycollege.edu
Foreign Student Adviser Counseling Office
701 South Mount Vernon Avenue
San Bernardino, CA 92410
E-mail: admissions@valleycollege.edu
Phone: (909) 384-4401

San Diego Christian College
www.sdcc.edu
2100 Greenfield Drive
El Cajon, CA 92019-1157
Fax: (619) 201-8749
E-mail: nrcraig@sdcc.edu
Phone: (619) 201-8748

San Diego City College
www.sdccd.edu
International Student Admissions
1313 Park Boulevard
San Diego, CA 92101-4787
Fax: (619) 388-3505
E-mail: dmeza@sdccd.edu
Phone: (619) 388-3476

San Diego Mesa College
www.sdmesa.edu
International Admissions
7250 Mesa College Drive
San Diego, CA 92111
Fax: (619) 388-2960
E-mail: csawyer@sdccd.edu
Phone: (619) 388-2717

San Diego Miramar College
www.sdmiramar.edu
International Student Advisor
10440 Black Mountain Road
San Diego, CA 92126-2999
Fax: (619) 388-7914
E-mail: mhollman@sdccd.edu
Phone: (619) 388-7840

San Diego State University
www.sdsu.edu
International Student Center
5500 Campanile Drive
San Diego, CA 92182-7455
Fax: (619) 594-1973
E-mail: isc.reception@sdsu.edu
Phone: (619) 594-1982

San Francisco Art Institute
www.sfai.edu
Office of Admissions
800 Chestnut Street
San Francisco, CA 94133-2299
Fax: (415) 749-4592
E-mail: admissions@sfai.edu
Phone: (415) 749-4500

San Francisco Conservatory of Music
www.sfcm.edu
Director of Admission
50 Oak Street
San Francisco, CA 94102
Fax: (415) 503-6299
E-mail: mcocco@sfcm.edu
Phone: (415) 503-6207

San Francisco State University
www.sfsu.edu
Office of International Programs
1600 Holloway Avenue
San Francisco, CA 94132
Fax: (415) 338-6234
E-mail: oip@sfsu.edu
Phone: (415) 338-1293

San Jacinto College
www.sanjac.edu
Call Center
8060 Spencer Highway
Pasadena, TX 77505-5999
Fax: (281) 478-2720
E-mail: information@sjcd.edu
Phone: (281) 998-6150

San Joaquin Delta College
www.deltacollege.edu
International Student Program Specialist
5151 Pacific Avenue
Stockton, CA 95207-6370
Fax: (209) 954-5769
E-mail: mblack@deltacollege.edu
Phone: (209) 954-5641

San Joaquin Valley College
www.sjvc.edu
8400 West Mineral King Avenue
Visalia, CA 93291-9283
Fax: (559) 651-0574
Phone: (559) 651-2500

San Jose City College
www.sjcc.edu
International Admissions
2100 Moorpark Avenue
San Jose, CA 95128-2798
Fax: (408) 297-3924
E-mail: Elaine.burns@sjcc.edu
Phone: (408) 288-3750

San Jose State University
www.sjsu.edu
International Programs & Services
One Washington Square
San Jose, CA 95192-0011
Fax: (408) 924-5976
E-mail: hstevens@sjsu.edu
Phone: (408) 924-5916

San Juan College
www.sanjuancollege.edu
Admissions
4601 College Boulevard
Farmington, NM 87402-4699
Fax: (505) 566-3500
E-mail: admissions@sanjuancollege.edu
Phone: (505) 566-3300

Sandhills Community College
www.sandhills.edu
Admissions
3395 Airport Road
Pinehurst, NC 28374
Fax: (910) 695-3981
E-mail: mcallisterr@sandhills.edu
Phone: (910) 695-3729

Sanford-Brown College
www.sbcfenton.com
1345 Smizer Mill Road
Fenton, MO 63026-1583
Phone: (636) 349-4900

Sanford-Brown College: Hazelwood
www.sanford-brown.edu
75 Village Square
Hazelwood, MO 63042
Fax: (314) 731-0550
Phone: (314) 687-2900

Sanford-Brown College: Houston
www.sanfordbrown.edu/Houston
9999 Richmond Avenue
Houston, TX 77042
E-mail: vsmith@sbhouston.com
Phone: (713) 779-1110

Sanford-Brown College: St. Peters
www.sbcstpeters.com
100 Richmond Center Boulevard
St. Peters, MO 63376
E-mail: dgoodwin@sbc-stpeters.com
Phone: (636) 696-2300

Sanford-Brown Institute: Jacksonville
www.sbjacksonville.com
Admissions
10255 Fortune Parkway, Suite 501
Jacksonville, FL 32256
E-mail: tahmed@sbjacksonville.com
Phone: (904) 363-6221

Sanford-Brown Institute: Monroeville
www.sanfordbrown.edu
777 Penn Center Boulevard
Building Seven
Pittsburgh, PA 15235
Fax: (412) 374-0863
Phone: (412) 373-6400

Santa Ana College
www.sac.edu
International Students Office
1530 West 17th Street
Santa Ana, CA 92706
Fax: (714) 667-0751
E-mail: gitonga_kanana@rsccd.edu
Phone: (714) 564-6047

Santa Barbara Business College
www.sbbcollege.edu
506 Chapala Street
Santa Barbara, CA 93101
Fax: (805) 967-4248
Phone: (805) 967-9677

Santa Barbara Business College: Bakersfield
www.sbbcollege.edu
5300 California Avenue
Bakersfield, CA 93304
Phone: (866) 749-7222

Santa Barbara Business College: Palm Desert
www.sbbcollege.edu
75-030 Gerald Ford Drive, Building 2
Palm Desert, CA 92211
E-mail: hollyo@sbbcollege.edu
Phone: (866) 749-7222

Santa Barbara Business College: Santa Maria
www.sbbcollege.edu
303 East Plaza Drive
Santa Maria, CA 93454
Fax: (805) 346-1862
Phone: (866) 749-7222

Santa Barbara Business College: Ventura
www.sbbcollege.edu
4839 Market Street
Ventura, CA 93003
Fax: (805) 339-2994
Phone: (866) 749-7222

Santa Barbara City College
www.sbcc.edu
International Student Office
721 Cliff Drive
Santa Barbara, CA 93109-2394
Fax: (805) 965-0781
E-mail: smithc@sbcc.edu
Phone: (805) 965-0581 ext. 2243

Santa Clara University
www.scu.edu
Undergraduate Admissions
500 El Camino Real
Santa Clara, CA 95053
Fax: (408) 554-5255
E-mail: mmrubio@scu.edu
Phone: (408) 554-4700

Santa Fe College
www.sfcollege.edu
International Student Office
3000 NW 83rd Street, R-112
Gainesville, FL 32606-6210
Fax: (352) 395-4484
E-mail: james.schwartz@sfcollege.edu
Phone: (352) 395-5504

Santa Fe Community College
www.sfcc.edu
Admissions
6401 Richards Avenue
Santa Fe, NM 87508-4887
Fax: (505) 428-1237
E-mail: anna.tupler@sfcc.edu
Phone: (505) 428-1273

Santa Monica College
www.smc.edu
International Student Center
1900 Pico Boulevard
Santa Monica, CA 90405-1628
Fax: (310) 434-3645
Phone: (310) 434-4217

Santa Rosa Junior College
www.santarosa.edu
International Admissions
1501 Mendocino Avenue
Santa Rosa, CA 95401-4395
Fax: (707) 527-4791
E-mail: khunt@santarosa.edu
Phone: (707) 524-1751

Santiago Canyon College
www.sccollege.edu
International Students
8045 East Chapman Avenue
Orange, CA 92869
Fax: (714) 667-0751
E-mail: gitonga_kanana@sac.edu
Phone: (714) 564-6047

Sarah Lawrence College
www.slc.edu
Undergraduate Admissions
1 Mead Way
Bronxville, NY 10708-5999
Fax: (914) 395-2515
E-mail: slcadmit@slc.edu
Phone: (914) 395-2510

Sauk Valley Community College
www.svcc.edu
Counseling
173 Illinois Route 2
Dixon, IL 61021-9112
Fax: (815) 288-3190
E-mail: breedt@svcc.edu
Phone: (815) 835-6390

Savannah College of Art and Design
www.scad.edu
Office of Admission
PO Box 2072
Savannah, GA 31402-2072
Fax: (912) 525-5986
E-mail: admission@scad.edu
Phone: (912) 525-5100

Savannah State University
www.savannahstate.edu
Admissions
Office of Admissions and Recruitment
Box 20209
Savannah, GA 31404
Fax: (912) 356-2256
E-mail: admissions@savannahstate.edu
Phone: (912) 356-2181

Savannah Technical College
www.savannahtech.edu
Admissions
5717 White Bluff Road
Savannah, GA 31401-5521
Fax: (912) 443-5705
E-mail: mstump@savannahtech.edu
Phone: (912) 443-5706

Schenectady County Community College
www.sunysccc.edu
Admissions Office
78 Washington Avenue
Schenectady, NY 12305
Fax: (518) 346-1477
E-mail: sampsodg@gw.sunysccc.edu
Phone: (518) 381-1366

Schiller International University
www.schiller.edu
Admissions Office
8560 Ulmerton Road
Largo, FL 33771
Fax: (727) 736-3920
E-mail: admissions@schiller.edu
Phone: (877) 748-4338 ext. 410

School of the Art Institute of Chicago
www.saic.edu
Office of Student Affairs/International
36 South Wabash Avenue
Chicago, IL 60603
Fax: (312) 629-6831
E-mail: intaff@saic.edu
Phone: (312) 629-6830

School of the Museum of Fine Arts
www.smfa.edu
Admissions
230 The Fenway
Boston, MA 02115
Fax: (617) 369-4264
E-mail: admissions@smfa.edu
Phone: (617) 369-3626

School of Urban Missions: Oakland
www.sum.edu
Academic Dean
735 105th Avenue
Oakland, CA 94603
Fax: (510) 568-1024
E-mail: lbartley@sum.edu
Phone: (510) 567-6174

School of Visual Arts
www.sva.edu
Admissions Office
209 East 23rd Street
New York, NY 10010-3994
Fax: (212) 592-2242
E-mail: admissions@sva.edu
Phone: (212) 592-2100

Schreiner University
www.schreiner.edu
Admissions
2100 Memorial Boulevard
Kerrville, TX 78028-5697
Fax: (830) 792-7226
E-mail: admissions@schreiner.edu
Phone: (830) 792-7217

Scott Community College
www.eicc.edu
Admissions
500 Belmont Road
Bettendorf, IA 52722-6804
Fax: (563) 441-4101
E-mail: sbergren@eicc.edu
Phone: (563) 441-4004

Scottsdale Community College
www.scottsdalecc.edu
International Education Program
9000 East Chaparral Road
Scottsdale, AZ 85256-2626
Fax: (480) 423-6099
E-mail: therese.tendick@sccmail.maricopa.edu
Phone: (480) 423-6590

Scripps College
www.scrippscollege.edu
Admissions
1030 Columbia Avenue
Claremont, CA 91711-3905
Fax: (909) 607-7508
E-mail: admission@scrippscollege.edu
Phone: (909) 621-8149

Seattle Central Community College
www.seattlecentral.org
International Education Programs
1701 Broadway
Seattle, WA 98122
Fax: (206) 587-3868
E-mail: admiss@sccd.ctc.edu
Phone: (206) 587-3893

Seattle Pacific University
www.spu.edu
Admissions
3307 Third Avenue West, Suite 115
Seattle, WA 98119-1997
Fax: (206) 281-2544
E-mail: jhawkins@spu.edu
Phone: (800) 366-3344

Seattle University
www.seattleu.edu
Assistant Director of Admissions
901 12th Avenue
Seattle, WA 98122-4340
Fax: (206) 296-5656
E-mail: frangia@seattleu.edu
Phone: (206) 296-5812

Selma University
www.selmauniversity.org
1501 Lapsley Street
Selma, AL 36701
Fax: (334) 872-7746
E-mail: selmau.admissions@bellsouth.net
Phone: (334) 872-2533 ext. 18

Seminole State College of Florida
www.seminolestate.edu
Office of Admissions
100 Weldon Boulevard
Sanford, FL 32773-6199
Fax: (407) 708-2395
E-mail: smitha@seminolestate.edu
Phone: (407) 708-2041

Sessions College for Professional Design
www.sessions.edu
398 South Mill Avenue, Suite 300
Tempe, AZ 85281
E-mail: admissions@sessions.edu
Phone: (480) 212-1704

Seton Hall University
www.shu.edu
Office of Undergraduate Admissions
400 South Orange Avenue
South Orange, NJ 07079-2680
Fax: (973) 275-2321
E-mail: thehall@shu.edu
Phone: (973) 313-6146

Seton Hill University
www.setonhill.edu
Office of Admissions
1 Seton Hill Drive
Greensburg, PA 15601
Fax: (724) 830-1294
E-mail: admit@setonhill.edu
Phone: (724) 838-4255

Shasta Bible College and Graduate School
www.shasta.edu
Registrar
2951 Goodwater Avenue
Redding, CA 96002
Fax: (530) 221-6929
E-mail: registrar@shasta.edu
Phone: (530) 221-4275 ext. 26

Shasta College
www.shastacollege.edu
Admissions and Records
Box 496006
Redding, CA 96049-6006
Fax: (530) 225-4995
E-mail: cprice@shastacollege.edu
Phone: (530) 242-7665

Shaw University
www.shawu.edu/
Office of Admissions
118 East South Street
Raleigh, NC 27601
Fax: (919) 546-8271
E-mail: sclifton@shaw.edu
Phone: (919) 546-8275

Shawnee State University
www.shawnee.edu
Admissions
940 Second Street
Portsmouth, OH 45662
Fax: (740) 351-3111
E-mail: rmerb@shawnee.edu
Phone: (740) 351-3576

Shelton State Community College
www.sheltonstate.edu
International Student Liaison
9500 Old Greensboro Road
Tuscaloosa, AL 35405-8522
Fax: (205) 391-3910
E-mail: tbranch@sheltonstate.edu
Phone: (205) 391-2342

Shenandoah University
www.su.edu
Admissions
1460 University Drive
Winchester, VA 22601-5195
Fax: (540) 665-4627
E-mail: admit@su.edu
Phone: (540) 665-4520

Shepherd University
www.shepherd.edu
Admissions
PO Box 5000
Shepherdstown, WV 25443-5000
Fax: (304) 876-5165
E-mail: szimmerm@shepherd.edu
Phone: (304) 876-5212

Shepherds Theological Seminary
www.shepherdsseminary.org
6051 Tryon Road
Cary, NC 27518
Fax: (919) 573-1438
E-mail: info@shepherds.edu
Phone: (919) 573-1555

Sheridan College
www.sheridan.edu
Student Services
PO Box 1500
Sheridan, WY 82801-1500
Fax: (307) 674-3373
E-mail: ccolnar@sheridan.edu
Phone: (307) 674-6446 ext. 2011

Shimer College
www.shimer.edu
Office of Admissions
3424 South State Street
Chicago, IL 60616
Fax: (312) 235-3501
E-mail: admissions@shimer.edu
Phone: (847) 623-8400

Shippensburg University of Pennsylvania
www.ship.edu
Associate Dean, Admissions
1871 Old Main Drive
Shippensburg, PA 17257-2299
Fax: (717) 477-4016
E-mail: whwash@ship.edu
Phone: (717) 477-1231

Shor Yoshuv Rabbinical College
www.shoryoshuv.org
One Cedar Lawn Avenue
Lawrence, NY 11559
E-mail: info@shoryoshuv.org
Phone: (516) 239-9002

Shoreline Community College
www.shoreline.edu
International Student Office
16101 Greenwood Avenue North
Seattle, WA 98133
Fax: (206) 546-7854
E-mail: isp@shoreline.edu
Phone: (206) 546-6940

Shorter University
www.shorter.edu
Admissions
315 Shorter Avenue
Rome, GA 30165
Fax: (706) 233-7224
E-mail: jhead@shorter.edu
Phone: (706) 233-7310

Siena College
www.siena.edu
Assistant Director of Admissions
515 Loudon Road
Loudonville, NY 12211-1462
Fax: (518) 783-2436
E-mail: theffernan@siena.edu
Phone: (888) 287-4362 ext. 4206

Siena Heights University
www.sienaheights.edu
1247 East Siena Heights Drive
Adrian, MI 49221-1796
Fax: (517) 264-7745
E-mail: jhanson@sienaheights.edu
Phone: (517) 264-7001

Sierra College
www.sierracollege.edu
International Students Office
5000 Rocklin Road
Rocklin, CA 95677
Fax: (916) 630-4522
E-mail:
internationalstudents@sierracollege.edu
Phone: (916) 660-7374

Sierra Nevada College
www.sierranevada.edu
Admissions
999 Tahoe Boulevard
Incline Village, NV 89451-4269
Fax: (775) 831-6223
E-mail: admissions@sierranevada.edu
Phone: (866) 412-4636

Silver Lake College
www.sl.edu
Admissions
2406 South Alverno Road
Manitowoc, WI 54220-9319
Fax: (920) 686-6322
E-mail: admslc@silver.sl.edu
Phone: (920) 686-6186

Simmons College
www.simmons.edu
Undergraduate Admissions
300 The Fenway
Boston, MA 02115-5898
Fax: (617) 521-3190
E-mail: alexandra.krol@simmons.edu
Phone: (617) 521-2504

Simpson College
www.simpson.edu
Office of Admissions
701 North C Street
Indianola, IA 50125
Fax: (515) 961-1870
E-mail: gwen.schroder@simpson.edu
Phone: (515) 961-1624

Simpson University
www.simpsonu.edu
Enrollment Management
2211 College View Drive
Redding, CA 96003-8606
Fax: (530) 226-4861
E-mail: admissions@simpsonu.edu
Phone: (530) 226-4606

Sinclair Community College
www.sinclair.edu
Registration/Student Records
444 West Third Street
Dayton, OH 45402-1460
Fax: (937) 512-3456
E-mail: intladm@sinclair.edu
Phone: (937) 512-3024

Sinte Gleska University
www.sintegleska.edu
Box 105
Mission, SD 57555
Fax: (605) 747-4258
Phone: (605) 747-2263

Sisseton Wahpeton College
www.swc.tc
BIA 700, Box 689
Sisseton, SD 57262-0689
Fax: (605) 698-3132
E-mail: dredday@swc.tc
Phone: (605) 698-3966

Skagit Valley College
www.skagit.edu
International Programs
2405 East College Way
Mount Vernon, WA 98273
Fax: (360) 416-7868
E-mail: ganeson@skagit.ctc.edu
Phone: (360) 416-7734

Skidmore College
www.skidmore.edu
Admissions
815 North Broadway
Saratoga Springs, NY 12866
Fax: (518) 580-5584
E-mail: admissions@skidmore.edu
Phone: (518) 580-5570

Skyline College
www.skylinecollege.edu
Admissions and Records
3300 College Drive
San Bruno, CA 94066-1662
Fax: (650) 738-4200
E-mail: zepedak@smccd.edu
Phone: (650) 738-4251

Slippery Rock University of Pennsylvania
www.sru.edu
International Services
1 Morrow Way
Slippery Rock, PA 16057-1383
Fax: (724) 738-2289
E-mail: genevieve.bordogna@sru.edu
Phone: (724) 738-2603

Smith College
www.smith.edu
Admission
7 College Lane
Northampton, MA 01063
Fax: (413) 585-2527
E-mail: kkristof@smith.edu
Phone: (413) 585-2500

Snow College
www.snow.edu
International Students Admissions
150 East College Avenue
Ephraim, UT 84627
Fax: (435) 283-7438
E-mail: diane.ogden@snow.edu
Phone: (435) 283-7430

Sojourner-Douglass College
www.sdc.edu
500 North Caroline Street
Baltimore, MD 21205
Fax: (410) 675-1811
Phone: (410) 276-0306 ext. 248

Soka University of America
www.soka.edu
Admission and Financial Aid
One University Drive
Aliso Viejo, CA 92656-8081
Fax: (949) 480-4151
E-mail: cbrown@soka.edu
Phone: (949) 480-4048

Solano Community College
www.solano.edu
4000 Suisun Valley Road
Fairfield, CA 94534-3197
Fax: (707) 646-2053
E-mail: admissions@solano.edu
Phone: (707) 864-7171

Somerset Community College
www.somerset.kctcs.edu
Student Affairs Admissions
808 Monticello Street
Somerset, KY 42501
Fax: (606) 679-4369
E-mail: tina.whitaker@kctcs.edu
Phone: (606) 451-6636

Sonoma State University
www.sonoma.edu
Academic Records Specialist/Evaluator
1801 East Cotati Avenue
Rohnert Park, CA 94928-3609
Fax: (707) 664-2060
E-mail: inquiryi@sonoma.edu
Phone: (707) 664-3030

South Arkansas Community College
www.southark.edu
Enrollment Services
Box 7010
El Dorado, AR 71731-7010
Fax: (870) 864-7137
E-mail: dinman@southark.edu
Phone: (870) 862-8131

South Carolina State University
www.scsu.edu
Admissions and Recruitment
300 College Street NE
PO Box 7127
Orangeburg, SC 29117
Fax: (803) 536-8990
E-mail: aboyle@scsu.edu
Phone: (803) 536-8407

South Central College
www.southcentral.edu
Admissions
1920 Lee Boulevard
PO Box 1920
North Mankato, MN 56003
Fax: (507) 388-9951
E-mail: admissions@southcentral.edu
Phone: (507) 389-7336

South Coast College
www.southcoastcollege.com
2011 West Chapman Avenue
Orange, CA 92868
E-mail: requestinfo@southcoastcollege.com
Phone: (714) 867-5009

South College
www.southcollegetn.edu
Admissions
3904 Lonas Drive
Knoxville, TN 37909
Fax: (865) 470-8737
E-mail: admissions@southcollegetn.edu
Phone: (865) 251-1800

South Dakota School of Mines and Technology
www.sdsmt.edu
Ivanhoe International Student Center
501 East St. Joseph Street
Rapid City, SD 57701
Fax: (605) 394-6883
E-mail: susan.aadland@sdsmt.edu
Phone: (605) 394-6884

South Dakota State University
www.sdstate.edu
International Student Affairs
Box 2201 SAD 200
Brookings, SD 57007-0649
Fax: (605) 688-4355
E-mail: sdsu.intlstud@sdstate.edu
Phone: (605) 688-5585

South Florida Community College
www.southflorida.edu
University Relations
600 West College Drive
Avon Park, FL 33825
Fax: (863) 453-2365
E-mail: laura.white@southflorida.edu
Phone: (863) 453-6661 ext. 7154

South Georgia College
www.sgc.edu
Admissions office
100 West College Park Drive
Douglas, GA 31533-5098
Fax: (912) 260-4441
E-mail: admissions@sgc.edu
Phone: (912) 260-4207

South Louisiana Community College
www.southlouisiana.edu
Admissions
320 Devalcourt
Lafayette, LA 70506-4124
Fax: (337) 262-2101
E-mail: agillis@southlouisiana.edu
Phone: (337) 521-8943

South Mountain Community College
www.southmountaincc.edu
7050 South 24th Street
Phoenix, AZ 85042
Fax: (602) 243-8199
E-mail: della.garcia@smcmail.maricopa.edu
Phone: (602) 243-8124

South Plains College
www.southplainscollege.edu
Admissions
1401 South College Avenue
Levelland, TX 79336
Fax: (806) 897-3167
E-mail: aruiz@southplainscollege.edu
Phone: (806) 894-9611 ext. 2371

South Puget Sound Community College
www.spscc.ctc.edu
International Student Programs Office
2011 Mottman Road, SW
Olympia, WA 98512-6218
Fax: (360) 664-0780
E-mail: hlukashin@spscc.ctc.edu
Phone: (360) 596-5247

South Seattle Community College
www.southseattle.edu
International Programs Office
6000 16th Avenue, SW
Seattle, WA 98106-1499
Fax: (206) 764-5836
E-mail: ip@ssccd.ctc.edu
Phone: (206) 764-5360

South Texas College
www.southtexascollege.edu
Admissions
3201 West Pecan Boulevard
McAllen, TX 78502
Fax: (956) 872-8321
E-mail: romerol@southtexascollege.edu
Phone: (956) 872-2250

South University: Columbia
www.southuniversity.edu
Registrar
9 Science Court
Columbia, SC 29203
Fax: (803) 799-5009
Phone: (803) 935-4305

South University: Savannah
www.southuniversity.edu
Admissions office
709 Mall Boulevard
Savannah, GA 31406
Fax: (912) 201-8070
E-mail: dmaddox@southuniversity.edu
Phone: (912) 201-8018

South University: Tampa
www.southuniversity.edu
Admissions Office
4401 North Himes Avenue
Tampa, FL 33614
Phone: (813) 393-3800

South University: West Palm Beach
www.southuniversity.edu
Admissions
9801 Belvedere Road
University Centre
Royal Palm Beach, FL 33411
Fax: (561) 273-6420
E-mail: smohammed@southuniversity.edu
Phone: (561) 273-6500

Southeast Arkansas College
www.seark.edu
Admissions
1900 Hazel Street
Pine Bluff, AR 71603
Fax: (870) 543-5957
E-mail: bdunn@seark.edu
Phone: (870) 543-5957

Southeast Kentucky Community and Technical College
www.southeast.kctcs.edu
Admissions
700 College Road
Cumberland, KY 40823
Fax: (606) 589-5423
E-mail: cookie.baldwin@kctcs.net
Phone: (606) 589-2145

Southeast Missouri Hospital College of Nursing and Health Sciences
www.southeastmissourihospitalcollege.edu
2001 William Street, Second Floor
Cape Girardeau, MO 63703
Fax: (573) 339-7805
E-mail: dpugh@sehosp.org
Phone: (573) 334-6825 ext. 23

Southeast Missouri State University
www.semo.edu
Office of International Education and Services
One University Plaza
MS 3550
Cape Girardeau, MO 63701
Fax: (573) 986-6866
E-mail: intadmit@semo.edu
Phone: (573) 986-6863

Southeastern Baptist College
www.southeasternbaptist.edu
4229 Highway 15 North
Laurel, MS 39440
Fax: (601) 426-6347
E-mail: admissions@southeasternbaptist.edu
Phone: (601) 426-6346

Southeastern Baptist Theological Seminary
www.sebts.edu
PO Box 1889
Wake Forest, NC 27588
Fax: (919) 556-0998
E-mail: admissions@sebts.edu
Phone: (919) 761-2280

Southeastern Bible College
www.sebc.edu
Admissions
2545 Valleydale Road
Birmingham, AL 35244-2083
Fax: (205) 970-9207
E-mail: jbarber@sebc.edu
Phone: (205) 970-9209

Southeastern Community College
www.sccnc.edu
Admissions Office
4564 Chadbourn Highway
PO Box 151
Whiteville, NC 28472-0151
Fax: (910) 642-5658
E-mail: jfowler@sccnc.edu
Phone: (910) 642-7141 ext. 265

Southeastern Community College: North Campus
www.scciowa.edu
Enrollment Services
1500 West Agency Road
PO Box 180
West Burlington, IA 52655-0605
Fax: (319) 758-6725
E-mail: kthorarinsdottir@scciowa.edu
Phone: (319) 752-2731 ext. 5026

Southeastern Illinois College
www.sic.edu
Academic Advising
3575 College Road
Harrisburg, IL 62946
Fax: (618) 252-3062
E-mail: tyler.billman@sic.edu
Phone: (618) 252-5400 ext. 2430

Southeastern Louisiana University
www.selu.edu
Office of Admissions
SLU 10752
Hammond, LA 70402
Fax: (985) 549-5882
E-mail: admissions@selu.edu
Phone: (985) 549-2360

Southeastern Oklahoma State University
www.se.edu
Office of Admissions and Enrollment Services
1405 North Fourth Avenue, PMB 4225
Durant, OK 74701-0607
Fax: (580) 745-7502
E-mail: ttollett@se.edu
Phone: (580) 745-2166

Southeastern Technical College
www.southeasterntech.edu
Admissions
3001 East First Street
Vidalia, GA 30474
Fax: (912) 538-3156
E-mail: amcrae@southeasterntech.edu
Phone: (478) 289-2259

Southeastern University
www.seuniversity.edu
International Admission Counselor
1000 Longfellow Boulevard
Lakeland, FL 33801-6034
Fax: (863) 667-5200
E-mail: jfarul@seuniversity.edu
Phone: (863) 667-5018

Southern Arkansas University
www.saumag.edu
International Student Admissions
Box 9382
Magnolia, AR 71754-9382
Fax: (870) 235-5096
E-mail: cjlyons@saumag.edu
Phone: (870) 235-4082

Southern Arkansas University Tech
www.sautech.edu
Vice Chancellor for Student Services
PO Box 3499
100 Carr Road
Camden, AR 71711-1599
Fax: (870) 574-4478
E-mail: rcooper@sautech.edu
Phone: (870) 574-4504

Southern California Institute of Architecture
www.sciarc.edu
Admissions
960 East Third Street
Los Angeles, CA 90013
Fax: (213) 613-2260
E-mail: sandy@sciarc.edu
Phone: (213) 356-5320

Southern California Institute of Technology
www.scitech.edu
Admissions Director
222 South Harbor Boulevard, Suite 200
Anaheim, CA 92805-3758
Fax: (714) 300-0310
E-mail: jpinesett@scitech.edu
Phone: (714) 300-0300

Southern California Seminary
www.socalsem.edu
International Admissions
2075 East Madison Avenue
El Cajon, CA 92019
Fax: (619) 590-2133
E-mail: dmullen@socalsem.edu
Phone: (619) 590-2140

Southern Connecticut State University
www.southernct.edu
Admissions
131 Farnham Avenue
New Haven, CT 06515-1202
Fax: (203) 392-5727
E-mail: belchert1@southernct.edu
Phone: (203) 392-5726

Southern Crescent Technical College
www.sctech.edu
501 Varsity Road
Griffin, GA 30223
Fax: (770) 229-3227
E-mail: tkinard@sctech.edu
Phone: (706) 646-6160

Southern Illinois University Carbondale
www.siuc.edu
International Students and Scholars
Mailcode 4701
Carbondale, IL 62901-4701
Fax: (618) 453-7660
E-mail: admrec@siu.edu
Phone: (618) 453-2979

Southern Illinois University Edwardsville
www.siue.edu
International Programs Specialist
Campus Box 1600, Rendleman Hall, Rm 2120
Edwardsville, IL 62026-1600
Fax: (618) 650-2081
E-mail: satamar@siue.edu
Phone: (618) 650-3781

Southern Maine Community College
www.smccme.edu
Enrollment Services
2 Fort Road
South Portland, ME 04106
Fax: (207) 741-5760
E-mail: jlane@smccme.edu
Phone: (207) 741-5880

Southern Methodist University
www.smu.edu
International Center
PO Box 750181
Dallas, TX 75275-0181
Fax: (214) 768-1051
E-mail: mclarke@smu.edu
Phone: (214) 768-4475

Southern Nazarene University
www.snu.edu
International Student Services
6729 NW 39th Expressway
Bethany, OK 73008
Fax: (405) 717-6270
E-mail: rgraves@snu.edu
Phone: (405) 491-6624

Southern New Hampshire University
www.snhu.edu
International Student Admission
2500 North River Road
Manchester, NH 03106-1045
Fax: (603) 645-9603
E-mail: s.harvey@snhu.edu
Phone: (603) 645-9629

Southern Oregon University
www.sou.edu
Admissions
1250 Siskiyou Boulevard
Ashland, OR 97520-5032
Fax: (541) 552-8403
E-mail: admissions@sou.edu
Phone: (541) 552-6411

Southern Polytechnic State University
www.spsu.edu
Admissions
1100 South Marietta Parkway
Marietta, GA 30060-2896
Fax: (678) 915-7292
E-mail: bcoleman@spsu.edu
Phone: (678) 915-6864

Southern Union State Community College
www.suscc.edu
Admissions
750 Roberts Street
PO Box 1000
Wadley, AL 36276
Fax: (256) 395-2215
E-mail: cstringfellow@suscc.edu
Phone: (256) 395-2215

**Southern University and Agricultural and
Mechanical College**
www.subr.edu
Admissions Office
T.H. Harris Hall
PO Box 9426
Baton Rouge, LA 70813
Fax: (225) 771-2500
E-mail: yvonne_roberson@cxs.subr.edu
Phone: (225) 771-2430

Southern University at New Orleans
www.suno.edu
Admissions
6801 Press Drive
New Orleans, LA 70126
Fax: (504) 284-5481
E-mail: rgpratt@suno.edu
Phone: (504) 286-5314

Southern University at Shreveport
www.susla.edu
3050 Martin Luther King, Jr. Drive
Shreveport, LA 71107
Fax: (318) 674-3489
Phone: (318) 674-3342

Southern Utah University
www.suu.edu
351 West Center Street
Cedar City, UT 84720
Fax: (435) 865-8223
E-mail: adminfo@suu.edu
Phone: (435) 586-7740

Southern Vermont College
www.svc.edu
Admissions
982 Mansion Drive
Bennington, VT 05201-6002
Fax: (802) 447-6313
E-mail: admissions@svc.edu
Phone: (802) 447-6304

Southern Virginia University
www.svu.edu
Admissions Office
One University Hill Drive
Buena Vista, VA 24416-3097
Fax: (540) 261-8559
E-mail: brett.garcia@svu.edu
Phone: (540) 261-4503

Southern Wesleyan University
www.swu.edu
Admissions
PO Box 1020
Central, SC 29630-1020
Fax: (864) 644-5972
E-mail: ayoung@swu.edu
Phone: (864) 644-5550

Southwest Baptist University
www.sbuniv.edu
Admissions
1600 University Avenue
Bolivar, MO 65613-2597
Fax: (417) 328-1808
E-mail: cstandley@sbuniv.edu
Phone: (417) 328-1810

Southwest Florida College
www.swfc.edu
1685 Medical Lane
Ft. Myers, FL 33907-1108
Fax: (239) 936-4040
E-mail: ballen@swfc.edu
Phone: (239) 939-4766

Southwest Georgia Technical College
www.southwestgatech.edu
15689 US Highway 19N
Thomasville, GA 31792
Fax: (229) 227-2666
E-mail: info@southwestgatech.edu
Phone: (229) 225-5089

Southwest Minnesota State University
www.smsu.edu
Admissions
1501 State Street
Marshall, MN 56258-1598
Fax: (507) 537-7154
E-mail: andrew.hlubek@smsu.edu
Phone: (507) 537-6286

Southwest Tennessee Community College
www.southwest.tn.edu
PO Box 780
Memphis, TN 38101-0780
Fax: (901) 333-4523
E-mail: vdowdy@southwest.tn.edu
Phone: (901) 333-4804

Southwest Texas Junior College
www.swtjc.edu
2401 Garner Field Road
Uvalde, TX 78801
Fax: (830) 591-7396
E-mail: luana.rodriguez@swtjc.cc.tx.us
Phone: (830) 278-4401

Southwest University
www.southwest.edu
Office of Admissions
2200 Veterans Memorial Boulevard
Kenner, LA 70062-4005
Fax: (504) 468-3213
E-mail: admissions@southwest.edu
Phone: (800) 433-5923

Southwest Virginia Community College
www.sw.edu
Admissions
PO Box SVCC
Richlands, VA 24641-1101
Fax: (276) 964-7716
E-mail: jim.farris@sw.edu
Phone: (276) 964-7300

Southwest Wisconsin Technical College
www.swtc.edu
Student Services
1800 Bronson Boulevard
Fennimore, WI 53809
Fax: (608) 822-6019
E-mail: pwegner@swtc.edu
Phone: (608) 822-2354

Southwestern Adventist University
www.swau.edu
International Admissions
Box 567
Keene, TX 76059
Fax: (817) 556-4744
E-mail: martinezm@swau.edu
Phone: (817) 645-3921 ext. 6083

Southwestern Assemblies of God University
www.sagu.edu
Admissions
1200 Sycamore Street
Waxahachie, TX 75165
Fax: (972) 937-0006
E-mail: pthompson@sagu.edu
Phone: (972) 937-4010 ext. 1229

Southwestern Baptist Theological Seminary
www.swbts.edu
PO Box 22000
Fort Worth, TX 76122
E-mail: admissions@swbts.edu
Phone: (800) 792-8701

Southwestern Christian College
www.swcc.edu
Admissions
Box 10
200 Bowser Circle
Terrell, TX 75160
Fax: (972) 563-7133
E-mail: rhodr@swcc.edu
Phone: (972) 524-3341 ext. 161

Southwestern Christian University
www.swcu.edu
Academic Affairs
Box 340
Bethany, OK 73008
Fax: (405) 495-0078
E-mail: jean.perdue@swcu.edu
Phone: (405) 789-7661 ext. 3458

Southwestern College
www.swccd.edu
Admissions Center Evening Lead
900 Otay Lakes Road
Chula Vista, CA 91910-7297
Fax: (619) 482-6489
E-mail: amora@swccd.edu
Phone: (619) 482-6584

Southwestern College
www.sckans.edu
100 College Street
Winfield, KS 67156
Fax: (620) 229-6344
E-mail: leslie.grant@sckans.edu
Phone: (620) 229-6269

Southwestern College: Tri-County
www.swcollege.net
149 Northland Boulevard
Cincinnati, OH 45246
E-mail: rkimble@swcollege.net
Phone: (513) 874-0432

Southwestern Community College
www.swcciowa.edu
Admissions Coordinator
1501 West Townline Street
Creston, IA 50801
Fax: (641) 782-3312
E-mail: carstens@swcciowa.edu
Phone: (641) 782-7081 ext. 453

Southwestern Community College
www.southwesterncc.edu
447 College Drive
Sylva, NC 28779
Fax: (828) 586-3129
Phone: (828) 586-4091 ext. 352

Southwestern Illinois College
www.swic.edu
Admissions
2500 Carlyle Avenue
Belleville, IL 62221-5899
Fax: (618) 222-9768
E-mail: janice.sanders@swic.edu
Phone: (618) 235-2700 ext. 5444

Southwestern Michigan College
www.swmich.edu
Academic Support
58900 Cherry Grove Road
Dowagiac, MI 49047-9793
Fax: (269) 782-1331
E-mail: szovich@swmich.edu
Phone: (269) 782-1348

Southwestern Oklahoma State University
www.swosu.edu
Registrar's Office
100 Campus Drive
Weatherford, OK 73096
Fax: (580) 774-3795
E-mail: klaassb@swosu.edu
Phone: (580) 774-3777

Southwestern Oregon Community College
www.socc.edu
International Student Services
1988 Newmark Avenue
Coos Bay, OR 97420-2956
Fax: (541) 888-7247
E-mail: chockman@socc.edu
Phone: (541) 888-7408

Southwestern University
www.southwestern.edu
Admission
1001 East University Avenue
Georgetown, TX 78626
Fax: (512) 863-9601
E-mail: navarroa@southwestern.edu
Phone: (512) 863-1200

Spalding University
www.spalding.edu
Dean of Enrollment Management
845 S Third Street
Louisville, KY 40203
Fax: (502) 992-2418
E-mail: chart@spalding.edu
Phone: (502) 585-9911 ext. 2228

Spartan College of Aeronautics and Technology
www.spartan.edu
8820 East Pine Street
PO Box 582833
Tulsa, OK 74158-2833
Fax: (918) 831-5234
E-mail: spartan@mail.spartan.edu
Phone: (918) 836-6886 ext. 228

Spartanburg Community College
www.sccsc.edu
Box 4386
Spartanburg, SC 29305-4386
Fax: (864) 592-4642
E-mail: rogersp@sccsc.edu
Phone: (864) 592-4816

Spartanburg Methodist College
www.smcsc.edu
Admissions
1000 Powell Mill Road
Spartanburg, SC 29301-5899
Fax: (864) 587-4355
E-mail: admiss@smcsc.edu
Phone: (864) 587-4213

Spelman College
www.spelman.edu
Office of International and Commuter
Students
350 Spelman Lane SW, Campus Box 277
Atlanta, GA 30314
Fax: (404) 270-5201
E-mail: ldenard@spelman.edu
Phone: (404) 270-5137

Spencerian College: Lexington
www.spencerian.edu
Admissions
1575 Winchester Road
Lexington, KY 40505
Fax: (859) 224-7744
E-mail: cdouglas@spencerian.edu
Phone: (859) 223-9608

Spokane Community College
www.scc.spokane.edu
Program Coordinator
1810 North Greene Street
Spokane, WA 99217-5399
Fax: (509) 533-8860
E-mail: TAllen@scc.spokane.edu
Phone: (509) 533-8659

Spoon River College
www.src.edu
Advisor
23235 North County Road 22
Canton, IL 61520
Fax: (309) 833-6062
E-mail: patrick.denecke@src.edu
Phone: (309) 833-6022

Spring Arbor University
www.arbor.edu
106 East Main Street
Spring Arbor, MI 49283-9799
Fax: (517) 750-6620
E-mail: sharonh@arbor.edu
Phone: (517) 750-6468

Spring Hill College
www.shc.edu
Admissions Office
4000 Dauphin Street
Mobile, AL 36608-1791
Fax: (251) 460-2186
E-mail: admit@shc.edu
Phone: (251) 380-3030

Springfield College
www.springfieldcollege.edu
International Center
263 Alden Street
Springfield, MA 01109
Fax: (413) 731-1681
E-mail: dalm@spldcol.edu
Phone: (413) 748-3215

Springfield Technical Community College
www.stcc.edu
Admissions
One Armory Square
PO Box 9000, Suite 1
Springfield, MA 01102-9000
Fax: (413) 746-0344
E-mail: admissions@stcc.edu
Phone: (413) 755-4202

Stanbridge College
www.stanbridge.edu
2041 Business Center Drive, Suite 107
Irvine, CA 92612
E-mail: eriepma@stanbridge.edu
Phone: (949) 794-9090 ext. 5116

Stanford University
www.stanford.edu
Undergraduate Admission
Montag Hall
355 Galvez Street
Stanford, CA 94305-6106
Fax: (650) 723-6050
E-mail: admissions@stanford.edu
Phone: (650) 723-2091

Stark State College of Technology
www.starkstate.edu
Admissions
6200 Frank Avenue NW
North Canton, OH 44720
Fax: (330) 497-6313
E-mail: info@starkstate.edu
Phone: (330) 494-6170

State College of Florida, Manatee-Sarasota
www.scf.edu
Foreign Student Coordinator
Box 1849
Bradenton, FL 34206-1849
Fax: (941) 727-6179
E-mail: hekkinw@scf.edu
Phone: (941) 752-5418

State Fair Community College
www.sfccmo.edu
Admissions/Recruitment
3201 West 16th Street
Sedalia, MO 65301-2199
Fax: (660) 596-7472
E-mail: mcarter@sfccmo.edu
Phone: (660) 596-7221

Stenotype Institute: Jacksonville
www.stenotype.edu
3563 Phillips Highway, Building E, #501
Jacksonville, FL 32207
Fax: (904) 398-7878
E-mail: info@thestenotypeinstitute.com
Phone: (904) 398-4141

Stenotype Institute: Orlando
www.stenotype.edu
1636 West Oakridge Road
Orlando, FL 32809
Phone: (407) 816-5573

Stephen F. Austin State University
www.sfasu.edu
Admissions Counselor
Box 13051, SFA Station
Nacogdoches, TX 75962-3051
Fax: (936) 468-3849
E-mail: feltskr1@sfasu.edu
Phone: (936) 468-2504

Stephens College
www.stephens.edu
Admissions
1200 East Broadway
Box 2121
Columbia, MO 65215
Fax: (573) 876-7207
E-mail: apply@stephens.edu
Phone: (800) 876-7207

Sterling College
www.sterling.edu
Admissions
125 West Cooper
Sterling, KS 67579
Fax: (620) 278-4416
E-mail: admissions@sterling.edu
Phone: (620) 278-4275

Sterling College
www.sterlingcollege.edu
Director of Admissions
PO Box 72
Craftsbury Common, VT 05827-0072
Fax: (802) 586-2596
E-mail: lbirdsall@sterlingcollege.edu
Phone: (802) 586-7711 ext. 135

Stetson University
www.stetson.edu
Admissions
Campus Box 8378
DeLand, FL 32723
Fax: (386) 822-7112
E-mail: admissions@stetson.edu
Phone: (386) 822-7100

Stevens Institute of Business & Arts
www.siba.edu
Admissions
1521 Washington Avenue
St. Louis, MO 63103
Fax: (314) 421-0304
E-mail: admissions@siba.edu
Phone: (314) 421-0949 ext. 1119

Stevens Institute of Technology
www.stevens.edu
Undergraduate Admissions
1 Castle Point on Hudson
Wesley J Howe Center, 8th Floor
Hoboken, NJ 07030-5991
Fax: (201) 216-8348
E-mail: Ilona.Castro@stevens.edu
Phone: (201) 216-8349

Stevens-Henager College: Boise
www.stevenshenager.edu
Campus Director
1444 S Entertainment Avenue
Boise, ID 83709
Fax: (208) 345-6999
E-mail: shane.reeder@stevenshenager.edu
Phone: (208) 383-4540

Stevens-Henager College: Logan
www.stevenshenager.edu
755 South Main
Logan, UT 84321
Fax: (435) 755-7611
Phone: (435) 792-6970 ext. 5002

Stevens-Henager College: Orem
www.stevenshenager.edu
Salt Lake Campus International Students
1476 South Sand Hill Road
Orem, UT 84058
Fax: (801) 375-9836
E-mail: jesse.hafen@stevenshenager.edu
Phone: (800) 233-9762

Stevenson University
www.stevenson.edu
Admissions Office
1525 Greenspring Valley Road
Stevenson, MD 21153-0641
Fax: (443) 352-4440
E-mail: admissions@stevenson.edu
Phone: (443) 352-4410

Stillman College
www.stillman.edu
Admissions
3600 Stillman Boulevard
PO Box 1430
Tuscaloosa, AL 35403
Fax: (205) 247-8156
E-mail: mfinch@stillman.edu
Phone: (205) 366-8814

Stonehill College
www.stonehill.edu
Admissions Office
320 Washington Street
Easton, MA 02357-0100
Fax: (508) 565-1545
E-mail: ssmith@stonehill.edu
Phone: (508) 565-1373

Stratford University: Falls Church
www.stratford.edu
7777 Leesburg Pike
Falls Church, VA 22043
Fax: (703) 734-5339
E-mail: fkhan@stratford.edu
Phone: (703) 821-8570

Stratford University: Woodbridge
www.stratford.edu
International Student Office
14349 Gideon Drive
Woodbridge, VA 22192
Fax: (703) 734-5335
E-mail: fkhan@stratford.edu
Phone: (703) 821-8570 ext. 3231

Suffolk County Community College
www.sunysuffolk.edu
Central Admissions
533 College Road
Selden, NY 11784
Fax: (631) 451-4415
E-mail: spagnoe@sunysuffolk.edu
Phone: (631) 451-4000

Suffolk University
www.suffolk.edu
Undergraduate Admissions
8 Ashburton Place
Boston, MA 02108
Fax: (617) 557-1574
E-mail: admission@suffolk.edu
Phone: (617) 573-8460

Sul Ross State University
www.sulross.edu
International Admissions
PO Box C-2
Alpine, TX 79832
Fax: (432) 837-8431
E-mail: coleman@sulross.edu
Phone: (432) 837-8050

Sullivan College of Technology and Design
www.sctd.edu
Admissions
3901 Atkinson Square Drive
Louisville, KY 40218-4524
Fax: (502) 456-2341
E-mail: kriperdan@louisvilletech.edu
Phone: (502) 456-6509

Sullivan County Community College
www.sullivan.suny.edu
112 College Road
Loch Sheldrake, NY 12759-5151
Fax: (845) 434-0923
E-mail: admissions@sullivan.suny.edu
Phone: (845) 434-5750 ext. 4287

Sullivan University
www.sullivan.edu
Front Desk Personnel
3101 Bardstown Road
Louisville, KY 40205
Fax: (502) 456-0040
E-mail: admissions@sullivan.edu
Phone: (502) 456-6505

SUNY College at Brockport
www.brockport.edu
Admissions
350 New Campus Drive
Brockport, NY 14420-2915
Fax: (585) 395-5291
E-mail: bvalento@brockport.edu
Phone: (585) 395-5453

SUNY College at Buffalo
www.buffalostate.edu
International Student Affairs
1300 Elmwood Avenue, Moot Hall
Buffalo, NY 14222-1095
Fax: (716) 878-6100
E-mail: burnhasl@BuffaloState.edu
Phone: (716) 878-5522

SUNY College at Cortland
www.cortland.edu
Admissions
PO Box 2000
Cortland, NY 13045-0900
Fax: (607) 753-5998
E-mail: admissions@cortland.edu
Phone: (607) 753-4711

SUNY College at Fredonia
www.fredonia.edu
Office of Admissions
178 Central Avenue
Fredonia, NY 14063-1136
Fax: (716) 673-3249
E-mail: admissions@fredonia.edu
Phone: (716) 673-3251

SUNY College at Geneseo
www.geneseo.edu
International Student Services
1 College Circle
Geneseo, NY 14454-1401
Fax: (585) 245-5405
E-mail: hope@geneseo.edu
Phone: (585) 245-5404

SUNY College at New Paltz
www.newpaltz.edu
Center for International Programs
100 Hawk Drive
New Paltz, NY 12561-2443
Fax: (845) 257-6903
E-mail: intadmissions@newpaltz.edu
Phone: (845) 257-3040

SUNY College at Old Westbury
www.oldwestbury.edu
Enrollment Services
Box 307
Old Westbury, NY 11568-0307
Fax: (516) 876-3307
E-mail: enroll@oldwestbury.edu
Phone: (516) 876-3073

SUNY College at Oneonta
www.oneonta.edu
Office of International Education
Admissions Office, 116 Alumni Hall
State University College
Oneonta, NY 13820-4016
Fax: (607) 436-2475
E-mail: mandzicl@oneonta.edu
Phone: (607) 436-3369

SUNY College at Oswego
www.oswego.edu
Office of Admissions
229 Sheldon Hall
Oswego, NY 13126-3599
Fax: (315) 312-3260
E-mail: oberst@oswego.edu
Phone: (315) 312-2250

SUNY College at Plattsburgh
www.plattsburgh.edu
International Student Services
Kehoe Administration Building
Plattsburgh, NY 12901
Fax: (518) 564-3292
E-mail: iss@plattsburgh.edu
Phone: (518) 564-3287

SUNY College at Potsdam
www.potsdam.edu
Office of Admissions
44 Pierrepont Avenue
Potsdam, NY 13676
Fax: (315) 267-2163
E-mail: admint@potsdam.edu
Phone: (315) 267-2180

SUNY College at Purchase
www.purchase.edu
Admissions Office
735 Anderson Hill Road
Purchase, NY 10577-1400
Fax: (914) 251-6314
E-mail: barbaraw@purchase.edu
Phone: (914) 251-6300

SUNY College of Agriculture and Technology at Cobleskill
www.cobleskill.edu
International Programs
Knapp Hall
Cobleskill, NY 12043
Fax: (518) 255-5113
E-mail: jagends@cobleskill.edu
Phone: (518) 255-5558

SUNY College of Agriculture and Technology at Morrisville
www.morrisville.edu
Admissions Office
PO Box 901
Morrisville, NY 13408-0901
Fax: (315) 684-6427
E-mail: admissions@morrisville.edu
Phone: (315) 684-6046

SUNY College of Environmental Science and Forestry
www.esf.edu
Undergraduate Admissions
106 Bray Hall
One Forestry Drive
Syracuse, NY 13210
Fax: (315) 470-6933
E-mail: esfinfo@esf.edu
Phone: (315) 470-6600

SUNY College of Technology at Alfred
www.alfredstate.edu
International Education
Huntington Administration Building
10 Upper College Drive
Alfred, NY 14802-1196
Fax: (607) 587-4340
E-mail: jiangs@alfredstate.edu
Phone: (607) 587-4059

SUNY College of Technology at Canton
www.canton.edu
Admissions
34 Cornell Drive
Canton, NY 13617-1098
Fax: (315) 386-7929
E-mail: lassiale@canton.edu
Phone: (315) 386-7123

SUNY College of Technology at Delhi
www.delhi.edu
Admissions
2 Main Street
Delhi, NY 13753-1190
Fax: (607) 746-4104
E-mail: enroll@delhi.edu
Phone: (607) 746-4550

SUNY College of Technology at Farmingdale
www.farmingdale.edu
Admissions
2350 Broadhollow Road
Farmingdale, NY 11735-1021
Fax: (631) 420-2633
E-mail: admissions@farmingdale.edu
Phone: (631) 420-2200

SUNY Empire State College
www.esc.edu
Admissions
Two Union Avenue
Saratoga Springs, NY 12866
Fax: (518) 587-9759
E-mail: melanie.kaiser@esc.edu
Phone: (518) 587-2100 ext. 2447

SUNY Institute of Technology at Utica/ Rome
www.sunyit.edu
Admissions Office
100 Seymour Road
Utica, NY 13502
Fax: (315) 792-7837
E-mail: international@sunyit.edu
Phone: (315) 792-7500

SUNY Maritime College
www.sunymaritime.edu
6 Pennyfield Avenue
Throggs Neck, NY 10465-4198
Fax: (718) 409-7465
E-mail: mvargas@sunymaritime.edu
Phone: (718) 409-2223

SUNY University at Albany
www.albany.edu
Office of Undergraduate Admissions,
University Hall 112
1400 Washington Avenue
Albany, NY 12222
Fax: (518) 442-5383
E-mail: ugadmissions@uamail.albany.edu
Phone: (518) 442-5435

SUNY University at Binghamton
www.binghamton.edu
Admissions
Box 6001
Binghamton, NY 13902-6001
Fax: (607) 777-4445
E-mail: nforcier@binghamton.edu
Phone: (607) 777-2171

SUNY University at Buffalo
www.buffalo.edu
International Admissions
12 Capen Hall
Buffalo, NY 14260-1660
Fax: (716) 645-2528
E-mail: intladmit@buffalo.edu
Phone: (716) 645-2368

SUNY University at Stony Brook
www.stonybrook.edu
International Admissions
118 Administration Building
Stony Brook, NY 11794-1901
Fax: (631) 632-9898
E-mail: enrollintl@stonybrook.edu
Phone: (631) 632-6868

SUNY Upstate Medical University
www.upstate.edu
International Student Advisor
766 Irving Avenue
Syracuse, NY 13210
Fax: (315) 464-8857
E-mail: abbottj@upstate.edu
Phone: (315) 464-8817

Susquehanna University
www.susqu.edu
Office of Admissions
514 University Avenue
Selinsgrove, PA 17870-1164
Fax: (570) 372-2722
E-mail: ryans@susqu.edu
Phone: (570) 372-4260

Sussex County Community College
www.sussex.edu
Senior Vice President of Student Services
One College Hill Road
Newton, NJ 07860
Fax: (973) 579-5226
E-mail: hdamato@sussex.edu
Phone: (973) 300-2219

Swarthmore College
www.swarthmore.edu
Director of International Recruitment
500 College Avenue
Swarthmore, PA 19081
Fax: (610) 328-8580
E-mail: jsawyer1@swarthmore.edu
Phone: (610) 328-8300

Swedish Institute
www.swedishinstitute.edu
226 West 26th Street, 5th Floor
New York, NY 10001-6700
Fax: (212) 924-7600
E-mail: admissions@swedishinstitute.edu
Phone: (212) 924-5900

Sweet Briar College
www.sbc.edu
Admissions
PO Box 1052
Sweet Briar, VA 24595-1502
Fax: (434) 381-6152
E-mail: admissions@sbc.edu
Phone: (434) 381-6142

Syracuse University
www.syr.edu
Office of Admissions
100 Crouse-Hinds Hall
900 South Crouse Avenue
Syracuse, NY 13244-2130
Fax: (315) 443-4226
E-mail: orange@syr.edu
Phone: (315) 443-3611

Tabor College
www.tabor.edu
Enrollment Management
400 South Jefferson
Hillsboro, KS 67063-1799
Fax: (620) 947-6276
E-mail: admissions@tabor.edu
Phone: (620) 947-3121 ext. 1721

Tacoma Community College
www.tacomacc.edu
International Student Office
6501 South 19th Street
Tacoma, WA 98466-9971
Fax: (253) 566-6027
E-mail: admit@tacomacc.edu
Phone: (253) 566-5166

Taft College
www.taftcollege.edu
Registrar, Director of Admissions
29 Emmons Park Drive
Taft, CA 93268
Fax: (661) 763-7758
E-mail: bmckee@taft.org
Phone: (661) 763-7843

Talladega College
www.talladega.edu
Admissions
627 West Battle Street
Talladega, AL 35160
Fax: (256) 362-0274
E-mail: mthornton@tallladega.edu
Phone: (256) 761-6219

Tallahassee Community College
www.tcc.fl.edu
International Student Services
444 Appleyard Drive
Tallahassee, FL 32304
Fax: (850) 201-8474
E-mail: jensenb@tcc.fl.edu
Phone: (850) 201-8235

Talmudical Institute of Upstate New York
www.tiuny.org
769 Park Avenue
Rochester, NY 14607
Fax: (585) 442-0417
Phone: (585) 473-2810

Talmudical Seminary Oholei Torah
667 Eastern Parkway
Brooklyn, NY 11213-3397
Phone: (718) 774-5215

Tarleton State University
www.tarleton.edu
International Academic Programs
Box T-0030
Stephenville, TX 76402
Fax: (254) 968-9618
E-mail: iap@tarleton.edu
Phone: (254) 968-9632

Tarrant County College
www.tccd.edu
International Admissions Services
1500 Houston Street
Fort Worth, TX 76102-6599
Fax: (817) 515-55021
E-mail: vikas.rajpurohit@tccd.edu
Phone: (817) 515-5232

Taylor Business Institute
www.tbiil.edu
318 West Adams Street, 5th Floor
Chicago, IL 60606
Phone: (312) 658-5100

Taylor University
www.taylor.edu
Admissions Office
236 West Reade Avenue
Upland, IN 46989-1001
Fax: (765) 998-4925
E-mail: drkamwesa@taylor.edu
Phone: (765) 998-5564

Technical Career Institutes
www.tcicollege.edu
Student Affairs
320 West 31st Street
New York, NY 10001
Fax: (212) 629-3937
E-mail: admissions@tcicollege.edu
Phone: (212) 594-4000 ext. 5216

Telshe Yeshiva-Chicago
3535 West Foster Avenue
Chicago, IL 60625
Fax: (773) 463-2894
Phone: (773) 463-7738

Temple Baptist College
www.templebaptist.edu
11965 Kenn Road
Cincinnati, OH 45240
E-mail: infotbc@templebaptist.edu
Phone: (513) 851-3800

Temple University
www.temple.edu
Office of Undergraduate Admissions
103 Conwell Hall
1801 North Broad Street
Philadelphia, PA 19122-6096
Fax: (215) 204-5694
E-mail: janusz.baran@temple.edu
Phone: (215) 204-7200

Tennessee State University
www.tnstate.edu
Foreign Student Adviser
3500 John A. Merritt Boulevard
Nashville, TN 37209-1561
Fax: (615) 963-5051
Phone: (615) 963-5639

Tennessee Technological University
www.tntech.edu
Office of Admissions
Box 5006
Cookeville, TN 38505-0001
Fax: (931) 372-6111
E-mail: cwilkerson@tntech.edu
Phone: (931) 372-3634

Tennessee Wesleyan College
www.twcnet.edu
Vice President of Enrollemnt Services
204 East College Street
P O Box 40
Athens, TN 37371-0040
Fax: (423) 744-9968
E-mail: sharrison@twcnet.edu
Phone: (423) 745-7504 ext. 5310

TESST College of Technology: Beltsville
www.tesst.com
4600 Powder Mill Road
Beltsville, MD 20705
E-mail: dedmonds@tesst.com
Phone: (301) 937-8448

Texas A&M International University
www.tamiu.edu
Admissions Office
5201 University Boulevard
Laredo, TX 78041-1900
Fax: (956) 326-2199
E-mail: adms@tamiu.edu
Phone: (956) 326-2200

Texas A&M University
www.tamu.edu
International Admissions
PO Box 30014
College Station, TX 77842-3014
Fax: (979) 458-1808
E-mail: admissions@tamu.edu
Phone: (979) 845-1079

Texas A&M University-Commerce
www.tamu-commerce.edu
International Student Services
Box 3011
Commerce, TX 75429-3011
Fax: (903) 468-6036
E-mail: John_Jones@tamu-commerce.edu
Phone: (903) 468-6034

Texas A&M University-Corpus Christi
www.tamucc.edu
Admissions
6300 Ocean Drive, Unit 5774
Corpus Christi, TX 78412-5774
Fax: (361) 825-5887
E-mail: karin.griffith@tamucc.edu
Phone: (361) 825-2624

Texas A&M University-Galveston
www.tamug.edu
Office of International Admissions
PO Box 1675
Galveston, TX 77553-1675
Fax: (979) 845-6979
E-mail: iss@iss.tamu.edu
Phone: (979) 845-1071

Texas A&M University-Kingsville
www.tamuk.edu
International Student Adviser
MSC 105
Kingsville, TX 78363-8201
Fax: (361) 593-3984
E-mail: diana.lozano@tamuk.edu
Phone: (361) 593-3317

Texas A&M University-Texarkana
www.tamut.edu
Student Services
7101 University Avenue
Box 5518
Texarkana, TX 75505-5518
Fax: (903) 223-3118
E-mail: carl.greig@tamut.edu
Phone: (903) 223-3062

Texas Christian University
www.tcu.edu
International Admissions
TCU Box 297013
Fort Worth, TX 76129
Fax: (817) 257-5256
E-mail: frogworld@tcu.edu
Phone: (817) 257-7871

Texas College
www.texascollege.edu
Admissions Office
2404 North Grand Avenue
PO Box 4500
Tyler, TX 75712-4500
Fax: (903) 593-8311
E-mail: jroberts@texascollege.edu
Phone: (903) 593-8311 ext. 2251

Texas County Technical Institute
www.texascountytech.edu
6915 South Highway 63
P.O. Box 314
Houston, MO 65483
Fax: (417) 967-4604
E-mail: info@texascountytech.edu
Phone: (417) 967-5466

Texas Lutheran University
www.tlu.edu
Enrollment Services
1000 West Court Street
Seguin, TX 78155-5999
Fax: (830) 372-8096
E-mail: mowen@tlu.edu
Phone: (830) 372-8057

Texas Southern University
www.tsu.edu
International Student Affairs
3100 Cleburne Street
Bell Building 225
Houston, TX 77004
Fax: (713) 313-1878
E-mail: luckettph@tsu.edu
Phone: (713) 313-7930

Texas State Technical College: Harlingen
www.harlingen.tstc.edu
Admissions and Records
1902 North Loop 499
Harlingen, TX 78550-3697
Fax: (956) 364-5117
E-mail: paula.arredondo@harlingen.tstc.edu
Phone: (956) 364-4322

Texas State Technical College: Marshall
www.marshall.tstc.edu
2650 East End Boulevard South
Marshall, TX 75672
Phone: (903) 935-1010

Texas State Technical College: Waco
www.waco.tstc.edu
Director of College Records
3801 Campus Drive
Waco, TX 76705
Fax: (254) 867-2250
E-mail: brenda.montemayor@tstc.edu
Phone: (254) 867-3061

Texas State Technical College: West Texas
www.westtexas.tstc.edu
Admissions and Records Office
300 Homer K Taylor Drive
Sweetwater, TX 79556
Fax: (325) 235-7443
E-mail: oretha.pack@sweetwater.tstc.edu
Phone: (325) 235-7377

Texas State University: San Marcos
www.txstate.edu
International Undergraduate Admissions
Center
429 North Guadalupe Street
San Marcos, TX 78666-5709
Fax: (512) 245-8044
E-mail: admissions@txstate.edu
Phone: (512) 245-2364

Texas Tech University
www.ttu.edu
Admissions
Box 45005
Lubbock, TX 79409-5005
Fax: (806) 742-0062
E-mail: admissions@ttu.edu
Phone: (806) 742-1480

**Texas Tech University Health Sciences
Center**
www.ttuhsc.edu
3601 Fourth Street
Lubbock, TX 79430
Phone: (806) 743-2300

Texas Wesleyan University
www.txwes.edu
International Programs Coordinator
1201 Wesleyan Street
Fort Worth, TX 76105-1536
Fax: (817) 531-4980
E-mail: nvallejo@txwes.edu
Phone: (817) 531-5868

Texas Woman's University
www.twu.edu
International Student Office
Box 425589
Denton, TX 76204-5589
Fax: (940) 898-3157
E-mail: intloffice@twu.edu
Phone: (940) 898-3338

Thiel College
www.thiel.edu
Director of Admissions
75 College Avenue
Greenville, PA 16125-2181
Fax: (724) 289-2013
E-mail: abecher@thiel.edu
Phone: (724) 589-2182

Thomas College
www.thomas.edu
Admissions
180 West River Road
Waterville, ME 04901
Fax: (207) 859-1114
E-mail: admiss@thomas.edu
Phone: (207) 859-1101

Thomas Edison State College
www.tesc.edu
Admissions
101 West State Street
Trenton, NJ 08608-1176
Fax: (609) 984-8447
E-mail: admissions@tesc.edu
Phone: (888) 442-8372

Thomas More College
www.thomasmore.edu
Admissions Office
333 Thomas More Parkway
Crestview Hills, KY 41017-3495
Fax: (859) 344-4444
E-mail: jodee.mcelfresh@thomasmore.edu
Phone: (859) 344-3332

Thomas More College of Liberal Arts
www.thomasmorecollege.edu
Admissions
Six Manchester Street
Merrimack, NH 03054-4818
Fax: (603) 880-9280
E-mail: admissions@thomasmorecollege.edu
Phone: (800) 880-8308

Thomas Nelson Community College
www.tncc.edu
Admissions and Records
PO Box 9407
Hampton, VA 23670
Fax: (757) 825-2763
E-mail: admissions@tncc.edu
Phone: (757) 825-2800

Thomas University
www.thomasu.edu
Executive Director of Enrollment Management
and Student Affairs
1501 Millpond Road
Thomasville, GA 31792-7499
Fax: (229) 227-6919
E-mail: mwest@thomasu.edu
Phone: (229) 226-1621 ext. 214

Three Rivers Community College
www.trcc.edu
Admissions
2080 Three Rivers Boulevard
Poplar Bluff, MO 63901-1308
Fax: (573) 840-9058
E-mail: mfields@trcc.edu
Phone: (573) 840-9675 ext. 675

Tidewater Community College
www.tcc.vccs.edu
International Student Services
7000 College Drive/Portsmouth Campus
Portsmouth, VA 23703
Fax: (757) 822-7544
E-mail: iss@tcc.edu
Phone: (757) 822-7342

Tiffin University
www.tiffin.edu
International Admissions
155 Miami Street
Tiffin, OH 44883
Fax: (419) 443-5006
E-mail: admissions@tiffin.edu
Phone: (800) 968-6446 ext. 3332

Toccoa Falls College
www.tfc.edu
Admissions
PO Box 800899
Toccoa Falls, GA 30598-0368
Fax: (706) 282-6012
E-mail: admissions@tfc.edu
Phone: (888) 785-5624

Tohono O'odham Community College
www.tocc.cc.az.us
PO Box 3129
Sells, AZ 85634-3129
Fax: (520) 383-0029
E-mail: lluna@tocc.cc.az.us
Phone: (520) 383-8401 ext. 35

Tompkins Cortland Community College
www.TC3.edu
Enrollment Services Center
170 North Street
Box 139
Dryden, NY 13053-0139
Fax: (607) 844-6541
E-mail: armstrc@tc3.edu
Phone: (607) 844-6580 ext. 4320

Torah Temimah Talmudical Seminary
555 Ocean Parkway
Brooklyn, NY 11218
Phone: (718) 853-8500

Tougaloo College
www.tougaloo.edu
Office of Admissions
500 West County Line Road
Tougaloo, MS 39174
Fax: (601) 977-4501
E-mail: jjacobs@tougaloo.edu
Phone: (601) 977-7768

Touro College
www.touro.edu
Registrar
1602 Avenue J
Brooklyn, NY 11230
Fax: (212) 627-9542
E-mail: eddies@touro.edu
Phone: (212) 463-0400 ext. 607

Touro College Los Angeles
www.touro.edu/losangeles
1317 North Crescent Heights Boulevard
West Hollywood, CA 90046
E-mail: tourolaadmissions@touro.edu
Phone: (323) 822-9700 ext. 85155

Towson University
www.towson.edu
International Admissions
8000 York Road
Towson, MD 21252-0001
Fax: (410) 704-6070
E-mail: intladm@towson.edu
Phone: (410) 704-6069

Transylvania University
www.transy.edu
Admissions Counselor
300 North Broadway
Lexington, KY 40508-1797
Fax: (859) 233-8797
E-mail: kkolb@transy.edu
Phone: (859) 233-8242

Treasure Valley Community College
www.tvcc.cc
Admissions
650 College Boulevard
Ontario, OR 97914
Fax: (541) 881-2721
E-mail: sromans@tvcc.cc
Phone: (541) 881-5757

Trevecca Nazarene University
www.trevecca.edu
Office of Admissions
333 Murfreesboro Road
Nashville, TN 37210
Fax: (615) 248-7406
E-mail: admissions_und@trevecca.edu
Phone: (615) 248-1320

Tri-County Community College
www.tricountycc.edu
21 Campus Circle
Murphy, NC 28906
Fax: (828) 837-3266
E-mail: jchambers@tricountycc.edu
Phone: (828) 837-6810

Tri-County Technical College
www.tctc.edu
Admissions
Box 587
Pendleton, SC 29670
Fax: (864) 646-1890
E-mail: info@tctc.edu
Phone: (864) 646-1550

Tri-State Bible College
www.tsbc.edu
506 Margaret Street
PO Box 445
South Point, OH 45680-0445
Fax: (740) 377-0001
E-mail: cmark@zoominternet.net
Phone: (740) 377-2520

Triangle Tech: Bethlehem
www.triangle-tech.edu
31 South Commerce Way, Lehigh Valley
Industrial Park IV
Bethlehem, PA 18017
Fax: (610) 691-7525
Phone: (610) 691-1300

Triangle Tech: Greensburg
www.triangle-tech.edu
222 East Pittsburgh Street, Suite A
Greensburg, PA 15601-3304
Fax: (724) 834-0325
Phone: (724) 832-1050

Trident Technical College
www.tridenttech.edu
International Admissions Coordinator
Box 118067, AM-M
Charleston, SC 29423-8067
Fax: (843) 574-6483
E-mail: ben.mwaura@tridenttech.edu
Phone: (843) 574-6325

Trident University International
www.tuiu.edu
Attn: Office of the Registrar
5665 Plaza Drive, 3rd Floor
Cypress, CA 90630
Fax: (714) 827-7407
E-mail: registration@tuiu.edu
Phone: (800) 375-9878

Trine University
www.trine.edu
Admissions
One University Avenue
Angola, IN 46703
Fax: (260) 665-4578
E-mail: admit@trine.edu
Phone: (260) 665-4100

Trinidad State Junior College
www.trinidadstate.edu
Admissions
600 Prospect Street
Trinidad, CO 81082
Fax: (719) 846-5620
E-mail: bernadine.degarbo@trinidadstate.edu
Phone: (719) 846-5621

Trinity Baptist College
www.tbc.edu
800 Hammond Boulevard
Jacksonville, FL 32221
E-mail: admissions@tbc.edu
Phone: (800) 786-2206

Trinity Christian College
www.trnty.edu
Admissions Counselor
6601 West College Drive
Palos Heights, IL 60463
Fax: (708) 239-3980
E-mail: kellyjo.beezhold@trnty.edu
Phone: (708) 239-4592

Trinity College
www.trincoll.edu
Admissions
300 Summit Street
Hartford, CT 06106
Fax: (860) 297-2287
E-mail: mandi.haines@trincoll.edu
Phone: (860) 297-2551

Trinity College of Florida
www.trinitycollege.edu
Office of Admissions
2430 Welbilt Boulevard
Trinity, FL 34655-4401
Fax: (727) 569-1410
E-mail: msawyer@trinitycollege.edu
Phone: (727) 569-1412

Trinity College of Nursing and Health Sciences
www.trinitycollegeqc.edu
2122 25th Avenue
Rock Island, IL 61201
Fax: (309) 779-7748
E-mail: perezlj@ihs.org
Phone: (309) 779-7814

Trinity International University
www.tiu.edu
Undergraduate Admissions
2065 Half Day Road
Deerfield, IL 60015
Fax: (847) 317-8097
E-mail: tcadmissions@tiu.edu
Phone: (847) 317-7000

Trinity Lutheran College
www.tlc.edu
Registrar's Office
2802 Wetmore Avenue
Everett, WA 98201
Fax: (425) 392-0404
E-mail: registrar@tlc.edu
Phone: (425) 961-5513

Trinity University
www.trinity.edu
Admissions
One Trinity Place
San Antonio, TX 78212-7200
Fax: (210) 999-8164
E-mail: eric.maloof@trinity.edu
Phone: (210) 999-7207

Trinity Valley Community College
www.tvcc.edu
Student Affairs
100 Cardinal Drive
Athens, TX 75751
Fax: (903) 675-6316
Phone: (903) 675-6220

Trinity Washington University
www.trinitydc.edu
125 Michigan Avenue, NE
Washington, DC 20017
Fax: (202) 884-9403
E-mail: peppind@trinitydc.edu
Phone: (202) 884-9019

Triton College
www.triton.edu
Record Evaluator
2000 North Fifth Avenue
River Grove, IL 60171
Fax: (708) 583-3147
E-mail: vhoward@triton.edu
Phone: (708) 456-0300 ext. 3444

Trocaire College
www.trocaire.edu
Admissions
360 Choate Avenue
Buffalo, NY 14220
Fax: (716) 828-6107
E-mail: lesinskic@trocaire.edu
Phone: (716) 826-1200 ext. 1218

Troy University
www.troy.edu
Dean of International Students
University Avenue, Adams Administration 111
Troy, AL 36082
Fax: (334) 670-3735
E-mail: dstewart@troy.edu
Phone: (334) 670-3335

Truckee Meadows Community College
www.tmcc.edu
Admissions and Records
7000 Dandini Boulevard
MS RDMT 319
Reno, NV 89512
Fax: (775) 673-7028
E-mail: csteppat@tmcc.edu
Phone: (775) 674-7042

Truett-McConnell College
www.truett.edu
Admissions
100 Alumni Drive
Cleveland, GA 30528
Fax: (706) 865-3110
E-mail: csienkiewicz@truett.edu
Phone: (706) 865-2134 ext. 110

Truman State University
www.truman.edu
International Student Affairs Office
100 East Normal Avenue
Kirksville, MO 63501
Fax: (660) 785-5395
E-mail: intladmit@truman.edu
Phone: (660) 785-4215

Tufts University
www.tufts.edu
Undergraduate Admissions
Bendetson Hall
Medford, MA 02155
Fax: (617) 627-3860
E-mail: admissions.inquiry@ase.tufts.edu
Phone: (617) 627-3170

Tulane University
www.tulane.edu
Undergraduate Admissions
6823 St. Charles Avenue
New Orleans, LA 70118-5680
Fax: (504) 862-8715
E-mail: undergrad.admission@tulane.edu
Phone: (504) 865-5731

Tulsa Community College
www.tulsacc.edu
Northeast Campus Counseling and Testing
Center
6111 East Skelly Drive
Tulsa, OK 74135
Fax: (918) 595-7598
E-mail: dklingha@tulsa.cc.ok.us
Phone: (918) 595-7533

Tulsa Welding School
www.weldingschool.com
2545 East 11th Street
Tulsa, OK 74104-3909
Fax: (918) 587-8170
E-mail: tws@ionet.net
Phone: (918) 587-6789 ext. 240

Tunxis Community College
www.tunxis.commnet.edu
Admissions
271 Scott Swamp Road
Farmington, CT 06032-3187
Fax: (860) 255-3559
E-mail: pmccluskey@txcc.commnet.edu
Phone: (860) 255-3555

Turabo University
www.suagm.edu/ut
Admissions and Marketing
PO Box 3030
Gurabo, PR 00778
Fax: (787) 743-7940
E-mail: ut_vgonzalez@suagm.edu
Phone: (787) 743-7979 ext. 4453

Tusculum College
www.tusculum.edu
International Student Admissions Counselor
60 Shiloh Road
Box 5097
Greeneville, TN 37743
Fax: (423) 798-1622
E-mail: mripley@tusculum.edu
Phone: (423) 636-7300 ext. 5374

Tuskegee University
www.tuskegee.edu
102 Old Administration Building
Tuskegee, AL 36088
Fax: (334) 724-4402
E-mail: adm@tuskegee.edu
Phone: (334) 727-8953

U.T.A. Mesivta-Kiryas Jocl
9 Nickelsburg Road, #312
Monroe, NY 10950-2169
Phone: (845) 783-9901

Ulster County Community College
www.sunyulster.edu
Admissions
Cottekill Road
Stone Ridge, NY 12484
Fax: (845) 687-5090
E-mail: admissions@sunyulster.edu
Phone: (845) 687-5022

Umpqua Community College
www.umpqua.edu
Student Services
1140 College Road
PO Box 967
Roseburg, OR 97470-0226
Fax: (541) 440-7713
E-mail: LaVera.Noland@umpqua.edu
Phone: (541) 440-7743

Union College
www.unionky.edu
Admission
310 College Street, Box 005
Barbourville, KY 40906
Fax: (606) 546-1667
E-mail: jgjackson@unionky.edu
Phone: (606) 546-1221

Union College
www.ucollege.edu
Enrollment Services
3800 South 48th Street
Lincoln, NE 68506-4300
Fax: (402) 486-2895
E-mail: ucenroll@ucollege.edu
Phone: (800) 228-4600

Union College
www.union.edu
Office of Admissions
Grant Hall
Schenectady, NY 12308-3107
Fax: (518) 388-6986
E-mail: admissions@union.edu
Phone: (518) 388-6112

Union County College
www.ucc.edu
Registrar
1033 Springfield Avenue
Cranford, NJ 07016-1599
Fax: (908) 709-7125
E-mail: davis@ucc.edu
Phone: (908) 709-7127

Union Institute & University
www.myunion.edu
Enrollment Management
440 East McMillan Street
Cincinnati, OH 45206
Fax: (802) 828-8855
E-mail: jon.mays@myunion.edu
Phone: (800) 486-3116

Union University
www.uu.edu
Enrollment Counselor
1050 Union University Drive
Jackson, TN 38305-3697
Fax: (731) 661-5017
E-mail: cbrunson@uu.edu
Phone: (731) 661-5006

United States Merchant Marine Academy
www.usmma.edu
Admissions
300 Steamboat Road, Admissions Center
Kings Point, NY 11024-1699
Fax: (516) 773-5390
E-mail: derosam@usmma.edu
Phone: (516) 773-5391

United States Naval Academy
www.usna.edu
Naval Attache in the United States Embassy
of home country
117 Decatur Road
United States Naval Academy
Annapolis, MD 21402-5018
Fax: (410) 293-1815
E-mail: webmail@usna.edu
Phone: (410) 293-4361

United States Sports Academy
www.ussa.edu
One Academy Drive
Daphne, AL 36526
Fax: (251) 625-1035
E-mail: admissions@ussa.edu
Phone: (251) 626-3303

United Talmudical Seminary
82 Lee Avenue
Brooklyn, NY 11211
Phone: (718) 963-9260

United Tribes Technical College
www.uttc.edu
Admission Department
3315 University Drive
Bismarck, ND 58504
Fax: (701) 530-0640
E-mail: vgillette@uttc.edu
Phone: (701) 255-3285 ext. 1334

Unity College in Maine
www.unity.edu
Dean of Enrollment Management
P.O. 532
Unity, ME 04988-0532
Fax: (207) 948-2928
E-mail: ajohnson@unity.edu
Phone: (207) 948-3131 ext. 203

Universal Technical Institute
www.uti.edu
Campus Admissions
10695 West Pierce Street
Avondale, AZ 85323
Fax: (623) 245-4605
E-mail: info@uticorp.com
Phone: (623) 245-4600

Universidad Adventista de las Antillas
www.uaa.edu
PO Box 118
Mayaguez, PR 00681-0118
Fax: (787) 834-9597
E-mail: rdelvalle@uaa.edu
Phone: (787) 834-9595 ext. 2213

Universidad del Este
www.suagm.edu/une
PO Box 2010
Carolina, PR 00984-2010
Fax: (787) 257-8601
E-mail: ue_rfuentes@suagm.edu
Phone: (787) 257-7373 ext. 3330

Universidad FLET
www.flet.edu
13024 SW 120th Street
Miami, FL 33186
Fax: (305) 232-5832
E-mail: admisiones@flet.edu
Phone: (305) 378-8700

Universidad Metropolitana
www.suagm.edu/umet
Director of Admissions
Apartado 21150
San Juan, PR 00928
Fax: (787) 751-0992
E-mail: yrivera@suagm.edu
Phone: (787) 766-1717 ext. 6657

Universidad Pentecostal Mizpa
www.colmizpa.edu
Dean of Students
PO Box 20966
San Juan, PR 00928-0966
Fax: (787) 720-2012
E-mail: decanatoestudiantes@colmizpa.edu
Phone: (787) 720-4476 ext. 228

Universidad Politecnica de Puerto Rico
www.pupr.edu
Admissions Office
PO Box 192017
San Juan, PR 00919-2017
Fax: (787) 764-8712
E-mail: tcardona@pupr.edu
Phone: (787) 622-8000 ext. 309

University College of San Juan
www.cunisanjuan.edu
Admissions Office
180 Jose R. Oliver Avenue
San Juan, PR 00918
Fax: (787) 274-1388
E-mail: sanrivera@sanjuancapital.com
Phone: (787) 480-2424 ext. 2399

University of Advancing Technology
www.uat.edu
Manager of Marketing
2625 West Baseline Road
Tempe, AZ 85283-1056
Fax: (602) 383-8228
E-mail: ahromas@uat.edu
Phone: (800) 658-5744

University of Akron
www.uakron.edu
International Programs
Simmons Hall
302 Buchtel Common
Akron, OH 44325-2001
Fax: (330) 972-8604
E-mail: international@uakron.edu
Phone: (330) 972-6349

University of Akron: Wayne College
www.wayne.uakron.edu
1901 Smucker Road
Orrville, OH 44667-9758
Fax: (330) 684-8989
E-mail: wayneadmissions@uakron.edu
Phone: (330) 683-2010

University of Alabama
www.ua.edu
Undergraduate Admissions
Box 870132
Tuscaloosa, AL 35487-0132
Fax: (205) 348-9046
E-mail: international.admissions@ua.edu
Phone: (205) 348-5666

University of Alabama at Birmingham
www.uab.edu
Undergraduate Admissions
HUC 260, 1530 Third Avenue South
Birmingham, AL 35294-1150
Fax: (205) 934-8664
E-mail: carola@uab.edu
Phone: (205) 934-3328

University of Alabama in Huntsville
www.uah.edu
Office of Undergraduate Admissions
UAH Office of Undergraduate Admissions
301 Sparkman Drive
Huntsville, AL 35899
Fax: (256) 824-6073
E-mail: willias@uah.edu
Phone: (256) 824-2744

University of Alaska Anchorage
www.uaa.alaska.edu
Enrollment Management, Division of
International and Study Abroad
PO Box 141629
3915 Old Seward Highway
Anchorage, AK 99514-1629
Fax: (907) 786-4888
E-mail: doni@uaa.alaska.edu
Phone: (907) 786-1573

University of Alaska Fairbanks
www.uaf.edu
Office of International Programs
PO Box 757480
Fairbanks, AK 99775-7480
Fax: (907) 474-5979
E-mail: fyoip@uaf.edu
Phone: (907) 474-5327

University of Alaska Southeast
www.uas.alaska.edu
Admissions
11120 Glacier Highway
Juneau, AK 99801-8681
Fax: (907) 796-6365
E-mail: joe.nelson@uas.alaska.edu
Phone: (907) 796-6100

University of Arizona
www.arizona.edu
Dean of Admissions
Robert L. Nugent Building
Box 210073
Tucson, AZ 85721-0073
Fax: (520) 621-9799
E-mail: kohn@email.arizona.edu
Phone: (520) 621-3705

University of Arkansas
www.uark.edu
International Admissions
232 Silas Hunt Hall
Fayetteville, AR 72701
Fax: (479) 575-5055
E-mail: mosesso@uark.edu
Phone: (479) 575-5346

University of Arkansas at Fort Smith
www.uafortsmith.edu
Admissions
PO Box 3649
Smith-Pendergraft Campus Center 219
Fort Smith, AR 72913-3649
Fax: (479) 788-7402
E-mail: mlloyd@uafortsmith.edu
Phone: (479) 788-7635

University of Arkansas at Little Rock
www.ualr.edu
Office of International Services
2801 South University Avenue
Administration South, Room 208
Little Rock, AR 72204
Fax: (501) 683-7567
E-mail: admissions@ualr.edu
Phone: (501) 683-7566

University of Arkansas at Monticello
www.uamont.edu
Admissions
Box 3600
Monticello, AR 71656
Fax: (870) 460-1926
E-mail: whitingm@uamont.edu
Phone: (870) 460-1026

University of Arkansas at Pine Bluff
www.uapb.edu
International Program Adviser/Admissions
Officer
1200 North University Drive, Mail Slot 4981
Pine Bluff, AR 71601-2799
Fax: (870) 575-4607
E-mail: owasoyop@uapb.edu
Phone: (870) 575-8732

University of the Arts
www.uarts.edu
Office of Admissions
320 South Broad Street
Philadelphia, PA 19102
Fax: (215) 717-6045
E-mail: admissions@uarts.edu
Phone: (215) 717-6039

University of Baltimore
www.ubalt.edu
International Service's Office
1420 North Charles Street
Baltimore, MD 21201-5779
Fax: (410) 837-4793
E-mail: admissions@ubalt.edu
Phone: (410) 837-4756

University of Bridgeport
www.bridgeport.edu
International Admissions
126 Park Avenue
Bridgeport, CT 06604
Fax: (203) 576-4941
E-mail: admit@bridgeport.edu
Phone: (203) 576-4552

University of California: Berkeley
www.berkeley.edu
110 Sproul Hall, #5800
Berkeley, CA 94720-5800
Phone: (510) 642-6000

University of California: Davis
www.ucdavis.edu
Associate Vice Chancellor, Student Affairs
One Shields Ave
178 Mrak Hall
Davis, CA 95616
Fax: (530) 752-2565
E-mail: ljbossio@ucdavis.edu
Phone: (530) 752-6449

University of California: Irvine
www.uci.edu
International Specialist
204 Aldrich Hall
Irvine, CA 92697-1075
Fax: (949) 824-2711
E-mail: kerry.lekutai@uci.edu
Phone: (949) 824-9344

University of California: Los Angeles
www.ucla.edu
UCLA Undergraduate Admissions
1147 Murphy Hall
Box 951436
Los Angeles, CA 90095-1436
Fax: (310) 206-1206
E-mail: ugadm@saonet.ucla.edu
Phone: (310) 825-3101

University of California: Merced
www.ucmerced.edu
International Programs
5200 North Lake Road
Merced, CA 95343-5603
Fax: (209) 228-4244
E-mail: admissions@ucmerced.edu
Phone: (209) 228-4667

University of California: Riverside
www.ucr.edu/
Office of Undergraduate Admissions
Admissions Office
3106 Student Services Building
Riverside, CA 92521
Fax: (951) 827-6344
E-mail: admin@ucr.edu
Phone: (951) 827-3411

University of California: San Diego
www.ucsd.edu
International Admissions, 0021
9500 Gilman Drive, 0021
La Jolla, CA 92093-0021
Fax: (858) 534-5629
E-mail: admissionsreply@ucsd.edu
Phone: (858) 534-4831

University of California: Santa Barbara
www.ucsb.edu
Associate Director of Admissions
1210 Cheadle Hall
Santa Barbara, CA 93106-2014
Fax: (805) 893-7132
E-mail: donna.coyne@sa.ucsb.edu
Phone: (805) 893-8551

University of California: Santa Cruz
www.ucsc.edu
Admissions
Cook House, 1156 High Street
Santa Cruz, CA 95064
Fax: (831) 459-4163
E-mail: myapplication@ucsc.edu
Phone: (831) 459-2131

University of Central Arkansas
www.uca.edu
Office of International Programs
201 Donaghey Avenue
Bernard 101
Conway, AR 72035
Fax: (501) 450-5095
E-mail: afaulkner@uca.edu
Phone: (501) 450-3442

University of Central Florida
www.ucf.edu
International Student Services
Box 160111
Orlando, FL 32816-0111
Fax: (407) 823-2526
E-mail: admission@mail.ucf.edu
Phone: (407) 823-2337

University of Central Missouri
www.ucmo.edu
Office of International Programs
WDE 1400
Warrensburg, MO 64093
Fax: (660) 543-4201
E-mail: intladmit@ucmo.edu
Phone: (660) 543-8502

University of Central Oklahoma
www.uco.edu
International Office
100 North University Drive
Edmond, OK 73034-0151
Fax: (405) 974-3842
E-mail: ddunham1@uco.edu
Phone: (405) 974-2390

University of Charleston
www.ucwv.edu
Admissions
2300 MacCorkle Avenue, SE
Charleston, WV 25304
Fax: (304) 357-4781
E-mail: amandapritt@ucwv.edu
Phone: (304) 357-4750

University of Chicago
www.uchicago.edu
1101 East 58th Street
Rosenwald Hall, Suite 105
Chicago, IL 60637
Fax: (773) 702-4199
E-mail: mhetlage@uchicago.edu
Phone: (773) 702-8658

University of Cincinnati
www.uc.edu
Admissions Office
PO Box 210091
Cincinnati, OH 45221-0091
Fax: (513) 556-1105
E-mail: international.admissions@uc.edu
Phone: (513) 556-1100

University of Cincinnati: Clermont College
www.ucclermont.edu
Senior Enrollment Adviser
4200 Clermont College Drive
Batavia, OH 45103
Fax: (513) 732-5303
E-mail: blaine.kelley@uc.edu
Phone: (513) 732-5301

University of Cincinnati: Raymond Walters College
www.rwc.uc.edu
Enrollment Services
9555 Plainfield Road
Cincinnati, OH 45236-1096
Fax: (513) 745-5768
E-mail: jenny.young@uc.edu
Phone: (513) 745-5700

University of Colorado at Boulder
www.colorado.edu
Office of Admissions
552 UCB
Boulder, CO 80309-0552
Fax: (303) 735-2501
E-mail: intladm@colorado.edu
Phone: (303) 492-6301

University of Colorado at Colorado Springs
www.uccs.edu
Admissions and Records
1420 Austin Bluffs Parkway
Colorado Springs, CO 80918
Fax: (719) 255-3116
E-mail: smorehea@uccs.edu
Phone: (719) 255-4316

University of Colorado at Denver
www.ucdenver.edu
Admissions and Records
Box 173364, Campus Box 167
Denver, CO 80217-3364
Fax: (303) 556-4838
E-mail: constance.costa@ucdenver.edu
Phone: (303) 556-2704

University of Connecticut
www.uconn.edu
Office of Undergraduate Admissions
2131 Hillside Road, Unit 3088
Storrs, CT 06269-3088
Fax: (860) 486-1476
E-mail: beahusky@uconn.edu
Phone: (860) 486-3137

University of the Cumberlands
www.ucumberlands.edu
Office of International Relations
6178 College Station Drive
Williamsburg, KY 40769
Fax: (606) 549-4238
E-mail: rick.fleenor@ucumberlands.edu
Phone: (606) 539-4154

University of Dallas
www.udallas.edu
Admissions
1845 East Northgate Drive
Irving, TX 75062-4736
Fax: (972) 721-5017
E-mail: ugadmis@udallas.edu
Phone: (972) 721-5266

University of Dayton
www.udayton.edu
International Admission
300 College Park
Dayton, OH 45469-1300
Fax: (937) 229-4729
E-mail: goglobal@notes.udayton.edu
Phone: (937) 229-4351

University of Delaware
www.udel.edu
Admissions Officer
210 South College Avenue
Newark, DE 19716
Fax: (302) 831-6905
E-mail: ehinson@udel.edu
Phone: (302) 831-8123

University of Denver
www.du.edu
Office of International Admission
2197 South University Boulevard
Denver, CO 80208
Fax: (303) 871-3522
E-mail: intladm@du.edu
Phone: (303) 871-2790

University of Detroit Mercy
www.udmercy.edu
International Services Office
4001 West McNichols Road
Detroit, MI 48221-3038
Fax: (313) 993-1192
E-mail: isoffice@udmercy.edu
Phone: (313) 993-1205

University of the District of Columbia
www.udc.edu
Office of Institutional Research
4200 Connecticut Avenue NW
Washington, DC 20008
Fax: (202) 274-6180
E-mail: dhayes@udc.edu
Phone: (202) 274-6088

University of Dubuque
www.dbq.edu
Admissions
2000 University Avenue
Dubuque, IA 52001-5099
Fax: (563) 589-3690
E-mail: jjames@dbq.edu
Phone: (800) 722-5583

University of Evansville
www.evansville.edu
Office of International Admission
1800 Lincoln Avenue
Evansville, IN 47722
Fax: (812) 488-6389
E-mail: bf28@evansville.edu
Phone: (812) 488-2146

University of Findlay
www.findlay.edu
Office of International Admissions and
Services
1000 North Main Street
Findlay, OH 45840-3653
Fax: (419) 434-5507
E-mail: gerdeman@findlay.edu
Phone: (419) 434-4558

University of Florida
www.ufl.edu
Office of Admissions
201 Criser Hall-PO Box 114000
Gainesville, FL 32611-4000
Fax: (352) 392-2115
E-mail: cmitche@ufl.edu
Phone: (352) 392-1365

University of Georgia
www.uga.edu
Office of Undergraduate Admission
Office of Undergraduate Admissions
Terrell Hall
Athens, GA 30602-1633
Fax: (706) 542-1466
E-mail: undergrad@admissions.uga.edu
Phone: (706) 542-8776

University of Great Falls
www.ugf.edu
Assistant Director of Admissions
1301 20th Street South
Great Falls, MT 59405
Fax: (406) 791-5209
E-mail: aclutter01@ugf.edu
Phone: (406) 791-5200

University of Hawaii at Hilo
www.uhh.hawaii.edu
Admissions
200 West Kawili Street
Hilo, HI 96720-4091
Fax: (808) 974-7691
E-mail: pgrossma@hawaii.edu
Phone: (808) 974-7414

University of Hawaii at Manoa
www.manoa.hawaii.edu
Admissions and Records
2600 Campus Road, QLC Rm 001
Honolulu, HI 96822
Fax: (808) 956-4148
E-mail: ar-info@hawaii.edu
Phone: (808) 956-8975

**University of Hawaii: Hawaii Community
College**
www.hawcc.hawaii.edu
200 West Kawili Street
Hilo, HI 96720-4091
Fax: (808) 974-7692
E-mail: loeding@hawaii.edu
Phone: (808) 974-7662

**University of Hawaii: Honolulu Community
College**
www2.honolulu.hawaii.edu
Admissions
874 Dillingham Boulevard
Honolulu, HI 96817
Fax: (808) 847-9872
E-mail: admissions@hcc.hawaii.edu
Phone: (808) 845-9129

**University of Hawaii: Kapiolani
Community College**
www.kcc.hawaii.edu
4303 Diamond Head Road
Honolulu, HI 96816-4421
Fax: (808) 734-9896
E-mail: liantmei@hawaii.edu
Phone: (808) 734-9312

**University of Hawaii: Kauai Community
College**
http://kauai.hawaii.edu
Admissions and Records Office
3-1901 Kaumualii Highway
Lihue, HI 96766-9500
Fax: (808) 245-8297
E-mail: loride@hawaii.edu
Phone: (808) 245-8225

**University of Hawaii: Leeward Community
College**
www.lcc.hawaii.edu
96-045 Ala Ike
Pearl City, HI 96782
Fax: (808) 454-8804
E-mail: lccar@hawaii.edu
Phone: (808) 455-0217

University of Hawaii: Maui College
www.maui.hawaii.edu
Student Services
310 West Kaahumanu Avenue
Kahului, HI 96732-1617
Fax: (808) 242-9618
Phone: (808) 984-3517

University of Hawaii: West Oahu
www.uhwo.hawaii.edu
Admissions Specialist
96-129 Ala Ike
Pearl City, HI 96782
Fax: (808) 453-6075
E-mail: ralynnn@hawaii.edu
Phone: (808) 454-4700

**University of Hawaii: Windward
Community College**
www.wcc.hawaii.edu
Admissions and Records
45-720 Kea'ahala Road
Kaneohe, HI 96744
Fax: (808) 235-9148
E-mail: wccinfo@hawaii.edu
Phone: (808) 235-7432

University of Houston
www.uh.edu
International Admissions
Welcome Center
4400 University Drive
Houston, TX 77204-2023
Fax: (713) 743-7542
E-mail: mtthomas@central.uh.edu
Phone: (713) 743-1010

University of Houston-Clear Lake
www.uhcl.edu
Associate Director, Admissions - International
2700 Bay Area Boulevard
Houston, TX 77058-1098
Fax: (281) 283-2522
E-mail: kabasele@uhcl.edu
Phone: (281) 283-2500

University of Houston-Downtown
www.uhd.edu
International Admissions
One Main Street, Suite 350-S
Houston, TX 77002
Fax: (713) 221-2718
E-mail: internationaladmissions@uhd.edu
Phone: (713) 221-8048

University of Houston-Victoria
www.uhv.edu
Admissions/Enrollment Services
3007 North Ben Wilson
Victoria, TX 77901-4450
Fax: (361) 580-5500
E-mail: kraatze@uhv.edu
Phone: (361) 570-4112

University of Idaho
www.uidaho.edu
Admissions - Undergraduate
PO Box 444264
Moscow, ID 83844-4264
Fax: (208) 885-9119
E-mail: admappl@idaho.edu
Phone: (208) 885-9422

University of Illinois at Chicago
www.uic.edu
Admissions and Records
PO Box 5220
Chicago, IL 60680-5220
Fax: (312) 413-7628
E-mail: uicadmit@uic.edu
Phone: (312) 996-4350

University of Illinois at Urbana-Champaign
www.illinois.edu
International Admissions
901 West Illinois
Urbana, IL 61801-3028
Fax: (217) 244-4614
E-mail: gperry@uiuc.edu
Phone: (217) 333-0302

University of Illinois: Springfield
www.uis.edu
Admissions
One University Plaza, MS UHB 1080
Springfield, IL 62703
Fax: (217) 206-6620
E-mail: admissions@uis.edu
Phone: (217) 206-4847

University of the Incarnate Word
www.uiw.edu
International Admissions
4301 Broadway
CPO #285
San Antonio, TX 78209-6397
Fax: (210) 805-5701
E-mail: adestefa@uiwtx.edu
Phone: (210) 805-5707

University of Indianapolis
www.uindy.edu
International Student Admissions
1400 East Hanna Avenue
Indianapolis, IN 46227-3697
Fax: (317) 788-3300
E-mail: kgunyon@uindy.edu
Phone: (317) 788-3600

University of Iowa
www.uiowa.edu
Admissions
107 Calvin Hall
Iowa City, IA 52242-1396
Fax: (319) 335-1535
E-mail: rebecca-hanson@uiowa.edu
Phone: (319) 335-3847

University of Kansas
www.ku.edu
International Student and Scholar Services
1502 Iowa Street
Lawrence, KS 66045-7576
Fax: (785) 864-3404
E-mail: issapps@ku.edu
Phone: (785) 864-2616

University of Kansas Medical Center
www.kumc.edu
Varies by academic school
3901 Rainbow Boulevard
Kansas City, KS 66160-7116
Fax: (913) 588-4697
E-mail: kumcregistrar@kumc.edu
Phone: (913) 588-7055

University of Kentucky
www.uky.edu
100 W.D. Funkhouser Building
Lexington, KY 40506-0054
Fax: (859) 257-3823
E-mail: mlkrin0@uky.edu
Phone: (859) 257-4708

University of La Verne
www.laverne.edu
Undergraduate Admissions
1950 Third Street
La Verne, CA 91750
Fax: (909) 392-2714
E-mail: mckinney@laverne.edu
Phone: (909) 392-2800

University of Louisiana at Lafayette
www.louisiana.edu
Box 41210
Lafayette, LA 70504-1210
Fax: (337) 482-6195
E-mail: admissions@louisiana.edu
Phone: (337) 482-6467

University of Louisiana at Monroe
www.ulm.edu
Associate Director of Admissions
700 University Avenue
Monroe, LA 71209-1160
Fax: (318) 342-6764
E-mail: schmeer@ulm.edu
Phone: (318) 342-5259

University of Louisville
www.louisville.edu
Admissions
2211 South Brook Street
Louisville, KY 40292
Fax: (502) 852-6526
E-mail: admitme@louisville.edu
Phone: (502) 852-4953

University of Maine
www.umaine.edu
Office of International Programs
5713 Chadbourne Hall
Orono, ME 04469-5713
Fax: (207) 581-2920
E-mail: umintprg@maine.edu
Phone: (207) 581-2905

University of Maine at Augusta
www.uma.edu
Admissions
46 University Drive
Augusta, ME 04330
Fax: (207) 621-3333
E-mail: trask@maine.edu
Phone: (207) 621-3140

University of Maine at Farmington
www.farmington.edu
Associate Director Admissions
246 Main Street
Farmington, ME 04938
Fax: (207) 778-8182
E-mail: ellrich@maine.edu
Phone: (207) 778-7050 ext. 7054

University of Maine at Fort Kent
www.umfk.maine.edu
Admissions
23 University Drive
Fort Kent, ME 04743
Fax: (207) 834-7609
E-mail: jillb@maine.edu
Phone: (207) 834-7602

University of Maine at Machias
www.umm.maine.edu
Admissions Office
116 O'Brien Avenue
Machias, ME 04654-1397
Fax: (207) 255-1363
E-mail: mahmoud.sowe@maine.edu
Phone: (207) 255-1332

University of Maine at Presque Isle
www.umpi.edu
Admissions
181 Main Street
Presque Isle, ME 04769
Fax: (207) 768-9450
E-mail: bonnie.devaney@umpi.edu
Phone: (207) 768-9750

University of Management and Technology
www.umtweb.edu
1901 N Fort Myer Drive/Suite 700
Arlington, VA 22209
Fax: (703) 516-0985
E-mail: info@umtweb.edu
Phone: (703) 516-0035

University of Mary
www.umary.edu
Enrollment Services
7500 University Drive
Bismarck, ND 58504-9652
Fax: (701) 255-7687
E-mail: mcheitkamp@umary.edu
Phone: (701) 355-8190

University of Mary Hardin-Baylor
www.umhb.edu
Office of International Student Services
900 College Street
UMHB Box 8004
Belton, TX 76513
Fax: (254) 295-4535
E-mail: etanaka@umhb.edu
Phone: (254) 295-4949

University of Mary Washington
www.umw.edu
Admissions
1301 College Avenue
Fredericksburg, VA 22401-5300
Fax: (540) 654-1857
E-mail: admit@umw.edu
Phone: (540) 654-2000

University of Maryland: Baltimore
www.umaryland.edu
Office of Records and Registration
620 West Lexington Street
Baltimore, MD 21201
Fax: (410) 706-4053
E-mail: tday@umaryland.edu
Phone: (410) 706-7480

University of Maryland: Baltimore County
www.umbc.edu
Office of Undergraduate Admissions
1000 Hilltop Circle
Baltimore, MD 21250
Fax: (410) 455-1094
E-mail: massey@umbc.edu
Phone: (410) 455-6705

University of Maryland: College Park
www.maryland.edu
Office of International Services
Mitchell Building
College Park, MD 20742-5235
Fax: (301) 314-3280
E-mail: internationalservices@umd.edu
Phone: (301) 314-7740

University of Maryland: Eastern Shore
www.umes.edu
Student Development Center, Suite 1140
Princess Anne, MD 21853
Fax: (410) 651-8386
E-mail: snacquah@mail.umes.edu
Phone: (410) 651-6079

University of Maryland: University College
www.umuc.edu
Admission Office
1616 McCormick Drive
Largo, MD 20774
Fax: (240) 684-2151
E-mail: enroll@umuc.edu
Phone: (800) 888-8682

University of Massachusetts Amherst
www.umass.edu
Undergraduate Admissions Office
University Admissions Center
37 Mather Drive
Amherst, MA 01003-9291
Fax: (413) 545-4312
E-mail: mail@admissions.umass.edu
Phone: (413) 545-0222

University of Massachusetts Boston
www.umb.edu
Undergraduate Admissions
100 Morrissey Boulevard
Boston, MA 02125-3393
Fax: (617) 287-5999
E-mail: enrollment.info@umb.edu
Phone: (617) 287-6000

University of Massachusetts Dartmouth
www.umassd.edu
Undergraduate Admissions Office
285 Old Westport Road
North Dartmouth, MA 02747-2300
Fax: (508) 999-8755
E-mail: skesman@umassd.edu
Phone: (508) 999-9107

University of Massachusetts Lowell
www.uml.edu
Admissions Office
883 Broadway Street, Room 110
Lowell, MA 01854-5104
Fax: (978) 934-3086
E-mail: admissions@uml.edu
Phone: (978) 934-3931

University of Medicine and Dentistry of New Jersey: School of Nursing
www.sn.umdnj.edu
Office of International Students
65 Bergen Street, Room 149
Newark, NJ 07101-1709
Fax: (973) 972-7453
E-mail: snadmissions@umdnj.edu
Phone: (973) 972-6138

University of Medicine and Dentistry of New Jersey: School of Health Related Professions
www.shrp.umdnj.edu
Office of International Services - Office of the University Registrar
65 Bergen Street
Room 149
Newark, NJ 07101-1709
Fax: (973) 972-8260
E-mail: shrpadm@umdnj.edu
Phone: (973) 972-6138

University of Memphis
www.memphis.edu
Office of Admissions
101 Wilder Tower
Memphis, TN 38152
Fax: (901) 678-3053
E-mail: gmoore@memphis.edu
Phone: (901) 678-2111

University of Miami
www.miami.edu
Office of International Admission
132 Ashe Building
Box 248025
Coral Gables, FL 33124-4616
Fax: (305) 284-6811
E-mail: mreid@miami.edu
Phone: (305) 284-2271

University of Michigan
www.umich.edu
Office of Undergraduate Admissions
1220 Student Activities Building
515 East Jefferson Street
Ann Arbor, MI 48109-1316
Fax: (734) 936-0747
E-mail: tsz@umich.edu
Phone: (734) 764-7433

University of Michigan: Dearborn
www.umd.umich.edu
Admissions
4901 Evergreen Road, 1145 UC
Dearborn, MI 48128-1491
Fax: (313) 436-9167
E-mail: dmalin@umd.umich.edu
Phone: (313) 593-5100

University of Michigan: Flint
www.umflint.edu
Admissions
303 East Kearsley Street
245 UPAV
Flint, MI 48502-1950
Fax: (810) 762-0006
E-mail: ic@umflint.edu
Phone: (810) 762-0867

University of Minnesota: Crookston
www1.crk.umn.edu/
International Programs Office
2900 University Avenue
170 Owen Hall
Crookston, MN 56716-5001
Fax: (218) 281-8588
E-mail: gillette@umn.edu
Phone: (218) 281-8442

University of Minnesota: Duluth
www.d.umn.edu
Office of Admissions
25 Solon Campus Center
1117 University Drive
Duluth, MN 55812-3000
Fax: (218) 726-6724
E-mail: pokeefe@d.umn.edu
Phone: (218) 726-7531

University of Minnesota: Morris
www.morris.umn.edu
Office of Admissions
600 East 4th Street
Morris, MN 56267
Fax: (320) 589-1673
E-mail: taraw@morris.umn.edu
Phone: (320) 589-6490

University of Minnesota: Rochester
www.r.umn.edu
Student Affairs
111 South Broadway
Rochester, MN 55904
Fax: (507) 258-8021
E-mail: frid0014@umn.edu
Phone: (507) 258-8077

University of Minnesota: Twin Cities
www.umn.edu/tc
Admissions
240 Williamson Hall, 231 Pillsbury Drive SE
Minneapolis, MN 55455-0115
Fax: (612) 626-1693
Phone: (800) 752-1000

University of Mississippi
www.olemiss.edu
Office of International Programs
145 Martindale
PO BOX 1848
University, MS 38677-1848
Fax: (662) 915-7486
E-mail: ktyler@olemiss.edu
Phone: (662) 915-7404

University of Missouri: Columbia
www.missouri.edu
International Student Admissions
230 Jesse Hall
Columbia, MO 65211
Fax: (573) 882-7887
E-mail: inter@missouri.edu
Phone: (573) 882-3754

University of Missouri: Kansas City
www.umkc.edu
International Student Affairs Office
5100 Rockhill Road, AC120
Kansas City, MO 64110-2499
Fax: (816) 235-6502
E-mail: gaults@umkc.edu
Phone: (816) 235-6234

University of Missouri: St. Louis
www.umsl.edu
Office of International Student and Scholar
Services
One University Boulevard
351 Millennium Student Center
St. Louis, MO 63121-4400
Fax: (314) 516-5636
E-mail: westdav@umsl.edu
Phone: (314) 516-5229

University of Mobile
www.umobile.edu
Admissions
5735 College Parkway
Mobile, AL 36613-2842
Fax: (251) 442-2498
E-mail: kristies@umobile.edu
Phone: (251) 442-2273

University of Montana
www.umt.edu
Admissions
Lommasson Center 103
Missoula, MT 59812
Fax: (406) 243-5711
E-mail: jalcala@mso.umt.edu
Phone: (406) 243-2049

University of Montana: Western
www.umwestern.edu
Admissions
710 South Atlantic Street
Dillon, MT 59725
Fax: (406) 683-7493
E-mail: j_jones@umwestern.edu
Phone: (406) 683-7331

University of Montevallo
www.montevallo.edu
Admissions
Palmer Hall, Station 6030
University of Montevallo
Montevallo, AL 35115-6000
Fax: (205) 665-6032
E-mail: admissions@montevallo.edu
Phone: (205) 665-6030

University of Mount Union
www.mountunion.edu
International Admissions
1972 Clark Avenue
Alliance, OH 44601-3993
Fax: (330) 829-8204
E-mail: IntlAdms@mountunion.edu
Phone: (330) 823-3296

University of Nebraska - Kearney
www.unk.edu
International Education Admissions
905 West 25th
Kearney, NE 68849
Fax: (308) 865-8160
E-mail: intladmin@unk.edu
Phone: (308) 865-8157

University of Nebraska - Lincoln
www.unl.edu
International Affairs
1410 Q Street
Box 880417
Lincoln, NE 68588-0417
Fax: (402) 472-5383
E-mail: hturner1@unl.edu
Phone: (402) 472-5358

University of Nebraska - Omaha
www.unomaha.edu
International Admissions
6001 Dodge Street
Omaha, NE 68182-0005
Fax: (402) 554-2949
E-mail: emaloley@mail.unomaha.edu
Phone: (402) 554-2293

University of Nevada: Las Vegas
www.unlv.edu
4505 Maryland Parkway, Box 451021
Las Vegas, NV 89154-1021
Fax: (702) 895-4046
E-mail: isssc@unlv.edu
Phone: (702) 774-8658

University of Nevada: Reno
www.unr.edu
Office of International Students & Scholars
Mail Stop 120
Reno, NV 89557
Fax: (775) 327-5843
E-mail: bender@unr.edu
Phone: (775) 784-6874

University of New England
www.une.edu
Admissions
Hills Beach Road
Biddeford, ME 04005
Fax: (207) 221-4898
E-mail: admissions@une.edu
Phone: (800) 477-4863 ext. 4208

University of New Hampshire
www.unh.edu
Admissions Office
Grant House
4 Garrison Avenue
Durham, NH 03824
Fax: (603) 862-0077
E-mail: admissions@unh.edu
Phone: (603) 862-1360

University of New Hampshire at Manchester
www.unhm.unh.edu
Admissions
400 Commercial Street
Manchester, NH 03101-1113
Fax: (603) 641-4342
E-mail: unhm.admissions@unh.edu
Phone: (603) 641-4150

University of New Haven
www.newhaven.edu
Office of International Admissions
300 Boston Post Road
West Haven, CT 06516
Fax: (203) 931-6093
E-mail: jspellman@newhaven.edu
Phone: (203) 932-7134

University of New Mexico
www.unm.edu
Office of International Admissions
Office of Admissions
PO Box 4895
Albuquerque, NM 87196-4895
Fax: (505) 277-6686
E-mail: goglobal@unm.edu
Phone: (505) 277-5829

University of New Orleans
www.uno.edu
Admissions
Administration Building, Room 103
New Orleans, LA 70148
Fax: (504) 280-6552
E-mail: admissions@uno.edu
Phone: (504) 280-6595

University of North Alabama
www.una.edu
Office of International Affairs
One Harrison Plaza, UNA Box 5011
Florence, AL 35632-0001
Fax: (256) 765-4960
E-mail: czhang@una.edu
Phone: (256) 765-4626

University of North Carolina at Asheville
www.unca.edu
Admissions
CPO#1320, UNCA
One University Heights
Asheville, NC 28804-8502
Fax: (828) 251-6482
E-mail: lmcbride@unca.edu
Phone: (828) 251-6481

University of North Carolina at Chapel Hill
www.unc.edu
Undergraduate Admissions
Jackson Hall
CB# 2200
Chapel Hill, NC 27599-2200
Fax: (919) 962-3045
E-mail: afelder@admissions.unc.edu
Phone: (919) 843-6156

University of North Carolina at Charlotte
www.uncc.edu
Office of International Admissions
Undergraduate Admissions- Cato Hall
9201 University Boulevard
Charlotte, NC 28223-0001
Fax: (704) 687-2897
E-mail: intnladm@uncc.edu
Phone: (704) 687-5503

University of North Carolina at Greensboro
www.uncg.edu
Undergraduate Admissions
1400 Spring Garden Street
PO Box 26170
Greensboro, NC 27402-6170
Fax: (336) 334-4180
E-mail: admissions@uncg.edu
Phone: (336) 334-5243

University of North Carolina at Pembroke
www.uncp.edu
Associate Director for International
Recruitment
Box 1510
One University Drive
Pembroke, NC 28372
Fax: (910) 521-6497
E-mail: lela.clark@uncp.edu
Phone: (910) 521-6262

University of North Carolina at Wilmington
www.uncw.edu
Admissions Coordinator
601 South College Road
Wilmington, NC 28403-5904
Fax: (910) 962-3038
E-mail: byrnesl@uncw.edu
Phone: (910) 962-7779

University of North Carolina School of the Arts
www.uncsa.edu
Coordinator of International Student
Admissions
1533 South Main Street
Winston-Salem, NC 27127-2188
Fax: (336) 770-3370
E-mail: hollidays@uncsa.edu
Phone: (336) 770-1471

University of North Dakota
www.und.edu
Undergraduate Admissions Office
Twamley Hall, Room 205
264 Centennial Drive, Stop 8357
Grand Forks, ND 58202-8357
Fax: (701) 777-2721
E-mail: debmelby@mail.und.edu
Phone: (701) 777-3821

University of North Florida
www.unf.edu
International Center
1 UNF Drive
Jacksonville, FL 32224-7699
Fax: (904) 620-3925
E-mail: trobinso@unf.edu
Phone: (904) 620-2768

University of North Texas
www.unt.edu
Office of International Admissions
1401 West Prairie, Suite 309
1155 Union Circle #311277
Denton, TX 76203-5017
Fax: (940) 565-4822
E-mail: Robert.Prather@unt.edu
Phone: (940) 565-2405

University of Northern Colorado
www.unco.edu
Graduate School
501 20th Street, Campus Box 10
Greeley, CO 80639
Fax: (970) 351-2371
E-mail: grad.school@unco.edu
Phone: (970) 351-1811

University of Northern Iowa
www.uni.edu
Admissions
1227 West 27th Street
Cedar Falls, IA 50614-0018
Fax: (319) 273-2885
E-mail: kristi.marchesani@uni.edu
Phone: (319) 273-2281

University of Northwestern Ohio
www.unoh.edu
1441 North Cable Road
Lima, OH 45805
Fax: (419) 229-6926
E-mail: info@unoh.edu
Phone: (419) 998-3120

University of Notre Dame
www.nd.edu
Admissions
220 Main Building
Notre Dame, IN 46556
Fax: (574) 631-8865
E-mail: admissions@nd.edu
Phone: (574) 631-7505

University of Oklahoma
www.ou.edu
Office of Admissions
1000 Asp Avenue
Norman, OK 73019-4076
Fax: (405) 325-7124
E-mail: admrec@ou.edu
Phone: (405) 325-2252

University of Oregon
www.uoregon.edu
International Affairs
1217 University of Oregon
Eugene, OR 97403-1217
Fax: (541) 346-1232
E-mail: intl@uoregon.edu
Phone: (541) 346-3206

University of the Ozarks
www.ozarks.edu
415 North College Avenue
Clarksville, AR 72830-2880
Fax: (479) 979-1239
E-mail: rjcasey@ozarks.edu
Phone: (479) 979-1232

University of the Pacific
www.pacific.edu
Assistant Director of Admission
3601 Pacific Avenue
Stockton, CA 95211-0197
Fax: (209) 946-2413
E-mail: ksanpei@pacific.edu
Phone: (209) 346-2211

University of Pennsylvania
www.upenn.edu
1 College Hall
Room 1
Philadelphia, PA 19104-6376
Fax: (215) 898-9670
E-mail: intl@admissions.upenn.edu
Phone: (215) 898-7507

University of Phoenix: Atlanta
www.phoenix.edu
8200 Roberts Drive, Suite 300
Sandy Springs, GA 30350

University of Phoenix: Augusta
www.phoenix.edu
3152 Perimeter Pkwy
Augusta, GA 30909-4583

University of Phoenix: Austin
www.phoenix.edu
10801-2 North MoPac, Suite 300
Austin, TX 78759-5459

University of Phoenix: Bay Area
www.phoenix.edu
3590 North First Street
San Jose, CA 95134-1805

University of Phoenix: Birmingham
www.phoenix.edu
100 Corporate Drive, Suite 150
Birmingham, AL 35242-2982

University of Phoenix: Boston
www.phoenix.edu
19 Granite Street, Suite 300
Braintree, MA 02169-1744

University of Phoenix: Central Florida
www.phoenix.edu
2290 Lucien Way, Suite 400
Maitland, FL 32751

University of Phoenix: Central Valley
www.phoenix.edu
45 River Park Place West
Fresno, CA 93720-1562

University of Phoenix: Charlotte
www.phoenix.edu
3800 Arco Corporate Drive, Suite 100
Charlotte, NC 28273-3409

University of Phoenix: Chattanooga
www.phoenix.edu
1208 Pointe Centre Drive
Chattanooga, TN 37421-3983

University of Phoenix: Cheyenne
www.phoenix.edu
6900 Yellowtail Road
Cheyenne, WY 82009-6112

University of Phoenix: Chicago
www.phoenix.edu
1500 McConnor Parkway
Schaumburg, IL 60173

University of Phoenix: Cincinnati
www.phoenix.edu
9050 Centre Point, Ste 250
West Chester, OH 4874

University of Phoenix: Cleveland
www.phoenix.edu
5005 Rockside Road, Suite 130
Independence, OH 44131-6808

University of Phoenix: Columbia
www.phoenix.edu
1001 Pinnacle Point Drive, Suite 200
Columbia, SC 29223-5727

University of Phoenix: Columbus Georgia
4747 Hamilton Road
Columbus, GA 31904

University of Phoenix: Columbus Ohio
www.phoenix.edu
8415 Pulsar Place
Columbus, OH 43240-4032

University of Phoenix: Dallas Fort Worth
www.phoenix.edu
12400 Coit Road, Suite 200
Dallas, TX 75251-2004

University of Phoenix: Denver
www.phoenix.edu
10004 Park Meadows Drive
Lone Tree, CO 80124-5453

University of Phoenix: Des Moines
www.phoenix.edu
6600 Westown Parkway
West Des Moines, IA 50266-7724

University of Phoenix: Fairfield County
www.phoenix.edu
535 Connecticut Avenue
Norwalk, CT 06854-1700

University of Phoenix: Harrisburg
www.phoenix.edu
4050 Crums Mill Road
Harrisburg, PA 17112-2894

University of Phoenix: Hawaii
www.phoenix.edu
745 Fort Street, Suite 2000
Honolulu, HI 96813

University of Phoenix: Houston Westside
www.phoenix.edu
11451 Katy Freeway
Houston, TX 77079-2004

University of Phoenix: Idaho
www.phoenix.edu
1422 South Tech Lane
Meridian, ID 83642-3014

University of Phoenix: Indianapolis
www.phoenix.edu
7999 Knue Road
Indianapolis, IN 46250-1932

University of Phoenix: Jersey City
www.phoenix.edu
100 Town Square Place
Jersey City, NJ 07310

University of Phoenix: Kansas City
www.phoenix.edu
901 East 104th Street, Suite 200
Kansas City, MO 64131-3459

University of Phoenix: Las Vegas
www.phoenix.edu
7455 West Washington Avenue
Las Vegas, NV 89128-4340

University of Phoenix: Little Rock
www.phoenix.edu
10800 Financial Center Parkway
Little Rock, AR 72211-3552

University of Phoenix: Louisiana
www.phoenix.edu
One Galleria Boulevard, Suite 725
Metairie, LA 70001-2082

University of Phoenix: Louisville
www.phoenix.edu
10400 Linn Station Road
Louisville, KY 40223-3839

University of Phoenix: Madison
www.phoenix.edu
2310 Crossroads Drive
Madison, WI 53718-2416

University of Phoenix: Maryland
www.phoenix.edu
8830 Stanford Boulevard, Suite 100
Coumbia, MD 20145

University of Phoenix: Memphis
www.phoenix.edu
65 Germantown Ct, Ste 100
Cordova, TN 38018-7290

University of Phoenix: Metro Detroit
www.phoenix.edu
5480 Corporoate Drive, Suite 240
Troy, MI 48098-2623

University of Phoenix: Milwaukee
www.phoenix.edu
20075 Watertower Road
Brookfield, WI 53045-3573

University of Phoenix: Minneapolis-St. Paul
www.phoenix.edu
435 Ford Road, Suite 1000
Saint Louis Park, MN 55426-4915

University of Phoenix: Nashville
www.phoenix.edu
616 Marriott Drive, Ste 150
Nashville, TN 37214-5048

University of Phoenix: New Mexico
www.phoenix.edu
5700 Pasadena NE
Albuquerque, NM 87113-8711

University of Phoenix: North Florida
www.phoenix.edu
4500 Salisbury Road N, Suite 200
Jacksonville, FL 32216

University of Phoenix: Northern Nevada
www.phoenix.edu
10345 Professional Circle, Suite 200
Reno, NV 89521-5862

University of Phoenix: Northern Virginia
www.phoenix.edu
11730 Plaza America Drive, Suite 200
Reston, VA 20190-4750

University of Phoenix: Northwest Arkansas
www.phoenix.edu
903 North 47th Street
Barrington Centre 2
Rogers, AR 72756-9615

University of Phoenix: Oklahoma City
www.phoenix.edu
6501 North Broadway, Suite 100
Oklahoma City, OK 73116-8244

University of Phoenix: Omaha
www.phoenix.edu
13321 California Street, Suite 200
Omaha, NE 68154-5258

University of Phoenix: Oregon
www.phoenix.edu
13221 Southwest 68th Parkway, Suite 500
Tigard, OR 97223-8328

University of Phoenix: Philadelphia
www.phoenix.edu
1170 Devon Park Drive
Wayne, PA 19087-2121

University of Phoenix: Phoenix-Hohokam
www.phoenix.edu
University of Phoenix: On-Line Campus
4035 South Riverpoint Parkway
Mail Stop CF-L501
Phoenix, AZ 85040-0723
E-mail: Heather.Tsui@west.edu
Phone: (602) 429-1127

University of Phoenix: Pittsburgh
www.phoenix.edu
Penn Center West, Building 6, Suite 100
Pittsburgh, PA 15276-0119

University of Phoenix: Puerto Rico
www.phoenix.edu
B7 Calle Tabonuco
Guaynabo, PR 00968-3003

University of Phoenix: Raleigh
www.phoenix.edu
5511 Capital Center Drive, Suite 390
Raleigh, NC 27606-3380

University of Phoenix: Richmond
www.phoenix.edu
6600 West Broad Street
Richmond, VA 23230-1709

University of Phoenix: Sacramento Valley
www.phoenix.edu
2860 Gateway Oaks Drive, Suite 200
Sacramento, CA 95833-4334

University of Phoenix: San Antonio
www.phoenix.edu
8200 IH010 West, Suite 910
San Antonio, TX 78230-3876

University of Phoenix: San Diego
www.phoenix.edu
3890 Murphy Canyon Road, Suite 100
San Diego, CA 92123-4403

University of Phoenix: Savannah
www.phoenix.edu
8001 Chatham Center Drive, Suite 200
Savannah, GA 31405

University of Phoenix: South Florida
www.phoenix.edu
600 North Pine Island Road, Suite 500
Plantation, FL 33324

University of Phoenix: Southern Arizona
www.phoenix.edu
300 South Craycroft Road
Tucson, AZ 85711-4574

University of Phoenix: Southern California
www.phoenix.edu
3100 Bristol Street, Suite 500
Costa Mesa, CA 92626-3099

University of Phoenix: Southern Colorado
www.phoenix.edu
5725 Mark Dabling Boulevard
Colorado Springs, CO 80919-2221

University of Phoenix: Springfield
www.phoenix.edu
1343 East Kingsley Street
Springfield, MO 65804-7216

University of Phoenix: St. Louis
www.phoenix.edu
13801 Riverport Drive, Suite 102
St. Louis, MO 63043-4828

University of Phoenix: Tulsa
www.phoenix.edu
14002 East 21st Street, Suite 1000
Tulsa, OK 74134-1412

University of Phoenix: Utah
www.phoenix.edu
5373 South Green Street
Salt Lake City, UT 84123-4642

University of Phoenix: Washington DC
www.phoenix.edu
25 Massachusetts Avenue NW
Washington, DC 20001-1431

University of Phoenix: West Florida
www.phoenix.edu
12802 Tampa Oaks Boulevard, Suite 200
Temple Terrace, FL 33637-1920

University of Phoenix: West Michigan
www.phoenix.edu
318 River Ridge Drive NW
Grand Rapids, MI 49544-1683

University of Phoenix: Western Washington
www.phoenix.edu
7100 Fort Dent Way
Tukwila, WA 98188-8553

University of Phoenix: Wichita
www.phoenix.edu
3020 North Cypress Drive, Suite 150
Wichita, KS 67226

University of Pittsburgh
www.pitt.edu
Office of International Services
4227 Fifth Avenue, 1st Floor, Alumni Hall
Pittsburgh, PA 15260
Fax: (412) 624-8184
E-mail: intladm@pitt.edu
Phone: (412) 624-7128

University of Pittsburgh at Bradford
www.upb.pitt.edu
Office of Admissions
300 Campus Drive
Bradford, PA 16701
Fax: (814) 362-5150
E-mail: admissions@upb.pitt.edu
Phone: (814) 362-7555

University of Pittsburgh at Greensburg
www.greensburg.pitt.edu
Office of Admissions and Financial Aid
150 Finoli Drive
Greensburg, PA 15601
Fax: (412) 648-8815
E-mail: intladmin@pitt.edu
Phone: (412) 624-4096

University of Pittsburgh at Johnstown
www.upj.pitt.edu
Office of International Services
450 Schoolhouse Road, 157 Blackington Hall
Johnstown, PA 15904-1200
Fax: (814) 269-7044
E-mail: jskist@pitt.edu
Phone: (814) 269-7049

University of Pittsburgh at Titusville
www.upt.pitt.edu
Office of Admissions and Student Aid
UPT Admissions Office
Box 287
Titusville, PA 16354-0287
Fax: (412) 624-7105
E-mail: uptadm@pitt.edu
Phone: (412) 624-7125

University of Portland
www.up.edu
Office of Admissions
5000 North Willamette Boulevard
Portland, OR 97203-5798
Fax: (503) 943-7315
E-mail: mcdonaja@up.edu
Phone: (503) 943-7147

University of Puerto Rico: Aguadilla
www.uprag.edu
Admissions Office
Box 6150
Aguadilla, PR 00604-6150
Fax: (787) 890-4543
E-mail: melba.serrano@upr.edu
Phone: (787) 890-2681 ext. 280

University of Puerto Rico: Arecibo
www.upra.edu
PO Box 4010
Arecibo, PR 00614-4010
Fax: (787) 880-4972
E-mail: mmendez@upra.edu
Phone: (787) 815-0000 ext. 4110

University of Puerto Rico: Bayamon University College
www.uprb.edu
174 Street #170 Minillas Industrial Park
Bayamon, PR 00959-1919
Fax: (787) 993-8929
E-mail: cmontes@uprb.edu
Phone: (787) 993-8952

University of Puerto Rico: Carolina Regional College
www.uprc.edu
Admissions Office
PO Box 4800
Carolina, PR 00984-4800
Fax: (787) 750-7940
E-mail: celia.mendez@upr.edu
Phone: (787) 757-1485

University of Puerto Rico: Cayey University College
www.cayey.upr.edu
Admissions Office
Oficina de Admisiones UPR- Cayey
205 Antonio Barcelo Avenue
Cayey, PR 00736
Fax: (787) 738-5633
E-mail: wilfredo.lopez3@upr.edu
Phone: (787) 738-2161 ext. 2233

University of Puerto Rico: Humacao
www.uprh.edu
Acting Director of Admissions
100 Road 908 CUH Station
Humacao, PR 00791
Fax: (787) 850-9428
E-mail: elizabeth.gerena@upr.edu
Phone: (787) 850-9301

University of Puerto Rico: Mayaguez
www.uprm.edu
International Students Office
Admissions Office
PO Box 9000
Mayaguez, PR 00681-9000
Fax: (787) 265-5432
E-mail: gildreth@uprm.edu
Phone: (787) 265-3896

University of Puerto Rico: Medical Sciences
www.rcm.upr.edu
PO Box 365067
San Juan, PR 00936-5067
Fax: (787) 282-7117
E-mail: margarita.rivera4@upr.edu
Phone: (787) 758-2525 ext. 5211

University of Puerto Rico: Ponce
www.uprp.edu
Director of Admissions
Box 7186
Ponce, PR 00732
Fax: (787) 840-8108
E-mail: avelazquez@uprp.edu
Phone: (787) 844-8181 ext. 2530

University of Puerto Rico: Rio Piedras
www.uprrp.edu
Box 23344
San Juan, PR 00931-3344
Fax: (787) 764-3680
E-mail: admisiones@uprrp.edu
Phone: (787) 764-0000 ext. 85700

University of Puerto Rico: Utuado
www.uprutuado.edu
Admissions
PO Box 2500
Utuado, PR 00641
Fax: (787) 894-2891
Phone: (787) 894-2828 ext. 2240

University of Puget Sound
www.pugetsound.edu
Admission
1500 North Warner Street
CMB #1062
Tacoma, WA 98416-1062
Fax: (253) 879-3993
E-mail: admission@ups.edu
Phone: (253) 879-3211

University of Redlands
www.redlands.edu
International Student Adviser
1200 East Colton Avenue
PO Box 3080
Redlands, CA 92373-0999
Fax: (909) 335-4089
E-mail: admissions@redlands.edu
Phone: (909) 793-2121 ext. 4583

University of Rhode Island
www.uri.edu
Office of Admission
Newman Hall
14 Upper College Road
Kingston, RI 02881-1322
Fax: (401) 874-5523
E-mail: nancys@uri.edu
Phone: (401) 874-7100

University of Richmond
www.richmond.edu
Brunet Memorial Hall: 28 Westhampton Way
University of Richmond, VA 23173
Fax: (804) 287-6535
E-mail: intladm@richmond.edu
Phone: (804) 289-6531

University of Rio Grande
www.rio.edu
Student Services
218 North College Avenue
Box F-30
Rio Grande, OH 45674
Fax: (749) 245-7341
E-mail: aquinn@rio.edu
Phone: (740) 245-7126

University of Rochester
www.rochester.edu
Office of Admissions
300 Wilson Boulevard
Box 270251
Rochester, NY 14627-0251
Fax: (585) 461-4595
E-mail: jennifer.blask@rochester.edu
Phone: (585) 275-3221

University of Rochester School of Nursing
www.son.rochester.edu
Box SON
601 Elmwood Avenue
Rochester, NY 14642
E-mail: son_admissions@urmc.rochester.edu
Phone: (585) 275-2375

University of San Diego
www.sandiego.edu
Admissions Office
5998 Alcala Park
San Diego, CA 92110
Fax: (619) 260-6836
E-mail: msmalloy@sandiego.edu
Phone: (619) 260-4506

University of San Francisco
www.usfca.edu
Director, Asia, International Relations
2130 Fulton Street
San Francisco, CA 94117-1046
Fax: (415) 422-2217
E-mail: admission@usfca.edu
Phone: (415) 422-6563

University of Science and Arts of Oklahoma
www.usao.edu
Office of Admissions
1727 West Alabama
Chickasha, OK 73018-5322
Fax: (405) 574-1220
E-mail: usao-admissions@usao.edu
Phone: (405) 574-1357

University of the Sciences in Philadelphia
www.usp.edu
Student Affairs
600 South 43rd Street
Philadelphia, PA 19104-4495
Fax: (215) 895-1100
E-mail: w.perry@usp.edu
Phone: (215) 596-8890

University of Scranton
www.scranton.edu
Director of International Student Affairs
800 Linden Street
The Estate
Scranton, PA 18510-4699
Fax: (570) 941-5928
E-mail: blazespl@scranton.edu
Phone: (570) 941-7575

University of Sioux Falls
www.usiouxfalls.edu
Admissions Office
1101 West 22nd Street
Sioux Falls, SD 57105-1699
Fax: (605) 331-6615
E-mail: admissions@usiouxfalls.edu
Phone: (800) 888-1047

University of the South
www.sewanee.edu
Associate Dean of Admission
Office of Admission
735 University Avenue
Sewanee, TN 37383-1000
Fax: (931) 598-3248
E-mail: lwburns@sewanee.edu
Phone: (800) 522-2234

University of South Alabama
www.southalabama.edu
Office of International Services
Meisler Hall, Suite 2500
307 University Boulevard North
Mobile, AL 36688-0002
Fax: (251) 414-8213
E-mail: intlserv@jaguar1.usouthal.edu
Phone: (251) 460-6050

University of South Carolina: Aiken
web.usca.edu
Admissions Office
471 University Parkway
Aiken, SC 29801-6399
Fax: (803) 641-3727
E-mail: admit@usca.edu
Phone: (803) 641-3366

University of South Carolina: Beaufort
www.uscb.edu
Admissions Office
One University Boulevard
Bluffton, SC 29909
Fax: (843) 208-8290
E-mail: mrwilli5@uscb.edu
Phone: (843) 208-8112

University of South Carolina: Columbia
www.sc.edu
Admissions Office
Office of Undergraduate Admissions
Columbia, SC 29208
Fax: (803) 777-0101
E-mail: bbutler@sc.edu
Phone: (803) 777-7700

University of South Carolina: Lancaster
usclancaster.sc.edu
Admissions
Box 889
Lancaster, SC 29721
Fax: (803) 313-7116
E-mail: kfaile@mailbox.sc.edu
Phone: (803) 313-7000

University of South Carolina: Sumter
www.uscsumter.edu
Admissions
200 Miller Road
Sumter, SC 29150-2498
Fax: (803) 938-3901
E-mail: kbritton@uscsumter.edu
Phone: (803) 938-3882

University of South Carolina: Union
uscunion.sc.edu
PO Drawer 729
Union, SC 29379
Fax: (864) 427-3682
Phone: (864) 429-8728

University of South Carolina: Upstate
www.uscupstate.edu
Admissions
800 University Way
Spartanburg, SC 29303
Fax: (864) 503-5727
E-mail: dstewart@uscupstate.edu
Phone: (864) 503-5280

University of South Dakota
www.usd.edu
International Student Advising Office
414 East Clark Street
Vermillion, SD 57069-2390
Fax: (605) 677-6679
E-mail: jacy.fry@usd.edu
Phone: (605) 677-5332

University of South Florida
www.usf.edu
International Admissions
4202 East Fowler Avenue, SVC 1036
Tampa, FL 33620-9951
Fax: (813) 974-8271
E-mail: taylor@iac.usf.edu
Phone: (813) 974-5102

University of Southern California
www.usc.edu
Dean of Admission
Office of Admission
University Park
Los Angeles, CA 90089-0911
Fax: (213) 740-1556
E-mail: admdean@usc.edu
Phone: (213) 740-6753

University of Southern Indiana
www.usi.edu
Admission
8600 University Boulevard
Evansville, IN 47712
Fax: (812) 465-7154
E-mail: eotto@usi.edu
Phone: (812) 464-1765

University of Southern Maine
www.usm.maine.edu
Rachel Morales, Associate Director
PO Box 9300
Portland, ME 04104
Fax: (207) 780-5640
E-mail: rmorales@usm.maine.edu
Phone: (207) 780-5670

University of Southern Mississippi
www.usm.edu
Office of International Student and Scholar
Services
118 College Drive #5166
Hattiesburg, MS 39406-0001
Fax: (601) 266-4898
E-mail: isss@usm.edu
Phone: (601) 266-4841

University of Southern Nevada
www.usn.edu
Registrar and Director of Student Services
11 Sunset Way
Henderson, NV 89014-2333
Fax: (702) 968-2097
E-mail: abigby@usn.edu
Phone: (702) 968-2046

University of the Southwest
www.usw.edu
Office of Admissions
6610 Lovington Highway #506
Hobbs, NM 88240
Fax: (575) 392-6006
E-mail: admissions@usw.edu
Phone: (575) 392-6563 ext. 1047

University of St. Francis
www.stfrancis.edu
Director Undergraduate Admissions
500 Wilcox Street
Joliet, IL 60435
Fax: (815) 740-5032
E-mail: jmarlatt@srfrancis.edu
Phone: (800) 735-7500

University of St. Francis
www.sf.edu
Admissions
2701 Spring Street
Fort Wayne, IN 46808
Fax: (260) 434-7590
E-mail: jtownsend@sf.edu
Phone: (260) 399-8000

University of St. Mary
www.stmary.edu
Office of Admission
4100 South Fourth Street Trafficway
Leavenworth, KS 66048
Fax: (913) 758-6307
E-mail: admiss@stmary.edu
Phone: (800) 752-7043

University of St. Thomas
www.stthomas.edu
Director, International Recruiting and
Admissions
2115 Summit Avenue, 32F
St. Paul, MN 55105
Fax: (651) 962-5199
E-mail: hilp5533@stthomas.edu
Phone: (651) 962-6454

University of St. Thomas
www.stthom.edu
Office of Director of International Student and
Scholar Services
3800 Montrose Boulevard
Houston, TX 77006-4626
Fax: (713) 525-3896
E-mail: alsarrf@stthom.edu
Phone: (713) 525-3503

University of Tampa
www.ut.edu
Office of Admissions
401 West Kennedy Boulevard
Tampa, FL 33606-1490
Fax: (813) 258-7398
E-mail: admissions@ut.edu
Phone: (813) 253-6211

**University of Tennessee Health Science
Center**
www.uthsc.edu
Office of Enrollment Services
910 Madison Avenue
Memphis, TN 38163
Fax: (901) 448-7772
E-mail: rpatte10@uthsc.edu
Phone: (901) 448-5560

University of Tennessee: Chattanooga
www.utc.edu
International Student Advisor
615 McCallie Avenue
Guerry Hall, Dept 5105
Chattanooga, TN 37403
Fax: (423) 425-2292
E-mail: nancy-amberson@utc.edu
Phone: (423) 425-2110

University of Tennessee: Knoxville
www.utk.edu
Office of Undergraduate Admissions
320 Student Services Building, Circle Park
Knoxville, TN 37996-0230
Fax: (423) 974-4784
E-mail: admissions@utk.edu
Phone: (865) 974-2184

University of Tennessee: Martin
www.utm.edu
International Programs Office
200 Hall Moody Administration Building
Martin, TN 38238
Fax: (731) 881-7322
E-mail: cwilson@utm.edu
Phone: (731) 881-7340

University of Texas at Arlington
www.uta.edu
Admissions
Box 19088
Arlington, TX 76019
Fax: (817) 272-3435
E-mail: jrussel@uta.edu
Phone: (817) 272-3252

University of Texas at Austin
www.utexas.edu
Graduate and International Admission Center
PO Box 8058
Austin, TX 78713-8058
Fax: (512) 475-7395
E-mail: pat.ellison@mail.utexas.edu
Phone: (512) 475-7398

University of Texas at Brownsville - Texas Southmost College
www.utb.edu
Admissions Office
80 Fort Brown
Brownsville, TX 78520
Fax: (956) 882-7810
E-mail: admissions@utb.edu
Phone: (956) 882-8295

University of Texas at Dallas
www.utdallas.edu
Enrollment Services
Office of Admissions
800 West Campbell Road, Mailstop ROC11
Richardson, TX 75080-3021
Fax: (972) 883-2599
E-mail: interest@utdallas.edu
Phone: (972) 883-2270

University of Texas at El Paso
www.utep.edu
Office of International Programs
500 West University Avenue
El Paso, TX 79968-0510
Fax: (915) 747-8893
E-mail: oip@utep.edu
Phone: (915) 747-5664

University of Texas at San Antonio
www.utsa.edu
International Programs
One UTSA Circle
San Antonio, TX 78249-0617
Fax: (210) 458-7222
E-mail: charles.crane@utsa.edu
Phone: (210) 458-7240

University of Texas at Tyler
www.uttyler.edu
Admissions
3900 University Boulevard
Tyler, TX 75799
Fax: (903) 566-7068
E-mail: acrockett@mail.uttyl.edu
Phone: (903) 566-7230

University of Texas Health Science Center at Houston
www.uth.tmc.edu
Office of International Affairs
Box 20036
Houston, TX 77225
Fax: (713) 500-3189
E-mail: admissions@uth.tmc.edu
Phone: (713) 500-3176

University of Texas Health Science Center at San Antonio
www.uthscsa.edu
Registrar
7703 Floyd Curl Drive
MSC 7702
San Antonio, TX 78229-3900
Fax: (210) 567-2685
E-mail: mcgilvraya@uthscsa.edu
Phone: (210) 567-2621

University of Texas Medical Branch at Galveston
www.utmb.edu
301 University Boulevard
Galveston, TX 77555-1305
Fax: (409) 772-4466
E-mail: enrollment.services@utmb.edu
Phone: (409) 772-1215

University of Texas of the Permian Basin
www.utpb.edu
Admissions
4901 East University
Odessa, TX 79762
Fax: (432) 552-3605
E-mail: admissions@utpb.edu
Phone: (432) 552-2608

University of Texas Southwestern Medical Center at Dallas
www.utsouthwestern.edu
International Affairs
5323 Harry Hines Boulevard
Dallas, TX 75390-9162
Fax: (214) 648-2102
E-mail: admissions@utsouthwestern.edu
Phone: (214) 648-2780

University of Texas: Pan American
www.utpa.edu
Office of International Admissions
1201 West University Drive
Edinburg, TX 78539-2999
Fax: (956) 665-2281
E-mail: pchapa1@utpa.edu
Phone: (956) 665-2922

University of Toledo
www.utoledo.edu
Office of Undergraduate Admissions for Adult, Transfer and International Students
2801 West Bancroft Street
Toledo, OH 43606-3398
Fax: (419) 530-1202
E-mail: cathi.kwapich@utoledo.edu
Phone: (419) 530-5704

University of Tulsa
www.utulsa.edu
International Student Services
800 South Tucker Drive
Tulsa, OK 74104-3189
Fax: (918) 631-3322
E-mail: pamela-smith@utulsa.edu
Phone: (918) 631-2329

University of Utah
www.utah.edu
Admissions Office
201 South 1460 East, Room 250 S
Salt Lake City, UT 84112-9057
Fax: (801) 585-7864
E-mail: swayment@sa.utah.edu
Phone: (801) 581-3091

University of Vermont
www.uvm.edu
Admissions
194 South Prospect Street
Burlington, VT 05401-3596
Fax: (802) 656-8611
E-mail: admissions@uvm.edu
Phone: (802) 656-4620

University of Virginia
www.virginia.edu
Office of Undergraduate Admission
Box 400160
Charlottesville, VA 22904-4160
Fax: (434) 924-3587
E-mail: undergradadmission@virginia.edu
Phone: (434) 982-3200

University of Virginia's College at Wise
www.uvawise.edu
Chancellor for Enrollment Management
1 College Avenue
Wise, VA 24293-4412
Fax: (276) 328-0251
E-mail: rdn2f@uvawise.edu
Phone: (276) 328-0104

University of Washington
www.washington.edu
Office of Admissions
1410 Northeast Campus Parkway, Box 355852
Seattle, WA 98195-5852
Fax: (206) 685-3655
E-mail: intladm@u.washington.edu
Phone: (206) 543-9686

University of Washington Bothell
www.uwb.edu
Admissions
18115 Campus Way NE
Box 358500
Bothell, WA 98011-8246
Fax: (425) 352-5455
E-mail: smoss@uwb.edu
Phone: (425) 352-3601

University of Washington Tacoma
www.tacoma.washington.edu
International Student Services
Campus Box 358404
1900 Commerce Street
Tacoma, WA 98402-3100
Fax: (253) 692-4788
E-mail: uwtiss@uw.edu
Phone: (253) 692-4695

University of the West
www.uwest.edu
Office of Admissions
1409 North Walnut Grove Avenue
Rosemead, CA 91770
Fax: (626) 571-1413
E-mail: admission@uwest.edu
Phone: (626) 656-2120

University of West Alabama
www.uwa.edu
Registrar's Office
Station 4
Livingston, AL 35470
Fax: (205) 652-3708
E-mail: sgt@uwa.edu
Phone: (205) 652-3587

University of West Florida
www.uwf.edu
Office of Admissions
11000 University Parkway
Pensacola, FL 32514-5750
Fax: (850) 474-3360
E-mail: admissions@uwf.edu
Phone: (850) 474-2230

University of West Georgia
www.westga.edu
Admissions
1601 Maple Street
Carrollton, GA 30118
Fax: (678) 839-4747
E-mail: khubbell@westga.edu
Phone: (678) 839-4168

University of Wisconsin-Baraboo/Sauk County
www.baraboo.uwc.edu
Associate Registrar
1006 Connie Road
Baraboo, WI 53913-1098
Fax: (608) 356-0752
E-mail: lori.turner@uwc.edu
Phone: (608) 356-8351 ext. 255

University of Wisconsin-Barron County
www.barron.uwc.edu
Associate Registrar
1800 College Drive
Rice Lake, WI 54868
Fax: (715) 234-8024
E-mail: lori.turner@uwc.edu
Phone: (715) 234-8024

University of Wisconsin-Eau Claire
www.uwec.edu
Center for International Education
111 Schofield Hall
Eau Claire, WI 54701
Fax: (715) 836-4948
E-mail: markgraf@uwec.edu
Phone: (715) 836-4411

University of Wisconsin-Fox Valley
www.uwfox.uwc.edu
Associate Registrar
1478 Midway Road
Menasha, WI 54952-2850
Fax: (920) 832-2850
E-mail: lori.turner@uwc.edu
Phone: (920) 832-2620

University of Wisconsin-Green Bay
www.uwgb.edu
Office of International Student Services
2420 Nicolet Drive
Green Bay, WI 54311-7001
Fax: (920) 465-2949
E-mail: oie@uwgb.edu
Phone: (920) 465-2889

University of Wisconsin-La Crosse
www.uwlax.edu
Office of International Education
1725 State Street, Cleary Center
La Crosse, WI 54601
Fax: (608) 785-8923
E-mail: uwlworld@uwlax.edu
Phone: (608) 785-8922

University of Wisconsin-Madison
www.wisc.edu
Undergraduate Admissions Office
Armory & Gymnasium
702 West Johnson Street, Suite 101
Madison, WI 53715-1007
Fax: (608) 262-7706
E-mail: onwisconsin@admissions.wisc.edu
Phone: (608) 262-3961

University of Wisconsin-Marathon County
www.uwmc.uwc.edu
Associate Registrar
518 South Seventh Avenue
Wausau, WI 54401-5396
Fax: (715) 261-6331
E-mail: lori.turner@uwc.edu
Phone: (715) 261-6100

University of Wisconsin-Marinette
www.marinette.uwc.edu
Associate Registrar
750 West Bay Shore Street
Marinette, WI 54143
Fax: (715) 735-4304
E-mail: lori.turner@uwc.edu
Phone: (715) 735-4301

University of Wisconsin-Marshfield/Wood County
www.marshfield.uwc.edu
Associate Registrar
2000 West Fifth Street
Marshfield, WI 54449
Fax: (608) 265-9473
E-mail: lori.turner@uwc.edu
Phone: (608) 262-9652

University of Wisconsin-Milwaukee
www.uwm.edu
International Admissions
Box 749
Milwaukee, WI 53201
Fax: (414) 229-0521
E-mail: isss@uwm.edu
Phone: (414) 229-4846

University of Wisconsin-Oshkosh
www.uwosh.edu
Dean of Students
800 Algoma Boulevard
Oshkosh, WI 54901-8602
Fax: (920) 424-1098
E-mail: gogginm@uwosh.edu
Phone: (920) 424-3100

University of Wisconsin-Parkside
www.uwp.edu
Admissions
PO Box 2000
Kenosha, WI 53141-2000
Fax: (262) 595-2008
E-mail: admissions@uwp.edu
Phone: (262) 595-2355

University of Wisconsin-Platteville
www.uwplatt.edu
Admissions
One University Plaza
Platteville, WI 53818
Fax: (608) 342-1122
E-mail: admit@uwplatt.edu
Phone: (608) 342-1125

University of Wisconsin-Richland
www.richland.uwc.edu
Coordinator of International Education
1200 Highway 14 West
Richland Center, WI 53581
Fax: (608) 265-6784
E-mail: kathy.neckar@uwc.edu
Phone: (608) 890-3005

University of Wisconsin-River Falls
www.uwrf.edu
Admissions Counselor
410 South 3rd Street
112 South Hall
River Falls, WI 54022-5001
Fax: (715) 425-0676
E-mail: carolyn.j.brady@uwrf.edu
Phone: (715) 425-3500

University of Wisconsin-Rock County
www.rock.uwc.edu
Associate Registrar
2909 Kellogg Avenue
Janesville, WI 53546-5699
Fax: (608) 758-6579
E-mail: lori.turner@uwc.edu
Phone: (608) 262-9652

University of Wisconsin-Sheboygan
www.sheboygan.uwc.edu
Student Services
One University Drive
Sheboygan, WI 53081
Fax: (920) 459-6662
E-mail: rcampopi@uwc.edu
Phone: (920) 459-6633

University of Wisconsin-Stevens Point
www.uwsp.edu
International Students and Scholars Office
Student Services Center
1108 Fremont St. Room 102
Stevens Point, WI 54481
Fax: (715) 346-3819
E-mail: isso@uwsp.edu
Phone: (715) 346-3849

University of Wisconsin-Stout
www.uwstout.edu
International Education
1 Clocktower Plaza
Menomonie, WI 54751
Fax: (715) 232-2500
E-mail: rosth@uwstout.edu
Phone: (715) 232-2132

University of Wisconsin-Superior
www.uwsuper.edu
International Admissions Coordinator
Belknap and Catlin, PO Box 2000
Superior, WI 54880
Fax: (715) 394-8363
E-mail: MMACLEAN@uwsuper.edu
Phone: (715) 394-8052

University of Wisconsin-Washington County
www.washington.uwc.edu
Associate Registrar
400 University Drive
West Bend, WI 53095
Fax: (262) 335-5274
E-mail: lori.turner@uwc.edu
Phone: (608) 263-9652

University of Wisconsin-Waukesha
www.waukesha.uwc.edu
International Education Coordinator
1500 North University Drive
Waukesha, WI 53188
Fax: (608) 265-9473
E-mail: kathy.neckar@uwc.edu
Phone: (608) 890-3005

University of Wisconsin-Whitewater
www.uww.edu
International Education and Programs
800 West Main Street
Whitewater, WI 53190-1790
Fax: (262) 472-1491
E-mail: smithh@uww.edu
Phone: (262) 472-5178

University of Wyoming
www.uwyo.edu
Associate Director
Dept 3435
1000 E. University Avenue
Laramie, WY 82071
Fax: (307) 766-4053
E-mail: uwglobal@uwyo.edu
Phone: (307) 766-5193

Upper Iowa University
www.uiu.edu
International Programs office
Parker Fox Hall
PO Box 1859
Fayette, IA 52142
Fax: (563) 425-5833
E-mail: moreb@uiu.edu
Phone: (563) 425-5831

Urbana University
www.urbana.edu
Graduate/International Admissions
579 College Way
Urbana, OH 43078
Fax: (937) 652-6871
E-mail: rsnow@urbana.edu
Phone: (937) 484-1256

Ursinus College
www.ursinus.edu
Admissions
PO Box 1000
601 Main Street
Collegeville, PA 19426-1000
Fax: (610) 409-3662
E-mail: admissions@ursinus.edu
Phone: (610) 409-3200

Ursuline College
www.ursuline.edu
Admission
2550 Lander Road
Pepper Pike, OH 44124-4398
Fax: (440) 684-6114
E-mail: jhanna@ursuline.edu
Phone: (440) 449-4203

Utah State University
www.usu.edu
International Students and Scholars
0160 Old Main Hill
Logan, UT 84322-0160
Fax: (435) 797-3522
E-mail: jeannie.pacheco@usu.edu
Phone: (435) 797-1124

Utah Valley University
www.uvu.edu
International Admissions and Immigration Affairs
800 West University Parkway
Orem, UT 84058-5999
Fax: (801) 225-4677
E-mail: whaleyco@uvu.edu
Phone: (801) 863-8466 ext. 8475

Utica College
www.utica.edu
Dean of International Education
1600 Burrstone Road
Utica, NY 13502-4892
Fax: (315) 792-3003
E-mail: lroberts@utica.edu
Phone: (315) 792-3340

Utica School of Commerce
www.uscny.edu
201 Bleecker Street
Utica, NY 13501
Fax: (315) 733-9281
E-mail: admissions@uscny.edu
Phone: (315) 733-2307

Valdosta State University
www.valdosta.edu
International Programs
1500 North Patterson Street
Valdosta, GA 31698-0170
Fax: (229) 245-3849
E-mail: ibmcclel@valdosta.edu
Phone: (229) 333-7410

Valencia College
www.valenciacollege.edu
Admissions and Records
PO Box 3028
Orlando, FL 32802-3028
Fax: (407) 582-1403
E-mail: rsimpson@valenciacc.edu
Phone: (407) 582-1506

Valley City State University
www.vcsu.edu
Enrollment Services
101 College Street SW
Valley City, ND 58072-4098
Fax: (701) 845-7299
E-mail: joy.smith@vcsu.edu
Phone: (701) 845-7552

Valley Forge Christian College
www.vfcc.edu
Admissions
1401 Charlestown Road
Phoenixville, PA 19460
Fax: (610) 917-2069
E-mail: bachenco@vfcc.edu
Phone: (800) 432-8322

Valley Forge Military Academy and College
www.vfmac.edu
1001 Eagle Road
Wayne, PA 19087
Fax: (610) 688-1545
E-mail: jlambert@vfmac.edu
Phone: (610) 989-1561

Valparaiso University
www.valpo.edu
Division of Enrollment Management
Kretzmann Hall, 1700 Chapel Drive
Valparaiso, IN 46383-6493
Fax: (219) 464-6898
E-mail: Timothy.Tesar@valpo.edu
Phone: (219) 464-5011

Vance-Granville Community College
www.vgcc.edu
Registrar
Box 917
Henderson, NC 27536
Fax: (252) 430-0460
E-mail: waddlet@vgcc.edu
Phone: (252) 492-2061

Vanderbilt University
www.vanderbilt.edu
Undergraduate Admissions
2305 West End Avenue
Nashville, TN 37203-1727
Fax: (615) 343-8326
E-mail: admissions@vanderbilt.edu
Phone: (615) 936-2811

VanderCook College of Music
www.vandercook.edu
Admissions
3140 South Federal Street
Chicago, IL 60616-3731
Fax: (312) 225-5211
E-mail: admissions@vandercook.edu
Phone: (312) 225-6288 ext. 230

Vanguard University of Southern California
www.vanguard.edu
Undergraduate Admissions
55 Fair Drive
Costa Mesa, CA 92626-9601
Fax: (714) 966-5471
E-mail: nichole.wike@vanguard.edu
Phone: (714) 556-3610

Vassar College
www.vassar.edu
Office of Admissions
Box 10, 124 Raymond Avenue
Poughkeepsie, NY 12604-0077
Fax: (845) 437-7063
E-mail: admissions@vassar.edu
Phone: (845) 437-7300

Vatterott College: Berkeley
www.vatterott-college.edu
8580 Evans Avenue
Berkeley, MO 63134
Fax: (314) 522-6174
E-mail: adm@vatterot-college.edu
Phone: (314) 264-1040

Vatterott College: Des Moines
www.vatterott-college.edu
7000 Fleur Drive
Des Moines, IA 50321
Fax: (515) 309-0366
E-mail: desmoines@vatterott-college.edu
Phone: (515) 309-9000

Vatterott College: Joplin
www.vatterott-college.com
809 Illinois Avenue
Joplin, MO 64801
Phone: (417) 781-5633

Vatterott College: Kansas City
www.vatterott-college.edu
8955 East 38th Terrace
Kansas City, MO 64129
Fax: (816) 861-1400
E-mail: kc@vatterott-college.edu
Phone: (816) 861-1000

Vatterott College: O'Fallon
www.vatterott-college.edu
3350 West Clay Street
St. Charles, MO 63301
Fax: (636) 978-5121
E-mail: ofallon@vatterott-college.edu
Phone: (636) 978-7488

Vatterott College: Oklahoma City
www.vatterott-college.com
4621 NW 23rd Street
Oklahoma City, OK 73127
Fax: (405) 945-0788
Phone: (405) 945-0088

Vatterott College: Quincy
www.vatterott-college.edu
3609 North Marx Drive
Quincy, IL 62305
Fax: (217) 223-6771
Phone: (217) 224-0600

Vatterott College: Sunset Hills
www.vatterott-college.com
12900 Maurer Industrial Drive
Sunset Hills, MO 63127
E-mail: jessalyn.mckeown@vatterott-college.com
Phone: (314) 843-4200

Vatterott College: Tulsa
www.vatterott-college.edu
4343 South 118th East Avenue
Tulsa, OK 74146
Fax: (918) 836-9698
E-mail: tulsa@vatterott-college.edu
Phone: (918) 835-8288

Vaughn College of Aeronautics and Technology
www.vaughn.edu
International Student Admissions
86-01 23rd Avenue
Flushing, NY 11369
Fax: (718) 779-2231
E-mail: celso.alvarez@vaughn.edu
Phone: (718) 429-6600 ext. 117

Ventura College
www.venturacollege.edu
Admissions & Records
4667 Telegraph Road
Ventura, CA 93003
Fax: (805) 654-6357
E-mail: sbricker@vcccd.edu
Phone: (805) 654-6457

Vet Tech Institute
www.vettechinstitute.edu
125 Seventh Street
Pittsburgh, PA 15222-3400
Fax: (412) 232-4348
E-mail: admissions@vettechinstitute.edu
Phone: (412) 391-7021

Victor Valley College
www.vvc.edu
Admissions and Records
18422 Bear Valley Road
Victorville, CA 92392-5850
Fax: (760) 843-7707
E-mail: millenb@vvc.edu
Phone: (760) 245-4271 ext. 2668

Victoria College
www.victoriacollege.edu
Admissions and Records Office
2200 East Red River
Victoria, TX 77901
Fax: (361) 582-2525
E-mail: registrar@victoriacollege.edu
Phone: (361) 572-6400

Victory University
www.victory.edu
Admissions
255 North Highland Street
Memphis, TN 38111-1375
Fax: (901) 320-9791
E-mail: sdunn@victory.edu
Phone: (800) 960-9777

Villa Maria College of Buffalo
www.villa.edu
Admissions
240 Pine Ridge Road
Buffalo, NY 14225-3999
Fax: (716) 896-0705
E-mail: admissions@villa.edu
Phone: (716) 896-0700 ext. 1870

Villanova University
www.villanova.edu
Admission
800 Lancaster Avenue
Villanova, PA 19085-1672
Fax: (610) 519-6450
E-mail: gotovu@villanova.edu
Phone: (610) 519-4000

Vincennes University
www.vinu.edu
Admissions
1002 North First Street
Vincennes, IN 47591
Fax: (812) 888-5707
E-mail: intstudent@vinu.edu
Phone: (812) 888-4313

Virginia College at Jackson
www.vc.edu
4795 Interstate 55 North
Jackson, MS 39206
Fax: (601) 977-2719
E-mail: mtlittle@vc.edu
Phone: (601) 977-0960

Virginia College Gulf Coast
www.vc.edu/gulfcoast/index.cfm
920 Cedar Lake Road
BIloxi, MS 39532
Phone: (228) 392-2994

Virginia Commonwealth University
www.vcu.edu
Office of International Admissions
Box 842526
821 West Franklin Street
Richmond, VA 23284-2526
Fax: (804) 828-1829
E-mail: bwbrown@vcu.edu
Phone: (804) 828-6016

Virginia Intermont College
www.vic.edu
Admissions Office
1013 Moore Street
Campus Box D-460
Bristol, VA 24201
Fax: (276) 466-7855
E-mail: viadmit@vic.edu
Phone: (276) 466-7892

Virginia Military Institute
www.vmi.edu
Admissions
VMI Office of Admissions
319 Letcher Avenue
Lexington, VA 24450-9967
Fax: (540) 464-7746
E-mail: admissions@vmi.edu
Phone: (540) 464-7211

Virginia Polytechnic Institute and State University
www.vt.edu
201 Burruss Hall
Blacksburg, VA 24061-0202
Fax: (540) 231-3242
E-mail: vtadmiss@vt.edu
Phone: (540) 231-6267

Virginia State University
www.vsu.edu
Orientation and Advisement
One Hayden Drive
PO Box 9018
Petersburg, VA 23806
Fax: (804) 524-5466
E-mail: fmarshall@vsu.edu
Phone: (804) 524-5562

Virginia Union University
www.vuu.edu
Office of Admissions
1500 North Lombardy Street
Richmond, VA 23220
Fax: (804) 342-3511
E-mail: admissions@vuu.edu
Phone: (804) 342-3571

Virginia University of Lynchburg
www.vul.edu
Registrar
2058 Garfield Avenue
Lynchburg, VA 24501-6417
Fax: (434) 528-2705
E-mail: dsmith@vul.edu
Phone: (434) 528-5276 ext. 102

Virginia Wesleyan College
www.vwc.edu
Admissions Office
1584 Wesleyan Drive
Norfolk, VA 23502-5599
Fax: (757) 461-5238
E-mail: admissions@vwc.edu
Phone: (757) 455-5717

Visible School - Music and Worship Arts College
www.visible.edu
1015 South Cooper Street
Memphis, TN 38104
Fax: (901) 377-0544
E-mail: seeyourself@visible.edu
Phone: (901) 377-2992

Vista College
www.vistacollege.edu
775 South 2000 East
Clearfield, UT 84015
Phone: (801) 774-9900

Viterbo University
www.viterbo.edu
Office of Global Education
900 Viterbo Drive
La Crosse, WI 54601-8804
Fax: (608) 796-3050
E-mail: globaled@viterbo.edu
Phone: (608) 796-3172

Volunteer State Community College
www.volstate.edu
Assistant Director of Records & Registration
1480 Nashville Pike
Gallatin, TN 37066
Fax: (615) 230-3645
E-mail: pam.carey@volstate.edu
Phone: (615) 452-8600 ext. 3558

Voorhees College
www.voorhees.edu
Office of Admissions
213 Wiggins Road
PO Box 678
Denmark, SC 29042
Fax: (803) 780-1444
E-mail: williej@voorhees.edu
Phone: (803) 780-1049

Wabash College
www.wabash.edu
Coordinator of International Admissions
PO Box 352
Crawfordsville, IN 47933
Fax: (765) 361-6437
E-mail: weaverl@wabash.edu
Phone: (765) 361-6254

Wade College
www.wadecollege.edu
Director of Financial Services
Dallas Market Center, PO Box 421149
Dallas, TX 75342
Fax: (214) 637-0827
E-mail: lhoover@wadecollege.edu
Phone: (214) 637-3530

Wagner College
www.wagner.edu
Admissions
One Campus Road
Pape Admissions Building
Staten Island, NY 10301-4495
Fax: (718) 390-3105
E-mail: kmuller@wagner.edu
Phone: (718) 390-3144

Wake Forest University
www.wfu.edu
Associate Director of Admissions
PO Box 7305
Winston-Salem, NC 27109-7305
Fax: (336) 758-3613
E-mail: admissions@wfu.edu
Phone: (336) 758-3614

Wake Technical Community College
www.waketech.edu
International Student Coordinator
9101 Fayetteville Road
Raleigh, NC 27603
Fax: (919) 661-0117
E-mail: pmsolomon@waketech.edu
Phone: (919) 866-5426

Walden University
www.waldenu.edu
Admissions
650 South Exeter Street, 8th Floor
Baltimore, MD 21202
E-mail: internationaladmissions@waldenu.edu
Phone: (800) 925-3368

Waldorf College
www.waldorf.edu
Admissions
106 South Sixth Street
Forest City, IA 50436-1713
Fax: (641) 585-8125
E-mail: international@waldorf.edu
Phone: (641) 585-8112

Walla Walla Community College
www.wwcc.edu
Admissions
500 Tausick Way
Walla Walla, WA 99362-9972
Fax: (509) 527-3661
E-mail: sally.wagoner@wwcc.edu
Phone: (509) 527-4283

Walla Walla University
www.wallawalla.edu
Admissions
204 South College Avenue
College Place, WA 99324-3000
Fax: (509) 527-2397
E-mail: dallas.weis@wallawalla.edu
Phone: (800) 541-8900 ext. 2608

Wallace State Community College at Hanceville
www.wallacestate.edu
PO Box 2000
Hanceville, AL 35077-2000
Fax: (256) 352-8228
Phone: (256) 352-8278

Walsh College of Accountancy and Business Administration
www.walshcollege.edu
Admissions and Academic Advising
PO Box 7006
Troy, MI 48007-7006
Fax: (248) 823-1611
E-mail: admissions@walshcollege.edu
Phone: (248) 823-1235

Walsh University
www.walsh.edu
Admissions
2020 East Maple Street
North Canton, OH 44720-3396
Fax: (330) 490-7165
E-mail: admissions@walsh.edu
Phone: (330) 490-7172

Walters State Community College
www.ws.edu
Enrollment Development
500 South Davy Crockett Parkway
Morristown, TN 37813-6899
Fax: (423) 585-6786
E-mail: sherry.watson@ws.edu
Phone: (423) 585-2691

Warner Pacific College
www.warnerpacific.edu
2219 SE 68th Avenue
Portland, OR 97215-4026
Fax: (503) 517-1352
E-mail: smackey@warnerpacific.edu
Phone: (503) 517-1024

Warner University
www.warner.edu
Admissions
13895 Highway 27
Lake Wales, FL 33859
Fax: (863) 638-7290
E-mail: jason.roe@warner.edu
Phone: (863) 638-7213

Warren Wilson College
www.warren-wilson.edu
Office of Admission
Box 9000
Asheville, NC 28815-9000
Fax: (828) 298-1440
E-mail: admit@warren-wilson.edu
Phone: (828) 771-2073

Wartburg College
www.wartburg.edu
Office of Admissions
100 Wartburg Boulevard, PO Box 1003
Waverly, IA 50677-0903
Fax: (319) 352-8579
E-mail: global.admissions@wartburg.edu
Phone: (319) 352-8511

Washburn University
www.washburn.edu
International Student Services
1700 SW College Avenue, Morgan 114
Topeka, KS 66621
Fax: (785) 670-1067
E-mail: heidi.staerkel@washburn.edu
Phone: (785) 670-2087

Washington & Jefferson College
www.washjeff.edu
Admission Office
60 South Lincoln Street
Washington, PA 15301
Fax: (724) 223-6534
E-mail: tlewisking@washjeff.edu
Phone: (724) 503-1001 ext. 2644

Washington Adventist University
www.cuc.edu
Associate Dean of Admissions
7600 Flower Avenue
Takoma Park, MD 20912
Fax: (301) 891-4230
E-mail: ejohn@wau.edu
Phone: (301) 891-4005

Washington and Lee University
www.wlu.edu
Admissions
204 West Washington Street
Lexington, VA 24450-2116
Fax: (540) 458-8062
E-mail: admissions@wlu.edu
Phone: (540) 458-8710

Washington Bible College
www.bible.edu
Admissions
6511 Princess Garden Parkway
Lanham, MD 20706-3599
Fax: (301) 552-2775
E-mail: iadmissions@bible.edu
Phone: (301) 552-1400 ext. 1208

Washington College
www.washcoll.edu
300 Washington Avenue
Chestertown, MD 21620-1197
Fax: (410) 778-7287
E-mail: tlittlefield2@washcoll.edu
Phone: (410) 778-7700

Washington County Community College
www.wccc.me.edu
Admissions
One College Drive
Calais, ME 04619
Fax: (207) 454-1092
E-mail: dmcgaw@wccc.me.edu
Phone: (207) 454-1000

Washington State University
www.wsu.edu
International Programs, Enrollment
370 Lighty Student Services Bldg
PO Box 641067
Pullman, WA 99164-1067
Fax: (509) 335-2373
E-mail: international@wsu.edu
Phone: (509) 335-4508

Washington University in St. Louis
www.wustl.edu
Office of Undergraduate Admissions
Campus Box 1089, One Brookings Drive
St. Louis, MO 63130-4899
Fax: (314) 935-4290
E-mail: admissions@wustl.edu
Phone: (314) 935-6000

Washtenaw Community College
www.wccnet.edu
Enrollment Services
4800 East Huron River Drive
Ann Arbor, MI 48105-4800
Fax: (734) 677-5414
E-mail: studrec@wccnet.org
Phone: (734) 973-3315

Watkins College of Art, Design & Film
www.watkins.edu
Admissions Office
2298 Rosa L. Parks Boulevard
Nashville, TN 37228
Fax: (615) 383-4849
E-mail: admissions@watkins.edu
Phone: (615) 383-4848 ext. 7458

Waycross College
www.waycross.edu
Admissions
2001 South Georgia Parkway
Waycross, GA 31503
Fax: (912) 449-7610
E-mail: rwing@waycross.edu
Phone: (912) 449-7600

Wayland Baptist University
www.wbu.edu
Admissions
1900 West Seventh Street, CMB #712
Plainview, TX 79072
Fax: (806) 291-1960
E-mail: admityou@wbu.edu
Phone: (806) 291-3500

Wayne County Community College
www.wcccd.edu
801 West Fort Street
Detroit, MI 48226
E-mail: oodegba1@wcccd.edu
Phone: (313) 496-2756

Wayne State College
www.wsc.edu
Admissions Office
1111 Main Street
Wayne, NE 68787
Fax: (402) 375-7204
E-mail: admit1@wsc.edu
Phone: (402) 375-7234

Wayne State University
www.wayne.edu
Office of Admissions
P.O. Box 02759
Detroit, MI 48202-0759
Fax: (313) 577-7536
E-mail: admissions@wayne.edu
Phone: (313) 577-3577

Waynesburg University
www.waynesburg.edu
Admission Counselor
51 West College Street
Waynesburg, PA 15370-1222
Fax: (724) 627-8124
E-mail: kwhite@waynesburg.edu
Phone: (724) 852-3216

Weatherford College
www.wc.edu
225 College Park Drive
Weatherford, TX 76086
Fax: (817) 598-6205
E-mail: lhines@wc.edu
Phone: (817) 598-6468

Webber International University
www.webber.edu
Admissions
1201 North Scenic Highway
PO Box 96
Babson Park, FL 33827-0096
Fax: (863) 638-1591
E-mail: mattisonmb@webber.edu
Phone: (863) 638-2910

Weber State University
www.weber.edu
Director of International Student Services
1137 University Circle
Ogden, UT 84408-1137
Fax: (801) 626-7693
E-mail: memami@weber.edu
Phone: (801) 626-7534

Webster University
www.webster.edu
International Recruitment and International
Services
470 East Lockwood Avenue
St. Louis, MO 63119-3194
Fax: (314) 968-7122
E-mail: intlstudy@webster.edu
Phone: (314) 968-7138

Wellesley College
www.wellesley.edu
Admissions Office
106 Central Street
Wellesley, MA 02481
Fax: (781) 283-3678
E-mail: mmareva@wellesley.edu
Phone: (781) 283-2270

Wells College
www.wells.edu
Admissions
170 Main Street
Aurora, NY 13026
Fax: (315) 364-3227
E-mail: admissions@wells.edu
Phone: (315) 364-3264

Wentworth Institute of Technology
www.wit.edu
Admissions Office
550 Huntington Avenue
Boston, MA 02115
Fax: (617) 989-4010
E-mail: hincheyr@wit.edu
Phone: (617) 989-4030

Wentworth Military Junior College
www.wma.edu/college
1880 Washington Avenue
Lexington, MO 64067-1799
Fax: (660) 259-3395
E-mail: admissions@wma1880.org
Phone: (660) 259-2221 ext. 517

Wesley College
www.wesley.edu
120 North State Street
Dover, DE 19901-3875
Fax: (302) 736-2301
E-mail: jacobsar@wesley.edu
Phone: (302) 736-2428

Wesleyan College
www.wesleyancollege.edu
Admissions
4760 Forsyth Road
Macon, GA 31210-4462
Fax: (478) 757-4030
E-mail: admission@wesleyancollege.edu
Phone: (478) 757-5206

Wesleyan University
www.wesleyan.edu
Office of Admission
70 Wyllys Avenue
Middletown, CT 06459-0260
Fax: (860) 685-3001
E-mail: toverton@wesleyan.edu
Phone: (860) 685-3000

West Chester University of Pennsylvania
www.wcupa.edu
Center for International Programs
Messikomer Hall
100 West Rosedale Avenue
West Chester, PA 19383
Fax: (610) 436-2436
E-mail: international@wcupa.edu
Phone: (610) 436-3515

West Coast University
www.westcoastuniversity.edu
12215 Victory Boulevard
North Hollywood, CA 91606
Phone: (877) 505-4928

West Hills College: Coalinga
www.westhillscollege.com
300 Cherry Lane
Coalinga, CA 93210
Fax: (559) 935-2788
E-mail: danieltamayo@whccd.edu
Phone: (559) 934-2432

West Hills College: Lemoore
www.westhillscollege.com/lemoore
Daniel Tamayo
555 College Avenue
Lemoore, CA 93245
Fax: (559) 925-3837
E-mail: danieltamayo@whccd.edu
Phone: (559) 934-2000 ext. 2432

West Liberty University
www.westliberty.edu
PO Box 295
West Liberty, WV 26074-0295
Fax: (304) 336-8403
E-mail: admissions@westliberty.edu
Phone: (304) 336-8076

West Los Angeles College
www.wlac.edu
Dean
9000 Overland Avenue
Culver City, CA 90230
Fax: (310) 287-4327
E-mail: IchonE@wlac.edu
Phone: (310) 287-4305

West Tennessee Business College
www.wtbc.edu
1186 Highway 45 Bypass
Jackson, TN 38301
E-mail: ann.record@wtbc.edu
Phone: (731) 668-7240

West Texas A&M University
www.wtamu.edu
International Student Office
2501 Fourth Avenue, WTAMU Box 60907
Canyon, TX 79016-0001
Fax: (806) 651-2071
E-mail: kcombs@mail.wtamu.edu
Phone: (806) 651-2073

West Valley College
www.westvalley.edu
Counseling Center - Foreign Student Adviser
14000 Fruitvale Avenue
Saratoga, CA 95070-5698
Fax: (408) 867-5033
E-mail: Sara_Patterson@wvm.edu
Phone: (408) 741-2009

West Virginia Junior College: Bridgeport
www.wvjcinfo.net
Director of Admissions
176 Thompson Drive
Bridgeport, WV 26330
Fax: (304) 842-8191
E-mail: dwebster@wvjcinfo.net
Phone: (304) 842-4007 ext. 110

West Virginia Northern Community College
www.wvncc.edu
Dean of Enrollments Management
1704 Market Street
Wheeling, WV 26003
Fax: (304) 232-8187
E-mail: jfike@northern.wvnet.edu
Phone: (304) 233-5900 ext. 4363

West Virginia State University
www.wvstateu.edu
Office of Admissions
Campus Box 197
PO Box 1000
Institute, WV 25112-1000
Fax: (304) 766-5182
E-mail: sweeneyt@wvstateu.edu
Phone: (304) 766-4345

West Virginia University
www.wvu.edu
International Admissions
Admissions and Records Office
PO Box 6009
Morgantown, WV 26506-6009
Fax: (304) 293-8832
E-mail: internationaladmissions@mail.wvu.edu
Phone: (304) 293-2124

West Virginia University at Parkersburg
www.wvup.edu
Enrollment Management
300 Campus Drive
Parkersburg, WV 26104-8647
Fax: (304) 424-8332
E-mail: Christine.Post@mail.wvu.edu
Phone: (304) 424-8221

West Virginia University Institute of Technology
www.wvutech.edu
Director of Admissions & Recruiting
405 Fayette Pike
Montgomery, WV 25136-2436
Fax: (304) 442-3097
E-mail: tech-admissions@mail.wvu.edu
Phone: (304) 442-3146

West Virginia Wesleyan College
www.wvwc.edu
Admission
59 College Avenue
Buckhannon, WV 26201-2998
Fax: (304) 473-8108
E-mail: admission@wvwc.edu
Phone: (304) 473-8510

Westchester Community College
www.sunywcc.edu
International and Immigrant Student Affairs
75 Grasslands Road
Valhalla, NY 10595
Fax: (914) 606-5629
E-mail: Anne.Verini@sunywcc.edu
Phone: (914) 606-8567

Western Carolina University
www.wcu.edu
International Programs and Services
102 Camp Building
Cullowhee, NC 28723
Fax: (828) 227-7080
E-mail: lmwaniki@email.wcu.edu
Phone: (828) 227-7494

Western Illinois University
www.wiu.edu
International Programs
One University Circle
115 Sherman Hall
Macomb, IL 61455-1390
Fax: (309) 298-2245
E-mail: international-ed@wiu.edu
Phone: (309) 298-2426

Western International University
www.west.edu
Associate Director of Admissions
9215 North Black Canyon Highway
Phoenix, AZ 85021-2718
Fax: (602) 944-1831
E-mail: susan.caldwell@west.edu
Phone: (602) 429-1081

Western Iowa Tech Community College
www.witcc.com
Enrollment Services
Box 5199
Sioux City, IA 51102-5199
Fax: (712) 274-6412
E-mail: rogers_pitts254@witcc.edu
Phone: (712) 274-8733 ext. 3236

Western Kentucky University
www.wku.edu
Assistant Director of International Student & Scholar Services
1906 College Heights Boulevard
Bowling Green, KY 42101
Fax: (270) 745-6144
E-mail: isss@wku.edu
Phone: (270) 745-4857

Western Michigan University
www.wmich.edu
International Services and Student Affairs
1903 West Michigan Avenue
Kalamazoo, MI 49008-5211
Fax: (269) 387-5899
E-mail: rebecca.solomon@wmich.edu
Phone: (269) 387-5876

Western Nebraska Community College
www.wncc.edu
Registrar
1601 East 27th Street
Scottsbluff, NE 69361
Fax: (308) 635-6732
E-mail: rhovey@wncc.edu
Phone: (308) 635-6013

Western Nevada College
www.wnc.edu
Admission and Records
2201 West College Parkway
Carson City, NV 89703-7399
Fax: (775) 887-3147
E-mail: dianne@wnc.nevada.edu
Phone: (775) 445-3288

Western New England College
www.wnec.edu
Admissions
1215 Wilbraham Road
Springfield, MA 01119-2684
Fax: (413) 782-1777
E-mail: ugradmis@wnec.edu
Phone: (413) 782-1321

Western Oklahoma State College
www.wosc.edu
2801 North Main Street
Altus, OK 73521
Fax: (580) 477-7723
E-mail: lana.scott@wosc.edu
Phone: (580) 477-7720

Western Oregon University
www.wou.edu
International Students and Scholar Affairs
345 North Monmouth Avenue
Monmouth, OR 97361
Fax: (503) 838-8067
E-mail: yangn@wou.edu
Phone: (503) 838-8590

Western State College of Colorado
www.western.edu
International Student Programs
600 North Adams Street
Gunnison, CO 81231
Fax: (970) 943-2212
E-mail: bsamter@western.edu
Phone: (970) 943-2176

Western Technical College
www.westerntech.edu
9624 Plaza Circle
El Paso, TX 79927
Phone: (915) 532-3737

Western Technical College
www.westerntc.edu
Counseling Center
PO Box 908
La Crosse, WI 54602-0908
Fax: (608) 785-9094
E-mail: wellsj@westerntc.edu
Phone: (608) 785-9575

Western Technical College: Diana Drive
www.westerntech.edu
9451 Diana Drive
El Paso, TX 79924
Phone: (915) 566-9621

Western Texas College
www.wtc.edu
International Studies
6200 College Avenue
Snyder, TX 79549
Fax: (325) 573-9321
E-mail: jsentell@wtc.edu
Phone: (325) 574-7650

Western Washington University
www.wwu.edu
Office of Admissions
516 High Street
Bellingham, WA 98225-9009
Fax: (360) 650-7369
E-mail: admit@wwu.edu
Phone: (360) 650-3440

Western Wyoming Community College
www.wwcc.wy.edu
Admissions
Box 428
Rock Springs, WY 82902-0428
Fax: (307) 382-1636
E-mail: admissions@wwcc.wy.edu
Phone: (307) 382-1647

Westfield State University
www.wsc.ma.edu
Office of Admission
577 Western Avenue
PO Box 1630
Westfield, MA 01086-1630
Fax: (413) 572-0520
E-mail: internationaladmission@wsc.ma.edu
Phone: (413) 572-5218

Westminster College
www.westminster-mo.edu
Office of Off-Campus and International
Programs
501 Westminster Avenue
Fulton, MO 65251-1299
Fax: (573) 592-5255
E-mail: pat.kirby@westminster-mo.edu
Phone: (573) 592-5147

Westminster College
www.westminstercollege.edu
Admissions Office
1840 South 1300 East
Salt Lake City, UT 84105
Fax: (801) 832-3101
E-mail: admission@westminstercollege.edu
Phone: (801) 832-2200

Westmont College
www.westmont.edu
Assistant to the Dean of Admission/
International Student Advisor
955 La Paz Road
Santa Barbara, CA 93108-1089
Fax: (805) 565-6234
E-mail: slyon@westmont.edu
Phone: (805) 565-6226

Westwood College: Anaheim
www.westwood.edu
International Admissions
1551 South Douglass Road
Anaheim, CA 92806
E-mail: smccloskey@westwood.edu
Phone: (303) 930-2516

Westwood College: Annandale
www.westwood.edu
7619 Little River Turnpike, Suite 500
Annandale, VA 22003
Phone: (703) 642-3770

Westwood College: Arlington Ballston
www.westwood.edu
7619 Litlle River Turnpike, Suite 500
Arlington, VA 22203
Phone: (703) 243-3900

Westwood College: Chicago Loop
International Admissions
17 North State Street, Third Floor
Chicago, IL 60602
Fax: (312) 739-1004
E-mail: smccloskey@westwood.edu
Phone: (303) 930-2516

Westwood College: Dallas
www.westwood.edu/locations/texas/dallas-
campus
International Admissions
8390 LBJ Freeway
Dallas, TX 75243
E-mail: smccloskey@westwood.edu
Phone: (303) 930-2516

Westwood College: Denver North
www.westwood.edu/locations/colorado/denver-
north-campus
International Admissions
7350 North Broadway
Denver, CO 80221
Fax: (303) 487-0214
E-mail: smccloskey@westwood.edu
Phone: (303) 930-2516

Westwood College: Denver South
www.westwood.edu/locations/colorado/denver-
south-campus
International Admissions
3150 South Sheridan Boulevard
Denver, CO 80227-5507
Fax: (303) 934-2583
E-mail: smccloskey@westwood.edu
Phone: (303) 930-2516

Westwood College: DuPage
www.westwood.edu
International Admissions
7155 Janes Avenue
Woodridge, IL 60517
Fax: (630) 743-0667
E-mail: smccloskey@westwood.edu
Phone: (303) 930-2516

Westwood College: Houston South
www.westwood.edu
International Admissions
7322 Southwest Freeway
One Arena Place, Suite 110
Houston, TX 77074
Fax: (713) 219-2088
E-mail: smccloskey@westwood.edu
Phone: (303) 930-2516

Westwood College: Los Angeles
www.westwood.edu/locations/california/los-
angeles-campus
International Admissions
3250 Wilshire Boulevard, Suite 400
Los Angeles, CA 90010
E-mail: smccloskey@westwood.edu
Phone: (303) 930-2516

Westwood College: Northlake
www.westwood.edu
International Admissions
2220 Parklake Drive, Suite 175
Atlanta, GA 30345
E-mail: smccloskey@westwood.edu
Phone: (303) 930-2516

Westwood College: O'Hare Airport
www.westwood.edu
International Admissions
8501 West Higgins Road
Suite 100
Chicago, IL 60631
Fax: (773) 714-0828
E-mail: smccloskey@westwood.edu
Phone: (303) 930-2516

Westwood College: Online
www.westwood.edu
10249 Church Ranch Way
Broomfield, CO 80021
Phone: (800) 281-2978

Westwood College: River Oaks
www.westwood.edu
International Admissions
80 River Oaks Center Drive, Suite D-49
Calumet City, IL 60409-5802
E-mail: smccloskey@westwood.edu
Phone: (303) 930-2516

Westwood College: South Bay
www.westwood.edu
International Admissions
19700 South Vermont Avenue #100
Torrance, CA 90502
Fax: (310) 516-8232
E-mail: smccloskey@westwood.edu
Phone: (303) 930-2516

Wharton County Junior College
www.wcjc.edu
Admissions Office
911 Boling Highway
Wharton, TX 77488-0080
Fax: (979) 532-6494
E-mail: maryanng@wcjc.edu
Phone: (979) 532-6454

Whatcom Community College
www.whatcom.ctc.edu
International Programs Office
237 West Kellogg Road
Bellingham, WA 98226
Fax: (360) 752-6767
E-mail: ied@whatcom.ctc.edu
Phone: (360) 676-2170 ext. 3910

Wheaton College
www.wheaton.edu
Undergraduate Admissions
501 College Avenue
Wheaton, IL 60187-5593
Fax: (630) 752-5285
E-mail: becky.wilson@wheaton.edu
Phone: (630) 752-5011

Wheaton College
www.wheatoncollege.edu
Office of Admission
26 East Main Street
Norton, MA 02766
Fax: (508) 286-8271
E-mail: admission@wheatoncollege.edu
Phone: (508) 286-8251

Wheeling Jesuit University
www.wju.edu
International Student Advisor's Office
316 Washington Avenue
Wheeling, WV 26003-6295
Fax: (304) 243-2243
E-mail: eileenv@wju.edu
Phone: (800) 624-6992 ext. 2346

Wheelock College
www.wheelock.edu
Office of Admission
200 The Riverway
Boston, MA 02215-4176
Fax: (617) 879-2449
E-mail: undergrad@wheelock.edu
Phone: (617) 879-2206

**White Earth Tribal and Community
College**
www.wetcc.org
202 South Main Street
PO Box 478
Mahnomen, MN 56557
E-mail: molson@wetcc.org
Phone: (218) 936-5731

White Mountains Community College
www.wmcc.edu
Admissions
2020 Riverside Drive
Berlin, NH 03570
Fax: (603) 752-6335
E-mail: mlaflamme@ccsnh.edu
Phone: (603) 752-1113 ext. 3005

Whitman College
www.whitman.edu
Admission
345 Boyer Avenue
Walla Walla, WA 99362-2046
Fax: (509) 527-4967
E-mail: thatchac@whitman.edu
Phone: (509) 527-5176

Whittier College
www.whittier.edu
Admissions
13406 East Philadelphia Street
Box 634
Whittier, CA 90608-0634
Fax: (562) 907-4870
E-mail: dfoy@whittier.edu
Phone: (562) 907-4238

Whitworth University
www.whitworth.edu
Undergraduate Admissions
300 West Hawthorne Road
Spokane, WA 99251-0002
Fax: (509) 466-3758
E-mail: hdonkor@whitworth.edu
Phone: (509) 777-4571

Wichita Area Technical College
www.watc.edu
4004 North Webb Road, Suite 100
Wichita, KS 67226
E-mail: info@watc.edu

Wichita State University
www.wichita.edu
Office of International Education
1845 Fairmount, Box 124
Wichita, KS 67260-0124
Fax: (316) 978-3777
E-mail: international@wichita.edu
Phone: (316) 978-3232

Widener University
www.widener.edu
Office of Admissions
One University Place
Chester, PA 19013
Fax: (610) 499-4676
E-mail: eshyde@widener.edu
Phone: (610) 499-4595

Wilberforce University
www.wilberforce.edu
Academic Affairs
1055 North Bickett Road
PO Box 1001
Wilberforce, OH 45384-1001
Fax: (937) 376-4751
E-mail: admissions@wilberforce.edu
Phone: (937) 708-5705

Wiley College
www.wileyc.edu
711 Wiley Avenue
Marshall, TX 75670
Fax: (903) 927-3366
E-mail: smasenda@wileyc.edu
Phone: (903) 927-3242 ext. 3242

Wilkes Community College
www.wilkescc.edu
1328 South Collegiate Drive
PO Box 120
Wilkesboro, NC 28697-0120
Fax: (336) 838-6547
E-mail: mac.warren@wilkescc.edu
Phone: (336) 838-6135

Willamette University
www.willamette.edu
Office of Admission
900 State Street
Salem, OR 97301-3922
Fax: (503) 375-5363
E-mail: thudkins@willamette.edu
Phone: (503) 370-6303

William Carey University
www.wmcarey.edu
Admissions
498 Tuscan Avenue
WCC Box 13
Hattiesburg, MS 39401
Fax: (601) 318-6765
E-mail: etoledo@wmcarey.edu
Phone: (601) 318-6103 ext. 564

William Jessup University
www.jessup.edu
Director of Admission
333 Sunset Boulevard
Rocklin, CA 95765
Fax: (916) 577-2220
E-mail: admissions@jessup.edu
Phone: (916) 577-2222

William Jewell College
www.jewell.edu
Office of Admission
500 College Hill
Liberty, MO 64068
Fax: (816) 415-5040
E-mail: grovesj@william.jewell.edu
Phone: (816) 415-7502

William Paterson University of New Jersey
www.wpunj.edu
Admissions
300 Pompton Road
Wayne, NJ 07470
Fax: (973) 720-2910
E-mail: admissions@wpunj.edu
Phone: (973) 720-2763

William Penn University
www.wmpenn.edu
Admissions Office
201 Trueblood Avenue
Oskaloosa, IA 52577
Fax: (641) 673-2113
E-mail: strongk@wmpenn.edu
Phone: (641) 673-1012

William Woods University
www.williamwoods.edu
Office of Enrollment Services
One University Avenue
Fulton, MO 65251-2388
Fax: (573) 592-1146
E-mail: admissions@williamwoods.edu
Phone: (573) 592-4221

Williams Baptist College
www.wbcoll.edu
Admissions
PO Box 3665
Walnut Ridge, AR 72476
Fax: (870) 886-3924
E-mail: admissions@wbcoll.edu
Phone: (870) 759-4120

Williams College
www.williams.edu
Admissions Office
33 Stetson Court
Williamstown, MA 01267
Fax: (413) 597-4052
E-mail: admission@williams.edu
Phone: (413) 597-2211

Williamson Christian College
www.williamsoncc.edu
200 Seaboard Lane
Franklin, TN 37067
Fax: (615) 771-7810
E-mail: mkelley@williamsoncc.edu
Phone: (615) 771-7821

Williston State College
www.willistonstate.edu
Admission and Records Office
1410 University Avenue
Williston, ND 58801
Fax: (701) 774-4211
E-mail: Lacey.Madison@wsc.nodak.edu
Phone: (701) 774-4585

Wilmington College
www.wilmington.edu
Student Life
Box 1325 Pyle Center
Wilmington, OH 45177
Fax: (937) 382-7077
E-mail: mark_denniston@wilmington.edu
Phone: (937) 382-6661 ext. 264

Wilson College
www.wilson.edu
Admissions
1015 Philadelphia Avenue
Chambersburg, PA 17201-1285
Fax: (717) 262-2546
E-mail: lbrittain@wilson.edu
Phone: (717) 262-2002

Wilson Community College
www.wilsoncc.edu
Student Services
Box 4305
902 Herring Avenue
Wilson, NC 27893-0305
Fax: (252) 246-1384
E-mail: jebison@wilsontech.edu
Phone: (252) 246-1230

Wingate University
www.wingate.edu
Admissions Counselor
Campus Box 3059
Wingate, NC 28174-0157
Fax: (704) 233-8110
E-mail: nick@wingate.edu
Phone: (704) 233-8206

Winona State University
www.winona.edu
Director of International Students
Office of Admissions
PO Box 5838
Winona, MN 55987
Fax: (507) 457-5620
E-mail: jskranka@winona.edu
Phone: (507) 457-5303

Winston-Salem State University
www.wssu.edu
International Student Affairs
601 Martin Luther King Jr Drive
PO Box 19413
Winston-Salem, NC 27110
Fax: (336) 750-2079
E-mail: admissions@wssu.edu
Phone: (336) 750-2306

Winthrop University
www.winthrop.edu
701 Oakland Avenue
Office of Admissions
Rock Hill, SC 29733
Fax: (803) 323-2340
E-mail: edwardsa@winthrop.edu
Phone: (803) 323-2133

Wiregrass Georgia Technical College
www.wiregrass.edu
4089 Val Tech Road
Valdosta, GA 31602
E-mail: admissions@wiregrass.edu
Phone: (229) 259-5195

Wisconsin Indianhead Technical College
www.witc.edu
Registrar
505 Pine Ridge Drive
Shell Lake, WI 54871
Fax: (715) 468-2819
E-mail: shane.evenson@witc.edu
Phone: (715) 468-2815 ext. 2280

Wisconsin Lutheran College
www.wlc.edu
Center for International Education
8800 West Bluemound Road
Milwaukee, WI 53226-4699
Fax: (414) 443-8535
E-mail: cie@wlc.edu
Phone: (414) 443-8551

Wittenberg University
www.wittenberg.edu
Admission Office
Ward Street and North Wittenberg
PO Box 720
Springfield, OH 45501-0720
Fax: (937) 327-6379
E-mail: admission@wittenberg.edu
Phone: (877) 206-0332

Wofford College
www.wofford.edu
Admission
429 North Church Street
Spartanburg, SC 29303-3663
Fax: (864) 597-4147
E-mail: admission@wofford.edu
Phone: (864) 597-4130

Wood Tobe-Coburn School
www.woodtobecoburn.edu
8 East 40th Street
New York, NY 10016-0190
Fax: (212) 686-9171
Phone: (212) 686-9040

Woodbury University
www.woodbury.edu
Admissions
7500 Glenoaks Boulevard
Burbank, CA 91510-7846
Fax: (818) 767-7520
E-mail: admissions@woodbury.edu
Phone: (800) 784-9663

Worcester Polytechnic Institute
www.wpi.edu
Admissions
100 Institute Road
Worcester, MA 01609-2280
Fax: (508) 831-5875
E-mail: intl_admissions@wpi.edu
Phone: (508) 831-5286

Worcester State University
www.worcester.edu
Associate Director of Admissions
Office of Undergraduate Admission
486 Chandler Street
Worcester, MA 01602-2597
Fax: (508) 929-8183
E-mail: sara.grady@worcester.edu
Phone: (508) 929-8040

World College
www.cie-wc.edu
Lake Shore Plaza, 5193 Shore Drive
Suite 105
Virginia Beach, VA 23455-2500
E-mail: instruct@cie-wc.edu
Phone: (800) 696-7532

World Mission University
www.wmu.edu
Admissions Department
500 Shatto Place
Los Angeles, CA 90020
Fax: (213) 385-2332
E-mail: wmuoffice@gmail.com
Phone: (213) 385-2322

Wright State University
www.wright.edu
University Center for International Education
3640 Colonel Glenn Highway
Dayton, OH 45435
Fax: (937) 775-5776
E-mail: claudia.espinoza@wright.edu
Phone: (937) 775-5745

Wright State University: Lake Campus
www.wright.edu/lake
University Center for International Education
7600 State Route 703
Celina, OH 45822-2952
Fax: (937) 775-5776
E-mail: claudia.espinoza@wright.edu
Phone: (937) 775-5745

WyoTech: Blairsville
www.wyotech.edu
500 Innovation Drive
Blairsville, PA 15717
Fax: (724) 459-6499
E-mail: whauser@wyotechstaff.edu
Phone: (724) 459-9500

WyoTech: Fremont
www.wyotech.edu
200 Whitney Place
Fremont, CA 94539
Fax: (510) 490-8599
Phone: (510) 490-6900

WyoTech: Laramie
www.wyotech.edu
Admissions
4373 North Third Street
Laramie, WY 82072
Fax: (307) 742-4354
E-mail: admissions@wyotech.com
Phone: (307) 742-3776

WyoTech: Long Beach
www.wyotech.edu/campus/long_beach
2161 Technology Place
Long Beach, CA 90810
Fax: (562) 437-8111
Phone: (562) 624-9530

WyoTech: Sacramento
www.wyotech.edu
980 Riverside Parkway
West Sacramento, CA 95605
E-mail: scoffee@wyotechstaff.edu
Phone: (916) 376-8888

Xavier University
www.xavier.edu
Undergraduate Admission for ESL and
Undergraduate Programs
3800 Victory Parkway
Cincinnati, OH 45207-5311
Fax: (513) 745-4319
E-mail: goodloe@xavier.edu
Phone: (513) 745-3163

Xavier University of Louisiana
www.xula.edu
Dean of Admissions
1 Drexel Drive
New Orleans, LA 70125-1098
Fax: (504) 520-7920
E-mail: wbrown@xula.edu
Phone: (504) 520-7587

Yakima Valley Community College
www.yvcc.edu
Manager, Housing and International Students
PO Box 22520
Yakima, WA 98907-2520
Fax: (509) 574-4882
E-mail: bmugleston@yvcc.edu
Phone: (509) 574-4880

Yale University
www.yale.edu
International Admissions
Box 208234
New Haven, CT 06520-8234
Fax: (203) 432-9392
E-mail: student.questions@yale.edu
Phone: (203) 432-9300

Yavapai College
www.yc.edu
Registration
1100 East Sheldon Street
Prescott, AZ 86301
Fax: (928) 776-2151
E-mail: Marianne.Doyle@yc.edu
Phone: (928) 776-2144

Yeshiva and Kolel Bais Medrash Elyon
73 Main Street
Monsey, NY 10952
Phone: (845) 356-7064

Yeshiva and Kollel Harbotzas Torah
1049 East 15th Street
Brooklyn, NY 11230
Phone: (718) 692-0208

Yeshiva Derech Chaim
1573 39th Street
Brooklyn, NY 11218
Phone: (718) 438-3070

Yeshiva D'Monsey Rabbinical College
2 Roman Boulevard
Monsey, NY 10952
Phone: (845) 352-5852

Yeshiva Gedolah Imrei Yosef D'Spinka
1466 56th Street
Brooklyn, NY 11219
Phone: (718) 851-1600

Yeshiva Gedolah Zichron Moshe
84 Laurel Park Road
Box 580
South Fallsburg, NY 12779
Fax: (845) 434-1009
Phone: (845) 434-5240

Yeshiva Karlin Stolin
1818 54th Street
Brooklyn, NY 11204-1545
Phone: (718) 232-7800

Yeshiva of Nitra
Pine Bridge Road
Mount Kisco, NY 10549
Phone: (718) 387-0422

Yeshiva of the Telshe Alumni
4904 Independence Avenue
Riverdale, NY 10471
Phone: (718) 601-3523

Yeshiva Shaar Hatorah
117-06 84th Avenue
Kew Gardens, NY 11418
Phone: (718) 846-1940

Yeshiva Shaarei Torah of Rockland
91 West Carlton Road
Suffern, NY 10901
Phone: (845) 352-3431

Yeshivas Novominsk
1569 47th Street
Brooklyn, NY 11219
Phone: (718) 438-2727

Yeshivat Mikdash Melech
www.mikdashmelech.net
1326 Ocean Parkway
Brooklyn, NY 11230
Fax: (718) 998-9321
E-mail: mikdashmelech@verizon.net
Phone: (718) 339-1090

Yeshivath Viznitz
25 Phyllis Terrace
Monsey, NY 10952
Phone: (914) 356-1010

York College
www.york.edu
1125 East 8th Street
York, NE 68467
Fax: (402) 363-5623
E-mail: willie.sanchez@york.edu
Phone: (402) 363-5620

York College of Pennsylvania
www.ycp.edu
Admissions
441 Country Club Road
York, PA 17403-3651
Fax: (717) 849-1607
E-mail: iramirez@ycp.edu
Phone: (717) 815-1786

York County Community College
www.yccc.edu
Director of Admissions
112 College Drive
Wells, ME 04090
Fax: (207) 641-0837
E-mail: fquistgard@yccc.edu
Phone: (207) 646-9282

Young Harris College
www.yhc.edu
Admissions
PO Box 116
Young Harris, GA 30582-0116
Fax: (706) 379-3108
E-mail: tgibson@yhc.edu
Phone: (706) 379-3111 ext. 5176

Youngstown State University
www.ysu.edu
International Undergraduate Admissions
One University Plaza
Youngstown, OH 44555-0001
Fax: (330) 941-2338
E-mail: jcdavis05@ysu.edu
Phone: (330) 941-2336

YTI Career Institute: Altoona
www.yti.edu
2900 Fairway Drive
Altoona, PA 16602
E-mail: altoonaadmission@yti.edu
Phone: (814) 944-5643

YTI Career Institute: Capital Region
www.yti.edu
401 East Winding Hill Road, Suite 100
Mechanicsburg, PA 17055
Phone: (800) 338-8037

YTI Career Institute: Lancaster
www.yti.edu
3050 Hempland Road
Lancaster, PA 17601
Fax: (717) 295-1135
E-mail: thomas.driscoll@yti.edu
Phone: (717) 295-1100

Yuba Community College District
www.yccd.edu
Director, Admissions and Enrollment Services
2088 North Beale Road
Marysville, CA 95901
Fax: (530) 741-6872
E-mail: kmagnuso@yccd.edu
Phone: (530) 741-6989

Zion Bible College
www.zbc.edu
Admissions Office
320 South Main Street
Haverhill, MA 01835
Fax: (978) 478-3406
E-mail: admissions@zbc.edu
Phone: (978) 478-3400 ext. 3432

EducationUSA Advising Centers

Afghanistan

Kabul
Public Affairs Section, US Embassy
EducationUSA Afghanistan
The Great Massoud Road
Kabul 24000, Afghanistan
Tel: 93-799-608-776
E-mail: MujaddediMA@state.gov
Web: //kabul.usembassy.gov/educational_
  exchange.html

Albania

Tirana
EducationUSA Advising Center
US Embassy
Rruga e Elbasanit No. 103
Tirana, Albania
Tel: 355-4-269 955
E-mail: acie_albania@yahoo.com
Web: //tirana.usembassy.gov/education_
  exchange.html

Algeria

Algiers
US Embassy Public Affairs Section
Educational Advising Center
4 Chemin Cheikh Bachir Ibrahimi
Algiers 16035, Algeria
Tel: 213-770-082-000 ext.4294
E-mail: algiers@educationusa.info
Web: //algiers.usembassy.gov/ edu_training.
  html

Angola

Luanda
Educational Advising Center
US Embassy Public Affairs Section
Rua Houari Boumedienne, 32, Miramar
Luanda 6484, Angola
Tel: 244-222-641122; 445727
E-mail: Luandapas1@yahoo.com
Web: //angola.usembassy.gov/study_usa.
  html

Anguilla, British West Indies

The Valley
Anguilla Library Service
Schools Librarian
The Valley
Anguilla, British West Indies
Tel: 264-497-2441
E-mail: meadsbayqueen@yahoo.com

Argentina

Buenos Aires
ICANA-Instituto Cultural
Argentino Norteamericano
Centro de Asesoria Estudiantil
EducationUSA
Maipu 672
Buenos Aires C1006ACH
Argentina
Tel: 54-351-423-6396
E-mail: advising@icana.org.ar;spalmer@
  icana.org.ar
Web: www.icana.org.ar

Buenos Aires
Fulbright Commission
Educational Adviser
Viamonte 1653, 2 piso
Buenos Aires C1055ABE
Argentina
Tel: 54-11-4814-3561
E-mail: info@fulbright.com.ar
Web: www.fulbright.edu.ar/eng/servicios_4.
  asp

Cordoba
Instituto de Intercambio Cultural
Argentino Norteamericano
IICANA Dept de Orientacion Educacional
Dean Funes 454
Cordoba 5000, Argentina
Tel: 54-351-4236396
E-mail: iicanaeduusa@fibertel.com.ar
Web: www.iicana.org/asesoria.html

Mendoza
Asociacion Mendocina de Intercambio
  Cultural
Argentino Norteamericano (AMICANA)
Chile 987
Mendoza 5500, Argentina
Tel: 54-261-4236271
E-mail: aeducacional@amicana.com
Web: www.amicana.com

Rosario
Asociacion Rosarina de Intercambio
  Cultural
Argentino Norteamericano (ARICANA)
Buenos Aires 934
Rosario S2000, Argentina
Tel: 54-341-4217664
E-mail: advising@aricanabnc.com.ar
Web: www.aricanabnc.com.ar/
  contenidos/2008/03/19/Editorial_2590.
  html

Salta
Instituto Salteno de Intercambio
Cultural Argentino-Norteamericano
(ISICANA)
Santiago del Estero 865
Salta 4400, Argentina
Tel: 54-387-431-4040
E-mail: isicana-dir@arnet.com.ar
Web: www.isicana.org.ar/eng/servicios.aspx

Santa Fe
ALICANA Santa Fe
San Martin 2293
Santa Fe 3000, Argentina
Tel: 54-34-2453-7597
E-mail: alicana@arnet.com.ar

Tucuman
Asociacion Tucumana de Intercambio
  Cultural Argentino-Norteamericano
  (ATICANA)
Avda. Salta no. 581
Tucuman 4000, Argentina
Tel: 54-381-303070
E-mail: aticana@arnet.com.ar
Web: www.aticana.com

Ushuaia
USHICANA Ushuaia
Roca 470
Ushuaia, Argentina
Tel: 54-2901-1560-4660
E-mail: vivian@impsat1.com.ar

Armenia

Yerevan
Yerevan ACIE Educational Advising Center
American Councils
Baghramyan Ave. 1, Apt.1
Yerevan 0019, Armenia
Tel: 374-10-54-40-12; 54-40-15
E-mail: gayane@americancouncils.am
Web: www.americancouncils.am

Australia

Barton ACT (Canberra)
EducationUSA Center
US Embassy Public Affairs Section
National Press Club Building
16 National Circuit
Barton ACT 2606, Australia
Tel: 61-2-6214-5766
Web: //canberra.usembassy.gov

Melbourne VIC
EducationUSA Center
U.S. Consulate General General Level 6/553
   St. Kilda Road
Melbourne VIC 3004, Australia
Tel: 61-3-9526-5966
E-mail: melbourne@educationusa.info
Web: // www.educationusa.info/melbourne

Perth WA
EducationUSA Perth
U.S. Consulate General
16 St. Georges Terrace, 4th FL
Perth WA 6000, Australia
Tel: 61-8-9225-6839
E-mail: edusaperth@gmail.com;
   perth@educationusa.info
Web: //canberra.usembassy.gov/studying_
   intheusa.html

Sydney NSW
EducationUSA Advising Center,
US Consulate General
Level 59, MLC Center
19-29 Martin Place
Sydney NSW 2000, Australia
Tel: 61-2-9373-9230
E-mail: sydney@educationusa.info
Web: //sydney.usconsulate.gov/sydney/
   student.html

Austria

Vienna (Wien)
Centre International Universitaire
EducationUSA Adviser
Schottengasse 1, Mezzanin
Vienna 1010, Austria
Tel: 43-1-533 65 33
E-mail: advising@ciu.at
Web: www.ciu.at

Vienna (Wien)
Austrian-American Educational
Commission (Fulbright)
quartier21/MQ
Museumsplatz 1
Vienna 1070, Austria
Tel: 43-1-236 7878 0
E-mail: Aenzi@fulbright.at
Web: www.fulbright.at/austrians/beratung_
   intro.php

Azerbaijan

Baku
Baku Education Information
Center - BEIC
71 Alovsat Guliyev str.
Baku AZ 1009, Azerbaijan
Tel: 994-12-448-28-45
E-mail: bhaji-zada@beic.az
Web: www.beic.az

Ganja
Ganja Education Information Center
Mirali Gashgay 10
Ganja AZE 2000, Azerbaijan
Tel: 994-22-563025
E-mail: hhuseynli@geic.osi-az.org
Web: www.gitc.aznet.org

Sumgait
Sumgait Education Information Center
Kosmos Maishet Evi, 1st floor
3d microdistrict
Sumgait AZE 5006, Azerbaijan
Tel: 994-12-448 28 45
E-mail: sevamamedova@hotmail.com

Bahrain

Manama
US Embassy Public Affairs Section
Bldg 979, Road 3119, Block 331
Zinj District
Manama, Bahrain
Tel: 973-17-242767
E-mail: hasansaf@state.gov
Web: //bahrain.usembassy.gov/resources/
   education-advising.html

Bangladesh

Dhaka
The American Center
House # 110, Road # 27
Banani Model Town
Dhaka 1213, Bangladesh
Tel: 880-2-883-7150 ext.4
E-mail: dhakapa@state.gov
Web: //dhaka.usembassy.gov

Barbados

St. Michael
Counselling & Placement Centre
Barbados Community College
"Eyrie" Howell's Cross Road
Two Mile Hill
St. Michael, Barbados
Tel: 246-426-3278
E-mail: clicorish@bcc.edu.bb
Web: www.bcc.edu.bb/EducationUSA.cfm

Belgium

Brussels
Commission for Educational Exchange
Boulevard de l'Empereur, 4
Keizerslaan
Brussels B-1000, Belgium
Tel: 32-2-519.57.72
E-mail: adviser@fulbright.be
Web: www.fulbright.be/General_Info/
   Advising_Center.htm

Benin

Cotonou
Centre Culturel Americain
Boulevard de France
Pres du Conseil de l'Entente
Cotonou, Benin
Tel: 229-21-30 03 12
E-mail: demagbout@state.gov
Web: //cotonou.usembassy.gov/advising_
   office.html

Bolivia

Cochabamba
Centro Boliviano Americano,
   Asesoramiento Educativo
EducationUSA Info & Advising Center
Calle 25 de Mayo N-0365
Cochabamba, Bolivia
Tel: 591-4-422-9934
E-mail: rribera@cbacoch.org;info@cbacoch.
   org
Web: www.cbacoch.org/adv/advising.html

La Paz
US Embassy Public Affairs Section
Fulbright Office
Av. Arce 2780
La Paz, Bolivia
Tel: 591-2-2168471
E-mail: BallivianDI@state.gov
Web: //bolivia.usembassy.gov/advising.html

La Paz
Centro Boliviano Americano
Centro de Informacion y Asesoria Educativa
Avenida Arce-Parque Zenon
Iturralde No.121
La Paz, Bolivia
Tel: 591-2-2430998
E-mail: romeror.eduusa@cba.edu.bo
Web: www.educationusabolivia.org/
   advising/index.html

Santa Cruz de la Sierra
Centro Boliviano Americano
Asesoria Educativa
Calle Cochabamba No. 66
Santa Cruz de la Sierra, Bolivia
Tel: 591-3-3342299
E-mail: amelgar@cba.com.bo
Web: www.cba.com.bo

Sucre, Chuquisaca
Centro Boliviano Americano-Sucre
Calle Calvo #301
or Calle Potosi #201
Sucre, Chuquisaca, Bolivia
Tel: 591-4-644-1608
E-mail: cba@entelnet.bo;cba@mara.scr.
   entelnet.b
Web: //lapaz.usembassy.gov/cbasucre/cba.
   htm

Tarija
Centro Boliviano Americano-Tarija
Tarija, Bolivia
Tel: 591-511-445-4746
E-mail: rarens@reac.org.pe

Bosnia & Herzegovina

Sarajevo
SUS BiH-US Educational Advising Center
Zmaja od Bosne bb
Kampus Univerziteta u Sarajevu
Sarajevo 71000
Bosnia & Herzegovina
Tel: 387-33-200 070
E-mail: useac.adviser@sus.ba;useac@sus.ba
Web: www.sus.ba/useac

EducationUSA Advising Centers

Brazil

Belem PA
Centro Cultural Brasil-Estados Unidos
  (CCBEU)
Travessa Padre Eutiquio, 1309
Batista Campos
Belem PA 66023-710, Brazil
Tel: 55-91-3242-9455 ext.240-211
E-mail: cultural@ccbeu.com.br
Web: www.ccbeu.com.br

Belo Horizonte MG
Instituto Cultural Brasil-Estados Unidos
  ICBEU
Educational Advising
Rua da Bahia, 1723-Lourdes
Belo Horizonte MG 30160-011
Brazil
Tel: 55-31-3271-7255 ext.223
E-mail: advising@icbeu.com.br;icbeu012@
  terra.com.br
Web: www.icbeu.com.br

Brasilia DF
Casa Thomas Jefferson
Escritorio de Consultas Educacionais
SGAN 606-Conj. B
Brasilia DF 70840-060, Brazil
Tel: 55-61-3347-4040 ext.46
E-mail: eao@thomas.org.br
Web: www.thomas.org.br

Campinas SP
Centro Cultural Brasil-Estados Unidos-
  Campinas
Consultas Educacionais
Av. Julio de Mesquita, 606
Campinas SP 13025-061, Brazil
Tel: 55-19-3794-9700
E-mail: consedu@ccbeuc.com.br
Web: www.ccbeuc.com.br

Curitiba, Parana
Interamericano EBC
Educational & Business Center
Av. Munhoz da Rocha, 490, Cabral
Curitiba PR 80035-000, Brazil
Tel: 55-41-3229-3064
E-mail: eac_curitiba@interamericano.com.br
Web: www.interamericano.com.br

Curitiba, Parana
UniFAE Centro Universitario
Escritorio de Consultas Educacionais ECE
Avenida Silva Jardim, 1499-Reboucas
80.250-200 Curitiba, Parana
Brazil
Tel: 55-41-2105-4444
E-mail: aretagalat@fae.edu
Web: www.fae.edu/ece/index.as

Fortaleza, Ceara
IBEU-Ceara
Orientacao Educacional
Rua Nogueira Acioly, 891
Fortaleza CE 60110-140, Brazil
Tel: 55-85-2533-400-69941
E-mail: adviserusa@yahoo.com
Web: www.ibeuce.com.br

Goiania, Goias
Centro Cultural Brasil-Estados Unidos
  (CCBEU)
Av. T-5, 441
Setor Bueno
Goiania, Goias 74015-050
Brazil
Tel: 55-62-3533-1415, 1416
E-mail: ies@ccbeu.com
Web: www.ccbeu.com

Joinville SC
Centro Cultural Brasil-Estados Unidos-
  Joinville
Consultas Educacionales
Rua Tijucas, 370-America
Joinville SC 89204-020, Brazil
Tel: 55-47-3433-4110
E-mail: adviser@ccbeuj.com.br
Web: www.ccbeuj.com.br

Londrina PR
Instituto Cultural Brasil Estados Unidos
Escritorio de Consultas Educacionais
Rua Professor Joao Candido, 1114-Centro
Londrina PR 86010-001, Brazil
Tel: 55-43-3324-5372
E-mail: advising@culturalweb.com.br
Web: www.culturalweb.com.br

Manaus, Amazonas
Instituto Cultural Brasil-Estados Unidos
Servico de Orientacao
Av. Joaquim Nabuco, 1286
Manaus AM 69020-030, Brazil
Tel: 55-92-3232-5919
E-mail: coord.cult@icbeu.com
Web: www.icbeu.com

Porto Alegre RS
Instituto Cultural Brasileiro Norte-
  Americano ICBNA
Rua Riachuelo, #1257 2nd floor
Porto Alegre RS 90010-271
Brazil
Tel: 55-51-4009-2321
E-mail: culturalgrad@icbna.com.br
Web: www.cultural.org.br

Recife, Pernambuco
Associacao Brasil-America (ABA)
Servicos de Orientacao
Av. Rosa e Silva,1510-Aflitos
Recife, Pernambuco 52050-220
Brazil
Tel: 55-81-3427-0200
E-mail: intercambio@abaweb.org
Web: www.abaweb.org

Rio de Janeiro RJ
Fulbright Office of Educational Advising,
  PUC Rio
Av. Marques de Sao Vicente, 225
Ed. Pe. Leonel Franca, sala 55, Gavea
Rio de Janeiro RJ 22451-041
Brazil
Tel: 55-21-2294-1177
E-mail: fulbrightrio@fulbright.org.br
Web: www.fulbright.org.br

Rio de Janeiro RJ
Instituto Brasil-Estados Unidos-IBEU/BNC
Av. Nossa Senhora de Copacabana,
  690 - Room 1004
Rio de Janeiro RJ 22050-001
Brazil
Tel: 55-21-3816-9445
E-mail: neidemonteiro@ibeu.org.br
Web: www.ibeu.org.br

Salvador, Bahia
ACBEU-Salvador
Consultas Educacionais
Av. Prof. Magalhaes Netto, 1520 - Stiep
Salvador, Bahia 41820-140, Brazil
Tel: 55-71-3340-5400
E-mail: mgsantos@acbeubahia.org.br
Web: www.acbeubahia.org.br

SantosSP
Centro Cultural Brasil-Estados Unidos
Servico de Orientacao, studos nos EUA
Rua Jorge Tibirica, 5/7
Santos SP 11055-250, Brazil
Tel: 55-13-3281 3999/3993
E-mail: advising@ccbeunet.br
Web: www.ccbeunet.br/educationusa/index.
  html

Sao Jose dos Campos SP
ICBEU Sao Jose dos Campos
Av. Dr. Adhemar de Barros,
  464 Vila Ady'Anna
Sao Jose dos Campos 12243-610 SP
Brazil
Tel: 55-12-3941-4978; 3924-1000
E-mail: advising@icbeusjc.com.br
Web: www.icbeusjc.com.br

Sao Paulo SP
Associacao Alumni
Dep. de Consultas Educacionais
Alameda Jau 1.208– Cerqueira Cesar
Sao Paulo SP 01420-001, Brazil
Tel: 55-11-3067-2916
E-mail: advising@alumni.org.br
Web: www.alumni.org.br

Sao Paulo SP
Uniao Cultural Brasil Estados Unidos
Rua Coronel Oscar Porto, 208
Paraiso
Sao Paulo SP 04003-000, Brazil
Tel: 55-11-2148-2912
E-mail: studentadvising@uniaocultural.com.
  br
Web: www.uniaocultural.com.br

Brunei

Bandar Seri Begawan
EducationUSA Brunei
US Embassy Public Affairs Section
Simpang 336-52-16-9, Jalan Kebangssan,
  Bandar Seri Begawan BS8675 Brunei
Tel: 673-2384616
E-mail: studyusa_bsb@state.gov
Web: //brunei.usembassy.gov/educational_
  exchanges2.html

Bulgaria

Sofia
Bulgarian-American Fulbright Commission
17, Alex. Stamboliiski Boulevard
Sofia 1000, Bulgaria
Tel: 359-2-981 6830
E-mail: steneva@fulbright.bg
Web: www.fulbright.bg

Burkina Faso

Ouagadougou
EducationUSA Center
Centre Culturel Americain
674, Avenue John F. Kennedy, Koulouba
Ouagadougou 01, Burkina Faso
Tel: 226-50-30 67 23
E-mail: ouagaPASeducation@state.gov
Web: //ouagadougou.usembassy.gov/
  educationusa_advising _center.html

Burma (Myanmar)

Rangoon (Yangon)
EducationUSA Burma
The American Center
14, Tawwin Road
Dagon Township
Yangon, Burma (Myanmar)
Tel: 95-1-223140 ext. 323
E-mail: lwintmm@state.gov
Web: //rangoon.state.gov

Burundi

Bujumbura
English Language Center
PAS Bujumbura
Chausse PL Rwagasore
Bujumbura, Burundi
Tel: 257-22-207-229
E-mail: sunstrumb@state.gov
Web: //burundi.usembassy.gov/educational_
  exchange.html

Cambodia

Phnom Penh
EducationUSA Cambodia
University of Phnom Penh
Rm 103, Faculty of Science Bldg.
Blvd. Confederation of Russia
Khan Tuol kok, Phnom Penh
Cambodia
Tel: 855-23-216-163
E-mail: caradvchthon@online.com.kh
Web: www.eacc-edu-kh.com

Cameroon

Yaoundé
American Embassy Yaounde
Public Affairs Section
Avenue Rosa Parks
Yaounde, Cameroon
Tel: 237-220-1500
E-mail: yaoundeEdu@state.gov
Web: //yaounde.usembassy.gov/educational_
  advising.html

Cape Verde

Praia
EucationUSA-US Embassy
Public Affairs Section
Rua Abilio Macedo 6
Praia, Cape Verde
Tel: 238-260-8900
E-mail: britomt@state.gov
Web: //praia.usembassy.gov/resources/
  academic-advising.html

Cayman Islands BWI

George Town
Department of Employee Relations (MOE)
Paddington Place, Suite 309-310
Godfrey Nixon Way
George Town, Grand Cayman
Cayman Islands BWI
Tel: 345-945-1199
E-mail: Jennifer.Smith@gov.ky
Web: //employmentservices@gov.ky

Central African Republic

Bangui
US Embassy - EducationUSA
Avenue David Dacko
Bangui, Central African Republic
Tel: 236 21 61 02 00
E-mail: balifiors@state.gov

Chad

N'Djamena
US Embassy, Public Diplomacy Section
Information Resource Center
Avenue Felix Eboue
N'Djamena 235, Chad
Tel: 235-51 70 09
E-mail: roasser@state.gov;roassre@yahoo.fr
Web: //ndjamena.usembassy.gov/
  educational_advising.html

Chile

Antofagasta
Instituto Chileno Norteamericano de
  Antofagasta
Carrera 1445
Antofagasta, Chile
Tel: 56-55-266268; 263 520
E-mail: inchafta@chilesat.net
Web: www.norteamericano.cl

Chillan
Instituto Chileno Norteamericano de
  Cultura Chillan - Asesoria
Dieciocho de Septiembre 253
Chillan, Chile
Tel: 56-42-221-414
E-mail: mainsa@entelchile.net

Concepcion
Instituto Chileno Norteamericano de
  Cultura - Asesora Academica
Caupolican 315
Concepcion, Chile
Tel: 56-40-225506
E-mail: mtvilla@norteamericanoconcepcion.
  cl
Web: www.norteamericanoconcepcion.cl

Curico
Instituto Chileno Norteamericano de
  Cultura - Asesora Academica
Estado 563
Curico, Chile
Tel: 56-75-311129
E-mail: edusacurico@gmail.com
Web: www.inchinor.cl

Santiago
Centro de Asesoria Academica
EducationUSA
Instituto Chileno Norteamericano de
  Cultura
San Pío X 2485, Providencia
Santiago 7510602, Chile
Tel: 56-2-677-7157
E-mail: advising@norteamericano.cl
Web: www.norteamericano.cl

Valparaiso
Instituto Chileno Norteamericano de
  Cultura
2 Oriente 385, Vina del Mar, Chile
Tel: 56-32-2686191;2450400
E-mail: ccarmona@chilenonorteamericano.cl
Web: www.chilenonorteamericano.cl

China

Beijing
EducationUSA China
ACEE American Center for Educational
  Exchange
Suite 2801 Jingguang Center
Hu Jia Lou, Chaoyang District
Beijing 100020, China
E-mail: educationUSAchina@state.gov
Web: www.educationusa.info/china

Colombia

Armenia, Quindio
BNC Colombo Americano Educational
  Advising Center
Avenida Bolivar 1-55
Armenia, Quindio, Colombia
Tel: 57-67-463-588
E-mail: advising@educationusacolombia.
  com
Web: www.educationusacolombia.com

Barranquilla, Atlantico
Centro Cultural Colombo
Americano de Barranquilla Asesoria
Carrera 43 No. 51-95
Barranquilla, Colombia
Tel: 57-5-379 3951
E-mail: colombolibrary@caribemovil.com
Web: www.colomboamericano.org/
  counseling.htm

Bogota
Centro Colombo Americano
Centro de Asesoria Educativa
Calle 19 No. 2-49
Bogota 1101, Colombia
Tel: 57-1-334-7640 ext 231
E-mail: advising@colombobogota.edu.co
Web: www.colombobogota.edu.co

Bogota
COLFUTURO
Consejeria Academica
Carrera 15 No. 37-15, Barrio
Teusaquillo
Bogota, Colombia
Tel: 57-1-340-5394 PBX
E-mail: yosoyfuturo@colfuturo.com.co
Web: www.colfuturo.com.co

Bogota
Fulbright Commission
Consejeria Academica
Calle 37 # 15-73
Bogota, Colombia
Tel: 57-1-2859467
E-mail: consejeria@fulbright.edu.co
Web: www.fulbright.edu.co

Cali, Valle
Centro Cultural Colombo
Americano Cali
Asesoria Estudiantil
Calle 13 Norte, # 8-45
Cali, Colombia
Tel: 57-2-667-3539 ext.114
E-mail: asesoria@colomboamericano.edu.co
Web: www.colomboamericano.edu.co

Cartagena, Bolivar
Centro Colombo Americano de Cartagena
- Biblioteca
Calle de la Factoria No. 36-27
Cartagena 28-31, Colombia
Tel: 57-5-6641-714 ext.102
E-mail: information@colombocartagena.
com
Web: www.colombocartagena.com

Manizales, Caldas
Centro Colombo Americano de Manizales
- Asesoria
Carrera 24 B No. 61A-50
Manizales, Caldas, Colombia
Tel: 57-6-881-1525
E-mail: studyusa@colombomanizales.com
Web: www.colombomanizales.com

Medellin, Antioquia
Centro Colombo Americano
Educational Advising Office #901
Carrera 45 # 53-24, Maracaibo/El Palo
Medellin, Colombia
Tel: 57-4-513 4444 ext. 227
E-mail: studyusa@colomboworld.com
Web: www.colomboworld.com

Pereira, Risaralda
Centro Colombo Americano
Asesoria Estudiantil
Carrera 6 # 22-26
Pereira, Colombia
Tel: 57-6-335-9767; 325-4032
E-mail: educationaladvisor@
colombopereira.com
Web: www.colombopereira.com

Congo, Rep. (Brazzaville)

Brazzaville
US Embassy
Maya Maya Blvd
Brazzaville, Republic of Congo
Tel: 242 6122 181
E-mail: moukouboukaln@state.gov
Web: brazzaville.usembassy.gov/

Congo, Democratic Republic

Kinshasa
Congo American Language Institute
Complex Utexafrica
Avenue Colonel Mondjiba
Kinshasa, Dem. Republic of Congo
Tel: 243-81-7152350
E-mail: edadvisor@cali.cd
Web: www.calidrc.org

Costa Rica

San José
Centro Cultural Costarricense-
Norteamericano
Asesoria Educacional
150 metros norte de Gasolinera los Yoses
San Jose, Costa Rica
Tel: 506-2-207-7566
E-mail: mlopez@cccncr.com
Web: www.cccncr.com

Côte d'Ivoire

Abidjan
US Embassy
Centre Culturel Americain
rue des Ambassades
Cocody, Riviera Golf
Abidjan 01, Cote d'Ivoire
Tel: 225-22-49 41 45
E-mail: educationusa_abidjan@state.
gov;educationusa_abidjan@yahoo.com
Web: //abidjan.usembassy.gov/study_in_
the_us.html

Croatia

Zagreb
Institute for the Development of Education
IRO
EducationUSA adviser
Preradoviceva 33/I
Zagreb 10000, Croatia
Tel: 385-1-4817-195
E-mail: iro@iro.hr
Web: www.iro.hr

Cyprus

Nicosia
Cyprus Fulbright Commission -
Koskluciftlik
5A Server Somuncuoglu Street
Koskluciftlik
Nicosia, Cyprus
Tel: 90-392-2271800
E-mail: fulbright@superonline.com
Web: www.fulbright.org.cy

Nicosia
Cyprus Fulbright Commission
Educational Adviser
2 Egypt Ave.
Nicosia 1097, Cyprus
Tel: 357-2-22 669757
E-mail: cfc@fulbright.org.cy
Web: www.fulbright.org.cy

Czech Republic

Prague
J. W. Fulbright Commission
Educational Adviser
Taboritska 23
Prague 130 87, Czech Republic
Tel: 420-222718452
E-mail: advisor@fulbright.cz
Web: www.fulbright.cz

Denmark

Copenhagen
Denmark-America
Foundation/Fulbright Commission
Fiolstraede 24, 3rd floor
Copenhagen K DK-1171, Denmark
Tel: 45-33-12 82 23
E-mail: advising@daf-fulb.dk
Web: www.wemakeithappen.dk

Djibouti

Djibouti
EducationUSA-US Embassy
Public Affairs Section
Avenue de Marechal Joffre
Djibouti, Djibouti
Tel: 253-35-39-95
Web: //djibouti.usembassy.gov/
educational_advising_center.html

Dominica, Commonwealth

Roseau
Educational Advising Unit
Public Library
Victoria Street
Roseau
Commonwealth of Dominica
Tel: 767-266-3409/3341
E-mail: dominicaedadvise@gmail.com

Dominican Republic

Santiago de los Caballeros
Centro Cultural Dominico-Americano
Avda. Salvador Estrella Sahdala
La Rinconada
Santiago de los Caballeros
Dominican Republic
Tel: 809-582-1244
E-mail: CCDAlibrary@yahoo.com

Santo Domingo
Instituto Cultural Dominico-Americano
Educational Advising Office
Ave. Abraham Lincoln #21, Sector Mata
  Hambre
Santo Domingo 10102
Dominican Republic
Tel: 809-535-0665 ext. 263
E-mail: eco@icda.edu.do
Web: www.icda.edu.do/espanol/eco

East Timor (Timor-Leste)

Dili
American Studies Center
Embaixada EUA
Avenida de Portugal Praia dos Coqueiros
Dili, Timor-Leste
E-mail: padili@state.gov

Ecuador

Quito
Comision Fulbright del Ecuador
Centro de Asesoria Academica
EducationUSA
Almagro N25-41 y Av. Colon
Quito, Ecuador
Tel: 593-2-222-2103
E-mail: advisorecuador@fulbright.org.ec
Web: www.fulbright.org.ec/asesoria.htm

Egypt

Alexandria
AMIDEAST
American Center Alexandria
3 Pharana Street, Azarita
Alexandria, Egypt
Tel: 20-3-486-9091
E-mail: rrateb@amideast.org
Web: www.amideast.org

Cairo (Giza)
AMIDEAST
23, Mossadak St.
Dokki
Giza, Egypt
Tel: 20-2-3332-0411
E-mail: Hal-Hawary@amideast.org;
  jsabeh@amideast.org
Web: www.amideast.org/egypt/ advising/
  advising-services-cairo

El Salvador

San Salvador
Centro Cultural Salvadoreno
Student Advising Office
Avenida los Sisimiles, Costado
norte de Metrocentro
San Salvador, El Salvador
Tel: 503-260-3911 ext. 141
E-mail: stadvisor@hotmail.com
Web: www.ccsa.edu.sv/23.php

Eritrea

Asmara
American Center
Public Affairs Section
Ala Street, #179
Asmara, Eritrea
Tel: 291-1-12-06-37
E-mail: AregahegnS@state.gov
Web: //eritrea.usembassy.gov/educational_
  advising.html

Estonia

Tallinn
EducationUSA Advising Center
Tallinn Technical University
Ehitajate tee 5, III korpus, room 211a
Tallinn 19086, Estonia
Tel: 372-2-620 3543
E-mail: EducationUSA@ttu.ee
Web: www.eac.ttu.ee

Tartu
EducationUSA Advising Center
Tartu University Library
W. Struve 1-325
Tartu 50091, Estonia
Tel: 372-7-427 243
E-mail: educentre@lists.ut.ee
Web: www.ut.ee/ameerika

Ethiopia

Addis Ababa
US Embassy, Public Affairs Section
Entoto Street
Woreda 11, Kebele 10
Addis Ababa, Ethiopia
Tel: 251-1-5174223
E-mail: alhadisj@state.gov
Web: //ethiopia.usembassy.gov/educational_
  advising_services.html

Fiji

Suva
U.S. Embassy Public Affairs
31 Loftus Street
Suva, Fiji
Tel: 679-3314466 ext. 8204
E-mail: usembsuva@gmail.com
Web: //suva.usembassy.gov/educational_
  exchange.html

Finland

Helsinki
Fulbright Center
Kaisaniemenkatu 3 B, 5th floor
Helsinki 00100, Finland
Tel: 358-9-5494 7400
E-mail: office@fulbright.fi
Web: www.fulbright.fi

France

Paris
Centre Education USA
Franco-American Commission for
  Educational Exchange
9, rue Chardin
Paris 75016, France
Tel: 33-1-44 14 53 60
E-mail: doc@fulbright-france.org
Web: www.fulbright-france.org/htm/centred.
  asp

Gabon

Libreville
U.S. Embassy
Blvd. du Bord de Mer
Libreville, Gabon
Tel: 241-76-2003
E-mail: diakitemf@state.gov

Gambia, The

Banjul
US Embassy, Public Affairs Section
Kairaba Avenue
Fajara
Banjul, The Gambia
Tel: 220-439-2856 ext 2166
E-mail: NjieMM@state.gov
Web: //banjul.usembassy.gov/about_the_
  embassy/public-affairs-section2.html

Georgia

Batumi
Center for International Education
International Student Advising Center
23 Ninoshvili Street
Batumi 6010, Georgia
Tel: 995-222-75817
E-mail: nino_inaishvili@osgf.ge
Web: www.cie-batumi.org;
  //batumi.osgf.ge

Kutaisi
International Student Advising Center
University of Law and Economics
Tsereteli str., 13
384000 Kutaisi, Georgia
Tel: 995-331-4-11-40
E-mail: isac-kutaisi@mail.osgf.ge

Tbilisi
Center for International Education
Open Society Georgia Foundation
ul. Chovelidze,10
0108 Tbilisi, Georgia
Tel: 995-32-25-04-63; 252615
E-mail: natia@isac.osgf.ge;
  nino@isac.osgf.ge
Web: www.cie.ge;
  www.osgf.ge/isac

Tbilisi
Educational Advising Center Kvali
3, Chavchavadze Avenue
Tbilisi State University
Tbilisi 0128, Georgia
Tel: 995-32-91 24 31
E-mail: eac@kvali.com
Web: www.kvali.org/center

EducationUSA Advising Centers

Germany

Berlin/all cities
US Embassy Virtual Education Info Service
Di, Mi, Do von 14-17 Uhr
Web chat with a Virtual Advisor
Tel: 49-030-31 80 08 99
E-mail: austausch@state.gov
Web: www.educationusa.de

Frankfurt/all cities
EducationUSA Frankfurt
Virtual Education Info Service
Di, Mi, Do von 14-17 Uhr
Tel: 49-030-31 80 08 99
E-mail: austausch@state.gov
Web: www.educationusa.de

Freiburg im Breisgau
Carl-Schurz-Haus
German-American Institute
Eisenbahnstrasse 62
Freiburg im Breisgau 79098
Germany
Tel: 49-761-55652716
E-mail: studienberatung@carl-schurz-haus.de
Web: www.carl-schurz-haus.de

Hamburg
Amerikazentrum Hamburg
Am Sandtorkai 5
Hamburg 20457, Germany
Tel: 49-40-70 38 36 88
E-mail: info@amerikazentrum.de
Web: www.amerikazentrum.de

Hannover-Linden
Fachhochschule Hannover
Studienberatung USA
Hanomagstrasse 8, Zi.122
Hannover-Linden 30449, Germany
Tel: 49-511-9296-2154
E-mail: usa@fh-hannover.de
Web: www.fh-hannover.de/usa/

Heidelberg
German American Institute
Deutsch-amerikanisches Institut
Sofienstrasse 12
Heidelberg 69115, Germany
Tel: 49-6221-607315
E-mail: biblio@dai-heidelberg.de
Web: www.dai-heidelberg.de

Kiel
Kennedy Infozentrum Kiel
Amerika-Gesellschaft Schleswig-Holstein
Olshausenstrasse 10
Kiel 24118, Germany
Tel: 49-431-586 999 3
E-mail: info@amerika-gesellschaft.de
Web: www.amerika-gesellschaft.de

Leipzig
Generalkonsulat der USA Leipzig
Amerika Haus
Wilhelm-Seyfferth-Strasse 4
Leipzig 04107, Germany
Tel: 49-341-213 84 65
E-mail: ircLeipzig@state.gov
Web: //leipzig.usconsulate.gov/leipzig/
meetusa.html

Munich
Bavarian American Center - Amerika Haus
Munich
Section Education & Exchange
Karolinenplatz 3
Munich 80333, Germany
Tel: 49-89-55 25 37 17
E-mail: education@amerikahaus.de
Web: www.amerikahaus.de

Nürnberg
Deutsch-Amerikanisches Institut
GAI Nuernberg
Gleissbuhlstrasse 13
90402 Nuernberg, Germany
Tel: 49-911-2306912
E-mail: mail@dai-nuernberg.de
Web: www.dai- nuernberg.de/
DAIFrameStudy.htm

Stuttgart
Deutsch-Amerikanisches Zentrum
James-F.-Byrnes Institut e.V.
Charlottenplatz 17
Stuttgart 70173, Germany
Tel: 49-711-22 81 80
E-mail: info@daz.org
Web: www.daz.org

Tübingen
German American Institute
Karlstrasse 3
Tuebingen 72072, Germany
Tel: 49-7071-795-2617
E-mail: roswitha.degenhard@dai-tuebingen.de
Web: www.dai-tuebingen.de

Ghana

Accra
Educational Advising Center, US Embassy
Public Affairs Section
No. 24, Fourth Circular Road
Cantonments-Accra
Accra, Ghana
Tel: 233-302-741 531
E-mail: affoteyb@state.gov
Web: //ghana.usembassy.gov/educational_
advising.html

Kumasi
EducationUSA Advisory Center
ACE CONSULT
3rd FL Top Martin's Complex,
Asokwa
Kumasi, Ghana
Tel: 233-51-0244-369027
E-mail: ace_consult2006@yahoo.com
Web: //ghana.usembassy.gov/educational_
advising.html

Greece

Athens
The Fulbright Foundation in Greece-Athens
EducationUSA adviser
6 Vassilissis Sophias Avenue
Athens 10674, Greece
Tel: 30-210-7241811
E-mail: advisor@fulbright.gr;
info@fulbright.gr
Web: www.fulbright.gr/frameset.html

Thessaloniki
The Fulbright Foundation-Thessaloniki
EducationUSA adviser
4 Venizelou Str., 3rd floor
Thessaloniki 54625, Greece
Tel: 30-2310-242-904
E-mail: edadthes@fulbright.gr
Web: www.fulbright.gr/frameset.html

Guatemala

Guatemala City
Instituto Guatemalteco Americano
Walt Whitman Library
Ruta 1, 4-05, Zona 4, 1st Fl, Of.108
Guatemala City 01004, Guatemala
Tel: 502-2422-5590
E-mail: educationUSA@iga.edu
Web: www.iga.edu

Quetzaltenango
Instituto Guatemalteco Americano _ Xela
EducationUSA Quetzaltenango
14 avenida "A" 2-36, zona 1
Quetzaltenango, Guatemala
Tel: 502-7765-8160
E-mail: wcalva@iga.edu
Web: //xela.usvpp.gov/educationusaxela.
html

Guinea

Conakry
Conakry Educational Advising Center
Centre d'Etudes de la Langue Anglaise
CELA
Universite GLC de Sonfonia, Rte Donka
Conakry 4027, Guinea
Tel: 224-60-26 19 67
E-mail: marudaka@yahoo.fr
Web: //conakry.usembassy.gov/study_in_
the_us1.html

Guyana

Georgetown
United States Embassy, Public Affairs
Section
99-100 Young and Duke Streets
Kingston
Georgetown, Guyana
Tel: 592-225-4900 ext.235
E-mail: DuncanJR@state.gov
Web: //georgetown.usembassy.gov

Haiti

Port au Prince
US Embassy
Information Resource Center
Boulevard 15 Octobre, Tabarre 41
Port au Prince, Haiti
Tel: 509-2229-8000
E-mail: GardereNM@state.gov
Web: //haiti.usembassy.gov

Honduras

San Pedro Sula
Centro Cultural Sampedrano-Benjamin
  Franklin Library
4ta Avenida, entre 5ra y 4ta calles,
detr.del Gran Hotel Sula, Cortes
San Pedro Sula, Honduras
Tel: 504-553-3911
E-mail: biblioteca@centrocultural-sps.com
Web: www.centrocultural-sps.com

Tegucigalpa
Instituto Hondureno de Cultura
  Interamericana
Blvd. Morazan 1/2 cuadra antes del Mall El
  Dorado
Edificio IHCI Primera Planta
Tegucigalpa, Honduras
Tel: 504-221-3981
E-mail: educationusaihci@yahoo.com
Web: www.ihcihn.org/education_usa.html

Hong Kong

Hong Kong
EducationUSA Advising Center
Public Affairs Section U.S. Consulate
  General
26 Garden Road Central,
Hong Kong SAR, Hong Kong
Tel: 852-2841 2333
E-mail: hkeducationusa@state.gov
Web: //hongkong.usconsulate.gov/ studyusa.
  html

Hungary

Budapest
Fulbright EducationUSA Advising Center
Hungarian-American Fulbright Commission
Baross u. 62
Budapest 1082, Hungary
Tel: 36-1-462-8044;462-8050
E-mail: advising@fulbright.hu
Web: www.fulbright.hu/advising

Pecs
American Corner
EducationUSA Advising Center
International House/Europa Haz
Maria u. 9
Pecs 7621, Hungary
Tel: 36-72-514817
E-mail: pecs@americancorner.hu
Web: //pecs.americancorner.hu/htmls/
  study_in_the_usa.html

Szeged
American Higher Education
Information Center AFIK
University of Szeged, University Library
Ady ter 10
Szeged 6722, Hungary
Tel: 36-62-546-625
E-mail: ficzko@bibl.u-szeged.hu
Web: www.bibl.u-szeged.hu/afik/

Veszprem
American Corner-EducationUSA Advising
Eotvos Karoly Megyei Konyvtar
Komakut ter 3.
Veszprem 8200, Hungary
Tel: 36-88-560-600
E-mail: veszprem@americancorner.hu
Web: www.fulbright.hu/advising

Iceland

Reykjavik
Iceland-US Educational Commission
Laugavegur 59
Reykjavik 101, Iceland
Tel: 354-551-0860
E-mail: advisor@fulbright.is
Web: www.fulbright.is

India

Ahmedabad
Indo-American Education Society, USIEF
  Satellite Ctr
C/o Calorx Admn. Office, Ground Floor,
  Opp Sanjivani Hospital, Nr. Sonal
  Complex,Bodakdev Road, Vastrapur,
Ahmedabad 3800054, Gujarat, India
Tel: 91-79-26765694
E-mail: eduadviser@gmail.com
Web: www.iaesgujarat.org

Bangalore
Yashna Trust-USIEF Satellite Centre
102 Park View
40 Haines Road, Frazer
Bangalore 560005, India
Tel: 91-80-4125-1922
E-mail: swetha_muthanna@lycos.com;
  info@yashnatrust.org
Web: www.yashnatrust.org

Chennai
United States India Educational Foundation
  (USIEF)
American Consulate Building, Anna Salai
220 Mount Road
Chennai 600006, India
Tel: 91-44-2811-2049
E-mail: usiefchennai@usief.org.in
Web: www.usief.org.in/Scripts/
  StudyinUSAOverview.aspx

Hyderabad
UNITI Foundation-USIEF Satellite Center
702 Paigah Plaza
Basheerbagh
Hyderabad 500063, India
Tel: 91-40-6666-8435
E-mail: info@unitifoundation.org
Web: www.unitifoundation.org

Kolkata (Calcutta)
United States India Educational Foundation
  (USIEF)
American Center
38A, Jawaharlal Nehru Road
Calcutta 700071, West Bengal, India
Tel: 91-33-3984-6310
E-mail: usiefkolkata@usief.org.in
Web: www.usief.org.in/Scripts/
  StudyinUSAOverview.aspx

Mumbai (Bombay)
United States India Educational
Foundation (USIEF) Regional Office,
Maker Bhavan 1, Floor 2, New Marine
  Lines, Churchgate
Mumbai 400020, India
Tel: 91-22-2262-4603
E-mail: usiefmumbai@usief.org.in
Web: www.usief.org.in/Scripts/
  StudyinUSAOverview.aspx

New Delhi
United States India Educational Foundation
  (USIEF)
Fulbright House
12 Hailey Road-City
New Delhi 110001, India
Tel: 91-11-4209-0909
E-mail: rupali@usief.org.in;
renuka@usief.org.in
Web: www.usief.org.in/Scripts/
  StudyinUSAOverview.aspx

Indonesia

Jakarta
EducationUSA - AMINEF
CIMB Niaga Plaza 3rd Floor,
Jalan Jenderal Sudirman Kav 25
Jakarta 12920, Indonesia
Tel: 62-21-52962138/39 ext 300
E-mail: infoeas@aminef.or.id
Web: www.educationusa.or.id

Malang
EducationUSA Malang
Universitas Muhammadiyah
Gedung Perpustakaan, 1st FL
Jl. Raya Tlogomas no. 246
Malang 65144, Indonesia
Tel: 62-341-463 345
E-mail: malangeas@aminef.or.id
Web: www.educationusa.or.id

Medan
EducationUSA Medan
YPPIA Medan
Jalan Dr. Mansur III No. 1A
Medan 20121, North Sumatra
Indonesia
Tel: 62-61-821 1074
E-mail: medaneas@aminef.or.id

Surabaya
AMINEF/EAS
International Village 2nd Floor
Universitas Surabaya
Surabaya 60293, Indonesia
Tel: 62-31-8471809
E-mail: eas_sby@rad.net.id
Web: www.aminef.or.id/eusa.ph

Iran

All cities
EducationUSA Student Advising Services -
  online only
E-mail: adviser@educationusairan.com
Web: www.educationusairan.com

EducationUSA Advising Centers

Iraq

Baghdad
Education Adviser, Cultural Affairs U.S.
  Embassy Baghdad
U.S. Office: 1-240-553-0581, ext. 3733
Iraqi Mobile: +964-0770-443-0876
E-mail: baghdadeducationadv@state.gov
Web: iraq.usembassy.gov/studyintheusa.html

Ireland

Dublin
US Embassy, Office of Public Diplomacy
42 Elgin Road, Ballsbridge
Dublin 4, Ireland
Tel: 353-1-668-8777
E-mail: edudublin@state.gov
Web: //dublin.usembassy.gov/educational_
  exchange.html

Israel

Tel Aviv
U.S. Israel Educational Foundation
Fulbright Educational Adviser
1 Ben Yehuda Street
Tel Aviv 61261, Israel
Tel: 972-3-517-2131
E-mail: adviser@fulbright.org.il
Web: www.fulbright.org.il

Italy

Milano
EAC Milan, US Consulate General
Public Affairs Section
Via Principe Amedeo 2/10
Milano 20120, Italy
Tel: 39-2-2903-5503
E-mail: fulbrightmilan@fulbright.it
Web: //milan.usconsulate.gov/studyusa.asp

Naples (Napoli)
US Consulate General Naples
Public Affairs Section
Piazza della Repubblica, 2
Naples 80122, Italy
Tel: 39-81-669-989
E-mail: fulbrightnaples@fulbright.it
Web: www.fulbright.it

Palermo
US Consulate General Palermo
Public Affairs Section
Via Vaccarini 1
Palermo 90143, Italy
Tel: 39-91-346036
E-mail: fulbrightpalermo@fulbright.it
Web: www.fulbright.it

Rome
Commission for Educational and Cultural
  Exchange between Italy and the United
  States
Via Castelfidardo, 8
Rome 00185, Italy
Tel: 39-6-4888.211
E-mail: info@fulbright.it
Web: www.fulbright.it

Jamaica

Kingston
Office of Public Affairs,
EducationUSA Adviser
US Embassy
142 Old Hope Road
Kingston 6, Jamaica
Tel: 876-702-6172
E-mail: opakgn@state.gov
Web: //kingston.usembassy.gov/educational_
  exchange.html

Japan

Fukuoka
Fukuoka International Exchange Foundation
ACROS Fukuoka 3F
1-1-1, Tenjin, Chuo-ku
Fukuoka 810-0001, Japan
Tel: 81-92-725-9201
E-mail: eas@fulbright.jp
Web: www.kokusaihiroba.or.jp

Kyoto
Kyoto City International Foundation
2-1, Torii-cho, Awataguchi
Sakyo-ku
Kyoto 606-8536, Japan
Tel: 81-75-752-3511
E-mail: office@kcif.or.jp
Web: www.kcif.or.jp

Nagoya
The Nagoya International Center
Nagoya International Ctr Bldg. 3F
Nagono 1-47-1, Nakamura-ku
Nagoya 450-0100, Japan
Tel: 81-52-581-0100
E-mail: info@nic-nagoya.or.jp
Web: www.nic-nagoya.or.jp

Naha, Okinawa
Okinawa Int'l Exchange & Human
  Resources Dvpt Fndn
Higashicho Kaikan 9F
1-1, Higashimachi
Naha, Okinawa 900-0034, Japan
Tel: 81-98-941-6771
E-mail: ryugaku@oihf.or.jp
Web: www.oihf.or.jp

Osaka
Osaka International House
Information Center
8-2-6 Uenohonmachi, Tennoji-ku
Osaka 543-0001, Japan
Tel: 81-66-772-5931
E-mail: center@ih-osaka.or.jp
Web: www.ih-osaka.or.jp

Sapporo, Hokkaido
Sapporo International
Communication Plaza Foundation
Sapporo MN Bldg. 3F, Kita 1,
Nishi 3
Chuo-ku, Sapporo City,
Hokkaido 060-0001, Japan
Tel: 81-11-211-2105
E-mail: sicpfexc@plaza-sapporo.or.jp
Web: //plaza-sapporo.or.jp

Sendai, Miyagi
Sendai International Center
Aobayama, Aoba-ku
Miyagi-ken
Sendai 980-0856, Japan
Tel: 81-22-265-2471
E-mail: info@sira.or.jp
Web: www.sira.or.jp

Tokyo
Japan-U.S. Educational Commission
Sanno Grand Bldg. #207, 2-14-2
Nagata-cho
Chiyoda-ku
Tokyo 100-0014, Japan
Tel: 81-3-3580-3231
E-mail: eas@fulbright.jp
Web: www.fulbright.jp/eng/study/index.html

Jordan

Amman
AMIDEAST Jordan
Rodeo Plaza, 3rd Fl near Café la Noisette
6, Nuh Al-Rumi Street, Sweifiyeh
Amman 11118, Jordan
Tel: 962-6-581-0930 ext. 112
E-mail: jordan@amideast.org;
mnhussein@amideast.org
Web: www.amideast.org/programs_services/
  advising/jordan/default.htm

Kazakhstan

Aktobe
Aktobe Educational Advising Center
  AKEAC
ul. 101 Strelkovoi Brigady 6-A
Aktobe 030000, Kazakhstan
Tel: 7-3132-514 331
E-mail: info@akeac.org
Web: www.akeac.org

Almaty
Bilim-Central Asia
83 Masanchi Street
Almaty, Kazakhstan 050022
Tel: 7-727-259 76 20/22
E-mail: gissakhanova@bilim.kz
Web: www.bilim.kz

Almaty
EducationUSA Almaty
531 Seifullin, Office 604
Almaty 050004, Kazakhstan
Tel: 7-7272- 72 08 03/ 09 04
E-mail: educationusa@americancouncils-kz.
  com
Web: //americancouncils-kz.com/

Astana
Astana ACIE Educational Advising Center
American Councils for International
  Education
Ul. Beibitshilik, 18, office 409
Astana 010000, Kazakhstan
Tel: 7-7172-91 00 68
E-mail: astana_eac@americancouncils-kz.
  com
Web: www.kz.vco-edusa.net

Karaganda
BILIM Educational Center
20 Bukhar Zhyrau Avenue
office 228-230
Karaganda 100000, Kazakhstan
Tel: 7-7212-42 0761
E-mail: abekishev61@gmail.com
Web: //www.bilim.kz

Shymkent
BILIM Educational Center
Shymkent
25, Gani Ilyaev Street
Shymkent 160012, Kazakhstan
Tel: 7-7252-211981
E-mail: aturdaliyev@gmail.com
Web: //www.bilim.kz

Kenya

Nairobi
American Educational Advising Center
Maksons Plaza, 2nd floor
Parklands Road
Nairobi 00606, Kenya
Tel: 254-2-3740759
E-mail: info@educationusa.co.ke;
  aeac@accesskenya.co.ke
Web: //nairobi.usembassy.gov/ resources/
  education-usa/

Korea, South (ROK)

Seoul
Korean-American Educational Commission
  (Fulbright)
U.S. Education Center
168-15 Yomni-dong Mapo-Gu
Seoul 121-874, South Korea ROK
Tel: 82-2-3275-4000; 3275-4011
E-mail: usec@fulbright.or.kr
Web: www.educationusa.or.kr/en/usec/
  index.php

Kosovo

Prishtina
American Advising Center-Kosova
American School of Kosova
Rr. Luan Haradinaj n.n. (Pallati i Rinise-
  Sportit)
Prishtina 10000, Kosovo
Tel: 381-38-227277; 228288 ext107
E-mail: info@aacks.org
Web: //pristina.usmission.gov/exchange_
  programs.html

Kuwait

Sharq, Kuwait City
AMIDEAST Kuwait
Sharq Ahmed Al-Jaber Street, Opposite
  Al-Awadhi Mosque, Commercial Bank
  Building, 2 Fl Sharq, Kuwait
Tel: 965-2247-0091
E-mail: rfadlallah@amideast.org
Web: www.amideast.org/

Kyrgyzstan

Bishkek
Bishkek Resource Center
Soros Foundation Kyrgyzstan
55a Logvinenko Str.
Bishkek 720040, Kyrgyzstan
Tel: 996-312-66-34-75
E-mail: ajamasheva@soros.kg;
  ajamasheva@gmail.com
Web: www.eac.kg

Karakol, Issyk-Kul
Steps to Success
T. Satylganov School
uL. Esenina, 1
Karakol 722200, Issyk-Kul
Kyrgyzstan
Tel: 996-3922 50193
E-mail: ersalta@gmail.com

Naryn
Naryn Education Center
47 Sagynbay Orozbak uulu Str.
Naryn 722600, Kyrgyzstan
Tel: 996-3522-5-04-27
E-mail: naryn.edu.center@gmail.com
Web: //bishkek.usembassy.gov/educational_
  advising.html

Osh
EAC "Education for All" Osh
Educational Advising Center
Kurmanjan-Datka str. 271
Osh 723500, Kyrgyzstan
Tel: 996-322-25-66-62
E-mail: educforall@rambler.ru
Web: //bishkek.usembassy.gov/educational_
  advising.html

Laos

Vientiane
US Embassy Public Affairs Section
Rue Bartholonie
That Dam
Vientiane, Laos
Tel: 856-21-26 7055
E-mail: vimolDX@state.gov
Web: //laos.usembassy.gov/fulbright_pro-
  gram.html

Latvia

Riga
EducationUSA Advising Center
at RTU Riga Business School
Skolas 11
Riga LV-1010, Latvia
Tel: 371-7217921
E-mail: educationusa@rbs.lv
Web: www.educationusa.lv

Lebanon

Beirut
AMIDEAST
Bazerkan Building, 1st fl,
Riad el Solh ST
Nijmeh Square
Beirut 2011 5601, Lebanon
Tel: 961-1-989901 ext 161
E-mail: lebanon@amideast.org
Web: www.amideast.org/offices/lebanon/

Lesotho

Maseru
US Embassy Maseru
Public Affairs
254 Kingsway Ave.
Maseru 100, Lesotho
Tel: 266-22-312-666
E-mail: fanyanemr@state.gov
Web: //maseru.usembassy.gov

Liberia

Monrovia
US Information Resource Center
Office of Public Affairs, US Embassy
111 United Nations Drive
Mamba Point, Monrovia, Liberia
Tel: 231-7-705-4826
E-mail: MassaquoiBB@state.gov
Web: //monrovia.usembassy.gov/
  informationandadvising.html

Libya

Tripoli
United States Embassy
Public Affairs Section
Jaraba Street-Ben Ashoor/ behind
Libyan-Swiss Diagnostic Center
Tripoli, Libya
Tel: 218-21-362-1005; 335-1831
E-mail: elmahrougna@state.gov;
  educationusalibya@state.gov
Web: //libya.usembassy.gov/edu_advising.
  html

Lithuania

Kaunas
Youth Career and Advising Center
Vytautas Magnus University
S.Daukanto 27-310
Kaunas LT-44249, Lithuania
Tel: 370-37-228151
E-mail: jkc@jkc.vdu.lt
Web: www.vdu.lt/jkc/index.
  php?id=66&lang=en

Vilnius
International Education and Career
  Advising Center
European Humanities University
Tauro St. 12
Vilnius LT-01114, Lithuania
Tel: 370-5-263 9650
E-mail: advising@ehu.lt
Web: //vco-edusa.net; www.ehu.lt

Vilnius
Vilnius Educational Information Center
Sauletekio 9
VU Skaiciavimo Centras room 107
Vilnius 10222, Lithuania
Tel: 370-5-2366274
E-mail: eac@cr.vu.lt
Web: //eac.osf.lt

Vilnius
American Center Vilnius
Educational Advising Center
Akmenu gatve 7
Vilnius 10133, Lithuania
Tel: 370-5-266-5470
E-mail: webemailvilnius@state.gov
Web: www.usembassy.lt

Luxembourg

Luxembourg
Centre de Documentation et d'Information
    sur l'Enseignement Supérieur- CEDIES
211, route d'Esch
Luxembourg L-1471, Luxembourg
Tel: 352-478-8650
E-mail: cedies@mcesr.etat.lu
Web: www.cedies.public.lu/index.html

Macau

Macau
University of Macau
American Corner
International Library, T404 Tai
Fung Building
Av. Padre Tomas Pereira S.J.,
Taipa Island, Macau
Tel: 86-853-397-8191
E-mail: BillyL@umac.mo
Web: www.umac.mo

Macedonia

Bitola
American Corner Bitola
House of Culture (Dom na Kulturata)
Marshal Tito bb
Bitola 7000, Macedonia
Tel: 389-47-203-326
E-mail: acmbitola@t-home.mk
Web: //skopje.usembassy.gov/american_
    corner_bitola.html

Skopje
American Educational Center
City Library "Braka Miladinovci"
blvd Partizanski Odredi 22
Skopje 1000, Macedonia
Tel: 389-2-3224-970
E-mail: aec.mof@gmail.com
Web: www.mof.org.mk/aec

Madagascar

Antananarivo
EducationUSA Center
22, Làlana Rainitovo Antsahavola
    Antananarivo 105, Madagascar
Tel: 261-32 02 275 59
E-mail: raharijaf@etp.mg
Web: www.antananarivo.usembassy.gov/

Malawi

Lilongwe
USA Education Advising Center
US Embassy Public Affairs Section
Old Mutual Building, City Center
Lilongwe, Malawi
Tel: 265-1-772222
E-mail: mphepotr@state.gov;
    cohense@state.gov
Web: //lilongwe.usembassy.gov/advising_
    services.html

Malaysia

Kuala Lumpur
Malaysian-American Commission on
    Educational Exchange
MACEE 18th Floor, Menara
Yayasan Tun Razak
200, Jalan Bukit Bintang
Kuala Lumpur 50200, Malaysia
Tel: 60-3-21668878
E-mail: mea@macee.org.my
Web: www.macee.org.my

Malacca
EducationUSA Library Malacca
Perbadanan Perpustakaan Awam Melaka
    242-1, Jalan Bukit Baru
E-mail: mea@macee.org.my
Tel: 606-2824859
Web: www.macee.org.my

Penang
SEBERANG JAYA: Penang Public Library
    Corporation JKR 2118, Jalan Perpustakaan
    Seberang Jaya, 13700 Perai, Penang,
    Malaysia
GEORGE TOWN: Penang Public Library
    George Town Branch JKR 2936, Jalan
    Scotland 10450, Penang, Malaysia
E-mail: adviser.penang@macee.org.my
Tel: 60-4-019-611-2463
Web: www.macee.org.my

Sarawak
EducationUSA Library
Yayasan Sarawak, Ting. 9 & 10, Wisma
    Satok, Jalan Satok,
93400 Kuching, Sarawak, Malaysia
Tel: 60-3-21668878
E-mail: mea@macee.org.my
Web: www.macee.org.my

Maldives

Malé
Male National Library
American Corner
Majeedi Magu
Male, Maldives
Tel: 092-322-4462459
E-mail: oconstantinescu@yahoo.com
Web: //maldives.usvpp.gov

Mali

Bamako
American Cultural Center
ACI 2000
Hamdallaye Rue 243, Porte 297
Bamako, Mali
Tel: 223-270-2419
E-mail: Syab@state.gov
Web: //mali.usembassy.gov/resources2.html

Malta

Msida
Reference Department
University of Malta Library
University of Malta
Msida, MSD 06, Malta
Tel: 356-2340-2050
E-mail: anton.abela@um.edu.mt
Web: www.lib.um.edu.mt

Marshall Islands

Majuro
U.S. Embassy Majuro
EducationUSA Advising Center
Public Affairs/Cultural & Education
Majuro, Marshall Islands 96960
Tel: 692-247-4011 ext.228
E-mail: majuropd@state.gov
Web: //majuro.usembassy.gov/higher_
    education2.html

Mauritania

Nouakchott
US Embassy
rue 42-100 (Rue Abdallaye)
Nouakchott, Mauritania
Tel: 222-525-2660 ext 4733
E-mail: syab@state.gov
Web: //mauritania.usembassy.gov/
    educational_and_exch.html

Mauritius

Port-Louis
Educational Advising Center, US Embassy
4th Floor, Rogers House
John Kennedy Avenue
Port-Louis, Mauritius
Tel: 230-202 4445
E-mail: usinfo@intnet.mu
Web: //mauritius.usembassy.gov/eduadv_
    center.html

Mexico

Chihuahua, Chihuahua
Scholarships and Studies Abroad
Bogota No. 1905
Venusiano Carranza Building of
    Revolutionary Heroes
Chihuahua 31139, Mexico
Tel: 52-614-442-56-07
E-mail: provisionalactual@hotmail.com
Web: www.chihuahua.gob.mx

Guadalajara, Jalisco
Instituto Cultural Mexicano Norteamericano
Enrique Diaz de Leon Sur 300
Colonia Moderna
Guadalajara 44170, Mexico
Tel: 52-33-3825-5838;
    3825-4101
E-mail: advisingguad@yahoo.com
Web: www.institutocultural.com.mx

Hermosillo, Sonora
Secretaria de Educacion y Cultura de Sonora
Direccion General de Intercambios
Educativos y Asuntos Internacionales
Guerrero #39 y Luis Donaldo
Colosio; Edif.Antiguo Cuartel
Hermosillo, Sonora 83000, Mexico
Tel: 52-662-289-7600 x2381
E-mail: arline.araiza@gmail.com
Web: www.sec-sonora.gob.mx

Merida, Yucatan
Instituto Benjamin Franklin de Yucatan, A.C.
Calle 57 No. 474-A
X 52 X 54 Centro
Merida, Yucatan 97000, Mexico
Tel: 52-999-928-6005;
    928-0097
E-mail:franklin@benjaminfranklin.com.mx
Web: www.benjaminfranklin.com.mx/
    informacion.htm

Mexicali, Baja California
Centro de Orientacion Educativa-EUA
CETYS Universidad, Programas
Internacionales
Calzada CETYS s/n, Colonia Rivera
Mexicali B.C. 21259, Mexico
Tel: 52-686-567-3745
E-mail: coe@cetys.mx
Web: www.mxl.cetys.mx/coe-eua

Mexico D.F
Institute of International Education
    -EducationUSA
U.S. Trade Center, Colonia Juarez
Calle Liverpool 31 (entre Berlin y
    Dinamarca)
Mexico D.F. 06600, Mexico
Tel: 52-55-5703-0167
E-mail: info@iielatinamerica.org
Web: www.iielatinamerica.org

Monterrey, Nuevo Leon
Biblioteca Benjamin Franklin de Monterrey,
    ABP
Porfirio Diaz 949 Sur, Col. Centro
Monterrey CP 64000, Mexico
Tel: 52-81-8343-3907
E-mail: biblioteca@relacionesculturales.edu.
    mx
Web: www.relacionesculturales.edu.mx/bbf/

Morelia, Michoacan
Preparatoria Gregorio Torres Fraga
Belisario Domínguez 156
Centro
Morelia 58000, Mexico
Tel: 52-443-313-3041
E-mail: moreliaadviser@yahoo.com
Web: www.gtf.com.mx/educationusa

Oaxaca, Oaxaca
US Consular Agency
Plaza Santo Domingo, planta alta
Alcala 407, int. 20
Oaxaca, Oaxaca 68000, Mexico
Tel: 52-951-514-3054
E-mail: mleyes49@hotmail.com

Oaxaca, Oaxaca
Universidad Autonoma Benito
Juarez de Oaxaca (UABJO)-Biblioteca PB
Oficina de Educacion
Internacional; Unidad de Atencion a
    Estudiantes Indigenas
C.U. ex-Hacienda de Cinco Senores
Oaxaca, Oaxaca 68120, Mexico
Tel: 52-951-502-0763
E-mail: ebautista@iielatinamerica.org
Web: www.iielatinamerica.org

Saltillo, Coahuila
Instituto Mexicano
Norteamericano de Relaciones Culturales
Av. Presidente Cardenas 840
Zona Centro
Saltillo, Coahuila 25000, Mexico
Tel: 52-844-414 8422
E-mail: cenasi_imarc@hotmail.com

San Luis Potosi SLP
Universidad Autonoma de San Luis Potosi
Centro de Asesoria Educativa,
Centro de Idiomas
Zaragoza 410
San Luis Potosi 78000, Mexico
Tel: 52-444-812-8676; 812-4955
E-mail: salomonvalles@yahoo.com.mx
Web: //cidiomas.uaslp.mx

Tijuana, Baja California
Universidad Autonoma de Baja California
Faculdad de Idiomas 2nd Floor
Calz. #14418, Mesa de Otay
Tijuana, Baja California 22390
Mexico
Tel: 52-664-979-7500 3403
E-mail: aquintanaeducationusa@gmail.com
Web: www.uabc.mx

Tuxtla Gutierrez, Chiapas
Universidad Autonoma de Chiapas, Depto
    de Intercambio Academico
Unidad Cultural Benito Juarez,
Biblioteca Central
Blvd Belisario Dominguez km1081
Tuxtla Gutierrez, Chiapas 29020
Mexico
Tel: 52-961-615-3533
E-mail: velia@altamira.ms
Web: www.unach.mx

Xalapa, Veracruz
Centro de Asesoria, Escuela para
    Estudiantes Extranjeros
Universidad Veracruzana
Zamora #25 Centro
Xalapa, Veracruz 91000, Mexico
Tel: 52-228-817-7380; 817-8687
E-mail: movilidad_eee@uv.mx;
    movilidaduv@yahoo.com.mx
Web: www.uv.mx/eee/caeuv

Micronesia FSM

Palikir, Pohnpei
College of Micronesia
Palikir, Pohnpei, Micronesia FSM
Tel: 691-320-2481
E-mail: msantos@comfsm.fm
Web: //kolonia.usembassy.gov

Moldova

Chisinau
Educational Advising Center
148 Stefan cel Mare si Sfant Blvd., of. 22
Chisinau MD 2012, Moldova
Tel: 373-22-22 11 67
E-mail: eac@eac.md; amuset@eac.md
Web: www.eac.md

Mongolia

Darkhan City
Educational Advising Center
Darkhan Library
Darkhan City 213800, Mongolia
Tel: 976-1-372-27937
E-mail: darkhanadvising@yahoo.com
Web: //mongolia.usembassy.gov/study_in_
    the_u.s

Dornod-Choibalsan
Educational Advising Center
Public Library of Dornod
Dornod
Choibalsan 212600, Mongolia
Tel: 976-1-582-23259
E-mail: dornodadvising@yahoo.com
Web: //mongolia.usembassy.gov/study_in_
    the_u.s

Erdenet
Educational Advising Center
Mongolian National University in Erdenet
Erdenet Book Center
Erdenet, Orkhon province
Mongolia
Tel: 976-1-352-21064
E-mail: erdenetadvising@yahoo.com
Web: //mongolia.usembassy.gov/study_in_
    the_u.s

Khovd
American Corner Hovd
Public Library, Khovd, Mongolia
Tel: 976-99439969
E-mail: khovdadvising@yahoo.com
Web: //mongolia.usembassy.gov/study_in_
    the_u.s

Ulaanbaatar
Educational Advising Resource Center
MKM 24th Building, 1st Floor
8th khoroo Student's Street,
Sukhbaatar district
Ulaanbaatar 210648, Mongolia
Tel: 976-11-319016
E-mail: info@earcmn.org
Web: www.earcmn.org;
    //mongolia.usembassy.gov/study_in_
    the_u.s

Morocco

Casablanca
AMIDEAST Casablanca
3 Boulevard Al Massira Al Khadra
Maarif
Casablanca, Morocco
Tel: 212-22 25 61 32
E-mail: advise-morocco@amideast.org
Web: www.amideast.org

Rabat
AMIDEAST
35, Zanqat Oukaimeden
Agdal
Rabat 1000, Morocco
Tel: 212-37-67 50 81
E-mail: advise-morocco@amideast.org
Web: www.amideast.org

Mozambique

Maputo
US Embassy-Public Affairs Section
Martin Luther King, Jr. Library
Av. Mao Tse Tung, 542
Maputo, Mozambique
Tel: 258-21-49 19 16
E-mail: massavanhaneab@state.gov
Web: //maputo.usembassy.gov/educational_
   exchange.html

Namibia

Windhoek
American Cultural Center
154 Independence Avenue
3rd Floor, Sanlam
Windhoek, Namibia
Tel: 264-61-229801
E-mail: nassauwch@state.gov
Web: //windhoek.usembassy.gov/featured_
   programs.html

Nepal

Kathmandu
US Educational Foundation in
Nepal (USEF-Nepal)
American Center
Gyaneshwor
Kathmandu, Nepal
Tel: 977-1-4414598
E-mail: adviserusef@fulbrightnepal.org.np
Web: www.fulbrightnepal.org.np

Netherlands

Amsterdam
Fulbright Center
Herengracht 472
Amsterdam 1017 CA, Netherlands
Tel: 31-20-5315930
E-mail: info@fulbright.nl
Web: www.fulbright.nl

New Zealand

Auckland
US Consulate General-Public Affairs
   Assistant
3rd Floor, Citibank Building
23 Customs St.
Auckland, New Zealand
Tel: 64-9-303 2724 ext.2966
E-mail: aucklandeducation@state.gov
Web: //newzealand.usembassy.gov/

Wellington
Fulbright New Zealand
Level 8, 120 Featherston Street
Wellington, New Zealand
Tel: 64-4-472 2065
E-mail: wellington@educationusa.info
Web: www.fulbright.org.nz/education/index.
   html

Nicaragua

Managua
Centro Cultural Nicaraguense
   Norteamericano
Centro Comercial Nejapa, detras del Banco
   Popular
Contiguo a los Juzgados
Managua, Nicaragua
Tel: 505-265-2578
E-mail: advise@ccnn.org.ni
Web: www.ccnn.org.ni/educationusa.html

Niger

Niamey
Centre Culturel Americain
Educational Advising Center
Rue de la Tapoa, Plateau
Niamey, Niger
Tel: 227-733169
E-mail: adamamaigao@state.gov
Web: //niamey.usembassy.gov

Nigeria

Abuja
EducationUSA Advising Center
Plot 1075, Diplomatic Drive
Central Area District
Abuja, Garki, Nigeria
Tel: 234-9-4614000
E-mail: usabuja@state.gov
Web: //nigeria.usembassy.gov/educational_
   advising.html

Lagos
EAC Lagos
Public Affairs Section
2, Broad Street, Lagos Island
Lagos, Nigeria
Tel: 234-1-263-0933
E-mail: eaclagos@yahoo.com;
   esclagos@state.gov
Web: //abuja.usembassy.gov/wwwhescc.html

Norway

Oslo
US-Norway Fulbright Foundation for
   Educational Exchange - Arbinsgate 2
Oslo 0253, Norway
Tel: 47-22 01 40 10
E-mail: fulbright@fulbright.no
Web: www.fulbright.no

Oslo
EducationUSA Advising,
US Embassy Public Affairs
Henrik Ibsensgate 48
0244 Oslo, Norway
Tel: 47-21 30 89 26
E-mail: osloedu@state.gov

Oman

Muscat
AMIDEAST Muscat
11 Fahood Street
Qurum, Sultanate of Oman
Muscat 115, Oman
Tel: 968-24-56-1727
E-mail: kconrad@amideast.org
Web: www.amideast.org/oman/

Pakistan

Islamabad
US Educational Foundation in Pakistan
Islamabad 44000, Pakistan
Tel: 92-51-8431300
E-mail: advising@usefpakistan.org
Web: www.usefpakistan.org

Karachi
World Educational Services
Suite 505, Marine Pride
Block-7 Clifton
Karachi 75600, Pakistan
Tel: 92-21-5361322
E-mail: wes@cyber.net.pk
Web: www.wes.edu.pk

Karachi
USEF Pakistan Karachi Center
F-47 Park Lane
Clifton Block 5
Karachi 74800, Pakistan
Tel: 92-21-581-0671-5
E-mail: fhussain@usefpakistan.org
Web: www.usefpakistan.org

Lahore
US Consulate Lahore
Public Affairs Section
50, Sharah-e-Abdul Hameed Bin Badees
   (old Empress RD)
Lahore 54000, Pakistan
Tel: 92-42-36034256
E-mail: anwarl@state.gov
Web: lahore.usconsulate.gov

Lahore
USEF Pakistan Lahore Center
Hose # 19, FC College
Gulberg
Lahore 56400, Pakistan
Tel: 92-42-5762466/67
E-mail: lahoreadvising@usefpakistan.org
Web: www.usefpakistan.org

Palestinian Territories

Gaza
AMIDEAST Gaza
Shaheed Raja St.
Besiso Bldg, 8 fl. Opposite Arab
Bank, Rimal Branch, Al Jonjdi Sq.
Gaza, Palestinian Territories
Tel: 972-8-2824635
E-mail: abaghdadi@amideast.org
Web: www.amideast.org

El-Bireh, Ramallah
AMIDEAST West Bank
Al-Watanieh Towers, 1st Floor
34 El-Bireh Municipality St.
El-Bireh, Ramallah District
Palestinian Territories
Tel: 972-2-240-8023 ext.103
E-mail: sitayim@amideast.org;
   westbank-gaza@amideast.org
Web: www.amideast.org/programs_services/
advising

Panama

Panama
EducationUSA Advising Center-USMA
Edificio de Postgrado e Investigacion (Planta
   baja)
entrada hacia Canal TV 5, El Dorado
Panama zona 6, Panama
Tel: 507-230-8398; 230-8373
E-mail: educationusa@usma.ac.pa
Web: www.usma.ac.pa

Papua New Guinea

Port Moresby
University of Papua New Guinea
Port Moresby N.C.D.
Papua New Guinea
Tel: 675.321.1544 ext.2128
E-mail: iveck@state.gov; turians@state.gov
Web: //portmoresby.usembassy.gov

Paraguay

Asuncion
Centro Cultural Paraguayo Americano
Asesoria Estudiantil
Avda Espana 352
Asuncion 1401, Paraguay
Tel: 595-21-224-831
E-mail: asesoria@ccpa.edu.py
Web: www.ccpa.edu.py

Peru

Arequipa
Centro Cultural Peruano Norteamericano de
   Arequipa-Asesoria Educacional
Melgar 109, Cercado
Arequipa, Peru
Tel: 51-54-391022, ext.226
E-mail: smolina@cultural.edu.pe
Web: www.cultural.edu.pe

Chiclayo
Instituto Cultural Peruano Norteamericano
   de Chiclayo-Asesoria Educativa
Manuel Maria Izaga 807
Chiclayo, Peru
Tel: 51-74-231241
E-mail: jmblanco@icpnachi.edu.pe
Web: www.icpnachi.edu.pe

Cusco
Instituto Cultural Peruano Norteamericano
   de Cusco
Asesoria Educativa
Av. Tullumayo 125
Cusco, Peru
Tel: 51-84-224112 ext. 119; 239451
E-mail: asesoriaedu@icpnacusco.org
Web: www.icpnacusco.org

Huancayo
ICPNA Region CentroAsesoria Educacional
Jr. Ayacucho 171, 2do piso
Huancayo, Peru
Tel: 51-64-211873
E-mail: csotomayor@icpnarc.edu.pe
Web: www.icpnarc.edu.pe/academico/
   asesoria_educacional.html

Ilo
Centro Cultural Peruano Norteamericano
   Ilo
Asesoria Educacional
Urb. Villa del Mar D-1,
Moquegua 01
Ilo, Peru
Tel: 51-53-484102
E-mail: yobando@cultural.edu.pe
Web: www.cultural.edu.pe

Lima
Instituto Cultural Peruano Norteamericano
   Asesoria Educacional
Av. Angamos Oeste 160, Miraflores
Lima 18, Peru
Tel: 51-1-7067001 ext.9060
E-mail: educational_advising@icpna.edu.pe
Web: www.icpna.edu.pe

Lima
Educational Advising Center, Fulbright
   Commission
Juan Romero Hidalgo 444
San Borja, Lima 41, Peru
Tel: 51-1-476-0666
E-mail: info@fulbrightperu.info
Web: www.fulbrightperu.info

Piura
Instituto Cultural Peruano Norteamericano-
   RG-Piura
Educational Advisory Office
Piura, Peru
Tel: 51-73-33-1360
E-mail: carlos-card@hotmail.com

Tacna
Centro Cultural Peruano Norteamericano
Asesoria Educacional
Coronel Bustios 146
Tacna 054, Peru
Tel: 51-52-24 44 06
E-mail: ragarcia@cultural.edu.pe
Web: www.cultural.edu.pe

Trujillo
Centro Peruano Americano
Asesoria Educacional
Av. Venezuela 125 Urb. El Recreo
Trujillo, Peru
Tel: 51-44-261944
E-mail: aeusa@elcultural.com.pe
Web: www.elcultural.com.pe

Philippines

Bacolod City
EducationUSA Advising Center, ASRC
University of St. La Salle
American Studies Resource Ctr,
La Salle Ave.
Bacolod City 6100, Philippines
Tel: 63-34-433-0078
E-mail: tvjochico@usls.edu.ph
Web: www.usls.edu.ph

Baguio City
EducationUSA Advising Center,
   Guidance Center
St. Louis University
Bonifacio ST
Baguio City 2600, Philippines
Tel: 63-74-444-8246 ext.222
E-mail: slu_gc_dir@yahoo.com
Web: www.slu.edu.ph

Batac, Ilocos Norte
EducationUSA Advising Center,
   Mariano Marcos State University
   American Studies Resource Ctr,
   ASRC Main Library
Batac 2906, Ilocos Norte
Philippines
Tel: 63-77-792-2615
E-mail: mmsu_asrc@hotmail.com;
   lucena_felipe@yahoo.com
Web: www.paef.org.ph

Davao City
EducationUSA Advising Center, ASRC
Ateneo de Davao University
American Studies Resource Ctr,
E. Jacinto ST
Davao City 8016, Philippines
Tel: 63-82-221-2411 ext.8242
E-mail: educationusa.addu@gmail.com
Web: www.fulbright.org.ph

Dumaguete City
SU - EducationUSA
Silliman University ASRC
Hibbard Avenue
Dumaguete City 6200, Negros
Oriental, Philippines
Tel: 63-35-422-6002 ext. 361
E-mail: shokoy@gmail.com;
reganj68@yahoo.com
Web: www.fulbright.org.ph

Ilo-ilo City
EducationUSA Advising Center, ASRC
Central Philippine University
Henry Luce III Library, Lopez
Jaena ST, Jaro
Iloilo City 5000, Philippines
Tel: 63-33-329-1971 ext.1019
E-mail: cpupaef@gmail.com
Web: www.cpu.edu.ph

Makati, Manila
Philippine-American Educational
   Foundation (PAEF)
10/F Ayala Life FGU Center
6811 Ayala Avenue
Makati City 1226, Philippines
Tel: 63-2-812-0945
E-mail: educationusa@fulbright.org.ph
Web: www.fulbright.org.ph

Zamboanga City
EducationUSA Advising Center, ASRC
Ateneo de Zamboanga University,
   La Purisima Street
Zamboanga City 7000, Philippines
Tel: 63-62-992-1478
E-mail: ben_adzu@yahoo.com
Web: www.fulbright.org.ph

Poland

Krakow
US Consulate General Krakow
Public Affairs
ul. Stolarska 9
Krakow 31-043, Poland
Tel: 48-12-424 5140
E-mail: brzostekmr@state.gov
Web: //krakow.usconsulate.gov/krakow/
   studyus.html

Warsaw
Polish-U.S. Fulbright Commission
   Educational Advising Center
Nowy Swiat 4
Warsaw 00-497, Poland
Tel: 48-22- 628 7950
E-mail: ola.augustyniak@fulbright.edu.pl
Web: www.fulbright.edu.pl

Warsaw
US Embassy Public Affairs IRC
ul. Piekna 14a
Warsaw, Poland 00540
Tel: 48-22-504 23 63
E-mail: waciszmd@state.gov
Web: //poland.usembassy.gov/poland/
   programs/education-advising-center.html

Portugal

Lisboa
Fulbright Information Center
Edificio da Reitoria, Universidade
   de Lisboa
Cidade Universitaria, Campo Grande
Lisboa 1649-0004, Portugal
Tel: 351-21-7611130
E-mail: studyusa@fulbright.pt
Web: www.fulbright.pt

Qatar

Doha
US Embassy Public Affairs Section
22 February Road
Doha, Qatar
Tel: 974-496-6749
E-mail: educationusaDoha@state.gov
Web: //qatar.usembassy.gov

Romania

Bucharest
Fulbright Educational Advising Center
Fulbright Commission
Str. Ing. Costinescu nr 2, sector 1
Bucharest 011878, Romania
Tel: 40-21-231 9015
E-mail: feac@fulbright.ro
Web: www.fulbright.ro/educational-
   advising-center.html

Russia

Kazan
Kazan State University International Office
ul. Kremlyovskaya 18, room 17
Kazan, Tatarstan 420008, Russia
Tel: 7-8432-92-76-00
E-mail: olya@ksu.ru
Web: www.ksu.ru/umc1/index.
   php?id=17&idm=42

Moscow
EducationUSA Advising Center
American Councils
Ulitsa Nikoloyamskaya, dom 1,
3rd floor, EAC
Moscow 109189, Russia
Tel: 7-495-777 65 32
E-mail: eic@useic.ru
Web: www.useic.ru

Nizhny Novgorod
Nizhny Novgorod Linguistics University –
   American Corner
ul. Minina 31a
Nizhny Novgorod 603155, Russia
Tel: 7-831-436-22-21
E-mail: kms@lunn.ru
Web: amcorners.ru/contacts/ac147/

Novosibirsk
Educational Advising Center-EducationUSA
American Councils for International
   Education
pr. Lavrentiaeva 17, 2nd Building
Novosibirsk 630090, Russia
Tel: 7-383-330-92-94
E-mail: eac@ieie.nsc.ru
Web: //actr.nsk.ru

St. Petersburg
American Councils for International
   Education
Nab. Moiki, 58, office 401
St. Petersburg 190000, Russia
Tel: 7-812-326-1803
E-mail: adviser@americancouncils.spb.ru
Web: www.americancouncils.spb.ru

Tomsk
Tomsk State University
American Center
34a, Lenin Pr.
Tomsk 634050, Russia
Tel: 7-3822-53-42-75
E-mail: tomsk@amcorners.ru
Web: //amcorners.ru/contacts/ac316/

Vladimir
Vladimir Educational Advising Center
Regional Scientific Library
ul. Dzerzhinskogo 3
Vladimir 600000, Russia
Tel: 7-922-32-32-02, 32-26-08
E-mail: vladimireac@lib33.ru
Web: library.vladimir.ru/ otdeli_mo_00.htm

Vladivostok
Vladivostok Educational Advising Center
American Councils
Okeanskiy pr-t, 15A, 3 floor
Vladivostok 690091, Russia
Tel: 7-4232-408071
E-mail: useac@vlad.ru
Web: //americancouncils-vlad.ru/

Volgograd
EducationUSA Center Volgograd
Volgograd Regional Scientific Library
Ulitsa Mira 15, office 4-02
Volgograd 400066, Russia
Tel: 7-8442-90-30-93
E-mail: volgogradeac@gmail.com
Web: www.acv.vipcentr.ru

Voronezh
Voronezh Regional Educational Advising
   Center
ul. Kukolkina 3, office 203
Voronezh 394018, Russia
Tel: 8-951 552 3163
E-mail: adviser@vreac.org.ru
Web: www.vreac.org.ru

Yekaterinburg
American Information Center
ul. Mamina-Sibiryaka, 193
Yekaterinburg 620055, Russia
Tel: 7-3432-61-53-38
E-mail: tbabkina@yandex.ru
Web: www.ac-ekb.info/education.html

Rwanda

Kigali
US Embassy-Public Affairs Section
Educational Advising Center
2756 Rue de la Gendarmerie,
Kacyiru, Gasabo
Kigali, Rwanda
Tel: 250-252596 400
E-mail: kaburenterx@state.gov
Web: //rwanda.usembassy.gov/educational_
advising.html

Saudi Arabia

Dhahran
US Consulate General Dhahran
Public Affairs Section next to KFUPM
Dhahran 31942, Saudi Arabia
Tel: 966-3-330-3200 ext 3044
E-mail: edudhahran@state.gov
Web: //dhahran.usconsulate.gov/dhahran/
resources.html

Jeddah
US Consulate General Jeddah
Public Affairs Section
Falasteen Street, Al Ruwais District
Jeddah, Saudi Arabia
Tel: 966-2-667-0080 ext 4151
E-mail: EduJeddah@state.gov
Web: //jeddah.usconsulate.gov/educational-
advising.html

Riyadh
Education Advising Office
US Embassy-Riyadh
Diplomatic Quarter
Riyadh 11693, Saudi Arabia
Tel: 966-1-488 3800 ext 4505
E-mail: eduriyadh@state.gov
Web: //riyadh.usembassy.gov/saudi-arabia/
resources.html

Senegal

Dakar
US Embassy Public Affairs Section
Avenue Jean XXIII x rue Bugnicourt
Immeuble Kleber II
Dakar, Senegal
Tel: 221-33-829 23 81
E-mail: DiengAX@state.gov
Web: //dakar.usembassy.gov/resources/
education-advising-service.html

Serbia

Belgrade
International Academic Center
Decanska 12, prvi sprat
Belgrade 11003, Serbia
Tel: 381 11 334 9639
E-mail: office@iacbg.org
Web: www.iacbg.org

Sierra Leone

Freetown
Educational Advising Center
US Embassy Public Affairs Section
Southridge-Hill Station
Freetown, Sierra Leone
Tel: 232-22-515-363
E-mail: RoweAA@state.gov
Web: //freetown.usembassy.gov/
educational_advising_services.html

Singapore

Singapore
United States Education Information Center
12 Prince Edward Road
01-03 Bestway Building Podium A
Singapore 079212, Singapore
Tel: 65-6223 4193
E-mail: inquiry@useic.org
Web: www.useic.org

Slovakia

Bratislava
Fulbright Commission Advising Center
Levicka 3
Bratislava 821 08, Slovakia
Tel: 421-2-5542 5606
E-mail: office@fulbright.gov.sk
Web: www.fulbright.sk

Banska Bystrica
Slovak Academic Information
Agency SAIA, N.O.
Tajovskeho 51
Banska Bystrica, Slovak Republic 974 00
Tel: 421-48-4137810
E-mail: saia.bbystrica@saia.sk
Web: www.saia.sk

Slovenia

Ljubljana
Slovene Human Resources Developmt &
Scholarship Fund
Dunajska 22, 5th FL
1000 Ljubljana, Slovenia
Tel: 386-1-434 10 88
E-mail: EducationUSA@sklad-kadri.si
Web: www.sklad-kadri.si/si/izobrazevanje-
v-tujini/svetovalnica-za-izobrazevanje-v-
tujini/educationusa/

South Africa

Cape Town
US Consulate General
EducationUSA Advising Center
2 Reddam Ave., Westlake 7945
Cape Town, Western Cape
South Africa
Tel: 27-21-702-7362
Web: //southafrica.usembassy.gov/
educational-advising.html

Durban
US Consulate General
Educational Advising Center
30th Fl, 303 West Street
Old Mutual Bldg
Durban 4001, South Africa
Tel: 27-31-305-7600 ext.3135
E-mail: knowlesSD@state.gov
Web: //southafrica.usembassy.gov/
educational-advising.html

Johannesburg
US Consulate General
American Culture and Information Center
1 Sandton Drive
Johannesburg, South Africa
Tel: 27-11-838-2231
E-mail: educationusajhb@state.gov
Web: //southafrica.usembassy.gov/
educational-advising.html

Spain

Barcelona
Institut Nord-America
Academic Advising Office/IEN Library
Via Augusta, 123
Barcelona 08006, Spain
Tel: 34-93-240.51.10
E-mail: jmoya@ien.es
Web: www.ien.es

Madrid
Comision Espana-EE.UU.
Fulbright Program-Educational Adviser
Po General Martinez Campos, 24 bis
Madrid 28002, Spain
Tel: 34-91-319 1126
E-mail: adviser@comision-fulbright.org
Web: www.fulbright.es/

Sri Lanka

Colombo
US-Sri Lanka Fulbright Commission
Educational Advising Center
7, Flower Terrace
Colombo 7, Sri Lanka
Tel: 94-11-256 4176
E-mail: advising@isplanka.lk
Web: www.fulbrightsrilanka.com/edu_
advising_centre.html#edu

St. Kitts and Nevis

Charlestown
Nevis Public Library
EducationUSA Advising Center
Prince William Street
Charlestown, St. Kitts and Nevis
Tel: 869-469-0421 x2055
E-mail: nepublib@sisterisles.kn

St. Lucia, West Indies

Castries
Students Services Centre
Sir Arthur Lewis Community College
Morne Fortune
Castries, St. Lucia, West Indies
Tel: 758-452-5507
E-mail: larybynoe@hotmail.com
Web: www.salcc.edu.lc

St. Vincent & Grenadines

Kingstown
National Archives & Documentation Center
Richmond Hill
Kingstown
St. Vincent & the Grenadines
E-mail: document@vincysurf.com
Web: www.nalis.gov.tt/IFLA/stvincent1.htm

Sudan

Khartoum
EducationUSA Advising
U.S. Embassy Khartoum
Kilo 10, Soba Khartoum, Sudan
E-mail: educationusasudan@state.gov
Tel: 249-187-022-851

Suriname

Paramaribo
Business Education Resource Center,
  US Embassy
Dr. Sophie Redmondstraat 129
Paramaribo, Suriname
Tel: 597-472900 ext.2267
E-mail: dijksjb@state.gov
Web: //suriname.usembassy.gov/resources.
  html

Swaziland

Mbabane
US Embassy
Ryan House, Cnr Sir Robert Croydon
  Avenue & Jubela Street
Mbabane H100, Swaziland
Tel: 268-404-1158
E-mail: balarinMN@state.gov
Web: //swaziland.usembassy.gov

Sweden

Malmö
Malmö Borgarskola
EducationUSA Advising Center
Regementsgatan 36
Malmö SE-200 10, Sweden
Tel: 46-40-34 70 20
E-mail: andreas.lejon@pub.malmo.se
Web: www.malmoborgarskola.se/
  edukationusa.aspx

Stockholm
Swedish Fulbright Commission
Vasagatan 15-17, 4th floor
Stockholm SE-111 20, Sweden
Tel: 46-8-534 818 80
E-mail: fulbright@fulbright.se
Web: www.fulbright.se/

Switzerland

Bern
US Embassy
Public Affairs Office
Bern CH-3001, Switzerland
Tel: 41-31-357-7011
E-mail: bernpa@state.gov
Web: //bern.usembassy.gov/ study_usa.html

Syria

Damascus
Education Advising Office
American Cultural Center
87 Ata Al-Ayoubi St., Abou
Rumaneh
Damascus, Syria
Tel: 963-11-3391-4171
E-mail: educationusa.syria@gmail.com
Web: //damascus.usembassy.gov/eato2.html

Taiwan

Taipei
AIT - Public Affairs Section
Suite 2101, 21F, No. 333 Keelung
Road - Section I
Taipei 110, Taiwan
Tel: 886-2-2723-3959
E-mail: application@mail.ait.org.tw
Web: www.educationusa.org.tw

Taipei
Foundation for Scholarly Exchange
U.S. Education Information Center
3F, 45 Yanping S. Road
Taipei 10043, Taiwan
Tel: 886-2-2388-7600
E-mail: feedback@fulbright.org.tw
Web: www.educationusa.org.tw

Tajikistan

Dushanbe
American Councils for International
  Education: ACTR/ACCELS
EducationUSA Advising Center
86 Tolstoy Street
Dushanbe 734003, Tajikistan
Tel: 992-37-221 2103
E-mail: educationusa@americancouncils-tj.
  org
Web: www.americancouncils-tj.org

Khujand
Khujand Education Advising Center
183a Lenin Street
(inside Real Comfort LLC building)
Khujand 735700, Tajikistan
Tel: 992-91-909 0091
E-mail: naimjon@gmail.com
Web: www.americancouncils-tj.org

Tanzania

Dar es Salaam
US Embassy-Office of Public Affairs
Educational Advising Center
686 Old Bagamoyo Road, Msasani
Dar es Salaam, Tanzania
Tel: 255-22-2668001
E-mail: eadar@state.gov
Web: //tanzania.usembassy.gov/educational_
  advising.html

Thailand

Bangkok
Civil Service Commission Office
Education Counseling Center
Siam Square Soi 7, Rama I Road,
Pathumwan
Bangkok 10330, Thailand
Tel: 66-2-2820876
E-mail: vatchara01@gmail.com
Web: www.ocsc.go.th

Bangkok
EducationUSA @Knowledge Plus
Silom Shanghai Bldg, 2nd fl
(opp.Silom Village)
807 Silom 17, Silom Road
Bangkok 10500, Thailand
Tel: 66-2-238-3933
E-mail: siriporn@knowledgeplus.ac.th
Web: www.knowledgeplus.ac.th

Bangkok
American University Alumni (AUA)
  Language Center
Library, 2nd Fl -Educational Counseling
  Unit
179 Rajdamri Road, Lumpini, Pathumwan
Bangkok 10330, Thailand
Tel: 66-2383933-4 ext4006
E-mail: counseling@auathailand.org
Web: www.auathailand.org/rajdamri/
  counseling.php

Bangkok
Bangkok Bank Public Co., Ltd.
Educational Advisory Service
333 Silom Road (2nd Floor)
Bangkok 10500, Thailand
Tel: 66-2-230-1329
E-mail: indira.are@bbl.co.th
Web: www.bangkokbank.com

Bangkok
Public Affairs Section
U.S. Embassy
95 Wireless Road
Bangkok 10330, Thailand
Tel: 66-2-205-4596
E-mail: preeyawan@state.gov
Web: //bangkok.usembassy.gov/

Chiang Mai
ACE! Academy for EducationUSA
Chiang Mai University
IC-Uniserv Bldg
239 Nimmanhaemin RD, A.Muang
Chiang Mai 50200, Thailand
Tel: 66-86.6703777
E-mail: hub.ace@gmail.com
Web: //acethai.weebly.com/

Hat Yai
E-mail: hatyai@educationusa.info

Togo

Lomé
US Embassy-Public Affairs Section
U.S. Student Advising Center Boulevard
  Eyadema
Lomé, Togo
Tel: 228-261-5470
E-mail: Sewonukk@state.gov
Web: //togo.usembassy.gov/educational_
  advising.html

Tonga

Nukuʻalofa
EducationUSA Tonga
Tupou Tertiary Institute
Lavinia Rd, Fasi moe Afi, Nuku'alofa 22007,
  Tonga
E-mail: educationusatonga@yahoo.com
Tel: 676-862-8890

Trinidad & Tobago, WI

Port of Spain
US Embassy Public Affairs Section
Information Resource Center
7-9 Marli Street
Port of Spain,
Trinidad & Tobago, WI
Tel: 868-822-5576
E-mail: ircpos@state.gov
Web: //trinidad.usembassy.gov/public_
  affairs_information.html

Tunisia

Tunis
AMIDEAST Tunisia
22 Rue Al Amine Al Abassi
Cite les Jardins
Tunis, Belvedere 1002, Tunisia
Tel: 216-71-790559; 71-841488
E-mail: lzahmoul@amideast.org
Web: www.amideast.org

Turkey

Ankara
Fulbright Commission
Sehit Ersan Caddesi 28/4
Cankaya
Ankara 06680, Turkey
Tel: 90-312-4284824
E-mail: advising@fulbright.org.tr
Web: www.fulbright.org.tr

Istanbul
Fulbright Istanbul Ofisi
Dumen Sokak 3/11, Gumussuyu
Taksim-Beyoglu
Istanbul 34437, Turkey
Tel: 90-212-244 1105
E-mail: fulb-ist@fulbright.org.tr
Web: www.fulbright.org.tr

Turkmenistan

Ashgabat
EAC/American Councils for International
  Education in Turkmenistan
Gerogly Street 48/A, 2nd floor
Ashgabat 744000

Turkmenistan
Tel: 993-12-33-10-15/33-10-16
E-mail: eacashgabat@inbox.ru
Web: //americancouncilstm.org

Dashoguz
Dashoguz American Corner
Educational Adviser
Turkmenbashy str. 7/2
746300 Dashoguz, Turkmenistan
Tel: 993-322-5-03-81
E-mail: acdashoguz@gmail.com
Web: //americancornerstm.org

Mary
Mary American Corner
Educational Adviser, 2nd floor
42a Agziberlik Avenue
Mary 745400, Turkmenistan
Tel: 993-522-7-38-65
E-mail: macorner@rambler.ru
Web: //americancornerstm.org/ac-mary-r20.
  htm

Turkmenabat
Turkmenabat American Corner
3rd floor, Shatlyk Building
33 Pushkinà Avenue
Turkmenabat 746100
Turkmenistan
Tel: 993-422-3 37 71; 6-37-71
E-mail: acturkmenabat@rambler.ru
Web: //americancornerstm.org

Turkmenbashy
Turkmenbashy American Corner
Educational Adviser
13 Dostluk Street, Balkan Velayat
Turkmenbashy City 745000
Turkmenistan
Tel: 993-243-7-45-83; 2-13-95
E-mail: tbashy@americancornerstm.org
Web: //americancornerstm.org

Uganda

Kampala
US Embassy-Public Affairs Section
Educational Advising Center
Plot 1577 Ggaba Road
Nsambya-Kampala, Uganda
Tel: 256-41-259-795
E-mail: MutazindwaCB@state.gov
Web: //kampala.usembassy.gov/educational_
  exchange.html

Ukraine

Dnipropetrovsk
"Osvita" Educational Information and
  Advising Center
K. Marksa 60, office 74, 75
Dnipropetrovsk 49000, Ukraine
Tel: 380-56-744-62-42
E-mail: center.osvita@gmail.com
Web: www.center-osvita.dp.ua

Kharkiv
Kharkiv "Osvita" Educational Advising
  Center
13 Chernyshevskogo Str, office 701 Kharkiv
  61057, Ukraine

Tel: 380-57- 756-7562
E-mail: bulgakovanb@gmail.com
Web: www.osvita.kharkiv.org

Kyiv
EducationUSA Advising Center
American Councils for International
  Education
vul. Esplanadna 20, (6th floor),
Kyiv 01001, Ukraine
Tel: 380- 44-289-3952
E-mail: edusa@americancouncils.org.ua
Web: www.americancouncils.org.ua

Lviv
Osvita Educational Advising Center
prospekt Chornolova, 4, room 1
Lviv, Ukraine
Tel: 380-32-243-4738
E-mail: info@osvita.org
Web: www.osvita.org/ukr/

Simferopol
Center for Promotion of International
  Education
ul. Pavlenko 5, korp. 2, komn.110
  Simferopol 95006, Ukraine
Tel: 380-652-54-6033
E-mail: eacosvita@pop.cris.net;
  malii@mail.ru

Simferopol
Crimean Engineering and Pedagogical
  University library (Window on America
  center)
ul.Sevastopolskaya, 21, per.Uchebniy, 8,
Simferopol 95015, Ukraine
Tel: 380-50 134 59 18
E-mail: nataliakrasnobayeva@gmail.com

United Arab Emirates

Abu Dhabi
US Embassy Public Affairs Section
Embassies District, Al Karama Street
Abu Dhabi, United Arab Emirates
Tel: 971-2-414 2245
E-mail: educationusaad@state.gov
Web: //abudhabi.usembassy.gov

United Kingdom

London, England
US-UK Fulbright Commission Fulbright
  Advisory Service
Battersea Power Station
188 Kirtling Street
London SW8 5BN United Kingdom
Tel: 09014880162
Web: www.fulbright.co.uk

Uruguay

Montevideo
Fulbright Commission
Centro de Asesoramiento Educativo
Colonia 810, Suite 703
Montevideo 11100, Uruguay
Tel: 598-2-901 41 60
E-mail: fulbrigh@chasque.apc.org
Web: www.fulbright.org.uy/web/
  asesoramiento.htm

EducationUSA Advising Centers

Uzbekistan

Tashkent
US Embassy
Educational Advising Center
3 Moyqorghon Street, 5th Block
Yunusobod District
100093 Tashkent, Uzbekistan
Tel: 998-71-120-54-50
E-mail: Tashkent-advising@state.gov
Web: //uzbekistan.usembassy.gov/advising

Venezuela

Caracas
Asociacion Venezolano Americana de
   Amistad
Ave. Libertador, Multicentro
Empresarial del Este
Torre Libertador A, piso 10
Ofic.A-103.
Chacao, Caracas 1060, Venezuela
Tel: 58-212-2637601
E-mail: info@avaa.org
Web: www.avaa.org

Maracaibo
Centro Venezolano Americano del Zulia
   CEVAZ
Departamento de Estudios en Estados
   Unidos
Calle 63, #3E-60, Sector Las Mercedes
Maracaibo 4001, Venezuela
Tel: 58-61-793-4517
E-mail: estudiosusa@cevaz.com
Web: www.cevaz.org/es/servicios_oficaseso-
   ria.asp

Merida
Centro Venezolano Americano de Merida
Urbanizacion El Encanto
Avenida 2 (Lora) Esq. Calle 43
No. 1-55
Merida 5101, Venezuela
Tel: 58-74-263-1362
E-mail: cevam@interlink.net.ve
Web: www.cevam.org

Vietnam

Hanoi
EducationUSA Advising Center
US Embassy
1st Floor, Rose Garden Tower, 170 Ngoc
   Khanh, Ba Dinh District
Hanoi, Vietnam
Tel: 84-4-3850-5000
E-mail: hanoieducationusa@gmail.com
Web: vietnam.usembassy.gov/ educationusa.
   html

Ho Chi Minh City
EducationUSA
US Consulate General
Diamond Plaza 8th Floor,
34 Le Duan, District 1
Ho Chi Minh City, Vietnam
Tel: 84-8-3821-6400
E-mail: hcmcedusa@state.gov
Web: www.educationusa.info/hcmc

Yemen

Sana'a
AMIDEAST Yemen
66, Algiers Street
(near the Sana'a Trade Center)
Sana'a, Yemen
Tel: 967-1-400279
E-mail: advising-sanaa@amideast.org
Web: //www.amideast.org/yemen

Zambia

Lusaka
American Center
COMESA Building, Zone F
Ben Bella Road
Lusaka 10101, Zambia
Tel: 260-1-227993
E-mail: paslusaka@state.gov
Web: //zambia.usembassy.gov

Zimbabwe

Bulawayo
Bulawayo Educational Advising Center
Bulawayo Public Library
100 Fort Street & 8th Avenue
Bulawayo, Zimbabwe
Tel: 263-9-60965
E-mail: advisingzw@yahoo.com
Web: //harare.usembassy.gov/educational_
   advising.html

Harare
US Educational Advising Center,
US Embassy-PAS
Eastgate Mall, 7th Fl, Goldbridge
2nd Street
Harare, Zimbabwe
Tel: 263-4-758800/1/5
E-mail: useaczim@gmail.com
Web: //harare.usembassy.gov/educational_
   advising.html

More College Planning Resources
from the College Board

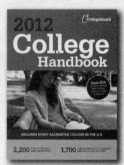

College Handbook 2012

The only guide listing all accredited universities, two-year and four-year colleges, and technical schools in the United States — more than 3,900 in total.

2,300 pages, paperback
ISBN: 978-0-87447-967-6
$29.99

Book of Majors 2012

Explore in-depth descriptions of 200 majors, and see where over 1,100 majors are offered at colleges nationwide.

1,350 pages, paperback
ISBN: 978-0-87447-968-3
$26.99

Applying to College?

Know what to do, how to do it, and when — with the new edition of

Get it together
for College

Packed with:

- **Checklists** to know what to do

- **Journal pages** to record what you learn

- **Tips** to keep it simple

- **Timelines** to keep on track

- **PLUS:** special tips for art portfolios, music auditions, student athletes and home-schooled applicants

240 pages, paperback | ISBN: 978-0-87447-974-4 | $15.99

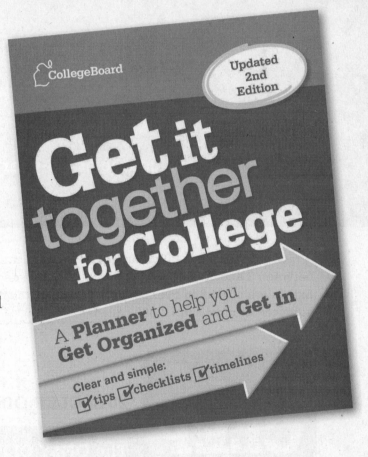

Don't get overwhelmed — get organized.